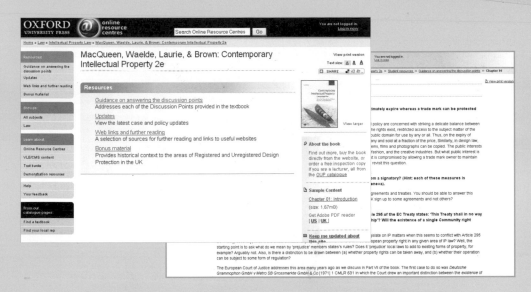

 online resource centre
www.oxfordtextbooks.co.uk/orc/macqueen2e/

When you visit the **Online Resource Centre** you will find a wealth of resources and bonus material to help further your study of intellectual property law, including:

For students:

- Guidance on answering discussion points
- Updates
- Web links
- Further reading
- Bonus material

! Remember to check the Online Resource Centre regularly for updates on recent developments and major events in law.

See the **Guide to the Online Resource Centre** on page xix for full details.

Contemporary Intellectual Property

Law and Policy

Second edition

Hector MacQueen

Charlotte Waelde

Graeme Laurie

Abbe Brown

OXFORD

UNIVERSITY PRESS

OXFORD
UNIVERSITY PRESS

Great Clarendon Street, Oxford OX2 6DP

Oxford University Press is a department of the University of Oxford.
It furthers the University's objective of excellence in research, scholarship,
and education by publishing worldwide in Oxford New York

Auckland Cape Town Dar es Salaam Hong Kong Karachi
Kuala Lumpur Madrid Melbourne Mexico City Nairobi
New Delhi Shanghai Taipei Toronto

With offices in

Argentina Austria Brazil Chile Czech Republic France Greece
Guatemala Hungary Italy Japan Poland Portugal Singapore
South Korea Switzerland Thailand Turkey Ukraine Vietnam

Oxford is a registered trade mark of Oxford University Press
in the UK and in certain other countries

Published in the United States
by Oxford University Press Inc., New York

© Hector MacQueen, Charlotte Waelde, Graeme Laurie, and Abbe Brown 2011

The moral rights of the authors have been asserted

Crown copyright material is reproduced with the permission of the Controller,
HMSO (under the terms of the Click Use licence)

Database right Oxford University Press (maker)

First published 2008

British Library Cataloguing in Publication Data

Data available

Library of Congress Cataloging in Publication Data

Data available

Typeset by Newgen Imaging Systems (P) Ltd., Chennai, India
Printed in Great Britain on acid-free paper by
Ashford Colour Press Ltd, Gosport, Hampshire

ISBN 978–0–19–957532–9

10 9 8 7 6 5 4 3 2 1

For Bill and Lovety Cornish,
with sincere thanks for all the support and inspiration over the years

We can scarcely believe that we have now produced the second edition of this book. It is only three (short) years since the first edition appeared and yet so much has happened in the field of intellectual property law that a new edition was increasingly overdue. It is the challenge of any contemporary legal academic to keep up with developments in his or her field, but this seems to be particularly true of intellectual property law. The task is complicated by the inherently international nature of the subject and this book has only been possible as a truly collaborative effort. In recognition of this, we are delighted to welcome our colleague Abbe Brown as full author on the project; thanks must also go to those colleagues who have given us invaluable research assistance: Michael Dizon, Yolande Stolte and Stephen Wright. We continue to enjoy unparalleled support from colleagues in the SCRIPT research centre—generously supported by the Arts and Humanities Research Council—and from the School of Law at the University of Edinburgh. Life, like law, moves inevitably forward. Hector MacQueen is now a Scottish Law Commissioner and Charlotte Waelde has recently joined the School of Law at the University of Exeter. Notwithstanding, we sincerely hope to continue our collaboration in years to come.

It was our original aim when this book was first conceived to provide a fresh and new approach to teaching and learning intellectual property law. We have been delighted by the positive response which the first edition received and we have been heartened that our approach is useful to both students and teachers alike. Accordingly, the format of this second edition largely follows that of the first and we explain this further in the walk-through guide. As with the previous edition, an Online Resource Centre accompanies this volume where readers can find regular updates on legal developments as well as outline answers to some of the questions posed in our substantive chapters.

We endeavour to state the law as accurate as of 30 November 2009 although we have included more recent updates in the text where this has been possible. The House of Lords was replaced by the Supreme Court in October 2009 and the Lisbon Treaty came into force on 1 December 2009. This last instrument brought about extensive amendment of the Treaty on European Union, and the EC Treaty was superseded by the Treaty on the Functioning of the European Union (TFEU) with consequential renumbering of Articles. The Court of First Instance is now the General Court. Our practice with respect to these changes is the same throughout the book, viz, we retain old names and numbering in cases decided prior to the reforms but have adopted new names and numbering for events or commentary post-reforms.

This edition is dedicated to Bill Cornish and his wife Lovety. Bill has been a source of support and inspiration to us over many years and we are sure that we speak for many generations of intellectual property lawyers when we say, quite simply, thank you.

Hector MacQueen
Charlotte Waelde
Graeme Laurie
Abbe Brown
May 2010

Contents

This book is unlike any other on intellectual property law. It does not attempt a simple trawl through the legal provisions that make up this discipline. Rather, it sets intellectual property protection within its wider social context and explains the tensions and dynamics that operate in that world and which shape the law over time. We are particularly interested in the contemporary challenges to modern intellectual property law; hence the title of our book. We have sought to produce a text which both introduces students, primarily undergraduates, to the laws in this area, and which at the same time helps them to understand the policies that lead those laws to be the way they are. The world of intellectual property is full of contradictions, competing interests, political agenda, and, sometimes, ideology. Our aim has been to help students understand these tensions by explaining how law is shaped within their contours. It is, in other words, to help students appreciate intellectual property law within the 'real' world.

There is no denying that intellectual property law can be difficult. The law can sometimes seem dense and impenetrable, and it is a challenge in itself just to keep up with developments. We have divided the responsibility for writing this book among four authors because of the enormity of the task, but we each share a common vision which is to make the study of intellectual property law accessible, engaging and fun. The challenge should not be difficult to meet: intellectual property law is an amazingly vibrant and dynamic discipline which has a bearing on the daily lives of each and every one of us. We want the students who use this book to engage with the subject and we have written it accordingly. We explain below the various elements used in the text to achieve this. It is another feature of the book that is unique.

Intellectual property law is an extremely diverse and expanding field and it has not been possible to offer complete coverage of all areas which make up the discipline while meeting our objectives outlined above. We do not believe that one book can serve both ends, and we prefer innovation and difference. This having been said, the book offers critical analysis of all of the main areas of intellectual property law, both under statute and at common law, and ensures that every issue is considered from each of the national, European and international perspectives.

A further and final feature of this book which helps it to stand out is its contemporary presentation and layout, and its use of images. No other legal subject can be understood or come alive in quite the same way as intellectual property law because so much of the field is concerned with visualisations of creations. And no other intellectual property textbook contains so many images to illustrate key issues. In a pertinent demonstration of the power of intellectual property law in practice, it proved not possible to include all the images we wanted. Sometimes locating the copyright owner was not straightforward and sometimes our publishers' requests for permission to reproduce an image were refused even though it was for use in an educational text. As you will come to appreciate, this is but one example of the legal and political complexities of the subject. Where we have not obtained illustrative material for use in the book itself, we have sometimes been able to provide references to where it may be found, or to give a relevant link in the book's Online Resource Centre (see further below).

Distinguishing features of this book

This book embodies an holistic account of intellectual property law as an organic and developing discipline. Its key features include:

- An in-depth and up-to-date account of the current law with particular emphasis on the contemporary challenges in each of the main areas of the discipline.
- A consideration of the underlying policies which have shaped each of the areas of the law to date.
- Critical analysis of the forces that drive these policies with a view to predicting how intellectual property law might develop in the future.
- Identification of the tensions that arise for intellectual property law as a result of influences from other policy areas, such as the single European market, competition law and human rights discourse.
- Evaluation of the 'success' with which intellectual property law has responded to new challenges as these have arisen, including the Internet, the advent of the new genetics, and calls for better protection of the personality.
- A broad contextualisation of the discussion in domestic, European and international spheres, ensuring that students understand that intellectual property law is truly a global discipline.

Walk-through guide to the educational features of this book

This book is full of features that are designed to help students engage with the subject-matter, to acquire and refine critical and reflective skills, and to remain up-to-date with the fast-paced developments that typify intellectual property law. This guide is a step-by-step walk through these features and you should pay close attention to ensure that you get the most out of the book.

Parts

The book is divided into parts, each of which deals with a discrete area of intellectual property law. The beginning of each part contains an overview of what will be covered and an account of the key sources of law. Internet links to the actual text of these instruments are also provided.

Learning objectives

Each chapter gives an account of the learning objectives that you should be able to meet once you have worked through the chapter. For example, the first learning objective in Chapter 2 states: 'By the end of this chapter you should be able to describe and explain the development of copyright, and its rationale.' If you cannot meet the objectives, then you need to work through the chapter again!

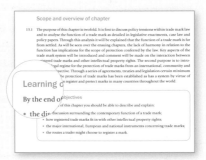

Key points

Every chapter uses key points to highlight essential features of the chapter or area of law that you need to know. These help to focus your study and serve as valuable milestones as you move through the different parts of the book.

Key extracts from cases and materials

Every legal case tells a story, and we have designed the format of the book to ensure that crucial extracts and legal points are clearly communicated to the reader.

Important websites

We highlight systematically important web pages where you can check out the most up-to-date developments in your chosen area of study. Website addresses themselves will be updated on the book's Online Resource Centre www.oxfordtextbooks.co.uk/orc/macqueen2e/

Questions

We ask questions throughout each chapter to help you assess your developing knowledge. These will usually be factual questions or 'reminder' questions and the answer can normally be found within the text itself.

Discussion points

These points are designed to encourage you to think more widely about particular ideas and legal issues raised in a chapter. Guidance on answering discussion points will appear on the Online Resource Centre at www.oxfordtextbooks.co.uk/orc/macqueen2e/

Exercises

Exercises can be used to help you with coursework and assignments that require you to undertake further research and read more widely about particular topics.

Further reading

Every chapter ends with suggestions for additional reading which are specially selected to highlight key areas of the chapter and to help you to take your learning further.

Guide to the Online Resource Centre

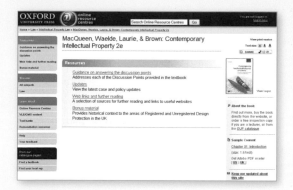

This book is accompanied by a dynamic Online Resource Centre (ORC) which is designed to enhance your learning experience and which contains the following features:

Updates

Documenting recent developments, changes in law and policy, and other information relevant to your study of intellectual property law.

Further reading and web links

Recently published sources for further reading will be added to the ORC, to help you in your research. New and updated web links will be provided together with links to images which can help your understanding of the law.

Guidance

Guidance on addressing each of the discussion points in the book will be provided in the ORC to aid your understanding of the subject-matter and help to refine your analytical skills.

Bonus material

Two short chapters from the author team provide historical context to the areas of registered and unregistered design protection in the UK.

Table of cases

Table of legislation

European Legislation
Treaties and Conventions

Regulations

Directives

List of illustrations

Abbreviations

ACTA	Anti Counterfeiting Trade Agreement
ADNDRC	Asian Domain Name Dispute Resolution
aff'd	affirmed
APIG	All Party Parliamentary Internet Group
BAILII	British and Irish Legal Information Institute
BECS	British Equity Collecting Society
CAFC	US Court of Appeals for the Federal Circuit
CBD	Convention on Biological Diversity
CC	Creative Commons
ccTLD	Country code Top Level Domain
CD	compact disc
CDPA 1988	Copyright, Designs and Patents Act 1988
CDR	Community Design Regulation
CFI	Court of First Instance
CIPIH	Commission on Intellectual Property Rights, Innovation and Public Health
CLA	Copyright Licensing Authority
Cm	Command Number
COMPAT	Community patent (now EU patent)
CPC	Community Patent Convention
CSS	Content scramble system
CT	Copyright Tribunal
CTM	Community Trade Mark
CTMR	Community Trade Mark Regulation
DACS	Design and Artists' Copyright Society
DCA	Department of Constitutional Affairs
DD	EU Directive on Legal Protection of Designs
DO	Designation of Origin
DRM	Digital rights management
DSB	Dispute Settlement Body (WTO)
DSU	Dispute Settlement Understanding (WTO)
DVD	digital versatile disk
EBA	Enlarged Board of Appeal (EPO)
EC	European Community
ECHR	European Convention on Human Rights
ECJ	European Court of Justice (now Court of Justice of the European Union)
ECtHR	European Court of Human Rights
EEA	European Economic Area
EEC	European Economic Community

EEUPC	European and European Union Patents Court
EGE	European Group on Ethics in Science and New Technologies
EPC	European Patent Convention
EPLA	European Patent Litigation Agreement
EPO	European Patent Office
eRes	eResolution
ESTs	Expressed Sequence Tags
EU	European Union
FAC	Facultative Advisory Council
FACT	Federation Against Copyright Theft
FAST	Federation Against Software Theft
GATT	General Agreement on Tariffs and Trade
GI	Geographical Indication
gTLD	Generic top level domain
HCA	High Court of Australia
HRA 1998	Human Rights Act 1998
ICANN	Internet Corporation for Assigned Names and Numbers
IDN	Internationalised Domain Name
IFPI	International Federation of Phonographic Industry
IGC	Intergovernmental Committee on Intellectual Property and Genetic Resources, Traditional Knowledge and Folklore
IGWG	Intergovernmental Working Group
InfoSoc	Directive Copyright in the Information Society Directive
IP	Intellectual property
IPL	International Private Law
IPRs	intellectual property rights
LDCs	Least Developed Countries
MCPS	Mechanical Copyright Protection Society
MMC	Monopoly and Mergers Commission
MR	Master of the Rolls
NAF	National Arbitration Forum
NZCA	New Zealand Court of Appeal
OD	Opposition Division (EPO)
OFT	Office of Fair Trading
OECD	Organisation for Economic Co-operation and Development
OHIM	Office for Harmonization in the Internal Market
OPSI	Office of Public Sector Information
OUP	Oxford University Press
P2P	peer-to-peer
PCT	Patent Cooperation Treaty
PDO	Protected Designations of Origin
PGI	Protected Geographical Indication
PPL	Phonographic Performance Limited
PRS	Performing Right Society
R&D	research and development
RDA 1949	Registered Designs Act 1949
rev'd	reversed

RMI	Rights management information system
SABIP	Strategic Advisory Board for Intellectual Property Policy
SI	Statutory Instrument
SPC	Supplementary Protection Certificate
SNPs	Single Nucleotide Polymorphisms
TCEs	traditional cultural expressions
TFEU	Treaty on the Functioning of the European Union
TK	traditional knowledge
TLD	top level domain
TLT	Trade Mark Law Treaty
TM	trade mark
TMA 1994	Trade Marks Act 1994
TPM	Technical Protection Measure
TRIPS	(Agreement on) Trade-Related Aspects of Intellectual Property Rights
TSG	Traditional Specialty Guaranteed
TTBE	Technology Transfer Block Exemption
TTBER	Technology Transfer Block Exemption Regulation
UCITA	Uniform Computer Information Transaction Act (USA)
UDR	Unregistered Design Right
UDRP	(ICANN) Uniform Domain Name Dispute Resolution Policy
UK–IPO	United Kingdom Intellectual Property Office
UPOV	International Union for the Protection of New Varieties of Plants
USC	United States Code
USPTO	US Patent and Trademark Office
VABE	Vertical Agreement Block Exemption
VC	Vice Chancellor
WCT	WIPO Copyright Treaty
WHO	World Health Organization
WIPO	World Intellectual Property Organization
WPL	Working Party on Litigation (EPO)
WPPT	WIPO Performances and Phonograms Treaty 1996
WTO	World Trade Organization

Law Reports, Journals etc

AC	Law Reports, Third Series, Appeal Cases
All ER	All England Law Reports
ALR	Adelaide Law Review
ALR	Aden Law Reports
ALR	Argus Law Reports (Aust.)
ALR	Australian Law Reports
App Cas	Appeal Cases
BCLC	Butterworths Company Law Cases
Beav	Beavan
BPIR	Bankruptcy and Personal Insolvency Reports

Ch	Law Reports, Third Series, Chancery Division
Ch D	Law Reports, Second Series, Chancery Division
CIPAJ	Chartered Institute of Patent Agents Journal
CLJ	Cambridge Law Journal
CLR	Canada Law Reports
CLR	Common Law Reports
CLR	Commonwealth Law Reports (Aus.)
CLSR	Computer Law and Security Report
CMLR	Common Market Law Reports
COM	European Commission Document
CP	Rep Civil Procedure Reports
CPR	Canadian Patent Reporter
Cr App Rep	Criminal Appeal Reports
Crim LR	Criminal Law Review
CSOH	Court of Session (Outer House)
CTLR	Computer and Telecommunications Law Review D Session Cases, 2nd Series [Dunlop] (Sc.)
EBL Rev	European Business Law Review
ECC	European Commercial Cases
ECDR	European Copyright and Design Reports
ECL&P	E-Commerce Law & Policy
ECLR	European Competition Law Review
ECR	European Court Reports
EHRLR	European Human Rights Law Review
EHRR	European Human Rights Reports
EIPR	European Intellectual Property Review
EL Rev	European Law Review
EMLR	Entertainment and Media Law Reports
EntLR	Entertainment Law Review
EPOR	European Patent Office Reports
ER	English Reports
ETMR	European Trade Mark Reports
EWCA	Media neutral citation from the Court of Appeal
EWCA Civ	Media neutral citation from the Court of Appeal (Civil Division)
EWHC	Media neutral citation from the High Court
EWPCC	Media neutral citation from the Patent County Court Ex Exchequer Reports
Ex CR	Exchequer Court Reports
F	Session Cases, 5th Series [Fraser] (Sc.)
FC	Federal Court
FCA	Federal Court of Australia
FSR	Fleet Street Reports
GRUR	Gewerblicher Rechtsschutz und Urheberrecht
GWD	Green's Weekly Digest (Sc.)
HC	House of Commons
HKC	Hong Kong Cases

HL	Law Reports, First Series, English and Irish Appeals
HL	House of Lords
HLR	Harvard Law Review
HMSO	Her Majesty's Stationery Office
HR	House of Representatives (US)
ICLT	Information & Communications Technology Law
IIC	International Review of Industrial Property and Copyright Law
IJL & IT	International Journal of Law and Information Technology
ILR	International Law Reports
Int TLR	International Trade Law and Regulation
IPQ	Intellectual Property Quarterly
IPR	Intellectual Property Reports
JBL	Journal of Business Law
JIEL	Journal of International Economic Law
JILT	Journal of Information, Law and Technology
JIPLP	Journal of Intellectual Property Law & Practice
JR	Juridical Review
K & J	Kay & Johnson's Vice Chancellor's Reports
KB	Law Reports, Third Series, King's Bench
LJPC	Law Journal Reports, Privy Council
LMCLQ	Lloyds Maritime and Commercial Law Quarterly LQR Law Quarterly Review
LR	(QB) Law Reports, Queens Bench
LT	Law Times Reports
M	Session Cases, 3rd Series [Macpherson] (Sc.)
MCC	Macgillivray's Copyright Cases
MLR	Modern Law Review
Mor	Morison's Dictionary of Decisions of the Court of Session
NZLR	New Zealand Law Reports
OJ	Official Journal of the European Communities
OJEPO	Official Journal of the European Patent Office
OJLS	Oxford Journal of Legal Studies
PC	Privy Council
PD	Law Reports, Second Series, Probate Division
QB	Queen's Bench
QBD	Law Reports, Second Series, Queen's Bench Division
R	Session Cases, 4th Series [Rettie] (Sc.)
RPC	Reports of Patent Design and Trade Mark Cases S Session Cases, [Shaw] (Sc.)
S	Senate
SALR	South African Law Reports
SC	Session Cases (Sc.)
SCLR	Scottish Civil Law Reports
SCR	Supreme Court Reports, Canada

SEC	(European) Commission Staff Working Document
SLT	Scots Law Times
TLR	Times Law Reports
TW	Trademark World
UKHL	Media neutral citation from the House of Lords
US	United States Supreme Court Reports
USPTO	US Patent and Trademark Office
VR	Victorian Reports (Aust.)
WL	WestLaw
WLR	Weekly Law Reports

Part I

Introduction

1

Intellectual property law: an introduction

Introduction

Scope and overview of chapter

1.1 This chapter is an introduction to the discipline of intellectual property (IP) law. You will examine the nature of IP and the aims and content of IP law. A brief overview will be given of the main rights and actions which make up IP law, together with an analysis of the various themes which underpin this area of law. The importance of the European and international dimensions to IP law will be emphasised. Here we lay the groundwork for the rest of this book, and you should use this chapter as a platform for further in-depth study.

1.2
> ### Learning objectives
>
> By the end of this chapter you should be able to:
>
> - define IP and the broad church that is IP law;
> - articulate the aims and objectives of IP law and to place it in its wider commercial setting;
> - give a brief account of the range and type of IPRs which exist;
> - appreciate the relationships between different levels of IP law (a) nationally, (b) at the European level, and (c) on the international stage; and
> - understand the various influences on the formation, justifications for and development of IP law, as well as the tensions that arise when the law seeks to protect IP.

The rest of the chapter looks like this:

- What is intellectual property law? (1.3–1.16)
- What is intellectual property? (1.17–1.44)
- Developing intellectual property law (1.45–1.72)

Exercise

Before reading this chapter, ask yourself, what is 'intellectual property'? Do you think that it should receive legal protection? What form should that legal protection take? Try to justify your responses and then compare your views with what we say below.

What is intellectual property law?

1.3   This is a book about the law that protects IP. Let us begin, then, with a very brief overview of the various elements of this area of law, which at first will seem disconnected. We will then go on to explore the themes that tie these elements together, and to consider the influences that shape and form modern IP law.

1.4   IP law comprises a wide range of forms of protection for IP. It encompasses statutory and common law arrangements and has aspects which are shaped by international, European and national considerations. Under the umbrella of IP, a significant number of intellectual property rights (IPRs) exist; each is tailored to protect a particular example of IP.

The statutory rights

1.5   There are four principal forms of IP, and in the UK these are protected by statute. They are as follows.

Patents: Patents Act 1977

1.6   Patent law protects *inventions*, which can be described as technical solutions to technical problems. An invention can be a product or a process. An invention is the paradigmatic example of 'industrial property'—a concept which we will explore further below. The Intellectual Property Office (UK–IPO) in Newport in Gwent is responsible for the grant of patents in the UK.[1] The European Patent Office in Munich is responsible for the grant of 'European' patents.[2] There is no such thing as a world patent.[3]

Copyright: Copyright, Designs and Patents Act 1988

1.7   Copyright law is designed to protect aesthetic and artistic creations such as literary, musical, dramatic and artistic works, known as *original works*, together with *derivative works* such as films, sound recordings, cable programmes, broadcasts and the typographical arrangement of a published work (ie the way the material is laid out). Copyright was expanded considerably throughout the course of the 20th century to protect new and emerging forms of IP such as computer software and databases. Copyright protection arises on the creation of a protectable work. There is no need to register the right (cf patents).

---

[1] http://www.ipo.gov.uk/pro-home.htm   [2] http://www.european-patent-office.org/
[3] Other important patent offices are the US Patent and Trademark Office http://www.uspto.gov/ and the Japanese Patent Office http://www.jpo.go.jp/

Designs: Registered Designs Act 1949 and Copyright, Designs and Patents Act 1988

1.8   Design law protects the way a commercially produced article 'looks' and/or 'functions'. Designs can either be protected by registration (in the case of aesthetic designs) or automatically on the creation of a design document or an article embodying the design (primarily for functional designs). The two forms of protection are not mutually exclusive. There is also much potential for overlap between copyright protection for artistic works and design protection. The UK–IPO is responsible for the grant of UK registered designs and for maintaining the Design Register. Unregistered and registered European Community design rights have also been available since 2002 and 2003 respectively. Oversight of this system and the registration process is handled by the Office for Harmonization in the Internal Market (OHIM) in Alicante, Spain.[4]

Trade marks: Trade Marks Act 1994

1.9   Trade marks operate to distinguish the goods and services of one enterprise from those of another. They exist as badges of origin and help the consumer to avoid confusion between goods or services of variable quality. Trade marks can assist greatly in bolstering protection for goods already protected by another form of IP law. For example, patent-protected drugs will invariably carry their own trade mark, eg 'Viagra' is the trade mark for the drug sildenafil citrate, the patent on which will expire in the next few years. The advantage of trade marks on patented products is, however, that the trade mark can continue long after the patent has expired, eg 'Valium'. Trade mark protection is awarded by registration. In the UK, this is handled by the Trade Mark Registry, once again, at the UK–IPO in Newport. A Community trade mark is also available, awarded by the OHIM.

Common law actions

1.10   Beyond these statutory rights a number of common law actions are also considered to make up the body of IP law in the UK. We examine these in full depth in Chapters 17 and 18. For now, it is only important that you understand the ambit of the two main actions.

Passing off

1.11   Passing off protects the reputation or 'goodwill' of traders in respect of their product 'get-up', name or trading style. The action becomes relevant when traders copy a rival's 'get up' and when this leads to, or is likely to lead to, public confusion between the competing products. There is much scope for overlap between trade mark protection and passing off. Often both actions are brought in the same dispute.

Breach of confidence

1.12   The common law action of breach of confidence is often included in the definition of IP law. The action provides ancillary support in the protection of the interests of IP producers, especially when information about registered IP must be kept out of the public domain prior to registration, for example, as with patents and registered designs. By its protection of trade secrets, breach of confidence also provides an alternative means to protect valuable knowledge. Breach of confidence is concerned with keeping valuable information out of the public domain; in

---

[4] http://oami.europa.eu/ows/rw/pages/index.en.do

contrast, registrable IPRs require full public disclosure in the course of the application process.

Sui generis rights

1.13   In more recent years a series of new IPRs has been introduced, usually because of the success of arguments that existing forms of protection are inadequate to accommodate emerging technologies, and/or because political agenda have desired a novel and unique form of protection. Some key examples include the following:

Semi-conductor topography: Design Right (Semiconductor Topographies) Regulations 1989 (SI 1989/1100)

1.14   Semi-conductor topography concerns the layout of computer circuit boards. The UK originally created a 'topography right' in 1989 to comply with a European Directive.[5] Since then topographies have been protected as a special form of unregistered design right. The move to protect this form of IP came after pressure was brought to bear by the United States which threatened to exclude foreign nationals from protection under its law if equivalent provisions did not exist in their own countries.

Plant breeders' rights: Plant Varieties and Seeds Act 1964 and Plant Varieties Act 1997

1.15   New varieties of plants and seeds can be protected by a right of protection under UK legislation which complies with a European Community Regulation from 1994.[6] Moreover, protection of the rights in question is required by the UPOV Convention of 1961, as amended in 1991.[7]

Database rights: Copyright and Rights in Databases Regulations 1997 (SI 1997/3032), now incorporated into Copyright, Designs, Patents Act 1988

1.16   Compilations of data can receive protection in Europe as a *database* in two separate ways. First, if the structure of the compilation is original, then the structure is protected by copyright. If it is not, then secondly, the underlying material can be protected if sufficient investment has been made in its compilation. 'Investment' is broadly defined and includes both investment of time and money. This material is protected by a 'database right' which entitles the 'maker' of the database to prevent another from extracting the whole or a significant part of the database without permission. This is a *sui generis* form of protection which is not required under international obligations. It will therefore only be accorded to foreign nationals whose country accords similar degrees of protection. Copyright protection in the contents of the database is not precluded by the existence of the new right.

 Question

What could possibly unite the disparate areas of protection which have been considered so far? Can you see any common themes that might link them together?

---

[5] Council Directive 87/54/EEC of 16 December 1986 on the legal protection of topographies of semiconductor products.
[6] Council Regulation (EC) No 2100/94 of 27 July 1994 on Community plant variety rights.
[7] UPOV Convention for the Protection of New Varieties of Plants 1961, 1991.

What is intellectual property?

1.17   In this section we will attempt to make sense of this seemingly disparate collection of legal rights. Let us begin by asking, what really is 'intellectual property'?

1.18   IP is frequently referred to as 'the novel products of human intellectual endeavour'. Yet, the use of the term 'property' to describe intellectual products implies the existence of rights and, perhaps more importantly, remedies in respect of the property and any unwarranted interference with it. A property paradigm, in turn, implies a system of control to be exercised by the right holder, that is, control of the subject matter of his property right. What makes a book *your* book in legal terms is the fact that no one can take, use or otherwise interfere with your property without your permission. At this level, IP protection operates in a similar fashion to other forms of property. IP is concerned with identifying and controlling permissible and impermissible dealings with intellectual products, usually by reference to the consent of the right holder, at least in the first instance. However, in many other respects an analogy with tangible property rights—that is, property rights over physical entities— does not help us to understand what we mean by *intellectual* property. For example, your book will not stop being your book at midnight tonight, yet in most cases IPRs eventually expire, leaving the subject matter without an owner and so free to be used or exploited by anyone. Similarly, no one can require you to lend your book to others so that they might benefit from it, whereas with certain forms of IP compulsory licences can be granted to third parties to exploit the property in question. Finally, for all forms of IP to exist, stringent criteria must be met, with these varying with the kind of IP protection that is sought. This is not true of other forms of property which assume the quality of *property* by sheer dint of their existence.

1.19   In order to understand how and why IP is treated in this way we must first appreciate that at the broadest level of abstraction IP is concerned with protection of information. Beyonce's songs, Margaret Atwood's latest poem, the website that supports this textbook, Jean Paul Gaultier's designer labels, OUP's electronic databases of authors, the chemical formulae for new cancer drugs, and the shape of Volvic's newest mineral water bottle, are all protectable as IP; but equally they are all simply classes of information. Thus, unlike many forms of property, IPRs protect intangibles. This gives rise to considerable problems over the control of the property and its protection. For example, unlike tangible property, interference with IP can occur without exhaustion of the property itself. If I borrow your book you are automatically precluded from using it, but if I copy your process for refining sugar this in no way precludes you from using the process for your own ends, or indeed, from passing it to others. This makes protection and exploitation potentially problematic. It is largely for this reason that rights and remedies are not available for intellectual products in the abstract. Protectable IP does not exist, therefore, in unspecific and ill-defined ideas alone. Such ideas must be reduced to some tangible embodiment before rights and remedies will accrue.[8]

1.20   But this does not explain why IPRs expire, nor why the scope of these rights can be limited in certain circumstances. To understand these features of IP protection we must ask:

 Question

> Which interests are furthered, or compromised, by the protection of IP? Revisit your thoughts after you have considered the rest of this chapter.

---

[8] A possible variation on this occurs with the protection of confidential information, which need not be in written form to be protected, but must nevertheless be sufficiently identifiable to merit protection. See Chapter 18, below.

A wide range of arguments can be put forward to justify IP. These will now be explored—and as will be seen, they are not necessarily consistent with each other.

Moral interests

1.21 A wise and now long-dead Scottish lawyer once wrote: 'Of all things, the produce of a man's intellectual labour is most peculiarly distinguishable as his own'.[9] This neatly sums up the moral argument as to why IP is protected. Intellectual products are produced by the efforts of people who have contributed from within themselves to the creation of the new entity, and so it is thought that IP reflects a moral connection between the property and its creator. Thus, in theory at least, to protect the property is also to protect certain crucial personal interests. Such interests can be compromised, for example, when control is relinquished to a third party and the property is subjected to some form of derogatory treatment. And, while a creator might happily renounce his economic stake in his property, for example by selling it, this does not mean that his moral interests are also abandoned. This sort of reasoning is directly reflected in the law of copyright, as we discuss in Chapter 3.

1.22 Another common moral reason to protect IP is because it would be unjust for others to benefit from a creator's time, labour and expenditure if it were possible simply to copy new intellectual products without fear of reprisal. The standard example is the experience of the pharmaceutical company. It is estimated that it costs upwards of $800 million to bring a new drug to market.[10] Most of this is spent in research and development and in gaining regulatory approval for the drug's safety and efficacy. However, once a drug is available it is incredibly easy to copy at a tiny fraction of this original cost. Would it be fair if rival companies were allowed to do so? Moreover, in that situation would any company go to the bother and expense of being the first to develop and market a new drug? These arguments focus, of course, on the investor or employers in respect of the innovation, rather than the individual innovator. It can also be argued that IP can lead to inefficient work to avoid existing rights, and can slow down the future innovation of others. Further, it could be said, at least in some sectors (software being a notable example) that there would be innovation without IP, and that even in pharmaceuticals there are other means, such as prizes, which would support innovation without the need for IP. This brings us to the all important issue of social interests which can be met, and hindered, by IP.

Social interests

1.23 Considerable social benefit can arise from IP. Indeed, it is precisely this argument that is advanced by pharmaceutical companies: 'give us protection for our drugs and we will have an incentive to produce them: deprive us of that protection and the incentive is gone'. This may be true, but it is also important to appreciate that social interests can be significantly compromised if IP is protected too strongly. For example, if too much market control is given to a creator then a paradigm may be established which will interfere with healthy competition which will operate to the detriment of competitors and consumers alike. Similarly, an inventor might choose to suppress a significant technological development or refuse to license it to third parties, thereby compromising social interests which could benefit from access to the technology.

---

[9] Bell, *Commentaries*, I, 103.

[10] CP Adams and VV Branter, 'Estimating The Cost Of New Drug Development: Is It Really $802 Million?' (2006) 25(2) Health Affairs 420.

Indeed, these arguments help to explain why limits are placed on IPRs, and we explore them further below.

1.24   In addition, the granting of IPRs over certain novel creations can give rise to social consternation about the morality of certain acts of creation and the legal protection of them. This has been most notable in recent years in the context of the patentability of the products of the biotechnology industry. Patents have been granted for the creation of genetically engineered human gene fragments and the development of transgenic animals which contain genetic material from foreign species, including humans. Many voices have been raised in Europe in objection to this as a fundamentally immoral practice. We explore this debate and its outcome in Chapter 12. It should be noted, however, that questions of morality in the granting of IPRs potentially impinges on all of the statutory forms of IP.[11] This is because IPRs are granted at the behest of the state. The courts are also most unwilling to treat iniquitous information as 'confidential' for the purposes of the common law.[12]

Economic interests

1.25   The economic interests of the producer of IP *and* his competitors *and* his customers will be affected when that property is exploited in the marketplace. The degree to which this occurs depends on the rights and remedies which are accorded to the property in question. It is here that we find one of the most serious areas of tension in IP protection. When IP is introduced into a market (as part of a product or through a licence to another person to make a product), it can have profound effects on the market's overall economic balance, as well as on the economic well-being of the whole geographical area in which it is exploited. There is, therefore, considerable room for dispute between the legitimate boundaries of IP protection and the encouragement of a free market economy. Indeed, this is most acutely felt within the confines of the European Union (EU), where the commitment of member states to a single market in which goods can circulate freely between states is threatened by the exercise of IPRs, which, by their nature, potentially erect barriers to such free trade. We discuss this further below.

1.26   Considering all of these interests, it should be clear that what is required is a balance that seeks to ensure that no one interest or group of interests dominates, while at the same time ensuring a fair and just degree of protection for any IP that has been produced. It is the over-arching role and aim of IP law to achieve such a balance.

Policies and tensions in intellectual property

1.27   Consistent with the range of justifications for IP, the ongoing protection of IP is also driven by a number of important, and at times competing, policies. The outcome of any tussle between these policies ultimately shapes the nature and scope of IPRs and determines the future direction of IP law. Let us consider in more depth the various interests and policies at stake.

---

[11] See, eg, *Glyn v Weston Feature Films* [1916] 1 Ch 261 (copyright); *Re Masterman's Application* [1991] RPC 89 (registered designs); *Re Hack's Application* (1941) 58 RPC 91 (trade marks).
[12] See *Coco v AN Clark (Engineers) Ltd* [1969] RPC 41, and *Attorney General v Guardian Newspapers (No 2)* [1990] 1 AC 109.

The protection of private interests through property rights

1.28   Property rights generally support and promote private interests, paramount among which is the interest of the owner to enjoy his property. Thus, these rights usually include exclusive control of the property and the right to exclude others from unauthorised use. Only in rare circumstances are the private rights of an owner curtailed to further a public interest, for example, through the compulsory acquisition of land. The enjoyment of one's property is guaranteed as a matter of individual human rights,[13] and it is a fundamental tenet of European Union law that national systems of property law should not be influenced by European measures.[14]

Reconciling public and private interests

1.29   The mere existence of IP can, however, significantly influence a number of public interests, as we have seen above. All forms of IP contribute something new to the sum total of human knowledge, and this can occur across every conceivable realm of human experience; from the development of new pharmaceuticals to treat cancer and AIDS, to the design of more comfortable office chairs; from the creation of beautiful (and not so beautiful) works of art, literature, music, or dance, to the introduction of distinctive packaging to assist consumers in distinguishing between the ever-burgeoning range of soft drinks on offer; from the splicing of genetic material to create a new strain of rose, to the improvement in processing times of computer board circuitry. All of these innovations can be the subject of IPRs, and their introduction to the public realm can surely only enrich the human condition.

1.30   It should be self-evident, then, that innovations such as these are to be encouraged, and the so-called *reward theory* of IP (see Diagram 1.1 below) seeks to promote this by engendering a cyclical pattern of social interaction whereby those who innovate are rewarded by the grant of property rights, which in turn act as an incentive to others to innovate, who are rewarded in their turn, and so on.

Diagram 1.1 The cyclical pattern of intellectual property production and protection

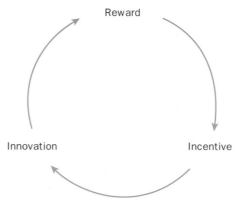

---

[13] European Convention for the Protection of Human Rights and Fundamental Freedoms, 1950, Protocol 1, Art 1: 'Every natural person is entitled to the peaceful enjoyment of his possessions. No one shall be deprived of his possessions except in the public interest and subject to the conditions provided for by law and by the general principles of international law'.

[14] Art 345 of the Treaty on the Functioning of the European Union states: 'The Treaties shall in no way prejudice the rules in Member States governing the system of property ownership'.

1.31   This model only serves its purpose, however, if the intellectual products find their way into the public domain, and it is one of the paradoxes of the IP regime that it seeks to promote public interests by granting private rights which—as we have seen above—under a classic property model imply exclusive control over the subject matter. The public interest can, therefore, be jeopardised if private rights are exercised in a way that means that the property in question is not used or exploited in a public setting.

1.32   A further paradox arises from the particular type of property right that is granted. This is an exclusive right of control of what use can be made of, say, new technologies. The IP holder can exclude others from a variety of activities for example, direct copying of their property by rivals or importation of samples of the property from a country where the price is lower, thereby stopping the importer from undercutting their prices. The potential for adverse influence from the exercise of IPRs can therefore extend across a number of public interests. Not only might various technological, scientific, artistic or consumer ends be thwarted, but over-zealous use of these rights can lead to a distortion in competition, which in turn impacts on wider economic interests, including those of the individual consumer who might have to pay higher prices to obtain new products, and those of competitors who must find another way to compete.

1.33   This is not to say that the existence of exclusive rights necessarily leads to these outcomes. Indeed, economists and others argue endlessly about whether exclusive rights hinder or promote competition, in that the rights can also serve as an incentive to others to engage in their own innovation and go on to obtain their own exclusive rights. What can be said with certainty, however, is that some exercise of power can have adverse outcomes. We see this most obviously in the context of Articles 101 and 102 of the Treaty on the Functioning of the European Union (TFEU), which respectively prohibit practices amounting to anti-competitive agreements (cartels) or abuses of a dominant market position, where these are likely to affect trade between member states. Each of these prohibitions has a potential direct bearing on the ways in which IP owners can exercise their rights, and the relationship between IP and competition has been receiving increasing attention from courts, regulators and academics. We revisit these provisions below, as well as in more detail in Chapter 20.

1.34   In other contexts the matter distils, once again, into a question of striking a balance between the potentially competing public and private interests. It is in this respect that IPRs differ most significantly from traditional property rights. Consider, for example, the following features that are found in the domain of IPRs.

- In some contexts an IP owner cannot simply refuse to exploit, or prevent others from exploiting, his property once he has received protection for it. The fear is that if this were so, certain technological developments would never make it into the public domain and further innovation would be stifled under the threat of a law suit for infringement of IPRs. Thus, in the context of patents and design law, compulsory licences can be granted to third parties who apply to the relevant authority[15] if the right holder does not exploit his property within a certain period of time (three years from the date of grant as in the case of patents),[16] or when the IPR is nearing the end of its term (the last five years of protection in the case of unregistered design right).[17] These measures have the effect of removing the exclusive control of the IPR subject matter from the right holder; they are

---

[15] This is the UK–IPO Office in the United Kingdom.   [16] Patents Act 1977, s 48.
[17] Copyright, Designs and Patents Act 1988, s 237.

compensated to the extent that the third parties' entitlements are akin to those that would have been granted under a reasonable licence agreement, with a 'just' licence fee to be paid to the owner of the IP. A variation on this theme is the right of a government department to engage in otherwise infringing acts in relation to a patented invention without the consent of the proprietor 'for services of the Crown'.[18] Here too compensation is payable to the IP owner (or an exclusive licensee) for 'any loss resulting from his not being awarded a contract to supply the patented product or...to perform the patented process or supply a thing made by means of the patented process'.[19]

- In other contexts, an IP owner may not be able to prevent certain uses of his property by others when these uses serve another valuable public interest. For example, copyright is not infringed when a third party engages in 'permitted acts' with respect to the work. These acts include copying done for the purposes of research or private study,[20] dealings with the work for the purposes of criticism, review or news reporting,[21] and things done for the purposes of instruction, examination or education.[22] The permitted acts in copyright law are considered to be fair dealings with the work, in that they serve independent and worthwhile interests without unduly compromising the individual (economic) interests of the copyright holder. However, the question of what is 'fair' is a matter of endless dispute, as we discuss in Chapter 5. Similarly, a trade mark owner cannot prevent the use of its trade mark by a rival who simply engages in comparative advertising, ie compares its goods or services with those of the trade mark owner, if this is done in an accurate and honest manner.[23] This latter practice is thought to encourage competition by raising consumer awareness about the range and quality of products available on the market. This is discussed in Chapter 15.

- In all cases, as has been noted for intellectual products to qualify for protection, they must satisfy certain pre-determined criteria in order to assume the quality of *property*. The stringency of the qualification criteria for each IPR will be seen to be aligned to the strength and length of the exclusive right that might ultimately be granted or obtained.

1.35   The balance which the law strikes between all these competing interests and ideas is endlessly controversial, with the result that proposals for reform, and actual reforms, are continuously occurring. In the UK, the Government ordered a review of the IP system in December 2005, headed by Mr Andrew Gowers. The review was published in December 2006 and made recommendations under seven headings: Balance, Coherence, Flexibility, Award, Use, Enforcement and Governance.[24] Many of the report's conclusions, recommendations and steps which were then taken will be discussed later in this book.

 Exercise

Compare and contrast the following forms of IP.

1.36   *Patents* protect inventions which must display *novelty*, ie the invention must never previously have been made available to the public by any means anywhere in the world. This is the strictest

---

[18] Patents Act 1977, ss 55–58.   [19] Patents Act 1977, s 57A.
[20] Copyright, Designs and Patents Act 1988, s 29.   [21] Copyright, Designs and Patents Act 1988, s 30.
[22] Copyright, Designs and Patents Act 1988, ss 32–36.   [23] Trade Marks Act 1994, s 10(6).
[24] Gowers Review of Intellectual Property, available at http://webarchive.nationalarchives.gov.uk/+/http://www.hm-treasury.gov.uk/d/pbr06_gowers_report_755.pdf

requirement of its kind in IP law. However, if it and the other patentability criteria are met, the reward is the strongest type of IPR available. This is the right for the holder to prevent every unauthorised use of his invention in the marketplace. Thus, rivals cannot make and sell illicit copies of the protected invention, nor import any such copies, nor indeed sell the invention in a kit form without fear of an infringement action.[25] There is no requirement of 'copying'—the patent owner has the power to control any use of the invention, howsoever that arises. Thus, even if Abraham has no idea that Jacob already holds a patent for a vacuum cleaner that employs cyclone technology, and even when there is no suggestion whatsoever of any copying, Abraham can nevertheless be prevented from entering the public arena with his independently-created version of the machine if it effectively embodies the kernel of Jacob's invention.

1.37   *Copyright* protects works that demonstrate *originality*. Here, originality simply means that there must be some evidence of independent skill or intellectual endeavour on the part of the creator, and that the work is not simply copied from an existing work. Thus, if we take our class on an outing to Princes Street Gardens in Edinburgh and every member of the class sketches Edinburgh Castle, each and every sketch will attract copyright protection from the moment that it is created. It does not matter that the subject is the same because the drawings themselves are original works deserving legal protection. Moreover, if half of the class also takes a photograph of the castle, each photograph will also be protected by copyright. The originality requirement is met by the simple act of holding the camera at a certain angle and the independent exercise of judgment by each person as to when they release the shutter. In the realm of copyright, it does not matter that millions of photographs have already been taken of Edinburgh castle: *originality* does not mean *novelty* in the same sense we find in patent law. There is a good reason why different terminology is used because the threshold to qualify for protection is set at a very different level. Furthermore, none of the people who has previously photographed or sketched the castle can prevent our students from doing so. The right received in copyright law is, as the name suggests, merely a right to prevent unauthorised copying or interference with one's own work. It is not a right to control all use of the underlying subject matter. As we explain in Chapter 2, copyright relates to the particular *expression* that the IP creator gives to their work. This is just as well, for were it otherwise copyright monopolies could significantly hinder the production of works in the fields of literature and the arts. Human beings are not very imaginative creatures. We always explore the same basic themes through our stories: birth, death, love, betrayal, revenge, hate, reconciliation and salvation. Copyright does not prevent anyone writing about these subjects, it merely protects the ways in which particular stories are told.

Question

What do 'novelty' and 'originality' mean in the context of design law? How, if at all, do these concepts dove-tail with the above definitions? What is the threshold criterion in trade mark law?

1.38   We can see, then, that the rights conferred by a copyright are much weaker than those conferred by a patent. Not only does this affect the nature and scope of the private rights of the property owner, but it also means that each of these IPRs will have a very different impact on the public sphere where it is exercised. Differential time limits are employed to minimise these effects. For

---

[25] Patents Act 1977, s 60.

example, a patent will initially only be granted for four years, although it can be renewed in successive years on the payment of a steadily increasing renewal fee,[26] up to a maximum of 20 years.[27] Compare this with copyright protection which, in the context of original works, lasts for the life of the author plus 70 years after their death. The compromise that is achieved balances, on the one hand, short and strong protection with, on the other, longer and weaker protection. In all cases when an IPR expires, however, the property enters the public sphere unconditionally, where it is free to be used by anyone.

1.39   Registration of IP is a common, although not universal, feature of protection regimes. Patents, trade marks and some design rights must be registered. In contrast, copyright protection arises whenever a work which satisfies the qualification criteria is created and unregistered design right exists whenever a design document is produced,[28] or an article is made to the design. Registration serves a number of functions, including identification of the subject matter to be protected, and a means to test whether the putative property is indeed 'new' (since a search of the relevant register can be carried out to determine if a similar or identical piece of property is already protected). Registers are public documents and provide a single point of reference for third parties to consider the current state of play in a particular field of innovation.

 Discussion point   For answer guidance visit www.oxfordtextbooks.co.uk/orc/macqueen2e/

Look at the table below. Why do each of patents, copyright and design rights ultimately expire whereas a trade mark can be protected for all time so long as it is re-registered every 10 years?

1.40   When a right must be registered it is important to bear in mind that, as has been noted, the qualification criteria can be fairly stringent, and can call for no prior disclosure of the creation. The classic example of this is patent law, which requires that an invention must never have been made available to the public prior to the filing of an application for patent protection. This is also true, in the realm of registered design law.

What protection do intellectual products receive prior to registration?

1.41   Here, as noted, the importance of common law protection through the action of breach of confidence can become important. As we discuss in Chapter 18, the law of confidence protects confidential information, ie information which is not part of the public domain. The action provides a remedy against those who disclose confidential information into that domain or are

---

[26] Patents (Fees) Rules 2007 (SI 2007/3292).

[27] A notable exception to this is the Supplementary Protection Certificate (SPC). These certificates can be granted in respect of 'medical products' and 'plant protection products' to extend legal protection for a further five years at the end of the initial 20-year period of patent protection. The market lead-in time for such products is often prolonged because of the requirement to subject them to regulatory and safety controls in the public interest. This results in a net reduction in the effectiveness of any patent that is granted, and an SPC is a means to redress this imbalance in favour of the intellectual property producer. Both forms of SPC were introduced by European Regulation (Regulation 1768/92 (medicinal products) 1992 OJ L182/1; Regulation 1610/96 (plant protection products) 1996 OJ L198/30).

[28] Defined in Copyright, Designs and Patents Act 1988, s 263(1).

Diagram 1.2 Core features of the statutory intellectual property rights

	Qualification criterion	Length of protection period	Strength of monopoly
Patents	Novelty	20 years max	Absolute monopoly
Copyright	Originality	Life of the author + 70 years for original works	Monopoly only over the expression of one's own creation
Registered designs	Novelty and with individual character	25 years max (five 5-year renewal periods)	Monopoly over use of design as it is applied to articles for which protection has been sought and granted
Unregistered designs	Originality and not commonplace in the design field	15 years max (more limited if design exploited)	Monopoly of use and against copying of design
Trade marks	Capacity to distinguish goods or services of right holder from those of another trader	10-year periods in perpetuity (with re-registration)	Monopoly over use of mark in respect of goods or services for which it is registered
	+ No conflict with 'earlier trade mark'	Loss of right if no use for 5 consecutive years	If mark is 'well known' right holder can prevent use on 'dissimilar' goods

likely to do so. Thus, the threat of an action of breach of confidence can assist considerably in protecting the interests of IP producers in the period between the initial conception of their idea for a new creation and the time when they file for registration.

1.42   However, in order to receive any protection at all, you must be able to express your idea with a sufficient degree of specificity to make it realisable as a final product.[29] This does not necessarily mean that you should write it down, although you would be wise to do so, but it does require that you can give sufficient substance to the information for which you wish to claim protection. Above all, you must keep the information secret and only disclose it to those persons upon whom you can impose a duty of confidence.

 Question

If you write your idea down you will receive a form of IP protection in addition to what may be pursued using breach of confidence. Which protection will this be? How far will this protection extend?

---

[29] *De Maudsley v Palumbo and Others* [1996] FSR 447.

C Geiger, 'Fundamental Rights—A Safeguard for the Coherence of Intellectual Property Law' (2004) 35 IIC 268

EC Hettinger, 'Justifying Intellectual Property' (1989) 19 Philosophy and Public Affairs 31

A Kur, 'A New Framework for Intellectual Property Rights—Horizontal Issues' (2004) 35 IIC 1

Sir H Laddie, 'National IP Rights: A Moribund Anachronism in a Federal Europe?' (2001) 23(9) EIPR 402

K Maskus and J Reichman, 'The Globalisation of Private Knowledge Goods and the Privatization of Global Public Goods' (2004) 7 JIEL 279–320

T Rychlicki, 'GPLv3: new software licence and new axiology of intellectual property law' (2008) 30(6) EIPR 232–243

PK Yu, 'Currents and crosscurrents in the International Intellectual Property Regime' (2004) 38 Loyola of Los Angeles Law Review 323

Ongoing updates

The IPkat blog: http://ipkitten.blogspot.com/

Part II

Copyright

Introduction

This part of the book explains and discusses the law of copyright. It has six chapters. The first considers the scope of copyright in the UK against the background of international, EU and comparative law on the subject as well as its historical development. This also throws light on the rationales or justifications for copyright. The chapter then discusses the subject matter of copyright, that is to say, those things—or works—which come under its protection. The second chapter goes on to explain which persons can claim the benefits of copyright and the length of time for which the protection endures. The next chapter explains what constitutes infringement of copyright, and is followed by one discussing the exceptions to copyright. A crucial point is that the forms of infringement—or restricted acts—also define how copyright may be exploited to obtain financial returns for its owner. Other persons who wish to do one or more of these acts will have to obtain the copyright owner's permission—or licence—to do so, and usually that permission will come at a price unless an exception applies. The fifth of the copyright chapters examines recently introduced rights very similar to, but different from copyright—the sui generis database right and performers' rights. The final chapter deals with some of the most important contemporary issues affecting the development of copyright law, including the Internet, the concept of the public domain, and the impact of human rights law.

Sources of the law: key websites

- Copyright, Designs and Patents Act 1988 as amended. The UK–IPO provides a consolidated text of the copyright sections (as at 3 May 2007) at
  http://www.ipo.gov.uk/cdpact1988.pdf
- Decisions of the courts in the various jurisdictions of the UK, for which see BAILII
  http://www.bailii.org/
- EU Copyright Directives, for which see the Commission's Internal Market Directorate General's website
- http://ec.europa.eu/internal_market/copyright/index_en.htm

- Berne Convention for the Protection of Literary and Artistic Works, for which see the WIPO website
  http://www.wipo.int/treaties/en/ip/berne/trtdocs_wo001.html
- Rome Convention for the Protection of Performers, Producers of Phonograms and Broadcasting Organizations, for which see the WIPO website
  http://www.wipo.int/treaties/en/ip/rome/index.html
- The UK–IPO website has a useful section devoted to copyright
- http://www.ipo.gov.uk/copy.htm

Copyright 1: history, rationale and subject matter

Introduction

Scope and overview of chapter

2.1 This chapter considers the scope and subject matter of modern copyright law against a background of its historical development in the UK and the international and European contexts in which that historical development has been increasingly set since the 19th century. Having thus set the scene, the chapter examines the matter in which copyright subsists. This centres on the concept of the 'protected work', and makes use of a distinction between what are sometimes known as 'author works' (literary, dramatic, musical, artistic and film works) and 'media works' (typographical arrangements, sound recordings, broadcasts, cablecasts and adaptations).

2.2 **Learning objectives**

By the end of this chapter you should be able to describe and explain:

- the development of copyright, and its rationale;
- the subject matter that copyright protects, and the different categories of work used by the law.

2.3 The chapter explores the history and rationales of copyright, before turning to consider the subject matter which the law protects. So the rest of the chapter looks like this:

- History (2.4–2.16)
- Rationale of copyright (2.17–2.21)
- Subject matter of protection (works, fixation, originality) (2.22–2.48)
- Author works (literary, dramatic, musical, artistic, film) (2.49–2.89)
- Media works (sound recordings, broadcasts, published editions) (2.90–2.96)

History

Early history

2.4   In most European countries the origins of copyright law lie in the efforts of government to regulate and control the output of printers once the technology of printing had been invented and become established in the 15th and 16th centuries. Whereas before printing a writing, once created, could only be physically multiplied by the highly laborious and error-prone process of manual copying out, printing made it possible to have as many exact copies of a work as there were persons who wanted and could afford to buy them. This meant much more rapid and widespread circulation of ideas and information. While the state and church thought this was to be encouraged in many aspects (eg dissemination of material such as Bibles and government information), it also meant that undesirable content—dissent and criticism of government and established religion, for example—could circulate too quickly for their comfort. So, all over Europe, government established controls over printing, by requiring printers to have official licences to be in business and produce books. These licences typically gave the printer the exclusive right to print particular works for a fixed period of years, enabling him to prevent others doing so during that period. Although the official licences could only grant rights to print in the territory of the state that had granted them, and therefore could not prevent printing of the same works in other territories, they did usually prohibit the import of such foreign printings into the territory where the licence had been granted. In England, the printers (then termed 'stationers') formed a collective organisation, known as the Stationers' Company, which in the 16th century was given the power to require the entry in its register of all lawfully printed books. Further, only members of the Company could enter books in the register. As a result the Company achieved a dominant position over publishing in 17th century England. But there was no equivalent in contemporary Scotland or Ireland.[1] However, in 1694 the English Parliament deprived the Stationers' Company of its powers of control, creating uncertainty about regulation of the printing industry at a critical juncture in British history.[2]

 Question

How was the printing of books regulated in England before 1707?

2.5   In 1707 the Parliaments of England and Scotland were united in a single body as the result of the Anglo-Scottish Union finally agreed that year, after much debate. The new Parliament was enjoined to respect the separate identities of the English and Scottish legal systems, but was enabled to change the laws of both countries as part of an overall project that today might be described as the creation of a single market in the UK. An important early piece of legislation to

---

[1] On the pre-history of copyright in Scotland see A J Mann 'Scottish copyright before the Statute of 1710' [2000] Juridical Review 11; also the same author's *The Scottish Book Trade 1500–1720* (2000), Ch 4 and App 1; and 'Some property is theft': copyright law and illegal activity in early modern Scotland', in R Myers, M Harris and G Mandelbrote (eds), *Against the Law: Crime, Sharp Practice and the Control of Print* (2004).

[2] See in general M Rose, *Authors and Owners* (1993); J Greene, *The Trouble with Ownership: Literary Property and Authorial Liability in England, 1660–1730* (2005).

this end was the Copyright Act of 1709,[3] which created a single regime for application in both England and Scotland. The Act marks an important shift of emphasis in the law, because it gave the 'sole right and liberty of printing books', not to printers, but to the authors of the books. This is the first formal legal recognition that a reason for conferring exclusive or property rights in this area was the work of its creator or originator. It may reflect the theories of contemporary philosophers such as John Locke, who held that rights of property flowed first from the labour of the person who created the thing to be owned. But the 1709 Act also enabled the author to transfer his rights to 'assigns', who would typically be the printer, without whom the author would be unable to disseminate and profit from his creation. Further, a pre-condition of the right was registration of the work at Stationers' Hall; something of a disadvantage for Scottish and Irish printers, since the Hall was in London. The right lasted for 14 years from first publication and if at the end of that time the author was still alive, it was renewed for another 14 years.[4]

Question

When was the first copyright statute passed? What changes did it make to the previous regime described in para 2.4?

2.6 The next critical stage in the early history of British copyright came from the 1730s on, as the first copyrights created under the 1709 Act began to expire. Did those who had held statutory rights to prevent unauthorised copies also have an underlying right at common law which now revived to enable them to continue to control printing and publication of their work? There was intense controversy and much litigation in both England and Scotland on this question.[5] Matters were not resolved until the great cases of *Hinton v Donaldson*[6] in Scotland in 1773 and *Donaldson v Beckett*[7] in England in 1774. In these decisions, the Court of Session and the House of Lords respectively held that there was no copyright at common law in works which had been published and enjoyed copyright under the 1709 Act. While the common law of both England and Scotland went on to develop with regard to *unpublished* works (only the author or his licensee could authorise publication), the development of copyright would henceforth be principally through statute. The common law copyright in unpublished work remained significant until the beginning of the 20th century, however, because unlike the statutory copyrights, it

---

[3] Often known to copyright lawyers as 'the Statute or Act of Anne', after Queen Anne, who reigned 1702–1714. The Act entered into force in 1710 and is sometimes given that date rather than 1709.

[4] See further R Deazley, *On the Origin of the Right to Copy – Charting the Movement of Copyright Law in Eighteenth Century Britain (1695–1775)* (2004); JC Ginsburg, "'Un chose publique?' The author's domain and the public domain in early British, French and US copyright law" (2006) 16 CLJ 636.

[5] In addition to works already cited, see WR Cornish, 'The author's surrogate: the genesis of British copyright' in K O'Donovan and GR Rubin (eds), *Human Rights and Legal History: essays in honour of Brian Simpson* (2000); W St Clair, *The Reading Nation in the Romantic Period* (2004); W McDougall, 'Copyright litigation in the Court of Session, 1738–1749, and the rise of the Scottish book trade' (1987) 5 Edinburgh Bibliographical Society Transactions 2–31; H MacQueen, 'Intellectual property and the common law in Scotland c1700-c1850' in L Bently, C Ng and G D'Agostino (eds), *The Common Law of Intellectual Property: essays in honour of David Vaver* (2010).

[6] 1773 Mor 8307. Full text of the judicial opinions in the case can be found in J Boswell, *The Decisions of the Court of Session upon the Question of Literary Property in the Cause of John Hinton of London, Bookseller, against Alexander Donaldson and John Wood, Booksellers in Edinburgh, and James Meurose, Bookseller in Kilmarnock* (1774). See further MacQueen, 'Intellectual property and the common law', 33–38.

[7] (1774) 2 Bro PC 129. See further R Deazley, *Rethinking Copyright: History, Theory, Language* (2006).

had no specific time limit, and lasted until lawful publication (ie it could go on for ever if publication never occurred).

Question

What was the effect of the decisions in *Donaldson v Beckett* and *Hinton v Donaldson?*

2.7   The primary development of copyright after *Donaldson v Beckett* was by statute. Engravings had been given copyright by statutes in 1734 and 1766, and further Acts for this subject matter were passed in 1777 and 1836;[8] sculptures joined books as copyright subject matter in 1798;[9] and paintings, drawings and photographs (the last a form of art recently made possible by technological development) were added by the Fine Arts Copyright Act 1862. Plays were protected against unauthorised public performance as well as printing by the Dramatic Copyright Act 1833, and public lectures were given limited protection by the Lectures Copyright Act 1835. The length of the copyright term began to increase, moved by ideas that, if the basis of copyright was the recognition and encouragement of authorship, its duration should be extended for the benefit of family and descendants who might otherwise suffer for their relative's art.[10] In 1814 the term for books became the longer of 28 years or the author's lifetime, while in 1842 there was a further extension, inspired by the lawyer-playwright Thomas Talfourd, to the longer of 42 years or the author's lifetime plus seven years. These extensions of copyright did not have an easy passage through Parliament: for example, the debates on the 1842 Act include TB Macaulay's famous criticism that copyright was 'a tax on readers for the purpose of giving a bounty to authors'.[11] In general, however, it was accepted that if authorship in literature, drama, music and art was to be rewarded, then the protection of copyright was essential.[12]

Key points on the early history

- Modern copyright begins in the 18th century, mainly for printed books
- It is decided that copyright is primarily a statutory right, which endures only for the period laid down by the statute
- Unpublished works have a common law copyright which lasts for as long as the work is unpublished
- In the 19th century, copyright is extended to works of art and drama, and the period of protection gets longer

---

[8] Engraving Copyright Acts 1734, 1766, 1777 and 1836.

[9] Sculpture Copyright Act 1798; replaced by Sculpture Copyright Act 1814.

[10] Particularly significant writers in this regard were William Wordsworth and Sir Walter Scott.

[11] See for a very full account of the genesis of the 1842 Act, C Seville, *Literary Copyright Reform in Early Victorian England* (1999).

[12] On the 19th-century 'crystallisation' of copyright in the UK, see B Sherman and L Bently, *The Making of Modern Intellectual Property* (1999), pp 111–28, 137–40.

International developments: Berne Convention 1886

2.8   The major problem which domestic legislation alone could not solve was unauthorised activity outside the UK. Copyright remained, like the old licensing systems from which it sprang, entirely limited to the territory in which it was granted, leaving authors and publishers unprotected beyond their home shores. As international markets for creative output began to take off in the course of the 19th century, so states began to enter into negotiations for the mutual recognition and enforcement of foreigners' copyrights. This culminated in 1886 in the multinational arrangement known as the *Berne Convention*, although the treaty also underwent important revisions at Paris in 1896, Berlin in 1908, Rome in 1928, Brussels in 1948, Stockholm in 1967 and Paris in 1971.[13] The Convention relates to literary and artistic works, amongst which are included films, and requires its member states to provide protection for every production in the literary, scientific and artistic domain.

 Question

When did the Berne Convention come into being, and how often has it been revised? What is the policy objective of the Convention?

The other *main features of the Berne Convention* which have emerged from the international activity of the last 120 years are:

- The principle of *national treatment*: each member state of the Convention would give citizens of other member states the same rights of copyright that it gave to its own citizens (Articles 3–5).

- *Minimum standards for national copyright legislation* – each member state agreed to certain basic rules which their national laws must contain, although it could if it wished increase the amount of protection given to right holders. One of these minimum rules was that copyright should arise with the creation of a work and not depend upon any formality such as a system of public registration (Article 5(2)). This entailed the end of the British system of registration at Stationers' Hall when the UK finally implemented the Berne Convention in the Copyright Act 1911. Another important Berne rule, also implemented in the 1911 Act, was that the term of copyright was to be a minimum of the author's lifetime plus 50 years.

- *A focus on the author* as the key figure in copyright law: apart from the prohibition of registration requirements and the extension of the copyright term, the Berne Convention emphasised in other ways the centrality of authorship in copyright. Its purpose was 'the protection of the rights of authors in their literary and artistic works' (Article 1), not the protection of publishers and other actors in the process of disseminating works to their public. In the 1928 revision the concept of moral rights was introduced (Article 10bis), giving authors the right to be identified as such and to object to derogatory treatment of their works. These rights, unlike those which have become known as the economic rights to prevent

---

[13] See in general S Ricketson and J Ginsburg, *International Copyright and Neighbouring Rights: The Berne Convention and Beyond* (2006); C Seville, *The Internationalisation of Copyright Law: Books, Buccaneers and the Black Flag in the Nineteenth Century* (2006).

reproduction, public performance and, in due course, broadcasting, could not be transferred to others.

- The possibility of exceptions to copyright, enabling the reproduction of literary and artistic works without the right holder's prior permission. The precise nature of these exceptions was for national legislation: the guiding principle stated in Article 9 of the Convention was that such exceptions were permitted 'in certain special cases, provided that such reproduction does not conflict with a normal exploitation of the work and does not unreasonably prejudice the legitimate interests of the author'. Free use of works was expressly permitted in the cases of quotation from lawfully published works, illustration for teaching purposes, and news reporting (Article 10).

2.9   The importance of the Berne Convention cannot be overstated. It remains the basis for international copyright relations and domestic copyright law. Originally a mainly European instrument, it now extends to most of the world, including since 1989 the USA. Under the TRIPS Agreement of 1994 (see below, para 2.13), states wishing to participate in international trade must join and comply with the Berne Convention.

Recent history: Copyright Acts 1911–1988; European and international law

Copyright Acts 1911–1988

2.10   As already noted, the UK implemented the Berne Convention in the Copyright Act 1911, which came into force on 1 July 1912. The Act swept away all the particular copyrights which had grown up over the previous century (see above, para 2.7), and replaced them with a much more general approach. It also abolished the common law copyright in unpublished works, replacing that with a statutory scheme for such material. The Act also responded to technological development by conferring a copyright on a new subject not mentioned in Berne, namely, sound recordings. Yet more new technology underlay the 1911 Act's replacement with the Copyright Act 1956, which came into force on 1 June 1957, and extended protection to films and broadcasts, and also to the typographical arrangements of published editions of works. Between them the two statutes brought under the umbrella of copyright works which, apart from films, were seen in continental European systems as belonging to a distinct category of their own. They were not author works, but rather technological media works by which entrepreneurs brought such works to new audiences in a different form. While they deserved copyright-like protection, the substance of the protection did not need to be as great as with author works. The continental European systems thus developed systems for the protection of what were termed 'neighbouring rights' quite distinct from those for author works. The approach was reinforced by the creation in 1961 of a Berne-like treaty for such neighbouring rights, the Rome Convention on the Protection of Performers, Producers of Phonograms and Broadcasting Organisations. But in the UK the 1956 Act followed the distinction between author and media works only in a modified form: one part of the Act gave copyright to literary, dramatic, musical and artistic works, while a second part gave a somewhat modified form of what was still called copyright to sound recordings, films, broadcasts and published editions.

Question

What are the differences in subject matter of the Berne and Rome Conventions?

2.11   The Copyright, Designs and Patents Act 1988 (CDPA 1988), which came into force on 1 August 1989, was also a response to technological development. Again new ways of creating and disseminating works – for example, computer programs, or software, and cable and satellite broadcasting – were recognised. But even more important in giving rise to the replacement of the 1956 Act were expansions in the ways by which copies might be made of works, notably photocopying, re-recording sound recordings on audio cassettes, and videoing broadcasts. Advances in copying technology meant that not only could individuals make copies for their personal or business use, but so too could so-called 'pirates', that is, persons who made copies in great quantities for commercial resale at prices significantly lower than those of the copyright owner. The Act continued to apply the concept of copyright generally to both author and media works, but it also moved towards the continental European model by recognising moral rights for authors in literary, dramatic, musical and artistic works and films.

 Question

List and date the three UK copyright statutes of the 20th century, and give the dates when each of the Acts came into force.

European developments

2.12   In the 1980s the European Community began to become more interested in copyright as an element in the creation of a single market. In 1991 there began a programme of Directives on copyright, designed to harmonise the national laws of the member states in certain key areas (computer programs, databases, the Internet) and to reduce the potential for differences to cause unjustified obstacles to the free movement of goods and services (rental rights, satellite broadcasting, copyright duration, resale rights in works of art). These Directives led to significant amendment of the CDPA 1988, generally by way of regulations. The process has made it clear that the initiative for copyright reform legislation taking effect in the UK now lies mainly in Brussels rather than Westminster.[14]

 Question

What topics have been dealt with in the EU's copyright directives?

[14] See further S Fitzpatrick, 'Prospects of further copyright harmonisation' [2003] EIPR 215; P Kamina, 'Towards new forms of neighbouring rights within the EU' in D Vaver and L Bently (eds), *Intellectual Property in the New Millennium* (2004).

International developments

2.13   Looking even further afield than Europe, there were important developments in the international protection of copyright in the 1990s. The TRIPS Agreement 1994 contains a number of provisions on copyright, compliance with which is required of states wishing to be members of the World Trading Organisation (WTO). They have to:

- sign up to the Berne Convention, apart from its provisions on moral rights (Article 9(1));

- protect computer programs and databases (Article 10);

- provide for rental rights in at least computer programs and films (Article 11);

- where the duration of copyright is calculated other than by reference to the life of a natural person, give a minimum term of 50 years calculated from, as the case may be, the date of authorised publication or of the work being made.[15]

Further, TRIPS makes explicit what had previously been an underlying principle of copyright law, namely, that it protects expression rather than ideas.[16] The agreement also states that member states must 'confine' limitations or exceptions to copyright to 'certain special cases which do not conflict with a normal exploitation of the work and do not unreasonably prejudice the legitimate interests of the right holder'.[17] The verb 'confine', not found in this context in the Berne Convention, is significant, hinting as it does at a hostile attitude towards copyright exceptions and limitations. Finally, there is provision for the protection of performers, producers of sound recordings and broadcasting organisations.[18]

 Question

What does TRIPS add to the Berne and Rome Conventions?

2.14   In 1996 two further treaties supplementing the Berne Convention were agreed at the World Intellectual Property Organisation (WIPO). The WIPO Copyright Treaty (WCT) followed TRIPS in:

- providing that copyright protected only the form in which a work was expressed and not its underlying ideas (Article 2);

- requiring copyright protection for computer programs and databases (Articles 4 and 5);

- recognising rental right in relation to computer programs and films, and extending it to sound recordings (Article 7);

- adopting the language of 'confining' copyright exceptions and limitations (Article 10 WCT).

2.15   But where TRIPS was driven by concerns about international trade, the WCT was primarily concerned to respond to the problems created by the rise of the Internet, and hence it added rights to deal with distribution and public communication of works and to support the use of technological measures in the protection from unauthorised use of works recorded digitally.[19] The other WIPO Treaty concluded in 1996 was for the further protection of performers and

---

[15] TRIPS, Art 12.   [16] TRIPS, Art 9(2).   [17] TRIPS, Art 13.   [18] TRIPS, Art 14.
[19] WCT, Arts 6, 8, 11, 12.

producers of sound recordings, significantly supplementing the provisions of the Rome Convention 1961 (see above, para 2.10) in this regard.

 Question

What did WCT 1996 add to previous international agreements on copyright? What was its main policy goal?

2.16 All this international activity in the 1990s, in particular the WCT, had significant effects upon copyright law in the UK. While the 1988 Act had granted copyright to computer programs and databases, and had introduced rental rights, the EU's need to respond to international developments in these areas led to Directives which required significant amendments to the Act. The 1996 Treaty led to the introduction in 1997 of the first draft of what eventually became, after much debate and controversy, the Copyright in the Information Society (InfoSoc) Directive 2001; and the implementation of this Directive in the UK made necessary major surgery on the 1988 Act by way of amending regulations which came into force on 31 October 2003.[20] An appreciation of the international as well as the European background is therefore vital to full understanding of the present law in the UK.

Key points on modern developments

- Copyright extended further, to photographs, films, sound recordings, broadcasts and computer technology (software and databases)

- Copyright internationalised from the late 19th century on – today there is both a global and a European dimension to law-making, meaning that scope for purely national initiatives is limited

- There is a division apparent in most legal systems between the copyright treatment of 'author works' (covered by the Berne Convention) and 'neighbouring' or 'media works' (covered by the Rome Convention) – see further below, para 2.47

Rationale of copyright

2.17 Copyright first developed in the early modern period as a response to the growth of the printing technology that facilitated the rapid multiplication and distribution of copies of written works. As shown by the history just described, change in the law has continued to be driven by technological advance in the means by which works can be presented to the public at large, and protection has been extended and adapted to cover photography, cinematography, sound recording, broadcasting, cable transmissions, computer programs and, most recently, the Internet. The practical benefit of developing protections within the copyright mould is the applicability of the international regime under the Berne Convention and other treaties which ensure potentially worldwide protection for right holders.

---

[20] Copyright and Related Rights Regulations 2003 (SI 2003/2498).

2.18 Despite the harmonising effects of the Berne Convention and other more recent international instruments, two distinct major conceptualisations of the functions of copyright can still be identified in the world's legal systems.[21] The Anglo-American or Common Law tradition emphasises the *economic role of copyright*. Protection of copyright subject matter against unauthorised acts of exploitation enables right holders either to go to market themselves with a product based on the material, or to grant others, by outright transfer or, more typically, by licence, the right to do so for whatever seems an appropriate price. In the absence of copyright, which would enable free- riding by would-be users, it is unlikely that producers of the material would earn any return for their work, and without that incentive production would dry up or slacken significantly. Copyright is thus essentially a response to market failure, a means by which socially beneficial activities can be made financially worthwhile for those engaging in them. It rests ultimately upon the general or public interest in having works containing ideas, information, instruction and entertainment made available, and in rewarding those – publishers as well as the creators of the works – who perform this function in society in accordance with the public demand for their efforts.[22] In contrast, the Continental European or Civil Law tradition sees copyright as springing from the *personality rights of the individual creator* of the subject matter. This perception is reflected in the name 'author-law' given to the topic by the various Continental systems – *droit d'auteur, urheberrecht*, and so on. Protection is given out of respect for the individual's creative act of production, and extends beyond the merely economic to the so-called 'moral rights': the right to be identified as the creator of a work, the right to have the integrity of a work preserved, and others. Copyright is thus rooted in protection of the individual personality and interests of the author as expressed in his work. Companies and organisations as such cannot be creators.

2.19 The distinction between the two conceptualisations is sometimes summarised by saying that the Anglo-American tradition is centred on the entrepreneur, the Continental one on the author. It is reflected in various rules. For example:

- where the Anglo-American tradition gives copyright protection to media works such as sound recordings and broadcasts, the Continental tradition uses a separate group of 'neighbouring rights' for these non-author works;

- where the Anglo-American tradition vests first ownership of copyright in the employer of an author making a work in the course of employment, the Continental tradition gives it to the author;

- where the Anglo-American tradition operates a relatively low threshold of 'originality' for works to enjoy copyright, based mainly upon the author's effort in not copying previous work, the Continental tradition tends to require a higher level of creativity before works will be protected.

 Question

Explain with illustrative examples the differences between the Anglo-American and Continental European conceptions of what copyright is for.

[21] For a comparative overview see G Davies, *Copyright and the Public Interest* (2nd edn, 2003), especially Chs 5–7. See also B Sherman and A Strowel (eds), *Of Authors and Origins: Essays on Copyright Law* (1994).

[22] The economics of copyright are explored in eg W Landes and R Posner, *The Economic Structure of Intellectual Property Law* (2003), Chs 2– 6, 8–10; R Towse (ed), *Copyright and the Cultural Industries* (2002); MA Einhorn, *Media, Technology and Copyright: Integrating Law and Economics* (2004). Many classic earlier studies are reprinted in R Towse and R Holzhauer (eds) *The Economics of Intellectual Property* (2002), vol 1 (Introduction and Copyright).

2.20   A further significant aspect of the distinctness of the two traditions is their stances in relation to the *copyright limitations and exceptions* allowed under the Berne Convention (see above, para 2.8); that is, those activities in which members of the public may engage with regard to copyright works without any authorisation from the right holders concerned. The Anglo-American tradition has traditionally allowed 'fair dealing' or 'fair use' for free in areas where it is thought that the public interest in the dissemination of information and ideas outweighs the interest of the right holder in earning reward from the exploitation of the work and the public interest in encouraging the author's activities. In contrast, although the Continental traditions typically permit private copying, the author still receives remuneration by way of levies imposed upon the sale of the equipment that enables the copying to take place. There is generally a less expansive approach to exceptions and limitations based upon wider interests than those of the author and the publisher.

2.21   The significance of such distinctions should not be over-emphasised. Continental copyright laws are also a basis for market operations with regard to ideas, information and entertainment, while, as we shall see (below, paras 3.4–3.30), the author plays a fundamental role in Anglo-American copyright laws, where moral rights are now also developing (see below, paras 3.31–3.46). Membership of the Berne Convention has embraced countries from both traditions for most of its history and since 1989 has included the USA. The convergence promoted by the Convention's minimum standards has been further advanced by TRIPS and the WIPO Treaties of 1996, as well as the copyright Directives of the EU. Nonetheless the deep-seated differences in basic concepts have an effect upon international discussions, the outcomes of which occasionally reflect a somewhat uneasy compromise between the competing schools of thought.

Key points on rationales

- Copyright has an economic function, enabling the production of information, ideas and entertainment to be rewarding for their authors and publishers

- Copyright also has a non-economic function, related in some legal systems to the idea of recognising creativity as an aspect of individual personality

- Copyright rewards individuals for their contributions; but this is offset by recognition of the interests – if not the rights – of the wider public in the free dissemination of material in certain circumstances

- Different legal systems give different emphases to these functions, making it sometimes difficult to achieve European or global harmonisation

---

Subject matter

2.22   Under the Copyright Designs and Patents Act 1988, as now several times amended, the following subject matter is protected by copyright:[23]

- original literary, dramatic, musical and artistic works (literary work including computer programs, databases and compilations other than databases);
- films;
- sound recordings;

---

[23] CDPA 1988, ss 1–8.

- broadcasts;

- the typographical arrangement of published editions of literary, dramatic or musical works.

The Act thus meets the requirements of the Berne Convention (protection for literary and artistic works, to include every production in the literary, scientific and artistic domain, including films – see above para 2.8), the Rome Convention as supplemented in 1996 (protection for sound recordings and broadcasts – see above, para 2.10) and the WCT (computer programs and databases – see above, para 2.14). A number of general points may be made covering all the categories listed, before turning to the detailed law of each one.

Products may have more than one copyright

2.23   A very important point is that any product in the domain of the subject matter listed in the previous paragraph (above, para 2.22) is quite likely to have more than one copyright in it. Thus a book will have copyright as a literary work, but there will also be a copyright in its typographical arrangement, as would also be the case with printed dramatic scripts and musical scores. A database has copyright in the selection and arrangement of its contents,[24] but this does not affect any copyright those items of content may have in their own right. A sound recording of a piece of music will involve copyrights, not only in the sound recording as such, but also, separately, one in the music. And if the work recorded is a song, there will be a further copyright in the song lyrics.[25] A broadcast of a film or sound recording will have copyright as a broadcast, but this will leave unaffected the copyrights in the film or sound recording. While the sound track accompanying a film is treated as part of the film for copyright purposes, a copyright may also subsist in the sound track as a sound recording.[26] With the advent of digital technology, the multimedia product (eg a computer game, the Microsoft Encarta encyclopaedia), which consists of digitised material combining audio, video, text and images still and moving played through a computer, and with which the user may interact, has become commonplace, raising difficult questions about the mixture of copyrights which such a product may have.[27]

 Question

Explain what it means to say that a product may have more than one copyright, and give some examples.

Need for a work

2.24   Copyright protects works. To paraphrase TRIPS and the WCT (see above, paras 2.14–2.15), the concern is, not with ideas as such, but with their expression.[28] There can be difficult issues,

---

[24] 1988 Act, s 3A.
[25] Note how CDPA 1988, s 3(1) defines 'musical work' as excluding any words intended to be spoken or sung with the music.   [26] CDPA 1988, s 5B(2), (5).
[27] See I Stamatoudi, *Copyright and Multimedia Works: A Comparative Analysis* (2002); T Aplin, *Copyright Law in the Digital Society* (2005).
[28] The classic discussion of this distinction is the US case of *Baker v Selden* 101 US 99 (1879). See also *University of London Press v University Tutorial Press* [1916] 2 Ch 601 and J Pila, 'An intentional view of the copyright work' (2008) 71 MLR 535.

however, in knowing when an expression, in whatever medium, reaches the level of a work capable of copyright protection. In a case about the copyright in law reports, Canadian judges argued that a work is something which generally is whole, complete or able to stand on its own, and that

> 'if a production is dependent upon surrounding materials such that it is rendered meaningless or its utility largely disappears when taken apart from the context in which it is disseminated, then that component will instead be merely a part of a work.'[29]

With this approach, they were nonetheless able to conclude that component parts of a law report, such as its key words and headnote, were, like the full report itself, works that attracted copyright. The idea that, when an expression is 'able to stand on its own' there is a work, presumably covers the many well-known examples of incomplete productions such as Schubert's Unfinished Symphony and Samuel Taylor Coleridge's poem 'Kubla Khan', the composition of which was famously interrupted by a person on business from Porlock, with the consequence that the poet's inspiration was lost and the work never completed.

■ *Sweeney v Macmillan Publishers Ltd* [2002] RPC 35

This complex case concerned the copyright in James Joyce's novel *Ulysses*, first published in 1922, and the publication of a new edition of that work in 1997, edited by DR. The novel was written over a long period, and considerably revised and rewritten in the process. Joyce's manuscripts and other preparatory material, such as corrected and amended typescripts and proofs, continued to exist. As originally published, the book contained many typographical errors. Some of these were corrected in later editions, which, however, also introduced new ones. Facsimiles of the Joyce manuscripts and other materials were published from 1975 on. The 1997 edition was based on a collation of all this material with the published editions, and sought the publication of the text intended by Joyce. The Joyce estate, which owned the copyright in *Ulysses* and the preparatory material, claimed infringement of copyright by the new edition. It was held that copyright subsisted in each chapter and perhaps each page or even sentence of *Ulysses* as it was written; but as each passage was incorporated into the larger work, copyright should be regarded as residing in that rather than in its constituent parts.[30] Copyright thus subsisted in Joyce's fair copy manuscript. Copyright also subsisted in earlier drafts of the work and in successive typescripts and proofs. DR had copied parts of this material, and its copyright had been infringed.

2.25 Nor is there a requirement of minimum length or substance to constitute a work: musical copyright was found to exist in the four notes constituting the Channel 4 television theme, for example,[31] although on the other hand single words, titles, the catch-phrases of a TV personality, headings on computer menus, and individual command names in a computer program[32] have been held to be too insubstantial to be literary works.

[29] *CCH Canadian Ltd v Law Society of Upper Canada* [2002] 4 FC 213 (CA) at 260 (para 66) per Linden JA. See also ibid at 308 (paras 197–9) per Rothstein JA. The court's conclusion was upheld by the Supreme Court of Canada, which did not find it necessary, however, to dwell on the meaning of 'work' in this context: see *Law Society of Upper Canada v CCH Canadian Ltd* [2004] 1 SCR 339.
[30] Contrast *Robin Ray v Classic FM plc* [1998] FSR 622, where a catalogue was subsumed into a database, but Lightman J rejected an argument that as a result the copyright of the first work was also subsumed into that of the second.
[31] *Lawton v Lord David Dundas*, The Times, 13 June 1985. Another example might be the Intel Inside theme.
[32] *Navitaire Inc v EasyJet Airline Co Ltd* [2006] RPC 3.

■ *Case C 5/08 Infopaq International A/S v Danske Dagblades Forening* [2009] ECDR 16

For the facts of this case, which related to an electronic news cuttings service, see below, para 4.15. The European Court of Justice stated that 'words, considered in isolation, are not as such an intellectual creation of the author who employs them' (para 45); but ' the possibility may not be ruled out that certain isolated sentences, or even certain parts of sentences ... may be suitable for conveying to the reader the originality of a publication such as a newspaper article, by communicating to that reader an element which is, in itself, the expression of the intellectual creation of the author of that article' (para 47).

 Discussion point   For answer guidance visit www.oxfordtextbooks.co.uk/orc/macqueen2e/

Can '4 Minutes 33 Seconds', by the composer John Cage, be held to be a work? In this composition, an orchestra is on stage at the outset, but does not start to play any of its instruments. Instead, the members of the orchestra silently sit on the platform for a period of just over four and a half minutes. If it is a work, does the fact that its author is generally regarded as a composer of music make the work musical? Are there any other possibilities? See further Cheng Lim Saw, 'Protecting the sound of silence in 4'33': a timely revisit of basic principles in copyright law' [2005] 12 EIPR 467.

2.26   While the general principle, that copyright protects the expression of a work rather than its ideas, is central, it is also important not to be misled as to its scope. In considering the concept, bear in mind what constitutes infringement of copyright, for example (see further below para 4.10 ff). Analysis of this part of the law shows it to be misleading to say that copyright protects no more than the form of expression. Otherwise it would not be possible for the author of a book to be able to control the exploitation of his work in other media such as film and broadcasting. Such adaptations will almost certainly adopt a distinct mode of expression, yet must be authorised by the author to be legitimate.[33] The author of a two-dimensional artistic work may challenge a three-dimensional reproduction, and vice-versa.[34] Editors of anthologies and collections of material produced by others have a copyright, not so much in the words gathered together by them, as in the arrangement and ordering of the material.[35] Of course this is a form of expression, but it shows that we should not take 'form of expression' in any narrow sense coloured by the idea that copyright prevents only slavish imitation. Thus a particular interpretation of historical events has been held capable of copyright protection.[36] The best view seems to be that there is no copyright in ideas while they remain just that, but that once the ideas have been expressed in some form it would be wrong to assume that a different expression of the same ideas must necessarily be a new work with its own copyright, or cannot be an infringement of the earlier work.

---

[33] CDPA 1988, ss 16(1)(e) and 21.   [34] CDPA 1988, s 17(3). See further below, para 4.26.

[35] *Macmillan v Suresh Chunder Deb* (1890) ILR 17 Calc 951; *Macmillan v Cooper* (1923) 93 LJPC 113. Note also Berne Convention, Art 2(5): 'Collections of literary or artistic works such as encyclopaedias and anthologies which, by reason of the selection and arrangement of their contents, constitute intellectual creations shall be protected as such, without prejudice to the copyright in each of the works forming part of such collections.'

[36] *Harman Pictures NV v Osborne* [1967] 1 WLR 723 (Charge of the Light Brigade); see further below, para 4.32.

Question

Give some examples to illustrate the difference between protectable expression and unprotectable ideas.

2.27 Lord Hoffmann said the following on this topic in *Designers Guild Ltd v Russell Williams (Textiles) Ltd*:[37]

'Plainly there can be no copyright in an idea which is merely in the head, which has not been expressed in copyrightable form, as a literary, dramatic, musical or artistic work, but the distinction between ideas and expression cannot mean anything so trivial as that. On the other hand, every element in the expression of an artistic work (unless it got there by accident or compulsion) is the expression of an idea on the part of the author. It represents her choice to paint stripes rather than polka dots, flowers rather than tadpoles, use one colour and brush technique rather than another, and so on. The expression of these ideas is protected, both as a cumulative whole and also to the extent to which they form a 'substantial part' of the work. [para 24] ... My Lords, if one examines the cases in which the distinction between ideas and the expression of ideas has been given effect, I think it will be found that they support two quite distinct propositions. The first is that a copyright work may express certain ideas which are not protected because they have no connection with the literary, dramatic, musical or artistic nature of the work. It is on this ground that, for example, a literary work which describes a system or invention does not entitle the author to claim protection for his system or invention as such. The same is true of an inventive concept expressed in an artistic work. However striking or original it may be, others are (in the absence of patent protection) free to express it in works of their own: see *Kleeneze Ltd v DRG (UK) Ltd* [1984] FSR 399. The other proposition is that certain ideas expressed by a copyright work may not be protected because, although they are ideas of a literary, dramatic or artistic nature they are not original, or so commonplace as not to form a substantial part of the work. *Kenrick & Co v Lawrence & Co* (1890) 25 QBD 99 is a well known example. It is on this ground that the mere notion of combining stripes and flowers would not have amounted to a substantial part of the plaintiff's work. At that level of abstraction, the idea, though expressed in the design, would not have represented sufficient of the author's skill and labour as to attract copyright protection [para 25]'.

2.28 Lord Hoffmann here connects the translation of unprotectable idea into copyright expression with the degree of originality, skill and labour shown by the author, and more will be said of that below (at para 2.39).[38] Clearly each case will turn on its own facts in this area, although it can perhaps be said that the higher the level of generality, or abstraction, of the idea of a work, the less likely it is to be protected as such.[39]

■ *Interlego AG v Tyco Industries Inc* [1989] AC 217 (PC)

Artistic copyright was claimed in engineering drawings modifying an earlier design by the same author (the Lego company). The visual impression from the two sets of drawings was much the same; the distinction lay mainly in the technical information as to dimensions and tolerances. It was held that the later drawings were not new works for the purposes of artistic copyright: the new ideas in the second drawings were not artistic, but literary. 'Nobody draws a tolerance, nor can it be reproduced three-dimensionally' (per Lord Oliver at p 258). This was

---

[37] [2001] FSR 11, paras 24, 25.

[38] See further M Spence and T Endicott, 'Vagueness in the scope of copyright' (2005) 121 LQR 657.

[39] *Plix Products v Winstone* [1986] FSR 63 per Prichard J at 92–4 (aff'd [1986] FSR 608); *Nova Productions Ltd v Mazooma Games Ltd* [2007] RPC 25 (CA), paras 31–55 (Jacob LJ).

important because literary copyright knows no equivalent to artistic copyright's concept of three-dimensional infringement (see main text above, para 2.26).

2.29   Another celebrated dictum in this area is as follows:

> 'You do not infringe copyright in a recipe by making a cake.' (*J & S Davis (Holdings) Ltd v Wright Health Group* [1988] RPC 403 per Whitford J at p 414).

Key points so far on subject matter

- Copyright protects expressions rather than ideas and information as such
- Before copyright can arise, there must be a *work* of a relevant kind: literary, dramatic, musical, artistic, film, sound recording, broadcast, published edition

---

Fixation

2.30   One way of establishing whether or not there is a work is to find a recording, or fixation, of the expression which constitutes the work.

> The *Berne Convention* says that copyright subsists in literary and artistic works 'whatever may be the mode or form of its expression' (Article 2(1)), but then allows national law 'to prescribe that works in general or any specified categories of works shall not be protected unless they have been fixed in some material form' (Article 2(2)). Note this means that member states have a choice as to whether to require fixation.
>
> In the UK, the *CDPA 1988* provides that copyright does not subsist in a literary, dramatic or musical work unless and until it is recorded in writing or otherwise (s 3(2)). 'Writing' includes any form of notation or code, whether by hand or otherwise, and regardless of the method by which, or medium in or on which, it is recorded (s 178). No definition of otherwise!

2.31   The UK thus opts for an explicit requirement of fixation before any literary, dramatic or musical work may enjoy copyright protection. The main form of fixation mentioned in the 1988 Act is writing; but the definition quoted above is very broad and obviously capable of covering, for example, the use of shorthand.[40] In any event, writing is not the only possible method of recording literary, dramatic and musical works, nor does the 1988 Act so limit its requirement. The electronic storage of work in digital form on discs and in computer memories is well known. Literary work means work which is spoken and sung as well as written,[41] while music and drama can be created in improvised performances as well as based upon scores and scripts. So far as concerns speech, singing and music, the tape and cassette recorder have been familiar ways of making recordings for a long time, and film, video and digital recording, including voice recognition software, can now be added to the list of methods of fixation sufficient to confer copyright on the work recorded. A further possibility might arise through lip reading what a speaker is saying on a film without a sound track, as for example with closed circuit TV cameras.

---

[40] See *Pitman v Hine* (1884) 1 TLR 82.   [41] CDPA, s 3(1).

2.32 The requirement of fixation still means, however, that there is no copyright in the unrecorded spoken word, ad lib stage performance, or aleatory musical composition. Since the copyright does not come into existence unless and until the recording is made, copyright confers no right on a speaker to stop people making recordings of what is said. If there is any right at all to prevent recording of one's words, it must be sought in other branches of the law.[42] However, the 1988 Act expressly provides that, for the purposes of conferring copyright on a work by recording it, it is immaterial whether the work is recorded by or with the permission of the author, ie the speaker.[43] Thus, while I may eavesdrop on and record other people's telephone conversations without infringing copyright in what they say, as soon as the recording is made, the words have copyright and the subsequent reproduction and publication of these words elsewhere may be controlled by the speaker.[44]

Question

What will constitute fixation of a work so that it can enjoy copyright?

■ *Norowzian v Arks Ltd (No 2)* [1999] FSR 79; aff'd [2000] FSR 363

N produced a film called *Joy*. It showed a man dancing to music. Use of the editing technique known as 'jump cutting' made it appear that the man was making sudden changes of position not possible as successive movements in reality. An issue in the case was whether the film was a recording of a dramatic work. Rattee J held not, in the following passage later approved by the Court of Appeal:

> 'Joy, unlike some films, is not a recording of a dramatic work, because, as a result of the drastic editing process adopted by Mr Norowzian, it is not a recording of anything that was, or could be, performed or danced by anyone...It may well be, in the case of Joy, that the original unedited film of the actor's performance, what I believe are called "the rushes", was a recording of a dramatic work, but Mr Norowzian's claim is not in respect of copyright in them or their subject matter. His claim is in respect of the finished film.' ([1999] FSR at pp 87–88, approved [2000] FSR at p 367).[45]

Discussion point For answer guidance visit www.oxfordtextbooks.co.uk/orc/macqueen2e/

How exact or good must a recording be to confer copyright on unscripted speech (such as a lecture), drama or music? Do a student's non-verbatim lecture notes make the lecturer's extempore words protectable? Or a bootlegger's poor-quality and unauthorised recording of a live 'jamming' session by a musician?

2.33 There is no explicit requirement of fixation in the 1988 Act with regard to artistic works, but it seems clear from the definitions within the category (see further below paras 2.69–2.86) that copyright will not exist until the work is recorded in either tangible or visible form. Similarly

---

[42] For example, the Regulation of Investigatory Powers Act 2000 or breach of confidence.
[43] CDPA 1988, s 3(3).
[44] See for further discussion HL MacQueen, ' "My tongue is mine ain": copyright, the spoken word and privacy' (2005) 68 MLR 349.
[45] See further on the *Norowzian* case, A Barron, 'The legal properties of film' (2004) 67 MLR 177.

films and sound recordings must both be 'recordings' on some medium from which sounds or moving images, as the case may be, can be reproduced.[46] Broadcasts, however, are electronic transmissions of visual images, sounds or other information which need only be visible and/or audible to their intended audience.

 Question 1

What is the significance of having an explicit fixation requirement for literary, dramatic and musical works, but not for the other categories of copyright works?

Question 2

Is it possible to have copyright works which have not been 'fixed' in the sense just discussed?

Originality

2.34   Another important test of whether or not a work protected by copyright has been created is the requirement of originality. The 1988 Act says that to have copyright, literary, dramatic, musical and artistic works must all be original.[47] There is no express requirement of originality as such in relation to films, sound recordings, broadcasts, and typographical arrangements of published editions,[48] but copyright does not subsist in a sound recording or film or typographical arrangement of a published edition which is, or to the extent that it is, respectively, a copy taken from a previous sound recording or film, or reproduces the typographical arrangement of a previous edition.[49] This certainly also captures at least one aspect of 'originality' in the context of literary, dramatic, musical and artistic works, namely, that to have copyright they must not be copies of preceding works. The underlying idea is still best expressed in the classic words of Peterson J:

> 'The word "original" does not in this connection mean that the work must be the expression of original or inventive thought. Copyright Acts are not concerned with the originality of ideas, but with the expression of thought. ... The originality which is required relates to the expression of the thought. But the Act does not require that the expression must be in an original or novel form, but that the work must not be copied from another work – that it should originate from the author.'[50]

 Question

Which kinds of work must be 'original' to enjoy copyright protection?

2.35   Originality, in other words, is not a high standard for entry into copyright protection. It imposes no requirement of aesthetic or intellectual quality: even the most mundane of works, rehearsing old ideas and information, has copyright if expressed in the author's own way. This is reinforced by other provisions of the copyright legislation: for example, that certain artistic works are protected 'irrespective of artistic quality', or that tables and compilations are to be

---

[46] CDPA, ss 5A and 5B.   [47] CDPA 1988, s 1(1)(a).   [48] CDPA 1988, s 1(1)(b).
[49] CDPA 1988, ss 5A(2), 5B(5), 8(2). For broadcasts, see below, para 2.46.
[50] *University of London Press v University Tutorial Press* [1916] 2 Ch 601 at 608.

counted as literary works.[51] Another theme found in discussions of originality is the test of the effort, skill and labour which the author has invested in the work. Where this test is satisfied, there is likely to be a copyright in the result. Finally, there is the point succinctly made by Peterson J himself: 'What is worth copying is worth protecting'.[52] This is not in itself a test of the originality of the work that has been copied, but if someone has copied another's work, that tends to suggest the value of the latter and its possible need for copyright protection to ensure that the return goes to its author.

 Question

What are the main elements of originality for copyright purposes?

2.36   All these themes require some qualification, however. While what is worth copying is worth protecting, it is not always clear that copyright is the appropriate form of protection. With regard to ideas, 'as the late Professor Joad used to observe, it all depends on what you mean by ideas'.[53] Although copyright may not specify intellectual or aesthetic qualities as essential for its protection, nonetheless works must fall into the designated categories under the legislation, the identification of which may involve assessment of just such qualities. Similarly, the mere expenditure of effort, skill and labour may not be sufficient to give rise to copyright if the end result is not a work within the statutory categories. The appropriate conclusion seems to be that originality is not definable in terms of a single, simple test but should rather be considered as a combination of factors, the relative importance of which may vary according to the nature of the case.[54]

■ *Estate of Willem Endstra v New Amsterdam,* May 30, 2008 (HR (NL))[55]

In this case the Netherlands Supreme Court considered whether recorded interviews between police officers and a witness were sufficiently original to qualify as copyright works. It was alleged that the asserted copyright was infringed when transcripts of the interview were published in a book after the witness was murdered. The case was brought by the heirs to the estate of the deceased witness. The Supreme Court held that originality required two separate things, namely (a) a work had to have its own character; and (b) bear the stamp of the author. The first requirement meant that a work should not be derived from another work. The second meant that the work must have come from a creative human effort with creative choices, being a product of the human mind. This should be judged with reference to the work itself, rather than the intentions of the author. The court also noted that the work does not need to have the character of an intended coherent creation, thus covering accidental photographs or subconscious scribbles on a pad of paper.

---

[51] CDPA 1988, ss 3(1)(a) and 4(1)(a).   [52] *University of London Press*, above n 49, at p 610.

[53] Lord Hailsham in *LB Plastics* at p 629. Professor Cyril Joad (1891–1953) was a professor of philosophy at Birkbeck College London, who became famous through appearances on a BBC show, *The Brains Trust*, and the catch-phrase with which he prefaced the answer to any question, 'Well, it depends what you mean by ....' This is also quite a useful phrase for a lawyer's conversational armoury.

[54] For a discussion of the standards of originality for copyright protection, and whether all protected works have elements in common or are different in nature, see A Waisman, 'Revisiting originality' [2009] EIPR 370.

[55] See [2008] EIPR N73–74.

? Question

How would a UK court have decided this case?

No requirement of quality or merit

2.37 It is easy to misunderstand the absence of any requirement that a work possess intellectual or aesthetic merit. What is clear is that, in determining whether or not a work has copyright, the court is not called upon to judge the work on standards of good or bad in its field. This would be much too subjective to be acceptable. On the other hand, the court must decide whether a work falls into one or other of the categories found in the copyright legislation, and this is bound to involve some effort to judge what objective qualities constitute a work of this kind.

■ *George Hensher Ltd v Restawile Upholstery (Lancashire) Ltd* [1976] AC 64

An example is the difficulty in which the House of Lords found itself in this case where it had to determine whether a rough prototype for a suite of furniture was a work of artistic craftsman-ship (see further below paras 2.83–2.85). This required an understanding of how such a work might be identified – how to distinguish it from a sculpture, for example – which called for some sort of aesthetic judgement. It was held that the prototype was not a work of artistic craftsmanship.

■ *Green v Broadcasting Corp of New Zealand* [1989] 2 All ER 1056 (PC)

Similarly in this case (see further para 2.66 below) the Privy Council had to grapple with the question of whether a few catch phrases used constantly by the host of a television talent show ('Opportunity Knocks') constituted a dramatic work. The phrases included: 'For [*competitor's name*], opportunity knocks!'; 'This is your show, folks, and I do mean you'; and 'Make up your mind time'. The show also used a device called the 'clapometer' to measure the levels of applause attracted by each act. It was held that this did not amount to a dramatic work.

2.38 In both these cases, the works in question were excluded from copyright, not on the grounds of lack of merit, but on the grounds that they lacked the intellectual qualities of the categories under which copyright was claimed. Similarly, the use of unimaginative titles –'The Lawyer's Diary' for a diary for lawyers, for example – or of commonplace phrases in advertising will not give rise to copyright in those collections of words.[56] Here there is some overlap with the require-ment that effort, skill and labour should be employed by the author to gain copyright: is the work one which needed such qualities to be brought into existence?

Effort, skill and labour

2.39 The expenditure of independent effort, skill and labour by the author is often seen as the essence of originality in the field of copyright. It has been much stressed in justifying the copy-right which may be held in a compilation, particularly where it is of information or material which was available before the publication of the work. It is the skill and labour of the compiler

---

[56] *Rose v Information Services Ltd* [1987] FSR 254; *Kirk v J & R Fleming* [1928–35] MCC 44; *Sinanide v La Maison Kosmeo* (1928) 139 LT 365.

in arranging the material which receives protection.[57] If this has occurred, it is unlikely that the resulting work will be merely derivative. In *Cramp v Smythson*,[58] on the other hand, it was held that tables and information printed on part of a pocket diary had no copyright because their selection and arrangement had not required the exercise of any judgement or taste by the compiler. Behind all this lies the idea that simple copying does not involve the requisite degree of activity to justify the award of copyright. This is so even though copying may require at least effort and labour, and often skill as well, as Lord Oliver pointed out in *Interlego AG v Tyco Industries Inc*:

> 'Take the simplest case of artistic copyright, a painting or a photograph. It takes great skill, judgment and labour to produce a good copy by painting or to produce an enlarged photograph from a positive print, but no one would reasonably contend that the copy painting or enlargement was an "original" artistic work in which the copier is entitled to claim copyright. Skill, labour or judgment merely in the process of copying cannot confer originality ... A well-executed tracing is the result of much labour and skill but remains what it is, a tracing.'[59]

 Question

Why are effort, skill and labour not *necessarily* enough for originality?

2.40 In the *Interlego* case the subject of the copyright claim was the design of Lego bricks which included modifications of some technical importance in relation to earlier designs but where the visual impression was much the same. Skill and labour had been expended on the technical changes but these did not change the artistic or visual character of the drawings. Accordingly the later drawings were not original. Another case in which it was accepted that much effort, skill, labour and investment of money had gone into the creation of the work in question, yet its author was not entitled to a copyright, is *Exxon Corporation v Exxon Insurance*.[60] The claim was to literary copyright in the single word 'Exxon'. Here the failure was to achieve a literary work,[61] rather than originality as such, but the point to be stressed in the context of the present discussion is that *effort, skill and labour by itself is not necessarily enough for the result to have copyright*. It would seem that, while the presence of effort, skill and labour will often be very important, it should not be adopted as a universal test of originality, and that it is also necessary to consider exactly what type of skill and labour has been involved in relation to the nature of the copyright claimed.[62]

Derivative works

2.41 The concept of originality may be further qualified by considering the many examples of works (*derivative works*) drawing on, even copying from, other works, which nonetheless can have their own copyright. The obvious examples in the material already discussed in this section are compilations and anthologies. Other straightforward instances in the literary world would be books and articles quoting or summarising source material, as for example in a legal textbook.

---

[57] Macmillan & Co Ltd v K & J Cooper (1923) 93 LJPC 113.
[58] [1944] AC 329. Compare the decision of the US Supreme Court in *Feist Publications Inc v Rural Telephone Service Co Inc* 499 US 340 (1991), where it was held that there was no copyright in a telephone directory organised by alphabetical listing of surnames. But see further below, paras 7.24–31. [59] [1989] AC at 262–3.
[60] [1982] Ch 119 (CA). [61] See further below, para 2.51 ff.
[62] *Interlego AG v Tyco Industries Inc* [1989] AC 217 at 262.

Originality is not simply a matter of not copying, therefore. In all the examples given, it is clear that while the author is copying, he is also exercising independent skill and labour, both in the selection of sources and quotations, and in the choice of words in which to express the material, so that the work is not entirely derivative. Less straightforward may be the cases where a new edition of a text is published. If a new copyright is to be created, the alterations to the text must be extensive and substantial. If a text is printed unaltered from a previous edition and the editorial matter consists of annotations or appendices, then again, so long as these have independent value, there will be a new copyright, independent of that of the text, if any.[63]

■ *Black v Murray* (1870) 9 M 341

B had published an edition of the poetry of Sir Walter Scott which had gone out of copyright. B published a second edition of the texts together with amendments, alterations and editorial notes. M published what purported to be a reprint of B's first edition, but which included material taken from the second edition as well. It was held that the changes made in B's second edition had their own copyright, but that M's takings were substantial, and infringed copyright, only in relation to the editorial notes.

2.42   Translations, adaptations and dramatisations will attract their own copyright, even though manifestly derivative, as do arrangements, orchestrations and transcriptions of musical works.[64] In the computer world, many programs are developed from existing ones, either by the creators themselves or by competitors engaging in 'reverse engineering', but it seems to be accepted that even when the end result is very close to the original work a new copyright has come into existence.

■ *Walter v Lane* [1900] AC 539

The House of Lords allowed *The Times* newspaper copyright in its reporter's verbatim transcript of a speech by Lord Rosebery, a leading politician of the day. Clearly the reporter's work was derivative, but its creation had involved the expenditure of individual skill and effort. Since the case was decided before originality became a statutory requirement, it has been questioned whether the copyright would be accepted now, as otherwise an audio typist would acquire rights in dictated material.[65] However, the current judicial view appears to favour the reporter's copyright established in *Walter v Lane*.[66]

    Question

Is there a relevant difference between a typist taking dictation or typing from material recorded on a dictaphone, on the one hand, and a transcriber such as the journalist in *Walter v Lane*?

---

[63]   *Black v Murray* (1870) 9 M 341 (editorial material in the works of Sir Walter Scott).

[64]   See also Berne Convention, Art 2(3): 'Translations, adaptations, arrangements of music and other alterations of a literary or artistic work shall be protected as original works without prejudice to the copyright in the original work.' And see the UNESCO Nairobi Recommendation: the Translator's Charter (1994), accessible at http://www.fit-ift.org/download/referencebil.pdf.   [65]   *Roberton v Lewis* [1976] RPC 169 per Cross J at pp 174–5.

[66]   See *Express Newspapers plc v News (UK) Ltd* [1990] FSR 359 per Sir Nicolas Browne-Wilkinson V-C at pp 365–6, preferring the views expressed in *Sands McDougall Pty Ltd v Robinson* (1917) 23 CLR 49 to those of Cross J. See further MacQueen, (2005) 68 MLR 349, at pp 369–73.

■ *Eisenman v Qimron* (2000) 54(3) PD 817; [2001] ECDR 6 (Supreme Court of Israel)

Q deciphered and put together a text from 67 fragments of an ancient Dead Sea scroll known as 4QMMT. Publication was planned but not yet accomplished when S published in the archaeology journal he edited a copy of the text as edited by Q. S had been critical of the long delays in publishing the Dead Sea scrolls, and this publication formed part of his campaign. Q sued for infringement of his copyright. The defendant contended that Q's editorial labours amounted to no more than an attempt to reproduce as faithfully as possible what had been originated by the scribe who wrote 4QMMT, and therefore lacked the originality required for copyright. It was held that Q's work had copyright and that S had infringed. Q's work was original in the sense that he 'used his knowledge, expertise and imagination, exercised judgement and chose between different alternatives'.[67]

■ *Sawkins v Hyperion Records Ltd* [2005] RPC 32 (CA)

S edited the work of a late 17th/early 18th-centuries composer, L. The editing involved the insertion of notes missing or inaccurately recorded in L's original scores, the addition or correction of flourishes and other performing indications, and the supply of figuring which, in relation to the bass line of baroque works, was the foundation of the work. The expert evidence was that without this last the works could not have been performed in a modern recording session using the original sources. HR produced CDs of the music using S's editions but without a licence. It was held that HR had infringed S's copyright in the work. S's work was original, involving skill and labour over a considerable period of time, going beyond mere transcription.

Discussion point   For answer guidance visit www.oxfordtextbooks.co.uk/orc/macqueen2e/

Consider whether *Walter v Lane*, *Interlego v Tyco* and *Sawkins v Hyperion Records* are correctly decided on the originality point. See further J Pila, 'An intentional view of the copyright work' (2008) 71 MLR 535 and NP Gravells, 'Authorship and originality: the persistent influence of Walter v Lane' [2007] IPQ 267.

2.43   In the *Interlego* case, Lord Oliver recognised that a derivative artistic work might be original where there was '*some element of material alteration or embellishment*' in it by comparison with the previous work.[68]

■ *Baumann v Fussell* [1978] RPC 485 (CA)

A photograph of two cocks fighting each other was used as the basis of a painting. The composition of the subject matter was followed closely but the painter employed different colouring to heighten the dramatic effect of the representation. It was held that there was no infringement. It seems likely, therefore, that the painting would have been held to be original and so qualified for its own copyright.

---

[67] For an English translation of the judgments in this case and discussion of its content, see TH Lim, HL MacQueen and CM Carmichael (eds), *On Scrolls, Artefacts and Intellectual Property* (2001). The extensive discussion of this case is critically reviewed in HL MacQueen, 'The legal definition of authorship and the scrolls', in JJ Collins and TH Lim (eds), *Oxford Handbook of the Dead Sea Scrolls* (2010).   [68] [1989] AC 217 at p 263.

Contrast the New York case of:

■ *Bridgeman Art Library Ltd v Corel Corp* 25 Fed Supp 421 (1999)

Kaplan J found that he was obliged to apply UK law in a case where the question was whether photographs of public domain works of art were the subject of copyright so that their unauthorised digitisation and inclusion in the defendants' CD-ROMs was infringement. It was held that, since the photographs aspired to create as accurate as possible a copy of the subject of the photograph, their work lacked originality under UK law and could not be protected.

 Discussion point   For answer guidance visit www.oxfordtextbooks.co.uk/orc/macqueen2e/

Is this decision a correct application of the concept of originality? Compare with *Eisenman v Qimron*, described above (para 2.42). See further K Garnett 'Copyright in photographs'[2000] EIPR 229; R Deazley, 'Photographing paintings in the public domain: a response to Garnett' [2001] EIPR 229; S Stokes, 'Photographing paintings in the public domain: a response to Garnett' [2001] EIPR 354; and R Arnold, 'Copyright in photographs: a case for reform' [2005] EIPR 303.

Consider further:

■ *Antiquesportfolio.com plc v Rodney Fitch & Co Ltd* [2001] FSR 345

It was held that a photograph of a single static item was an original artistic work, because it could be said that the positioning of the object, the angle at which it was taken, the lighting and the focus were all matters of personal judgement, albeit in many cases at a very basic level.

 Discussion point   For answer guidance visit www.oxfordtextbooks.co.uk/orc/macqueen2e/

Do the auto-focus, portrait, landscape and action shot functions in a digital camera mean that there is insufficient input from the user of the camera to make his or her photographs with the camera original for copyright purposes?

Independent but similar works

2.44   As indicated by the dictum of Peterson J quoted at the outset of this section (above, para 2.34), 'the Act does not require that the expression must be in an original or novel form, but that the work must not be copied from another work'.[69] Thus, if two works are similar, it does not follow that one cannot be original in the sense of copyright law. Unless there is derivation of one from another, a link between them beyond the similarity, the question cannot arise. The point is perhaps most significant in the field of artistic works, particularly paintings and photographs, where certain subjects and themes (for example, representations of well-known

---

[69]   *University of London Press v University Tutorial Press* [1916] 2 Ch 601 at 608.

scenes, landmarks and buildings) are or become well-worn. Probably there is often some indirect derivation – influence may be a better word – in relation to earlier works in such cases, but it may well be difficult if not impossible to establish the absolute originality of a particular view, even in the limited copyright sense of the originator as the person who first gave expression to it.

 Question

List again all the elements to be considered in dealing with issues about originality. Which do you consider the most significant?

Key points on originality

- Literary, dramatic, musical and artistic works must be *'original'* to attract copyright
- Originality is not a high standard, or a requirement of quality/merit/creativity/ novelty
- Although individual facts and circumstances are always significant, the following factors are often cumulatively of use in assessing originality:– work not copied– work is product of author's own effort, skill and labour
- But derivative works may nevertheless be original

Originality in sound recordings, films, published editions

2.45   With regard to sound recordings, films, and the typographical arrangements of published editions, there is no express requirement of originality; but no copyright arises in such a work to the extent that it reproduces another work in the same category. This is regardless of whether or not the earlier work had, or is still in, copyright. Thus a photographic reprint of an out-of-copyright book does not preclude others from making another edition of the same work using the same technique, although any additional editorial matter in the first work would have its own copyright in accordance with *Black v Murray*.[70] The matter is becoming ever more important in the film and recording industries, where digital technology has made it possible to re-record old material with greatly enhanced quality of sound and visual reproduction, with the possibility of embellishments such as colorisation of black-and-white films, or the stripping out of production effects in the original which are no longer wanted.[71] Although such re-recordings are derivative works, it may well be that the further technological input will be enough to mean that the new version is not merely a copy of the old but gains a new copyright.

---

[70] (1870) 9 M 341 (discussed above, para 2.41).
[71] See for examples the colorisation of John Huston's film, *The Maltese Falcon* and, more recently, the removal from a 2003 re-release of The Beatles' final album, *Let It Be*, of effects added in the original by the producer Phil Spector.

Exercise

Through use of a 'sampler', a digital recorder converts small samples of sound from other records into digits and stores them in microchips. These samples are then capable of electronic manipulation – for example, by slowing down or speeding up – and the results are then mixed to produce a new record. In effect, it is equivalent to a compilation of extracts from previous records. Quite apart from the question of the extent to which such activities infringe the copyrights in the original recordings, is the collection of samples itself a subject of copyright? (See further LC Bently, 'Sampling and copyright: is the law on the right track?' [1989] JBL 113 and 405.)

Broadcasts

2.46   The position of broadcasts with regard to requirements of originality is different from that of sound recordings, films and typographical arrangements. The 1988 Act provides that copyright does not subsist in a broadcast which infringes, or to the extent that it infringes, the copyright in another broadcast.[72] The background to this is that merely broadcasting a programme which has already been put out has the effect of creating a new copyright. This is clear from the provisions of what is now s 14(5) of the 1988 Act, which states that 'copyright in a repeat broadcast expires at the same time as the copyright in the original broadcast'. As the sub-section goes on to say, however, 'accordingly no copyright arises in respect of a repeat broadcast which is broadcast after the expiry of the copyright in the original broadcast'. It is also clear from this that only unauthorised repeats infringe the original copyright and are therefore unable to claim copyright themselves. This seems obvious, but it makes an important contrast with the forms of work discussed in the previous paragraph (above para 2.45), where no copy, authorised or unauthorised, can bring a new copyright into existence.

Author works and media works

2.47   For convenience, in the remainder of this chapter, literary, dramatic, musical and artistic works and films will be collectively referred to as *'author works'*, and the other categories will be grouped as *'media works'*. The distinction has already been discussed in so far as it can be derived from the international structure of copyright (see above, para 2.16): the Berne Convention for literary and artistic productions, broadly conceived (see above, para 2.8), and the Rome Convention for sound recordings and broadcasts (see above, para 2.10). The distinction rests on a number of points, of which the most important conceptually is the idea that the second group relies essentially on the operation of machinery and technology where the first depends upon one or more individuals as creator. The nature of authorship, as understood in the law of copyright, is dealt with further below (para 3.4–3.30). Another element may be that in author works *content* is protected, whereas with media works it is the *medium* itself, or the *signal*, that is protected rather than the material embodied within it. So a song or music have author copyright, while the sound recording and broadcast containing them are purely media ones. Note also that the distinction has some difficulties in dealing with photographs and films, although in the law

---

[72] CDPA 1988, s 6(6).

and in this book both are included in the author rather than the media work category. The point here is that anyone can get a result by wielding a camera, but does that make the person an author with protection for the content of the result?[73]

2.48   The distinction between author and media works has practical consequences in differences in the rules applying to the two groups. The first owner of the copyright in an author work is generally the author,[74] whereas in the media work it is the person by whose investment (to be conceived more widely than the kind of investment that is authorship or composition) the work was produced. Only author works need be original to be protected,[75] meaning that they must be independent forms of expression achieved through their author's judgement, skill and labour.[76] Author works alone attract moral rights.[77] Author work copyright lasts significantly longer than media work copyright: with the former, it normally lasts for the lifetime of the author plus 70 years, while for sound recordings and broadcasts it is 50 years from making, release or transmission, as the case may be.[78]

Key points on author and media works

- The distinction between *author* and *media* work, resting in principle on the degree of individual as opposed to technological creativity involved
- The difference in rules applying to each of the groups, explained in detail below
- The borderline nature of photographs and films in this distinction

---

Author works

2.49   The following are the categories of author work:

- literary
- dramatic
- musical
- artistic
- films

The distinctions between these groups of author works are not without importance, but in a number of recent cases the English courts have held that a work may belong to more than one of the categories. So for example circuit diagrams have been held to be both literary and artistic

---

[73] See for interesting discussion of this point R Arnold, 'Copyright in photographs: a case for reform' [2005] EIPR 303.

[74] In the case of films in the UK, joint authorship is attributed to the principal director and the producer (CDPA1988, s 9(2)(ab)). Note also (1) the British concept of a computer-generated work where there is no human author (CDPA 1988, ss 9(3), 178); and (2) that copyright in a work produced in the course of employment falls to the employer unless otherwise agreed (CDPA 1988, s 11(2)). Employment should be distinguished from a commission, where the copyright would remain with the author unless otherwise agreed.

[75] But note that there is no express requirement that a film be original (see CDPA 1988, s 1(1)(b), and above para 2.45).

[76] See further above, paras 2.34–43.

[77] Apart from computer programs (CDPA 1988, s 79(2)(a)); see further below para 3.38.

[78] See further below, para 3.49 ff, for copyright terms.

works,[79] while a film has been held to be also a dramatic work.[80] As Laddie J has pointed out, this is a different point from the one made earlier in this chapter (above para 2.23), that one product may embody several copyrights:

> '[A]lthough different copyrights can protect simultaneously a particular product and an author can produce more than one copyright work during the course of a single episode of creative effort, for example a competent musician may write the words and the music for a song at the same time, it is quite another thing to say that a single piece of work by an author gives rise to two or more copyrights in respect of the same creative effort. In some cases the borderline between one category of copyright work and another may be difficult to define, but that does not justify giving to the author protection in both categories. The categories of copyright work are, to some extent, arbitrarily defined. In the case of a borderline work, I think there are compelling arguments that the author must be confined to one or other of the possible categories. The proper category is that which most nearly suits the characteristics of the work in issue'.[81]

 Exercise

Explain clearly the difference between copyright in a work and the several copyrights which may co-exist in a product such as a CD. Why does this distinction matter? Consider in particular the multimedia product (eg the Encarta encyclopaedia, computer game), which consists of digitised material combining audio, video, text and images still and moving played through a computer, and with which the user may interact.

2.50   From a taxonomic point of view there must be much to be said for the approach of Laddie J; what after all is the point of having categories if they are not mutually exclusive? And if they are not mutually exclusive, or fail to capture particular types of work adequately, should the categorisation not be abandoned or re-thought? The principle of Occam's razor might usefully be applied:[82] categories are not to be multiplied unnecessarily in copyright law, and perhaps the present UK statute is guilty of that offence (see further on this theme para 7.19 below).[83]

Literary works

2.51   The 1988 Act defines 'literary work' as follows:

> 'any work other than a dramatic or musical work which is written, spoken or sung, and accordingly includes a table or compilation other than a database, a computer program, preparatory design material for a computer program, and a database (s 3(1))'.

This statutory definition is not exhaustive and there are a number of cases in which the courts have had to give an opinion one way or the other as a matter of impression. Standard examples of literary works protected by copyright would include novels, short stories, poetry, song-lyrics,

---

[79] *Anacon Corp Ltd v Environmental Research Technology Ltd* [1994] FSR 659; *Electronic Techniques (Anglia) Ltd v Critchley Components Ltd* [1997] FSR 401; *Sandman v Panasonic UK Ltd* [1998] FSR 651.

[80] *Norowzian v Arks Ltd (No 2)* [2000] FSR 363.

[81] *Electronic Techniques (Anglia) Ltd v Critchley Components Ltd* [1997] FSR 401 at 413.

[82] For Occam's razor see http://en.wikipedia.org/wiki/Occam's_Razor

[83] See further A Christie, 'A proposal for simplifying UK copyright law' [2001] EIPR 26; I Stamatoudi, *Copyright and Multimedia Works: A Comparative Analysis* (2002); T Aplin, *Copyright Law in the Digital Society* (2005), Ch 6; B Bandey, 'Over-categorisation in copyright law: computer and internet programming perspectives' [2007] EIPR 461.

nonfiction books, and periodical articles. But, as already noted in the discussion of originality (above, para 2.34), the law does not require works to possess, or even to aspire to possess, aesthetic merit before they can be the subject of copyright as literary works. Trade catalogues,[84] examination papers,[85] a grid containing 25 letters and two separate rows of five letters each,[86] and the critical apparatus or annotations attached to an edition of another work[87] may all be literary works. Moreover, while the work must have some meaning,[88] it is not necessary for it to be expressed in a conventional way, so that a work written in shorthand or in code may be a literary work.[89] A knitting guide consisting of 'various words and numerals…which constitute detailed instructions intelligible to anyone who understands the production of knitwear'[90] would presumably be a literary work.

Single words and phrases

2.52   On the other hand, the courts usually have great difficulty in according copyright to single words and phrases as literary works.

■ *Exxon Corporation v Exxon Insurance Consultants* [1982] Ch 119

Copyright was claimed in the invented single word 'Exxon', which had been developed as a new company name with great expenditure of time and money by the company in question. The court held that a literary work must be 'intended to afford either information and instruction or pleasure in the form of literary enjoyment',[91] and that this could not be the case with a single word, even though research and effort had been involved in its creation.

Similarly it has been said that in general the title of a work by itself does not have copyright,[92] while advertising slogans consisting of stock phrases or a few commonplace sentences have also been denied copyright as literary works.[93] It has been held in a number of cases that there is no copyright in the names of computer program commands, since they are merely 'triggers' for a set of instructions to be given effect by the computer.[94] The same might seem to follow with regard to words and phrases used as hypertext links on websites.

2.53   But there are occasional departures from the generally negative view of short works of this kind.[95] The *Infopaq* case accepted the possibility that isolated sentences, or even parts of sentences, might be intellectual creations, for example (above, para 2.25).

■ *Shetland Times v Wills* [1997] FSR 604

The *Shetland Times* home page used its newspaper headlines as links to the material deeper within the site. The headline texts were used by *The Shetland News* website to act as the deep

---

[84] *Harpers v Barry Henry & Co* (1892) 20 R 133.

[85] *University of London Press v University Tutorial Press* [1916] 2 Ch 601.

[86] *Express Newspapers plc v Liverpool Daily Post & Echo plc* [1985] FSR 306.

[87] *Black v Murray* (1870) 9 M 341.   [88] *Fournet v Pearson* (1897) 14 TLR 82.

[89] *Pitman v Hine* (1884) 1 TLR 82; *Anderson & Co v Lieber Code Co* [1917] 2 KB 469.

[90] *Brigid Foley Ltd v Ellott* [1982] RPC 433 at 434 per Sir Robert Megarry V-C.

[91] Phrasing derived from *Hollinrake v Truswell* [1894] 3 Ch 420.

[92] *Francis Day & Hunter Ltd v Twentieth Century Fox Corp Ltd* [1940] AC 112 (PC) per Lord Wright at p 123; *Rose v Information Services Ltd* [1987] FSR 254; cf *Dicks v Yates* (1881) 18 ChD 76 per Jessel MR at p 89.

[93] *Kirk v J & R Fleming* [1928–35] MCC 44; *Sinanide v La Maison Kosmeo* (1928) 139 LT 365 (CA).

[94] *Powerflex Services Pty Ltd v Data Access Corporation* (1996) 137 ALR 498 (Fed Ct Aus); aff'd (1999) 202 CLR 1 (HCA); *Navitaire Inc v EasyJet Airline Co Ltd* [2006] RPC 3 (Pumfrey J).

[95] See also P Sumpter, 'Copyright in slogans: another bald spot exposed' [2009] EIPR 287.

links on to the relative *Times* stories. But, in a prima facie view granting interim interdict, Lord Hamilton held that the headline texts had copyright, so that the actions of the *News* in copying them for reproduction on its own website was infringement. In defence of Lord Hamilton's view, the creation of a headline does involve skill and labour, in that the reader's attention has to be attracted, information about the relevant item conveyed, and (at least in the case of the tabloid press, which much favours punning and jokey headlines) entertainment provided.

The protection of such works, if any, must be very 'thin', however, given the necessarily limited scope of the genre,[96] and it is certainly unlikely to extend to the typical bald hypertext link. More difficult might be the question of slightly more elaborate texts, such as notes on what will be found through using a link, or material on help menus, 'frequently asked questions' facilities, and the like.

 Question

What is needed for there to be a literary work?

Computer programs as literary works[97]

2.54   The 1988 Act states that a computer program and its preparatory design material are literary works.[98] The Act does not otherwise define the meaning of computer program. Jacob LJ has pointed out that the Software Directive implemented by the 1988 Act envisages one rather than two separate copyrights in the program *and* its preparatory material.[99] In general a computer program is a set of instructions to a computer to perform certain tasks. The production of a program is a complex process involving first the expression of an analysis of the functions to be performed as a set of algorithms (often most simply represented by means of a flowchart or some other logical flow diagram); second its restatement (usually by a programmer, but also often by a computer) in a computer language (the source code); and finally the translation by a computer running under a compiler program of the source code into a machine-readable language (the object code). The 'preparatory design material for a computer program' mentioned in the 1988 Act as a literary work must be such that a computer program can result from it at some stage.[100] Such matter as the logic, algorithms and programming languages lying behind the source code may well comprise unprotectable ideas and principles.[101] Source code is clearly protectable as part of the computer program.[102] The lack of a definition of a computer program is to avoid failure to cover advances in the technology; arguments that object code is incapable of copyright protection are no longer

---

[96] Ie, not very much variation from the first work would be required to evade a charge of infringement.

[97] See generally S Lai, *The Copyright Protection of Computer Software in the UK* (2000); S Gordon, 'The very idea! Why copyright law is an inappropriate way to protect computer programs' [1998] EIPR 10.

[98] CDPA 1988, s 3(1)(b). Note also the possibility of software patents, discussed below, para 11.33 ff.

[99] *Nova Productions Ltd v Mazooma Games Ltd* [2007] RPC 25 (CA), para 28.

[100] CDPA 1988, s 3(1)(c). See for an example *Nova Productions Ltd v Mazooma Games Ltd* [2007] RPC 25 (CA).

[101] Software Directive 1991, recitals 7, 13, 14 and 15; see *Navitaire Inc v EasyJet Airline Co Ltd* [2006] RPC 3 (Pumfrey J), for an example of denial of copyright to programming languages comprised by defined user command interfaces (despite its ad hoc character) and a collection of commands.

[102] *Ibcos Computers v Barclays Mercantile Highland Finance* [1994] FSR 275.

sustainable.[103] It has been held in Australia that a 'hardware lock' enabling a computer program to run is itself a computer program,[104] while in the USA codes embedded in microchips within the computer have also been found to be copyrightable subject matter.[105] A video game simulating a game of pool has been held to be a computer program in the UK.[106]

Question

What is the difference between source code and object code? Are they both protected by copyright?

Tables and compilations

2.55 Tables and compilations may be literary works. Thus import and export lists,[107] railway timetables,[108] television programme schedules,[109] and football fixture lists[110] have been held to be literary works, as have poetry anthologies[111] and football pools coupons.[112] Character-based screen displays used for online booking of tickets on a 'ticketless' airline, providing a static framework within which the dynamic data supplied by customers caused the booking software to operate, were also held to be copyright tables, but in the same case a collection of computer programs was held not to be a compilation since there was no overall design underlying the collection, simply an accretion of material over time.[113] The component parts of a compilation may be out of copyright, but the compilation will still enjoy copyright as such.[114] But such material has always to be subjected to the test of originality before copyright can be claimed and its construction must be shown to be the product of some skill and labour by the author.[115]

Question

What is it that copyright protects in relation to tables and compilations?

Databases[116]

2.56 Until 1 January 1998, databases were thought to be protected under UK law as 'compilations'; but from that date the position was changed as a result of the implementation of the EU's

---

[103] This argument succeeded in the Australian case of *Apple Computer Inc v Computer Edge Pty Ltd* [1986] FSR 537. In New Zealand the object code achieved copyright as a translation of the source code: *IBM Corp v Computer Imports Ltd* [1989] 2 NZLR 395.

[104] *Autodesk Inc v Dyason and Kelly* [1992] RPC 575 (HCA); criticised in *Cantor Fitzgerald v Tradition UK* [2000] RPC 95.

[105] *NEC Corp v Intel Corp* 835 F 2d 1546 (1988). See also recital 7 of the Software Directive 1991.

[106] *Nova Productions Ltd v Mazooma Games Ltd* [2006] RPC 14 (Kitchin J) affd [2007] RPC 25 (CA).

[107] *Walford v Johnston* (1846) 20 D 1160; *Maclean v Moody* (1858) 20D 1154.

[108] *Leslie v Young* (1894) 21 R (HL) 57.

[109] *Independent Television Publications Ltd v Time Out Ltd* [1984] FSR 64. For the Australian approach, see [2009] EIPR N63.

[110] *Football League v Littlewoods Pools* [1959] Ch 637.

[111] *Macmillan v Suresh Chunder Deb* (1890) ILR 17 Calc 951.

[112] *Ladbroke (Football) Ltd v William Hill (Football) Ltd* [1964] 1 WLR 273 (HL).

[113] *Navitaire Inc v EasyJet Airline Co Ltd* [2006] RPC 3 (Pumfrey J).

[114] *Ashmore v Douglas Home* [1987] FSR 553.   [115] See above, paras 2.39–40.

[116] See generally E Derclaye, *The Legal Protection of Databases* (2008); T Aplin, *Copyright Law in the Digital Society: the Challenges of Multimedia* (2005), pp 41–73.

Database Directive 1996.[117] 'Compilation' now expressly does not include databases.[118] Databases are defined as:

> 'collections of independent works, data or other materials arranged in a systematic or methodical way and individually accessible by electronic or other means (1988 Act, s 3A)'.

This definition means that, unlike traditional compilations, database protection is not confined to collections the basic form of which is written, as distinct from other forms of expression (eg graphic). Databases include:

> 'literary, artistic, musical or other collections of works or collections of other materials such as texts, sounds, images, numbers, facts, and data' (Database Directive 1996, recital 17).

That is, they can be *multimedia works*. So the elements of a database may be works in their own right, or simply items of information in textual, visual or audio form. Many websites are database-driven, for example, particularly where they are inter-active. But databases are not merely electronic compilations or collections; they can also be created in non-electronic media. The Court of Justice has indicated that a broad approach is intended by the Union legislature.[119] The definition is capable of including football fixture lists,[120] telephone directories,[121] trade directories[122] and news websites.[123]

Special requirement of originality

2.57   Not all databases are protected by copyright. There is a special definition of the level of originality that a database must show, introduced as a result of the Database Directive 1996:

> 'if, and only if, by reason of the *selection or arrangement of the contents* of the database the database constitutes the *author's own intellectual creation*' author's emphasis (CDPA 1988, s 3A(2).)

This is generally taken to be a higher level of originality than the traditional 'skill, effort and labour' UK originality test (see above, paras 2.39–40). One result is that many databases which would previously have been protected by copyright in the UK are no longer. For this reason the Database Directive also introduced a special, or *sui generis*, database right for the protection of databases not covered by copyright. An account of this special right is given in paras 6.4–6.20 below. Another consequence of the special definition of originality is to make clear that database copyright covers, not the contents of the database, but their *selection or arrangement* – that is, the way in which the contents are structured. Further, the structure must be the author's *own intellectual creation*, not some standard method. See further para 2.63 below.

 Question

What is protected by the copyright (if any) in a database?

---

[117] Parliament and Council Directive 96/9/EC, Art 3(1), implemented in the UK by the Copyright and Rights in Databases Regulations 1997 (SI 1997/3032).   [118] CDPA 1988, s 3(1)(a).
[119] C-444/02 *Fixtures Marketing Ltd v OPAP* [2004] I-ECR 10549, paras 20–24.
[120] C-444/02 *Fixtures Marketing Ltd v OPAP*, paras 23, 33–36 (ECJ).
[121] *Unauthorised reproduction of telephone directories on CD-Rom* [2002] ECDR 3 (6 May 1999).
[122] *Societe Tigest SARL v Societe Reed Expositions France* [2002] ECC 29 (12 September 2001).
[123] *SA Prline v SA Communication & Sales and Sal News Investment* [2002] ECDR 2 (Trib de Comm); *Danske Dagblades Forening v Newsbooster* [2003] ECDR 5.

Databases and computer programs

2.58 The Database Directive provides that its protection does not apply to computer programs used in the making or operation of databases accessible by electronic means,[124] raising the sometimes difficult question of when and whether an electronically operated database might or might not also be a computer program. In *Navitaire Inc v EasyJet Airline Co Ltd*[125] Pumfrey J held that schemas or material directly entered by the compiler of a database which changed its structure by adding or subtracting fields, or adding or removing datasets, were computer programs rather than databases in their own right. On the other hand, he held with some hesitation that the metadata created by this activity, defining the fields and datasets in the database, fell to be protected, since this related to the structure and arrangement of the data in the database.

 Question

What are the differences between (1) a database and a compilation; (2) a database and a computer program?

2.59 The complex definition of a database protectable by copyright requires further analysis of four specific elements:

(1) independence of the constituent elements
(2) systematic or methodical arrangement of the elements
(3) individual accessibility of the elements
(4) intellectual creation in selection and arrangement of contents

The meaning of each of these elements has been the subject of a ruling of the European Court of Justice in a case referred to it by a Greek court; and guidance is also obtainable from the opinions of the Advocate General on this and other parallel references.[126]

Defining databases: (1) Independence of the constituent elements

2.60 The Advocate General said this means that 'the data or materials must not be linked or must at least be capable of being separate without losing their informative content'.[127] So films as such are not databases, because there *is* interaction between script, music, sound recordings and the moving images.[128] But an entry in a telephone directory can be understood standing alone, and so the directory is a database. Sports fixtures, the subject of the European Court reference, provide more complex examples. Is the information, 'X v Y', an item which can be understood on its own? Is it separate from the date information without which 'X v Y' is probably meaningless? Or is 'X v Y, 1 January 2010' the single item of information which can be understood on its own and which therefore renders the whole collection of such items a potentially copyright database? The European Court held that the materials have to be separable from one another

---

[124] Art 1(3). Computer programs have copyright as such (see above, para 2.54).

[125] [2006] RPC 3 (Pumfrey J).

[126] C-444/02 *Fixtures Marketing Ltd v OPAP*, [2004] I-ECR 10549; C46/02 *Fixtures Marketing Ltd v Oy Veikkaus Ab* [2004] ECR I-10365.

[127] C-444/02 *Fixtures Marketing Ltd v OPAP*, para 39 (AG); C-46/02 *Fixtures Marketing Ltd v Oy Veikkaus Ab*, AG, para 36.

[128] See also Database Directive, recital 17: 'a recording or an audio visual cinematographic, literary or musical work as such does not fall within the scope of this Directive'.

without their informative, literary, artistic, musical or other value being affected. Data relating to sporting activity was not precluded from recognition as a database. The date and time of, and the identity of two teams playing in, both home and away matches were covered by the concept of independent materials with autonomous informative value.[129]

Defining databases: (2) Systematic or methodical arrangement of the elements

2.61   The Advocate General said that the purpose of this requirement is 'to exclude random accumulations of data and ensure that only planned collections of data are covered, that is to say, data organised to specific criteria'.[130] The arrangement required here need not be a physical one,[131] but the European Court stated that the condition implies that the collection should be contained in a fixed base of some kind. Such a base may be technical (eg electronic, electro-magnetic or electro-optical processes), or something else (eg an index, table of contents, or a particular plan or method of classification), to allow retrieval of any independent material contained within it.[132] Thus the arrangement involved is *conceptual*, that is to say, it is about the way in which the contents are presented to and retrievable by the user of the database. Alphabetical, chronological or subject arrangements will be enough (although subject to the requirement of 'intellectual creation', for which see further below, para 2.63).

Defining databases: (3) Individual accessibility of the elements

2.62   This requirement was not clarified in the Advocate General's opinions, despite its ambiguity. Does it mean that the works or items comprising the database must be separately retrievable by the user, and if so, how must that access work? The European Court stated that a means of retrieving each of a database's constituent materials, technical or otherwise (as described in the previous paragraph), was what made it possible to distinguish a protected database from a mere collection.[133]

 Exercise

Take a printed telephone directory or sports fixture list. When you access an item of information therein (eg a person's telephone number you want to call, a match you want to attend), is it 'individually accessible by electronic or other means' simply because you can read it and ignore the rest of what is visible on the printed page? Or is it accessible only alongside the other information on the page, and therefore not individually or separately retrievable? Compare what happens if you search an electronic telephone directory for a particular person, or a fixtures database for the match on a particular date, or for the date your team plays its local 'derby' game on its home ground. Should there be a different result according to whether the information is collected in print or electronic form?

---

[129] Case C-444/02, *Fixtures Marketing Ltd v OPAP* [2004] I-ECR 10549, paras 23, 32–35.
[130] C-444/02 *Fixtures Marketing Ltd v OPAP*, para 40 (AG); C-46/02 *Fixtures Marketing Ltd v Oy Veikkaus Ab*, para 37 (AG).
[131] Database Directive, recital 21.
[132] Case C-444/02, *Fixtures Marketing Ltd v OPAP* [2004] I-ECR 10549, para 30 (ECJ).
[133] Case C-444/02, *Fixtures Marketing Ltd v OPAP* [2004] I-ECR 10549, paras 31–32 (ECJ).

Defining databases: (4) Intellectual creation of selection and arrangement

2.63   Finally, to attract copyright, the database must be the author's own intellectual creation by reason of the selection or arrangement of its contents.[134] The use of the phrase 'intellectual creation' means that the selection and arrangement of the database contents must show more than the traditional skill and labour which make compilations original (see above, paras 2.39–40). The protection is offered to the selection and arrangement of the database, rather than to its contents as such, although the latter may attract copyright – or several copyrights – in their own right. The European Court of Justice held it irrelevant whether the collection is made up of materials from a source or sources other than the person making up the collection, materials created by that person, or a combination of the two.[135] The 'intellectual creation' requirement seems particularly likely to *exclude* some compilations from copyright protection as databases. For example, would an alphabetical ordering, as in the telephone directory, or a chronological one, as in a fixture list, be enough?[136] The Database Directive says that, as a rule (ie normally), the compilation of several recordings of musical performances on a CD does not attract copyright protection as a database.[137]

Key point on absence of intellectual creation

The lack of intellectual creation does not mean that the collection fails to be a database, however. Rather the database does not have copyright; but it may still be protected by sui generis database right, for which see further below, para 6.4–6.20.

? Question

Are the following databases: (a) newspapers; (b) websites; (c) multimedia works? If so, how far is the database covered as such by copyright?

Discussion point   For answer guidance visit www.oxfordtextbooks.co.uk/orc/macqueen2e/

Imagine a compilation which is not a database for legal purposes, ie is not a collection of independent works or items of information, systematically arranged and individually accessible. Would the work you have thus imagined be protectable by copyright?

---

[134] CDPA 1988, s 3A. See also for use of this formulation Council Directive on the legal protection of computer programs 91/250/EEC, Art 1(3); but in the implementation of this Directive the UK did not see fit to use the phrase. See further Ch 7.   [135] Case C-444/02, *Fixtures Marketing Ltd v OPAP* [2004] ECR I-10549, para 25.
[136] See *Van Dale v Romme* [1991] Ned Jur 608, [1994] Ned Jur 58 (Hoge Raad, Netherlands), denying the choice of words in a dictionary (as distinct from the definitions thereof) copyright protection as a database.
[137] Database Directive, recital 19.

Crossing categories: circuit diagrams

2.64   Electronic circuit diagrams have been held to be literary works without excluding the possibility that they also incorporate artistic works.[138] Electronic circuits incorporate a number of interconnected components, such as resistors, transistors and capacitators, and the diagrams show the way in which these components are connected as well as stating in relation to each component the rating or value that that component should have for the circuit to work. The components themselves are shown in the diagrams by way of conventional symbols. The diagrams are not visual representations of the way the circuit is linked up in reality, but are simply 'topological', 'schematic' or 'architectural' indications of the inter-relationship of the components in the completed circuit. Such diagrams may also form part of the information accompanying individual components when sold, in order to indicate the kinds of circuit in which the component in question will give its best performance.[139]

2.65   The question of category is important for this reason. The typical act of alleged infringement is the production of a circuit, and generally this will not look particularly like the original diagram. Although copyright in a two-dimensional artistic work (the diagram) can be infringed by a three-dimensional reproduction (the circuit) (see para 4.26), this will only be so if the latter is visually similar to the former. This is why artistic copyright is not very useful to stop circuits being copied. But the second circuit will incorporate the information shown in the diagram, and may well be based on a 'net list' of all the components and their interconnections in the first circuit, made from that circuit and then fed into a computer to produce the second, allegedly infringing circuit. The production of the second circuit thus potentially involves an infringing indirect copy of the literary elements of the diagram underlying the first circuit.

 Question

To which category of copyright works do electronic circuit diagrams belong?

Dramatic works

2.66   The distinction between literary, dramatic and musical works is not of much practical significance in terms of its consequences for copyright, and this may explain a lack of definition of dramatic works. The 1988 Act defines 'dramatic work' as including a work of dance or mime.[140] It has been said that a dramatic work must be such that 'for its proper representation, acting, and possibly scenery, formed a necessary ingredient'.[141] The Privy Council has stated that a dramatic work must have sufficient unity to be capable of performance, leading to a decision that the stock phrases and other aspects of the format of a television talent show did not constitute a dramatic work in themselves, being merely accessory to the show.[142] On the other hand, where the format of a television show had been worked out in sufficient detail in a written document supported by a feasibility study, the New Zealand courts were prepared to hold that this was a dramatic

---

[138] *Anacon Corp Ltd v Environmental Research Technology Ltd* [1994] FSR 659; *Electronic Techniques (Anglia) Ltd v Critchley Components Ltd* [1997] FSR 401; *Sandman v Panasonic UK Ltd* [1998] FSR 651.

[139] An illustration of an electronic circuit diagram is in *Electronic Techniques (Anglia) Ltd v Critchley Components Ltd* at p 405.   [140] CDPA 1988 s 3(1). For an example see *Norowzian v Arks Ltd (No 2)* [2000] FSR 363 (CA).

[141] *Fuller v Blackpool Winter Gardens & Pavilion Co Ltd* [1895] 2 QB 429 at p 442 per AL Smith LJ.

[142] *Green v Broadcasting Corp of New Zealand* [1989] 2 All ER 1056, per Lord Bridge of Harwich at p 1058.

work.[143] In the latest case, it was said that 'a dramatic work is a work of action, with or without words or music, which is capable of being performed before an audience.'[144] Thus a scene created to be part of the cover for a forthcoming album by the pop group Oasis was held not to be a dramatic work, since it involved no action.[145] The sequence of images produced by a computer video game was also not a dramatic work, because it varied too much each time the game was played and lacked the unity for it to be a work capable of performance.[146]

Question

How may a dramatic work be defined for copyright purposes?

2.67   The 1988 Act omits from its definition of dramatic work some words which appeared in the 1956 Act, that the phrase does not include a cinematograph film as distinct from a scenario or script for a cinematograph film.[147] Did this change mean that films, which retain their own copyright under the 1988 Act,[148] can now also be protected as dramatic works? In *Norowzian v Arks Ltd (No 2)*,[149] the Court of Appeal concluded that a film which was a work of action and which could be performed before an audience could as a result also be a dramatic work. A film might be both a recording of a dramatic work and a dramatic work in itself; sometimes it might not be a recording of a dramatic work but would none the less itself be a dramatic work. The questions arising from overlapping categories are reduced inasmuch as films and dramatic works both attract moral rights, have more or less the same duration of copyright,[150] and enjoy the same categories of restricted acts.

Discussion point 1   For answer guidance visit www.oxfordtextbooks.co.uk/orc/macqueen2e/

Is a television commercial a dramatic work? See *Marblehead Trading Ltd v The Stroh Brewery Co* 1988 GWD 20–885.

Discussion point 2

How should works which contain a musical element but are intended for stage performance or to be made as a film – for example an opera, a ballet or the type of entertainment known as a 'musical' – be characterised for the purposes of copyright?

[143] *Wilson v Broadcasting Corp of New Zealand* [1990] 2 NZLR 565.
[144] *Norowzian v Arks Ltd (No 2)* [2000] FSR 363 (CA) per Nourse LJ at 367.
[145] *Creation Records Ltd v News Group Hewspapers Ltd* [1997] EMLR 444.
[146] *Nova Productions Ltd v Mazooma Games Ltd* [2006] RPC 14 (Kitchin J); point not discussed in the Court of Appeal ([2007] RPC 25).   [147] 1956 Act, s 48(1).
[148] CDPA 1988, s 1(1)(b).
[149] [2001] FSR 363 (CA); see above para 2.32. See further A Barron, 'The legal property of film' (2004) 67 MLR 177; I Stamatoudi, 'Joy for the claimant: can a film also be protected as a dramatic work?' [2000] IPQ 117; R Arnold, 'Joy: a reply' [2001] IPQ 10.
[150] Note however that the only relevant author for a dramatic work is the dramatist, whereas for a film it is not only the screenplay writer and dialogue author but also the principal director and the composer of any special music, and the duration of the copyright is determined by the death of the last of these to die. A film may thus enjoy copyright for longer as such than it does as a dramatic work.

Musical works[151]

2.68   A musical work is a work consisting of music, exclusive of any words or action intended to be sung, spoken or performed with the music.[152] Words written to be sung to music thus do not form part of any musical work but have their own literary or dramatic copyright. Music, it might be thought, consists of sounds other than words, recorded in writing or otherwise. Otherwise the limits of the definition of music are unclear. It seems to go beyond the notes on a score to include the combination of melodies and harmonies, the figuring of the bass, ornamentation and performance directions.[153] Music also covers the sampling and scratching of tracks by DJ's of works composed by other artists which create a new work. Another problem is the example of John Cage's '4 Minutes 33 Seconds', which has already been mentioned on the question of what constitutes a work (above, para 2.25): is a deliberately created silence in a concert hall, lasting for a fixed period, a musical work?[154] Most other gaps in the definition can probably be filled by the categories of literary, dramatic and artistic work, or by sound recording copyright. Cage's work might be regarded as a dramatic one, for example, inasmuch as it involves a performance before an audience.

 Question

What is the definition of a musical work? Can you define music?

Artistic works[155]

2.69   An artistic work is defined[156] as:

- a graphic work, photograph, sculpture or collage, irrespective of artistic quality;
- a work of architecture, being either a building or a model for a building;
- works of artistic craftsmanship.

Graphic work, photograph, sculpture or collage

2.70   The 1988 Act defines most, but not all, of these works:

- Graphic work includes any painting, drawing, diagram, map, chart or plan, and any engraving, etching, lithograph, woodcut, print or similar work.

---

[151] See generally S Frith and L Marshall, *Music and Copyright* (2nd edn, 2004); A Rahmatian, 'Music and creativity as perceived by copyright law' [2005] IPQ 267.   [152] CDPA 1988, s 3(1).

[153] See *Sawkins v Hyperion Records Ltd* [2005] RPC 32 (CA).

[154] See Cheng Lim Saw, 'Protecting the sound of silence in 4'33": a timely revisit of basic principles in copyright law', [2005] EIPR 467.

[155] See generally P Kearns, *The Legal Concept of Art* (1998); D McClean and K Schubert (eds), *Dear Images: Art, Culture and Copyright* (2002); S Stokes, *Art and Copyright* (2003); A Barron, 'Copyright law and the claims of art' [2002] IPQ 369; D Booton, 'Framing pictures: defining art in UK copyright law' [2003] IPQ 38; Landes and Posner, *Economic Structure of Intellectual Property Law* (2004) Ch 9 ('The legal protection of postmodern art'); S Stokes, 'Art and copyright: some current issues' (2006) 1 JIPLP 272.

[156] CDPA 1988, s 4(1). See further T Rychlicki, 'Legal questions about illegal art' [2008] 3 JIPLP 393.

- Photograph means a recording of light or other radiation on any medium on which an image is produced or from which an image may by any means be produced, and which is not part of a film.
- Sculpture includes any cast or model made for purposes of sculpture.

Graphic works

2.71　The first point to note is that the definition of graphic work is non-exclusive, so that it may catch works other than those listed. Thus the screen layouts of websites have been held to be graphic works, even although only recorded as such in digital code. The same case found that icons used in the displays were also graphic works, but as drawings.[157] But the Court of Appeal has held that a common feature of graphic works as defined in the 1988 Act is their static and non-moving character. So video games are not graphic works, while a series of drawings is a series of graphic works, not a single one.[158]

Paintings

2.72　The word 'painting' is not defined by the Act. There has been a judicial attempt to do so:

■ *Merchandising Corporation of America v Harpbond* [1983] FSR 32

It was held that a painting required a surface before it could be a protected work. Paint without a surface is not a painting. From this premise it was concluded that a flamboyant style of facial make-up forming part of the distinctive image of Adam Ant, a well-known popular musician, could not be a painting for copyright purposes.[159] Works of graffiti could, under the above definition, fall within the purview of artistic works for the purposes of copyright protection.[160]

Question

Does the fact that the surface in question in the Adam Ant case was a person's face take the work out of the judge's definition of a painting?

Drawings

2.73　The most significant of the categories of artistic work in terms of reported litigation is that of drawings. Examples of works held to be drawings include architects' plans,[161] sketches of garments,[162] engineering and machine part drawings,[163] cartoon characters,[164] and trade mark and label designs.[165] The rudimentary nature of a drawing is no objection to its being copyright;

---

[157] *Navitaire Inc v EasyJet Airline Co Ltd* [2006] RPC 3 (Pumfrey J).
[158] Nova Productions Ltd v Mazooma Games Ltd [2007] RPC 25 (CA).
[159] For more about Adam Ant, see http://en.wikipedia.org/wiki/Adam_Ant.
[160] T Rychlicki, 'Legal questions about illegal art' (2008) 3 JIPLP 393, at 396.
[161] See eg *Robert Allan & Partners v Scottish Ideal Homes* 1972 SLT (Sh Ct) 32.
[162] See eg *Howard Clark v David Allan & Co Ltd* 1987 SLT 271.
[163] See eg *British Leyland v Armstrong Patents* [1986] AC 577.
[164] *King Features Syndicate Inc v O M Kleeman Ltd* [1941] AC 417 (Popeye the Sailorman).
[165] *KARO STEP Trade Mark* [1977] RPC 255.

thus for example a drawing of three concentric rings has been held to have artistic copyright.[166] Many of the cases concerning design drawings should now be read with caution, however. While such drawings retain copyright under the 1988 Act, the scope of infringement has been severely restricted in relation to them, and the principal mode of protection is likely to be under design right. (See further Part III of this book, below.)

Diagrams, maps, charts, plans

2.74   The special feature of all these kinds of work is that, while they have a strong visual dimension, at the very least literary matter also found on the work (words and numbers) is necessary for its full meaning to be comprehended or utilised. Indeed between the 1911 and the 1956 Acts they were treated as literary works, and the appearance of the phrase 'irrespective of artistic quality' in the provision about graphic works (see below, para 2.81) is to be explained by the inclusion of this then new subject matter in the category of artistic works.[167] One important effect of the change, in particular with regard to plans, is that as artistic works these two-dimensional works can be infringed by three-dimensional reproductions, which would not be so if they were literary works.[168] This rule then had rather disastrous knock-on effects with regard to the protection of industrial designs (see Online Resource Centre), and the scope of copyright infringement by three-dimensional reproductions in this context is now carefully restricted (see paras 9.85–9.99). But the rule remains in full effect outside industrial design protection.

Photographs

2.75   There is relatively little authority on this subject.[169] With regard to photographs, the 1988 Act's definition (see above para 2.70) is clearly intended to cover continuing development in the technology of photography. The replacement of film by digital recording as the ordinary mode of photography well demonstrates the need for definitional flexibility of this kind.

Discussion point   For answer guidance visit www.oxfordtextbooks.co.uk/orc/macqueen2e/

Does the definition of a photograph cover the case whereby the camera records the image digitally and the photographer then adjusts the result electronically, for example to insert other images, as by putting the head of the Prime Minister on what is otherwise an image of a footballer; or merely editing out unwanted parts of the image captured? Is there still a photograph where the image has been digitally enhanced, for example, by sharpening contrasts, or heightening/ lowering colours?

Sculptures

2.76   Sculptures are plainly three-dimensional works and must be distinguished from works of architecture and of artistic craftsmanship. Casts and models for the purposes of sculpture are

---

[166]   *Solar Thomson Engineering v Barton* [1977] RPC 537. For the drawing see p 540.

[167]   For a Singaporean case concerning copyright in an online street map, see *Virtual Map (Singapore) Pte Ltd v Singapore Land Authority and Anr* [2009] SGCA 2, noted in B Ong, 'Copyright and cartography: mapping the boundaries of infringement liability' [2009] EIPR 17.   [168]   See para 4.26.

[169]   See generally Y Gendreau, *Copyright and Photographs: an International Survey* (1999); C Mihalos, *The Law of Photography and Digital Images* (2004); K Garnett, 'Copyright in photographs' [2000] EIPR 229; R Deazley, 'Photographing paintings in the public domain: a response to Garnett' [2001] EIPR 229; S Stokes, 'Photographing paintings in the public domain: a response to Garnett' [2001] EIPR 354; and R Arnold, 'Copyright in photographs: a case for reform' [2005] EIPR 303.

included in the category.[170] The vagueness of the statutory definition has been used by those seeking copyright protection for industrial designs.

■ *Wham-O Manufacturing Co v Lincoln Industries Ltd* [1985] RPC 127[171]

It was held that wooden model prototypes for the Frisbee toy were sculptures.[172] The New Zealand court held that sculpture could no longer be confined to the process of carving and modelling representations using natural materials, but should simply be thought of as the three-dimensional expression of an idea of its creator. The model fitted this conception, but not, the court held, the Frisbee itself. A plastic injection process for mass production could not give rise to a sculpture.

2.77   Similar arguments were rejected in England, however, in respect of prototypes of plastic dental impression trays,[173] and in Australia in respect of moulds used for casting pulleys, plates and a drive mechanism for a ride-on mower used in parks and gardens.[174] In the English case, Whitford J stressed that the prototypes were merely a stage in the production of the trays, and were not intended to have permanent existence, and so in his view fell outside the category of sculpture. Nor could the prototypes be considered 'casts or models for the purposes of sculpture'. In the Australian case Pinkus J commented that:

> 'it is true, as was pointed out in the course of argument, that some modern sculptures consist of or include parts of machines, but that does not warrant the conclusion that all machines are and parts thereof are properly called sculptures and similar reasoning applies to moulds'.[175]

English cases have construed 'sculpture' narrowly, in accordance with its ordinary dictionary meaning, but while as a result moulds for making functional cartridges were denied protection, scallop-shaped ones for use in toasted sandwich-makers were not.[176] The authorities were reviewed in a powerful judgment by Mann J in the "Star Wars" case subsequently approved in the Court of Appeal:

■ *Lucasfilm Ltd v Ainsworth* [2009] FSR 2; [2009] EWCA Civ 1328

A established a website in 2004 selling replica helmets and body armour used in the Star Wars films. Working from general designs prepared by L, A had previously created the moulds used to create the various pieces of armour used in the original 1977 film for the Imperial Stormtroopers and other characters. These included white helmets as well as armour referred to as the 'cheesegrater', 'jawbone', 'X-wing fighter pilot', 'rebel troop', 'Tie fighter' helmets and a 'chest box' worn by the Tie fighter pilots. L's claim of copyright infringement against A was met with a counterclaim to enforce A's alleged copyright in the helmets and armour as sculptures. The following points of guidance were found useful in deciding this point:

(1)   Regard was to be had to the normal use of the word.

(2)   Nevertheless, the concept could be applicable to things going beyond what would normally be expected to be art in the sense of the sort of things expected to be found in art galleries.

(3)   It was inappropriate to stray too far from what would normally be regarded as sculpture.

(4)   No judgement was to be made about artistic worth.

---

[170] CDPA 1988, s 4(2).   [171] See also *Plix Products v Winstone* [1985] 1 NZLR 376.
[172] For more on the Frisbee, see http://en.wikipedia.org/wiki/Frisbee
[173] *J & S Davis (Holdings) Ltd v Wright Health Group* [1988] RPC 403.
[174] *Greenfield Products Pty Ltd v Rover-Scott Bonar Ltd* [1990] 95 ALR 275.   [175] ibid, at 284.
[176] *Breville Europe v Thorn EMI* [1995] FSR 77; *Metix v Maughan* [1997] FSR 718.

(5) Not every three-dimensional representation of a concept could be regarded as a sculpture, otherwise every three-dimensional construction or fabrication would be a sculpture.

(6) It was of the essence of a sculpture that it should have, as part of its purpose, a visual appeal in the sense that it might be enjoyed for that purpose alone, whether or not it might have another purpose as well. The purpose was that of the creator and it was this underlying purpose that was important.

(7) The fact that the object had some other use did not necessarily disqualify it from being a sculpture, but it still had to have the intrinsic quality of being intended to be enjoyed as a visual thing.

(8) The process of fabrication was relevant but not decisive. There was no reason why a purely functional item, not intended to be at all decorative, should be treated as a sculpture simply because it had been (for example) carved out of wood or stone.

It was held that the Imperial Stormtrooper helmet was not a sculpture within the meaning of the Act. It was a mixture of costume and prop, but its primary function was utilitarian. The judge indicated that while it had an interest as an object, and while it was intended to express an idea, it had not been conceived, or created, with the intention that it should do so other than as part of character portrayal in the film. Furthermore, he opined that it was not that it lacked artistic merit, but that it lacked artistic purpose. The same reasoning applied to the armour. Toy models marketed by L after the film became successful were also not deemed to be sculptures for the reason that their primary purpose was for play. The *Wham-O* decision was disapproved for similar reasons: the purpose of the model for the Frisbee was not artistic.[77] The Court of Appeal approved the judge's reasoning and held that he had correctly applied his 'multi-factorial approach' (para 77) finding that '[n]either the armour nor the helmet are sculpture' (para 80). With regard to the toy stormtroopers: 'We are not dealing here with highly crafted models designed to appeal to the collector but which might be played with by his children. These are mass produced plastic toys. They are no more works of sculpture than the helmet and the armour which they reproduce' (para 82).

 Discussion point   For answer guidance visit www.oxfordtextbooks.co.uk/orc/macqueen2e/

Should ice sculptures be protected as sculptures? Is the snowman you make during a white Christmas so protected?

Discussion point 2

Kinetic sculptures are sculptures with moving parts, or in which motion is incorporated as part of the design, so that the form or colour of the work may change continuously or from time to time. Does mobility or motion within the sculpture take it out of the dictionary definition of 'sculpture'? See also the case of *Komesaroff v Mickle* [1988] RPC 204, discussed below (para 2.85) for a similar issue with works of artistic craftsmanship.

---

77 See further S Clark, 'Lucasfilm Ltd and Others v Ainsworth and Another: the force of copyright protection for three-dimensional designs as sculptures or works of artistic craftsmanship' [2009] EIPR 384; A Hobson, 'Imperial stormtroopers, art works, and copyright defences' (2009) 4 JIPLP 16.

Engravings

2.78 The *Wham-O* case (above, para 2.76)[178] is also an authority on engravings, which the New Zealand court held the markings on the surface of the Frisbee to be, along with the plastic injection mould. Engraving is first a process of cutting or incising images into material such as wood or metal, and then using the result for the purpose of producing prints of the image.[179] In the 1956 Act it was defined to include etchings, lithographs, woodcuts, and prints, but photographs were expressly excluded.[180] Using this, it was held that an engraving included both the original engraved plate and the resulting print, and further that, given the apparent need to exclude the process of producing prints known as photography, engraving was not confined to processes involving cutting into material to produce the plate.[181] This approach enabled the court in *Wham-O* to hold that the mould was a plate and the Frisbee disc a 'print' thereof.[182]

 Exercise

Compare the *Wham-O* case with *George Hensher Ltd v Restawile Upholstery (Lancs) Ltd* [1976] AC 64, discussed below, para 2.83 ff. What, if any, policy reasons justify the different results reached in these cases with regard to the protection of models to be used in the mass production of consumer objects?

2.79 As already noted, however, the 1988 Act differs somewhat from the 1956 Act in respect of engravings. In particular the word 'print' no longer appears either in juxtaposition (as with etchings, lithographs and woodcuts) or in any definition. Nor is photography mentioned.[183] It is not clear whether this excludes the reasoning of the *Wham-O* decision, given that mere changes of expression in the 1988 Act do not necessarily entail departure from the previous law.[184] But considering the Act's overall policy of excluding copyright from the field of industrial design, it is suggested that the result in *Wham-O* should now be treated with caution, although its general discussion of both engravings and sculptures remains helpful. With regard to both categories of work, the case may be an example of a court anxious to protect the skill and labour of the plaintiff from piracy and forcing the facts rather uneasily into unsuitable concepts. Design rights probably offer more satisfactory solutions to such problems now.[185] In *Greenfield Products Pty Ltd v Rover-Scott Bonnar Ltd*,[186] an argument that a mould of a lawnmower engine was an engraving was rejected. Pincus J said:

'It is not all cutting which is engraving ... The term does not cover shaping a piece of metal or wood on a lathe, but has to do with marking, cutting or working the surface – typically the flat surface – of an object ... '[187]

---

[178] [1985] RPC 127.   [179] For an example see *Martin v Polyplas* [1969] NZLR 1046.
[180] 1956 Act, s 48(1).
[181] *James Arnold & Co v Miafern Ltd* [1980] RPC 397 esp at pp 403–4: rubber stereos for printing designs on ties held to be engravings.   [182] [1985] RPC 127.
[183] CDPA 1988, s 4(2).   [184] CDPA 1988, s 172(2).   [185] For design rights, see Part III (Ch 8 and 9) below.
[186] (1990) 95 ALR 275.
[187] ibid, at 285. See also *Talk of the Town v Hagstrom* (1991) 19 IPR 649, 655.

Collages

2.80   The last item specifically mentioned is the collage. A collage is an artistic equivalent to the literary compilation. The creator assembles diverse fragments of material, some of which may be extracts from other copyright or formerly copyright works, artistic and others, some of which may be incapable of copyright at all (for example, a piece of string), and places them either on a single surface or in some other form of juxtaposition, often with incongruous effect. Without this specific reference in the 1988 Act, there is an obvious danger that such works may fail to attract copyright on the grounds of lack of originality or the inherent nature of the material used. Collage has been held not to be constituted by ephemeral collocation, whether or not with artistic intent, of random, unrelated and unfixed elements.[188]

Artistic quality of graphic works, etc

2.81   An artistic work in any of the categories just discussed need not have aesthetic appeal or be a work of fine art in the ordinary sense, for it is provided that the copyright subsists 'irrespective of its artistic quality'.[189] The phrase 'artistic work' is rather to be taken as an indication of the methods by which the work must be produced. Some recent decisions suggest that it may be necessary to show that the work is intended to be permanent, insofar as anything can be, or at least not transient in form.[190] On the other hand, with a very simple drawing, it may be difficult to show infringement of the copyright.[191] As a consequence, however, there can be difficult questions of definition where there is some overlap with other forms of work. Although it is clear that plain lettering cannot be the subject of artistic copyright,[192] fancy lettering, for example in a greeting card, a label or a trade mark, may well be a drawing. In relation in particular to maps, charts, diagrams and plans, lettering, words and figures may form an integral part of the representation and would fall to be protected by artistic rather than literary copyright; but where a drawing is merely an explanatory adjunct to written material, the latter has literary copyright.[193]

Works of architecture[194]

2.82   Works of architecture are either buildings or models for buildings and do not include architects' plans, which are dealt with as drawings for copyright purposes.[195] A building includes any fixed structure,[196] and it would appear from the use of the word 'any' that no consideration need be given to the question of artistic quality in determining whether or not a work of architecture has copyright, a view supported by an obiter dictum of Lord Reid.[197] The meaning of 'structure' has not been judicially discussed since the passage of the 1956 Act, but in an earlier case it had been held that a garden layout including stone walls, steps and ponds had copyright as a

---

[188]   *Creation Records Ltd v News Group Newspapers Ltd* [1997] EMLR 444. See further below, para 2.86.

[189]   CDPA 1988, s 4(1)(a).

[190]   *Merchandising Corp of America v Harpbond* [1983] FSR 32; also *Komesaroff v Mickle* [1988] RPC 204. Note that there is no explicit requirement of fixation with artistic works, unlike literary, dramatic and musical works (see above, para 2.30–33).   [191]   *Kenrick v Lawrence* (1890) 25 QBD 99.

[192]   *Miller & Lang Ltd v Macniven & Cameron Ltd* (1908) 16 SLT 56.

[193]   *Duriron Co Inc v Hugh Jennings & Co Ltd* [1984] FSR 1; *British Leyland v Armstrong Patents* [1986] RPC 279 per Oliver LJ at 289–96; *Interlego AG v Tyco Industries Inc* [1989] AC 217 per Lord Oliver at 264–5.

[194]   See further A Adrian, 'Architecture and copyright: a quick survey of the law' (2008) 3 JIPLP 524.

[195]   CDPA 1988, s 4(1)(b).   [196]   CDPA 1988, s 4(2).

[197]   *Hensher v Restawile* [1976] AC 64 per Lord Reid at p 78.

structure;[198] department store buildings[199] and semi-detached villas[200] have also been accorded copyright. It may be suggested that a building is an artificial structure attached to land, but difficult questions of definition can be seen by examining some of the leading cases on fixtures.[201]

> ### Exercise
>
> Consider eg the Scottish case of *Christie v Smith's Executrix* 1949 SC 572, which raised the question whether a summerhouse which rested on specially laid foundations on land by virtue of its considerable weight was sufficiently attached to the land to be a fixture (answer: yes). Was the summerhouse also a work of architecture for copyright purposes?

Works of artistic craftsmanship

2.83   The phrase 'artistic craftsmanship' is not defined in the 1988 Act and no single clear meaning has emerged from the cases on the subject.[202] Considering the phrase in the context of the section on artistic works as a whole, it would appear to cover works in three dimensions which are not sculptures or buildings; since the decision of the House of Lords in *George Hensher Ltd v Restawile Upholstery (Lancs) Ltd*,[203] it has also been accepted that for a work to be one of artistic craftsmanship it must be of a quality making it capable of being described as artistic. The problem which is fully but inconclusively discussed in *Hensher* is how the court may test the issue of artistic quality without becoming involved in subjective discussion of the merits of a work.

■ *George Hensher Ltd v Restawile Upholstery (Lancs) Ltd* [1976] AC 64

H produced popular suites of furniture deploying a boat-shaped theme. Expert witnesses described the shape as 'flashy', 'horrible', 'middle of the road', 'mediocre' and 'slightly vulgar', although obviously quite a good commercial design, and a 'winner' in terms of its appeal to the market.[204] R, competitors of H, produced similar-looking suites, and H sued for infringement of copyright, relying, not on any right in the finished articles, but in the original three-dimensional prototype of the design made before the furniture went into production. Their claim was that the prototype was a work of craftsmanship, artistic quality was not necessary for protection and therefore the adjective 'artistic' added nothing to the legal meaning of the subject matter to be protected; accordingly the prototype fell within the scope of copyright. All the judges in the House of Lords agreed with those of the Court of Appeal that the prototype was not a work of artistic craftsmanship, but there was considerable disagreement as to the reasons wh~ should be so.

2.84   In *Hensher* the House of Lords rejected the view expressed by the Cou~ that the test was whether the work would be purchased for its aesthet~

[198] *Vincent v Universal Housing Co* [1928–35] MCC 275.   [199] *Meikle v Maufe* [1941] 3 A~
[200] *Blake v Warren* [1928–35] MCC 268.
[201] For the English and Scots law of fixtures, see *Halsbury's Laws of England*, vol 27(1), pa~
Scotland: Stair Memorial Encyclopaedia, vol 18, paras 578–587.
[202] See also M Rushton, 'An economic approach to copyright in works of artistic craftsmanshi~
[203] [1976] AC 64.
[204] Three slightly fuzzy black and white photographs of the plaintiff's suites are available in [197~

its utility, but their Lordships differed among themselves about what the test should be and about whether it was a test of fact depending on the evidence or a test of law for the court. One view was that the intention of the author of the work to produce a work of art was the critical factor, and this is supported in other earlier cases.[205] A second view was to ask whether a substantial part of the public would regard the work as artistic, this being distinct from the question of whether or not the primary reason for purchasing it was its aesthetic appeal. But the most cogent speech in *Hensher* is that of Lord Simon of Glaisdale, who argued that works of artistic craftsmanship first came to be copyright subjects under the Copyright Act 1911 as a consequence of the influence of the Arts and Crafts movement of the 19th century, which emphasised the necessary connection between form and function. The phrase 'artistic craftsmanship' should therefore be construed as a whole rather than by separate examination of its constituent words. So the question to be asked of a work in which copyright was claimed under this heading is: is this the work of one who was in this respect an artist-craftsman? The artistic merit of the work was thus not an issue to be considered. The question was to be answered on the evidence, and the best evidence was likely to be that of acknowledged artist-craftsmen or those concerned with training artist-craftsmen.[206]

2.85   The test of the creator's intention seemed to gain ground in decisions holding that a baby's raincape and a plastic dental impression tray were not works of artistic craftsmanship.[207] But it remains far from clear exactly what works will come under this head of artistic copyright. If Lord Simon's historical analysis in *Hensher* is correct, then we should begin with articles which have some function to perform, for example, furniture, crockery, cutlery, clothing, and it should not necessarily be an objection that the article is the subject of industrial production, or that its function is industrial, or indeed merely decorative.

■ *Komesaroff v Mickle [1988] RPC 204* (Sup Ct of Victoria)

K developed and marketed a product named 'moving sand pictures', which was made by enclosing inside glass panels a mixture of liquid, coloured sands and a layer of air bubbles. Miniature sand landscapes were brought about when the sands trickled through the bubbles under the influence of gravity. The process could be repeated by shaking the product. M copied and commenced marketing an identical product. It was held that K's product was not a work of artistic craftsmanship because her activity did not directly bring about the sand landscapes which resulted from shaking the product, and there was no craftsmanship in what she had done.

■ *Burge v Swarbrick [2007] FSR 27* (High Court of Australia)

The question in this case was whether a model known as a "plug" from which a mould for a yacht hull could be derived was a work of artistic craftsmanship. Following Lord Simon in *Hensher*, the Court held that artistic craftsmanship is not limited to artistic handicraft and so can include machine production items and indeed prototypes such as the "plug". There was no antithesis between utility and beauty. A conclusion on the question of the "plug's" character was not controlled by the creator's intentions, but was one for objective determination by the

---

[205] *Burke v Spicers Dress Design* [1936] Ch 400 per Clauson J at 407–8; *Cuisenaire v Reed* [1963] VR 719 per Pape J at 730; *Cuisenaire v South West Imports* [1968] 1 Ex CR 493 per Niel J at 574.

[206] Lord Simon's approach was preferred by the Federal Court of Australia in *Coogi Australia v Hysport International* (1999) 157 ALR 247 and by the High Court of Australia in *Burge v Swarbrick* [2007] FSR 27.

[207] *Merlet v Mothercare* [1986] RPC 115; *J & S Davis (Holdings) Ltd v Wright Health Group* [1988] RPC 403.

court. Matters of visual and aesthetic appeal were but one element in the design, and were sub-ordinated to the achievement of the purely functional aspects of the design. The determination of artistic craftsmanship turns on assessing the extent to which the work's artistic expression is unconstrained by functional considerations. The more substantial the latter, the less the scope for real or substantial artistic effort. The evidence in this case was that the designer had been constrained to such an extent that his work was not that of an artist-craftsman.

2.86   A difficult question is whether there must be an individual artist-craftsman whose concept the work is; it has been suggested that where the idea and the execution are separated there can be no work of artistic craftsmanship.[208] But this may be too restrictive, as has been held in the New Zealand case of *Bonz Group v Cooke*,[209] which involved the production of hand-knitted woollen sweaters where the designer and the hand-knitters were different persons. *Bonz Group* was applied in the English case of *Vermaat and Powell v Boncrest Ltd*,[210] which was concerned with sample patchwork bedspreads and matching cushion covers made by seam-stresses to a design produced by another. It was finally held, however, that while the work of the seamstresses might have involved craftsmanship, the result was not a work of artistic craftsmanship.

■ *Lucasfilm Ltd v Ainsworth* [2009] FSR 2

See also para 2.77 for the facts of this case. Mann J held that the intention of the creator was relevant in determining whether a work was one of artistic craftsmanship. *Bonz Group (Pty) Ltd v Cooke* (above) was approved and applied, with the judge stating that the artist and the crafts-man did not have to be the same person but there had to be a proper nexus between them. The producer of the helmets in this case was a craftsman producing high quality products with justifiable pride in his work. However, his works could not be described as works of artistic craftsmanship. They did not have the purpose of being aesthetically appealing. Instead, they were used to provide an impression in a film. Unlike a work of artistic craftsmanship, they were not intended to sustain close scrutiny.[211]

Discussion point   For answer guidance visit www.oxfordtextbooks.co.uk/orc/macqueen2e/

(1) Are the designer and the hand-knitters in the *Bonz Group* case joint authors? See below, paras 3.7–3.14.
(2) Could and should a recipe constitute a work of artistic craftsmanship? See TSL Cheng, 'Copyright protection of haute cuisine: recipe for disaster?' [2008] EIPR 93.

Exercise

Consider the two following cases and how, if at all, they may be reconciled (or distinguished).

---

[208] *Burke v Spicers Dress Design* [1936] Ch 400.   [209] [1994] 3 NZLR 216.
[210] [2001] FSR 5.   [211] There was no appeal on this point: *Lucasfilm Ltd v Ainsworth* [2009] EWCA Civ 1328.

■ *Shelley Films Ltd v Rex Features Ltd* [1994] EMLR 134

SF was making a film called 'Mary Shelley's Frankenstein'. RF took an unauthorised photograph of a scene from the film as it was being shot. The picture was later published in *The People* newspaper. SF claimed infringement of copyright in the actors' costumes and the set as works of artistic craftsmanship, and in the latex prostheses being worn by the star of the film (Robert de Niro), as either a sculpture or a work of artistic craftsmanship. In preliminary proceedings all the claims of copyright were held to be arguable and an injunction granted against RF.

■ *Creation Records Ltd v News Group Newspapers Ltd* [1997] EMLR 444

CR devised a scene (a white Rolls Royce in a swimming pool with various other props, none of them made for the purpose) to be the background for a photograph of a pop group (Oasis) to appear on the cover of their forthcoming album. An unauthorised photograph of the scene was taken and published in *The Sun* newspaper, which also intended to market the picture as a poster. CR claimed copyright in the scene as a sculpture or work of artistic craftsmanship. It was held that the scene was not a sculpture, since its making involved no carving, modelling or other techniques of sculpture. Nor was such an assemblage of *objets trouvés* a work of artistic craftsmanship, since neither subject nor result involved craftsmanship.

Films[212]

2.87   A film is:

> 'a recording in any medium from which a moving image may by any means be reproduced' (s 5B(1)).

Again there is apparent in this broad definition the effort of the 1988 Act to retain the ability to offer copyright protection whatever technical changes may occur in the film industry. Thus the recording embodied in a video, a CD-Rom or a DVD, or captured by a closed circuit TV camera, has copyright just as much as if it was recorded on traditional translucent film. The sound track accompanying a film is part of the work for copyright purposes, although it may also have an independent copyright as a sound recording.[213] Computer games can be protected as films,[214] but it is very doubtful whether images consisting purely of written text and/or still pictures can ever be treated as film, even if the reader is able to move the material around on her screen by use of scroll bars, cursors and other control mechanisms.[215]

2.88   Questions of overlap with other copyright works and subject matter may sometimes arise with films. It has already been noted that a film may be a dramatic work.[216] The definition of a photograph excludes any part of a film,[217] so that there is no possibility of a film claiming copyright as a set of photographs; but modern still cameras may include motor drive units which enable photographs to be taken in very rapid sequence. If these are capable of being shown as moving

---

[212] See generally P Kamina, *Film Copyright in the EU* (2002); I Stamatoudi, *Copyright in Multimedia Products: a Comparative Analysis* (2002).   [213] CDPA 1988, s 5B(2) and (5).

[214] See *Sega Enterprises Ltd v Galaxy Electronics Pty Ltd* (1997) 145 ALR 21 (Fed Ct of Australia); *Golden China TV Game Centre v Nintendo Co Ltd* 1997 (1) SA 405 (A). *Nova Productions Ltd v Mazooma Games Ltd* [2007] RPC 25 (CA). The computer program incorporated in the game will also have its own copyright as a literary work.

[215] cf *WGN Continental Broadcasting Co v United Video Inc* 693 F.2d 622 (7th Circuit, 1982), where teletext accompanying a TV programme but broadcast from a different channel was held to be an audiovisual work.

[216] See *Norowzian v Arks Ltd (No 2)* [2000] FSR 363; and see above, para 2.67.   [217] CDPA 1988, s 4(2).

images then there may be a film for copyright purposes. The converse case is the camera which is fixed on one place, for example, part of the sky, or the ground, and captures images at intervals; which when played in sequence at normal speed show speeded-up and striking images of cloud movement or plant growth.

2.89   For the purposes of infringement, a photograph may be a copy of a film.[218] It would seem to follow from this, and the exclusion of parts of a film from the definition of a photograph that a publicity poster using an image from the film would not have a copyright in that image as such. The protection would be that of a film, and it would be achieved through the concept of indirect copying (see below, para 4.21). It has also been suggested that a completed set of drawings intended for use in a cartoon film will by itself be a film because it is capable of being shown as a moving picture.

 Question

What is a film for copyright purposes? Is there an overlap with other categories of copyright work?

Media works

Sound recordings

2.90   A sound recording is defined as:

> '…either
>
> (a) a recording of sounds, from which the sounds may be reproduced, or
>
> (b) a recording of the whole or any part of a literary, dramatic or musical work, from which sounds reproducing the work or part may be reproduced' (s 5A(1)).

Sounds in category (a) might include, for example, bird-song or sound effects for use in a dramatic production, while category (b) includes readings as well as, most importantly from a commercial point of view, music. The Act seeks to retain coverage against technical development in sound recording by providing that there will be copyright regardless of the medium on which the recording is made or the method by which the sounds are reproduced or produced.[219] Copyright subsists in every sound recording that is not a copy taken from a previous sound recording.[220] Accordingly, copyright will not subsist in the records, cassettes and CDs as such as sold to the public, since these are merely copies of the producer's master recording. But to copy from such copies will still be infringement of the master recording's copyright.[221]

 Question

Looking at the statutory definition of a sound recording above, what in essence is protected by the copyright in this subject matter?

---

[218] CDPA 1988, s 17(4).   [219] CDPA 1988, s 5A(1).   [220] CDPA 1988, s 5A(2).
[221] See further below, para 4.21.

Broadcasts

2.91   This embraces both television and radio. There is no significant difference in the technology involved in radio and television broadcasting, merely in the end result, television embracing visual images as well as sound. Under the law until 2003 a distinction was drawn between the wireless technology of broadcasting and the supply of programme services by cable, but this has been dropped as a result of the implementation of the Information Society Directive. A broadcast is now defined as:

> 'an electronic transmission of visual images, sounds, or other information, either
>
> (a) transmitted for simultaneous reception by members of the public and is capable of being lawfully received by them;
>
> or
>
> (b) transmitted at a time determined solely by the person making the transmission for presentation to members of the public' (CDPA 1988, s 6(1)).

The purpose of distinguishing between (a) and (b) is to accommodate the phenomenon of satellite alongside more traditional terrestrial wireless and cable broadcasting. The latter are covered by (a); (b) requires some explanation of satellite technology in broadcasting.

Satellite broadcasting

2.92   There are two main forms of satellite broadcasting:

(1) point-to-point or fixed satellite broadcasts; and

(2) direct broadcasting by satellite.

The former involves the transmission of signals to a satellite by one broadcaster, which are then transmitted to another broadcaster who includes the signals in his own transmissions. Familiar examples of this include the broadcasting by the BBC and IBA of sports events taking place in other countries, where the initial signal is sent by a broadcaster in the other country. With direct broadcasting by satellite, the signal of the originating broadcaster is transmitted through the satellite direct to the receivers of the public. These receivers may require special equipment to receive the signal, for example, satellite dishes, and to decode it for the purposes of viewing. Signals broadcast from satellites may be encrypted or scrambled in order to ensure that only those so equipped – that is, subscribers to the service – can receive the signal in intelligible form. Sky Television provides an example of this technology currently familiar in Britain.

2.93   This simplified account of broadcasting technology helps in understanding some of the problems underlying the provisions in the 1988 Act defining broadcasting. Doubts as to whether a signal directed initially only to a satellite (the 'up-leg') could be a broadcast are removed, because it is an electronic transmission of visual images and sounds made at a time determined solely by the person making the transmission for presentation to members of the public. The purpose of the transmission is such a presentation, although as such the signal is not capable of lawful reception by the public. There were similar doubts as to whether the signal from the satellite (the 'down- leg') could be a broadcast if it was encrypted. The 1988 Act provides that an encrypted transmission shall be regarded as capable of being lawfully received by members of the public (and therefore a broadcast) only if decoding equipment has been made available to the public by or with the authority of the person making the transmission or the person providing the contents of the transmission.[222]

■ *Network Ten Pty Ltd v TCN Channel Nine Pty Ltd* **(2004) 205 ALR 1 (HCA)**[223]

Ten broadcast a TV programme which included short excerpts from programmes previously broadcast by Nine. Nine claimed infringement of copyright in that each visual image capable of being observed as a separate image on the TV screen was a broadcast in which copyright subsisted. Ten argued that a broadcast was constituted rather by a programme than by the images making up the programme. The importance of the point in the case was whether or not Nine's actions amounted to 'substantial' copying for the purposes of infringement. It was held that a broadcast was more than the transmission of a single image for the purposes of copyright, and that Ten's activities had to be related to Nine's programmes for the purposes of infringement. A television commercial in the middle of a programme was itself a discrete TV broadcast. Kirby J dissented on the ground that the court was going beyond the language of the copyright statute (which was similar to that of the 1956 Act in the UK).

Question

Does the amended language of the 1988 Act make clear the answer to the question raised by this Australian case?

Teletext and Internet transmissions

2.94   The definition of broadcasting makes clear that broadcasting is not restricted to the transmission of sounds and visual images, but can include other material such as teletext information services.[224] Internet transmissions are in general *not* to be treated as broadcasts,[225] however, since in general they are neither transmitted simultaneously to their audience, nor does the transmitter decide the time of transmission (the recipient generally does that). However, an Internet transmission can fall within the definition of a broadcast if:

(1) the transmission takes place simultaneously on the Internet and by other means, such as conventional TV or radio ('streaming');

(2) it is a concurrent transmission of a live event; or

(3) it is a transmission of recorded moving images or sounds forming part of a programme service offered by the person responsible for making the transmission, being a service in which programmes are transmitted at scheduled times determined by that person.[226]

---

[222] CDPA 1988, s 6(2); and see s 6(1)(b) and 6(4).
[223] The judgment is applied by the Federal Court of Australia at (2005) 216 ALR 631.
[224] CDPA 1988, s 6(1).
[225] So the decision in *Shetland Times v Wills* [1997] FSR 604 that a website was a cable programme service could not now be reached. None of the exceptions to the general rule would have applied either.   [226] CDPA 1988, s 6(1A).

Discussion point 1   For answer guidance visit www.oxfordtextbooks.co.uk/orc/macqueen2e/

Consider 'podcasting', a method of distributing audio or audio-visual material on the Internet, for playback on personal computers or mobile devices at a time chosen by the user. This technique is increasingly being used by broadcasting companies to allow viewers/ listeners to see/hear programmes or other material at a time convenient to them. Is a 'podcast' a broadcast for copyright purposes?

Discussion point 2

Consider also the possibility increasingly deployed in digital broadcasting, where the viewer may 'pause and record' a programme as it is transmitted, thereby allowing him to answer the doorbell or telephone without missing any part of the programme. What are the implications for the distinction between broadcasts and other forms of transmission?

Repeats

2.95   Many broadcasts on television and radio are repeated once or more. Such repeats have a copyright separate from or additional to that of the original broadcast,[227] unless it infringes the copyright in another broadcast or in a cable programme.[228]

Published editions of literary, dramatic and musical works

2.96   Copyright subsists in the typographical arrangement of every published edition of a literary, dramatic, or musical work.[229] A new edition is not a reprint of the work reproducing the typographical arrangement of a previous edition, but some new mode of presenting the work. The concept of 'edition' as here should be distinguished from the use of the word in describing versions of, say, a textbook, where each successive edition involves a change, not only in the typographical arrangement but also in the content of the text thus presented. The same text may be published several times, but so long as each publication adopts a different typographical arrangement, there will be separate copyrights for the publishers.[230] Equally the text itself may be out-of-copyright, but there will be a copyright in the typographical arrangement of any edition which is not a reproduction, in whole or in part, of a previous typographical arrangement.[231]

■ *Newspaper Licensing Agency Ltd v Marks and Spencer plc* [2003] 1 AC 551

M&S subscribed to a press cutting service which provided a daily supply of photocopies of items of interest appearing in national and daily newspapers. The press cutting service had a licence from the newspapers' collecting society, the NLA. M&S copied the photocopies for distribution to individuals within its organisation, but had no licence for this. The NLA sued for infringement

---

[227] See CDPA 1988, s 14(2) and (5) (note duration of copyright in a repeat cannot exceed that of the original transmission).
[228] CDPA 1988, s 6(6).   [229] CDPA 1988, s 1(1)(c) and 8(1).
[230] See further discussion of this point by Lord Hoffmann in *Newspaper Licensing Agency Ltd v Marks and Spencer plc* [2003] 1 AC 551, paras 11, 16.   [231] CDPA 1988, s 8(2).

of a copyright in the typographical arrangement of the published editions of the newspapers. The issue was whether the copyright subsisted only in the whole newspaper, or separately in each article within the newspaper. Giving the main speech, Lord Hoffmann said: 'In my opinion, the frame of reference for the term 'published edition' is the language of the publishing trade. The edition is the product, generally between covers, which the publisher offers to the public.' (para 14). While the articles each had literary copyright in their own right, this did not mean that each article as printed was a separate published edition, and a newspaper a collection of such editions. Lord Hoffmann added: 'In the case of a modern newspaper, I think that the skill and labour devoted to typographical arrangement is principally expressed in the overall design. It is not the choice of a particular typeface, the precise number or width of the columns, the breadth of margins and the relationship of headlines and straplines to the other text, the number of articles on a page and the distribution of photographs and advertisements but the combination of all of these into pages which give the newspaper as a whole its distinctive appearance … I find it difficult to think of the skill and labour which has gone into the typographical arrangement of a newspaper being expressed in anything less than a full page. The particular fonts, columns, margins and so forth are only, so to speak, the typographical vocabulary in which the arrangement is expressed.' (para 23).

Further reading

Books

Copinger & Skone James on Copyright (15th edn, 2005), Chs 2 and 3

Laddie Prescott & Vitoria, *Modern Law of Copyright* (3rd edn, 2000), Chs 3–9, 34

Bently & Sherman, *Intellectual Property Law* (3rd edn, 2009), Chs 2, 3 and 4.

Cornish & Llewelyn, *Intellectual Property* (6th edn, 2007), Chs 10, 20

History

R Deazley, *On the Origin of the Right to Copy* (2004)

C Seville, *Literary Copyright Reform in Early Victorian England* (1999)

B Sherman and L Bently, *The Making of Modern Intellectual Property* (1999)

C Seville, *The Internationalisation of Copyright Law: Books, Buccaneers and the Black Flag in the Nineteenth Century* (2006)

Economics

R Towse and R Holzhauer (eds), *The Economics of Intellectual Property* (2002), vol 1 (Introduction and Copyright)

W Landes and R Posner, *The Economic Structure of Intellectual Property Law* (2003), Chs 2–6, 8–10

R Towse (ed), *Copyright and the Cultural Industries* (2002)

M A Einhorn, *Media, Technology and Copyright: Integrating Law and Economics* (2004)

Computer programs

S Lai, *The Copyright Protection of Computer Software in the UK* (2000)

Multimedia

I Stamatoudi, *Copyright and Multimedia Products: a Comparative Analysis* (2002)

T Aplin, *Copyright Law in the Digital Society: the Challenges of Multimedia* (2005)

Musical works

S Frith and L Marshall, *Music and Copyright* (2nd edn, 2004)

Artistic works

S Stokes, *Art and Copyright* (2003)

Y Gendreau, *Copyright and Photographs: an International Survey* (1999)

C Mihalos, *The Law of Photography and Digital Images* (2004)

Articles

Works

J Pila, 'An intentional view of the copyright work' (2008) 71 MLR 535

Originality

HL *MacQueen*, 'The legal definition of authorship and the scrolls', in JJ Collins and TH Lim (eds), *Oxford Handbook of the Dead Sea Scrolls* (2010)

A Waisman, 'Revisiting originality' [2009] EIPR 370

Musical works

A Rahmatian 'Music and creativity as perceived by copyright law' [2005] IPQ 267

Artistic works

M Rushton 'An economic approach to copyright in works of artistic craftsmanship' [2003] IPQ 255

T Rychlick, 'Legal questions about illegal art' (2008) 3 JIPLP 393

Copyright 2: first ownership, moral rights and term

Introduction

Scope and overview of chapter

3.1 This chapter initially considers the identification of the first owner of the copyright when it comes into existence. Normally this is the author of the work; but this concept is not so easily applied to media works. This difficulty involves further analysis of the difference between 'author' and 'media' copyright works, first explored in the previous chapter. The highlighting of the author's position makes this also the appropriate chapter in which to consider the author's 'moral rights': that is, the right to be identified as the author of the protected work, and to have that work's integrity respected by others. Copyright (including moral rights) is generally a right of limited duration, however, and the final section of the chapter expounds the various periods of time for which it lasts.

3.2 **Learning objectives**

By the end of this chapter you should be able to describe and explain:

- who is the first owner of copyright in a protected work (usually the author or equivalent);
- the moral rights of the author to be identified and to have the work's integrity respected;
- how long the protection of copyright lasts in relation to each of the categories of its subject matter.

3.3 Copyright is a form of property which comes into existence with the creation of its subject matter (no registration process is required, unlike patents, trade marks or designs), so there are some important rules to identify the first owner of the right thus created. This is usually the author with author works, and an equivalent in the case of media works. The author's moral rights to be identified and to have the integrity of a work respected are treated next, along with other rights akin to moral rights, such as the artist's resale right, the right to prevent false attribution, and the special right of privacy in relation to certain commissioned photographs. These and the other rights conferred by copyright also exist for a specified period of time, varying according to the subject matter protected. In sum, the chapter explains who is the first to benefit from the protection of copyright; some of the rights which authors gain along with first ownership; and for how long the protection lasts. So the rest of the chapter looks like this:

- First ownership (3.4–3.30)
- Author's moral rights (3.31–3.48)
- Duration of copyright and moral rights (3.49–3.61)

First ownership

Introduction

3.4   It is necessary to consider ownership of copyright in two parts:

(1)   the *initial ownership* of the copyright, which in general pertains to the *author or creator* of the work in question;

(2)   given that copyright is an item of property, ownership of which may be transferred and which may also endure beyond the author's lifetime, the *transfer of copyright and consequent rights*.

This section considers only the first of these issues. The second issue is covered in the chapter on exploitation of intellectual property in general (Chapter 21).

3.5   The *author* of a work is usually the *first owner* of the copyright in the work (CDPA 1988, s 11(1)). There is *no requirement of registration*, in contrast with most other forms of intellectual property, and *copyright will arise automatically with the creation of the work*. An *author is the person who creates the work* (s 9(1)), a concept readily applicable to most literary, dramatic, musical, and artistic works. However the 1988 Act gives explicit definitions of who is to be taken as the author of sound recordings, films, broadcasts, cable programmes and computer-generated works. Further, an *employer will be the first owner of copyright in any literary, dramatic, musical or artistic work or film authored by an employee in the course of employment unless there is an agreement to the contrary* (s 11(2)). In these provisions can be most clearly seen the UK's attribution of authorship to the entrepreneur as distinct from the creator. Finally there are *special rules relating to Crown and Parliamentary copyright*, and copyright vested in certain international organisations.

Author of literary, dramatic, musical or artistic work

3.6   With literary, dramatic, musical and artistic works which are not computer-generated (for which see below, para 3.22), the author is the person who creates the work.[1] There is a statutory

---

[1] CDPA 1988, s 9(1).

presumption that, where a name purporting to be that of the author appears on copies of a literary, dramatic, musical or artistic work when published, or when made, the person whose name so appears is the author of the work, and that the work was made in circumstances not involving that person's course of employment, Crown or Parliamentary copyright, or the copyright vested in certain international organisations. Like any presumption, this may be rebutted by contrary proof.[2] In general, the author is the person by whose skill and labour, or intellectual creativity, the work took on its final material form, and the broad principle that copyright subsists, not in ideas but in the way in which ideas are expressed (see above, paras 2.26–2.28) should also be borne in mind. Copyright law has thus not taken up the post-modern deconstructionist critique, which rejects what it calls 'the Romantic concept of the author', and argues that works are not so much the expression of an individual as of the whole society and culture in which they are made.[3] Such analysis can be taken to undermine the individual author's claim to ownership of rights in the work and to highlight instead the claims that society as a whole is entitled to make. The foundation of copyright law remains, however, its recognition of the author's contribution against anyone or anything else.

 Question

Who may be treated as the author of a literary, dramatic, musical or artistic work?

Joint authorship

3.7   However, the law does recognise that a work may have more than one author. There may be joint authorship of a work where it is

> 'a work produced by the collaboration of two or more authors in which the contribution of each is not distinct from the contribution of the other author or authors' (CDPA 1988, s 10(1)).

Works of joint authorship are usually readily identifiable as such because the names of all authors appear on the work and no effort is made to separate their contributions. The presumption of authorship in favour of those whose names appear on copies of literary, dramatic, musical or artistic works[4] applies also to works of joint authorship.

3.8   Complexities may arise, however, where there is no express attribution to joint authors.[5] In an old case the test of joint authorship was said to be whether the authors had a 'preconcerted joint design' or cooperated in the design or execution of the work so that one who improved or

---

[2] CDPA 1988, s 104(2).

[3] The classic analyses are: M Foucault, 'Qu'est ce qu'un auteur?' (1969) 64 *Bulletin de la Société française de Philosophie* 73 (translated as 'What is an author?', in JV Harris (ed), *Textual Strategies: Perspectives in Post-Structuralist Criticism* (1979)); R Barthes, 'The death of the author', in *Image Music Text* (1977); and J Derrida, 'Limited Inc a b c', in *Limited Inc* (1988). The literature in English is immense: see eg L Zemer, *The Idea of Authorship in Copyright* (2007). See too JC Ginsburg, 'The concept of authorship in comparative copyright law' (2003) 52 De Paul LR 1063; J Pila, 'An intentional view of the copyright work' (2008) 71 MLR 535; J Phillips, 'Authorship, ownership, wikiship: copyright in the twenty-first century' (2008) 3 JIPLP 788; WR Cornish, 'Conserving culture and copyright: a partial history' (2009) 13 Edinburgh Law Review 8; HL MacQueen, 'The legal definition of authorship and the scrolls', in JJ Collins and TH Lim (eds), *Oxford Handbook of the Dead Sea Scrolls* (2010).   [4] CDPA 1988, s 104(2).

[5] See generally L Zemer, 'Contribution and collaboration in joint authorship: too many misconceptions' (2006) 1 JIPLP 283.

touched up the work of another was not a joint author of the eventual production.[6] In *Beckingham v Hodgens*,[7] however, the Court of Appeal held that the existence of a common intention to produce a joint work was not a requirement for a work of joint authorship. The essence of joint authorship is collaboration or cooperation between the authors in the *execution* of the work.[8] The decision as to whether or not there is joint authorship will turn on the nature of each of the contributions, linked to the fundamental concept of copyright pertaining to the form of expression rather than to ideas and information. Did one person supply only ideas and material which were translated into a work by the other, or did the former's contribution amount to a part in formulating the expression, ie, authorship?

■ *Brown v Mcasso Music* [2005] FSR 40

M had drafted lyrics for a rap song to be used in a TV commercial. B had then amended the lyrics to give them a greater authenticity as a rap song, changing idiomatically incorrect language, using appropriate Jamaican English to match word rhythm to the music, and adding extempore exclamations. It was held that B was a joint author of the song. His contribution to the writing was an active one, involving skill and judgement to obtain the authentic feel of rap. Although he made use of standard elements of rap culture, his work satisfied the copyright test of originality (above, paras 2.34–2.46).[9]

Question

When may a person be identified as a joint author?

3.9   In cases where clearly one person supplies ideas and information and another puts these into literary or artistic form, the latter is author and owner of the copyright. So a person who supplied the ideas for the plot of a play,[10] a director who added ideas during the rehearsals and development of a play's script,[11] and a person who had had the idea of using an outline drawing of a human hand as an indicator on a ballot paper,[12] were all held not entitled to the copyright in the resultant works, while in *Donoghue v Allied Newspapers*[13] the ghost writer of a jockey's memoirs was held to be the owner of the copyright therein as the person responsible for the language in which the work was cast.

■ *Robin Ray v Classic FM plc* [1998] FSR 622

RR, an individual with wide knowledge of classical music, entered a consultancy arrangement with Classic FM under which he provided a catalogue of 50,000 items to be in the radio station's music library, categorised in a way which would enable it to be used to establish the station's playlists. A database incorporating RR's work was established by Classic FM, which then sought to license its use by overseas radio stations without RR's consent. RR claimed copyright in the

---

[6] *Bagge v Miller* [1917–23] MCC 179.   [7] [2003] EMLR 18.
[8] *Cala Homes (South) v Alfred McAlpine Homes East* [1995] FSR 818 at 835.
[9] Leave to appeal was refused by the Court of Appeal: [2006] FSR 24.
[10] *Tate v Thomas* [1921] 1 Ch 503; also *Wiseman v Weidenfeld & Nicolson* [1985] FSR 525.
[11] *Brighton v Jones* [2005] FSR [16] 288.   [12] *Kenrick v Lawrence* (1890) 25 QBD 99.
[13] [1938] Ch 106; also *Evans v Hulton & Co* (1924) 131 LT 534.

catalogue and its categorisation, and argued that Classic FM were infringing. Classic FM replied that they were joint authors. It was held that RR was the sole author of the catalogue; Classic FM had supplied ideas, suggestions and materials for RR's use, but he alone composed the catalogue.

Some particular examples of joint authorship issues

3.10   There have been a number of difficult cases where parties were working together in the production of new software.

■ *Fylde Microsystems Ltd v Key Radio Systems Ltd* [1998] FSR 449

The parties were cooperating (without a contract) in the development of radios. FM wrote software for installation in KRS's radios, which the latter then sold. The parties fell into dispute over ownership of the copyright in the software. KRS admitted that F was the writer but argued that it was a joint author by setting the specification for the software, reporting errors and bugs, making suggestions as to the cause of faults, and providing technical information about the hardware in which the software had to operate. It was held that although KRS's activities involved much skill and labour, it was not of the nature of authorship, and the parties were not joint authors.

■ *Cyprotex Discovery Ltd v University of Sheffield* [2004] RPC 4[14]

The University and a company (C) were engaged together under a contract in the development for practical application of software initially created by the University. The relationship broke down and an issue emerged as to whether the parties were joint authors of the software which had been developed under the contract. It was held that the University's contribution to the new software—provision of background information about the initial software, assistance in compilation of the technical specifications of what the new software should contain, and vetting the suggestions of third-party sponsors of the work—was not that of an author but of a client wishing to ensure the functionality of the new software when completed. It therefore had no claim to the copyright in the new software.

 Exercise

Consider the case of two sets of solicitors negotiating and drafting written contracts on behalf of their respective clients. Is the contractual document which results a work of joint authorship or not? See David Vaver, 'Copyright in legal documents' (1993) 31 Osgoode Hall LJ 661.

3.11   Another quite common situation is the development of musical work by a group working together but developing the ideas by playing them on their instruments rather than writing

---

[14] On appeal the decision was affirmed in other grounds: [2004] RPC 44 (CA).

mode of expression or execution. A straightforward example would be where someone is dictating to an amanuensis, in which case he is plainly the sole author. It also appears certain that a builder cannot claim copyright in a work of architecture, where the architect is regarded as the author.[18]

■ *Najma Heptulla v Orient Longman Ltd* [1989] FSR 598 (High Court of India)

MA, a leader of the Indian independence movement, dictated his memoirs to HK, with whom he also discussed the content. MA was not confident writing in English (the language of the memoirs) and this was why he worked with HK. MA read the whole manuscript, made many corrections and ordered a deletion. It was held that HK was not the sole author of the book. In a literary work both language and subject matter are important. Joint authorship arose where there was an intellectual contribution by two or more persons in pursuit of a pre-concerted joint design.

Nature of joint ownership: common property

3.14   In cases of joint authorship all the authors own the copyright in the work.[19] The main consequence of joint authorship for a work is that there is only one copyright in the whole work, the duration of which is tied to the death of the last-surviving author alone.[20] The copyright is held by the authors as common property, each having a title to his own share which he can alienate and which passes to his estate on death.[21] It would also follow that each co-owner is entitled to share in the management of the common property, meaning in this case that the consent of all must be obtained before any licence is granted.[22] In any event it is provided that where copyright is owned jointly any requirement of the licence of the copyright owner requires the licence of all the owners.[23] It has been held, however, that a co-author may sue for infringement of copyright without the other authors.[24]

> ### Key points on joint authorship
>
> - Arises where more than one person collaborates in the *execution* of a work (ie in formulating the expression) and the contributions are indistinguishable in the final work
> - Supply of ideas/information insufficient to make one a joint author
> - Improvement/amendment/editing of another's work not enough to make one a joint author
> - Giving another directions/instructions as to the mode of expression may lead to one becoming at least a joint author
> - Dictation makes one the sole author
> - Ownership is common, not joint: ie there is one copyright, each party owning a share of the whole which passes to his estate on death; each may share in management, sell the share

---

[18] *Meikle v Maufe* [1941] 3 All ER 144.   [19] CDPA 1988, ss 10(3) and 11(1).
[20] CDPA 1988, s 12(4); and see below, para 3.54.
[21] See *Lauri v Renad* (1892) 3 Ch 402. The point is not entirely free from doubt and it still might be open, at least to a Scottish court, to hold that this was a case of joint property, in which case all the rights would ultimately accresce in the estate of the last-surviving author. Possibly, however, this would be unfair. On joint and common property, see *Halsbury's Laws of England* vol 9(2), para 122; *Laws of Scotland: Stair Memorial Encyclopaedia*, vol 18, paras 22–36.
[22] *Powell v Head* (1879) 12 Ch D 686; *Mail Newspapers v Express Newspapers* [1987] FSR 90.
[23] CDPA 1988, s 173(2).   [24] *Waterlow Publishers v Rose*, The Times, 8 December 1989 (CA).

Collective works

3.15   The definition of joint authorship makes it possible to distinguish what may be called 'collective works',[25] that is, works produced by collaboration where the contributions of the collaborators are separate from each other. A common example of the latter would be a song in which the words were written by one person and the music by another.[26] In a collective work each contributor has a separate copyright as the author of his part of the work, and the terms of copyright in each part will vary according to the longevity of each contributor.

Discussion point 1   For answer guidance visit www.oxfordtextbooks.co.uk/orc/macqueen2e/

Can you give any other examples of 'collective works' which are not works of joint authorship?

Discussion point 2

What is the position where a work is produced as apparently one of joint authorship within the meaning of the CDPA 1988, but the authors indicate, perhaps in a prefatory statement, that responsibility has in fact been divided along certain lines?

Compilations and authorship

3.16   Compilations must also be distinguished from both collective works and works of joint authorship: compilations have copyright and the compiler is an author even though there may be several different works by other authors represented in the compilation. The borderline can be unclear: thus *Who's Who*, which is compiled from returns completed by the subjects of each entry, has been held to be a compilation rather than a collection of autobiographies with the subjects each having copyright in their own contributions.[27]

Authors of films

3.17   The authors of a film are its producer and principal director,[28] and the film will be treated as a work of joint authorship unless these two are the same person.[29]

Sound recordings

3.18   The first copyright in a sound recording is owned by the producer.[30]

---

[25] Although note that CDPA 1988, s 178 unhelpfully defines 'collective work' so as to include works of joint authorship as well as the category of work discussed in this paragraph.

[26] See *Redwood Music Ltd v Feldman & Co Ltd* [1979] RPC 385 esp at 400–3 (a decision on the 1911 Act).

[27] *A & C Black Ltd v Claude Stacey Ltd* [1929] 1 Ch 177.   [28] CDPA 1988, s 9(2)(ab).

[29] CDPA 1988, s 10(1A). On joint authorship, see above, paras 3.7–3.14.

[30] CDPA 1988, ss 9(2)(aa), 11(1).

Broadcasts

3.19   The first copyright in every broadcast is owned by the person making the broadcast or, in the case of a broadcast which relays another broadcast by reception and immediate re-transmission, the person making that other broadcast.[31] The person making the broadcast is the person transmitting the programme, if he has any responsibility for its contents, or any person providing the programme who makes with the person transmitting it the arrangements necessary for its transmission; a programme is any item included in a broadcast.[32] An example of a situation where the transmitter has no responsibility for the contents is when he is simply transmitting a signal received from a satellite.

Published editions

3.20   The copyright in a published edition of a literary, dramatic or musical work belongs to its publisher.[33]

Joint authorship and the media copyrights

3.21   There is no restriction of the concept of joint authorship to literary, dramatic, musical and artistic works. As already noted, joint authorship arises with films; and there is express provision for joint authorship in broadcasts when a person provides a programme having made arrangements with the person actually transmitting it which are necessary for the programme's transmission.[34] Joint authorship might also arise with sound recordings produced by joint ventures or other collaborations over arrangements needed to make the record.

Using computers: computer-generated works

3.22   Problems may arise with computers. It is obvious that a person composing a computer program is author and (subject to the rules of employment discussed below, paras 3.25–3.28) first owner of the copyright in the work. In *Express Newspapers v Liverpool Daily Post and Echo*[35] it was held that the copyright in a work produced by a computer pertained to the programmers who had written the software to enable the computer to this function. Where someone other than the programmer deploys a program such as a word-processing package in the production of another work, however, the appropriate analogy would appear to be with a person using a pen, typewriter or paint brush to create something, where the copyright would plainly be in the user of the tool rather than in its maker. The 1988 Act introduces a further complication into this difficult area, the *computer-generated work*. This means that the work is generated by computer in circumstances such that there is no human author of the work.[36] In such circumstances, the author is taken to be the person by whom the arrangements necessary for the creation of the work are undertaken.[37] It seems that a distinction now requires to be made between works thus *generated* and those which are computer-*aided*. A work seems likely to be treated as computer-generated when the machine is merely provided with data by its operators which it analyses and converts into output. Where the operator has some role in the formulation of the output beyond the

---

[31] CDPA 1988, ss 9(2)(b), 11(1)   [32] For all this see CDPA 1988, s 6(3).   [33] CDPA 1988, s 9(2)(d).
[34] CDPA 1988, ss 10(2) and 6(3).   [35] [1985] FSR 306.   [36] CDPA 1988, s 178.
[37] CDPA 1988, s 9(3).

supply of data, then the work is more likely to be computer-aided only. The sequence of images generated in playing a computer video game has been held to be a computer rather than author-generated work; the person playing the game was merely a player, not an author.[38] There are several grey areas, as for example whether material obtained from a database[39] by means of a user's questioning (an example of this would be a search on a particular topic in a library cata-logue or in Lexis[40]) is computer- or user-generated. Resort to the traditional test of whose skill and labour is more significant may be necessary in such cases. The importance of the point is that the user may well be distinct from the person by whom the arrangements necessary for the creation of the work were undertaken. With computers, relevant factors may include ownership or possession of the machine, control of access and degree of input in terms of programming and data.

 Question

What is a computer-generated work? Can you give an example?

Anonymous and pseudonymous works

3.23   A literary, dramatic, musical or artistic work may be composed in such circumstances that it is not possible to identify any author. The work is thus *anonymous*. Alternatively authors may choose to use names or badges of identity other than their true names in connection with their works. The works will then be *pseudonymous*. Both are what the CDPA 1988 terms 'works of unknown authorship'.[41] In both cases, copyright in the work remains with the author whoever that may be, because where the identity is ascertainable by reasonable inquiry,[42] the term of copyright is determined by reference to the date of that person's death.[43] But there is a statutory presumption that, where no name purporting to be that of an author appears upon a published literary, dramatic, musical or artistic work, and a name purporting to be that of the publisher does appear on copies of the work as first published, the person whose name appeared is pre-sumed, until the contrary is proved, to have been the owner of the copyright at the time of publication.[44] The presumption operates even in cases where the publisher is not a party.

■ *Warwick Film Productions v Eisinger* [1969] 1 Ch 508

WFP claimed that the executor of the author of an anonymous book had assigned its copyright to them. It was held that, as WFP had not rebutted the presumption that the publisher owned the copyright, their case on this point failed. Plowman J also said that it would not have helped WFP to prove who the author was; the presumption could only be rebutted by evidence that the publishers did not own the copyright. This seems to go too far: the basic position under the Copyright Acts is that the author is the first owner of copyright and, in the case of published

---

[38] *Nova Productions Ltd v Mazooma Games Ltd* [2006] RPC 14 (Kitchin J).
[39] Which will have its own copyright or database right.
[40] Especially where the user can obtain a print-out of the results of the search.
[41] CDPA 1988, s 9(4).   [42] CDPA 1988, s 9(5).   [43] CDPA 1988, s 12(2).
[44] CDPA 1988, s 104(3). For an example see *Waterlow Publishers v Rose*, The Times, 8 December 1989 (CA). Note here the author's moral right to be identified as such (below paras 3.35–3.38), and a person's right not to have a work falsely attributed to him (below, para 3.47).

anonymous and pseudonymous works, if his identity can be established his date of death determines the term of the copyright. Viewed in this context, the presumption that the publisher owns the copyright must be rebuttable by evidence of who the author was.

3.24   The presumption does not deal with either the unpublished work or the work where the name that appears as author is a pseudonym, and the identity of the author is not reasonably discoverable in either case. Ownership may then hang in something of a void in both cases; but the effects of this are mitigated by the provision that where it is reasonable to assume that copyright has expired or that the author died 70 years or more before the beginning of the current calendar year, then no act can constitute infringement of copyright.[45]

 Discussion point   For answer guidance visit www.oxfordtextbooks.co.uk/orc/macqueen2e/

What advice would you give to someone who wished to include in an anthology of verse a poem published in a student magazine in 1900 under the name 'John Smith', but who had no idea who John Smith was?

Employment

3.25   In general, where a literary, dramatic, musical or artistic work is made in the course of the author's employment by another person, the employer is entitled to the copyright in the work.[46] The converse is of course that unless any contract under which a literary, dramatic, musical or artistic work is made is one of employment, the author will always be the first owner of the copyright.[47] This is particularly important with respect to *commissions*, one of the two points in this area where the 1988 Act departed from its predecessor's position. Under the 1956 Act, the commissioner was the first owner of copyright in respect of a limited class of artistic works; now in every case an assignation from the author will be needed to achieve this result.[48] The other change wrought by the 1988 Act was the removal of any claim by an employee-journalist to copyright in his work.[49]

 Question

When is an employer entitled to the copyright in an employee's work?

3.26   The 1988 Act's general provisions on the effect of employment on copyright are subject to any agreement to the contrary, and it is worth noting that there are no formal requirements with respect to such agreements.[50] Agreements can be implied from actings, as for example where

---

[45] CDPA 1988, s 57(1).   [46] CDPA 1988, s 11(2).

[47] For the meaning of employment see *Halsbury's Laws of England*, vol 16; *Laws of Scotland: Stair Memorial Encyclopaedia*, vol 9.

[48] 1956 Act, s 4(3). See CDPA 1988, Sch 1, para 11 for transitional provisions. For an example of the copyright in a commissioned work vesting in the author see *Oilfield Publications Ltd v MacLachlan* 1989 GWD 26–1128.

[49] 1956 Act, s 4(2); not replaced in CDPA 1988.   [50] CDPA 1988, s 11(2).

universities have generally not claimed copyright in their academic employees' works even though the production of such works might be said to be in the course of employment.[51]

■ *Noah v Shuba* [1991] FSR 14 (Mummery J)

N was employed as an epidemiologist at the Public Health Laboratory Scheme (PHLS). He wrote a book entitled *A Guide to Hygienic Skin Piercing*. In accordance with the usual practice of the PHLS, under which employees retained copyright in works written by them, the book showed N as the author and copyright owner. In an action for copyright infringement which N brought against third parties, Mummery J stated *obiter* that the long-standing practice of PHLS with regard to employees' copyright works meant that N's contract contained an implied term against the application of the employment rule in the 1988 Act.

There are no express provisions on commissions as such, and so general principles will apply. If the parties agree that the commissioner is to have the copyright in the commissioned work, the agreement will have to take the form of an assignation by the author, which the 1988 Act requires to be in writing.[52]

In the course of employment

3.27   Before the employer can claim any copyright in his employee's literary, dramatic, musical or artistic work, it must be shown to have been made in the course of the author's employment.[53]

■ *Stephenson Jordan and Harrison v Macdonald and Evans* (1952) 69 RPC 10

A former employee of the plaintiffs had published a book made up of the texts of public lectures composed and delivered by him before various audiences, and also of a report prepared by him for a client of the plaintiffs. Both parts had been written during the period of his employment. It was held that copyright in the report belonged to the employers, because the author wrote it as part of what he was employed to do; but with regard to the text of the lectures, even though the employers had encouraged the author to give the lectures and had met his resultant expenses, it was held that the employers had no copyright. An analogy was drawn between the employee and a university lecturer, and it was said to be 'both just and commonsense' (per Lord Evershed at p 18) that the latter rather than his university, had copyright in his lectures. The grounds for this view do not clearly appear in the case but it has been suggested that the employee was only employed to deliver and not to write the lectures. However this appears inconsistent with the observation of Morris LJ that it had not been shown that the employee could have been ordered either to write or to deliver the lectures (at p 24).

■ *Byrne v Statist Co* [1914] 1 KB 622

A member of the editorial staff of a newspaper made a translation into English of a speech reported in a foreign language for publication in the paper. The work was commissioned and paid for by his employers, but he carried it out in his own time and independently of his normal

---

[51] See further on universities and copyright ownership A Monotti with S Ricketson, *Universities and Intellectual Property: Ownership and exploitation* (2003); C McSherry, *Who Owns Academic Work? Battling for Control of Intellectual Property* (2001); and D Bok, *Universities in the Marketplace: the Commercialisation of Higher Education* (2003) Chapters 4, 5, 8, 9.

[52] CDPA 1988, s 90(3).   [53] CDPA 1988, s 11(2).

duties. It was held that he was the owner of the copyright, not having made the translation in the course of his employment.

■ *King v The South African Weather Service* [2009] FSR 6 (Supreme Court of Appeal, Republic of South Africa)

An employee created a computer program working both from home and in the office, over which he asserted his own copyright. His employer, a weather forecasting service, argued that the program was created 'in the course of employment' and so the copyright belonged to it. This was despite the fact that the employee's duties as a meteorologist did not include computer programming. The program assisted him in his duties to collect, collate and transmit weather data. The court held that the creation of the program, which fitted into the service's automated weather system, had been to the advantage of the employer. The employment had been the *causa causans* of the programs. A format for the program had been prescribed by the employer which also had to approve the program prior to its installation on the system. Furthermore, the appellant's job description was initially not intended to be comprehensive and was later amended to state that work outside the terms of the contract could still be created 'in the course of employment'. The scope of the employment could change either explicitly or implicitly.[54]

 Discussion point   For answer guidance visit www.oxfordtextbooks.co.uk/orc/macqueen2e/

Discuss whether a schoolteacher who writes and publishes a text for use in schools would have the copyright in it. Is there any difference in the position of the university lecturer who writes a book or articles? What about the composition of a database or a computer program by the same lecturer?

Presumption against employer

3.28   Where the name of a person purporting to be that of the author appears on a published copy of a literary, dramatic, musical or artistic work, or on a work when it is made, it is presumed that he is the author and that he did not make that work in the course of his employment. The contrary must therefore be proved.[55]

Crown copyright[56]

3.29   The monarch is entitled to copyright in every work made in the copyright area by the monarch or an officer or servant of the Crown in the course of his duties.[57] It seems that, for the most part, the position of the Crown is little different from that of any other employer, apart from the much longer duration of the copyright. It may have some unusual rights in respect of the works

---

[54]   See further L Tong, 'South African Supreme Court of Appeal interprets "course of employment" for copyright' (2009) 4 JIPLP 323.

[55]   CDPA 1988, s 104(2).

[56]   See further the website of the Office of Public Sector Information (OPSI), which administers Crown copyright: http://www.opsi.gov.uk/advice/crown-copyright/index.htm

[57]   CDPA 1988, s 163(1).

of former intelligence officers where these breach the lifelong duty of confidentiality owed to the Crown by such persons. According to some of the judges in *Attorney-General v Guardian Newspapers Ltd (No 2)*,[58] copyright in such works may vest in the Crown even though their creation occurs after the employment has ceased and cannot in any event be said to be in the course of the author's employment. The monarch is also entitled to copyright in every Act of Parliament, Act of the Scottish Parliament, Act of the Welsh and Northern Ireland Assemblies, or Measure of the General Synod of the Church of England.[59] Works made by the monarch also include any sound recordings, films, live broadcasts or cable programmes of the proceedings of the Welsh Assembly.[60] Finally, the monarch has copyright in works made in his private capacity. This is presumably affected by the special provisions as to the term of Crown copyrights, on the basis that such works are made by the monarch in terms of the section. Members of the royal family who make copyright works have the usual rights[61] and are not affected by any aspect of Crown copyright, since their works are not made by the monarch.[62]

Question

Who has the copyright in sound recordings, films or broadcasts of the Westminster and Scottish Parliaments?

Parliamentary copyright[63]

3.30   The first ownership of copyright in works made by or under the direction or control of the House of Commons or the House of Lords falls to the relevant House, or, if it made by or under the direction and control of both Houses, jointly to the two Houses.[64] The CDPA 1988 also provides that the copyright of every Bill introduced into the UK Parliament is vested in one or both of the Houses.[65] Copyright in a public Bill belongs in the first instance to the House in which the Bill is introduced, and after the Bill has been carried to the second House to both Houses jointly.[66] Copyright in a private Bill belongs to both Houses jointly.[67] Copyright in a personal Bill belongs in the first instance to the House of Lords, and after the Bill has been carried to the House of Commons to both Houses jointly.[68] Copyright in a Bill ceases when it receives Royal Assent (in which case it becomes an Act and subject to Crown copyright) or on the withdrawal or rejection of the Bill.[69] There are similar provisions for the Bills of the Scottish Parliament (first copyright belongs to the Scottish Parliamentary Corporate Body) and the

---

58   [1988] 3 All ER 545 per Scott J at p 567, per Dillon LJ at p 621 (CA) and per Lords Keith and Griffiths at pp 645 and 654 (HL). The argument is dependent on notions of equitable ownership which it would be impossible to apply in the Scottish context.

59   CDPA 1988, s 164(1); Scotland Act 1998, s 92(3). For the Bill stage, see para 3.30 below.

60   CDPA 1988, s 163(1A).

61   *Prince Albert v Strange* (1848) 2 De G & Sm 652 (64 ER 293) aff'd (1849)1 Mac & G 25 (41 ER 1171); *HRH The Prince of Wales v Associated Newspapers Ltd (No 3)* [2006] EWHC 522 (Ch, Blackburne J).

62   For a valuable discussion of the recent development and contemporary significance of Crown copyright, see S Saxby, 'Crown copyright regulation in the UK—is the debate still alive?' (2005) 13(3) International Journal of Law and Information Technology 299.

63   See generally the OPSI website, http://www.opsi.gov.uk/advice/parliamentary-copyright/index.htm, and N Cox, 'Copyright in statutes, regulations and judicial decisions in common law jurisdictions: public ownership or commercial enterprise?' (2006) 27(3) Statute Law Review 185.

64   CDPA 1988, s 165(1).   65   CDPA 1988, s 166(1).   66   CDPA 1988, s 166(2).

67   CDPA 1988, s 166(3).   68   CDPA 1988, s 166(4).

69   CDPA 1988, s 166(5). For the Crown copyright in an Act, see above, para 3.29.

Welsh and Northern Ireland Assemblies (first owner the Welsh and Northern Ireland Assembly Commissions respectively).[70]

Question

Why was there no provision for Welsh Assembly copyright before the coming into force of the Government of Wales Act 2006, Sch 10, para 28?

Author's moral rights

International background[71]

3.31   As noted in the historical introduction (above, para 2.8), the Berne Convention developed the concept of *non-transferable (inalienable) moral rights* (to claim authorship and to object to derogatory treatment of the work prejudicial to the author's honour or reputation [Article 6*bis*]. Moral rights thus recognise certain non-economic interests which an author (but no-one else) may continue to exercise in respect of a work even though no longer owner of the copyright or of the physical form in which the work was first created and recorded, this last being particularly important in respect of artistic works. The rights are reinforced by their recognition in the 1948 Universal Declaration of Human Rights: 'everyone has the right to the protection of the moral and material interests resulting from any scientific, literary or artistic production of which he is the author' (Article 27(2)).[72] The Berne Convention also provides (Article 14*ter*) for an author's inalienable resale right (*droit de suite*) in works of art and original manuscripts, giving him a right to a share of the proceeds of any sale of the work after the first transfer by the author. This latter right is however optional for Berne states.

3.32   EU Directives have nothing substantive to say about moral rights.[73] In 2001 however a Directive was enacted on the subject of artists' resale rights (*droit de suite*), to be implemented in the member states for the benefit of living artists by 2006 and for those dead before then by 2012 at latest.[74] It applies only to works of art and not (unlike the Berne Convention, see above, para 3.31) to literary or musical manuscripts, thus taking partial advantage of the option of resale rights under the Convention. The Directive gives the artist a right to a share of the proceeds of any resale of the original of his work after the sale by the artist to a first purchaser. While the Directive's objective is primarily economic, its content owes much to moral right ideas. The Directive was enacted against British opposition, but the majority of the then EU member states already had such a system in place and perceived distortion in the European art market resulting

---

[70]   CDPA 1988, ss 166A, 166B, 166C and 166D.

[71]   See in general E Adeney, *The Moral Rights of Authors and Performers: an International and Comparative Analysis* (2006) Chs 5–7.

[72]   Note also the International Covenant on Economic, Social and Cultural Rights 1966, Art 15(1): 'the States Parties to the present covenant recognize the right of everyone . . . to benefit from the protection of the moral and material interests resulting from any scientific, literary or artistic production of which he is the author'.

[73]   See the Database Directive 1996, recital 28 ('whereas the moral rights of the natural person who created the database belong to the author and should be exercised according to the legislation of the Member States and the provisions of the Berne Convention for the Protection of Literary and Artistic Works; whereas such moral rights remain outside the scope this Directive').

[74]   EC Directive 2001/84/EC.

from the variability of the national laws, as well as an injustice to the artist who gained no benefit from the value others came to place on the original of his work.

The law in the UK[75]

3.33   The two principal moral rights introduced in the UK by the CDPA 1988 are:

> Paternity: *the right to be identified as author* of a literary, dramatic, musical or artistic work, or as director of a copyright film (CDPA 1988, s 77)
>
> Integrity: the *right* of such *authors and directors to prevent derogatory treatment of their work* (CDPA 1988, s 80)

Under the heading of 'moral rights', the 1988 Act also deals with *prevention of false attributions* to one of literary, dramatic, musical or artistic works and films,[76] and a *right of privacy in certain photographs and films.*[77] It should be noted, however, that these are not usually seen as moral rights in other legal systems, or under the Berne Convention. In contrast, the Regulations implementing the *artist's resale right* in the UK do not characterise the rights as moral rights, although many of the characteristics of such rights are present, notably their inalienability from the author of the work to which they attach (see further below, para 3.34). The right is not usually included amongst the moral rights in other systems, as a result of its highly economic character.

  Question

What moral rights are now recognised in the UK?

Characteristics of moral rights

3.34   As will be explained in more detail later in the chapter, moral rights last as long as the other rights conferred by copyright (see below, para 3.51). This contrasts with the position in some Continental European countries, where the moral rights are of indefinite duration.[78] Being conceived as highly personal to the author, moral rights are not assignable[79]—that is, transferable to third parties—but they can be waived by an instrument in writing signed by the person giving up the right.[80] It is also not an infringement of the moral rights to do anything to which the person entitled to the right has consented.[81] In these ways, UK moral rights are significantly weaker than their Continental counterparts. Infringements of the rights are treated as breaches

---

[75] See Adeney, *Moral Rights*, Chs 13 and 14.   [76] CDPA 1988, s 84.   [77] CDPA 1988, s 85.
[78] Eg France (Adeney, *Moral Rights*, Ch 8); cf Ch 9 (Germany). Compare Canada, the USA and Australia, also discussed in Adeney, Chs 11, 12, 16 and 18.
[79] CDPA 1988, s 94.   [80] CDPA 1988, s 87(2)–(4).
[81] CDPA 1988, s 103. Note that an injunction may prohibit the doing of any act infringing the right of integrity unless a disclaimer is made dissociating the author or director from the treatment of the work (s 103(2)).

of statutory duty, giving rise to remedies such as injunction and damages.[82] Note that moral rights do not extend to the authors of computer programs.

 Question

May the owner of moral rights choose not to enforce them?

Key points about moral rights in general

The main moral rights are the rights of paternity and integrity

These moral rights last for the same length of time as the economic rights (see para 3.51)

The rights are inalienable, but can be waived, while the holder may consent to acts which would otherwise be infringements

---

Paternity right

3.35 The precise extent of the right to be identified as the author of a copyright work varies according to the nature of the work. When it is required, the identification must be clear and reasonably prominent so as to bring the identity of the author or director to the attention of the public.[83] The right applies to the whole or any substantial part of a work.[84] Identification is required in the following circumstances:

Literary and dramatic works (excluding song lyrics)

Whenever the work is published commercially, performed in public, or communicated to the public, or whenever copies of a film or sound recording including the work are issued to the public, or when any of these events occur in relation to an adaptation of the work.

Musical work and song lyrics

Whenever there is commercial publication, or copies of a sound recording are issued to the public, or where it is the soundtrack of a film available to the public, or when any of these events occur in relation to an adaptation.

Artistic work

Whenever there is commercial publication or public exhibition, or when a visual image is communicated to the public, or included in a film available to the public. In the case of three-dimensional artistic works, the author must be identified when copies of graphic works representing them or photographs of them are issued to the public. The author of a work of architecture in the form of a building has the right to be identified on the building as constructed, by appropriate means visible to persons entering or approaching the building.

---

[82] CDPA 1988, s 77(7).   [83] CDPA 1988, s 89(1).   [84] CDPA 1988, s 87(1).

Film

Whenever the film is shown in public, communicated to the public, or copies of the film are issued to the public.

Question

When must the author of a work be identified?

Paternity must be 'asserted'

3.36   There is no infringement of the right of paternity unless it has been previously *asserted* by the author.[85] Assertion is by *statement in writing* to that effect, either in any assignation of copyright in the work, or in any other instrument in writing signed by the author (for example, in a licence or in a warning letter to an infringer, actual or potential).[86] The requirement may well offend against the Berne Convention provision that the enjoyment and exercise of rights under the Convention (which include moral rights) shall not be subject to any formality.[87] The assertion may be general or in relation to any specified act or acts. A statement that the right has been asserted will commonly be found in the prelim pages of books, usually saying something like, 'The right of XYZ to be identified as the author of this work has been asserted in accordance with the Copyright, Designs and Patents Act 1988.' The Act contains *no requirement that paternity be asserted before the publication of a work*; but any delay in asserting the right is to be taken into account by a court in deciding whether or not to grant a remedy for breach of the right.[88]

■ *Sawkins v Hyperion Records* [2005] RPC 32 (CA)

For the facts see para 2.42 above. Hyperion issued the CD of Lalande music with the statement 'With thanks to Dr Lionel Sawkins for his preparation of performance materials for this recording'. Since this did not identify Sawkins as the author of a copyright work, the attribution right was held infringed. Sawkins had previously asserted his right with a letter during pre-recording negotiations with Hyperion in which he stated that the CD sleevenotes should bear the legend '© Copyright 2002 by Lionel Sawkins'.

Question

How and when must 'paternity' be asserted to be effective?

Exercise

Have the authors of this book asserted their rights of paternity? If not, why not?

---

[85] CDPA 1988, s 78(1).   [86] CDPA 1988, s 78(2).   [87] Berne Convention, Art 5(2).
[88] CDPA 1988, s 78(5).

Public exhibition of artistic works

3.37   There are some special provisions in respect of the *public exhibition of artistic works*. If the author affixes his name to the original or a copy when he parts with possession of it, he has asserted the moral right to be identified as its author against any subsequent possessors, whether or not the original identification is still present or visible on the work.[89] Further, where the author licenses the making of copies, moral rights to be identified where in pursuance of the licence there is an exhibition of a copy of the work may be asserted in the licence.[90] This affects the licensee and anyone into whose hands a copy made in pursuance of the licence comes, regardless of whether or not he has notice of the assertion.[91]

Exercise

A city council commissions a large bronze statue of a phoenix to stand in the city's main square, symbolising its post-industrial renaissance. The sculpture is erected and becomes a great popular success. However, no information is provided at the site about the identity of the sculptor, although it is publicised in newspapers at the time of the commission and again at the unveiling ceremony. The sculptor also identifies herself as the creator on her website, and her name is mentioned in official tourist and business guides. The commissioning contract contained no provisions about identification of the sculptor at the site, but it did give the council merchandising rights such as the reproduction and sale of miniatures of the sculpture, and the marketing of T-shirts bearing its image. Now the sculptor has approached the council, requesting that she be identified at the site of the sculpture and on merchandising material. Must the council comply with this request?

Limits on the right to be identified as author or director

3.38   The right to be identified as author does not exist in respect of computer programs, the design of typefaces, or computer-generated works.[92] Where copyright first vested in an employer, nothing done or authorised by him infringes the author's moral right.[93] Certain acts permitted in respect of the copyright in a work—fair dealing, for example—are not to be taken as infringements of the moral right to be identified as author.[94] The right does not apply to works in which Crown or Parliamentary copyright subsists, unless the author or director has previously been identified as such on or in published copies of the work.[95] Nor does it apply to publications in newspapers, magazines or similar periodicals, or in an encyclopaedia, dictionary, yearbook or other collective works of reference where the work was made for the purposes of such publication.[96]

Discussion point   For answer guidance visit www.oxfordtextbooks.co.uk/orc/macqueen2e/

What is the reason for the above limitations on the right of paternity?

---

[89] CDPA 1988, s 78(3)(a) and (4)(c).   [90] CDPA 1988, s 78(3)(b).   [91] CDPA 1988, s 78(4)(d).
[92] CDPA 1988, s 79(2).   [93] CDPA 1988, s 79(3).   [94] CDPA 1988, s 79(4)–(5).
[95] CDPA 1988, s 79(7).   [96] CDPA 1988, s 79(6).

> ### Key points about the moral right of paternity
>
> Paternity is the right to be identified as the author of a work
>
> It applies in varying ways to literary, dramatic, musical and artistic works and films but not to computer programs
>
> The right must be asserted by a statement in writing
>
> An employer who owns the copyright in a work cannot infringe the employee-author's moral rights

Right of integrity

3.39   The author of a work or director of a film has the right to object to *derogatory treatment* of his work. This moral right does not need to be asserted in any formal way. The right applies to the treatment of the whole or any part (without a requirement that it be a substantial part) of the work.[97] Derogatory treatment will occur when there is:

> 'addition to, deletion from or alteration to or adaptation of a work which amounts to distortion or mutilation of the work or is otherwise prejudicial to the honour or reputation of the author or director' (CDPA 1988 s 80(2)).

The potential scope of this can be illustrated with well-known decisions from other jurisdictions: for example, the French decision that the moral rights of the film director John Huston were infringed by the colourisation of his black-and-white film *The Asphalt Jungle*, even although the colouriser had a contractual right to do so and there was no right of integrity in Huston's home territory of the USA.[98] In a Canadian case it was held that the integrity of a sculpture in a public place was infringed by festooning it with Christmas decorations.[99] But the 1988 Act provides that a translation of a literary or dramatic work will not amount to derogatory treatment, nor will an arrangement or transcription of a musical work involving no more than a change of key or register.[100]

3.40   The right affects those who:

- publish commercially, perform in public, or communicate to the public, or issue to the public copies of a film or sound recording of, or including, a literary, dramatic or musical work (CDPA 1988, s 80(3));

- publish commercially, exhibit in public, communicate to the public, show or issue to the public copies of a film including images of, an artistic work (CDPA 1988, s 80(4)(a) and (b));

- issue to the public copies of a graphic work or photograph of works of architecture in the form of models, sculptures or works of artistic craftsmanship (CDPA 1988, s 80(4)(c)). Note that the author of a building has only the right to require that his identification be removed from it in the event of derogatory treatment (s 80(5));

- show in public, communicate to the public, or issue to the public copies of, a film (CDPA 1988, s 80(6)).

---

[97] CDPA 1988, s 89(2).   [98] *Huston v Turner Entertainment Inc* (1992) 23 IIC 702.
[99] *Snow v Eaton Centre Ltd* (1982) 70 CPR (2d) 105 (Ont).   [100] CDPA 1988, s 80(2)(a).

If any of these activities includes a derogatory treatment of a work to which the right pertains, the right of integrity has been infringed.[101] Further, dealing in an article which infringes this right will also attract a secondary infringement liability.[102]

Question

Identify the common features of the various situations in which the moral right of integrity may be infringed.

Discussion point   For answer guidance visit www.oxfordtextbooks.co.uk/orc/macqueen2e/

How far may the right of integrity be compared to one of private censorship?

3.41   There have been few cases to date in the UK courts about the right of integrity, and they exhibit a cautious approach.

■ *Morrison Leahy Music Ltd v Lightbond Ltd* [1993] EMLR 144

L produced a sound recording entitled 'Bad Boys Megamix' which took bits of the music and words from five George Michael compositions (the copyright of which MLM owned) and put them together in snatches lasting from 10 to 65 seconds, where the works from which they were taken lasted from three minutes, 22 seconds to six minutes, 45 seconds. It was held that it was plainly arguable that such relatively short snatches did alter the character of the original works by removing them from their original context and creating a new one.

■ *Tidy v Natural History Museum Trustees* (1995) 37 IPR 501

T, a cartoonist, produced large-scale dinosaur cartoons to hang in the Museum. It was held that the right of integrity did not entitle T to prevent the republication of the cartoons on a much smaller scale in a book being published by the Museum Trustees.

■ *Pasterfield v Denham* [1999] FSR 168

P was commissioned by Plymouth City Council in 1988 to design promotional leaflets for the Plymouth Dome, a tourist attraction. The leaflet used devices of a satellite, a German bomber formation, and a detailed cut-away drawing of the Dome interior. In 1994 the Council commissioned D to produce a new leaflet for the Dome: this included copies of the satellite and bomber formation, along with a smaller and altered version of the cut-away drawing. The alterations included the omission of features on the edge of the original drawing and a variation in colouring. It was held that these differences were so trivial that they could only be seen by close inspection, and so could not amount to derogatory treatment. Such treatment had also to be

---

[101] CDPA 1988, s 80(1).   [102] CDPA 1988, s 83.

prejudicial to the author's honour or reputation as an artist; it was not enough that the artist felt aggrieved.

■ *Confetti Records v Warner Music UK Ltd* [2003] EMLR 35

The composer of a musical work called 'Burnin' sued for derogatory treatment by way of mixing it on a compilation album with rap material referring to violence and drugs. It was held that merely distorting or mutilating a work did not infringe the right of integrity; prejudice to the author's honour and reputation was also required. In giving evidence the composer made no complaint about the treatment of 'Burnin', and the court should not infer prejudice for him. The words of the rap were for practical purposes in a foreign language the content of which was not proved, and they were anyway hard to decipher. All this went against any conclusion that the treatment infringed the right of integrity.

 Exercise

A local authority commissions a new concert hall and paintings to be hung in its entrance hall. The paintings are unpopular and much criticised in the local media for their abstract character. Following an election leading to a change of party in control of the authority, and amidst much publicity, the council orders the removal of the paintings to storage, and their replacement with cartoons humorously depicting aspects of local life. Can either the architect of the hall or the painter object to the council's action on the basis of their rights of integrity? You may find it helpful in thinking about this problem to consider the Indian case of *Sehgal v Union of India* [2005] FSR 39.

Limits on the right of integrity

3.42   The limits on the kinds of work affected by the right of integrity are similar to those operative in the right of paternity:[103] for example, computer programs, computer-generated works,[104] publications in collective works,[105] and works where the employer, Crown or Parliament has the first copyright.[106] There are some important further limits on the integrity right, however. It does not apply in relation to any work made for the purpose of reporting current events, since otherwise the traditional sub-editing process could be severely hampered.[107] In the case of anonymous and pseudonymous works where it is reasonable to suppose that copyright has expired,[108] no act will infringe the right of integrity if it would not infringe copyright.[109] The right is not infringed by anything done for the purpose of avoiding the commission of an offence, or complying with a duty imposed by or under an enactment.[110] Finally, anything done by the BBC for the purpose of avoiding the inclusion in a programme of anything which offends against good taste or decency or which is likely to encourage or incite to crime or to lead to disorder or to be offensive to public feeling will not infringe the right of integrity.[111]

---

[103] See generally CDPA 1988, ss 81 and 82, and above, para 3.38.
[104] CDPA 1988, s 81(2). But there is a right of integrity in a typeface.   [105] CDPA 1988, s 81(4).
[106] CDPA 1988, s 82.   [107] CDPA 1988, s 81(3).   [108] CDPA 1988, s 57 and see below, para 3.53.
[109] CDPA 1988, s 81(5).   [110] CDPA 1988, s 81(6)(a) and (b).
[111] CDPA 1988, s 81(6)(c). There is no specific exemption for commercial broadcasters, who will therefore have to rely on the general exemption in respect of avoiding the commission of offences or breach of a statutory duty (see previous note).

Exercise 1

Before the 1988 Act came into force, the author of a play about the Falklands War to be broadcast on the BBC strenuously objected to the Corporation's cutting of passages that presented the Prime Minister Mrs Thatcher in an unfavourable light.[112] Would that author now be able to make a claim under the right of integrity, and would the BBC be able to plead its privileged position (described above) in its defence?

Exercise 2

Would Elinor Glyn have been able to argue that the film satire 'Pimple's Three Weeks (without the option)' infringed the moral rights in her novel *Three Weeks* (see *Glyn v Weston Feature Film Co* [1916] 1 Ch 261)?

Exercise 3

To what extent are authors able to use the right to control the way in which their works are presented to the world—for example, through distasteful association, packaging or advertising, or through adaptations in other media which travesty their work (at least in their view)?

Exercise 4

Consider the case of *Galerie d'Art du Petit Champlain inc v Théberge* [2002] 2 SCR 336 (Supreme Court of Canada), discussed below, para 4.29. Was the artist's right of integrity infringed in that case?

Exercise 5

Could an author who had become dissatisfied with the quality of his work demand its withdrawal from public circulation, on the basis that its continued availability would damage his honour and reputation?[113] Consider in this connection the old Scottish case of *Davis v Miller* (1855) 17 D 1166.

Exercise 6

Consider the French case of *Hugo v SA Plon* [2007] ECDR 9 (Cour de Cassation, France) in which the moral right of Victor Hugo (1802–1885) in his famous novel *Les Misérables* (published 1862 and out of copyright) was held not infringed by the publication in 2001 of two works purporting to be sequels to the novel and using characters from it. French law requires respect for the author's name, title and work. Apart from the questions of location, term, and assertion, would it have been possible to sue on these facts for infringement of the UK moral rights of paternity or integrity?

---

[112] cf *Frisby v British Broadcasting Corporation* [1967] Ch 932, where a similar complaint was dealt with as a matter of interpreting the author's contract.

[113] The example is drawn from the well-known French case of *Eden v Whistler* DP 1900, I 497, where the famous artist was allowed to refuse to deliver a portrait to its commissioner, despite previously exhibiting it himself. The permission was conditional on Whistler repaying his fee and undertaking not to exhibit the painting again. On honour, see E Adeney, 'The moral right of integrity: the past and future of "honour" ' [2005] IPQ 111.

Meaning of publishing commercially

3.43   Both the rights of paternity and integrity arise, inter alia, when a work is published commercially. Commercial publication means issuing copies of the work to the public at a time when copies made in advance of the receipt of orders are generally available to the public (eg through a retail outlet), or making the work available to the public by means of an electronic retrieval system.[114]

> **Key points on the moral right of integrity**
>
> The right is to prevent derogatory treatment of copyright works when they are published or otherwise put before the public
>
> Derogatory treatment is distortion or mutilation of a work or treatment which is otherwise prejudicial to the honour or reputation of the author
>
> The UK courts have not given the right expansive scope in their decisions on the matter

Artists' resale rights

3.44   A further right was introduced in the UK on 14 February 2006, in implementation of a European Parliament and Council Directive of 2001.[115] The author of a work of graphic or plastic art in which copyright subsists has a right to a royalty on any sale of a work that is a resale subsequent to the first transfer of ownership by the author.[116] The right subsists so long as the copyright subsists,[117] one effect of this being that 'only the originals of works of modern and contemporary art…fall within the scope of the resale right'.[118] In general, and in the fashion of a moral right, this right cannot be assigned,[119] waived,[120] or shared[121] by the author, although it can be transmitted on death, whether by will or the rules of intestate succession,[122] and the right may be transferred to a charity.[123] But the right can be exercised *only* through a collecting society.[124] The holder of the right can choose which such collecting society to mandate for this purpose,[125] but in the absence of such a transfer of management, the collecting society managing copyright on behalf of artists (eg the Design and Artists' Copyright Society [DACS])[126] is deemed mandated to manage the right[127]—that is, collect the resale royalty in return for a fixed percentage or fee of the money so ingathered.[128] The amount of the royalty is calculated in relation to the resale price,[129] the resale price being taken to be the price obtained for the sale net of any tax payable on the transaction and converted into euro at the European Central Bank reference rate prevailing at the contract date.[130] The (not especially generous) royalty rates are as follows:[131]

---

[114] CDPA 1988, s 175(2).

[115] Artist's Resale Right Regulations 2006 (SI 2006/346), implementing Directive 2001/84/EC of the European Parliament and Council on the resale right for the benefit of the author of an original work of art. See generally C Lewis, 'Implementing the artist's resale right directive' (2007) 2 JIPLP 298.

[116] Reg 3(1). A sale is a transfer of ownership of the work from seller to buyer under a contract in exchange for a money consideration called the price (Sale of Goods Act 1979, s 2 and reg 2 (definition of 'sale')). The author is the person who creates the work (reg 2, definition of 'author'). For a presumption that the author is the person whose name appears on the work as such, see reg 6.

[117] Reg 3(2).   [118] Resale Right Directive 2001, recital 17.

[119] Reg 7(1). Any charge on a resale right is void (reg 7(2)).   [120] Reg 8(1).

[121] Reg 8(2). Note however the provisions for cases of joint authorship, where resale right is owned in common unless otherwise agreed in writing (reg 5).

[122] Reg 9. The person into whose hands the right is transmitted may likewise transmit it.   [123] Reg 7(3)–(5).

[124] Reg 14(1).   [125] Reg 14(3).   [126] See the DACS website: http://www.dacs.org.uk/   [127] Reg 14(2).

[128] Reg 14(5)(b).   [129] Reg 3(3).   [130] Reg 3(4).   [131] Schedule 1.

Diagram 3.1 Royalty rates table

Portion of the sale price	Percentage amount
From 0 to 50,000 euro	4%
From 50,000.01 to 200,000 euro	3%
From 200,000.01 to 350,000 euro	1%
From 350,000.01 to 500,000 euro	0.5%
Exceeding 500,000 euro	0.25%

A resale becomes liable to the royalty where the buyer or the seller or the agent of either is acting in the course of a business of dealing in works of art, and the sale price is not less than 1,000 euro.[132] The persons liable to pay the royalty are the seller *and*, if acting in the course of a business of dealing in works of art, the seller's agent, the buyer's agent if there is no seller's agent, and, where there are no such agents, the buyer.[133] The liability of these parties is joint and several.[134] The liability to make the payment arises on completion of the resale.[135]

3.45   A number of other points should be made about the artist's resale right:

- The royalty is only payable on the *resale of works of art*. Works of graphic or plastic art include, for example, a picture, collage, painting, drawing, engraving, print, lithograph, sculpture, tapestry, ceramic, glassware item or photograph.[136] The work sold must be the one which the artists created. The resale of a *copy* of a work of art is not subject to the royalty right unless it is one of a limited number made by the author or under his authority.[137]

- The royalty is only payable on a resale *after* the *first transfer of ownership of the work of art by the author*. While the author's first transfer of ownership will typically be a sale to another person, the transaction need not be for any consideration,[138] and so might be a gift. Transfer also includes transmission on death by will or by intestate succession, and disposal of the work by the author's personal representatives for estate administration purposes, as well as disposal by the administrator of the author's insolvent estate.[139]

- Where the seller previously acquired the work directly from the author less than three years before the resale *and* the sale price now does not exceed 10,000 euro, there is no liability to a resale royalty.[140]

- There are complex *transitional* provisions.[141] Resale royalties are not payable in respect of contracts concluded before 14 February 2006, but the right does otherwise apply to works made before that date. Where the artist died before 14 February 2006, three scenarios are possible:

  (1) *artist owned copyright*: resale right deemed transmitted to person beneficially entitled to that copyright;

  (2) *artist owned work but not copyright*: resale right deemed transmitted to person beneficially entitled to the work;

---

[132] Reg 12(2), (3).   [133] Reg 13(1), (2).   [134] Reg 13(1).
[135] Reg 13(3). The liable person may withhold payment until evidence of entitlement to be paid the royalty is produced (Reg 13(3)).
[136] Reg 4(1).   [137] Reg 4(2).   [138] Reg 12(1).   [139] Reg 3(5).   [140] Reg 12(4).   [141] Reg 16.

(3) *artist owned neither copyright nor work*: resale right deemed transmitted to person beneficially entitled to residue of personal estate.

Resale rights so transmitted, or actually transmitted on or after 14 February 2006, may not be exercised in respect of any sale where the contract date precedes 1 January 2010.[142] Thus the UK took advantage of a provision in the Directive intended 'to enable the economic operators in those Member States [which do not, at the time of the adoption of this Directive, apply a resale right] to adapt gradually to the aforementioned right whilst maintaining their economic viability'.[143] In September 2008 the UK–IPO published a consultation document proposing that the UK exemption be extended for a further two years until January 2012.[144] Ninety per cent of respondents stated that the derogation should not be extended. Despite this, the UK Government has written to the European Commission informing it of its intention to extend the derogation for two years.[145]

3.46 The purpose of an artist's resale right is succinctly summarised in one of the recitals to the Resale Right Directive: 'to ensure that authors of graphic and plastic works of art share in the economic success of their original works of art…to redress the balance between the economic situation of authors of graphic and plastic works of art and that of other creators who benefit from successive exploitations of their works'.[146] Crudely, the model is one of the impecunious artist forced to sell his creations, only to see others later earning riches from dealings in those creations. As already noted, the right did not exist in the UK before 14 February 2006, but it was found in the majority of other EU member states, albeit with variable rules. The harmonisation of the Directive was thus intended to eliminate the differences found in the EU, in order to remove an obstacle to the operation of a single European market in this field. The Directive was highly contested, because the resale right is not widely found outside Europe, and there was significant concern that what is effectively a form of tax on dealings in art would drive business away from Europe to other centres such as the USA (in particular New York).[147] The UK was particularly concerned because the success of its international art market could be attributed, some thought, to the absence of any artists' resale right. More fundamentally, it can be argued against the right that those who make successful businesses through dealing in art are not necessarily merely enriching themselves on the back of the artist, but play a significant independent role in ensuring that art works generate wealth.[148]

 Discussion point   For answer guidance visit www.oxfordtextbooks.co.uk/orc/macqueen2e/

Why should resale royalty right be limited to works of art? Why are there no equivalent right for authors of literary, dramatic and musical works in relation to their manuscripts, as provided in the Berne Convention, Article 14*ter* (above para 3.31)? (Note recital 19 of the Resale Right Directive: 'the harmonisation brought about by this Directive does not apply to original manuscripts of writers and composers').

[142] Reg 17. [143] Recital 17. [144] http://www.ipo.gov.uk/press-release-20080630
[145] http://webdb2.patent.gov.uk/press-release-20081219-letter.pdf
[146] European Parliament and Council Directive 2001/84/EC, recital 3.
[147] California has an artists' resale royalty right, and has lost much art business to New York.
[148] J Merryman, 'The proposed generalization of the droit de suite in the European Communities' [1997] IPQ 16.

> ## Key points about artists' resale rights
>
> The aim of the right is to enable artists to take a share of the profit made by others from sales of their original art works
>
> The right lasts for the same period as the copyright in the work
>
> The right is inalienable, although it transmits on death

False attribution of authorship

3.47   A person has a moral right not to have a work attributed to him.[149] This is the counterpart of the right to be identified as the author. There is a potential secondary liability for dealers in copies which infringe this right.[150] The right applies to the whole or any part (without any requirement of substantiality) of the work.[151]

■ *Clark v Associated Newspapers Ltd* [1998] 1 All ER 959[152]

The London *Evening Standard* published a series of articles entitled 'Alan Clark's Secret Election Diary' or 'Alan Clark's Secret Political Diary' and set beside a photograph of Clark, a prominent Conservative politician and an author well-known for the publication of his personal diaries, which were 'malicious, lecherous and self-pitying, and…enormous fun'. The *Standard* articles sought to parody or spoof the real diaries, and contained a statement that 'Peter Bradshaw…imagines what a new diary might contain'. The statement was in a font bigger than that of the main text but much smaller than the heading and title. It was held that there had been a false attribution. The statement of attribution had to have a clear single meaning, but the law did not require proof of damage, nor was there a cure for the attribution in the 'counter-messages' about Bradshaw's contribution. If 'counter-messages' are to be effective, they have to be as bold, precise and compelling as the false statement.

Right of privacy of certain photographs and films

3.48   A person who for private and domestic purposes commissions the taking of a photograph or the making of a film has, where copyright subsists in the resulting work, the right not to have copies of the work issued to the public, the work exhibited or shown in public, or the work communicated to the public.[153] The statutory right applies in relation to the whole or any substantial part of the photograph or film.[154] Any person doing or authorising one of these acts is liable as an infringer. An example would be the display of wedding photographs in the photographer's shop window where that was not authorised contractually or otherwise.[155] The right is not infringed where the act occurs in the context of one of the permitted acts in respect of the copyright in the work.[156]

---

[149]   CDPA 1988, s 84.   [150]   CDPA 1988, s 84(3)–(7).   [151]   CDPA 1988, s 89(2).
[152]   See also on the passing off aspects of this case, paras 17.39, 17.56.   [153]   CDPA 1988, s 85(1).
[154]   CDPA 1988, s 89(1).
[155]   An example drawn from the author's own experience with his wedding photographer; but see also *McCosh v Crow & Co* (1903) 5F 670 and *Pollard v Photographic Co* (1889) 40 Ch D 345.
[156]   CDPA 1988, s 85(2).

Duration of copyright and moral rights

Introduction

3.49 The rights conferred by copyright generally endure for a limited period of time only. The Berne Convention provides for a *minimum* period of the author's lifetime plus 50 years for the works to which it applies (Article 7), while the Rome Convention lays down another minimum of at least 20 years for sound recordings and broadcasts (Article 14). Various formulae are used in the UK legislation, generally involving a period of either 70 or 50 years from the end of the calendar year in which a given event occurred. The present position is the result of an EU Directive first enacted in 1993 and implemented in the UK in 1995.[157] In the following paragraphs, references to the 70- or 50-year periods should be understood as references to these formulae. The use of 'the end of the calendar year' as part of the formula is to avoid disputes as to precisely when the event in question occurred. With literary, dramatic, musical and artistic works, the copyright period is tied first to the lifetime of the author, with the 70-year period added on after his death (*post mortem auctoris*). This reflects recognition of the author's 'natural' right of property in his work, but it continues to be the period even where the copyright in the work is in other hands.[158] The extension of copyright beyond the author's lifetime was initially conceived as a form of protection for his family and descendants, but again the period applies even when the copyright has been transferred to others. With the media copyrights, there is a 50-year period, not tied to any particular lifetime, but rather to the making or publication of the work; reflecting views that works of this kind involve a lesser creative endeavour on the part of the individuals concerned; that the first owner will usually be a company, making it impossible to calculate the term by reference to a human life; and that the protection is essentially to support investment rather than creativity. The UK position parallels the rest of the EU, since the rules on copyright terms were harmonised by the 1993 Directive, but outside the Union, different copyright terms may apply in other jurisdictions. This can have the effect that a work which is in copyright in the EU may not have it in other countries, and vice-versa. This can create problems for the international flow of copyright products.

Economic rights in literary, dramatic, musical and artistic works

3.50 All literary, dramatic, musical and artistic works, published or unpublished, enjoy the economic rights conferred by copyright—that is, the rights of reproduction, distribution, rental and lending, public performance, broadcasting and adaptation (see further para 4.10 below)—until the end of the 70-year period after the author's death.[159]

---

[157] Council Directive 93/98/EEC of 29 October 1993 harmonising the term of protection for copyright and certain related rights; Duration of Copyright and Rights in Performances Regulations 1995 (SI 1995/3297). The Directive now exists in a consolidated version: European Parliament and Council Directive 2006/116/EC.

[158] On economic justifications for the copyright terms see Landes and Posner, *Economic Structure of Intellectual Property Law* (2004), Ch 8. See also the still thought-provoking K Puri, 'The term of copyright protection: is it too long in the wake of new technologies?' [1990] EIPR 12.

[159] CDPA 1988, s 12(1).

Diagram 3.2 Author copyright table

70 years

Creation - Author's death – year end - Copyright
expires

Under the pre-1988 Act law, unpublished works could enjoy copyright for as long as they remained unpublished, which might mean in perpetuity. But under the 1988 Act there is now no possibility of a *new* perpetual copyright coming into existence. The perpetual copyrights which existed under pre-1988 legislation have had dates of expiry placed upon them (generally the end of the 50-year period from the end of the year when the 1988 Act came into force, meaning that there could be a sort of copyright bonanza on 1 January 2040).[160] There is one exception to this, found in provisions added at a very late stage of the Parliamentary progress of the 1988 Act, giving the Hospital for Sick Children, Great Ormond Street, London, a right without limit of time to a royalty in respect of public performances, commercial publications, broadcasting or use in a cable programme service of JM Barrie's *Peter Pan*, notwithstanding that the copyright therein expired on 31 December 1987. Although the 1988 Act does not preserve the work's copyright in so many words, the effect is much as though it had.[161]

Question

If the author of a book published in 2010 was born in June 1956, when will the copyright in the book expire?

Moral rights

3.51   The rights of paternity and integrity (see above, paras 3.35–3.43) subsist as long as copyright in the works in question, as does the artist's resale right (above, para 3.44). The right to prevent false attributions (see further para 3.47 above) subsists until 20 years after the author's or director's death.[162] This creates the curious possibility of false attribution being lawful 20 years and one day after the death of the author or the director. In these respects, UK moral rights are weaker than those of some other countries, such as France, where they are of indefinite duration.

Computer-generated works

3.52   Where a literary, dramatic, musical or artistic work is computer-generated (see above para 3.22), the copyright expires at the end of the period of 50 years from the end of the calendar year in which the work was made,[163] as there is no reason to attach the work to the lifetime of any particular person.

---

[160] CDPA 1988, Sch 1, para 12.   [161] CDPA 1988, s 301 and Sch 6.   [162] CDPA 1988, s 86.
[163] CDPA 1988, s 12(7).

Anonymous and pseudonymous works

3.53 Anonymity and pseudonymity (see above paras 3.23–3.24) affect only the period for which the copyright endures. The copyright continues until the end of the 70-year period following the end of the calendar year in which either (a) the work was made, or (b) the work was first made available to the public.[164] But if the identity of the author becomes known before the end of those periods, then the usual period of that person's lifetime plus 70 years applies.[165] Literary, dramatic and musical works are made available to the public by performance in public or by being communicated to the public, although this definition does not exhaust the possible ways in which such works are made available to the public.[166] In the case of an artistic work, making available to the public includes exhibition in public, showing in public a film including the work, and communication to the public.[167] No account is taken, however, of any unauthorised act.[168]

Discussion point For answer guidance visit www.oxfordtextbooks.co.uk/orc/macqueen2e/

A person is copying and collecting with a view to publication the verses engraved on tombstones in local churchyards, most of which appear to have been erected in the 19th or early 20th centuries. The verses are otherwise unpublished and of unknown authorship. What steps should the collector take to avoid any danger of being sued for copyright infringement?

Works of joint authorship

3.54 The term of copyright for a work of joint authorship (see above paras 3.7–3.14) is determined by reference, where appropriate, to the date of death of the author who died last.[169] Copyright in the jointly authored work will therefore expire 70 years from the end of the calendar year in which there occurred the death of the author who died last of the group of joint authors. Where the identity of one or more of the authors is known, and the identity of one or more is not, copyright expires 70 years from the end of the calendar year in which died the last of the authors whose identity is known.[170]

Question

When will the copyright in this book expire? How do the rules above affect moral rights?

Term of Crown copyright in literary, dramatic, musical and artistic works

3.55 Where the monarch is entitled to the copyright in a literary, dramatic, musical or artistic work, it subsists until the end of the period of 125 years from the end of the calendar year in which

---

[164] CDPA 1988, s 12(2).   [165] ibid.   [166] CDPA 1988, s 12(2)(a).   [167] CDPA 1988, s 12(2)(b).
[168] CDPA 1988, s 12(5) proviso.   [169] CDPA 1988, s 12(8)(a)(i).   [170] CDPA 1988, s 12(8)(a)(ii).

the work was made, or, if the work is published commercially before the end of the period of 75 years from the end of the calendar year in which it was made, until the end of the period of 50 years from the end of the calendar year in which it was first so published.[171] The 125-year period is therefore a maximum which may be shortened by commercial publication during the first 75 years after the work is made. Commercial publication consists in issuing copies of the work to the public at a time when copies made in advance of the receipt of orders are generally available to the public, or when the work is made available to the public by means of an electronic retrieval system.[172] Crown copyright in sound recordings and films is of the same duration as for other owners.

 Discussion point   For answer guidance visit www.oxfordtextbooks.co.uk/orc/macqueen2e/
Why is Crown copyright in literary, dramatic, musical and artistic works not subject to the usual rules on duration?

Crown copyright in Acts and Measures

3.56   The Crown copyright in Acts of Parliament, the Scottish Parliament and the Welsh and Northern Ireland Assemblies and Measures of the General Synod of the Church of England subsists from Royal Assent until the end of the period of 50 years from the end of the calendar year in which Royal Assent was given.[173]

Term of Parliamentary copyright

3.57   Copyright in literary, dramatic, musical or artistic works made by or under the direction or control of the Houses of Parliament subsists until the end of the period of 50 years from the end of the calendar year in which the work was made.[174] Where copyright has subsisted in a Parliamentary Bill, it ceases when the Bill receives the Royal Assent or is withdrawn or rejected or at the end of the Parliamentary Session.[175] There are similar provisions for Bills of the Scottish Parliament and the Northern Ireland and Welsh Assemblies.[176] If a Bill is rejected by the House of Lords but may be presented for Royal Assent by virtue of the Parliament Acts 1911 and 1949, copyright will continue to subsist in it notwithstanding the Lords' rejection.[177]

Films

3.58   Film copyright expires at the end of the period of 70 years from the end of the calendar year in which the death occurs of the last to die of (a) the principal director, (b) the screenplay author,(c) the dialogue author, or (e) the composer of music specially created for and used in the film.

---

[171] CDPA 1988, s 163(3).   [172] CDPA 1988, s 175(2).   [173] CDPA 1988, s 164(2).   [174] CDPA 1988, s 165(3).
[175] CDPA 1988, s 166(5).   [176] CDPA 1988, ss 166A(2), 166B(2), 166C(2), 166D(2).
[177] CDPA 1988, s 166(5) proviso.

If the identity of one or more of these persons is unknown, but the identity of another is not, the relevant death date is that of the last whose identity is known. If the identity of none of these persons is known then the film copyright subsists as follows:

(a) until the end of the 70-year period from the end of the calendar year in which the work is first made, or

(b) if, during period (a) it is made available to the public by being shown in or communicated to the public, 70 years from the end of the calendar year in which it is first so made available.[178]

In determining whether a film has been made available to the public, no account is taken of any unauthorised act.[179] Finally, if there is no principal director, screenplay or dialogue author or composer of music specially for the film, copyright expires at the end of 50 years from the end of the calendar year in which the film was made.[180]

 Question

Remind yourself of who is to be treated as the author of a film (above, para 3.17). Are there any anomalies when you compare these rules with the rules about the duration of film copyright?

Sound recordings

3.59   The copyright in a sound recording subsists:

(a) until the end of the 50-year period from the end of the calendar year in which the work is first made, or

(b) if it is published before the end of period (a), 50 years from the end of the calendar year in which it is first published, or

(c) if, during period (a) it is not published but is made available to the public by being played in or communicated to the public, 50 years from the end of the calendar year in which it is first so made available.[181]

Diagram 3.3 50 years table

---

[178] CDPA 1988, s 13B(2)–(4).   [179] CDPA 1988, s 13B(6), proviso.   [180] CDPA 1988, s 13B(9).
[181] CDPA 1988, s 13A(2).

In determining whether a sound recording has been published, played in, or communicated to the public, no account is taken of any unauthorised act.[182] In July 2008 the European Commission published a proposal for a Directive to extend the term for sound recordings from 50 to 95 years.[183]

Broadcasts

3.60   Copyright in a broadcast expires 50 years from the end of the year in which the broadcast is made.[184] Copyright in a repeat broadcast expires at the same time as the copyright in the original broadcast.[185]

Published editions

3.61   The publisher's copyright in the typographical arrangement of published editions of literary, dramatic and musical works expires 25 years from the end of the calendar year in which the edition was first published.[186]

 Discussion point   For answer guidance visit www.oxfordtextbooks.co.uk/orc/macqueen2e/

Why is the publisher's copyright in its typographical arrangement so much shorter than other copyrights?

Further reading

Books

Bently & Sherman, *Intellectual Property Law* (3rd edn, 2009), Chs 5, 7, 10, 13.7
Copinger & Skone James on Copyright (15th edn, 2005), Chs 4, 6, 11 and 12
Cornish & Llewelyn, *Intellectual Property* (6th edn, 2007), Chs 11.6, 12.6, 13.1
Laddie, Prescott & Vitoria, *Modern Law of Copyright* (3rd edn, 2000), Chs 10, 10A, 13, and 21.

Authorship

L Zemer, *The Idea of Authorship in Copyright* (2007)

Employment and universities

A Monotti with S Ricketson, *Universities and Intellectual Property: Ownership and Exploitation* (2003)

---

[182] CDPA 1988, s 13A(2), proviso.
[183] The proposal is accessible at http://eur-lex.europa.eu/LexUriServ/LexUriServ.do?uri=COM:2008:0464:FIN:EN:PDF. See further below, paras 7.5, 7.44–7.46.
[184] CDPA 1988, s 14(2).   [185] CDPA 1988, s 14(5). See above para 2.95 for copyright in repeats.
[186] CDPA 1988, s 15.

Moral rights

E Adeney, *The Moral Rights of Authors and Performers: An International and Comparative Analysis* (2006)

FW Grosheide, 'Moral Rights', in E Derclaye (ed), *Research Handbook on the Future of EU Copyright* (2009), Ch 10

Term

W Landes and R Posner, *Economic Structure of Intellectual Property Law* (2004), Ch 8

Articles

Authorship and ownership

WR Cornish, 'Conserving culture and copyright: a partial history' (2009) 13 Edinburgh Law Review 8

HL MacQueen, 'The legal definition of authorship and the scrolls', in JJ Collins and TH Lim (eds), *Oxford Handbook of the Dead Sea Scrolls* (2010)

J Pila, 'An intentional view of the copyright work' (2008) 71 MLR 535

J Phillips, 'Authorship, ownership, wikiship: copyright in the twenty-first century' (2008) 3 JIPLP 788

D Vaver, 'Copyright in legal documents' (1993) 31 Osgoode Hall Law Journal 661

Crown copyright

S Saxby, 'Crown copyright regulation in the UK—is the debate still alive?' (2005) 13(3) International Journal of Law and Information Technology 299

Parliamentary copyright

N Cox, 'Copyright in statutes, regulations and judicial decisions in common law jurisdictions: public ownership or commercial enterprise?' (2006) 27(3) Statute Law Review 185

Artists' resale rights

J Merryman, 'The proposed generalization of the droit de suite in the European Communities' [1997] IPQ 16

Copyright 3: economic rights and infringement

Introduction

Scope and overview of chapter

4.1 This chapter considers the rights which the owner of copyright enjoys while the copyright endures, apart from the moral rights discussed in the previous chapter. The rights to be considered here are usually known as *'economic rights'*, because, unlike the moral rights, they may be exploited by transferring them to others or licensing others to use them for a price. The basic scheme of the CDPA 1988 is to define a group of what it calls *'acts restricted by copyright'*. This concept has two functions:

- one is to define those acts by others in relation to the copyright work which the rightholder can challenge and stop by *court action*;

- the other is to tell persons who wish to use works the copyright in which is owned by another whether or not that use requires the permission of the right holder. In other words, the restricted acts define the ground on which right holder and would-be user will *negotiate the terms and conditions* on which the use will be permitted.

An important point of which we need to remind ourselves constantly is that in practical terms copyright is useless to its owner unless others want to perform the various restricted acts, whereupon it becomes the basis upon which a bargain may be struck between the two sides. It may be that the owner has no wish to bargain, and expressly or impliedly gives *carte blanche* to users. On the other hand, the owner who does not wish to bargain may simply want to prevent any one else from disseminating the work, in which case the would-be user's remedy, if any, lies in competition law (for which, see Chapter 20).

4.2

Learning objectives

By the end of this chapter you should be able to describe and explain:

- the general nature of the economic rights conferred by copyright upon its owners;
- the distinction between moral and economic rights;
- the specific economic rights (to make copies, issue copies to the public; rent or lend commercially to the public; perform, show or play in public; broadcast; make adaptations).

4.3   The chapter opens with a general discussion of the rights flowing from ownership of copyright and the international framework which underpins them, noting in particular the influence upon UK law of a number of EU Directives. The chapter next elaborates upon what distinguishes economic from moral rights, before turning to the detailed rules on the former category in the CDPA 1988. So the rest of the chapter looks like this:

- International background (4.4–4.9)
- Economic rights in general (4.10–4.12)
- Economic rights and primary infringements: general principles (4.13–4.22)
- Restricted acts and primary infringement: detail (4.23–4.67)
- Authorisation of infringement (4.68–4.75)
- Secondary infringement of copyright (4.76–4.78)

International background

Berne Convention

4.4   In addition to the non-transferable moral rights discussed in the previous chapter (above, paras 3.31–3.46), the Berne Convention recognises *transferable economic rights* enabling copyright owners to control the following activities in relation to their works:

- translation (Article 8)
- reproduction (Articles 9, 14)
- public performance and communication of dramatic and musical works (Articles 11, 11*ter*, 14)
- broadcasting (Article 11*bis*)
- adaptation (Article 12)

4.5   Economic rights are so known because it is essentially through these rights that copyright can become a source of income for its owner, by selling them or licensing others to perform the acts restricted by the rights. Moral rights, on the other hand, cannot be transferred to persons other than the author of the work, and are essentially linked to the author's interests in the work as an expression of an individual's personality. Resale rights admittedly occupy something of a middle ground between the economic and moral, in that through them the author earns an income; but this is entirely contingent on the activities of others over which the author has no control.

 Question

How may economic and moral rights be distinguished?

TRIPS and WCT

4.6   Modern international activity has, unsurprisingly, focused almost entirely on economic rights, and the TRIPS Agreement of 1994 expressly states that its members have no rights or obligations under Article 6*bis* of Berne,[1] that is, the moral rights article. TRIPS did require members to provide commercial rental rights in respect of 'at least' computer programs and films,[2] and this was also laid down in the WIPO Copyright Treaty of 1996 (WCT).[3] The Treaty further provided for a *distribution, or first sale, right*,[4] and a *public communication right*. This was to be without prejudice to the relevant provisions of Berne.[5]

Rome Convention, TRIPS and WPPT

4.7   Economic rights in neighbouring or media works were initially dealt with in the Rome Convention, which enables producers of phonograms (sound recordings) to authorise or prohibit direct or indirect reproduction of their products.[6] Broadcasters have likewise the right to authorise or prohibit re-broadcasting, fixation, reproduction of fixations in certain circumstances, and public communication, again in certain circumstances, of broadcasts.[7] TRIPS and the WIPO Performances and Phonograms Treaty 1996 (WPPT) restated these minimum rights for phonogram producers,[8] while the WPPT added distribution, commercial rental and 'making available to the public' rights.[9]

EU Directives

4.8   The following EU Directives contain provisions relevant to copyright ownership economic rights:

- Software Directive 1991 (Article 4)

- Rental and Lending Right Directive 1992 (consolidated 2006)

- Satellite Broadcasting Directive 1993

- Database Directive 1996 (Article 5)

- InfoSoc Directive 2001 (Articles 2–4)

---

[1] TRIPS, Art 9(2).   [2] TRIPS, Art 11.   [3] WCT, Art 7.   [4] WCT, Art 6.
[5] WCT, Art 8, referring to Berne Convention, Arts 11, 11*ter* and 14—see above para 4.4.
[6] Rome Convention, Art 10.   [7] Rome Convention, Art 13.   [8] TRIPS, Art 14(2), (3); WPPT, Art 11.
[9] WPPT, Arts 12–14.

Essentially these implement in Europe the policies also apparent in the development of the international instruments described in the previous two paragraphs (paras 4.6–4.7), requiring member states to have distribution, rental and public communication rights. All made necessary significant changes to the UK CDPA 1988, as will emerge from the account of UK law later on in this chapter.

4.9   A specifically European initiative is the inclusion of temporary or transient reproduction as an act restricted by copyright, which as yet has not been agreed at the global level. Attempts to include a provision of this kind in the WCT 1996 failed. First introduced in the EU in respect of software, so that copyright owners could regulate the use of programs in computers,[10] it was extended next to databases,[11] and now covers all author works, phonograms, films and broadcasts.[12] But the UK did not have to make any change here, as the concept of infringement by transient copying had already been introduced in the 1988 Act.[13] See further below para 4.36.

Key points on international background

- The Berne Convention recognises two groups of rights:
  - the economic (basis on which copyright can be used to make money)
  - the moral (recognition of author's personality claims)

- The Berne Convention has been supplemented with respect to media works by the Rome Convention

- The economic rights have been the subject of most international activity in modern times, through TRIPS, the WCT and the WPPT

- Much of this more recent international activity has been concerned with new technology subject matter such as computer programs and databases, and new rights such as rental right

- Within the EU the developing global framework has been reflected and sometimes led by initiatives embodied in Directives aimed at harmonising the laws of the member states

- Apart from the special case of artists' resale rights in the EU, there has been no recent international development with regard to moral rights

---

Economic rights in general

Primary restricted acts

4.10   There are six major exclusive economic rights arising from ownership of the copyright in any protected work. The restricted acts for which a licence must be sought if they are to be lawfully carried out by a person other than the copyright owner may be listed as follows:[14]

- copying (reproduction right)
- issuing copies of the work to the public (first sale or distribution right)

---

[10] Software Directive 1991, Art 4(a).   [11] Database Directive 1996, Art 5(a).
[12] InfoSoc Directive, Art 2.   [13] CDPA 1988, s 17(6).   [14] CDPA 1988, s 16(1).

Although there was a striking similarity of style and technique, no copyright subsisted in these elements. A choreographer also gave evidence that there was no particular similarity in the dance movements of the two films.[28]

4.20   It is specifically provided that copying in relation to a film or broadcast includes making a photograph of the whole or any substantial part of any image forming part of the work.[29] The emphasis on quality rather than quantity of taking does not mean that the latter is irrelevant, however.[30] There is some authority to the effect that separate acts of copying of what are in themselves insubstantial parts may be taken as a whole to constitute substantial taking, either as acts in relation to a serial work such as a newspaper treated as a single copyright work, or as simply a single act spread over time.[31]

General principles: (b) doing a restricted act directly or indirectly

4.21   The doing of a restricted act is infringement whether carried out directly or indirectly.[32] In other words, it is no answer to a claim of infringement to say that the restricted act was carried out, not in relation to the original work, but to some other work which was derived from it.

■ King Features Syndicate Inc v Kleeman Ltd [1941] AC 417

Copyright in drawings of Popeye the Sailorman was held to be infringed although the defendant had copied not the drawings, but the plaintiffs' licensed dolls and brooches based on these drawings.

■ Sony Music v Easyinternetcafé Ltd [2003] FSR 48

Internet cafés operated by E provided a CD burning service for customers, which could include sound recordings downloaded from the Internet by the customers. Fees were payable for this service. The owners of the copyright in sound recordings sued E for copyright infringement. It was held that E was guilty of indirect infringement by copying the copies which its customers had made. It was not an involuntary copier like an Internet service provider or the recipient of a fax. It was irrelevant that the customer might be going on to use the CD for private and domestic purposes; E was in business for commercial gain.

Reverse engineering

4.22   'Reverse engineering' can thus be an infringement of copyright. This involves a party working back from a finished product to the copyright work which underlies it, and then evolving a work of his own. Formerly of greatest significance in the field of industrial design (see Part III), it also raises problems for the software industry, where competitive development is commonly achieved by such endeavours in relation to the embodiment of the program in a disk.[33] Often

---

[28] See further A Barron, 'The legal properties of film' (2004) 67 MLR 177.

[29] CDPA 1988, s 17(4); see *Spelling Goldberg v BPC Publishing* [1981] RPC 280 (CA).

[30] *Sillitoe v McGraw Hill Book Co* [1983] FSR 545.

[31] *Cate v Devon and Exeter Constitutional Newspaper Co* (1889) 40 Ch D 500; *Electronic Techniques (Anglia) Ltd v Critchley Components Ltd* [1997] FSR 401. See also the provisions for such infringement of the *sui generis* database right (below, paras 6.15–6.16).

[32] CDPA 1988, s 16(3)(b).

[33] For an example, see *Autodesk Inc v Dyason and Kelly* (1990) 96 ALR 57. Note however that 'decompilation' of a computer program in low level language (ie the object code) is not infringement if certain conditions are met: CDPA 1988, s 50B,

'reverse engineering' will be carried out through a process of *'redesign'* or *'clean-room' procedure*, where the analysis of the original product and the briefing of the designers of the new one are kept rigorously apart within the organisation carrying out the work. It has been held that a defender cannot escape liability by showing that the copy was made by a third party if the third party acted in accordance with the defender's instructions;[34] but there have been successful arguments that redesign is not copying.[35] In considering whether a restricted act has been carried out indirectly, it is immaterial whether any intervening acts themselves infringe copyright, as for example might be the case in the preparation of a redesign brief.

 Question

What is the difference between direct and indirect infringement? Give an example of each form of infringement.

Key points on general principles applicable to all restricted acts

- The restrictions apply whether the act in question relates to the whole of the copyright work or only part of it
- Where the act relates to only part of the copyright work, it must be a substantial part of the work to be an infringement of the copyright
- Substantiality depends more on the quality than on the quantity being used; how far is the author's skill and labour appropriated? Or is the part taken the part of the copyright work that really matters to its user?
- A restricted act may infringe copyright whether performed directly or indirectly, via some intermediate work

Restricted acts and primary infringement: detail

4.23 We now turn to detailed discussion of each of the restricted acts, viewed primarily through the lens of infringement actions.

(1) Copying (reproduction)

4.24 Two basics need to be established in any action for infringement based on a claim of copying:

- *similarity* of the alleged infringing work with that of the copyright owner
- *the similarity is caused by copying* the copyright owner's work.

implementing Software Directive 1991, Art 6; discussed further below, para 5.44.

[34] *Solar Thomson Engineering Co Ltd v Barton* [1977] RPC 537; *Howard Clark v David Allan & Co Ltd* 1987 SLT 271.

[35] *Merlet v Mothercare* [1986] RPC 115 (CA); *Rose Plastics GmbH v Wm Beckett & Co* [1989] FSR 113.

When are two works similar?

4.25   The starting point is the similarity of two works. In many of the most important instances of infringement, this is not a problem. The development of modern copying technology has made the production of *exact copies* in the fields of reprography, software and other digital works, and audio-visual works increasingly easy, and this is one of the major policy issues which copyright law has to confront. From a conceptual rather than a policy point of view, however, identifying the use of such technology as potentially infringing copying is not difficult.

Works similar but not the same

4.26   Generally, problems begin to arise when *works are similar but not the same*. It is clear from the law on substantial copying (above, paras 4.15–4.20) that the later work need not be identical to the earlier in order to infringe the latter's copyright, although the limits of this, given the basic principle that copyright subsists in modes of expression rather than ideas, are uncertain. The issue is perhaps most acute where it is alleged that a work has been reproduced in a different medium from the original. Copying in relation to a literary, dramatic, musical or artistic work means reproducing the work in any material form, including storing the work in any medium by electronic means.[36] This certainly includes reproduction in the form of a record or a film,[37] as well as reproduction in a broadcast or in a computer, computer disk or on the Internet. In the case of an artistic work, a version produced by representing a two-dimensional work in three dimensions is a reproduction, as is a version produced by the reverse process.[38] An example illustrating the second instance might be a photograph of a work of artistic craftsmanship.[39] Not being exhaustive, these statutory definitions are but particular instances showing the general principle that the reproduction need not be in the same form as the original to be an infringement. Other examples might include a painting of a photograph.[40] However there may be a difficulty where a literary work is translated into an artistic or quasi-artistic form: for example, the conversion of statistical data into drawings and graphs. Arguably, in the absence of express provision, reproducing the literary work is confined to reproductions which have some literary form in the sense of using words.

■ *Cuisenaire v Reed* [1963] VR 719

It was held here that coloured rods used for arithmetical calculations did not reproduce a literary work describing such rods.

■ *Brigid Foley v Ellott* [1982] RPC 433

It was held here that garments did not reproduce the words and numerals constituting a knitting guide. A reproduction of a literary work must be, according to Sir Robert Megarry V-C, 'some copy of or representation of the original' (at p 434).[41]

---

[36] CDPA 1988, s 17(2).   [37] As was specifically provided in s 48 of the 1956 Act.
[38] CDPA 1988, s 17(3).   [39] If not situated in a public place—see CDPA 1988, s 62.
[40] See *Bauman v Fussell* [1978] RPC 485.
[41] See also *Interlego AG v Tyco Industries Inc* [1989] AC 217 per Lord Oliver at 265 (PC); also *J & S Davis (Holdings) Ltd v Wright Health Group* [1988] RPC 403 per Whitford J at 414.

■ *Anacon Corporation Ltd v Environmental Research Technology Ltd* [1994] FSR 659

ACL were held to have both literary and artistic copyright in electronic circuit diagrams relating to an electronic dust meter. See above, para 2.64, for a description of electronic circuit diagrams. ERTL produced circuit boards using information derived from ACL's boards, involving the creation of a 'net list' of all the components in ACL's circuits, and the connections between them; by feeding such lists into a computer, a new circuit diagram could be produced and a scheme for producing a printed circuit board. It was held, with regard to the artistic copyright, that ACL's claim of infringement failed, because the alleged infringement did not look like the copyright work. With regard to the literary copyright, however, the claim succeeded so far as the net lists reproduced the information which was the literary work contained in the diagram. Jacob J preferred not to decide whether the ERTL circuits themselves, 'because in relation to each of the components there is also a written or coded indication of what it is' (at p 663), were also infringements.

■ *Electronic Techniques (Anglia) Ltd v Critchley Components Ltd* [1997] FSR 401

Another case about infringement of copyright electronic circuit diagrams in which Laddie J too held that they were literary works but that the defendant's taking might be insufficiently substantial to be infringement.

■ *Sandman v Panasonic UK Ltd* [1998] FSR 651

A final case on whether the copyright in electronic circuit diagrams was infringed by electronic circuits. It was held that the diagrams had both artistic and literary copyright. The artistic copyright would only be infringed if the circuit reproduced from a circuit diagram was visually similar to the latter, at least when laid out on the circuit. With regard to the literary copyright, there was no equivalent to the artistic infringement of two-dimensional by three-dimensional works, but it was possible for a circuit itself to contain the content of the literary aspects of the circuit diagram.

 Discussion point   For answer guidance visit www.oxfordtextbooks.co.uk/orc/macqueen2e/

How may the copyright in electronic circuit diagrams be infringed?

Causal connection between two works

4.27   It is necessary to show the causal connection of copying between two works, since there may be many other explanations for a similarity between them which do not involve infringement of the right holder's copyright: eg mere chance, a common source, the nature of the subject matter or, that the claimant copied the other party's work.[42]

---

[42]   *Corelli v Gray* (1913) 29 TLR 570 per Sargent J at 570 (Ch D).

■ *Purefoy v Sykes Boxall* (1955) 72 RPC 89

P produced a trade catalogue containing illustrations of its products. SB's products copied P's. SB produced a catalogue of its imitative products, and P sued for infringement of the copyright in the catalogue. It was held that these facts by themselves were not enough to establish that SB's *catalogue* was a copy, direct or indirect, of P's catalogue. SB's copying of the *products* was not indirect copying of P's catalogue. (However, other evidence showed that SB had copied certain advertisements and tables in P's catalogues; there was also indirect copying, since SB had copied certain tables from sheets prepared with P's consent by its customer, H, who had supplied them to SB.)

4.28   In general, it may be said that if two works are strikingly alike, if the claimant's work pre-dates that of the defendant, and if the latter had access to it, then the court will be ready to infer that copying took place.[43] '[I]n most copyright cases…infringement can only be established by inference because there is no evidence of anyone being present and looking over the defendants' shoulder'.[44] But before proceeding to make that inference the court must consider when it can be displaced by other evidence.[45] This is not a matter of the copyright owner shifting the evidential burden to the alleged infringer but rather of making 'a prima facie case for [him] to answer'.[46]

? Question

When will a court infer that copying has taken place?

4.29   But consider the problem confronted in a Canadian case:[47]

■ *Galerie d'Art du Petit Champlain inc v Théberge* [2002] 2 SCR 336 (Supreme Court of Canada)

T, a well-known painter, assigned to a publisher the right to publish cards, posters and other stationery products for sale to art galleries. The appellant galleries had purchased copies of these licensed products and then transferred the images on them to canvas by means of a technique for lifting the ink from the card or poster and shifting it to the canvas. The end result was to leave the original card or poster blank, so that there was no increase in the overall number of reproductions. The artist sued for infringement of copyright by reproduction. By a majority of 4:3 the Supreme Court of Canada held that there was no infringement. What the galleries had done was within their rights as the owners of the physical posters and cards. Substitution of a new backing was not reproduction, which for purposes of infringement required the production of new or further copies of the original work. In this literal, physical, mechanical *transfer* no multiplication took place. The artist was asserting moral rights in the guise of economic rights.

---

[43] See *Designers Guild Ltd v Russell Williams (Textiles) Ltd* [2001] FSR 11 (HL).
[44] *Sifam Electrical Instrument Co Ltd v Sangamo Weston Ltd* [1971] 2 All ER 1074 at 1076 per Graham J.
[45] *LB (Plastics) Ltd v Swish Products Ltd* [1979] RPC 537 at 621 per Lord Wilberforce.
[46] Per Willmer LJ, *Francis Day & Hunter v Bron* [1963] Ch 587, at 612.
[47] See further S Stokes, 'Copyright and the reproduction of artistic works' [2003] EIPR 486.

The dissenting minority view was that copyright protected the work, and that the work in this case included its material support. Reproduction did not have to entail the multiplication of copies, since the concept included, not just reproduction of the work, but of a substantial part of the work (see above, paras 4.15–4.20). This made it necessary to consider reproduction qualitatively and not just quantitatively.

 Discussion point For answer guidance visit www.oxfordtextbooks.co.uk/orc/macqueen2e/

Which of the competing views in the Théberge case do you prefer, and why? Why is the painter's moral right claim to the integrity of his work (see above paras 3.39–3.43) unlikely to be successful on the above facts?

Relevance of knowledge

4.30   So far as the issue of whether or not there has been infringement is concerned, it is irrelevant that the defendant did not know or was unaware of the existence of the original work (as might be the case, for example, where he was copying from a copy of it) or of the fact that the original work had copyright. All that matters is the causal chain between the original and the derivative work and that chain may have several links. Even where the defender produces a work apparently independently it has been said that he may be liable if subconscious copying can be established by the usual tests of similarity, dating and access.[48]

■ *Francis Day & Hunter Ltd v Bron* [1963] Ch 587 (CA)

FDH owned the copyright in a musical work 'In a Little Spanish Town' (published in 1926 and performed in a 1955 recording by Bing Crosby), and claimed that it was infringed by the conscious or unconscious taking of its first eight bars in another work, 'Why', published by B in 1959.

There was considerable similarity, but the composer (Peter de Angelis) gave evidence, accepted by the judge (Wilberforce J), that he had not consciously copied or indeed heard 'In a Little Spanish Town', and that his main musical influences were Puccini, Ravel and Debussy; if he had heard 'In a Little Spanish Town', this had probably occurred when he was young. It was held that there was no infringement, although subconscious copying was a possibility which might amount to infringement. But, 'if subconscious copying is to be found, there must be proof (or at least a strong inference) of de facto familiarity with the work alleged to be copied. In the present case, on the findings of Wilberforce J, this element is conspicuously lacking' (per Willmer LJ at p 613).

■ *Jones v Tower Hamlets London Borough* [2001] RPC 23

J, an architect, was instructed by ADL, a property development company, to produce plans for a housing development commissioned by THLB and to be carried out by ADL. After starting

---

[48] *Francis Day & Hunter v Bron* [1963] Ch 587. See also *Industrial Furnaces Ltd v Reaves* [1970] RPC 605 at 623–4 per Graham J.

work, ADL was dismissed by THLB, which continued the development but developing its own plans. J had not been paid his fees of £219,000 by ADL and remained unpaid when ADL went into liquidation. In an action against THLB, J claimed that the 'footprint' of the houses as built on the site and some interior floor plans infringed the copyright in his plans. The claim was largely rejected save in respect of a 'wrap around' bathroom partition. Although the THLB official concerned could not remember seeing J's plan for this, it was so striking that the only possible inference was that there had been copying, J's plans having possibly remained subconsciously in the official's mind.

 Question

What is the relevance of knowledge in a question about copying?

Copying and adaptation

4.31   Adaptation of a work is a form of infringement distinct from copying, applying only to literary, dramatic and musical works.[49] Adaptation is given a restricted meaning—it covers dramatisations and translations, for example—and it is specifically provided that no inference as to what does or does not amount to copying a work should be drawn from the definition of adaptation.[50] There may well be overlap, but copying is wider in scope.

Ideas and impressions

4.32   Even where both works are in the same medium or form of expression, it can be difficult to determine whether one reproduces another. Reproduction must be substantial rather than exact or complete,[51] and so the substance of a work must be determined in order to judge the scope of the copyright owner's rights. In some cases this has extended well beyond expression in the simple sense of words used, to touch on the ways in which information and ideas have been arranged by the author.

■ *Harman Pictures NV v Osborne* [1967] 1 WLR 723

It was held here that similarities of incidents and situations suggested that a film screen play by John Osborne infringed the copyright in a historical book (*The Reason Why* by Mrs Cecil Woodham Smith), even though there were also many dissimilarities between the two works and both were based upon historical events (the Charge of the Light Brigade in the Crimean War).

■ *Ravenscroft v Herbert* [1980] RPC 193

R had written *The Spear of Destiny*, a non-fiction book on an ancient spear held in the Hofburg Museum, Vienna. He had researched the provenance of the spear and identified it as the one which pierced the side of Christ at the Crucifixion, and which was later used by legendary figures, and inspired Nazi Germany. The research had combined orthodox historical methods

---

[49] See CDPA 1988, s 21 and generally paras 4.66–4.67 below.   [50] CDPA 1988, s 21(4).
[51] CDPA 1988, s 16(3)(a).

with mystical meditation. H, who had read R's book, wrote a novel called *The Spear* about what happened to the spear after the Second World War, but the prologues to each section retold the story of the Hofburg spear from the Crucifixion on. It was held that while a novelist might use the facts derived from a historical work, he was not entitled to adopt the language, selection and arrangement of the latter. 'In the prologues . . . [H] had deliberately copied the language of the plaintiff on many occasions. To a more significant extent he has adopted wholesale the identical incidents of documented and occult history which the plaintiff used in support of his theory of the ancestry and attributes of the spear, of Hitler's obsession with it and also General Patton's. He did this in order to give his novel a backbone of truth with the least possible labour to himself. In so doing he annexed for his own purposes the skill and labour of the plaintiff to an extent which is not permissible under the law of copyright' (per Brightman J at p 207).

Several other cases demonstrate that where the question is whether or not one dramatic or musical or artistic work reproduces another of the same kind, account may be taken of factors other than the similarity of the respective modes of expression. With dramatic works the essence of the copyright may be not so much in the words used as in the characterisation and sequence of incidents and events and where that is taken there is infringement of copyright.[52] With musical works, 'infringement of copyright . . . is not a question of note for note comparison', but falls to be determined 'by the ear as well as by the eye'.[53]

4.33   But there are limits to how far this approach can be taken, since it can make unacceptable inroads upon the basic principle that copyright does not protect ideas and information, which are available for all to use in their own work.

■ *Bauman v Fussell* [1978] RPC 485

A photograph of two cocks fighting each other was used as the basis of a painting. The composition of the subject matter was followed closely but the painter employed different colouring to heighten the dramatic effect of the representation. It was held that it was appropriate to consider the different effects of each work on the viewer in assessing whether there had been an infringement of artistic copyright (answer in this case, no).

■ *Baigent v Random House Group Ltd* [2006] EMLR 16 (Peter Smith J) aff'd [2007] FSR 24 (CA)

This case was based on a claim that the best-selling novel, *The Da Vinci Code* (DVC) by Dan Brown, infringed copyright in an earlier, non-fictional work called *The Holy Blood and the Holy Grail* (HBHG), written by B and others. The claimants relied on *Ravenscroft v Herbert*, arguing that Dan Brown had used the central theme and argument of HBHG in constructing the plot of DVC, and so infringed their copyright. The evidence showed that Dan Brown had used HBHG while working on DVC, and there was some limited textual copying. It was held that DVC did not infringe any copyright in HBHG. The central theme or argument claimed for HBHG was not made out in the book itself, but was an artificial creation put together for the purposes of raising the claim. DVC did not copy any central theme of HBHG, and the textual copying was insub-

---

[52] *Rees v Melville* [1911–16] MCC 168.
[53] *Austin v Columbia Gramophone Co Ltd* [1917–23] MCC 398 at 409 and 415, quoted with approval by Willmer LJ in *Francis Day & Hunter Ltd v Bron* [1963] Ch 587 at 608.

stantial. While the way in which facts, themes or ideas were put together could be protected by copyright, because this was the result of the skill and labour of the author, the facts, themes and ideas in themselves were open to anyone else.

 Discussion point　For answer guidance visit www.oxfordtextbooks.co.uk/orc/macqueen2e/

How useful is the distinction between idea and expression? How does it work in relation to, say, poetry, music or art?

Computer programs and infringement

4.34　Particular problems have arisen with copyright programs. It is clearly infringement to make an exact copy of a program.[54] More complex, however, is the situation often arising as a result of 'reverse engineering',[55] where the aim of the second party is to produce a program which can perform the same functions on the same machines as the first program (ie compatibility or inter-operability). This functional similarity can be achieved with quite distinct underlying codes. Thus the reverse engineer's product may not be an exact or literal copy of the original program, and the question which arises is how far the first programmer's copyright may be pressed in challenging such non-literal copies as infringements of a substantial part of his work. In the USA, there were controversial decisions to the effect that the 'structure, sequence and organisation', and the 'look and feel' of a program might be protected by copyright, taking account of the similarity of the results (including the appearance of screen displays) produced by running the two programs in question.[56] One interlocutory decision of the English High Court hinted at a similar approach.[57] Did this carry copyright beyond the protection of expression into the protection of ideas? As already noted (above, paras 4.32–4.33), copyright protection is not confined to literal copying, and can extend to sequences of ideas and effects. But the Software Directive provides that ideas and principles which underlie any element of a computer program, including those which underlie its interfaces, are not to be protected.[58] In the USA the very broad early approach was reined back in *Computer Associates v Altai*.[59] Instead the copyright program was analysed back from its object code to its conception, to filter out those elements which had come from the public domain or which could be expressed only in one way (the merger of idea and expression). What was then left was the core of protectable expression, which could not be copied without infringing.

The scope of infringement of software copyright by copying has continued to create unresolved difficulties for the English courts, although the US 'look and feel' test has not been adopted. The leading cases are all decisions at first instance.

---

[54] Note however CDPA 1988, s 50A, implementing the Software Directive 1991, Art 5(3), providing that the making of a back-up copy of a computer program necessary for the purposes of lawful use is not infringement, and may not be prevented by contract (below, para 5.44).

[55] For this phrase, see above, para 4.22.

[56] *Whelan Associates Inc v Jaslow Dental Laboratory Inc* 797 F 2d 1222 (3rd Cir 1986); *Apple Computer Inc v Microsoft Corp*, 709 F Supp 925, 717 F Supp 1428 and 759 F Supp 1444 (1989, 1991); *Lotus v Paperback Software* 740 F Supp 37 (1990).

[57] *MS Associates v Power* [1988] FSR 242.　　[58] Art 1(2).　　[59] 982 F 2d 693 (1992).

■ *John Richardson Computers Ltd v Flanders* [1993] FSR 497 (Ferris J)

F worked for JRC, first as employee, then as consultant, and had contributed to the development of JRC's program for stock control in a pharmacy. F left JRC, set up on his own, and produced a stock control program which JRC challenged as an infringement of the copyright in the first program. The first program had been developed for a BBC computer, the second for an IBM-compatible one. The making of the second program had not involved any use of JRC's source code, but it allegedly followed the scheme of the first, and included specific details of its particular routines. Ferris J followed *Computer Associates v Altai* in tackling the question of what would constitute infringement. As Ferris J remarked, 'this means that consideration is not restricted to the text of the code' (at p 527). In the particular case, he held that F had infringed three elements of JRC's program (the line editor, the amendment routines and the dose codes.

■ *Ibcos Computers v Barclays Mercantile* [1994] FSR 297 (Jacob J)

The reliance of Ferris J on US authority was criticised by Jacob J in this case, emphasising that the wording of the US and the UK statutes was not the same. But he agreed that testing infringement was not limited to literal copying of the source code: 'That must be right: most literary copyright works involve both literal matters (the exact words of a novel or computer program) and varying levels of abstraction (plot, more or less detailed, of a novel, general structure of a computer program). I therefore think it right to have regard in this case not only to… 'literal similarities' but also to… 'program structure' and 'design features' (at p 302). Taking this approach to a set of facts similar to the *Richardson* case, but involving accountancy packages for agricultural dealers, Jacob J held that the second program infringed the first, involving as it did both line-by-line literal copying of certain routines and substantial copying of structural elements.

■ *Cantor Fitzgerald International v Tradition UK Ltd* [2000] RPC 95 (Pumfrey J)

This case involved two inter-dealer bond brokers, C and T. A group of C ex-employees joined T, bringing with them a program which they had designed for C. This code was loaded into T's system, and was then used by the ex-employees for reference while writing and testing a system being designed for T. Copying in producing T's system was eventually admitted, but only to the extent of 2 per cent of C's system, which T submitted was insubstantial. An additional 1.3 per cent of T's code was questionable. It was held that there had been no copying of anything not admitted to be copied. Further, a computer program's only purpose was to make a machine function in a particular way. Only at a very high level of abstraction, such as its overall structure, or the allocation of functions between different programs, might the analogy with the plot of a play or novel be helpful. Copyright protected the author's skill and labour; entirely mechanical labour, involving no skill, might be saved by copying something produced only by entirely mechanical labour. Neither system in this case had anything exceptional or unusual in its overall design, and the architectural similarities were no more than might be attributable to both being written by the same programmers. The substantiality of what had been taken had to be judged in relation to the criteria for the originality of the copied work, namely the extent to which the skill and labour of the first author had been taken.

■ *Navitaire Inc v EasyJet Airline Co Inc* [2006] RPC 3 (Pumfrey J)

EJ had taken a licence from N to use their 'OpenRes' copyright software for an online 'ticketless' airline booking system and another program ('TakeFlight') for the web user interface accompanying it. EJ moved on to another web interface and B wrote for them the code for a new booking system ('eRes'). N alleged that its 'OpenRes' copyright was infringed by 'eRes'. There was no dispute that the underlying software was different, that EJ had wanted a new system substantially indistinguishable from 'OpenRes' in respect of its user interface, and that 'eRes' acted upon identical or very similar inputs and produced very similar results. N argued that there was non-textual copying, akin to that involved in copying the plot of a book, or copying of the 'business logic' of the programme. It was held that there was no infringement by non-textual copying. The analogy with infringement of the copyright in a plot was inapt, because a computer program did not have a theme, events or narrative flow, but was rather a series of pre-defined operations to produce a result in response to a user's requests or commands. 'Business logic' fell within the scope of unprotectable ideas and principles.

 Discussion point   For answer guidance visit www.oxfordtextbooks.co.uk/orc/macqueen2e/

Consider the difference of view between Jacob and Pumfrey JJ as to the analogy between a computer program and the plot of a play or novel. Which view is better, and why? Is Pumfrey J's suggested approach through linking the concepts of originality and substantiality of taking a helpful one in the context of computer programs?

4.35   Even where the form of expression in computer language is distinct from the first version, there may still be infringement by adaptation.[60] With regard to screen displays, a problem may be the idea that a literary work (which includes a computer program) cannot be infringed by a visual representation.[61] On the other hand, the display may have an independent artistic copyright of its own, which would be infringed by substantially similar displays.

Transient copies: computer programs, databases and the Internet

4.36   Copying in relation to any description of work includes the making of copies which are transient or are incidental to some other use of the work.[62] This again has particular significance in relation to computer programs. When a program is loaded into a computer, it is generally copied from the source into the computer's random access memory and central processing unit. This may well be transient or incidental, but is nonetheless infringement unless authorised. Similarly, in accessing a database via a computer, a user may bring up momentarily on screen copies of material contained in the work. If a substantial part is taken—and again the basic test of quality rather than quantity will be important—unauthorised access to a database will infringe its copyright. This can be readily extended to a browser on the Internet who calls up a webpage on his computer screen. Theoretically it also covers the reproduction which occurs on the various computers and servers through which the various packages comprising the webpage travel as they thread their way across the networks to the user's machine. But this is probably now allowed as the permitted act of being an integral and essential part of a technological process the sole purpose of which is to enable a transmission of the work in a network between third parties by an intermediary.[63] Otherwise the remarkable result would be that the technical

---

[60] See CDPA 1988, s 21(3)(a)(i) and (4), discussed below.   [61] See above, para 4.26.
[62] CDPA 1988, s 17(6).
[63] CDPA 1988, s 28A, inserted after the InfoSoc Directive 2001, Art 5(1). See further below, paras 5.14–5.16.

basis of the operation of the Internet itself is illegal. The concept of transient reproduction also embraces activities such as proxy server caching where, by deploying appropriate software technology Internet service providers, librarians, archivists and others make and store on their own servers temporary and regularly updated copies of materials contained on other servers with the purpose of making the information more readily available to their own clients by avoiding congestion at the 'live' site. Such operations may also amount to the infringing act of storage by electronic means.[64] It is not clear how far they may be saved by the permitted acts in relation to transient copies. The same is true of 'data scraping', the use of programs to copy data from a website or database, whether only the information available on-screen or the code which underlies it (eg an airline company having its pricing information copied and displayed by a price comparison company's website).[65]

■ Case C-5/08 *Infopaq International A/S v Danske Dagblades Forening* [2009] ECDR 16

For the facts see para 4.15 above. The ECJ held that the reproductions of electronic news articles involved in the preparation of an electronic 'cuttings' service by an agency were not 'transient' copies.

Common source material; admittedly derivative work

4.37   Difficult questions can also arise with compilations where the same generally available information or material is conveyed in a different way; but if it is shown that in fact the second work was based on the first then it will be held to infringe copyright.

■ *Alexander v Mackenzie* (1847) 9 D 748

A, a solicitor, published a work entitled *An Analysis of the Heritable Securities and Infeftment Acts with an Appendix, containing Practical Forms of the Writs and Instruments thereby introduced*. The Acts, which had been passed in 1845, were aimed at the simplification of conveyancing, and gave general directions and descriptions of the styles to be used henceforth by conveyancers. A used industry and his knowledge as a conveyancer to produce 19 new styles. A committee of the Society of Writers to the Signet (a society of solicitors in Edinburgh) prepared and circulated amongst its membership Reports on the two Statutes, which also had an appendix containing a number of forms. The forms were largely based on those in A's work; A, who was a member of the committee, objected to this way of proceeding. It was held that the styles, being the creation of industry and knowledge rather than a mere reproduction of what was in the statutes, were copyright subject matter; the committee's alterations in its forms were of a trivial and unimportant nature; the committee styles were presented in the same order as A's; actual copying was acknowledged; and A's copyright was infringed.

■ *Elanco Products Ltd v Mandops (Agrochemical Specialists) Ltd* [1980] RPC 213 (CA)

EP invented, patented and marketed a weed-killer. The product was accompanied by an instruction leaflet. The information contained in this leaflet was also available by way of scientific

---

[64] CDPA 1988, s 17(2).
[65] See F Jennings and J Yates, 'Scrapping over data: are the data scrapers' days numbered?' (2009) 4 JIPLP 120.

an audience which watches or listens: for example, the members' sing-song in a club,[104] or labourers playing music on a radio at a building site.[105] The same would seem to apply to playing a sound recording on a personal stereo which can be overheard by persons close to the wearer of the equipment. Note that performance of a literary, dramatic or musical work in the course of the activities of an educational establishment (school, college, university) before an audience of teachers, pupils and other persons directly connected with the establishment's activities[106] is not in public if the performers are teachers or pupils or if the performance is for the purpose of instruction.[107] The rule is the same for playing or showing a sound recording, film or broadcast to such an audience in the course of instruction at an educational establishment.[108]

Discussion point   For answer guidance visit www.oxfordtextbooks.co.uk/orc/macqueen2e/

Would the old case of *Duck v Bates* (1884) 13 QBD 843, in which a performance of a dramatic work by a group of amateurs before an audience of nurses and others in Guy's Hospital, London, was held not to be in public, be followed today?

Use of apparatus for receiving visual images or sounds conveyed by electronic means

4.59   One of the most important ways of performing, playing or showing a work may be through a television screen or radio set situated in a public place, on which a literary, dramatic or musical work may be being performed, or a sound recording, film, broadcast or cable programme played or shown. It is provided that in such cases, the person by whom the images or sounds are sent is not an infringer, and, in the case of a performance, nor is any performer;[109] but there is nothing to define who the primary infringer is in such cases; or, to put it another way, who should be seeking the licence for the performance in question. The 1956 Act provided that the occupier of the premises where the apparatus was situated would be taken as giving the performance, playing or showing, if he also provided the apparatus itself.[110] This may still be the most useful guide. It should be noted, however, that an occupier of premises who merely gave permission for the apparatus to be brought onto the premises can only be liable as a secondary infringer,[111] and that where there is no charge for admission to the premises, there is no infringement of any copyright in a broadcast or cable programme, or any sound recording or film included in it, by showing or playing in public a broadcast or cable programme.[112] There are also special exceptions for hotels, guest houses and similar facilities, as well as for clubs and societies where the provision of facilities for seeing or hearing broadcasts or cable programmes is only incidental to the organisation's main purposes.[113]

---

[104] See *PRS v Rangers FC Supporters Club*, at 55 per Lord Stott.

[105] See however *PRS v Kwik-Fit Group Ltd* [2008] ECDR 2, where it was held arguable that employees using personal radios at their place of work in such a way that members of the public and customers of the employer could hear the music being played might be guilty of infringing public performances.

[106] A parent of a pupil is not as such directly connected (CDPA 1988, s 34(3)).   [107] CDPA 1988, s 34(1).

[108] CDPA 1988, s 34(2).   [109] CDPA 1988, s 19(4).

[110] 1956 Act, s 48(6). See also *Phonographic Performance Ltd v Lion Breweries* [1980] FSR 1 (NZ).

[111] CDPA 1988, s 26(3); and see further below, paras 4.76–4.77.

[112] CDPA 1988, s 72(1). See also below para 4.76.   [113] CDPA 1988, ss 67, 72(3). See also below, para 4.76.

Exercise

Find out whether a pub or bar which has a 'big screen' on which are shown broadcasts of football matches, but which does not charge its customers for anything other than the drinks which they buy at the bar, has to have a copyright licence in respect of its displays. What is the effect of CDPA 1988, s 72(2) on this situation?

Key points on public performance

Whether a performance, playing or showing of a work is in public depends on a number of factors:

- is the audience paying, in some form or another, to attend the performance?
- is the person responsible for the performance engaged in profit-making activity?
- the audience must consist of members of the public, but restrictions on who may attend do not prevent the performance being in public
- the performance need not be simultaneous for each member of the audience

---

(5) Public communication right

4.60 The communication to the public of the work is an act restricted by the copyright in literary, dramatic, musical and artistic works, sound recordings, films and broadcasts.[114] This right was introduced in implementation of the InfoSoc Directive, which in turn implemented for the EU the WCT 1996.[115]

Public communication for these purposes means *electronic transmission* (CDPA 1988, s 20(2)).

It includes:

(1) *broadcasting* the work (CDPA 1988, s 20(2)(a)).
electronic transmission of visual images, sounds or other information,
transmitted for simultaneous reception by members of the public
capable of being lawfully received by members of the public
transmitted at a time determined solely by the person in question for presentation to members of the public (CDPA 1988 s 6(1) and above, paras 2.91–2.94).

Public communication also includes:

(2) *making available to the public of the work by electronic transmission in such a way that members of the public may access it from a place and at a time individually chosen by them* (s 20(2)(b)).

---

[114] CDPA 1988, s 20(1).
[115] See above, paras 4.6, 4.8. See further J Ginsburg, 'The (new?) right of making available to the public', in D Vaver and L Bently (eds), *Intellectual Property in the New Millennium* (2004).

Question

What are the differences between 'broadcasting' and 'making available' in the above definitions?

4.61   *Internet transmission* is public communication under the 'making available' head, and only the copyright owner or its licensee may so transmit a work. Accordingly those who make copyright material such as sound recordings or films available for Internet transmission without authorisation will infringe copyright under this category of restricted act. This is the chief purpose of the new right. Uploaders in peer-to-peer networks or on bulletin boards would be examples of such infringers.[116] Transmissions of copyright material on TV to different persons in individual hotel bedrooms also require copyright licences as public communications, according to the Court of Justice.[117] The distribution of a signal amounted to communication even though the provision of physical facilities did not. The hotel was intervening and transmitting the broadcasts to a new public consisting of a rapid turnover of guests who could decide whether to watch the TVs. In the case of broadcasting, the infringer will be the person transmitting the programme, if he has responsibility to any extent for its contents, or the person providing the programme who made with the person transmitting it the arrangements necessary for its transmission.[118] An important limitation on this form of infringement applies where a wireless broadcast is included in a cable programme service by reception and immediate re-transmission. Neither the copyright in the broadcast or in any work included in the broadcast is infringed by this if the inclusion is in pursuance of certain statutory requirements under the Broadcasting Act 1990.[119]

 Exercise

Consider the case of *Shetland Times v Wills* [1997] FSR 604. Would the defender's activities in this case (providing hyperlinks from his website to the pursuer's one, and bypassing the latter's home page) be an infringement of the pursuer's public communication right?

Key points on public communication right

* The right is concerned with electronic transmission of works to the public
* The right covers broadcasting and Internet transmissions of works
* The right covers both transmissions where the transmitter decides when the transmission takes place and those where the recipient decides

---

[116] On peer-to-peer (P2P) networks, see further below, paras 4.72–4.75. For a case decided against individual file-sharers as copyright infringers, see BBC News Online, 27 January 2006, http://news.bbc.co.uk/1/hi/entertainment/4653662.stm

[117] Case C-306/05 *SGAE v Rafael Hoteles SL* [2006] ECR I-11519.   [118] CDPA 1988, s 6(3).

[119] CDPA 1988, s 73.

4.62   What else does this right cover? In *SGAE v Rafael Hoteles SL*[120] the ECJ said that it:

> 'must be interpreted broadly. Such an interpretation is moreover essential to achieve the principal objective of that Directive, which, as can be seen from its ninth and tenth recitals, is to establish a high level of protection of, inter alios, authors, allowing them to obtain an appropriate reward for the use of their works' (para 36).

Although the case is concerned with broadcasting, it is also relevant for Internet transmission. So the Court observed that the public or private nature of the place where the communication took place was immaterial. The essence of 'making available' was the recipient's ability to choose the place and time of the communication, and this would be rendered meaningless if her choice of a private place made a difference. Even more clearly, it would seem, it does not matter that the communicator is working from a private space in making the work available to the public. That the communication might be made only to a limited number of the public—for example, subscribers to a website or members of a network who gained access through user names and passwords—probably does not matter either. As with the public performance right, it is the nature of the audience that counts—are they members of the public?—not whether anyone without restriction may choose to receive the communication. The Court identified hotel customers as 'a public' distinct from other 'publics', when holding that the copyright author's licence to the TV broadcasters to communicate its work to the public covered only 'direct' users of the broadcasts, ie 'owners of reception equipment who, either personally or within their own private or family circles, receive the programme'. This did not extend to occupants of hotel bedrooms receiving the work by way of a further transmission process inside the hotel, who were a new and different public for the work; a further licence was needed before the material could be communicated to them. A 'public' is constituted by 'a fairly large number of persons', and in determining the relevant numbers it is relevant to consider 'the fact that, usually, hotel customers quickly succeed each other' (para 38), ie it is not a matter of 'freezing' the audience at any particular moment in time.

4.63   Moreover, whether or not customers switch on the TVs is unimportant; or, putting the point more generally, whether or not members of the public actually access the communication. The language of the Directive—'may access'—makes clear that creation of the possibility of reception of the communication is sufficient. In the Internet context, this must raise the question whether inserting hypertext links to other sites without permission of the latter's owner is potentially an infringement of that person's public communication right. The ECJ noted that the seemingly very wide potential liability is somewhat restricted by a statement in the InfoSoc Directive recitals: 'the mere provision of physical facilities for enabling or making a communication does not in itself amount to communication within the meaning of this Directive.'[121] Thus, according to the Court, merely installing TV sets in the bedrooms would not be enough for liability, whereas transmitting signals to be picked up by those TVs would complete the infringement. Hyperlinks seem to provide an intermediate case: neither a physical facility nor a transmission, but undoubtedly something which enables communication to the public. The answer to this may be that in many cases the public enabled to receive the communication by the hyperlink is anyway part of the public at which the linked site is already aimed, rather than a new public in the sense discussed in the preceding paragraph. But the matter may be finely

---

[120] Case C-306/05 *SGAE v Rafael Hoteles SL* [2006] ECR I-11519.

[121] InfoSoc Directive, recital 27; Case C-306/05 *SGAE v Rafael Hoteles SL* [2006] ECR I-11519, paras 45–47.

balanced in many cases, especially those of deep-linking, which evades home pages and other original controls on access.[122]

4.64   Litigation in the Netherlands, Belgium and Ireland has raised the question of whether an Internet service provider (ISP) can be liable as a person 'making available' infringing material even although that material is placed upon its servers by others.[123] An argument might again be advanced about whether merely providing facilities for communication amounts to 'making available', and about whether the facilities offered by an ISP amount to the 'physical' kind explicitly excluded from liability in the InfoSoc Directive and discussed in the *Rafael Hoteles* case.[124]

4.65   Some other points mentioned in the *Rafael Hoteles* case may be more briefly treated to conclude this section on public communication right. Just as it did not matter there whether or not customers switched on the TVs, whether or not they received the same communications by way of the transmission, or whether they were received simultaneously or at different times, was also unimportant. But the Court did not decide whether the unlicensed communicator had to make a profit or receive some other benefit from the activity to be liable for it, but held that the hotel clearly did do so in the case before it, since it affected both the hotel's standing and the price of its rooms.[125] The view of the Commission, that profit or other benefit is not a pre-condition of liability, is borne out by the absence of any reference to such a requirement in the Directive, and may also be supported, at least in the UK, by the fact that no such requirement exists in relation to public performance right either.

(6) Infringement by adaptation

4.66   Making any adaptation of a literary, dramatic or musical work infringes its copyright.[126] An adaptation is made when it is recorded in writing or otherwise.[127] Copying such an adaptation in any material form, issuing it to the public for the first time, performing it in public, broadcasting it, including it in a cable programme, or further adapting it, also infringes the copyright in the original work.[128] In relation to *literary works other than computer programs or databases*, or to dramatic works, adaptation means any of the following things:

- a *translation* of the work (eg from French into English);
- in the case of a dramatic work, *conversion* into a non-dramatic work, or, in the case of a non-dramatic work, a *dramatisation*;
- a *version* of the work in which the story or action is conveyed wholly or mainly by means of *pictures* in a form suitable for reproduction in a book, or in a newspaper, magazine, or similar periodical (CDPA 1988, s 21(3)(a)).

---

[122] See further T Aplin, *Copyright Law in the Digital Society* (2005) 147–51.

[123] See *Stichting Bescherming Rechten Entertainment Industrie Nederland (BREIN) v Techno Design Internet Programming BV* [2006] ECDR 21 (Court of Appeal of Amsterdam); *SABAM v SA Tiscali (Scarlet)* [2007] ECDR 19, District Court of Brussels. Note also *EMI v Eircom*, High Court of Ireland 2008/1601 P, settled in January 2009 on the basis that the ISP defendant would henceforth operate a 'three strikes and you're out' policy against file-sharers using its facilities.

[124] The ISP will however have available the defences discussed at para 4.74 below.

[125] Case C-306/05 *SGAE v Rafael Hoteles SL* [2006] ECR I-11519, para 44. Advocate General Sharpston had likewise felt it not necessary to decide this particular point (paras 56–57 of her Opinion).

[126] CDPA 1988, s 21(1).   [127] CDPA 1988, s 21(1).   [128] CDPA 1988, s 21(2).

4.67   In relation to *computer programs and databases*, adaptation means an arrangement or altered version, or a translation.[129] Translation is given a particular meaning in relation to computer programs, where it is to include a version of the program in which it is converted into or out of a computer language or code or into a different computer language or code.[130] This is of particular importance in respect of 'reverse engineering' activities, which may well be caught by this provision if not by the prohibition on copying.[131]

Discussion point   For answer guidance visit www.oxfordtextbooks.co.uk/orc/macqueen2e/

What does 'adaptation' add to the concept of 'copying' (above, paras 4.24–4.42)? Is there adaptation or copying when a book is made into a film, or when a film is made into (a) a book, or (b) a play?

Key point on adaptation

• Adaptation deals with specific cases not clearly within the concept of 'copying'

Authorisation of infringement

4.68   The copyright in a work is infringed by:

'any person who, without the licence of the copyright owner, authorises another person to do any of the restricted acts [author's emphasis]' (CDPA 1988, s 16(2)).

There cannot be infringement by authorisation unless there has been an infringement of the primary rights of the copyright owner; or to put it another way, only if authorisation comes from the copyright owner is there no primary infringement. To authorise an infringement is to 'sanction, approve, or countenance' it,[132] a formulation capable of a very wide meaning, especially when conjoined with the apparent willingness of the courts to treat indifference as capable of being authorisation.[133] However, the concept has been applied in a relatively restricted way, by employing a test of the degree of authority, or control, which the defender had over those who actually carried out the infringement.

■ *CBS v Ames Records and Tapes* [1982] Ch 91

The defendants owned a chain of record shops and began to operate record lending libraries in them. This facilitated infringing copying of records by borrowers from the libraries and the plaintiffs argued that this was 'countenancing' infringement in such a way as to authorise it.

---

[129] CDPA 1988, s 21(3)(ab), (ac).   [130] CDPA 1988, s 21(4).   [131] See above, para 4.22, for reverse engineering.
[132] This definition of 'authorise' was first stated in *Monckton v Pathe Freres Pathephone Ltd* [1914] 1 KB 395 and *Evans v Hulton & Co Ltd* [1924] WN 130.
[133] *PRS v Ciryl Theatrical Syndicate* [1924] 1 KB 1; *Moorhouse v University of New South Wales* [1976] RPC 151 (High Ct of Australia); *CBS v Ames Record & Tapes* [1982] Ch 91; *PRS v Kwik-Fit Group Ltd* [2008] ECDR 2.

Whitford J refused to grant an injunction: 'an authorisation can only come from somebody having or purporting to have authority … an act is not authorised by somebody who merely enables or possibly assists or even encourages another to do that act, but does not purport to have any authority which he can grant to justify the doing of the act' (at p 105).

■ *RCA Corp v John Fairfax & Sons Ltd* [1982] RPC 91 (NSW Supreme Court)

Publishing a newspaper article or advertisement referring to the possibility of tape recording records by use of machinery does not authorise infringement because the authors cannot control what individuals do with the machinery once they have bought it.

■ *Vigneux v Canadian PRS* [1945] AC 108 (PC)

A company which rented a juke box to restauranteurs was held not to authorise infringement of the copyright in musical works by performance because it 'had no control over the use of the machine [and] … no voice as to whether at any particular time it was to be available to the restaurant customers or not' (at p 123 per Lord Russell of Killowen).

■ *CBS Songs Ltd v Amstrad Consumer Electronics plc* [1988] 1 AC 1013

The manufacture, distribution and supply of machines capable of use by buyers for copying copyright works at high speed cannot be by themselves authorisations of infringement, since again the manufacturer lacks control over the uses to which the machine is put, and it is also capable of legitimate use.

4.69   Compare the leading case on the US copyright law equivalent of infringement by authorisation, contributory infringement:

■ *Universal City Studios Inc v Sony Corp of America* 464 US 417 (1984, US Supreme Court)

It was held here that the manufacture and sale of video tape recorders for use to copy broadcasts and films being shown on TV did not give rise to contributory infringement liability, although Sony knew that the machines were being used to commit infringements. A claim of contributory infringement would be defeated if, as in this case, the product in question was shown to be capable of substantial or commercially significant non-infringing uses. Constructive knowledge of infringing activity could not be imputed from a general awareness that the machine could be used for infringement.

 Discussion point   For answer guidance visit www.oxfordtextbooks.co.uk/orc/macqueen2e/

Would a UK court have reached the same decision in a case like *Sony*?

Cases finding authorisation to have taken place

4.70   The decisions just discussed may be compared with those where there has been held to be authorisation. Supply of a film of a play for exhibition at a cinema was held to authorise infringement of the copyright in the play in *Falcon v Famous Players Film Co.*[134] Ordering spare parts from a manufacturer authorised him to infringe the copyright in drawings of those spare parts.[135] The prior approval by a local authority of the list of musical works to be played on a public bandstand was held to be an authorisation of infringement.[136] In all these cases there was a direct and immediate link between the act of the defendant and the infringement which followed. They differ, too, from most of the cases cited in the previous paragraph where what was really being complained of was the fact that the defendant had created an opportunity for others to infringe which had probably, even certainly, been taken up, but specific instances of this were not brought to the court's attention.[137] However where the complaint is about the provision to others of opportunity to infringe and it can be coupled with the necessary degree of control over those others and specific instances of infringement, then there may be liability for authorisation.

■ *Moorhouse v University of New South Wales* [1976] RPC 151 (High Court of Australia)

The High Court of Australia held that a university had authorised infringement by students (and, presumably, staff) by providing photocopying facilities in the university library without adequate supervision of what was copied. A notice near the photocopiers warning against copyright infringement was insufficient to avoid liability. Specific incidents of infringing copying were established and the court stressed that authorisation might be implied from indifference to infringement where it was likely that such infringement would occur. Here the University also had power to control the access of students to photocopying facilities, either by not providing them or by ensuring through supervision that no infringing copying was done and accordingly it was liable.[138]

Notices and statements as defences against claims of authorisation

4.71   A further significant point in the *Moorhouse* case concerned the use of notices as a defence to a claim of authorisation. The university issued guides for library users which made incomplete reference to the provisions of the copyright legislation on copying and stated that a copy of the Act was available in the photocopying room. It was held that these were insufficient to rebut authorisation, but that an invitation to use copying facilities might be so restricted as to avoid liability.[139] But even the fullest possible notices will be inadequate if, despite their existence, infringing copying continues and the person able to control its occurrence remains indifferent to this.[140] The placing of copyright warning notices in the premises and on the copies of records lent was an important (but not the sole) factor in the *Ames Records & Tapes* case, where it was held that there had been no authorisation.[141] See most recently:

---

[134] [1926] 2 KB 474.   [135] *Standen Engineering v Spalding & Sons* [1984] FSR 554.
[136] *PRS v Bray UDC* [1930] AC 377 (PC).
[137] See in particular the discussion of the problem of 'home copying', which was the real issue in *CBS Songs Ltd v Amstrad Consumer Electronics plc* [1988] 1 AC 1013.
[138] Compare *CBS v Ames Records & Tapes* [1982] Ch 91, where no copying machines were provided. Under the CDPA 1988, the Moorhouse situation would now be avoided through the limited scope of the permitted acts (see in particular CDPA 1988, ss 29, 36–39) and reprography licensing (ss 130, 136–141). The Copyright Licensing Agency plays a significant role here (see further below, at para 21.19ff).
[139] *Moorhouse v University of New South Wales* [1976] RPC 151 (HCA).
[140] *Moorhouse v University of New South Wales* [1976] RPC 151 per Jacobs J at 166.
[141] *CBS v Ames Record & Tapes* [1982] Ch 91.

■ *Law Society of Upper Canada v CCH* [2004] 1 SCR 339 (Supreme Court, Canada)

The Law Society of Upper Canada maintained its Great Library at Osgoode Hall in Toronto. The library was for reference and research and had one of the largest collections of legal material in Canada. A self-service photocopier was located in the library for the use of patrons (Law Society members, the judiciary and other authorised researchers), alongside a notice warning that the library would not be responsible for any copies made in infringement of copyright. Law publishers challenged these practices as authorisation of infringement. It was held that the Law Society did not authorise copyright infringement. Authorisation could be inferred from indirect acts and omissions, but the authorisation of use of equipment which could be used to infringe copyright was not enough. Posting a notice warning against infringement was not an express acknowledgement that the machines would be used in an illegal manner. Authorisations should be presumed given to lawful acts only, this being rebuttable if a relationship or degree of control existed between the authoriser and persons who infringed copyright. This was not the case here, and there was no evidence of actual infringements. *Moorhouse* was criticised as shifting the balance in copyright too far in favour of the owner's rights, unnecessarily interfering with the proper use of copyrighted works for the good of society as a whole.

Discussion point   For answer guidance visit www.oxfordtextbooks.co.uk/orc/macqueen2e/

Is the criticism of *Moorhouse* in this case justified? Consider the implications for Internet service provider liability, discussed in the next paragraph (para 4.72).

Key points on authorisation

- Authorisation of infringement is sanctioning, countenancing or approving another person's primary infringement where one has authority or control over a primary infringer

- Creating opportunities for others to infringe, eg by means of machinery, is not by itself authorisation, especially where legitimate activities are also made possible by the action

- Notices warning against infringement may be a factor in preventing authorisation, but are not usually enough by themselves

Authorisation and Internet file-sharing

4.72   Liability by authorisation has obvious importance for commercial Internet service providers, universities, and other bodies which enable access to the Internet for customers, students and others by means of which infringing Internet activity can take place, whether by way of copying or the public communication right. Can such bodies be liable for authorising such infringing use? The *Amstrad* and *Ames Records & Tapes* cases held the providers of facilities not liable despite the fact that their services and products rendered infringement easy and probable,[142] the crucial factors being that lawful activity is possible with the facilities provided, and that the defendants had given express warnings to customers against use for infringing copying. This might seem encouraging for those whose facilities enable others to make use of the Internet: the facilities are capable of many lawful as well as infringing uses, and the providers generally give warnings to users against unlawful activity with the service.

4.73   Specific situations in which service providers and site operators on the Internet may nonetheless be liable for authorisation of infringement may appear from consideration of some of the substantial body of US case law before the Digital Millennium Copyright Act 1998 (for which see further below, para 4.74). This case law focuses upon the US equivalent of authorisation, the concept of contributory infringement, and its application to cases of 'file-sharing' on peer-to-peer (P2P) networks on the Internet.[143]

■ *A&M Records v Napster* 239 F 3d 1004 (2001)

The arrival of MP3 software in the late 1990s enabled the conversion of digitally recorded (or remastered) material (in particular music) into highly compressed computer files postable on and downloadable from the Internet. Napster Inc was a company which made available for downloading from the Internet its proprietary MusicShare software. This uploaded to the Napster servers a list of all MP3 files on the hard disk of the user's computer, while that person was enabled to search the servers, which contained master indices of the locations of music files on the hard disks of all users of the service. Using these indices, users might then freely download to their own computers copies of the files they wanted, directly from the hard disks of other users. These one-to-one networks were also described as 'peer-to-peer' (P2P). It was held that Napster was guilty of contributory and vicarious infringement. Napster's liability was founded, not upon their own infringement of copyright, but rather upon the holding that through their provision of indices they enabled, knew of, and could prevent, such infringement by others.

■ *Metro-Goldwyn-Mayer Studios Inc v Grokster Ltd*, 380 F 3d 1154 (9th Cir, 2004); 545 US 913 (2005, US Supreme Court)

The plaintiffs were companies in the film and music recording and publishing industries, and sought an injunction against the defendants' contributory and vicarious infringement of copyright by free distribution of software enabling users to exchange digital media via a peer-to-peer transfer network. Multiple transfers to or from other users could occur simultaneously to and from a single user's computer. The defendants argued that they merely provided software to users over whom they had no control, and that they had no liability for copyright infringement.

The lower courts held for the defendants. That there was infringing end-use by at least some users was undisputed, but for contributory infringement it had to be shown that the defendants knew or had reason to know of the direct infringement, and had materially contributed to it by personal conduct giving encouragement or assistance. But the knowledge had to be of specific acts of infringement; awareness in general that there could be infringement using the

---

[142] *CBS Inc v Ames Records & Tapes Ltd* [1982] Ch 91; *CBS Songs Ltd v Amstrad Consumer Electronics plc* [1988] 1 AC 1013.
[143] Under US law, contributory infringement results when somebody knows of the direct infringement of another and substantially participates in that infringement, such as inducing, causing, or materially contributing to the infringing conduct. This is a common law concept in the USA, and is not found in the US Copyright Act.

third party content.[148] A Dutch court has held that a file-sharing website is not an Internet service provider entitled to the benefit of these 'safe harbour' provisions.[149] In the *Promusicae v Telefónica* case in 2008, the ECJ applied the Communications Directive 2002 to refuse to order ISPs to disclose personal details of illegal downloaders to right-holders on privacy grounds (although noting that there might be exceptions to this to prevent crime, unauthorised use of electronic communication systems and the destruction of others' rights and freedoms, including intellectual property rights).[150]

 Discussion point   For answer guidance visit www.oxfordtextbooks.co.uk/orc/macqueen2e/

Would the orders made against Napster in the US have been possible under the E-Commerce Directive?

Key points on authorisation and Internet file-sharing

● The provider of a service by means of which otherwise unauthorised sharing of copyright files takes place will probably be liable for authorisation if, knowing that such sharing is taking place on a large scale, it appears to encourage the sharing to continue rather than taking possible steps to stop it

● The E-Commerce Directive provides a procedure by which the provider may avoid liability by acting expeditiously to remove infringing material once aware of its existence

Secondary infringement of copyright

4.76   'Secondary' infringements[151] of copyright are distinguished from 'primary' infringements because the defender is not liable unless he knew or had reason to believe that he was handling infringing copies, or that the performances would infringe copyright.[152] The following acts in relation to infringing copies of works constitute 'secondary' infringements of copyright:

● importing otherwise than for the importer's private and domestic use;

● possessing in the course of a business;

● selling or hiring or offering or exposing for sale or hire;

● exhibiting or distributing in the course of a business;

---

[148] E-Commerce Directive, Art 15.
[149] *Stichting Bescherming Rechten Entertainment Industrie Nederland (BREIN) v Techno Design Internet Programming BV* [2006] ECDR 21 (Court of Appeal of Amsterdam). See further HL MacQueen, 'Appropriate for the digital age? Copyright and the Internet', in L Edwards and C Waelde (eds), *Law and the Internet* (3rd edn, 2009), 197.
[150] Case C-275/06 *Productores de Música de España v Telefónica de España SAU* [2008] ECR I-271.
[151] See the heading to the relevant sections of the CDPA 1988, ss 22–26.
[152] See ss 22, 23, 24, 25(1) and 26(2)–(4).

- distribution otherwise in the course of a business to such an extent as to affect prejudicially the copyright owner.

 Discussion point For answer guidance visit www.oxfordtextbooks.co.uk/orc/macqueen2e/

What is the common feature of the above list of secondary infringements?

4.77 Also categorised as secondary infringements are:

- providing the means for making infringing copies;
- permitting the use of premises for infringing performances;
- provision of apparatus for infringing performances.

Where no charge is made for admission to the premises, however, there is no infringement of any copyright in a broadcast or cable programme, or any sound recording or film included in it, by showing or playing in public a broadcast or cable programme.[153] An audience has paid for admission to premises if (1) it has to pay for admission to *part* only of the premises; (2) it pays prices for goods or services on the premises either (a) *substantially* attributable to the facilities afforded for hearing or seeing the broadcast, or (b) exceeding those usually paid there and *partly* attributable to the facilities.[154] There are also special exceptions to copyright restrictions for hotels, guest houses and similar facilities, as well as for clubs and societies where the provision of facilities for seeing or hearing broadcasts or cable programmes is only incidental to the organisation's main purposes.[155]

 Discussion point For answer guidance visit www.oxfordtextbooks.co.uk/orc/macqueen2e/

How do these rules interact with those on public performance, showing or playing as a primary infringement (above, paras 4.53–4.59)?

Importance of secondary infringement

4.78 Claims of secondary infringement are of great importance in preventing commercial piracy, in particular the circulation of infringing sound recordings, videos, CDs and DVDs, where it is not possible to identify or take action against the person actually making the copies. The question of the degree and amount of knowledge required to make someone liable as a secondary infringer is one on which there is little clear authority. The 1988 Act requires that only 'reason to believe' need be shown to impose the liability.[156] The latest case law suggests that this is an objective test, requiring knowledge of facts from which a reasonable person would, after the

---

[153] CDPA 1988, s 72(1).

[154] CDPA 1988, s 72(2). On this test, the employer was probably not guilty of secondary infringement under this head in *PRS v Kwik-Fit Group Ltd* [2008] ECDR 2 (allowed employees to play personal radios at work so that music could be heard by customers of the employer).

[155] CDPA 1988, s 72(3).   [156] See ss 22, 23, 24, 25(1) and 26(2)–(4).

passage of a reasonable amount of time, arrive at the relevant belief; facts giving rise only to suspicion would not be enough.[157] In practice the safest approach where a possible infringement is discovered will be to send the defendant a warning letter as a first step; this will fix him with actual knowledge sufficient to justify action should the activities continue. The copyright owner should allow a reasonable time after receipt of the letter to enable the defender to consider his position, before further action is taken.[158]

Key points on secondary infringements

- Secondary infringements are essentially those of dealing commercially in products the making of which was a primary infringement of copyright, or which enable such products to be made

- The infringer must know or have reason believe that infringing copies were being handled

---

Further reading

Books

General

Bently & Sherman, *Intellectual Property Law* (3rd edn, 2009), Chs 6 and 8

Copinger & Skone James on Copyright (15th edn, 2005), Chs 7 and 8

Cornish & Llewelyn, *Intellectual Property* (6th edn, 2007), Chs 12.1–2, 12.5.

Laddie, Prescott & Vitoria, *Modern Law of Copyright* (3rd edn, 2000), Chs 14–19

Art

W Landes and R Posner, *Economic Structure of Intellectual Property Law* (2004), Ch 5

File-sharing

A Strowel (ed), *Peer-to-Peer File Sharing and Secondary Liability in Copyright Law* (2009)

Articles

Film

A Barron, 'The legal properties of film' (2004) 67 MLR 177

Art

S Stokes, 'Copyright and the reproduction of artistic works' [2003] EIPR 486

---

[157] *ZYX Music GmbH v King* [1997] 2 All ER 129 (CA); *Pensher Security Door Co Ltd v Sunderland City Council* [2000] RPC 249 (CA); *Vermaat and Powell v Boncrest (No 2)* [2002] FSR 21.
[158] *Van Dusen v Kritz* [1936] 2 KB 176; *Vermaat and Powell v Boncrest (No 2)* [2002] FSR 21.

Parody

E Gredley and S Maniatis, 'Parody: a fatal attraction?' [1997] EIPR 339

F W Grosheide, 'Some observations with regard to the parody-exception in copyright law', in E Philippin and others (eds), *Mélanges en l'honneur de Francois Dessemontet* (2009), 217–232

C Rütz, 'Parody: a missed opportunity?' [2004] IPQ 284

M Spence, 'Intellectual property and the problem of parody' (1998) 114 LQR 594

Public communication right

J Ginsburg, 'The (new?) right of making available to the public', in D Vaver and L Bently (eds), *Intellectual Property in the New Millennium* (2004)

HK Larusson, 'Uncertainty in the scope of copyright: the case of illegal file-sharing in the UK' [2009] EIPR 124

Copyright 4: exceptions, technical protection measures and contracts

Introduction

Scope and overview of chapter

5.1   This chapter first considers exceptions and limitations to the rights of the copyright owner described in the previous chapter. Copyright law establishes many such exceptions and limitations, listed in the CDPA 1988 as what it calls the *'permitted acts'*. These are acts which can be carried out in relation to the copyright work *without* the owner's permission or, in some cases, which can be performed subject to terms and conditions specified by the statute rather than by the copyright owner. As a result it is sometimes suggested that they are *user rights*. A controversial potential challenge to copyright exceptions and any concept of 'user rights' is however posed by the technical protection measures (TPMs) which right holders use to prevent unauthorised access to and use of copyright digital works. Arguably such TPMs are also capable of preventing use under the copyright exceptions and, indeed, when a work has fallen out of copyright altogether (eg at the expiry of its term). Yet copyright law gives protection to TPMs which makes their circumvention illegal so long as the protected work is made available by way of contractual terms. So TPMs also set up a world in which right holders and would-be users *contract* for the use of the copyright work, raising complex questions about the inter-relationship between exceptions to copyright, TPMs and contract rights.

5.2   ### Learning objectives

By the end of this chapter you should be able to describe and explain:

- the exceptions to the rights conferred by copyright;
- the legal protection of technical protection measures placed upon digital copyright works;
- the possibilities created by technology for the creation of direct contracts between right-holders and would-be users;
- the interaction between exceptions, technical protection measures, and contract law.

5.3   The chapter analyses each of the 'permitted acts', raising the question whether these exceptions can be regarded as 'user rights', and how far they may be set aside as a result of the application of the technological protection measures discussed in the previous chapter, or by contractual provision. So the rest of the chapter looks like this:

- The public domain and copyright exceptions in general (5.4–5.7)

- International background (5.8–5.11)

- Copyright exceptions in the UK (5.12–5.46)

- Other limitations upon copyright (5.47–5.49)

- Technical protection measures and rights management information systems (5.50–5.57)

- Copyright exceptions, TPMs, RMIs and contract (5.58–5.66)

The public domain and copyright exceptions in general

5.4   This chapter deals with what people may do with works without the authorisation or permission of the copyright owner.[1] Some material, of course, is never in copyright—for example, a single word because it is not a literary work,[2] or an unoriginal artistic work.[3] Some material which once was copyright is no longer because the term of copyright has expired, for example, sound recordings made over 50 years ago. In both cases people are free to do all the things which in other cases copyright would restrict: ie copy the work, issue copies to the public whether for sale, rental or commercial lending, perform the work in public, communicate it to the public, or adapt it. Some uses of copyright works do not fall within the scope of the restricted acts and may be freely carried out: for example, reselling a book of which you were the first purchaser, or performing a work of music in private. This copyright-free zone is sometimes known as the *public domain*.[4] It has been argued that there is a 'virtuous circle' between copyright and the public domain, with the latter feeding the creation of new copyright works which in turn fall bit by bit into the public domain, the process becoming complete when the copyright expires.[5]

 Question

How may the 'public domain' be defined in relation to copyright?

5.5   Further, and most importantly for the purposes of this section of the chapter, people may do certain things with copyright material without the licence of the copyright owner which *would* otherwise fall within the scope of the restricted acts, for example, make a copy for private study and research, perform the work in private, record a film on TV to watch it at a more convenient

---

[1] See in general G Davies, *Copyright and the Public Interest* (2nd edn, 2003); LMCR Guibault, *Copyright Limitations and Contracts: an Analysis of the Contractual Overridability of Limitations on Copyright* (2002); M Senftleben, *Copyright, Limitations and the Three-Step Test: an Analysis of the Three-Step Test in International and EC Copyright Law* (2004); R Burrell and A Coleman, *Copyright Exceptions: the Digital Impact* (2005).

[2] See *Exxon Corp v Exxon Insurance* [1982] Ch 119.   [3] *Interlego AG v Tyco Industries Inc* [1989] AC 217.

[4] See generally C Waelde and HL MacQueen (eds), *The Many Faces of the Public Domain* (2007), and references therein.

[5] W Davies and K Withers, *Public Innovation: Intellectual Property in a Digital Age* (Institute of Public Policy Research, 2006).

time, or quote a work for purposes such as criticising it or reporting the news. This is because British copyright law contains extensive and detailed provisions by which various carefully specified 'acts which would otherwise be infringements of copyright are made lawful'.[6] They are described in the CDPA 1988 under the general heading, 'Acts Permitted in Relation to Copyright Works'. Such acts do not require any licence from the copyright owner and may be freely performed by others.

5.6 The contents of the list of permitted acts reflect a legislative perception that certain interests in certain circumstances outweigh the interest in conferring and enforcing copyright. Some of the items on the list of permitted acts are grouped together as 'fair dealing', but there is no general principle that 'fair dealing' beyond the listed acts or for other than the listed purposes is allowed. (Note, however, the rather uncertain principle that copyright may be limited by what is known as the defence of 'public interest', discussed further below, at para 5.47.)

5.7 In this avoidance of a general principle and concentration upon a specific list of permitted acts, there is a contrast with US law, which provides a general 'fair use' defence covering purposes 'such as' criticism, comment, teaching, scholarship and research, and indicating that factors to be taken into account 'include' such matters as whether the use is of a commercial nature or for non-profit educational purposes, the amount and substantiality of the portion used in relation to the whole work, and the effect of the use upon the market or value of the copyright work.[7] The argument against such a general approach is that it creates uncertainty by contrast with the more specific approach in the UK; on the other hand, the flexibility of a general approach may enable the law to deal better with changing ways of producing and exploiting copyright works. There is also a different contrast between the UK and many of the Continental laws, which tend to exclude private non-commercial copying from the scope of copyright, although a concomitant in many of these systems is levies on blank audio cassettes and reprography, the proceeds from which are routed back ultimately to copyright owners via their collecting societies.[8] Thus the permitted use is nonetheless one for which the copyright owner ultimately receives remuneration, whether paid directly or indirectly by the user. The UK, on the other hand, has resisted both a general exemption for private use and the correlative deployment of levies on materials and machinery used for copying purposes. The European Commission is investigating whether such levies should be introduced on a harmonised Union-wide basis.[9]

 Question

What contrasts exist between UK, US and Continental European approaches to permitted acts?

---

[6] CDPA 1988, ss 28–76.   [7] US Copyright Act 1976, s 107.

[8] See eg the French Intellectual Property Code of 1 July 1992, L122–5, L211–3, L212–10, and L311; and German Copyright Act 1965, §§ 53, 54 and 54a-h.

[9] See the European Commission Internal Market DG website at http://ec.europa.eu/internal_market/copyright/levy_reform/index_en.htm

> ### Key points on permitted acts (introduction)
>
> - Works never in copyright, or the copyright in which has expired, are often said to be 'in the public domain'
> - The permitted acts are ones which would be infringements of copyright but are made lawful by specific statutory provision
> - UK law takes a specific rather than a general 'fair use' or 'private use' approach to this subject
> - The UK approach is not really consistent with the idea that the permitted acts are 'user rights'

International background

Berne Convention ('three-step test'), TRIPS and WCT

5.8   Under Article 9(2) of the Berne Convention members of the Union may:

> 'permit the reproduction of [literary and artistic] works in certain special cases, provided that such reproduction does not conflict with a normal exploitation of the work and does not unreasonably prejudice the legitimate interests of the author.'

Article 10, under the heading 'Certain Free Uses of Works', goes on to permit quotation from work lawfully made available to the public, provided that this is 'compatible with fair practice' and is not in excess of what is 'justified by the purpose'. The Article also allows members of the Union to permit 'utilisation, to the extent justified by the purpose' of literary and artistic works by way of illustration for teaching, so long this is 'compatible with fair practice'. In both cases, the source and the name of the author must be identified. Article 10*bis* of the Convention adds 'Further Possible Free Uses of Works' for the reporting of current events. The TRIPS Agreement of 1994 notes that limitations or exceptions to copyright are to be 'confined' to 'certain special cases which do not conflict with a normal exploitation of the work and do not unreasonably prejudice the legitimate interests of the right holder'.[10] For some reason, Article 10 of the WCT 1996 repeats this formula no less than twice, but, like TRIPS, where the Berne Convention talks of 'permitting' such acts, the WIPO Article speaks of 'confining' them. In 2000 a Dispute Panel of the WTO issued an opinion on the scope of the three-step test in 2000, holding that section 110(5) of the US Copyright Act 1976 violated the test by allowing public performance of works received from broadcasts. All three steps had to be complied with in any copyright exception. While minor or *de minimis* departures from the test were permissible, section 110(5) did not fall into that category.[11]

---

[10]   TRIPS, Art 13.
[11]   Report of the WTO Panel dated June 15, 2000, WT/DS160/R. See further C Geiger, J Griffiths and RM Hilty, 'Towards a balanced interpretation of the 'three-step test' in copyright law' [2008] EIPR 489.

Question

The Berne Convention regulation of exceptions to copyright is sometimes known as 'the three-step test'. What are these three steps?

Discussion point   For answer guidance visit www.oxfordtextbooks.co.uk/orc/macqueen2e/

Why do TRIPS and the WCT 1996 want to 'confine' exceptions to copyright?

European Union

5.9   The InfoSoc Directive 2001, the EU's implementation of the WCT 1996, made provision for what it called 'Exceptions and Limitations' to copyright. During the prolonged gestation of the Directive there was great controversy as to whether its extension of owner rights was sufficiently (or indeed at all) balanced by the exceptions to the restricted acts of reproduction and public communication set out in Article 5; and whether these in turn were set at naught by the rules in Article 6 supporting the use of technical measures of copyright protection in digital products, and enabling the right holder to deny access until paid by the would-be user, whether or not the proposed use fell within the scope of copyright or the exceptions. The importance of the debate was that, at least with regard to reproduction and public communication rights in the digital context, these exceptions were to replace entirely existing national rules on the subject.[12] However, all but one of the exceptions listed in Article 5 is permissive—that is, the member states may (and therefore need not) introduce them. The result is that an unharmonised scheme of exceptions and limitations continues to exist in the EU.

5.10   A generally restrictive approach to the exceptions is visible in the recitals:

> 'the provision of . . . exceptions [to copyright] . . . should . . . duly reflect the increased economic impact that such exceptions . . . may have in the context of the new electronic environment. Therefore the scope of certain exceptions may have to be even more limited when it comes to certain new uses of copyright works . . . ' (recital 44).

The Directive also seems to suggest that in at least some circumstances contractual provision may eliminate copyright exceptions. The fourth paragraph of Article 6(4) appears to give pre-eminence to contractual terms over the exceptions where works are made available in such a way that they may be accessed from places and at times individually chosen by users. Since this condition applies to everything found on the Internet, the provision seems to have the potential to eliminate the exceptions to copyright altogether in that context. Such apocalyptic conclusions need to be modified, however, because such elimination should only occur if a contract to that effect is *previously* in place between right holder and user. On the other hand, this

---

[12] COM(1997) 628 final, 28 (para 2); see also recital 22 and Art 5(3)(p), the latter of which permits member states to provide for 'use in certain other cases of minor importance where exceptions already exist under national law, *provided that they only concern analogue uses* [emphasis supplied] and do not affect the free circulation of goods and services within the Community [now Union]'.

reinforces the position of the right holder barring access in order to create an opportunity to establish a contractual nexus under which the user pays for his use; and it is really only against the right holder who wishes to deny access in order to be paid for the privilege that exceptions and limitations giving access regardless of the right-holder's wishes are of any significance.[13]

Exercise

Why do copyright exceptions have 'increased economic impact' in the electronic environment? Why should contract prevail over exceptions in that electronic environment?

5.11 It should also be noted that the Software and Database Directives made provision for exceptions to the rights which they conferred,[14] and that these are largely unaffected by the InfoSoc Directive. The Software Directive notably lays down that most of the exceptions to copyright in computer programs—in particular, making back up copies, decompilation, and observation, studying and testing—cannot be overcome by contractual agreement.[15] But there is nothing of this kind in the Database Directive.[16]

Copyright exceptions in the UK

5.12 The UK implemented the InfoSoc Directive provisions on copyright exceptions and limitations with effect from 31 October 2003,[17] and the account below is based upon the law as so amended. In negotiating and implementing the Directive, the UK Government's policy was to maintain as far as possible the previously existing regime, adjusting it as necessary. No new rights allowed under the Directive were introduced; but none of the existing rights made permissive by the Directive were eliminated, although some have been narrowed significantly in scope. The account which follows will therefore make use of authorities from the pre-Directive law as far as possible. It also deals with the implementation of the Software and Database Directives' provisions on exceptions and limitations, although only the former has truly distinct issues needing to be addressed.

(1) Making temporary copies

Introduction

5.13 As noted above (para 4.36), copying in relation to any description of work includes the making of copies which are transient or incidental to some other use of the work.[18] Major examples of what may therefore be infringement of copyright without the licence of the copyright owner are

---

[13] See further C Geiger, 'From Berne to national law, via the Copyright Directive: the dangerous mutations of the three-step test' [2007] EIPR 486.

[14] Software Directive, Arts 5, 6; Database Directive, Arts 6, 9.

[15] Software Directive, Arts 5(2), (3), 6(1). See CDPA 1988, ss 50A, 50B(4), 50BA and 296A, and below, para 5.44.

[16] However, see CDPA 1988, ss 50D(2) and 296B.

[17] Copyright and Related Rights Regulations 2003 (SI 2003/2498).   [18] CDPA 1988, s 17(6).

Diagram 5.1 Exceptions to copyright

Exceptions	Subject matter to which applicable	Relevant restricted acts
Temporary reproduction (general)	Author works apart from computer programs and databases	Temporary reproduction
Temporary reproduction (special)	Computer programs and databases	Temporary reproduction
Fair dealing (1): Non-commercial research	LDMA works	All
Fair dealing (2): Private study	LDMA works	All
Fair dealing (3): Criticism or review	LDMA works, films, sound recordings, broadcasts	All
Fair dealing (4): Reporting current events	LDMA works, films, sound recordings, broadcasts	All
Educational establishments	LDMA works	Copying; performing, playing, showing in public
Libraries and archives	LDM works	Copying; issuing to the public; lending
Disability	LDM works, broadcasts	Copying
Public administration	All; work done for public service, open to public inspection under statute, communicated to Crown in course of public business, public records	Copying; issuing to public
Incidental inclusion	All	Copying; issue to the public
Computer programs: back up; decompilation; observe, study, test; adapt for lawful use/error correction.	Computer programs	Copying; adaptation
Time-shifting	Broadcasts	Copying

Note: LDMA – literary, dramatic, musical and artistic works

This is an extremely simplified representation of the main exceptions recognised in UK copyright law, and should not be relied upon as a detailed analysis (for which the reader is referred to the text below as well as, of course, the relevant parts of CDPA 1988).

loading a computer program into a computer's RAM, or accessing an online database or website, where again copies are made in the RAM of the machine being used for the purpose. Indeed, the actual operation of the Internet, which involves the transmission of data in small packets from computer to computer across a network, also involves the making of temporary copies in each of the computers through which the packages are forwarded on their way. However, there are also important provisions amongst those on the permitted acts which prevent such temporary copying being infringement in certain, carefully defined circumstances, and so stop copyright becoming an impediment to perfectly reasonable, indeed often necessary, activities.

Temporary reproduction exception

5.14 The most general exception flows from the InfoSoc Directive. Copyright in author works (apart from computer programs and databases) and in typographical arrangements of a published edition, sound recordings or films is not infringed by the making of a temporary copy which is transient or incidental, so long as:

(1) the making is an *integral and essential part of a technological process, and*

(2) the *sole purpose* is to enable *either*—
 (a) a *transmission of the work in a network* between third parties by an intermediary; *or*
 (b) a *lawful use* of the work *and*

(3) the temporary copy has no *independent economic significance.*

5.15 The operation of the Internet and the making of copies of packets in transmission, typically by Internet service providers, provide the clearest example of this exception in action. The technology works by the making of these copies, and its only purpose is to play a role in the transmission of the information from a website to the person accessing it. The copy has no independent economic significance, both because normally no-one has any awareness of its existence and because on its own it has no utility or value to anyone; only when the packets are re-united at the accessing computer does the material become intelligible to a user.

5.16 Recital 33 of the InfoSoc Directive comments that 'this exception should include acts which enable browsing as well as acts of caching to take place, including those which enable transmission systems to function effectively'. The temporary reproduction exception covers the copy made in the RAM of the recipient's computer in order for that person to see the page on the screen when that enables a 'lawful use'. Given that making a temporary copy as such is infringement of copyright, such use can only become lawful as a result of an express or implied licence from the copyright owner, or as a result of some other permitted act, such as research for non-commercial purposes, private study or certain educational uses.

5.17 It is a moot point whether the temporary reproduction exception covers what is known as 'proxy server caching', where by deploying appropriate software technology Internet service providers, universities, librarians, archivists and others make and store on their own servers temporary and regularly updated copies of materials contained on other servers with the purpose of making the information more readily available to their local clients by avoiding congestion at the 'live' site.[19] Such copies are thus temporary, transient and incidental, arguably form an integral and essential part of a technological process the purpose of which is to enable transmissions between other parties and lawful uses (whether licensed or permitted), while having no independent economic significance (unless perhaps users are charged for the enhanced service thus made available). The European Parliament sought to prevent the exception extending so far, but such a limitation was rejected by the Commission on the ground that if right owners' authorisation was required for cache copies, the effective operation of the Internet would be seriously hindered.[20] The InfoSoc Directive also provides that there may be exceptions for:

'use by communication or making available, for the purpose of research or private study, to individual members of the public by dedicated terminals on the premises of [publicly accessible libraries,

---

[19] Such operations may also amount to the infringing act of storage by electronic means.
[20] See COM(1999) 250 final, para 4(1).

educational establishments or museums, or by archives] of works and other subject-matter not subject to purchase or licensing terms which are contained in their collections' (Art 5(3)(n)).

■ Case C-5/08 *Infopaq International A/S v Danske Dagblades Forening* [2009] ECDR 16

For the facts see para 4.15 above. The ECJ held that the reproductions of electronic news articles involved in the preparation of an electronic 'cuttings' service by an agency were not 'transient' copies. As a derogation from general principle (ie, reproduction is infringement), the exception was to be interpreted restrictively.

Question

Under what conditions is temporary reproduction a permitted act rather than an infringement? Give some illustrative examples.

Temporary reproduction of databases and computer programs

5.18   The Database Directive[21] and, following it, s 50D of the 1988 Act provide in effect that temporary reproduction of a database which is necessary for the purpose of access to and normal use of the contents of a database, or part thereof, by a person with a right to use the database, does not require the authorisation of the author of the database. A person will have a right to use through licence, express or implied, or by way of the generally permitted acts so far as they apply to databases. Any term or condition of an agreement purporting to prohibit an act permitted under this provision of the 1988 Act is void.[22] The Software Directive[23] and, following it, s 50C of the 1988 Act also provide in effect that temporary reproduction or adaptation of a computer program necessary for a lawful user's lawful use of the program is permitted. But, in an example of contract prevailing over exceptions (unlike the position with databases just described), a term of any contract regulating the circumstances in which the user's use is lawful, and prohibiting the copying or adaptation in question, will make those acts infringements. There are however a number of other acts in relation to computer programs which may be undertaken by a lawful user thereof, and which cannot be over-ridden by contract—making a back-up copy of the program, decompilation in terms of s 50B(2), and observing, studying or testing the functioning of the program in accordance with s 50BA. And for the owner of copyright in a computer program to put it on the market without granting a licence, express or implied, to enable the purchaser to load it into a computer's RAM and run it (thereby making the purchaser a lawful user) would seem an absurd scenario.

---

[21] Database Directive, reading Art 6(1) in conjunction with Art 5(a).
[22] CDPA 1988, s 50D(2) and 296B. For an example of a clause being held void under s 50D, see *Navitaire Inc v EasyJet Airline Co Inc* [2006] RPC 3.
[23] Software Directive, reading Art 5(1) in conjunction with Art 4(a).

> **Key points on exceptions for temporary reproduction**
>
> - The general exception, which does not apply to computer programs and databases, is for copying as an integral part of a technological process enabling either a network transmission or a lawful use of the work, and having no independent economic significance
>
> - This is intended to allow 'browsing' on the Internet and 'caching'
>
> - There are special exceptions for computer programs and databases, most of which cannot be contractually overridden

(2) Fair dealing

5.19   No fair dealing with a literary, dramatic, musical or artistic work will constitute infringement of the copyright in the work if it is carried out for one of the permitted purposes. Fair dealing for any other purpose, or dealing which is only fair in general, is not permitted as such, and if there is not to be liability for infringement of copyright the activity will have to be shown to fall within some other category of permitted act. But dealing for one of the statutory purposes and also for some other purpose may still be fair dealing.[24] The permitted statutory purposes for all literary, dramatic, musical and artistic works are:

- *research for a non-commercial purpose* accompanied by a sufficient acknowledgement, unless such acknowledgement is impossible for reasons of practicality or otherwise (CDPA 1988, s 29(1), as amended by 2003 Regulations);

- *private study* (CDPA 1988, s 29(1));

- *criticism or review*, whether of the work whose copyright is said to be infringed or of some other work or of a performance of a work, which is accompanied by a sufficient acknowledgement (CDPA 1988, s 30(1));

- *reporting current events* (CDPA 1988, s 30(2) and (3)).

In addition, fair dealing for purposes of criticism and review and reporting current events can extend to sound recordings, films, and broadcasts. But in these cases, where current events are being reported, there is no need for a sufficient acknowledgement.[25]

> **Question**
>
> Does fair dealing for purposes of non-commercial research or private study extend to films, sound recordings and broadcasts?

Fairness and the 'three-step test'

5.20   The dealing with the copyright work must be fair; but the Act, both before and after the 2003 amendments, contains no elaboration of what is or is not fair. Contrast the list of factors to be

---

[24] *Sillitoe v McGraw-Hill Book Co Ltd* [1983] FSR 545.   [25] See *BBC v BSB Ltd* [1992] Ch 141.

taken into account under the fair use provisions of the US Copyright Act, which 'include' such matters as whether the use is of a commercial nature or for non-profit educational purposes, the amount and substantiality of the portion used in relation to the whole work, and the effect of the use upon the market or value of the copyright work (see above, para 5.7). Some of these (eg commercial use) are built into the structure of the specific exceptions in the UK, and others have emerged in the case law, as will appear from the account below. But the question of fairness is still to at least some extent at large. An important element now, however, is the express reference to the Berne 'three-step test' (above, para 5.8), not in the amended text of the 1988 Act, but in the underlying Software, Database and InfoSoc Directives, that the exceptions and limitations are to be applied:

(1) only in certain special cases;

(2) not conflicting with normal exploitation; and

(3) not unreasonably prejudicing the legitimate interests of the copyright owner.[26]

At least one implication of this must be that the impact of the activity upon the market for the right holder's work, if any, is a relevant factor in assessing the fairness of that activity and whether it should be allowed as an exception to the copyright.

Fair dealing: (a) research for non-commercial purposes[27]

Meaning of research

5.21   The meaning of the word 'research' appears never to have been judicially considered in the UK. Prior to the 2003 amendments it was linked to 'private study', but the two have now been severed, so must each have a separate rather than a cumulative meaning. The Oxford English Dictionary defines research as a process of search or investigation undertaken to discover facts and reach new conclusions by the critical study of a subject or by a course of scientific inquiry; or as a systematic investigation into and study of materials, sources and so on, to establish facts or collate information. Study, on the other hand, is more about the application of the mind to the acquisition of knowledge, or reading a book or text with close attention.[28] Research may therefore be thought of as having some end product in view, a contribution to knowledge and understanding; while study is more about acquiring knowledge and understanding that already exists. But on these definitions it must also be admitted that research is hardly conceivable without study, and that any distinction between the two is difficult to maintain. In the university context, research would be the characteristic activity of the PhD student and study that of the first year undergraduate; but between the two levels there is a wide spectrum, indeed a progression, of activity partaking of both study and research. Thus the undergraduate will study for exams and research for essays or dissertations, while the postgraduate will have studied for an undergraduate degree and to establish the base from which the subject of the doctoral research can be identified. The professor or lecturer, on the other hand, will research to write learned articles in scholarly journals, perhaps merely study in order to give lectures and tutorials, and be somewhere in between in writing a student textbook. It is not clear whether the professor

---

[26] Database Directive, Art 6(3); InfoSoc Directive, Art 5(5). The Software Directive also refers to the three-step test in permitting decompilation of computer programs (Art 6(3)): see further below, para 5.44.

[27] See generally Burrell and Coleman, *Copyright Exceptions*, pp 115–20.

[28] For these definitions see the Oxford English Dictionary; note also the Australian and New Zealand cases of *De Garis v Neville Jeffress Pidler* (1990) 18 IPR 292 (Fed Ct Aus); *Television New Zealand v Newsmonitor Services* [1994] 2 NZLR 91 (High Ct NZ); and *Copyright Licensing v University of Auckland* (2002) 53 IPR 618 (NZ).

merely keeping up-to-date in his field—for example, reading and making copies of new publications and filing them for possible future use—can be said to be carrying out research: on the definitions above, probably not, but perhaps it amounts to private study. Whether research includes the publication of research results (ie quotation from research materials in the resulting publication) is perhaps a moot point. But it is difficult to see how one accompanies research carried out in one's own office, or in a library, archive or gallery, with the 'sufficient acknowledgement' required by the statute. The use of that phrase with regard to the research exception (but not that for private study) at least suggests that the former *does* cover quotation from research materials (with appropriate citation) in the publication of the researcher's results.[29] The Directive talks of 'scientific research', but this does not mean that only research in what would generally be thought of as science (as opposed to arts, humanities or social sciences) is covered; rather it means research directed to the development of knowledge and understanding (*scientia*) in whatever discipline.

Discussion point For answer guidance visit www.oxfordtextbooks.co.uk/orc/macqueen2e/

Does the research exception extend to quotation from research materials in a subsequent publication? What is the implication of CDPA 1988, s 29(3)(b) in this connection?

Non-commercial purpose

5.22 The really crucial change to UK law which was made by the Directive and the 2003 Regulations was the restriction of the exception or permission for research to research carried out for a *non-commercial purpose*. Thus, for example, the copying which might have been involved in a lawyer carrying out legal research on behalf of a client now requires authorisation from—and probably the payment of a fee to—the copyright owner.[30] On the other hand, the research carried out by an undergraduate writing an essay for assessment is clearly for a non-commercial purpose, as would be that carried out by a civil servant while preparing an internal report for a government minister. Unfortunately, however, there is a large amount of ambiguity in the distinction between commercial and non-commercial research. To pursue the university context as an example: what is the position of the professor writing a learned monograph which will be published by a commercial publisher, and from which the professor will earn royalties?[31] Is it different if the product is for a professional journal or conference for which the professor will receive a fee? Or suppose research which is initially published in an academic journal, for no fee, but which subsequently becomes the basis for the development of a commercial product? The language of the statute seems to suggest that the purpose of the research is to be tested at the time it is carried out, and that it is sufficient if there is 'a' non-commercial purpose, that is to say, where the researcher has multiple purposes, the presence of a non-commercial one will suffice

---

[29] Burrell and Coleman, *Copyright Exceptions*, p 117, argue the opposite view, supporting it by reference to CDPA 1988, s 29(3)(b). Guidance has been promulgated by the British Academy and the Publishers Association in April 2008, entitled 'Joint Guidelines on Copyright and Academic Research', available at http://www.publishers.org.uk/images/stories/AboutPA/Joint_Guidelines_on_Copyright_and_Academic_Research.pdf

[30] So the comment in *Law Society of Upper Canada v CCH Canadian* [2004] 1 SCR 339, para 51 ('Lawyers carrying on the business of law for profit are conducting research') may be literally true, but that would probably not enjoy the benefit of any exception in the UK.

[31] Contrary to popular belief amongst students, academic authors do earn royalties!

pertinence to law students and lawyers, will be given here. Anything done for the purpose of reporting parliamentary or judicial proceedings does not infringe copyright; but this does not authorise the copying of a work which is itself a published report of the proceedings (eg Hansard, a law report).[97]

Incidental inclusion

5.43   Copyright in a work is not infringed by its incidental inclusion in an artistic work, sound recording, film, or broadcast:[98] for example, the inclusion in the background of an informal photographic portrait of a painting or sculpture, or its appearance in the background of a television broadcast. Alongside this rule may be mentioned another one, permitting certain acts in respect of buildings, sculptures, models for buildings and works of artistic craftsmanship which are situated permanently in a public place or in premises open to the public: they may be made the subject of a graphic work, a photograph or film, or included in a broadcast as a visual image without their copyright being infringed thereby.[99] In neither case is the copyright infringed by the issue to the public of copies (for example, videos of the broadcast), or the playing, showing, or broadcasting of such a work.[100] A musical work, words spoken or sung with music, or so much of a sound recording, broadcast or cable programme as includes a musical work or such words, is not to be regarded as incidentally included in another work if it is deliberately included[101]—for example, as part of background noise in a film or television production; thus copyright permission will be required.

■ *FA Premier League v Panini* [2004] FSR 1 (CA)

P distributed an unofficial football sticker album and a sticker collection of pictures of players from Premier League clubs wearing team strips showing the Premier League logo or the logo of a Premier League club. FAPL, acting on behalf of the clubs, had granted exclusive rights to T, to use and reproduce the official team logos in stickers and albums. It was held at first instance that there was infringement. The use of the logos was not incidental, meaning casual or of secondary importance, but integral to showing the footballer in his current strip. An appeal was dismissed. 'Incidental' did not mean only unintentional or non-deliberate inclusion, and the question had to be answered by considering the circumstances in which the relevant artistic work was created. There was no necessary dichotomy between 'incidental' and 'integral'. Where a copyright artistic work appeared in a photograph because it was part of the setting in which the photographer found his subject, it could properly be said to be an integral part of that photograph. In order to test whether the use of one work in another was incidental, it was proper to ask why it had been included in the other, considering both commercial and aesthetic reasons. Applying that test, it was evident that the use of the team and Premier League logos in the stickers was not incidental. Further, the defence would probably not apply to the albums since they were arguably literary works.

Question

What does 'incidental' mean in this context?

[97] CDPA 1988, s 45(2), (3).
[98] CDPA 1988, s 31(1). See generally Burrell and Coleman, *Copyright Exceptions*, pp 64–6.
[99] CDPA 1988, s 62.   [100] CDPA 1988, ss 31(2) and 62(3).   [101] CDPA 1988, s 31(3).

Discussion point 1   For answer guidance visit www.oxfordtextbooks.co.uk/orc/macqueen2e/

Is 'incidental inclusion' really an exception to copyright? Or does it just follow from the definitions of copyright and infringement thereof?

Discussion point 2

If I take a photograph of my family against the background of a statue in a city square in order to create a striking overall image, is the sculptor's copyright infringed? Is it any different from taking a picture of a well-known actor against the background of a sculpture in his home because I think the statue symbolises something of the actor's personality?

Lawful uses of computer programs

5.44   A lawful user of a computer program (meaning someone who has a right to use it, whether under a licence or otherwise, eg under a fair dealing exception) who does the following things with the program is not infringing copyright:

- makes a *back up* copy necessary for his lawful use (CDPA 1988, s 50A);

- *decompiles* the program (ie converts it from a low level language (object code) to a high level one, incidentally copying it in the process), for the sole purpose of obtaining the information necessary to enable the creation of another program which will be inter-operable with the original one (CDPA 1988, s 50B);

- *observes, studies or tests* the functioning of the program to determine its underlying ideas and principles, while loading, displaying, running, transmitting or storing the program as entitled to do (CDPA 1988, s 50BA);

- *copies or adapts as necessary for lawful use,* and so far as not contractually prohibited, in particular for the purpose of *error correction* (CDPA 1988, s 50C).

Only the last of these is subject to any overriding contractual clause; in the other three cases, such clauses are void.[102]

 Discussion point   For answer guidance visit www.oxfordtextbooks.co.uk/orc/macqueen2e/

To what extent may the exceptions for lawful use of computer programs be compared with fair dealing for purposes of private study and non-commercial research in relation to literary, dramatic, musical and artistic works?

Time-shifting

5.45   The development of the video recorder as a consumer item has made it normal for individuals to be able to make copies of television programmes which can be viewed later at a more conven-ient time than that scheduled by the broadcasting authority. This is commonly known as

---

[102] CDPA 1988, s 296A.

'time-shifting'. Such activities do not constitute infringement of copyright either in the broadcast or in any work included in it—for example, a film—so long as carried out in domestic premises for private and domestic use.[103] The provision also applies to audio taping of a radio broadcast. Similarly, the making for private and domestic use of a photograph of the whole or any part of an image forming part of a television broadcast, or a copy of such a photograph, does not infringe any copyright in the broadcast or in any film included in it.[104] Selling or otherwise dealing with a copy made under these provisions may become a secondary infringement of copyright (see above, paras 4.76–4.78).[105]

5.46   There would seem clearly to be no room, however, for an argument under the present legislation such as that advanced, unsuccessfully, in the *MP3.com* case in the USA:[106] that since the company's activities, in enabling CD owners to make additional copies in MP3 format, allowed users to listen to the music, not only at the time but also in the place most convenient to them ('space- or place-shifting'), a fair use defence was available. Thus, copying a computer program from one's PC to a laptop, or a CD into an MP3 player, do not fall within the scope of any current copyright exception in the UK.

 Discussion point   For answer guidance visit www.oxfordtextbooks.co.uk/orc/macqueen2e/

Is 'place-shifting' as legitimate as 'time-shifting'? Ought there to be such an exception to copyright?

Other limitations on copyright

Public interest and public policy

5.47   The 1988 Act saves various rights and privileges in general terms as unaffected by its provisions.[107] It is also provided that nothing in the Act affects the law on breach of trust or confidence,[108] or any rule preventing or restricting the enforcement of copyright on grounds of public interest or otherwise.[109] The *public policy* concept is that certain types of work—pornography or material published in breach of a lifelong obligation of secrecy, for example—are undeserving of the protection of copyright.[110] A second limitation is one which allows otherwise infringing acts—or encourages dissemination—on the grounds that they are in the *public interest*.[111] The scope and, indeed, existence of this defence remain uncertain,[112] although in twice affirming it in 1999 Jacob J formulated the test as being one of reasonable certainty that no right-thinking member of society would quarrel with the validity of the defence in the circumstances.[113] The public interest defence in the law of confidential information has been applied in relation to the

---

[103] CDPA 1988, s 70.   [104] CDPA 1988, s 71.   [105] CDPA 1988, ss 70(2), (3), 71(2), (3).

[106] *UMG Recordings Inc and others v MP3.com Inc*, 2000 WL 1262568 (SD NY).

[107] CDPA 1988, s 171(a)–(d).   [108] CDPA 1988, s 171(e).   [109] CDPA 1988, s 171(3).

[110] See eg *Glyn v Weston Feature Film Co* [1916] 1 Ch 261; *Attorney-General v Guardian Newspapers Ltd (No 2)* [1990] 1 AC 109. See also A Sims, 'The denial of copyright on public policy grounds' [2008] EIPR 189.

[111] *Beloff v Pressdram* [1973] RPC 765. See generally Davies, *Copyright and the Public Interest*, passim; Burrell and Coleman, *Copyright Exceptions*, pp 80–112.

[112] A Sims, 'The public interest defence in copyright law: myth or reality?' [2006] EIPR 335.

[113] *Hyde Park Residence Ltd v Yelland* [1999] RPC 655; *Mars UK Ltd v Teknowledge Ltd* [2000] FSR 138.

unauthorised publication of information and material generated but kept secret by public authorities. If the authority's motivation in preventing publication is improper—for example, to conceal the failings of its officials—then an unauthorised publication, including one on the Internet, may be justified.[114]

■ *Hyde Park Residence Ltd v Yelland* [1999] RPC 655 (Jacob J); [2000] RPC 604 (CA)

Jacob J took a similar approach to copyright, holding that the public interest defence was applicable against a private individual (Mohammed al-Fayed), enabling the defendant to counter misleading public statements about how much time Princess Diana and Dodi al-Fayed had spent at the 'House of Windsor' in Paris on the day of their deaths. But this was overturned by the Court of Appeal,[115] the majority (Aldous LJ and Stuart-Smith LJ) holding that (1) there was no public interest defence separate from that of public policy; (2) the circumstances in which copyright would not be enforced must derive from the work itself (ie its immoral character or deleterious effects) rather than from the conduct of the owner of copyright; and (3) the considerations arising in breach of confidence cases, where the courts balanced the public interest in maintaining confidentiality against the public interest in knowledge of the truth and freedom of expression, were different from copyright ones, where property rights were involved and the legislation already provided fair dealing defences in the public interest. It should not be possible for public interest to uphold as legitimate an act that had been found, as in this case, not to be fair dealing (see above, para 5.35).[116] While generally agreeing with this approach, the third member of the Court, Mance LJ, indicated that there might be cases where a public interest dimension did arise from the ownership of the work, although this was not such a case.[117]

■ *Ashdown v Telegraph Group Ltd* [2002] Ch 149 (CA)

The approach of Mance LJ was preferred by a subsequent Court of Appeal in this case (see para 5.35), emphasising in particular the public interest in freedom of expression under Article 10 of the European Convention on Human Rights, albeit that on the facts of the case it was held that the defence was not made out, since the newspaper had extracted from Mr Ashdown's diaries 'colourful passages...likely to add flavour to the article and thus to appeal to the readership of the newspaper...for reasons that were essentially journalistic in furtherance of the commercial interests of the Telegraph Group' (para 82) rather than in the public interest.

■ *HRH The Prince of Wales v Associated Newspapers Ltd (No 3)* [2008] Ch 57 (CA)

For the facts see above, para 5.32. It was held that the unauthorised publication in a newspaper of extracts from the Prince's unpublished journals was not justified by any public interest defence, such as making more widely known the political views of the heir to the throne in relation to an important foreign power (the People's Republic of China). It would be rare for a case on public interest to succeed where the fair dealing defences had been found inapplicable (see also para 5.35). Public interest also rarely justified copying content rather than simply referring to the information therein.

---

[114] See paras 18.59–18.62.   [115] [2000] RPC 604.   [116] See paras 55, 58, 64–7.   [117] Paras 79–83.

Exercise 1

Explain the distinction between 'public policy' and 'public interest', if any. What difference does it make?

Exercise 2

Should pornography be unprotected by copyright? Does this encourage or discourage freedom of expression?

No derogation from grant

5.48   In *British Leyland v Armstrong Patents*,[118] the House of Lords declared that a copyright owner could be deprived of his rights where their exercise was in 'derogation from grant'. The context was the manufacture and supply to consumers of spare parts for cars, to which the car manufacturers took objection by means of copyright. The House found that car owners had a right to repair their vehicles, and that the car manufacturers could not exercise their copyright so as to prevent third parties enabling the owners to exercise their own separate and pre-existing rights as cheaply as possible. This was founded on the general legal principle of 'no derogation from grant', established in the context of leases, sales of goodwill and easements or servitudes. It had never been previously applied to copyright, and the reasoning of the House on the point is unsatisfactory. The Privy Council has since indicated that the principle should be interpreted very narrowly in copyright law, and that it is really based on public policy.[119] Nonetheless, it is therefore still applicable,[120] and may find some application in the context of the Internet, perhaps in relation to the questions about activities such as downloading and the construction and deployment of search engines.

Exercise

How might the 'no derogation from grant' principle apply to Internet copyrights?

Human rights and exceptions to copyright[121]

5.49   In *Ashdown v Telegraph Group*,[122] the Court of Appeal held that exceptions to copyright must be read in the light of the European Convention on Human Rights. The *Sunday Telegraph* newspaper had published unlicensed extracts from the diaries of Paddy Ashdown, the former Liberal Democrat leader. The issue concerned the impact of the Article 10 right to freedom of expression

---

[118] [1986] AC 577 gives the House of Lords' speeches only.
[119] *Canon Kabushiki Kaisha v Green Cartridge Co (Hong Kong) Ltd* [1997] AC 728.
[120] See in particular *Mars UK Ltd v Teknowledge Ltd* [2000] FSR 138 (Jacob J), a case about reverse engineering of computer programs and databases. The defence was rejected, however.
[121] See generally J Griffiths and U Suthersanen (eds), *Copyright and Free Expression* (2005); P Torremans (ed), *Copyright and Human Rights: Freedom of Expression, Intellectual Property, Privacy* (2004); C Ryan, 'Human rights and intellectual property' [2001] EIPR 521; PB Hugenholtz, 'Copyright and freedom of expression in Europe' in RC Dreyfuss, DL Zimmerman and H First (eds), *Expanding the Boundaries of Intellectual Property* (2001), 343–64.
[122] [2001] 2 WLR 967 (Morritt VC); rev'd [2002] Ch149 (CA).

upon the fair dealing defences to claims of infringement under the CDPA 1988. At first instance Sir Andrew Morritt VC held that the fair dealing provisions of the statute in themselves satisfied the requirements of Article 10 and that there was no need to bring into play s 3 of the Human Rights Act 1998 (which requires statutes to be interpreted as far as possible in consistency with Convention rights):

> 'the balance between the rights of the owner of the copyright and those of the public has been struck by the legislative organ of the democratic state itself in the legislation it has enacted. There is no room for any further defences outside the code which establishes the particular species of intellectual property in question.'[123]

The Court of Appeal concluded, however, that:

> 'rare circumstances can arise where the right of freedom of expression will come into conflict with the protection afforded by the Copyright Act, notwithstanding the express exceptions to be found in the Act. In these circumstances, we consider that the court is bound, insofar as it is able, to apply the Act in a manner that accommodates the right of freedom of expression.'[124]

This view must be correct under s 3 of the Human Rights Act 1998. The court went on to observe that, at least in this case, the approach required could be fulfilled, not so much through examination of the statutory language as such, as by way of the remedies granted to enforce the legislation: in the particular case, by withholding the discretionary relief of an injunction and leaving the copyright owner to a damages claim or an account of profits.[125] Further, while the statutory defences and the judicial precedents elaborating upon their application fell to be reconsidered in the light of Article 10, this did not require the defendant to be able to profit from the use of another's copyright material without paying compensation. The political interest of the matters discussed and freedom of expression under Article 10 of the European Convention on Human Rights did not justify deliberate filleting of and selection of the most colourful passages from the Ashdown diary.

 Exercise

What other ECHR rights apart from freedom of expression (Article 10) might be relevant to copyright exceptions?

Technical protection measures and rights management information systems

Introduction

Technical protection measures

5.50   In its original form, s 296 of the CDPA 1988 provided that where copies of a copyright work were issued to the public in an electronic copy-protected form—that is, could not be copied or could only be copied with poor quality reproduction—the copyright owner had a secondary

---

[123] [2001] 2 WLR 967, para 20.   [124] [2002] Ch 149, para 45.   [125] [2002] Ch 149, paras 46 and 59.

infringement claim against a person dealing in any device specifically designed or adapted to circumvent the form of copy-protection employed, or publishing information intended to enable or assist persons to circumvent that form of copy-protection. The Software Directive 1991 also provided that there should be appropriate remedies in national legislation against a person putting into circulation, or possessing for commercial purposes, any means the sole intended purpose of which was to facilitate the unauthorised removal or circumvention of any technical device applied to protect a computer program.[126] The aim of this legislation was to support the pragmatic answer to the problems of protecting electronic or digital works deployed to ensure that users and consumers paid for their access and use. That answer had been provided by the technology itself: products could be locked behind technological barriers (or 'walls' or 'fences'), for example encryption, passwords, activation codes, and so on, requiring payment and/or authorisation by electronic means before they could be opened up or set aside. Other examples operate through interaction between software and hardware: the former is encrypted and will only operate if the latter contains a device or key with which decryption is possible. Such devices protecting against unauthorised access are commonly known as *technical protection measures* (TPMs).[127]

5.51   The New York case of *Universal Studios Inc v Corley*[128] provides an explanation of one well-known such technical protection measure, the 'content scramble system' (CSS) protecting DVDs:

> 'CSS is an encryption scheme that employs an algorithm configured by a set of "keys" to encrypt a DVD's contents. The algorithm is a type of mathematical formula for transforming the contents of the movie file into gibberish; the "keys" are in actuality strings of 0's and 1's that serve as values for the mathematical formula. Decryption in the case of CSS requires a set of "player keys" contained in compliant DVD players, as well as an understanding of the CSS encryption algorithm. Without the player keys and the algorithm, a DVD player cannot access the contents of a DVD. With the player keys and the algorithm, a DVD player can display the movie on a television or a computer screen, but does not give a viewer the ability to use the copy function of the computer to copy the movie or to manipulate the digital content of the DVD.'[129]

From 1989, making and supplying devices to enable such technical protection measures to be evaded was, as we have just seen, made equivalent to infringement of copyright itself and, in the UK, also invited criminal penalties. In the early days, the primary kind of protected work was the computer program; but databases, CDs, commercial websites on the Internet and DVDs quickly joined the ranks of works technologically protected against unauthorised copying.

Rights management information systems

5.52   The WCT 1996 and the InfoSoc Directive 2001 contained further provisions designed to support and strengthen the rules against circumvention devices and their use, and also extended protection to 'electronic rights management information systems' (RMIs). The latter are electronic tags or fingerprints included in copies of digital products, enabling them to be traced and identified electronically wherever they may be in use, lawfully or otherwise. The

---

[126] Software Directive, Art 7(1)(c).

[127] See further G Davies, 'Technical devices as a solution to private copying', in IA Stamatoudi and PLC Torremans (eds), *Copyright in the New Digital Environment* (2000); *Digital Rights Management; Report of an Inquiry by the All Party Internet Group* (June 2006), accessible at http://www.apcomms.org.uk/apig/current-activities/apig-inquiry-into-digital-rights-management/DRMreport.pdf. For an international perspective, see P Akester, *A Practical Guide to Digital Copyright* (2008), ch 6.

[128] *Universal City Studios Inc v Corley* 273 F 3d 429 (2d Cir 2001).   [129] ibid at 436–7.

systems typically identify the software, the copyright owner, and the rights held by that party and the users of the work respectively. The information in the system may well often appear on the computer screen when the work is installed or run. Such systems are of particular importance in the Internet context, through which most tracing and identification activity is likely to be conducted.[130] The generic term for such systems together with TPMs is *digital rights management* (DRM). As a result of the InfoSoc Directive, UK law on the protection of DRMs has been substantially amended and added to, and it is to the present position that we now turn.

 Question

Explain the difference between technological protection measures and electronic rights management systems.

Technical protection measures: computer programs

5.53   There are still specific provisions for computer programs since the Software Directive was not superseded on this point by the InfoSoc Directive.[131] Any device that is intended to prevent or restrict acts unauthorised by the copyright owner *and* restricted by copyright is protected. Making, dealing in, or possessing for commercial purposes a circumvention device while knowing or having reason to believe that it will be used to make infringing copies makes the person in question liable as an infringer of copyright in his own right.

■ *Sony Computer Entertainment v Owen* [2002] EMLR 34 (Jacob J)

S made 'PlayStation 2' computer games consoles. O imported a computer chip which bypassed the process which otherwise ensured that only authorised copies of discs could be used in the machine and which also ensured that discs purchased in one region could not be played in another. O argued that the chip could be used legitimately, for example to make back up copies of discs, or play a disc from another licensed region. It was held, giving summary judgment for S, that (1) O's chip was a device specifically designed to circumvent the copy protection; (2) it was not a defence that the chip also enabled the machine to play software from another region; copyright was inherently territorial, and if a disc was 'for Japan only', there was no reason to suppose it was licensed for use elsewhere.

Contrast:

■ *Kabushiki Kaisha Sony Computer Entertainment v Stevens* (2005) 224 CLR 193 (HCA)

This Australian case also concerned Sony's PlayStation games. Insertion of a PlayStation CD into the PlayStation console enabled the game to be played. There was an 'access code' on

---

[130] See further P and R Akester, 'Digital rights management in the 21st century' [2006] EIPR 159; *Digital Rights Management; Report of an Inquiry by the All Party Internet Group* (June 2006), above note 127.

[131] CDPA 1988, s 296 as amended by the Copyright and Related Rights Regulations 2003, reg 24.

each CD, and a chip described as a 'Boot ROM' was located on the circuit board of the PlayStation console. In consequence of their interaction a game could be played only with the authority of the owner or licensee of the copyright. An unauthorised copy of a Sony PlayStation CD did not replicate the access code and therefore the Boot ROM of the console denied it access. S sold 'mod chips' or 'converter chips' and installed them in PlayStation consoles. Their purpose and effect was to overcome Sony's device. It was held that Sony's device was not a 'technological protection measure' within the wording of the Australian statute. It was necessary that, in order to be a technological protection measure within the meaning of the legislation, a device must be designed to prevent or inhibit post-access infringement of copyright. The purpose of S's chips was not to reproduce the computer games but to permit access to them. The court also decided that the temporary reproduction of the program embodying the game in the PlayStation console was not an infringement of copyright under Australian law. This probably provides an important point of distinction for a court in the UK, where unauthorised temporary reproduction *is* an infringement (see above, para 4.36), and it would be difficult to support a distinction between 'reproduction' and 'access'. Note, however, that the UK legislation also requires that the technological protection measure prevent or restrict acts which are infringements of copyright, rather than access per se.[132]

Technical protection measures: other copyright works

5.54   The rules are similar in respect of copyright works that are not computer programs (eg broadcasts, databases, sound recording CDs, film DVDs, websites), but wider in scope. Here there is a provision that the person who circumvents an effective technological measure, knowing or having reasonable grounds to know that he is pursuing that objective, is to be treated as a copyright infringer.[133] So now we are dealing with actual circumvention, and not just the manufacture of, dealing in, or commercial possession of, a circumvention device. The rules apply to protect not just technical devices, but effective technological measures applied to the work. This covers any technology, device or component designed in the normal course of its operation to protect a copyright work, that is, to prevent or restrict acts unauthorised by the copyright owner *and* restricted by copyright.[134] These measures are 'effective' if use of the work within the scope of the acts restricted by copyright is controlled by the copyright owner through either (a) an access control or protection process such as encryption, scrambling or other transformation of the work; *or* (b) a copy control mechanism.[135]

 Question

What are the differences between the protection of technical protection measures for computer programs and the protection of those for other kinds of copyright work?

---

[132] For commentary on this case see T Ciro and M Fox, 'Competition v Copyright Protection in the digital age' [2006] EIPR 329.

[133] CDPA 1988, s 296ZA.   [134] CDPA 1988, s 296ZF(1).   [135] CDPA 1988, s 296ZF(2).

Discussion point   For answer guidance visit www.oxfordtextbooks.co.uk/orc/macqueen2e/

Technical protection systems being developed by the entertainment industries include ones built into the hardware used to access and copy digital works, such as DVD players and games consoles. For instance, an encryption code in the work that prohibits access is more effective if the work has to be run through a chip embedded in a computer which decrypts the work, rather than simply relying on the code itself. Are systems so constructed in the hardware subject to the protection for 'effective technological measures'? See *Sony v Ball* below.

■ *Sony v Ball* [2005] FSR 9

This was another case about the territorially-based protection of Sony's 'Playstation 2'. The protection system was in two parts, one in the console and the other in the DVD carrying the game to be played. An unauthorised copy of a game would therefore not play on the console, nor would a game from a different region. B produced an electronic chip to fit the console and trick it into believing that unauthorised or foreign DVDs being played had the necessary embedded code. It was held that summary judgment could be granted to prevent sales of B's chips in the UK (but not elsewhere). It did not matter that the protection system was partly in the hardware (the console) and only partly in the software (the games DVD).[136]

There are, however, limits to the protection offered by the 'effective technological measure' provision in s 296ZF.

■ *R v Higgs (Neil Stanley)* [2008] FSR 34

The facts were similar to those of *Sony v Ball* (above). H ran a business selling 'modchips', which circumvented the embedded codes in a games console and allowed 'pirated' games to be played. The Crown charged H under CDPA 1988, s 296ZB. It was held that to fall within the meaning of 'effective technological measure' in s 296ZF it was not sufficient for the TPM to be merely a discouragement or general commercial hindrance to copyright infringement. Instead, the TPM either had to deny access to a copyright work or limit a person's ability to make copies of the work. A person must therefore be physically prevented from committing acts of infringement by the TPM.

Rights management information systems

5.55   The approach to the protection of rights management systems (for the definition of which see above, para 5.52) is likewise to make it akin to infringement of copyright knowingly and without authority to remove or alter digital rights management information associated with a copy of a copyright work or which appears in connection with a communication of the work to the public.[137] Also caught is the person who knowingly and without authority distributes, imports for distribution or communicates to the public copies of a copyright work from which the RMI has been removed or altered. In both cases the person so acting must know, or has reason to

---

[136] For discussion of this and the other PlayStation cases described above (para 5.53), see A Macculloch, 'Game over: the "region lock" in video games' [2005] EIPR 176.
[137] CDPA 1988, s 296ZG(1), (3).

believe, that the action induces, enables, facilitates or conceals an infringement of copyright.[138] A crucial difference between this and the protection of technological protection measures is that only for the former are the circumvention wrongs tied to actual copyright infringement. Nothing similar limits the protection of technological protection measures; and from this it seems to follow that circumvention of such a measure not aimed at copyright infringement but at the exercise of a copyright exception, such as private study or non-commercial research, will still be caught as infringement of the technological protection measures right. Indeed, technological protection measures could go even further and prevent access to a work which had either fallen out of copyright at the end of its term, or had never had copyright at all in the first place. None of this would apply, however, to rights management information protection.

Persons enjoying the anti-circumvention rights

5.56   The people who can sue under any of the anti-circumvention rights are:

- those who have issued copies of the protected work, or communicated it, to the public;
- the copyright owner or his exclusive licensee.[139]

In addition, with regard to devices protecting computer programs, the owner/exclusive licensee of any intellectual property right in the protection device itself may take action.[140]

Dealing in apparatus for unauthorised reception of transmissions

5.57   A person who makes charges for the reception of broadcasts provided from a place in the UK, or who sends encrypted transmissions of any other description from a place in the UK, has the same rights and remedies as a copyright owner in respect of infringement against a person dealing in any apparatus or device designed or adapted to enable or assist persons to receive the programmes or other transmissions when they are not entitled to do so, or publishing information calculated so to enable or assist them.[141]

■ *BBC Enterprises Ltd v Hi-Tech Xtravision Ltd* [1990] FSR 217 (Scott J and CA)

H, a manufacturer of decoders used to unscramble encrypted satellite transmissions for the purpose of television viewing, argued that this provision did not avail the BBC, operators of a satellite television service, in their efforts to stop H supplying decoders to persons who were not subscribers to the BBC service. The basis for this argument was that the provision did not in terms disentitle persons from receiving transmissions, and, there being in consequence no person disentitled, H had committed no wrong in supplying decoders. Having been upheld at first instance, the argument was overturned in the Court of Appeal, which held that the rule created a substantive right not to have transmissions received as well as the right to stop the supply of decoders.

The provisions may also be applied in relation to services provided from outside the UK.[142] There are criminal law sanctions against manufacturing, dealing in or with, or installing, maintaining or repairing unauthorised decoders; punishments include imprisonment and/or fines.[143]

---

[138] CDPA 1988, s 296ZG(2).   [139] CDPA 1988, ss 296(2), 296ZA(3), 296ZG(3), (4).
[140] CDPA 1988, s 296(2)(c).   [141] CDPA 1988, s 298(1) and (2).
[142] CDPA 1988, s 299(1)(b). See SI 1989/2003. Note that s 299(2) was repealed by the Broadcasting Act 1990, s 179(2).
[143] CDPA 1988, s 297A. See *Murphy v Media Protection Services Ltd* [2008] FSR 15 and 33 (Admin Ct) and *Football Association Premier League Ltd v QC Leisure* [2008] FSR 22 (Ch).

> ## Key points on TPM and RMI protection
>
> - Technical protection measures (TPMs) are any technological means within a copyright product designed to prevent acts restricted by copyright unless the authorisation of the copyright owner is obtained, usually by electronic means provided within the system
>
> - Rights management information systems (RMIs) are electronic systems built into digital products which record information about the identity and use of the product, thus enabling their tracing and the pursuit of unauthorised uses
>
> - TPMs and RMIs are sometimes known generically as digital rights management (DRM) systems
>
> - Copyright legislation prohibits circumvention of TPMs and removal or alteration of RMIs, treating these as infringements of copyright if carried out with knowledge, or reasonable grounds to know. The law is more limited with regard to computer programs
>
> - The legislation also treats as a form of infringement manufacturing or dealing in devices designed to circumvent TPMs or in products whose RMIs have been removed or altered.

Copyright exceptions, TPMs, RMIs and contract

TPMs v copyright exceptions and the public domain?

5.58 The previous section (paras 5.50–5.57, above) has shown that producers of digital works may be able to deploy technical protection measures to prevent users gaining access to them. At least theoretically, this is possible even if the users in question wish to perform acts that are permitted if the works have copyright—and, indeed, even if the works never had or have passed out of copyright. Thus technology has the potential to create protection akin to copyright for works which have never had, or have ceased to have, copyright, as well as to extend protection beyond the scope of copyright where that exists.[144] There has been little discussion in Britain to compare with a US and Canadian debate as to whether the rules on permitted acts merely provide defences to claims of infringement or are free-standing user or public rights.[145] The difference is important because, if the permitted acts are substantive rights, then the copyright owner should not be able to prevent actions designed to exercise them. But if the permitted acts are merely defences, then they can be invoked only when the copyright owner sues for infringement. The 1988 Act does say that its provisions on permitted acts:

> 'relate only to the question of infringement of copyright and do not affect any other right or obligation restricting the doing of any of the specified acts' (CDPA 1988, s 28(1)).

This is clearly against the notion that the permissions are to be seen as user rights.

---

[144] N Braun, 'The interface between the protection of technological measures and the exercise of exceptions to copyright and related rights: comparing the situation in the US and the EU' [2003] EIPR 496; W Davies and K Withers, *Public Innovation: Intellectual Property in a Digital Age* (Institute of Public Policy Research, 2006), 46–8, 84–7.

[145] The language of 'user rights' features strongly in *Law Society of Upper Canada v CCH Canadian Ltd* [2004] 1 SCR 339, following D Vaver, *Essentials of Canadian Law: Copyright Law* (2000), 171. For a different perspective see H Cohen Jehoram, 'Restrictions on copyright and their abuse' [2005] EIPR 359.

Contracting out of the exceptions?

5.59   There has also been little British discussion of whether the fair dealing provisions to be discussed below prevail over contrary contractual provision, contained for example in a copyright
licence. To put it another way, can one contract out of fair dealing?[146] Following the case of
ProCD v Zeidenberg[147] and the passage in 1999 of what is now the Uniform Computer Information
Transactions Act, however, the matter has become controversial in the USA.[148]

■ *ProCD v Zeidenberg* 86 F 3d 1447 (7th Cir, 1996)

ProCD compiled information from more than 3,000 telephone directories (which do not have
copyright under US law) into a computer database. The company sold a version of the database,
called SelectPhone, on CD-ROM discs in packages covered in plastic or cellophane 'shrinkwrap'.
A proprietary method of compressing the data served as effective encryption too. Customers
decrypted and used the data with the aid of an application program written by ProCD. This
program, which had copyright, searched the database in response to users' criteria, and the
resulting lists could be read and manipulated by other software, such as word processing programs. The database cost more than $10 million to compile and was also expensive to keep cur-
rent. ProCD charged consumers a much lower price for the product than commercial customers,
but every box containing its consumer product declared that the software came with restrictions
stated in an enclosed license. The licence was encoded on the CD-ROM disks as well as printed
in the manual; it also appeared on a user's screen every time the software ran. The licence limited
use of the application program and listings to non-commercial purposes. Z bought a consumer
package of the database from a retail outlet, but decided to ignore the licence. He formed a company to resell the information in the database over the Internet, at prices undercutting those of
ProCD. ProCD sought an injunction against further dissemination, based on a claim of breach
of the licence conditions by Z. It was held that the licence was enforceable, even although it in
effect gave protection, as between ProCD and Z, to the non-copyright contents of the database.
(Note that this is not a case of contract overriding copyright exceptions, but rather one of contract providing protection where there was no copyright at all.)

■ *Uniform Computer Information Transactions Act* (UCITA)

UCITA is a uniform model law for adoption in the states of the USA (so far taken up in only two
states). The Act makes 'shrink-wrap' and 'click-on' licences enforceable in what it calls 'mass
market transactions', ie those involving consumers. Information transactions thus move away
from the model of selling copies (the model on which copyright is based) to one of licensing
information in its electronic transmission to the consumer. This may give the supplier more
control of access to and use of information, whether or not the information itself and the use
thereof is protected by copyright.

5.60   The un-argued assumption in the UK, however, was that fair dealing prevails over contract. But
on closer examination this assumption appears ill-founded, at least as a generalisation. For
example, the exception enabling educational establishments to make a limited quantity of copies of works for purposes of instruction, does not apply if a licence for such activity is available

---

[146] See Guibault, *Copyright Limitations and Contracts*, passim; Burrell and Coleman, *Copyright Exceptions*, pp 67–70,
269–70, 306–10.

[147] 86 F 3d 1447 (7th Cir, 1996).

[148] See P Samuelson and K Opsdahl, 'The tensions between intellectual property and contracts in the information age:
an American perspective', in FW Grosheide and K Boele-Woelki (eds), *Molengrafica: Europees Privaatrecht 1998* (1999).

(above para 5.38).[149] There is also the provision quoted above (in para 5.58), which might be read as meaning that beyond the permitted acts may lie, unaffected, other rights or obligations restricting the doing of any of the specified acts.[150] Another example of contract prevailing over exceptions relates to the permitted act of temporary reproduction or adaptation of a computer program necessary for a lawful user's lawful use of the program: a term of any contract regulating the circumstances in which the user's use is lawful, and prohibiting the copying or adaptation in question, will make those acts infringements.[151]

5.61   On the other side of the coin (ie suggesting that contract does *not* prevail over exceptions and limitations) are the following specific provisions. Any term or condition of an agreement purporting to prohibit the permitted act of temporary reproduction of a database necessary for the purpose of access to and normal use of the database contents by a person with a right to use the database is void.[152] A number of other acts in relation to computer programs which are permitted to a lawful user thereof cannot be overridden by contract: ie making a back-up copy of the program,[153] decompilation in terms of CDPA 1988, s 50B(2),[154] and observing, studying or testing the functioning of the program in accordance with CDPA 1988, s 50BA.[155]

5.62   Overall, there seems much to support the view of Burrell and Coleman that it is:

'generally possible to contract out of the permitted acts. There is, however, a growing list of circumstances in which it is not possible to contract out of the permitted acts, Parliament and the European legislator having recognised that it ought not to be possible to exclude the exceptions in certain circumstances.'[156]

They argue that such a piecemeal approach is preferable to the inflexibility which would arise from a blanket prohibition on contractual exclusion of the permitted acts.[157] It would be better, in their view, to distinguish types of fair use, those excludable by contract and those not.[158]

 Discussion point 1   For answer guidance visit www.oxfordtextbooks.co.uk/orc/macqueen2e/

Is there a real difference between acts which are not within the scope of copyright at all, and acts which are permitted as exceptions to copyright? Is this important in the context of the idea of 'user rights'?

Discussion point 2

Can you distinguish between 'fair dealing' and 'public interest' exceptions to copyright?

Discussion point 3

How would the case of *ProCD v Zeidenberg* be decided in the UK? Are shrink-wrap and click-on licences enforceable under either English or Scots contract law?

Discussion point 4

Do you agree with the analysis of Burrell and Coleman?

---

[149] CDPA 1988, s 36(3).   [150] CDPA 1988, s 28(1).
[151] CDPA 1988, s 50C, implementing Software Directive 1991 (reading Art 5(1) in conjunction with Art 4(a)).
[152] CDPA 1988, ss 50D(2) and 296B.   [153] CDPA 1988, s 50A.   [154] See further above, para 5.44.
[155] See further above, para 5.44.   [156] Burrell and Coleman, *Copyright Exceptions: The Digital Impact*, p 69.
[157] ibid, p 70.   [158] ibid, pp 269–70, 306–10.

Controlling TPMs and RMIs

5.63 Concerns that the legal protection of TPMs had the potential to deprive copyright exceptions of their content and value led to Article 6(4) of the Infosoc Directive. This requires Member States to take:

> 'appropriate measures to ensure that right-holders make available to the beneficiary of an exception or limitation provided for in national law [in accordance with the Directive] the means of benefiting from that exception or limitation, to the extent necessary to benefit from that exception or limitation and where that beneficiary has legal access to the protected work or subject-matter concerned.'

The UK has implemented Article 6(4) in the following rather complex fashion. Where the application of any effective technological measure to a copyright work other than a computer program prevents a person from carrying out a permitted act in relation to that work, then that person (or a person who is a representative of a class of persons prevented from carrying out a permitted act) may complain to the Secretary of State (ie the relevant Government Minister). The Secretary of State may thereupon issue written directions to the copyright holder, with which the latter must comply. Failure to do so gives the complainant a civil right of action. The directions may be to establish whether any voluntary measure or agreement subsists with regard to the copyright work in question, *or* to ensure that the copyright owner or exclusive licensee makes available to the complainant the means of carrying out that permitted act, to the extent necessary to benefit from that permitted act. The direction can be subsequently revoked or varied. The complainant must be somebody who has lawful access to the protected copyright work.[159]

5.64 The above only applies to certain (and not all) permitted acts.[160] This includes, for example, research and private study as well as making a copy available for a visually impaired person. It is noteworthy, however, that it does not apply to criticism, review and news reporting, despite the particular importance which the courts have attributed to these exceptions in the interests of freedom of speech and expression (see above, paras 5.30, 5.35, 5.49).

5.65 None of this is applicable, however, where the copyright work in question has been 'made available to the public on agreed contractual terms in such a way that members of the public may access them from a place and at a time individually chosen by them'.[161] So, for example, there can be no complaint about TPMs and RMIs attached to music files downloaded from the iTunes service.[162] This would seem to suggest that the only complaint likely to be successful is one where access is completely blocked. A party making material available for a price, however exorbitant, is unlikely to be on the receiving end of government directions to change its ways. Thus it appears that in a digital network environment the exceptions and limitations to copyright may be overridden by contract, or at the least that the procedure described above will not be available where *contract* limits the availability or use of the exceptions. The limits on this may arise from the phrase 'agreed contractual terms'. Does 'agreed' mean that the terms must in some way be negotiated ones, rather than the standard forms normally used in online transactions? If the word does not have this meaning, its use alongside 'contractual' would appear rather tautologous.

---

[159] CDPA 1988, s 296ZE.   [160] CDPA 1988, Sch 5A, Part 1.   [161] CDPA 1988, s 296ZE(10).
[162] Example suggested in W Davies and K Withers, *Public Innovation: Intellectual Property in a Digital Age* (Institute of Public Policy Research, 2006), 23.

5.66   There does not seem to have been any use so far of these provisions, or of any agreements between relevant associations.[163]

 Question 1

Who may apply to the Secretary of State that the application of a TPM is preventing the exercise of an exception to copyright?

Question 2

What kinds of order may the Secretary of State make?

Question 3

What must be shown before the Secretary of State will issue an order?

Further reading

Books

General

Bently & Sherman, *Intellectual Property Law* (3rd edn, 2009), Ch 9, 11.8, 13.4–13.5

Copinger & Skone James on Copyright (15th edn, 2005), Chs 9 and 15

Cornish & Llewelyn, *Intellectual Property* (6th edn, 2007), 12.3, 12.4, 14.1, 14.2

Laddie, Prescott & Vitoria, *Modern Law of Copyright* (3rd edn, 2000), Ch 20

Copyright exceptions and public interest

R Burrell and A Coleman, *Copyright Exceptions: the Digital Impact* (2005)

G Davies, *Copyright and the Public Interest* (2nd edn, 2003)

LMCR Guibault, *Copyright Limitations and Contracts: an Analysis of the Contractual Overridability of Limitations on Copyright* (2002)

G Mazziotti, *EU Digital Copyright Law and the End-User* (2008)

M Senftleben, *Copyright Limitations and the Three-Step Test: an Analysis of the Three-Step Test in International and EC Copyright Law* (2004)

C Waelde and H L MacQueen (eds), *The Many Faces of the Public Domain* (2007)

Exceptions and human rights

J Griffiths and U Suthersanen (eds), *Copyright and Free Expression* (2005)

P Torremans (ed), *Copyright and Human Rights: Freedom of Expression, Intellectual Property, Privacy* (2004)

---

[163] As of 31 November 2009.

Technological protection measures and rights management information

P Akester, *A Practical Guide to Digital Copyright* (2008), Chapter 6

P Akester, *Report on the Impact of Technological Accommodation of Conflicts between Freedom of Expression and DRM: the first empirical assessment* (2009), accessible at http://www.law.cam.ac.uk/faculty-resources/summary/technological-accommodation-of-conflicts-between-freedom-of-expression-and-drm-the-first-empirical-assessment/6286

Articles

Copyright exceptions and public interest

H Cohen Jehoram, 'Is there a hidden agenda behind the general non-implementation of the EU three-step test?' [2009] EIPR 408

J Espantaleon, 'Does private copying need an update in the UK?' (2008) 3 JIPLP 115

A Sims, 'The denial of copyright on public policy grounds' [2008] EIPR 189

A Sims, 'The public interest defence in copyright law: myth or reality?' [2006] EIPR 335

Technical protection measures and rights management information systems

P and R Akester, 'Digital rights management in the 21st century' [2006] EIPR 159

N Braun, 'The interface between the protection of technological measures and the exercise of exceptions to copyright and related rights: comparing the situation in the US and the EU' [2003] EIPR 496

G Davies, 'Technical devices as a solution to private copying', in IA Stamatoudi and PLC Torremans (eds), *Copyright in the New Digital Environment* (2000)

Rights akin to copyright: database right and performers' rights

Introduction

Scope and overview of chapter

6.1 This chapter considers two rights closely akin to copyright in many ways, in terms of both subject matter and the substantive contents of the rights. Both rights have also been relatively recently introduced into the armoury of intellectual property law. The rights in question are (1) the special or *sui generis* database right, which operates alongside the copyright in databases (for which see paras 2.56–2.63); and (2) performers' rights. The chapter gives an account of each of these rights, comparing them with copyright, but also underlining the differences between the regimes, and the reasons behind these differences.

6.2 **Learning objectives**

- By the end of this chapter you should be able to describe and explain:
- the special or sui generis database right;
- performers' rights;
- the ways in which each of these rights compares with copyright;
- the reasons why these rights have been created and are distinct from copyright.

6.3 The chapter first explores the *sui generis* database right, explaining the reasons for its introduction by the Database Directive 1996 and considering in detail its exposition by the ECJ in the leading cases which, grouped together, were decided in 2004. The chapter then turns to performers' rights, again providing background to the introduction of the rights in their present form, and considering also developments now in prospect. So the rest of the chapter looks like this:

- *Sui generis* database right (6.4–6.20)
- Performers' rights (6.21–6.39)

Sui generis database right

Reasons for introduction of the *sui generis* right

6.4   The Database Directive not only harmonised the copyright protection of databases in the EU, but also introduced an additional, special (*sui generis*) database right to protect those commercially valuable and expensively created databases henceforth to be excluded from copyright in some member states (notably the UK) by the higher originality requirement now imposed under the Directive (see above, para 2.57). The UK implemented the Directive in the Database Regulations 1997.[1] The *sui generis* database right has met with mixed results.[2] A Commission Working Paper noted that decisions of the ECJ had substantially curtailed the right.[3] There have been problems defining key terms within the right. Furthermore, there are a number of textual ambiguities between national legislatures implementing the Directive, confusion about the parallel availability of copyright and the *sui generis* right, and consequent reluctance to use the right due to its complexity by national courts. The Commission also noted that there are difficulties understanding the legal nature of the right due to it being framed in non-legal language.

Criteria for protection to arise

6.5   The definition of database applying for copyright purposes (above, paras 2.56, 2.59, 2.62) also applies for the *sui generis* right apart from the requirement of 'intellectual creation'. While to enjoy the special right the database contents must still be organised in a systematic or methodical way, the system or method need not be a personal intellectual creation.[4] A copyright database is not precluded from also enjoying database right, the relevance of this being that database right confers protection against extraction and reutilisation of the contents of the database rather than the copyright protection for the selection and arrangement of the contents (see further below, paras 6.12–6.16). The principal substantive ground for database right protection is the creator's *substantial investment in obtaining, verifying or presenting the contents of the database*, and it is immaterial whether or not the database is also a copyright work, ie is an intellectual creation of the compiler in its selection or arrangement.[5]

 Question

Can a copyright database also be protected by the *sui generis* right? Will a database protected by the *sui generis* right also have copyright?

---

[1] Copyright and Rights in Databases Regulations 1997 (SI 1997/3032). See generally E Derclaye, *The Legal Protection of Databases: A Comparative Analysis* (2008); T Aplin, *Copyright Law in the Digital Society: the Challenges of Multimedia* (2005), pp 41–73.

[2] See E Derclaye, *The Legal Protection of Databases: A Comparative Analysis* (2008).

[3] See European Commission Working Paper, First Evaluation of Directive 96/9/EC (2005). See further para 6.6 below.

[4] So eg an arrangement of surnames in alphabetical order would attract database right.

[5] Copyright and Rights in Databases Regulations 1997, reg 13.

Obtaining, verifying, or preserving the contents of the database

6.6   Database right arises where there has been substantial investment in 'obtaining, verifying or preserving the contents of the database'. The first question to which this has given rise is whether, if the investment is in *creating* rather than *obtaining* data, database right is excluded. In other words, must the data exist before the investment is made? The ECJ's answer to this question surprised many.[6]

■ *British Horseracing Board v William Hill Organization Ltd* [2001] CMLR 12 (Laddie J); [2002] ECDR 4 (CA); Case C-203/02, [2004] ECR I-10415 (ECJ);[2005] RPC 35 (CA)

BHB administered British horse-racing, creating the fixture lists each year, and distributing information about races to subscribers. WHO were subscribers who used the BHB data in relation to their betting services. An issue arose between the parties about whether WHO's unauthorised use of the BHB data in its new Internet betting service infringed BHB's database right. Laddie J held that investment in creating data (the racing fixtures) did not count towards the investment needed to obtain the data. The Court of Appeal referred the question of whether 'obtaining' covered 'creating' as well as 'compiling' to the ECJ. The Advocate General opined that 'obtaining' extended to the creation or generation of data only when 'the creation of the data took place at the same time as its processing and was inseparable from it' (para 157). The ECJ held that merely creating data did *not* amount to obtaining it, or to its verification or preservation. 'Obtaining' involved the seeking out and collecting of existing independent materials, and verification and presentation had generally to relate to such material (paras 29–33). The Court of Appeal then applied this interpretation of the law to deny the existence of database right in BHB's database, since BHB created the data rather than collecting it from existing independent sources.

The same result was reached by the ECJ in a group of cases concerned with football fixture lists (the *Fixtures* cases).[7] The decision appears to restrict considerably the scope of protection given by the *sui generis* right.[8]

 Discussion point   For answer guidance visit www.oxfordtextbooks.co.uk/orc/macqueen2e/
Explain why the exclusion of *creation* from *obtaining* limits the scope of *sui generis* database right.

6.7   However, since 'obtaining' data is only one of three alternative ways in which an investment may be rewarded with database right—the others being 'verification' and 'presentation'—there may still be protection by way of these other two heads for the creator of data *later* put into a database. So checking the accuracy, completeness and reliability of the data *once in the database*

---

[6] For a useful analysis of the legal outcomes of the whole litigation see J Jenkins, 'Database rights' subsistence: under starter's orders' (2006) 1 JIPLP 467.

[7] Cases C-338/02 *Fixtures Marketing Ltd v Svenska Spel AB* [2004] ECR I-10497, paras 24–6; C-444/02 *Fixtures Marketing Ltd v OPAP* [2004] ECR I-10549, para 40; and C-46/02 *Fixtures Marketing Ltd v Oy Veikkaus Ab* [2004] ECR I-10365, para 34.

[8] See MJ Davison and PB Hugenholtz, 'Football fixtures, horseraces and spin-offs: the ECJ domesticates the database right' [2005] EIPR 113; T Aplin, 'The ECJ elucidates the database right' [2005] IPQ 204.

is verification, while presentation is about giving the database its function of processing information; that is, the resources used for the systematic or methodical arrangement of the data and the organisation of their individual accessibility.[9] So the concept includes materials necessary for the operation or consultation of the database by users such as thesaurus and indexation systems, as well as the structuring of the contents (the conceptual as distinct from the external format of the database). What is crucial is that, to be relevant for the establishment of *sui generis* protection, investment in verification and presentation must be subsequent to and not part of the process of creation of the data. None of this could, however, avail the creators of the data in the horseracing and *Fixtures* cases.

Discussion point   For answer guidance visit www.oxfordtextbooks.co.uk/orc/macqueen2e/

Consider the derivation of data from naturally occurring phenomena such as the weather or the genetic sequences of living creatures. Is that derivation an act of creation or obtaining for the purposes of *sui generis* database right? Compare on this the views of E Derclaye, 'Database *'sui generis'* right: should we adopt the spin-off theory?' [2004] EIPR 402, and MJ Davison and PB Hugenholtz, 'Football fixtures, horseraces and spin-offs: the ECJ domesticates the database right' [2005] EIPR 113 at 115.[10]

Substantial investment

6.8   The investment necessary for the existence of database right need not be merely financial, but can include human, technical and professional resources as well as the expenditure of time, effort and energy.[11] The substantiality of an investment may be measured qualitatively and/or quantitatively.[12] In her opinion in *Fixtures Marketing v Svenska*, the Advocate General said that the substantiality of an investment is to be assessed 'first in relation to costs and their redemption and secondly in relation to the scale, nature and contents of the database and the sector to which it belongs'. But she added that substantiality is not only a relative matter: 'the Directive requires an absolute lower threshold for investments worthy of protection as a sort of de minimis rule.'[13] This was justified by reference to recital 19 of the Directive, which states that, as a rule (ie usually), the compilation of several recordings of musical performances on a CD does not represent a substantial enough investment to be eligible for the *sui generis* right.[14] The difficulty is in using this rather specific example as a basis for determining what is the minimum threshold making an investment substantial, or indeed that there is such a requirement. The ECJ did not comment on this aspect of the Advocate General's opinion.

---

[9] Cases C-338/02 *Fixtures Marketing Ltd v Svenska Spel AB*, para 27 (ECJ); C-444/02 *Fixtures Marketing Ltd v OPAP*, para 43; C-46/02 *Fixtures Marketing Ltd v Oy Veikkaus Ab*, para 37; and C-203/02 *British Horseracing Board Ltd v William Hill Organization Ltd* [2004] ECR I-10415, paras 34–41. See also recital 20 of the Database Directive.

[10] Further on scientific databases see C Waelde, 'Creating a scientific research commons: practical experience' [2004] Molengrafica 155.

[11] Database Directive, recitals 7, 39, 40; Cases C-338/02 *Fixtures Marketing Ltd v Svenska Spel AB*, para 28 (ECJ); C-444/02 *Fixtures Marketing Ltd v OPAP*, para 44; and C-46/02 *Fixtures Marketing Ltd v Oy Veikkaus Ab*, para 38.

[12] Database Directive, Art 7(1); and see references in n 11 above.

[13] C-338/02, *Fixtures Marketing Ltd v Svenska Spel AB* [2004] ECR I-10497, para 39 (AG) (for both quotations).

[14] Database Directive, recital 19.

'Spin-off' databases

6.9   The Advocate General took the view in the *Fixtures* cases that the substantial investment need not be aimed primarily or only at creating the database, since the Directive imposes no such requirement. So for example investing in the creation of sports fixture lists is not done just to build a database, but to structure the season of the sport in question and provide advance information for participants, the media and potential spectators. The ECJ held, however, that investment is to be understood in relation to the database as such and refers to the resources used to seek out and collect existing independent materials and to ensure their reliability and/or accuracy. This is consistent with its view that creating data is not obtaining data of the kind necessary to achieve a protectable database (above, para 6.6). Thus *'spin-off' databases*—databases created as a sort of side effect of activity and investment of resources which had other aims primarily in mind, such as the organisation of a football season or a horse-racing calendar— will not be protected by the *sui generis* right unless there is additional substantial investment directed specifically at the database, most probably in the verification or presentation of the data contained within it.[15]

> ### Question
>
> What is a 'spin-off' database? Is such a database protected by the *sui generis* right?

Key points on sui generis database right

- For databases (collections of independent data, arranged systematically, individually accessible)
- Selection and arrangement need not be intellectual creation (contrast copyright protection)
- Needs substantial investment in:
  - obtaining (*not* creating—*Fixtures* and *William Hill* cases)
  - verifying
  - preserving
    - contents of database (problems of 'spin-off')
- Substantial investment financial/human/technical/professional; qualitative and/or quantitative

---

First ownership

6.10   The maker of a database is the first owner of the *sui generis* database right in it.[16] There is a presumption that a name appearing on copies of a database as its maker is the maker unless the

[15] Cases C-338/02 *Fixtures Marketing Ltd v Svenska Spel AB*, paras 29–36 (ECJ); C-444/02 *Fixtures Marketing Ltd v OPAP*, paras 45–52; and C-46/02 *Fixtures Marketing Ltd v Oy Veikkaus Ab*, paras 39–48.

[16] Copyright and Rights in Databases Regulations 1997, reg 15.

obtain BHB's licence to use the data in the Internet service. The following points emerge from the Court's judgment:

- Extraction is not removal: for the Court it meant the transfer of contents of database to another medium and covered any unauthorised act of appropriation. It does not mean that the contents in question must be removed from the database altogether; there is extraction even when afterwards the contents remain on the database. So, for example, a printout from a database is an extraction.

- Re-utilisation is making available to the public the database contents and covers any unauthorised distribution to the public. It therefore embraces both on-line transmission and distribution or rental/lending of the database, and is not limited to a right to first publication of the contents. Exhaustion only arises in relation to the sale of physical copies of the database (eg on CD and DVD).

- Extraction and re-utilisation can be either direct or indirect; that is, either from the database itself, or from a copy of the database. The context is provided by the facts of the case, where the defendants had obtained the data, not from BHB's database, but from one of BHB's licensed distributors.

- Substantiality of the part of the database extracted or re-utilised can be assessed both quantitatively and qualitatively. A quantitative measure is the volume of data extracted compared to the volume of the contents of the whole database; while a qualitative measure is the scale of the investment required in relation to the material extracted or re-utilised. The intrinsic value of the data, as distinct from the cost of the investment, is not a relevant consideration for the qualitative measurement of the substantiality of a part. Finally, 'it must be held,' said the Court, 'that any part which does not fulfil the definition of a substantial part, evaluated both quantitatively and qualitatively, falls within the definition of an insubstantial part of the contents of a database' (para 73).

6.14   While the ECJ only gives guidance to national courts on the interpretation of Union law, it did make the following comment in *British Horseracing Board v William Hill Organization Ltd* on how, in the light of its opinion, summarised above, on the meaning of the infringement provisions of the Database Directive, this case should be decided. Thus, so far as concerned the quantitative measure of whether a substantial part of the database had been extracted or re-utilised:

> '[T]he materials displayed on William Hill's internet sites, which derive from the BHB database, represent only a very small proportion of that database. . . . It must therefore be held that those materials do not constitute a substantial part, evaluated quantitatively, of the contents of that database.'[32]

With regard to qualitative measurement:

> 'The intrinsic value of the data affected . . . does not constitute a relevant criterion for assessing whether the part in question is substantial, evaluated qualitatively. The fact that the data extracted and re-utilised by WH are vital to the organisation of the [BHB] horse races . . . is thus irrelevant to the assessment [of] substantial part.'[33]

---

[32] [2004] ECR I-10415, para 74.

[33] [2004] ECR I-10415, para 78. This and the preceding issue were not considered when the case returned to the Court of Appeal, since there it was decided that the database in question was not protected by the *sui generis* right ([2005] EWCA Civ 863).

■ Case C-304/07 *Directmedia Publishing GMBH v Albert-Ludwigs-Universitat Freiburg* [2008] ECR I-7565

This case concerned alleged infringement of a university's *sui generis* database right in a list of poetry titles. D used the database as a guide to the creation of its CD-ROM entitled '1,000 poems everyone should have', omitting certain poems, adding others and critically examining each selection made by the professor who created the original database. Despite D taking the texts of each poem from its own resources, the ECJ held that the concept of 'extraction' covered the transfer of material from a protected database to another database following an on-screen consultation of the first database and an individual assessment of the extracted contents. Extraction, therefore, is to be given a wide meaning. The concept is not limited to physical taking, and also includes taking that is preceded by the taker's critical evaluation of the material. The Court noted that such a database was created through substantial human, financial or technical resource investment; the Directive allowed for a return on the investment involved without unauthorised appropriation of the results at a fraction of the cost needed to design it independently. The information 'extracted' from the database could be transferred in any way to another medium, such as eg, manual recopying, photocopying or downloading. It was irrelevant that the copied information was adapted into a different format. The objective pursued in the act of transfer was also immaterial. Mere consultation of a database, however, was not included in the definition of 'extraction'.

■ C-545/07 *Apis-Hristovich EOOD v Lakorda AD* [2009] 3 CMLR 3 (ECJ)

A, which operated a legal database, claimed that L, which had been set up by two ex-employees of A, infringed its database rights by extracting without A's consent substantial parts of two modules of the database. These extracted elements, it was argued, were used by the defendants to develop a similar system. L argued that it had invested significant independent time and money in the new database. Any similarities to the two modules were argued to be due to the fact that the legal sources relied upon were publicly available. The Court held that protection could be claimed in database sub-groups provided that each sub-group qualified as a protected database. If they did, the level of extraction was compared against the amount of data in the sub-group. If they did not, the level of extraction was measured against the entire database, rather than its constituent parts. The purpose of extraction was irrelevant, as was the unique feature of the new database. Furthermore, the Court noted that the public availability of materials did not preclude protection as long as there had been qualitative and/or quantitative substantial investment when obtaining, verifying or presenting the contents of the database. Additionally, the use of hyperlinks or other such similar features in both databases could be indicative, though not determinative, of extraction, as could such materials not available to the public. The Court reiterated that the term 'extraction' should be given a broad definition.

■ *Exchange Communications Ltd v Masheder* [2009] CSOH 135

The case was again one of a departing employee who, it was claimed by the erstwhile employers, had extracted from their database contact details for a potential customer, and details of the telephony and related equipment to be offered to that customer along with prices and discounts. The ex-employee had entered the employ of a competitor which had subsequently won the contract with the prospective customer. The employers' averments did not however detail the precise means of the extraction which would constitute infringement of the database right, and the defender therefore argued that the case on this point was irrelevant, ie should not be allowed to go to proof (trial). The judge, although thinking the issue 'finely balanced' (para 45), sent the case for proof. Quoting the ECJ cases on database right for the proposition that the concept of 'extraction' is to be approached widely, the judge noted: 'The clear aim of the Regulations and the Directive they implement is to protect those who have applied time and resources and effort to collating data often with significant commercial importance' (para 48).

Repeated and systematic extraction/re-utilisation of insubstantial parts

6.15   Repeated and systematic extraction/re-utilisation of insubstantial parts of database contents may amount to the extraction/re-utilisation of a substantial part of those contents.[34] In the *British Horseracing Board* case,[35] Laddie J held that the defendant's daily use of the BHB database was caught by this provision, but the issue of its meaning was referred to the ECJ by the Court of Appeal. The Advocate General made clear that the provision need not be invoked where a single act of extraction or re-utilisation affects a substantial part of the database. Repetition and system are cumulative rather than alternative requirements, and imply acts at regular intervals. The Court noted that the purpose of the rule was to prevent circumvention of the basic exclusive right conferred by the Directive by a series of insubstantial acts which would cumulatively cause serious prejudice to the investment of the maker of the database. It went on to hold that the prohibition affected repeated and systematic acts leading to the reconstitution of the whole database or a substantial part of it, whether or not the acts were carried out to create such a database. Third parties were also prevented from repeated and systematic making available to the public of insubstantial parts of the database.

6.16   The Directive says that the repeated and systematic acts must either (a) conflict with normal exploitation of the database, or (b) unreasonably prejudice the legitimate interests of its maker.[36] The Court held that this refers to serious prejudice to the database maker's investment by unauthorised acts the cumulative effect of which is (1) the reconstitution or (2) making available to the public, of the whole or a substantial part of the contents of a protected database.[37] The court concluded that the defendant's acts in this case would not result in the reconstitution of the BHB database, or in making it available to the public, so the prohibition did not apply.

Key points on infringement of sui generis database right

- The right is infringed by unauthorised extraction or re-utilisation of all or a substantial part of the database
- Extraction is transfer of database contents to another medium (but removal not needed)
- Extraction is to be given a wide meaning
- Re-utilisation is making database contents available to the public by any form of distribution
- The extraction/re-utilisation may be direct or indirect
- Substantiality is measured both quantitatively and qualitatively, but the intrinsic value of the data is not a factor in this assessment
- Repeated and systematic extraction/re-utilisation of insubstantial parts may cumulatively amount to extraction/re-utilisation of a substantial part

---

[34] 1997 Regulations, reg 16(2), implementing Database Directive, Art 7(5).
[35] [2001] CMLR 12 (Laddie J); [2002] ECDR 4 (CA).
[36] Database Directive, Art 7(5); not transposed as such in the 1997 Regulations.
[37] [2004] ECR I-10415, para 89.

Exceptions

6.17   The Database Directive made some provision for exceptions to the rights which it conferred,[38] and these were left largely unaffected by the subsequent InfoSoc Directive. But there is nothing in the Database Directive[39] to compare with the rules in the Software Directive that contractual agreement cannot overcome exceptions to copyright in computer programs—in particular, making back up copies, decompilation, and observation, studying and testing.[40] So it would seem that in this area contract will prevail over exceptions. The Database Regulations 1997 make it clear that a lawful user of a database which has been made available to the public in any manner shall be entitled to extract or re-utilise an *insubstantial* part of the contents of the database for any purpose,[41] and that any term in an agreement purporting to limit this entitlement shall be void.[42] This illustrates that contract provisions may not be used to extend the scope of the *sui generis* right itself; it is infringed only by taking of a *substantial* part of the database contents (see above, paras 6.12, 6.13 (fourth bullet point)).

Exception for non-commercial research

6.18   There is an exception permitting extraction for non-commercial research purposes from a database protected, not by copyright, but by the *sui generis* database right.[43] The database must have been made available to the public, and the person making the extraction must be already a lawful user apart from the exception. The source must be acknowledged. The exception covers only extraction of a substantial part of the database, so presumably extraction of an insubstantial part, not being infringement, requires no exception. It is worth noting that the ECJ has said that mere consultation of a database is not extraction of the database.[44] No similar exception exists for the other act restricted by database right, re-utilisation.

Teaching exception

6.19   There is also an exception to allow extraction (but, again, not re-utilisation) from a database made available to the public, by one already a lawful user of the database, for the purpose of illustration for teaching and not for any commercial purpose, so long as the source is indicated.[45]

 Discussion point   For answer guidance visit www.oxfordtextbooks.co.uk/orc/macqueen2e/

Why do the non-commercial research and teaching exceptions apply only to extraction of content from a database and not to its re-utilisation?

 Exercise

Compare the exceptions to *sui generis* database right with the exceptions to copyright in a database (see paras 5.12–5.46). Are the two systems compatible?

---

[38] Software Directive, Arts 5, 6; Database Directive, Arts 6, 9.
[39] However, see CDPA 1988, ss 50D(2) and 296B.
[40] Software Directive, Arts 5(2), (3), 6(1). See CDPA 1988, ss 50A, 50B(4), 50BA and 296A, and above, para 5.44.
[41] Reg 19(1).   [42] Reg 19(2).
[43] Copyright and Rights in Databases Regulations 1997, reg 20; implementing Database Directive 1996, Art 9. cf the equivalent copyright exception, discussed at para 5.22.
[44] Case C-203–02 *British Horseracing Board Ltd v Wiliam Hill Organization Ltd* [2004] ECR I-10415, para 54.
[45] Copyright and Rights in Databases Regulations 1997, reg 20; implementing Database Directive 1996, Art 9.

224

Deposit libraries

6.20   There is a deposit library exception for *sui generis* database right.[46]

Key points on exceptions to sui generis database right

- The principal exceptions are for non-commercial research and teaching
- The exceptions are only in relation to extraction and not to re-utilisation
- It seems to be possible to exclude the exceptions by contractual agreement between the right holder and the user of the database

---

Performers' rights[47]

Historical background to performers' protection

6.21   Performers were, historically, not well protected in the UK. Only in 1925 were criminal sanctions provided by the Dramatic and Musical Performers' Protection Act 1923 against making recordings of dramatic and musical performances without consent ('bootlegging'). The law was consolidated and extended over the years, notably by encompassing performances of literary, dramatic, musical and artistic works in the Performers Protection Act 1963, and in 1972 when another Performers Protection Act extended the penalties available. The Rome Convention for the Protection of Performers, Producers of Phonograms and Broadcasting Organizations 1961 provided the international basis for such protection.

6.22   The UK Acts appeared to give rise to criminal liability, but not to any civil cause of action, for either the performer or those who held recording contracts with the performer. Despite this, in *Rickless v United Artists Corporation*[48] a civil cause of action was accorded to *performers*. In that case, United Artists made a film using out-takes from previous films in the Pink Panther series starring the late Peter Sellers. Rickless, as the owner of the rights of Peter Sellers' services as an actor, sued for infringement of s 2 of the Dramatic and Musical and Performers' Protection Act 1958 because United Artists had failed to obtain permission for its activities. The Court of Appeal upheld the lower court's ruling that the Performers Acts *did* give civil remedies to a performer whose performance had been exploited without consent, in addition to the criminal penalties under the Act. This was although earlier, in *RCA v Pollard*,[49] the Court of Appeal had found that the Acts did *not* give rise to civil remedies for *recording companies* with whom performers had exclusive recording contracts.

6.23   The Rome Convention only gives performers the possibility of 'preventing' a list of acts, rather than a right to authorise and prohibit them in advance.[50] Thus, it was argued that the approach through the criminal law could continue.[51] However, in 1977 the Whitford Committee[52] recom-

---

[46] Copyright and Rights in Databases Regulations 1997, reg 20A. On deposit library exceptions to copyright, see para 5.40.

[47] See generally R Arnold, *Performers' Rights* (4th edn, 2008).

[48] *Rickless v United Artists Corp* [1988] QB 40.   [49] [1983] Ch 135.   [50] Arts 7, 10 and 13.

[51] Cornish & Llewelyn, para 14.30.   [52] Cmnd 6732.

mended that performers should be given a civil right of action for injunctions and damages, but that this should not amount to copyright. The CDPA 1988 introduced two distinct rights in performances. One right was a personal, non-assignable right for performers, while the other was for those making exclusive recording contracts with performers. The latter right could be assigned.[53]

Key points on historical background

- Between 1925 and 1988 performers were protected against unauthorised reproduction of their performances only through the criminal law

- A civil right of action was recognised by the courts in 1983 but the statutory change took place five years later

- The 1988 Act creates two kinds of civil right for performers: one personal and non-assignable, the other for those making recording contracts, which is assignable

---

European reforms

6.24   A number of EU Directives have now further changed the position for performers. Measures affecting the position of performers are to be found in the following:

- Rental Right Directive;[54]
- Satellite and Cable Directive[55] (which applies these requirements to satellite broadcasting);
- Term Directive;[56] and
- Infosoc Directive.[57]

Each of these resulted in significant amendments to the CDPA 1988.[58]

Current law on performers' rights

6.25   A *performer* is not defined in the Act, but a *performance* means a dramatic performance (including dance or mime), a musical one, a reading or recitation of a literary work or a performance of a variety act or any similar presentation.[59]

---

[53] Cornish & Llewelyn (para 14.31) argue that this in effect gave performers no entitlement to any protection of their own distinct from that of their recording company, except in relation to bootlegging.

[54] Originally Council Directive 92/100/EEC on rental right and lending right and on certain rights related to copyright in the field of intellectual property; now in a consolidated version, European Parliament and Council Directive 2006/115/EC. For a challenge to the UK implementation of the Rental Right Directive see *Phonographic Performance Limited v Department of Trade and Industry and Another* [2004] 3 CMLR 31 [2004] EWHC 1795 (Ch) Ch D.

[55] Council Directive 93/83/EEC on the coordination of certain rules concerning copyright and rights related to copyright applicable to satellite broadcasting and cable retransmission.

[56] Originally Council Directive 93/98/EEC harmonising the term of protection of copyright and certain related rights; now in a consolidated version, European Parliament and Council Directive 2006/116/EC.

[57] Directive 2001/29/EC of the European Parliament and of the Council on the harmonisation of certain aspects of copyright and related rights in the information society.

[58] The current law is to be found in the CDPA 1988, Part II, as amended by the Duration of Copyright and Rights in Performances Regulations 1995 (SI 1995/3297), the Copyright and Related Rights Regulations 1996 (SI 1996/2967), and the Copyright and Related Rights Regulations 2003 (SI 2003/2498). For a case about the legislation's application to pre-Act performances see *Experience Hendrix LLC v Purple Haze Records Ltd and others* [2007] FSR 31 (CA).

[59] CDPA 1988, s 180(2).

> **? Question**
>
> The Edinburgh Festivals, which take place every year from July to September, see a plethora of interesting, diverse and ingenious individuals engaged in all manner of behaviour. Under the definition, would the following be performances?
>
> - An individual dressed as a Greek Goddess standing stock still on an upturned bucket in the middle of the Royal Mile.
> - A group of individuals attentively engaged in drawing collaborative pictures on the pavement.
> - A group of individuals in Princes Street Gardens intently following instructions given by a keep fit expert, the purpose of which is to teach the elderly to keep fit.
> - An individual juggling with balls of fire whilst on top of a monocycle.
> - A fortune teller seated in a gypsy caravan gazing into a crystal ball.
> - A group of models parading around Edinburgh Castle showing off the latest collections by up-and-coming Scottish designers.
> - A heated debate between Professor Alexander McCall Smith and audience over whether the latest course of action taken by Precious Ramotswe was morally justifiable.

Categories of performers' rights

6.26   Performers' rights are divided into two main categories:

- *performers' non-property rights:* rights against bootlegging (recordings of live performances made without performers' consent);
- *performers' property rights:* rights in *authorised copies* of performances.

The main distinctions between the non-property and property rights are:

- non-property rights cannot be assigned, although they are transmissible on death, whereas the property rights are capable of transfer and assignation;

- infringements of non-property rights are actionable only as breach of statutory duty, whereas infringement of property rights are actionable in the same way as other property rights, including copyright.

Performers' rights in respect of live performances

6.27   Diagram 6.3 shows performers' rights in respect of live performances by reference to the CDPA 1988.

Diagram 6.3 Performer's rights in live performances

Property rights in recordings of performances	Non-property rights against 'bootlegging'	Remuneration right	Secondary infringement rights (wrongdoer must have knowledge that recording illicit) (183–4)
reproduction (182A)	fixation and live broadcasting (182)	on any public playing or broadcasting of commercially published sound recording (182D)	showing or playing performance in public
distribution (182B)	public performance and broadcasting of recording made without consent (183)		broadcasting the performance
rental (182C)	dealings in illicit recordings (184)		importing a recording or copy for other than private or domestic use
lending (182C)			selling, hiring, distributing or otherwise dealing in copies
making available (182CA)			

The extent of performers' rights

(1) Performers' property rights

6.28   A performer's property rights are infringed by the following (compare with the economic rights conferred by copyright: see above, paras 4.23–4.67):

- **Reproduction**

If a person, without consent, either directly or indirectly makes a copy of a recording of the whole or any substantial part of a qualifying performance. This does not apply to copies made for private and domestic use.[60]

- **Distribution**

By a person who, without consent, issues to the public copies of a recording of the whole or any substantial part of a qualifying performance. The rights are exhausted once copies are placed into circulation within the European Economic Area (EEA) by or with the consent of the performer (but note consent is still required for rental or lending).[61]

- **Rental and lending**

By a person who, without consent, rents or lends to the public copies of a recording of the whole or any substantial part of a qualifying performance.[62] *Rental* means the making of a copy of a recording available for use, on terms that it will or may be returned for direct or indirect economic or commercial advantage, and *lending* means making a copy of a recording available for use on terms that it will or may be returned otherwise than for direct

---

[60] CDPA 1988, s 182A.   [61] CDPA 1988, s 182B.   [62] CDPA 1988, s 182C.

or indirect economic or commercial advantage through an establishment which is accessible to the public.[63]

- **Public performance; communication to the public**

By a person who, without consent, makes available to the public a recording of the whole or any substantial part of a qualifying performance by electronic transmission in such a way that members of the public may access the recording from a place and at a time individually chosen by them (the making available right).[64]

 Discussion point   For answer guidance visit www.oxfordtextbooks.co.uk/orc/macqueen2e/

Which of the economic rights conferred by copyright (above, para 4.10) is not to be found in the above list? Why not?

(2) Performers' non-property rights

6.29   A performer's non-property rights are infringed by the following (again, compare with the economic rights conferred by copyright: see above, para 4.10):

- **Fixation**

By a person who, without consent:

(1)   makes a recording of the whole or any substantial part of a qualifying performance directly from the live performance;

(2)   broadcasts live, or includes in a cable program service, the whole or any part of a qualifying performance;

(3)   makes a recording of the whole or any substantial part of a qualifying performance directly from a broadcast of, or cable program including the live performance.[65]

There is, however, no infringement if such a copy was made purely for private or domestic use.[66] Further, no damages will be awarded against a defendant who shows that at the time of the recording he believed on reasonable grounds that consent had been given.[67]

- **Distribution**

Where a recording made without consent is imported into the UK otherwise than for private or domestic use, or is exposed for sale or for hire in the course of a business.[68]

- **Public performance; communication to the public**

Where a person, without consent, shows or plays in public the whole or any substantial part of a qualifying performance, or broadcasts the whole or any substantial part of a qualifying performance where the person knows or has reason to believe the recording was made without the performer's consent.[69]

---

[63] CDPA 1988, s 182C(2)(a),(b). There are other definitions in this section. For example, the terms rental and lending do not include making available for the purpose of public performance, playing or showing in public or broadcasting. In addition, the expression lending does not include making available between establishments which are accessible to the public (CDPA 1988, s 182C(3), (4)).

[64] CDPA 1988, s 182CA(1).   [65] CDPA 1988, s 182(1).   [66] CDPA 1988, s 182(2).
[67] CDPA 1988, s 182(3).   [68] CDPA 1988, s 188(1)(a), (b).   [69] CDPA 1988, s 183(a), (b).

Non-property rights and exclusive recording contracts

6.30   Where a performer enters into an exclusive recording contract with another person under which that person is entitled to the exclusion of all other persons (including the performer) to make a recording of one or more of his performances with a view to their commercial exploitation,[70] consent of *both* the person having exclusive recording rights and the performer is necessary for:

- recording of the performance, otherwise than for private or domestic purposes;[71]

- for showing or playing in public the whole or any substantial part of the performance;

- including it in a broadcast;[72] and

- importing it into the UK or selling or letting for hire the performance in the course of a business.[73]

Exercise

Why are performers' rights classified into property and non-property rights? Are there coherent policy objectives underlying this aspect of the law? What would you do to reform the law in this area and what would be your underlying objectives in suggesting such reform?

Restrictions on the scope of performers' property and non-property rights

6.31   The CDPA 1988 details various permitted acts in relation to performers' property and non-property rights. These may be compared with the exceptions to copyright (above, Chapter 5, especially at paras 5.29, 5.37–5.38). The permitted acts relate to the question of infringement of the rights. They include such matters as things done for purposes of criticism, review or news reporting,[74] or instruction or examination;[75] recording of broadcasts by educational establishments;[76] recording of folksongs;[77] and recording for the purpose of time shifting.[78] The exceptions largely cover the same ground as those to be found in the 1988 Act as defences to an action of infringement of copyright.

Duration of rights

6.32   The rights conferred in relation to a performance expire at the end of the period of 50 years from the end of the calendar year in which the performance takes place.[79] If a recording of a performance is released during that period, the rights expire 50 years from the end of the calendar year

---

[70] CDPA 1988, s 185(1).   [71] CDPA 1988, s 186(1).   [72] CDPA 1988, s 187(1)(a), (b).
[73] CDPA 1988, s 188(1)(a)(b).   [74] CDPA 1988, Sch 2, para 2.   [75] CDPA 1988, Sch 2, para 4.
[76] CDPA 1988, Sch 2, para 6.   [77] CDPA 1988, Sch 2, para 14   [78] CDPA 1988, Sch 2, para 17A.
[79] In July 2008 the European Commission published a proposal (accessible at http://eur-lex.europa.eu/LexUriServ/LexUriServ.do?uri=COM:2008:0464:FIN:EN:PDF) for an extension of this term to 95 years.

in which the recording is released.[80] A recording is released when it is first published, played or shown in public or broadcast.[81] The duration of the rights is thus comparable with that for the media works in copyright (see paras 3.59–3.60). Where a performer is not a national of an EEA state, the duration of rights is that to which the performer is entitled in the country of which he is a national provided this does not extend the period to which he would be entitled if he were an EEC national.[82] In *Sony Music Entertainment (Germany) GmbH v Falcon Neue Medien Vertrieb GmbH*,[83] the ECJ held that the term of protection of 50 years for copyright held by producers of Bob Dylan performances before 1966 captured on phonograms could apply to such work in a member state that at the time of performance gave no such protection. Such protection arose where the work was, on 1 July 1995, protected in at least one other member state and where the rightholder, being a national of a non-member state, benefited at that date from the protection provided by those national provisions.

 Discussion point   For answer guidance visit www.oxfordtextbooks.co.uk/orc/macqueen2e/

Why are performers not given rights lasting for the same duration as authors of works protected by copyright? Should they be?

Moral rights

6.33   It was only with the adoption of the WIPO Performances and Phonograms Treaty 1996 (WPPT) that the question of moral rights arose for performers in the UK. Article 5 of the WPPT states:

'Moral Rights of Performers
(1) Independently of a performer's economic rights, and even after the transfer of those rights, the performer shall, as regards his live aural performances or performances fixed in phonograms have the right to claim to be identified as the performer of his performances, except where omission is dictated by the manner of the use of the performance, and to object to any distortion, mutilation or other modification of his performances that would be prejudicial to his reputation'

The UK Patent Office carried out an extensive consultation exercise on the implementation of these rights,[84] asking also whether the provisions should be extended to audiovisual performers (ie those whose performances are captured in television broadcasts, films, DVDs and the like), who are not included within the WPPT. Predictably, the responses fell into two broad camps:

- performers, authors and film directors favoured a broad implementation of the rights and an extension to audiovisual performers;
- film and television producers, film distributors, cinema exhibitors, broadcasters, record producers, theatres and music argued for narrow implementation restricted to the obligations under the WPPT with no extension to audiovisual performers.

---

[80] CDPA 1988, s 191(2).   [81] No account is to be taken of any unauthorised act (CDPA 1988, s 191(3)).
[82] CDPA 1988, s 191(4).
[83] C-240/07, [2009] ECDR 13. See N Owers, 'Term of protection of copyright-related rights in the EC' (2009) 4 JIPLP 321.
[84] http://www.ipo.gov.uk/moralrights.pdf

The UK Regulations[85] came into force on 1 February 2006 and extend only as far as required under the WPPT, in some respects giving weaker protection to performers than might have been the case. The rights endure for the same period as the performers' economic rights.[86]

Right to be identified

6.34   A performer will be given the right to be identified as performer whenever a person:

- produces or puts on a qualifying performance that is given in public;
- broadcasts live a qualifying performance;
- communicates to the public a sound recording of a qualifying performance; or
- issues to the public copies of such a recording.[87]

The right to be identified is one:

- in the case of a performance that is given in public, to be identified in any programme accompanying the performance or in some other manner likely to bring his identity to the notice of a person seeing or hearing the performance;
- in the case of a performance that is broadcast, to be identified in a manner likely to bring his identity to the notice of a person seeing or hearing the broadcast;
- in the case of a sound recording that is communicated to the public, to be identified in a manner likely to bring his identity to the notice of a person hearing the communication;
- in the case of a sound recording that is issued to the public, to be identified in or on each copy or, if that is not appropriate, in some other manner likely to bring his identity to the notice of a person acquiring a copy.[88]

However, the right to be identified will not be infringed unless it has first been asserted,[89] and is also hedged with a number of exceptions including:

- where it is not reasonably practicable to identify the performer (or, where identification of a group is permitted);
- in relation to any performance given for the purposes of reporting current events;
- in relation to any performance given for the purposes of advertising any goods or services.[90]

In addition the right will not be infringed by an act which is covered by provisions relating to inter alia:

- news reporting;
- incidental inclusion of a performance or recording;
- things done for the purposes of examination.[91]

---

[85] Copyright Rights in Performances (Moral Rights, etc) Regulations 2006 (SI 2006/18), amending CDPA 1988 (to which references below are made).
[86] CDPA 1988, s 205I.   [87] CDPA 1988, s 205C(1)   [88] CDPA 1988, s 205C(2).
[89] CDPA 1988, s 205D(1).   [90] CDPA 1988, s 205E.   [91] CDPA 1988, s 205E(5).

Right to object to derogatory treatment

6.35   A performer has a right to object where a performance:

- is broadcast live, or
- by means of a sound recording the performance is played in public or communicated to the public,

with any distortion, mutilation or other modification that is prejudicial to the reputation of the performer.[92] Again this right is subject to a number of exceptions. Thus it does not apply or is not infringed:

- in relation to any performance given for the purposes of reporting current events;[93]
- by modifications made to a performance which are consistent with normal editorial or production practice.[94]

A performer may also waive the rights to be identified and to object to derogatory treatment.[95]

 Exercise

Compare and contrast a performer's rights of attribution and to object to derogatory treatment with those conferred on authors under ss 77–82 of the CDPA 1988 (see above, paras 3.31–3.43). Has the UK successfully implemented its obligations under the WIPO Performances and Phonograms Treaty 1996 with respect to the moral rights of performers?

Key points on performers' moral rights

Moral rights exist for performers only in respect of their live aural performance and performances fixed in phonograms. Audiovisual performers do not have moral rights.

The moral rights conferred are:

- the right to be identified;
- the right to prevent derogatory treatment of one's performance.

Audiovisual performers

6.36   As indicated above, the provisions in the WPPT concerning moral rights covers only performers in respect of their live aural performance and performances fixed in phonograms. This has engendered a debate concerning moral rights for audiovisual performers (ie those appearing in films and TV broadcasts). WIPO convened a diplomatic Conference in December 2000, to

---

[92] CDPA 1988, s 205F(1).   [93] CDPA 1988, s 205G(2).   [94] CDPA 1988, s 205G(3).
[95] CDPA 1988, s 205J.

discuss the protection of audiovisual performances.[96] The Conference came to the following wording as suitable for inclusion in a protocol of the WPPT:

(1) Independently of a performer's economic rights, and even after the transfer of those rights, the performer shall have the right:

    (i) to claim to be identified as the performer of his performances, except where omission is dictated by the manner of the use of the performance; and

    (ii) to object to any distortion, mutilation or other modification of his performances that would be prejudicial to his reputation. Modifications consistent with the normal exploitation of a performance in the course of a use authorized by the performer shall not be considered prejudicial to the performer's reputation.

As can be seen from the wording, delegates, particularly from the producer countries had concerns over the extent to which moral rights of audiovisual performers might hinder the exploitation of collective works. Hence the reference in the draft provision to permitting modifications consistent with the normal exploitation of a performance (such as the editing of a film).

The nature of a performer's right

6.37   As will be evident from the preceding summary, the characterisation of performers' rights within the UK statutory regime now is far from clear. One writer is of the opinion that performers' rights should *not* be considered as falling under the head of copyright,[97] while admitting that, since the inclusion of performers' property rights in the legislation, those rights have now 'inched...close to copyright.'[98] Others have said that although the performers' property rights granted by the 1988 Act were not described as copyright, 'in effect a new copyright was conferred on performers.'[99]

6.38   Nor is it easy to classify performers' rights as neighbouring or media rights as traditionally understood in the UK. Although UK legislation does not formally distinguish between authorial and other works, that distinction still underlies a good part of the assumptions on which the legal framework is built. In this context, authors' rights are understood to refer to the works created by authors such as books, plays, music and art. By contrast, neighbouring or entrepreneurial or media rights are derivative, and in general it is the investment in technical and organisational skill that is being protected, rather than the creative effort. Perhaps in response to this conundrum, performers' non-property rights which are personal and non-assignable right have been described as 'a form of neighbouring right to copyright.'[100] The Act makes clear that the rights conferred in relation to performers are independent of any copyright in, or moral rights relating to, any work performed or any film or sound recording of, or broadcast including the performance.[101] For these reasons some have referred to performers' rights as 'related rights',[102] which is perhaps the most suitable terminology to use. Yet performers

---

[96] For a full discussion see S von Lewinski, 'The WIPO Diplomatic Conference on Audiovisual Performances: a first resumé' [2001] EIPR 333.
[97] Cornish & Llewelyn, para 11.02.   [98] Cornish & Llewelyn, para 14.36.
[99] Copinger & Skone James, para 12.01.   [100] Cornish & Llewelyn, para 14.32.   [101] CDPA 1988, s 180(4)(a).
[102] Bently & Sherman, Ch 13.

appear rather closer to authors as figures with a claim to the law's protection, and the introduction of moral rights for the former as well as the latter makes the analogy even closer.

 Question

How should performers' rights be characterised in relation to copyright?

Performers' remuneration rights

6.39   An aspect of performers' rights which appears to be distinctive is the right to equitable remuneration. Two such rights are available to performers, introduced as a result of the Rental and Lending Rights Directive:

- A performer can claim equitable remuneration from the owner of the copyright in the sound recording[103] where a commercially published sound recording of a performance (but not a film) is played in public or communicated to the public otherwise than under the 'making available to the public' right.[104] The right may not be assigned except to a collecting society for the purpose of enabling it to enforce the right on the performer's behalf.[105] The amount payable is as agreed by the parties,[106] or, failing agreement, application may be made to the Copyright Tribunal to determine the amount payable.[107] Any agreement purporting to exclude or restrict the right to equitable remuneration, or purporting to prevent a person questioning the amount of equitable remuneration or to restrict the powers of the Copyright Tribunal is of no effect.[108]

- A performer retains a right to equitable remuneration where she transfers (or is presumed to transfer) her rental right in a film or sound recording to the producer.[109] Any agreement purporting to exclude or restrict the right to equitable remuneration is of no effect.[110] The right may not be assigned by the performer except to a collecting society for the purpose of enabling it to enforce the right on her behalf.[111] The Copyright Tribunal has jurisdiction to determine the amount payable failing agreement[112]

In the UK, the British Equity Collecting Society (BECS) deals with management of performers' equitable remuneration rights, including ingathering monies due from exploitation in other member states.

---

[103] CDPA 1988, s 182D.   [104] CDPA 1988, s 182CA(1).   [105] CDPA 1988, s 182D(2).
[106] CDPA 1988, s 182D(3).
[107] CDPA 1988, s 182D(5). The Tribunal may order any method of calculation and paying equitable remuneration it may determine to be reasonable in the circumstances taking into account the importance of the contribution of the performer to the sound recording (CDPA 1988, s 182D(6)).
[108] CDPA 1988, s 182D(7).   [109] CDPA 1988, s 191 F–H.   [110] CDPA 1988, s 191G(5).
[111] CDPA 1988, s 191G(2), (6). The collecting society must be an organisation which has as its main object, or one of its main objects, the exercise of the right to equitable remuneration on behalf of more than one performer.
[112] Remuneration shall not be considered inequitable merely because it was paid by way of a single payment or at the time of the transfer of the rental right (CDPA 1988, s 191H(4)).

> ## Key points on equitable remuneration right
>
> - A performer can claim equitable remuneration from the copyright owner in a commercially published sound recording of a performance (but not a film) when it is played in public or communicated to the public
> - A performer retains a right to equitable remuneration where she transfers (or is presumed to transfer) her rental right in a film or sound recording to the producer
> - These rights cannot be excluded by contract
> - The rights are not assignable except to a collecting society

 Exercise

What other areas of copyright and related rights contain provisions for equitable remuneration? Should such schemes be extended more generally across the area of copyright and related rights? Why do we not move from the 'property' system we have at present to one which is merely a right to remuneration for exploitation?

Further reading

Books

General

T Aplin, *Copyright Law in the Digital Society: the Challenges of Multimedia* (2005)

R Arnold, *Performers' Rights* (4th edn, 2008)

Bently & Sherman, *Intellectual Property Law* (3rd edn, 2009), Ch 13

Copinger & Skone James on Copyright (15th edn, 2005), Chs 12 and 18

Cornish & Llewelyn, *Intellectual Property* (6th edn, 2007), Ch 14.4 and 20.2

E Derclaye, *The Legal Protection of Databases: A Comparative Analysis* (2008)

Laddie, Prescott & Vitoria, *Modern Law of Copyright* (3rd edn, 2000), Chs 12 and 30

Articles

S von Lewinski, 'The WIPO Diplomatic Conference on Audiovisual Performances: a first resumé' [2001] EIPR 333

Websites

The Database Right File (website maintained by the Institute for Information Law, University of Amsterdam http://www.ivir.nl/files/database/index.html).

Contemporary issues in copyright

Introduction

Scope and overview of chapter

7.1 This chapter considers a number of issues of current concern in copyright. Its starting point is the several copyright reform initiatives under way as the book was completed. Copyright featured prominently among the issues addressed by the Gowers Review of intellectual property published in 2006.[1] Its remit included, in particular, whether the 'infringement framework reflects the digital environment'; whether 'fair use' (*sic*) provisions for citizens are reasonable; and what the term of protection for sound recordings should be.[2] This followed the Labour Party manifesto commitment with which it entered and won the 2005 general election:

> 'Copyright in a digital age: We will modernise copyright and other forms of protection of intellectual property rights so that they are appropriate for the digital age.'[3]

The EU had also been at work. A Commission staff working paper on the review of EU legislation on copyright and related rights (henceforth Commission Copyright Paper) was issued in July 2004.[4] This assessed, in particular, whether inconsistencies between the different Directives hamper the operation of EU copyright law or damage the balance between right holders' interests, those of users and consumers and those of the European economy as a whole. The Commission Paper appeared to envisage a future 'Copyright Code' for Europe, in which the present piecemeal collection of Directives enacted at various times since 1991 would be consolidated and, presumably, the gaps between them filled.[5] Little detail was given on this project, and to date its only manifestations are the issue late in 2006 of the consolidated versions of the Rental Right and Term Directives.[6]

---

[1] Gowers Review of Intellectual Property, HM Treasury, December 2006, accessible at http://www.hm-treasury.gov.uk/gowers_review_index.htm

[2] Press release available on the Treasury website, http://www.hm-treasury.gov.uk/press_102_05.htm

[3] *Britain Forward Not Back: The Labour Party Manifesto 2005*, p 95.

[4] *Commission Staff Working Paper on the review of the EC legal framework in the field of copyright and related rights*, SEC(2004) 995 (http://ec.europa.eu/internal_market/copyright/docs/review/sec-2004-995_en.pdf).

[5] ibid, para 1.3 (last internal paragraph).

[6] Parliament and Council Directives 2006/115/EC and 2006/116/EC respectively.

It has been said, however, that the continuing existence of many national copyright laws within the EU makes life very complicated for would-be users of works because so many permissions have to be sought for the use. The only solution to that would be a Community Copyright Regulation replacing the existing Directives and at least partially pre-empting national systems.[7]

7.2   The present chapter surveys some of the major issues to which the initiatives just described are directed, as well as some which, perhaps significantly, are not mentioned. The importance of doing this is above all to understand why reform of copyright is such an important question at present.[8] This also enables one to come to grips with the policy issues with which copyright law has to deal, recognising the sometimes sharply opposed views that exist on these matters. The issues chosen for discussion vary, however, in the likelihood that they will be addressed in any reform process which may flow in the coming years from the initiatives launched by the UK Government and the European Commission in 2004–2005. At the best of times law reform is a slow process; and the chapter shows how difficult it is in relation to copyright. The approach taken here is to consider specific issues against the general background of recent technological development (the 'digital environment'), while looking towards solutions that might be possible under a Europe-wide 'copyright code' rather than in a merely UK context. This recognises that significant reform in the future will generally stem from the EU or even more widely based international institutions.

7.3   ## Learning objectives

- By the end of this chapter you should be able to describe and explain:
- major policy issues relating to the reform of copyright law;
- the significance of the increasingly digital environment for copyright law;
- possible European solutions to some particular problems in copyright law.

7.4   The chapter begins by identifying some of the specific issues which have brought copyright reform to the forefront in recent times. What holds many of these together is the development of digital, mobile and interactive technology as the means of delivering ideas, information and entertainment to their users. The chapter then proceeds to look at the difficulties which this new environment presents for copyright, the rules of which were mostly created in a world where material came to users in the form of single copies or performances put on the market by intermediaries of one kind or another, such as publishers, broadcasters, and film and sound recording producers. A running theme, picking up from Chapter 5 in particular, is how far in the digital world copyright may be replaced or superseded by contract. Having thus surveyed the scene in general, the chapter turns to a number of specific topics where either the digital

---

[7] This is the conclusion of a European Commission DG Internal Market Study prepared by the Institute for Information Law, University of Amsterdam and published in November 2006, *The Recasting of Copyright & Related Rights for the Knowledge Economy*. But the authors of the report also recommend that there be no further harmonisation initiatives unless a clear need can be demonstrated.

[8] See HL MacQueen, 'Copyright law reform: some possible options', in F Macmillan (ed), *New Directions in Copyright, vol 3* (2007).

environment, or national differences of approach within Europe, or both, present reformers with particular challenges. Altogether, then, the rest of the chapter looks like this:

- Context (7.5–7.11)
- Purpose of copyright (7.12–7.17)
- Specific issues (7.18–7.61)

Context

7.5   Amongst the many particular developments which have brought copyright reform to the fore in the UK and Europe may be included the following:

- *File-sharing through unlicensed peer-to-peer networks*, especially with regard to sound recordings, but also in relation to computer software and games, and increasingly in relation to films as well.[9] The music and other entertainment industries claim that this unlicensed activity is having a significant impact upon the 'legitimate' market for their products. The major developments since the phenomenon first became prominent through the *Napster* case in the USA in 2000–2001 (see above, para 4.73) are the growth of licensed downloading sites, increased numbers of actions against individual downloaders, and several court decisions around the world, including the UK, against the operators and users of unlicensed file-sharing networks as infringers of copyright.[10] The sound recording industry has also had some success in pressing for some form of liability for Internet service providers through whose services file-sharing takes place, partly through successful court claims,[11] partly through negotiation with bodies representing internet service providers,[12] and partly through legislation proposed and actual.[13] In the UK the Government published a Bill on the subject in November 2009, following up the 'Digital Britain' debate of 2008–2009.[14]

- *Sound recording industry pressure to replace the term for the protection of sound recordings* (currently 50 years from release) with a term the same as that in the USA (that is, 95 years from the year of first publication). In July 2008 the European Commission published a proposal for a Directive to extend the term for sound recordings from 50 to 95 years.[15] The measure has so far failed to gain the whole-hearted support of the member states or of the European Parliament, which has recommended extension to 70 years only. The importance of

---

[9] See C Waelde and H MacQueen, 'From entertainment to education: the scope of copyright' [2004] IPQ 259; R Clark, 'Illegal downloads—sharing out online liability. Sharing files, sharing risks' [2007] 2 JIPLP 402.

[10] Eg the US Supreme Court in *MGM v Grokster* 545 US 913 (2005), and the Federal Court of Australia in *Universal Music Australia Pty Ltd v Sharman License Holdings Ltd* [2005] FCA 1242; and for UK cases see BBC News Online 27 January 2006 http://news.bbc.co.uk/1/hi/entertainment/4653662.stm, and 30 January 2006 http://news.bbc.co.uk/1/hi/technology/4663388.stm. See further P Akester, 'Copyright and the P2P challenge' [2005] EIPR 106, and P Ganley, 'Surviving *Grokster*: innovation and the future of peer-to-peer' [2006] EIPR 14.

[11] See eg *SABAM v SA Tiscali (Scarlet)* [2007] ECDR 19, District Court of Brussels.

[12] See http://news.bbc.co.uk/1/hi/technology/7486743.stm and http://news.bbc.co.uk/1/hi/technology/7522334.stm

[13] http://news.bbc.co.uk/1/hi/technology/7110024.stm (France), http://news.bbc.co.uk/1/hi/technology/7495085.stm (EU).

[14] The proposal is entitled the Digital Economy Bill. See further for background, HL MacQueen, ' "Appropriate for the digital age?" Copyright and the Internet', in L Edwards and C Waelde (eds), *Law and the Internet* (3rd edn, 2009), 189–90, 201.

[15] The proposal is accessible at http://eur-lex.europa.eu/LexUriServ/LexUriServ.do?uri=COM:2008:0464:FIN:EN:PDF See further 'Creativity stifled? A joint academic statement on the proposed copyright term extension for sound recordings' [2008] EIPR 341.

this is that many of the most popular sound recordings made in the 1950s and (soon) the 1960s are falling into the public domain and so becoming available for unlicensed Internet transmission.

- The *Google Books Settlement.* In the USA the Association of American Publishers and a number of authors began court action in the autumn of 2005 to stop the implementation of Google's arrangements with a number of leading academic libraries to digitise their collections of books in order to make the full texts thereof available to users of the Google service. The claim was that copyright was bound to be infringed in the execution of the scheme, even although Google and the participating libraries declared that digitisation would be confined to works either out of copyright or whose authors had not opted out of the scheme. A settlement was proposed in late 2008 subject to the approval of the court, which after much controversy and renegotiation had still not been granted by the end of 2009, although a fairness hearing was scheduled for 18 February 2010.[16]

- The use of *rights management information systems* (RMIs) and *technical protection measures* (TPMs) to build into products such as CDs, DVDs, databases and websites—and also into the hardware needed to use these products—mechanisms that prevent unauthorised access and use unless and until such contractual conditions as the producer imposes (typically payment by way of credit card or fund transfer systems such as Paypal, and carefully restricted re-use of the product), are met by the would-be user. As noted above (see paras 5.50–5.57), these mechanisms are intensely controversial.[17]

- *The establishment of Creative Commons UK* (building on a US model), with the aim of developing forms of licence under which copyright is retained but users are given advance permission to copy and distribute the work for their own purposes, so long as due credit is given to the original work and similar conditions are imposed upon any further sub-users; this being, it is argued, the most appropriate way to support and encourage creativity and innovation in the online and digital environments.[18] The licensor can indicate those types of use which remain restricted; but the starting point is that use is free and restrictions on use have to be stated, whereas the underpinning assumption of traditional licences is that no use is allowed unless expressly permitted. Creative Commons was inspired originally by the 'open source' movement which began in connection with computer software and was conceived in opposition to the existence of copyright in such material. The credo was that software should be made available in such a way that others might use and build upon it, especially in developing new software, as this was the best way to facilitate further such innovation. This does not necessarily mean that the software must be made available free of charge, but rather that copyright should not be used to block further development of what already exists.

- *The publication of the Adelphi Charter on creativity, innovation and intellectual property* in October 2005,[19] calling upon governments to maintain a balance between public domain and private right, and between competition and monopoly, with regard to intellectual property rights in general; to ensure in particular that the copyright term is limited in time and does not extend beyond what is proportionate and necessary; and to facilitate a wide range of

---

[16] See http://www.googlebooksettlement.com/.

[17] See *Digital Rights Management: Report of an Inquiry by the All Party Internet Group* (June 2006), accessible at http://www.apcomms.org.uk/apig/current-activities/apig-inquiry-into-digital-rights-management/DRMreport.pdf.

[18] See http://creativecommons.org/projects/international/uk/; there is also a site for Scotland (http://creativecommons.org/international/scotland/).

[19] Accessible at http://www.adelphicharter.org/.

policies to stimulate access and innovation, including non-proprietary models such as open source software licensing and open access to scientific literature.

There are also widespread perceptions of copyright as complex, inaccessible, productive of difficulty and uncertainty in relation to otherwise lawful activities, and sometimes absurd.[20] On the other hand, piracy—the unlicensed mass reproduction of copyright material such as sound recordings, films and computer games for resale at prices far undercutting those of the copyright owner—continues undoubtedly to be a serious issue for the affected industries, as it was also for most of the second half of the 20th century.

7.6   As the examples in the previous paragraph show, a huge range of areas of activity is affected by copyright: government, entertainment, education, creativity, technology and international development, to name but a few. The shortlist of major issues shows that much of the current debate has arisen in the context of the ever-expanding scope and possibilities of using digital, wireless and mobile technologies for the creation, dissemination and reproduction of ideas, information and entertainment. The context for policy thinking in the areas traditionally covered by copyright has been transformed by the ability to make material available so that it is potentially always accessible to users at times and places chosen by them; especially when it has gone along with expanding possibilities of, and demand for, interactivity between suppliers and users who, starting on the basis of what already exists, may themselves become creators, developers and suppliers of further material.[21] It is also clear that increasing amounts of material from both the digital and pre-digital era are going to become available electronically: not only sound recordings, films and broadcasts, but also works of art and literature of all kinds and all periods. The idea of the digital environment as a cultural jukebox, always on and available for use, shifts the traditional relationships between users and consumers, on the one hand, and creators and repositories such as libraries, archives, museums and galleries, and publishers and broadcasters, on the other. Further, because the digital environment does not know jurisdictional and national frontiers, the law's approach has to be an international one, moving beyond the traditional international approach of setting minimum standards of copyright protection (which does not entail the law and rights being the same everywhere), and according to foreigners whatever protection the national law affords its own nationals (see above, para 2.8).

 Exercise

Can you give any other examples of copyright policy issues like those mentioned in para 7.5, arising from attempts to create, disseminate and reproduce ideas, information and entertainment in the digital environment?

7.7   Debate is sparked, however, by varying visions of what the Internet and, following it, the 'information superhighway' through wireless and mobile communication systems should be about. For *government and commercial interests*, it is primarily a means of economic development. Technology now provides an information, marketing and selling device capable of reaching an ever-widening number of citizens, consumers and buyers. All kinds of producers can in effect

---

[20] Even judges can be critical: see eg H Laddie, 'Copyright: over-strength, over-regulated, over-rated?' [1996] EIPR 253.
[21] See generally T Dreier, 'Copyright in the age of digital technology' (1993) 24 IIC 481; A Christie, 'Reconceptualising copyright in the digital age' [1995] EIPR 522; PB Hugenholtz (ed), *The Future of Copyright in a Digital Environment* (1996).

set up electronic shops and information resources. Some simply sell goods and services that are already available (but usually more expensively) through traditional outlets. Good examples are Amazon, the online bookshop, offering books, CDs and DVDs, and easyJet, offering airline services; and each contracting with customers principally by way of electronic communication across the web. Ebay, the online auction site, is a slightly different example of the same thing, electronically putting sellers in contact with potential buyers of whatever they have to sell.[22] In another world altogether, courts have websites where their judgments can be read and, increasingly, aspects of their process carried out.

7.8   But digital technology also creates the possibility of new types of purely electronic products and services that can be traded primarily through communication systems. Computer programs and games were the most familiar type of digital product before the Internet took off; these could now be made available on the Internet for downloading directly to computers linked to the relevant website. Familiar also by the end of the 1980s were the digital CD-ROMs which were largely replacing analogue cassettes and the still-surviving vinyl record as the primary means of disseminating recorded musical performances. The Internet opened up the possibility, soon realised by Napster and others, of the global jukebox from which music enthusiasts could at any time download to a local computer, a mobile telephone or other device (such as an iPod) whatever took their fancy at the time. From music it was but a short step to films, albeit that a full-length feature requires far more digital capacity in both the carrier and the player—a technical problem solved for the moment by the technique of compression, and the development of the 'digital versatile disk' (DVD) and broadband. Broadcasting has also moved into the digital era via 'podcasting', so that viewers and listeners can increasingly choose when to watch and hear programmes, and interrupt, pause and replay them to suit their own rather than the broadcaster's convenience. Digitisation also enabled the rapid development of the multi-media product, combining writing, sounds, and images still and moving. Finally, the most obviously new kind of service made both necessary and possible in the digital environment was the search engine provided by such organisations as Google and Yahoo!, through which users of the Internet could find their way most speedily to the material they wanted.

7.9   The key point in all this for copyright is that, by contrast with the analogue world in which, although copying was easy, the copy was invariably less good than the original, the digital work will always copy perfectly. The downloader gets as good a version as the master copy on the original site—and gets it increasingly easily and quickly as the technology moves on. Nor does the user necessarily have to have, keep or find space for the products involved: access by way of streaming and podcasting may replace acquisition of anything other than the devices which provide the means of access. The Internet and subsequent developments in mobile communications systems thus provide a tremendous new way to reach consumers of information and entertainment products in the comfort of their own homes and social patterns. But the difficulty also facing those minded to exploit these opportunities is precisely the ease and speed of digital reproduction and transmission. How can consumers be made to pay for the material they download or receive in this way? How can pirates, those making copies and providing access for their own commercial gain without the authority of the originator, be stopped from exploiting the technology and thereby undercutting the latter's market?

[22] See more generally C Ramberg, *Internet Marketplaces: the Law of Auctions and Exchanges Online* (2002).

7.10   A further question is raised, however, from the perspective of those who see the new technology as raising other exciting possibilities of ever-greater and wider access to, and expression and circulation of ideas and information. In this perspective, the ease and speed of digital communication and reproduction is an opportunity rather than a problem; a real step forward in allowing the realisation of both individual and societal goals. This is the perspective which lies behind the idea of 'open source', in which material is made freely available to others—'free' here meaning, as it has famously been put, 'free' as in 'free expression' rather than as in 'free beer'.[23] By their very nature, information and ideas want to be free in the same sense as a prisoner or a caged wild animal might do.[24] As economists point out, information and ideas are 'public goods', meaning that their availability is not diminished no matter how many people have enjoyed or employed them.[25] Insofar as copyright is a barrier to the free flow of information and ideas, it is mis-used. Some go so far as to say that copyright is always such a barrier; the purpose of others, such as Creative Commons, however, is to recognise the value possessed by copyright provided that it is not used simply to obstruct otherwise beneficial further activity and creativity.[26]

7.11   File-sharing (above, paras 4.72ff, 7.5) provides a good example for argument about the different perspectives. The sound recording industry sees the transfer of music recordings from user to user without charge as the main reason, apart from piracy, behind a significant decline in the sale of music CDs since 2000 (the year in which the Napster operation first took off). The industry argues that without profit its investment in new talent will necessarily decline, with the end result being less opportunity for, and so overall less, new recorded music. Those supporting a more 'open' approach argue that the sound recording industry failed to move quickly enough to meet the potential of the Internet as a means of distributing music, and that users of the unlicensed file-sharing services actually did continue to buy CDs, turning to the services only for hard-to-obtain or actually unavailable material. The sound recording industry had only itself to blame for its financial woes, having been exposed by others more innovative and better attuned to the ways in which consumers wished to acquire and use their music in the digital environment, and who made that pay in different ways (eg by selling advertising space on their services).

 Exercise

Discuss the perspectives about file-sharing in the previous paragraph with reference to the more general perspectives explained in paras 7.7–7.10. What conclusions would be drawn about the correct use of copyright here by (a) the commercial sound recording industry; and (b) advocates of an 'open' approach to the distribution and circulation of recorded music? See also W Davies and K Withers, *Public Innovation: Intellectual Property in a Digital Age* (Institute of Public Policy Research, 2006), 43–4.

---

[23] See the GNU website, http://www.gnu.org/philosophy/free-sw.html

[24] Note also the concept of 'freedom of information' in constitutional law: Freedom of Information Act 2000 and Freedom of Information (Scotland) Act 2002.

[25] Hence it is not clear that the 'tragedy of the commons' (G Hardin, (1968) 162 Science 1243) befalls information and ideas.

[26] See generally JP Barlow, 'Selling without bottles: the economy of mind on the global Net', in PB Hugenholtz (ed), *The Future of Copyright in a Digital Environment* (1996), especially at pp 176–82; and the works of Lawrence Lessig: *Code and Other Laws of Cyberspace* (1999); *The Future of Ideas: the Fate of the Commons in a Connected World* (2001); and *Free Culture: How Big Media Uses Technology and the Law to Lock Down Culture and Control Creativity* (2004). See also M Farley, 'Web 2.0, wikis, and the IP community' [2007] 2 JIPLP 251; S Holmes and P Ganley, 'User-generated content and the law' [2007] 2 JIPLP 338.

Purpose of copyright

7.12   A fundamental question in thinking about these issues is the purpose, or purposes, of copyright. Only with clear ideas of what we are trying to achieve will clear, coherent and principled law emerge.[27] We have already discussed at some length many of copyright's underlying ideas:

- The *economic role* (para 2.18)—incentivising and rewarding, in accordance with market demand, those involved in the creation and publication of certain kinds of work. Economic interests therefore include, not only creators, but also entrepreneurs who convert what is created into products for the marketplace. Copyright is a response to market failure; without it, the *expression* of ideas and information, creativity and innovation would be available to all, without reward for those who invested in the creation and dissemination of the works thereby produced, either personally or financially. With copyright, the way is open for the reward of creative individuals and those who convert their creative work into products that the public will buy or otherwise spend money on.

- Protection of the *creative individual's personality rights* (para 2.19), most evident in the moral rights, and their recognition of inalienable, non-economic interests that an author (but no-one else) may continue to exercise in respect of a work even though no longer owner of the copyright or of the physical form in which the work was first created and recorded. This aspect of copyright is also apparent in the copyright terms, much longer than a strict economic analysis would suggest is necessary for the fulfilment of the economic goal. There may also be a link between moral rights and the fundamental human rights that underlie many personality rights in general. Human rights to dignity and respect seem particularly apt to support the right to be identified in connection with one's work and to have that work treated appropriately by others.[28] Copyright can also protect the individual's interest in *privacy*. There is no obligation to publish or make available one's work, and copyright serves to protect that position should that be the author's wish.[29]

- The *rights of users, or the public domain* (paras 2.20, 5.4). By placing various limitations upon what it protects on the producer side, copyright also protects, directly or indirectly, non-producer interests. Thus:

  – freedom of expression and information are protected by the limitation of copyright to forms of expression, as distinct from the ideas and information which are expressed;

  – copyright is not unlimited in duration, and works which fall out of copyright at the end of their term are available to all for any purpose;

  – works which fall below the threshold requirement of 'originality' do not have copyright, even if in other respects they come within one of the categories of protected work (eg being written, they are literary);

---

[27] A useful if not entirely uncontentious analysis is W Davies and K Withers, *Public Innovation: Intellectual Property in a Digital Age* (Institute of Public Policy Research, 2006).

[28] See further on this theme I Stamatoudi, 'Moral rights of authors in England: the missing emphasis on the role of the creator' [1997] IPQ 478; and two papers by MT Sundara Rajan: 'Moral rights in the digital age: new possibilities for the democratization of culture' (2002) 16 Intl Rev of Law Computers & Technology 187; 'Moral rights in information technology: a new kind of 'personal right'?' ((2004) 12 Intl J of Law and Information Technology 32; also LK Treiger-Bar-Am, 'The moral right of integrity: a freedom of expression', in F Macmillan (ed), *New Directions in Copyright Law, vol 2* (2006).

[29] See HL MacQueen, ' "My tongue is mine ain": copyright, the spoken word and privacy' (2005) 68 MLR 349.

– works which do not fit into the expressed categories of the law do not receive copyright protection;[30]

– copyright exceptions, whether general, eg fair dealing, or for specific types of work, eg 'time-shifting' of TV broadcasts, reflect a recognition that certain non-producer interests outweigh producer ones in at least some circumstances; or at any rate the impracticability of certain kinds of copyright enforcement; and

– the *product* embodying the protected work can generally be dealt with freely by the first and subsequent purchasers apart from integrity/ commercial rental/ lending/ public communication rights.

We might also take note of a further dimension:

• The *cultural purposes* of copyright: this dimension is apparent in the nature of what copyright protects—literary, dramatic, musical and artistic works, films, sound recordings and broadcasts—and also in the length of time for which it gives that protection, which, as noted above, is not necessarily (or at all) driven by economic analysis.

7.13   It is not suggested here that current UK law does anything other than reflect a mixture of these various purposes, which attempts to provide a *balance* between the different interests involved. Nor is it suggested that the present balance is satisfactory, or that it was at any time in the past. The interests inevitably come into conflict, especially those related to economic and personality interests in works, on the one hand, and those reflecting the public domain dimension, on the other. All that law-makers can do is be sensitive to all the interests involved, make choices between options from time to time, and be prepared to act should it become apparent that a solution, old or new, is not working as it should, or has become inappropriate in changing circumstances.

7.14   The digital environment now raises the question whether the economic interests of the creator and entrepreneur, or of society, still actually require copyright. In the pre-digital world, an author and a person wishing to use the author's work would have very little opportunity or incentive to meet and negotiate the terms and conditions of the latter's use; hence the need for copyright law to set down some general social bargain, as it were, and also for intermediaries such as publishers to enable works to find their markets and audiences. But in the digital environment it is potentially much easier for author and audience to find each other directly, and for them to use technology to conclude their own bespoke bargain about terms and conditions of use of the author's work. As already noted (para 5.58), TPMs and RMIs (henceforth collectively 'DRMs') can prevent access to and use of a work unless and until such contractual conditions as the producer imposes are met by the would-be user. Usually such technologies are seen by critics hostile to current legal developments in the field as the manifestation of the worst of current copyright rules, since the law protects them against circumvention by third parties even although their use can enable, not only the prevention of activities falling within the exceptions to copyright, but, indeed, the protection of works no longer or never in copyright. The position of the right owner thus appears to be considerably strengthened at the expense of the user, since money can be made even from a work without copyright, so long as it is technologically protectable.[31] Equally,

---

[30] Eg the format and catchphrases of the TV show 'Opportunity Knocks' did not amount to a dramatic work and so did not receive copyright protection (*Green v Broadcasting Corp of New Zealand* [1989] 2 All ER 1056 (PC); above para 2.37).

[31] LMCR Guibault, *Copyright Limitations and Contracts* (2002); R Burrell and A Coleman, *Copyright Exceptions: the Digital Impact* (2005), pp 67–70, 269–70, 306–10.

however, through contracts such as the forms provided by Creative Commons, an author can indicate in advance, as it were, those uses of the work by others which, although within the scope of copyright protection, are nonetheless permitted; further, the author can require those using this permission to apply those terms and conditions to further downstream sub-users. So in this context technology can operate in support of widespread use and later creativity with existing works. There is some evidence that in response to consumer demand right owners are beginning to explore the possibilities of DRMs enabling consumers to make use of their products other than by simply playing them (for example, making additional copies to store on personal computers or playback machines).[32] Further market pressures may lead to more such developments, particularly if different consumers might be prepared to pay variable prices for different packages of permissions made available through DRMs.[33] Contract will therefore often be automated and 'standard form' in this context, rather than the result of individual negotiation and bargaining; especially if the Internet does develop into the global digital jukebox already referred to (para 7.6), in which the user simply has to locate the material wanted, pay and play. But nonetheless, given contract's enormous flexibility, can it replace copyright, and would that be a good thing?[34]

7.15   An obvious tricky point is that it is copyright, for the most part, which, at least initially, creates the subject matter around which contracting parties can subsequently bargain. In the absence of copyright at the point of creation there might be no room for bargaining at all. In particular, the individual author/creator without access to the means of sophisticated technological protection, dissemination and online payment methods (and such persons will continue to exist for a long time, even in the digital environment) would be at a serious disadvantage without copyright in dealing with the entrepreneur who will convert the work into a marketable product. One could of course try to create some sort of 'fair contract' or 'minimum terms' regime for such authors, perhaps akin to the German publishers' contract law found in that country's Copyright Act and significantly amended as recently as 2002.[35] But that instrument assumes the existence of copyright; and the 'minimum contract' that would have to be created in the absence of copyright might end up looking remarkably similar to copyright.

7.16   Further, the economic interests protected by copyright are not limited to those of the author/creator of the work and the entrepreneur who first takes it to market. Since the economic rights protected by copyright are freely transferable to third parties, the person who at any given moment owns the copyright and reaps the economic returns it gives, may well be someone who had no hand in the original production of the work or the product flowing from it. How far such investors in works may deserve the same level of protection as the originators of the work is a nice question: after all, they are risk-takers to a greater extent than those from whom they bought the rights, and they have helped to ensure that the author/creator/first producer does indeed earn reward from their work.[36] Outright transfers of copyright could be banned,[37] but licensing would still be necessary to secure the author's reward; while a licensee would certainly require some incentive in its own right to make the investment in a licence worthwhile.

---

[32] P and R Akester, 'Digital rights management in the 21st century' [2006] EIPR 159.

[33] See further MA Einhorn, *Media, Technology and Copyright: Integrating Law and Economics* (2004); P Akester and F Lima, 'The economic dimension of the digital challenge: a copyright perspective' [2005] IPQ 69; JGH Griffin, 'The changing nature of authorship: why copyright law must focus on the increased role of technology' [2005] IPQ 135.

[34] There are of course issues about such matters as the equivalents to copyright term and exceptions in this model: these are dealt with below, paras 7.45–7.47, 7.51–7.56.

[35] See discussion in WR Cornish, 'The author as risk-taker' (2002–2003) 26 Columbia-VLA J L & Arts 1.

[36] cf F Macmillan, 'Copyright and corporate power', in R Towse (ed), *Copyright in the Cultural Industries* (2002).

[37] As with moral rights: see below, paras 7.38–7.41.

7.17   Contracts, whether between the author/producer and the user of a work, or between authors
and their publishers, are clearly important in the digital world. Many such contracts will be
in non-negotiable standard forms provided on a 'take it or leave it basis'. In general contract
law such standard contracts are well recognised as promoting economic efficiency but as
also requiring policing against the potential for abuse: see for example, the Unfair Contract
Terms Act 1977 and the Unfair Terms in Consumer Contracts Regulations 1999 (implementing an EU Directive of 1994).[38] The English and Scottish Law Commissions published
a report in 2005 recommending general reforms to the law on unfair contract terms:[39] is
something more specific required for copyright contracting? There are already provisions in
the copyright legislation regulating contract terms.[40] The common law on restraint of trade
and undue influence has often been deployed against publishing contracts.[41] But copyright
contracts could be more closely vetted for general unconscionability. There might be protection for copyright exceptions against contractual exclusion (see above, paras 5.59–5.62, and
below, paras 7.58–7.60). Compulsory equitable remuneration provisions, such as already
exist in relation to performers' rights (see para 6.39), could be extended to publishing contracts more generally, as in France and Germany.[42] The jurisdiction of the Copyright Tribunal
to regulate the licensing practices of collecting societies (see para 21.24) could be extended
to cover the activities of all those who engage in 'mass-marketing licensing' (see above para
5.59): that is, put their copyright product on the marketplace for access to anyone prepared to
pay the licence fee or meet any other conditions imposed. An important question is whether
contract law, consumer protection law and competition law deal adequately with copyright
contracting of all kinds, a matter the detailed investigation of which lies beyond the scope
of this chapter.[43] It may be noted that, while users of copyright products can often be at least
analogised with consumers, authors are often persons whose work is being consumed by
their publishers; in a sense, therefore, their claim to protection from market forces is more
like that of the employee in labour law than the consumer. Further, however, and like the
employee who is a member of a trade union or professional association, the author has some
possibility of self-protection through collective action by way of copyright management
societies and pressure groups. But should copyright be displaced altogether by contract in
a digital environment, specifically targeted controls over these contracts would probably
become essential.[44]

 Discussion point   For answer guidance visit www.oxfordtextbooks.co.uk/orc/macqueen2e/

Can contract (often automated in this context) replace copyright in the digital
environment?

---

[38] Council Directive (EEC) 93/13 on unfair terms in consumer contracts.

[39] Report on Unfair Terms in Contracts (Law Com No 292, Scot Law Com No 199: February 2005).

[40] See eg CDPA 1988, s 50A(3), 50B(4), 50D(2), all safeguarding exceptions against contractual exclusion.

[41] See Cornish and Llewelyn, paras 13.28–13.33.

[42] See WR Cornish, 'The author as risk-sharer', (2003) 26 Columbia Journal of Law and the Arts 1.

[43] See further, from a US perspective, P Goldstein, 'Paternalism and autonomy in copyright contracts', in D Vaver and
L Bently (eds), *Intellectual Property in the New Millennium* (2004).

[44] See further L Bently, *Between a Rock and a Hard Place: the Problems Facing Freelance Creators in the UK Media Market-
Place* (2002).

Specific issues

Introduction

7.18   In this section, we turn to look at some more specific issues of copyright law where reform seems necessary, likely or desirable as a result of either (1) the impetus created by the Europeanisation of the subject and international harmonisation, or (2) the impact of technological development, or, quite often, (3) both. The topics are generally treated in the order in which they were dealt with in the preceding five chapters, to facilitate the cross-reference needed in studying the section.

Categories of copyright work

7.19   The initial questions under this heading arise from the process of Europeanisation. Where Continental countries have a strong tradition of distinguishing between authors' rights and neighbouring rights in substance as well as form, and this distinction is reflected in international conventions (Berne and Rome), the UK has awarded copyright to both authors and entrepreneurial producers of works, albeit with differentiated content of rights—for example, clearly distinct copyright terms (see para 2.47). The law purports to draw its distinctions here on the basis of the nature of the work—literary, dramatic, musical, artistic, film, sound recording, broadcast and so on—rather than by way of a distinction between works of authorship and work to do with the media in which the products of authorship are conveyed to their public (if any). In a process of European harmonisation, which of the two approaches is to be preferred? Or is there some third way? The digital environment may suggest that there should be. If increasingly all kinds of work are carried out and fixed (insofar as they are ever fixed) in digital media, is the distinction between authorship and medium increasingly obsolescent? Further, in the post-modern world of culture generally, authors and artists are rejecting past understandings of their respective disciplines and consequent self-imposed limitations, to seek more and more to cross boundaries and use the huge flexibility of digital technology to convey their message, whatever it may be, to the world?[45]

7.20   It seems most likely, however, that for the time being the basic distinction between author and other works will continue to be drawn, if only because it also underlies some of the basic international infrastructure which will not be easily shifted. But nonetheless there may still be questions about the way in which UK law gives effect to the distinction. Only in the 1990s, for example, were films brought into author rather than media work protection in the UK, as a result of the Term Directive (Art 2). As noted in paras 2.49–2.50, the categorisation of author works into literary, dramatic, musical and artistic (not to mention the sub-categorisation within that of artistic works) is problematic, creating the possibility of a single work of authorship being protected in more than one category, or causing uncertainty about the category to which it belongs. None of this is required under the Berne Convention: only protection of 'literary and artistic work',[46] which includes 'every production in the literary, scientific and artistic domain, whatever may be the mode or form of its expression'.[47] The Convention provides an illustrative list of works, while elsewhere, and only so to speak incidentally, it refers to dramatic, musical

[45] See further A Christie, 'A proposal for simplifying UK copyright law' [2001] EIPR 26.
[46] Berne Convention, Art 1.   [47] ibid, Art 2(1).

and cinematographic works.[48] French law speaks of 'works of the mind whatever their kind, form of expression, merit or purpose' and gives thereafter an illustrative list.[49] This approach reduces the need to struggle with categories, albeit it may carry its own obvious uncertainties. But these uncertainties also have the attractive feature of being perhaps more flexible than narrower categories in meeting the emergence of new kinds of work. It also limits the possibility of giving the categories unnecessary or cumbersome substantive content: that is, having rules making it matter whether a work is literary or artistic, musical or dramatic.

7.21   This point can be extended in a return to the distinction between author and media works, where there are major differences in substantive content. An effect of these differences is that many *products* in the copyright domain are likely to enjoy more than one copyright – the basic media right, depending on which medium the product is using, and the right or rights which subsist in the work or works embodied in the product. Each one of these rights may then have a different owner as well as different content (see para 2.47 for examples). This variability of the copyrights which may exist in a single product can mean that while one element of the product is in the public domain, another is not. Several undesirable effects are possible: damage to the remaining copyright interest in the work in question; inhibition of perfectly lawful and appropriate free use of the product; or simply confused people. The issue is focused by the debate about the copyright term in sound recordings, the importance of which in the digital environment is already clear from the controversy about file-sharing and peer-to-peer networks (above, para 7.5). While the right in recordings made in, say, 1959 will expire from 1 January 2010, the rights in the recorded music and song lyrics will continue until 70 years after the deaths of the respective authors. There is thus no danger at all of a rash of unauthorised issues of copies of old recordings of Elvis Presley or Cliff Richard recordings from the 1950s, since that would also involve copying and issuing to the public works that are still in copyright (further, copyrights that presumably would often be held by the recording companies rather than the original authors). Note too, in the context of Europeanisation, that some EU member states treat songs as works of joint authorship between lyricist and composer, meaning that the copyright term in such material is extremely variable across the EU. The Commission paper raises the possibility that the term for songs as a whole should always be calculated in relation to the last-surviving author.[50]

7.22   A question of policy may therefore be whether, when a product enjoys multiple copyrights, these ought to stand and fall together, at least in relation to products of the kind in question; and this, whatever the duration of the rights may finally be.

Fixation

7.23   As noted in paras 2.30–2.33, the Berne Convention allows national law 'to prescribe that works in general or any specified categories of works shall not be protected unless they have been fixed in some material form'.[51] The UK in general requires fixation of a work before copyright can come into existence, leading to some peculiar, even absurd, rules, the effect of which is that while unauthorised recording of my ad lib speech or aleatory musical creation cannot be prevented by

---

[48] ibid, Arts 4, 11, 13 and 14*bis*.

[49] Intellectual Property Code, Art L 112–1, 2. More specific provision has to be made for the neighbouring rights of performers, and producers of phonograms, videograms and audiovisual communications (see Book II of the Code).

[50] Commission 2004 working paper (n 4 above), para 2.2.3.2. See also Institute for Information Law, University of Amsterdam, *The Recasting of Copyright & Related Rights for the Knowledge Economy* (November 2006), Ch 4.

[51] Berne Convention, Art 2(2).

copyright, I can nonetheless control the subsequent reproduction and publication of the recording which has made those words or music the subject of copyright. Other legal systems within the Berne Union exercise their discretion to avoid the imposition of any requirement of fixation. In the UK the requirement in relation to literary, dramatic and musical works appears intended to serve a mainly evidential purpose, but to be cast in a right-constituting form. Consideration might therefore be given to dropping the requirement of fixation in UK law, and to leaving the question of the existence of a literary, dramatic or musical work as a matter of evidence (in which the existence of a recorded form is always likely to be the best kind of evidence).

Originality

7.24 One of the major issues in harmonising copyright in Europe has been the different traditions of the UK and the Continent with regard to originality (see paras 2.34–2.46). Speaking very generally, Continental systems require works to manifest *'intellectual creation'*, and this is the standard which has so far been applied in those EU Directives referring to the matter.[52] The CDPA 1988 still says, however, that to have copyright, literary, dramatic, musical and artistic works must all be original,[53] a threshold generally taken to be less demanding than that of intellectual creation although it is left undefined by the statute. There is no express requirement of originality as such in relation to films, sound recordings, broadcasts, and typographical arrangements of published editions,[54] but copyright does not subsist in any such work which is, or to the extent that it is, respectively, a copy taken from a previous film or sound recording, or reproduces the typographical arrangement of a previous edition, as the case may be.[55] The basic idea apparent in these rules certainly also captures at least one aspect of 'originality' in the context of literary, dramatic, musical and artistic works, namely, that to have copyright they must *not be copies of preceding works*. Another theme found in discussions of originality is the test of the *effort, skill and labour* which the author has invested in the work. Where this test is satisfied, there is likely to be a copyright in the result. But the production of a copy of a work may involve considerable labour and no little skill; yet in that case there will be no originality and no copyright.[56]

7.25 The question of how to choose between the two standards in developing a copyright law suitable for the digital environment seems so far to have been resolved in favour of the Continental approach. In 1991 the Software Directive declared that 'a computer program shall be protected if it is original in the sense that it is the author's own intellectual creation'.[57] However the UK took no action to implement the formula in its resultant legislation, and the Commission took no action to suggest that this failure involved non-compliance with the Directive. A different result occurred, however, in the implementation of the Database Directive, which again used the phrase *'the author's own intellectual creation'* in defining the object of protection.[58] The phrase now appears in s 3A of the CDPA 1988 with regard to database copyright:

> 'A literary work consisting of a database is original if, and only if, by reason of the selection or arrangement of the contents of the database the database constitutes *the author's own intellectual creation*.' (emphasis added)

---

[52] Software and Database Directives, see further below, para 7.25.   [53] Section 1(1)(a).
[54] CDPA 1988, s 1(1)(b).
[55] CDPA 1988, ss 5A(2), 5B(5), 8(2). The 1988 Act provides that copyright does not subsist in a broadcast which infringes, or to the extent that it infringes, the copyright in another broadcast. The background to this is explained at para 2.46.
[56] *Interlego AG v Tyco Industries Inc* [1989] AC 217.   [57] Software Directive, Art 1(3).
[58] Database Directive, Art 3(1).

7.26   Thus the test of originality *for databases* in the UK is not the same as for other literary works. As a result, many databases which would have been protected by copyright before s 3A was introduced are no longer. This is why the *sui generis* database right was created, establishing a special new and additional form of protection for databases even if they did not attract copyright under the more rigorous originality test (see para 6.4). The aim was clearly to provide an alternative for those who would have had copyright in places such as the UK before the Directive. But this development raises questions at least about the lack of express implementation of the higher standard of originality with regard to computer programs; and more widely with regard to what a genuinely Europe-wide and comprehensive test of originality should be for, not just digital, but all copyright purposes (assuming that there should be such a test, which may also be a question suitable for investigation). The Commission Consultation Paper of 2004 concluded that, in the absence of contrary evidence, the difference between UK and Continental standards is not creating a problem for the functioning of the Internal Market and therefore there is no need for legislative action 'at this stage'.[59]

7.27   There have, however, been relevant developments in the Common Law world outside England, seeming to elevate 'skill' over 'labour' in the traditional test of originality. In the USA, the standard of 'originality' was raised by the Supreme Court in 1991, in *Feist v Rural Telephone Service Company Inc*, a case concerned with whether a telephone directory enjoyed copyright.[60] In answering the question negatively, *Feist* recast the originality requirement in US law, from a 'sweat of the brow' test to one of 'spark of creativity'. But *Feist* must be seen in the context of its own facts, namely, once again, the protection of a compilation or database. In this context, what copyright protects is, in the language of the Berne Convention, the 'selection and arrangement' of the contents of the work, and since all subscribers were included in the directory, and alphabetical listing was the only possible usable way of presenting the results, the originality of the selection and arrangement was indeed negligible.

7.28   The decision equivalent to *Feist* in Canada is *Tele-Direct (Publications) Inc v American Business Information*.[61] The case concerned the yellow pages section of a telephone directory, and again it was held that there was insufficient originality for copyright. But a later court confined *Tele-Direct* to the compilation/database area, saying that difficulties arose there 'because such works are not likely to exhibit, on their face, indicia of the author's personal style or manner of expression'.[62] *Tele-Direct* has also been the subject of criticism by the Federal Court of Appeal in *CCH Canadian Ltd v Law Society of Upper Canada*,[63] a case about the copyright in law reports rather than databases. On appeal in that case the Supreme Court took up a mid-position, emphasising that originality lay, not in either labour and 'sweat of the brow' or 'sparks of creativity', but in the author's exercise of skill and judgement.[64] In Australia, the Federal Court held in *Telstra Corporation Ltd v Desktop Marketing Systems Pty Ltd*,[65] after a full analysis of the English, Australian, Canadian and US authorities, that both yellow and white pages directories involved sufficient originality to attract copyright. Finkelstein J emphasised the need to consider each directory as a whole and highlighted the importance of the directories' 'information pages', which included such things as lists of emergency telephone numbers and information about the cost of calls and international calls. In other words, originality involved something extra

---

[59] Para 3.1.   [60] 499 US 340 (1991).   [61] [1998] 2 FC 22 (CA); leave to appeal to SCC denied [1998] 1 SCR xv.
[62] *Hager v ECW Press Ltd* [1999] 2 FC at 311 (para 42).   [63] [2002] 4 FC 213 (CA).
[64] *Law Society of Upper Canada v CCH Canadian Ltd* [2004] 1 SCR 339, paras 14–25, per McLachlin CJ.
[65] [2001] FCA 612.

beyond the mere labour of listing the names of subscribers; perhaps best described as decision-making about arrangement of the material.

7.29 Adoption of a higher threshold criterion of originality (or equivalent) might remove from the ambit of copyright some of the relatively trivial and ephemeral material currently within its scope. The disadvantage would be that someone (ultimately the courts) would have to take the decision as to which side of the line any given work fell on. The possibility of seeming absurdity would be replaced by perhaps dangerous uncertainty. It should be noted, moreover, that nearly all of the discussion of a higher standard in the Common Law world has been in the probably special context of databases where already the UK is applying a higher standard for copyright purposes (although not for the *sui generis* right).

7.30 An alternative approach would be to drop any threshold test whatsoever. Possibly this might sit best in a world where copyright had been displaced by contract, with the material which its producer did not want disseminated to a wider world being protected by laws of confidentiality and privacy (for which see Chapter 18). The protection afforded by contract would be relevant for any item for which a buyer was prepared to pay; that of confidentiality and privacy for material which was indeed confidential or private and which the producer was not prepared to sell or give away.

7.31 The policy issue here is the desirability of threshold tests such as 'originality' or 'intellectual creation', in particular in the digital environment, and what the consequences would be if (1) a higher threshold was adopted generally, beyond the subject matter of databases? or (2) there was no threshold test at all?

Databases: other issues

7.32 There are still more fundamental issues about the *sui generis* right protecting databases. Since the right protects the *contents* of the database, and not just the *selection and arrangement* thereof, does it go beyond the traditional exclusion of information as such from the scope of copyright protection? Does it preclude access to that which in the past has circulated freely amongst would-be users? An example which has been much discussed is scientific information, now commonly held on databases.[66] The Commission published a Communication on database rights in December 2005.[67] This notes that decisions of the ECJ have limited the protection conferred by the *sui generis* right.[68] The Commission's research suggests that the *sui generis* right has anyway failed to achieve its objective of boosting the global competitiveness of the European database industry (although the UK continues to be the leading member state in the field). Abolition of the right is accordingly one of the options under consideration by the Commission, along with amendment of the Directive to reverse the effects of the Court decisions, repeal of the whole Directive, or doing nothing, simply awaiting further judicial decisions. The last always looked

---

[66] See the Report of the Royal Society (London), *Keeping Science Open* (2003), Ch 5 (accessible at http://royalsociety.org/Report_WF.aspx?pageid=9842&terms=open; C Waelde, 'Creating a scientific research commons: practical experience' (2004) Molengrafica: Intellectual Property Law 155.

[67] *First Evaluation of Directive 96/9/EC on the Legal Protection of Databases* Brussels 12.12.2005, accessible at http://ec.europa.eu/internal_market/copyright/docs/databases/evaluation_report_en.pdf.

[68] The decisions are Case C-46/02 *Fixtures Marketing Ltd v Oy Veikkaus AB* [2004] ECR I-10365; Case-C 203/02 *British Horseracing Board v William Hill Organization Ltd* Case [2004] ECR I-10415; Case C-338/02 *Fixtures Marketing Ltd v Svenska Spel AB* [2004] ECR I-10497; and Case C-444/02 *Fixtures Marketing Ltd v OPAP* [2004] ECR I-10549; and the aftermath of the *BHB v Hill* case in the Court of Appeal, reported at [2005] RPC 35. See above, paras 6.4–6.20.

the likeliest outcome, and the cases that have emerged have shown a broader view being taken of the right's scope.[69]

7.33   The policy issue that remains here, however, is fundamental: does the *sui generis* database right serve any useful purpose, and if it does, should it be amended in any way in particular following the decisions of the ECJ in the fixtures and horse-racing cases?[70]

Ownership: employment

7.34   Under UK (but not Continental) laws, where an employee creates a work in the course of employment, the employer gets first ownership of the resulting copyright.[71] Given that the employer is an investor who is backing the production of copyright works, his gaining the copyright (at least in its economic aspects) and the return therefrom does not seem so dreadful as is sometimes suggested by those from systems more focused on copyright as reflecting more of personality rights than economic interests. The Software Directive laid down that the economic rights in a computer program should go to the employer unless otherwise provided by contract,[72] thus pointing Europeanisation for the digital environment in a UK or Anglo-American direction; but there has been no similar provision in any subsequent Directive.

7.35   Were a European copyright law to follow the UK model and give an employer the first copyright in an employee's work, a question might arise as to how to compensate the latter for the loss of the right that would otherwise have fallen to him. Patent law provides a possible example: the employer is entitled to patent inventions by employees working in the course of their employment, but the employee has a right to participate in the economic benefit which the work brings to the employer.[73] However, that scheme does not appear to have been regularly used and is not easy to apply.[74] But this may also be because well-advised employers put in place suitable or satisfactory schemes of their own devising as part of the contract of employment. Another model of possible relevance is the artists' resale right, introduced into UK law on 14 February 2006 (see paras 3.44–3.46). The right guarantees the original artist a share of the returns being earned from sales of the original art work, regardless of whether the artist still owns the copyright in the work in question.

7.36   Were an employee reward scheme along this or similar lines to be introduced into copyright, the question of whether it should be a default scheme subject to contract would have to be addressed; the precedent of the Software Directive suggests that it would be such a scheme.

Ownership: orphan works

7.37   One further issue related to the ownership of copyright is of considerable practical significance. Since copyright in author works extends well after the death of the author (and the date of that event may be difficult to ascertain), would-be users and re-publishers of works who wish to comply with the law frequently find it impracticable or impossible to take the necessary steps to do what they want to do lawfully, that is, find out whether a work is still in copyright and, if so, who is now the owner. At present the law offers certain protections to such persons only where authors have made it very difficult to identify themselves, by means of anonymity or pseudonymity.[75] These protections themselves cause certain difficulties in many cases. The

---

[69] See above, para 6.14.   [70] See further A Mazumdar, 'Information, copyright and the future' [2007] EIPR 180.
[71] Above, paras 3.25–3.28.   [72] Software Directive, Art 2(3).   [73] Patents Act 1977, ss 39–43.
[74] See further paras 11.160–11.165 below.   [75] CDPA 1988, s 9(4), (5), 12(3)–(5); above, paras 3.23–3.24, 3.53.

British Academy identified the issue as one of significance for academic research in the humanities and social sciences,[76] and the issue was also sharply focused in the debate about the Google Book Settlement. The US Register of Copyrights published a Report on Orphan Works on 31 January 2006, broadly recommending that 'if the user has performed a reasonably diligent search for the copyright owner but is unable to locate that owner, then that user should enjoy a benefit of limitations on the remedies that a copyright owner could obtain against him if the owner showed up at a later date and sued for infringement';[77] this was implemented in the Shawn Bentley Orphan Works Act of 2008. The Gowers Review supported the introduction of a copyright exception permitting the use of genuine orphan works provided the user had made a reasonable search and, where possible, given attribution.[78] One alternative solution would be a copyright registration system, but that would presumably be a radical step too far, since it is inconsistent with the Berne Convention.[79] In July 2008 the European Commission published a Green Paper entitled *Copyright in the Knowledge Economy*,[80] which discussed orphan works within the context of the best dissemination of knowledge in the digital environment for the purposes of research, science and education, and raised the possibility of Community legislative intervention in order to ensure a harmonised cross-border approach by member states. This would build on a recommendation of the Commission,[81] encouraging member states to create mechanisms to facilitate the use of orphan works, as well as the Final Report and Memorandum of Understanding produced by a High Level Expert Group on Digital Libraries on Digital Preservation, Orphan Works and Out-of-Print Works and signed by representatives of libraries, archives and rightholders. The Memorandum contains a set of guidelines on diligent search for rightholders and general principles concerning databases of orphan works and rights clearance mechanisms, leaving detailed solutions for development at national level.[82] In the UK, the Digital Economy Bill presented to Parliament in November 2009 contains a provision enabling the Secretary of State to make regulations under which a licensing body could either do or grant licences to do acts in relation to an orphan work which would otherwise require the consent of the copyright owner.[83]

Question

Ought the law to provide that where it is impossible to identify by reasonable inquiry whether a work is still in copyright or who the owner of any copyright is, the performance of the restricted acts will not be infringement of copyright provided that the original work receives due acknowledgement, attribution, and respect for its integrity in the new one?

---

[76] British Academy Review, *Copyright and Research in the Humanities and Social Sciences* (2006), para 43.

[77] From the report's executive summary (accessible at http://www.copyright.gov/orphan/).

[78] Gowers Review, Ch 4.91–4.99, recommendation 13. See also Institute for Information Law, University of Amsterdam, *The Recasting of Copyright & Related Rights for the Knowledge Economy* (November 2006), Ch 6; S Teng, 'The orphan works dilemma and museums: an uncomfortable straitjacket' (2007) 2 JIPLP 30.

[79] Berne Convention, Art 5(2) ('the enjoyment and exercise of [copyright] shall not be subject to any formality'). Note however Gowers Review, recommendation 14b: '*The Patent Office should establish a voluntary register of copyright; either on its own, or through partnerships with database holders . . .*' See also ibid, para 4.101.

[80] Brussels, COM(2008) 466/3, accessible at http://ec.europa.eu/internal_market/copyright/copyright-infso/copyright-infso_en.htm#Communication_Copyright_in_the_Knowledge_Economy.

[81] 2006/585/EC, L 236/28.

[82] See http://ec.europa.eu/information_society/activities/digital_libraries/experts/hleg/index_en.htm). See also the Joint Copyright Guidelines produced in the UK in April 2008 by the British Academy and the Publishers Association (http://www.britac.ac.uk/policy/joint-copyright-guide.cfm), section 8.

[83] Digital Economy Bill, clause 42. The regulations would define orphan works, presumably more widely than the present limited provisions.

Further reading

Books

General

Cornish & Llewelyn, *Intellectual Property* (6th edn, 2007), Ch 20.3

Laddie, Prescott & Vitoria, *Modern Law of Copyright* (3rd edn, 2000), Chs 1 and 34A

Debating the role of copyright in the digital environment: current issues

L Bently, *Between a Rock and a Hard Place: the Problems Facing Freelance Creators in the UK Media Market-Place* (2002)

WR Cornish, *Intellectual Property: Omnipresent, Distracting, Irrelevant?* (2004), Chapter 2

W Davies and K Withers, *Public Innovation: Intellectual Property in a Digital Age* (Institute of Public Policy Research, 2006)

European Commission Staff Working Paper on the review of the EC legal framework in the field of copyright and related rights, SEC (2004) 995

Gowers Review of Intellectual Property (HM Treasury, 2006), Chapter 4.

PB Hugenholtz (ed), *The Future of Copyright in a Digital Environment* (1996)

Institute for Information Law, University of Amsterdam, *The Recasting of Copyright & Related Rights for the Knowledge Economy* (European Commission DG Internal Market Study, November 2006)

J Litman, *Digital Copyright* (2001)

L Lessig, *Free Culture: How Big Media Uses Technology and the Law to Lock Down Culture and Control Creativity* (2004)

Articles

Debating the role of copyright in the digital environment: current issues

A Christie, 'Reconceptualising copyright in the digital age' [1995] EIPR 522

T Dreier, 'Copyright in the age of digital technology' (1993) 24 IIC 481

Part III

Design protection

Introduction

This Part follows on from the Copyright Part of the book, to consider a particular kind of work that might have been protected by copyright alone but for which there has been—sometimes instead of, sometimes as well as, copyright—a special regime or set of regimes since the 19th century. Traditionally the works in question were the designs of industrial products, meaning very broadly either the three-dimensional shape or configuration of a product, or the two-dimensional pattern, colouring or ornamentation applied to the surface of a product. The context in which this right developed was industrial and commercial; the concern was typically with the end results of mass production rather than the individual creative efforts which were seen as the essence of copyright. In any event, in the 19th century copyright had still not been generalised, and there were several different statutes each covering particular types of work—literature, sculpture, fine art, and so on. The system of design protection which was created alongside copyright survived the great generalisation of the Copyright Act 1911 because it was used and found useful in several industries. It also reflected what had become general government policy in the course of the 19th century, namely the support of good design, which was supposed to give products a competitive edge in the market place.

The basic form of design protection depended upon registration of the design in a public register maintained by government. In this feature design protection was like that provided by patents and trade marks, but unlike copyright from the 1911 Act on. Registration provided publicity, not only about who owned a design, but also about designs in general. Any member of the public could study design at the registry, just as inventions and trade marks could be studied. Registration continues to be a major feature of design protection down to the present day, and although its future has sometimes been questioned, at present the system appears secure. Chapter 8 thus deals in detail with protection of designs by way of registration. A key point is that to be registered, a design must meet certain criteria.

A difficulty, however, is and always has been the design that is not registered. A design may be unregistered for a variety of reasons: the designer did not know about the registration system; or chose not to register; or the design did not meet the criteria for registration laid down by the law. Many such unregistered designs might however attract copyright protection. This created an anomaly. Registered design protection was different from copyright protection: it was shorter in terms of time, although it gave a monopoly right rather than simple protection against copying. So the law-makers have had to make decisions about whether to allow, exclude or restrict copyright in the context of unregistered designs.

As Chapter 9 explains, views have changed from time to time on this question. By the time of the Copyright, Designs and Patents Act 1988, however, it had become clear that while copyright could not be excluded altogether from the field, it should be severely restricted; and the Act sets out to do this. The 1988 Act also introduced a new right, the unregistered design right, by which it was sought to give appropriately limited protection to such designs. The protection had to be less than that available through registration, since otherwise the latter would become completely unattractive to users, but had to provide enough value to make the inappropriate use of copyright completely unnecessary.

A further layer of complexity came about in the 1990s, however, when the EU set about the creation of a system of registered design protection for the whole Union, and decided that this should be supplemented by a system of unregistered design protection. This was achieved by way of a Regulation on Community designs in 2001. A Directive was also promulgated in 1998 under which the national systems of design registration were harmonised with each other and the new EU-wide system; but this contained no measure to harmonise unregistered design protection. The UK has chosen to continue with its unregistered design system, which is very different from the EU-wide one.

Thus Chapter 9, which considers unregistered design protection, has to deal with three different sets of rules, viz:

- Copyright so far as it has a role in relation to unregistered designs
- UK unregistered design right
- EU unregistered design right

Sources of the law: key websites

- UK–IPO
  http://www.ipo.gov.uk/design.htm
- OHIM
  http://oami.europa.eu/en/design/default.htm
- European Commission Internal Market Directorate-General
  http://ec.europa.eu/internal_market/indprop/design/index_en.htm
- Decisions of the courts in the various jurisdictions in the UK are available at BAILII
  http://www.bailii.org/

Registered designs

Introduction

Scope and overview of chapter

8.1 This chapter deals with the law of registered designs, leaving the protection of unregistered designs for Chapter 9. It considers which designs may be made the subject of registration and the nature of the rights conferred, including some important limitations upon them. The rules on these matters are the same whether one is seeking registration in the UK or throughout the EU, so both these aspects are treated together. The chapter does not provide a detailed description or analysis of the registration process, which lies beyond the scope of this book. That information should be sought instead in one of the practitioner works on the subject.

8.2 ### Learning objectives

By the end of this chapter you should be able to describe and explain:

- the international context for modern design law;
- the criteria designs must meet to be registered;
- the special rules dealing with the designs of complex products and spare parts for such products;
- the basic elements of the registration process;
- how a registration may be challenged as invalid;
- the rights given as a result of a valid registration;
- the defences available to a party sued for infringement of a registered design.

8.3 The chapter begins by explaining the international context of design law, which is more fragmentary and less detailed than for copyright law. International agreements allow designs to have special protection over and above that which they may also receive from copyright. In the UK there is a long history of using a registration process as the primary means of protecting product designs, although the current shape of the law is largely the outcome of EU-driven reforms introduced early this century. The chapter then proceeds to look at the substantive law of registered designs: what designs may be registered (including the difficult problem of 'complex products' and 'spare parts'), what is involved in the registration process, challenging the validity of a registration, the rights conferred by a valid registration, and the defences available to a party sued for infringement of a registered design. So the rest of the chapter looks like this:

- The international background to the current law (8.4–8.9)
- Development of UK and EU law (8.10–8.14)
- Designs that can be protected by registration (8.15–8.48)
- Complex products and spare parts (8.49–8.69)
- Registration (8.70–8.85)
- Declarations of invalidity (8.86–8.88)
- Rights given by registration (8.89–8.102)
- Defences (8.103–8.107)

The international background to the current law

8.4   Unlike copyright law, with its long-established Berne Convention, there is no international treaty setting out the minimum substantive content of protection for industrial designs. The Paris Convention does provide that: 'industrial designs shall be protected in all countries of the Union' (Article 5 *quinquies*) but leaves open how that protection is to be given. Thus designs may be protected through a registration system or not; or indeed through a combination of the two. The Berne Convention opened up the possibility of copyright protection for industrial designs, referring to works of applied art and to industrial designs and models; but this merely gave its members freedom to determine the application (or not) of their copyright laws to such works (Article 2(7)) and to decide the term of protection for 'works of applied art in so far as they are artistic works', subject to a minimum of 25 years from the making of the work (Article 7(4)). Berne adds the following, however, ensuring that a distinction is drawn between copyright and design protection where systems for the latter exist:

> 'Works protected in the country of origin solely as designs and models shall be entitled in another country of the Union only to such special protection as is granted in that country to designs and models; however, if no such special protection is granted in that country, such works shall be protected as artistic works' (Article 2(7)).

Thus international law allows copyright protection for industrial designs, but tends to exclude it for foreigners in countries where special non-copyright rules exist.

 Question

In what ways does international law allow designs to be protected?

8.5   Consistently with its general approach to industrial property protection based on registration (national treatment for non-nationals), the Paris Convention also requires its member states to allow foreigners access to national design registration systems, with an application in one Union country giving a priority in the others (that is, meaning that the applicant was to be treated as the first applicant in all Paris states and not just the one in which the application happened to be made). The Hague Agreement concerning the International Deposit of Industrial Designs (1925, revised 1960) simply provided a means whereby a deposit in Geneva gave rise to protection in the Agreement's member states, and contained no substantive provisions on the content of design protection. On 2 July 1999 consensus was reached on a New Act of the Hague Agreement, known as the Geneva Act, and it entered into force on 23 December 2003. The Geneva Act enhances the international registration system by making it more compatible with the systems in countries where, as in the UK, applications are subject to examination before registration. Countries must process international registrations according to their own legislation within a period of six months which may be extended by a further six months for those countries whose law requires examination. The Act also modifies the fee system, and gives the possibility of deferring publication of a design for up to 30 months as well as the ability to file samples of the design rather than photographs or other graphic reproductions.[1]

8.6 In 1968 the Locarno Agreement Establishing an International Classification for Industrial Designs (the *Locarno Classification*) was concluded. The Classification currently consists of 32 classes and 223 sub-classes of design together with a list of over 6,800 kinds of goods incorporating industrial designs indicating into which class or sub-class they fall. The lists are updated every five years, and the current edition (the ninth) was promulgated on 1 January 2009. Designs registries of the contracting states must include in the file for the deposit or registration of industrial designs the numbers of the classes and sub-classes of the Classification into which the goods incorporating the designs belong. The UK is one of the contracting parties, along with 42 other states and the European Union. MARQUES, an association of trade mark proprietors, has proposed that the Locarno system be updated to ensure that when searches are conducted, the classification considers what the design looks like, instead of exclusively what it does.[2]

? Question

What are the major international agreements regarding design registration, and what is their effect?

8.7 TRIPS contains two Articles on design protection (Articles 25, 26). These deal with substantive matters of design law in a little more detail than previous instruments, and may be taken to reflect a degree of international consensus as to the minimum content of design law. States are to provide for the protection of independently created industrial designs that are new or original. They may provide that designs are not new or original if they do not significantly differ from known designs or combinations of known design features. It may also be provided that protection is not to extend to designs dictated essentially by technical or functional

---

[1] The EU acceded to the Geneva Act of the Hague Agreement in 2008, linking the Community Registered Design to the international system.

[2] See MARQUES, 'Position Paper on Proposed Changes to the Locarno Classification System for Industrial Designs', 23 October 2008, available at http://www.marques.org/Downloads/Locarno%20Classificaton%20Position%20Paper. pdf. See further J Phillips, 'Locarno in the limelight' (2009) 4 JIPLP 1. It appears that the ninth edition of the system has not taken up the proposals. In its guidance to classification, it states: 'In principle, goods are classified first according to their purpose and subsidiarily, if this is possible, according to the object that they represent. This latter classification is optional.'

considerations. The costs and requirements for obtaining protection should not unreasonably impair the opportunity to seek or obtain such protection. Members are free to meet this last obligation through industrial design law or copyright. The owner of a protected industrial design must have the right to prevent unauthorised others making, selling or importing articles bearing or embodying a design which is a copy, or substantially a copy, of the protected design, when such acts are undertaken for commercial purposes. There may be limited exceptions to design rights, so long as they do not unreasonably conflict with normal exploitation or unreasonably prejudice the legitimate interests of the owner. However this adoption of the Berne formula for restricting the scope of exceptions is qualified, because account must also be taken of the legitimate interests of third parties. Finally, the protection must last for at least 10 years.

 Question

What is the minimum content of design protection law under TRIPS?

Key points on international framework of designs law

- The international framework of designs law has had, until relatively recently, very little substantive content

- Individual states have considerable discretion as to how to protect industrial designs

- Protection may be by means of copyright, although the Berne Convention then imposes some possible limits as to the term of protection

- Alternatively states may adopt a special system for the protection of designs

- There is no need for that system to be one of registration; but where a registration system exists non-nationals must be given access to it, and in general its costs and procedural requirements must not be such as to deter applicants

- TRIPS has increased the minimum content of designs protection, without limiting the options as to whether it is achieved through registration, a non-registration system, copyright or some combination of these

---

8.8   The essence of the minimum content as found in TRIPs can be put like this:

- Designs to be new/original/independently created
- Designs dictated by technical/functional considerations do not have to be protected
- Exclusive right is to manufacture/sell/import commercially articles bearing/embodying the design
- Exceptions allowed if consistent with normal exploitation/do not prejudice owner's legitimate interests
- Exceptions can take account of legitimate interests of third parties
- Duration at least 10 years (note also Berne minimum of 25 years for works of applied art in so far as works of art)

8.9 The low demands made of states by international law in the field of design protection led to very variable national protection, with each country tending to develop its own idiosyncratic system. However, the relatively recent achievement of the minimum standard set down in the TRIPS Agreement may be the first step towards a better harmonised global picture. In the EU, as will be seen in more detail below, further steps were taken with a Directive in 1998 which harmonised the registration systems of protection found in member states; while a Regulation which entered into force in 2002 has created an EU-wide system which offers protection for designs similar to that now found in each of the member states (see further below, paras 8.11–8.13).

 Question

What were the main objectives of the EU legislation on design protection?

Development of UK and EU law

UK law: history

8.10 Only the briefest reference to the development of registered design law in the UK is possible here; a fuller account may be found on this book's Online Resource Centre. The UK has had a registration process for the legal protection of product designs since the 18th century. The latest piece of primary legislation is the Registered Designs Act 1949 (RDA 1949) although, as we shall see, that has been extensively amended. The key points to note are as follows. For most of the 20th century, the legislation sought to exclude purely functional designs from registration. The period of protection was much shorter than copyright, while the rights conferred by registration were essentially those of a commercial monopoly of the exploitation of the design; it was not necessary to show that an infringer had copied from the registered design.

EU Regulation and Directives

8.11 In the late 1980s the EU began to take a serious interest in design law as part of its efforts to ensure that different national intellectual property laws did not pose unnecessary barriers to the creation of a single market in Europe. The ECJ had held in 1982 that a design registration system (in the case, the Benelux system) was 'industrial and commercial property', the rights in which might be exercised in derogation from the free movement of goods within the European Community, provided that the goods in question had not already been put on the market in the exporting member state by or with the consent of the right holder.[3] Thus a national design right might be used to prevent the import of goods lawfully produced in their territory of origin even if that was another member state. Further, given that the national laws varied considerably across the member states, a party who had rights in a design in one member state might have lost (for example, because they had expired), or be unable to obtain, equivalent rights in another member state.

---

[3] Case 144/81, *Keurkoop v Nancy Kean* [1982] ECR 2853.

8.12   Although agreement on the matter took a decade and more to achieve, the EU did finally settle on two steps with regard to the protection of industrial designs: (1) harmonisation of the different national laws of member states, achieved under a Directive promulgated in 1998; and (2) creation of a European system of design protection alongside the harmonised national laws, which took effect by way of a Regulation which came into effect on 6 March 2002. Both steps were founded on registration systems as the principal way of protecting designs, although as will be discussed further in Chapter 9, some provision was made in the Regulation for the protection of unregistered designs. In the UK, the effect of the Directive was the substantial amendment of the RDA 1949, by way of the Registered Design Regulations which came into force on 9 December 2001.[4] The Community Designs Register began to receive applications for registration at the Office for Harmonisation in the Internal Market (OHIM) in Alicante, Spain, and at various national offices, on 1 January 2003.[5]

8.13   For the purposes of the present chapter, the important point about the two pieces of European legislation was that they created a basically unified substantive law of registered designs in the EU. The rules on protectable designs, infringement and defences for the harmonised national laws and for the new Europe-wide system are the same, meaning that they can be treated together in this chapter. This means that it will be necessary in Britain to follow closely, not only the decisions of the Designs Registry and the courts in the UK, but also those of OHIM, the Court of Justice of the European Union, and the courts of other member states, in order to ensure that the aim of the legislation—a unified and harmonious approach to design protection in Europe—is fulfilled. Probably the easiest way to do this is via the OHIM website http://oami.europa.eu/ows/rw/pages/RCD/caseLaw/caseLaw.en.do.

  Question

What was the effect upon UK law of the EU legislation on design protection?

Key points on EU developments

- The intervention of the EU in designs law came about to prevent differences in national laws creating an obstacle to the single European market by preventing the free movement of goods

- There are two major European instruments:
  - The 1998 Directive, harmonising the registered design laws of the EU member states
  - The 2001 Regulation, setting up an EU-wide register, but using the same rules as the Directive

- The result is that there are EU-wide and member state systems of registered designs running in parallel.

---

[4] SI 2001/3949. A complex question challenging the constitutional validity of the Regulations was answered in the negative by the Court of Appeal in *Oakley Inc v Animal Ltd* [2006] RPC 9.

[5] The UK Community Designs Regulations (SI 2005/2339) make supplemental provisions ensuring that Community designs have the same protections as UK registered designs (eg against groundless threats of infringement).

8.14   The treatment which follows is based upon the RDA 1949 in its current form, but reference is made where appropriate to the 1998 Directive, the 2001 Regulation, and the approach being taken within the EU.

Designs that can be protected by registration

8.15   Before a product design can be registered, it must meet the following criteria:

- the design must fall within the definition of design given by the legislation (below, para 8.16);
- the design must be new and have individual character;
- features of the design's appearance which are solely dictated by the product's technical function cannot be protected by registration;
- design rights do not subsist in designs contrary to public policy or to accepted principles of morality.

Each of these criteria will now be discussed in turn. The first two may be described as positive requirements—features that a design must have to be registered—while the other two are exclusionary in character—either the design should be refused registration or should not have been registered (see further below, paras 8.86–8.88) or, if a registered design consists in part of such features, the right conferred by registration does not extend to those features. It is important to note that the Registrar is effectively obliged to accept applications for registration unless the Act's requirements are not met, or the applicant is not the owner of the design, or the application has otherwise not followed the correct procedures.[6]

Definition of design

8.16   Design means:

> 'the *appearance* of the whole or a part of a product resulting from the features of, in particular, the lines, contours, colours, shape, texture or materials of the product or its ornamentation' (RDA 1949, s 1(2); DD, Art 1(a); CDR, Art 3(a)).

8.17   The essence of this definition is that design is about the *appearance* of a *product*. The lawyer is at once led to two questions:

- What is a product?
- Does appearance mean that design is confined to what is visible in a product, and what does that mean?

Product

8.18   Product is defined as:

> 'any industrial or handicraft item other than a computer program; and in particular includes packaging, get-up, graphic symbols, typographic typefaces and parts intended to be assembled into a complex product' (RDA 1949, s 1(2); DD, Art 1(b); CDR, Art 3(b)).

---

[6] RDA 1949, s 3A as amended by Regulatory Reform (Registered Designs) Order 2006, Art 5 (note also that Art 3 repealed the former s 1A of the RDA 1949).

8.19   An immediately striking feature of this definition is its inclusion of 'handicraft' items as well as those produced by industrial process, so that the design of single or unique items may be protectable as well as the results of mass production processes.

8.20   Further, the inclusion of matter such as get-up and graphic symbols as products represents at least a change in the way in which the subject is approached. In the pre-Directive UK law, these might have been seen as designs applied to a product—pattern or ornamentation, in the original words of the RDA 1949. But now they are to be seen as products themselves. In other words, products may be two-dimensional.[7] Similarly under the pre-Directive law typefaces could not be registered as designs because it was not thought possible to regard each character as an 'article' (the concept equivalent to 'product'), nor the whole collection of characters as satisfying the former test for a registrable *set* of articles, because not all the articles bore the same design or had the same design with modifications or variations insufficient to alter the character or substantially affect the identity of the design.[8] Now however typefaces are expressly included in the definition of product and the designs may be registered for protection.[9] The old law also contained at least some doubt as to whether designs for packaging could be registered,[10] but it is now clear that this is so.

 Question

Explain how we can tell from the legislation that two-dimensional designs are now protectable by registration.

8.21   The new law's coverage of two-dimensional products raises issues about overlap with copyright protection which the old law used to avoid by denying registration to items of a primarily literary or artistic character where the article was no more than a carrier for the design. Copyright was expected to provide the necessary protection (as it certainly did with typefaces). The test of excluding products which had no other function than to carry the designs for which registration was sought derived from *Littlewood's Pools Ltd's Application*,[11] where it was held that the pattern of words and lines on a football pools coupon was not a registrable design, since the paper which constituted the article to which the design was applied had no function other than to carry the design. The result would now be different, even although the pools coupon also has copyright.[12] On the other hand the design applied to wallpaper, chair covers or bed linen would have been registrable under the old law and continues to be so now.

---

[7] See for examples of invalidity decisions on two-dimensional products (labels for vodka bottles, and logos), *Monika Barber v J & J Décor and Hee Jung Kim v Zellweger Analytics Ltd*, both OHIM Invalidity Division, 1 and 29 March 2006 respectively. See also A Kur, 'No logo!' (2004) 35 IIC 184. The registration of such designs raises overlap questions in respect of trade marks: see further A Carboni, 'The overlap between registered Community designs and Community trade marks' (2006) 1 JIPLP 259.

[8] 'The point is that "A" is different from "B" ' (*Copyright and Designs Law: Report of the Committee to consider the Law on Copyright and Designs* (the Whitford Report) (Cmnd 6732, 1977), para 521).

[9] For an example of an OHIM Invalidity Division decision on typefaces, see *Heidelberger Druckmaschinen AG v Microsoft Corp*, 6 Feb 2006.

[10] See *H Klarmann Ltd v Henshaw Linen Supplies* [1960] RPC 150, where the design of a disposable plastic bag covered with advertising matter was held prima facie excluded from registration.

[11] (1949) 66 RPC 309.   [12] *Ladbroke (Football) Ltd v William Hill (Football)Ltd* [1964] 1 WLR 273 (HL).

Exercise

Consider whether the following are products the appearance of which may constitute a registrable design:

- Book dustjacket
- Calendar
- Dress making pattern
- Map
- Playing cards
- Painting
- Typographical arrangement of this book
- Computer screen icons[13]
- A web page
- Tattoos

8.22 Similar questions can arise with three-dimensional products which may fall within the scope of artistic copyright, such as sculptures, works of artistic craftsmanship and, perhaps most significant of all, works of architecture. The indeterminate word 'item' which appears in the definition of 'product' certainly does not by itself limit the concept to goods or corporeal moveables. Under the old law, buildings were excluded because they were not items of manufacture; it might be rather a difficult question whether or not modern buildings are 'industrial or handicraft items'. Even the old law did allow registration of designs for structures such as poultry and animal sheds which are prefabricated and portable in that they are delivered to purchasers as a whole, even although they may still require erection in a simple operation on site; but an airraid shelter cast in reinforced concrete on site was denied registration.[14]

 Discussion point   For answer guidance visit www.oxfordtextbooks.co.uk/orc/macqueen2e/

May the design of a building be registered?

8.23 Sculptures (but not works of artistic craftsmanship) were definitely excluded from registration under the old law, but seem to epitomise handicraft under the new law. Casts or models used or intended to be used as models or patterns to be multiplied by any industrial process were registrable under the old law, however, and continue to be so in the new.

8.24 Computer programs are specifically excluded from the definition of product, so here at least is one copyright subject matter which cannot also be the subject of a registered design. However,

---

[13] See under the pre-2001 law *Apple Computer Inc v Design Registry* [2002] FSR 38 (held that computer screen icons not articles to which design applied; but computer with operating system displaying the icons was an article for these purposes).

[14] *Concrete Ltd's Application* (1940) 57 RPC 121.

the scope of this exclusion has been questioned. Is it limited to the extent of the copyright protection—that is, the source and object codes and the preparatory design material? Or does it go further, to include the 'look and feel' of the program in operation: user interfaces, screen displays and so on? The designs of computer screen icons are potentially registrable, whether in their own right as two-dimensional products, or as designs applied within the computer when in use.[15]

 Discussion point   For answer guidance visit www.oxfordtextbooks.co.uk/orc/macqueen2e/

To what extent does the definition of 'product' mean that there are overlaps between registered design and copyright subject matter?

Key points on the meaning of product

- 'Product' extends to the two- as well as the three-dimensional
- 'Product' also includes items of handicraft
- This means that there are issues about overlap with the subject matter of copyright, apart from computer programs, which are excluded from registration

---

Appearance

8.25   Appearance is the second essential element in the definition of design. It is defined as that:

> 'resulting from the features of, in particular, lines, contours, colours, shape, texture or materials of the product or its ornamentation' (RDA 1949, s 1(2)).

Given that a product may be two- as well as three-dimensional, there is not much need to highlight the difference with regard to appearance. Lines, contours and of course shape may be taken to refer to the three-dimensional, while lines (again), colours and ornamentation seem to be equivalent to the former 'pattern and ornament'. But discussions which used to cause trouble in the old law, about articles which had contoured surfaces (for example, the 'ribs' on a hot water bottle,[16] or the grooves moulded into the back and seat of a plastic chair),[17] and whether this was shape, configuration, pattern or ornament, seem unlikely to arise under the new law, where the list of design characteristics is 'in particular' and so not exclusive.

8.26   The really interesting question, however, is what, if anything, is added by the reference to 'texture and materials'. Does this mean that the 'feel' as well as the 'look' of a product is a protectable part of its design? Is the difference between silk and cotton something which registered design law can now recognise? Or does the very concept of 'appearance' imply that the only relevant human sense is that of sight?[18]

---

[15] See *Apple Computer Inc v Design Registry* [2002] FSR 38 (decided under pre-2001 law; icons would probably now be treated as products—see above, paras 8.20–8.21).

[16] *P B Cow & Co Ltd v Cannon Rubber Manufacturers Ltd* [1959] RPC 347 (CA).

[17] *Sommer Allibert (UK) Ltd v Flair Plastics Ltd* [1987] RPC 599 (CA).

[18] Although note the Elton John/Bernie Taupin lyric, 'Japanese Hands': 'Flesh on silk *looks* different/Than on a cotton sheet back home' (emphasis supplied).

8.27   The argument that 'appearance' concentrates on what can be seen and not at all upon what can be touched (or for that matter heard, smelled or tasted) may be supported by:

- the ordinary meaning of the word, not only in English but also in the versions found in the other language versions of the underlying Directive;
- the reference in recital 11 of the Directive to registration conferring protection upon design features shown *visibly* in an application; and
- the reference in recital 13 of the Directive and recital 14 of the Regulation, on the assessment of a design's individual character (for which see below paras 8.33–8.35), to 'the overall impression produced on an informed user *viewing* the design'.

Further, texture and material are at least to some extent discernible to the eye as well as to other human sensory organs.

Exercise 1

Are there any arguments which you can think of to counter the view that 'appearance' is solely concerned with what can be seen? Can you think of any examples of where 'feel' is an important element in product design? Should that element be protectable, and if so, how would you formulate the protection? Is 'feel' only a matter of texture and materials?

Exercise 2

Consider the case of *Interlego v Tyco Inc* [1989] AC 217, which concerned the copyright in the designs of two generations of Lego bricks. The second generation looked much like the first; the difference between them lay mainly in technical information as to 'tolerances', or durability; a very important feature commercially in a toy for children. But, as Lord Oliver remarked (at 258), 'nobody draws a tolerance, nor can it be reproduced three-dimensionally.' Should this innovative feature therefore be beyond the scope of design protection? Is there any other available form of intellectual property protection that could be relevant?

8.28   In general, the interpretation of 'appearance' as being about what can be seen does not mean that the features in question must at all times be visible to the customer or user. Thus the designs of the interior of chocolate eggs,[19] or for liquid crystal displays only made visible by pressing a button on the machine containing them,[20] or of computer screen icons only visible when the related software is running on the computer,[21] can continue to be registered as they were under the old law, and it will be no objection to registering the design of a terminal inside a washing machine,[22] or the underside of a shower tray,[23] that it will not normally be seen by the machine's owner or users. What will be important is that the designs are capable of being seen.[24]

---

[19] See *Ferrero and CSPA's Application* [1978] RPC 473.   [20] See *KK Suwa Seikosha's Application* [1982] RPC 168.
[21] *Apple Computer Inc v Design Registry* [2002] FSR 38.
[22] See *Amp v Utilux* [1972] RPC 103 (HL). The terminal may still fall foul of the functionality exclusion—see further below para 8.39ff.
[23] See *Gardex Ltd v Sorata Ltd* [1986] RPC 623 (also subject to the functionality exclusion).
[24] Note however the special rule on the novelty and individual character of a component part of a complex product in RDA 1949, s 1B(8), discussed below, para 8.51ff.

8.29   There is also still no need for the design to be of a fixed or rigid shape for the product; an important point, for example, for clothing, in particular dresses and skirts.[25] The possibility of a design having a kinetic or changing appearance might be important if, for example, the design of a web page containing moving or flashing elements can be registered.

> **? Question**
>
> What features of a design are relevant to consideration of its appearance?

> **Key points about 'appearance'**
>
> - 'Appearance' is concerned with what can be *seen* in a product and not, despite the legislation's reference to 'texture or materials', with what can be perceived with human sensory organs other than the eye
> - The concern with what can be seen does not mean that the design feature in question has to be visible all the time
> - The appearance could be of a changing or unfixed nature

The requirements of novelty and individual character

8.30   The determination of whether a design has the required novelty and individual character for registration is made by way of a comparison with other designs that have been made available to the public before the date on which the application for the registration of the design was made.[26]

Diagram 8.1 Determining novelty and individual character: chronology

Designs available to public————Application————Comparison

Novelty

8.31   A design is 'new':

'if no identical design, or no design whose features differ only on immaterial details, has been made available to the public before the date of application' (RDA 1949, s 1B(2); DD, Art 4; CDR, Art 5).

8.32   To be 'new', therefore, a design must differ from previous designs at least in material details. Some further guidance on what this might mean can be obtained from old case law as well as from the decisions of the OHIM Invalidity Division and the Registrar in the UK IPO.

---

[25] See *S Traver's Ltd's Application* (1951) 68 RPC 255; and for an OHIM invalidity decision on bottle carriers, the shape of which varied according to whether or not they were carrying bottles, see *Built NY Inc v I-Feng Kao*, 8 May 2006 (discussed in more detail, below, paras 8.32, 8.35).

[26] See generally the decisions of the OHIM Invalidity Division, accessible at http://oami.europa.eu/ows/rw/pages/RCD/caseLaw/caseLaw.en.do, at which cases cited below may be consulted, along with images of the designs in contention. For analysis of many of the early decisions, see JJ Izquierdo Peris, 'Registered Community Design: first two-year balance from an insider's perspective' [2006] EIPR 146 and R Bird, 'Registered Community Design: early decisions of the OHIM Invalidity Division' [2006] EIPR 297. Decisions of the Registrar at the UK IPO are available at http://www.ipo.gov.uk/d-decisions.htm.

■ *Built NY Inc v I-Feng Kao*, OHIM Invalidity Division, 8 May 2006

The design of a bottle carrier was registered as, inter alia, Community design No 00387584–0003. It was argued that this design was anticipated by a prior registered Community design, namely No 000359922–0001. It was held that while the two designs had many features in common, they also differed in a number of features apparent even when the carriers had bottles inside and so had a volume: for example, the ratio between width and height was about 1:1.3 in the challenged design, 1:1 in the prior one; the body part in the challenged design encompassed its bottom half and in the prior design its bottom two-thirds; the handle part in the challenged design encompassed its top half and in the prior design its top third; and the hole in the handle part had a circular shape in the challenged design and an oval one in the prior design. These were not immaterial differences, so the challenge on novelty failed.

■ *Le May v Welch* (1884) 28 Ch D 24

A design for detachable shirt collars, which differed from previous designs in the height of the collar above the stud which fastened it in front, and a wider cutting away of the corners in a segment of a circle.[27] It was held that that the second design was not new within the meaning of the registered designs legislation, and its removal from the register was ordered.

■ *Re Vlisco BV's Application* [1980] RPC 509 (Designs Registry)

Indian-style design applied to textile piece goods.[28] It was held that that a reduction in size compared to previous designs was an immaterial difference.

Discussion point   For answer guidance visit www.oxfordtextbooks.co.uk/orc/macqueen2e/

Is this approach always applicable? Is the increasingly small size of, for example, mobile phones, palmtop computers and headsets for personal music players, an immaterial difference in their design or not?

■ *Pitacs Ltd v Kamil Korhan Karagülle*, OHIM Invalidity Division, 26 April 2006

This case concerned Community Design No 000330402–0003, which related to radiators for heating. Its novelty was challenged on the basis of a prior registered Community Design No 000313572–0013, also related to radiators for heating. The designs had the same pattern of arrangement of features and similar shape and contours: both had a simple vertical rectangle shape with straight contours and the same pattern of arrangement of the elements, and both consisted of the same number of heating bars placed horizontally, grouped identically and fixed on two identical supporting elements placed vertically. However, the two designs differed slightly in their proportions. The ratio between the width and the height is 1:2 in the challenged design and 1:2.5 in the prior design. The challenged design thus looked wider and lower and the prior design narrower and higher. It was held that that the challenged design did not produce a different overall impression, and it was found invalid.

---

[27] Drawings of the competing shirt collars are available at p 25 of the report.
[28] Full-colour photographs of the designs are available at p 510 of the report.

In another decision between the same parties, concerning Community Design No 000330402–0002 and its anticipation by Community Design No 000313572–0012 it was found that the designs were mirror images, that is, the same but in reverse of each other. Again it was held that the designs did not create a different overall impression, and the challenged design was found invalid.

■ *Cook and Hurst's Design Application* [1979] RPC 197

This case concerned colour changes. Registration allowed for football jersey striped in red, white and blue, because the colouration had a special effect, was distinctive and clearly recognisable.

■ *Clarke v Julius Sax & Co Ltd* [1896] 2 Ch 38 (CA)

This was a case about the recombination of existing design elements in a different setting. C registered a design for a lamp shade intended for use with electric lighting, the apparatus to be placed outside shopfronts so as to throw light through the window on to the goods displayed in it. The design used a reflecting screen and ventilation top not materially different from the shading used in previous gaslighting systems. However, a chimney required for gaslight systems, but not for electric ones, was omitted. It was held that there was no novelty. The court did say that a combination of old shapes can produce a new shape; but a combination of old patterns has to result in something different as a whole. Merely removing a useless feature from an existing design was not enough for novelty.

> **Key point on novelty**
>
> To be registered, design must differ from previous designs in material details

Individual character

8.33   A design is said to have individual character if:

> 'The overall impression it produces on the informed user differs from the overall impression produced on such a user by any previous publicly available design' (RDA 1949, s 1B(3); DD, Art 5(1); CDR, Art 6(1)).

In assessing the extent to which a design has individual character:

> 'the degree of freedom of the author in creating the design is to be taken into consideration' (RDA 1949, s 1B(4); DD, Art 5(2); CDR, Art 6(2)).

> **Question**
>
> What factors must be considered under the legislation in assessing the 'individual character' of a design?

8.34   These requirements have no real parallel in the prior UK case law. We are therefore required to consider the matter in the light of what can be gleaned from the pre-legislative and other material, and one's sense of the meaning of the legislative wording.

- *Overall impression*—the comparison is not a matter of examining each design in its details (as would be done in the novelty test), but of considering each as a whole and judging whether in that impressionistic sense they are different. Recital 13 of the Directive and recital 14 of the Community Design Regulation indicate that the impression must be one of 'clear difference' between the two designs.

- *Informed user*—this notional person is clearly not merely any consumer or customer for the product, since he is 'informed'; equally clearly, as a 'user' rather than a designer, the person is not someone who is professionally engaged or expert in design activity.[29] To be informed, the user should know the existing design corpus, taking into consideration the nature of the product to which the design is applied or in which it is incorporated, and in particular the industrial sector to which it belongs.[30]

- *Designer freedom*—this probably refers primarily to the fact that the designer is designing a product which will in the end perform some function and must therefore have certain features. Trousers must have a waist band and legs; a cutlery knife must have a cutting edge; a printer has to have a paper feeder. The nature of the product being designed, or in which the design will be incorporated, imposes certain constraints which are not to be a factor in assessing the overall impression on the informed user.

■ *Rolawn Ltd v Turfmech Machinery Ltd* [2008] ECDR 13 (Mann J)[31]

R registered a design under the category of mowers for its own wide-area grass mower. R contended that T had infringed this registered design by creating a grass mower with a folding arms mechanism which was sufficiently similar as not to produce a different overall impression to the informed user when compared to R's design. T unsuccessfully challenged the validity of R's registration. Held that the informed user was not one familiar only with mowers, but rather one using machines in the turf-growing industry. The R machine had individual character, as there was a manifest and clear difference between it and the prior art:

> 'So far as folding configuration is concerned, the Jerry Clipper does not have one. It does not fold in any relevant way at all—it is moved by raising the cutters a bit, and then moving the tractor to what is the side of the mower in its cutting configuration and towing it from there. In its fully deployed form it gives an obviously different impression from the Rolawn machine. The Kesmac has some superficial similarity in the deployed form, but one does not have to look at it for long to appreciate that the Rolawn machine gives a very different overall impression. It does retract itself, but it does not have anything like the same central beam mechanism for suspending the cutters as the Rolawn machine has, and its folded-up position has a bunching, dangling effect. There is no sensible level of generality at which one can say that the Rolawn machine does not give a clearly different impression in all its configurations.' (para 117)

There was also considerable scope for design freedom according to expert evidence.[32]

8.35 While it is possible to imagine these matters being the subject of survey and even expert evidence, as in other fields of intellectual property law, in the end one suspects that most will depend on the individual judge deciding any case in which these matters arise as an issue. The judge will in all probability become equivalent to an informed user during the case, because the parties will lead evidence as to the state of the art. Further, the judge will understand the difference to be drawn between attention to details to test novelty and the overall impression with which individual character is to be assessed, and will be in a good position to decide the

---

[29] Although arguably a designer might be a user of other people's designs in the sense of researching them in search of ideas and inspiration for further new designs.

[30] DD, recital 13; CDR, recital 14.

[31] The appendix to the report contains several photographs of the prior art as well as the competing designs.

[32] R's infringement action was also unsuccessful, however: see further below, para 8.90.

matter. Consequently, any case is very likely to turn on its own facts and circumstances, and more general understandings of the meaning of the law in this area may take time to develop.[33] In *Procter & Gamble Co v Reckitt Benckiser (UK) Ltd* Jacob LJ said:

> 'A place for evidence is very limited indeed. By and large it should be possible to decide a registered design case in a few hours. The evidence of the designer, e.g. as to whether he/she was trying to make, or thought he/she had made, a breakthrough, is irrelevant. The evidence of experts, particularly about consumer products, is unlikely to be of much assistance: anyone can point out similarities and differences, though an educated eye can sometimes help a bit.'[34]

■ *Procter & Gamble Co v Reckitt Benckiser (UK) Ltd* [2008] FSR 8 (CA)

This was a case about the design of 'sprayers' used for air freshening and air conditioning. In finding the claimant's registration valid, the Court of Appeal held that the informed user was one 'fairly familiar' with design issues, whose experience of other similar articles made him or her reasonably discriminatory in being able to appreciate enough detail to decide whether a design creates an overall impression having an individual character. The informed user was not the same as the 'average consumer' of trade mark law (see para 15.32ff below). What matters is what strikes the mind of the informed user when the product is carefully viewed, not what is half-remembered about it. The informed user is also taken to know when design freedom is constrained by the product's function (here, eg, the product had to be gripped by the user and the spray operated by the user's finger). Smaller differences might be enough to create a different overall impression where design freedom was limited. But the protection given by the registration might be less for products only incrementally different from the prior art, so that while the registration was valid, it might not be too difficult for subsequent designers to avoid infringement. See further para 8.90 below on the infringement aspects of this case.

■ *Built NY Inc v I-Feng Kao*, OHIM Invalidity Division, 8 May 2006

The design of a bottle carrier was registered as, inter alia, Community design No 00264130–0001. It was argued that this design was anticipated by a prior registered Community design, namely No 000210679–0001. It was held that the informed user was aware that bottle carriers have the function of holding bottles and enabling their carriage, so must have a compartment for the bottle and at least one handle. Design freedom was limited, since the body of the carrier had to follow the generally cylindrical shape of bottles. There was greater freedom with regard to the handle. The two designs here produced the same overall impression on the informed user, both having a simple and the same overall shape, with almost the same contours and very close proportions. Their proportions of width to height were slightly different. But when the products were in use, differences in contour apparent in their flattened mode disappeared. Since the overall impression on the informed user was not different, the challenged design lacked individual character and was held invalid. (Contrast the decision on novelty in another dispute between the same parties over different designs, above, para 8.32.)

---

[33] For an approach to the overall impression question leading to the invalidation of a Community registered design see *Armmet SL's CD* [2004] ECDR 24.

[34] [2008] FSR 8 (CA) para 4.

■ *Rodi Comercial SA v Vuelta Internatonal SpA*, OHIM Invalidity Division,
20 December 2005

This case concerned a Community Design No 000107115–0002 for bicycle wheels. It was challenged on grounds of lack of novelty and individual character on the basis of a 2002 international patent application containing the figure of a bicycle wheel. It was held that the informed user was aware of the functional requirements of bicycle wheels and of the prior art known in the normal course of business to the circles specialising in the sector concerned. Design freedom was limited by the need to lace the wheel with spokes between hub and rim. So the informed user would pay more attention to features where the designer's creativity was less limited, such as the pattern of distribution of the spokes around the hub. Here, there was the same number of spokes and the same symmetrical and orderly arrangement and pattern, producing the same overall impression on the informed user. The challenged design thus lacked individual character and was found invalid.

■ *Aktiebolaget Design Rubens Sweden v Marie Ekman Bäcklund*, OHIM Invalidity Division, 20 December 2005

Community Design No 000093356–0010 related to dolls. The registration was challenged on grounds of lack of novelty and individual character, with reference to published newspaper photographs. Evidence was also submitted that the clothing of the applicant's dolls could be removed, leaving them looking quite different. The holders of the registered design argued that they had added features making the dolls look more human (for example, nose, belly button), and that the dolls felt more baby-like when held in the arms (important for the therapeutic and educational use of the dolls). It was held that the two sets of dolls had many features in common, but the differences were enough to give the challenged design novelty. However, it lacked individual character. The informed user was not limited to the therapeutic field, and there was considerable design freedom. The behaviour of the dolls in use was not part of the product's appearance and so was irrelevant. The dolls produced the same overall impression on the informed user, and the registration of the design was invalid.

■ *Case 196/2006-3 (Underwater motive device)*, OHIM Invalidity Decision (Third Board of Appeal), 28 November 2006

The Board considered individual character, upholding the Invalidity Division's declaration of invalidity. An underwater motive device was registered in 2004. Another model was exhibited at a fair in 2002 and a patent application was submitted for it in 2004. The Division held that the two designs were identical except for differences to the handle of the device. Though these were not immaterial differences, they were not sufficient to create a different overall impression on an informed user. It was held that the design lacked individual character. Although novelty and individual character overlap somewhat, they are separate concepts. Restyling or modifying a design where it is identical to a previous design but for immaterial details will produce the same overall impression. However, two designs cannot be identical where they create a different overall impression. There are differences between the tests for novelty and individual character. The former, it held, was an objective test as to whether the designs were identical, allowing for 'immaterial details'. As to the latter test, it is more complex and subjective, with consideration being given to the overall impression on the 'informed user'. The freedom of the designer will be considered in the light of technical limitations, with the consequence that a highly techni-cal product with little scope for innovation is more likely to allow for the finding of individual character than one which is less complex, where more design innovation will be required. It was held in this case that the only updated element of the underwater motive device was the handle. However, in comparing the two designs, the entirety of both designs is looked at.[35] Applying the law to the facts, the Board held that the overall impression was the same when considering also the rest of the machine. The Board rejected the argument that more consideration should be given to the handle of the machine as this was where design was not limited by technical necessity. A number of elements in the device could have been altered whilst still allowing the machine to undertake its function. But neither the Invalidity Division nor the Board of Appeal felt it necessary to decide on who the informed user was in this case.

■ Case 250/2007-3 (Tavoli), OHIM Invalidity Decision (Third Board of Appeal), 18 September 2007

The Board upheld the Division's decision that an invalidity challenge against the design for a table on the ground of lack of novelty and individual character was unfounded. As to 'indi-vidual character', the informed user was held not to be the designer but a person choosing a table having visited a number of shops, read magazines or conducted a search on the Internet. It was clear that both tables shared the same concept. However, the Board took the view that the legs of the RCD were more dynamic whereas the legs of the prior design were more compact and static; this did create a different overall impression. There were further differences in the metal arms. On this basis, the RCD was not declared invalid. On the lack of novelty point, the Board concluded that due to the same differences, the designs were not identical.

■ Karen Millen Ltd v Dunnes Stores (Limerick) Ltd [2007] IEHC 449 (Ireland)[36]

KML alleged that DS copied various clothing designs for which Community Design Rights were claimed. The court held that KML had only to indicate what it considered to be the design's individual character. This did not extend to producing proof that the design was new and that it had individual character, only that there was a *prima facie* design, whereupon the burden switched to the defendants to prove invalidity. Having considered *Procter & Gamble v Reckitt Benckiser* (above), the court went on to hold that the 'informed user' is an end user of products with a knowledge of design issues, better informed than the 'average consumer' in trade mark law, yet not quite as well informed as a designer would be. In the present case, this meant a woman 'with a keen sense of fashion, a good knowledge of designs of women's tops and shirts previously made available to the public, alert to design and with a basic understanding of any functional or technical limitations on designs for women's tops and shirts' (para 73). In decid-ing on overall impression, it was unnecessary and irrelevant for the court to consider the overall impression created on a witness. The assessment was solely for the court. Finally, in considering the individual character of the design, the design's overall impression must be compared to that of an actual identifiable prior design, rather than an amalgam of a number of different prior designs in the 'design corpus' (see recitals to CDR). As DS had not submitted any singular actual

---

[35] Case 196/2006-3 (*Underwater motive device*), OHIM Invalidity Decision (Third Board of Appeal), 28 November 2006.

[36] This case concerned unregistered Community designs, but the substantive criteria of protectability are the same whether or not the design is registered (see further para 9.101 below).

prior design in evidence, each KML design was held to have individual character as separate pieces of 'prior art'.[37]

Key points about individual character

- Individual character is about overall impression rather than differences in detail
- The overall impression in question is that of the informed user
- The informed user is neither a consumer nor a design professional
- Account must be taken of design freedom in relation to the design

---

 Discussion point   For answer guidance visit www.oxfordtextbooks.co.uk/orc/macqueen2e/

Now that you have considered some cases as well as the legislative wording, what factors do you think are to be taken into account in assessing a design's 'individual character'?

What designs are 'available to the public'?

8.36   Assessing novelty and individual character is about comparing the design for which registration is sought with designs already available to the public (the state of the art, in patent terms). Designs are already available to the public if they have been previously:

- published (whether or not registered);
- exhibited;
- used in trade (for example, design has already been applied to a product which is available in the commercial marketplace);
- otherwise disclosed (see for all this RDA 1949, s 1B(5); DD, Art 6(1); CDR, Art 7(1)).

The evidence which may be considered on this matter can be widely varied: the OHIM Invalidity Division has accepted material found as a result of a Google search, for example.[38] But it is important that it be dateable: in some cases material discovered on the Internet the posting of which could not be dated has been dismissed as irrelevant.[39]

 Question

Why is the dating of designs important in considering 'availability to the public'?

8.37   The disclosure will not count (that is, the design for which registration is sought could still be novel or of individual character even if the same or similar design has already been disclosed

---

[37] For comment see D Brophy, 'Clothing fashion designs protected against deliberate imitation in Ireland' (2008) 3 JIPLP 628–9. The case is understood to be under appeal to the Irish Supreme Court.
[38] See *Leng d'Or v Crown Confectionery Co Ltd*, 20 September 2005.
[39] *Holding C Vlemmix BV v Van Hellenberg Hubar* and *Dryson AB v Birger Olsson*, 13 and 17 March 2006 respectively.

somewhere else) if that disclosure:[40]

> '(1) could not reasonably have become known before the application date in the normal course of business to persons carrying on business in the European Economic Area and specialising in the sector concerned;'

This 'safeguard clause' means that the novelty and individual character are assessed by comparison with what is or could reasonably be known to the relevant specialised industry in Europe; thus for example, a disclosure in the Americas, Asia or Africa might not affect novelty or individual character in the European context.

Discussion point   For answer guidance visit www.oxfordtextbooks.co.uk/orc/macqueen2e/

Who is being 'safeguarded' by this rule?

■ *Green Lane Products Ltd v PMS International Group Ltd* [2008] FSR 1 (Patents Court)

The products in issue in this case were spiky plastic balls. D had from 2001 imported such balls from China and sold them as massage balls in the UK and from 2002 in the EU. In August 2004 C registered four Community designs for such balls, describing the class of products to which the designs were to be applied as 'flatirons and washing, cleaning and drying equipment'. The designs were also used in practice for laundry balls that could be put in a tumble dryer to soften fabric. In October 2006 D proposed to market his products inter alia as laundry dryer balls, hand exercisers, easy-catch toys and dog trainer balls. C argued that D would infringe its design rights by use for anything other than massage balls. D contended that C's registration was invalid for lack of novelty, arguing that the prior uses by D 'could not reasonably have become known in the normal course of business to the circles specialised in the sector concerned', which was the sector determined by the product class in his application for registration. At first instance it was held that the relevant sector was that consisting of or including the sector of the alleged prior art, and was not limited to the sector specified in the application for registration. The test was not the informed user, but what the informed user is looking at. Only once the prior art has been identified can the informed user do his job. This approach was upheld by the Court of Appeal. Jacob LJ said: 'The right gives a monopoly over any kind of goods according to the design. It makes complete sense that the prior art available for attacking novelty should also extend to all kinds of goods, subject only to the limited exception of prior art obscure even in the sector from which it comes' (para 79). The Court of Appeal looked at the 'travaux preparatoires', which indicated that the geographical limitation had been the result of industry lobbying intended to protect rights against being invalidated by claims of antecedents in remote places about which the European industry could not have known.

> '(2) made to a person other than the designer (or any successor in title of his) under conditions of confidentiality (whether express or implied);'

---

[40] For what follows see RDA 1949, s 1B(6); DD, Art 6; CDR, Art 7.

For example, designer creates a design for a product and shows it under conditions of confidentiality to potential manufacturers; this will not affect the possibility of later registration of the design by the designer.[41]

> '(3) made by the designer (or any successor in title of his) during the period of 12 months immediately preceding the application date (*grace period*)'

The purpose of this is to enable exhibition or market-testing of a design before undertaking the costs and process of registration.

> '(4) made by a person *other* than the designer (or any successor in title of his), during the period of 12 months immediately preceding the application date in consequence of information provided or other action taken by the designer (or any successor in title of his);'

This covers the cases where the designer authorises another party to manufacture a product according to the design to enable it to be market-tested, or where the designer has been commissioned to produce the design by the party who will manufacture the product and put it on the market.

> '(5) made during the period of 12 months immediately preceding the application date as a consequence of an abuse in relation to the designer (or any successor in title of his).'

For example, a third party obtains the design by way of industrial espionage or a disgruntled employee/ex-employee of the designer, or someone to whom the design has been disclosed in confidence breaks that confidence and publishes the design.

8.38 The 12-month *grace periods* can be seen as extremely important here. They cover the designer's own disclosure by way of publication, exhibition, trade use or other disclosure not in confidence. But also covered is third party disclosure, whether or not that results from the designer's own activity. Even if the disclosure is an abuse of the designer's interests by the third party, the designer still has only a grace period of 12 months within which to protect the claim to novelty and individual character.

Key point on previous disclosure to the public

- Previous design:
    (1) disclosed
    (2) for more than 12 months (unless disclosure in confidence)
    (3) in such a way that it could reasonably be known about
    (4) in the relevant industry/business/trade sector
    (5) within the EEA, and
    (6) later design lacks either or both novelty and individual character in relation to that previous design—application refused

---

Discussion point   For answer guidance visit www.oxfordtextbooks.co.uk/orc/macqueen2e/

Once a design has been disclosed, whether with or without the consent of the designer, what advice would you give the designer with regard to the registration of that design?

---

[41] See for another example *Grupo Promer Mon-Graphic SA v Pepsico Inc*, OHIM Invalidity Division, 1 July 2005.

8.43   The interpretation of the 'functionality' exclusion offered in these paragraphs was supported by the Court of Appeal in the unregistered Community design case of *Landor & Hawa International Ltd v Azure Designs Ltd*,[49] although the Court said that the *Philips v Remington* case discussed at para 8.42 is not decisive in reaching this view. But the difficulty with which the suggested interpretation confronts the law is that under it the functionality exclusion becomes virtually toothless. There are very few objects whose function is such that only one design will do. Even bricks, whose main function is generally to be connected with other bricks and so require straight edges and smooth surfaces, can be varied in the way in which the connections are made, as demonstrated by the *Interlego* case (see above, para 8.27). One has only to visit different houses or restaurants and compare the simple everyday objects found there, such as knives, forks, spoons, spouts and plates, to confirm that commonplace functions can be achieved in a wide variety of different ways.

8.44   Cornish and Llewelyn raise a different problem, however, based on the *Cow v Cannon* example. While there may be more than one way of designing the insulating ribs of a hot-water bottle, there may not be very many in reality; so an astute designer needs 'only a couple more registrations covering the obvious alternatives and he or she would have a monopoly on the practicable ways of giving effect to a clever technical idea without having to satisfy the requirements for a patent'.[50]

8.45   The attraction of the *Amp* approach was that the functionality exclusion took on some meaning, and monopoly, or the possibility of monopoly, in purely functional but non-inventive features was avoided; but the problem arose, at least for designers and manufacturers of products, of finding some other means of protecting commercially valuable designs. It was this that led to efforts to use copyright and then, in the UK, the development of unregistered design right. The policy of the European legislation is to give designs protection primarily through the registration system, and, as will be explored in more detail in the next chapter, to minimise the role to be played by other, unregistered rights. Limiting the exclusionary power of functionality supports this policy.

Discussion point   For answer guidance visit www.oxfordtextbooks.co.uk/orc/macqueen2e/

Would the policy of protecting design primarily through the registration system be even better supported by dropping the functionality exclusion altogether?

8.46   The exclusion from protection of designs which are solely functional probably reflects another policy hinted at in the quotation above from Cornish and Llewelyn: purely technological or technical innovation should be protected by patents, with the innovation at the relatively high level of inventiveness (see below, Chapter 10) rather than the mere novelty and individual character of a design.[51] However, with the very narrow interpretation of 'solely dictated' having the consequence that design protection is available for an innovation which is no more than a different way of performing a technical function, technological innovation could often find itself 'hampered' (in the words of the recital already quoted) by intellectual property rights falling well below the standards required for a patent.

---

[49] [2007] FSR 9 (CA).   [50] Cornish and Llewelyn, para 15.19.   [51] Bently and Sherman, chapter 25.4.1.1.

■ *Ampel 24 Vertriebs-GmbH & Co KG v Daka Research Inc*, OHIM Invalidity Division, 1 December 2005

This case concerned Community Design No 000225073–0001 for an 'underwater motive device'. An invalidity challenge was mounted based on novelty (in relation to a US design patent) and also because, it was claimed, most of the features of the design were necessary for the technical function of the device. It was held that, although novel, the design lacked individual character and its registration was invalid. The designer's freedom was limited by the need for an underwater motive device to have an overall shape of a longitudinal extension and handle elements attached to the body. 'However, the [Community Design] does not subsist in features of appearance solely dictated by the technical function of the underwater motive device. The device would still fulfil its function with a body of different shape. For instance, the designer could have chosen a more symmetrical shape for the body of the device such as a cylinder instead of the asymmetrical form realized in the [Community Design]. Likewise, the handle element could have been formed by two separated grips on the sides of the body instead of the unique piece attached on top of the body of the [Community Design]' (para 14). For the Invalidity Division, however, these facts told against the individual character of the design rather than leading to the exclusion from registration of functional features as such. On the face of it, since there were several ways to design this product so that it could perform this function, the method chosen could not be excluded from registration on that ground alone.

Exercise

Consider how *Amp v Utilux* and *Interlego v Tyco* (above, para 8.27, Exercise (2)) would be decided today in the event of an application for registration of the designs under discussion in those cases. Then, explain whether an application for the registration of the design of the triple razor-heads in *Philips v Remington* (above, para 8.42) would be successful.

Exclusions: public policy and morality

8.47   Rights in a registered design do *not* subsist in:

'designs contrary to public policy or to accepted principles of morality' (RDA 1949, s 1D; DD, Art 8; CDR, Art 9).

The content of public policy or accepted principles of morality is not spelled out in the legislation, and recital 16 of the Designs Directive is careful to say that 'this Directive does not constitute a harmonisation of national concepts of public policy or accepted principles of morality'. Thus each member state is free to bring to bear its own established approach (if any) to this exclusion. The pre-Directive law of the UK also contained an exclusion of designs which, in the opinion of the Registrar, would be contrary to law or morality.[52] The limited case law on this provision probably continues to be relevant under the new rule. On the whole, the courts take a restrictive approach to the exclusion.[53]

---

[52] Former Registered Designs Act 1949, s 43(1).
[53] Note, in addition to the case mentioned below, *In re La Marquise Footwear Inc's Application* (1947) 64 RPC 27, a trade mark decision that 'Oomphies' could be registered for shoes despite concern that 'Oomph' was slang for sex appeal and that the mark might therefore be taken as encouraging male fetishism about women's shoes.

■ *Masterman's Design* [1991] RPC 89

Application to register the design of a furry doll representing a Highlander-like figure wearing a sporran, the lifting of which revealed his genitalia (illustrative drawing at p 108 of the report). An objection on the grounds of immorality was refused, and registration allowed. The test was not whether some section of the public would be offended, but whether right-thinking members of the public, applying their moral principles, would think it very wrong to grant protection.

Discussion point   For answer guidance visit www.oxfordtextbooks.co.uk/orc/macqueen2e/

Can you think of any immoral designs, or designs contrary to public policy?

Key points on designs capable of registration

- Designs are the appearance of all or part of products (itself a concept of wide scope for these purposes)

- Such designs can gain legal protection against unauthorised commercial use by virtue of registration

- To be registered, a design must be different in detail and in general impression from previous product designs

- Features of the design's appearance solely dictated by the product's technical function are not protected by registration; but this is probably only a very limited exclusion

- Design rights do not subsist in designs contrary to public policy or to accepted principles of morality; but this too is not a very far-reaching exclusion from protection

---

8.48   You should by this stage have grasped the points noted above. If you are clear about these points, you are ready to move on to the next section of this chapter, which deals with the problem of complex products and spare parts.

Complex products and spare parts

Introduction

8.49   As a result of the European legislation, the Registered Designs Act 1949 now contains a rather complicated series of provisions dealing with what it calls 'complex products'. A *complex product* is a product (see above, paras 8.18–8.24) which is:

> 'composed of at least two replaceable component parts permitting disassembly and reassembly of the product' (RDA 1949, s 1(3); DD, Art 1(c); CDR, Art 3(c)).

There are special rules for such complex products with regard to novelty, individual character and functionality.

Question

What are the key elements of the definition of a 'complex product'?

Example of a complex product

8.50   It may be helpful to understanding what follows to have in mind an example of a complex product. A good one is a car. The vehicle's body will be made up of a number of parts—the basic shell, the wings, the doors, the lids of the bonnet and boot, perhaps a spoiler or fins. There will also be the engine, probably a complex product in its own right, as well as necessary attachments such as the fuel and exhaust pipes. There will be fittings—external ones, such as wheels, lights, bumpers and wing-mirrors, and internal ones, such as steering wheel, seats, dashboard and other features. The process of building a car is a process of assembling all the parts, and most if not all of these are replaceable; indeed, whole industries thrive on the business of manufacturing and supplying replacement parts for cars. Often such parts are sold to be added on to cars; and many car owners take great pleasure in disassembling and reconstructing their vehicles to improve, or at least change, their appearance and performance.

Discussion point   For answer guidance visit www.oxfordtextbooks.co.uk/orc/macqueen2e/

Can you give any other examples of complex products?

Novelty and individual character

8.51   A design applied to or incorporated in a product which constitutes a component part of a complex product can only have novelty and individual character if two conditions *over and above* those already stated generally (above, paras 8.31, 8.33) are both met:[54]

- Once incorporated in the complex product, the *component part must remain visible* while the complex product is *in normal use*.

- These *visible parts* of the component part *must in themselves be new and of an individual character.*

'Normal use' means use by the end user; but this does not include any maintenance, servicing or repair work in relation to the product.[55]

***

Key points on novelty and individual character of complex products

- *Only features of the component* that are *visible during normal use of the complex product* can be protected through registration, and then only if these visible features have novelty and individual character

***

[54] RDA 1949, s 1B(8); DD, art 3(3); CDR, art 4(2).   [55] RDA 1949, s 1B(9); DD, art 3(4); CDR, art 4(3).

> • While design is about appearance, this does not mean that it is only about features which are ordinarily visible; the normal rule is that a design feature need only be capable of being seen (see above, para 8.28). Thus the visibility requirement for component parts is an exception to the general rule

8.52   If we take our example of a car, let us consider the position with regard to an exhaust pipe.[56] This is clearly a component part of a complex product. When the complex product—the car—is in normal use (that is, being driven along, idling in traffic queues, parked, or being unloaded), only a very small part of the component part is visible. The fact that much of the pipe could be seen if its owner or a mechanic went underneath the car to inspect it (whether by lying down on the ground beneath the car, raising it on a lift, or parking it over a service pit) would be irrelevant, because that kind of maintenance or servicing activity is excluded from normal use. Likewise if the exhaust pipe had to be replaced: repair is not normal use either, and the fact that a pipe could be seen in full once removed or that the replacement was also wholly visible during the process would be irrelevant. Only the normally visible parts of the exhaust pipe are of significance for registered design rights, and it is to these that the tests of novelty and individual character have to be applied. Probably the average visible part of an exhaust pipe does not qualify, but there are some more extravagant examples on the road—the exhaust pipes of some long-distance trucks, for instance—which might come within the scope of protection.[57]

8.53   More likely to attract interest for registration is a car body part such as a door or a wing. The shape of a car is much more important in the attraction of buyers, by and large, than the design of its exhaust pipe. The external elements of the part, that which can be seen when the car is in normal use, will certainly be capable of attracting protection through registration provided that they are new and of an individual character; but the parts which face into the car rather than on to the outside world will be excluded.

8.54   The features within the driving and passenger section of the car may raise a question about to whom features should be visible to make them protectable. From outside the car, features such as the steering wheel, the seats, the dashboard and the rear-view mirror are only wholly visible with the expenditure of significant effort; but since they are wholly visible (more or less) to the driver and any passengers, that is presumably enough to make the complete design open for registration.

 Exercise

Discuss how far the following items may be protected as simple products in their own right, or whether they are to be seen as component parts of complex products:

- Roof rack bars
- Bicycle carriers, whether fitted to the roof or rear of a car
- Roof boxes
- Head rests
- Mud flaps
- Spoilers fitted to the car by an owner rather than as part of the original manufacturing and assembly process

---

[56] For the example see *British Leyland v Armstrong Patents* [1986] AC 577; and para 9.10ff.
[57] On visibility see further D Musker, 'Hidden meaning? UK perspectives on invisible in use designs' [2003] EIPR 450.

Functionality: 'must fit' elements

8.55   The rules on component parts of complex products must be read in the further light shed by the exclusion of rights in 'must fit' features of a registered design. These rules appear in the section dealing with the functionality exclusion.[58] It will be recalled that the functionality exclusion is a very narrow one; only if the design is the only one possible by which the product in question may perform its function may it not be registered (see above, para 8.41).[59] This is supplemented by the 'must fit' exclusion, which is couched in the following terms:

> 'A right in a registered design shall not subsist in features of appearance of a product which must necessarily be reproduced in their exact form and dimensions so as to permit the product in which the design is incorporated or to which it is applied to be mechanically connected to, or placed in, around or against, another product so that either product may perform its function' (RDA 1949, s 1C(2)).

 Question

What are the key elements in the 'must fit' exclusion?

8.56   Although this rule is not expressed in terms of complex products and component parts, it is easiest to understand first in that context, and to use our example of an exhaust pipe in a car once again. An exhaust pipe for a given model of car is a product which must be of an exact form and dimensions to take its place in that model—that is, to be mechanically connected to, placed in, around or against the car. Both products are needed for either to perform its function: the car cannot run without the exhaust pipe, and the exhaust pipe cannot discharge fumes unless connected to the car.

8.57   The cumulative effect of these rules taken with the 'complex product' rules discussed earlier is certainly that the design for a car exhaust pipe is extremely unlikely to gain registration, on the grounds of either invisibility in normal use or its 'must fit' nature. On the other hand, a body part is likely to fall foul of the 'must fit' exclusion only in respect of those aspects of its design which are there specifically to connect it to the immediately proximate parts of the vehicle, leaving the greater part of its external appearance still eligible for protection through registration.

8.58   The application of the 'must fit' rules outside the context of the complex product is perhaps best understood through the idea of a product which is an accessory to rather than a component of another product. This can be illustrated with the example of roof rack bars. These are not usually component parts of complex products, it is suggested, since they are not normally part of the assembly of the car to which they are later attached. They are however products made to be fitted to other products: they are accessories which many car owners will opt to add to their vehicles. Those parts of the bars which enable their connection to the roof of the car are excluded from protection by the 'must fit' exception. The remainder of the bars is eligible for protection provided that the other requirements for registration, notably novelty and individual character, are met.

---

[58] RDA 1949, s 1C(2); DD, art 7(2); CDR, Art 8(2).
[59] When the UK functionality exclusion was wider in scope, in accordance with the *Amp* case (see above, para 8.40), there was no explicit 'must fit' exception in registered designs law, since it was thought 'must fit' features were solely dictated by function and therefore excluded anyway.

> ### Key points on 'must fit' exclusion for complex products
>
> * A feature of a product which is part of a larger complex product will be not be registrable if the feature is necessary to enable the product to be fitted to the complex product
>
> * Only those parts of the product which are there for the purpose of fitting are excluded under this rule—other parts of the product may be registrable if they otherwise meet the criteria of registrability

> ### Exercise
>
> Consider again the possibility of registered design protection for the following items, but this time in the light of the 'must fit' exception:
>
> * Bicycle carriers, whether fitted to the roof or rear of a car
> * Roof boxes
> * Head rests
> * Mud flaps
> * Spoilers fitted to the car by an owner rather than as part of the original manufacturing and assembly process

Policy question 1: a free market in spare parts

8.59 What are the 'complex product' and 'must fit' rules trying to achieve? The essential issue was about replacement or spare parts—components in complex products which could be replaced, either because they were exhausted (for example, a spent bulb in a headlight), needed repair (for example, an exhaust pipe with a hole in it), or the owner took a fancy for doing so (for example, replacing a conventional steering wheel with a racing one). To what extent should design rights arise in such components, which in general had useful life only when installed within whatever the complex product might be? On the other hand, there clearly was a very significant market in such components, whether it arose through necessary replacement and repair, or as a result of self-indulgence. Should that secondary market be subject to the control of the manufacturers of the complex products, who could then tie in customers initially attracted to them in the primary market for the complex product? The policy issue arose with especial acuteness in relation to spare parts for cars:

> 'should manufacturers have intellectual property rights the effect of which would be to tie in consumers to their products, or should they be subjected to the competitive rigours of a free market untrammelled by intellectual property?'

This would enable third party providers to provide the goods and services at a much lower price to the consumer.

8.60 The answer produced in the European legislative process is not a simple one. Complex products have produced complex law.

Key points on component parts and 'must fit' exception

- In essence, the law denies protection to:
  - those features of component parts of complex products that are ordinarily invisible, and
  - the 'must fit' elements of products that, whether or not they are components, are to be connected to other products—that is, those elements which enable connection or fitting to take place.
- But this does not mean that spare or replacement parts are beyond protection through the registration process
- Features which are visible in normal use, or which are not there to permit connection or fitting, can enjoy the rights subsisting in a registered design
- Similarly, products which are essentially accessory to other products (for example, roof rack) rather than component parts can have registered design rights apart from those elements by which they are attached to the product to which they are accessory

---

The protection of such accessory products is, however, not limited to what is visible in normal use, since that restriction applies only to component parts. Thus, if a car roof box is accessory rather than component, for example, there may be registered design protection, not only for the external, but also for the internal design features of the box.

Policy question 2: Repair or 'must match' parts: the 'freeze/standstill plus'

8.61 A further element in the debate about spare parts leading up to the European Directive and Regulation was a proposed exclusion from protection for what were usually called *'must match'* designs. The name came from the British legislation on unregistered design right, to be discussed in detail in the next chapter (see paras 9.52–9.58). For present purposes, it suffices to note that:

> 'unregistered design right does not subsist in features of shape or configuration of an article which are dependent upon the appearance of another article of which the article is intended by the designer to form an integral part' (CDPA 1988, s 213(3)(b)(ii)).

The exception was designed to ensure that car body parts would not enjoy unregistered design rights, and followed competition investigations in the 1980s by both the UK and the European Community, the subject of which was the Ford motor company's refusal to grant licences to third parties to enable them to compete in the market for replacement body parts. A replacement wing or door for, say, a Ford Mondeo must match the remainder of the car; and Ford's refusal to license potential competitors left them free to control the market and set prices for such parts. The denial of unregistered design rights for such parts in the UK was therefore part of an attempt to open up this market to competition for the benefit of consumers. The 1988 legislation also extended this 'must match' exception into registered designs law.

 Question

What are the key elements in the definition of 'must match' designs?

8.62   However, a 'must match' or 'repair' exception in the original draft of the European Directive did not survive the debate about spare parts, despite its extremely limited scope—much narrower than that established in the UK in the 1988 Act. The original idea was that three years after the first marketing of the product to which a protected design had been applied, third parties might reproduce the design to effect repairs of complex products of which the protected product was part and upon the appearance of which the protected design was dependent. During the debate the European Parliament proposed a system of compulsory licences, under which third parties would have the right to make parts for repair purposes provided that the right holder would receive 'fair and reasonable remuneration' taking account of its investment in developing the design, so ensuring that competitor/imitators would contribute to the recouping of the costs. But this was rejected by the European Council.

> 'The point to note is that "must match" or "repair" rights reach far more of a product's design than "must fit" can.'

So the objection of the original manufacturers to such free use is understandable, whether or not sound as a matter of public policy. Equally, the compulsory licence proposal of the Parliament was so hedged around with bureaucratic requirements—for example, the third party was to notify the rightholder of the intended use and to provide regular and reliable information as to the scale of the use—that the objections of the manufacturer lobby were entirely comprehensible.

8.63   Following a Conciliation procedure between Parliament and Council, however, nothing appeared in the Directive other than what has been called an *'apology'*[60] in recital 19:

> 'the rapid adoption of this Directive has become a matter of urgency for a number of industrial sectors...full-scale approximation...cannot be introduced at the present stage'

—and two Articles providing for future action which have become known as the *'freeze or standstill plus'* solution to the problem of 'must match' designs. Article 14, which is the 'freeze' or 'standstill' element, states:

> 'Until such time as amendments to this Directive are adopted on a proposal from the Commission in accordance with the provisions of Article 18, Member States shall maintain in force their existing legal provisions relating to the use of the design of a component part used for the purpose of the repair of a complex product so as to restore its original appearance and shall introduce changes to those provisions only if the purpose is to liberalise the market for such parts.'

8.64   In the UK this was taken, for reasons which are not immediately apparent, to require the repeal of the former 'must match' exception introduced in registered designs law by the 1988 Act; but unregistered designs law was left untouched. However, as will be discussed in more detail later in this chapter (see para 8.66), a new defence to claims of infringement of a registered design was introduced, allowing use of a component part to *repair* a complex product so as to restore its appearance.[61]

8.65   Article 18 of the Directive provided the 'plus' element of the compromise. It required the Commission to submit at the end of October 2004 'an analysis of the consequences of the provisions of this Directive for Community industry, in particular the industrial sectors which are most affected, particularly manufacturers of complex products and component parts, for consumers, for competition and for the functioning of the internal market'. Within one further

---

[60] Cornish & Llewelyn, p 590, n 28.   [61] RDA 1949 as amended, s 7A(5).

year any necessary changes to the Directive would be proposed. Recital 19 mentioned possibilities such as a remuneration system and a limited term of exclusivity.

8.66   The Regulation of 2001 also took up the 'freeze plus' position,[62] and its original Article 23 providing for a 'must match' or 'repair' clause was deleted. But Article 110(1) provides that during the interim period protection as a Community design will not exist for a design constituting a component part of a complex product used for the purpose of the repair of that complex product so as to restore its original appearance—the same solution as that used in UK registered designs law.

Key points on 'must match'/repair exceptions to registered designs

- There is currently *no* exclusion in registered design law like the 'must match' exception found in UK unregistered design law (see para 9.52ff on this)
- However, the UK and Community Registered Design rules do provide for a right of repair in relation to the component parts of complex products

---

8.67   On 14 September 2004 the Commission issued a proposal for an amendment to the Designs Directive.[63] Following a study which was said to show that prices for car spare parts were higher in countries granting them design protection than in countries which did not, the Commission concluded that the internal market was distorted: 'vehicle manufacturers as the right holders exercise considerable market power in these Member States to the detriment of consumers'. Therefore the market should be liberalised by removing protection for spare parts in the context of the 'after market'. The present 'freeze or standstill' Article 14 of the Directive would be replaced as follows:

(1)   Protection as a design shall not exist for a design which constitutes a component part of a complex product used within the meaning of Article 12(1) of this Directive, for the purpose of the repair of that complex product so as to restore its original appearance.

(2)   Member states shall ensure that consumers are duly informed about the origin of spare parts so that they can make an informed choice between competing spare parts.

8.68   This proposal has been inching its way through the formal legislative procedure of the EU, and has also been the subject of a Patent Office consultation in the UK. It remains unclear, however, where all this will lead. In November 2007, a report to the European Parliament committee on legal affairs recommended as follows:

'[T]he solution proposed by the Commission, which means that design protection for spare parts ceases immediately, fails to take sufficient account of…tension between the various interested parties. [A] transitional solution, whereby those "Member States under whose existing legislation protection as a design exists for a design which constitutes a component part of a complex product used within the meaning of Article 12(1) of Directive 98/71/EEC for the purpose of the repair of that complex product so as to restore its original appearance" may retain this design protection for another five years after the entry into force of the directive, [is proposed].'[64]

---

[62] CDR, recital 13.

[63] COM(2004) 582 final, accessible at the Internal Market Directorate-General website, http://eur-lex.europa.eu/LexUriServ/LexUriServ.do?uri=COM:2004:0582:FIN:EN:PDF

[64] See   http://www.europarl.europa.eu/sides/getDoc.do?pubRef=-//EP//TEXT+REPORT+A6-2007-0453+0+DOC+XML+V0//EN#title1 for the full report and the earlier (2005) opinions of the committees on Economic and Monetary Affairs and on Internal Market and Consumer Affairs.

There is no proposal for the amendment of the Community Design Regulation's provision giving a 'repair defence' to use of a registered design with the aim of restoring the appearance of a complex product, so should the Directive be amended, the UK would seem to have the options of leaving the Registered Designs Act as it is or of going back to its 'must match' exception to the subsistence of a right.[65]

Modular systems and the 'must fit' exception

8.69   The 'must-fit' exception does not prevent a right in a registered design subsisting in a design serving the purpose of allowing multiple assembly or connection of mutually interchangeable products within a modular system (s 1C(3)).[66] The Directive's recital 15 offers the explanation that 'the mechanical fittings of modular products may nevertheless constitute an important element of the innovative characteristics of modular products and present a major marketing asset and therefore should be eligible for protection'. Modular means 'involving or consisting of modules or discrete units as the basis of design, construction, or operation' (the Oxford English Dictionary). So a modular product is one built up from separate units. The background clarifies the provision somewhat. During the negotiations and lobbying leading up to the Directive, Denmark was anxious to protect the position of the Lego company with regard to its toy bricks, a key feature of which is the interconnecting elements. Other toy manufacturers, for example Meccano, were supportive, and the provision entered European designs law. Its scope remains unclear.

Registration

Registration in the UK[67]

Where and to whom?

8.70   Registration is carried out at the Designs Registry. It is part of the UK–IPO, which was relocated to Newport, Gwent, in 1991, although it retains a London address.

Who may apply?

8.71   The applicant must claim to be the proprietor of the design.[68] The original proprietor of a design is its author, the person who created the design,[69] unless the design was created:

(1) in pursuance of a commission for money or money's worth, in which case the commissioner is the original proprietor;[70] or

---

[65] For critical discussion of the Commission's proposal see J Straus, 'Design protection for spare parts gone in Europe? Proposed changes to the EC Directive: the Commission's mandate and its doubtful execution' [2005] EIPR 391; and J Drexl, RM Hilty and A Kur, 'Design protection for spare parts and the Commission's proposal for a repairs clause' (2005) 36 IIC 448.

[66] RDA 1949, s 1C(3); DD, Art 7(3); CDR, Art 8(3).

[67] For detailed regulation see the Registered Designs Rules 2006 (SI 2006/1975), which replaced the previous Rules of 1995 with effect from 1 October 2006.

[68] RDA 1949, s 3(2).

[69] RDA 1949, s 2(1), (3). Note also RDA 1949, s 2(4): author of computer-generated design is person who makes arrangements necessary for creation of design.

[70] RDA 1949, s 2(1A).

(2) by an employee in the course of his employment, in which case the employer is the original proprietor.[71]

If unregistered design rights subsist in the design, the application must be made by the owner of that unregistered design right.[72]

How?

8.72 Applications are made on a form which is accessible on the UK–IPO website but has to be posted if not submitted in person. There is no online application system, because the application has to enclose two identical representations or specimens of the design to be registered.

How much?

8.73 £60 per application. Costs will increase, of course, if one uses a patent or a trade mark agent (since they charge fees), or if the application runs into difficulties.

What happens next?

8.74 Registration procedure is much more of a formality than once it was, because unless requested to do so, the Registry does not conduct a search of the register to see whether, for example, the design is new (although it will object to registration where it knows or it is obvious that the design is not new). An applicant can request a search, for which a fee will be charged. If everything is in order with the application when it arrives, the interval before registration may be as short as six to eight weeks; otherwise it may take three to four months. That timescale may be extended if complications arise, for example if a third party objects to the registration.

Modification of applications, and partial disclaimers

8.75 The applicant may be allowed to make modification of the application as it proceeds.[73] Modifications may be effected by making partial disclaimers, for example by stating that only some aspects of the design of a product are claimed under the registration.

Date of registration

8.76 The date of registration is the date of application unless international priority is claimed, or there has been such a modification of the application that only from the design's alteration is it new or of individual character (in which case the date of modification can be treated as the date of application).

Registration of transactions

8.77 When a registered design is assigned or otherwise transferred (for example, after the death or insolvency of the owner), the new owner can apply for the registration of his title. The title is then registered, and the owner thereafter has power to assign, grant licences or otherwise deal with the design. Similarly the grant of a security over the design, or of a licence, may be registered: the effect of this is that third parties have notice, via the register, of the interests of

---

[71] RDA 1949, s 2(1B).   [72] RDA 1949, s 3(3).   [73] RDA 1949, s 3B.

the security-holder or the licensee. An application for registration can be made by the assignor (cedent in Scotland), grantor of the security, or licensor, as the case may be.[74]

Statistics on use of the UK Register

8.78   There are many times fewer applications for design registrations each year than for patents and trade marks (see eg below, para 13.33).

Diagram 8.2 Applications and registrations under the Registered Designs Act 1949 2000–2008

Year	Applications	Registrations
2000	9380	9768
2001	8703	7828
2002	9505	9192
2003	5910	6470
2004	4174	3874
2005	3588	3432
2006	3086	3495
2007	4683	4683
2008	4037	4093

This suggests that registration of designs is not seen as so important as patents and trade marks, whatever may be the commercial significance of design itself.

 Question

What patterns can be detected in the use of the registered design system since 2000? Why do you think use of the UK systems appears to have more than halved since 2002?

Registration of Community designs[75]

Where and to whom?

8.79   Registration is carried out at the Office of Harmonization in the Internal Market (OHIM) at Alicante in Spain, or through the patent offices of member states (the UK–IPO in the UK).[76]

Who may apply?

8.80   Anyone may apply to register a Community design. But a person entitled to the Community design—that is, the designer or his successor in title, or the employer of the designer who has

---

[74] See for all this RDA 1949, s 19.
[75] See M Schlotelburg, 'The Community Design: first experience with registrations' [2003] EIPR 383.
[76] CDR, Art 38.

developed it in the execution of his duties or following the employer's instructions[77]—may claim to be recognised as the legitimate holder of the design for up to three years after the publication of the registration; and if the person who actually applied for the registration was in bad faith in doing so, then the entitled person may at any time claim recognition in the register.[78] The designer, whether or not the applicant for or the holder of the Community design, has a right to be cited as such before the Office and in the register.[79]

How?

8.81   An application may be made by post, by fax, electronically or in person at the Office. An application form should be completed and must be accompanied by a representation of the design suitable for reproduction. This representation may be a drawing or a photograph. The applicant can file as many designs as he wishes in one multiple application, the only condition being that the products to which the design is applied belong to the same Locarno class, that is, that they pertain to the same type of goods. This condition does not apply when an application concerns ornamentation.

How much?

8.82   The basic charge is 230 euros per single application, with further charges in multiple applications of 115 euros for each additional design from the second to the tenth and 50 euros per design from the eleventh one upwards. There is a further charge of 120 euros for publication of the application.[80]

What happens next?

8.83   Applications are mainly checked for formalities. An examination checks that formal requirements are met and that the design is not contrary to public policy or morality. An application not meeting the formal requirements may be amended, or rejected unless there is compliance. There is no opposition procedure. If there are no problems the design is registered and published immediately or after any deferment period.

Date of registration

8.84   The date of registration is from the date the application is filed.[81]

Registration of transactions

8.85   Transfers of the Community registered design must be, at the request of one of the parties (that is, either side of the transaction), entered in the register and published, before which time the new owner may not use the rights under the design.[82] The design may also be granted in security, and that transaction must likewise be registered to take effect.[83] Both transfers and grants

---

[77] CDR, Art 14. In *Fundación Española para la Innovación de la Artesanía (FEIA) v Cul de Sac Espacio Creativo, S.L. and Acierta Product & Position, S.A.* the ECJ held that Article 14(3) does not apply to Community designs produced as a result of a contract for commission. Furthermore, Article 14(1) meant that the right to the design vested in the designer, unless it was contractually assigned to a successor in title.

[78] CDR, Art 18.   [79] CDR, Art 18.

[80] For fees in OHIM in respect of designs in general see Commission Regulation (EC) No 2246/2002, OJ 2002, L341/54.

[81] CDR, Art 12.   [82] CDR, Art 28.   [83] CDR, Art 29.

in security only have effect in relation to third parties in all member states after entry in the register, and the same also applies to licences, exclusive or non-exclusive.[84] But a transaction can have effect before registration in relation to a third party who acquires rights after its date (that is, in a further, later transaction) who at the time of acquiring the rights knows of the earlier transaction.[85]

Diagram 8.3 Applications and registrations under the Community Designs Regulation 2001 2003–September 2009[86]

Year	Single design applications	Multiple design applications	Number of designs in multiple applications	Number of design registrations
2003	5004	5469	35,620	19,934
2004	6854	7177	46,953	57,764
2005	8375	8422	55,236	67,881
2006	8626	9002	Average per application 6.74	69,540
2007	9269	9944	6.90	74,424
2008	9267	9965	6.81	78,937
2009 (to 30/9/09)	6901	6934	6.54	54,358

Declarations of invalidity

8.86   As the foregoing brief account of the registration processes of OHIM and the UK Designs Registry shows, the offices do not engage in detailed examination of applications to test their compliance with the requirements of definition, novelty, individual character, functionality and public policy and morality discussed earlier in this chapter. Nor is there any provision for third party opposition such as is found in the registration of patents. Save in very exceptional cases, the application is likely to go through to registration.

8.87   But registered designs may still be subject to challenge because in fact they do not meet the requirements laid down by the law. The challenge may come from a defendant when the rightholder is seeking to enforce the design right in court; but it is also possible for 'any person interested' to make an application to the Registrar for a declaration of invalidity based on the nonregistrability of the design.[87] A registration may also be declared invalid on the grounds:

- of its non-registrability;[88]

---

[84]   CDR, Arts 32, 33(1).

[85]   CDR, Art 33(2). This rule does not apply where a Community registered design right is acquired by way of purchasing the whole of a company's undertaking (eg in a takeover) or by any other universal succession (eg transmission of a whole estate on death) (Art 33(3)). The effect of insolvency proceedings is governed by the national law of the place where such proceedings are first brought (Art 33(4)).

[86]   See further JJ Izquierdo Peris, 'Registered Community Design: first two-year balance from an insider's perspective' [2006] EIPR 146 at pp 146–9. Compare Community trade mark registrations (below, para 13.44).

[87]   RDA 1949, s 11ZB.

[88]   RDA 1949, s 11ZA(1) as amended by the Regulatory Reform (Registered Designs) Order 2006, Art 7(2).

- that it is not new or possessed of an individual character in comparison with a design made available to the public on or after the application for registration *but* which has priority nonetheless by virtue of earlier registration, whether in the UK or the Community Registry;[89]

- that the registered proprietor is not the proprietor of the design, and the real proprietor is objecting.[90]

If the design is either in copyright or involves the use of an earlier distinctive sign, then the registration may be declared invalid at the behest of the copyright owner and the holder of rights in the sign respectively.[91] If a ground is made out, the Registrar makes a declaration of invalidity, which can be one of partial invalidity;[92] a proprietor against whom a declaration of invalidity is to be made may also seek instead a modification of the registration, for example by the inclusion of a partial disclaimer.[93] An appeal lies against decisions of the Registrar.[94]

 Question

On what grounds may a design registration be declared invalid?

8.88 There are similar provisions in relation to the invalidity of registered Community designs.[95]

Key points on invalidity

- A registration may be challenged on the grounds that:
- The design does not meet the statutory criteria
- The registered owner is not the owner of the design
- The design infringes copyright or a trade mark right

Invalidity may be partial; OR a registration may be modified.

Rights given by registration

Exclusive right to use the design

8.89 The principal right conferred by registration is quite simply stated as follows:

'the exclusive right to *use* the design . . .' (RDA, s 7(1); DD, Art 12(1); CDR, Art 19(1))

---

[89] RDA 1949, s 11ZA(1A), added by the Regulatory Reform (Registered Designs) Order 2006, para 7(3).
[90] RDA 1949, s 11ZA(2).
[91] RDA 1949, s 11ZA(3) and (4). See for an OHIM Invalidity Division decision that a prior registered trade mark invalidated a Community Registered Design *Zellweger Analytics Ltd's Designs*, 1 March 2006 (commented upon critically by D Smyth, (2006) 1 JIPLP 509).
[92] RDA 1949, s 11ZC   [93] RDA 1949, s 11ZD.   [94] RDA 1949, s 11ZE.
[95] CDR, Title II, Section 5, Titles VI and VII. See further JJ Izquierdo Peris, 'Registered Community Design: first two-year balance from an insider's perspective' [2006] EIPR 146 at pp 149–57.

The Registered Designs Act adds:

'. . . and any design which does not produce on the informed user a different overall impression' (RDA, s 7(1)).

It is thus *a right, not only to the design itself, but to any other design which produces the same overall impression on the informed user.* 'Overall impression' and the 'informed user' are concepts we have already encountered when discussing the requirement of individual character (above, para 8.33); that is, we are not concerned with an examination detail by detail, while the impression that matters is neither that of the expert or the simple end user, but rather that of one who has some knowledge of the design field in question. Section 7(3) also repeats the admonition to have in mind, while assessing overall impression, the degree of freedom of the author in creating the design (above, para 8.33). In the discussion of individual character, it was suggested that the informed user was really the judge trying the case in which the overall impression was being tested, having the benefit of evidence on the subject. Thus in the end each case would tend to turn on its own facts and circumstances as determined by the judge. The same conclusion seems to hold good here. The crucial point for present purposes—considering the scope of the rights conferred—is that *protection extends beyond the exact design registered.*

 Question

What exclusive right is conferred upon the owner of a registered design?

8.90   The concepts of the informed user, design freedom and overall impression are deployed in the infringement case of *Procter & Gamble Co v Reckitt Benckiser (UK) Ltd*,[96] where the competing products were sprayers for air fresheners. The concepts for testing infringement are the same as those for registration (see para 8.33 above). In comparing the products in this case, colours and graphics were not taken into account since they were not part of the registered design. At first instance Lewison J found that there was infringement. The similarities between the overall visual impressions significantly outweighed the differences. The fact that the claimant's design was of far higher quality than the defendant's did not mean that the latter escaped infringement; otherwise a poor quality copy would not be infringement even if it created the same visual impression. The Court of Appeal disagreed and held there was no infringement. In assessing the overall impressions of the two designs, it was not necessary for the differences to be 'clear'. On the issue of quality, Jacob LJ said:

'We are here considering monopolies in designs, not trade marks. A "poor quality" imitation if it does not convey the same impression as the "original" will fail on its own design merits, or rather the lack of them. If it conveys the "same impression" then it can hardly be a "poor quality imitation" and will succeed for the same reason as the "original" ' (para 60).

■ *J Choo (Jersey) Ltd v Towerstone Ltd* [2008] FSR 19 (Ch)

This was a case on Community design right in a handbag. It was held that the informed user was someone with a knowledge of handbag design, rather than the woman in the street, or a

---

[96] [2007] FSR 13 (Patents Court, Lewison J); revd in part [2008] FSR 8 (CA). See for varying decisions elsewhere in Europe on whether the facts in this case amounted to infringement, D Stone, "Some clarity, some confusion: 12 P&G v Reckitt Benckiser decisions help explain registered Community designs" (2008) 3 JIPLP 376.

handbag designer. Such a person would know about the design constraints inherent in handbag design, what features were necessary and un-necessary, and so on.

■ *Rolawn Ltd v Turfmech Machinery Ltd* [2008] ECDR 13 (Mann J)

See also para 8.34. R registered a design under the category of mowers for its own wide-area grass mower. R contended that T had infringed this registered design by creating a grass mower with a folding arms mechanism which was sufficiently similar as not to produce a different overall impression for the informed user. Held that there was no infringement of the registered design right. In particular, differences between the R and T grass mowers emerged in relation to

'the triangular gantry of the Rolawn (missing from the Turfmech machine), the additional wheel on the Turfmech arm, the differences at the forward end of the machine (where it joins the tractor), the very striking differences in the fully folded position (the overall impression of girders in Rolawn vs the overall impression of distributed cutters in Turfmech) and the obvious differences in the shapes of the support structure and tank, both when viewed from the rear and when viewed from the side' (para 126).

8.91   As with other forms of intellectual property, the exclusive right conferred by registration has two main effects. As the Designs Directive and the Community Designs Regulation put it:

'the exclusive right to use [the design] and to prevent any third party not having his consent from using it' (DD, Art 12(1); CDR, Art 19(1)).

So the exclusive right is a basis for challenging—in court if necessary—unauthorised use of the design by others. The converse of that, of course, is that the right holder can authorise others to use the design by way of licences. But the right holder can decide not to do so, and to exploit the exclusive right in an exclusive way.

8.92   A further, fundamentally important, point is that *'use' is a very different concept from 'copying'*, which is the characteristic right to which we have become accustomed by our earlier discussion of copyright. 'Copying' involves a causal connection between an earlier and a later work (see above, para 4.27); an exclusive right to use does not.

Key point on the exclusive right conferred by a registered design

• 'Use' is what is sometimes called a 'monopoly' right
• The holder of a registered design can stop anyone else using the design for a product, regardless of whether or not that other's use was the result of copying

---

8.93   The broad nature of this exclusive right to use explains in part why the registration system exists. A person who proposes to use a design can always check the register to see if the same or a similar design has been registered; if it has, the person is then in a position to know that the proposed use is illegitimate. If however a design is unregistered, the only way a person can know whether someone else has produced the same or a similar design is by finding it already in use on a product in the market place; and, as we will see in the next chapter (below, paras 9.74–9.80), the person can only be liable to the existing user if the former has copied the latter's design. As the matter is put in recital 21 of the Community Design Regulation:

'The exclusive nature of the right conferred by the registered Community design is consistent with its greater legal certainty. It is appropriate that the unregistered Community design should, however, constitute a right only to prevent copying. Protection could not therefore extend to design products which are the result of a design arrived at independently by a second designer.'

 Question

How does design registration support greater legal certainty?

8.94   The legislation goes on to say that use includes (that is, is not limited to):

> 'making, offering, putting on the market, importing, exporting or using of a product in which the design is incorporated or to which it is applied; or stocking such a product for those purposes' (RDA, s 7(2); DD, Art 12(1); CDR, Art 19(1)).

Much of this will typically be *commercial or trading activity*—manufacture, sale, import, export, stocking—but there is no express limitation to a business context in the way the exclusive right of use is framed in the legislation. However, when we turn to the defences (see below, para 8.103–8.107), we find that the right in a registered design is not infringed by an act which is done privately and for purposes which are not commercial.[97] So, essentially, the exclusive right to use a registered design covers commercial use alone.

 Question

Why can we say that registered design protection is essentially about commercial or trading activity?

8.95   The right is a right to use the design; and the typical uses mentioned in the legislation (above) all involve incorporation in or application to a product. But there is no need for an infringer's product to be the same product as that of the right holder. The classic examples are use of wallpaper design on curtains, or of a car design on a toy model.[98]

Key points on exclusive right conferred by a registered design

- A right, not only to the design itself, but to any other design which produces the same overall impression on the informed user
- Protection thus extends beyond the exact design registered
- An exclusive right to use the design, generally commercially
- It is not necessary in an infringement action to show that the defendant copied the original design, just that he used it
- This can be characterised as a 'monopoly' right (see also patents and trade marks for an equivalent approach)
- Innocent infringers are not liable for damages

---

[97] RDA 1949, s 7A(2)(a); DD, Art 13(1)(a); CDR, Art 20(1)(a).
[98] Bently and Sherman, chapter 28.4.1.1.

Duration of rights

8.96   The initial right in a registered design lasts for five years beginning at the date of registration (which is the date of application).[99] The right can be renewed for up to four more periods of five years, making a maximum of 25 years in all.[100] Failure to renew leads to the right ceasing to have effect,[101] but a renewal application may be made up to six months after any such expiry of the right.[102] There are renewal fees which grow more expensive at each stage, as follows:

2nd period renewal	£130.00
3rd period renewal	£210.00
4th period renewal	£310.00
5th period renewal	£450.00
Late renewal fee, per month or part of:	No charge
not exceeding one month	
each succeeding month (up to six months)	£24.00

Diagram 8.4 Extensions of design protection under the Registered Designs Act 1949 2000–2008

Year	2nd period	3rd period	4th period	5th period
2000	3729	1583		
2001	3269	1385		
2002	3323	1319	640	
2003	3887	1675	715	
2004	4023	1689	869	
2005	4131	1786	755	
2006	4182	1848	792	84
2007	4309	2104	871	295
2008	2098	2364	946	402

8.97   These figures suggest that for many businesses, five years' worth of exclusive rights in a design is enough, and that for a very substantial majority 10 years is quite sufficient. Harder to detect from the figures alone are the reasons why renewals do not occur: cost, commercial failure of the design or of the rightholder's business, and simple administrative inefficiency are possibilities as well as conscious decisions that the purpose of protection has been achieved. It is unlikely, however, that having the possibility of protection for 25 years is a significant factor in the decision whether or not to register a design in the first place. But there is a discernible trend towards repeated renewals in every period.

8.98   In OHIM statistics about renewals are not readily available and probably it is still too early to determine any pattern anyway. The renewal charges are as follows (per design, whether or not originally included in a multiple application):[103]

---

[99] RDA 1949, ss 8(1), 3C; DD, Art 10; CDR, Art 12.   [100] RDA 1949, s 8(2).   [101] RDA 1949, s 8(3).
[102] RDA 1949, s 8(4).   [103] See Commission Regulation (EC) No 2246/2002, OJ 2002, L341/54.

Private and non-commercial acts

8.104   There is a similarly worded exception in patent law, which has caused difficulties of interpretation.[109] The acts must be both private *and* non-commercial; so a private act which was commercial would be infringement, as would a non-commercial act which was public. The difficulties in defining private and non-commercial are not inconsiderable. In patent law, private has been defined to mean for the actor's own use; it is not the same as secret. Where an act has both commercial and non-commercial aspects, the subjective intention of the actor is used to determine whether or not the defence is available.

Experimental use

8.105   There is again a similarly worded exception in patent law; and once more its interpretation is open to debate.[110] In the context of designs law, experiments are most likely to occur with a view to determining the best design by which particular functions of a product may be achieved; but one can also imagine experiments being conducted to find designs which were most attractive to consumers. Experimental purposes can also be commercial ones.

Teaching and citations

8.106   This defence seems closer to some of those familiar from copyright law, and it is also subject to conditions somewhat akin to those of the Berne and TRIPS 'three-step' test for copyright exceptions. The teaching defence certainly facilitates activities in relation to design instruction in schools, art and design colleges, and universities; but unlike the parallel copyright exception it is not confined to operations inside educational institutions and so might be applied in an industrial and commercial context as well. The citations defence appears to cover the use of designs in publications such as books of instruction for designers and, it is suggested, textbooks for intellectual property lawyers and students. This would seem perfectly compatible with fair trade practice and not to prejudice unduly the normal exploitation of the design—indeed not to do so at all. The source of the design has to be given in both teaching and citation activities if they are to enjoy the benefit of the defence; it has been said that this is in effect a moral right of paternity for designers.

Must match

8.107   The background to this defence in the long-running debate about the protection of spare parts and complex products under design law has already been discussed in some depth (above, paras 8.61–8.68).[111] Instead of creating a rule that registered design rights did not subsist in those features of a design which enabled it to match with the design of another product of which the first product was intended to form part, the legislators chose to have design right subsistent in such features subject to a defence. The keynote of that defence as stated in both the RDA 1949 and the Community Designs Regulation is repair of the complex product, implying that there must first have been damage to that product.

---

[109] Patents Act 1977, s 60(5)(a); see below para 11.214.   [110] Patents Act 1977, s 60(5)(b); see below, para 11.215.
[111] For a discussion of the application of the three-step test to the protection of spare parts, see A G de Borja, 'Exceptions to design rights: the potential impact of Article 26(2) TRIPS' [2008] EIPR 500.

Exercise

Contrast the 'must match' or 'repair' defence just discussed with the 'must match' exception found in the unregistered designs law of the UK (see above, para 8.61, and below, paras 9.52–9.58). What, if any, difference is there between them, and what, if any, practical effect follows? To what products may the defence apply?

Further reading

Books

General texts

Bently & Sherman, *Intellectual Property Law* (3rd edn, 2009), Part III, Chs 25–28

Copinger & Skone James on Copyright (15th edn, 2005), Ch 13

Cornish & Llewelyn, *Intellectual Property* (6th edn, 2007), Ch 15

M Howe, *Russell-Clarke and Howe on Industrial Designs* (7th edn, 2005)

Laddie, Prescott & Vitoria, *Modern Law of Copyright* (3rd edn, 2000), Ch 42–52

D Musker, *Community Design Law: Principles and Practice* (2002)

J Sykes, *Intellectual Property in Designs* (2005)

History

B Sherman and L Bently, *The Making of Intellectual Property Law* (1999), Chs 3, 4

Articles

Community registered design

R Bird, 'Registered Community Design: early decisions of the OHIM Invalidity Division' [2006] EIPR 297

A Carboni, 'The overlap between registered Community designs and Community trade marks' (2006) 1 JIPLP 256

JJ Izquierdo Peris, 'Registered Community Design: first two-year balance from an insider's perspective' [2006] EIPR 146

M Schlotelburg, 'The Community Design: first experience with registrations' [2003] EIPR 383

Registrability and validity

JJ Izquierdo Peris, 'OHIM practice in the field of invalidity of registered Community designs' [2008] EIPR 56

A Kur, 'No logo!' (2004) 35 IIC 184

D Musker, 'Hidden meaning? UK perspectives on invisible in use designs' [2003] EIPR 450

Spare part protection

J Drexl, RM Hilty and A Kur, 'Design protection for spare parts and the Commission's proposal for a repairs clause' (2005) 36 IIC 448

J Straus, 'Design protection for spare parts gone in Europe? Proposed changes to the EC Directive: the Commission's mandate and its doubtful execution' [2005] EIPR 391

9

Unregistered designs

Introduction

Scope and overview of chapter

9.1　This chapter deals with the various forms of protection available for designs that have not been registered. There are two main forms of protection: the unregistered design right established for the UK by Part II of the CDPA 1988 (UK UDR), and the Community unregistered design right created by the Designs Regulation 2001 (Community UDR). The chapter expounds each of these rights in turn and also considers the role still enjoyed by copyright in relation to the protection of designs.

9.2　**Learning objectives**

By the end of this chapter you should be able to describe and explain:

- the legal protection conferred upon unregistered designs in the UK and the EU, and the differences between the two systems;
- the exclusions of certain features of designs from protection;
- the differences between unregistered design rights and (a) registered design rights and (b) copyright;
- the interaction between unregistered design rights and both registered designs and copyright.

9.3　The chapter begins by setting unregistered design right in the international context described in more detail in the previous chapter. There then follows a detailed account and analysis of the UK unregistered design right (UDR), finishing with an assessment of the right's interaction with copyright. The chapter then examines Community unregistered design right, which is different in a number of important respects from UK unregistered design right, and discusses the issues arising from these differences. So the rest of the chapter looks like this:

- International context (9.4–9.8)
- Historical background of UK UDR (9.9–9.14)

International context

9.4   In the previous chapter (paras 8.4–8.9) we saw how the international framework for the protection of designs did not require that protection to be given through a registration system, and even allowed states to choose to protect designs through copyright law. Indeed the general permissiveness of the international framework extends to enabling states to use more than one form of protection for designs. The creation of UDRs alongside registered designs and copyright systems by, first, the UK, and then by the EU is therefore perfectly consistent with general international intellectual property law.

9.5   We also saw in the previous chapter that if there was a registration system the Paris Convention obliged its member states to give foreigners access to that system; and of course the Berne Copyright Convention requires member states to provide protection under their national law for persons and works from other Berne countries (para 2.8). However there is no equivalent international provision for a system of unregistered design rights separate from copyright; and this gap was used by the UK when it created its UDR in the late 1980s.

9.6   Instead of the usual principle of allowing access to persons and works from outside the country, UK UDR uses a system of *'reciprocity'*. Foreign nationals will only enjoy UK UDR where their own legal system provides equivalent protection for British nationals. The effect of the provision is that British companies are able to copy foreign products entering the UK without fear of litigation ensuing, unless they come from countries with equivalents to design right. The EU countries have been recognised as granting an equivalent protection to the designs of British nationals, but not the USA and Japan.[1]

 Question

How does 'reciprocity' differ from the usual international principle of 'national treatment'?

9.7   The US Semiconductor Chip Protection Act 1984 was the first piece of legislation to use this technique of 'reciprocity' to gain international compliance with a system of IP rights created to

---

[1] CDPA 1988 Act, s 217(3)(c); Design Right (Reciprocal Protection) Order, SI 1989/1294.

protect national rights. In this it was very successful. When the UK introduced UDR in 1988, it followed the US model.[2]

9.8   There is no equivalent limitation of access to the Community UDR.

> ### Key points on international context
>
> - Unregistered design rights are allowed under the international IP systems
> - There may also be more than one form of protection at a time for designs
> - However, foreigners may only access UK UDR if their national laws give equivalent protection in their countries to UK nationals. Under the Paris Convention, there is no requirement of national treatment outside the registration system

Historical background of UK UDR

9.9   UK UDR is a compromise between allowing copyright protection for designs alongside registered designs, as happened in the UK between 1968 and 1988, and only allowing registered design protection. To understand UK UDR, therefore, it is necessary to find out why some businesses thought copyright protection was more useful than registration of designs; and why policy-makers thought that this use of copyright protection was nevertheless a bad thing.

9.10   Once again, only the briefest reference to the development of unregistered design law in the UK is possible here; a fuller account may be found on this book's Online Resource Centre. Since the 19th century legislation has continually tried to prevent copyright protection for designs operating alongside the registration system. The form of the copyright legislation between 1956 and 1988 unintentionally allowed the courts to conclude that unregistered and unregistrable designs could be protected by copyright, however. This had particular importance in the car replacement part industry, where eventually the effects were found to be anti-competitive by the competition authorities in the Ford body parts case. The House of Lords then held in *British Leyland v Armstrong Patents*[3] in 1986 that the copyright in the design of a replacement part (in the case, a car exhaust pipe) could not be exercised 'in derogation from grant', thereby accepting the existence of the copyright, but denying it any practical effect.

Lessons of history to 1988: the correct policy?

9.11   In bringing forward the Copyright Designs and Patents Bill in parliamentary session 1987–88 in the immediate aftermath of the UK competition law investigation of Ford and the decision of the House of Lords in *British Leyland*, the basic policy of the Government was to provide a legal framework which would encourage innovation and competition. In design rights the encouragement of innovation meant, first, creating a legal structure in which investment in design would be rewarded by the grant of protection from unauthorised use of the design by others, and so give rise to advantage over competitors. Without protection there is less incentive to innovate; it is not cost-effective to invest in research and development of ideas if the end result

---

[2] See CDPA 1988, ss 217, 255, 258.   [3] [1986] AC 579. See above para 5.48.

immediately becomes common property. The existence of protection also forces competitors to engage in innovation if they wish to compete lawfully. Competition is fostered, however, by ensuring that this protection is not too strong; for example, in terms of the length of time for which it lasts. This care not to give over-powerful protection also provides a second level of encouragement for innovation, in that the owner of a right must continue to develop design ideas in order to retain or regain such competitive advantage as may have been gained by the initial design. There is a complex interaction between the protection and encouragement of innovation and competition, and a balance has to be struck if both are to be achieved.

9.12   A further general point was the way in which the various parts of intellectual property law should interact in this area. Inventive products should be protected through the patent system. Products whose designs had aesthetic qualities should receive their protection from the registered designs system. Products without either of these qualities should not receive a greater but rather a lesser protection from the law.

9.13   The problem of car spare parts as manifested by the *British Leyland* and *Ford* cases had made apparent the need to remove impediments to a competitive market. The new law certainly removed (or at least severely limited) protection from spare parts for cars. Accordingly, in this area the Government committed itself fully to the encouragement of competition rather than to finding a balance of interests. But this has not been achieved by legislating specifically for car spare parts but instead by the use of general words capable of covering many other situations (see below, paras 9.39–9.58). For a whole host of industries—the aerospace, electrical goods and motor manufacturing ones were most frequently mentioned in the parliamentary debates—the 1988 Act therefore seemed to open up the prospect of what they regarded as piracy of their ideas and investment in research and development without any possibility of control or redress.

 Question

What was the underlying policy of the 1988 Act with regard to unregistered design protection?

9.14   The 1988 Act deals with the problem of design protection on three fronts:

- by severely limiting the ways in which the copyright subsisting in designs may be infringed;
- by amending the RDA 1949 to make registration more attractive to users; and
- by creating a new unregistered design right of much more limited effect and duration than either copyright or registration.

The basic rules of the 1956 Act which led to *British Leyland v Armstrong* are, for the most part, still to be found in the 1988 Act. The belief was that as a result of new provisions in the 1988 Act artistic copyright would cease to be of major significance for industrial designs, although it has not been removed altogether. Copyright subsists in original artistic works. Artistic work includes what are now termed graphic works, irrespective of artistic quality and a graphic work includes any drawing, diagram, map, chart or plan (see above paras 2.69–2.81). In relation to an artistic work the restricted act of copying includes (i) reproduction in any material form, which can be in any way and for any purpose [again, still contrast the limited scope of infringement of a registered design (paras 8.89–8.95)]; and (ii) the making of a copy in three dimensions of a two-dimensional work (paras 4.24–4.33). The spare parts exception propounded by the House of Lords in *British Leyland* (that is, no derogation from grant) was not removed in so many words, and indeed CDPA 1988, section 171(3) provides that nothing in the Act affects any rule of law preventing or restricting the enforcement of copyright, on grounds of public interest or otherwise. Given the legal doctrine of precedent, it is therefore still possible to plead no derogation from grant against copyright enforcement. The hope was that, at any rate with regard to the problem of spare parts, it would not be necessary to do so, because other provisions of the Act took care of the matter. In fact, the defence was used after the entry into force of the 1988 Act, but its death sentence was pronounced by Lord Hoffmann in an appeal to the Privy Council in 1997.[4]

UK UDR: what is a design?

9.15   UK UDR is set out in Part III of CDPA 1988. We begin our analysis by considering the designs to which the UDR can apply, and noting how this differs from the definition of design already encountered in our earlier discussion of registered designs. This is set out in section 213 of CDPA 1988, of which Jacob LJ has memorably observed:

> 'It has the merit of being short. It has no other . . . It is not just a question of drafting (though words and phrases such as "commonplace", "dependent", "aspect of shape or configuration of part of an article" and "design field in question" are full of uncertainty in themselves and pose near impossible factual questions). The problem is deeper: neither the language used nor the context of the legislation give any clear idea of what was intended. Time and time again one struggles but fails to ascertain a precise meaning, a meaning which men of business can reasonably use to guide their conduct.'[5]

Thus forewarned, let us see what we can do to render the section's meaning more comprehensible.

Definition of design

9.16   To be protected by UDR a design must be:

> 'the design of any aspect of the shape or configuration (whether internal or external but excluding surface decoration) of the whole or part of an article' (CDPA 1988, s 213(2)).

9.17   Before turning to explain the different elements in this definition, however, we should also take note of section 213(6), which states that:

> 'design right does not subsist unless and until the design has been recorded in a design document or an article has been made to the design.'

So like copyright the mere idea of a design is not protected; it must be expressed in some tangible form.[6]

---

[4] *Canon Kabushiki Kaisha v Green Cartridge Co (Hong Kong) Ltd* [1997] AC 728 (Privy Council, appeal from Hong Kong). See above para 5.48.

[5] *Dyson Ltd v Qualtex (UK) Ltd* [2006] RPC 31, para 14.

[6] *Rolawn Ltd v Turfmech Machinery Ltd* [2008] ECDR 13, paras 79–83 per Mann J.

9.18   *Design document* is defined as:

> 'any record of a design, whether in the form of a drawing, a written description, a photograph, data stored in a computer or otherwise' (CDPA 1988, s 263(1)).

The scope of this definition is quite wide.

■ *Squirewood Ltd v H Morris & Co Ltd* 1993 GWD 20–1239 (Outer House, Court of Session)

The petitioners designed office furniture and produced brochures in which their furniture was described and illustrated by photographs and drawings. Lord Clyde granted interim interdict on the basis that the brochure was a design document. It could however have been made clearer in the opinion that UDR did not subsist in the brochure as such or as a design document. UDR subsists in the design, of which the design document is a record only. It is not necessary to refer to any design document to determine whether infringement of a UDR has taken place. As will be further discussed below (paras 9.71–9.81), all that is needed for infringement is to establish the causal link of copying between the original design and subsequent commercial reproduction of articles exactly or substantially to that design (CDPA 1988, section 226).

■ *Lambretta Clothing Co Ltd v Teddy Smith (UK) Ltd* [2005] RPC 6 (Court of Appeal)

It was held that a simple drawing of a track top showing its colours was a design document even although the colours were excluded from UDR protection as surface decoration.[7]

9.19   The role of computer technology in design work is recognised in the definition of design document. Data stored in a computer is capable of constituting a design document. Section 215 of CDPA 1988 also refers with the possibility of a computer generating a design without any significant human intervention (cf para 3.22).

> ### Key points on form and design document
>
> - There must be a design document before there will be UDR
> - A design document is any record of the design and can include the article itself as well as written descriptions and data stored in a computer

9.20   We now take each part of the definition of 'design' (above, para 9.16) in turn, although not in the order in which they appear in the statutory wording.

Design of the whole or part of an article

9.21   Despite the importance of component or spare parts in the history lying behind UDR, it is not limited to that kind of product. UDR applies to free-standing items of all kinds. In this way it gives protection from industrial copying to the product design which for whatever reason is unregistered (eg because it is unregistrable, or the owner has decided not to register, or has left it

---

[7] The significance of this was to limit how the copyright in the document might be infringed under CDPA 1988, s 51: see further below, paras 9.87–9.88. One implication might be that the well-advised designer makes two documents: one which is a design document and one which is not, the latter for the purpose of invoking full copyright protection where necessary.

too late, or was unaware of the possibility of registration at the time of creation). UDR certainly therefore helps the manufacturers of many different kinds of products. Products held protected by UDR have included pig fenders with roll bars, slurry separators, lawnmowers and clothing items; so the reach of the right is extensive.

9.22   As we will see in more detail later (paras 9.25–9.34), UDR concentrates on the appearance of the product rather than on the way it is made. But there is no requirement that the appearance of the product should appeal to the eye, either of the customer or of anyone else.[8] Indeed, it is clear from the section that the design feature need not be ordinarily visible in the finished article (below, para 9.30). Functional designs are not excluded from UDR either.[9] So there are significant contrasts with registered design law here (see above, paras 8.39–8.46).

9.23   But, as will be explored further below (below, para 9.59ff), the protection is not so extensive as under the amended 1949 Act, particularly in respect of scope of rights and duration. Accordingly, a manufacturer will have to make a choice whether or not to register his design. That choice will presumably depend on the resources of the designer and the expected market life of the product, and must be made within 12 months of putting the product on the market.[10] The manufacturer will as a matter of course have UDR and, for what it is worth in the light of CDPA 1988, sections 51 and 52 (below, paras 9.87–9.99), copyright from the time that there is a design document, but if a product made to that design is marketed for more than 12 months prior to registration, then the right to register will be lost.

9.24   There is no statutory definition of the meaning of the word 'article' in relation to unregistered design right, but it should be noted that the design protected may be of *part* of an article. So in principle component parts, including spare parts, can attract UDR; but this is subject to the 'must fit' and 'must match' exceptions, which are intended to exclude such articles from protection to at least some extent (see further below para 9.39ff). It is thus *not* quite right to say, as Mummery LJ did in *Farmers Build Ltd v Carier Bulk Materials Handling Ltd*, that 'the purpose of introducing the design right [is] ... in the case of spare parts, to remove protection from copying completely'.[11]

 Question

Why is it not right to say spare parts are excluded from UDR protection?

 Exercise

Consider whether the following case should be treated as relevant for defining 'article' in UDR. If so, what are the consequences for UDR? What reasons might there be for holding the decision not relevant?

---

[8] Cf the former requirement of 'eye appeal' in the RDA 1949, discussed in the historical outline of the subject accessible on this book's Online Resource Centre.

[9] *Landor & Hawa International Ltd v Azure Designs Ltd* [2007] FSR 9 (CA), noted by D Wilkinson 'Case closed: functional designs protected by design right' [2007] EIPR 118.

[10] As a result of the pre-registration grace period: see paras 8.36–8.38.   [11] [1999] RPC 461 at 480.

■ *R v Registered Designs Appeal Tribunal ex parte Ford Motor* Co [1995] 1 WLR 18 (HL)

This case was decided under the RDA 1949 as it stood between 1989 and 2001. The question was whether the designs of spare parts for cars had been 'applied to articles' as required by that version of the 1949 Act. The House of Lords held that in general such parts had no reality as articles of commerce apart from the vehicle itself; they applied the then definition of 'article' for registered design right as 'any article of manufacture [including] any part of an article if that is made and sold separately' (RDA 1949, s 46(1)). But applications in respect of the designs of a wing mirror, a vehicle seat, a steering wheel, wheels and wheel covers were allowed to proceed, these being features where substitutions of a character distinct from the part being replaced were possible, while leaving the general shape and appearance of the vehicle itself unaffected. The House held that there was an essential difference between an item designed for incorporation in a larger article, whether as an original component or a spare part, which would be unregistrable as an article, and an item designed for general use, albeit aimed principally at use with the manufacturer's own artefacts, which would be registrable as an article.

There might be an argument that 'whole or part' means that UDR is intended to arise for the overall design of products complete in themselves, or for those parts of the design which are not excluded by other words in the legislation, such as surface decoration (below, paras 9.32–9.33) and the 'must fit' and 'must match' exceptions (see further below, para 9.39ff). But in *Dyson Ltd v Qualtex (UK) Ltd*[12] Mann J and the Court of Appeal had no difficulty in holding that 'pattern parts' for Dyson vacuum cleaners attracted UDR in their own right and not simply as part of the overall design of the cleaners.

> ## Key points on meaning of design of whole or part of an article
>
> - UDR applies to free-standing items of all kinds as well as component and spare parts of other products
> - Functional designs are not excluded from UDR (but note must fit/must match exclusions later on)
> - There is no requirement that the article or part in question be visible in ordinary use

Shape or configuration

9.25   'Shape' and 'configuration' are concepts already familiar from registered design law (see above, para 8.25), where until the reforms triggered by the Designs Directive 1998 they were usually taken as referring to the three-dimensional aspects of a product, and as distinct from two-dimensional pattern or ornamentation applied to the surface of the article. Thus a feature of UDR which appeared distinctive in 1988 was that, unlike registered design protection, it did *not* apply to two-dimensional 'pattern and ornamentation'. This seemed also to be underlined by the exclusion of 'surface decoration' of an article from the scope of UDR. But, as we saw in the previous chapter, the distinction between the three- and the two-dimensional has been blurred by the European reforms of the 1990s and early 2000s (see above, para 8.20). Whether or not

---

[12] [2005] RPC 19 (Mann J); aff'd [2006] RPC 31. For commentary on the significance of this case see A Michaels, 'The end of the road for "pattern spare" parts? *Dyson Ltd v Qualtex (UK) Ltd*' [2006] EIPR 396; J Sykes, 'The unregistered design right: interpretation and practical application of the must-match exemption' (2006) 1 JIPLP 442.

under this influence, the UDR case law has demonstrated both the refinements possible in the concept of 'three-dimensional' and the ability to accommodate designs which are essentially two-dimensional, yet not 'surface decoration'.

9.26   The basis for this has been the legislation's apparent distinction between 'shape' *or* 'configuration'. While shape certainly refers to three-dimensional features, it has been suggested that configuration may cover at least some two- as well as three-dimensional designs. So electronic circuit diagrams[13] have been held covered by UDR as configurations.

■ *Mackie Designs v Behringer Specialised Studio Equipment (UK) Ltd* [1999] RPC 717 (Pumfrey J)

It was held that electronic circuit diagrams were covered by UDR, as 'configuration' rather than shape; 'configuration' should be broadly construed to cover 'the relative arrangement of parts or elements'.

9.27   The limits of this broad approach to 'configuration' are not clear, although the decision can probably be extended to mechanical engineering designs, such as pneumatic and hydraulic circuits, and chemical or process flow diagrams. Design right applies to semiconductor topographies, although these are essentially patterns fixed or etched upon semiconductor material, rather than shapes or configurations. The availability of the protection is however the result of express legislation, the Design Right (Semiconductor Topographies) Regulations 1989,[14] which apply the design right provisions of the 1988 Act to this subject matter.

9.28   The broad approach suggested in *Mackie* has been criticised: a merely schematic diagram[15] of something cannot be the design of an article, since it could be represented by any one of several different articles. Contrast the following case with *Mackie Designs*:

■ *Baby Dan AS v Brevi Srl and another* [1999] FSR 377

BD manufactured and sold child safety barriers in the UK, and BS distributed them in Italy. The barrier consisted of various component parts. When the distributorship ceased, BS started to manufacture child safety barriers in Italy, and the second defendant imported and sold these barriers in the UK. BD claimed that there was copying by BS and infringement by both defendants. It was held that the *relative locations* of inter-related functional parts of BD's safety barrier were not aspects of its configuration.

 Discussion point   For answer guidance visit www.oxfordtextbooks.co.uk/orc/macqueen2e/

Refer to the discussion in paras 2.64–2.65 about electronic circuit diagrams and copyright, then consider how such diagrams differ from the designs of child safety barriers as revealed in the *Baby Dan* case. Why are the relative locations of the component parts of the latter not 'configuration' when electronic circuit diagrams apparently are?

---

[13] On the nature of electronic circuit diagrams, and the definitional problems they pose for copyright law, see paras 2.64–2.65. See also, for penetrating analysis before the cases began to come before the courts, J Reynolds and P Brownlow, 'Increased legal protection for schematic designs in the UK' [1994] EIPR 398.

[14] SI 1989/1100 (amended by SI 1991/2237 and SI 1992/400).

[15] A schematic diagram is one which does not give an impression of the physical actuality of that which is represented. An example is the well-known map of the London Underground, from which it is not possible to determine the actual geographical position of the stations or of the exact routes followed by the tunnels; but you can tell what the relative positions are and the connections between them.

See further the case below:

■ *Lambretta Clothing Co Ltd v Teddy Smith (UK) Ltd* [2005] RPC 6 (Court of Appeal)

The product in question was L's track top, the shape of which was old (or 'retro'). The new fea-ture was the choice of colours ('colourways')—blue for the body, red for the arms, white for the zip. L claimed T was copying and selling these tops. T claimed that the colourways were pro-tected as configuration of the garment. It was held that UDR did not subsist in L's top. Giving the main judgment, Jacob LJ pointed out that, while it would not be an abuse of language to say that the colours of the top were configured together, registered designs law had never held colouration to constitute configuration, and ruled that even with the wide meaning of the word UDR does not subsist in the arrangement of colours (or in patterns, such as that of a patchwork quilt).

9.29   'Configuration' is therefore not excluded from the three-dimensional, even if the design in question essentially relates to the surface of the product in question.

■ *A Fulton Co Ltd v Grant Barnett & Co Ltd* [2001] RPC 16 (Park J)

Outward facing seams on the edge of a case for a compact umbrella accentuated a rectangular (rather than the more usual cylindrical) character for the product (see photographs at pp 290–2 of the report). It was held that the seams were protected as configuration (and not excluded as surface decoration), even although only marginally three-dimensional.

Further, 'shape' can reach down into very fine aspects of the three-dimensional. As Jacob LJ remarked in *Lambretta Clothing Co Ltd v Teddy Smith (UK) Ltd*:

> 'All articles (even thin flat ones) are 3 dimensional (using the practical Euclidean view of the world—not that of modern physics). There is no reason why a "design" should not subsist in what people would ordinarily call a "flat" or "2-dimensional" thing—for instance a new design of doily would have a new"shape" and could in principle have UDR in it.'[16]

The same judge has also drawn attention to the fact that the legislation confers UDR upon 'any aspect' of the shape or configuration of an article,[17] and held that this means any 'discernible' or 'recognisable' element of the shape or configuration.[18]

■ *Ocular Sciences Ltd v Vision Care Ltd* [1997] RPC 289 (Laddie J)

The products in this case were contact lenses (some 200 designs in total). The designs claimed related to the front surface dimensions of the lens, the rear surface dimensions, and the edge characteristics. The lenses differed from each other only in fine dimensional details, but the plaintiffs argued that these dimensions were a way of defining the shape or configuration. It was held that although these differences of dimension were indistinguishable by the human eye, that did not mean that the designs were not in fact different. So these dimensions could not be excluded from protection on the grounds that they were not designs. However, mere changes in scale did not amount to design differences.

---

[16] [2005] RPC 6, para 24.   [17] CDPA 1988, s 213(2).
[18] *A Fulton v Totes Isotomer (UK) Ltd* [2004] RPC 16, para 31; *Dyson Ltd v Qualtex (UK) Ltd* [2006] EWCA 166, paras 22–3.

> ### Key points on shape or configuration
>
> - The words 'shape or configuration' suggest that basically UDR protects the design of the three- rather than the two-dimensional
> - However, the courts have (controversially) given protection to electronic circuit diagrams under UDR
> - Protection has also been given to objects (eg contact lenses) where the three-dimensional character of the product was barely discernible to the human eye

Whether internal or external: visibility

9.30 UDR is expressly not limited to what is visible when the product is in use (contrast Community design rights for component parts of complex products: see above, para 8.51). The product could be one which spends its entire operative life concealed within or beneath another product, as with a terminal in a washing machine, or an exhaust pipe in a car; or it could be the internal parts of a product which also has external parts, such as the shape and configuration of the inside of a car roof box. In the *Farmers Build* case, the products in question were internal components, namely hoppers in slurry separators; in *A Fulton Co Ltd v Totes Isotomer (UK) Ltd*,[19] they were cases for umbrellas.

9.31 Another interesting possible subject of unregistered design right has been suggested by Sean Hird and Michael Peeters, namely synthesised molecules of DNA, the products of genetic engineering. They argue that 'each of the four classes of nucleotide which make up a DNA molecule has a unique shape which can be distinguished under an electron microscope. Therefore a recombinant DNA molecule will have a unique shape insofar as it consists of a unique sequence of nucleotides.'[20] Since there is no requirement that a design be visible, there seems no reason why a molecule should not be an article, and that accordingly the genetic engineer may claim UDR.[21]

> **Question**
>
> What is the difference between registered design protection and UDR with regard to the visibility of the product to which the design in question is applied?

Surface decoration exclusion

9.32 The exclusion of surface decoration is because generally such material—decoration on the surface of the article—will be the subject of copyright and so does not need the additional protection of UDR.[22] At first sight, the exclusion seems simply to reaffirm the concern of the right with

---

[19] [2004] RPC 18.

[20] S Hird and M Peeters, 'UK protection for recombinant DNA—exploring the options' [1991] EIPR 334.

[21] The claim might however fall foul of the exclusion of methods or principles of construction from UDR (for which see below para 9.34); this might be applicable to a nucleotide sequence.

[22] *Dyson Ltd v Qualtex (UK) Ltd* [2006] RPC 31 per Jacob LJ at para 78.

the three-dimensional; but the case law shows that the position is somewhat more complex, since the exclusion has been held to affect three-dimensional features of a design and, at least in a particular context (clothing), to reach below the actual surface of the product in question.

■ *Mark Wilkinson Furniture Ltd v Woodcraft Designs (Radcliffe) Ltd* [1998] FSR 63

This case concerned surface decoration on kitchen furniture. The parties were competitors in the design and manufacture of furniture for fitted kitchens. MW claimed UDR in the whole external appearance of a single wall unit or, alternatively, in two specific features, that is, (1) substantially curved quadrant corners between the front and side panels; and (2) shallow v-grooves running down the cornice and continuing down the vertical edge of the quadrant corners.[23] It was held that the *overall* design of MW's wall unit was one in which UDR could subsist, being for an aspect or aspects of the shape or configuration of the unit. But surface decoration was excluded from the design in which UDR can subsist. Surface decoration included both decoration lying on the surface of the article and decorative features of the surface itself, and was not confined to features that were essentially two-dimensional. It further included decorative features also serving a functional purpose. Applying this test, the v-grooves (and painted finish and cockbeading) were excluded from the design as aspects or features of surface decoration. But the quadrant corners were not excluded, as significant parts of the shape and configuration of the furniture.

■ *Jo Y Jo v Matalan Retail* [2000] ECDR 178

Embroidery on ladies' garments was surface decoration and so excluded; but not the choice of fabric, or edging.

■ *Hi-Tech Autoparts Ltd v Towergate Two Ltd (No 2)* [2002] FSR 16

Projections on a car floor mat were held to play an important function in the use of the mat, and so not excluded from protection as mere surface decoration.

■ *Lambretta Clothing Co Ltd v Teddy Smith (UK) Ltd* [2005] RPC 6 (Court of Appeal)

See previously para 9.28. T claimed that the colourways of the retro track tops were surface decoration; L responded that the colours ran right through the garment, not just its surface. It was held that UDR did not subsist in L's top. The exclusion of surface decoration applied to both the situation where the decoration was a thin layer covering the surface of the product and the one where it ran throughout the article. The court affirmed the approach of the judge in *Mark Wilkinson* (above) that surface decoration could be more than essentially flat, and could be three-dimensional. If such three-dimensional surface decoration was protected at all, it was by artistic copyright.

9.33   After analysis of the authorities on surface decoration in *Dyson Ltd v Qualtex (UK) Ltd*,[24] Mann J held that the distinction between overall shape and configuration was a useful one which was however dependent on facts and impressions in each case (in other words, a value judgment). If the aspect of the design in question was primarily functional, then it would not be 'mere' surface decoration; but if the functional purpose was subsidiary, then the exclusion might still bite.

---

[23] See pp 68–9 of the report for diagrams of the furniture, and Bently & Sherman, p 690, for a photograph of it.
[24] [2005] RPC 19, paras 36–8, aff'd [2006] RPC 31.

In assessing this issue, the intention of the designer is relevant. This approach was approved in the Court of Appeal.

Discussion point For answer guidance visit www.oxfordtextbooks.co.uk/orc/macqueen2e/

What is the difference between 'shape or configuration' and 'surface decoration'?

Key points on surface decoration exclusion

- Surface decoration is not limited to two-dimensional ornamentation of the article but can extend to three-dimensional features
- It can include features which run right through an article from its surface (eg colourways on a garment)
- If the feature performs or contributes to a function of the article, it is unlikely to be excluded from UDR protection as mere surface decoration

---

Methods or principles of construction

9.34 Methods and principles of construction are excluded from UDR as well, being protectable by patent if at all. In registered designs law before 2001 there was a similar exclusion, which had been judicially glossed as follows:[25]

> 'A mode or principle of construction is a process or operation by which a shape is produced as opposed to the shape itself.'

This definition has been used quite often in UDR cases.

■ *Baby Dan AS v Brevi Srl and another* [1999] FSR 377

The child safety barrier case (for facts, see above para 9.28). As already noted, it was held that the *relative locations* of inter-related functional parts of BD's safety barrier were not aspects of its configuration; they amounted rather to a method or principle of construction, and were therefore excluded from protection by UDR.

Question

Might electronic circuit diagrams be principles and methods of construction?

■ *Landor & Hawa International Ltd v Azure Designs Ltd* [2006] FSR 22 (PCC) affd [2007] FSR 9 (CA)

The arrangement of zippers and piping for the expander section of a suitcase design was held *not* to be a principle or method of construction. The exclusion was to prevent the creation of what

---

[25] *Kestos Ltd v Kempat Ltd* (1936) 53 RPC 139 per Luxmoore J at 151.

would be in effect petty or trivial patents; but here other designers could easily use the features in quite distinct designs, so the effect of the UDR would not be petty-patent-like.[26]

Original and not commonplace

9.35   Designs must be 'original' to attract design right.[27] But a later sub-section provides that:

'a design is not "original" for the purposes of [UDR] if it is commonplace in the design field in question at the time of its creation' (CDPA 1988, s 213(4)).

It might have been thought that this meant the test of originality in unregistered design right is *not* the same as in copyright. However the Court of Appeal has clearly accepted in several cases[28] a two-step approach to this question, asking:

(1) *whether the design is original in the copyright sense* of being independently produced as a result of the designer's own skill and labour, and not copied from the work of another.[29] In approaching the question of originality, the design should be approached as a whole, although some consideration of its individual features is often necessary as well.[30]

(2) The second stage is analysis of *whether or not the design is commonplace in the design field in question*, usually resulting in a subsidiary, but necessary, further analysis of what constitutes that design field.

Most of the decisions have been concerned with how to test 'commonplace-ness' rather than originality.

■ *C & H Engineering Ltd v F Klucznik & Sons Ltd* [1992] FSR 421 (Aldous J)

The subject matter for discussion in this case was pig fenders, devices to stop piglets leaving the sty while enabling the sow to step over into the field outside the sty. It is important that the fender be shaped so that the sow's teats are not scratched as she steps over it. The fender in the case solved this problem by having a two-inch rounded metal tube placed around its top edge (see p 423 of the report for photographs). Aldous J held that originality in design right is the same as in copyright. The test meant that the design must not be copied from another design but be the independent work of the designer (at 427). The judge went on to say: 'By 1990 pig fenders were commonplace and had been made in metal and wood. In essence [the farmer] wanted a commonplace pig fender with a metal roll bar on the top…the only part of the pig fender shown in the drawing which was not commonplace was the 2 inch tube on the top' (at 428). Aldous J then referred to the provision about commonplace designs and concluded that '*for the design to be original it must be the work of the creator and that work must result in a design which is not commonplace in the relevant field*' (at 428, emphasis supplied). Thus the issue concerned, not the whole of the pig fender, but just the roll bar. Under CDPA 1988, section 213 UDR subsists in designs, and a design may be the design of the whole *or part* of an article. UDR could therefore have subsisted in the roll bar alone. It is doubtful whether the rest of the pig fender had any design right.

[26] See also *Bailey v Haynes* [2007] FSR 10 (design of micromesh for bait bag covered by exclusion).
[27] CDPA 1988, s 213(1).
[28] The main Court of Appeal decision is *Farmers Build Ltd v Carier Bulk Materials Handling Ltd* [1999] RPC 461 (summarised below). See also *Dyson Ltd v Qualtex (UK) Ltd* [2006] RPC 31, per Jacob LJ at paras 85–99.
[29] On the copyright concept of originality see paras 2.34–2.44.   [30] *Guild v Eskander* [2003] FSR 3, para 53.

■ *Farmers Build Ltd v Carier Bulk Materials Handling Ltd* [1999] RPC 461 (CA)

The case concerned competing slurry separators (machines which separate manure into solid and liquid parts for use as fertiliser). The plaintiffs' slurry separator was in part based on the designs of two earlier separators, and internally the machinery was based around 'hoppers' which the respondents argued had long been in use for agricultural machinery. It was held: (1) the design was original in the sense of not being simply copied from the earlier machines; and that it was not commonplace; (2) given the already limited scope of UDR, the 'commonplace' exception should be given a narrow interpretation. It was not equivalent to the 'novelty' of registered designs; (3) a comparative exercise in the relevant design field was required: the closer the various designs in the field were to each other, the more likely it was that the design in question was commonplace. Coincidental similarity could well mean that there was only one way of designing the article. But if there were aspects of the design not found in any other design in the field, the court was entitled to conclude that the design was not commonplace. A commonplace *article* can have an un-commonplace shape or configuration,[31] and the legislation conferred the right on the design rather than the product. The hopper in this case was such a commonplace article but had a different shape or configuration from those in the previous slurry separators.

■ *Ocular Sciences Ltd v Vision Care Ltd* [1997] RPC 289 (Laddie J)

The products in this case were contact lenses (some 200 designs in total). The designs claimed related to the front surface dimensions of the lens, the rear surface dimensions, and the edge characteristics. The defendants argued that the designs were commonplace; the plaintiffs' response was that the combinations of dimensions had not been used before and were not commonplace. It was held that there was nothing out of the ordinary about the plaintiffs' contact lenses; either the lens designs as a whole were commonplace, or the combination of features therein so far as not excluded by the 'must fit' exception (see further below, paras 9.45–9.51). 'Any design which is trite, trivial, common-or-garden, hackneyed or of the type which would excite no particular attention in those in the relevant art is likely to be commonplace' (per Laddie J at 428–9). The closer the similarity of the designs in a particular field, the more likely it is that the designs are commonplace, especially if there is no causal connection (such as copying) between them. But a design made up of commonplace elements might still not be in the overall commonplace.

■ *Scholes Windows Ltd v Magnet Ltd* [2002] FSR 10 (Court of Appeal)

This case concerned decoratively shaped window frames made in unplasticated PVC. It was held that the design field was window frames generally. Design was defined in relation to shape and configuration, not to materials or nature/purpose of the article. The design field should therefore be defined in relation to the shape or configuration. In considering the design field, the court had to take account of what designs were in the field at the time of the creation of the design in question, including old designs. Victorian window frames were still in use and formed part of the design field.

---

[31] For a later illustration of this see *A Fulton Co Ltd v Grant Barnett & Co Ltd* [2001] RPC 16, para 54 (umbrella cases commonplace, but rectangular shapes not a commonplace design for such products).

■ *Lambretta Clothing Co Ltd v Teddy Smith (UK) Ltd* [2005] RPC 6 (Court of Appeal)

For the facts and other findings, see above, para 9.28. It was held that the choice of red, blue and white colourways was commonplace in the field of leisurewear design. A reasonably broad approach to 'the design field in question' was called for. What mattered was the sort of designs with which a notional designer of the article concerned would be familiar. In this case the design of well-known *actual* sportswear (whether strictly so-called or not) would be part of the background in the mind of a designer wishing to give a garment a sporty image.

■ *Rolawn Ltd v Turfmech Machinery Ltd* [2008] ECDR 13 (Mann J)

For the facts and other findings, see above, paras 8.34 and 8.90. The judge considered whether the design of a wide-area grass mower was excluded from protection for being commonplace in the design field in question. Whilst T argued that the correct design field was agricultural machinery generally, R maintained that it was the narrower field of mower design. R accepted that, given the evidence, a designer and an informed user would be aware of agricultural machinery in general. It was held that while many of the individual elements of the designs of the R mower could be found elsewhere in that general agricultural machinery field, nothing in that design field looked like the actual mower in the particular configurations claimed. According to the judge:

> '[I]t is (I find) commonplace to have staggered cutters, and commonplace to have a box structure made up of triangular sections. However, the particular combination of those features that one sees making up the overall designs of "the whole" in its extended, semi-retracted and fully retracted positions is not commonplace' (para 89)

 Discussion point   For answer guidance visit www.oxfordtextbooks.co.uk/orc/macqueen2e/

What is the difference between 'original' and 'not commonplace'?

9.36   The UDR requirement that a design be original and not commonplace in its design field looks like a compromise or half-way house between the registered design standard of 'novelty' and the copyright one of originality. Many of the questions which are asked in each of these two tests can usefully be asked again in the context of UDR. For example, from registered designs law we might draw the following:

> The *territorial question*: is the design field with which comparison is to be made limited to the UK (or possibly to England and Wales, or Scotland, or Northern Ireland, depending on which jurisdiction the parties are in), *or* should it extend more generally, to those designs of which the designer was or could reasonably have been aware, *or* should designs from across the world be taken into account?

9.37   In *Fulton v Totes*[32] it was held that the design field was limited to the UK ('What relevance to the UK market has a design which is commonplace in Vanuatu?').[33] In *Dyson Ltd v Qualtex (UK) Ltd*,[34] Mann J took a slightly broader approach: 'the design must be commonplace in the UK in the sense that UK designers in the field would have to be aware of the design to an extent sufficient to make it commonplace if the statutory exemption is to operate... [T]o [that] question the marketing of the other article or articles in which the design appears will be relevant but

---

[32] [2003] RPC 27 (Fysh QC), aff'd without comment [2004] RPC 16 (CA).
[33] [2003] RPC 27, para 73.   [34] [2005] RPC 19, paras 42–9.

not essential.' However in other cases global design fields have been used, or comparisons made with designs from other countries.[35]

> The *whose eye question*: in assessing the similarity of the design in question to other designs in the field, through whose eye is the court looking – the designer's or the customer's?

9.38 In *Ocular Sciences Ltd v Vision Care Ltd*,[36] Laddie J said that the comparative exercise must be conducted objectively, with the benefit of expert evidence in the field, but in the end the judgment was the court's. In *A Fulton Co Ltd v Grant Barnett & Co Ltd*[37] it was held that a design might well not be commonplace even if the public appeared not to like it. In *Lambretta Clothing Co Ltd v Teddy Smith (UK) Ltd*[38] the Court of Appeal said that what mattered was the sort of designs with which a notional designer of the article concerned would be familiar. The test therefore seems to be looking through the designer's eye.[39]

Key points on original and not commonplace

- The UDR test of originality is the same as in copyright
- The 'not commonplace' test is then applied, using the 'design field in question' as the basis of assessment
- It is the 'commonplace-ness' of the design, not the article, which is to be tested
- It is not fully settled whether the design field has any geographical limitations, or whether it is assessed from the point of view of designers or other people

---

 Exercise

Consider again the case of *Interlego v Tyco Inc* [1989] AC 217. If the design of the toy bricks had satisfied the originality test, to what extent would they have also been regarded as not commonplace in the design field in question? What about the design which is worked out over time through a series of drawings or other representations, or through successive generations of the product's design? Will the ultimate design in the series have to be visually different from its predecessors to be original as in the *Interlego* case? On this, see also the judgments of Mann J in *Dyson Ltd v Qualtex (UK) Ltd* [2005] RPC 19, paras 21–5, and of Jacob LJ on appeal, [2006] RPC 31, paras 98–110.

Exclusions: must fit, must match

9.39 Excluded from the protection of UDR are a number of aspects of designs that might otherwise fall within the scope of the right. These exclusions reflect some of the problem areas which

---

[35] *Guild v Eskander Ltd* [2001] FSR 38 (Rimer J, dealing with ladies' luxury fashion; defendant's argument that the field was a 'sensual/philosopher' one rejected); *Spraymiser Ltd & Snell v Wrightway Marketing Ltd* [2000] ECDR 349 (comparison with US design).
[36] [1997] RPC 289. [37] [2001] RPC 16, para 60.
[38] [2005] RPC 6. This aspect of the issue was not discussed in the Court of Appeal.
[39] cf *Bailey v Haynes* [2007] FSR 10 (design of bait bag: notional addressee an angler).

developed as a result of the availability of copyright protection before the CDPA 1988. In particular, the exceptions to UDR protection considered in this section are the main way in which the spare parts problem manifested by the *British Leyland* case is now dealt with by the law.

'Must fit and must match' exceptions

9.40   Two features of designs may be excluded from the protection of design right—the *'must fit'* and *'must match'* exceptions, concerning which there was considerable debate as the measure passed through Parliament. The design of features of shape or configuration of an article which are there to enable the article to fit with, or match, the appearance of another article is excluded from unregistered design protection.

9.41   *'Fit'* is an encapsulation of the statutory formula, which is:

> 'features of shape or configuration of an article which enable the article to be connected to or placed in, around or against another article so that either article may perform its function' (CDPA 1988, s 213(3)(b)(i)).

9.42   *'Match'* summarises:

> 'features of shape or configuration of an article which are dependent upon the appearance of another article of which the article is intended by the designer to form an integral part' (CDPA 1988, s 213(3)(b)(ii)).

 Question

What are the key elements in the above definitions of 'must fit' and 'must match' designs?

9.43   The aim of the exceptions, as the Government made clear in Parliament when it brought them forward, was to tackle the problem of the spare parts for motor cars which had been at the heart of the *British Leyland* case and the Monopolies Commission report on Ford (see above, para 9.10). The legislation was not confined to those specific situations, however, and, as a result, the precise scope of its application is far from clear. Plainly the *British Leyland* case is covered: an exhaust pipe is an excellent example of a design with features of shape and configuration which are there to enable it to fit another article (ie a car). The decisions of the lower courts and tribunals in the *Ford* case (below, para 9.53) also confirmed that motor vehicle body panels could not be registered as a result of the 'must match' exception.[40]

 Question

What was the main objective of the 'must fit' and 'must match' exceptions to UDR?

9.44   What then is the scope of the exceptions apart from those cases to which it was a direct response, and more generally outside the motor industry? The 1988 Act itself provides that both the 'must

---

[40] *Ford Motor Co Ltd and Iveco Fiat SpA's Applications* [1993] RPC 399, affd sub nom *Ford Motor Co Ltd's Design Application* [1994] RPC 545 (DC).

match' and the 'must fit' exceptions apply to kits of parts which when assembled form a complete article[41] (a common example is an item of self-assembly furniture, such as a desk, bed or wardrobe). The case law now allows us to say quite a bit more about both exceptions.

Must fit

9.45 A large number of the cases about 'must fit' have not involved cars or other motor vehicles.

■ *Electronic Techniques (Anglia) v Critchley Components* [1997] FSR 401

This case concerned the design of transformers, electrical equipment which could increase or decrease the voltage of an alternating electric current. The transformers in question were very small and fitted inside electronic equipment such as computers and telephone modems. They were used extensively in equipment to be connected to telephone lines. The plaintiffs, E, argued that since their claim was to UDR in the complete transformers, the 'must fit' exception could only apply to those parts of the design of the whole transformer by which it was enabled to interface with some other article. The defendants, C, argued that the 'must fit' exception also applied to the interconnecting parts of the components which made up the transformers. Laddie J upheld C's argument. The law was concerned with design rather than with protecting particular articles. 'Must fit' was an exclusion of protection for interconnecting features, and there was no reason in the legislation why it should not apply merely because the two interfitting articles were assembled together and formed the whole or part of another, larger article.

■ *Ocular Sciences Ltd v Vision Care Ltd* [1997] RPC 289 (Laddie J)

The products in this case were contact lenses (some 200 designs in total). The designs claimed related to the front surface dimensions of the lens, the rear surface dimensions, and the edge characteristics. The defendants argued that a number of the features of the lenses were present to enable the lens to fit another article—the wearer's eyeball—and to correct the wearer's vision, that is, perform its function. The plaintiffs responded that the eyeball, as a part of the human body, was not an 'article' to which the lens was to be fitted. It was held (*obiter*)[42] that any feature performing an interconnection function was excluded from protection by the 'must fit' exception, even if it performed another function (for example, if it was attractive). The word 'article' did not have a restricted meaning, and could apply to animate (living and formerly living) as well as inanimate things. The back radius, diameter, CN bevel and parallel peripheral carrier of a contact lens enabled it to fit against the eyeball and to perform its function of correcting vision while remaining stable in the eye.[43] These features were excluded from UDR under the 'must fit' exception.

9.46 The scope of this characterisation of the human body—and indeed animate things in general—as articles to which other articles may be fitted raises several interesting questions. What about clothes, for example? If clothes can come within the exception, is there a relevant difference between individually tailored and off-the peg garments? Some of the possible issues arose in the slightly different context provided by the following case.

---

[41] CDPA 1988, s 260(1). But this does not affect the question whether design right subsists in any aspect of the design of the components of a kit as opposed to the design of the assembled article (s 260(2)).

[42] Because it was held that in any event the designs were commonplace and there was no infringement.

[43] For diagrams of how the contact lenses were fitted to the eye see the report at pp 426–7.

■ *Amoena v Trulife* **unreported, 25 May 1995, Chancery Division, Deputy Judge**
Jonathan Sumption QC

This case concerned claims of UDR in breast prostheses for mastectomy patients. The aim of a
prosthesis designer is to emulate the appearance of a woman's breast, not in its natural state but
in a bra. The shapes of bras, governed in part by fashion, are much less variable than those of
breasts. It was argued that the shape of the front of the prosthesis was determined by the need
to enable it to be placed in and against the bra so that both objects performed their functions.
It was held, rejecting the argument, (1) the shape of the bra did not determine the details of the
prosthesis; (2) the prosthesis was highly flexible and could fit a number of different bras; 'must
fit' was concerned with a much more precise correspondence between two articles, such as a
rigid plug and socket.

9.47   Deputy Judge Sumption's approach has been criticised, however, on the basis that nothing in
the statutory language requires a feature to be the only way to achieve an interface between
two products for it to fall within the exclusion. If a number of 'fits' are possible, in other
words, the feature is still 'must fit'.[44] For clothes, then, whether tailored or not, at least those
parts of the design which were next to the body when worn would seem to be within the
exception.

Question

> To what extent do articles meant to be worn with or attached to the human body fall
> within the 'must fit' exception?

9.48   Another tricky and potentially far-reaching example can be found in *Dyson Ltd v Qualtex (UK)*
Ltd,[45] where the product in question was the handle of a Dyson vacuum cleaner. Despite the
Ocular Sciences precedent, it was *not* argued that some parts of the handle, such as certain triggers and a catch, being designed to interface with the human finger or thumb, were excluded
from UDR as 'must fit' features. But should it have been? A final example from the UDR case law
is provided by the mobile phone:[46] are those features of the design which enable such instruments to interact with the human hand, fingers and ears 'must fit' in nature and therefore
excluded from UDR?

Discussion point   For answer guidance visit www.oxfordtextbooks.co.uk/orc/macqueen2e/

> What if any parts of an artificial human limb or joint (e.g. artificial knee), or of a heart
> pacemaker, might be considered as protectable by UK UDR? Are there any other examples
> of such products?

9.49   'Must fit' also applies to semiconductor topographies, and so the pattern of the interfacing area
of a semiconductor is unprotected.

---

[44] *Ocular Sciences Ltd v Vision Care Ltd* [1997] RPC 289 per Laddie J at 424.
[45] [2005] RPC 19; [2006] RPC 31.   [46] See *Parker v Tidball* [1997] FSR 680.

Exercise

Consider the application of the 'must fit' exception to (1) the case of an oven to be built into a waist-high kitchen unit; and (2) the Lego brick. With regard to (2), bear in mind that *Interlego v Tyco Inc* [1989] AC 217 held that the design of the original Lego brick was registrable. Is it possible still for a design to be registrable and yet unable to attract UDR?

9.50   By itself, however, the must fit exception does not altogether deprive spare parts of UDR protection: only features which permit the spare part to be fitted to the original piece of equipment are unprotected as a result. The Government Minister piloting the CDPA through the House of Commons in 1988 provided the example of an agitator for a Hoover vacuum cleaner to illustrate this point. The agitator was connected to the cleaner by fittings at either end and only these features were caught by the exception. The remainder of the agitator—some 80 per cent of it—was protected by UDR.[47] The courts have on a number of subsequent occasions confirmed the point.

■ *Baby Dan AS v Brevi Srl and another* [1999] FSR 377

The child safety barriers case (above, para 9.28). The barriers were made up of component parts. It was held that the 'must fit' exception did not exclude the shape or configuration of component parts of a larger article from the protection of UDR, and here the design of parts of the barrier, such as the cam housing and the spindle retainer, were protected.

■ *Ultraframe UK Ltd v Clayton* [2003] RPC 23

'When the legislature included the must fit provisions in the Act, was it intending to ensure that competitors were to be able to supply the same component, or merely something which fitted into the composite article of which it was a part? If the latter, then it is only the interface which is excluded from protection, not the rest of the design. If it is the latter, the competitor has to do his own design work except for the interface. In my judgment it is tolerably clear that the legislature only wanted to deprive the interface feature of protection' (per Laddie J at para 73).

9.51   In the light of the Parliamentary example, the most significant of the cases is perhaps one about spare or pattern parts for Dyson vacuum cleaners.

■ *Dyson Ltd v Qualtex (UK) Ltd* [2005] RPC 19 (Mann J); aff'd [2006] RPC 31 (CA)

As already noted (above, para 9.24), Mann J and the Court of Appeal upheld the existence of UDR in component parts in general. While the parties agreed that large numbers of these parts were affected by the 'must fit' exception—such as the stop on the main wand handle of the cleaner which interacted with the stop on the release catch and the inside of the tubular boss which received the cable winder and the inner pocket with the snap detail[48]—the judge ruled that many others were not: for example, a semi-circular or curved part of the handle which lay underneath the handle release catch. While the curved under-surface of the release catch was 'must fit' in relation to the handle, the upper surface of the handle was not in relation to the

---

[47] *Parliamentary Debates*, 14 June 1988, HC Standing Committee E, col 532.
[48] The full and lengthy list can be found, together with photographs of the machines in issue, in a schedule to Mann J's judgment.

catch, because it was not necessary for the handle to be that shape to enable the catch to perform its function. The design history showed that the handle was designed first, and the catch later, suggesting that the latter was made to fit the former, but not the other way round.[49] The example is also interesting because the two parts did not actually touch each other, even when the catch was pressed; yet this did not prevent the operation of the 'must fit' exception. Earlier in his judgment, Mann J had warned that the *'shorthand description'*, 'must fit', did not appear in the statutory wording, and could be misleading as to the nature of the juxtaposition of parts needed for the operation of the exception.[50] So in the example of the handle and the catch, the relevant part of the statutory wording was not 'connected' but rather 'placed in around or against another article'. The findings were confirmed on appeal (see paras 27–52 of the judgment of Jacob LJ).

 Exercise

Consider in the light of the foregoing (1) the view of Robert Englehart QC in *Parker v Tidball* [1997] FSR 680 that a leather carrying case for a mobile phone is caught by the 'must fit' exception; and (2) the contrasting view of Park J in *A Fulton Co Ltd v Grant Barnett & Co Ltd* [2001] RPC 16, paras 72–5 that an umbrella case, designed to fit around an umbrella, is not. Which view is correct as a matter of the interpretation of CDPA 1988, section 213(3) (b)(i)? In the umbrella case, might the umbrella to be placed into the purpose-built case with which it is sold be caught by the exception?

Key points on must fit exception

- The must fit exception applies only to the interconnecting parts of an article, whether it is a component or a spare (replacement) part of another article, or simply an article which can be fitted to another article (eg a roof rack)
- The article to which the features connect may be a living creature
- The fact that the connection may work in several different ways (eg how clothes fit a person) does not prevent the connecting features being subject to the 'must fit' exception

---

Must match

9.52   By contrast with 'must fit', 'must match' was always intended as a blanket exclusion of protection for spare parts falling within its scope. Thus, for example, the Minister when the CDPA was passing through Parliament in the House of Lords:

> 'The must match exception is intended to prevent monopolies arising in the first place, and to preserve the benefits of competition. Although design right is only a right to prevent copying, it is quite clear that in circumstances where a competitor has no choice but to copy if he is to produce a part which will match, then if there were no must match exception he would be completely shut out of the market. This is not a question of abuse but of basic policy. And I have to say that this Government does not wish to create monopolies in this way in any sector of industry...And we should be quite clear about this: the

---

[49] See para 84 of the judgment.   [50] At para 31.

absence of a must match exception would enable competition in certain kinds of product to be totally frozen out. In our view that is not the way that the markets should operate.'[51]

This made it clear that where 'must match' applied there was no question of partial protection for the part in question. All of it was open to the copyist.

Question

Why is 'must match' more of a blanket exclusion for the design in question than 'must fit'?

9.53   The judgments of the lower courts in the *Ford* case (above, para 9.24) offer some helpful discussion of the 'must match' exception. The most important points to emerge are that 'must match' is not a blanket exclusion of all accessory parts, and that the requirement of dependency upon the appearance of another article of which the article in question is to be an integral part restricts the scope of the exception. Deputy Judge Jeffs in the Registered Designs Appeal Tribunal found the amended provisions of the 1949 Act on 'must match' 'undoubtedly ambiguous and obscure'.[52] He therefore invoked the ruling of the House of Lords in *Pepper v Hart*[53] and found guidance in the Parliamentary debates on the legislation.[54] As we have seen, the debates made it quite clear that the intention of Parliament had been to deny design protection to car body panels. While such panels might be sold as independent items, they had necessarily to be the same in appearance as those which they replaced. The design of the panel was subordinate to the design of the vehicle as a whole. Some other items such as wheel covers, steering wheels, seats and wing mirrors were, however, ones where an owner of a vehicle might choose between alternatives, for example, to give a car a sportier appearance or increase its comfort. Thus the appearance of parts such as these was not integral to the appearance of the vehicle as a whole, and the designs fell outside the scope of the 'must match' exception. The Divisional Court rejected the need to invoke *Pepper v Hart*, McCowan LJ commenting that he did 'not consider that in this case the ministerial statements clearly disclose the mischief aimed at or the legislative intention. In fact I have sympathy with Mr Silverleaf's [counsel for the Registrar] description of them as "long and diffuse and varied" '.[55] It was nevertheless held, in agreement with Judge Jeffs, that in considering whether or not an article's features were dependent upon the appearance of another article, the whole of the latter article should be considered, and not that article minus the part in issue (the 'n-1' approach).

Key points on must match exception

- The requirement of dependency upon the appearance of another article of which the article in question is to be an integral part restricts the scope of the exception
- The 'must match' exception catches designs of articles which are subordinate to the overall design of another article
- In considering whether one design is subordinate to another, consider the second article as a whole (including the first article)

---

[51] *Parliamentary Debates*, 29 March 1988, HL, col 699.   [52] [1993] RPC at 421.   [53] [1993] AC 534.
[54] [1993] RPC at 413–14, 421–2.   [55] [1994] RPC at 554.

9.54   A number of motor vehicle accessories apart from body panels were thus held to fall outside the exceptions in the *Ford* case. Such accessories would therefore also receive protection from UDR if registration was for any other reason not used or achieved. It can accordingly be seen that the exceptions do not wholly remove such protection for spare parts for motor vehicles.

9.55   There is a difficulty, however, which the *Ford* judgments do not fully address. The statutory wording shows that the intention of the designer must be taken into account in considering the issue of one design's dependency on another. As Mann J pointed out in *Dyson Ltd v Qualtex Ltd*:[56]

> '[M]ost consumer goods are likely to have been produced from a designer's pen (or CAD package). If made up of more than one part (which, again, most will have been) then each of those parts is likely to have been designed with the others in mind and to fit in. . . . [T]he design of each will be dependent on the appearance of the whole because that is how the designer will have intended it.'

This analysis would however have the effect of exempting most external aspects of a product's design from UDR, a conclusion Mann J found unacceptably wide. Instead he took from the *Ford* judgments a test of design dependency, which made the 'must match' exception bite only where changing the appearance of the article for which UDR was claimed would make the appearance of the overall article 'radically different'.[57] In assessing this, the saleability of the replacement article would be useful evidence or a cross-check, since consumers would probably not buy something which radically changed the appearance of the overall product. Applying this test, Mann J held that the design features of the Dyson vacuum cleaner handle were not caught by 'must match', because they could be changed without radically affecting the appearance of the vacuum cleaner, and there was no evidence to show that consumers required this utilitarian household product to retain its overall appearance.[58] The test was essentially approved in the Court of Appeal, where Jacob LJ said:

> 'Dependency must be viewed practically. . . [U]nless the spare parts dealer can show that as a practical matter there is a real need to copy a feature of shape or configuration because of some design consideration of the whole article, he is not within the exclusion. . . . The more there is design freedom the less is there room for the exclusion.'[59]

 Question

What is meant by the 'dependency' test for a 'must match' design?

9.56   As the *Dyson* case exemplifies, the courts have not often found 'must match' removing the protection of UDR, probably because it has such sweeping effects where it does apply.

■ *A Fulton Co Ltd v Grant Barnett & Co Ltd* [2001] RPC 16

The rectangular umbrella decision (see above, para 9.29). It was held that the design of the flat rectangular cuboid shape or configuration of the umbrella handle was not dependent upon, or constrained by, the equivalent appearance of the umbrella.

---

[56] [2005] RPC 19, para 60.   [57] Ibid, paras 63–4.
[58] Mann J had however earlier in his judgment (para 71) accepted the status of Dyson machines as 'design icons', with the carefully thought-out designs contributing to a very successful marketing operation over a 10-year period, and some of the designs having also achieved the status of exhibits in design museums. It may be, however, that he took this to support the view that the designers had earned the reward of UDR, of which they should not be deprived by giving the exceptions too wide scope.
[59] [2006] RPC 31, para 64.

■ *Ultraframe UK Ltd v Fielding* [2003] RPC 23 (Laddie J)

A conservatory roof system, the parts of which were said to give a 'consistent theme' to the roof. It was held that the designs of each part were not dependent upon the design of the remainder of the system.

9.57 However, it has been held (albeit in a registered designs case), that the second article upon which the design of the first must depend to come within the 'must match' exception need not be in existence at the time of the creation of the first. In *Valeo Vision SA v Flexible Lamps*,[60] the first articles were rear light clusters for use on trucks, to which they were attached via bases which had yet to be designed at the relevant time. It was held that the 'must match' exception could still apply.

9.58 The exception does not apply to 'families' of items such as dinner services and crockery sets. As originally drafted, it appeared that 'must match' would permit the manufacture and supply of replacement plates or crockery without the consent of the manufacturer of the set. The requirement that the replacement article should be an 'integral part' of the other article whose appearance it is to match is intended to prevent this result. Take the example of a cup and saucer in a tea set: while the two items are undoubtedly meant to 'match', the appearance of neither is integral to the other.

■ *Mark Wilkinson Furniture Ltd v Woodcraft Designs (Radcliffe) Ltd* [1998] FSR 63

The kitchen furniture case (see above, para 9.32). It was held that the 'must match' exclusion did not apply to the plaintiff's furnishings because the complete fitted kitchen unit was a series of matching articles, none of which formed an integral part of another article.

 Discussion point   For answer guidance visit www.oxfordtextbooks.co.uk/orc/macqueen2e/

How do the UK UDR 'must fit/must match' exceptions differ from those applying to Community designs (see above, paras 8.55–8.69)?

Duration

Length of protection

9.59 Design right lasts for 15 years from the end of the year in which the design was recorded, or in which an article was made to the design, whichever of these is earlier in time. In addition, the right is restricted further if, within five years of the earlier of these two events, an article made to the design is made available for sale or hire anywhere in the world by or with the licence of the design right owner. The right will then expire 10 years from the end of the calendar year in which the marketing took place. Accordingly, the 15-year period is a maximum which will be reduced by commercial exploitation of the design during the first five years of its existence.

[60] [1995] RPC 208.

Diagram 9.1 Duration of UK UDR

```
                              15 years
(a) Design record - - - - - - - - - - - - - - - - - - - - - - - - - - - - - - - - - - - - - - - - - - - - - - EXPIRY

         OR - - - - - - - -  <5 yrs - - - - - - -  Article lawfully  - - - - - - -  +10 yrs- - - - - - - - - - - - - EXPIRY
                                                   made and
                                                   marketed
(b) Article made
    to design - - - - - - - - - - - - - - - - - - - - - - - - - - - - - - - - - - - - - - - - - - - - - - - - - - - - EXPIRY
                              15 years
```

9.60   UK UDR is significantly shorter than both registered design right's maximum period (25 years) and copyright (lifetime of the author plus 70 years). This reflects a key policy decision, that UDR should be a lesser right in general than others available in this field. Further, the term for which there is an *exclusive* right may be shortened by licences of right available during the last five years of the UDR term (see below, para 9.62).[61] The clear policy is to encourage registration where that is possible.

> **?   Question**
>
> What is the maximum period of UDR protection?

Commencement

9.61   Three events are of importance with regard to starting time periods running:

    (1) recording the design;
    (2) making an article to the design;
    (3) lawfully marketing an article lawfully made to the design.

(1) or (2), whichever is the earlier, starts the 15-year period, while (3), if within five years of the earlier of (1) or (2), starts a 10-year period.

 Dyson Ltd v Qualtex (UK) Ltd [2005] RPC 19 (Mann J); [2006] RPC 31

D made a prototype for its vacuum cleaner in 1992, but actual production machines for sale were not made or actually available until after 1 January 1993. However customers who had been shown the prototype ordered the product before 31 December 1992. It was held that the statutory words 'made available for sale' connoted something that was actually in existence, and that merely taking orders was not making available. Prototypes or samples were definitely not available for sale. Mann J noted however that his view was based on the statutory wording: '[o]ne could make a logical case for saying that in the context of the Act commercial exploitation starts when articles are offered for sale, whether manufactured or not; and one could make a case for saying that it starts when articles are offered having been made, or when they are first made after an offer [*recte* order?]' (para 307). On appeal, this approach was approved by Jacob LJ (paras 115–19).

---

[61] CDPA 1988, s 239.

Licences of right during last five years

9.62 A further limit on the duration of design right is to be found in the provision of CDPA 1988, s 237 for licences of right to be obtainable during the last five years of the design right term. In effect, this means that the design right owner has an exclusive claim to the design only for five years after his initial exploitation of it. Diagram 9.1 above illustrating duration needs to be adjusted as shown in Diagram 9.2 to take account of this:

Diagram 9.2 Duration of UK UDR with licences of right during last five years

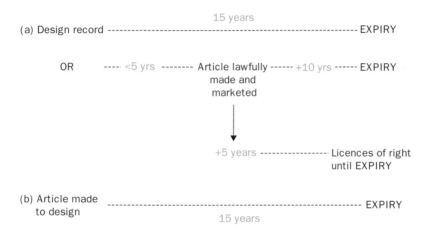

The short term is clearly designed to foster the competitive environment in respect of unregistered designs generally. It contrasts sharply with the potential length of the protection arising through registration and therefore encourages the use of that system.

 Question

How do licences of right promote competition?

9.63 A licence of right is one which the licensee is entitled to have from the owner of the UDR in question, but for which negotiation about terms and conditions (including royalties) is permissible. If however the parties cannot agree, the terms will be settled by the Comptroller-General of Patents, Designs and Trade Marks (the chief executive of the UK–IPO). The remuneration of the right owner will in either case take account of his investment and development costs. A statutory instrument made under the Act gives these as factors to be considered by the Comptroller in disputed cases, along with quality and safety.[62]

9.64 An example of proceedings before the comptroller in a licence of right case is as follows:

■ *NIC Instruments Ltd's Licence of Right (Design Right) Application* [2005] RPC 1

N had been infringing A's UDRs in bomb disposal kits, and having ceased to do so, now sought a licence of right (in order to limit the damages it would have to pay in respect of the

---

[62] Design Right (Proceedings before Comptroller) Rules, SI 1989/1130, as amended by Design Right (Proceedings before Comptroller) (Amendment) Rules, SI 1992/618.

infringements—see further below, para 21.107ff). The parties having failed to agree terms, the matter was referred to the comptroller. It was agreed that the comptroller should approach the matter on the basis of what willing parties would have agreed. It was held that willing parties do not negotiate by way of demands but by taking account, not only of their own, but also of the other side's interests, so that the agreement gives fair benefits on each side, achieving a half-way house or compromise. In the absence of comparable licences, the approach would be through splitting of the profits available to the licensee. A 50:50 per cent split would not be appropriate outside the pharmaceuticals field (in which research and development costs greatly exceeded manufacturing ones); in the field of bomb disposal kits, where R&D costs were unlikely to be high, the parties would have chosen a 25:75 per cent split, with the 75 per cent going to the licensee. The comptroller also held that he would not include terms (1) prohibiting sub-licensing (no jurisdiction to do so); (2) requiring N to mark the goods as those of A (evidence that disadvantageous in the market); (3) providing a warranty that the UDR existed, was owned by A, and would expire on 31 December 2005 (inappropriate when licence being determined by comptroller rather than parties); or (4) providing for termination on breach (because licensee could immediately demand a new licence). The full text of the licence imposed appears at the end of the report of the case.[63]

9.65 The availability of licences of right has one other important aspect under section 239 of CDPA 1988. When a right owner raises proceedings for *infringement at a time when a licence of right is available under the statute*, the defendant may undertake to take a licence of right at any time before a final order is made in the proceedings. This may be done without any admission of liability, and has three important effects in relation to the remedies which the court may grant:

- no injunction or interdict may be granted against the defendant (in other words, he may carry on with his hitherto infringing activities);

- no order for delivery up of infringing articles or of the means of making infringing articles may be made against the defendant; and

- the amount recoverable against the defendant by way of damages or on an account of profits shall not exceed double the amount payable by him as licensee if such a licence (ie a licence of right) on those terms had been granted before the earliest infringement.

9.66 This provision does not apply to infringements committed before licences of right were available; so the situation may arise where a defendant was infringing UDR before and after the date on which licences of right became potentially available (that is, five years before the right would have anyway expired). All relevant remedies would apply to the pre-licence availability infringements; but they would be quite severely restricted for the post-licence availability ones.

9.67 The potential significance of this capacity to cut down the remedies available to the right owner is well shown by the following case.

■ *Ultraframe (UK) Ltd v Eurocell Building Plastics* [2005] EWCA Civ 761

The case concerned findings of infringement of UDR in kits of parts for making lowpitch conservatory lean-to roof assemblies, after which judgment the defendant offered to take a licence of right, thereby limiting the damages payable in accordance with CDPA 1988, s 239 (above,

---

[63] For commentary see J Reed, 'Royalties for design right "licences of right" ' [2005] EIPR 298.

para 9.65). The UDR had expired as the proceedings continued, and the claimant argued that therefore a licence of right was no longer available. It was held that a licence of right could be obtained to restrict damages liability for infringement even after the UDR had expired. The licence under section 239 was a licence, not of the UDR as such, but for the infringements that had been committed, and there was nothing in the section meaning that the undertaking had to be given within any particular period so long as there were proceedings for infringement.

Diagram 9.3 Effect of availability of licence of right in infringement proceedings

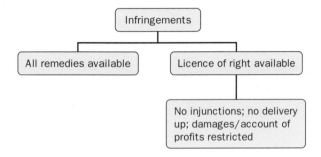

9.68   However, it would seem that the limitation of damages after a licence of right is taken has no effect to restrict the amount of the royalty that may be agreed or imposed under the licence.

■ *NIC Instruments Ltd's Licence of Right (Design Right) Application* [2005] RPC 1

For the facts and other findings in this case, see above, para 9.64. The comptroller also held that he should not take account of any damages payable for infringement in fixing the royalty rate under the licence, since he had no jurisdiction on the damages question.

 Discussion point For answer guidance visit www.oxfordtextbooks.co.uk/orc/macqueen2e/

> In the light of the two decisions just described, what would your advice be to a party sued for infringement of a UDR who wished to dispute the existence of the right, its scope in relation to his or her product, and that there had been infringement; and therefore to fight the action in all respects and continue his or her trading activities?

Rights in a UK UDR

Ownership

9.69   *Authorship* of a design is the basic test for ownership of the design right. There are, however, three circumstances in which authorship does not lead to ownership:

(1) where a design is created in pursuance of a *commission*;
(2) where a design is created by an *employee in the course of his employment*;
(3) where a design is *computer-generated*.

9.70   In the first two cases, design right belongs to the commissioner and the employer respectively. In the case of a computer-generated design, the design right belongs to the person 'by whom the arrangements necessary for the creation of the design are undertaken'.[64] Although this phrase is not wholly clear, it seems likely that the owner or possessor (say under a lease or conditional sale contract) of the computer will be owner of the design right. The situation should be distinguished from that where a human designer uses the computer as a tool towards the creation of the design, when it will not be computer-generated within the meaning of the Act and the other rules as to authorship, employment and commissions will apply.

■ *Ultraframe UK Ltd v Fielding* [2003] RPC 23 (Laddie J)

D, who had created the designs in issue in the case, was the controlling shareholder and managing director of the claimant company but also had a contract of employment with the company at the time the designs were made. It was held that the company owned the UDR as D's employer. The rule covers cases in which the designer does the design work within the scope of his employment, in his employer's time and with his employer's equipment and facilities, even if the designer wants to keep the product for himself. 'As a rough and ready rule of thumb, if designs are created and paid for by another, the statutory rights under the Act should belong to that other' (per Laddie J at para 43).

■ *Intercase Ltd v Time Computers Ltd* [2003] EWHC 2988 (Ch) (Patten J)

B was director, controlling shareholder and employee of MW Ltd, a furniture manufacturing company. The company supplied worktops to a college, and B learned of difficulties for the college with computer desks. B designed the I-Desk to deal with these problems, with the MW Ltd logo appearing in most of the design drawings. B set up another company (I Ltd) to market the new product and assigned all IPR in the desk to it. MW Ltd manufactured the I-Desk. TCL began to market a competitor to the I-Desk, and I Ltd sued for infringement of UDR. TCL defended on the basis that B had carried out his design work in the course of his employment with MW Ltd, which was therefore the owner of the UDR. B argued that he had done the design work in his own time. It was held that the test to be applied was whether the work done fell within the employee's duties, not whether it was done during normal office hours or with the employer's materials or equipment, or at the employer's expense. Although B's design work for the I-Desk went beyond anything previously done by MW Ltd, that company's business included the design of furniture, and the work was within the scope of B's duties as its employee. MW Ltd was therefore the first owner of the UDR in the I-Desk, and not B.

 Question

Who is the first owner of an UDR?

Infringement

9.71   The exclusive right under an UDR is to *reproduce the design for commercial purposes*:

(1) by making articles to the design;

---

[64] CDPA 1988, s 214(2).

(2) by making design documents to enable such articles to be made (CDPA 1988, s 226(1)).

UDR is infringed by doing either (1) or (2) without the licence of the owner, or by authorising another to do so.[65] It thus draws on two copyright concepts: copying (above para 4.24ff) and authorisation (above, para 4.68ff). The requirement of a causal link of copying between the design and the article that has been produced by the defendant for infringement means that UDR, unlike the rights conferred by a patent or a registered design, is *not a monopoly right in the design* in question. This is a limitation of UDR by comparison with the protection conferred by registration. Again, therefore, the policy of encouraging registration of designs is apparent.

 Question

What is the difference between the exclusive right under a registered design and that under UDR?

9.72   Like a registered design, however, UDR is *a commercial right*, protecting only commercial interests. Non-commercial interests in a design fall into the sphere of copyright in so far as they receive IPR protection at all.

Key points about infringement of UDR

- Infringement is *copying by making an article* to the design, or by making design documents to enable such an article to be made
- The right is therefore *not a monopoly right*, unlike registered design right
- But the *infringing act must be for commercial purposes* (like registered design right)

9.73   The exclusive rights just described are said to give rise to 'primary' infringement of UDR. There are also 'secondary' infringements, like those in copyright (above, para 4.76), by possessing or dealing in for commercial purposes an article which is, and which the defendant concerned knows or has reason to believe is, an infringing article.[66] An infringing article is one the making of which infringed UDR or, in the case of an imported article, would have infringed UDR had it been made in the UK, that is, it was made without the permission of the owner of the UK UDR.[67] The key distinction between primary and secondary infringements, as in copyright, is that the latter depends on knowledge where the former depends on copying, regardless of whether or not the copyist knew or had reason to know that this was infringement.

Reproduction by making articles to the design

9.74   Reproduction means copying the design, directly or indirectly, so as to produce articles exactly or substantially to that design.[68] The copyright test of copying applies and so 'reverse engineering' and 'redesign' will continue to be caught as infringements (see above, para 4.22). Semiconductor topographies, however, have been taken to be a special case in this regard ever since the original legislation in the USA, since it is understood that most development in this

---

[65] CDPA 1988, s 226(3).   [66] CDPA 1988, s 229.   [67] CDPA 1988, s 228.   [68] CDPA 1988, s 226(2), (4).

area, as with much other computer-related technology, is based upon 'reverse engineering' in relation to existing products, and it is therefore regarded within the industry as a legitimate competitive technique rather than as an infringement of rights. Accordingly reverse engineering is not an infringement of topography right.[69]

9.75   Another aspect of the copyright approach to 'reproduction' which has been used in UDR cases has been the inference of copying based on sufficient similarity between the claimant's design and the allegedly infringing article and opportunity for the alleged copier to have access to the design.[70] This should however be treated with care, as the following case illustrates:

■ *Virgin Atlantic Airways Ltd v Premium Aircraft Interiors Group Ltd and Premium Aircraft Interiors UK Ltd* [2009] EWHC 26 (Pat) (Lewison J)[71]

V alleged that its design in a business-class aircraft seat had been copied. The claim centred on whether the allegedly copying seats were 'articles exactly or substantially reproduced to the design', with mere similarity between them being held insufficient to establish this in the context of the highly competitive airline industry, where the competitors closely watched each other's developments and sought to build upon them by doing similar things better. Lewison J found 'helpful' the approach of Lord Millett in the copyright case, *Designers Guild Ltd v Russell Williams* (above, para 4.16): similarities had to be sufficiently close, numerous or extensive as to be more likely the result of copying than coincidence. The inquiry is to be directed to similarities rather than differences, although both should be taken into account. The function of experts providing evidence on the question of copying is not to evaluate, but instead to inform the court about similarities and differences and their significance. Held under this approach that there was no copying, and that P's seats had been independently designed; at most what had been taken was a general idea (ie inward 'herringbone'configuration of seats).

9.76   However, reproduction for UDR is significantly different from reproduction in copyright in one crucial respect: where copyright is infringed by reproduction of any substantial part of a work in any material form,[72] UDR is only infringed by making articles substantially to the design for commercial purposes.[73] The difference this can make is illustrated by the following case:

■ *L Woolley Jewellers Ltd v A & A Jewellery Ltd* [2003] FSR 15 (Court of Appeal)

The product in question here was a pendant on a chain worn around the neck, with a 'bail' on the pendant through which the chain was threaded. Obsolete and imitation coins were inserted in the pendant and held in place by 'lugs'; these could also be formed within a bezel (a captive ring with lugs placed over the circumference of the insert). The area around the insert contained an outline of three hearts into which the bail had been inserted, while the bail itself had been cut into a heart shape. The first instance judge found that the bail had been copied but without

---

[69] Design Right (Semiconductor Topographies) Regulations 1989, reg 8(4).

[70] Eg *Mark Wilkinson Furniture Ltd v Woodcraft Designs (Radcliffe) Ltd* [1998] FSR 63 at 74; *A Fulton Co Ltd v Grant Barnett & Co Ltd* [2001] RPC 16, para 95; *Guild v Eskander* [2003] FSR 3, para 70 (a case, however, alleging *conscious* copying, to which this test is not relevant); *Bailey v Haynes* [2007] FSR 10 (design produced by third party from China, no other evidence of copying).

[71] Design issues were not considered when this case later reached the Court of Appeal on patent questions: see [2009] EWCA (Civ) 1062.

[72] CDPA 1988, ss 16(3)(a), 17(2); above, para 4.26.

[73] Note also that by virtue of CDPA 1988, s 51, making articles to a design is not an infringement of the copyright in the design.

the repeating heart motif; he held that nonetheless this amounted to copying a substantial part of the design. It was held that this was the wrong approach. There was a difference between an enquiry whether the *whole* design containing the copied element was substantially the same as that enjoying UDR, and the copyright one about whether the item copied formed a substantial part of a copyright work. The case was remitted back to the judge to apply the correct test. Doing so, Fysh J found there was substantial similarity between the designs of the two pendants, and thus infringement.[74]

Question

Explain the difference between reproduction of any substantial part of a work in any material form (copyright), and making articles substantially to a design (UDR).

9.77 Since design continues to be defined primarily in terms of visual features, questions arise about how to determine when an article has been made to a design. In the language made familiar by registered designs law, through whose 'eye' do we judge this and the closely related question of *substantial* similarity? The *Klucznik* case on pig fenders was the first to discuss how to approach these matters.

■ *C & H Engineering Ltd v F Klucznik & Sons Ltd* [1992] FSR 421 (Aldous J)

The allegedly infringing pig fender had a rounded tube or roll bar on top but it differed from the first fender in having flaring sides which enabled it to be stacked with other fenders. The claim of infringement failed. Although there was substantial similarity in respect of the roll bars, the overall designs of the fenders were different. Aldous J said (at p 428):

'Whether or not the alleged infringing article is made substantially to the plaintiff's design must be an objective test to be decided through the eyes of the person to whom the design is directed. Pig fenders are purchased by pig farmers and I have no doubt that they purchase them taking into account price and design. In the present case, the plaintiff's alleged infringing pig fenders do not have exactly the same design as shown in the defendant's design document. Thus it is necessary to compare the plaintiff's pig fenders with the defendant's design drawing and, looking at the differences and similarities through the eyes of a person such as a pig farmer, decide whether the design of the plaintiff's pig fender is substantially the same as the design shown in the drawing.'

9.78 This reasoning can be criticised. In *Klucznik* it was established that the designer of the second fender had seen the first one and had used it towards his own design; Aldous J had no doubt 'that the idea of having a tube as the roll bar came from the defendant's pig fender and therefore copying did take place'.[75] That, it is submitted, should have been enough to establish a prima facie case of infringement of the UDR in the first fender. Indeed, to be more precise, given that only the roll bar was not of commonplace design in pig fenders (see above, para 9.35), the infringement was of its UDR rather than that of the fender as a whole. Further, although it is right to say that the comparison between a design and an allegedly infringing article must be objective, the 'pig farmer' test—or, more generally, the reference to the eye of the person to whom the design is directed—appears to be an unjustified gloss on the statutory provisions. There is no reason, once the causal link between design and article is established, to go on to

---

[74] *L Woolley Jewellers Ltd v A & A Jewellery Ltd (No 2)* [2004] FSR 49.   [75] [1992] FSR at 429.

test whether the article is made to the design by reference to the person to whom the design is directed. The question is simply whether a design has been copied and an article made to it. The only possible relevance of such a test might be when using an appearance of similarity to draw an inference of copying, just as such tests for similarity are deployed when assessing whether a design is commonplace in its field.

■ *Rolawn Ltd v Turfmech Machinery Ltd* [2008] ECDR 13 (Mann J)

See also para 9.35. The degree of generality in relation to the alleged copying of an unregistered design right was central to the dispute in this case concerning wide-area grass mowers with a folding arm mechanism designed to cut grass in wide areas such as playing fields and public parks. R claimed that an UDR existed in numerous aspects of the configuration and shape of the mower. It sought protection for the actual designs of the machine itself and its overall shape in much the same way that a playwright is entitled to protect not only the words of the play but also the overall plot. R claimed that the defendants had copied aspects of its wide-area grass mower, thereby infringing its unregistered design rights. The R machines were not available for purchase. Nor were they reasonably open for inspection as they stayed on the R farms with only limited visibility from adjoining roads and a small possibility of unauthorised inspection at night when they were sometimes left out.

It was held that there was no evidence that the design was copied. Instead, only generalised ideas were taken by T. On the evidence, only the photographs were seen by T and they could not have allowed for any detailed copying. Copying only persisted insofar as T's designers took the idea of a grass mower with wings that could fold in half and cutters disposed underneath from the R photographs. Once these ideas had been taken as inspiration, the other alleged similarities could flow naturally without copying.

R was not entitled to claim design right in such abstract ideas or concepts as the folding wings. Rather than the underlying design concept, which was an idea and so governed by patent law, R would be allowed only to claim design right in aspects or the configuration of the physical manifestation. Thus while R was not entitled to claim design right in the concept of a grass mower with arms folding back on themselves at the mid-way point, they could claim design right in their particular mower, or an aspect of the shape or configuration of it. It was held that there was no infringement of the unregistered design right. Though overall ideas were copied, 'the design' itself was not. Certain methods or principles of construction were taken, but these are excluded from being design rights.

 Question

How may it be determined that an allegedly infringing article has been made to a design?

9.79   An 'eye' test has also been deployed in cases where the issue has been the 'substantial similarity' of an allegedly infringing product to a design in which UDR is claimed, with the eye being taken as that of the relevant customer as 'the person to whom the design is directed'.[76] The eye

---

[76] See eg *Mark Wilkinson Furniture Ltd v Woodcraft Designs (Radcliffe) Ltd* [1998] FSR 63 at 74–75; *A Fulton Co Ltd v Grant Barnett & Co Ltd* [2001] RPC 16, at para 89.

of a person interested in the design of articles of the kind in question may also be taken into account.[77] The problems inherent in such an anthropomorphic test begin to emerge, however, in those cases where the key features of the design and the offending article are too fine to be picked up by anyone's unaided eye, as for example with contact lenses;[78] and the difficulties are reinforced where the design is not essentially about visual features at all, as with electronic circuit diagrams.[79]

> ## Key points on reproduction by making article to the design
>
> - Since the reproduction may be indirect, 'reverse engineering' can be an infringement of UDR (except for semiconductor topographies)
> - The correct approach to the question of 'substantial reproduction' is to ask whether the *whole* design containing the copied element was substantially the same as that enjoying UDR, not the copyright one about whether the item copied formed a substantial part of a copyright work
> - Similarity is tested through the eyes of the person to whom the design is directed

Reproduction of the design document for purpose of making articles to the design

9.80 This exclusive right goes further than the Registered Designs Act in giving exclusive rights to the reproduction of the design document where that reproduction is for the purpose of making articles to the design. Registration only protects against the use of articles in which the design is incorporated or to which it has been applied (see above, paras 8.89–8.95). Design documents may also have copyright, but it is not infringement of that copyright to make an article to the design or copy an article made to the design (unless it is design for an artistic work or typeface).[80]

■ *Societá Esplosivi Industriali SpA v Ordnance Technologies (UK) Ltd* [2008] RPC 12 (Lindsay J)

This case arose from what was at first a joint venture between the parties to design multiple warhead systems. The designs were very complex, created first on computers, then tested physically. After the joint venture broke down, the defendant used joint venture designs as starting points in later projects, and the claimant sued for infringement of UDR by way of reproducing design documents for the purpose of making articles to the design. It was held that there had been infringement in one project where the defendant's use of the documents had gone beyond design study and evaluation, and moved to manufacture; but not in another, which had never reached the manufacturing stage or been intended to do so. The judge held that a design document had to have been made for the purpose of enabling articles to be made, and that it was necessary to show that an alleged infringer had had that purpose in mind at the relevant time. It was not necessary however to show that the infringer had the intention of manufacturing

---

[77] *Baby Dan AS v Brevi SRL and another* [1999] FSR 377 at 388.
[78] *Ocular Sciences Ltd v Vision Care Ltd* [1997] RPC 289 (Laddie J).
[79] *Mackie Designs v Behringer Specialised Studio Equipment (UK) Ltd* [1999] RPC 717 (Pumfrey J). This may simply reinforce doubts about the correctness of the decision that such diagrams enjoy UDR.
[80] CDPA 1988, s 51(1); and see further below, paras 9.87–9.88.

himself, or of authorising third parties to do so; all that was required was an intention of enabling manufacture. The use of a protected document as a starting point for the making of further design documents which were variations upon the protected original, even where that making had been in the course of a commercial purpose, did not without more constitute an infringement.[81]

Other points of comparison with infringement of registered designs

9.81 The UDR holder has all the usual remedies for infringement, including damages, injunctions and interdicts, accounts of profits, and delivery up of infringing articles and the means of making them.[82] As with registered designs, damages liability is excluded in cases of innocent infringement: that is, where it is shown at the time of the infringement the defendant did not know, and had no reason to believe, that design right subsisted in the design to which the action relates.[83] There is no defence of innocent infringement, however, in respect of registered or unregistered Community design.[84]

Exceptions to exclusive rights

9.82 There are no exceptions to UDR like those for registered designs (private and non-commercial use, experimental purposes, citation and teaching). This is because what constitutes infringement of UDR is much less extensive. If for example I wanted to use an unregistered design for the purposes of teaching design or the law on the subject, there would be no question of my infringing either of the exclusive rights since I am not making or intending to make articles to the design. Again, UDR is expressly limited to acts for commercial purposes, so there is no need for a private and non-commercial exception. UDR's exclusivity is also quite significantly limited by the availability of licences of right five years after the first marketing of the article to which the design was applied (above, paras 9.62–9.68). The Secretary of State also has power, in respect of designs where the Competition Commission reports that the conduct of the UDR owner in licensing the right may be expected to operate, or has operated, against the public interest, to order the cancellation or modification of licences, or to order the provision of licences of right.[85] This meets the problem encountered following the Monopolies Commission report on Ford in 1985 (see above, para 9.10), that there were no effective remedies available under the existing legislation to deal with the situation there disclosed.

 Question

Why are there no exceptions to UDR for private and non-commercial use, experimental purposes, citation and teaching?

---

[81] See further the note on this case by S Vousden, 'Societa Esplosivi Industriale SpA: on confidences, copying designs and directors' [2008] EIPR 332. See also S. Yavorsky, 'Negotiating an IP minefield: infringing design documents' (2008) 3 JIPLP 361.

[82] CDPA 1988, ss 229, 230. On remedies see further Chapter 21 (enforcement).   [83] CDPA 1988, s 233(1).

[84] *J Choo (Jersey) Ltd v Towerstone Ltd* [2008] FSR 19 (Ch). See also J Fitzgerald, '"Innocent infringement" and the Community unregistered design right: the position in the UK and Ireland' (2008) 3 JIPLP 236.

[85] CDPA 1988, s 238.

Assessing UK UDR

9.83 Much of the policy which appears to guide the formulation of the specific rules of UK UDR apart from topography right is drawn from the law relating to patents and registered designs rather than copyright. This is evident in a number of features discussed above.

> UDR depends rather more on ideas of novelty (through the 'commonplace' test) than on originality in the copyright sense of independent production.
>
> Again, although UDR is not a monopoly right, being dependent on copying, infringement is primarily the manufacture and marketing of industrial products, as with patents and registered designs.
>
> The provisions on licences of right also are more reminiscent of patent law (where there are provisions for compulsory licences to be granted in certain circumstances) than of anything found in copyright, where involuntary licences are frowned upon.
>
> A final aspect of the new right, also obviously taken from patent and registered design law and without parallel in copyright, is the unrestricted right of the Crown to make use of an unregistered design without requiring authorisation from the owner.

Overall, then, UK UDR is more of an industrial property right, less concerned to protect the creativity inherent in design than to help realise the commercial value which a successful design will have.

9.84 It is also apparent that UK UDR is hedged around with considerable limitations, often of uncertain scope, in respect of its existence, duration and remedies for infringement. When the right was first introduced, the Government was clearly reluctant to accept any modification to extend the right. This left open to question how far, if at all, commercial enterprises would seek to make use of it, since it might be seen as at best a fair-weather friend. Such reluctance might be reinforced by the Secretary of State's powers to make far-reaching orders in respect of licences (above, para 9.82). While this recognises that the essence of the whole problem in this area is the regulation of competition in the marketplace, where competitors are armed with the ability to seek the use of such extensive executive powers, the exercise of rights becomes a matter fraught with a very high level of uncertainty. Nevertheless, as shown by the now extensive case law (much of it already cited and discussed in this chapter), UDR has been deployed, with varying degrees of success, across a wide range of industries, and it cannot be said to be useless, or even not very useful to these industries.

 Exercise

Is UK UDR useful?

Interaction between UK UDR and copyright

9.85 A design which is no more than a design—for example, a drawing on a piece of paper, or in a computer—may well also be a copyright work. This section explores how UDR interacts with copyright, given the general policy that copyright should be excluded from operation in the field of product design.

When will there be copyright in a design?

9.86   To find the existence of copyright in a design requires no extraordinary application of the principles of copyright. A design may begin life as a drawing, a set of calculations or verbal ideas, material stored in a computer or on a computer disk, or as a model. All such works may fall within the scope of copyright subject matter, typically as an artistic work. Because there is no requirement of quality, copyright can cover all designs, no matter how functional or simple, so long as there is sufficient originality. Copyright can be infringed by the making of products to the design, because the copyright in a two-dimensional work could be infringed by a three-dimensional reproduction. If the copyist copied, not the design, but a product lawfully made from the design, there was, until the CDPA 1988, still infringement, because copyright prevents indirect as well as direct copying. Under the 1988 Act, however, the scope of infringement of the copyright in a design is severely cut back, with the aim of ensuring that, for the most part, copyright becomes a marginal form of protection in this field.

 Question

When will a product design have copyright?

Restricting copyright

No infringement of copyright in design document or model by making articles to the design

9.87   Copyright is restricted principally through CDPA 1988, sections 51–52. Section 51 says what is *not* infringement of copyright in a design document or model recording or embodying a design for anything other than an artistic work or a typeface. A design document for these purposes is defined as:

> 'any record of a design, whether in the form of a drawing, a written description, a photograph, data stored in a computer or otherwise' (CDPA 1988, s 51(3)).

The *ejusdem generis* principle of statutory interpretation suggests that the 'otherwise' covers only two-dimensional design records like the others actually mentioned in the definition. Three-dimensional prototypes of the kind discussed by the House of Lords in *George Hensher Ltd v Restawile Upholstery (Lancs) Ltd*[86] (see above para 2.83), insofar as they have copyright at all, are covered by the earlier words in the section referring to 'models' embodying a design. There remains the question of what constitutes a design: it is defined in CDPA 1988 as:

> 'the design of any aspect of the shape or configuration (whether internal or external) of the whole or part of an article, other than surface decoration' (CDPA 1988, s 51(3)).

– that is, the kind of design that is protected by UDR (see above, para 9.16ff).

 Question

What constitutes infringement of the copyright in a design?

---

[86] [1976] AC 64.

9.88 It is important to grasp that section 51 recognises copyright in design documents (where it exists). But the significance of this is carefully restricted. It is not infringement of the copyright to make an article to the design or to copy an article made to the design. This has the effect, broadly, that the unauthorised making of three-dimensional articles by copying either directly or indirectly from a design document cannot give rise to a copyright action. The only claim available is under UDR (see above, paras 9.74–9.78). But the wording of section 51 is not without its difficulties of interpretation.

■ *Lambretta Clothing Co Ltd v Teddy Smith (UK) Ltd* [2005] RPC 6 (Court of Appeal)

This is the track top case (for the facts see above, para 9.28). Although UDR did not apply to the colourways of the top, there was a design document drawn by a director of the plaintiffs. So the defendants' top might have been treated as copied (indirectly) from this document and as therefore infringing its copyright. It was held that section 51 barred any claim to artistic copyright infringement by the defendants' garment. But Mance LJ dissented, on a close reading of section 51, as follows:

> '[I]n order "to make an article to the design" or "to copy an article made to the design" embodied in a drawing, it is, because of the definition in s 51(3), still necessary to conclude that the article was made, or was a copy of an article made, to the design, meaning "the design [as embodied in the drawing] of any aspect of the shape or configuration...of the whole or part of an article, *other than surface decoration*" [emphasis supplied]. Only if it was, does s 51 prevent there being any copyright infringement' (para 80).

In this case, only the colourways and the surface decoration of the track tops had been copied, and these were not shape or configuration; so they were incapable of being protected by UDR (see above paras 9.28, 9.32). Therefore, Mance LJ argued, they had artistic copyright which could be infringed by three-dimensional reproductions; since the surface decoration was not part of the 'design' as defined by the legislation, the limitation of copyright under section 51 did not apply. For the majority, however, this made for an impossible result, divorcing the colourways from the shape and configuration of the garment which provided both their borders and the means of their juxtaposition. Jacob LJ also pointed out the 'bizarre oddity' (para 40) that would arise if there was a much longer period of protection for mere colouring than there would be if the garment had UDR.

■ *Flashing Badge Co Ltd v Groves* [2007] FSR 36 (Ch)

This case was about design drawings for flashing novelty badges with messages such as '40 Today', 'Let's Party' and 'Happy Birthday' presented on them in a stylised way along with images such as balloons and cakes with candles. An artistic design for these was thus applied to the badge surfaces, with the shape of the badges also following that of the relevant artistic designs. The question was whether CDPA 1988, section 51 applied to prevent the claimant's action for copyright infringement against an importer of virtually identical badges from China. Granting summary judgment for copyright infringement, Rimer J held:

(1) Each drawing was a design document incorporating (a) a design for an artistic work and (b) a design for something other than an artistic work, namely an article in the nature of a badge in the same outline shape as the artistic work. Section 51 applied only to (b). The only 'design' to which the section 51(1) defence could apply was a design for the shape or configuration of the whole or part of an article *other* than surface decoration. It followed that the section 51(1) defence applied, if at all, only to a copyright claim in the design

minus the surface decoration. It provided no defence in respect of an infringement of copyright in the graphic design which provided the surface decoration of the badges.

(2) Whilst it was true that the design of the shape of the badge followed the outline of the design for the artistic work on the face of the badge, the latter design was in the nature of a graphic design which was in no sense something which could only exist as part of the shape of the badge. It was a design which could be applied to any other substrate and which, if so applied, would enjoy copyright protection for the infringement of which section 51 afforded no defence. Distinguishing *Lambretta*, Rimer J thought his position was akin to that of Mance LJ:

'The decision of the majority in *Lambretta* on the s 51 point therefore appears to have turned on its special facts. . . . It is true that the design of the shape of the badge follows the outline of the design for the artistic work on the face of each badge. But the latter design is in the nature of a graphic design which is in no sense something which (unlike the *Lambretta* colourways) can only exist as part of the shape of the badge. It is a design which can be applied to any other substrate and which, if so applied, would enjoy copyright protection for the infringement of which s 51 would afford no defence' (para 22).[87]

Key points on CDPA 1988, s 51

- The section restricts the ways in which copyright in a design document or model can be infringed.

- In particular, making an article to the design recorded in the document does not infringe copyright—only UDR can be infringed in this way.

Design documents for artistic works

9.89   If, however, there is a design document for an artistic work—for example, an architect's plans for a building or a design for a work of artistic craftsmanship such as certain types of clothing, furniture, sculpture, or photographs—or for a typeface, then under section 51 that design enjoys the full protection of artistic copyright. The protection will last for the lifetime of the author plus the post mortem period of protection. The author and his successors will be able to take action throughout that period to stop reproduction of all kinds, including the making of three-dimensional copies. Artistic copyright also covers surface decoration applied to an industrial product.

9.90   It will therefore be vital to distinguish when a drawing or model is the design of an artistic work and when it is simply the design of an article. Only in the latter case will the full protection of copyright be unavailable. The most crucial things to keep in mind in approaching the question are:

which three-dimensional works attract copyright (ie works of architecture and artistic craftsmanship, sculptures and casts and moulds made for purposes of sculpture); and

the distinction between shape and configuration on the one hand and surface decoration on the other (UDR only applies to the former).

■ *Lucasfilm Ltd v Ainsworth* [2009] FSR 2 (Mann J)

This case was concerned with the designs for Imperial Stormtrooper helmets and armour featured in the film *Star Wars*. A had made the helmets and armour used during filming, from

---

[87] See further the note on this case by E Derclaye, 'Flashing Badge Co Ltd v Groves; a step forward in the clarification of the copyright/design interface' [2008] EIPR 251.

initial designs prepared for L in which L enjoyed copyright. The drawings or models conveyed the look or feel to be created, but were not definitive. They were held to constitute design documents. Mann J summarised the consequences of this conclusion as follows:

> 'The section [51] is therefore capable of barring a copyright claim in relation to the design document if it is for "anything other than an artistic work". If the items were not artistic works, the section works in Mr Ainsworth's favour and prevents his acts being infringements. The designs could only be for artistic works in this case if they were for a sculpture or a work of artistic craftsmanship. I have held that they were not artistic works in either of the two candidate senses [*for which see para 2.86 above*]. Therefore the designs were for something other than an artistic work and s.51 operates in Mr Ainsworth's favour to prevent his copying of the work being an infringement of copyright.'[88]

 Discussion point For answer guidance visit www.oxfordtextbooks.co.uk/orc/macqueen2e/

Why do designs for artistic works retain full copyright?

Exploiting artistic works as commercial products

9.91 Questions arose even before the CDPA 1988 as to whether commercial products may have copyright in themselves as artistic works. It is recognised that certain types of furniture, clothing and toys can claim the status of artistic works; but in general such questions have been answered in the negative by the courts where the product has been intended for a mass market, as was the case in *Hensher* (above, para 2.83) and *Merlet v Mothercare*.[89] Prototypes of plastic dental impression trays have been refused copyright as either sculptures or models;[90] on the other hand, in New Zealand it has been held that the Frisbee toy was an artistic work as an engraving and that wooden mould prototypes for the toy were sculptures.[91]

9.92 Consider this paean of praise for the modern car emanating from Mr Richard Page MP during the Parliamentary debates:[92]

> 'I trained as a mechanical engineer and to me an exhaust system is a thing of beauty. It has an artistic ability of its own, it is not simply a functional piece of apparatus... Have hon Members seen how, in the latest racing cars, the exhaust systems blend to make a harmonious whole? They may not appreciate them, but to a mechanical engineer they are things of beauty and artistic design... How can anyone not admit that a car body shell is a thing of beauty? Design teams spend fortunes on producing harmonious shapes and ensuring that they are pleasing and artistic and have popular appeal. It always seems that something that is useful is not artistic, but that if it cannot be used it is artistic. Sir William Lyons, the creator of Jaguar cars—who sadly has now passed away—always had delivered to his home the latest sculpted model; he put it in the garden, spent hours looking at it and then sent it back for the shape to be altered. Only after hours and hours of studying it could he feel that he had something that represented the peak of artistic ability and that would appeal to the public. It is incredible to me that a sculpted body shell is not regarded as a thing of beauty. In Italy Ferina, Ital and Bertona have design studios that are trying to create body shells which are sufficiently attractive to be purchased by the manufacturer and then by the public.'

---

[88] This aspect of the decision was not challenged on appeal: *Lucasfilm Ltd v Ainsworth* [2009] EWCA Civ 1328, para 87.
[89] [1986] RPC 115.
[90] *J & S Davis (Holdings) Ltd v Wright Health Group* [1988] RPC 403.
[91] *Wham-O Manufacturing Co v Lincoln Industries* [1985] RPC 127. See however *Lucasfilm Ltd v Ainsworth* [2009] FSR 2, paras 104–19 (Mann J).
[92] 24 May 1988, HC Standing Committee E, cols 238–9.

is done for the purpose of manufacturing articles commercially. On the other hand, section 51 ensures that copyright is not infringed by the making of articles to the design. However where the design document does not have copyright, copying it will infringe UDR if the purpose of the copyist is to manufacture articles commercially to the design.

■ *Squirewood Ltd v H Morris & Co Ltd* 1993 GWD 20–1239 (Outer House, Court of Session)

In this case UDR in office furniture was upheld (see above, para 9.18). S's designs for office furniture were contained in drawings and brochures, which as noted above, were held to be design documents. S claimed that M were manufacturing and selling office furniture which was in substance a reproduction of the designs. Interim interdict was granted on the basis of both copyright and UDR in the brochure (see para 9.18 for criticism on the UDR point). Lord Clyde also held the brochure to be a literary work also containing artistic works in the form of the photographs and drawings. But the copyright was almost certainly not infringed by the manufacture and sale of office furniture. While the copyright in a two-dimensional artistic work may be infringed by making a copy in three dimensions (CDPA 1988, s 17(3)), this is limited by section 51 of the 1988 Act. To make furniture to someone else's design without permission is not an infringement of copyright unless the furniture is an artistic work in its own right. Furniture can constitute artistic work: as a sculpture or a work of artistic craftsmanship, for example. But this is not very likely when the work is intended for mass industrial production, as was probably the situation in this case. The copyright in the brochure therefore only prevented other parties from making two-dimensional reproductions of its contents.

Summary

9.99   Sections 4 and 17(2) and (3) of CDPA 1988 have the effect that copyright can subsist in a design. This means that in many cases *both* copyright and UDR will subsist alongside each other. However, CDPA 1988, sections 51–53 limit the scope of that copyright, so that making articles to the design is generally not an infringement of copyright. In other words, the owner of the design must, if wanting to stop someone else making articles to the design without licence to do so, use UDR to achieve that objective. Contrariwise, where a design has copyright, it is not an infringement of UDR to do anything which is an infringement of copyright in that work.[95]

Community UDR

About this topic

9.100   Now we turn to the second major form of UDR, Community UDR.[96] As explained in the introduction to Part III of this book, this form of intellectual property was introduced nearly 15 years after the UK UDR, and co-exists with it, with the two rights being quite different from each other in a number of respects. Community UDR is really primarily an adjunct of Community registered design right, whereas UK UDR is a fully fledged independent right. The existence of the Community UDR is expressly without prejudice to national laws relating to unregistered designs

---

[95] CDPA 1988, s 238.   [96] See generally VM Saez, 'The unregistered Community design right' [2002] EIPR 588.

(such as UK UDR), or indeed to trade marks or other distinctive signs, patents and utility models, typefaces, civil liability (that is, tort or delict) and unfair competition (passing off in the UK).[97] A design protected by Community UDR may also be protected by copyright under the national laws of the member states; but the extent and conditions of such protection is left to each member state. Thus CDPA 1988, sections 51 and 52 could apply to a Community UDR in the UK to restrict the ways in copyright in the design could be infringed (see further above, paras 9.87–9.99).

> ### Key point on Community UDR
>
> - Community UDR is a supplement to Community registered design rights, and is quite different from UK UDR

 Question

What are the major distinctions between UK UDR and Community UDR?

Designs to which Community UDR applies

9.101   The designs to which Community UDR applies are defined just as for Community registered designs. Thus the discussions of the following key points in connection with Community registered designs apply as much to unregistered as to registered designs:

- Design as the *appearance* of the whole of part of a product (see paras 8.25–8.29).
- *Products* as any industrial or handicraft item (see para 8.18).
- *Complex products* as products composed of multiple, replaceable components (see para 8.49).
- Possession of *novelty* (see paras 8.31–8.32).
- Possession of *individual character* (see paras 8.33–8.35).
- Exclusion of *designs solely dictated by the technical function* of the product (see paras 8.39–8.46).
- *Must fit* exclusion (see paras 8.55–8.58, 8.69).
- *Must match* or *repair* defence (see paras 8.61–8.68).
- Scope of protection is the *overall impression made on the informed user,* taking account of the designer's freedom to develop the design (see paras 8.33–8.34, 8.89–8.90).

9.102   Notice that all this necessarily implies that *Community UDR cannot apply to any design which is incapable of registration under the Community registered design system.* This is an important contrast with the UK UDR. Thus there may be unregistered designs which enjoy UK UDR in the UK but which will not have Community UDR. The best example would be a product whose design was dictated solely by function in the sense that it was the only possible design by which the product in question might perform its function. In so far as it was not caught by the UK UDR 'must fit' or any of the other exceptions, then that product would be protected in the UK, but not under the Community UDR.

[97] CDR, Art 96(1).

> ### ? Question
>
> Explain why Community UDR cannot apply to a design incapable of registration as a
> Community registered design.

Commencement and duration of Community UDR

9.103   The key differences between Community UDR and the Community registered design right are
as follows:

> Rather obviously, perhaps, there is no need for the design to be registered for the right to arise. Instead,
> Community UDR arises *when the design is first made available to the public within the European Union*, by
> way of publication, exhibition, use in trade or other disclosure in such a way that, in the normal course
> of business, these events could reasonably have become known to the circles specialised in the sector
> concerned, operating within the Union. But there is no such making available by disclosing the design
> to a third person subject to express or implied terms of confidentiality.

9.104   Note how the second of these points parallels what constitutes such disclosure as to prevent
registration of the design unless application for registration is made within 12 months of that
disclosure (the grace period—see above, paras 8.37–8.38). *Community UDR thus protects, inter
alia, the design which is or may be on its way to registration but is being first market-tested.*

9.105   Disclosure having occurred, the Community UDR then lasts for *three years* from the date on
which the design was first made available to the public. This period is significantly shorter than
both the UK UDR, even at its shortest, and Community registered design right, which lasts for
an initial period of five years and is renewable for four more such periods, so permitting a maximum period of protection of 25 years. The main purpose of this short form of protection apart
from the protection of the design on its way to registration can be gleaned from the recitals to
the Community Design Regulation (emphasis supplied):

> '(15) A Community design sector should, as far as possible, serve the needs of all sectors of industry in
> the Community. (16) Some of those sectors produce large numbers of designs for products frequently
> having a *short market life* where protection without the burden of registration formalities is an advantage
> and the duration of protection is of lesser significance. On the other hand, there are sectors of industry
> which value the advantages of registration for the greater legal certainty it provides . . . (17) This calls for
> two forms of protection, one being a short-term unregistered design and the other being a longer term
> registered design.'

The best example of an industrial sector with short market-life products is the clothing fashion
industry, where designs are turned over on a seasonal basis, for which registration would probably not have much point.

Rights conferred

Ownership

9.106   So far as appropriate, the same rules about ownership apply as in the Community registered
design. The first owner of a Community UDR is the *designer* or his successor in title. If two or
more persons develop a design jointly, the right vests in them jointly. If a design is developed by
an *employee* in the execution of his duties or following the instructions given by his employer,
the right to the design vests in the employer unless otherwise agreed or specified by national

law.[98] In *Fundación Española para la Innovación de la Artesanía (FEIA) v Cul de Sac Espacio Creativo, S.L. and Acierta Product & Position, SA*[99] the ECJ considered whether the employer-employee relationship (by which designs vested in the employer) extended to a design for a wall clock for which there was a contract for commission, with reference to Article 14(3) of the Community Design Regulation 6/2002. Article 14(1) of the Regulation states that the right to the Community design vests in the designer or his successor in title. The Court held that Article 14(3) does not apply to Community designs that have been produced as a result of a contract for commission. Furthermore, Article 14(1) meant that the right to the design vested in the designer, unless it was contractually assigned to a successor in title. If an unregistered Community design is disclosed or claimed by a person not entitled to it, the entitled person may claim to be recognised as the legitimate holder of the design. Such a claim will become barred three years after the disclosure, unless the party making the disclosure was in bad faith.[100]

9.107   Community UDRs may be treated as objects of property, with transfers of ownership, or in security; or by way of licences to others to use the right, exclusively or non-exclusively.[101]

Exclusive right

9.108   A Community UDR confers on its holder the *exclusive right to use the design and to prevent any third party not having his consent from using it*. The uses covered are as with Community registered designs, that is, in relation to a product in which the design is incorporated or to which it is applied, and in particular (that is, non-exclusively):

- making
- offering
- putting on the market
- importing
- exporting
- otherwise using
- stocking (CDR, Article 19(1))

These rights do not extend to acts done privately and for non-commercial purposes, so the use must be public (in the sense of non-private) and for a commercial purpose.[102] So, as with registered design rights in general and the UK UDR, *the right is essentially a commercial one, concerned with commercial activity.*

9.109   But unlike the registered design, which confers a monopoly, so that the right is available even against a party who is unaware of the existence of the prior design, this right of exclusive use in the commercial setting can only be enforced if the contested use arises from *copying* the protected design. The contested use will not be deemed to result from copying if it results from an independent work of creation by a designer who may be reasonably thought not to be familiar with the design made available to the public by the holder. The justification for this difference is that a party proposing to put a design into the marketplace can check the register for any similar prior registered designs; but cannot do so for unregistered ones. Fairness requires that such a person be liable only if that person knows, or ought reasonably to know, of that prior

---

[98] CDR, Art 14.   [99] Case C-32/08, [2009] ECDR 19.   [100] CDR, Art 18.   [101] See generally CDR, Title III.
[102] CDR, Art 20(1)(a).

unregistered design and right. There may also be the difficulty of knowing whether or not the right is still subsistent, but it may well not be difficult to establish when a design was first made available to the public in such a way as to start the Community UDR running. In any event, in the short market life industries at which Community UDR is chiefly aimed, it may well be worthwhile for a second party to use the design over the short period while the design is still in fashion. The policy is summarised thus in recital 21 of the CDR:

> 'The exclusive nature of the right conferred by the Community registered design is consistent with its greater legal certainty. It is appropriate that the unregistered Community design should, however, constitute a right only to prevent copying. Protection could not therefore extend to design products which are the result of a design arrived at independently by a second designer.'

With the limitation of the exclusive right being to copying, Community UDR is like UK UDR.

Key points about Community UDR

- Design is defined as for the Community registered design
- The term of Community UDR is only three years. It is aimed at the protection of designs on their way to being registered, or to be applied to articles with a short market-life
- The right protects only against copying in relation to the commercial exploitation of articles

---

Defences

9.110   The Community UDR does not prevent any of the following uses of the design:

- Acts done privately and for non-commercial purposes.
- Acts done for experimental purposes.
- Acts of reproduction to make citations or teaching purposes, provided that such acts are compatible with fair trade practice and do not prejudice the normal exploitation of the design, with mention being made of the source.

These are the same as the exceptions applying to registered designs and reference should be made to paras 8.103–8.106 for relevant discussion. The exceptions there mentioned in respect of equipment and repairs on foreign ships and aircraft temporarily in the EU also apply in Community UDR.

 Discussion point   For answer guidance visit www.oxfordtextbooks.co.uk/orc/macqueen2e/

- What is the purpose of this UDR?
- To what products will the Community UDR typically apply?
- How do the main features of Community UDR (designs to which applicable, duration, rights, defences) compare, contrast, and interact with Registered Design protection?
- Likewise, how does Community UDR contrast with the UK UDR?
- Why does UK UDR continue to exist despite the introduction of Community UDR?

Summary overview of Part III

9.111   This section draws together the strands of this and the previous chapter on design law, to clarify in particular the co-existence of four distinct design regimes along with copyright.

There are four forms of design right available to those who wish to protect their designs from unauthorised commercial use by others:

(1) Community registered design right
(2) UK registered design right

Note that the substance of what these rights protect is the same following the Designs Directive 1998 and the Community Designs Regulation 2001.

(3) UK unregistered design right
(4) Community unregistered design right

The unregistered rights are, however, unharmonised with, and indeed significantly different from, each other. It is unclear how they interact. But Community unregistered design right has a considerable overlap in substance with Community registered design: the main differences are the requirement of registration, duration, and the nature of the exclusive right (registered monopoly versus unregistered protection against copying only). Because it can protect functional designs (whether as defined in old UK registered design law or as now more narrowly defined under the current regime—see paras 8.39–8.46), the UK unregistered design right reaches a wider range of designs than either registered design law or Community unregistered design law; but the practical effects of this, given that the first of these rights is also limited by a 'must fit' exception, is probably limited.

In addition, in the UK, designs still receive protection, albeit limited, from

(5) copyright.

But in relation to artistic or other works which are or which become designs for products, what constitutes infringement of copyright is significantly restricted.

Further reading

Books

General

Bently & Sherman, *Intellectual Property Law* (3rd edn, 2009), Chs 29 and 30

Copinger & Skone James on Copyright (15th edn, 2005), Ch 13

Cornish & Llewelyn, *Intellectual Property* (6th edn, 2007), Ch 15

Laddie, Prescott & Vitoria, *Modern Law of Copyright* (3rd edn, 2000), Ch 53–59

History and policy

HL MacQueen, *Copyright, Competition and Industrial Design* (2nd edn, 1995)

Articles

Applications of UDR

A Coulthard and L Bently, 'From the commonplace to the interface: five cases on unregistered design right' [1997] EIPR 401

S Hird and M Peeters, 'UK protection for recombinant DNA—exploring the options' [1991] EIPR 334

J Reynolds and P Brownlow, 'Increased legal protection for schematic designs in the UK' [1994] EIPR 398

Spare parts

A Michaels, 'The end of the road for "pattern spare" parts? *Dyson Ltd v Qualtex (UK) Ltd*' [2006] EIPR 396

J Sykes, 'The unregistered design right: interpretation and practical application of the must-match exemption' (2006) 1 JIPLP 442

Licences of right

J Reed, 'Royalties for design right "licences of right" ' [2005] EIPR 298

Community UDR

C-H Massa & A Strowel, 'Community Design: Cinderella revamped' [2003] 2 EIPR 68VM Saez, 'The unregistered Community design right' [2002] EIPR 585

Part IV

Patents

Introduction

This Part of the book explores the law of patents over three chapters. Chapter 10 considers the nature of patents and patentability in the context of the various patent regimes that operate at the national, European and international levels. We will examine current developments within these regimes against the background of the justifications that are commonly advanced for patent protection. We also consider the nature of the patent application process. Chapter 11 then explains what is required in order to obtain a patent, what it means to have a patent, and what constitutes patent infringement. Crucial to this exercise is a discussion of exceptions to patentability. An important issue in this respect is patent revocation, that is, the claim that a patent is somehow invalid and should be struck down. This is a common response to actions for infringement and we will examine how it operates together with defences for alleged infringers. Finally, Chapter 12 deals with two of the most pressing contemporary challenges to patent law, being biotechnological inventions and software patents. We will use these examples to explore how well patent law adapts to new technological advances and challenges and we will consider whether reforms to patent regimes are required.

Sources of the law: key websites

- Patents Act 1977, as amended to 1 January 2010, available at
  http://www.ipo.gov.uk/patentsact1977.pdf
- The patents related sections of the Copyright, Designs and Patents Act 1988, as amended to 1 January 2010, available at
  http://www.ipo.gov.uk/pdact1988.pdf
- European Patent Convention 2000, available at
  http://www.epo.org/patents/law/legal-texts/epc.html
- TRIPS Agreement 1994, as amended, available at
  http://www.wto.org/english/tratop_e/trips_e/t_agm0_e.htm
- Paris Convention for the Protection of Industrial Property 1883, as amended
  http://www.wipo.int/treaties/en/ip/paris/trtdocs_wo020.html

- Patent Cooperation Treaty 1970, as amended
  http://www.wipo.int/pct/en/texts/articles/atoc.htm
- Patent Law Treaty (2000)
  http://www.wipo.int/treaties/en/ip/plt/trtdocs_wo038.html
- Decisions of the courts in the various jurisdictions of the UK, for which see BAILII
  http://www.bailii.org/
- WIPO Standing Committee on the Law of Patents
  http://www.wipo.int/scp/en/

10

Patent regimes and the application process

Introduction

Scope and overview of chapter

10.1 This chapter examines the architecture and procedures of contemporary patent systems as they currently operate in the UK, within the European patent system, and through international agreements, instruments and procedures. The first section will lay out the framework of these patent regimes, explaining their origins and current remits. All patent regimes operate through a registration process, meaning that patent protection is only granted after rigorous consideration of the criteria for patentability as applied to each putative invention. For present purposes, a valid patent normally lasts for 20 years and provides the patent holder (the patentee) with an 'absolute' monopoly over his invention. This is the strongest of all monopolies available in intellectual property law, and it makes patent protection one of the most sought after of intellectual property rights (IPRs).

10.2 **Learning objectives**

By the end of this chapter you should be able to describe and explain:

- the subject matter of patent protection and the various justifications offered for the existence of patent regimes;
- the nature of the various patent regimes as well as their similarities and differences;
- the current challenges for patent law and options for reform;
- the processes and procedures for obtaining patent protection.

10.3 The chapter explains the different kinds of patent regime that exist at national, regional and international levels and helps the reader to understand those systems by setting the discussion against a background of the various arguments advanced to support patent protection.

Thereafter, we consider the registration system used in the UK to obtain a patent. Unlike copyright, patent protection does not come into existence with the creation of the relevant subject matter, but rather must be granted by an intellectual property office after an application and examination process. These processes will be described, including the issue of who is entitled to apply for, and receive, a patent. So the chapter looks like this:

- Patent regimes: past and present (10.4–10.13)
- Rationales of patent protection (10.14–10.21)
- The European dimension (10.22–10.36)
- The international dimension (10.37–10.70)
- Further reform: patent regimes in the future (10.71–10.94)
- Patent procedures (10.95–10.127)

Patent regimes: past and present

Early history

10.4   The essential features of the modern patent system can be seen in the earliest origins of that system which began, in Europe at least, as a form of state or monarch grace and favour. Monopolies over trade practices or production were initially used as a reward for loyalty or as a form of privilege, done through the grant of *letters patent* (an 'open letter') as proof that the privilege—the monopoly—had been bestowed. The first recorded patent in England was for a method of making stained glass given to John of Utynam by King Henry VI in 1449.[1] From the very beginning, however, there has been an expectation of reciprocity as between the granter of the monopoly—be it monarch or state—and the grantee. Thus the monopoly holder would be expected to undertake certain obligations to his monarch, or, as typified by the Venetian Republic, the grantee would undertake to disclose the elements of his new 'craft' in return for the privilege of a market monopoly of 10 years. Venice was the first state to establish a patent system, done by decree in 1474, in an attempt to attract tradesmen to introduce products and processes not known in Venice at that time. This encouraged innovation in the Republic while avoiding conflict with the powerful guilds that held considerable sway over the markets.[2] Other states followed suit, each using the device of monopoly as the incentive to inventors to enter the social contract with the state. But the terms of this contract have been in dispute since the earliest of times, and the courts have always been willing to strike a monopoly down if the balance of interests has not been appropriately struck. Thus, in *Darcy v Allin*[3] a monopoly from Queen Elizabeth I over trade in playing cards was overturned, partly on the basis that there was no discernible advantage to the public of allowing such a state of affairs to continue. Parliament, too, has shown antipathy towards monopolies since early times, especially those which were, in effect, at the unfettered discretion of the Crown. This culminated in the 1624 Statute of Monopolies which had the general aim of preventing Crown monopolies. Section 6, however, stated:

> 'Provided also (and be it declared and enacted) that any declaration before mentioned shall not extend to any letters patent and grants of privilege for the term of fourteen years or under, hereafter to be made,

---

[1] HM Treasury, *Gowers Review of Intellectual Property*, December 2006, para 1.13.
[2] See, CM Belfanti, 'Guilds, Patents and the Circulation of Technical Knowledge: Northern Italy During the Early Modern Age' (2004) 45 Technology and Culture 569.
[3] (1602) 77 ER 1131.

of the sole working or making of any manner of new manufacture within this realm, to the true and first inventor and inventors of such manufactures which others at the time of making such letters patent and grants shall not use, so as also they be not contrary to the law or mischievous to the state, by raising prices of commodities at home, or hurt of trade, or generally inconvenient.'

10.5   This provides an exception to the rule, and then stipulates an exception to the exception. The exception to the rule that Crown monopolies should not be granted is the proviso that the 'true and first inventor' of 'any manner of new manufacture' could receive a 14-year-long privilege over his invention, but the exception to this is that this monopoly should not be abusive or abused in ways contrary to law, state interests, trade and economic interests, or indeed, if it were 'generally inconvenient'.

 Discussion point   For answer guidance visit www.oxfordtextbooks.co.uk/orc/macqueen2e/

Why do you think that a period of 14 years was chosen, as opposed to 13 or 15 or some other figure?

10.6   We see, then, elements in the early history of patents which we can still recognise in our modern system. These are:

- the patent system as a mechanism to encourage innovation;
- the notion of social contract between state and patentee, with corresponding obligations on both sides;
- the centrality of monopoly to the regulation of that contract;
- the desire for a balance of interests as between society and the patentee;
- the idea that the monopoly should rightly go to the inventor of the new creation.

10.7   Other matters have changed. Patents are now granted for a maximum of 20 years,[4] and the law in the UK no longer talks of 'manner of new manufacture'.[5] We thus have to look elsewhere for some guidance on what constitutes an invention.[6] The search for a just balance is, however, a constant.

10.8   It is important to note that the grant of patents remained discretionary under the Statute of Monopolies of 1624. It was not until the 19th century that procedural form and a degree of certainty of process was introduced to the British patent system. The Patent Office was not established until 1852,[7] and it did not begin thorough examination of patent applications, in the sense of a proper scrutiny of the existing art, until 1905.[8] Prior to this it was sufficient merely to lodge a specification—a description of the invention—with the Patent Office to

---

[4] The average life of a patent in the United Kingdom has been estimated to be 10–11 years, see Gowers Report, n 1 above, para 6.19. A recent World Intellectual Property Organization report has found that only a minority of patents are maintain for the full 20-year term, see WIPO, *World Patent Report: A Statistical Review* (2008), p 24.

[5] The laws in the United States, Canada, Australia and New Zealand still refer to this concept in some form or another betraying their colonial roots.

[6] The UK law changed with the passing of the Patents Act 1977 which brought the UK into line with the European Patent Convention 1973.

[7] Patent Law Amendment Act 1852. Initially there existed Commissioners who were replaced by the Office itself in 1883. The Office is currently located in Newport, Gwent but its original home was in Southampton Buildings, London where it shared space with the Secretaries of Bankrupts and Lunatics!

[8] As a result of the Patents Act 1902.

obtain protection.[9] Reforms brought about by the Patents, Designs and Trade Marks Act 1883 introduced a more robust procedure for examining applications, but even then it was largely a matter of checking for deficiencies in the formalities of an application and for insufficiency in the description of the invention itself.[10]

10.9   There were certain adverse social consequences of such lax procedures. It meant, for example, that patents of dubious or no worth could be obtained relatively easily and then waived over competitors as a threat; it also generated considerable uncertainty as to where the boundaries of legitimate trading lay. Movements in various European countries took up against the patent system around this time,[11] and the Dutch actually abolished their system in the period 1869 to 1912. In the UK, many trade organisations railed against patents in the 18th and 19th centuries, and bodies such as the Royal Society of Arts lobbied governments against the worst excesses of patent monopolies.[12] Indeed, the Society created an alternative scheme to the patent system in an attempt to achieve the same social ends but without the restrictions that monopolies can bring. The Society offered cash *premiums* for innovations in certain areas, and published *Lists* advertising these widely. The Lists set questions or problems requiring resolution, thereby providing a partly directed policy of innovation for British society. Importantly, from 1765, no person was to be considered as a candidate for a premium if they had previously obtained a patent for the invention for which the premium was offered. The premium acted as an incentive to innovators to disclose their inventions early and to allow others to build on their expertise. No monopoly over the invention was given.

 Discussion point   For answer guidance visit www.oxfordtextbooks.co.uk/orc/macqueen2e/

What are the advantages of the premium system compared to the patent system? Equally, can you think of any disadvantages?

10.10   The premium system did not survive, but the Royal Society continues its struggle against inappropriate monopolies. A contemporary example of this is the Adelphi Charter.[13] This instrument was drawn up by a distinguished group of interested individuals and parties concerned about the ever-expanding nature of intellectual property rights and the possible consequences for the public domain of their aggressive enforcement. The Charter calls on governments and other bodies to adopt new strategies for thinking about, and protecting, intellectual property and the public interest. It consists of nine statements of principle which could be taken to guide intellectual property policy in the future in ways that might result in the striking of a different balance of interests to that which exists today. Three of the principles give a flavour of the tone of the document:

'(1) Laws regulating intellectual property must serve as means of achieving creative, social and economic ends and not as ends in themselves . . .

---

[9] This system was introduced by the Patent Law Amendment Act 1852.

[10] Interestingly, this reflects many utility models systems which exist elsewhere in Europe, see paras 10.75ff.

[11] Various countries have gone without patent systems at one time or another, see HC Wegner, *Patent Harmonisation* (1993) at 17, and E Schiff, *Industrialization without National Patents: The Netherlands, 1869–1912, Switzerland, 1850–1907* (1971).

[12] Royal Society for the Encouragement of Arts, Manufactures and Commerce: http://www.thersa.org/. The Society itself points out that in many ways the broad aim of the Society is not entirely dissimilar to that of the patent system.

[13] Royal Society of Arts Adelphi Charter: http://www.adelphicharter.org/

...(3) The public interest requires a balance between the public domain and private rights. It also requires a balance between the free competition that is essential for economic vitality and the monopoly rights granted by intellectual property laws..., and

...(9) There must be an automatic presumption against creating new areas of intellectual property protection, extending existing privileges or extending the duration of rights'.

 Exercise

> Visit the Adelphi Charter site at http://www.adelphicharter.org/ to find out more. Critically assess the terms of the Charter. It is nice rhetoric, but is there much chance of it becoming reality?

10.11   The establishment of a patent registration system was a move to create a gate-keeping device. Such a system provides a relatively clear indication of thresholds that have to be met in order for patent protection to be granted, that is, that the invention must be new, involve inventive step and be capable of industrial application. It also serves to ensure that the obligation of the applicant to disclose his invention in a way that furthers the public interest is fully discharged.[14] Moreover, and just as importantly, it is a mechanism for weeding out innovations that have been deemed not to be inventions, such as discoveries, or which are to be excluded on a number of policy grounds, for example, that they offend against common decency or morality. We should be very clear, therefore, that the process of examining a patent application is not some technical box ticking exercise. Indeed, the examination of a patent application involves the assessment of a plethora of policy considerations which are designed to reflect the policy objectives of the patent system itself. How well this is achieved is another question.

Internationalisation of patent protection

10.12   We have already seen in the context of copyright and designs that intellectual property rights started their life as creatures of national territorial effect only, meaning that protection was only afforded to innovators in their own country. The same was true, and remains true, of patents. But patents have always had an international dimension. From earliest times, part of the reason for granting a monopoly to a national was for fear that foreigners might otherwise dominate a domestic market. By the same token, as we have seen, the Venetian Republic used its own system of encouraging innovation to attract those from outside the Republic to bring new crafts and methods of manufacture to the city. Indeed, the prospect of international trade has been inherently bound up with the development of patent protection over the years. This was particularly acute in the 19th century with the advent of the industrial revolution and at a time when various European patent systems were developing along similar lines and cross-jurisdictional influence was common. The vagaries of international trade meant that there was a growing urgency to ensure that intellectual property was recognised and mutually protected across national boundaries for the benefit of all. Thus, just as we had the emergence of the Berne

---

[14] This was one of the major criticisms of the system during the pre-registration period, see generally on this period B Sherman and L Bently, *The Making of Modern Intellectual Property Law* (1999) pp 101–110.

Convention in respect of copyright in 1886 (see Chapter 2), so too the international community (or much of it) foresaw a unmet need for an instrument to protect other forms of intellectual property, specifically patents, but far more broadly and crudely, *industrial property*.[15] In this way the Paris Convention of 1883 was born,[16] obliging signatory states to provide appropriate protection for the range of interests subsumed under the rubric of 'Industrial Property', being 'patents, utility models, industrial designs, trademarks, service marks, trade names, indications of source or appellations of origin, and the repression of unfair competition'.[17] This Convention says nothing specific about the substantive elements of patent law for its signatory countries—beyond the obligation to provide protection—but it did bring about various important reforms.

The *main features of the Paris Convention* perform, in numerous ways, similar functions as the Berne Convention does for copyright. In other ways, it distinguishes industrial property as a class apart from copyright and its related rights. Thus:

- The principle of *national treatment* was established in the Paris Convention, ensuring that each signatory state will afford the same rights to foreigners of other signatory states as to its own nationals (Article 2). Nationals of non-contracting states are also entitled to national treatment under the Convention if they are domiciled in a contracting state or if they have a 'real and effective industrial or commercial establishment' in a contracting state (Article 3).

- An applicant enjoys a *12-month right of priority from the date of first filing of a patent in a signatory country* (Article 4). This means that no subsequent filing of related applications in other countries within this period will be invalidated by the earlier filing, nor will any publication or use of the invention affect patentability. It also means that the novelty of all such applications will be tested by reference to the period before the first filing. We discuss the significance of this below (paras 11.76–11.92).

- *National patents remain independent of each other*, therefore the granting of a patent in one contracting state does not oblige the other contracting states to grant a patent; a patent cannot be refused, annulled or terminated in any contracting state on the ground that it has been refused or annulled or has terminated in any other contracting state (Article 4*bis*).

- The *focus is on the inventor* who has the right to be named as such in the patent (Article 4*ter*). The primary right holder, in the first instance, is the inventor. While this may be varied by contract or by the existence of an employer/employee relationship, such modifications to the general rule are left to domestic laws.

10.13   The Paris Convention remains of central significance in the protection of patents, and it is allied to the more recent TRIPS Agreement 1994, see below at paras 10.44–10.47, in that a signatory state to the latter instrument must also comply with the core provisions of the Paris Convention, notably Articles 1–12, and 19.[18]

---

[15] Paris Convention for the Protection of Industrial Property (1883), revised at Brussels on 14 December 1900, at Washington on 2 June 1911, at The Hague on 6 November 1925, at London on 2 June 1934, at Lisbon on 31 October 1958, and at Stockholm on 14 July 1967, and as amended on 28 September 1979.
[16] There are currently 173 contracting parties to the Convention (March 2010).   [17] ibid, Art 1(2).
[18] Agreement on Trade-related Aspects of Intellectual Property Rights (1994), Art 2.

> ## Key points on the early history
>
> - Contemporary patent law began as a system of grace and favour, but a central feature from early on has been the idea of the patent as a form of 'social contract' with obligations on both sides
> - In return for patent protection, then, a patentee must make his invention public
> - The monopolistic effects of patents have always been viewed with suspicion, and attempts to minimise these include limiting the duration of a patent (currently to 20 years in most cases)
> - In the 19th century, and throughout the 20th century, the process of internationalisation of patent law gathers pace, making it today one of the most harmonised areas of law at least in terms of substantive law.

Rationales of patent protection

10.14   There is no single rationale for the patent system—indeed some claim that it makes little sense at all. But its 400-year-long history speaks to the fact that it must be achieving some useful purpose(s), and a recent WIPO report on patenting activity worldwide reveals an average annual growth rate in patent filings of 5.3 per cent between 1995 and 2006, though this was lower than the overall increase in economic activity around the globe.[19] Internationalisation of patent filing by non-residents has also increased dramatically with an 8.0 per cent average annual increase in the same period. This in turn is linked to a marked rise in the use of the international application mechanism as a conduit to foreign markets.[20] Patents are, it would seem, a big success worldwide.

10.15   There has, however, always been a need to justify the patent system. Its existence is not self-evidently in the public good and its approach of offering a market monopoly is not manifestly the best means to strike a balance of potentially competing interests. The interests at stake include those of inventors, their competitors, consumers, researchers, and the state itself. As we have seen, a patent is often described as a form of social contract between the patentee and the state, whereby the award of a patent monopoly is given in return for public disclosure of the invention. This reveals an irony in the way that the patent system operates: an exclusionary private property right is given in return for public dissemination of the details of the invention. Why so?

10.16   Various rationales for patents have been advanced over the years, and it is probably the case that each has held sway at one time or another in the development of patent law policy. The idea of the patent as a *reward* for inventive activity is difficult to sustain, however, because the need for a reward does not require that a monopoly be given. Rewards can take many forms such as

---

[19] World Intellectual Property Organization, *World Patent Report: a Statistical Review* (2008), available here: http://www.wipo.int/export/sites/www/ipstats/en/statistics/patents/pdf/wipo_pub_931.pdf

[20] This was established by the Patent Co-operation Treaty 1970 (see below paras 10.39–10.40). International applications through the PCT grew dramatically until 2001, with a yearly growth rate in excess of 10 per cent; since then it has been slowing down to an increase of 5.9 per cent year on year see (. . .), see *World Patent Report* (2008), ibid.

prizes or one-off payments without any risk of adverse effects on the market.[21] Rather, the most commonly advanced rationale for the social contract approach is the *incentive* function that it is thought to represent. This is the view that the prospect of a monopoly is so attractive that it will encourage innovation and that it represents the best means to secure adequate returns for intellectual endeavour; moreover, the public disclosure requirement acts as a further spur to others to invent around a particular invention and to receive their own protection. This rationale rests on certain assumptions, however. For example, it assumes that the value of innovative activity outweighs increased costs to consumers, and that any monopolies granted will not be used to block, rather than encourage, development in a particular field.[22] It also presupposes that citizens will be in a position to pay higher costs and that the necessary infrastructures are in place to support further innovation. Neither of these last two assumptions stands for many developing countries, calling into question the rationale and value of the patent system to those countries. A World Bank publication has indicated that patent rights over high-technology products are of most value in large, middle-income, developing countries where imitation of an invention is most likely, while export decisions to poorer countries often do not depend on the existence of IPRs in those countries since the threat of imitation is lower because of lack of infrastructure.[23]

10.17   The *public disclosure* requirement in patent law should not be underestimated. It is an essential feature of the arrangement between the patentee and the state, and a patent can be struck down on grounds of *insufficiency* if adequate disclosure is not made in a patent application.[24] Adequate disclosure requires that the essential features of the invention are made public and that the means to make or reproduce the invention are revealed in a way that would enable a person skilled in the particular field ('the art') to do so.[25] The European Patent Office claims that its searchable patent databases now provide the most efficient, detailed and up-to-date source of information in over 50 technical fields. The stringent disclosure requirements mean that 70 per cent of information contained in patents is not available anywhere else.[26]

10.18   It has also been argued that patents perform a *signalling* function, that is, indicating the innovative and productive capacity of the patent holder and signalling that he may be a sound investment for the future.[27] Patent portfolios are certainly a key consideration for venture capitalists.[28]

10.19   *Human rights discourse* has become more prevalent in recent years both in support of, and against, the existence and exercise of IPRs. On the one hand, it is important to note that the 1948 Universal Declaration of Human Rights provides that '[e]veryone has the right to the protection

---

[21] EC Hettinger, 'Justifying Intellectual Property' (1989) 18 Philosophy and Public Affairs 31–52.

[22] A survey funded by the European Commission found that about one third of European patents are not used for any commercial or industrial purposes, and that one half of these are used as 'blocking' patents, that is, to prevent competitors from using the protected technology, see 'Study on Evaluating the Knowledge Economy: What are Patents Actually Worth? The Value of Patents for Today's Economy and Society', Final Report, 23 July 2006, p 10. See also, I Troy and R Werle, *Uncertainty and the Market for Patents* (2008).

[23] C Fink and KE Maskus (eds), *Intellectual Property and Development: Lessons from Recent Economic Research*, (2005), Ch 2 by C Fink and CA Primo Braga, 'How Stronger Protection of Intellectual Property Rights Affects International Trade Flows'. See also, World Bank, *Global Economic Prospects 2008: Technology Diffusion in the Developing World (2008)*.

[24] Patents Act 1977, ss 14(3) and 72(1)—see further paras 11.201–11.212.

[25] See generally *Kirin-Amgen v Hoechst Marion Roussel No.2* [2005] RPC 9.

[26] See the Esp@cenet database at http://ep.espacenet.com/ and EPO, Global Patent Data Coverage (2009).

[27] Commission on Intellectual Property Rights, Innovation and Public Health, *Public health, innovation and intellectual property rights* (2006) p 21: http://www.who.int/intellectualproperty/documents/thereport/ENPublicHealthReport.pdf

[28] See generally, the Regional Comparative Advantage and Knowledge-Based Entrepreneurship Research Programme, London School of Economics, available at: http://www.lse.ac.uk/collections/RICAFE/

of the moral and material interests resulting from any scientific, literary or artistic production of which he is the author',[29] suggesting that individual creators have a human rights claim to IP. On the other hand the UN Sub-Commission on Human Rights has pointed to the potential inherent conflict which IPRs can generate *face-à-face* other economic, social or cultural rights and issued a Resolution to the effect that these latter rights should trump in any case of conflict.[30] But not everyone sees these two regimes as in inherent conflict.[31] Few rights, even human rights, are absolute. Limitations can be placed on the exercise of rights in an attempt either to protect the rights and freedoms of others, or to achieve an overall equitable balance of interests. In contemporary policy terms, it is clear that *balance* is the watchword of the day. The language of human rights might help us to frame the discussion, but it is unlikely to provide any universal solution.[32]

10.20   Human rights perspectives have not only had the effect of opening up dialogue about the nature of IPRs, but they have also led to a greater appreciation of relationships between the intellectual property world and other social realms. An example of this is the potential *regulation* function of the patent system. Just as the grant of a patent might encourage innovation, so it might follow that the denial of a patent might dissuade certain forms of innovation. In this sense, the patent system could be seen as a means to regulate or control undesirable inventions. Alternatively, undesirable uses of the monopoly which a patent provides might also be regulated through the patent system, for example, through greater use of compulsory licences or more generous interpretations of patent defences. Little work has been done to date on the interface between patent and regulation regimes,[33] but a few cautious comments can be offered here. First, the denial of a patent in no way prohibits innovation, it merely removes an incentive. Plenty of innovative behaviour carries on without the potential of a patent, and there is no guarantee that the denial of protection will have the desired dissuasive effect. The *efficiency* of this alleged regulatory function is therefore open to question. Secondly, the assessment of which inventions are undesirable is a complex matter, involving ethical and moral considerations which may be beyond the competence of a patent office examiner. Moreover, given the nature of the patent system in requiring secrecy about an invention prior to applying for a patent, there will have been little or no opportunity for broader social debate about an invention, thereby raising questions about the *legitimacy* of quasi-regulatory decisions about the value, or otherwise, of a particular invention. Notwithstanding, there has been increased reliance on the exclusions provisions in patent law in recent years, especially in the field of biotechnological inventions,[34] implying that the rationale of the patent system may, once again, be changing.[35]

10.21   It matters very much which of these rationales is promoted over any other in the development and implementation of patent policy. A public interest mandate will require evidence that the

[29] UN General Assembly Resolution 217A(III), UN Doc A/810, at 71, Art 27(2).

[30] UN High Commissioner for Human Rights, Sub-Commission on Human Rights, Intellectual Property Rights and Human Rights, Resolution 2000/7, 17 August 2000, available at: http://www.un.org/en/rights/

[31] See HL MacQueen, 'Towards Utopia or Irreconcilable Tensions? Thoughts on Intellectual Property, Human Rights and Competition Law' (2005) 2(4) SCRIPTed, 452–66 and L Helfer, 'Human Rights and Intellectual Property: Conflict or Co-existence?' (2003) 5 Minnesota Intellectual Property Review 47.

[32] PK Yu, 'Reconceptualizing Intellectual Property Interests in a Human Rights Framework' (2007) UC Davis Law Review 1039–1149.

[33] See GT Laurie, 'Patents, Patients and Consent: Exploring the Interface Between Regulation and Innovation Regimes' in H Somsen (ed), *The Regulatory Challenge of Biotechnology* (2007).

[34] See paras 12.43ff.

[35] cf, the collective reply of German patent attorneys to the European Commission's survey on IP policy, n 22 above, wherein they opined that '…there is no reason for a political debate on principles concerning patent protection in view of ethical behaviour, protection of the environment, health protection, or freedom of information', ibid, p 10.

dual aims of dissemination of knowledge and increased innovation can be achieved before there is any strengthening of IP rights, or indeed, the introduction of new rights. A focus on the individual inventor's claims would, however, promote new and more robust forms of protection.

> ### Exercise
>
> Consider which of these, or other, rationales are operating as you read more about the different regimes and features of patent law. Are we always striking the right balance?

The European dimension

10.22   Easily the most far-reaching reforms of the 20th century for UK patent law came in the period of 'Europeanisation', which produced the European Patent Convention (EPC, 1973, as amended) after long negotiations throughout the 1960s. The Patents Act 1977 incorporated these reforms into domestic law,[36] and in doing so swept away many of the vestiges of the uniquely British regime that had gone before.[37] We have already seen, for example, that the law no longer requires proof of 'a manner of manufacture', although the reforming measures did not provide us with a replacement definition of an invention. It is now assumed that if an applicant clears the hurdles of patentability then he has produced an 'invention'.[38] The EPC harmonised the substantive law on patentability and exclusions and it now represents the position in 37 European countries.[39] Judicial attitudes in the UK towards the interpretation of patents also had to change after the 1977 Act came into force. The traditional British perspective had been towards a *literal approach* to interpreting a patentee's claims for his invention, while the European tradition (as in many other areas of law) has been to adopt a *purposive approach*, that is, to seek to interpret the law in light of the ultimate purpose it was designed to achieve. This has been a difficult transition for the courts as we shall see in due course (see paras 11.182–11.198), and there is still discussion of the extent to which the UK takes its own path, despite further clarification from within the European system on how patent claims should be interpreted.[40] Most recently, the EPC has been revised and now takes the form of EPC 2000 which came into force in December 2007.

10.23   The European Patent Convention also established the European Patent Office (EPO), which is based in Munich, Germany, and which opened its doors on 1 June 1978 when the Convention came into force. The EPO grants 'European' patents, although this is something of a misnomer since there is no such thing (yet) as a European patent in the sense of one instrument effective throughout European territory. Rather, the EPO provides a single point of entry for the patent

---

[36] Relevant laws in the 20th century were the Patents Acts of 1902 and 1949. European laws had, nonetheless, been approximating over the years and in many respects patent laws were very similar.

[37] Consider the early 20th-century proposals for a 'British Empire patent', see C Wadlow, 'The British Empire Patent 1901–1923: The "Global Patent" that Never Was' (2006) Intellectual Property Quarterly 311.

[38] cf the discussion on the need for an 'invention' in *Biogen v Medeva* [1997] RPC 1, especially per Lord Mustill at 31, where the door was not firmly closed on the issue but neither their Lordships nor counsel could think of a pertinent example.

[39] As of 1 May 2010.

[40] See now Art 2 to the Additional Protocol on the Interpretation of Art 69, inserted by EPC 2000.

applicant to lodge only one application, and be subject to only one examination process, but in respect of any number of signatory countries that he might designate. If successful, the EPO grants collections of patents for the designated countries, and each patent has full effect in the country for which it was sought as if it was granted by the domestic intellectual property office.[41]

Diagram 10.1 Internal structure of European Patent Office[42]

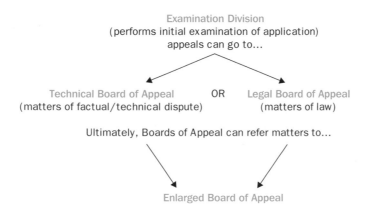

10.24 The President of the European Patent Office can also perform a 'declaratory' function[43] and issue opinions on cases of import.[44] He or she[45] can refer questions to the Enlarged Board of Appeal to clarify matters in particular areas of law, as can Boards of Appeal.

10.25 An important feature of the European patent system is the existence of *Opposition Proceedings*.[46] These allow any party who objects to the grant of a patent—for example, on evidence that it did not, in fact, meet the criteria for patentability or because it offends *ordre public* or morality[47]—to petition the Opposition Division of the Office within nine months of publication of the grant of the patent.[48] The Division has the power to revoke the patent.[49] This mechanism has been used increasingly in recent years in the context of biotechnological inventions, as we discuss in Chapter 12. It is a valuable social device which gives access to the patent system to groups who may have legitimate concerns about how well the granting authorities are striking the balance of interests at stake.[50]

[41] The terminology is of European Patent (UK) or European Patent (France).

[42] See here for ongoing discussions of reform of the Boards of Appeal http://www.epo.org/patents/law/legislative-initiatives.html

[43] See G3/95 *Inadmissable referral* (1996) OJEPO 169 and EPC 2000, Art 112(1)(b).

[44] See, for example, G2/06 Comments by the President of the European Patent Office (September 2006), available here: http://www.cipa.org.uk/download_files/epo_warf.pdf

[45] Alison Brimelow, former Director of the UK Patent Office, took over the Presidency of the EPO in July 2007 and was succeed by Benoît Battistelli from France on 1 July 2010.

[46] EPC 2000, Part V.

[47] EPC 2000, Art 100 outlines the grounds for opposition. These are (a) the subject matter of the European patent is not patentable within the terms of the EPC; (b) the patent does not disclose the invention in a manner sufficiently clear and complete for it to be carried out by a person skilled in the art; (c) the subject matter of the European patent extends beyond the content of the relevant application.

[48] EPC 2000, Art 99.   [49] EPC 2000, Art 102.

[50] S Harmon, 'The Rules of Re-Engagement: The Use of Patent Proceedings To Influence the Regulation of Science (What The Science Does When The Salmon Comes Back Downstream)' (2006) 4 Intellectual Property Quarterly 378–403.

10.26   Note that the EPO is a granting body only. There is no European body (as yet) on questions of infringement or enforcement. Domestic and 'European' patents are therefore enforced in individual jurisdictions. A result of this is that it can lead to the unusual scenario where a patent may be held to be valid and infringed in one country and yet invalid in another even although they relate to the very same invention.[51] This is because judicial attitudes towards interpretation of patents can vary as between jurisdictions and to that extent the harmonisation process remains far from complete.

A new European appeal body?

10.27   There have been proposals circulating for a decade to create a new international organisation, the European Patent Judiciary, which would be composed of the European Patent Court and its Administrative Council.[52] The Court would have the power to settle litigation on matters of validity and infringement over European patents effective in contracting states. There is also provision for an appeal mechanism.[53] Interestingly, as an important harmonising feature, the Court of Appeal would also perform the role of the Facultative Advisory Council (FAC) which would be to deliver non-binding opinions on points of law concerning European *or* harmonised national patent law.[54] Thus a national court or a quasi-judicial authority could refer such matters to the FAC in an attempt to achieve some clarity and consistency in the applicable law. Note, however, the Working Party under whose auspices these proposals were developed has recognised that these reforming measures must be paused in light of initiatives within the European Union to establish the EU patent (formerly termed the Community patent) and a European patent court of its own (see para 10.29ff below).[55]

10.28   It is important at this juncture to clarify a point which often causes confusion. The European Patent Convention is *not* an instrument of the European Union (EU). The European Patent Organisation is an entirely separate entity which administers the EPC through its Administrative Council. There are 37 signatory states to the EPC, including all 27 member states of the European Union, as well as non-EU countries.[56] But any coordination of effort between the European Patent Organisation and the European Union is on an entirely voluntary basis. This is not to imply that the EU has not been active in the realm of intellectual property law—indeed, quite the opposite is true as we demonstrate in every chapter of this book—but its successes in the patent law field have been more modest than elsewhere.[57] This may be set to change with the latest proposals to emerge from the EU Competitiveness Council in December 2009. Before consider these, however, it is helpful to provide some background on proposals (and failures) to date.

---

[51]   *Improver Corporation v Remington Consumer Products Ltd* [1990] FSR 181.

[52]   See the work of the Working Party on Litigation set up by the contracting states of the European Patent Organisation in June 1999: http://www.epo.org/patents/law/legislative-initiatives/epla.html. In particular, consider the proposals on a Draft Agreement on the establishment of a European patent litigation system (aka European Patent Litigation Agreement) (December 2005).

[53]   Draft Agreement, above, Part V.   [54]   ibid, Part Va.

[55]   Working Party on Litigation, Declaration, 20 November 2003: http://documents.epo.org/projects/babylon/eponet.nsf/0/9F8870AD4D54AE4DC125723D004AF178/$File/declaration_en.pdf

[56]   Figure accurate as at 1 July2009.

[57]   Examples of harmonising measures that have failed include utility models and computer-implemented inventions.

A unitary patent right for Europe?

10.29   An early initiative from the late 1950s pre-empted the negotiations towards the EPC, and this was an attempt to create a unitary patent right for the, then, European Economic Community (EEC). The rationale for such an initiative takes us back to the fundamental tensions that IPRs can create in a market: the problem for the EEC—committed as it was to a single European market—was how to prevent the exercise of national patent monopolies partitioning the market. If only a single right subsists throughout that market then the problem of partition largely disappears. This proposal did not come to fruition, but the idea of a single European patent survived into the 1960s negotiations,[58] where two core proposals were on the table: a European Patent Convention (to deal with harmonisation of substantive criteria and to create a centralised granting body) and a Community Patent Convention (CPC, to produce a single, truly European patent effective throughout the Community). The former, as we have seen, became a reality in 1973. A Community Patent Convention was also signed in Luxembourg in 1975,[59] but failed to receive sufficient ratifications to come into force, as did a second attempt in 1989.[60] One of the biggest problems has been that of translation. The official languages of the EPO are English, French and German, but the European Union currently has 23 official languages, and the Convention provided that a patent had to be translated into every Community language. Self-evidently, the costs of this exercise would be prohibitive, especially when one considers that it is not unusual for a patent to run to over 20 pages in length.[61]

10.30   Notwithstanding these problems, the European Commission has not been willing to give up on the idea of a unitary patent.[62] It insists that a single right makes economic sense, would reduce the costs of patenting and would provide more legal certainty.[63] Accordingly, it introduced another proposal in 2000[64] and further steps towards agreement were taken in December 2009 when Ministers in the Competiveness Council agreed on a draft Regulation on the EU patent and a set of conclusions on (a) features of the unified patent litigation system, (b) renewal fees arrangements and (c) a system of Enhanced Partnership between central industrial property offices and the EPO.[65] No agreement was reached on language arrangements. The draft regulation envisages the EU— now a legal entity in its own right after the coming into force of the

---

[58] An early output from these negotiations was the Council of Europe Convention on the Unification of Certain Points of Substantive Law on Patents for Invention, 27 November 1963 (the Strasbourg Convention) wherein signatory states agreed the substantive criteria for invention, being novelty, inventive step, and capability of industrial application (Art 1) as well as exclusions from patentability when an invention or its publication is contrary to *ordre public* or morality (Art 2).

[59] Convention for the European Patent for the Common Market, 15 December 1975.

[60] Agreement relating to Community Patents, 15 December 1989.

[61] The European Commission estimated this was the average length of a patent application in its proposal for a Community patent, n 22 above, para 2.4.3.1.

[62] Commission's Green Paper on the Community patent and the European patent system COM(97) 314 final, of 24 June 1997.

[63] See the EU's Industrial Property website at: http://ec.europa.eu/internal_market/indprop/patent/index_en.htm

[64] Proposal for a Council Regulation on the Community patent COM/2000/0412 final—Official Journal C 337 E, 28/11/2000 P 0278–0290. This received support from the EU Council of Ministers in a Common Political Approach in 2003 which laid out an agreed framework for the scheme. See Council of the European Union, Community Patent— Common Political Approach (2003) 7159/03, adopted following meetings of the Council (Competitiveness) on 3 March 2003 and of the Council (Employment, Social Policy, Health and Consumer Affairs) on 6 March 2003. This instrument achieved agreement in four key areas: jurisdiction, languages and costs, the role of national patent offices and the question of distribution of fees.

[65] Proposal for a Council Regulation on the Community Patent—General Approach, 16113/09, 27 November 2009.

Lisbon Treaty[66]—becoming a signatory to the EPC and with the EPO having the power to grant EU patents. A European and European Union Patents Court (EEUPC) would be created with exclusive jurisdiction over infringement and validity issues concerning European and EU patents. It would be made up of a Court of First Instance, a Court of Appeal and a Registry. There are clear parallels here with the proposals already made by the EPO and indeed that organisation has responded favourably to this latest development. At the time of writing the Council had submitted a request to the Court of Justice of the European Union on the compatibility of the draft proposals with the EU Treaties. The EU patent system would coexist with the national and European systems.

> ### Reminder
>
> The European Union does not have authority to interfere with property rights in member states (Article 345 of the Treaty on the Functioning of the European Union (TFEU)). Any Europe-wide reforms can only *add* to national property rights, they cannot take them away.

10.31   It is envisaged that a symbiotic relationship would exist between the EU patent and the European patent system such that an applicant for a EU patent would simply apply to the EPO for a European patent designating the territory of the Union.[67] If granted by the EPO, the patent would then become an EU patent under the Regulation. It is further proposed that translation issues would be dealt with in a separate Regulation.[68] The Commission has previously acknowledged that: '[t]he costs of translating the patent into all the official languages of the [Union] would entail a risk of the entire [EU] patent project foundering, placing as it would too heavy a burden on inventors, above all small and medium sized enterprises'. See further below para 10.35 for proposals to address the language issue emanating from the EPO.

10.32   As we have seen, this unified scheme also envisages a single body to oversee questions of infringement and validity of EU patents. This is the European and European Union Patents Court (EEUPC) and the proposals are in the draft Agreement produced by the Council (Competitiveness) in 2009.[69] As stated above, the proposal is that the EEUPC would consist of a Court of First Instance, a Court of Appeal and a Registry. All would be subject to the supervision of the Court of Justice of the European Union and there would be no prejudice to the jurisdiction of that court to hear referrals from domestic courts. The Court of First Instance would comprise both a central division and local and regional divisions, drawing on local patent judicial and practitioner expertise. Direct actions for revocation of a patent would be brought before the central division, while regional and local divisions could hear counterclaims

---

[66] See Article 118 Treaty of the Functioning of the European Union: '...the European Parliament and the Council, acting in accordance with the ordinary legislative procedure, shall establish measures for the creation of European intellectual property rights to provide uniform protection of intellectual property rights throughout the Union and for the setting up of centralised Union-wide authorisation, coordination and supervision arrangements.'

[67] Applications would also be possible through national patent offices but could only be granted by the EPO. Countries which shared an EPO official language could also perform searches on behalf of the EPO.

[68] During the Slovenian Presidency in 2008 a proposal was put to addresses translation issues, including the introducing of an automated service for translation into all official languages. See Council of the European Union (Slovenian Presidency), Community patent: translation of claims and distribution of revenue from fees (28 February 2008, 6985/08). This was further developed later that year by the Working Party on Intellectual Property (Patents), (28 April 2008, 8928/08).

[69] Council of the European Union (Competitiveness 2982nd), Conclusions on an enhanced patent system in Europe (2009). See too Draft Agreement on the European and Community Patents Court (Document 7928/09 of 23 March 2009).

for revocation. Cases could be referred to the central division with the agreement of all parties.

Discussion point   For answer guidance visit www.oxfordtextbooks.co.uk/orc/macqueen2e/

Given the co-existence of national patents and EU patents, and roles for domestic courts as well as the divisions of the EEUPC, are we likely to see a convergence or divergence of approach to patent protection as between member states and EU bodies? In particular, would domestic courts be required to follow decisions of the EEUPC?

10.33   These are significant reforms for Europe, requiring important legal changes both within the Union (eg concerning the jurisdiction of the Court of Justice) and beyond (changes will be required to the EPC).[70] Moreover, the European Union will, itself, have to become a signatory of the European Patent Convention. But where do we stand on these becoming tangible reforms?

10.34   Recently, in January 2006, the Commission mounted a public consultation on the future of patent policy in Europe, and one of the key agenda items was the Community patent, as it was then known. This initiative has been set against the Commission's programme for a new integrated industrial policy for Europe in which IPRs play a central part.[71] A central part of that vision undoubtedly remains the idea of a unitary patent for Europe but the preliminary findings from the consultation suggested that this will not become a reality any time soon.[72] While there is widespread support for a unitary patent through most sectors of industry and other interest groups,[73] there was strong resistance to the current proposal that stood at the time (and which was not terribly different to the one that has emerged more recently). This seems to have been for two main reasons: (1) dissatisfaction over the language regime, and (2) inadequate arrangements on jurisdiction of the unitary Court.[74] The position on language seems increasingly polarised, with one camp supporting a one-language (English) regime and another unwilling to compromise on anything short of full translation into all official EU languages upon grant. Views divide, broadly, depending on the size of an enterprise, and also down territorial lines, with countries such as Greece, Italy, Poland, Portugal, Spain, and some stakeholders in France supporting a multi-language regime. The stalemate is such that it even led to some stakeholders to urge the Commission to put its original proposal from the 1970s back on the table!

10.35   Public consultation is an important part of the European legislative process, and the European Parliament is particularly minded to listen to public opinion when it comes to intellectual

---

[70] Preparation of the meeting of the Council on 26 and 27 November 2003, Community patent—Proposal for amendments to the European Patent Convention, Doc no 15088/03.

[71] Commission Communication, 'Implementing the Community Lisbon Programme: A Policy Framework to Strengthen EU Manufacturing—towards a more integrated approach for Industrial Policy', COM(2005) 474 final of 5.10.2005.

[72] Public Hearing on Future Patent Policy in Europe (July 2006), available at: http://ec.europa.eu/internal_market/indprop/patent/hearing_en.htm

[73] This support is, however, by no means universal as the study indicates, particularly among certain advocacy groups such as those supporting Open Source.

[74] Jurisdictional concerns range from the consequences of having a single Europe-wide right and problems of proving infringement to the need to have judges with solid legal and technical training exercising the jurisdiction in question.

property laws.[75] If these results accurately reflect broader concerns about a unitary patent in European society then the reform measures outlined above are unlikely to succeed. Yet it becomes increasingly more difficult to see what further reform might end up satisfying the various parties that adopt such opposing views on how to proceed. Some consultees went as far as to suggest that the Commission should abandon its plans and concentrate its efforts elsewhere. This has not proved to be the case, as the events of 2009 reveal. The issue of language has, however, been sidelined for now to be dealt with in a separate Regulation. It is difficult not to see this a mere political manoeuvring to remove a particular hurdle from an otherwise intractable process.

Wait a minute...

If language is such a problem, how have we managed to have an effective *European Patent Office* for over 30 years and which has granted almost 800,000 patents?

How are language issues addressed by the European Patent Office?

Consider the provisions of the *London Agreement* from 2000[76] which you can find here:

http://archive.epo.org/epo/pubs/oj001/12_01/12_5491.pdf

This Agreement allows signatory parties that share an official language with the EPO to waive, wholly or partially, the translation requirement under the EPC (Article 65) that a patent be filed in their national language. Countries that do not share a language with the EPO can also waive this requirement, so long as the patent has been granted in an official EPO language. The Agreement came into force in May 2008 when France ratified the agreement. This Agreement can reduce the costs of patenting in Europe up to 45 per cent when the countries designated by the patentee have signed up to the agreement. The approximate cost of the translation of an average length patent into one other language lies around 1,100 euros. This results in 5,500 euros for five translations, which is the average number of foreign states for which protection is sought and around 30.000 euros for the translations which you would need to obtain patent coverage in all 37 EPC countries under the current regime.

10.36   We can sum up the European scene as follows:

European Patent Organisation	European Union
• European Patent Convention (2000)	• Programme of harmonising measures
• 37 signatory countries	• 27 members
• European Patent Office—grants 'European' patents for designated countries—enforced domestically	• EU Patent proposal—would create one right enforceable throughout the Union with a single dispute settlement body—the European And European Union Patents Court.
• No appeal body from signatory states	
• No single 'European' patent (for now...)	

---

[75] The European Parliament used its veto for the first time in March 1995 in respect of the draft Biotechnology Directive after intense lobbying from a range of stakeholder groups.

[76] European Patent Organisation, Agreement dated 17 October 2000 on the application of Art 65, EPC (London Agreement), (2001) 12 OJEPO 549. An informative guide has been produced by the EPO here: http://www.epo.org/patents/law/legal-texts/london-agreement.html.

The international dimension

10.37   The World Intellectual Property Organization (WIPO) and the World Trade Organisation (WTO) are each responsible for administering important treaties on patent protection at the international level. These perform a harmonising or approximating function for both formal and substantive aspects of patent law.

WIPO – streamlining the patent application process

10.38   Two instruments are currently administered by WIPO which considerably facilitate the process of applying for a patent.

10.39   The *Patent Cooperation Treaty (1970, as amended)* (PCT) is another product of fervent patent reform emerging from the 1960s, this time at the initiative of the United States.[77] The Treaty is designed to facilitate the process when an applicant is applying for patents simultaneously in numerous jurisdictions worldwide.[78] It is *not* a granting procedure and merely provides a conduit whereby a single application can be processed and searched by a qualified international body before being sent to national or regional intellectual property offices for full consideration. Anyone who is a national or resident of a contracting state[79] can file a single international patent application, either in his national office, or at the EPO if the state is also a signatory to the EPC, or at the International Bureau of WIPO in Geneva.[80] This single application is then subject to an 'international search' from which an international research report is prepared. This contains details of published documents that might cause problems for an invention in terms of its patentability, that is, because they may demonstrate that the invention is not 'new' (see below, paras 11.76ff). It is also possible for applicants to request an international preliminary examination which results in a non-binding written opinion on patentability.[81] If an applicant does not withdraw his application at this point, the report becomes a public document,[82] although the written opinion does not.

10.40   The application is then sent for consideration to national or regional offices as designated by the applicant.[83] While the results of the international search do not guarantee that an invention will be 'novel' for all purposes in the designated countries, it does provide the applicant with 'reasonable probability' of receiving patent protection, according to WIPO. Moreover, the procedure not only greatly limits costs, but it can also speed up the process for obtaining patent protection, especially in countries which do not have adequate search facilities. Applicants also have time within the PCT process—up to 18 months—to amend their application before proceeding to designated foreign offices, and, indeed, to decide whether to proceed at all, weighing

---

[77]   You can read the current text of the PCT here: http://www.wipo.int/pct/en/texts/articles/atoc.htm

[78]   Full details are available here: http://www.wipo.int/pct/en/

[79]   There were 142 contracting states to the PCT as of 1 February 2010. See also World Intellectual Property Organization, *The International Patent System in 2008: PCT yearly review* (May 2009), available here: http://www.wipo.int/pct/en/activity/pct_2008.html.

[80]   See further WIPO, *History of the PCT Regulations (June 19, 1970–January 1, 2009)*, 2009, available at: http://www.wipo.int/pct/en/

[81]   PCT, Ch II.   [82]   This is published by the International Bureau.

[83]   An application through PCT automatically constitutes an election of all contracting states in the first instance, but in reality applicants are selective about the countries they wish to target. See Rule 53.7 of the Regulations under the PCT (1 July 2009): http://www.wipo.int/pct/en/texts/rules/rtoc1.htm

up the various considerations such as appointing local patent agents, preparing translations and paying national fees. It is also claimed that this process furthers the public interest in that the systematic publication of international reports—carried out by approved authorities[84]—means that third parties are better placed to assess the patentability of any given invention and to assess the state of the art at any given time. The importance of the quality of searches is crucial to the success and efficiency of any patent system.[85] The success of the PCT is demonstrated by the fact that it had received a million applications from around the world by the end of 2004.

10.41   WIPO established the *Standing Committee on the Law of Patents* in 1998 with a remit to take debate and international patent reform forward into the 21st century. The Committee's membership is broad, including all members of WIPO itself as well as non-members, and various intergovernmental and non-governmental agencies. It aims to contribute both to formal and substantive reforms of patent law, and in this regard has two core projects:

- Patent Law Treaty (2000). This treaty harmonises patent procedures and formalities for filing, obtaining and maintaining patent protection. It entered into force on 28 April 2005 and had been ratified by 24 contracting parties as of May 2010. This includes the UK where it entered into force on 22 March 2006 and which resulted in some changes to domestic law.[86]

- Substantive Patent Law Treaty (2001–present). This draft treaty is aimed at harmonising the substantive elements of patent law, such as novelty, inventive step/non-obviousness and industrial applicability/utility[87] with a view to streamlining of application documentation, greater legal certainty on an international level and, as always, a reduction in costs. Negotiations are ongoing and we discuss the substance further below (para 10.72).

10.42   The *Patent Law Treaty* (2000) mandates a maximum number of formal requirements that can be imposed on patent applications, although individual contracting parties can be more generous if they wish.[88] Important features that have been harmonised include the standardisation of requirements to obtain a filing date on the fulfilment of three criteria: (i) an indication that the elements received by the Office are intended to be an application for a patent for an invention;(ii) indications that would allow the Office to identify or to contact the applicant (or both); (iii) a

---

[84] International searches are carried out by approved International Searching Authorities (PCT, Art 16) and there also exist International Preliminary Examination Authorities (PCT, Art 32). Regulations under the PCT impose minimum requirements on authorities appointed by the PCT Union (Rule 36 and Rule 63). These now require that International Preliminary Examining Authorities must '...have in place a quality management system and internal review arrangements in accordance with the common rules of international preliminary examination...' and it must hold an official appointment as an International Searching Authority.

[85] This point was made very clearly by industry and patent attorneys alike in the recent public consultation on the future of the patent system in Europe carried out by the European Commission, see n 22 above.

[86] The United Kingdom passed the Regulatory Reform (Patents) Order 2004 to make the necessary changes to domestic law.

[87] This variation in terminology reflects current different approaches to the criteria for patentability around the globe. Thus, while European patent law talks of 'inventive step' and 'industrial applicability', US law employs the terms 'non-obviousness' and 'utility'. This is not merely a question of semantics because the terms are interpreted quite differently meaning that access to patent protection is variable (it is generally far easier in the United States). Note, that in Art 27(1), TRIPS which requires 'patents shall be available for any inventions, whether products or processes, in all fields of technology, provided that they are new, involve an inventive step and are capable of industrial application' there is a caveat which provides: 'For the purposes of this Art, the terms "inventive step" and "capable of industrial application" may be deemed by a Member to be synonymous with the terms "non-obvious" and "useful" respectively.'

[88] Patent Law Treaty, Art 2. The exception to this relates to Art 5 and mandatory requirements about obtaining a filing date.

part which appears to be a description of the invention (this part can be filed in any language or could even merely be a drawing).[89]

10.43 More than 60 countries had signed the Treaty by March 2010, indicating their intention to ratify in due course; 24 of these countries have already done so. Signatories include the United States and the European Patent Organisation on behalf of the European Patent Office. Other countries representing the remaining members of the top five patent offices of the world[90]—China, Japan, South Korea—will doubtless follow suit. The effect of the Patent Law Treaty therefore will be near-global harmonisation of procedures for obtaining patent protection.

WTO—the TRIPS Agreement (1994)

10.44 We have discussed the nature of the TRIPS Agreement in Chapter 1 and elsewhere in the book thus far. You will recall that the Agreement on Trade-related Aspects of Intellectual Property Rights was concluded in 1994 as part of the Uruguay Round of the General Agreement on Tariffs and Trade (GATT). It is administered by the World Trade Organization (WTO) and parties to the Agreement are subject to WTO's dispute settlement system.[91] This entails the possible imposition of trade sanctions for non-compliance. The linking of obligations to protect intellectual property with the attractiveness of trade privileges available under GATT was a stroke of genius by those parties frustrated by the fact that many countries had not signed up to previous international instruments such as the Paris and Berne Conventions and were openly infringing intellectual property on an unprecedented scale. Many of these countries were, however, also developing countries desperate for increased trade to improve their economic circumstances. Few could resist the trade attractions of the Uruguay Round, and TRIPS was the bitter pill they had to swallow.

10.45 The implications for patent law from TRIPS are, first and foremost, that the agreement represents the first international measure to harmonise substantive patent provisions. Article 27(1) TRIPS provides:

'Subject to the provisions of paragraphs 2 and 3, patents shall be available for any inventions, whether products or processes, in all fields of technology, provided that they are new, involve an inventive step and are capable of industrial application.'

10.46 There are two points to note about this. First, it makes clear that there are three common criteria for patentability, and second, signatory states are obliged to make protection available for *any* inventions in *all* technological fields. This has required significant changes to law in numerous states which previously did not have a robust patent system or specifically excluded certain types of invention from protection, such as pharmaceuticals.[92] It has also given rise to charges against the UK or even the European Union itself that continued resistance to patents in certain fields such as software can no longer be sustained and may even be illegal.

10.47 TRIPS permits, but does not require, exclusions from patentability, providing in Article 27(2) and (3) that:

'2. Members may exclude from patentability inventions, the prevention within their territory of the commercial exploitation of which is necessary to protect *ordre public* or morality, including to protect human,

---

[89] Patent Law Treaty, Art 5(1) and (2).

[90] These five offices account for a large majority share of all patent applications. See *WIPO Patent Report* (2008), p 14 (see n 19 above).

[91] See here for an account of the Dispute Settlement System: http://www.wto.org/english/thewto_e/whatis_e/tif_e/disp1_e.htm

[92] China and India are obvious examples.

animal or plant life or health or to avoid serious prejudice to the environment, provided that such exclusion is not made merely because the exploitation is prohibited by their law.

3. Members may also exclude from patentability: (a) diagnostic, therapeutic and surgical methods for the treatment of humans or animals; (b) plants and animals other than micro-organisms, and essentially biological processes for the production of plants or animals other than non-biological and microbiological processes. However, Members shall provide for the protection of plant varieties either by patents or by an effective *sui generis* system or by any combination thereof.'

Note the judicious use of the term 'may' here. These are not mandatory exclusions and were, in fact, included largely at the behest of European states and the European Union which already have such provisions in their patent law (see paras 11.47ff below). There are no such exclusions in the United States, although a surprisingly high number of countries have some form of morality exclusion in their law.

Patents and international development

10.48   Many discussions on reform of TRIPS have been directly bound up with the morality of the Agreement itself. The current round of negotiations are part of the *Doha Development Agenda*, and date back to the Fourth Ministerial Conference in Doha, Qatar in November 2001 with halting progress ever since. This resulted, inter alia, in the Doha Declaration which serves as the template and mandate for further negotiations in a number of subjects central to improved international trade, one of which is the protection of IPRs. The Ministerial Declaration to emerge from the Fourth Conference stressed once more the importance of balance in achieving this protection, stating in Article 17 that the implementation and interpretation give to TRIPS must be in a manner '…supportive of public health, by promoting both access to existing medicines and research and development into new medicines…' Further articulation of this came in a separate instrument—the Declaration on the TRIPS Agreement and Public Health[93]—which stressed the need to recognise that the WTO and TRIPS are part of the wider global, social public health crisis affecting developing and least-developed countries, most particularly in terms of securing access to affordable medicines to treat conditions such as HIV/AIDS, malaria and tuberculosis.

10.49   All of this was prompted by an attempt by South Africa to address its own chronic public health problems through changes to patent law. The South African Medicines and Medical Devices Regulatory Authority Act 1998 allowed the Ministry of Health '[to] determine that the rights with regard to any medicine under a patent granted in the Republic shall not extend to act in respect of such medicine which has been put onto the market by the owner of the medicine, or with his or her consent' (Article 15C).[94] Inter alia, this would give the South African state the power to manufacture patented pharmaceuticals under compulsory licence and/or import cheaper generic drugs from abroad. The reaction by the pharmaceutical industry and the United States was immediate, with the latter imposing economic sanctions through the removal of preferential tariff treatments (making import from the US economically unviable). Pharma, for its part, filed a law suit against the law. The Act never saw the light of day.

10.50   The resulting international response through the World Trade Organization was the Public Health Declaration.[95] It is agreed therein that TRIPS does not and should not prevent members

---

[93] 14 November 2001: http://www.wto.org/english/thewto_e/minist_e/min01_e/mindecl_trips_e.htm
[94] This is effectively a use of the 'exhaustion principle' which we discuss further in Chapter 19.
[95] Declaration on the TRIPS Agreement and Public Health, 20 November 2001, Doc No WT/MIN(01)/DEC/2.

from taking measures to protect public health, and that WTO members have the right to use, 'to the full', the flexible provisions found in the Agreement itself to support the right to public health and promote access to medicines for all. What are these flexible provisions? These are articulated in Article 5 and include the right of each member to grant compulsory licences on the grounds that they consider appropriate, and the freedom of each member to determine its own regime of exhaustion of rights. In other words, the same mechanisms as deployed by South Africa are available under TRIPS. There are, however, certain restrictions, most notably that the compulsory licence provisions in the 1994 Agreement are solely concerned with producing drugs for a domestic market. This causes an immediate problem for countries which do not have domestic manufacturing capacity, and means, potentially, that the least developed countries, which may also experience the most severe public health crises, are the ones most disadvantaged under the law. They are, indeed, doubly disadvantaged because it would also mean that another country could not rely on the provisions to come to their aid since an *export* of drugs made under compulsory licence would be a violation of TRIPS. By the same token, a solution is not immediately apparent from the perspective of developed countries which have a concern that too liberal an approach to compulsory licensing may result in their own markets being flooded. The Declaration instructed the TRIPS Council to pursue a solution[96] which was eventually reached in August 2003.[97]

10.51   The solution is effectively a form of waiver over the obligations of members under Article 31(f) TRIPS.[98] This provides that any compulsory licensing system should be '...authorized predominantly for the supply of the domestic market of the Member authorizing such use.' The Council Decision allows an exporting member to waive these obligations when exporting to a 'eligible importing member', being any least-developed country member, and any other member that has made a notification to the Council for TRIPS of its intention to use the system as an importer.[99] The waiver operates to the extent *necessary* for the purposes of production of a pharmaceutical product(s) and its export. Further conditions include notification of specific needs for drugs and the tailoring of licence terms accordingly, labelling requirements to set these products apart from others in the market, and a public disclosure requirement, via the internet, informing of quantities and distinguishing features to be exported. The TRIPS Council plays a key role in the operation of this system: it is charged with receiving and administering all notifications and with producing an annual report on the system as a whole.

[96] Para 6 provides: 'We recognize that WTO members with insufficient or no manufacturing capacities in the pharmaceutical sector could face difficulties in making effective use of compulsory licensing under the TRIPS Agreement. We instruct the Council for TRIPS to find an expeditious solution to this problem and to report to the General Council before the end of 2002.'

[97] General Council Decision of 30 August 2003 on the Implementation of Paragraph 6 of the Doha Declaration on the TRIPS Agreement and Public Health: WT/L/540 and Corr.1, 1 September 2003.

[98] There are, in fact, three waivers: (1) exporting countries are not bound by the provisions of Art 31(f); (2) importing countries are not bound to pay reasonable remuneration to the patent holder (this is borne by the exporter); and (3) exporting restrictions are waived for developing and least-developed countries which are members of a regional trade agreement, when at least half of the members are classed as least-developed countries when the export decision is made.

[99] Para 2. It is possible to notify that the system will only be used in a limited way, eg only in the case of a national emergency or other circumstances of extreme urgency or in cases of public non-commercial use. Indeed, some countries and trading blocks have notified that they will not be using the system as an importer to protect domestic markets. These include the United States, the United Kingdom and many other European states.

10.52   A 2006 Oxfam report claimed that little had changed in the first five years after the adoption of the Doha Declaration.[100] This is partly because the provisions and protections of TRIPS can be circumvented in bilateral or regional agreements between countries when there is an imbalance of bargaining power and weaker states agree to so-called TRIPS-plus obligations—tying them further into intellectual property protection—in return for economic or trade benefits. The United States relies heavily on such an approach. Oxfam has called on poorer states to resist these moves and recommends that G8 countries provide the necessary technical, political and economic support to allow poorer states to enact TRIPS safeguards.[101] It also recommends that the WTO carry out a thorough review of the impact of TRIPS on access to medicines, supported (or not) by independent studies from bodies such as the World Health Organization.

10.53   Work has nonetheless been ongoing at WTO since the 2003 Decision. A General Council decision from 6 December 2005 will replace the 2003 decision in due course;[102] this will effectively embody the 2003 scheme permanently into the TRIPS Agreement. It is, in fact, the first official amendment of a WTO Agreement.[103] The Amendment is designed to reflect the terms of the original waiver as closely as possible because there are strong political reasons not to re-open the issues. Thus, as with the 2003 waiver, any member country can manufacture and export pharmaceutical products under compulsory licence for public health reasons. Changes will be required in domestic law. The European Commission had presented a proposal for a Council Decision accepting the Amendment in April 2006 and in May 2006 the European Parliament and the Council adopted Regulation No 816/2006 on compulsory licensing of patents relating to the manufacture of pharmaceutical products for export to countries with public health problems.[104]

10.54   The Amendment[105] creates Article 31bis and a new annex to the TRIPS Agreement. This re-iterates the core principle that it is lawful to produce pharmaceutical products under compulsory licence for export to countries lacking production capacity. It then goes on to specify further matters such as an obligation on an importing member to take 'reasonable measures' within their means to prevent re-exportation, and a duty on all members to ensure that effective legal means are in place to prevent the import of goods made under the scheme which have been unlawfully diverted to their market.[106] The annex specifies the terms for using the system and

[100] Oxfam International, *Patents v Patients: Five Years After the Doha Declaration* (2006): http://www.oxfam.org.uk/resources/policy/health/downloads/bp95_patents.pdf

[101] The White Paper, 'Eliminating World Poverty: Making Globalisation Work for the Poor' pointed to the need for intellectual property regimes to work better for poor people. See UK–IPO: http://www.dfid.gov.uk/Documents/publications/whitepaper2000.pdf

[102] This will happen when two-thirds of the membership accepts the amendment. It was originally hoped that this would happen by 1 December 2007 but this deadline was not met and was extended until 31 December 2009 '…or such later date as may be decided by the Ministerial Conference': WTO WT/L/711. This amendment remains in limbo at the time of writing (March 2010).

[103] The Sixth Ministerial Conference which took place in Hong Kong in December 2005 reaffirmed the importance of the 2003 Council decision and endorsed the work of the Council on an Amendment of the TRIPS Agreement, Draft Ministerial Declaration, 18 December 2005, WT/MIN(05)/W/3/Rev 2.

[104] See Proposal for a Regulation of the European Parliament and of the Council on compulsory licensing of patents relating to the manufacture of pharmaceutical products for export to countries with public health problems COM/2004/0737 final, and ultimately, Regulation (EC) No 816/2006 of the European Parliament and of the Council of 17 May 2006 on compulsory licensing of patents relating to the manufacture of pharmaceutical products for export to countries with public health problems (2006) OJ EU, 9 June 2006, L157/1.

[105] General Council, Doc No WT/L/641, 8 December 2005, Amendment of the TRIPS Agreement, Decision of 6 December 2005.

[106] Other provisions include the prohibition on a patent holder receiving 'reasonable remuneration' from both an exporting and an importing state, the release of developing country members from Art 31(f) obligations when involved

includes definitions, obligations of notification to TRIPS Council, and an ongoing duty of the Council to carry out annual reviews. Finally, an appendix to the annex lays out criteria to assess whether a country lacks manufacturing capacity such that it can rely upon the Amendment. There are 153 members of the WTO, and less than a third of the member states had accepted this Amendment at the time of writing. Two-thirds of members must accept before the Amendment can replace the 2003 Decision.

10.55   It should be further noted that an additional outcome of these ongoing negotiations is that Least-Developed Countries (LDCs) have until 2016 to provide patent protection for pharmaceuticals, and until 1 July 2013 to provide protection for other IPRs.

New provision for the TRIPS Agreement, Article 31*bis*

'1. The obligations of an exporting Member under Article 31(f) shall not apply with respect to the grant by it of a compulsory licence *to the extent necessary* for the purposes of production of a pharmaceutical product(s) and its export to an eligible importing Member(s) in accordance with the terms set out in paragraph 2 of the Annex to this Agreement.' [emphasis added]

 Discussion point   For answer guidance visit www.oxfordtextbooks.co.uk/orc/macqueen2e/

How much flexibility do the words '…to the extent necessary' provide for those who would reply on this provision, or indeed, who would object to others relying on this provision?

10.56   Critics assessing the success of the Doha Declaration in 2006 have argued that it is largely a failure. It is suggested that the requirements of the system such as notification of specific type and quantity of drugs, labelling requirements, or the need to negotiate directly with the patent holder are too onerous.[107] It is essentially a protectionist system—in that it allows countries to act as exporters while blocking access to their own markets—and thereby undermines the economies of scale for developing countries with manufacturing capacity but no access to high-income markets. That said, it is acknowledged that the problem is not simply with the WTO or its Agreements. Bilateral agreements often mean that developing countries are willing to give up reliance on the TRIPS provisions for other economic advantages, such as reduced trade barriers. A 2006 World Bank report on the economics of HIV/AIDS treatment in Thailand suggested that such concessions come at significant cost.[108] It estimated that reliance on the compulsory licensing scheme could reduce the costs of second-line therapy by 90 per cent, cutting the Thai government future budgetary obligations by US$3.2 billion to 2025 and reducing by half the costs of life-years saved under its National Access to Antiretroviral Program for People Living with HIV/AIDS. Thailand issued a compulsory licence to manufacture a generic

---

in a regional agreement with countries facing the same public health crisis, and the retention of existing TRIPS flexibilities.

[107] Médicins Sans Fronitières, Campaign for Access to Essential Medicines, (1999–present http://www.msfaccess.org/
[108] The World Bank, *The Economics of Effective AIDS Treatment: Evaluating Policy Options for Thailand* (2006), p xxxl–xl. Available via: http://www.worldbank.org/

version of the HIV/AIDS drug Efavirenz in November 2006[109] which has since been followed by several more compulsory licences for a number of different drugs.[110]

10.57   Other hurdles for developing and least-developed countries are that they are often ill-equipped to amend national laws to take full advantage of TRIPS flexibilities, and international bodies, such as UN agencies or the World Health Organization (WHO), are often under-resourced to provide the necessary technical support.

10.58   This having been said, the WHO has taken a strong interest in the issue—possibly as a direct result of the Doha Declaration—and it established a Commission on Intellectual Property Rights, Innovation and Public Health (CIPIH) in 2004.[111] Its 2006 report[112] called for a holistic approach to crises in public health: 'The market alone, and the incentives that propel it, such as patent protection, cannot by themselves address the health needs of developing countries.'[113] Furthermore, the Commission questioned whether current regimes of intellectual property protection have led to innovation or better access to medicines, particularly because market mechanisms and incentives do not lead to research and development that is directed towards the needs of developing countries. The Commission issued 60 recommendations, key among which was the call for a Global Plan to examine the challenges at each of the stages of discovery, development and delivery of pharmaceuticals and other health products needed to secure public health. The World Health Organization responded swiftly and the World Health Assembly adopted Resolution WHA59.24 in May 2006 calling on the Director-General to establish an Intergovernmental Working Group (IGWG) to draw up a strategy with contributions from member states and the global community.[114] A public consultation then took place by which time proposals had already started to emerge from the IGWG. The suggested elements of the strategy range across (1) prioritising and promoting R&D needs, (2) capacity building, (3) improving delivery and access,(4) securing sustainable financing, and (5) instituting effective monitoring systems. A particular proposal for patents is the recommendation to promote patent pools which allow for the collective management of IPRs directed towards specific ends such as the promotion of innovation in products relating to priority diseases in developing countries. Patent pools can reduce costs and ensure uniformity of approach towards licensing, allowing countries to work together towards common goals. The IGWG presented its Global Strategy and plan of action to the World Health Assembly at its Sixty-First Meeting in 2008, which adopted the plan by resolution WHA 61.21.[115]

Evolutionary law and policy

10.59   This ambitious WHO strategy to develop a Global Plan for addressing crises in public health demonstrates very well that although patents may be a part of the problem they can also only

---

[109] D Schuettler, 'Activists hail Thai move to make generic AIDS drug' (2006) Reuters UK, 30 November, available at: http://www.reuters.com/article/healthNews/idUSBKK5661020061130

[110] F Rozanski, *Developing Countries and Pharmaceutical Intellectual Property Rights: Myths and Reality* (2007) and Cm Correa (ed) *A Guide to Pharmaceutical Patents* (2008, vols 1 and 2).

[111] WHO Resolution (WHA 56.27, 2003), see http://apps.who.int/gb/archive/pdf_files/WHA56/ea56r27.pdf

[112] CIPIH, *Public Health, Innovation and Intellectual Property Rights* (WHO, 2006): http://www.who.int/intellectualproperty/documents/thereport/ENPublicHealthReport.pdf

[113] ibid, p 17.

[114] A Special Issue of the Bulletin of the World Health Organization (Vol 84(5), May 2006, 337–424) is dedicated to the topic. Available here: http://www.who.int/bulletin/volumes/84/5/en/index.html

[115] For details see WHA Resolution 61.21, available at: http://apps.who.int/gb/ebwha/pdf_files/A61/A61_R21-en.pdf

be a part of the solution. Multilevel strategies will be required and part of the challenge is to understand how the operation of the world's patent systems interacts with other systems of regulation, health promotion, development, environmental protection, and even notions of justice. This approach embraces the interconnectedness of these systems and seeks solutions through those connections. Intellectual property cannot be seen as a regime in isolation. This is accepted by the WTO. The TRIPS Agreement itself required review of the provisions of Article 27(3)(b) as to the patentability of plants and animals other than micro-organisms, and essentially biological processes for the production of plants or animals other than non-biological and microbiological processes.[116] This began four years after the Agreement came into force (1999) and is ongoing.[117] The permissiblity of plant and animal patents remains in dispute with lobbying on opposite sides arguing, on the one hand, that these are necessary to promote innovation and aid technology transfer, and on the other that patenting causes problems of access, especially for farmers in gaining access to seed, excessively broad patents can lead to the misappropriation of genetic material, and that this in turn may lead to breaches under the Convention on Biological Diversity (see para 10.64 below).

Proposed solutions

10.60   These include: (1) removal of the provisions, (2) retention of the provisions with clarification as to definitions, (3) a complete ban on plant and animal patenting. Such polar opposite views have given rise to concern that the Review remains inconclusive, and the TRIPS Council has recently moved to find common ground for agreement with a view to producing a Council Decision, but this has yielded no results so far

Possible areas of consensus

10.61   These include: (1) acceptance of every member state's right to adopt appropriate regimes to protect plant varieties by an effective *sui generis* system; (2) that the TRIPS Agreement and the CBD should be implemented in a mutually supportive and consistent manner; (3) that the TRIPS Agreement, being a minimum standards agreement, does not prevent members from protecting traditional knowledge; (4) the importance of documentation of genetic resources and traditional knowledge to help better patent examination.[118]

Outstanding issues

10.62   These include: (1) the proposal to eliminate patent availability for all life forms (including micro-organisms), the need to clarify the terms in Article 27(3)(b);[119] (2) the protection of traditional knowledge;[120] and (3) consideration of ways to make the TRIPS Agreement and the CBD mutually supportive.[121] There have also been proposals to consider the ethical provisions of

---

[116] Note, however, that TRIPS Art 27(3)(b) obliges its members to provide effective protection for plant varieties either under patent law or in some *sui generis* form (or a combination thereof). See generally, LR Helfer, *Intellectual property rights in plant varieties: International legal regimes and policy options for national governments* (FAO, 2004), and for the European perspective, M Llewelyn and M Adcock, *European Plant Intellectual Property* (2006), and G Wurtenberger et al, *European Community Plant Variety Protection* (2006).

[117] TRIPS Council, Review of the Provisions of Art 27(3)(b), Paper IP/C/W/369/Rev 1, revised 9 March 2006, see further for a current overview of the related issues: http://www.wto.org/english/tratop_e/trips_e/art27_3b_background_e.htm

[118] African Group, IP/C/W/404, p 2; Zimbabwe, IP/C/M/36/Add 1, para 201.

[119] Zimbabwe, IP/C/M/37/Add 1, para 197.   [120] African Group, IP/C/W/404, p 4.

[121] African Group, IP/C/W/404, p 5.

Article 27(2) as part of this review process given the obvious and inherent connections between the two Articles.

Beyond Doha?

10.63   The Doha Declaration further extended the remit of the TRIPS Council to consider the interconnectedness of TRIPS to other regimes. Paragraph 19 requires the Council to consider the relationship between TRIPS and the UN Convention on Biological Diversity (CBD), as well as the challenges of protecting traditional knowledge and folklore.

10.64   World leaders agreed on a strategy for sustainable development at the World Summit in Rio de Janeiro in 1992. The CBD, signed at that time, is a central element of that strategy with three principal objectives:

(1) the conservation of biological diversity,
(2) the sustainable use of its components, and
(3) the fair and equitable sharing of the benefits arising out of the utilisation of genetic resources.

10.65   There are concerns in some quarters that the provisions of the CBD and TRIPS are fundamentally incompatible. The two main arguments are, first, the TRIPS Agreement actually requires that certain genetic material—such as micro-organisms—be patentable under Article 27(3)(b), as we have seen. This therefore allows private parties to gain private property rights over material which is guaranteed by the CBD to be the exclusive sovereign domain of signatory countries.[122] Secondly, TRIPS allows patent and other IPRs over genetic material without providing that certain core provisions of the CBD—such as the need for prior informed consent and benefit sharing—are complied with.[123] While this is disputed in other quarters,[124] these issues have set the agenda for the TRIPS Council discussion in this field of reform. Opinion has largely divided along economic lines, with developing countries arguing that TRIPS should be amended to bring the two treaties into line. These arguments, in turn, split into two camps: those that argue that TRIPS should exclude genetic patents altogether (this view is mostly advanced by the African Group),[125] and those who argue that there is insufficient provision in TRIPS to achieve an appropriate balance as between the objectives of the two treaties, for example requirements of consent, disclosure of the origin of genetic material and benefit sharing. Strong proponents of this view are Brazil and India. Options range from:

• do nothing to amend the treaties, but implement in a mutually supportive manner;

• implement in a mutually supportive manner and seek further evidence of the extent to which conflict arises in practice and might require changes to the patent system;

• accept that there is no inherent conflict but seek ways to ensure or enhance the mutual supportiveness of both Agreements (with to without amendment to TRIPS);

• accept that there is inherent conflict and amend TRIPS accordingly.

[122] For example, African Group, IP/C/W/404, IP/C/W/206, IP/C/W/163, IP/C/M/40, paras 76–9; Kenya, IP/C/M/47 para 68, IP/C/M/36/Add 1, para 233, IP/C/M/28, para 144.
[123] For example, African Group, IP/C/W/404, IP/C/W/206, IP/C/W/163; Brazil, IP/C/W/228, IP/C/M/48, para 37, IP/C/M/29, paras 146 and 148; IP/C/M/28, para 135, IP/C/M/27, para 122; Brazil et al, IP/C/W/429/Rev 1, IP/C/W/356.
[124] See the summary of discussion on these issues in IP/C/W/369/Rev 1 and IP/C/W/370/Rev 1.
[125] The Africa Group is an alliance of all African states.

10.66   No resolution has emerged as yet. Arguments continue to be put from all quarters, although by far the most likely outcome will be some compromise on the specifics related to disclosure of genetic origin and/or benefit sharing. There is considerable resistance to amendment of TRIPS itself.

10.67   The United States favours national action, whereby it would be left to individual states to use national legislation and contractual arrangements to impose obligations of disclosure or benefit sharing as they saw fit.[126] Switzerland has also proposed focusing on domestic law and has advocated amendment to the Patent Cooperation Treaty to allow signatory states to require disclosure of genetic origin or traditional knowledge in patent applications when the invention is 'directly based' on genetic resources.[127] The consequences of doing so could include invalidity of the patent if non-disclosure was fraudulent. The EU proposal suggested that all patent applications should be required to disclose the genetic source of an invention, but that sanctions would be found outside the patent system,[128] that is, non-disclosure would not affect the validity of the patent.[129] Finally, a group of eight developing countries (including Brazil, China and India) put forward a proposal to amend TRIPS itself with a new Article 29*bis* on disclosure of origin of biological resources. This proposal has been co-sponsored by several other countries since it was first drafted in May 2006.[130] The proposal states:[131]

Proposed Article 29*bis* TRIPS

Disclosure of Origin of Biological Resources and/or Associated Traditional Knowledge

1. For the purposes of establishing a mutually supportive relationship between this Agreement and the Convention on Biological Diversity, in implementing their obligations, Members shall have regard to the objectives and principles of this Agreement and the objectives of the Convention on Biological Diversity.

2. Where the subject matter of a patent application concerns, **is derived from or developed with biological resources and/or associated traditional knowledge**, Members **shall require applicants to disclose the country providing the resources and/or associated traditional knowledge**, from whom in the providing country they were obtained, and, as known after **reasonable inquiry**, the country of origin. Members shall also require that applicants provide information including evidence of compliance with the applicable legal requirements in the providing country **for prior informed consent for access and fair and equitable benefit-sharing** arising from the commercial or other utilization of such resources and/or associated traditional knowledge...

...5. Members shall put in place effective enforcement procedures so as to ensure compliance with the obligations set out in paragraphs 2 and 3 of this Article. In particular, **Members shall ensure that administrative and/or judicial authorities have the authority to prevent the further processing of an application or the grant of a patent and to revoke,** subject to the provisions of Article 32 of this Agreement, **or render unenforceable a patent when the applicant has, knowingly or with reasonable grounds to know, failed to comply with the obligations in paragraphs 2 and 3 of this Article or provided false or fraudulent information.**

---

[126] United States, IP/C/W/257.

[127] Switzerland, IP/C/W/433, IP/C/W/423, IP/C/W/400/Rev 1, IP/C/M/49, para 115, IP/C/M/46, para 22, IP/C/M/45, paras 47–8, IP/C/M/44, para 25, IP/C/M/42, paras 97 and 99, IP/C/M/40 para 71.

[128] It would be for individual countries to determine the appropriate sanctions, eg civil or criminal, but that in each case they should be 'effective, proportionate and dissuasive.'

[129] EC IP/C/W/383, IP/C/M/49, paras 123–4, IP/C/M/46, paras 43–9; Norway, IP/C/W/293, IP/C/M/47, paras 64–5.

[130] Amongst others by South Africa, for a full list of countries see IP/C/W/24 add. 1-9

[131] WT/GC/W/564, 31 May 2006 (emphasis added).

Exercise

Critically assess this proposal in light of the alternatives offered by other countries or alliances. The highlighted passages are likely to be most controversial. In particular, what do you think of the proposal to link non-disclosure to revocation or unenforceability of the patent?

10.68   Matters are complicated further by the fact that parallel discussions on the disclosure of origin obligation and the protection of traditional knowledge are ongoing in the World Intellectual Property Organization (WIPO). WIPO established an Intergovernmental Committee on Intellectual Property and Genetic Resources, Traditional Knowledge and Folklore (the IGC) in 2001 and its programme of work continues. It has produced two sets of draft provisions for the protection of traditional cultural expressions/folklore (TCEs) and for the protection of traditional knowledge (TK) against misappropriation and misuse.[132]

Weblink

WIPO: Traditional Knowledge, Genetic Resources and Traditional Cultural Expressions/Folklore— http://www.wipo.int/tk/en/

10.69   The discussion on genetic resources includes the Swiss and EU proposals referred to above. The broader political question, however, is that of the legitimacy of either WTO or WIPO to initiate change in these areas. Certainly, it is only for the WTO to seek to amend TRIPS, but broader issues are at stake such as relationships with CBD and the protection of traditional knowledge. Moreover, it was the Conference of the Parties of the CBD that invited WIPO to carry out a technical study on disclosure requirements in patent applications,[133] from which additional work has been undertaken by WIPO.[134] The IGC continues to work on its current mandate.

10.70   While WIPO probably has more technical expertise in the field, it has been argued that the WTO mandate in the Doha Declaration has a specific development remit, making it the better body to take matters forward.[135] Either way, WTO only has authority over the TRIPS Agreement, while reforms to formal aspects of patent law— such as the creation of a genetic origin disclosure requirement—will require changes to WIPO instruments such as the Patent Cooperation Treaty or the Patent Law Treaty (see paras 10.41–10.43 above).[136]

Further reform: patents regimes in the future

10.71   The above descriptions of the current architecture of our patent systems did not survive the lifetime of the first edition of this book; nor will they survive this one. Some matters will

---

[132] Available here: http://www.wipo.int/tk/en/consultations/draft_provisions/draft_provisions.html
[133] Available here: http://www.wipo.int/tk/en/publications/technical_study.pdf
[134] Full details available here: http://www.wipo.int/tk/en/genetic/proposals/index.html
[135] For example, Brazil, IP/C/M/49, para 155, IP/C/M/42, para 101, IP/C/M/36/Add 1, para 199.
[136] The latest IGC meeting in July 2009 proved inconclusive on ways forward.

already have changed by the time you read this. As with all areas of intellectual property law, patent law moves fast and it is important to keep an eye on what is coming next. Here is an overview of proposed or actual reforming measures as we went to press. As above, let us consider these at the international, European and national (UK) levels, this time beginning where we left off in the last section with the work of WIPO.

International reforms—WIPO's ongoing programme of harmonisation

10.72   We have already seen that WIPO's Standing Committee on the Law of Patents has enjoyed success with the coming into force of the Patent Law Treaty (2000). It now hopes to bring about harmonisation in respect of a number of elements of substantive law with its draft Substantive Patent Law Treaty, discussion on which began in May 2001. The scope of the Treaty has been slowly extended over the years to cover more issues, with the result that it has been harder to reach consensus with all delegations. The first draft provisions focused on issues directly pertinent to the grant of patents, such as the definition of prior art, novelty, inventive step/non-obviousness, industrial applicability/utility, the drafting and interpretation of claims and the requirement of sufficient disclosure of the invention. This was then expanded to a proposal that the Standing Committee on Patents consider prior art, grace period, novelty and inventive step, and the Intergovernmental Committee on Intellectual Property and Genetic Resources, Traditional Knowledge and Folklore (IGC) should consider sufficiency of disclosure and genetic resources.[137] Brazil, however, issued a statement[138] on behalf of the Group of Friends of Development[139] recalling that WIPO has undertaken to develop a proposal to establish a development agenda for the organisation and requesting that the continuation of the negotiations of the Treaty be on the basis of the draft treaty as a whole, including all the above elements and also questions of provisions on the transfer of technology, anti-competitive practices, and the safeguarding of public interest flexibilities to ensure that appropriate balance in brought to the content of the instrument.[140] Current work of the Standing Committee is based on a working document on issues relating to the international patent system covering the different needs and interests of all Member States.[141]

European reforms: the European Union and the European Patent Organisation

10.73   You will recall that the European Patent Organisation is not a body of the European Union and that each institution is at liberty to pursue its own initiatives. This having been said, the 27 member states of the European Union are all signatories to the European Patent Convention

---

[137] WIPO, Standing Committee on the Law of Patents, Eleventh Session, Geneva, 1 and 2 June, 2005 (SCP/11/3), available here: http://www.wipo.int/edocs/mdocs/scp/en/scp_11/scp_11_3.pdf

[138] WIPO, Standing Committee on the Law of Patents, Statement Received from Brazil, Eleventh Session, Geneva, June 1 and 2, 2005 (SCP/11/4), available here: http://www.wipo.int/edocs/mdocs/scp/en/scp_11/scp_11_4.pdf

[139] The Group of Friends of Development consists of Argentina, Brazil, Bolivia, Cuba, Dominican Republic, Ecuador, Egypt, Iran, Kenya, Peru, Sierra Leone, South Africa, Tanzania and Venezuela.

[140] Some countries and regions such as the US, EU, Japan and the European Patent Organisation undertook to convene future meetings on the basis of an earlier proposal (WIPO Document WO/GA/31/10) to continue future discussions: see Statement of Intent from the Participants of the Exploratory Meeting Concerning the Future of Substantive Patent Law Harmonisation which took place at the United States Patent and Trademark Office, Alexandria, Virginia, 3–4 February 2005: http://ec.europa.eu/internal_market/indprop/docs/patent/docs/harmonisation_en.pdf

[141] Document SPC/12/3/Rev.2, available here: http://www.wipo.int/meetings/en/doc_details.jsp?doc_id=116324

and it is in no-one's interests for the EPO and the EU to pursue different patent agenda. In practice the bodies work closely together to ensure complementarity. We see evidence of this below.

European Union

10.74   The Green Paper on the Community patent and patent system in Europe (1997)[142] was a response to The Action Plan for the Single Market, adopted by the European Council in Amsterdam in June 1997, and in which industrial property was highlighted as a sector where action was required to realise the full benefits of the Internal Market in the field of innovation. The Green Paper's aim was to initiate dialogue on the need for new initiatives in the field, and its adoption coincided with a public consultation of all interested parties. The Commission responded in turn with the publication of a Communication detailing its agenda and priorities for reform.[143]

10.75   Other initiatives, started before the Green Paper, have had variable success. A proposal to approximate laws around the Union concerning utility models was proposed after a Green Paper from 1995.[144] A utility model can be seen as a form of patent-like protection but which usually does not last as long (6–10 years) and which is subject to far less stringent criteria, especially concerning the equivalent notion of inventive step which will not require as high a level of inventiveness as we find in patent law. Utility model protection is variable around the Union, with some countries such as the UK having no such protection. The proposal[145] was not well received, and even after amendment[146] and a consultation exercise the majority of respondents (75 per cent) was against the introduction of a new scheme.[147] Arguments included a lack of clarity or agreement on the qualifying criteria, a concern that the scheme would not help small to medium-sized enterprises, as promised, but would rather open an avenue for big business to corner yet another area of the market. Moreover, it was felt that while utility model protection might be helpful for those operating in a local market it could not be justified at a Community level. Nothing has happened in this field since 2002.

10.76   The Biotechnology Directive was eventually adopted in July 1998 after 10 years in the European legislative process.[148] It has always been a controversial piece of law and the European Parliament in fact exercised its power of veto over a draft of the Directive in March 1995. Nonetheless, the Directive survived and has now been implemented in all member states. We discuss its implications in Chapter 12.

[142]   Green Paper of 24 June 1997 on the Community patent and the patent system in Europe, COM(97) 314 final.

[143]   European Commission Communication, 'Promoting innovation through patents: The follow-up to the Green Paper on the Community Patent and the Patent System in Europe', 12 February 1999, available at: http://ec.europa.eu/internal_market/indprop/docs/patent/docs/8682_en.pdf

[144]   Commission Green Paper of 19 July 1995 on the Protection of Utility Models in the Single Market COM (1995) 370 final.

[145]   Proposal for a European Parliament and Council Directive approximating the legal arrangements for the protection of inventions by utility model, COM (1997) 691 final, and Amended proposal, 12.07.1999 COM (1999) 309 final /2.

[146]   European Commission, 'Summary report of replies to the questionnaire on the impact of the Community utility model with a view to updating the Green Paper on protection by the utility model in the internal market' (SEC(2001)1307).

[147]   WIPO explains utility models here: http://www.wipo.int/sme/en/ip_business/utility_models/utility_models.htm

[148]   Directive 98/44/EC of the European Parliament and of the Council of 6 July 1998 on the legal protection of biotechnological inventions, available here: http://ec.europa.eu/internal_market/indprop/invent/index_en.htm

10.77   In 2005 the Commission issued a communication containing a Europe-wide strategy to strengthen industrial policy.[149] IPRs are acknowledged to be of key importance in this process and it is stated that more can be done to ensure that the regulatory framework meets the needs and challenges of industries. But lessons from past failures have made the Commission cautious and it announced a dialogue on IPRs in 2006 to determine how balance of interests can be achieved within a sound IP framework. This was followed by a Communication in 2008 in which the Commission emphasised the need to take action in the near future.[150] A public consultation on the future of patent policy that took place in 2006[151] indicated, inter alia, that the then proposal for a Community patent was unlikely to proceed in its current form and that many in industry and the patent attorney profession saw the future of successful European reform coming not from the Union, but from initiatives from the European Patent Organisation. This will be discussed below in para 10.79.

10.78   As we have seen, in 2007, the Commission redoubled its efforts to create a Unified Patent Litigation System (UPLS) which would establish a court system with jurisdiction concerning the infringement and validity of European and EU patents. The Commission has adopted a Recommendation regarding the negotiation and adoption of the Agreement that would create a UPLS,[152] while the Council of the European Union has adopted conclusions on this system in December 2009.[153] The creation of the UPLS could result in total private cost savings up to 289 million euro per year by 2013.[154] In parallel, the Council has most recently issued a Resolution on the enforcement of IPRs in the internal market (1 March 2010).[155]

European Patent Organisation

EPC 2000

10.79   The signatory states of the European Patent Organisation met in 2000 to revisit and revise the provisions of the European Patent Convention. The aim was to modernise the Convention for the 21st century and to ensure its fitness for purpose within the European integrated economy and its compliance with international agreements, such as TRIPS. Controversial issues such as biotechnological inventions[156] and the patenting of computer programs[157] were, however, left unchanged by the 2000 Diplomatic Conference, and the view was expressed that these would require the attention of a future Conference in due course. We consider these topics separately in Chapter 12. The revised version of the Convention (EPC 2000) was adopted by the

---

[149] Communication from the Commission, Implementing the Community Lisbon Programme: A policy framework to strengthen EU manufacturing—towards a more integrated approach for industrial policy COM (2005) 474 final.

[150] Communication from the Commission: An Industrial Property Rights Strategy for Europe (COM 2008 465/3), available here: http://ec.europa.eu/internal_market/indprop/docs/rights/communication_en.pdf

[151] 'Public Hearing on Future Patent Policy in Europe' (July 2006), available at: http://ec.europa.eu/internal_market/indprop/patent/hearing_en.htm

[152] Commission Recommendation SEC (2009) 330 final, available here: http://ec.europa.eu/internal_market/indprop/docs/patent/recommendation_sec09-330_en.pdf

[153] IP/09/1880 (4 December 2009).

[154] D Harhoff 'Economic Cost-Benefit Analysis of a Unified and Integrated European Patent Litigation System' (2009) available here: http://ec.europa.eu/internal_market/indprop/docs/patent/studies/litigation_system_en.pdf

[155] Available here: http://ec.europa.eu/internal_market/iprenforcement/docs/council/20100401_resolution_ipr_enforcement_en.pdf

[156] This matter was not on the Conference Agenda largely because of efforts within the EU to harmonise the law on these inventions.

[157] Proposals to remove the computer program exception from the provisions of Art 52 EPC were not taken up.

Administrative Council of the EPO on 28 June 2001 and came into force December 2007.[158] Key changes in the law were:

- **Patentability:** Article 52(1) EPC now states that 'European patents shall be granted for any inventions, in *all* fields of technology…(emphasis supplied)' This reflects the provisions of Article 27(1) TRIPS (see above).

- **Exclusions:** Article 53(c) EPC now provides that methods for treatment of the human or animal body by surgery or therapy and diagnostic methods practised on the human or animal body are expressly excluded from patentability. Previously, these were considered not to demonstrate industrial applicability.[159] (See further paras 11.60ff.)

- **Novelty:** Article 54(3) EPC extends the scope of the 'state of the art' when testing the novelty of an invention. As we discuss in para 11.80, an invention is only new if it was not part of the state of the art—that is, publicly available—before the patent application was filed (normally). This reform widened the scope of what constitutes the state of the art in that it now includes the content of all European patent applications filed prior to the filing date of the instant application.

- **Interpretation:** Textual revisions to Article 2 of the Protocol on the Interpretation of Article 69 EPC now make it clear that the 'due account' should be taken of equivalents as part of the law in determining the extent of protection for an invention. This, however, is simply to confirm a long-standing approach and is not intended as a reform of the substantive law (see further para 11.189).

- **Judicial review:** New Article 112a states that: '[a]ny party to appeal proceedings adversely affected by the decision of the Board of Appeal may file a petition for review by the Enlarged Board of Appeal'. This provides a limited form of judicial review in that the only grounds upon which this procedure can be used is if there was a fundamental procedural defect in Board of Appeal proceedings or if a criminal act may have had an impact on the Board's decision.

- **Procedure:** Numerous revisions have been adopted in an attempt to streamline processes for gaining and maintaining a patent. Important changes include: (a) applicants can file in any language and do not need to submit an EPO official language translation until later in the process (Article 14(2)); (b) applicants may request 'further processing' of their application if they fail to comply with time limits (Article 121(1)); (c) the EPO will move to a system of search and examination of an application by the same examiner when previously these have been separate systems. This was designed to improve the efficiency of the Office.

- **Post-grant amendments:** EPC 1973 only allowed amendments to patent claims as part of Opposition Proceedings. Thus unilateral action could not be taken by a patentee to limit protection voluntarily and so avoid lengthy and costly litigation in cases of dispute. Article 105a EPC 2000 allows a patent proprietor to request revocation or limitation of his patent before the EPO and Article 105b(3) makes it clear that any such amendments

---

[158] The Implementing Regulations of EPC 2000 are available here: http://www.epo.org/patents/law/legal-texts/archive/epc2000/regulations.html

[159] Note the text of Art 53(a) has been brought into line with Art 27(2) TRIPS which reads: 'Members may exclude from patentability inventions, the prevention within their territory of the commercial exploitation of which is necessary to protect *ordre public* or morality'. EPC 1973 talked of '*publication* or exploitation' as being offensive to morality or *ordre public*. 'Publication' has now been deleted.

will have effect in all countries for which the European patent was designated. This, in effect, creates a centralised amendment system. Article 138 also gives a proprietor a right to limit his claims in national proceedings questioning the validity of his patent. It has been stated that these reforms 'will act as an incentive to amend incorrectly granted patents quickly and at low cost'.[160]

10.80   The Conference also laid the groundwork for future agreements between member states on translation issues and the creation of a centralised judicial body as discussed above. The Administrative Council is now charged with the authority to revise the EPC in accordance with international treaties or European Union legislation, and it has the power to conclude agreements with states, non-governmental bodies and with documentation centres set up by virtue of agreements with such organisations.[161]

European Patent Litigation Agreement

10.81   Revisions to the European Patent Convention can do nothing to address what is arguably the biggest hurdle to achieving true European integration in patent protection. This is the absence of a centralised litigation system with a single judicial body able to rule definitely on the validity and infringement of European patents. The co-existence of a plethora of national enforcement mechanisms is not only extremely costly and lengthy but leads to forum shopping, complex cross-border litigation and considerable legal uncertainty. We have already considered European Union proposals for an EU Patent and associated court, and we have also seen that the European Patent Organisation has offered its own proposals for reform. These come in the form of the draft *European Patent Litigation Agreement* which is the product of the EPO's Working Party on Litigation (WPL) established in 1999. Its original remit was to present a draft text for an optional Protocol to the European Patent Convention for the establishment and running of a common appeal court and standardised procedures. Importantly, the WPL had to address the logistics of the enterprise to demonstrate the viability of any proposal to signatory states. Years of discussion and negotiation[162] eventually resulted in a Draft Agreement on the Establishment of a European Patent Litigation System[163] as an associated Draft Statute on a European Patent Court.[164] This would establish a European Patent Court with a Court of First Instance in several Divisions and a Court of Appeal with the further power to act as Facultative Advisory Council in offering non-binding opinions on points of law to national courts involved in actions about the validity or infringement of European patents.

10.82   The WPL is acutely aware of the need to dovetail any proposal with parallel efforts in the European Union. Inter alia, then, the substantive law in the draft Agreement is closely allied to

---

[160] Statement by Dr Roland Grossenbacher, Chairman of the Administrative Council of the European Patent Organisation, 29 November 2000.

[161] Act Revising the Convention on the Grant of European Patents, 29 November 2000, Art 10.

[162] See the Working Party on Litigation, Declaration, 20 November 2003 in which the WPL affirms its belief that its drafts form a 'suitable basis for an intergovernmental conference to establish a judiciary for the European Patent Organisation', available here: http://documents.epo.org/projects/babylon/eponet.nsf/0/9F8870AD4D54AE4DC125723 D004AF178/$File/declaration_en.pdf

[163] Working Party on Litigation, Draft Agreement on the Establishment of a European Patent Litigation System, December 2005, available here: http://documents.epo.org/projects/babylon/eponet.nsf/0/F4CF2F6008160AB4C12572 3D004B0707/$File/latest_draft_en.pdf

[164] Working party on Litigation, Draft Statute on a European Patent Court, February 2004, available here: http://documents.epo.org/projects/babylon/eponet.nsf/0/885CCB85F5CC33ABC125723D004B15F9/$File/statute_draft_en.pdf

certain core provisions of the European Union's 1989 proposal for a Community court.[165] This covers issues such as the definition of infringing acts and the meaning of indirect infringement. The proposed language scheme is based on that of the EPO and the London Agreement (see para 10.35 above).

10.83   There are two stumbling blocks for the European Patent Litigation Agreement (EPLA). The first is the need not only to reflect European Union efforts but also not to usurp them. Thus the stalled attempts in the Union to establish a common court have meant that the draft Agreement has been put temporarily on hold. The two models are not mutually exclusive, however. The European Commission had, in fact, taken the view that the EPLA is inconsistent with EU law, but as we have seen, the EU's proposals have undergone recent extensive revision and these are largely based on the model contained in the EPLA. This may be the initiative that finally bears fruit for both the EU and the EPO. An enduring concern about both proposals is that each leaves a variety of issues to national courts.

National reforms

10.84   The Patents Act 2004 embodies the most far-reaching reform to UK patent law since the passing of the Patents Act 1977, although the 1977 Act remains the primary piece of legislation in the field. The main instigation behind the 2004 Act was EPC 2000, and the reforms outlined above came fully into force in the UK at the same time as EPC 2000 took effect (December 2007). We deal with the particular measures in domestic law in due course.

10.85   The 2004 Act also addresses certain issues about enforcement of patents and introduces a UK–IPO dispute resolution mechanism in an attempt to avoid lengthy and costly litigation. The Act makes it clear that the owner of a patent can himself apply for revocation,[166] but co-owners must act jointly if they wish to amend or revoke their patent.[167] The Patent Opinions Service began on 1 October 2005 and offers an avenue for parties in dispute over the validity or infringement of a UK or European patent to make representations and receive a non-binding ruling from a patent examiner. It also provides an opportunity to test the strength of respective arguments before deciding whether to proceed to litigation.[168] The service costs £200 and issued its 100th Opinion in September 2009. A review was carried out in the same year, the results of which were awaited at the time of going to press. A final important feature of the 2004 Act is its reform of the employee inventor compensation scheme, which we discuss in detail at paras 11.160ff.

10.86   The day-to-day business and the formal procedures of the UK–IPO are governed by the Patents Rules 2007.[169] These rules completely replaced the 1995 rules, which were in need of serious overhaul, but major reforms were held back until the publication of the *Gowers Review of Intellectual Property* in 2006 (see below para 10.87ff). The rules had to be amended to keep pace with the UK's international obligations.

---

[165] See n 60 above.   [166] Patents Act 1977, s 72(4A), as amended by the Patents Act 2004, s 4.
[167] Patents Act 1977, s 36(3)(a), as amended by the Patents Act 2004, s 9.
[168] Patents Act 1977 ss 74A–B, as amended by the Patents Act 2004, s 13.
[169] SI 2007/3291, as amended.

Gowers Review: the future of the IP system in the United Kingdom

10.87   We have already mentioned the Gowers Review in previous chapters. While its remit was solely the IP system in the United Kingdom, its recommendations extend to international and European policy matters with advice to the UK Government and UK–IPO on how to achieve better IP enforcement, lower IP costs, and a system of balanced and flexible rights. We can therefore consider some of Gowers' key recommendations at the international, European and national levels as they relate to patents. Moreover, now that we have a few years distance from the publication of the report itself we are in a position to gauge whether the suggested reforms/ implemented changes are having the desired effect.

International relations

10.88   It is recognised that while international harmonisation of patent systems has been significantly slower than in other areas of IP law, there is much that can still be achieved through closer cooperation between countries and their respective intellectual property offices. It is important to appreciate, however, that different countries may use patent laws in different ways depending on their particular needs. Thus Gowers recommended the following:

- UK–IPO should work more closely with African patent offices to help them to take full advantage of flexibilities within the TRIPS Agreement.

- UK–IPO should encourage international re-consideration of time limits for compliance with TRIPS for least developed countries—currently 2016.

- UK Government should encourage WTO members to ratify the Amendment to Article 31*bis* on access to medicines (paras 10.54–10.55 above).

- UK Government and UK–IPO should pursue work sharing agreements with other intellectual property offices, for example, to avoid duplication of searches of the prior art.

- The UK–IPO has developed a helpful consolidated list of the Gowers recommendations and evidence of its progress to date in implementing them. In respect of most of the above, the recommendations remain in progress largely because of the need for interaction and action by other bodies such as the European Commission and the EPO.[170] In many other areas, especially at level of domestic policy, most of the recommendations have been taken on board (see further below).

Greater European collaboration and harmonisation

10.89   The current fragmented nature of Europe's patent systems creates legal uncertainty and drives up costs—it is presently five times more expensive to patent in Europe than in the United States.[171] The Gowers Review supported *both* the EU initiative to establish a unitary patent (COMPAT) *and* the European Patent Litigation Agreement towards the establishment of a single European patent court. The two initiatives are not seen as mutually exclusive.

---

[170] The list can be accessed via the UK-IPO website here: http://www.ipo.gov.uk/pro-policy/policy-information/policy-issues/policy-issues-gowers.htm

[171] B Pottelsberghe de la Potterie B. *Economic incongruities in the European patent system*, (Bruegel Working Paper 2009/01 and ECARES Working Paper 2009_003) available here: http://www.bruegel.org/uploads/tx_btbbreugel/economic_incongruities_BVP_MM_Jan2009_FINAL3_01.pdf

10.90   The Gowers Review also recommended that the UK Government support the London Agreement (para 10.35 above) as a valuable initiative in its own right as well as an interim measure towards COMPAT. The UK has now signed the London Agreement, which took effect in May 2008.

National considerations

10.91   Various aspects of the domestic system were scrutinised by Gowers, including granting procedures, training of examiners in new developments, raising awareness of firms and the public about IP, review of practice and reform of defences. In particular, the UK–IPO was encouraged to play a greater and more defined role in IP policy development, for example, by working more closely with industry and government departments. Some of the specific patent recommendations included and the progress since the publication of the Gowers Review are discussed below.

- **Accelerated grant.** Both UK–IPO and EPO now provide for a combined examination and search procedure. The Review recommended that this should be improved further to create an 'accelerated grant' mechanism since speed of access to the market is often the single biggest determinant of success for inventors. This was put out to consultation but the responses indicated that it was not welcome and the proposal has not been taken forward. Instead, more effort is being put into raising awareness of existing procedures.

- **Maintaining quality.** The Review stated that speed should not come at the expense of quality of examination to determine that an invention is truly new and sufficiently inventive.[172] It recommended that the UK–IPO should improve its system of 'section 21 observations' whereby anyone can comment on the viability of an invention when the patent application is published. Applications should be easier to view and objections should be easier to make; generally, the availability of the service should be publicised more widely. Following the Review, the UK–IPO has improved its web-interface for making observations.

- **Raising awareness.** The Review recommended that UK–IPO should develop further links with universities and industry to permit examiners to stay on top of developments. General public and industry awareness should be raised as to the existence and function of IPRs, and the UK–IPO should adopt more of an advisory role for innovators. Numerous initiatives have since been undertaken by UK–IPO in this regard.

- **Encouraging licences of right.** Patent law currently provides that a patentee can reduce his renewal fees by half by granting third parties a 'licence of right' to exploit the invention on mutually agreed terms.[173] The system has historically been poorly used, and the Review recommended that awareness of this facility be raised and that a model licence be adopted to encourage greater use. A Working Group has been established to take this work forward and guidance has been issued.

- **Clarifying defences.** There has been a lack of clarity as to the meaning of the research exemption in the Patents Act 1977, s 60(5). This has important implications for education, experimentation and innovation and reform is required to establish the parameters of the defence. The Review suggested the Swiss model as one which

---

[172] A 2006 UK–IPO consultation on inventive step showed that the current basic UK law regarding inventive step and its application are appropriate, available here: http://www.ipo.gov.uk/response-inventive.pdf
[173] Patents Act 1977, s 46. Gowers, n 1 above, para 3.20.

adequately balances interests. A public consultation was opened on this topic but the results had not reached the public domain at the time of writing. We discuss the issues in paras 11.213–11.220.

10.92 In policy terms, it was recommended, and accepted by the Chancellor, that a Strategic Advisory Board for IP Policy (SABIP) be established with external experts, a Secretariat and suitable funding to advise on the future direction of IP initiatives for the UK and its wider relations. This was established in June 2008 and is now fully operational.[174]

Do we need new IP rights?

10.93 An interesting discussion in the Review is whether new rights are required to meet the needs of new and emerging technologies. The patent system has been put to the test in recent decades with the advent of biotechnologies and information technologies, including software and electronic business methods, as we see in Chapter 12. But it has also been argued that patent law sets the threshold too high for protection, necessitating a system of 'petty patents' or 'utility models' which can protect less inventive, but no less valuable, innovations.[175] Length of protection and costs are also a factor—many new technologies may have a short shelf life, thus obviating the need for protection over 20 years, while high registration, translation and enforcement costs mean that many small to medium-sized enterprises are effectively excluded from the patent system. Notwithstanding, the Gowers Review rejected any special case for utility model patents, software patents, biotechnology and genetic patents and business methods patents. In fact, it is claimed to be a strength of the system that it has not responded with the creation of new rights for new developments which would mean added complexity and increased cost.

10.94 Economics play a large part in this. Not only are there significant costs in setting up and administering new rights, but there is precious little evidence that their establishment would improve the economic situation,[176] or that they are necessary to encourage innovation.[177] Indeed, there is evidence from the United States that business method patents and gene patents can have an anti-competitive effect which de-incentivises rather than encourages innovation.[178] The UK and EPO take a harder line on these kinds of patents than the US and the Gowers recommendation was that this should remain the position unless good economic cause can be shown to justify change. The point has been 'noted' by the UK–IPO.

 Discussion point For answer guidance visit www.oxfordtextbooks.co.uk/orc/macqueen2e/

What other costs would be involved with the introduction of new IPRs? How might these new rights impact on existing rights?

---

[174] You can find out more about SABIP here: http://www.sabip.org.uk/

[175] See para 10.75 above for discussion of attempts in the EU to approximate laws in this area.

[176] 'There seems to be no correlation between the existence of a utility model patent and innovation': Gowers Review, n 1 above, para 4.112.

[177] The example is given of the US software industry which 'grew expotentially without pure software patents', ibid, para 4.114.

[178] ibid, paras 4.118–4.121.

Exercise

Visit the UK–IPO to check which of the outstanding proposals for reform have, or have not, been initiated or implemented by the time you read this chapter. For those that have not been taken up, are you convinced by the reasons given? See: http://www.ipo.gov.uk

Patent procedures

The patenting procedure

10.95   We have already seen that there are various routes to obtaining patent registration, either via national (UK–IPO), European (EPO), or international (PCT) avenues. The net outcome is, how-ever, always the same—patents are granted with territorial effect only in the countries for which protection was sought, and this can be a very costly process if multiple filing is contemplated. There is therefore a great amount of strategic and economic thinking required in developing a patent strategy, including an assessment of one's actual and potential markets, a weighing-up of the costs of patenting against possible returns, a judgment on whether it is worth seeking protection in a country where imitation is unlikely, and a sense of future behaviour of com-petitors. Time is also against the prospective patentee. Any delay in registering an invention increases the likelihood that a rival might release their own version of the invention, thereby thwarting any chances of future protection; by the same token, seeking protection at too early a stage in the development of an invention can seriously limit the scope of monopoly obtained— the inventor is only entitled to protection for what he has actually contributed to the sum total of human knowledge (known as 'the state of the art', see further para 11.78 below).

10.96   The starting point to understanding the scope and content of a patent monopoly is the patent application itself. In this section we describe the patent application process for the UK, although this largely reflects the processes of the EPO and the PCT.[179] We also consider the constituent elements of a UK patent application.

10.97   The critical event in the process of any patent application is the obtaining of its priority date. Normally, this is the date when the application is filed with the UK–IPO,[180] but crucially it can be up to 12 months earlier if a patent has been filed in another World Trade Organization coun-try and the later application is 'supported by matter' contained in the earlier application.[181] The importance of the priority date cannot be underestimated because it is the date from which the novelty of an invention will be tested. Only if the invention was publicly available *prior* to the priority date is there a problem. It is therefore perfectly acceptable to disclose the invention after obtaining the priority date; indeed it is common practice to begin marketing at this point or after publication of the application (see para 10.119ff below). You may have seen the term *patent pending* attached to various products. This refers to products marketed in the time period between the priority date and the grant of the patent and it puts rivals on notice of the patent application.

---

[179] If the UK is designated in a European patent application the resulting patent is treated entirely as if it were a UK pat-ent, see Patents Act, ss 77–8, PR, Part 5, EPC 2000, Art 64.

[180] Patents Act 1977, s 5(1), as amended.

[181] Patents Act 1977, s 5(2), as amended. The Comptroller also has a discretion to allow an unintentional late filing, Patents Act 1977, ss 5(2A)–5(2C), as amended.

10.98 It is also possible to make an 'early filing' on provision of a few key pieces of information to the UK–IPO, being a written indication that a patent is sought, the identification of the person applying for the patent, a description of the invention, or a reference to an earlier relevant application.[182] This mechanism is far short of a full application, but allows the prospective applicant up to 12 months to ponder his patent strategy and to decide if a full application is merited. It also serves to secure an early priority date for the same reasons discussed above.

10.99 If a full application is to be made, the Patents Act 1977 lays down stringent criteria as to its form and content. Section 14(2) of the Act provides that every application must contain:

- a *request* for the grant of a patent;
- an *abstract* which gives technical information about the invention and the field to which it contributes; it also serves to facilitate future searches but does not form part of the state of the art;[183]
- a *specification* which is the part of the application that contains (i) a description of the invention, (ii) the claim or claims as to what has been invented and what a monopoly is sought for, (iii) any drawings referred to in the description or claims.

10.100 The inventor must sufficiently disclose his invention in the specification to allow effective examination of its suitability for a patent. The criterion is that 'the specification shall disclose the invention in a manner which is clear enough and complete enough for the invention to be performed by a person skilled in the art'.[184] If this has not happened but a patent in nonetheless granted, it can be a ground for subsequent revocation of the patent for *insufficiency*.[185] We consider this in Chapter 11 (paras 11.201ff).

10.101 An invention is described in words and pictures and, in the case of inventions involving living organisms, by a deposit of samples under the Budapest Treaty 1977.[186] Note, however, there is no obligation to describe the fastest, most efficient, or most economical way to perform the invention. Such knowledge—'know how'—invariably remains out of the public domain and provides the patentee with additional commercial advantage in the exploitation of her invention.

 Exercise

The best way to make sense of these arcane terms and to understand patent applications is to read them for yourself.[187] Various patent databases exist. One of the most comprehensive is Esp@cenet which is maintained by the European Patent Office: http://ep.espacenet.com/

10.102 Figure 10.1 shows an example of a patented invention from the United States for Animal Ear Protectors with the Patent Number US4233942.[188] Go to the Esp@cenet website and do a Quick Search for this patent using the Patent Number.

---

[182] Patents Act 1977, s 15(1).   [183] Patents Act 1977, s 14(7), as amended.
[184] Patents Act 1977, s 14(3), as amended.   [185] Patents Act 1977, s 72(1).
[186] Available at: http://www.wipo.int/treaties/en/registration/budapest/trtdocs_wo002.html
[187] Note, procedures and processes in the EPO and through the PCT do not use the term 'specification' but, simply, 'patent application'.
[188] Also published as GB2040663(A) and FR2448289(A1).

Figure 10.1 Patent application for Animal Ear Protectors

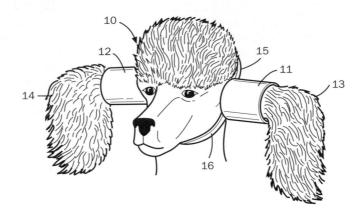

The first thing you will see is this picture and the *Abstract* of the patent which sums up the invention thus:

> 'This invention provides a device for protecting the ears of animals, especially long-haired dogs, from becoming soiled by the animal's food while the animal is eating. The device provides a generally tubular shaped member for containing and protecting each ear of the animal, and a member to position the tubular member and animal ears away from the mouth and food of the animal while it is eating.'

Now go to the *Description* section of the patent where we find more detail about the invention. Note, in particular, two features: (1) the applicant has described 'the prior art', that is, the existing state of knowledge before this invention, (2) the applicant describes how this invention solves a previously-unsolved problem, viz, protecting the ears of long-eared animals when they eat or drink. In other words, he is explaining how this device is *new* and *inventive*. We return to the specifics of the law on these points in the next chapter. A final point to note about the description is that it must support the claims, otherwise the patent may be denied or invalidated in due course.[189]

10.103 The *Claims* are arguably the most important part of a patent. Claims serve at least two vital functions. First, they describe in technical detail the essence of the invention; second, they establish the limits of the monopoly that a successful applicant will eventually enjoy. You can only legitimately claim for actual technical contribution to human knowledge—to the state of the art—and any claims which exceed the boundaries of your contribution can be struck out. Overly broad claims can be a problem when a new technology emerges and patent examiners are unfamiliar with the science and so unsure about what, precisely, has been added to the state of the art.[190] Section 14(5) of the Patents Act 1977 states that:

> 'The claim or claims shall—(a) define the matter for which the applicant seeks protection; (b) be clear and concise; (c) be supported by the description; and (d) relate to one invention or to a group of inventions which are so linked as to form a single inventive concept.'

---

[189] Patents Act 1977, s 14(5)(c).

[190] This description straddles two 'traditional' approaches to claim drafting: the 'central claiming system' whereby the objective is to define the kernel of the invention and the scope of protection flows from the precise contribution to the state of the art. This is still largely the approach in Continental Europe. It is to be contrasted with the 'peripheral claiming system' where the task is to demarcate the boundaries of the monopoly that is being claimed. This reflects more the position in the UK and the US.

10.104   Our invention for Animal Ear Protectors only has one claim. Here it is:

> '1. A device for protecting animal ears comprising: a pair of generally tubular protectors each of which is formed of a sheet of self-biasing material which in their free state tend to form themselves into said generally tubular protectors; each of said protectors being longitudinally openable to allow easy insertion of one of said animal ears; and positioning means for flexibly joining one end of one protector in spaced apart relationship with one end of the other protector and for securing said device to the head of said animal such that the longitudinal axis of each protector and a portion of each ear of said animal, are held generally horizontally and approximately perpendicularly to the head of said animal whereby the ends of said animal ears are separated by a distance greater than the width of the head of said animal.'

10.105   There are numerous points to observe about this passage. First, consider the use of language. It may strike you as a rather convoluted way of describing two tubes placed over a dog's ears. But the purpose of claims is to describe the specific *technical* contribution that this particular invention makes to the state of the art. Indeed, it is not written with the ordinary reader in mind, but rather the audience is the person skilled in the relevant art. The drafting of patent claims is in fact a highly-skilled enterprise, usually undertaken by patent agents or attorneys who specialise in particular fields of technology and who also provide advice and guidance on navigating the patent system.[191] While an applicant is not obliged to engage the services of a patent agent, the highly complex nature of the application and drafting processes indicates that it is strongly in his interests to do so.

10.106   The *precision* of the language in claims is also important because it must both distinguish the present invention from what has already been invented and describe the invention widely to secure as broad a monopoly as possible. Note the use of the term 'a pair of generally tubular protectors'—why 'generally'? Well, it may be because the applicant does not want to restrict his monopoly solely to 'tubular' protectors because then it would be easy to invent around his contribution, for example, by producing square protectors. This is an issue of *interpretation* of claims and the approach of the courts to this is a matter of considerable importance, especially in infringement proceedings which we examine in the next chapter.

10.107   Most patent applications have numerous claims, and the average length of a European patent is 22 pages. The general approach is to begin with the first claim as the broadest and to claim narrower features of the invention and/or to pick out particular features of the invention in subsequent claims. In this way, if some claims are struck out, for example, for being too broad, the applicant might still have a chance of receiving some, albeit narrower, protection through the remaining claims.

10.108   Let's consider another example. Do an Esp@cenet search for an invention relating to an insert for a cat litter box (EP1720404). Here are the first few claims:

> '1. An insert (1) which can be placed in a lower part (5) of a cat lavatory and is replaceable, characterised in that the blank of the insert (1) is substantially rectangular, the corners (7) of the insert (1) being sloped.
>
> 2. The insert as claimed in Claim 1, characterised in that the insert is a pouch (6).
>
> 3. The insert as claimed in either of Claims 1 or 2, characterised in that the blank of the insert (1) is substantially rectangular or square.'

---

[191] See, for example, the Chartered Institute of Patent Attorneys which was established in 1882: http://www.cipa.org.uk

Question

What is *inventive* about this insert compared to all the other available cat litter accessories? How would you find out?

Drafting of claims

10.109   The way in which a claim is drafted is of considerable importance for the scope of protection eventually received. The above claims in respect of the cat litter insert rely on the term 'characterised in . . .' to distinguish particular features of this invention from others already part of the state of the art. This is typical of the European approach. Various categories of claims exist and are used around the world. The UK has a fairly liberal approach to claim drafting and there is no prescription in law as to how claims should be drawn up.[192] In contrast, the European Patent Office has strict guidelines about drafting[193] and does not permit all kinds of claims, as we shall see below. Moreover, the European Patent Convention Guidelines impose a fee if an application has more than 15 claims,[194] and the number of claims cannot be indefinite because 'the number of the claims shall be reasonable in consideration of the nature of the invention claimed'.[195]

10.110   It is commonly said that an invention can be a *product* or a *process*. This is reflected in the categories of claims that are most commonly used—product or process claims—and it is important to distinguish between the two because the legal effects of a patentee's monopoly can be affected by the choice of claim category.[196] A *product claim* is often characterised by a claim to a device, substance, embodiment or compound, that is, to the physical entity making up the invention. A monopoly over the product itself is a strong one because it prevents all uses of the product by a competitor and it does not matter if the product was made by independent, non-rivalrous means. A *process claim* is as its name suggests—a claim to a means of producing something. Such claims are often characterised by language such as a method, use or system, for example, a 'system for storing information'. A simple process claim is additionally useful because it extends protection to the products directly obtained by the process itself.[197]

10.111   *Product-by-process claims* are to be distinguished from the last example. These are product claims where the product is described by reference to its process of manufacture rather than by its own characteristics. For example, 'the product obtained by the process described in claim 1'. There are a couple of advantages of using such claims. One is a way of distinguishing your product from other similar products already on the market. Your monopoly will only extend to products made by your particular process, and may not therefore interfere with other products made by different means. An additional advantage of a product-by-process claim comes when it is

---

[192] *Kirin-Amgen v Transkaryotic Therapies* [2003] RPC 3, CA, per Aldous LJ, paras 29–31.
[193] Guidelines for Examination in the European Patent Office, Part C, Chapter III, and Implementing Regulations to part III of the Convention, Rule 43, available here: http://www.epo.org/patents/law/legal-texts/html/epc/2000/e/rpiii. html.
[194] ibid, Rule 45.   [195] ibid, Rule 43(5).
[196] See the comments by the EPO in T378/86 MOOG/Change of category [1988] OJEPO 386.
[197] EPC 2000, Art 64(2).

difficult or impossible to describe your product by reference to its own characteristics, for example, if you have invented a useful compound but you do not yet know its structure or composition.

10.112 Despite these benefits, product-by-process claims are frowned on by the European Patent Office, while they have generally been acceptable in the UK. The EPO will only allow such claims when it is not possible to describe the product by any other means and when the product is patentable in its own right.[198] A product is not rendered novel merely by the fact that it is produced by means of a new process.[199] In 2005, the House of Lords ruled that 'it is important that the United Kingdom should apply the same law as the EPO' and signalled a change of practice for the UK.[200]

10.113 We may also know what a product does, that is, how its functions, without yet knowing its essential technical features, that is, how it is structured or constituted. Normally, it is the description of these technical features which is required for a successful patent application,[201] but in certain circumstances *functional claims* are acceptable 'provided that a skilled person would have no difficulty in providing some means of performing this function without exercising inventive skill',[202] and notably when the claimed features of the invention 'cannot otherwise be defined more precisely without restricting the scope of the claim'.[203]

Exercise

Can you think of any other advantage to drafting claims in terms of an invention's function rather than its technical features?

10.114 Article 82 of the European Patent Convention provides that a '…European patent application shall relate to one invention only or to a group of inventions so linked as to form a single general inventive concept.'[204] It is not unusual, however, and especially in the pharmaceutical and biotechnology industries, for one patent application to concern many different, yet related, embodiments of a single inventive concept. Examples include thousands of different variations on a particular chemical compound or related elements of a gene sequence. In such circumstances, patent agents will invoke *representative claims* which allow specific examples to be given of the invention's particular features which are held out to be present across the range of products claimed. It would be impractical and self-defeating for the patent system to require more specific details or separate patent applications for each and every product.

---

[198] Guidelines for Examination in the European Patent Office, Part C, Chapter III, para 4.12, and T150/82 IFF/Claim categories, [1984] OJEPO 309, paras 10–11.

[199] ibid.

[200] *Kirin-Amgen Inc and others v Hoechst Marion Roussel Ltd and others* [2005] 1 All ER 667, [2005] RPC 9.

[201] Guidelines for Examination in the European Patent Office, Part C, Chapter III, para 4.5 , and implementing regulation rule 43(1)

[202] EPC Guidelines for Examination, Part C, Chapter III, para 2.1.

[203] T694/92 MYCOGEN/Modifying plant cells [1998] EPOR 114, para 4.

[204] See also Rule 44 of the Implementing Regulations, which requires a 'technical relationship' among all claimed inventions involving the same or corresponding special technical features.

10.115   Similarly, the *Markush claim* is frequently used in the chemical industry where vast numbers of related entities can be claimed together. The distinguishing feature is that this type of claim allows 'alternatives' to be claimed as functional equivalents, that is, various permutations of different entities will produce the same inventive result and so are claimed to fall within the monopoly. This is acceptable so long as the alternatives are of a similar nature and can fairly be substituted for one another.[205] Markush claims contain symbols to refer to the sub-groups. This type of claim is named after the first inventor to successfully use it.[206]

10.116   *Swiss-type claims* were developed to get around problems of non-patentability of second or subsequent uses of existing compounds for medical treatment.[207] Consider, for example, that you find out that athlete foot cream is also good for curing acne: can you patent the product in these terms or for this second use? You cannot patent the product because it is already known and therefore not *new*. Medical use is also already known, and so what is new is the *method* of treatment, but there is a further problem because historically methods of treatment of the human or animal body have been excluded from patentability.[208] The EPO Enlarged Board of Appeal addressed this issue by following a practice first adopted by the Swiss Federal Intellectual Property Office and held that claims could be formulated in a certain way to be permissible.[209] That formulation is a claim to '*use of substance X in the manufacture of a medicament for the treatment of condition Y*'. The claim, then, is to the method of manufacture not to the method of treatment. Because of the origin of the formulation, this became known as a Swiss-type claim. This legal fiction has since been addressed by reforms introduced by EPC 2000.[210] It is now no longer necessary to adopt Swiss-type claims because '[i]n the case of an invention consisting of a substance or composition for a specific use in any such method, the fact that the substance or composition forms part of the state of the art shall not prevent the invention from being taken to be new if that specific use does not form part of the state of the art.'[211] This now allows a simple claim of 'substance X for use in treatment of disease Y'.

10.117   Finally, we can consider the role of *omnibus claims*. These claims rely on references to the description of the invention in respect of their technical features and are commonly used in the UK. An example is 'A process in accordance with claim 1 substantially as described in the foregoing Example I [from the specification]'. There is, however, an express prohibition against this practice in the EPO Guidelines,[212] and therefore omnibus claims are not allowed except where 'absolutely necessary'.[213] This could be, for example, when the invention has features which can only be expressed by means of drawings or graphs defining a particular shape.

10.118   *Disclaimers* can be used to define an invention in a way that avoids problems of patentability such as non-novelty,[214] for example by expressly excluding certain features of the invention because these are already part of the state of the art.[215] But what happens if you want to disclaim features of your patent after it has been granted? This was considered by the Enlarged Board of Appeal in two cases[216] wherein it was held that post-grant disclaimers are possible in limited

---

[205] Guidelines for Examination in the European Patent Office, Part C, Chapter III, paras 3.7 and 7.4.1
[206] Eugene Markush, US patent 1,506,316, granted on 26 August 1924.
[207] See Patents Act 1977, s 2(6) for first medical use.
[208] Art 52(4) EPC and Patents Act 1977, s 4(2)—note, now amended as we discuss at paras 11.60ff.
[209] G5/83 EISAI/Second Medical Indication [1985] OJEPO 64.
[210] Arts 53(c) and 54(4) and (5) EPC 2000.   [211] Patents Act 1977, s 4A(4), as amended.
[212] Rules 43(4) and 46(6).   [213] T0150/82 IFF/Claim categories [1984] OJEPO 309.
[214] See Guidelines, Part C, Chapter III, para 4.20.   [215] T 4/80, BAYER/disclaimer [1982] OJEPO 149.
[216] See G01/03 PPG INDUSTRIES/disclaimer [2004] OJEPO 413 and G02/03 GENETIC SYSTEMS CORP/Synthetic Antigens [2004] OJEPO 448.

circumstances, namely, (1) to restore novelty by delimiting a claim against the state of the art, (2) to restore novelty by delimiting a claim against an accidental anticipation, and (3) to disclaim subject matter that is non-technical and so, non-patentable.

From preparation to application

(Note: guidance on applying for a patent is available from the UK–IPO here: http://www.patent. gov.uk/p-apply.pdf)

10.119   Once you have completed your patent application form you can submit it to the UK–IPO for examination. Figure 10.2 is a diagram of the process, kindly provided by the patent attorneys, Murgitroyd & Company.

10.120   The stages in the process are:

(1) Submission of patent specification (description of invention as minimum) and application form and *request for grant of a patent* form. (Patents Form 1: £30 Paper; £20 e-Filed)
(2) Receipt issued from UK–IPO with application number and confirmation of *priority date.*[217]
(3) *Request search* and file appropriate fee (£150/130 (e-Filed) for search) within 12 months. Add claims and abstract if not present. (Patents Form 9A)
(4) *Preliminary examination* to ensure formal requirements of the application are met and *search* of the 'prior art' to determine if invention in *new* and *inventive*. A *search report* will be prepared and sent to the applicant highlighting any materials that may pose problems for patentability as well as other technical materials showing what has been done in the field.[218] (£100/80 (e-Filed))
(5) *Publication of the patent* happens 18 months after the priority date.[219]
(6) *Substantive examination* is a thorough consideration of the application by a skilled patent examiner to determine if it meets the requirements for patentability.[220] (Patents Form 10)
(7) *Substantive examination report* issued and period for *amendment*, if required
(8) If all criteria are met, the patent is *granted, the application is published in its final form, and the patent certificate is sent to the patentee.*[221]

10.121   In total, it costs around £250–300 in official fees to apply for a UK patent.[222] Professional patent attorney fees will be substantially more. Consider the diagram from Murgitroyd & Company on applying for protection internationally (Figure 10.3). Note how the domestic intellectual property office can act as a conduit into other patent systems.

Who can apply for a patent?

10.122   Anyone can apply for a patent,[223] and they do not need to be the inventor, although if this is the case they must have some entitlement in law to apply, for example through contractual arrangement, and the basis for this must be made clear at the time of application (see Patents Form 7).[224] The inventor is entitled to be named both in the application and the patent.[225] It

[217] Patents Act 1977, s 15.   [218] Patents Act 1977, s 15A and s 17.   [219] Patents Act 1977, s 16(1).
[220] Patents Act 1977, s 18.   [221] Patents Act 1977, s 18.
[222] Note: The Patents and Patents and Trade Marks (Fees) (Amendment) Rules 2010 (SI 2010/33) introduced new fees as of 6 April 2010.
[223] Patents Act 1977, s 7(1).   [224] Patents Act 1977, s 7(2).   [225] Patents Act 1977, s 13.

Figure 10.2 UK Patent Application Procedure

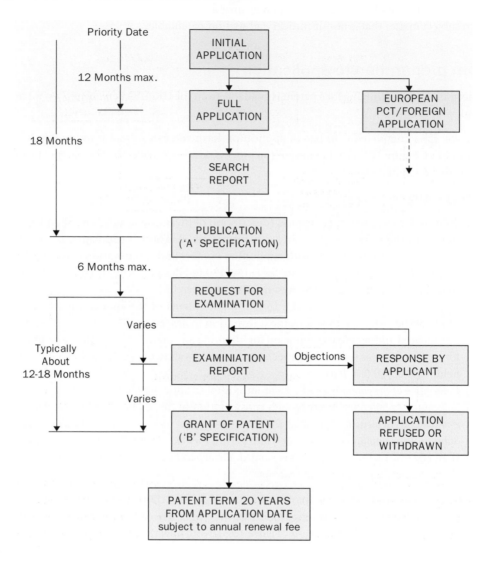

will be assumed that the applicant is entitled to apply until the contrary is proven.[226] Matters of dispute over entitlement to the patent are referred to the Comptroller in the first instance.[227]

10.123 The UK, Europe and most other countries of the world apply the so-called *first-to-file* approach to patent entitlement, that is, that priority of claim depends solely on who is first to submit a complete application to the patent office. The United States, in contrast, has operated a *first-to-invent* procedure which requires a far more nuanced examination of the processes leading up

---

[226] Patents Act 1977, s 7(4).   [227] Patents Act 1977, s 8. Post-grant disputes are handled under s 37.

Figure 10.3 International patent application procedure

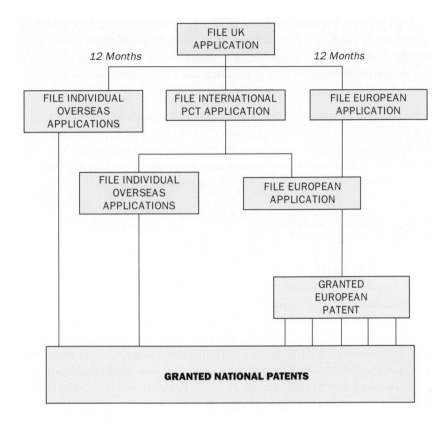

to a patent application and a need to determine at what point an 'invention' occurred. This is a two-stage process of (1) conception of the invention, and (2) reduction to practice of the invention. The best claim is that of an inventor who first conceived of the invention and then reduced it to practice and filed a patent application. Provided that he can prove this process, then he will have a stronger claim than someone who was first to file but cannot establish prior invention. But this can be a difficult and costly process. There has been recent and lengthy debate about reform of the US system including a move to a first-to-file approach. A series of proposals for patent reform has been made, the latest being the Patent Reform Act 2009 (HR1260). This Act and its predecessors have been through, and continue to go through, various iterations while argument rages on both sides as to the merits of such a radical change of US patent policy.

Discussion point For answer guidance visit www.oxfordtextbooks.co.uk/orc/macqueen2e/

What are the pros and cons of first-to-invent as opposed to first-to-file?

418

10.124 An application for a patent may be withdrawn at any time before the patent is granted and any withdrawal of such an application may not be revoked.[228] The publication of the patent is important for at least two reasons. First, at this time all correspondence and details of the invention are released into the public domain destroying the last vestiges of secrecy. Second, this is the date from which the patentee can sue for infringement.[229] If the patent is granted, the initial protection for the invention is for four years. Thereafter, the patent must be renewed annually on the payment of increasing fees up to a maximum of 20 years.[230]

10.125 A standard UK patent usually takes between two to three years to grant, but in some areas and in some other offices it is longer. For example, the EPO can take between four to six years to grant a biotechnology patent. An accelerated examination and search is now available from the UK–IPO. This involves collapsing both processes and paying both fees together. This means that a patent can be granted within a few months of publication.

Post-grant amendments

10.126 Sections 27(1) and 75(1) of the Patents Act 1977, as amended, provide the Comptroller and the courts with discretion to allow the amendment of a patent once it has been granted; the former section deals with circumstances when the request is from the proprietor himself, and the latter with cases when the validity of the patent is in dispute, for example, in infringement or revocation proceedings. EPC 2000 reforms found in Article 138(3) now mean that a proprietor, or consenting co-proprietors, can apply to amend or revoke a patent in *any* proceedings in which validity can be an issue, even if it is not an issue in the particular circumstances.[231] In exercising their discretion, the Comptroller and the courts must also now have regard to relevant principles in the European Patent Convention, for example, Regulations made under the Convention or EPO Guidelines or rulings from the EPO Boards of Appeal or Opposition Division. This is to ensure closer approximation and consistency of approach in signatory countries.[232] The UK–IPO offers a service whereby requests for amendments are made publicly available and those who may oppose them are given notice of the application to amend.[233] You cannot apply to amend your patent in favour of more subject matter or a broader monopoly.[234] Amendments can only maintain, or more usually restrict, the scope of protection originally received.

 Discussion point For answer guidance visit www.oxfordtextbooks.co.uk/orc/macqueen2e/

What sorts of factors do you think would influence the Comptroller or court one way or another in exercising its discretion to amend a patent?

10.127 In the next chapter we consider the criteria for patentability, the exclusions, rights conferred by a patent, revocation and defences.

---

[228] See Patents Act 1977, s 14(9).

[229] Patents Act 1977, s 69.

[230] This 20-year period is calculated from the filing date, see Patents Act 1977, s 25(1).

[231] Such circumstances are outlined in the Patents Act 1977, s 74.

[232] Patents Act 1977, s 75(5), as inserted by the Patents Act 2004, s 2(5). Art 105a EPC 2000 gives a discretion to the EPO to allow amendments to 'European' patents but not during opposition proceedings.

[233] Patent Office Amendment Service: http://www.ipo.gov.uk/p-pn-changespec.htm

[234] Patents Act 1977, s 76(2) and (3).

Diagram 10.2 UK patent renewal fees

Renewal year	New Renewal fees
5th Year	£70
6th Year	£90
7th Year	£110
8th Year	£130
9th Year	£150
10th Year	£170
11th Year	£190
12th Year	£210
13th Year	£250
14th Year	£290
15th Year	£350
16th Year	£410
17th Year	£460
18th Year	£510
19th Year	£560
20th Year	£600

Further reading

Books

CM Correa, *Trade Related Aspects of Intellectual Property Rights: A Commentary on the TRIPS Agreement* (2008)

PW Grubb and PL Thomsen, *Patents for Chemicals, Pharmaceuticals and Biotechnology: Fundamentals of Global Law, Practice and Strategy* (Fifth Edition, 2010)

MP Pugatch (ed), *The Intellectual Property Debate: Perspective from Law, Economics and Political Economy* (2006)

B Sherman and L Bently, *The Making of Modern Intellectual Property Law* (1999)

T Takenaka, *Patent Law and Theory: A Handbook of Contemporary Research* (2009)

Reports

Commission on Intellectual Property Rights, Innovation and Public Health, Public Health, Innovation and Intellectual Property Rights (2006)

European Commission, Pharmaceutical Sector Inquiry Report (2009)

Gowers Review of Intellectual Property (HM Treasury, 2006)

Articles and chapters

AF Christie, 'Non-overlapping Rights: A Patent Misconception' (2010) 32(2) EIPR 58.

E Derclaye, 'Patent Law's Role in the Protection of the Environment: Reassessing Patent Law and its Justifications in the 21st Century' (2009) 40(3) IIC 249.

AM Imam, 'How Does Patent Protection Help Developing Countries?' (2006) IIC 245

A Kur, RM Hilty, C Geiger and M Leister, 'The European Patent Litigation Agreement—Admissibility and Future of a Dispute Resolution for Europe' (2006) IIC 501

GT Laurie, 'Patents, Patients and Consent: Exploring the Interface Between Regulation and Innovation Regimes' in H Somsen (ed) The Regulatory Challenge of Biotechnology (2007)

D Matthews, 'The Lisbon Treaty, Trade Agreements and the Enforcement of Intellectual Property Rights' (2010) 32(3) EIPR 104.

J Straus and N-S Klunker, 'Harmonisation of International Patent Law?' (2007) 38 IIC 907, and the reply from C Health (2008) 39 IIC 210.

Patentability and infringement

Introduction

Scope and overview of chapter

11.1 This chapter is about obtaining and maintaining a patent. The first half deals with the issue of patentability and explores the criteria which are applied by an intellectual property office in examining a patent application. These are *novelty*, *inventive step* and *industrial applicability*. Equally important, however, are the exclusions from patentability and we will begin by considering these before moving on to consider the positive criteria for patenting. The second half of the chapter concerns the rights that a patentee enjoys, the circumstances in which infringement actions might be brought, and the defences that are available to rivals.

11.2
> ### Learning objectives
>
> By the end of this chapter you should be able to describe and explain:
>
> - the exclusions from patentability and their underlying rationales;
> - the meaning and operation of the criteria for patentability;
> - the range of rights conferred on an inventor by the grant of a patent as well as the limits of those rights;
> - the circumstances in which infringement proceedings can be brought and the common counter-claim of revocation;
> - the available defences to an action for patent infringement.

11.3 Patent law protects inventions, but interestingly there is no legal definition of *invention*.[1] Rather, the eligibility of a new product or process for patent protection is considered in a two-step process. First, a patent examiner will consider what is *not* an invention under the law, or at

---

[1] But see the Patents Act 1977, s 125(1).

least, what will not be entitled to patent protection. Well-established lists of exclusions from patentability exist in most legal systems and it is essential to understand both what is on such lists and why certain subject matter is excluded. The reasons are many and varied as we shall see. It is in these exclusions that many cultural and jurisdictional differences lie in the application of patent law. Secondly, an intellectual property office will test an invention against the positive criteria for patentability, which are *novelty* (does the invention already exist and is it in the public domain?); *inventive step* (is the invention sufficiently innovative to represent a significant move forward in the field?); and *industrial applicability* (can the invention be made or used in any kind of industry?). These criteria operate as threshold devices to determine if a particular invention makes a sufficient contribution to human knowledge and experience to merit the award of a monopoly. Article 27(1) of the TRIPS Agreement ensures that all countries are agreed that these are the relevant criteria for patentability.[2] But it is in the interpretation given to these criteria by national courts where differences emerge, and we will focus on the UK courts in this regard.

11.4   Once granted, a patent confers on the patentee a range of rights and the monopoly is arguably the strongest within intellectual property law. But as with all intellectual property rights, limits can be placed on that monopoly such as Crown use or compulsory licences. Moreover, what can be given can also be taken away, and patents are vulnerable throughout their life to a claim for revocation, that is, that the patent should be struck from the patent register because it was erroneously granted. Infringement proceedings are often met with a counter-claim for revocation. It is therefore necessary to consider infringement and revocation together. Finally, the chapter examines the available defences to an action for patent infringement. So the rest of the chapter looks like this:

- Excluded subject matter (11.5–11.74)
- Protectable subject matter (11.75–11.135)
- Patent rights and their limits (11.136–11.165)
- Infringement proceedings (11.166–11.199)
- Revocation (11.200–11.212)
- Defences (11.213–11.225)

Excluded subject matter

11.5   The final version of the revised European Patent Convention, known as EPC 2000, was issued by the European Patent Office in January 2007 and came into force December that year.[3] We have discussed its reforming measures in the previous chapter. Article 52(1) EPC 2000 now provides that: 'European patents shall be granted for any inventions, in all fields of technology, provided that they are new, involve an inventive step and are susceptible of industrial

---

[2] Art 27(1) TRIPS: 'Subject to the provisions of paragraphs 2 and 3, patents shall be available for any inventions, whether products or processes, in all fields of technology, provided that they are new, involve an inventive step and are capable of industrial application.'

[3] (2007) Special Edition No 1 OJEPO, available here: available here: http://archive.epo.org/epo/pubs/oj007/01_07/special_edition_1_epc_2000.pdf

application.' The relevant provisions which concern non-patentable subject matter are found in Articles 52(2), (3) and 53. These provide:

'**Article 52(2)**

The following in particular shall not be regarded as inventions within the meaning of paragraph 1:
(a) discoveries, scientific theories and mathematical methods;
(b) aesthetic creations;
(c) schemes, rules and methods for performing mental acts, playing games or doing business, and programs for computers;
(d) presentations of information.

(3) Paragraph 2 shall exclude the patentability of the subject-matter or activities referred to therein only to the extent to which a European patent application or European patent relates to such subject matter or activities **as such**. [emphasis added]

Article 53

Exceptions to patentability
European patents shall not be granted in respect of:
(a) inventions the commercial exploitation of which would be contrary to 'ordre public' or morality; such exploitation shall not be deemed to be so contrary merely because it is prohibited by law or regulation in some or all of the Contracting States;
(b) plant or animal varieties or essentially biological processes for the production of plants or animals; this provision shall not apply to microbiological processes or the products thereof;
(c) methods for treatment of the human or animal body by surgery or therapy and diagnostic methods practised on the human or animal body; this provision shall not apply to products, in particular substances or compositions, for use in any of these methods.'

11.6 The UK provisions equivalent to Article 52 EPC 2000 are found in s 1(2) of the Patents Act 1977,[4] while the terms of Article 53 EPC 2000 are reflected in s 1(3), (4) of, and Schedule A2 to, the 1977 Act. Schedule A2 deals with biotechnological inventions which are the subject of a European Directive[5] and which we explore in more depth in the next chapter. Finally, Article 53(c) is a new addition which is incorporated into domestic law through the Patents Act 2004 as s 4A of the Patents Act 1977.

 Question

What is the basis for excluding the respective categories of subject matter in Article 52 as opposed to Article 53? How are they different?

11.7 As Pumfrey J stated in *Shopalotto.com's Application:*[6] '[a] moment's thought will show that it is not possible to provide an exhaustive definition of "invention". The Convention does not attempt to interpret the word but provides a list of things which are excluded, whether or not they would be regarded as inventions.'[7]

---

[4] As amended by the Patents Act 2004.
[5] Directive 98/44/EC of the European Parliament and of the Council of 6 July 1998 on the legal protection of biotechnological inventions, available here: http://ec.europa.eu/internal_market/indprop/invent/index_en.htm (Biotechnology Directive).
[6] [2005] EWHC 2416 (Pat); [2006] RPC 293 at para 6.
[7] There was discussion in *Biogen v Medeva* [1997] RPC 1 of the need to prove an 'invention' over and above the established criteria for patentability, while this was not entirely ruled out no example could be given of where this would be required. See further J Pila, *The Requirement for an Invention in Patent Law* (2010).

■ *Aerotel Ltd v Telco Holdings Ltd & Others* [2006] EWCA Civ 1371, [2007] RPC 7

This case involved two appeals which raised issues about the interpretation of Article 52 and the approach of the British courts to considering excluded subject matter. The *Aerotel* appeal concerned a system and a method of making a telephone call from any available telephone station using a prepaid code.[8] An action for infringement was met with a counter-claim for revocation on the grounds that the invention was merely a method of doing business. Macrossan's invention related to an automated method of producing the necessary documents to incorporate a company.[9] This had been rejected by the Patent Office as unpatentable and the High Court agreed holding that it was as a method of performing a mental act by a computer.[10] The Court of Appeal similarly rejected Macrossan's appeal as a method of doing business and a claim to a computer program as such. Aerotel won, however, because the primary claim was to a new device while their second claim was to the use of the new device, and therefore not only to a method of doing business *as such*. In handing down this ruling the Court of Appeal sought to provide a 'definitive statement' on how the UK should approach the interpretation of Article 52.

11.8   The court began by distinguishing the class of excluded matter under Article 52 from the matter mentioned in Article 53. Article 52 deals with things that are not considered to be inventions, while Article 53 is concerned with exceptions to patentability. The importance of the distinction lies in the fact that exceptions should be construed narrowly,[11] but the same does not apply to non-inventions.[12] The correct approach towards the latter is to attempt to identify the underlying policy for each exclusion and to give effect to it through interpretation, although the court could find no single principle or rationale that unifies all of the examples in Article 52. Each must be considered on its own terms.[13]

Discussion point   For answer guidance visit www.oxfordtextbooks.co.uk/orc/macqueen2e/

What might be the various rationales that explain the inclusion of the specific examples in Article 52?

11.9   The approach in the UK historically has been to ask if the invention makes a 'technical contribution' to the state of the art—that is, to the sum total of human knowledge—and if so, it will be patentable so long as the contribution is not solely in the realm of excluded matter.[14] A technical contribution is one which produces a *technical effect*, and in most cases this means a real-world

---

[8] You can read Aerotel's claims here: http://v3.espacenet.com/textclam?DB=EPODOC&IDX=GB2171877&F=0& QPN=GB2171877

[9] You can read Macrossan's claims here: http://v3.espacenet.com/textclam?DB=EPODOC&IDX=GB2388937&F= 8&QPN=GB2388937

[10] [2006] EWHC 705 (Ch).

[11] See, eg, T19/90 HARVARD/Oncomouse [1990] OJEPO 376 and T356/93 PLANT GENETIC SYSTEMS/Glutamine Synthetase Inhibitors [1995] EPOR 357. Compare discussion at para 12.54ff.

[12] *Aerotel v Telco Holdings Ltd & Others* [2006] EWCA Civ 1371 para 12.

[13] For the impact on UK–IPO granting practice see Practice Notice (PO: Patents Act 1977: Patentable Subject Matter) (No 1) [2007] RPC 8 and Practice Notice (PO: Patents Act 1977: Patentable Subject Matter) (No 2) [2008] RPC 15. But for comment on a different approach in the EPO see, N Gardner and P England 'European Union: patents—exclusion from patentability' (2008) 30(1) EIPR N5-6.

[14] See *Merrill Lynch's Application* [1988] RPC 1, and also *Gale's Application* [1991] RPC 305 and *Fujitsu's Application* [1996] RPC 511. But see now Practice Note (PO: Patents Act 1977: Examining for Patentability) [2006] RPC 6.

change in the state, operation, or function of something tangible.[15] The problem is that the term *technical contribution* suffers from an 'inherent vagueness'[16], and its utility and limits were probably best summed up by Fox LJ in *Gale's Application*:

> 'If you look at the case law on the subject, both here and in Munich, you will find many references to "technical contribution", "technical result", and so on, being touchstones by which these cases are decided. The use of the word 'technical' as a short-hand expression in order to identify patentable subject-matter is often convenient. But it should be remembered that it was not used by the framers of the Patents Act 1977 or the European Patent Convention when they wanted to tell us what is or is not an 'invention'. In any case the word "technical" is not a solution. It is merely a restatement of the problem in different and more imprecise language. I am not claiming that it is wrong to decide cases with reference to the word "technical". It happens all the time. What I am saying is that it is not a panacea. It is a useful servant but a dangerous master.'

11.10   In fact, the need to find a *technical* contribution may have been down-graded by the Court of Appeal in *Aerotel*. The Court reviewed all of the existing UK and European Patent Office (EPO) rulings and opined that its ruling would be the 'definitive statement' on patentable subject matter. While confirming the authority of existing precedents,[17] the Court set about 'reformulating' the test to be applied into a four-step approach. This is:

(1)   properly construe the claim;
(2)   identify the actual contribution;
(3)   ask whether it falls solely within the excluded subject matter;
(4)   check whether the actual or alleged contribution is actually technical in nature.

The fourth criterion is merely a final check which should be deployed only when the application has passed the first three criteria.[18] The presence or absence of a technical effect is therefore only a subsidiary matter which speaks to patentability rather than exclusion.[19] This approach has been followed in various cases including *Astron Clinica Ltd and others v the Comptroller General of Patents*, where it was confirmed that the first three steps should answer whether the invention is excluded, with the fourth step being a final check.[20] However, since the ruling in *Aerotel* there has been some controversy over the exact implementation of the test, especially concerning the place of the fourth step. The court reviewed the *Aerotel* test in *Symbian Ltd's Application* and came to the conclusion that the four-step test encompasses all previously employed tests and the test is intended to be equivalent to the prior case law test of 'technical contribution'.[21] It did consider, however, that it may be necessary to fuse the third and the fourth step into a single step as it is not as important *when* the technical contribution is identified, as it is to consider whether the invention makes a relevant technical contribution to the art.[22] Most recently, Lord Walker noted the difference between the 'inventive concept' of a claimed invention and its 'technical contribution to the art' in *Generics (UK) Ltd & Others v H Lundbeck A/S*.[23] 'Inventive concept' is concerned with the identification of the core of the invention, that idea or principle that makes the invention inventive. The 'technical contribution to the art' is concerned with the evaluation of its inventive concept—what needs to be considered is how far forward has it carried the state of the art?[24]

---

[15] In this respect the UK broadly followed the EPO, see T208/84 VICOM/Computer-related inventions [1987] EPOR 74, but see further paras 12.94ff in Chapter 12.
[16] See *Aerotel*, n 12 above, para 124.   [17] See n 12 above.   [18] *Aerotel*, n 12 above, paras 46–47.
[19] See the ruling of the Hearing Officer in *John Lahiri Khan's Application* (BL O/356/06).
[20] *Astron Clinica Ltd and v the Comptroller General of Patents* [2008] EWHC 85, para 45.
[21] *Symbian Ltd's Application* [2008] EWCA Civ 1066, [2009] RPC 1
[22] *Symbian Ltd's Application* [2008] EWCA Civ 1066, [2009] RPC 1, at para 58   [23] [2009] UKHL 12.
[24] [2009] UKHL 12, para 30.

11.11   The UK–IPO has issued Practice Notices detailing the new approach to patentable subject matter and instructing patent examiners to follow them with immediate effect.[25] The first Notice from 2006 points out that construction of the claim is necessary to establish the nature of the monopoly, and it is the actual contribution to human knowledge in terms of the substance of the invention which is important and not the form of the claim. Thus, in *Macrossan* the fact that computer hardware elements formed part of the invention did not detract from the fact that the actual contribution was merely in the realm of a computer program and a method of doing business. The third criterion is the equivalent of the term 'as such' in Article 52 EPC. It means that an application is excluded from further consideration only if the subject matter falls wholly into one or more excluded category. If, when considering the test as a whole, a patent examiner believes that it would be fruitless to conduct a search then s/he can issue a report to this effect.[26] This Practice Note was amended on 7 February 2008 with regards to the permissible form of a claim[27] following the *Astron Clinica Ltd and others v The Comptroller General of Patents* judgment.[28] A claim to a computer program can be allowable 'if the claim reflects the features of the invention which would ensure the patentability of the method which the program is intended to carry out when it is run.' We discuss the implications of this in Chapter 12.

11.12   In *Aerotel* the Court of Appeal acknowledged the importance of decisions from the Boards of Appeal of the European Patent Office and that they have 'great persuasive authority' for the UK courts.[29] Notwithstanding, it did not follow the available rulings because it considered that the EPO jurisprudence is currently unstable. We explore this in the context of computer software inventions in the next chapter, but the Court did suggest that its different approach would probably not make much difference in practice.[30] The Court also looked beyond Europe to the United States and noted the contrasting approach to patentability where 'everything under the sun that is made by man' is patentable.[31] While this may overstate the position somewhat, it is clear that the American policy is to ensure that the categories of patentable invention are given wide scope.[32]

11.13   We have seen, however, that various examples are given in Europe of things that are not considered to be inventions and the Court of Appeal has indicated that the underlying rationales may be different depending on the example in question. Moreover, we find no real help from the *travaux préparatoires* of the European Patent Convention to assist us in understanding these exclusions.[33] We are left, then, to consider the existing case law on each example to appreciate the reasons for its exclusion from patent protection, and some additional help is provided by the EPC Guidelines for Examination.

---

[25] Practice Notice (PO: Patents Act 1977: Patentable Subject Matter) (No.1) [2007] RPC 8 and Practice Notice (PO: Patents Act 1977: Patentable Subject Matter) (No.2) [2008] RPC 15.

[26] Patents Act 1977, s 17(5).

[27] Amendment available here: http://www.ipo.gov.uk/pro-types/pro-patent/p-law/p-pn/p-pn-subjectmatter-20080207.htm

[28] *Astron Clinica Ltd and others v The Comptroller General of Patents* [2008] EWHC 85 (Pat).

[29] *Merrell Dow v Norton* [1996] RPC 76, per Lord Hoffmann at 82. See more recently, *Eli Lilly & Co v Human Genome Sciences Inc* [2010] EWCA Civ 33.

[30] But see T 154/04, *DUNS LICENSING ASSOCIATES*/Estimating Sales Activity OJ 2/2008, 46.

[31] Famously stated by the Supreme Court in *Diamond v Chakrabarty* (1980) 447 US 303, 100 S Ct 2204 in respect of the patentability of a man-made oil-eating bacterium.

[32] Confirmed by the Congress Committee Reports when patents laws were being re-codified in 1952: S Rep No 1979, 82d Cong, 2d Sess, 5 (1952); HR Rep No 1923, 82d Cong, 2d Sess, 6 (1952).

[33] J Pila, 'Art 52(2) of the Convention on the Grant of European Patents: What did the Framers Intend? A study of the Travaux Preparatoires (2005) 36 IIC 755 and ED Ventose, 'In the Footsteps of the Framers of the European Patent Convention: Examining the Travaux Preparatoires' (2009) 31(7) EIPR 353.

11.14 The Guidelines provide, for example, that the list of things which are not regarded as inventions includes items which are either too abstract (such as a discovery or scientific method) and/or which are non-technical (such as aesthetic creations). An invention can be in any field of technology but it must be concrete and have technical character.[34] Let us consider each of the categories of exclusion in turn.

Discoveries, scientific theories and mathematical methods

11.15 As mentioned, this category is thought to contain items which are too abstract or indistinct to be the proper subject of patent protection. The most interesting example is, however, discoveries. Anton van Leeuwenhoek of Holland (1632–1723) is credited as being the father of microscopy. His invention of new methods to grind and polish lenses led him to be the first person to see and describe bacteria. Clearly, he did not invent those bacteria but merely discovered them using an invention. Conversely, discoveries often lead to inventions. For example, Sir Alexander Fleming (1881–1955) was working in 1928 on colonies of the bacterium Staphylococcus Aureus, which can be dangerous to humans, when a batch accidentally became contaminated by a mould that killed off the bacterium. This was penicillin—the first antibiotic—and further work by Fleming and others led to production of penicillin in large, high quality doses. A patent was eventually granted in 1948 for a method of mass production of penicillin.[35]

Exercise

Fleming did not attempt to patent penicillin itself, but would he have been successful if he had tried? Do you think that the absence of a patent on the product contributed to the fact that it took 20 years to go from discovery to mass production?

11.16 One of the problems that has been thrown up for the biotechnology industry has been the objection that attempts to patent biotechnological products is nothing more than an attempt to patent a living thing, that is, something already pre-existing in nature and so merely a discovery. We explore the contours of these arguments in the next chapter, but the reality is that many biotechnology products are patented. Where then do we draw a line between a discovery and an invention? The answer is in the concept of *technical effect* which we have considered above. If human intervention can bring about a specific technical effect or application of discovery then the embodiment of that technical effect or application can be the subject of a patent. Consider the EPO Guidelines:

> 'If a new property of a known material or article is found out, that is mere discovery and unpatentable because discovery as such has no technical effect and is therefore not an invention within the meaning of Article 52(1). If, however, that property is put to practical use, then this constitutes an invention which may be patentable. For example, the discovery that a particular known material is able to withstand mechanical shock would not be patentable, but a railway sleeper made from that material could well be patentable.'[36]

---

[34] EPO Guidelines for Examination, Part C, Chapter IV, para 2.1.
[35] W Kingston, 'Antibiotics, Invention and Innovation' (2000) 29(6) Research Policy 679–710.
[36] Guidelines, Part C, Chapter IV, para 2.3.1.

11.17   Similarly, merely to find a naturally occurring substance is a pure discovery, but if you are able to put it to some tangible use, for example, as an antibiotic, then it may be patentable in respect of this particular technical effect. An invention requires some evidence of human ingenuity in realising a particular use for a discovery[37] or in making it available to the public in a form which previously it was not. An example of this last point is the case of *Howard Florey/Relaxin* before the Opposition Division of the EPO.[38] The patent in suit concerned a naturally occurring protein produced by women during childbirth to ease the passage of the child. Howard Florey had isolated and determined the chemical structure of the substance and was then able to produce it in a form which made it a marketable product, but the objection was that this remained a discovery. The Opposition Division, however, ruled otherwise holding that a newly isolated and characterised substance was not a mere discovery, but rather an industrially applicable technical solution to a pre-existing technical problem. A further relevant point in respect of a claim in the patent to the gene sequence itself was the fact that the form of the sequence claimed by the patentee was 'purer' than that found in nature and so sufficiently distinct to be patentable. These concepts are now embodied in the Biotechnology Directive which provides that '[a]n element isolated from the human body or otherwise produced by means of a technical process, including the sequence or partial sequence of a gene, may constitute a patentable invention, even if the structure of that element is identical to that of a natural element.'[39] Note, in particular, that such a patent would *not* give a patentee any claim over naturally occurring elements *within* the human body.

All of this has been confirmed by the House of Lords in *Kirin-Amgen v Hoechst Marion Roussel*[40] which summed up the current position thus:

(1) To find a new substance or micro-organism in nature is a discovery and not an invention;

(2) but if it is necessary to isolate and extract the substance—as will almost always be the case—then the relevant process, as well as the material obtained by this process, could both be patentable;

(3) furthermore, if the material had no previously recognised existence, and can be adequately identified without reference to the process by which it is obtained, then it may be patentable per se.

11.18   We see, then, that it is possible through human endeavour to take something from an excluded category such as discovery and make it an invention and so patentable. The same is true with respect to the other two exclusions in this category when we go from the abstract to the tangible. Thus, while a scientific theory about a fifth dimension is just an example of an abstract concept and unpatentable, the application of that theory to produce a device that could dematerialise and re-materialise objects through space would be patentable, as would any related processes.[41] Similarly, a mathematical method in itself is purely intellectual and intangible,

[37] The Court of Appeal in *Genentech Inc's Patent* [1989] RPC 147 confirmed that a claim to the practical application of a discovery did not related to the discovery as such.

[38] T741/91 *HOWARD FLOREY/Relaxin* [1995] EPOR 541.   [39] Art 5(2) of the Biotechnology Directive, see n 5 above.

[40] [2005] RPC 9. The case is also known as *Kirin-Amgen Inc v Transkaryotic Therapies Inc (No 2)*.

[41] EPO Guidelines, n 34 above, para 2.3.2.

for example, a shortcut method of long division, but a device which deploys this method may itself be patentable.[42] The distinction was considered by the EPO Technical Board of Appeal in *VICOM/Computer-related invention*[43] which related to an invention involving a mathematical method applied to data which resulted in an enhanced digital image on a computer. The core question was, which aspects of this invention were patentable and where should the line be drawn between a mathematical method *as such* and an invention which was an application of such a method? The Board defined 'mathematical method' as something which is carried out on numbers and which produces a result in numerical form, that is, it remains in an abstract form. On this interpretation the Board rejected claims to a means of filtering data digitally on a conventional computer as they involved processes indistinguishable from a mathematical method. Conversely, the Board upheld claims to the method of using the mathematical method to process images because the output of the method was a real world technical effect on the quality of the images.

Aesthetic creations

11.19   Examples of aesthetic creations which are excluded include literary, dramatic, musical and artistic works.[44] This should sound familiar as the realm of protection offered primarily by copyright. We have seen in the previous chapter how the international history of intellectual property protection has always drawn a division between industrial property on the one hand (Paris Convention 1883) and copyright and its related rights (Berne Convention 1886) on the other. The principal reason why aesthetic creations are excluded is because they are not technical in nature and do not, normally, represent a technical contribution to our experiences. Their contribution lies elsewhere and their appreciation is usually entirely subjective. This is not to say that inventions cannot have aesthetic features, merely that those features cannot form the basis of patent protection if their sole contribution is in the realm of aesthetics. If, however, an aesthetic feature produces a de facto technical effect, then it may be patentable. The classic example that is cited in this regard is *ITS Rubber Ltd's Application*,[45] in which the main claim simply read:

> '1. A squash ball having a surface of a blue colour.'

What possible difference could colour make to the functioning of a squash ball? Well, the claim was upheld on evidence that the particular colour chosen improved visibility of the ball during play. The contribution was therefore not merely aesthetic.[46] Note too that technical means which produce an aesthetic effect can be patentable even if the aesthetic effect itself cannot be. For example, a machine may be set to produce a beautiful wood carving (not patentable in itself) but the new machine or the technical process used to program may be patentable. Similarly, a new printing technique to reproduce designs on fabric could be protected while the designs themselves would fall to another domain of intellectual property law. As always, the intellectual property office will be concerned not with the form of a claim but with the question of whether the essential nature of the invention in solely aesthetic or contains technical features.

---

[42] ibid, para 2.3.3.   [43] T208/84 [1987] OJEPO 14.   [44] See the Patents Act 1977, s 1(2)(b).
[45] [1979] RPC 318.   [46] EPO Guidelines, n 34 above, para 2.3.4.

Schemes, rules and methods for performing mental acts, playing games or doing business, and programs for computers

11.20   Schemes, rules, and methods for performing mental acts, playing games or doing business are similarly excluded in the first instance because of their abstract or intellectual character.[47] Much has been made in recent years, however, of the patentability of computer programs in Europe with a raft of conflicting EPO decisions and even a failed attempt to harmonise the position in a European Directive.[48] The EPO Guidelines now make it clear, for example, that if a claim in a patent application 'specifies computers, computer networks or other conventional programmable apparatus, or a program therefor, for carrying out at least some steps of a scheme', it is to be examined as a 'computer-implemented invention',[49] therefore as a *sui generic* case. And yet, despite clarification and decades of jurisprudence, as at 30 November 2009 a referral to the Enlarged Board of Appeal on patenting software was pending.[50] For all of these reasons we pay particularly close attention to computer and software-implemented inventions in Chapter 12. We do no more here than lay out the general principles for exclusion.

Mental acts

11.21   Examples of methods of performing mental acts include schemes for doing arithmetic, learning to read or speaking a new language. Similarly, a claim which merely lays out the steps for decision-making or the performance of a particular task will be rejected.

■ *Halliburton Energy Services v Smith International (North Sea) Ltd* [2006] RPC 2

This dispute before the Patent Court related to two patents concerning various features of drill bits for drilling in rock. In particular, two claims related to 'a method of designing a roller cone bit' comprising steps which involve calculating measurements and making adjustments to parameters to achieve optimal effectiveness of the bit. Pumfrey J held that these claims were 'directed purely to the intellectual content of the design process and the criteria according to which decisions on the way to a design are made.' Accordingly, as framed, these were merely claims to a method for performing a mental act and would be excluded or require redrafting to take them outside the excluded category.[51]

---

[47] EPO Guidelines, n 34 above, para 2.3.5.

[48] Commission Proposal on the patentability of computer-implemented inventions COM (2002) 92 final, 20 February 2002.

[49] EPO Guidelines, n 34 above, and para 2.3.6.

[50] Case G3/08: Referral under Art.112(1)(b) EPC by the President of the EPO (Patentability of programs for computers) to the Enlarged Board of Appeal (22 October 2008).

[51] Note, the objection here was to the form of the claims not to the substance of the invention which could have industrial utility, see Pumfrey J at para 218. Note also that part of this case was appealed to the Court of Appeal for lack of sufficiency and we discuss this at para 11.203.

Question

Is a method of performing a mental act still excluded if it is performed by a computer rather than a human being?

■ *Fujitsu Ltd's Application* [1997] RPC 608

Applicants applied for a UK patent claiming priority from an earlier Japanese application in respect of an invention for a 'Method and Apparatus for creating synthetic crystal structure images'. The apparatus was a conventional computer programmed to allow an operator to select parameters, such as atoms or lattice vectors, to create pictorial representations of how the combined chosen structures would look. A Principal Examiner rejected the application, however, stating that it related both to a method for performing a mental act and to a program for a computer. The Court of Appeal similarly rejected the appeal stating that it is a question of fact whether a claim to an invention is to anything more than disqualified matter. It was relevant for the court that a significant amount of (human) input from an operator was required in order to carry out the task. Methods of solving a problem or providing advice remain examples of excluded methods of performing a mental act even if performed by a computer.[52]

11.22 This last point was doubted by the Court of Appeal in *Aerotel/Macrossan* but the comment was obiter and its authority remains in doubt.[53] This question was later answered in a new Practice Notice on Patentability of computer programs. The Notice followed the judgment of the Court of Appeal in *Symbian Ltd's Application*.[54] This case noted that one effect of the computer program exclusion is to prevent other excluded material becoming patentable merely by use of a computer in its implementation. The 'computerisation' of what would be a pure mental act if done without the aid of a computer would be objected to by examiners on the grounds of it being a mental act and a computer program as such.[55]

11.23 The EPO itself tends to draw a distinction between mental acts which human beings can perform and automated acts which go beyond human capacity, for example, in terms of the alacrity or difficulty of the task.[56] Thus, method claims were allowed in *IBM/Editable document form*[57] for a method for maintaining formats of documents transferred between word processors, and in *IBM/Rotating Displayed Objects*[58] for a method ensuring high precision rotation and manipulation of graphic images on screen. In other cases, however, text manipulation inventions have been denied protection for lack of technical contribution.[59] For example, the Technical Board of Appeal in *IBM/Document abstracting and retrieval*[60] rejected a computer system for creating and

[52] See also *Gale's Application*, para 11.32 below.

[53] '…we are doubtful as to whether the exclusion extends to electronic means of doing what could otherwise have been done mentally', per Jacob LJ, *Aerotel*, n 12 above, para 62.

[54] [2008] EWCA Civ 1066.

[55] UK Intellectual Property Office, Practice Notice: Patents Act 1977: Patentability of Computer Programs (2008), [2009] Bus LR 625; also available here: http://www.ipo.gov.uk/pro-types/pro-patent/p-law/p-pn/p-pn-computer.htm.

[56] See *Research in Motion UK Ltd v Inpro Licensing SARL* [2006] RPC 20 at para 186 where Pumfrey J found technical effect in 'computers running faster and transmitting information more efficiently…'. On appeal: [2007] EWCA Civ 51 (although the point here made at first instance was not contested).

[57] T110/90 [1995] EPOR 185.

[58] T59/93, unreported, available on the EPO website at: http://legal.european-patent-office.org/dg3/pdf/t930059eu1.pdf

[59] T38/86 *IBM/Text clarity processing* [1990] EPOR 606.   [60] T22/85 [1990] EPOR 98.

storing abstracts obtained from archives, inter alia, because the claims merely described an automated means of performing a task which could be carried out manually. It was not enough that the task was performed by technical means, that is, through a computer, the invention itself must make a technical contribution beyond that which can be done by humans.

Playing games

11.24   The rules on patentability of games were shaken up by the decision in *Shopalotto.com Ltd's Application*.[61] Strangely, the position had remained unchanged since an Official Ruling in 1926[62] despite the sweeping changes brought in by the Patents Acts of 1949 and 1977, not to mention innumerable revisions in the meantime.

■ *Shopalotto.com Ltd's Application* [2006] RPC 7

This was an appeal against a decision of the Deputy Director of the Patent Office that computer apparatus configured to provide a lottery playable via the Internet was unpatentable under s 1(2) of the Patents Act 1977. The appellant argued that he should benefit from the Official Ruling on board games handed down in 1926 and based on interpretation of the definition of an invention contained in s 93 of the Patents and Designs Acts 1907 and 1919. This was to the effect that board games are eligible for a patent if they involve apparatus for playing a game which include one or more playing pieces and a marked board together with instructions on how the game is played. The appellant argued that this should be applied by analogy to his online game. Pumfrey J made the powerful point that the 1926 Ruling cannot serve as a guide to the 1977 Act in light of the European Patent Convention (1973). The patentability of games should be assessed in the same manner as all other potential excluded categories, and a claim which falls wholly into an established category should be excluded. Moreover, in the instant case the claimed invention was, in effect, to a general purpose computer providing a web server which makes no original contribution to the art.

11.25   The UK–IPO has since issued a Practice Notice on patentability of games.[63] This follows the judgment in *Shopalotto* and confirms that the Official Ruling from 1926 will no longer be used.[64]

Methods of doing business

11.26   Innovative ways of tackling everyday business problems are not normally patentable. These include new methods of bar-coding banking materials to improve customer services,[65] display mechanisms on buses to let customers know if they are picking up or dropping off,[66] coding mechanisms to protect customers' identity,[67] a scheme to allow prisoners to trade sentence time for corporal punishment,[68] and a method to facilitate introductions between people wear-

---

[61] [2006] RPC 7.   [62] Official Ruling 1926(A), (1926) 43 RPC Appendix, p i.

[63] Practice Notice 'Patents Act 1977: Patentability of games' [2006] RPC 8, as amended in light of the judgment in *Aerotel/Macrossan*. The current version is available here: http://www.ipo.gov.uk/pro-types/pro-patent/p-law/p-pn/p-pn-games.htm

[64] See too *IGT's Applications* [2007] EWHC 1341 (Ch).

[65] *Good News Pty Ltd's Application* (Patent Office Hearing Officer: BL O/124/84).

[66] *Crawford v Jones* [2005] EWHC 2417.

[67] *Peter Williams' Application* (IPO Hearing Officer: BL O/038/07).

[68] *Melia's Application* (Patent Office Hearing officer: BL O/153/92).

ing mutually recognisable artefacts, such as rings.[69] Note how under the last two examples, 'business' enjoys a wide interpretation in law and does not necessarily have to imply commercial interests.

11.27   The mantra remains the same, however: does the invention solve a technical problem rather than merely tackle a business problem?

11.28   It was previously thought that the exclusion of a method of doing business referred to the conduct of an entire business endeavour,[70] but this has been rejected by the Court of Appeal in *AEROTEL/Macrossan* where it was held that there is no reason for such a narrow interpretation and that business methods should not be restricted to abstract matters or completed transactions. Double-entry bookkeeping is neither abstract nor an output of a business transaction, but it remains a method of doing business.[71] On this basis, then, the court rejected Macrossan's claim for an automatic method of providing the necessary documents to incorporate a company because this method was for the essence of the business itself, that is, to provide advice and documentation.

11.29   As we have seen elsewhere, the mere automation of a process or operation does not change its essential character. Thus in *Merrill Lynch's Application*[72] a known computer system was programmed in known computer language to provide a data-processing-based system for implementing an automated trading market for securities. The Court of Appeal held that if there was any contribution to human knowledge it was in the production of a trading system, that is, a method of doing business. Moreover, the fact that this may be an improvement on previous systems is irrelevant: 'the prohibition in section 1(2)(c) is generic; qualitative considerations do not enter into the matter.'

11.30   Methods of doing business which solve technical problems can be patentable. This was confirmed by the European Patent Office in *PENSION BENEFIT SYSTEMS/Controlling pension benefits systems*[73] which related to a computer system that performed a number of pension-related tasks, including calculations, speculation, and the control of the benefit system to ensure periodic payments to subscribers. Despite rejecting this particular appeal for want of technical character, the Technical Board of Appeal confirmed that a method claim that relates to a method of doing business can be patentable so long as it is technical, and that apparatus claims, even if they are programmed to function in a business environment, cannot be excluded because Article 52 EPC does not mention apparatus. A caveat to add to this is that it is dangerous to attempt to dress up a business method claim as an apparatus claim because the task of the patent offices and the courts is to examine the substance not for the form of the claim. Moreover, an attempt to get around a technical problem by modifying a business method—rather than by solving the problem by technical means—is insufficient to bring technical character to an invention.[74]

11.31   Many business method claims are linked to computer-implemented inventions, as the above example demonstrates. Because of this, we continue a fuller discussion of this category of exclusion at para 12.106ff.[75]

---

[69] *John Lahiri Khan's Appn* (Patent Office Hearing Officer: BL O/356/06).
[70] *Macrossan's Patent Application* [2006] EWHC 705.
[71] *Aerotel*, n 12 above, paras 69–70, citing the French and German texts of the EPC in support of this interpretation.
[72] [1988] RPC 1   [73] [2002] EPOR 52.   [74] See T258/03 *HITACHI/Auction method* [2004] 12 OJEPO 575.
[75] The Court of Appeal confirmed in *Bi Lothian Ltd's Application* [2009] RPC 1 that a business method implemented on a 'conventional computer system' would be excluded as a pure business method.

The UK–IPO Manual points out that many business arrangements implemented over the Internet have been refused protection. These include:

- a method for offering personalised financial products over the Internet,[76]
- a method of creating and distributing advertising material,[77]
- a system to allow a client to monitor progress made on a building site via the Internet,[78]
- a system for ordering food over the Internet.[79]

It seems clear that merely providing a service or assistance over the Internet will not be enough on its own to merit patent protection, but each innovation must be considered on its own merit to determine if it displays the necessary *technical effect*.

11.32   The UK–IPO has issued a Practice Notice in response to the increased number of applications relating to business method patents in recent years.[80] This provides a mechanism to invite an applicant to a hearing earlier in the application process than normal. If the application is refused it will be referred immediately to a Hearing Officer for a ruling on patentability and the applicant will be given an opportunity for an oral hearing. All other procedures are suspended at this time until the Hearing Officer gives a ruling. This need not be lengthy since the UK–IPO has articulated many times the reasons for refusal in such cases.[81] The applicant will be provided with a brief report that is intelligible and adequately explains the reasons for refusal[82] by reference to previous decisions. This procedure is designed to cut down lengthy and costly correspondence on matters which should be straightforward to settle.

Computer programs

■ *Gale's Application* [1991] RPC 305

The applicant discovered a means of calculating a square root with the assistance of a computer and modified a silicon chip (ROM) to perform this function. He claimed the ROM chip with its particular circuitry embodying the instructions. The examiner objected that this was no more than a computer program and the case eventually made its way to the Court of Appeal. It was held that instructions to be used for the operation of a computer were not patentable. Physical alterations to the chip itself were immaterial as mere conventional means to allow the chip to perform its function—which was the ordinary running of a computer. The appeal was denied.

11.33   We have already pointed out at several junctures that patents for computer programs and computer-implemented inventions have received special attention in recent years. The current approach to their patentability is probably best summed up by Pumfrey J in *Shopalotto.com's Application*:

'The real question is whether there is a *relevant* technical effect, or, more crudely, whether there is enough technical effect: is there a technical effect over and above that to be expected from the mere loading of a program into a computer? From this sort of consideration there has developed an approach

---

[76] *Accucard's Application* (BL O/145/03).   [77] *Adgistics Ltd's Application* (BLO/297/04).

[78] *Ashizawa's Application* (BL O/201/03).   [79] *Fujitsu'sApplication* (BL O/121/04).

[80] UK–IPO Practice Notice, 'Patent applications relating to methods of doing business', 24 November 2004, as amended, available here: http://www.ipo.gov.uk/pro-types/pro-patent/p-law/p-pn/p-pn-businessmethod.htm

[81] See Practice Notice 'Patents Act 1977: Interpreting section 1(2)' [2002] RPC 40. The Practice Notice Annex also gives some examples, available here: http://www.ipo.gov.uk/pro-types/pro-patent/p-law/p-pn/p-pn-businessmethod/p-pn-businessmethod-annex.htm

[82] See House of Lords in *South Bucks District Council and Another v Porter (No 2)* [2004] UKHL 33.

that I consider to be well established on the authorities, which is to take the claimed programmed computer, and ask what it contributes to the art over and above the fact that it covers a programmed computer. If there is a contribution outside the list of excluded matter, then the invention is patentable, but if the only contribution to the art lies in excluded subject matter, it is not patentable.'[83]

11.34   This is subject to the approach now laid down by the Court of Appeal in *AEROTEL/Macrossan*, although it has been emphasised that this should not make much practical difference. It is likely to mean, however, that claims to programs themselves, even if on a carrier, will fail at the third hurdle of the *Aerotel* test as specifically excluded matter. Macrossan's application failed because it was held that his contribution was the provision of a computer program which could be used to carry out his method of providing documentation. So the essence of the claim was entirely to excluded matter.[84]

11.35   A decision of the UK–IPO confirmed this and it was also one of the first decisions to apply the Court of Appeal's four-point test. In *Nintendo Co Ltd's Application*[85] the application concerned a game machine for a virtual kart race. The advance with this game lay in the fact that the computer would take over when a player crashed and run a sequence which ensured a smooth transition of the virtual vehicle back onto the track and facing in the correct direction. Existing machines did not do this. The Examiner took the view, however, that the contribution was concerned with moving the player from one game state to another and that this was executed wholly by computer program elements and therefore excluded from protection. There was accordingly no need to consider the fourth element of the test as to technical effect.[86]

11.36   The European Patent Office is slightly more cavalier in these matters. It maintains[87] that while 'programs for computers' are excluded as such, if the claimed subject matter has a technical character this will be sufficient to allow patentability. And so, '…if a computer program is capable of bringing about, when running on a computer, a further technical effect going beyond…normal physical effects, it is not excluded from patentability…' This is so even if the program itself is claimed or if it is claimed in tandem with its carrier.[88] This comes very close to saying that computer programs per se are patentable. It is almost a reversal of the approach in the United Kingdom which is concerned to know if the kernel of the invention falls wholly into a category of excluded matter. The EPO made clear in *Duns Licensing*[89] that it did not approve of the approach taken in the UK.

Discussion point   For answer guidance visit www.oxfordtextbooks.co.uk/orc/macqueen2e/

What is the underlying rationale for excluding computer programs in Europe especially when they are patentable in most other legal systems? Does the role of copyright in software protection make a difference? Can this approach be sustained?

11.37   Despite widespread patenting of inventions related to computer software throughout Europe, the *Gowers Review of Intellectual Property* in December 2006 recommended that the UK should

---

[83] *Shopalotto*, n 6 above, para 9.   [84] *Aerotel*, n 12 above, paras 73–4.   [85] BL O/377/06.
[86] See also *Astron Clinica and others v The Comptroller General of Patents* [2008] EWHC 85 (Pat).
[87] EPO Guidelines, n 34 above, para 2.3.6.
[88] T935/97 *IBM/Computer Programs* [1999] EPOR 301 and T1173/97 *IBM/Computer Programs* [2000] EPOR 219.
[89] *DUNS LICENSING ASSOCIATES/Estimating Sales activity* [2007] EPOR 38.

maintain its policy of not extending patent rights beyond their current limits. The review found mixed evidence of the success of 'pure' software patents, particularly from the US where the evidence actually seems to indicate that the software industry grew exponentially in the *absence* of patent protection. Other evidence suggests that where protection is available it is used negatively to restrict competitors rather than positively to encourage further innovation.[90]

11.38   Recently, the patentability of computer programs has been clarified in *Symbian Ltd's Application*, in which the Court of Appeal tried to find a way between the previous Court of Appeal authorities and the approach taken by the EPO. The main issue the court clarified was that the technical contribution of the invention to the state of the art must be considered. Whether this is done during the third or the fourth step of the test is less important. This ruling has led to a change in the UK–IPO Practice Notice for Patentable Subject Matter,[91] confirming that the four-step test will continue to be used. When dealing with computer programs, it must be considered what the program does as a matter of practical reality. Where a program results in a computer running faster or more reliably, it may be considered to provide a technical contribution even if the invention solely addresses a problem in the programming.[92] It is interesting that the UK Practice Notice confirms a point of divergence with the EPO. It is not sufficient merely to include claims to computer hardware to avoid the exclusion.

Presentations of information

11.39   The concern of this exclusion is the *content* of information. No claim will be sustained if it relates solely to the expression of information or the conveyance of meaning or decisions where and how to display information.[93] Patent law is not in the business of giving protection to pretty pictures, TV images, radio signals, books, sounds, diagrams, codes or symbols which derive their value from the meaning they convey to human beings. Thus in *Townsend's Patent Application*[94] the problem to be solved was the thorny issue of how to ensure fair distribution of the treats found behind the doors on an advent calendar and to prevent the early-riser in the family from scoffing the lot! Mr Townsend's solution was to put markings on the doors to indicate the turn of each user to open a door. He argued that this was not a presentation of information because the correct interpretation of the exclusion only covered *expression* of information and not *provision* of information, that is, it was restricted to *how* information is conveyed and not *what* is conveyed. It is the difference between the advent calendar being designed in the shape of a sleigh (how) and stating 'three more days to Christmas' (what). Laddie J disagreed and held that the exclusion covers both instances of presenting information on an ordinary interpretation of the provision. The calendar was refused protection.

11.40   This means that any method or means of conveying information which is characterised only by the content of the information will be excluded. It does not matter that some physical device or apparatus is used to convey the information nor that such a device or apparatus can be moved around.

---

[90] *Gowers Review of Intellectual Property* (HM Treasury, 2006), para 4.114, available here: http://webarchive.nationalarchives.gov.uk/+/http://www.hm-treasury.gov.uk/d/pbr06_gowers_report_755.pdf

[91] Practice Notice (PO: Patents Act 1977: Patentability of computer programs) [2009] Bus LR 625.

[92] ibid, para 5

[93] *Autonomy Corp Ltd v Comptroller General of Patents, Trade Marks and Designs* [2008] EWHC 146 (Pat).

[94] [2004] EWHC 482 (Pat).

■ *Crawford v Jones* [2005] EWHC 2417 (Pat)

The application related to a display system for buses to indicate to passengers whether the bus was in picking-up or setting-down only mode. The claims were to Boarding and Exit Bus Indicators, being visual or audible apparatus. Notwithstanding, the application was refused, inter alia, as solely a method of presentation of information. The only advance in the art was the nature of the information displayed on the front of the bus but this was not of a technical nature.

11.41　The implication of a decision like *Crawford* is that if a presentation of information *is* of a technical nature then it might be patentable, and this is indeed true. As we now know, solving a pre-existing problem by technical means is the way to make a technical contribution. In *Cooper's Application*[95] the problem was how to fold a newspaper without hindering reading, and the successful invention was to arrange the layout of text to allow this. Similarly, in *Fishburn's Application*[96] the particular arrangement of text on a ticket meant that information was not lost when the ticket was torn and the patent was upheld.

11.42　The European Patent Office Guidelines make it clear that if the presentation of information has new technical features then there could be patentable subject matter in the information carrier, or in the process or apparatus for presenting the information, or even in the manner of presentation itself.[97] Examples include a communication system using a particular code to represent characters (eg pulse code) or a gramophone record having a particular groove to allow stereo recordings. Put differently, an invention can function by presenting information and still be patentable so long as the sum and substance of that invention is not only found in the presentation of the information.

11.43　The general European approach is laid out in the decision of the Technical Board of Appeal in *KONINKLIJKE PHILIPS ELECTRONICS/Picture retrieval system*.[98] The invention related to a system of picture storage and retrieval and included a claim to a record carrier which provided recorded picture data to any part of the system and consisted of a picture access data structure which controlled the operation of the retrieval device. The data structure was the novel part of the invention but the claim to its record carrier was refused as a means of presenting information. The Technical Board of Appeal upheld the appeal against this, however, and found that the data structure provided the necessary technical nature to the invention. Moreover, it sought to draw a distinction between two types of information: cognitive data and functional data. In doing so it relied on an earlier decision of the Board in *BBC/Colour Television Signal*[99] which distinguished between the example of a TV signal solely characterised by the information per se, for example, the pictures and sound, and a TV signal which is defined in terms of the TV system through which it is transmitted. Both transmit (or present) data, but the former is cognitive data which convey meaning to human beings, while the latter is functional/technical data where meaning in a human sense is irrelevant. As the Board said 'information must not be confused with meaning'. The exclusion is concerned with subject matter which merely conveys cognitive or aesthetic content directly to a human.[100] The instant invention was patentable because the record carrier was concerned with functional data and the operation of a system which produced a new technical effect.

[95]　19 RPC 351.　　[96]　57 RPC 245.　　[97]　EPO Guidelines, n 34 above, para 2.3.7.
[98]　T1194/97 [2000] OJEPO 525, [2001] EPOR 25.　　[99]　T163/85 [1990] OJEPO 379.
[100]　See T603/89, *MARKER/Beattie* (1992) OJEPO 230 (visible marking of musical keys).

Exercise

This decision also contains an explanation of the rationale for this particular exclusion. Look this up and then consider it against all of the other possible rationales for the exclusions in Article 52 EPC.

Key points on exclusions under Article 52

- It is essential to read the provisions of the law carefully. If we look back at Article 52(2) it states: 'The following *in particular* shall not be regarded as inventions...'[101] and Article 52(3) states: 'The provisions of paragraph 2 shall exclude patentability of the subject-matter or activities referred to in that provision only to the extent to which a European patent application or European patent relates to such subject-matter or activities *as such*.' [emphasis added]

- This means that the list of exclusions is *non-exhaustive*, and indeed in the UK the Secretary of State has the power to expand it (s. 1(5) of the Patents Act 1977)

- The *as such* qualification is extremely important. It means that only claims which fall squarely within a category of excluded matter will be struck down. Inventions which straddle patentable and non-patentable matter can survive if the technical features meet the other criteria for patentability.

11.44   There is one example of the courts excluding matter from protection for something which is not in Article 52 EPC/section 1(2) of the Patents Act 1977. In *Lux Traffic Controls Ltd v Pike Signals Ltd and Faronwise Ltd*[102] the invention related to apparatus to control traffic through a system that detected non-motion in vehicles and responded by holding the traffic lights to allow drivers more time. Although the court allowed the apparatus claims, Aldous J had this to say:

> '...s.1(2) of the Act comprises a non-exhaustive catalogue of matters or things which are not patentable. Although not specifically mentioned, I believe a method of controlling traffic as such is not patentable, whether or not it can be said to be a scheme for doing business. The field expressly excluded by the section concerns mere ideas not normally thought to be the proper subject for patents which are concerned with manufacturing.'

11.45   This may do no more than express the common rationale underpinning many of the exclusions that abstracts, such as ideas, are not a suitable case for patenting. By the same token, it demonstrates that the categories of exclusions are not closed and policy in the future may expand the list of non-inventions. Legislative changes would, however, require to be initiated by the Secretary of State and laid before both House of Parliament for approval.

---

[101] The equivalent provision in s 1(2) of the Patents Act 1977 states: 'It is hereby declared that the following (*among other things*) are not inventions...'
[102] [1993] RPC 107.

Exceptions to patentability

11.46   Let us turn now to the exceptions to patentability contained in Article 53 EPC 2000 and reproduced in section 1(3) and (4) and Schedule A2 of the Patents Act 1977.

> '**Article 53**
>
> European patents shall not be granted in respect of:
> (a)   inventions the commercial exploitation of which would be contrary to 'ordre public' or morality; such exploitation shall not be deemed to be so contrary merely because it is prohibited by law or regulation in some or all of the Contracting States;
> (b)   plant or animal varieties or essentially biological processes for the production of plants or animals; this provision shall not apply to microbiological processes or the products thereof;
> (c)   methods for treatment of the human or animal body by surgery or therapy and diagnostic methods practised on the human or animal body; this provision shall not apply to products, in particular substances or compositions, for use in any of these methods.'

Morality, *ordre public* and plant and animal varieties

11.47   It has sometimes been claimed that morality has nothing to do with patent law, but this is clearly nonsense.[103] The decision whether or not to grant a patent is not some mechanistic process which merely involves a checklist of technical details. Rather, it entails many nuanced considerations and value judgments on whether the numerous criteria for patentability have been met. The entire intellectual property system is based on fundamental notions of merit and justice concerning the appropriateness or otherwise of granting protection in the form of a monopoly. This is what the morality provision in patent law is about.[104]

11.48   There is, however, a lot of confusion about the role and remit of the morality provision which has been fuelled in recent years by the advent of biotechnology patents. Indeed the provision had rarely been invoked before the arrival of this technology but a few decades on we have a rich literature on the topic, a series of EPO rulings and even a harmonising European Biotechnology Directive. We discuss the specifics of biotechnology in our next chapter. For now, we outline the nature of the morality provision and how it has been interpreted to date.[105]

11.49   EPC 2000 revised the text of Article 53 to bring it into line with Article 27(2) of TRIPS.[106] Previously, the provisions concerned 'inventions the publication or exploitation of which would be contrary to *ordre public* or morality'. Now the concern is with the commercial exploitation of the invention. It is arguable that much of the confusion which has surrounded the interpretation of these provisions has stemmed from a lack of clarity about the purpose of the law as well as its limits. The purpose of the law has been stated in the EPO Guidelines to be: 'to exclude from protection inventions likely to induce riot or public disorder, or to lead to criminal or other generally offensive behaviour.'[107] But the denial of a patent cannot prevent the use of an

---

[103]   We will not name the guilty; they know who they are.

[104]   For a good analysis, see L Bently & B Sherman, 'The Ethics of Patenting: Towards a Transgenic Patent System' (1995) 3 Medical LR 275.

[105]   See, generally, O Mills, *Biotechnological Inventions: Moral Restraints and Patent Law* (2005).

[106]   Art 27 TRIPS: 'Members may exclude from patentability inventions, the prevention within their territory of the commercial exploitation of which is necessary to protect *ordre public* or morality, including to protect human, animal or plant life or health or to avoid serious prejudice to the environment, provided that such exclusion is not made merely because the exploitation is prohibited by their law.'

[107]   EPO Guidelines, n 34 above, IV, para 4.1

Petroleum's Application[147] it was stated that the involvement of a surgeon necessarily meant that the procedure was surgical in nature; by the same token, it does not follow that the absence of a surgeon means that a method is not surgical if it still requires a degree of skill in its execution, for example by a nurse.[148]

 Question

Do you think that the work of tattoo or piercing artists would count as 'surgery' under the law?

11.67   The jurisprudence of the EPO has been in flux in recent years and we welcome a recent Enlarged Board of Appeal decision from February 2010 which seeks to clarify matters. Part of the problem lay is previous rulings which cast some doubt on the status of cosmetic interventions and indeed on the surgical exclusion generally. For example, in *GENERAL HOSPITAL/Hair removal method*[149] the invention concerned a method of hair removal from the skin by optical radiation and the Technical Board of Appeal felt the need to return to the *travaux préparatoires* of the EPC to determine the original purpose behind these provisions. It held that 'the intention of the legislator was that only those treatments by therapy or surgery are excluded from patentability which are suitable for or potentially suitable for maintaining or restoring the health, the physical integrity, and the physical well being of a human being or an animal and to prevent diseases.'[150] The Board opined that the therapeutic/non-therapeutic distinctions applied to 'therapy' should now also extend to 'surgery'. The appeal against exclusion was upheld on the basis that the hair removal method did not fulfil any of the purposes behind the exclusion.[151]

 Discussion point   For answer guidance visit www.oxfordtextbooks.co.uk/orc/macqueen2e/

What would the position in respect of breast augmentation surgery or correction of the shape of the nose? Are these always and necessarily 'cosmetic'?

11.68   The UK–IPO has stated that it will continue to follow its prior case law which draws no such distinction and is concerned only to know if the method is 'surgical'.[152] But in the particular circumstances of hair removal, this would probably not be considered as 'surgical' in the UK.[153] Most recently, the EPO Enlarged Board of Appeal has directly tackled this point holding that the therapeutic/non-therapeutic distinction does *not* apply in the case of 'treatment by surgery'. That is, if the claimed method is 'surgical' in nature then the exclusion will apply. The case is

---

[147] BL O/35/84, see UK–IPO Guidelines, para 48.
[148] *Allen's Application* BL O/59/92, ibid (method of inserting markers in body for NMR and CT scans).
[149] T383/03 [2005] OJEPO 159.   [150] ibid, p 4 of judgment.
[151] See further, T9/04, KONINKLIJKE PHILIPS ELECTRONICS NV/Medical diagnostic imaging [2007] EPOR 10, point 6 of the Reasons: where a method claim was not struck down because it was '... not a method suitable or potentially suitable for maintaining or restoring the health, the physical integrity, and the physical well-being of a human being or animal and to prevent diseases.' The claimed method allowed the use of CT scans and x-rays to gather information about positioning a catheter in patients. This simply yielded an 'intermediate result' of information to assist in treatment and did not involve treatment per se.
[152] UK–IPO Guidelines, para 47 citing *Unilever (Davis's) Application* [1983] RPC 219.
[153] See *Commonwealth Scientific & Industrial Research Organization's Application* BL O/248/04.

MED-PHYSICS/Treatment by surgery.[154] The main question was whether a single surgical step in an otherwise patentable method would bring the entire method under the surgical exclusion, even when the surgical step was not necessarily aimed at maintaining life and health. The procedure involved an method of obtaining images of patents requiring that a contrast agent be injected into the heart. Did this invasive element prove fatal to the entire claim, even although it was in no way treatment or curative in its own right? The case throws up numerous issues, the two most important of which for present purposes are: (1) what is the purpose of the 'surgical' exclusion in patent law? and (2) what counts as 'surgical' anyway? The EBA held that the rationale for the exclusion is 'to free [medical] practitioners from being potentially hampered by patents in the application of the best possible treatment on their patients'; moreover, there is nothing in the travaux préparatoires or in the EPC itself to suggest that this should be limited to therapeutic or curative surgery. The EBA then confirmed what it saw as the underlying principle of the law and the jurisprudence to date, viz, 'a method claim falls under the prohibition of patenting methods for treatment by therapy or surgery now under Article 53(c) EPC if it comprises or encompasses at least one feature defining a physical activity or action that constitutes a method step for treatment of a human or animal body by surgery or therapy.' It must be remembered that if a method is to be patentable it must be *neither* treatment *nor* surgical *nor* a diagnostic method (on this last point see further below). These are cumulative provisions and so even if something does not fall within the definition of 'treatment' or 'diagnostic method' it might still fall foul of the 'surgical' provision. This clearly begs the question of what is surgery? It is here that the EBA departed from existing case law in holding that the technical definition which has grown up over the years is too broad and does not appropriately reflect technical realities; these now mean that many interventions or manipulations of the human body can be carried out perfectly safely and without a (high) level of professional medical skills or risk to patients. A new concept of 'surgery' in patent law is therefore required. The EBA stopped short of providing a definition, but it did point to key elements that should be weighed in the balance at first instance. Thus the exclusion should operate to strike down claims (a) over the kinds of interventions for which the medical profession is specifically trained, (b) over physical interventions on the body which require professional medical skills, and (c) over methods which involve health risks even when carried out with requisite medical professional care and expertise. Other factors that might be of relevance include the degree of complexity involved and the degrees of intervention or risk involved but none is determinative and each case will have to be judged on its facts.

 Exercise

> What are the implications of this recent ruling from the EPO? It seems both broad and narrow at the same time—broad because it upholds a wide role for the exclusion of *any* method if it involves surgery, but also narrow in that it now purports to restrict what counts as 'surgery'. Can you think of examples of interventions that might fall on either side of the line? What about the facts in the instant case? Would this count as 'surgery'?

---

[154] Case G1/07: Referral under Art. 112 (1)(a) EPC by the Technical Board of Appeal T 992/03 (Methods for treatment by surgery) to the Enlarged Board of Appeal; Decision of the Enlarged Board of Appeal (15 February 2010).

11.69   Are there any further limitations to this exclusion? Well one further and important point dealt with by the EBA in *MED-PHYSICS/Treatment by surgery* was the role of disclaimers. The question is this: if you run the risk of falling foul of the surgery exclusion because one element of your procedure counts as 'surgery' is it possible simply to disclaim or exclude this as part of your claim for protection? The EBA confirmed that there is nothing to prevent you attempting to do so, but it will be a question of fact whether the resulting disclosure in sufficient as a matter of law. The EPC (Art 84) requires that patent claims must be clear and disclose all of the essential features of the invention needed to reproduce it. It will be a matter for first instance bodies to determine in each case whether this is so. A final point to note is that none of this affects claims to what are known as 'purely technical methods', that is, method claims about the operation of a device used in healthcare as opposed to claims to health-related methods which themselves involve treatment, surgery or diagnostic methods.[155] Let us now turn to consider the last of these.

Diagnostic methods practised on the body

11.70   There has been some confusion and dispute over the years about the precise meaning of the exclusion of diagnostic methods,[156] and this has now been considered by the EPO Enlarged Board of Appeal in an attempt to bring clarity to the subject.

■ **G01/04 *CYGNUS/Diagnostic methods***[157]

This case involved a referral on a point of law from the President of the EPO to the Enlarged Board of Appeal. In summary, the essential question was whether 'diagnostic methods practised on the human or animal body' excluded only those claims to methods containing *all* of the procedural steps necessary to a medical diagnosis—for example, the examination phase *and* the data collection phase *and* the comparison phase *and* the discovery of deviation phase *and* the deductive clinical decision phase—or whether the exclusion applied if any *one* of these steps could be used for diagnostic purposes or related to diagnosis? It was held that:

> 'The method steps to be carried out prior to making a diagnosis as an intellectual exercise . . . are related to examination, data gathering and comparison . . . If only one of the preceding steps which are constitutive for making such a diagnosis is lacking, there is no diagnostic method, but at best a method of data acquisition or data processing that can be used in a diagnostic method . . . '[158]

11.71   In other words, only claims which encompass all of the steps required to come up with a definitive diagnosis are excluded from protection. It means that methods which may represent interim steps in a differential diagnosis and which may be a value in diagnosis will be patentable in themselves so long as they do not lead directly to a diagnosis. Examples include the taking of a sample, methods of internal imaging (eg x-rays or MRI scanning) and methods for measuring temperature. This is a particularly narrow interpretation of the exclusion provisions, but one which the EBA felt able to adopt on the basis that it is a 'matter of principle' that European patents should be granted for inventions that meet the requirements of Article 52(1).

---

[155] T9/04, n 151 above, is an example of this. If, however, there is a functional link to the effects of the device on the body this will be excluded. Once again, this will fall to be considered on the technical circumstances of each case. See further para 11.74.

[156] Compare, eg, *BRUKER/Non-invasive measurement* T385/86 [1988] EPOR 357 and *CYGNUS/Device and method for sampling substances* T964/99 [2002] OJEPO 4.

[157] [2006] EPOR 15.   [158] ibid, para 6.2.2.

11.72   This does not mean that a claim must laboriously lay out all steps in a process; rather, it must adequately describe the invention to the extent of the monopoly claimed,[159] and if the method *in fact* allows a diagnosis to be made it will be excluded.

11.73   The exclusion is also subject to the proviso that the method is practised *on the human or animal body*. The EBA has decided that this means that the patient or animal must be present to perform the step in question. Furthermore, to be excluded *all* of the technical steps in the method must be performed on the body, but this does not include the final step of joining the dots and actually deciding on a diagnosis because this is a purely intellectual exercise and therefore not technical.[160]

Exercise

Is it possible to reconcile the decisions of the Enlarged Boards of Appeal in G01/04 (diagnostic methods) and G01/07 (treatment by surgery)? Hint: read G01/07 for that EBA's own take on the issues? Do these kinds of decisions point to the need for a single body of appeal as we discuss in Chapter 10?

11.74   Finally, what about implements or other apparatus that are used for the purposes of therapy, surgery or diagnosis—are these affected by the exclusion? Well, the exclusion relates to *method claims* and not *product claims*, and so normally medical devices should be as patentable as non-medical devices. But an invention which is characterised by its use—for example, 'in surgery'—will not be granted protection. For example, in *TELETRONICS/Cardiac pacing*[161] the principal claim was to a method of operating a pacer in accordance with the required cardiac output while a person is exercising, and the Technical Board of Appeal held that this was, in essence, a claim involving a step that was a method of treatment. This was enough to defeat the patent and amendment at the opposition stage was not permissible. Similarly, in *EXPANDABLE GRAFTS/Surgical device*[162] it was decided that claims to products which can only be assembled inside the human or animal body by means of a surgical step are not permissible. The lesson lies in careful drafting of claims in the first place. As we discuss in para 11.69, claims to 'purely technical methods' about the operation of a device should succeed.

Protectable subject matter

'S 1(1) of the Patents Act 1977:

A patent may be granted only for an invention in respect of which the following conditions are satisfied, that is to say—
    (a) the invention is new;
    (b) it involves an inventive step;
    (c) it is capable of industrial application;
    (d) the grant of a patent for it is not excluded by subsections (2) and (3) below . . .'

---

[159] Patents Act 1977, s 14(5)(a).
[160] See further T1197/02 *AUSTRALIAN NATIONAL UNIVERSITY/Detection of glaucoma* [2007] EPOR 9.
[161] T82/93 [1996] OJEPO 274.   [162] T775/97 [2002] EPOR 24.

11.75   We have already considered the extent and meaning of subsections (2) and (3) above. Let us now consider what we might call the 'positive criteria' for patentability. Each of these criteria sets a threshold hurdle that the prospective patentee must clear in order to secure a patent. The rationale for each criterion is different, but collectively they serve to ensure that only previously-unavailable, highly-innovative and useful inventions receive patent protection.

Novelty

11.76   The policies underpinning the novelty requirement are to prevent the disutility of re-inventing of the wheel, to ensure that matter which is already in the public domain is not brought (once again) under private monopoly control, and to protect parties who have been happily using a product or process publicly from being stopped from doing so on the grant of a patent over the same or substantially the same product or process.

11.77   There are certain key questions that we must ask in order to know whether an invention will be new. These are:

(1)   What constitutes the public domain for these purposes?
(2)   How much information about an invention must have been in the public domain before this becomes a problem for patent purposes?

11.78   Novelty is covered by section 2 of the Patents Act 1977, as amended, and the equivalent provisions are found in Articles 54 and 55 EPC 2000. Section 2(1) of the 1977 Act provides that '[a]n invention shall be taken to be new if it does not form part of the state of the art'. The state of the art is the public domain for patent purposes. It is defined in section 2(2) as:

'The state of the art in the case of an invention shall be taken to comprise all matter (whether a product, a process, information about either, or anything else) which has at any time before the priority date of that invention been made available to the public (whether in the United Kingdom or elsewhere) by written or oral description, by use or in any other way.'

11.79   This is clearly an extremely wide definition which is global in scope and which covers any manner by which information about an invention might be disclosed. Something becomes part of the state of the art on the day that it is made available to the public, and this does not even require that members of the public have actual sight of the information, merely that they can have access to the information, either freely or on payment of a fee.[163] An obscure article may, therefore, be published in a journal that no-one ever reads but it would still be part of the state of the art. Moreover, this publication can be anywhere in the world and in any language. Note too, by implication, it does not matter *who* makes a public disclosure, and this includes the prospective patentee himself. This is why it is so important to keep information about an invention out of the public domain until you have secured a *priority date*. You should recall from the previous chapter that the priority date is normally the filing date of the patent application with an intellectual property office, unless an earlier filing has taken place in another office within the previous 12 months, in which case that date becomes the priority date.[164] Novelty is only tested by reference to the state of the art *prior to* the priority date.

[163] See further the EPO Enlarged Board of Appeal in G1/92 *Availability to the Public* [1993] EPOR 241.
[164] See para 10.97 above.

11.80   The state of the art is forever expanding—we can only add to it; information, once added, always remains a part of it. It is dangerous to pass information to third parties without stipulating a confidentiality clause, ideally by contract; even communication to one individual can be enough to make information public.[165] Allowing the public an opportunity to examine the details of an invention in circumstances where a skilled person would become aware of the core technical features of the invention would amount to public disclosure.[166] It is even possible for something to become part of the state of the art if it is merely seen in public if a skilled person[167] on seeing it would be able to discern its core features with sufficient detail to reproduce the invention.[168] Finally, and for the purposes of testing novelty only, it is important to note that the state of the art includes the content of any patent applications designating the UK[169] published on or after the priority date of the invention in question.[170] Article 54(3) EPC 2000 makes the contents of European patent applications relevant to the state of the art.

11.81   If an invention already exists in the state of the art then we say that a subsequent patent application or invention is *anticipated*.

■ *Pall Corporation v Commercial Hydraulics (Bedford) Ltd* [1990] FSR 329

The patent in suit concerned 'hydrophilic microporous membranes' for filters. The membranes were capable of being wetted through in less than one second yet when heated to a temperature just below the softening temperature the membrane reverted to a hydrophobic material. An action of infringement was brought by the plaintiffs which was met with a counter-claim of revocation on grounds of lack of novelty. It was alleged that the plaintiff had anticipated their own invention by prior use. The plaintiff had given sight of the claimed product to a potential customer. No details of the nature or construction of the membranes were disclosed to the customer or the other suppliers represented at the test, and the nature of the membrane could not have been ascertained simply by sight of the membrane. The plaintiff also sent samples to other potential customers but these were sent under conditions of confidence and the customers knew that the membranes were experimental and secret. It was held that (a) the use of the membranes in the comparison test did not place the invention in the state of the art because the use was not a sale or supply in the course of trading nor did it make the samples available to the public; (b) the sending of samples to potential customers in confidence did not amount to anticipation because this did not make the samples available to the public. The obligation of confidence ensured that the relevant information was kept in the private, as opposed to the public, domain.

---

[165] *Bristol-Myers Co's Application* [1969] RPC 146. In T482/89 *TELEMECHANIQUE/single sale* [1992] OJEPO 646 a single sale was enough to anticipate.

[166] *Milliken Denmark AS v Walk Off Mats Ltd and Ano* [1996] FSR 292 (hire of mats to the public would allow an expert to discover its novel qualities and perform the invention).

[167] See *Folding Attic Stairs Ltd v Loft Stairs Co Ltd* [2009] FSR 24.

[168] See *Lux Traffic Controls Ltd v Pile Signals Ltd and Faronwise Ltd* [1993] RPC 107. Cf, *Kavanagh Balloons Pty Ltd v Cameron Balloons Ltd* [2004] RPC 5.

[169] It is important to remember that this can therefore cover applications via the UK–IPO, the European Patent Office and/or the Patent Cooperation Treaty. In this last regard the application must not only have been published under the PCT (Art 21) but it must also have entered the national phase for UK patents or the regional phase for European (UK) patents, ie that the necessary translation has been carried out and the appropriate fee paid: see ss 79, 89, 89A and 89B of the Patents Act 1977. The abstract of any patent application does not form part of the state of the art for these or any other purposes: Patents Act 1977 s 14(7).

[170] Patents Act 1977, s 2(3), as amended. Note, this does not apply to the test for inventive step, see Patents Act 1977, s 3, discussed at para 11.109.

11.82   The law of confidence can be an extremely important tool in the protection of information surrounding the development of an invention in the period prior to application and the award of a priority date. Unlike the US which provides for 'grace periods'—the period of one year prior to filing is exempt from consideration for the purposes of testing novelty—Europe will consider everything made available to the public up to the priority date. Compare the above decision with *Monsanto Co (Brignac's) Application*[171] in which a process patent was sought concerning the production of nylon having finely divided carbon black uniformly dispersed therein. Thirty or 40 copies of a *Technical Information Bulletin* containing details of pigmentation of synthetic fibres (including nylon) were given to salesmen of the company developing the process. Opposition to the grant of the patent on grounds of lack of novelty was successful because the salesmen were considered by the court to be members of the public and in the absence of a fetter on them this amounted to prior publication. No evidence was led that the brochures had in fact been distributed to customers, but this was not considered to be necessary in order for anticipation to have taken place.

11.83   There are strict rules about which kinds of document can anticipate an invention and in which circumstances. Many of these were established many years ago and remain relevant today.

■ *General Tire and Rubber Co v Firestone Tyre and Rubber Co* [1972] RPC 457

This was a decision by the Court of Appeal. The plaintiffs claimed infringement of their patent for oil-extended rubber by the defendants who counter-claimed for revocation of the patent, inter alia, on grounds of novelty. It was alleged that the patent had been anticipated by certain documents published prior to the priority date of 20 November 1970. The patent in suit was for a process for making a compound suitable for tyre treads by mixing synthetic rubber with oil and carbon black (a mixture referred to as 'oil-extended rubber') and for the product thus made. The earlier publications relied upon by the defendants were:

(1)   a Viennese patent dated 17 May 1943 for 'Semperit (a)' (compound with carbon black for tyres);

(2)   a Viennese patent dated 15 January 1945 for 'Semperit (c)' (extended synthetic rubber);

(3)   an English patent dated 2 August 1944 'Wilmington' (oil and latex invention);

(4)   two articles published in August 1947 and March 1950 in 'Rubber Age' (experiments using oil and carbon black to soften rubber).

It was held that:

• Alleged anticipatory matter must be interpreted at the date of its publication and without regard to subsequent events.[172]

• The alleged anticipatory material must be interpreted by a reader skilled in the relevant art at the relevant date. If the art is one having a highly developed technology, the notional skilled reader to whom the document is addressed can be a team, whose combined skills would normally be employed in that art in interpreting and carrying into effect instructions such as those contained in the document to be construed.

• Alleged anticipatory materials must be considered separately: it is not permissible to combine earlier unconnected publications to show anticipation[173] (compare with the concept of 'mosaicing' discussed below in terms of inventive step, para 11.109).

---

[171] [1971] RPC 153.
[172] The EPO authority on this is T/396/89 *UNION CARBIDE/high tear strength polymers* [1992] EPOR 312.
[173] *British Ore Concentration Syndicate Ltd v Mineral Separation Ltd* (1909) 26 RPC 124.

- If, in light of the above, the alleged anticipatory material contains a clear description of, or clear instructions to do or make something which would infringe the prospective patentee's patent if granted, the patent in suit will have been shown to lack the necessary novelty.[174]

- By corollary, if the prior publication contains a direction which is capable of being carried out in a manner which would infringe the patentee's claim, but would be at least as likely to be carried out in a way which would not do so, the patent in suit will not have been anticipated (although it might fail on grounds of obviousness, see below).

- 'A signpost, however clear, upon the road to the patentee's invention will not suffice. The prior inventor must be clearly shown to have planted his flag at the precise destination before the patentee.'[175]

- Given the above, the *General Tire and Rubber* patent had not been anticipated by the prior publications. None of the publications planted a flag at the spot of GTR's invention. They were concerned essentially with different aims and different means of realising those aims.

11.84 The test to be applied is the 'notional skilled reader', and we might see this as a similar policy device to that used in tort/delict, viz, the 'reasonable man'.

11.85 The need to plant a flag in the exact spot claimed by the patent in suit means that prior publications or prior uses of matter which incidentally disclose a future invention might not anticipate the invention. In fact, the House of Lords has considered what is required for anticipation and has confirmed that this comprises two elements: (1) prior disclosure, and (2) enablement.

■ *Synthon BV v Smithkline Beecham plc* [2006] RPC 10

The dispute related to a salt of Paroxetine which is used to treat depression. Although one salt form of the compound had been marketed for some time, both parties to the dispute discovered, more or less simultaneously, another salt form which was far more suitable for pharmaceutical use (PMS). Both applied for patent protection within a few months of each other. Synthon's application referred to a group of salts of which one was PMS. Before this was published, however, Smithkline claimed priority on its own application and was successful in receiving a patent for a particular form of crystalline PMS. Synthon brought proceedings claiming that the invention had been anticipated by their own patent application on the basis of section 2(3) of the Patents Act 1977. It was held that there had been anticipation and this required the proof of two matters: first, that the Synthon application disclosed the invention which had been patented (prior disclosure), and second, that an ordinary skilled man would be able to perform the disclosed invention if he attempted to do so by using the disclosed matter and common general knowledge (enablement).

11.86 This is a refinement on the approach to date. The court stressed that these are two separate, albeit related, matters. As we have seen above, a *prior disclosure* must be construed as it would have been understood by a skilled person at the date of the disclosure and not with the benefit

---

[174] Endorsed by the House of Lords in endorsed by the House of Lords in Synthon v SmithKline Beecham [2006] RPC 10 at paras 21–25. The prior art need not disclose exactly the same invention in all its facets, see *Glaverbel SA v British Coal Corporation* [1995] RPC 255, but it must normally disclose all of the technical features of the claim which is under scrutiny.

[175] See too *Koninkijke Philips Electronics NV v Princo Digital Disc GmbH; Koninkijke Philips Electronics NV v Chin-Shou Kuo* [2003] EWHC 1598.

of hindsight. Moreover, in order to anticipate, a prior disclosure must disclose subject matter such that, if performed by the skilled person, it would *necessarily* infringe the patent.[176] The prior disclosure must firmly plant the flag on the patentee's invention: '. . . the infringement must not merely be a possible or even likely consequence of performing the invention disclosed by the prior disclosure; it must be necessarily entailed. If there is more than one possible consequence, one cannot say that performing the disclosed invention will infringe.'[177] But note: the prior disclosure need not be expressed in the same form or by reference to the same parameters as the invention. Indeed, people do not even need to *know* what they are making[178]—the question is whether the relevant essential features of the invention are in the public domain.[179]

11.87   *Enablement* requires that the ordinary skilled person must be able to perform the invention from the information disclosed.[180] This is closely allied with the concept of sufficiency, which we discuss later in this chapter (para 11.201ff). In *Synthon*, Lord Hoffmann said that he accepted that enablement meant the same thing in that case as it means for sufficiency, but he also remarked that this might not always be so because the perspective of the skilled person can change. For example, when considering sufficiency the skilled person is attempting to reproduce the invention, while in a test for novelty the prior art may have disclosed the invention but not specifically identified it—the task of the skilled person is therefore different. In similar fashion, the role of the skilled person changes depending on whether we are discussing prior disclosure or enablement. With the former the role is to understand what is meant by the prior disclosure, while with enablement the concern is whether the skilled person can 'work' the invention. It is important, therefore, to see the two concepts as distinct.

Exercise

Can you envisage any circumstances where there would be prior disclosure but no enablement? Could the converse hold true?

11.88   The House of Lords had ruled on novelty on a number of occasions prior to this decision. Various elements of those decisions remain valid.

■ *Asahi Kasei Kogyo KK's Application* [1991] RPC 485

The patent claimed by Asahi Kasei Kogyo KK was for a human protein (Human Tissue Necrosis Factor) produced by genetic engineering and useful in the treatment of tumours. The application was rejected by the Patent Office on the grounds of lack of novelty under section 2(3) of the Patents Act 1977 because of information contained in another pending patent application filed by Dainippon. Although this second application had a filing date later than the application in

---

[176]   See most recently *Boegli-Gravures SA v Darsail-ASP Ltd* [2009] EWHC 2690 (Pat).

[177]   *Synthon*, para 11.85 above, per Lord Hoffmann at para 23.

[178]   T303/86 (*CPC Int*) [1989] 2 EPOR 95 (a process for the manufacture of flavour concentrates was anticipated because it could not be distinguished from known cooking and frying processes which, albeit incidentally, produced versions of the said flavour concentrates. It was irrelevant that the chefs in question had no idea that this was so).

[179]   *Merrell Dow Pharmaceuticals Inc & Another v HN Norton & Co Ltd and Others* [1996] RPC 76.

[180]   Note, Synthon made a mistake in describing PMS in its application but this was not a problem because it was held that the notional skilled person would nonetheless produce Smithkline's invention if he set out to make it using Synthon's instructions.

suit, it claimed priority from an earlier application which disclosed and claimed the protein but did not disclose any method of preparing it. The appeal went all the way to the House of Lords.

Key dates

- Asahi Kasei Kogyo KK filed in UK on 4 April 1985 (priority claimed US, 6 April 1984)
- Dainippon filed European patent on 26 February 1985 (priority claimed Japan, 6 March 1984)

It was held that matter comprised in the state of the art for the purposes of sections 2(2) *and* 2(3) had to be the subject of an *enabling disclosure*, that is, there must be enough information available to allow the skilled person to reproduce the invention. This is now refined in light of the two-part test in *Synthon*. The point remains, however, that an invention is not made available to the public merely by a published statement of its existence, unless the method of 'working' the invention is so obvious as to require no explanation. There was no anticipation because the Dainippon application did not disclose the means to make the protein.

11.89   The interpretation given to section 2(3) can lead, albeit in rare circumstances, to double patenting. Imagine the following scenario:

6 March 1984	6 April 1984	26 February 1985	4 April 1985
Japan	United States	Europe	UK
Not enabling	Priority claimed	Protein claim	Protein claim

If the UK application is not anticipated by the European application because the former can claim priority from the US application, and if the Japanese application is not an enabling disclosure, then the UK patent can be granted. However, because the European patent claims priority from the Japanese patent, the state of the art in respect of the European patent will be tested prior to 6 March 1984, and will thereby exclude the contents of the US patent application. In this way it is also possible for the European patent to be granted. The House of Lords recognised this possibility in *Asahi* but considered that it would occur only rarely.[181]

■ *Merrell Dow Pharmaceuticals Inc & Another v HN Norton & Co Ltd and Others* [1996] RPC 76

Merrell Dow obtained a patent in 1972 for terfenadine, an anti-histamine drug. When the patent expired in 1992 other companies (including Norton) began to manufacture and sell the drug. Merrell Dow had carried out extensive research into anti-histamines in the intervening period and discovered that, once ingested, terfenadine was rapidly metabolised by the human liver and a bi-product was produced: an acid metabolite. It was further discovered that this acid metabolite was almost exclusively responsible for the anti-histamine effects of terfenadine. Merrell Dow sought and received a patent over the acid metabolite in 1980. When after 1992 other companies began to produce terfenadine, Merrell Dow brought infringement proceedings against them in respect of the production of the acid metabolite inherent in the use of terfenadine. This was so even although the existence of the acid metabolite was not known to

---

[181] For a discussion of the issues on double patenting see *Synthon BV v Smithkline Beecham plc* [2003] RPC 607 and in the Court of Appeal at [2003] RPC 114. See also E Nettleton et al. 'EPO Decisions: Double Patenting' (2009) 38(4) CIPAJ 268.

the companies prior to the priority date of the patent over the acid metabolite. The defendants counter-claimed that the 1980 patent had been anticipated by the use of terfenadine in clinical trials and the specification of the appellant's earlier patent which had published information on the chemical composition of terfenadine and that it should be taken for its anti-histamine effect. The appeal was taken to the House of Lords.

It was held that:

- The appeal was dismissed. The House emphasised the need to interpret the 1977 Act to accord with the provisions of the European Patent Convention (EPC) and therefore felt able to refer to decisions of the European Patent Office (EPO) in interpreting the EPC. Although such decisions are not binding on UK courts they are highly persuasive.

- In essence the revocation claim was based on two arguments: anticipation by use and anticipation by disclosure. Regarding the former, it was held that use only makes an invention part of the state of the art if the use itself makes information about the details of the invention available to the public. Mere use is not enough. Thus, unlike the law prior to 1977 (Patents Act 1949), secret use of a product or process prior to a patent application cannot be part of the state of the art. The ingestion of the drug by those taking part in trials did not *in se* reveal any information to the public about the existence of the acid metabolite.

- The question of anticipation by disclosure, which concerned the specification in the 1972 patent over terfenadine and its uses, revealed information which led to the production of the acid metabolite. Merrell Dow had argued that they could not anticipate that which they did not know to exist but this referred to knowledge about the chemical composition of the acid metabolite. However, one can know the same thing under many different descriptions. Section 2(2) does not confine the state of the art to the chemical composition of products. It is the invention which must be known and in this case the invention in dispute is the acid metabolite. The terfenadine patent describes a chemical and its effects on the body, one such effect being the anti-histamine effect (which was caused by the acid metabolite): 'an invention is part of the state of the art if the information which has been disclosed enables the public to know the product under a description sufficient to work the invention.' Lord Hoffmann concluded that: 'if the recipe which inevitably produces the substance is part of the state of the art, so is the substance as made by the recipe.' Indeed, this was supported by the EPO in Decision T303/86 *CPC/Flavour Concentrates*[182] in which the EPO's Technical Board refused an application to patent flavour concentrates on the grounds that recipes in existing cook books, although not containing any references to flavour concentrates, nevertheless had the effect of making them.

11.90   Although the Patents Act provides that it is an infringement of a patent relating to a product to make the product without the patentee's authority (section 60(1)(a)), the individuals who took terfenadine and therefore automatically made the acid metabolite would not be infringers by virtue of section 60(5)(a) of the 1977 Act which provides that there is no infringement in respect of acts done privately and without commercial interest.

11.91   On one view this decision is consistent with those above such as *General Tire and Rubber Co* which held that if alleged anticipatory material contains a clear description of, *or clear instructions to*

---

[182] [1989] 2 EPOR 95.

do or make, something which would infringe the disputed patent (if valid), the disputed patent will have been shown to lack the necessary novelty.

11.92   The House of Lords' reservations on anticipation by use have since been distinguished by Pumfrey J in *Halliburton Energy Services Inc v Smith International (North Sea) Ltd*[183] in which is was stated that '…the law has always been that clear and unmistakable directions to do or make something within the claim will, if they form part of the state of the art, anticipate the claim.' The fact that *Merrell Dow* concerned a chemical produced inside the human body and so not analysable/available was thought to make a difference. In the instant case the invention was a mechanical drill bit which could serve as a 'dumb' anticipation by conveying sufficient information to enable it to be dumbly reproduced.[184] Notwithstanding, it remains the case that a prior use must give clear and precise directions to reproduce an invention before it will amount to anticipation.[185]

Novelty at the margins

11.93   There are two sets of circumstances where claims to products have required a specialised approach in order to secure protection and where the perspectives of the UK and the EPO have not always been in symmetry, although the process of approximation continues unabated as we see below. These are the cases of (a) product-by-process claims and (b) selection patents.

Product-by-process claims

11.94   The UK has traditionally allowed this kind of claim whereby a product could be claimed by reference to its process of manufacture rather than by its own technical features. The claim might read, for example, 'the product obtained by the process described in claim 1'. Although this would give a more restricted monopoly through the necessary link of the product and process, it could prove useful if someone manufactured products outside the country using a patented process and then imported the products—infringement proceedings could still be brought. Moreover, such a formulation is important when it is difficult to define the product by its own characteristics, for example, if you cannot discern its structure. The EPO, however, has always taken a restricted view of such claims and will only allow them when it is not possible to describe the product by any other means *and* when the product is patentable in its own right.[186] The UK has now followed suit in:

■ *Kirin-Amgen Inc and others v Hoechst Marion Roussel Ltd and others* [2005] 1 All ER 667, [2005] RPC 9

Amgen held a European patent for the production of erythropoietin (EPO) by genetic engineering (recombinant DNA technology). EPO is a protein that regulates the function of red blood cells in the body and has various therapeutic applications, including the treatment of anaemia. Hoecht developed its own method of making EPO and Amgen alleged infringement of its patent, while Hoecht argued that key parts of the patent were invalid, inter alia, for lack of novelty.

---

[183] [2006] RPC 2 affirmed by the Court of Appeal in [2006] EWCA Civ 1715, see n 208 below.
[184] See also *Evans Medical Ltd's Patent* [1998] RPC 517.
[185] *Quantel Ltd v Spaceward Microsystems Ltd* [1990] RPC 83.
[186] EPO Guidelines for Examination, Part C, Chapter III, para 4.11, and T150/82 IFF/Claim categories, [1984] OJEPO 309, paras 10–11.

In particular, claim 26 was challenged. This was to EPO as the product of the expression in a host cell of a DNA sequence according to claim 1. Claim 1 detailed a DNA sequence for use in securing the expression of EPO in a host cell, and so claim 26 was a product-by-process claim. The core novelty question was: what counts as a new product given that EPO had already been purified from urine by others? It was held that the UK has been singled out as the only signatory state to the EPC to accept product-by-process claims.[187] It is important that the UK should apply the same law as the EPO and the other member states when deciding what counts as new for the purposes of the EPC, and on the facts the product in itself was not new compared to the state of the art.

11.95   We should note, however, that the House of Lords did not consider that this change to practice for the UK would make much difference. In particular, it pointed out that a patentee can continue to rely on Article 64(2) EPC which provides that '[i]f the subject-matter of the European patent is a process, the protection conferred by the patent shall extend to the products directly obtained by such process.'

Selection patents

11.96   We have established that mere mention of the existence of a substance is not fatal in terms of novelty—the prior art must plant a flag at the specific spot of an invention, for example, by describing not only a substance's existence, but perhaps also its structure, its function, its special qualities and the means to make it. This is very useful in the chemical and biotechnological industries where many thousands of substances or compounds or groups thereof may be known to exist, but where their particular properties are yet to be discovered and put to use. The refining or particularising of knowledge from the general to the specific can be achieved through *selection patents*. These concern the selection of entities from a wider known class or group and an attempt to patent them for particular qualities such as improved performance or novel use. Selection patents can be obtained provided there is no anticipation as defined above. For example, in *Beecham Group's (Amoxycillin) Application*,[188] Beecham held a patent for a wide class of penicillins from which it identified nine as being particularly effective and for which a further patent was sought. The case concerned one type from the group of nine which, it had been established, was especially amenable to absorption in the blood. The question arose as to whether the mention of the penicillin in the previous patent amounted to anticipation. The Court of Appeal held that it did not because the mention in the previous patent of the penicillin did not disclose any details regarding the efficacy of the drug in humans (it concerned only mice). Similarly, in *EI Du Pont de Nemours (Witsiepe's) Application*[189] the House of Lords allowed a selection patent on a copolymer despite prior art which had suggested that copolymers of this type could be produced with a number of variants from what had already been invented in the field. Crucially, however, there was no evidence that these variants had been tried, let alone that they revealed the particular properties possessed by the invention in the instant patent. The mere raising of a possibility does not defeat novelty. The general rule which is accepted in the UK, and maybe in the EPO,[190] is that compounds are novel provided that no members of the sub-group are *specifically* described in the prior publication, even if they have been described

---

[187] T150/82 *International Flavors & Fragrances Inc* [1984] OJEPO 309.   [188] [1980] RPC 261.
[189] [1982] FSR 303 (HL).
[190] See *SANOFI/Enantiomer* T658/91 [1996] EPOR 24 but compare with T198/84 *HOECHST/Thio-chloroformates* [1985] OJEPO 209 and *PFIZER/Penem* T1042/92 [1995] EPOR 207.

in general terms.[191] If this has happened then even the discovery of a new property will not be enough to establish novelty. The later patent must state the precise advantage of the selected invention over the prior art, otherwise 'it is merely an arbitrary selection among things already disclosed, and will lack novelty'.[192] Moreover, the Court of Appeal has confirmed that giving clear and unmistakable directions to use the *common general knowledge* to produce a specific material is no answer to a challenge of novelty.[193]

What can be excluded from the state of the art?

11.97   The starting premise in testing novelty is that everything which is available to the public *as a matter of fact* is counted as part of the state of the art. This can be varied only in a few narrow circumstances and the onus is on the applicant to satisfy the intellectual property office or court that the exceptions should apply. These are detailed in section 2(4) of the Patents Act 1977 which provides that (a) disclosures about the invention which are made in breach of confidence or unlawfully, and (b) disclosures made by the inventor at a recognised international exhibition, can be excluded from the state of the art provided that the patent is applied for within six months of the disclosure in question. The relevant date for calculation purposes is the *filing date*. The applicant must prove on the balance of probabilities that there was a breach of confidence or unlawful act leading to disclosure, or in the case of exhibition, he must provide a statement on applying for the patent that this invention has been exhibited and provide a certificate from the exhibit organisers confirming the details of this within the next four months.[194] Only exhibitions which come under the terms of the Convention on International Exhibitions (1928, as amended 1951) can count, and this is unlikely to include regular industry trade fairs. The six-month window will be helpful to an inventor who is the victim of a breach of confidence only if the invention is at a sufficient stage of development to make it worth while applying for a patent. At best, it may mean that a more restrictive monopoly will be granted; at worst, it might preclude patent protection altogether if the invention is only in the idea or concept phase.

 Question

What must an international exhibition do to qualify under the 1928 provisions?

Exceptions to exceptions: the case of 'medical use' patents[195]

11.98   It has been a long-standing general principle of novelty in the UK that a known substance cannot be claimed for a new use, even if that use has never previously been described, unless the substance requires some form of transformation to make it suitable for that use. For example,

[191] See also *Dr Reddy's Laboratories (UK) Ltd v Eli Lilly and Co* [2008] EWHC 2345, where the court stated that a general formula in a patent with multiple substituents chosen from lists of some length would not normally take away the novelty of a subsequent claim to an individual compound.

[192] *Ranbaxy UK Limited and Another v Warner-Lambert Company* [2005] EWHC 2142 (Pat), at para 64 per Pumfrey J.

[193] See *Ranbaxy (UK) Ltd and another v Warner-Lambert Company* [2007] RPC 4 at para 41 quoting the court of first instance in this regard. The prior art here was an earlier co-pending application which explicitly pointed the way towards the invention under challenge and merely required the application of the common general knowledge to carry it out.

[194] See Patents Rules 2007, Rule 5   [195] For a helpful IP and Medicine blog see: http://ipmed.blogspot.com/

a public announcement system cannot be claimed for use in attracting dogs if all that happens is that high-pitched whistle sounds are played through the system. But if the system must be technically modified to broadcast high-frequency signals inaudible to human ears then it may be patentable in respect of that use. Thus, in *IG Farbenindustrie AG's Patents* it was stated: 'no man can have a patent merely for ascertaining the properties of a known substance'.[196] The strategy in such a case is then not to attempt to claim the *product* but to claim a new *method* of using a known material.

11.99   The EPO takes a different approach. The Enlarged Board of Appeal has held in two decisions[197] that a claim to a new use of a known product is possible, so long as the claim identifies the use as a technical effect and it was previously unknown to the public. The new technical effect can be the mere uncovering of a new use for the substance. For example, in G2/88 *MOBIL OIL III/ Friction Reducing Additive*[198] a product originally developed as a lubricant to prevent rust was found also to have qualities to reduce friction and a patent was allowed in this respect. The advice from the UK–IPO Office, however, is that this approach should not be followed.[199]

11.100   But the UK recognises an exception to its general rule and this is in the realm of substances or compositions for treatment of the human or animal body.[200] We have already seen that *method* patents in this field are exceptions to patentability, but also noted that this does not apply to compounds or substances *used* in those methods. This is specifically provided for by section 4A(3) of the Patents Act 1977, which states that in relation to a method of treatment of the human or animal body by surgery or therapy, or a method of diagnosis practised on the human or animal body:

> 'In the case of an invention consisting of a substance or composition for use in any such method, the fact that the substance or composition forms part of the state of the art shall not prevent the invention from being taken to be new if the use of the substance or composition in any such method does not form part of the state of the art.'

11.101   We observed above that usually the way around the 'no new use' rule is to claim a method of new use, but this could not apply in the case of methods for therapy, surgery or diagnosis because these are already specifically excluded from protection. Section 4A(3) therefore offers a way out of the problem: it operates as an exception to an exception.

 Discussion point   For answer guidance visit www.oxfordtextbooks.co.uk/orc/macqueen2e/

Look back at the definitions of the 'therapy' and 'surgery' in the previous section on method exclusions and in particular consider what we said about cosmetic methods of treatment. Are they 'therapeutic'? How does this affect the application of section 4A(3)? What about cosmetic surgery?

---

[196] (1930) 47 RPC 289 at 322.
[197] G2/88 *MOBIL OIL III/Friction Reducing Additive* [1990] OJEPO 93 and G6/88 *BAYER/Plant growth regulating agent* [1990] OJEPO 114.
[198] [1990] OJEPO 93.
[199] Patents Manual (2010), para 2.14. But compare the views of L Bently & B Sherman, *Intellectual Property Law* (3rd edn, 2008) who argue that 'novelty of purpose' claims have been accepted by the UK courts, p 469–471 quoting obiter comments in *Bristol*.
[200] Note this does not extend to apparatus (see para 11.74 above).

First medical use

11.102 A strict application of novelty from within the UK tradition should still impose limits on which medical uses can be claimed for a known substance. In particular, it would seem clear from section 4A(3) that only the first medical use can be claimed. Once a substance is deployed for a medical use this becomes part of the state of the art for any future additional medical uses and destroys novelty as a result.[201] Thus in *Bayer AG (Meyer's) Application*[202] a claim to 'Compound X for use in combating medical condition Y' was refused because compound X was already known as a therapy. But the influence from Europe is strong and the British courts are not always able to resist it.

Second medical use

11.103 Developments over the years now mean that in some circumstances a second medical use *can* be claimed. This (further) exception was invented by the Enlarged Board of Appeal in G05/83 *EISAI/Second Medical Indication* in which it held that limitations to patentability should be construed narrowly—a common mantra[203]—and that legislative purpose did not overtly preclude second and subsequent uses and therefore they should be allowed. The Enlarged Board of Appeal qualified this slightly, however, and required that such second or subsequent use claims should take a particular form following the practice of the Swiss Federal Intellectual Property Office. Because of this, they had been known as Swiss-type claims. The form is normally: *'use of substance X in the manufacture of a medicament for the treatment of condition Y'*, and we have seen this form of claim in the previous chapter. The focus, then, is to the method of manufacture of a new application of a known substance. This may be seen as one sophistic step too far. Nonetheless, the possibility of claiming second and subsequent medical uses has now been directly embraced by the EPO and EPC 2000 has removed the need to use Swiss-type claims.[204] Henceforth it will be possible to claim simply 'substance X for use in treatment of disease Y'.[205]

11.104 This reform is now found in section 4A(3) and (4) of the Patents Act 1977, as amended by the Patents Act 2004, section 1, and puts to bed any residual doubts that second medical use claims were valid in the UK.[206] In *Actavis UK Ltd v Merck*[207] the Court of Appeal held that a valid second medical use claim can be made for a new and inventive dosage regime, despite the fact that the substance in question had been used in the prior art to treat the same condition at a different dosage. In this case there was such a low expectation of a successful treatment by applying this dosage that it was a novel idea and the claim was granted. Most recently, the question of whether or not second medical use claims relating to dosage regimes are patentable under the EPC 2000 has been settled by the Enlarged Board of Appeal. In G02/08 *Abbott Respiratory/ dosage regime*[208] the EBA opined that there is no reason to consider dosage regimes differently

---

[201] Note, there must be actual evidence of prior *use* of the substance to destroy novelty for later medical applications; it is not enough that a possible medical use has been discussed: see Manual, para 4A.25

[202] [1984] RPC 11.   [203] Although see G1/07, n 154 above, para 3.1.

[204] This does not, however, preclude their use.

[205] See Art 54(5) EPC 2000: 'Paragraphs 2 and 3 shall also not exclude the patentability of any substance or composition referred to in paragraph 4 for any specific use in a method referred to in Article 53(c), provided that such use is not comprised in the state of the art.'

[206] Previously they had only been grudgingly accepted, see *Wyeth's Application* [1985] RPC 545 and *Bristol-Myers Squibb v Baker Norton Pharmaceuticals* [2001] RPC 1 in which the court refused to rule on the correctness of *Easai* but did indicate that there were 'strong reasons' to maintain the view expressed by the judges in *Wyeth* which followed *Easai* despite reservations.

[207] *Actavis UK Ltd v Merck* [2008] EWCA Civ 444.   [208] Decision of 19 February 2010.

to acceptable second medical uses. More far-reachingly, however, in determining what counts as an acceptable second medical use the EBA held that EPC 2000 (Art 54(5)) now permits the patenting of a further specific use of a known medicament *even for the same disease* so long as it is claimed in a method of therapy. Swiss-type claims should no longer be used.

Exercise

Consider the implications of these decisions allowing the patenting of dosage regimes. Is there a risk that this will lead to the extension of patent protection? Consider the scenario where, through usage of a patented medicine, it becomes clearly which dosage regime is most effective in the treatment of the disease and the dosage regime becomes patentable in its own right.

Inventive step

11.105   The policies underlying the inventive step requirement involve the need to show merit by reaching a sufficiently high level of inventive activity to justify the award of a strong monopoly. Also, an inventive step must demonstrate some advantage over what has gone before for the benefit of society; a departure from the prior art which has no advantages, or which represents a disadvantage, should be denied protection for lack of inventive step.[209] Finally, and as a parallel with the rationale behind novelty, the public should not be preventing from doing things which are simply obvious extensions or developments of what they were already doing.[210]

11.106   Inventive step is also referred to as non-obviousness—indeed, the US law uses this term.[211] Inventive step is defined in section 3 of the Patents Act 1977, as amended, and the equivalent provisions are found in Article 56 EPC 2000. Section 3 provides:

> 'An invention shall be taken to involve an inventive step if it is not obvious to a person skilled in the art, having regard to any matter which forms part of the state of the art by virtue only of section 2(2) above (and disregarding section 2(3) above).'

11.107   This raises three questions:

(1)   What is the state of the art for the purposes of testing inventive step?
(2)   What traits or qualities does the person skilled in the art possess?
(3)   How do we know when something is 'obvious' to the person skilled in the art?

State of the art

11.108   The starting point for assessing the state of the art for inventive step purposes is the same as that we use for testing novelty, namely the definition in section 2(2) of the Patents Act 1977—so it includes virtually the sum total of human knowledge that is available to the public anywhere in the world. It does not include, however, the content of any patent applications designating the UK and filed before the priority date of the current application under scrutiny (section 2(3)).

---

[209] T119/82 OJEPO 5/84.   [210] *Windsurfing International inc v Tabur Marine (GB)* [1985] RPC 59 at 77.
[211] 35 USC ¶103.

Question

Why are patent applications excluded from inventive step but not from novelty?

11.109   We saw that in order to defeat novelty a single piece of prior art must directly plant the flag on the applicant's invention and it is not possible to combine different pieces of prior art in order to say that something is not new.[212] This combining process is called *mosaicing* and, in contrast, it is perfectly permissible when testing inventive step so long as this is something that the person skilled in the particular art would have done. Whether this is so clearly varies from technology to technology and explains why the criterion of inventive step is something of a moveable feast—its application is very field-specific and resolution usually turns on the particular technical features of each case. The subtle relationship between inventive step and novelty was explained by Lord Hoffmann in *Synthon*: 'If performance of an invention disclosed by the prior art would not infringe the patent but the prior art would make it obvious to a skilled person how he might make adaptations which resulted in an infringing invention, then the patent may be invalid for lack of an inventive step but not for lack of novelty.'[213]

11.110   A feature of the state of the art which is not necessarily field-specific is *common knowledge*. The courts will often assume that certain features, practices or possibilities are so manifestly self-evident that they do not need to be spelt out in detail but can be assumed to be part of the skilled person's experience. This applies both to general common knowledge and to field-specific common knowledge.

11.111   While it is theoretically the case that the entire sum of publicly available information is at the fingertips of the skilled person, the intellectual property office or court will ask what was the particular skilled person in the field under scrutiny likely to come across and consider together. The more obscure the connections necessary across different fields, and the more documents that have to be mosaiced to come up with the invention, the more likely it is that the invention will be found to have an inventive step. Relevant factors include (a) the age of the documents, (b) the role of references in linking one document to others, (c) the proximity of fields from which the prior art comes, (d) the amount of effort or analysis required of the skilled person in identifying the relevant features in the prior art, and (e) the ubiquity of some documents in the field such that they form part of the common knowledge.[214] A good guide was offered by Lord Reid in *Technograph v Mills & Rockley*: 'In dealing with obviousness, unlike novelty, it is permissible to make a "mosaic" out of the relevant documents, but it must be a mosaic which can be put together by an unimaginative man with no inventive capacity.'[215]

11.112   The question of whether it is appropriate to look across and between technical fields is largely answered by the nature of the problem to be solved and whether the relevant skilled person would be expected to look for parallels in related fields where, perhaps, similar problems are encountered.[216] Similarly, it is also possible to consider that the skilled person might call upon

---

[212] See too EPO Guidelines, Chapter IV, Part C, para 11.4: 'it is fair to construe any published document in the light of subsequent knowledge and to have regard to all the knowledge generally available to the person skilled in the art the day before the filing or priority date valid for the claimed invention.'

[213] *Synthon*, para 11.85 above, at para 25.

[214] A good step-by-step illustration of what the skilled person might know and mosaic is found in *Ivax Pharmaceuticals UK Ltd v Akzo Nobel NV; Arrow Generics Ltd v Akzo Nobel NV* [2007] RPC 3.

[215] [1972] RPC 346 at p 355.   [216] T176/84 *MOBIUS/Neighbouring field* [1986] OJEPO 50.

the expertise of others in related fields in attempting to solve his problem. Indeed, the person skilled in the art might, in fact, be a team of different specialists and this should include those relevant to the field(s) of the invention.[217]

Conor Medsystems Inc v Angiotech Pharmaceuticals Inc and Another [2008] RPC 28

This case involved a challenge on the grounds of obviousness to a patent relating to a device used in coronary surgery called a *stent*. This is implanted into diseased arteries to keep them from collapsing. The problem facing the skilled person was how to develop stents that did not cause restenosis (closure of the artery channel)—a pre-existing problem for 33–50 per cent of patients treated with existing techniques. Here it was held to be the case that the person skilled in the art and trying to solve the pre-existing problem would be a team which would include, inter alia, an interventional cardiologist and someone familiar with drugs for treating cancer. All of the experts would bring their own knowledge to the problem. In the instant case where the invention involved coating the stent with taxol (an anti-angiogenic) it was held by the Court of Appeal to be obvious that the skilled man would consider taxol to be worth testing to see what its properties were. However, the House of Lords ruled that the prior art merely mentioned taxol as one of an undifferentiated (and large) number of drugs which could be tried and this was insufficient to make it obvious that taxol would prevent restenosis. The correct question to ask was whether it was obvious to use a taxol-coated stent to prevent restenosis. The patentee had disclosed a plausible invention which, if it worked, could be patentable so long as the solution itself was not obvious. It is the technical solution which must be tested for obviousness not the question of whether it was obvious to try taxol (among many other compounds).

> **? Question**
>
> Could this variability in the application of the inventive step test lead to unfairness in terms of the standards to which different technologies might be held?

The qualities of the person skilled in the art

11.113   The idea of the person skilled in the art is a device used by intellectual property offices and courts to assess the merits of any given innovation. We are concerned with the notional expert and the courts will hear evidence in each case on what that expert might be expected to know. He is an ordinary member of their field who is aware of everything in the state of the art[218] but, as we have seen above, is unimaginative and with no inventive capacity (para 11.111). The range of qualities of this person was helpfully summarised for us by Jacob LJ in *Rockwater v Technip France SA and another*:[219] he is, first and foremost, a nerd (not Lord Justice Jacob)! Beyond the traits we have just discovered, he is forgetful, in that he will not join the dots between different pieces of prior art unless it is obvious to do so, and unconnected matter will drift from his

---

[217] *Schlumberger Holdings Ltd v Electromagnetic Geoservices AS* [2009] RPC 19.
[218] See for example *W L Gore & Associates GmbH v Geox SpA* [2008] EWHC 2311 (Pat) in which the person skilled in the art was held to be a person or team with a practical interest in the functional aspects of shoe design.
[219] [2004] EWCA CIV 381, [2004] RPC 46.

memory as he moves through the literature. He can, however, have the prejudices of his field, which may be long-standing assumptions that a particular avenue of research will be fruitless. Those who prove otherwise have, therefore, a good chance of clearing the inventive step hurdle. Similarly, those who identify a problem for the first time and provide a means to overcome it should have few difficulties. For example, in *Dyson Appliances Ltd v Hoover*[220] the issue of prejudice was raised and held to be relevant in determining what the skilled person would consider obvious to do. The advent of the bagless vacuum cleaner was an innovation that came from the blue—no-one had even perceived a problem with conventional machines.

11.114   The skilled person is not expected to pursue avenues that he would regard as futile.[221] As the EPO Guidelines put it: 'There is an inventive step if the prior art leads the person skilled in the art away from the procedure proposed by the invention'.[222] Timing is also vitally important. We ask the skilled person to consider what was obvious at the time of the priority date and it is crucial to guard against the vagaries of ex post facto analysis—many things may appear obvious with hindsight.[223] It is not appropriate to define the class of expert so broadly that the specific knowledge and prejudices of those most closely involved in the actual field with which the patent is concerned do not form part of the prejudices and attributes of the skilled person.[224]

11.115   Evidence on what the skilled person would know or do is taken from relevant experts at first instance. Appeal courts do not have an opportunity to re-hear evidence and should not overrule a trial judge's findings of fact unless there is very good reasons to do so. The position was summed up by Lord Hoffmann in *Biogen v Medeva*:[225]

> 'The need for appellate caution in reversing the judge's evaluation of the facts is based upon much more solid grounds than professional courtesy. It is because specific findings of fact, even by the most meticulous judge, are inherently an incomplete statement of the impression which was made upon him by the primary evidence. His expressed findings are always surrounded by a penumbra of imprecision as to emphasis, relative weight, minor qualification and nuance (as Renan said, la vérité est dans une nuance), of which time and language do not permit exact expression, but which may play an important part in the judge's overall evaluation...Where the application of a legal standard such as negligence or obviousness involves no question of principle but is simply a matter of degree, an appellate court should be very cautious in differing from the judge's evaluation.'

The test for obviousness

11.116   The criterion of 'inventive step' can be thought of as a misnomer. It is not inventive for someone to take the next logical, obvious *step* in the develop of any given field of technology, rather what is required is a *leap* forward in ways that would not be obvious to others working in the field. It is an objective test. The classic approach to this question was laid down in:

■ *Windsurfing International Inc v Tabur Marine (GB) Ltd* [1985] RPC 59 (CA)

The patent in suit claimed a wind-propelled apparatus for use on water with a sail attached to a surf board and two arcuate booms attached to the sail—imagine an ordinary windsurf board. In an action for infringement of the patent the defendants counter-claimed that the patent was invalid both on grounds of novelty and obviousness. The novelty issue arose from prior use

---

[220] [2001] RPC 26.   [221] *Hallen Co v Barbantia (UK) Ltd* [1991] RPC 195.   [222] Chapter IV, Annex E.4.
[223] *Ferag AG v Muller Martini Ltd* [2007] EWCA Civ 15.
[224] *Mayne Pharma Ltd and another v Debiopharm SA and another* [2006] EWHC 1123 (Pat).
[225] [1997] RPC 1 at p 45.

of a similar device by a third party and obviousness was argued both in relation to this prior use and/or in view of a printed publication which appeared before the priority date of the patent. The publication was an article entitled, 'Sailboarding—Exciting New Water Sport' which described the basic concept as that of the patent except that the sail was square-rigged. The prior use was allegedly 10 years prior to the patent application by a 12-year-old boy who had built a sailboard and used it on public waterways on summer weekends over two consecutive seasons. This sail-board differed from that claimed only in that the booms were straight and not arcuate. It was held that the patent was invalid both on grounds of novelty and obviousness. As regards novelty it did not matter that prior use was by a private individual and in a non-commercial setting. Of relevance was the extent of the public nature of the use which, in the case, was considerable even although in relative terms the public use was of short duration. Obviousness is to be tested by asking what would have been obvious to a person skilled in the particular art at the time of the priority date of the patent.

Answering the question on obviousness was held to be a four-step process:

(1) identify the 'inventive concept' embodied in the patent;
(2) impute to a normally skilled but unimaginative addressee what was common general knowledge in the art at the priority date;
(3) identify the differences, if any, between the matter cited as part of the state of the art and the alleged invention;
(4) decide whether those differences, viewed without any knowledge of the alleged invention, constitute steps which would have been obvious to the skilled man or whether they require a degree of invention.

This has been reformulated more recently by the Court of Appeal in *Pozzoli SPA v BDMO SA.*[226] The following should be taken as accurate reflection of the current approach and *Windsurfing* and *Pozzoli* should be read together.

The *Windsurfing/Pozzoli* approach

(1)(a) Identify the notional 'person skilled in the art'.

(1)(b) Identify the relevant common general knowledge of that person.

(2) Identify the inventive concept of the claim in question or if that cannot readily be done, construe it.

(3) Identify what, if any, differences exist between the matter cited as forming part of the 'state of the art' and the inventive concept of the claim or the claim as construed.[227]

(4) Viewed without any knowledge of the alleged invention as claimed, do those differences constitute steps which would have been obvious to the person skilled in the art or do they require any degree of invention?

---

[226] [2007] FSR 37. An explanation of this reformulation can be found at paras 15 and 16.

[227] The Patents Manual (2010) offers the following helpful instruction: 'In determining whether an invention is obvious in the light of a given document combined with common general knowledge, other documents, or instances of prior use, there are two major considerations: (i) whether the skilled person could reasonably be expected to find the document in conducting a diligent search for material relevant to the problem in hand … and (ii) whether, if he had found the document, he would have given it serious consideration' (para 3.75.1).

Question

Before reading on ask yourself—what is the inventive concept involved with a windsurf board? Is it the sail? The boom? The board or something else?

11.117   The inventive concept in *Windsurfing* was the 'free-sail': a sail attached to an unstayed spar on one side which is connected to the board by a universal joint, that is, a joint having three axes of rotation. This allows the sail to be manipulated to power and control the board without the need for a rudder or other means. The inventive concept described in the publication was essentially that contained in the patent. The essential difference between the two was the shape of the sail: square in the publication, triangular in the patent. This, however, made no practical difference in the determination of obviousness. The prior use by the young boy was of a device essentially the same as the vehicle described in the patent in suit save that the booms were straight and not arcuate. It would have been obvious to anyone skilled in the art in 1958 on witnessing the boy's board that an improvement would be to replace the straight booms with arcuate booms. Indeed, the straight booms formed such a shape when the board was put to water.

11.118   Here is an old but valuable illustration of the importance of defining 'inventive concept'.

   ■ *Parks-Cramer Co v G W Thornton & Sons Ltd* [1966] RPC 407 (CA)

   This was an appeal to the Court of Appeal concerning a patent for a device used to clean the floor around textile machines of 'fly' (or lint) by the automatic and repeated passage of an overhead vacuum cleaner having vacuum tubes extending almost to the floor. An action for infringement was brought which was met with a counterclaim alleging invalidity on grounds of obviousness. Inter alia, it was alleged that the invention was obvious because of general knowledge of the problem about the collection of fly or lint in textile factories and the existence of certain patents previously granted which were aimed at alleviating the problem. Such patents included (a) overhead devices which blew the fly onto the floor for collection, (b) suction devices aimed at the parts of the machine where most fly accumulated. None of these machines sought to deal with the problem of accumulation of fly upon the floor of the factory generally or in particular with the accumulation of fly in the aisles. Finally (c) a number of devices were developed in an attempt to clean factory floors of fly and some were patented. They operated on the principle of directing air currents across the floor in one direction so as to blow the fly towards fixed collecting points where the fly was removed by suction into ducts or collecting chambers. None of these devices proved satisfactory in practice. On the basis of the above it was argued by the defendants that the extension of the basic ideas disclosed by the above devices and patents to using a vacuum device to clean factory floors of fly was obvious.

   It was held that:

   • The patent was valid. The inventive concept contained in the plaintiff's patent was this: if you pass a suction nozzle closely adjacent to the floor repeatedly at regular intervals over a fixed path along the aisles between and at the ends of rows of machines the suction will remove the fly from *the whole of the floor* and *not merely* that part of the floor which is in the relatively narrow direct track of the suction nozzle.

- It was not obvious that by passing such a machine over the floor in such a manner that the whole of the floor would be cleaned and not just a narrow tract.

- The problem which the plaintiff sought to solve had been a problem since the early 1950s. Many individuals and companies had sought to solve it but no one had been successful. It had occurred to no one that the solution lay in passing a suction tube repeatedly over a narrow track in the aisles.

- The evidence shows that the plaintiff's machine was an immediate commercial success and although this could be attributable to many other factors, this point fortified the view that it was not obvious to solve the problem in the way which the plaintiff did.

11.119 It would appear that the inventors themselves did not even appreciate the efficacy of their invention in cleaning the whole of the floor rather than a narrow tract. Yet, not only did this not affect the validity of the patent, it aided the court in determining that the invention was not obvious: the plaintiff was very experienced in the field of cleaning devices for use in textile mills.

11.120 It has been suggested that the *Windsurfing* four-point test is merely a tool to help decide obviousness and is not a mandatory approach,[228] but its appeal endures and it was found to have been applied by the trial judge, albeit obliquely, by the House of Lords in *Sabaf SpA v MFI Furniture Centres Limited and others*.[229] This ruling is significant for the point that before we consider whether an invention is obvious, we must first decide what the invention is or whether it is merely a collocation, that is, the juxtaposition of devices or inventions which do not make up a unified whole. The example offered by the EPO on this point is a machine for producing sausages consisting of a known mincing machine and a known filling machine disposed side by side.[230] In *Sabaf* it was held that two features in respect of gas burners for kitchen cookers were a mere collocation, being a means to drawn air in above the burner and a way of control flow under the burner which did not interact with each other—there were therefore two inventions, neither of which differed significantly from the prior art in line with the *Windsurfing* structure.

The importance of the *Windsurfing/Pozzoli* structured approach[231] is to get the court in the right frame of mind to test obviousness and to avoid the trap of applying hindsight.[232]

11.121 The Court of Appeal in *Conor* best summed up the position:[233]

> 'In the end the question is simply "was the invention obvious?" This involves taking into account a number of factors, for instance the attributes and common general knowledge of the skilled man, the difference between what is claimed and the prior art, whether there is a motive provided or hinted by the prior art and so on. Some factors are more important than others. Sometimes commercial success can demonstrate that an idea was a good one. In others "obvious to try" may come into the assessment. But such a formula cannot itself necessarily provide the answer. Of particular importance is of course the nature of the invention itself.'

---

[228] For an example of the court being invited to depart from *Windsurfing* see *Cipla Ltd and others v Glaxo Group Ltd* [2004] EWHC 477. From a comparative perspective, see *Aktiebologet Hassle v Alphapharm* (2002) 212 CLR 411 *(Australia) and Aventis v Apotex* [2005] FC 1504 *(Canada)*.

[229] [2004] UKHL 45, [2005] RPC 10.   [230] EPO Guidelines, n 34 above, Chapter IV, Annex E 2.1.

[231] Though the modified test of *Pozzoli* is now mainly used, the *Windsurfing* approach is still valid and used occasionally, for example in *Handi-Craft Co v B Free World Ltd* [2007] EWHC 10.

[232] *Wheatley v Drillsafe Ltd* [2001] RPC 7.

[233] *Conor Medsystems Inc v Angiotech In and Another* [2007] EWCA Civ 5, para 45.

11.122   The relevance of commercial success of an invention can be a *faux ami*.[234] Numerous factors can play a role in the success of an invention in the market and many of them may have nothing to do with inventiveness. Especially when dealing with the commercial success of a product subject to anterior patent protection, one should be cautious as there is a clear reason why no one else has ever launched a similar product.[235]

 Discussion point   For answer guidance visit www.oxfordtextbooks.co.uk/orc/macqueen2e/

How many different factors can you think of that might influence market success?

11.123   The key question in deciding if commercial success is a relevant factor in determining inventive step lies in being able to identify *why* there was commercial success and to assess whether this was because of inventiveness. In *Haberman v Jackel*[236] the invention was very simple and concerned the 'AnyWayUp Cup'—a cup especially designed to help babies make the transition from suckling to proper feeding (UK Patent 2,266,045—why not try to find this on Esp@cenet?)

11.124   The inventiveness was said to lie in the fact that the cup sealed between sips and so avoided drips. Rival companies had similar devices which worked through various mechanisms. It was argued that Haberman had not produced anything outside the normal workshop modifications which had long been available to those in the art. It was a simple solution to a known problem using known and readily available expedients.

11.125   Laddie J laid out a list of factors that might have a bearing on a determination of obviousness:

Inventive step: some of the considerations

(1) What was the problem which the patented development addressed?
(2) How long had that problem existed?
(3) How significant was the problem seen to be?
(4) How widely known was the problem and how many were likely to be seeking a solution?
(5) What prior art would have been likely to be known to all or most of those who would have been expected to be involved in finding a solution?
(6) What other solutions were put forward in the period leading up to the publication of the patentee's development?
(7) To what extent were there factors which would have held back the exploitation of the solution even if it was technically obvious?
(8) How well has the patentee's development been received?
(9) To what extent can it be shown that the whole or much of the commercial success is due to the technical merits of the development, that is, because it solves the problem?

This is not an exhaustive list but it is a helpful guide which may point either towards or away from inventiveness.[237]

---

[234] But neither is it altogether irrelevant: *Dyson Appliances Ltd v Hoover Ltd* [2002] RPC 22 '…commercial realities cannot necessarily be divorced from the kinds of practical outcome which might occur to the skilled addressee as worthwhile.'
[235] *Dr Reddy's Laboratories (UK) Ltd v Eli Lilly and Co* [2008] EWHC 2345, at 187.   [236] [1999] FSR 683.
[237] As stated in *Generics (UK) Limited and others v H Lundbeck A/S* [2009] UKHL 12, in the end the question of obviousness must be considered on the facts of each single case. The court must attach weight to any particular factor in taking into account all the relevant circumstances.

> **Exercise**
>
> Consider each of these factors and the ways in which they might influence a determination of obviousness.

11.126   In the end Mrs Haberman kept her patent. She took a step forward that many others in the field could have taken during the long period during which the problem was known but did not. Nor did the simplicity of the invention defeat inventiveness; indeed, rather the opposite—if it was so straightforward then why had it not be done before? Moreover, evidence to the court suggested strongly that the tremendous commercial success of the cup was due primarily to its technical quality and contribution to the state of the art—it did not leak.

11.127   Meeting an unmet need may be evidence of inventiveness, but it is not inventive merely to take advantage of an upturn in economic circumstances which create a market not previously existing (eg by making certain materials affordable when previously they were not). Similarly, it is not because it has taken a lot of time and expense to bring a product to market that this in any sense implies inventiveness.[238]

Obvious to try

11.128   We have mentioned above the idea of 'obvious to try' which is often offered as a gloss on the obviousness test.[239] But the Court of Appeal in *Saint-Gobain PAM SA v Fusion Provida Ltd and Another*[240] opined that the obvious-to-try test really only applies in circumstances where it is more or less self-evident that what is proposed will work. In this case, however, it was not possible for the skilled person to predict success and so the invention was non-obvious. Thus speculative inclusion of experiments in a research programme will not be defeated simply because you try—it is the obvious likelihood of success which presents a problem, not trying itself. In terms of strategy it is prudent, therefore, to lay out in the patent specification reasons why success is in doubt and far from guaranteed.[241] The House of Lords confirmed in *Conor Medsystems Inc v Angiotech Pharmaceuticals Inc*[242] that an invention can only be obvious if there is an expectation of success and noted that the expectation of success must be assessed in light of the purpose for which the invention is intended; that is the solution to the technical problem that it is intended to fix. Furthermore, when evaluating the reasonable expectation of success, one must consider without hindsight the attractiveness of the route at the time, taking into account all the surrounding circumstances.[243] Lord Hoffmann views on the question of 'obvious to try without any expectation of success' are worth noting: 'This oxymoronic concept has, so far as I know, no precedent in the law of patents.'

Reforms and the European approach

11.129   Having considered the broad approach in the UK to testing obviousness, it is important to highlight that the UK–IPO has recently conducted a consultation exercise on this criterion with a

---

[238]   *Teva v Gentili* [2003] EWHC 5 (Patent), [2003] EWCA Civ 1545.
[239]   Its origins are found in *Johns-Manville Corporations Patent* [1967] RPC 479.   [240]   [2005] EWCA Civ 177.
[241]   See *Conor Medsystems Inc v Angiotech Pharmaceuticals Inc and another* [2006] EWHC 260 (Pat).
[242]   *Conor Medsystems Inc v Angiotech Pharmaceuticals Inc* [2008] RPC 28.
[243]   See A Carter 'Conor Medsystems Inc v Angiotech Pharmaceuticals Inc and others: House of Lords judgment clarifying the assessment of "inventive step" ' (2008) 30(10) EIPR 429. See also *Generics (UK) Ltd v Daiichi Pharmaceutical Co Ltd* [2009] EWCA Civ 646.

view to possible reform. The motivation for this consultation was to know if the inventive step criterion best serves innovation by steering a middle way through the easy and hard extremes that could otherwise be adopted. If an intellectual property office sets the inventive threshold too low this can result in trivial patents and a surfeit of protection blocking innovation, but if the hurdle is too high this may also impede innovation.[244] The consultation showed that there is no need to change the basic law on testing obviousness, as the current application of the law is broadly thought to be appropriate. It was noted, however, that it is important to make sure that practice stays in line with the high technological environments in which inventions are made and that the test is applied consistently.[245]

 Exercise

Compare the UK approach to three alternatives considered by the UK–IPO. Should we test inventiveness by reference to:

(1) The person skilled in the art, having regard to any item(s) of prior art or common general knowledge, would have arrived at the claimed invention (the European approach)?
(2) Any item(s) of prior art or common general knowledge would have motivated a person skilled in the art to reach the claimed invention (the Japanese approach)?
(3) Any item(s) of prior art or common general knowledge would have motivated, with a reasonable expectation of success, a person skilled in the art to reach the claimed invention (the American approach)?

Which of these is a softer or harder option? What are the advantages and disadvantages of the UK maintaining its current approach?

EPO/UK differences

11.130   The EPO adopts a problem-and-solution approach. It asks what is the pre-existing technical problem and is it solved by a technical solution? The approach in the EPO and in the UK are much the same at this broad level. But the EPO has developed a three-point test which differs somewhat from the UK. Non-obviousness is determined by:

(1) determining the 'closest prior art',
(2) establishing the 'objective technical problem' to be solved; and
(3) considering whether or not the claimed invention, starting from the closest prior art and the objective technical problem, would have been obvious to the skilled person.[246]

11.131   The closest prior art often restricts the search to the same technical field as the invention and looks for the most promising point from which an obvious development towards the invention might be made. This is to be assessed on the day before the filing or priority date of the invention.[247] The objective technical problem is formulated by comparing the prior art with the distinguishing features of the invention. Occasionally, this formulation may be at odds with

---

[244] See further *Gowers Review of Intellectual Property* (HM Treasury, 2006), para 5.24.
[245] The outcome of the consultation is available here: http://www.ipo.gov.uk/response-inventive.pdf
[246] EPO Guidelines, n 34 above, Chapter C, IV, para 11.7   [247] ibid, para 11.7.1

472

how the applicant has framed the problem in the patent application and this requires a re-formulation of the problem in the application since the technical formulation is supposed to be the objective assessment of the problem to be solved. The technical problem can be interpreted broadly and may only cover an alternative means to produce the same or similar effects in the state of the art.

11.132   This test differs most significantly from the UK in its starting point of seeking (only) the closest prior art. As Pumfrey J said at first instance in *Ranbaxy*, 'its concentration on the closest prior art, which must stem from a belief that if an invention is not obvious in the light of the closest prior art it cannot be obvious in the light of anything further away. This runs the risk of offending against the principle that a skilled man must be permitted to do that which is obvious in the light of each individual item of prior art seen in the light of the common general knowledge.'[248] That said, Pumfrey J did not in the end consider that there are differences of principle at stake as between the jurisdictions.[249]

Question

Do you agree with Pumfrey J's assessment of these approaches? Consider your answer in light of the UK–IPO exercise discussed above. How did the same invention fare before the EPO?

Industrial applicability

11.133   This final criterion for patentability ensures that we maintain the industrial or technical nature of inventions. The relevant section of the Patents Act 1977, as amended, is section 4(1), with the equivalent provisions being found in Article 57 EPC 2000. Section 4(1) states:

> '...an invention shall be taken to be capable of industrial application if it can be made or used in any kind of industry, including agriculture.'

We have already covered the other provisions in section 4 and 4A (para 11.59ff above) when we discussed methods of treatment of the human and animal body and use claims. The concept of 'industry' is construed very widely and does not necessarily involve a for-profit purpose.[250] Note that the test is whether something can be *made* or used industry, so widening the scope further, and the requirement is only that the invention is *capable* of use in industry or agriculture; no actual evidence of effective use is required.

11.134   Something can be held to lack industrial applicability if its essential nature is aesthetic, artistic or intellectual. There is, therefore, some overlap with the kinds of considerations we saw above in respect of section 1(2) of the Patents Act 1977. The two tests are, however, distinct. An example of something being denied protection was a method of initiating introductions between people in *John Lahiri Khan's Application* which was also rejected under section 1(2) as a method of doing business.[251]

---

[248] [2005] EWHC 2142 (Pat) at para 69.
[249] For more recent discussion see Jacob LJ in *Actavis UK Limited v Novartis AG* [2010] EWCA Civ 82.
[250] *Chiron Corp v Murex Diagnostics Ltd and other* [1996] RPC 535 at 607.
[251] Patents Manual (2010), para 4.03 (BL O/356/06).

11.135 Beyond this, there is little else to say about this provision. It does not cause problems in the vast majority of cases. One area which has required refinement, however, is in respect of bio-technological inventions because of the need to show the *function* of any new gene sequences or fragments unearthed during scientific research. This has been dealt with separately through the Biotechnology Directive and we discuss this in detail in paras 12.47ff in the next chapter.

Patent rights and their limits

11.136 So, you have applied for your patent, your invention has not been excluded on one or more policy grounds, and you have satisfied a patent examiner that your invention is new, inventive and of a technical nature. What now?

11.137 Your patent[252] is a right to exclude everyone from the market, even the so-called innocent infringer, for a period up to a maximum of 20 years. It is a form of *personal property* in much the same way as any other thing you own. Thus, it can be sold, assigned, licensed, mortgaged or otherwise transferred to other parties.[253] A patent is an asset over which securities can be granted and so against which capital can be raised.

11.138 A patent will be granted initially for four years but can be extended annually for a maximum of 20 years. Supplementary Protection Certificates are available in the case of pharmaceutical inventions and agrochemicals inventions which permit an extension of the term for a further five years to compensate for the stringent regulatory approval mechanisms which these inventions are often subject to before given access to the market.[254] The European Parliament and Council adopted a Regulation on medicines for paediatric use which includes a further six-month extension to a Supplementary Protection Certificate as incentive to produce in the area in 2006.[255]

11.139 Like most intellectual property rights, patents are principally exploited through licences and sub-licences and, normally, these can be further assigned and mortgaged.[256] We deal with exploitation of patents in paras 21.39–21.48. Patents, applications, licences and sub-licences can vest in personal representatives on death in the same way as any other piece of personal property.[257] Some transfers of rights must be in writing and signed by or on behalf of the transferor,[258] otherwise all such transactions are void. This applies to assignments, mortgages and transfers

[252] This applies to patent applications as well.

[253] Patents Act 1977, s 30 for England, Wales and Northern Ireland and s 31 for Scotland where a patent is 'incorporeal moveable property'. Assignations or grants of security are subject to the provisions of the Requirements of Writing (Scotland) Act 1995.

[254] Regulation (EEC) No 1768/92 created a Supplementary Protection Certificate for medicinal products and it entered into force on 2 January 1993. Regulation (EC) No 1610/96 of the European Parliament and of the Council, created a Supplementary Protection Certificate for plant protection products, and entered into force on 8 February 1997. The UK–IPO provides a full guide to both: UK–IPO, *Supplementary Protection Certificates for Medicinal and Plant Products: A Guide for Applicants* (2009), available here: http://www.patent.gov.uk/patent/info/spctext.pdf. Disputes over SPCs arise in terms of the 'product' they are certified to cover and whether the invention and the product to be authorised are one in the same, see *Takeda Chemical Industries Ltd's SPC Applications* (No 3) [2004] RPC 3.

[255] Regulation (EC) No 1901/2006 of the European Parliament and of the Council of 12 December 2006 on medicinal products for paediatric use and amending Regulation (EEC) No 1768/92, Directive 2001/20/EC, Directive 2001/83/EC and Regulation (EC) No 726/2004. The amendments are incorporated in Regulation (EC) No 469/2009.

[256] Patents Act 1977, s 30(4)(a), subject to s 36(3) which deals with the need for consent of co-owners.

[257] Patents Act 1977, s 30(3) and (4)(b).

[258] It is no longer necessary for all parties to sign as of 1 January 2005, see Regulatory Reform (Patents) Order 2004, SI 2004/2357.

on death.[259] Licences do not need to be in writing and do not involve any transfer of property.[260] An assignment or an exclusive licence can give the right to bring infringement proceedings[261] or disputes over Crown use.[262] An exclusive licensee can bring independent infringement proceedings without the need to refer to the owner.[263]

11.140   Assignations and other transfers of rights can be entered in the Register of Patents with the effect that this will give priority over someone who claims an earlier transaction if, (i) the earlier transaction was not registered, and (ii) the person claiming under the later transaction was unaware of the earlier transaction.[264] Moreover, assignees or exclusive licensees who register within six months of the transfer can then claim damages or an account of profits for infringements of the patent prior to the transaction.[265]

 Question

What would happen if you have applied for registration but this has not taken place when someone comes forward with an earlier claim?

11.141   As well as entering specific one-to-one contracts for exploitation of a patent, a patentee has a mechanism at his disposal known as *licences as of right*.[266] We discuss these later in Chapter 21, and the principle here is largely the same: the patentee requests that an entry be made in the Register that licences are available as of right and this allows any party who wishes to take a licence on terms they are willing to accept through agreement or by intervention from the Comptroller.[267] A licensee of right can request that the patentee bring infringement proceedings to protect the invention and if nothing is done within two months can bring infringement proceedings herself.[268] A subsequent application can be made to have the patent removed from the Register in this respect, although at that stage the request can be opposed by any interested parties.[269] The UK–IPO maintains an open standards web database containing all patents issued under licence of right.[270]

 Exercise

Read the relevant provisions of the law and consider the pros and cons for a patentee of relying in this scheme. Note, in particular, how signing up to the scheme affects renewal fees.

---

[259] For a Scottish perspective on assignations and loss of rights to sue, see *Buchanan v Alba Diagnostics Limited* [2004] RPC 34. For comment, see RG Anderson, '*Buchanan v Alba Diagnostics*: Accretion of Title and Assignation of Future Patents' (2005) 9(3) Edinburgh LR 457.

[260] For discussion see *Allen & Hanburys Ltd v Generics (UK) Ltd and Gist-Brocades NV and others and the Comptroller-General of Patents* [1986] RPC 203 per Lord Diplock.

[261] Patents Act 1977, s 30(7).   [262] Patents Act 1977, s 58.   [263] Patents Act 1977, s 67.

[264] Patents Act 1977, s 33(1).   [265] Patents Act 1977, s 68.   [266] Patents Act 1977, s 46.

[267] See the Patents Manual (2007), s 46 for details on the scheme.   [268] Patents Act 1977, s 46(4).

[269] Patents Act 1977, s 47.

[270] This was following a recommendation in *Gowers Review of Intellectual Property* (HM Treasury, 2006), para 5.50.

Limits on patent rights

11.142 The core unifying feature of the various limits which are imposed on the exercise of patent rights is our old friend, the public interest. At the most general level and as with other IPRs, the European principle of free movement of goods and competition law can impose limits on the way patents are exploited. We discuss these in Chapters 19 and 20 respectively.

11.143 If we accept that the whole ethos behind the patent system is to encourage inventions that become available to the public, then this end is thwarted if someone seeks and receives patent protection but then does not exploit the invention and keeps the technical details out of the public domain. For these reasons we allow *compulsory licences* under ss 48 and 53 of the Patents Act 1977. Broadly, a common criterion is that a compulsory licence cannot be sought until three years after the grant of the patent to give the patentee a fair chance to exploit the invention himself. But if this has not happened the law provides for two avenues to apply for a compulsory licence to the Comptroller, and the relevant avenue depends on whether the patentee is from a WTO country or not. The criteria to be met are different and we detail them in paras 21.40–21.48 in our discussion of exploitation. The important point to note for now, however, is that this scheme is rarely used and much more could be done to further the public interest in this regard. The *Gowers Review of Intellectual Property* recommended, for example, that model licence templates be established to facilitate agreements on mutually-beneficial terms and obviate the need for difficult and protracted negotiation on a case-by-case basis or, indeed, the need to revert to compulsory licences at all.[271] The UK–IPO has since produced guidance *How Licensing Intellectual Property Can Help Your Business* (July 2008).

11.144 *Crown use* is a further limitation to a patent right.[272] This can happen when any government department or someone authorised by a government department (in writing) considers that it is in the services of the Crown to use and exploit an invention. Any act which would normally be considered an infringement is not so considered in these circumstances. 'Services of the Crown' includes supply of anything for foreign defence purposes, production or supply of specified drugs or medicines, and such purposes relating to the production or use of atomic energy or research into matter connected therewith as the Secretary of State thinks necessary or expedient.[273] Compensation is payable, however, to the patentee or exclusive licensee on the basis of the loss of profit of the contract that might have arisen for provision of the invention.[274] The Crown or its agents do not need to apply to the Comptroller to take action but any disputes will be resolved by the courts.[275]

Ownership and compensation

Ownership

11.145 We saw in Chapter 10 that anyone is at liberty to apply for a patent,[276] but who is entitled to be named as the inventor? It is important to know the answer to this because a patent is granted primarily to the inventor or joint inventors,[277] or to someone entitled to the invention by law or agreement, or ultimately a successor of either of these two categories.[278] It is the status of inventor and co-inventor that interests us here. The inventor is entitled to be named in the patent

---

[271] ibid, paras 5.48–5.49.   [272] Patents Act 1977, ss 55–59.   [273] Patents Act 1977, s 56(2).
[274] Patents Act 1977, s 57.   [275] Patents Act 1977, s 58.   [276] Patents Act 1977, s 7(1).
[277] Patents Act 1977, s 7(2)(a).   [278] Patents Act 1977, s 7(2)(b) and 7(2)(c).

application and resulting patent even if he is not the applicant.[279] Section 7(3) of the 1977 Act states that: '[i]n this Act "inventor" in relation to an invention means the actual deviser of the invention and "joint inventor" shall be construed accordingly.' The test to determine inventorship is twofold: (1) what is the inventive concept? and (2) who devised that concept?[280]

11.146   You will recall from previous sections that the inventive concept is the kernel of the invention—it is the essential technical heart of the new innovation and its inventor must do more than simply proffer an initial prompt or a mere idea about where to start. That said, it is not necessary to be the one to reduce the invention to practice. If you contribute an idea that consists of the essential elements of a claim— for example a proposal on the solution and the means to arrive at it—then this would qualify as inventorship.[281]

■ IDA Ltd & others v University of Southampton & others [2006] RPC 21

This was a dispute about who invented a cockroach trap. The existing art was provided by Professor Howse of Southampton University and involved a trap which worked by luring the insect into a box with bait whereupon its feet would become contaminated with electrostatic talcum powder. This caused the insect to slip onto fly paper and die. A member of IDA, specialists in magnetic powders, read about the invention and wondered if it would work with magnetic powder—an advantage because it would not lose its 'stickiness'. He shared his idea with Mr Metcalfe in a telephone conversation and the patent in dispute was one subsequently lodged by Metcalfe in which he claimed: '... a composition comprising particles containing or consisting of at least one magnetic material.' It was held: 'This was the sole key to the information in the patent. That key was provided solely by Mr Metcalfe. Putting it another way, insofar as there is anything inventive in the patent, it was provided only by him.' It did not matter that the inventive concept was an idea because the idea provided the entire technical solution (forever-sticky magnetic powder) to the technical problem (the ongoing effectiveness of a cockroach trap).

11.147   In a dispute over entitlement to a patent, the question is simply who has an entitlement to claim to be an inventor; each claimant must establish why he has a claim to a proprietary interest in the instant patent and/or why the patentee is not entitled to it if the challenger is seeking to be named as sole inventor.[282]

Co-owners

11.148   Inventions are frequently made up by a combination of multiple features, and if different people have contributed different features towards a unitary invention then each person is considered as a co-inventor.[283]

■ Staeng Ltd's Patent [1996] RPC 183

The invention in question had been devised in an incremental fashion by two employees of two separate companies—one providing an initial design, the other providing an idea for

---

[279] Patents Act 1977, s 13.

[280] *Henry Brothers (Magherafelt) Ltd v The Ministry of Defence and the Northern Ireland Office* [1999] RPC 442.

[281] *Stanelco Fibre Optics Ltd's Applications* [2005] RPC 15.

[282] See *Yeda Research and Development Co Ltd v Rhone-Poulenc Rorer International Holdings Inc and others* [2008] RPC 1 on seeking to be substituted as the sole inventor.

[283] It is not enough for one party merely to follow the instructions of another, see *Stanelco Fibre Optics Ltd v Biopress Technology Ltd* [2005] RPC 319.

improvement. It was held that this was an example of joint invention. The inventive concept lay in the use of a coiled spring to hold a cable to an adaptor—the idea of such a device came from the employee seeking to be named as sole inventor. However, the problem was solved by the other inventor, who also had expertise in the area, unlike the first employee who, it was found, would not have come up with the solution but for the role of the second employee.

11.149   Disputes such as these are resolved primarily on the basis of the evidence which the court is willing to accept. Reliable evidence of what was said, or agreed, or done, is of crucial importance. The most prudent thing to do is to begin a collaborative relationship with a written contract which addresses issues of ownership from the beginning.

11.150   The rights of co-inventors are dealt with by section 36 of the Patents Act 1977, as amended. The guiding principle is that each owner is entitled to an equal, undivided share of the property,[284] an equal share in benefits from the patent, and has an independent right to exploit the invention without the need to consult or involve co-owners.[285] This does not extend to the granting of licences, assignations or mortgages, however, which requires the consent of all co-owners.[286] Reforms from EPC 2000 allow owners to apply to amend or revoke their own patent after grant, but in the case of co-owners this must be with the consent of all owners.[287] It is possible, however, to vary some of these rights by agreement, for example, that one of the co-owners can grant licences unilaterally. Moreover, the Comptroller has the discretion to vary these provisions if it is thought that to do so would result in a fairer balance of interests.[288] Any disputes over who might have a valid proprietary interest in a patent are similarly determined by the Comptroller in the first instance.[289] This discretion has survived a human rights challenge when it was argued before the Court of Appeal that the discretion could not be legitimately exercised to require a co-owner to grant a licence: *Derek Hughes v Neil Paxman*.[290] The court disagreed, pointing out that it could not be the case that the legislator intended the exploitation of patents to be frustrated by deadlocks situations. Moreover, there was no breach of human rights so long as the Comptroller acted rationally, fairly and proportionately in light of all of the circumstances. The scope of the discretionary power was not so wide as to be arbitrary.

The employer/employee relationship

Patents Act 1977, s 39(1)

Notwithstanding anything in any rule of law, an invention made by an employee shall, as between him and his employer, be taken to belong to his employer for the purposes of this Act and all other purposes if—

   (a) it was made in the course of the normal duties of the employee or in the course of duties falling outside his normal duties, but specifically assigned to him, and the circumstances in either case were such that an invention might reasonably be expected to result from the carrying out of his duties; or

---

[284] Patents Act 1977, s 36(1).   [285] Patents Act 1977, s 36(2).
[286] Patents Act 1977, s 36(3)(b). In Scotland this also extends to the granting of a security.
[287] Patents Act 1977, s 36(3)(a), as amended by Patents Act 2004, s 9.   [288] Patents Act 1977, s 37(1).
[289] ibid, and Part 7 of the Patents Rules 2007 on proceedings heard before the Comptroller. Section 38 of the 1977 Act deals with the transfer of patents. Section 8 of the 1977 Act deals with the resolution of questions about entitlement to the patent which arise *before* grant.
[290] [2006] EWCA Civ 818.

> (b) the invention was made in the course of the duties of the employee and, at the time of making the invention, because of the nature of his duties and the particular responsibilities arising from the nature of his duties he had a special obligation to further the interests of the employer's undertaking.
>
> (2) Any other invention made by an employee shall, as between him and his employer, be taken for those purposes to belong to the employee.

11.151   Let's explore the elements of this provision. First, the default position is that inventions created by an employee belong to the employee and this cannot be varied by contract—such a term would be unenforceable.[291] Moreover, no one else who works with an employer, such as a consultant, need worry about their inventions (although this might give rise to problem of co-ownership, see para 11.158 below). It is important to know, therefore, when someone is an *employee*. This is determined on standard labour law principles[292] and the distinction is made between a contract of service (employee) and a contract of services (consultant or commissioned work).[293] Only in the specific circumstances outlined above can an employer lay claim to an employee's invention. 'Invention' in this case does not simply mean a patentable invention, that is, one that meets the patentability criteria in this chapter, but it extends to any invention in a broad sense made by an employee and satisfying the above criteria in s 39. So a claim may be made to an invention even if a patent will not, and could not, be sought.

11.152   The provisions apply when an employee has invented something *either* in the course of his normal duties *or* when specific duties are assigned to him and in *both* cases the nature of those duties is such that an invention is the likely result.[294] Moreover, in other contexts when an employee has a *special obligation* to further his employer's interests then resulting inventions may also be claimed. This class of employee usually includes managers or directors with over-arching responsibilities which necessarily encompass inventive activity within a business. The Court of Appeal in *Liffe Administration & Management v Pinkova*[295] ruled on the meaning of 'normal duties' under section 39(1) of the Patents Act 1977 and dismissed an employee's claim to an invention relating to an electronic trading system that he had devised while employed by Liffe. The ruling emphasised that the test under section 39(1)(a) is an objective one and that duties are not only established and set in the terms of the original contract, but may evolve over time as the job changes. It was also stated that the expectations an employer might have that an invention will result from an employee's normal duties should be directly linked to the person and the skills they possess; the reasonableness of the expectation should be judged accordingly. If a person is hired to innovate it would normally follow that the provisions of section 39(1) would be satisfied.

---

[291] See *Electrolux v Hudson* [1977] RPC 312. See too, Patents Act 1977, s 42(2) which makes unenforceable any attempt to derogate from the rights of the employee in respect of his own inventions, and Patents Manual (2007), paras 42.03–42.04.

[292] On the nature of the duty of fidelity between employee and employer see *Helmet Integrated Systems Ltd v Tunnard and others* [2007] FSR 16.

[293] In the design case of *Ultraframe UK Ltd v Fielding* [2004] RPC 24 (see also para 9.70) it was said that a contract of service is typified by (1) circumstances where the servant has agreed that, in consideration of a wage of other remuneration, he would provide his own work and skill in the performance of some service for his master, (2) he agreed, expressly or implied, that in the performance of that service, he would be subject to the other's control in a sufficient degree to make the other master, and (3) the provisions of the contract were consistent with it being a contract of service. Control is key.

[294] An early decision is *Harris' Patent* [1985] RPC 19 which considered the pre-1977 Act position where this area was governed by the common law.

[295] [2007] RPC 30.

■ *Greater Glasgow Health Board's Application* [1996] RPC 207

A Registrar employed by the health board in the Tennent Research Institute invented an optical spacing device for use with an indirect opthalmoscope. He conceived of this idea while at home and not during his professional duties. His job description stated that his duties were clinical in nature: he had a duty to serve in the out-patient department, and this included casualty, opthalmic and general care of in-patients and opthalmic surgery. His job description also included a number of other functions, which were not described as duties, and which included undergraduate and postgraduate teaching. He was also 'expected to avail himself of the facilities provided' for basic and clinical research. This having been said, his Head of Department did not consider that he was employed to carry out research. The health board argued that because of the very nature of his working environment in a research institute, he was expected to use his experiences of treating patients to produce novel forms of treatment and prevention. The patent was taken in the name of the board and the dispute arose when Dr Montgomery argued that he should be named as sole inventor. It was held that Dr Montgomery should be named as such. It was fallacious to expect that a person with clinical duties and responsibilities towards patients should necessarily be required by his contract to devise novel ways of diagnosing and treating patients. The fact that he was employed within a research institute was not, of itself, determinative of the issue. The focus must be on the terms of the employment contract as they stood, and these clearly revealed that his duties were clinical in nature and not innovative.

11.153   Another relevant factor in this case was that the creation of the invention had nothing to do with the carrying out of his duties. Dr Montgomery was a junior member of staff who spent nearly all of his time treating patients. He made the invention in his own time, he was not working to treat any particular patient or class of patients, indeed, he was concerned with the problem of eye examination generally—the invention could not be reasonably expected to result from his duties.

11.154   The importance of evidence in these cases is illustrated by *Liffe Administration and Management v Pinkava and another* which concerned inventions related to the trading of various types of financial instruments on an electronic exchange. Evidence to the court at first instance[296] showed that the inventions developed by the employee were not part of his normal duties as a product manager employed in the marketing and product management department, but that they did arise directly from a project he was assigned to work on to develop an exchange tradable contract and this was evidenced by the nature of the initial discussions and subsequent focus of the project. The employee tried to argue that the inventions were ones unlikely to arise from the discharge of his duties, inter alia, because the employer had no history of invention. This was held not to be necessary for section 39(1) to apply, as the employer (any employer?) had a clear interest in new developments and products. It was also relevant from the evidence that the employee was known as an 'ideas man' in the firm and the expectation was that he would be creative in the discharge of his duties. This was confirmed by the Court of Appeal in dismissing the appeal.[297]

---

[296] [2006] EWHC 595 (Pat).   [297] See also *Cinpres Gas Injection Ltd v Melea Ltd* [2008] RPC 17.

> **Key point on employee invention**
>
> - It is not sufficient merely to produce an invention which would assist an employer in tackling the problems which he faces in the course of his business or profession. This is an example of an *indirect* invention which, at best, builds on the general experience and stock of knowledge of the individual inventor, *qua* an individual and not *qua* employee. Rather, an invention which is to fall to an employer must result from the workings of an employee *qua* inventor. In other words, when his job of work *directly* requires him to invent or his duties *directly* lead him to invent; all as a *direct* consequence of doing his job of work.

11.155   Consider now *Staeng Ltd's Patent* (para 11.148 above). The circumstances of this dispute involved, inter alia, the question of whether an employee of company H, which was soon to be taken over by company S, could be named as the sole inventor of an invention which was not part of the business of his employer. The invention in suit related to a means of securing an electrical cable sheathing to the body portion of a 'connector backshell adaptor'. Company H was not in the business of backshell adaptors, but rather was concerned with developing products for the cable industry. All technology relating to backshell adaptors had to be bought in from company S. The employee argued that it was not reasonable to imply that an individual's obligations included the making of an invention if that invention was not within the business of the employer. The employer argued that its broader business interests included backshell adaptors, and indeed, it had marketed S's adaptors as though they were its own. The employee's duties involved innovation and the seeking out of novel uses for existing products. It was held that the invention belonged to the employer. The employee had made the invention in the course of his normal duties and the circumstances were such that the invention might reasonably be expected to results from the carrying on of his duties. The intimate connection between the products produced by the employer and the invention meant that the invention was within the broad field of the employer's business. Furthermore, the position of the employee as a senior executive with knowledge and insight into the business's future interests, viz, the merger, meant he had a *special obligation* under section 39(1).

11.156   Factors which might make a difference in these cases therefore include:

- Where was the invention produced (work or home)?
- Was the invention produced during working hours?
- What is the standing of the employee within the employer's hierarchy?
- What are the specific contractual duties and which other duties can reasonably be inferred?
- What role has the employee actually assumed in the discharge of his duties?

> **Question**
>
> Do you think it is relevant if materials from the workplace are used to create the invention?

11.157   We can easily imagine a situation where an employer might be entitled to an employee's invention, but that the employee's claim to the invention is partial because he has invented the product or process jointly with someone else who is not an employee. In such cases what should the employer do?

11.158   These questions were addressed by the Scottish Court of Session in *Goddin and Rennie's Application*.[298] In this case the patent concerned covers for circular tanks, in particular fish tanks. While the original design was conceived by G in respect of his salmon-rearing business, the design was improved by R, who was commissioned to make the net covers. Initially both contributors were named on the patent application but a dispute arose and G brought a claim that the patent application should proceed solely in the name of his company, W. The arguments were: first, R's contribution was merely ancillary to the inventive principle which had been discovered by G. Second, even if that were not the case, the contract of services contained an implied term that W was entitled to the exclusive benefit of what R devised in the course of his work. The Court held that G was entitled to the patent in his name alone. R's contract was clearly to produce an improved design, but the contract would not make business sense unless it contained an implied term that any improved design was the property of W. This having been said, certain features of the frame for the nets had been suggested by R prior to, and separately from, the contract and as such he was entitled to the benefit of the features introduced by them. As a consequence, while G was entitled to the patent, R was entitled to an irrevocable exclusive licence, with power to sub-license in respect of the features which he had added.

11.159   This ruling in respect of the intellectual property of the commissioned person, and the authorities on which it is based,[299] reflects some of the approaches we have seen in copyright law where there has been the recognition of *equitable interests* in respect of commissioned work (see paras 3.25ff). While the starting point is that a commissioned person retains the intellectual property of that which he creates, it is also true that it is illogical to enter a contract with someone to create a new entity if there is no underlying assumption that the entity will come within the control of the commissioner. It makes sound sense to read an implied clause into the contract in these circumstances. Note, however, the law does not specifically recognise equitable interests in the context. The practical answer is that the commissioned person should include an *express* term that any IPRs are to be retained if that is his intention. In practice, of course, it is unlikely that any such term will be accepted. More likely to survive is a term which specifically states that the invention is to be regarded as having been created jointly with licensing or other rights specified accordingly.

Compensation of employees for certain inventions

11.160   Sections 40 and 41 of the Patents Act 1977 provide for a compensation scheme for employees when the provisions of section 39 apply or when they have transferred their patent rights to their employer and the benefit in return is inadequate. These provisions have been reformed over the years to widen the circumstances in which compensation might be paid. Thus section 40(1) now provides:

> '**40(1)** Where it appears to the court or the comptroller on an application made by an employee within the prescribed period that—

---

[298] [1996] RPC 141.   [299] *Bogrich & Shape Machines Ltd's Application*, 4 November 1994, unreported.

(a)   the employee has made an invention belonging to the employer for which a patent has been granted,

(b)   having regard among other things to the size and nature of the employer's undertaking, the invention or the patent for it (or the combination of both) is of outstanding benefit to the employer, and

(c)   by reason of those facts it is just that the employee should be awarded compensation to be paid by the employer,

the court or the comptroller may award him such compensation of an amount determined under section 41 below.'

11.161   Note compensation can be triggered when the patent *or* the invention *or* both prove to be of outstanding benefit to the employer. Previously, the scheme could only be invoked when the *patent* was of outstanding benefit. Not only was this more difficult to prove, but it necessitated that a patent was granted. As we have seen, even non-patentable inventions can be claimed by employers and even those which are patentable might sometimes be better protected by other means, for example trade secrets (see Chapter 18). This anomaly has now been rectified. Notwithstanding, a serious hurdle still faces the employee because the qualifying threshold remains the same: there must be an *outstanding benefit* to the employer. How do we know when this has happened?

■ *British Steel plc's patent* [1992] RPC 117

In this case the employer contended that the benefit derived from the employee's invention of a new valve, for use in steel-making, should not be linked to the patented product itself but rather to the extensive development work expended on it by the employer after the application had been filed. This work had been carried out to remove what the Comptroller's hearing called 'major technical obstacles [which] stood in the way of the deployment of the rotary valve'. Thus, the employer had to incur considerable development costs before any tangible benefit accrued. This argument was, however, rejected by the hearing officer. This having been said, the employee's claim was refused because benefits had not (yet) flowed to the employer from the grant of the patent. Thus a real benefit must be shown and not merely the promise of benefit.

11.162   Is this 'just'? Were it otherwise the paradox would arise whereby the more an employee invention departs from traditional technology the less likely it would ever be that he would receive compensation because of the necessary development costs which would be incurred by the employer.

11.163   Benefit from a patent is readily provable if the employer is in receipt of royalty payments from licensees. If, however, the employer chooses to exploit the invention himself, it becomes harder to prove.

 Discussion point   For answer guidance visit www.oxfordtextbooks.co.uk/orc/macqueen2e/

How many reasons can you think of for an increased order book?

■ *Memco-Med's Patent* [1992] RPC 403

Did the employer's sales of a patented product to a single customer amount to the creation of an outstanding benefit? In this case the lift manufacturers Otis encouraged the employer, Memco-Med, to refine an existing patent which related to door detector units and two employees undertook the task. As an incentive Otis ordered 1,000 models of the new unit. However, the unit experienced problems and Otis changed their order to buy a new improved model. Nonetheless, in the overall period the employer earned £4 million. Unfortunately for the employees who claimed compensation, the Court considered that sales were due entirely to good relations between the companies and could not be attributable to the patent, even although the new model 'stood on the shoulders' of the work done by the employees.

■ *GEC's patent* [1992] RPC 107

The employer obtained a patent for a cockpit display unit which had been invented by their employee for use in military aircraft. The US Air Force placed substantial orders. Unfortunately, contracts could not be fulfilled because units had to be redesigned and tested. Further contracts were placed for non-patented equipment worth $75 million each. In 1986 the employer signed a main contract to supply redesigned equipment based on the patented invention. This contract was worth $72 million. The employee argued that the early sums of $75 million should be regarded as benefits deriving from the possession of a patent over the invention. It was argued that such contracts would not have been agreed but for the initial order based on the patent. It was held that the evidential burden falls on the shoulders of the employee. He was unable to discharge this given the overall size of the firm involved; in relative terms, the figures in question were not 'outstanding'.

■ *Kelly & Anor v GE Healthcare Ltd* [2009] RPC 12

This case is the first to award compensation to employees under section 40 of the 1977 Act. Two inventors sought a share of the profits under section 40 as compensation for the invention of a compound used in radioactive imaging which they developed while employed as research scientists. In deciding whether the patents were of 'outstanding benefit' to the company the court took all circumstances into consideration, including the size and nature of the employer's undertaking, and came to the conclusion that the benefits of the invention went far beyond anything which could normally be expected to arise from the sort of work the employees had undertaken. The benefit was not limited to profits from sales as the resulting patents also protected the business against generic competition and were highly influential in achieving corporate deals. The patents had recently expired which allowed the court to quantify more exactly the benefit those patents had brought to the employer. Courts had shown themselves unwilling in previous cases to speculate on future benefits that patents might bring, but as that was unnecessary here, this could not bar the award of compensation.[300]

> **What is an 'outstanding benefit'?**
>
> (1) Benefit in question must exist at time of employee's application (future possible benefits affect quantum of compensation only).
> (2) 'Outstanding' is much more than 'substantial' and 'valuable'.
> (3) 'Outstanding' must be assessed in light of all facts and circumstances. Thus, compensation is more likely from a smaller firm than a larger firm. Paradoxically, this is likely to mean that smaller firms will be liable to pay compensation which only larger firms can truly afford.

---

[300] See A Hobson and T Shafran, '*Kelly and Chiu v GE Healthcare Limited*: pharmaceutical companies at risk of successful employee inventor compensation claim following landmark ruling' (2009) 31(10) EIPR 523.

11.164   The scheme also applies when an employee retains an entitlement to his invention but has assigned it or granted an exclusive licence to his employer and when the benefit under the contract is 'inadequate' and it is 'just' that the employee should be awarded compensation.[301]

 Question

How would you assess what was 'inadequate' and 'just' in these circumstances? Could you get access to your employer's accounts to see what income had been generated?

11.165   Section 41 of the 1977 Act deals with the amount of compensation to be awarded.[302] This must obviously be decided on a case-by-case basis. The guiding parameters include the following: (1) the aim is to confer a *fair share* of the benefit of the invention and/or the patent; (2) *benefit* includes money and money's worth from exploitation of the invention and/or patent; (3) it is assessed by reference to the following, among other things; (4) nature of the employee's duties and any benefits from the invention; (5) the effort and skill he has displayed; (6) the efforts and skill of others in developing the invention; (7) the effort and skill of the employer in bringing the invention to fruition and market.

Infringement proceedings

11.166   It is all very well to have a range of sophisticated patent rights but these are worthless in the absence of a robust enforcement system. We consider broader issues of enforcement in Chapter 21; here we concentrate on enforcement of patents through infringement proceedings.

11.167   The first thing to note when you read the cases is that an action for infringement is often met with a counter-claim that the patent is invalid and should be revoked. We therefore deal with revocation in the next section. This possibility means that a patent is vulnerable throughout its life and it is a strategic question whether it is worth bringing infringement proceedings when this might result in the complete extinguishing of your property right in the long run.

11.168   If proceedings are brought, it ends up being an extremely costly business. The *Gowers Review of Intellectual Property* estimated, for example, that a firm challenging a patent can expect to pay £750,000 for a simple case, and if one loses, the costs of the other side could bring the total to over £1.5 million.[303]

11.169   This section is divided into two parts. In the first part we consider the grounds for infringement actions and the types of conduct which qualify. In the second part we consider how the courts approach the interpretation of patent claims because it is in this interpretation that we discover the fine lines between legitimate and illegitimate conduct with respect to patented inventions.

---

[301] Patents Act 1977, s 40(2).   [302] Amended by the Patents Act 2004, s 10(3).
[303] *Gowers Review of Intellectual Property* (HM Treasury, 2006), para 3.21.

What counts as patent infringement?

11.170   Article 64(3) EPC 2000 makes it clear that infringement proceedings are to be dealt with by national law. In the UK, the principal infringing acts are laid out in sections 60(1) and 60(2) of the Patents Act 1977.

> '**60(1)** Subject to the provision of this section, a person infringes a patent for an invention if, but only if, while the patent is in force, he does any of the following things in the United Kingdom in relation to the invention without the consent of the proprietor of the patent, that is to say—
> (a) where the invention is a product, he makes, disposes of, offers to dispose of, uses or imports the product or keeps it whether for disposal or otherwise;
> (b) where the invention is a process, he uses the process or he offers it for use in the United Kingdom when he knows, or it is obvious to a reasonable person in the circumstances, that its use there without the consent of the proprietor would be an infringement of the patent;
> (c) where the invention is a process, he disposes of, offers to dispose of, uses or imports any product obtained directly by means of that process.'

11.171   So, as we can see, it is important to know what kind of invention we are dealing with because what counts as infringement depends on this and, sometimes, on the knowledge of the alleged infringer. Note, however, in the context of a product there is no knowledge requirement. This means that even the so-called innocent infringer can be liable if he carries out any of the acts detailed in section 60(1)(a) which deals with product inventions or in section 60(1)(c) which deals with process inventions which result in a product. It is irrelevant whether the infringer knew of the patent or of the lack of owner consent. This is referred to as 'absolute' liability.[304]

 Question

Can we justify such a draconian approach to liability?

11.172   These are all examples of *direct* infringement which involve direct dealings with the invention itself. Section 60(2) is concerned with *indirect* infringement which arises when someone facilitates a directly infringing act by supplying or offering to supply any of the means, relating to an essential element of the invention, for putting the invention into effect *and* with actual or constructive knowledge that those means are suitable for putting, and are intended to put, the invention into effect in the UK.

11.173   Note this last point. We have already established that patents are creatures of territorial effect only, and so infringement proceedings in the UK can only be brought with respect to activities within its shores. It is also trite to note that the law is only concerned with acts done during the life of the patent. Infringement proceedings can be brought for any conduct from the date the patent application is published to the end of the patent's term.[305] Those who can bring infringement proceedings include the proprietor of the patent, co-proprietors[306] and exclusive licensees.[307]

---

[304]   *Merrell Dow v Norton* [1996] RPC 76, per Lord Hoffmann at 92.

[305]   Albeit that the right cannot be enforced until the patent is actually granted, see the Patents Act 1977, s 69.

[306]   Each co-proprietor can do any act independently with respect to the invention which would otherwise be an infringement: Patents Act 1977, s 66, and each can bring independent infringement proceedings without the consent of the others subject to the proviso that co-owners are made parties to the proceedings, s 66(2).

[307]   An exclusive licensee has the same right as the proprietor to bring infringement actions, see the Patents Act 1977, s 67(1).

11.174   Let us consider each of the infringing behaviours in turn.

Making the invention

11.175   It is clearly an infringement to make copies of someone else's existing invention, but what is the position if you buy the original item under patent and then modify it or repair it? This question was considered by the House of Lords in *United Wire Ltd v Screen Repair Services (Scotland) Ltd*[308] which involved mesh screen assemblies used in sifting and filtering machines. The defendants tried to enter the market by selling reconditioned versions of the plaintiffs' screens which had been stripped down and new mesh applied. They then tried to argue that this was mere 'repair' and not 'making' and so outside the scope of section 60(1). It was held that while 'genuine repair' is a legitimate activity, this conduct went far beyond and was equivalent to reproducing an infringing assembly. The concepts of 'repair' and 'making' are entirely distinct in patent law with the latter involving some form of manufacture. The right to repair is not an implied licence, but rather the residual right left over once the parameters of patent protection have been demarcated by the operation of section 60. In the instant case the disassembly of the product was so extreme that it effectively ceased to exist and its reconstitution with new elements was in effect a new infringing manufacture.

Disposing of, offering to dispose of, or using the invention

11.176   Manifestly it is not an infringement of a patent for someone who has bought an example of an invention to sell it on as a piece of personal property—this is another example of the residual rights that the purchaser enjoys; moreover, attempts by a patent proprietor to prevent the sale and circulation of goods that he himself has placed on the market will be faced with challenges under European law because the principle of exhaustion of rights will apply as will the principle of free movement of goods (see Chapter 19). Rather, this provision concerns the commercialisation of infringing copies of an invention, and must include, at least, selling.[309]

Importing the invention

11.177   Here we are concerned with the activities of someone who imports an invention in the course of their trade, for example, with a view to selling them on. A mere carrier or someone who arranges the importation on behalf of the owner of the goods is not considered to be a direct infringer because they have no legal or beneficial interest in those goods.[310] This is true even if this person has sold the goods to the now owner outside the UK.[311] It is possible for two or more parties involved in the importation business to be jointly liable as joint tortfeasors, but this requires a common design or concerted action on all parts. The mere supplying of goods outside the jurisdiction for sale within the jurisdiction is not constitutive of joint tortfeasorship. Nor is it illegal to pass on information to domestic regulatory authorities on behalf of another party who has an intention to receive approval to sell versions of the invention on the domestic market. This does not make the third party complicit in the seller's commercial venture.[312] In keeping with the fragmented territorial nature of patent protection, the ECJ has ruled

[308] [2001] RPC 24.   [309] *Kalman and another v PCL Packaging (UK) Ltd and another* [1982] FSR 406.
[310] *Sabaf* in the House of Lords, n 229 above.
[311] Compare the trade mark case of *Waterford Wedgwood PLC v David Nagli Ltd* [1998] FSR 92 in which the seller imported the goods into the UK while still retaining ownership rights. This constituted infringement.
[312] *Generics (UK) Ltd v H Lundbeck A/S* [2006] EWCA Civ 1261.

that it is not possible to bring patent infringement proceedings in one state against a group of allegedly infringing parties in various different states *even if* those parties belong to the same corporate group and *even if* they have been acting in an identical or similar manner with respect to infringing activity.[313]

Keeping the invention

11.178   Once again, we are concerned here with acts done in the course of trade; acting as a mere custodian of goods does not amount to 'keeping' within the terms of the Act which has been interpreted to mean 'keeping in stock' with a view to furthering business ends. In *McDonald and Another v Graham*[314] the invention in question was promotional 'Z cards' which were designed to fold out to show publicity material and to fold back down to the size of a credit card. Despite instructions to destroy any remaining copies in his possession, a business associate of the patentee was found to have a stock on his business premises. His argument that these were for private or experimental use did not hold on the evidence. Rather, he was 'keeping them in stock for the purposes of his business in order to make use of them as and when it would be beneficial to him to do so'. In contrast there was no finding of 'keeping' in *Smith, Kline and French Labs Ltd v Harbottle*[315] when a quantity of the drug Cimetidine was shipped through Heathrow on its way to Nigeria and held in British Airways's bonded warehouse under the custodianship of Harbottle. It was held that this was not an example of 'keeping' under the statutory provision. The Oxford English Dictionary reveals 26 nuanced meanings of this word and the correct approach for the court was to identify the mischief to be avoided and interpret the term accordingly. If the mere holding of material in a warehouse was intended to be caught by this law it would have been expressed in far stronger terms.[316]

11.179   Section 60(1)(c) confirms that a patent over a process gives monopoly control over any products derived from that process, and this can be a useful tool if, say, the process is performed outside the jurisdiction but the end products are imported into the UK—infringement proceedings could still be brought. The caveat, however, is found in the specific wording of the sub-section when it talks of '...any product obtained *directly* by means of that process'.

■ *Pioneer Electronics Capital Inc v Warner Music Manufacturing Europe GmbH* [1997] RPC 757

This case involved a patented process for manufacturing CDs. The rival company's imported versions of the product certainly seemed to involve the process, but had they been 'directly' obtained? It was held that the question fell to be decided by reference to Article 64(2) EPC, the terminology of which had its origin in German law. The German authorities were consistent in their approach, taking 'directly' (*unmittelbar*) to refer to the product with which the process ended. It was not correct to say that the finished disc was an identical copy of the master. The allegedly infringing devices in the instant case differed in material ways from the patented invention, notably for having gone through three further stages of production. A new and different product emerged from each stage. The Court of Appeal used the expression 'without

---

[313] Case C-539/03 *Roche Nederland BV and others v Primus and another* [2006] All ER (D) 186 (Jul), OJ C 224 of 16.09.2006, p 1.

[314] [1994] RPC 407.   [315] [1980] RPC 363.

[316] This is also a more accurate reflection of the sense in which the term is employed in the Community Patent Convention, Art 29(a) and the two instruments should be read in tandem where possible.

intermediary' implying, perhaps, that the result should be immediate and precluding any possibility of further processing. But the Patent Court has recently considered the issue and raised the possibility from German jurisprudence that it is not the number of intermediary stages which is important, but the question of whether they are material to the identity of the product—only if it emerges with the same identity as the invention will there be infringement.[317]

Indirect infringement

11.180 Section 60(2) deals with indirect or contributory infringement. It states: '…a person…also infringes a patent for an invention if, while the patent is in force and without the consent of the proprietor, he supplies or offers to supply in the United Kingdom a person…with any of the means relating to an essential element of the invention, for putting the invention into effect when he knows, or it is obvious to a reasonable person in the circumstances, that those means are suitable for putting, and are intended to put, the invention into effect in the United Kingdom.' The important issues are well-illustrated in the case of *Menashe Business Mercantile Ltd and another v William Hill Organisation Ltd*[318] which also tells us something about what is meant by infringement occurring in the UK. This is because the case involved an online gaming system linked to a central computer in the Caribbean. Customers were sent software on CDs which allowed their home computers to communicate with the host computer. The patentees owned an interactive gaming system with a host computer that operated in a similar fashion to that of the defendants, but could this system be infringed when the defendants' computer was off-shore? Moreover, could the supply of CDs to British customers amount to supply of the means for putting the invention into effect? It was held that the alleged infringers' host computer was 'used' in the UK by customers in a very real sense and it did not matter that it was physically located abroad. The key issue was whether persons in the UK had been supplied with the means of implementing the invention, and this was so through the supply of the CDs which allowed access to the host computer and so to the entire online gaming system. The supply of the CDs in the UK would be taken as intended to put the invention into effect and the patent was infringed.

11.181 The classic example of contributory infringement is the supply of kits for an invention which are assembled at a later date. Clearly, if you provide all of the necessary elements of an invention you are supplying the 'essential element' of the invention. By the same token, if you merely provide 'staple commercial products' which someone else takes and puts together into an infringing device or apparatus, you would not be liable for infringement, for example, if you merely provides the nuts and bolts and electrically circuits. By the same token, your level of knowledge, or indeed intention to be complicit, are relevant factors in whether infringement proceedings could be brought or would succeed.[319]

 Question

What counts as 'staple commercial products'?

---

[317] *Halliburton Energy Services Inc v Smith International and Others* [2005] EWHC 1623 (Pat).
[318] [2003] 1 All ER 279, [2003] 1 WLR 1462.   [319] Patents Act 1977, s 60(3).

Interpretation of patent claims

11.182 The question of whether there is infringement is far from straightforward when a rival has produced their own version of an invention aimed at the same technical problem and solving it in similar technical ways, perhaps with similar features. How do we know if such variants infringe an existing patent? This brings us to the complex question of *interpretation of patent claims*. We have already considered the importance of careful drafting of claims in the previous chapter, and we have made the point that it is imperative to choose the language of claims carefully because this will delineate the nature, breadth and scope of any monopoly granted. We now turn to consider the rules that apply when these claims have to be interpreted. It is probably in the realm of interpretation that EPC 1973 brought most changes to the law in the UK. Article 69(1) EPC 1973 provided that '[t]he extent of the protection conferred by a European patent or a European patent application shall be determined by the terms of the claims,' and the drawings and description shall also be used to interpret the claims. This remains unchanged in EPC 2000 and its UK equivalent is found in section 125 of the Patents Act 1977. Article 69 has, however, been accompanied by a Protocol on Interpretation of Article 69 because a variety of approaches were used around Europe at the time the EPC was drafted. The Protocol is designed to provide guidance to national courts on how to tackle interpretation in a uniform fashion that is in keeping with the spirit of the Convention. That spirit is grounded in the Continental legal tradition which favours a *purposive approach* to interpretation, that is, one that seeks to give effect to the underlying reasons for the particular legal provision.

11.183 This posed a challenge for the UK which had a very different tradition and was inclined to adopt a *literal approach* to claim interpretation, that is, to ask what is the literal meaning of the words used. What we have seen, then, in the last quarter century or so, is a shift of perspective among the UK judiciary in an attempt to accommodate a more purposive stance. It is a matter of ongoing discussion as to how well they have faired. This process actually began before Article 69 and its Protocol came about, as we see below, but for the sake of completeness here are the principal provisions of the Protocol as embodied in EPC 2000.

Protocol on Interpretation of Article 69 EPC—Article 1

'**Article 69** should not be interpreted as meaning that the extent of the protection conferred by a European patent is to be understood as that defined by the strict, literal meaning of the wording used in the claims, the description and drawings being employed only for the purpose of resolving an ambiguity found in the claims.

Nor should it be taken to mean that the claims serve only as a guideline and that the actual protection conferred may extend to what, from a consideration of the description and drawings by a person skilled in the art, the patent proprietor has contemplated.

On the contrary, it is to be interpreted as defining a position between these extremes which combines a fair protection for the patent proprietor with a reasonable degree of legal certainty for third parties.'

11.184 This clearly eschews a literal approach (which is thought to be too narrow), but equally it does not give carte blanche to discover a patentee's true purpose or intentions (which is thought to be too broad). The expectation is that a middle course should be steered; one which seeks both certainty and fairness of outcome. It is by no means an easy task and helps to explain why patent interpretation is a complex business. It is important that we begin by laying out the parameters of Article 69 and its Protocol because, as Lord Hoffmann indicated in *Kirin-Amgen v*

Hoechst Marion Roussel Ltd,[320] these embody the only compulsory question in claim interpretation, viz, 'what would the person skilled in the art have understood the patentee to have used the language of the claim to mean?' Everything else—that is, any approaches that have been developed over the years (see paras 11.188ff below)—are mere guidance towards an answer to this question. But Lord Hoffmann also said that it is important to have a sense of the origins of the English (British) rules of interpretation, so let us begin with the seminal House of Lords ruling that signalled the sea-change in this field.

■ *Catnic Components Ltd v Hill and Smith Ltd* [1982] RPC 183 (HL)

Catnic were the proprietors of a patent in respect of steel lintels of considerable commercial success. The defendants decided to enter the field and to copy Catnic's lintels. Catnic served a writ on the defendants for patent infringement and as a result the latter changed the design of their lintels by slanting the rear support member at 6°–8° from the vertical, compared to that of the plaintiffs which was perpendicular to the base (see below). Claim 1 of the patent required that the rear support member 'extend vertically'. The question therefore arose as to whether the new lintels made by the defendants infringed the patent of the plaintiffs. This would not be so on a literal interpretation of the words used.

It was held that:

- The patent had been infringed. A literal interpretation of the wording of claims in a patent is not the correct approach to adopt when interpreting claims unless this is clearly the intention of the patentee. The English tradition of applying a 'pith and marrow' perspective was no longer appropriate.[321] A purposive rather than literal approach to interpretation is appropriate.

- The effect of the angulation of the rear support member was negligible as regards the load bearing capacity of the lintel. At an angle of 6° the reduction is only 0.6%. At 8° the reduction is 1.2%. In other words, this had no material effect on how the lintel worked.

- The question to be asked in each case is as follows: would persons with practical knowledge and experience of the kind of work in which the invention is intended to be used, understand that strict compliance with the particular descriptive word or phrase appearing in the claim was intended by the patentee to be an essential requirement of the invention so that *any* variant would fall outside the monopoly claimed, even though it could have no material effect upon the way the invention worked?

- The question is to be answered in the negative only when it would be apparent to any reader skilled in the art that a particular descriptive word or phrase used in a claim cannot have been intended by a patentee, who was also skilled in the art, to exclude minor variations which, to the knowledge of both him and the readers to whom the patent is addressed, could have no material effect upon the way in which the invention worked.

- In this case no plausible reason was advanced why any rational patentee should want to place so narrow a limitation on his invention. To do so would render his monopoly worthless for all practical purposes.

---

[320] [2005] RPC 9.

[321] The 'pith and marrow' approach was invented by Lord Cairns in *Clark v Adie* (1877) 2 App Cas 315 at 320 and involved a rather vague approach of stripping the invention down by the removal of 'immaterial' or 'non-essential' features or integers to deter what, if anything, the infringer had taken.

Figure 11.1 Claimant's lintel

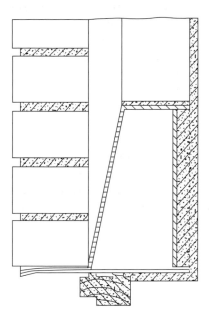

Figure 11.2 Defendant's lintel

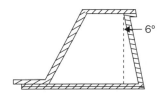

11.185 The decision has had a considerable role to play in changing the way in which patent monopolies function. It is now no longer possible (as it was pre-*Catnic*) to make minor changes in a product or process in an attempt to evade the terms of the monopoly. This also means that improvements in efficiency or speed of operation will not necessarily lead to a patentable invention and will infringe an existing patent if the essential idea embodied in the patent remains unchanged. By the same token, it does not follow that a purposive approach is necessarily more generous to the patentee. It is contingent on what the skilled person would consider the purpose to be, and this may be fairly narrow in scope.

11.186 An essential feature of this decision was the fact that the change of angulation in the rear support member made a negligible change to the load bearing capacity of the lintel. The House of Lords was emphatic in its assertion that the test laid down above does not apply where the variant does in fact have a material effect upon the way in which the invention works. If this is so then the variant will not infringe the particular claim. Furthermore, if the fact that a variant made no material difference to the way the invention works was not obvious to a person skilled in the particular art at the date of publication of the patent, then the variant will also fall outside the claim.

11.187   This case began to bring the UK into line with the approaches of the EPO and other continental patent courts which apply a purposive interpretation to patents as a matter of course.[322] This does not, however, mean that we have as yet achieved consistency across Europe.[323]

11.188   The case which illustrates this all too well, and which put the most important gloss on the *Catnic* decision, is *Improver Corporation v Remington Consumer Products Ltd*.[324] In this case litigation was conducted on the same matter in both England and Germany. The dispute concerned an electronic hair removing device for women called the 'Epilady'. The device functioned through the use of a high speed rotating arc-shaped spring which plucked hair from the skin. The alleged infringing device—the 'Smooth & Silky'—performed the same function by the use of a high speed rotating arc-shaped synthetic rubber rod into which were cut slits which captured the hairs. In England the court applied *Catnic* and came to the conclusion that the patent had not been infringed because although the variant made no material difference to the way in which the invention worked, and that to adopt the rubber rod was obvious to a person skilled in the art, the fact that the words of the relevant patent claim referred specifically to a 'helical spring' and made no mention of any other mechanism for working the invention meant that the interpretation of the term 'helical spring' could not be stretched to include a rubber rod. In the equivalent German decision the court came to the opposite conclusion. The German court was satisfied that the patent was clearly infringed because of the lack of material difference and the obviousness of replacing the spring with a rubber rod. It saw no reason to dwell on the actual words of the patent.

11.189   This is an issue of variants which amount to *equivalents* to a patented invention. That is, although they may differ in appearance, form, or even certain technical features, there can be infringement if they amount, in essence, to the embodiment of the same inventive concept and these modifications do not bring about a material change in the way the variant works. Note, however, while it is acceptable in the UK to talk of these variants as 'equivalents' this is not to be confused with the idea of a *doctrine of equivalents* which embodies a particular test for infringement, and is often used as a shorthand to refer to the approach in the United States.[325] This does not apply in the UK, nor, indeed, do we have a general doctrine of equivalents as the House of Lords has confirmed (see para 11.94).[326] The concern with the US doctrine of equivalents is that it has been interpreted to extend protection to things beyond the boundaries of the claims which perform substantially the same function in substantially the same way to obtain the same result.[327] This is precisely what *Catnic* set out to avoid—it is the claims which delimit the scope of monopoly, nothing more, and it is bad policy to allow a monopoly beyond the scope of claims as these have been drafted. Indeed, the UK courts have been generally very wary of discussion of equivalents, but this must change because EPC 2000 added a new Article 2 to the Protocol on Interpretation of Article 69 thus:

---

[322] The same purposive approach is employed in Scotland, see *Trunature Ltd v Scotnet (1974) Ltd and Others* [2006] CSOH 114.

[323] The House of Lords in *Kirin-Amgen Inc v Hoechst Marion Roussel Ltd* [2005] RPC 9 took the view that the purposive approach in *Catnic* is 'precisely in accordance with the Protocol', para 48. See further P England, 'Towards a single pan-European standard—common concepts in UK and continental European patent law: Part 1: scope of patent protection and inventive concept' (2010) 32(5) EIPR 195.

[324] [1990] FSR 181.

[325] As Lord Hoffmann said in *Kirin-Amgen*, n 323 above at para 37: 'it is frankly acknowledged that it allows the patentee to extend his monopoly beyond the claims.' See *Graver Tank & Manufacturing Co Inc v Linde Air Products Co* (1950) 339 US 605 at 607.

[326] cf J Brinkhof, 'Is there a European Doctrine of Equivalence?' (2002) 33 IIC 911.

[327] *Festo Corp v Shoketsu Kinzoku Kogyo Kabushiki Co Ltd* (2002) 535 US 722— Supreme Court upholding existing approach.

> ## Article 2—Equivalents
>
> For the purpose of determining the extent of protection conferred by a European patent, due account shall be taken of any element which is equivalent to an element specified in the claims.

11.190   The obvious question is what is meant by 'due account' and does the UK approach conform to this? Let's examine the specifics of *Improver* in more details since they have set the tone since their inception in 1989.[328] The value of the case lies in the articulation, per Hoffmann J, of the so-called Improver Questions[329] which act as a guide to determining when a variant will infringe. These can be depicted as shown in Diagram 11.1.

11.191   The importance, then, is to consider the language of the claims as these are drafted in the specification. Contrast this with *Kastner v Rizla and Another*[330] where the Court of Appeal seemed to take the purposive approach several stages further. This case involved a dispute over the patent for a device which interleaves and cuts cigarette papers for sale in small booklet form. The patent holder brought an action against market leader Rizla Ltd, for infringement of his patent and was met with a counterclaim of invalidity based, inter alia, on obviousness. The essential dispute concerned the cutting mechanism employed by each device. Kastner's machine used a platform to which was attached a knife and which moved backwards and forwards by piston rods as the paper was advanced, cutting the paper into strips of desired length. The Rizla machine used as a knife a wheel to which was attached a crescent-shaped blade. The axis of this knife was at a fixed distance from the paper strands. It worked by application of the 'velocity principle'. In holding that the patent was valid and infringed, the Court of Appeal sought to apply a purposive approach when interpreting the main claim of Kastner's patent. However, rather than focusing on 'a particular descriptive word or phrase appearing in the claim'—as Lord Diplock laid down in *Catnic*—the Court felt able to interpret several paragraphs of the claim which described the cutting mechanism to mean that *generally* the device included a 'means for achieving cutting of the interleaved strips using the equal velocity principle'. In other words, the Court took the view that interpretation at a general level of abstraction led to a conclusion of infringement. This, however, is to ignore the details of the invention and further, to ignore the patentee's own words as stated in his claim—words which have the function in law of staking out the limits of his monopoly. This approach goes beyond the intention of the House of Lords in *Catnic* and leans too far in the direction of protection of the patentee.

11.192   In *Hoechst Celanese Corporation v BP Chemicals Ltd and Another*[331] it was held that there is no presumption that words which can have a technical meaning should be given that meaning within the claims. While the courts are open to hear expert testimony of the technical meaning of words, in the final analysis it is for the courts to decide on the particular meaning of any word with regard to the context in which it is used. Where non-technical words are used, expert evidence will not be entertained: *Scanvaegt International A/S and Another v Pelcombe Ltd and Another*.[332] The purposive approach can only apply to descriptive words capable of more than one meaning. If numerals are used in a patent application, for example, to establish upper and

---

[328] Note in *PLG Research v Ardon* [1995] RPC 287 the Court of Appeal doubted if the UK approach was in conformity with interpretation of the Protocol in other European countries, especially Germany.

[329] Also known as the Protocol Questions: *Wheatley v Drillsafe Ltd* [2001] RPC 133 at 142.

[330] [1995] RPC 585.   [331] [1999] FSR 319.   [332] [1998] FSR 786.

Diagram 11.1 The Improver Questions

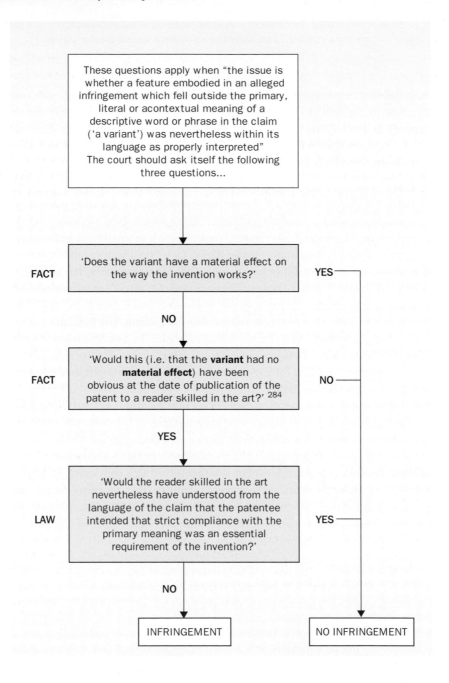

lower limits, these must be taken as the patentee's statement of an essential feature of the invention and there is no scope for considering anything which is not caught by such a numerical value or limit.[333]

11.193 The Improver Questions have been deployed ever since their conception by Hoffmann J, but their limitations have also been fully recognised by their progenitor, as he pointed out in the House of Lords *Kirin-Amgen v Hoechst* (para 11.94 above): they are not a rule of law, but merely a guide to assist a court in determining what the skilled person would understand.[334] Moreover, they apply in the case of equivalents to determine if these fall within the scope of claims and they should not be confused with, or detract from, the overarching principle of interpretation laid down in *Catnic*, being the principle of purposive construction. This, the court held, gives effect to the requirements of the Protocol,[335] and Lord Hoffmann expressly acknowledged the imminent impact of Article 2 of the Protocol, stating 'there is no reason why [equivalence] cannot be an important part of the background of facts known to the skilled man which would affect what he understood the claims to mean.' Note: The concern is to avoid any concept of equivalence that extends protection beyond the limits of the claims. There is no objection to the idea of equivalence as such.

11.194 Lord Hoffmann accepted the limits of the Improver Questions most notably when applied to fast-moving high-technology inventions such as genetic engineering as was the case in this appeal. The dispute concerned artificially made versions of erythropoietin (EPO)—a hormone that stimulates the production of red blood cells in the body. A crucial question in the case was what is the invention? Was it the discovery of the EPO gene sequence (a product) or the new means to make it (a process)? The trial judge held the former, but the Court of Appeal and the House of Lords opted for the latter. The problem, then, was how could Kirin-Amgen interpret their claims to a process broadly enough to cover their rival's product produced by a different and new process (gene activation) not known when Kirin-Amgen filed their patent? The Improver Questions ask a very difficult question at stage two: would it have been obvious to the person skilled in the art that the variant worked in the same way as the invention? Unless we imbue this person with considerable foresight, how can we expect them to envisage how a completely new technology would work sometime in the future? Indeed, it may not be obvious that it would work at all.[336] The Questions did not help in such cases,[337] and instead Lord Hoffmann fell back on the general principle: 'The question is always what the person skilled in the art would have understood the patentee to be using the language of the claim to mean.' On this basis the court held that the skilled person would not have understood the claims to be sufficiently general to encompass the future technology of gene activation. Note: this is not to say that the skilled person cannot foresee future developments, it is to state that the claims must be able to encompass new developments within their original terms. Conversely, if the claims do cover the new innovation then an action for infringement will still succeed even if the new variant is inventive in its own right.

---

[333] See *Auchincloss v Agricultural & Veterinary Supplies Ltd* [1997] RPC 649.

[334] See *Warheit and another v Olympia Tools Ltd and another* [2002] EWCA Civ 1161 for an example of an unsuccessful appeal which tried to argue that the first instance judge was wrong in law for failing to apply the Improver Questions.

[335] *Kirin-Amgen*, n 323 above, para 48.

[336] Lord Hoffmann suggested in passing that a better way to ask the second question would be to follow the German approach and ask if the variant solves the problem underlying the invention by means which have the same technical effect, para 75. This is certainly in keeping with the underlying rational of patent protection in Europe.

[337] In fact, they lead to the unusual outcome that the answer to Q1 might be 'no' (leading to an inference of infringement) but because the technology is new and non-obvious, the answer to Q2 might also be 'no' (which implies no infringement). This was the case in *Kirin-Amgen* and also in *Union Carbide v BP Chemicals Ltd* [1999] RPC 409.

11.195   Doubts of this kind about the limits of the Questions had already been raised by the Court of Appeal[338] when a similar approach was adopted. The Questions are helpful when inventions and modifications deal with figures, measurements and angles, as in *Catnic*, because these are measurable differences. As for other cases, the House of Lords had this to say:

> 'No doubt there will be patent lawyers who are dismayed at the notion that the Protocol questions do not provide an answer in every case. They may feel cast adrift on a sea of interpretative uncertainty. But that is the fate of all who have to understand what people mean by using language.'[339]

The distinct impression conveyed by the House of Lords is not only that this UK approach is in keeping with Article 69 EPC and its Protocol, but that it conforms to the new Article 2 to the Protocol, namely, that 'due account' is taken of equivalents. *Plus ça change . . .*

 Question

Is there any need for the first two Improver Questions in light of this ruling?

11.196   It has been suggested that the first two Improver Questions are merely a shortcut to answering the third question, and moreover, that an approach to asking this question which is more true to the spirit of *Catnic* is to ask: 'whether it would have been apparent to the skilled addressee from the wording of the claim that a limitation to exclude the variant could *not* have been intended by the patentee.'[340]

 Discussion point   For answer guidance visit www.oxfordtextbooks.co.uk/orc/macqueen2e/

Does it matter what way around we ask, or answer, the question?

11.197   Remember that the court must attempt to steer a middle way through claim interpretation. Here is what the House of Lords had to say on this in *Kirin-Amgen*:[341]

> '. . . the object is to combine a fair protection for the patentee with a reasonable degree of certainty for third parties. How is this to be achieved? The claims must be construed in a way which attempts, so far as is possible in an imperfect world, not to disappoint the reasonable expectations of either side. What principle of interpretation would give fair protection to the patentee? Surely, a principle which would give him the full extent of the monopoly which the person skilled in the art would think he was intending to claim. And what principle would provide a reasonable degree of protection for third parties? Surely again, a principle which would not give the patentee more than the full extent of the monopoly which the person skilled in the art would think that he was intending to claim. Indeed, any other principle would also be unfair to the patentee, because it would unreasonably expose the patent to claims of invalidity on grounds of anticipation or insufficiency.'[342]

---

[338] In particular, see *Wheatley*, n 232 above, and *Pharmacia Corp v Merck and Co* [2002] RPC 775.
[339] *Kirin-Amgen*, n 323 above, para 71.
[340] See *Telsonic AG's Patent* [2004] RPC 38 and *Merck & Co Inc v Generics (UK) Ltd* [2004] RPC 31.
[341] See also *Merck & Co Inc v Generics (UK) Ltd* [2004] RPC 31.
[342] Para 47. See H Laddie, 'Kirin Amgen—The End of Equivalents in England?' (2009) 40(1) IIC 3.

11.198   The principles of claim construction have since been summarised by Jacob LJ in *Mayne Pharma v Pharmacia Italia SpA*[343] re-iterating his early account in *Technip France SA's Patent*[344] which had been approved by the House of Lords in *Kirin-Amgen*, with one exception.[345] These embody the elements discussed above and you can read them for yourself.[346]

 Exercise

Read *Mayne Pharma* for a concise summary of the current UK position on claim interpretation.

Declaration or declarator of non-infringement

11.199   It is possible to apply under section 71 of the Patents Act 1977 to the Comptroller or the courts for a declaration (or declarator in Scotland) of non-infringement in respect of either past or future acts done with or to a patented invention. The procedure requires the person seeking the order first to apply to the proprietor in writing for a written acknowledgement of the declaration or declarator claimed;[347] the proprietor should also be furnished with the full particulars of the acts in question at this time.[348] Only if this acknowledgement is refused or simply not given, can the applicant then seek a formal declaration or declarator from the Comptroller in the first instance. The tests for infringement in such cases are those outlined above. Note that while it is possible to put the validity of the patent in issue in such proceedings, a finding of invalidity does not, in itself, result in revocation of the patent. For that we have to turn to our next section which deals with this particular procedure.

Revocation

11.200   We have seen in the previous sections how an action for infringement is often met with a counter-claim for revocation. This is dealt with by section 72(1) of the Patents Act 1977, as amended, with the equivalent provisions appearing as Article 138 EPC 2000. The fact that a revocation procedure exists stands in testament to the fact that the patent granting system is not infallible. Patents may be granted when one of the exclusions or exceptions should have applied (paras 11.5–11.74 above), they may be granted to someone who is not entitled to the patent (para 11.145 above), they may be granted when the patent application does not sufficiently disclose the invention to allow it to be performed by the skilled person (and thereby discharge the public disclosure obligation), they may be granted in terms which give too broad a monopoly compared to what the invention actually contributes to the state of the art[349] (para 10.107 above),

---

[343] [2005] EWCA Civ 137.   [344] [2004] RPC 46 at para 41(a)–(k).

[345] There is no presumption about the width of the claims when considering fairness to the patentee, *Kirin-Amgen*, n 323 above, para 33.

[346] See too, *Pozzoli SpA v BDMO SA* [2007] EWCA Civ 588, [2007] FSR 37.

[347] On the requirements, see *Mallory Metallurgical Products Limited v Black Sivalls and Bryson Incorporated* [1977] RPC 321.

[348] An incomplete written description can be saved by accompanying drawings: *MMD Design & Consultancy Ltd's Patent* [1989] RPC 131.

[349] See in particular, *Biogen Inc v Medeva plc* [1997] RPC 1 per Lord Hoffmann at pp 53–4.

factors to be considered include the vigilance of intellectual property offices in carrying out thorough searches of the prior art, an on-going review of the role for imaginative licensing options, and, as we have seen above, careful application of the criteria for patentability. The Organisation for Economic Co-operation and Development (OECD) has indicated the difficulty of finding common solutions because of the complexity of the area, but it has nevertheless recommended that a multi-strategy approach should be considered at governmental level requiring, inter alia, review of the policies within the IP system itself, the manner by which patents are administered, and changing the behaviour of patentees in the way they exploit their monopolies.[383] The Organisation noted in particular that the role of compulsory licences, although not popular to date, should be revisited.[384]

 Exercise

Look at the Gowers Review and the provisions of Swiss law. Critically assess this proposal to follow the Swiss model, considering the arguments that might be put from all sides on whether this is appropriate for the UK.

Farmers' privileges

11.222   New defences were introduced to the Patents Act 1977 as a result of negotiations on the Biotechnology Directive which we discuss in the next chapter. These are designed to ensure that farmers using traditional harvesting and livestock reproduction techniques are not hindered in their work by the existence and exercise of intellectual property rights relating to biological material. There are two particular defences.

11.223   Section 60(5)(g) concerns propagating material for plants, including material that may be the subject of a patent, which has been sold to a farmer by the patent owner for use in agriculture. The defence provides that the farmer may use the material for further propagation of the material on his own land without infringing any patent. This is not a catch-all provision, however; section 60(6A) of the Act provides that the defence is only available in respect of certain varieties of material, and these are detailed in paragraph 2 of Schedule A1 to the Act. Common harvest like wheat, oats and potatoes are covered. Moreover, if use is authorised under the Act, the farmer must still pay the patent owner 'equitable remuneration' for that use, although this cannot be more than what the farmer would pay to buy more material from the owner. 'Small farmers' are exempt from this payment, being, in the case of exempted varieties, a farmer who grows plants on an area not larger than necessary to produce 92 tonnes of material.[385]

11.224   Section 60(5)(h) provides a similar scheme for farmers who breed livestock or otherwise deal in reproductive material. The law does not restrict which animal varieties can be the subject of the exemption. The main prohibition, however, is that the farmer cannot sell on any animal or material derived from his 'use' as part of a 'commercial reproductive activity'.[386]

---

[383] Organisation for Economic Co-operation and Development, Genetic Inventions, Intellectual Property Rights and Licensing Practices: Evidence and Policies (2002), 80.

[384] ibid, 81.

[385] Council Regulation (EC) No 2100/94 of 27 July 1994 on Community plant variety rights, Art 14(3), third indent.

[386] Patents Act 1977, s 60(6B).

Bolar exemptions

11.225   Section 60(5)(i) is concerned with the conduct of clinical trials for the approval of therapeutic products based on patented inventions. It was introduced into domestic law as a result of two Directives concerning, respectively, veterinary[387] and human[388] medicinal products. These are known as 'Bolar' exemptions and they operate when generic drugs manufacturers are seeking regulatory approval for their products. They provide protection for acts done on generic medicines to demonstrate that they are bio-equivalent to a patented product; the point is, from the perspective of the generic manufacturer, he can rely on the patentee's prior regulatory approval if bio-equivalence can be shown. The problem is that while, clearly, generics can be produced once a patent expires, manufacturers do not want to have to wait until this time before carrying out trials and seeking regulatory approval. A Bolar exemption therefore works to allow this activity *before* a patent expires with a view to facilitating a wider market in generics *after* it expires. This is the European equivalent to the US Supreme Court ruling in *Merck* (para 11.219 above).

Exercise

Having reached the end of this chapter consider how many ways a person accused of patent infringement can respond—seeking a defence is only one option. What are the relative merits of any particular strategy?

Further reading

Books

CIPA, *Guide to the Patents Acts* (6th edn, 2009)

C Heath and L Petit (eds), *Patent Enforcement Worldwide* (2005)

R Miller et al, *Terrell on the Law of Patents* (17th edn, 2010/2011)

J Pila, *The Requirement for an Invention in Patent Law* (2010)

Reports

T Cook, *A European Perspective as to the Extent to Which Experimental Use, and Certain Other Defences to Patent Infringement, Apply to Differing Types of Research* (2006)

R Sagar and A Nagarsheth, *Ownership of Employee Inventions and Remuneration: a Comparative Overview* (2006)

Organisation for Economic Co-operation and Development, *Genetic Inventions, Intellectual Property Rights and Licensing Practices: Evidence and Policies* (2002)

---

[387] Art 13(6) of Directive 2001/82/EC on veterinary medicinal products.
[388] Art 10(5) of Directive 2001/83/EC on medicinal products for human use, amended by the Directive 2004/27, Art 10(6).

Articles and Chapters

DJ Brennan, 'Biogen Sufficiency Reconsidered' (2009) 4 IPQ 476

G Grant and D Gibbons, 'Inventive Concept—Is it a Good Idea?' [2005] EIPR 170

EC Hettinger, 'Justifying Intellectual Property' (1989) 18 Philosophy and Public Affairs 31–52

C Howell, 'Compensation at last for employee inventors: Kelly v GE Healthcare Ltd' [2010] J Bus Law 41

J Pila, 'Art 52(2) of the Convention on the Grant of European Patents: What did the Framers Intend? A study of the Travaux Preparatoires' (2005) 36 IIC 755

A Sims, 'The Case Against Patenting Methods of Medical Treatment' [2007] EIPR 43

ED Ventose, '"Farming" Out an Exception for Animals to the Method of Medical Treatment Exclusion under the European Patent Convention' (2008) 30(12) EIPR 509

C Von Drathen, 'Patent scope in English and German law under the European Patent Convention 1973 and 2000' (2008) 39(4) IIC 384

A Von Hellfeld, 'Patent Infringement in Europe: The British and the German Approaches to Claim Construction or Purposive Construction versus Equivalency' (2008) 30(9) EIPR 364

12

Contemporary issues in patent law

Introduction

Scope and overview of chapter

12.1   We have already identified a trend in intellectual property law and policy involving the expansion of the scope of a number of intellectual property rights and a corresponding restriction on the limitations on those rights. This trend equally typifies developments in the realm of patent law, and some contemporary examples are considered in this chapter. First, we shall examine the problem of biotechnological inventions which has proved to be a particularly controversial issue in Europe. Second, we shall consider the patentability of computer software and related inventions such as business method patents. The overarching aim of this chapter is to demonstrate the evolution in legal and policy thinking in these two fields as a means to assist you in making sense of developments in patent law.

12.2   **Learning objectives**

By the end of this chapter you should be able to:

- critically assess the exclusions from patentable subject matter, and in particular the meaning of the qualification *as such*;

- give an analytical account of the controversy surrounding the protection of biotechnological inventions, with particular emphasis on the role of the morality provision in European patent law;

- evaluate, by considering the strengths of opposing arguments, the acceptability of monopolies over biological material and consider strategies to temper the effects of such monopolies;

- comment in an informed manner on the application of patent law to software-related inventions, and in particular on the advisability of business method patents;

- critically compare the merits of patent and copyright protection for software products;

- assess attempts to reform patent protection for computer-implemented inventions in Europe.

Sources of law

12.3 Biotechnological inventions in most countries are not subject to special legal provisions and for the most part these have been accommodated by the standard patent law. In Europe, however, a disparity of approach existed between the member states, with some countries such as the Netherlands refusing to apply patent law to living biological material. The European Commission therefore proposed a harmonising Directive in 1988[1] as part of its wider strategy on completing the internal market.[2] The proposal proved to be one of the most controversial pieces of legislation ever to proceed through the European Institutions and in 1995 it provoked the European Parliament to use its newly established power of veto for the first time over an early version of the instrument.[3] The Directive was eventually adopted in 1998[4] but, as we will see, it remains controversial and the debate on its merits is far from over.

12.4 Despite a widely-held belief that patent law is a virtual irrelevancy to the protection of software in Europe, estimates indicate that over 30,000 software-related patents have been granted over the last quarter of a century. This is notwithstanding an express exclusion of computer programs from patent protection in the law: European Patent Convention (EPC) 2000, Article 52(2). The European Commission attempted to introduce a Directive to clarify the situation but this was defeated in the European Parliament in 2005. You can read more about it by following the link below.

> ### Weblinks
>
> Directive 98/44/EC of 6 July 1998 on the legal protection of biotechnological inventions, OJ L213/13:
>
> http://eur-lex.europa.eu/LexUriServ/LexUriServ.do?uri=OJ:L:1998:213:0013:0021:EN:PDF
>
> The history and defeat of the Commission Proposal on the patentability of computer-implemented inventions, COM (2002) 92 final, 20 February 2002:
>
> http://ec.europa.eu/internal_market/indprop/comp/index_en.htm
>
> UK–IPO, Examination Guidelines for Patent Applications relating to Biotechnological Inventions in the Intellectual Property Office (2009): http://www.ipo.gov.uk/biotech.pdf

12.5 The rest of the chapter looks like this:

- Background (12.6–12.7)
- Biotechnological inventions (12.8–12.71)
- Software-related inventions (12.72–12.152)

Background

Is the scope of excluded matter narrowing?

12.6 We have already seen in Chapter 11 that certain subject matter is excluded from patent protection. This is detailed in Article 52(2) EPC 2000, with equivalent provisions in section 1(2) of the

---

[1] COM (88) 496 final SYN 159, 17 October 1988; [1989] OJ C10/3.   [2] COM (85) 310 final, 14 June 1985.

[3] [1995] OJ C68, 20 March 1995.

[4] Directive 98/44/EC of the European Parliament and of the Council of 6 July 1998 on the legal protection of biotechnological inventions (Biotechnology Directive).

UK Patents Act 1977:

> '**Article 52(2)**—The following in particular shall not be regarded as inventions within the meaning of paragraph 1:
>
> (a) discoveries, scientific theories and mathematical methods;
> (b) aesthetic creations;
> (c) schemes, rules and methods for performing mental acts, playing games or doing business, and programs for computers;
> (d) presentations of information.
>
> (3) Paragraph 2 shall exclude the patentability of the subject-matter or activities referred to therein only to the extent to which a European patent application or European patent relates to such subject matter or activities *as such*'. [emphasis added]

12.7   We will concentrate on a number of these examples in this chapter, and in particular, the prohibition on patenting discoveries and the exclusion of computer programs. The most significant part of this section, however, lies in the two little words *'as such'*. The interpretation of these words by intellectual property offices and courts around Europe has had a profound impact on the scope of the exclusions from patentable inventions. The trend has been towards a narrowing interpretation of the provisions resulting in a corresponding expansion in the scope of patentable inventions in a number of controversial areas such as biotechnological inventions, computer software and business method patents. This may be set to change, however, with new challenges brought by new technologies, such as stem cell research and also pronouncements by the EPO's Enlarged Board of Appeal on the appropriateness of such a trend.[5] Let us consider each of these in turn.

Biotechnological inventions

12.8   The *Gowers Review of Intellectual Property* reported in 2006 that almost 20 per cent of human gene DNA sequences had been patented; 4,382 out of the 23,688 known human genes.[6] How can this be?

12.9   Several questions sit at the heart of the debate about the propriety of granting patents over genetic and biological materials. First, how can property rights be granted over genes or partial gene sequences which, after all, seem to be no more than mere discoveries? Second, how appropriate is it to grant a monopoly over the building blocks of life or, indeed, life itself in the form of genetically engineered organisms? Finally, if this is to happen, what is the optimal policy to ensure that research is not hindered by the grant of these patents and that individual (human and competing commercial) interests are also respected?

Biotechnology: the techniques

12.10   It is important to have a rudimentary understanding of the science that underpins biotechnology before we can embark on a study of the legal and ethical issues surrounding the patenting of biotechnological inventions.[7] You must understand some of the concepts and terminology in order to understand the legal cases.

---

[5] G1/07 *Med-Physics/Treatment by surgery*, Decision of 15 February 2010.
[6] *Gowers Review of Intellectual Property* (HM Treasury, 2006), para 2.30.
[7] See for example, CR Harwood and A Wipat, 'Genome Management and Analysis: Prokaryotes' in C Ratledge and B Kristiansen (eds), *Basic Biotechnology* (3rd edn, 2006), Ch 4.

biotechnological patents have been raised relying on the provisions of the law and we shall consider each of these in turn.

Discoveries

What is inventive about uncovering a naturally-occurring gene?

12.18   One of the most frequently raised objections to biotechnological patents is the challenge that the attempt to patent a sequence of DNA, or a part thereof, is simply an attempt to patent a discovery. It is argued that it is not an invention to uncover a pre-existing and naturally occurring entity.[13] However, the terms 'discovery' and 'invention' have particular technical legal meanings in patent law which reflect fundamental policy objectives including the encouragement of innovation and the reward of endeavour. You will remember from Chapter 11 that one way to think about an invention is that it is a technical solution to a pre-existing and as yet unresolved technical problem. While discoveries and inventions both contribute new knowledge to the sum total of human understanding, an invention does so through the *application* of that knowledge, for example, by making something available that was previously beyond our reach. Thus, the mere discovery of the base pair sequence of a gene cannot be the subject of a patent, but locating a previously unknown gene, determining its function and making it accessible for further exploitation is an example of a technical solution to the pre-existing problem of the inaccessibility of the genetic product.

12.19   This position has been reached by a restrictive interpretation of the qualifier—*as such*—in the exclusions from patent law. A discovery *as such*, that is, in and of itself, cannot be patented, but the use of that discovery in bringing about a technical contribution takes it into the realm of patentable subject matter. This is illustrated most clearly in the guidelines issued by the European Patent Office in respect of discoveries.

> ### EPO Guidelines on discoveries:
>
> If a new property of a known material or article is found out, that is mere discovery and unpatentable because discovery as such has no technical effect and is therefore not an invention . . . [i]f, however, that property is put to practical use, then this constitute an invention which may be patentable . . .
>
> To find a previously unrecognised substance occurring in nature is also mere discovery and therefore unpatentable. However, if a substance found in nature can be shown to produce a technical effect, it may be patentable. An example of such a case is that of a substance occurring in nature which is found to have an antibiotic effect. In addition, if a microorganism is discovered to exist in nature and to produce an antibiotic, the micro-organism itself may also be patentable as one aspect of the invention. Similarly, a gene which is discovered to exist in nature may be patentable if a technical effect is revealed, eg its use in making a certain polypeptide or in gene therapy.[14]

12.20   This means that an invention that happens to involve biological or genetic material can be patentable even although the material also exists in nature provided that the invention makes

---

[13] For arguments of this kind see Genewatch UK at http://www.genewatch.org/
[14] EPO Guidelines Part C, Chapter IV, para 2.3.1.

a technical contribution to the state of the art. This can be achieved by removing it from its natural environment and by characterising the contribution by the isolation of the substance and its new-found availability.

12.21 Patentees have also employed other techniques to ensure protection for their biotechnological inventions. These include the argument that the invention as claimed does not exist naturally in this form. For example, in the *Icos Decision*[15] the European Patent Office held that the production of a purified and isolated nucleic acid having a sequence that does not exist in nature is not a discovery.[16]

12.22 Numerous examples of natural products have accordingly been the subject of patents. These range from sequences or partial sequences of DNA, protein molecules and recombinant DNA molecules used as research tools, to purified forms of bacteria, vitamins and viruses. It has been argued, however, that merely to remove an entity from its natural environment and to produce it in a purer form towards an identified commercial end is insufficiently inventive and confuses the criterion of inventive step with the demonstration of function.[17] Moreover, the strength of monopoly over such an invention can be considerable. Often the breadth of a monopoly on a natural product invention can make it very difficult to invent around and this can have adverse consequences for further and future research in any number of fields requiring access to the material. This may be hindered by an unwillingness on the part of the patentee to license or by the imposition of unduly burdensome licence fees. Indeed, the threat of litigation may itself deter future research. We will return to the question of licensing in Part VIII.

12.23 For present purposes it is interesting to note that the Organisation for Economic Co-operation and Development (OECD) has produced guidelines for the licensing of genetic inventions used in health care systems.[18] These arose because of concerns about how some genetic inventions, especially those used in genetic testing, had been exploited to the detriment of patients principally because aggressive licensing practices had inhibited access to genetic tests.[19] The Recommendation lays out principles and best practices for achieving 'a balance between the delivery of new products and services, healthcare needs, and economic returns'.[20] The general spirit of the instrument is to foster openness, sharing, cooperation and further innovation through responsible licensing practices. An OECD Recommendation is by no means legally binding, but it does represent the views and political will of 30 of the most economically influential global democracies.[21]

---

[15] *Icos Decision* [2002] OJEPO 293. Available at: http://archive.epo.org/epo/pubs/oj002/06_02/06_2932.pdf

[16] It should be noted, however, that this patent failed on other grounds including lack of inventive step and lack of industrial applicability.

[17] LJ Demaine and AX Fellmeth, 'Natural Substances and Patentable Inventions' (2003) 300 Science 1375–6. See also MA Majumder et al, 'Ethical Challenges of Patenting "Nature": Legal and Economic Accounts of Altered Nature as Property' in BA Lustig et al (eds) *Altering Nature: Concepts of 'Nature' and 'The Natural' in Biotechnology Debates* (2008), ch 4.

[18] OECD, *Recommendation on the Licensing of Genetic Inventions* (2006), Council of the OECD, 23 February 2006, (2005)149/Rev1.

[19] See B Williams-Jones, 'History of a Gene Patent: Tracing the Development and Application of Commercial BRCA Testing' (2002) 10 Health Law Journal 123–46.

[20] See further, OECD, *Guidelines for the Licensing of Genetic Inventions*, (2006), available at: http://www.oecd.org/sti/biotechnology/licensing

[21] The OECD includes the United States and the United Kingdom but not China or India. cf KS Jayaraman, 'Is India's "Patent Factory" Squandering Funds?' (2006) 442 Nature 120.

Exercise

Critically assess the provisions of the OECD Recommendation and consider how its provisions might be implemented in practice.

Novelty

When is a naturally occurring substance new?

12.24   It might also be objected that a biotechnological invention cannot be patented because it is not new in the strict sense required by patent law because it can already be found in the natural world. You will remember, however, that novelty requires that the invention be available to the public before the priority date of the patent application. The key word here is *available*. It is not enough to anticipate an invention simply to know that a product exists in nature if it cannot also be accessed by human beings. At the very least, there must be evidence both if its availability and the means to reproduce it. Thus, in *Asahi Kasei Kogyo KK's Application*[22] the mere mention of the existence of human tissue necrosis factor in an earlier patent application in Japan was not enough to defeat the instant patent over a genetically engineered version of the protein which had been developed to assist in treating tumours. The House of Lords held that prior publication of existence does not mean that the invention is available to the public unless the method of working the invention is so obvious as to require no explanation. Mere speculation on how the invention might be useful is insufficient;[23] by the same token the prospective patentee need not show, by experiment, that the invention actually works, merely that it is plausible that it will work.[24]

Question

Does this imply that the product must already have been produced before it will anticipate a later patent? Is it enough merely to provide instructions on how to produce it?

12.25   Remember that an invention can be either a *product* or a *process*. In the realm of biotechnological inventions, it was previously the case in the UK that the novelty of a known biological product could be derived from demonstrating the novelty of the process used to produce the product—a so-called product-by-process claim.[25] This, however, put the UK at odds with every other signatory country to the European Patent Convention (EPC), and with the jurisprudence of the European Patent Office itself. The House of Lords has now addressed this anomaly, holding that the correct interpretation of the law is that found in Article 64(2) EPC that: 'If the subject-matter of the European patent is a process, the protection conferred by the patent shall extend to the products directly obtained by such process.'[26] The only circumstances in which the EPO will consider a product-by-process claim is when the product itself is new (that is, novelty is not

[22] *Asahi Kasei Kogyo KK's Application* [1991] RPC 485.
[23] See *Eli Lilly & Co. V Human Genome Sciences Inc* [2008] EWHC 1903.
[24] *Conor Medsystems Inc v Angiotech Pharmaceuticals Inc and Another* [2008] RPC 28.
[25] See the Court of Appeal in *Kirin Amgen Inc and others v Transkaryotic Therapies Inc and others (No 2)* [2003] RPC 3.
[26] See the appeal in the House of Lords: *Kirin Amgen Inc and others v Transkaryotic Therapies Inc and others (No 2) (aka Kirin-Amgen Inc v Hoechst and others)* [2005] 1 All ER 667 [2005] RPC 9.

derived from the novelty of the process), and when its novelty cannot be described in chemical or physical terms.[27]

12.26 Another technique that has been used to avoid problems of novelty is to claim the artificially manufactured version of the product. Higher life forms (eukaryotics) contain segments of DNA in their genetic make-up that do not code for proteins. These segments are called *introns*. Lower life forms (prokaryotics), such as bacteria, do not contain introns.[28] Genetic engineering techniques can remove these introns leaving only the 'purified' form of the DNA, which is known as copy or complimentary DNA (cDNA). cDNA does not exist in nature and so it is argued that a claim to cDNA products is not a claim to a naturally occurring entity.[29] You should note, however, that cDNA sequences perform exactly the same function as the natural version of the same sequences.

12.27 The European Directive on the protection of biotechnological inventions confirms that patents are available for:

> 'An element isolated from the human body or otherwise produced by means of a technical process, including the sequence or partial sequence of a gene, even if the structure of that element is identical to that of a natural element'.[30]

12.28 However, it also reiterates that patents are not available for 'the human body or its parts in their natural state or for the simple discovery of one of its elements'.[31] The equivalent provisions were incorporated into UK law by the Patents Regulations 2000.[32] The EPO Guidelines for Examination confirm that '[i]n principle, biotechnological inventions are patentable under the EPC',[33] while also incorporating the qualifications outlined above.

12.29 Nonetheless, a patent based on a naturally occurring entity is always open to the claim that the entity has already been extracted from its natural environment and utilised by man. This kind of challenge has been successful in two high-profile cases: the Mexican government and other parties secured the revocation of a patent over corn plants with improved oil composition in 2004 on the grounds that the patent lacked *novelty*, that is, that maize having the characteristics described in the patent was already known and available in Mexico.[34] A similar challenge saw the defeat of the Neem Tree Oil patent in 2000 for lack of novelty based on evidence from India.[35]

Inventive step (non-obviousness)

12.30 The biggest threat to the patentability of genetic and biological material does not come from the above criteria but rather from the requirement that the invention demonstrate 'inventive step', that is, that it represents a non-obviousness advance in the particular field of technology compared to what was known prior to the filing of the patent. You will recall once again from Chapter 11 that this criterion is tested by reference to the knowledge of persons skilled in

---

[27] Remember, however, that s 60(1)(c) of the Patents Act 1977 states that the protection given by a claim for a process extends to the product of that process. This provides some residual comfort to patentees. The same provision is found in Article 64(2) EPC.

[28] This information is important to bear in mind when you read *Biogen v Medeva* [1997] RPC 1.

[29] *HOWARD FLOREY/Relaxin* [1995] EPOR 541.   [30] Biotechnology Directive, Art 5(2), n 4 above.

[31] Biotechnology Directive, Art 5(1), n 4 above.

[32] Patents Regulations 2000, SI 2000/2037, incorporating Sch A2 into the Patents Act 1977.

[33] EPO Guidelines, para 2a.2.   [34] European Patent 0744888.

[35] European Patent 0436257.

the particular area.[36] In *Genentech Inc's Patent*[37] the Court of Appeal considered the validity of Genentech's patent for human tissue plasminogen activator (t-PA), a protein occurring naturally in the human body that assists in the dissolution of blood clots. Genentech was able to produce sufficient quantities of t-PA in a sufficiently pure form to market as a therapeutic agent through the application of standard recombinant DNA techniques. At least five other teams embarked on similar work at considerable expense and with a degree of uncertainty of success. Genentech was the first to succeed in establishing t-PA's genetic sequence and sought a patent for products that included t-PA produced by genetic engineering techniques and processes used in its production. Revocation of the patent was sought, inter alia, for lack of inventive step. It was held that:

- The patent was invalid for lack of inventive step. It was obvious to a person skilled in the art to set out to produce human t-PA by recombinant DNA technology. All steps taken by Genentech in establishing the composition of the relevant sequences and applying that knowledge to produce t-PA were applications of known technology towards a known end without any original step.

- The fact that at least five other teams embarked towards the same goal using the same techniques was a sign of obviousness. Being the first to succeed was not enough; but if no one else had set out to produce the invention this might be evidence that it was not obvious.

- Laborious and costly effort did not necessarily involve an inventive step even if it amounted to more than the exercise of proficiency.

12.31   In coming to this decision the Court of Appeal opined that the skilled person in such a hi-tech industry must possess a degree of ingenuity and inventiveness for otherwise they would not be part of the industry at all. Moreover, inventiveness could be assessed by reference to a research team where this is the standard working practice in a particular area.[38] It has been observed that this decision seems to set a higher standard of test of obviousness for hi-tech industries such as the biotechnology industry.[39] This could mean that problems which are encountered on the route to the end goal are more likely to be seen as everyday run-of-the-mill hiccups for the hi-tech skilled person and that their resolution is less likely to exhibit inventiveness. Invention is the norm in an industry such as biotechnology and as the law stands it is eminently sensible that the concept of the skilled person, used to test obviousness, should assume the traits of those working in the field in question. Overly zealous application of this view might, however, lead to a paradox in practice, namely, that those who make significant advances in the name of benefiting humanity and who spend considerable sums in the process, are less likely to be rewarded by the grant of a patent in recognition of their endeavour.

12.32   This, of course, depends entirely on the attitude and approach of the courts to interpreting these criteria. At the time of the *Genentech* decision there were concerns that a different standard was being laid down for the biotechnology industry and this was fuelled by the suggestion in that case that an additional requirement existed for patents involving biological material to show

---

[36] For guidance on relevant characteristics in the biotechnology field see T455/91 *GENENTECH ET AL/ Expression in yeast* [1995] OJEPO 684.
[37] [1989] RPC 147 (CA).
[38] ibid, at 278. Also *Eli Lilly & Co v Human Genome Sciences Inc* [2008] EWHC 1903 (Pat), at 31–32 and *Schlumberger Holdings Ltd v Electromagnetic Geoservices AS* [2009] RPC 19.
[39] See too *POLYMER POWDERS/Allied Colloids* T39/93 [1997] OJEPO 134, 149.

that there was an 'invention' over and above the basic criteria of patentability.[40] But there is no real evidence of the biotechnology industry suffering discriminatory treatment subsequent to *Genentech* and Lord Hoffmann was unconvinced by the additional criterion in delivering the House of Lords' ruling in *Biogen v Medeva*.[41] Although he did not rule out the possibility that in the future it might be possible for a novel creation to satisfy all statutory criteria and yet not be properly describable as an 'invention', he noted that neither the draftsmen of the European Patent Convention, nor those who drew up the 1977 Act, nor indeed counsel for the defendants could offer a single example of such a creation. For the time being then, to satisfy the standard criteria on patentability *is* to produce an invention.

12.33 The Nuffield Council on Bioethics has called for more stringent assessments of the criteria of patentability and most notably that of inventive step.[42] The Council conjectures that many patents have been granted for so-called inventions that do not meet these rigorous requirements. Moreover, it notes that the US and European interpretations of this criterion differ slightly but to a sufficient degree to make a real difference to a prospective patentee's chances of success. Thus, while in Europe we consider the need for 'inventive step', that is, that there must be evidence of non-obvious inventiveness of the part of the inventor, the US interpretation focuses on 'non-obviousness' so that so long as the particularities of the result were not obvious to an expert then the criterion is satisfied—for example, that the precise sequence of bases that would appear in a recombinant DNA molecule would not be obvious to an expert. This latter is a lower threshold and consequently means that genetically engineered products remains, potentially at least, more easily patentable in the US than in Europe. By the same token, it has been established in the EPO[43] and the UK–IPO[44] that it is obvious to claim a specific recombinant DNA sequence if all of the techniques necessary to produce it are known. The corollary is that the use of non-obvious techniques, perhaps involving bioinformatics tools, can overcome this objection.

Industrial applicability (utility)

Other differences between the US and Europe

12.34 The requirement of industrial applicability in Europe means that it must be shown that the invention can be made or used in any kind of industry, including agriculture.[45] In the United States, the equivalent criterion requires *utility*, an issue which has caused some controversy in the context of biotech patents over the years. Various attempts were made in the early 1990s to patent ESTs (Expressed Sequence Tags), being partial gene fragments with no known utility. The rationale, however, was that these might point the way to complete gene sequences and so may help to stake a claim to the full sequences once these were found. The US Patent and Trademark Office (USPTO) rejected such claims, and most notably those of the National Institutes of Health, for lack of utility: the function of the invention could not be sufficiently described. Since then the USPTO has revised its guidelines on utility (January 2001, updated December 2008).[46] An invention now must show a 'specific and substantial and credible utility', but it should be noted that 'credible' here includes a theoretical credible use, that is, it is

[40] *Genentech*, n 36 above, at 263.   [41] *Biogen v Medeva* [1997] RPC 1.
[42] Nuffield Council on Bioethics, *The Ethics of Patenting DNA* (2002).
[43] T886/91 *BIOGEN INC/Hepatitis B virus* [1999] EPOR 361.   [44] *Collaborative Research's Patent* BL O/86/94.
[45] Patents Act 1977, s 4(1) and EPC Art 57.
[46] http://www.uspto.gov/web/offices/pac/mpep/documents/2100_2107.htm#sect2107

not necessary to show that the invention actually works in order to obtain a patent. There is therefore no specific prohibition on the patenting of ESTs, or indeed, other gene variations such as SNPs,[47] so long as the criteria for patentability are met.

12.35   The EC Directive on the patentability of biotechnological inventions states that full or partial gene sequences with no known function will not be patentable,[48] and this has been confirmed by the ECJ.[49] It has also been endorsed by the UK–IPO[50] and the European Patent Office which has ruled that mere speculative function for a genetically engineered gene sequence cannot lead to the conclusion that it is capable of industrial application.[51] Indeed, the EPO indicated that uses must be 'specific, substantial and credible' to meet this criterion, thereby reflecting the wording of the US model and, potentially, approximating the legal standards on both sides of the Atlantic. Indeed, the EPO Guidelines now provide that '…the industrial application of a sequence or a partial sequence of a gene must be disclosed in the patent application. A mere nucleic acid sequence without indication of a function is not a patentable invention…'.[52]

12.36   The issue of biotechnology and industrial applicability has recently been considered for the first time by the English Court of Appeal in *Eli Lily & Co v Human Genome Sciences*.[53] This case concerned a patent for a polynucleotide sequence which Eli Lily sought to revoke on the grounds that, amongst other things, the specification failed to disclose an invention capable of industrial application. The argument was that the prediction of the uses of the sequence were purely speculative. The court noted that UK jurisprudence on industrial application is limited, but that the EPO jurisprudence does provide guidance;[54] the English courts will follow any principles of law clearly laid down by the TBAs of the EPO. This, however, does not preclude divergence on matters of fact based on the evidence presented to each judicial body (as happened in this case). Article 57 EPC states clearly that an invention is only patentable if it is 'susceptible of industrial application'. Any invention which does not comply should be revoked, and at national level this is according to the Patents Act 1977 section 72(1). Central to the question of industrial application for claims to gene sequences or proteins is adequate description of their function. A patent will not be given if it is not possible to disclose how the sequence or protein can be used. Merely describing existence and structure is not enough. The Court of Appeal rejected the appeal against revocation and confirmed the correctness of the approach of the judge at first instance. He had considered whether a skilled person could derive the capability of industrial application from the description of the invention, when it was read with the benefit of common general knowledge. Furthermore, the description must disclose in definite technical terms the purpose of the invention and show how it can be used to solve a given technical problem.[55] In this case the invention had been found using bioinformatics, which made the industrial application even less obvious than in other biotechnology cases, Notwithstanding, the use of bioinformatics is not necessarily a bar to patentability in and of itself.

---

[47] Single Nucleotide Polymorphisms (SNPs), as their name suggests, are sequences of identical DNA that vary from the norm in only a single base pair. Despite these extremely minor differences SNPs can be used as markers for particular genes and may play a key role in understanding the genetic basis for individual patient response to medicines.

[48] n 4 above, Art 5(3) read in conjunction with recitals 23 and 24. See too Patents Act 1977, Sch A2, para 6.

[49] Case C-377/98 *Kingdom of the Netherlands v Council of the European Union and the European Parliament* [2002] FSR 36 at para 74 of the judgment.

[50] UK–IPO *Examination Guidelines for Patent Applications relating to Biotechnological Inventions in the Intellectual Property Office* (2009), paras 51–60 and see *Aeomica Inc* BL O/286/05 31.

[51] *Icos Decision* [2002] OJEPO 293. http://archive.epo.org/epo/pubs/oj002/06_02/06_2932.pdf

[52] EPO Guidelines Part C, Chapter IV, para 5.4   [53] [2010] EWCA Civ 33.

[54] For a good illustration, see T898/05 *ZYMOGENETICS/Hematopoietic cytokine receptor* [2007] EPOR 2.

[55] See *Eli Lily & Co v Human Genome Sciences Inc* [2008] EWHC 1903, para 226.

12.37 These examples demonstrate how the restrictive interpretation of the exclusions from patent-ability has, in turn, led to an accommodation of the particularities of biotechnological inventions in the criteria for patentability. Only the volonté of the intellectual property offices and the courts has brought us to this position. Yet, each is also mindful of the need to balance interests in intellectual property law, weighing up the legitimacy of the claims of the prospective patentee with the interests of competitors to invent around and compete fairly with parties enjoying a monopolistic control of sectors of the market. It is helpful in this regard to examine a few examples of how this accommodation has been reached by the British courts.

 Exercise

You might like to consider the different approaches adopted in the United States, Europe, and Japan in these comparative studies of biotechnology patent practices:

http://www.trilateral.net/projects/biotechnology.html

The problem of excessively broad patents

12.38 The policy concerns surrounding biotechnological inventions were first aired in the British courts in the *Genentech* case, discussed above. Many matters were laid to rest, however, by the House of Lords in *Biogen v Medeva* which clarified the law and confirmed beyond doubt the patentability of biotechnological inventions as a matter of UK policy. The patent in *Biogen* related, inter alia, to the genetic sequence of the infective agent of the Hepatitis B virus (such an agent is referred to as displaying *antigen specificity*). Biogen was the only company to pursue this line of research and was granted a patent which was subsequently challenged. The court found that while the inventors claimed protection for *all* molecules showing Hepatitis B antigen specificity produced by *any* technique in *any* host, the actual contribution of the invention was a single means to express crude molecules displaying Hepatitis B antigen specificity in basic hosts when the relevant gene sequence was unknown. Indeed, once that sequence was uncovered—which happened very soon after the patent was first filed—there was no need to rely on the Biogen contribution, yet to uphold the patent in its original terms would have excluded much future work on the Hepatitis B virus. This is the problem of breadth of monopoly and undue scope of patent protection. It was held that the claimed monopoly was deemed to be excessively broad compared to the actual contribution that the inventors had made to the state of the art. Patent protection will only be awarded for the additional knowledge that inventors add to the sum total of human knowledge and no more.

12.39 It is a frequent problem with new and emerging technologies that early patents are granted broadly by intellectual property offices before the offices and the courts get to grips with the true nature of the technology. *Biogen* was an early attempt to keep the UK on a narrow path.

12.40 *Biogen* is also authority for the proposition that the subject matter described in the application must enable the invention to be worked *to the full extent* of the monopoly claimed. If the invention embodies a principle that is capable of general application across a wide range of products, then it is permissible to claim all such products and it is not necessary for the patentee to prove that his principle applies in all cases. However, if the patentee claims different products or processes in the same application, each must be described by a separate enabling disclosure.

Moreover, if no unifying principle links the claimed inventions together, then all that can be claimed is that which can be described.[56] It was held in *Dr Reddy's Laboratories* that where a previous patent discloses a general formula with multiple substituents chosen from lists of some length, this will not normally take away the novelty of a subsequent claim to a specific individual compound.[57]

> ## Weblink
>
> You can read more about the *Biogen* case and the corresponding dispute before the European Patent Office at the Textbook's website:
>
> www.oxfordtextbooks.co.uk/orc/macqueen2e/

12.41 In *Kirin-Amgen v Hoechst* the House of Lords invalidated the core claims of a patent over genetically engineered Erythropoietin (EPO)—a protein found in minute levels in the body which regulates the production of red blood cells—in large part because of the unsustainability of the breadth of the claims made by the patentee.[58] The patentees claimed, in essence, *any* way of making EPO by recombinant DNA technology and the resultant forms of EPO, but their patent specification did not disclose an invention which was capable of furnishing the person skill in the particular art with sufficient information to realise such a broad range of possibilities. Lord Hoffmann confirmed that it is possible to claim an invention discloses 'a principle capable of general application' and accordingly to have a monopoly over the entire class of products which flow from the application of that principle, but this case was not such an example.[59] Rather, Lord Hoffmann laid down a three-point test to determine sufficiency, that is, whether the claims are sustained by the actual contribution that the invention makes to human knowledge. This is:

- What exactly is the invention?
- What does the application claim to enable the skilled man to do?
- Does the specification actually enable him to do it?

This may seem trite, but the first question is of crucial importance. The patentees sought to have the court believe that they had invented a product, a form of EPO, but their Lordships took a different view holding that they had, in fact, invented a way of making EPO, that is, a process. Moreover, the process that was revealed was not one which taught a skilled expert *any* way of making EPO by recombinant DNA technology, nor did it reveal a way of making EPO in such general terms as to cover the process used by the defendants. A further point made by the court concerns the role of the skilled expert in interpreting the language used by the applicant in drafting his claims: 'what would a person skilled in the art have understood the patentee to have used the language of the claim to mean?'. In other words, the courts will use the notional expert as a device to limit ex post facto interpretations by a

---

[56] See *Chiron Corp and Others v Murex Diagnostics and Others* [1996] FSR 153 in which the patent in suit claimed, inter alia, Hepatitis C virus (HCV) polypeptides, antibodies, vaccines against HCV and methods of propagating HCV but it was shown that the principal claim as drafted '...covers an almost infinite number of polypeptides which are useless for any known purpose.' (at 177).

[57] *Dr Reddy's Laboratories (UK) Ltd v Eli Lilly and Co* [2008] EWHC 2345, para 91.

[58] *Kirin Amgen Inc and others Hoechst and others* [2005] 1 All ER 667, [2005] RPC 9.

[59] For an example of this see T 0292/85 *GENENTECH/Polypeptide expression* [1989] OJEPO 275 discussed by Lord Hoffmann at paras 112–113.

patentee in an attempt to broaden the scope of his monopoly. This is particularly pertinent when new technologies emerge and the patentee attempts to argue that they are also caught by his patent.

12.42 In another House of Lords decision their Lordships took the opportunity to clarify the law after *Biogen*. In *Generics (UK) Limited and others v H Lundbeck A/S*[60] the House of Lords upheld the patent on a product which was for the effective agent in an anti-depressant drug Citalopram (see further para 11.207). A challenge arose because the inventiveness of the product was claimed solely by reference to the means to make it. Only one such means had been disclosed but a product patent would give a monopoly that could prevent competition no matter how rival versions of the product were made. Was this an overly-broad monopoly? The answer was 'no' and *Biogen* was distinguished. *Biogen* was characterised as not dealing with a product claim but rather with an unusual product/process hybrid claim whose breadth was clearly too wide. *Generics* involved a product of which the means to make it was completely non-obvious. The technical contribution was 'to make available, for the first time, a product which had previously been unavailable, namely the isolated (+)-enantiomer of Citalopram. On that basis, it would appear to follow that the respondent was entitled to claim the enantiomer.'[61] It was no offence to UK or EPO case law that the monopoly which flowed from this extended to all rival products, however made.

Key points on biotechnological inventions

Biotechnological inventions are patentable as long as you remember:

- *Discoveries*—the claim should be to the (purified) entity isolated from its natural environment and should include a description of the technical effect brought about by its application/use

- *Novelty*—prior disclosure is always a risk, but mere knowledge of the existence of a naturally occurring product is not enough. Prior availability of the claimed invention must be shown

- *Inventive step*—intellectual property offices are likely to be tougher with this criterion if policy guidance is followed; using traditional genetic engineering techniques to isolate material is unlikely to be inventive

- *Industrial applicability*—the function of the invention should always be disclosed

- *Broad claims*—protection will only be given for the extent of the contribution made to human knowledge and no more

---

Morality

12.43 Thus far we have avoided mention of morality but this issue has proved to be one of the most controversial in the biotechnology patenting field. In stark contrast to the position in the United States where the Supreme Court has held that 'Congress intended statutory subject matter to include anything under the sun that is made by man',[62] Europe has long contemplated a role for

---

[60] [2009] UKHL 12.   [61] per Lord Neuberger, para 83.   [62] *Diamond v Chakrabarty* 447 US 303 (1980), 309.

moral concerns in the decision-making process about the grant of a patent.[63] Article 53 of the European Patent Convention 2000 provides that:

'(a) inventions the commercial exploitation of which would be contrary to "ordre public" or morality; such exploitation shall not be deemed to be so contrary merely because it is prohibited by law or regulation in some or all of the Contracting States;

(b) plant or animal varieties or essentially biological processes for the production of plants or animals; this provision shall not apply to microbiological processes or the products thereof;'[64]

(Recall that this reflects Article 27 TRIPS, and has been incorporated into domestic law by amendments to the Patents Act 1977 by the Patents Act 2004.)

12.44   The morality provisions in TRIPS appear largely at the insistence of European states and as a reflection of their history, but the morality provisions in European patent law mostly lay dormant until the advent of contemporary biotechnology patenting whereupon they were aggressively invoked by parties harbouring a plethora of doubts about biotechnology, of which patenting practices are merely a small part. The debacle has largely been played out on the European stage in the Opposition Division of the European Patent Office and more recently in the institutions of the European Union.

Exercise

Before reading any further, consider what is meant by 'inventions the commercial exploitation of which would be contrary to…morality'. How do we know when something is immoral? Note: It is the commercial exploitation of the invention which must be immoral, not necessarily the invention itself. Why is this so? What difference does this make?

Morality case law before the EPO

12.45   We saw in the last chapter that morality provisions before the EPO have been interpreted, in the main, narrowly. This is true in respect of each category of biotechnological inventions relating to plant,[65] animal[66] and human[67] material. The hurdle has been set very high at a level of abhorrence to the majority of the European publics, and the range of morality questions has been restricted to the term of Article 53(a)—the commercial exploitation of the invention (or previously, the publication or exploitation of the invention, EPC 1973).[68] Before we discuss more recent developments, however, we need to assess the role and impact of the Biotechnology Directive which interceded squarely in the middle of these developments.

12.46   The advent of the Biotechnology Directive was one of two events in 1998 which signalled a turning point in European patent granting practice. The other was the scientific breakthrough

---

[63] Strasbourg Convention 1963. For commentary, see O Mills, *Biotechnological Inventions: Moral Restraints and Patent Law* (2005).

[64] As we go to press two referral cases on the meaning of 'essentially biological' are pending before the EPO Enlarged Board of Appeal. For comment, see S Bostyn, 'How Biological is Essentially Biological? The Referrals to the Enlarged Board of Appeal G2/07 and G1/08' (2009) 31(11) EIPR 549.

[65] *PLANT GENETIC SYSTEMS/Glutamine Synthetase Inhibitors* [1995] EPOR 357.

[66] *HARVARD/Oncomouse* [1991] EPOR 525 and *HARVARD/Transgenic animal* [2005] EPOR 31.

[67] *HOWARD FLOREY/H2 Relaxin* [1995] EPOR 541.

[68] *Michigan State University/Euthanasia compositions*, available at http://legal.european-patent-office.org/dg3/biblio/t010866eu1.htm

of isolating human embryonic stem cells which hold great therapeutic promise in a number of areas including spinal cord injuries, Parkinson's disease, stroke and transplantation therapy.[69] The Biotechnology Directive was originally proposed in 1988, but suffered a very difficult passage and was vetoed by the European Parliament in 1995. While it was eventually adopted in 1998 and contains morality provisions that broadly reflect the jurisprudence of the EPO, there was no time to incorporate any mention of human embryonic stem cell technologies. The resulting controversy has beleaguered the Directive ever since and has brought about a sea-change in attitude in the European Patent Office. Let us begin with a consideration of the Directive itself.

The Biotechnology Directive

12.47   Objections to the European Biotechnology Directive based on moral grounds were primarily responsible for the delay in adopting the legislation; a process which, as we have noted, took 10 years. Even after its eventual adoption in July 1998, the Directive was challenged before the ECJ by the Netherlands, Italy and Norway. The Court took until October 2001 to uphold the validity of the law,[70] and eight member states were referred to the ECJ in July 2003 for failure to implement the Directive.[71] The UK implemented the provisions of the Directive in the Patents Regulations 2000 which amended the Patents Act 1977.[72]

12.48   The rationale behind the Biotechnology Directive[73] was elegantly simple. Europe was lagging behind other economic areas, and in particular the United States, and unevenness of approach towards biotechnological inventions throughout the member states was at odds with the Commission's plans for completion of the internal market. The aim of the Directive is equally straightforward: to harmonise the law throughout all member states, making it clear that biotechnological inventions are patentable, subject to certain narrowly defined exceptions and limitations.[74]

12.49   Thus, for example, Article 3(1) confirms that inventions which are new, which involve an inventive step and which are susceptible of industrial application shall be patentable 'even if they concern a product consisting of or containing biological material or a process by means of which biological material is produced, processed or used.' Moreover, Article 3(2) states that '[b]iological material which is isolated from its natural environment or produced by means of a technical process may be the subject of an invention even if it previously occurred in nature'.

---

[69] JA Thomson et al, 'Embryonic Stem Cell Lines Derived from Human Blastocysts' (1998) 282 Science 1145.

[70] C-377/98 *Kingdom of the Netherlands v Council of the European Union and the European Parliament* [2002] FSR 36. Subsequently the EPO Technical Board of Appeal confirmed that the absence of consent to patenting from the individuals who provide human material that is used to create a patentable invention is irrelevant in European patent law, see T1213/05 *University of Utah/Linked breast and ovarian cancer susceptibility gene*, unreported, Sept 2007. For comment see, A Odell-West, 'The absence of informed consent to commercial exploitation for inventions developed from human biological material: a bar to patentability?' [2009] 3 IPQ 273.

[71] A State of Play list which details the stages of implementation of member states as at January 2007 is available from the EU Internal Market: Industrial Property website: http://ec.europa.eu/internal_market/indprop/invent/index_en.htm

[72] Patents Regulations 2000, SI 2000/2037.

[73] A full copy of the text of the Directive is available at: http://eur-lex.europa.eu/LexUriServ/LexUriServ.do?uri=OJ:L:1998:213:0013:0021:EN:PDF

[74] See generally, G Kamstra, M Döring, N Scott-Ram, A Sheard, A and H Wixon, *Patents on Biotechnological Inventions: The EC Directive*, (2002).

12.50   This is a direct endorsement of the policy direction that had been rigorously pursued by the EPO.[75] Indeed the relevant provisions of the European Patent Convention were brought into line with the key Articles of the Biotechnology Directive by a Decision of the Administrative Council of the European Patent Organisation of 16 June 1999.[76] This was necessary to avoid confusion and disharmony because the Directive clearly only applies to the 27 member states of the EU, while the signatories to the EPC include these states and, currently, ten others.[77]

12.51   Notwithstanding, the specific provisions of the Directive continue to cause controversy and their interpretation in the EPO as applied to human embryonic stem cell technologies has called into question the entire approach of European intellectual property offices towards morality clauses in patent law.

12.52   Article 6 embodies the morality provisions of the Directive. It states:

'1. Inventions shall be considered unpatentable where their commercial exploitation would be contrary to ordre public or morality; however, exploitation shall not be deemed to be so contrary merely because it is prohibited by law or regulation.

2. On the basis of paragraph 1, the following, in particular, shall be considered unpatentable:

(a) processes for cloning human beings;

(b) processes for modifying the germ line genetic identity of human beings;

(c) uses of human embryos for industrial or commercial purposes;

(d) processes for modifying the genetic identity of animals which are likely to cause them suffering without any substantial medical benefit to man or animal, and also animals resulting from such processes.'

12.53   While morality per se is left undefined, specific examples have now been included as part of a non-exhaustive list.[78] The last is a modification of the test laid down in *Harvard/Oncomouse* albeit in a more rigorous fashion, now requiring substantial *medical* benefit to outweigh potential suffering to the animal. It remains, nonetheless, a crude felicific calculus and a questionable measure of morality from the philosophical perspective. Note too, the prohibition is now restricted to the immorality of the 'commercial exploitation' of the invention, and no longer refers to its 'publication' as was the case in Article 53 EPC 1973. This re-emphasises the fact that the moral dubiety of the patent grant should properly be focussed on the way in which the monopoly is exploited.

 Question

Why were these particular examples chosen? Have any important matters been left out? Is this an appropriate measure of 'morality' for the purposes of patent law? Should the morality provision remain in European patent law?

---

[75] Eg, the essence of the rulings in *Oncomouse* and *Plant Genetic Systems* is essentially reproduced in Art 4 which states: '1. The following shall not be patentable: (a) plant and animal varieties; (b) essentially biological processes for the production of plants or animals. 2. Inventions which concern plants or animals shall be patentable if the technical feasibility of the invention is not confined to a particular plant or animal variety. 3. Paragraph 1(b) shall be without prejudice to the patentability of inventions which concern a microbiological or other technical process or a product obtained by means of such a process'.

[76] http://archive.epo.org/epo/pubs/oj99/7_99/7_4379.pdf Note the Implementing Regulations are amended as of 1 April 2010 (not available at time of going to press).

[77] There are 37 signatory states to the European Patent Convention (as at May 2010).

[78] The exclusions from patentability in the UK regulations state: 'the following are not patentable', while the Directive makes it clear that the exclusions are mere examples of exclusions. Is the UK in breach of its obligations?

Human embryonic stem cell inventions

12.54   Although Article 6 excludes uses of human embryos from patenting, it says nothing about cells or cell lines derived from embryos.[79] Nor is it clear whether the prohibition on processes for cloning human beings relates only to reproductive cloning techniques or extends to cloning to produce stem cells for therapeutic purposes.[80] Human embryo research is ethically problematic for a number of reasons, all of which centre around the moral status of this organism. The particular concern surrounding embryonic stem cell technologies is that—*at the present time*—we must both use and destroy a human embryo to produce valuable embryonic stem cell cultures. The prospect of then patenting those cultures or other products derived from embryonic stem cells is all the more problematic for many groups. Although there have been claims to have produced human embryonic stem cell lines without the destruction of embryos,[81] and while this could end the ethical debate surrounding stem cell inventions, any such method will still need further research to verify the safety and reliability of the procedure before it can be widely used; moreover, it is far from clear that such alternative methods will be scientifically equivalent to or better than embryonic stem cells. Thus the debate is far from over.

Exercise

The EPO has granted patents in respect of stem cell technologies which claim not to destroy embryos? Can you find these patents using the Esp@cenet facility?

12.55   The European Group on Ethics in Science and New Technologies (EGE) reported that by 2002 over 2,000 patent applications had been lodged around the world involving both human and non-human stem cells; a quarter of which related to embryonic stem cells. Over a third of all stem cell applications had been granted, as had a quarter of those related to embryonic stem cells.[82] The European Group on Ethics urged a cautious approach and recommended 'excluding the patentability of the process of creation of a human embryo by cloning for stem cells'.[83] It also stated that unmodified stem cells with no use should not be patentable, and this is in keeping with the functional approach towards biotechnological patents already outlined above.

12.56   The EGE Opinion was, however, rejected *in toto* by the Opposition Division (OD) of the European Patent Office (EPO) when it heard the so-called 'Edinburgh Patent' case only a few

---

[79] Art 5(1) of the Directive provides: 'The human body, at the various stages of its formation and development, and the simple discovery of one of its elements, including the sequence or partial sequence of a gene, cannot constitute patentable inventions.'

[80] Stem cells are relatively undifferentiated cells of the same lineage (family type) that retain the ability to divide and cycle throughout postnatal life to provide cells that can become specialised and take the place of those that die or are lost.

[81] See, for example, iPS (Induced Pluripontent Stem cells) which are produced from reprogrammed adult somatic cells, argued by many to avoid the ethical dilemmas, see, SA Brockman-Lee 'Embryonic stem cells in science and medicine: An invitation for dialogue' (2007) 4 Gender Medicine 288 and LM Solomon and SA Brockman-Lee 'Embryonic stem cells in science and medicine, part II: Law, ethics, and the continuing need for dialogue' (2008) 5 Gender Medicine 3.

[82] European Group on Ethics in Science and New Technologies, *Ethical Aspects of Patenting Inventions Involving Human Stem Cells*, Opinion No 16, 17 May 2002, para 1.16.

[83] ibid, para 2.5.

months later. The patent in suit related to *animal* transgenic stem cells but numerous groups raised opposition proceedings to the grant of the patent, inter alia, on the grounds that 'animal' includes 'human' in the scientific taxonomy. In amending the patent to exclude mention of human or animal embryonic stem cells, the OD interpreted the Article 53(a) EPC morality clause and the EPO equivalent guidelines to Article 6 of the Biotech Directive very broadly and in a manner which was completely at odds with the existing EPO case law. The OD noted that the provisions could be interpreted in two ways: *narrowly*, to mean that only commercial uses of human embryos *as such* are excluded from patentability, or *broadly*, to mean that human embryonic stem cells—which as we have noted can only be obtained by destroying an embryo—are also not patentable. The OD preferred the latter approach, arguing that since embryos *as such* are already protected by Rule 23(e) (equivalent of Article 5(1) of the EC Directive), a similar interpretation of Rule 23(d)(c) (equivalent of Article 6(2)(c) of the EC Directive) would be redundancy and this could not have been the intention of the legislator.[84]

12.57   This approach has since been followed in the Examining Division of the EPO, most notably in respect of the application of the Wisconsin Alumni Research Foundation (WARF) which was responsible for developing the first techniques to isolate human embryonic stem cells in 1998. The application was for European patents in respect of 'primate embryonic stem cells', or more particularly, embryonic stem cell cultures, that is, stem cell *products* but the application also disclosed the means to make such products, as one would expect. Thus the application disclosed a method for preparing ES cells from primate blastocysts. It was accepted, but not demonstrated in the application, that this method was also enabling of the production of human ES cells. Moreover, the sole method of production of the stem cell cultures that was described involved the use, and destruction, of embryos. The Examining Division held that all of the claims which could be extended to human embryonic stem cells were invalid on grounds of immorality. It did so on the basis of an extremely literal and broad interpretation of Rule 23(d)(c): 'European patents are not to be granted in respect of...inventions which concern...uses of human embryos for industrial or commercial purposes.' In sum, the Division held that: 'The use of an embryo as starting material for the generation of a product of industrial application is considered equal to industrial use of this embryo'. The rationale here is that the claimed cultures are inseparable from the means to make them. It is, therefore, in a literal sense, necessary to 'use' embryos to create the claimed invention. The message from this ruling is that the moral concern goes far beyond patenting itself and extends to general instrumentalisation. It implies that mere involvement—use—of embryos in the research and development of an invention is sufficient to bar the patentability of that invention.

12.58   The matter was referred to the Enlarged Board of Appeal (EBA) in November 2005 for consideration. The above rulings represent such an extreme turnaround from previous EPO jurisprudence in this area that it leads us to wonder if the issue is not being forced from within the EPO itself to ensure that a body with standing such as the EBA brings full and final resolution to the issue. Four key questions were presented to the Board:

---

[84] See G Laurie, 'Patenting Stem Cells of Human Origin' [2004] European Intellectual Property Review 59.

Embryonic Stem Cell Patents: Questions for the EPO Enlarged Board of Appeal:

(1) Does Rule 23d(c) EPC apply to an application filed before the entry into force of the rule?

(2) If the answer to question 1 is yes, does Rule 23d(c) EPC forbid the patenting of claims directed to products (here: human embryonic stem cell cultures) which—as described in the application—at the filing date could be prepared exclusively by a method which necessarily involved the destruction of the human embryos from which the said products are derived, if the said method is not part of the claims?

(3) If the answer to question 1 or 2 is no, does Article 53(a) EPC forbid patenting such claims?

(4) In the context of questions 2 and 3, is it of relevance that after the filing date the same products could be obtained without having to recur to a method necessarily involving the destruction of human embryos (here: eg derivation from available human embryonic cell lines)?

Question

Before reading any further consider how would you answer questions 2–4? By reference to what moral matters would you justify your responses?

12.59   In something of a last minute intervention, the then President of the European Patent Office, Alain Pompidou, became involved, issuing a letter commenting on the questions put to the Board.[85] In his opinion, and contrary to practice to date,[86] Article 53 should not receive a restricted or narrow interpretation:

> 'A presumption in favour of a narrow interpretation of exceptions would unduly limit the significance of the moral jurisdiction under Article 53(a) and Rule23d(c) the purpose of which is the incorporation of higher ranking legal and moral principles into European patent law and would thus be in conflict with the general objective of said norms.'[87]

If this opinion was followed by the Enlarged Board of Appeal it would represent a major *volte face* by the EPO.[88] There is a fear in some quarters that this direction will further compound the confusions surrounding the morality provisions and result in a stifling of stem cell research around Europe. It is important to consider too the extent to which the patent system should purport to perform a regulatory function in respect of science. That is the legitimate role of state governments and it may be a role that is usurped by an unelected administrative body that is able to pass judgment on the morality of new technologies. This is particularly problematic

---

[85] G2/06 Comments by the President of the European Patent Office (September 2006), available here: http://www.cipa.org.uk/download_files/epo_warf.pdf

[86] See, eg, T356/93 *PLANT GENETIC SYSTEMS/Glutamine Synthetase Inhibitors*, n 66 above, T315/03 *HARVARD/ Transgenic animal*, n 66 above, and G1/04 *CYGNUS/Diagnostic Methods* [2006] EPOR 15.

[87] n 85 above, p 37. Such a rejection of a presumption in favour of narrow interpretation of exclusions was more recently expressed by the Enlarged Board of Appeal in Case G1/07 *MED-PHYSICS/Treatment by surgery*, Decision of 15 February 2010.

[88] For British judicial angst about not giving the exclusions too wide an interpretation, see *Research in Motion UK Ltd v Inpro Licensing SARL* [2006] EWHC 70 (Pat), [2006] RPC 20, affirmed by the Court of Appeal: [2007] EWCA Civ 51.

when one considers the example of the UK, which invests millions of pounds a year in support of stem cell research. Is it acceptable that these efforts might be thwarted by the EPO?

12.60   The Enlarged Board of Appeal delivered its decision in November 2008, stating that European patent law forbids the patenting of claims directed to products which, at the filing date of the application, could be prepared exclusively by a method which necessarily involved the destruction of the human embryo from which the products are derived, *even if* the method is not part of the claims.[89] Moreover, if after the filing date a method is discovered which allows the same products to be obtained without having recourse to a method which necessarily involves the destruction of human embryos, this will not 'fix' an application. There was a further issue of whether additional questions in this matter should be referred to the ECJ as it touched on the wording of the Biotechnology Directive, but it was ruled that there were no grounds for such a referral. This decision prompted the UK–IPO to reconsider its practice. It released a Practice Notice concerning Inventions involving Human Embryonic Stem Cells, which states that the Office will not grant patents for processes of obtaining stem cells from human embryos.[90] As for the other questions referred to the EBA, since the answer to the second question was yes, the third question concerning the interpretation of Article 53 was not considered and remains open to debate. The EBA did state, however, that: 'it is important to point out that it is not the fact of the patenting itself that is considered to be against *ordre public* or morality, but it is the performing of the invention, which includes a step (the use involving its destruction of a human embryo) that has to be considered to contravene those concepts' (para 41).[91]

Exercise

Consider the wider implications of these decisions to exclude patent protection in respect of inventions developed using embryonic stem cells. What are the social, ethical, scientific and economic issues at stake? In particular, where does this leave a country like the UK which actively encourages embryonic stem cell research? Do these rulings remove the incentive to research in Europe?

Synthetic biology

12.61   There has been growing discussion of late surrounding a new type of invention: inventions created by synthetic biology. Synthetic biology is a broad field that is hard to define, but it can roughly be seen as designing biological components, through engineering methods and principles, which have novel properties and functions that do not occur in nature.[92] A common shorthand is to talk about the creation of 'artificial life'. This type of invention has raised several

---

[89] Decision G2/06 *WARF/stem cells* [2009] EPOR 15.

[90] UK–IPO, *Practice Notice on Inventions involving Human Embryonic Stem Cells* (3 February 2009), available here: http://www.ipo.gov.uk/pro-types/pro-patent/p-law/p-pn/p-pn-stemcells-20090203.htm

[91] For commentary see, generally, A Plomer and P Torremans (eds), *Embryonic Stem Cell Patnts: European Law and Ethics* (2009), and P Treichel, 'G2/06 and the Verdict of Immorality' (2009) 40(4) IIC 450 and M Rowlandson, 'WARF/Stem cells (G2/06): The *ordre public* and Morality Exception and its Impact on the Patentability of Human Embryonic Stem Cells' (2010) 32(2) EIPR 67.

[92] For a good definition see M Schmidt, 'Diffusion of Synthetic Biology: A Challenge to Biosafety' (2008) 2(1–2) *Systems and Synthetic Biology* 1–6, at 1: 'Synthetic biologists use artificial molecules to reproduce emergent behaviour from natural biology, with the goal of creating artificial life or seek interchangeable biological parts to assemble them into devices and systems that function in a manner not found in nature.'

concerns in the scientific and public communities.[93] From early on there have been concerns regarding biosecurity and biosafety arising from potential misuse of such technology and the risk of artificial organisms getting out of control and becoming a danger to human life. A further issue concerns the meaning and scope of 'artificial life' and the value that should be assigned to this. But these inventions also raise interesting questions where patent law is concerned, such as, do these inventions consist of patentable subject matter?; are there reasons to exclude them on reasons of *ordre public* or morality?; are they novel?, and can they satisfy the requirement of inventive step? All these issues will need further consideration and many parallels can be draw with discussions that have taken place in the context of nanotechnology and genetics.

12.62 The EU is currently funding a project named SYNTH-ETHICS which will address a variety of ethical, legal and social aspects of synthetic biology. This might provide the basis for European policy making in the medium to long-term.[94] The first patent applications for synthetic biological inventions have been filed in the US by the Venter Institute,[95] but we will have to wait to see if these applications will go unchallenged.[96] The European Group on Ethics has issued the following Recommendations:[97]

> **Recommendation N°16:** The EGE proposes that debates on the most appropriate ways to ensure the public access to the results of synthetic biology is launched. These debates should include also what can be object of patent and what should be available through open access.

> **Recommendation N°17:** The EU Patent Directive (98/44/EC) defines the EGE as the Body to assess ethics implications related to patents. The Group urges the European Patent Office and the National Patent Offices to take account of Article 7 of the Patent Directive and refer contentious ethical issues of a general relevance to the EGE for consideration. This is particularly important if a class of inventions that ought not to be directly exploited commercially has to be defined.

 Exercise

Consider the possible challenges that might be created for the patent system by the advent of synthetic biology. What lessons might be learned from experiences with biotechnology patents to date?

Future action

12.63 Concern in Europe about reticence among the majority of member states to implement the Directive timeously and in full led to the establishment of a Group of Experts to monitor and advise on biotechnology and patenting in Europe, as was required by the Directive itself.[98] The remit of the Group is legal and technical aspects of biotechnological inventions. Ethical policy issues related to biotechnological patenting and social shaping are the remit of the European

---

[93] See, for example, European Group on Ethics, *Opinion 25: Ethics of Synthetic Biology* (2009).

[94] More information about this project can be found at: http://synthethics.eu/index.html

[95] For information on recent filings in this field see (2009) 27(12) *Nature Biotech* p.1127.

[96] See, for example, A Rai and James Boyle, 'Synthetic Biology: Caught between Property Rights, the Public Domain, and the Commons' (2007) PloS Biol PLoS Biol 5(3): e58. doi:10.1371/journal.pbio.0050058 and J Calvert, 'The Commodification of Emergence: Systems Biology, Synthetic Biology and Intellectual Property' (2008) 3 Biosocieties 383.

[97] n 93 above, para 4.5.

[98] Art 16. See generally, http://europa.eu/legislation_summaries/internal_market/businesses/intellectual_property/l26026_en.htm

Group on Ethics in Science and New Technologies,[99] which has, inter alia, already reported on ethical aspects of patenting inventions involving human stem cells, as we have mentioned above.[100]

12.64   The Group of Experts' programme was established in 2003 with two core issues for consideration:(1) 'the level of protection to be given to patents of sequences or partial-sequences of genes isolate from the human body'; and (2) 'the patentability of human stem cells and cell lines derived from them'. These are the two areas of most doubt and controversy to emerge from the public consultation and the Commission's negotiations with the member states.

12.65   Two reports have now been issued on the Biotech Directive and the work of the Group of Experts (2002 and 2005).[101] The first report reiterated the need to maintain competitiveness through full and proper implementation of the Directive, lest Europe lose out on the enormous potential of the biotechnology market. The report reflects the contents of a January 2002 communication from the Commission laying out a strategy for biotechnological development and protection within the European context and its regulatory frameworks.[102] This was followed by a public consultation highlighting ongoing areas of conflict regarding the biotechnology sector, including the prospect of patenting.[103] The European Parliament has also called for greater public engagement with the issues surrounding biotechnology, including its protection by legal means.[104] The second report considered the two controversial areas of gene sequence patents and stem cell patents. It is inconclusive on both counts. The Group of Experts did not favour adopting a 'purpose-bound protection' in respect of gene patents, that is, restricting protection only to the specific use disclosed in the application, although the Commission is aware of broader ethical and economic arguments and has commissioned a survey on gene patenting practice in Europe.[105] Another Commission survey on stem cell patents has recently culminated in a publication which is an invaluable source of commentary on the issues across various European perspectives.[106]

■ C- 34/10 *Oliver Brüstle v Greenpeace eV*

A case has been referred to the Court of Justice of the European Union for a preliminary ruling on the following questions:

1.   What is meant by the term 'human embryos' in Article 6(2)(c) of Directive 98/44/EC?
    (a)   Does it include all stages of the development of human life, beginning with the fertilisation of the ovum, or must further requirements, such as the attainment of a certain stage of development, be satisfied?
    (b)   Are the following organisms also included:
        1.   unfertilised human ova into which a cell nucleus from a mature human cell has been transplanted;

[99] http://ec.europa.eu/european_group_ethics/index_en.htm

[100] http://ec.europa.eu/european_group_ethics/docs/avis16_en.pdf

[101] Report from the Commission to the European Parliament and the Council, *Development and Implications of Patent Law in the Field of Biotechnology and Genetic Engineering*, COM (2002) 545 final, 7 October 2002, and COM (2005) 312 final, 14 July 2005, both available at: http://ec.europa.eu/internal_market/indprop/invent/index_en.htm

[102] For a summary of the strategy paper, see: http://ec.europa.eu/rapid/start/cgi/guesten.ksh?p_action.getfile=gf&doc=IP/02/122|0|AGED&lg=EN&type=PDF

[103] For the results of the public consultation: http://www.ec.europa.eu/research/press/2006/pdf/pr1906_eb_64_3_final_report-may2006_en.pdf

[104] http://ec.europa.eu/biotechnology/docs/com_2007_175_en.pdf

[105] The Patenting of Human DNA: Global Trends in Commercial and Public Sector Activity: http://www.lifecompetence.org/index.php/kb_1/io_483/io.html

[106] A Plomer and P Torremans (eds), *Embryonic Stem Cell Patents: European Law and Ethics* (2009)

    2. unfertilised human ova whose division and further development have been stimulated by parthenogenesis?

  (c) Are stem cells obtained from human embryos at the blastocyst stage also included?

2. What is meant by the expression 'uses of human embryos for industrial or commercial purposes'? Does it include any commercial exploitation within the meaning of Article 6(1) of the Directive, especially use for the purposes of scientific research?

3. Is technical teaching to be considered unpatentable pursuant to Article 6(2)(c) of the Directive even if the use of human embryos does not form part of the technical teaching claimed with the patent, but is a necessary precondition for the application of that teaching,

  (a) because the patent concerns a product whose production necessitates the prior destruction of human embryos,

  (b) or because the patent concerns a process for which such a product is needed as base material?

 Exercise

Consider these questions and how the possible outcomes might affect European patent law.

Monopoly concerns and licensing

12.66 It is possible to discern two main categories of objection to biotechnological inventions. There are those which find fault with the science itself and those which object to the grant of a private monopoly right over valuable resources that harbour considerable potential to further the public good. Only the latter are the proper subject of patent law. We must remind ourselves of the effect of a patent in order to appreciate the difference between the two kinds of objection. A patent merely provides a monopoly right to exclude competitors from the marketplace. It does not furnish the patentee with a right to exploit his invention— for he might be required to comply with a plethora of regulatory measures before the product or process can be introduced to the market—and it does not provide any means of curbing the way the invention might be exploited beyond limiting the impact or scope of the monopoly. We shall return to this last issue presently. For now, the point to take on board is that a patent is not a means to regulate or control developments in science, medicine or industry. Indeed, it cannot do so. Consider the effect of a successful challenge to a patent. What are the consequences of this in terms of who can then exploit the invention? If you object to the science itself or the availability of a particular invention will the denial of a patent further your cause? A patent is merely a right to control new information that has been contributed to the state of the art. In particular, it is only a right to prevent others from using this information in direct public competition. A biotechnology patent is not a property right over life as is so often claimed.

12.67 Sometimes, of course, free availability of the innovation is precisely what is sought and patents are seen to stand in the way of this. Consider the realm of health care where the public health benefits of freer access to medicines, therapies, diagnostic tools or even research tools is generally considered a public good. A number of strategies have been employed to achieve this end. For example, numerous patents have been granted or are pending in intellectual property offices around the world for inventions on, or related to, the SARS virus (Severe Acute Respiratory Syndrome) and it has been reported that some applicants seek patent protection in order to provide freer access to the material, which they propose to do through the grant of non-exclusive licences at reasonable costs.[107]

Question

If the true aim is to ensure free access then why not publish results of work on the SARS virus and thereby put the knowledge in the public domain? This would effectively nix any future patents. Is there any advantage to be gained for the research community by obtaining a patent and then licensing it on liberal and generous terms, beyond, of course, a possible financial benefit for the patentee?

12.68   Other examples of more aggressive uses of monopolies and licensing provisions can easily be found. Myriad Genetics has held patents worldwide for the BRCA1 and BRCA2 breast cancer genes, and in Europe for diagnostic uses of BRCA1. The Nuffield Council on Bioethics pointed out in 2002 that because of the breadth of the patents as they were originally granted 'there are currently no other methods of diagnosing the presence of the breast cancer susceptibility gene BRCA1 that can be used without infringing the patents'.[108] Myriad has a history of licensing its patents very restrictively and has established an exclusive market in testing in the United States. It insisted in Canada that all breast cancer screening using products derived from its patented invention be done it its own laboratories, potentially raising the costs for publicly funded bodies quite considerably. Indeed, British Columbia temporarily suspended its funding of public laboratory screening because of a fear of litigation.[109] Such measures prompted the European Parliament to issue a Resolution in October 2001 calling on the EPO to reconsider the grant of patents to Myriad Genetics over the genes,[110] and opposition proceedings instigated by the Institut Curie, the Assistance Publique-Hôpitaux de Paris and the Institut Gustave-Roussy led to one of the patents being revoked in 2004 (EP 0699754) and the scope of the other two being severely curtailed in 2005 (EP 0705902 and EP 0705903).[111] Note, however, the reasons for these decisions were not some moral judgment on Myriad's licensing practices, but rather on technical issues of novelty and inventive step.

Discussion point   For answer guidance visit www.oxfordtextbooks.co.uk/orc/macqueen2e/

As the Nuffield Council itself has asked: is it in the public interest that there is only one diagnostic test available for a particular disease? Will patents such as those that assert rights over BRCA1 inhibit further research, even in the context of other diseases? Or does the prospect of a strong reward act as a stronger incentive to innovate?

---

[107] 'Fight over Sars Virus Genes', No 153, Patent World, June 2003, p 8.

[108] Nuffield Council on Bioethics, *The Ethics of Patenting DNA* (2002), para 5.4.

[109] L Eggerston, 'Ontario Defies US Firm's Genetic Patent, Continues Cancer Screening' (2002) 166(4) Canadian Medical Association Journal 494.

[110] European Parliament *Resolution on the Patenting of BRCA1 and BRCA2 ('Breast Cancer') Genes* (4 October 2001, B5–0633, 0641, 0651, and 0663/2001). Available at: http://www.cptech.org/ip/health/biotech/eu-brca.html

[111] On appeal the patents were upheld but in a limited form, though this narrowing of the claim will likely have no significant commercial impact, see Appeal T80/05 (November 2008).

12.69   Concerns arising from this case study and others like it[112] led the Nuffield Council to recommend that intellectual property offices apply the criteria for patentability more rigorously, and indeed this may be what we have seen happen in the Opposition Division of the EPO. In particular, the Council doubted that the research and development process used to isolate and purify genetic materials today is sufficiently inventive. Many of the gene cases we have considered in this chapter relate to work done many years or decades ago. Now, much of the isolation work is relatively straightforward or even routine.[113] The Nuffield Council also questioned the wisdom of granting broad patents that effectively encompass *any* use of the genetic products. It advocated the granting of use patents for diagnostic inventions whereby the monopoly only extends to the use of the invention—ie a gene sequence—for the patentee's specific diagnostic test in relation to a single illness or condition. In this way other uses of the same core material would not be prohibited and, it is argued, a fairer balance of interests would be reached.[114]

12.70   A two-pronged strategy is advanced here. The first ensures that the integrity of the patent system is maintain and that only truly worthy inventions receive protection, the second seeks to limit any rights that are granted and thereby delimits the scope of the corresponding monopoly. The alternative all-or-nothing approach which aims to strike patents down completely is a dangerous strategy for a number of reasons. We are constantly told that patent protection is vital to encourage research and innovation generally, especially in the medical and pharmaceutical fields where development costs can be prohibitive. If this is true, why would an organisation embark on lengthy and costly research and development if there was not some measure of reward or indeed an opportunity to recoup its outlays in the long run?

12.71   A more balanced approach is to consider the second arm of the Nuffield Council's recommendations, namely, to refine the scope of a patent monopoly. Other complementary strategies are also available. One such measure that is attracting growing support, although not from industry, is the prospect of an increased role for compulsory licences.[115] We consider compulsory licences in more depth in Chapter 21, but for present purposes it is sufficient to note that a compulsory licence can be sought by a third party if a patent holder refuses to grant licences for use on reasonable terms and when the patentee is not exploiting the invention himself. The first European Commission report on the Biotech Directive pointed to a possible role for compulsory licences in the biotechnological sector but envisaged no expansion in that role, for example, by allowing compulsory licensing in circumstances other than three years non-use by the patentee.[116] Other bodies have been more ambitious. The Organisation for Economic Cooperation and Development (OECD) has sought to move beyond anecdotal accounts about biotechnology patenting to assess the real problems and concerns on the ground.[117] It concluded that while there does not seem to be a crisis within the licensing system, a few areas do cause

---

[112] Nuffield Council, n 108 above, Ch 4.   [113] ibid, paras 3.29—3.34.

[114] ibid, para 5.24. For more recent comment see K Liddell et al, 'Patents as Incentives for Translational and Evaluative Research: The Case of Genetic Tests and their Improved Clinical Performance' [2008] 3 IPQ 286.

[115] See, eg, Report from the Commission to the European Parliament and the Council, *Development and Implications of Patent Law in the Field of Biotechnology and Genetic Engineering*, COM (2002) 545 final, 7 October 2002, para 4.1.3; European Group on Ethics in Science and New Technologies, *Ethical Aspects of Patenting Inventions Involving Human Stem Cells*, Opinion No 16, 17 May 2002, para 2.9 and the House of Commons Science and Technology Committee, *Human Genetics: The Science and the Consequences*, Third Report (London, HMSO, 6 July 1995), paras 212–14.

[116] Report from the Commission to the European Parliament and the Council, *Development and Implications of Patent Law in the Field of Biotechnology and Genetic Engineering*, COM (2002) 545 final, 7 October 2002, para 4.1.3.

[117] Organisation for Economic Cooperation and Development, *Genetic Inventions, Intellectual Property Rights and Licensing Practices: Evidence and Policies*, 2002.

particular concern. These include the number and breadth of patents being granted, access to diagnostic genetic tests, and reach-through licensing whereby claims are made to future products developed using a patented invention. Reach-through clauses can cover a number of eventualities including: (1) royalties on the sales of future products; (2) options to take out exclusive or non-exclusive licences on future patents; and (3) full ownership of future inventions as a condition of the initial access.[118] The OECD recommended crucial policy guidance for a multi-strategy approach to be considered at governmental level requiring, inter alia, review of the policies within the IP system itself, the manner by which patents are administered, and changing the behaviour of patentees in the way they exploit their monopolies.[119] The OECD notes in particular that the role of compulsory licences, although not popular to date, should be revisited. It raises too the power of the threat of the compulsory licence which can, sometimes, be enough to force a patentee's hand to negotiation with potential licensees.[120] It turned this rhetoric into reality by producing an official Recommendation on Licensing Genetic Invention.[121]

Software-related inventions

'**Article 52(2)**—The following in particular shall not be regarded as inventions within the meaning of paragraph 1:

   (a) discoveries, scientific theories and mathematical methods;

   (b) aesthetic creations;

   (c) schemes, rules and methods for performing mental acts, playing games or doing business, and programs for computers;

   (d) presentations of information.

(3) Paragraph 2 shall exclude the patentability of the subject-matter or activities referred to therein only to the extent to which a European patent application or European patent relates to such subject matter or activities *as such*'. [emphasis added]

12.72   Although the domestic and European provisions are concerned with the same end, the majority of jurisprudence in the field of patenting software-related inventions has arisen in the European Patent Office and has thus been concerned with the interpretation of Article 52(2) EPC. For this reason, we shall use this Article as the primary reference point throughout this section.

A note on terminology

12.73   We use the term 'software-related invention' to describe inventions that employ software to perform their function and where the inventive contribution is embodied within the software itself. We avoid the term 'computer program related-inventions' to prevent confusion with the exclusion of computer programs as such, and we consider it unhelpful to employ the expression 'computer-implemented inventions', which has been deployed by the European Commission in its attempts at reform, because this does not cover all of the inventions discussed herein. The term 'software-related invention' should, therefore, be taken to encompass both (1) inventions that are described solely in terms of the software (eg the program(s) that it contains), and

[118] ibid (OECD), above p 92.   [119] ibid, p 80.   [120] ibid, p 81.

[121] OECD, *Recommendation on the Licensing of Genetic Inventions* (2006), Council of the OECD, 23 February 2006, (2005)149/Rev1. For comparative approaches and experiences see G van Overwalle (ed) *Gene Patents and Public Health* (2007).

(2) inventions that claim products or processes whose functionality depends on software (eg computers or methods for performing certain functions or tasks).

Computer programs *as such*

12.74   Article 52(2) excludes the patenting of computer programs *as such*, and we face the problem once again of establishing what this means in practice and as a matter of law. It is instructive, however, to begin with an understanding of the logic behind this exclusion. Indeed, prospective patentees of software-related inventions have faced a double offensive from Article 52(2). First, as we have seen with biotechnological patents, computer programs have been objected to because they embody one or more of the pre-existing exclusions, for example, it is sometimes argued that a program represents no more than an automated means to perform a mental act,[122] in the same way that it is argued that a biotechnological invention embodies little more than a discovery. However, unlike biotechnological inventions, computer programs are also the subject of a specific prohibition and can be objected to in their own right without the need to rely on other exclusions. Why is this so?

Why are computer programs excluded from patentability?

12.75   The drafting of the European Patent Convention (EPC 1973) was a long and arduous process lasting throughout the 1960s and into the early 1970s. Much of this time was taken up debating the need for, and the terms of, the exclusions from patentability. When the final version of the EPC was adopted in 1973 the specific prohibition on patenting computer programs had found its way into the instrument, but its inclusion was by no means a given.[123] Indeed, computer programs received no mention whatsoever in the outcome of the first round of negotiations. Opinion was greatly divided when the matter was eventually debated in the second round, with the UK showing most antipathy towards software-related inventions, calling them 'merely the mathematical application of a logical series of steps in a process which was no different from a mathematical method [already] excluded . . .'.[124] Moreover, there was concern about including a specific prohibition against computer programs lest genuinely inventive developments related to software also be excluded. Nonetheless, the provision found its way into law. The point to note, however, is the degree of ambivalence that has surrounded this particular exclusion from the start. We therefore began the modern European era of patentability with a tension over the patent protection of computer programs and a genuine desire to strike a balance between the exclusion such as it is and the imperative to protect well-deserving inventions irrespective of whether they are in some way connected to software. It is the resolution of this tension and the striking of this balance that has preoccupied the European Patent Office ever since.

12.76   It should not be thought that because Article 52(2) EPC seems to take a double swipe at patent applications relating to software that such patents are rarely granted. Indeed, the European Commission confirmed in 2002 that over 20,000 so-called computer-implemented

---

[122] See, eg, *Merrill Lynch's Application* [1989] RPC 561; *Gale's Application* 1991] RPC 305; *Fujitsu's Application* [1997] RPC 608, and more recently, *Aerotel Ltd v Telco Holdings Ltd* [2006] EWCA Civ 1371 and *Symbian Ltd v Comptroller General of Patents, Designs and Trademarks* [2009] RPC 1.

[123] It has even been suggested that its inclusion was a mistake, see G Kolle, 'The Patentable Invention in the European Patent Convention' (1974) 5 IIC 140–56.

[124] Taken from the report of discussions in Oct 1971. See too S Davis, 'Computer Program Claims: The Final Frontier for Software Inventions' [1998] 20 EIPR 429, n 11.

inventions had been granted by the EPO alone;[125] many thousands more have been awarded by national offices.[126] By corollary, commentators have indicated that only around 100 software-related inventions have experienced any problems before the EPO.[127] This gives rise to the obvious question: how is the exclusion being interpreted? In order to understand the answer to this question, it is first important to understand some essential features of computer software.

Computer software: the functions

12.77   The World Intellectual Property Organization defined a computer program in 1978 as: '...a set of instructions capable, when in a machine-readable medium, of causing a machine having information-processing capabilities to indicate, perform or achieve a particular function, task or result.'[128] This definition remains broadly accurate today, in that software is essentially a means of processing information in order to control the functioning of a computer, other device or a technical process. And, to the extent that there is a functional output from the operation of software, this technical end result may be the subject matter of a successful patent application.[129] Indeed, the Chief Executive of the UK–IPO has importantly drawn attention to the fact that as many as 15 per cent of all UK patents now being granted have a software element. Although the claimed invention in such cases would not normally be the program per se, the value of the invention will none the less be inherently bound up with the role of the software. This highlights the central role that software plays in technological development across a wide range of fields and it should lead us to question the desirability of attempting to separate patentable and non-patentable elements of an invention. Indeed, the EPO has repeatedly stressed the need to consider inventions 'as a whole' when assessing their patentability.[130] Nonetheless, from the patentee's perspective, it is in his interests to seek protection for as many separate elements of his invention as possible, giving rise to a multiplicity of monopolies each of which can be exploited and defended against a variety of competitors. Thus, while it may be reassuring that the inclusion of a software element in an invention will not necessarily be a bar to the patentability of that invention, the prudent patentee will also seek protection for the software element itself. We present no comment at this stage on the broader acceptability of this strategy but instead offer it as one of the reasons why there has been a sustained push from the software industry to extend protection in the realm of computer programs.

12.78   A number of analogies have been used over the years to describe software, some more helpful than others. The most obvious and ubiquitous parallel that is made is between the computer

[125]   European Commission, Proposal for a Directive of the European Parliament and of the Council on the patentability of computer-implemented inventions COM (2002) 92 final, 20.02.2002, p 2.

[126]   The overall figure from around Europe was estimated to exceed 30,000, in 2002, see 'Proposal for a Directive on the patentability of computer-implemented inventions—frequently asked questions', available at: http://ec.europa.eu/internal_market/indprop/comp/index_en.htm

[127]   L Cohen, 'The Patenting of Software' [1999] 12 European Intellectual Property Review 607. For an excellent account of European software patenting law and practice see K Beresford, *Patenting Software Under the European Patent Convention* (2nd edn, 2010/11).

[128]   See WIPO Model Provisions on the Protection of Computer Software, Geneva 1978, s 1(i).

[129]   See for example: *Raytheon Co v Comptroller General of Patents, Designs and Trade Marks* [2007] EWHC 1230. Here the court considered that where a claimed technical contribution exists independently of whether it is implemented by a computer, in the sense that it embodies a technical process lying outside the computer, the contribution will not be a computer program as such and can therefore be the subject of a patent application. This will be so even if the only practical way of implementing the invention will be on a computer.

[130]   See, in particular, T208/84 *VICOM/Computer related invention* [1987] EPOR 74 and T26/86 *KOCH AND STERZEL/X-ray apparatus* [1988] EPOR 72.

code[131] and 'literary works', as these are understood in copyright law. We have already explained the rudimentary operations of computers and the software used to run them in Chapter 2 where we discuss copyright protection of computer programs. But the protection that is afforded to computer code by copyright is simply in the expression of that code and does not extend to the functionality of the software, that is, to the effects that the software has when run on a computer, or to the underlying ideas and principles of the software. Yet, this is often where the true value of the software lies. It is this functionality which is the proper subject of patent protection.

 Question

What other differences can you think of between the protection afforded to software by copyright and that which might arise under patent law?

12.79   Further analogies about computer software being simply an automated means to perform mental acts vastly oversimplify the capabilities and complexities of contemporary software and probably have very little bearing on current practice, although this continues to be a problem where it has become enshrined in law. Moreover, there is no escaping the fact that the means by which software employs algorithms to perform its tasks—that is, through the application of a set of prescribed logical procedures to solve a particular problem—is in essence the deployment of mathematical formulae towards a particular end result. As we know, mathematical formulae cannot be patented but confusion has arisen because of a general failure to distinguish pure formulae on the one hand, from the application of those formulae to produce a technical outcome. It is the same distinction that must be drawn between computer software in itself and the effects that its operation brings about.

12.80   A common concern also underpins these examples, namely, the desire to exclude mere abstracts from protection, inter alia, because these are difficult to define, impossible to police and result in excessively broad monopolies. It has been argued that a computer program falls into this category, for where is the tangible embodiment of a computer program that consists of nothing more than a series of instructions? To the extent that these might be expressed in a written form, the program has a tangible expression which is protected by copyright. But beyond this, what *is* a computer program? This, however, simply reinforces the need to be clear about the difference between the abstract idea underlying the program and the products or processes that it influences. As Beresford has said, '...the wisest course is...to direct software claims clearly to a physical product or apparatus or a physical process'.[132]

12.81   Self-evidently, the primary effect of computer software is to make a computer work and it does this by controlling the processing of data within the computer's internal circuits. But, as the EPO

---

[131] As we explain in Chapter 2, computer code can take a variety of forms including 'source code', ie the alphanumerical code input to the computer by the programmer using an established language, and 'object code', ie the binary code read by the computer to control its functioning. Source code cannot be read by the computer and must first be converted to binary code by the computer's compiler. Both codes are potentially protectable by copyright by virtue of the inclusion of 'computer program' in the definition of 'literary work' in s 3(1) of the Copyright, Designs and Patents Act 1988. While 'computer program' is not defined by the 1988 Act, Art 10(1) of TRIPS confirms that '[c]omputer programs, whether in source or object code, shall be protected as literary works under the Berne Convention (1971)'. Moreover, Council Directive 91/250/EEC of 14 May 1991 on the legal protection of computer programs simply states in the preamble that 'the term "computer program" shall include program in any form...'.

[132] Beresford, n 127 above, para 1.41.

Guidelines for Examination make clear, '... such normal physical effects are not in themselves sufficient to lend a computer program technical character.'[133] Rather, '... if a computer program is capable of bringing about, when running on a computer, a *further technical effect* going beyond these normal physical effects, it is not excluded from patentability.' [emphasis added][134]

12.82   The architecture of software is a central feature of its protectability. In the realm of copyright, it has been confirmed that the originality requirement can be found in the overall structure and lay-out of the software thereby extending the protection to non-literal aspects of the work.[135] Software architecture can have a significant impact on the speed and efficiency of a program and novel architectures can result in considerable improvements in the operability of the software and the functions that it performs. To this extent, these technical features of the software may provide a means to bring about a technical effect susceptible to patent protection.

12.83   A final point to note about the central features of computer programs is that while software can only operate in the appropriate hardware, it can be stored separately in a variety of mediums such as CDs or USB sticks and it can be sent and received over the Internet or by attachment to email. In other words, software can be bought, sold and transferred free of any hardware apparatus. This can have important implications in terms of scope of protection and infringement proceedings as we shall see below.

The development of EPO jurisprudence

12.84   We are about to embark on an account of the evolution of thinking in the EPO towards software-related inventions. To make sense of this process you need to be aware of certain key features of the EPO's approach to patentability. At the broad level, and as we discussed in Chapter 11 on patenting, a European invention must provide a technical solution to a pre-existing and technical problem. More particularly, a patentee must show that he has an invention with *technical character* in the sense that it produces a *technical effect*.

12.85   The key term here, clearly, is *technical*, and we shall explore its meaning presently.[136] But the first thing you should ask yourself is, where do these requirements come from?

Exercise

Examine the European Patent Convention, Articles 52–57, the EPO Guidelines for Substantive Examination, Part C, Chapter IV and the EPC Implementing Regulations, Rules 27 and 29 (all available on the EPO website).[137] Where does the need for technical character and technical effect arise in European patent law?

---

[133] EPO Guidelines, Part C, Chapter IV, para 2.3.6 citing T1173/97 *IBM/Computer Programs* [2000] EPOR 219. See then T22/85 *IBM/Document abstracting and retrieving* [1990] EPOR 98.

[134] EPO Guidelines, Part C, Chapter IV, para 2.3.6.

[135] *Cantor Fitzgerald International v Tradition (UK) Ltd* [1999] Masons CLR 157; [2000] RPC 95 and *Nova Productions Ltd v Mazooma Games Ltd* [2007] RPC 25 (CA).

[136] The EPO provides helpful summaries of its jurisprudence http://documents.epo.org/projects/babylon/eponet. nsf/0/F7944E5E0AD5958DC12572BC004B2CB6/$File/clr_2006_en.pdf

[137] Note that the Guidelines and the Implementing Regulations are updated as of 1 April 2010.

12.86   The need to demonstrate *technical character* and *technical effect* permeates all of the jurisprudence of the EPO. While it is not stated explicitly in the criteria for patentability in Articles 54–57 EPC, *technical effect* is used to test inventive step: has the invention made a *technical contribution* to the art? Moreover, while neither the term *technical character* nor *technical effect* appears in Article 52 EPC regarding exclusions from patentability, the need to demonstrate *technical character* has become the single most important factor is restricting the scope of these exclusions.[138] Nowhere is this more true than in the context of computer programs. Indeed, the current position can be summed up as follows:

> **SUMMARY OF EPO POSITION:** So long as a software-related invention is of a technical character (in the sense of producing a technical effect) it will be eligible for patent protection. It does not matter that the essence of the invention falls into an excluded category, that is, that the technical character is found in a computer program.

Thus, we have the most recent version of the EPO Guidelines stating:

> 'The basic patentability considerations in respect of claims for computer programs are in principle the same as for other subject-matter. While "programs for computers" are included among the items listed in Art. 52(2), if the claimed subject-matter has a technical character it is not excluded from patentability by the provisions of Art. 52(2) and (3).'

What is the relationship between technical character and technical effect?

12.87   Technical character is demonstrated by bringing about a technical effect, that is, changes in the workings of apparatus, products or processes achieved by technical means. Relevant technical effects that lends technical character to a computer program include:

(1) the control of an industrial process;

(2) the processing of data which represent physical entities; and

(3) the control of the internal functions of a computer itself or its interfaces.[139]

The EPO Guidelines further state that technical effect can be found in a computer program that:

(1) affects the efficiency or security of a process;

(2) governs the management of computer resources; or

(3) regulates the rate of data transfer in a communication link.[140]

These are mere examples and the clear message to patent attorneys who must draft claims for software-related inventions is to focus their attentions on the possible technical effects which can be brought about by the computer program, for it is in these that protection will be secured.[141]

---

[138] Confirmed as a valid approach in T931/95 *PENSION BENEFIT SYSTEMS/Controlling pension benefits systems* [2002] EPOR 52 and see too T1227/05 *INFINEON TECHNOLOGIES/Circuit simulation I* [2010] EPOR 9.

[139] EPO Guidelines Part C, Chapter IV, para 2.3.6.   [140] ibid.

[141] Although see the comments in T1543/06 *Gameaccount* quoted in *AT&T Knowledge Ventures LP's Patent Application* [2009] FSR] 19: 'The Board is of the firm belief, that it cannot have been the legislator's purpose and intent on the one hand to exclude from patent protection such subject matter, while on the other hand awarding protection to a technical implementation thereof, where the only identifiable contribution of the claimed technical implementation to the state of the art is the excluded subject-matter itself. It is noted that here the term "contribution" encompasses both means (i.e. tangible features of the implementation) and effects resulting from the implementation. In that case Article 52(2) EPC would

12.88   The net effect of this position is that the seemingly absolutist prohibition on the patenting of computer programs *as such* is illusory. It is no longer a matter of interpreting the provisions of Article 52 EPC (albeit narrowly), for the emphasis has shifted from considering what is *not* patentable to considering what *is* patentable, the primary requirement being that the putative invention displays technical character.[142] Of course, this does not preclude the need to show that the invention is new, involves an inventive step and is capable of industrial application in the normal way, but it does leave us to question what, if anything, remains of the exclusion of computer programs from European patent law.

 Exercise

Before reading any further, consider whether there is any need to retain an exclusion of computer programs in Article 52 EPC. You might like to consider the discussions about possible removal of the provision at the Diplomatic Conference to revise the European Patent Convention in 2000: http://documents.epo.org/projects/babylon/eponet.nsf/0/a3d02ee ebea84306c12572ae00500cdc/$file/conference_proceedings_en.pdf

How have we arrived at this position?

12.89   We can plot the course of EPO thinking on software-related inventions in roughly three stages. First, the period from the establishment of the Office in 1978 until 1985 when the Examination Guidelines were changed in respect of computer programs. Second, the post-1985 period which is characterised by an increasingly liberal attitude towards these inventions when considerably fewer restraints applied, with some notable exceptions. Third, the modern era, which began in 1998/99 with the two important rulings in T935/97 *IBM/Computer Programs*[143] and T1173/97 *IBM/Computer Programs*.[144] This era ushered in the effective demise of the computer program exclusion, and the final nail was put in the coffin in 2001 when the EPO revised its Guidelines to bring practice into line with the *IBM* cases. The position since thereafter, as we shall see, has become unsustainable.

Stage 1: 1978–1985

12.90   We need not dwell on the national positions that prevailed prior to signing of the European Patent Convention in 1973 and the establishment of the European Patent Office in 1978, although it is suffice to say that patents had been granted for software-related inventions in a variety of countries.[145] But this was set to change somewhat by virtue of the exclusion of computer programs in the EPC and the requirement of signatory states to bring their laws into line with the Convention. All eyes looked to the EPO for an indication of how patenting practice in

be reduced to a mere requirement as to form, easily circumvented. The Board believes it is intended as substantive in nature, whatever considerations may have been the source of this exclusion at the time of its adoption.' This led the Board to conclude: 'It follows from the above that the mere technical implementation of excluded subject-matter *per se* cannot form the basis for inventive step. The Board concludes that inventive step can be based only on the particular manner of implementation.'

   [142] After T931/95 *PENSION BENEFIT SYSTEMS/Controlling pension benefits systems* [2002] EPOR 52 and T641/00 *COMVIK/Two identities* [2004] EPOR 10; followed most recently in T588/05 *WEST DIRECT/Computer assisted telemarketing* [2010] EPOR 12.
   [143] [1999] EPOR 301.   [144] [2000] EPOR 219.
   [145] See, eg, in the UK, *Slee and Harris's Applications* [1966] RPC 194; [1966] FSR 51 ('means' for controlling a computer were held to be prima facie patentable in themselves) and *Burroughs Corporation (Perkins') Application* [1974] RPC 147, [1973] FSR 439 (computer programs having the effect of controlling computers to operate in a particular way, and which are embodied in physical form, are the proper subject matter for patent law).

this new era would take shape. You will recall from Chapter 10, that while national intellectual property offices and courts are not bound by the rulings of the EPO, they do consider them to be highly persuasive, and for reasons that we have already examined it is preferable to keep discrepancies to an absolute minimum. We consider the efforts of the UK in this respect below (paras 12.137–12.143).

12.91   The original version of the EPO Guidelines had this to say about computer programs:

> 'If the contribution to the known art resides solely in the computer program then the subject matter is not patentable in whatever manner it may be presented in the claims'.[146]

Here the focus is firmly on the fact that the computer program is an example of an excluded category of invention and that if the essence of the claims in an application is to a computer program then those claims should be rejected, no matter the invention's actual technical contribution, function or effect.

12.92   Interestingly, there is precious little evidence of an antipathetic attitude from the Examining Division of the EPO towards inventions involving computer programs during this period, and the Board of Appeal did not even hear, let alone reject, any relevant appeal during this time. Nonetheless, after consultation on the Guidelines during which time the EPO came under considerable pressure to amend the provisions, the text was changed in 1985. It is possible that much of this pressure was brought to bear because of the widespread perception that the restriction on patenting was more stringent that was borne out by practice. The amended text—changed over numerous iterations—now contains the following features (April 2010):

- 'The basic patentability considerations in respect of claims for computer programs are in principle the same as for other subject-matter.'

- 'While "programs for computers" are included among the items listed in Art. 52(2), if the claimed subject-matter has a *technical character* it is not excluded from patentability by the provisions of Art. 52(2) and (3).'

- It follows also that, where the claimed subject matter is concerned only with the program-controlled internal working of a known computer, the subject matter could be patentable provided if it provides a *technical effect*.[147]

12.93   We see here a crucial shift in emphasis away from reasons to exclude protection towards reasons to extend protection to a claimed invention. The framework has thereby been established to allow the EPO more latitude in its interpretation of Article 52, a task to which it has taken with considerable gusto.

Stage 2: 1985–1998/99

12.94   The direction of EPO jurisprudence during this period was set by the first decision of the Board of Appeal to consider the exclusion of computer programs, T208/84 *VICOM/Computer related invention*.[148] This remained the most influential decision throughout this period and it continues to be a milestone of considerable significance. The case involved an appeal against the rejection by the Examining Division of claims related to (1) a method of digitally processing images with a view to enhancing their features, for example, the clarity of the image, and

---

[146] [1978] OJEPO 1.

[147] Note, previous editions of the Guidelines included the following statement: 'A computer program claimed by itself or as a record on a carrier, is not patentable irrespective of its content.' This has now been removed. Why?

[148] [1987] EPOR 74.

(2) specifically designed apparatus to carry out this method. It was a particular feature of the claimed invention that all of this could be done considerably faster and more efficiently than was possible in conventional computers of the time. The inventors acknowledged, however, that the invention itself could be implemented using a suitably programmed conventional computer. The Examining Board rejected the application on the grounds that it was for a mathematical method and/or a computer program as such.

12.95 The Board of Appeal disagreed on both counts holding:

- As regards the *method* of image processing:
    (i)   Methods of processing images, including simulated images, are susceptible of industrial application under Article 57 EPC, that is, they are sufficiently technical to be the proper subject of patent law.

    (ii) If the claim in question is directed towards a *technical process* which is carried out on a *physical entity*—here, an image (albeit one stored as an electric signal)—and that process brings about changes in that entity—here, the manipulation of the image to enhance or alter certain features—then this is a *technical effect* sufficient for the purposes of patent law.

    (iii) While it is true that such a process can be described in mathematical terms, for example, the operation of a mathematical algorithm on data, the effect of this operation is not merely to produce more abstract data but rather to produce a real change in a real image and therefore there is an effect beyond the simple execution of the mathematical method.

    (iv) It is irrelevant that the idea underlying the invention resides in a mathematical method so long as the process that is claimed goes beyond the mere mathematical method *as such*.

    (v)   It is also irrelevant that the technical means used to bring about the technical effect is by way of a computer program, since the claim is to the process carried out under the control of the program and not to the program *as such*.

- As regards the *apparatus* containing the software for processing the images, it was held that:

    '...claims which can be considered as being directed to a computer set up to operate in accordance with a specified program (whether by means of hardware or software) *for controlling or carrying out a technical process* cannot be regarded as relating to a computer program as such...'[149]

12.96 It is interesting and important to note that the need for specificity of claim was emphasised in *Vicom*. Thus, it was stated that:

'...a "method for digitally filtering data" remains an abstract notion not distinguished from a mathematical method so long as it is not specified what physical entity is represented by the data and forms the subject of the technical process...'[150]

This was an important qualification because the original claims before the Examining Division did not specify image manipulation and spoke only of a method of 'digitally filtering...data', which was a broad and unacceptable claim given the nature of the invention in question.

---

[149] ibid, at p 80 (para 15 of judgment).   [150] ibid, at p 90 (para 7 of judgment).

Discussion point For answer guidance visit www.oxfordtextbooks.co.uk/orc/macqueen2e/

Does the above comment about the exclusion of a method for digitally filtering data mean that such a claim could never succeed? Can you envisage examples where such a claim might be important to a prospective patentee? How might such a claim be successfully framed?

12.97   The net result from *Vicom* was that process *and* product claims involving both mathematical methods and computer programs became clearly patentable under the EPC. The essential lesson should be self-evident: the drafting of the claims should be to the process or product itself, emphasising the technical features used to bring about the technical effect and ensuring that any mention of a computer program (or mathematical method) is as a means to achieve the technical result not an end in itself. In particular:

- *process claims* are to a method of achieving a technical result by means of a computer program operating on appropriate hardware;
- *product claims* are to a computer, or similar device, incorporating a computer program.

Note: In both cases there is the need to link the software to hardware via the claims. This becomes important when we come to consider the third stage of EPO jurisprudence.

Successful examples that followed *Vicom* include:

(1)   A method claim for processes of regulating error messages within a computer system, T115/85 *IBM/Computer related invention*.[151]

(2)   A method claim for maintaining formats of documents transferred between word processors, T110/90 *IBM/Editable document form*.[152]

(3)   A method claim for precision rotation and manipulation of graphic images on screen, T59/93 *IBM/Rotating displayed object.s*[153]

(4)   An apparatus claim for an x-ray device controlled by a computer to monitor tube voltages to ensures optimal exposure while protecting against overload T26/86 *KOCH AND STERZEL/X-ray apparatus*.[154]

(5)   An apparatus claim for a device to monitor computer components to detect the cause of, and where possible improve the speed of, the computer's re-set procedure, T164/92 *BOSCH/Electronic computer components*.[155]

(6)   Method and apparatus claims for a system for providing product-specific data in a service station for recognition and editing of design and function states, T1242/04 *MAN/ Provision of product specific data*.[156]

Exercise

Consider each of these judgments and identify the all-important technical effect.

---

[151] [1990] EPOR 107.   [152] [1995] EPOR 185.
[153] Unreported, available on the EPO website at: http://legal.european-patent-office.org/dg3/pdf/t930059eu1.pdf
[154] [1988] EPOR 72.   [155] [1995] EPOR 585.   [156] [2007] EPOR 45.

12.98   It is interesting to note that in virtually all of these cases (and many more successful appeals to the Board of Appeal) the appellants amended their initial (rejected) claims after communication with the Board; indeed, this also happened in *Vicom*. Not only does this help to account for the high number of successful appeals to the Board of Appeal but it also re-emphasises the crucial point that careful drafting of claims is key.

Discussion point   For answer guidance visit www.oxfordtextbooks.co.uk/orc/macqueen2e/

Does it follow that skilful drafting can avoid Article 52 problems for any kind of method, device or software-related invention?

12.99   In each of the above examples the role of the computer program was as a *technical means* to realise the *technical effect* that was central to the invention. One might think as a result of these rulings that so long as a computer program is not claimed directly sufficient protection can be gained for any software-related invention. The reality has not been quite so straightforward and a number of hurdles have remained.

12.100   You will recall that a European patent application must disclose the following:

- a *technical* problem
- that is solved by *technical* means
- these means make a *technical* contribution to the state of the art.

12.101   It has been confirmed many times that a computer program on appropriate hardware can provide the necessary *technical means* in this equation, as each of the above cases demonstrates.[157] But problems remain as to what amounts to a *technical contribution* and, indeed, what is a *technical problem*? Two topics demonstrate the concerns. These are (a) software-related inventions in the field of textual processing, and (b) business method patents.

Software-related inventions and textual processing

12.102   The EPO Board of Appeal has held on a number of occasions that claims directed at processes or devices to assist the user in the processing or manipulation of text or language do not demonstrate a *technical* contribution to the art, but rather a contribution in non-technical areas such as aesthetic creations, methods of performing mental acts or mere presentations of information. Put another way, the EPO has found that if the sole contribution is in an excluded category protection will be denied. Thus, for example, in T22/85 *IBM/Document abstracting and retrieval*[158] the Board of Appeal rejected a claim relating to a system for creating and storing abstracts from archived documents by means of a key word search because:

(1)   the claims simply outlined an excluded category, namely, schemes, rules and methods for performing mental acts; in particular, it was considered that the claim merely described an automated means of key word search and abstract creation that could be carried out manually in essentially the same fashion;

---

[157]   See, in particular, *Koch & Sterzel/X-ray apparatus*, n 130 above.   [158]   [1990] EPOR 98.

(2) it was insufficient merely to show that technical means, that is, a computer program running on hardware, had been used to bring about the result because the contribution itself was non-technical; and

(3) '…the true problem to be solved was that of establishing a set of rules for document abstracting and retrieval on the basis of textual properties of the documents to be handled *which problem cannot be qualified as technical*'.[159]

12.103   Similarly, in T38/86 *IBM/Text clarity processing*, the Board stated that it would 'permit patenting only in those areas in which the invention involves a contribution to the art in a field not excluded from patentability'.[160] And, although the Board recognised that the EPO will grant patents for inventions which involve both technical and non-technical features so long as a technical contribution is realised by the invention when seen as a whole, here the problem was held to be nontechnical in nature—it related to the extraction of incomprehensible phrases from documents and their replacement with more comprehensible ones. This, once again, was seen as merely an automated means to execute a mental act (the act of assessing comprehensibility).

12.104   We need not see these cases, or others like them,[161] as a necessary departure from the general trend laid down in *Vicom*. Indeed, the position is well summed up in T121/85 *IBM/Spell Checker*[162] which involved an automatic spelling checking and correction system that was denied protection by the Board of Appeal. The central passage deserves quotation in full:

> 'Such spelling is basically not of a technical but of a linguistic nature. A correctly spelled word represents an abstract linguistic information and a correct spelling relates therefore to the correctness of an information and not to any physical entity. A wrong spelling can be detected by performing mental acts with no technical means involved.
>
> This does not necessarily mean that a system automatically performing, instead of a human being, the same spelling checking act is excluded from patentability. Rather, this will depend on whether the manner in which it is automated, involves features which make a contribution in a field outside the range of matters excluded from patentability under Art. 52(2) in connection with Art. 52(3) EPC.'

12.105   Note, once again, the stress on the need to show technicality. Has this become an overriding consideration? Consider, too, the reference to 'physical entity' which we also see appearing in *Vicom*. The indication seems to be that to bring about a change in a physical entity takes the claim more readily into the technical field, and 'physical entity' has been defined broadly to include non-tangible entities such as computer images[163] and television signals.[164]

Business method patents

12.106   Applications to patent business methods broadly come in two forms; those relating to methods of doing business involving computer software and those requiring no such input. We have already discussed the latter in Chapter 11 and therefore in this section we will focus on software-related business method patents.

---

[159] ibid, at 105.   [160] [1990] EPOR 606, at 611.

[161] Other failed appeals include T52/85 *IBM/Semantically related expressions* [1989] EPOR 454 (automated editing functions to list semantically connected expressions are linguistic not technical in character), T65/86 *IBM/Text processing* [1990] EPOR 181 (automated means to correct contextual errors in a document involved no technical steps that a human being would not also perform in the same task) and T1177/97 *SYSTRAN/Translating natural languages* [2005] EPOR 13 (the use of a 'longest word-stem match' system to assist in computer translation was based on linguistic considerations and did not solve a technical problem).

[162] Unreported, a summary is available at http://legal.european-patent-office.org/dg3/biblio/t850121du1.htm#txt

[163] *Vicom*, para 12.94 above and T643/00 *CANON/Searching image data* [2007] EPOR 1.

[164] T163/85 *BBC/Colour Television Signal* [1990] EPOR 599.

12.107   Much furore has surround the prospect of business method patents of both descriptions, particularly in the context of the internet where fears have arisen that patent thickets relating to e-commerce practices might considerably restrict the commercial viability and attractiveness of cyberspace as a place to do business. British Telecom claimed at the turn of the century that it had been granted a US patent over hyperlinking technology more than 20 years previously (US Pat No 4,873,662); it sought, and failed, to enforce rights against some American Internet Service Providers. But, perhaps the most famous Internet-related business method patent involves Amazon.com who devised a method for managing online orders and called it the 'One-Click' system (US Pat No 5,960,411). The method allows the customer to enter his personal and credit card details only once with the company and thereafter the customer can order products simply by clicking on the item on screen, whereupon Amazon can access the necessary billing information directly from the customer's account. Beyond customer convenience, the commercial advantage is that this effectively does away with the potential disincentive faced by customers who have to re-enter data for each purchase. Amazon was granted a patent on this business method in September 1999 but this was challenged by Barnes and Noble. In February 2001 the Federal US Court of Appeals in Washington, DC lifted a preliminary injunction that had barred Barnesandnoble.com from using the one-click technology. The matter was finally settled out of court in 2002 and the patent remains in the US. It was rejected by the EPO for lack of inventive step.

12.108   The EPO position was initially laid out in T769/92 *SOHEI/General purpose management system*[165] which concerned apparatus and method claims for a novel user interface allowing the input of management data across a broad spectrum of activities, including financial, inventory, personnel and construction management. The advantage of the system was that it allowed the user to input all of these data via one interface and for them to be processed automatically towards a variety of different ends via one medium. Previously different systems had to be learned for different spheres of management. The Examining Division rejected the application as (1) mere presentation of information, (2) a method of doing business, and (3) a computer program as such. In keeping with established case law, however, the Board of Appeal upheld the claims (albeit after amendment) on the following grounds:

- The program on the computer was merely the technical means to implement the invention and was not claimed as such; what was required was technical character and technical effect; similarly this would not be an example of the mere presentation of information if technical character was present.

- The 'user friendly' interface allowing multiple inputs of data and the structured execution of the method for automatically processing those data on the system provided sufficient technical character.

- The subject matter was not excluded if it involved, or implied, at least one aspect or component, which was not excluded from patentability.

- No objection could be raised that the claims related only to 'doing business' because the subject matter of the claims—which could be generalised across a range of possible uses and were not necessarily restricted merely to business ends—could not be said to be merely abstract and non-technical.

12.109   Beyond reiterating the rule in *Vicom*, this decision makes it clear that it is not problematic to an application to include aspects of business management in claims, that is, non-technical

---

[165] [1996] EPOR 253.

features, so long as the claims cannot be taken as solely directed to those ends and, of course, further technical effect is also represented.

12.110   Similarly, in T1002/92 *PETTERSSON/Queuing System*[166] an application was allowed for a system of managing queues of people in business establishments by allocating turn-numbers and displaying free service points automatically. The objection was raised in Opposition proceedings that this was simply a method of doing business, but this was rejected by the Board of Appeal which confirmed that the central claim was to technical apparatus that solved the technical problem of efficient queue management without the need for human input and by means of the interaction of various co-operating technical components. It was stressed that just because one practical application of such a system was in the service of customers of a 'business equipment' did not mean that the claimed subject-matter was a method of doing business *as such*. Moreover, while the Board accepted that one element of the claim probably was tantamount to a method of doing business— this being the means of 'deciding which particular turn-number is to be served at the particular free service point' (because it could equally be achieved by means of human intervention involving essentially the same steps)—the claim was to be viewed as a whole and a mix of technical and non-technical elements would not necessarily be excluded from patentability so long as the technical character resides in the technical elements, as was the case in the present application.

12.111   We must always bear in mind, however, that the claimed invention must be directed at a technical problem, which we have seen described in *Pettersson*, and which in *Sohei* was the problem of requiring multiple data inputs into various systems which was solved by the unique and convenient single user interface. In both cases, the fact that the invention assisted the user in the conduct of his business was incidental, and not fatal to the claim.

12.112   But, to the extent that the problem to be solved is solely a way of automating business practices, the problem to be solved here is non-technical in character and will remain unpatentable in Europe. This was held to be the case in T931/95 *PENSION BENEFIT SYSTEMS/Controlling pension benefits systems*[167] in which the Technical Board rejected an appeal for lack of technical character. In doing so, it confirmed a number of crucial points:

  • A *technical* invention does not loose its technical character simply because it is used for a non-technical purpose (such as a method of doing business).

  • A method claim, so long as it is *technical*, may relate to a method of doing business and still be patentable.

  • An apparatus claim, even if the apparatus is programmed for use in fields such as business or economy, cannot be an example of excluded subject matter since such products (ie apparatus) are not mentioned in Article 52(2) EPC.

12.113   Nonetheless, the appeal failed for the method claims because the claimed invention only described steps in a process for controlling a pension benefit scheme which were for administrative, actuarial or financial purposes; typically non-technical purposes. It was not enough to point to data processing and computer means employed to execute these purposes since there was no corresponding disclosure of a technical problem requiring a solution nor of a solution that represented a technical effect. The Technical Board of Appeal later modified the earlier position in *Pension Benefit Systems* in the decision of *Hitachi* (T258/03) wherein it was held that

---

[166] [1996] EPOR 1.   [167] [2002] EPOR 52.

it is not a display of technical character to circumvent a technical problem by modifying a business method as opposed to finding some truly technical means to resolve the problem.[168]

12.114   In T154/04 *DUNS LICENSING ASSOCIATES/Estimating sales activity* it was accepted that claims can contain both technical and non-technical features and this will not necessarily be fatal to the eligibility of the invention for protection. However, non-technical features will be ignored if they do not contribute to the resolution of the technical problem; indeed, there must be such a *technical* problem in the first place; this is defined as a problem which an expert in the field might be asked to solve. There was no technical problem in the instant case—it concerned merely a means to gather information about sales activities in various outlets and then to apply statistical methods to estimate future sales. This was quintessential business research and using a computer to generate the result did not make it *technical*. In similar fashion we have the Technical Board of Appeal in T388/04 *PITNEY BOWES/Undeliverable mail*[169] finding that the claims of the invention revealed 'no technical means…at all' to carry out the activities for which protection was sought (the claim was to a method of responding to a message that electronic mail was 'undelivered'). The mere possibility of using technical means to carry out the activity is not enough. Claims must specifically be directed to producing a technical effect. This has since been translated into the EPO Guidelines thus: 'A method of doing business is excluded from patentability even where it implies the possibility of making use of unspecified technical means or has practical utility.'[170]

12.115   Other recent examples of unsuccessful business method applications include:

> Claims to a method for running 'what if' scenarios in business databases for the purposes of business planning and information modelling (lack of technical character and the reference to their use in databases was not enough), T1149/06 *IBM/Database back-solving*.[171]

> A system to estimate environmental impact had no overall technical character because the tools were typical of operational/business management, T1029/06 *TOSHIBA/Environmental impact estimation*.[172]

> A system to gauge potential reduction of environmental impact of products was, in essence, a management tool to decide between investment strategies and as such lacked sufficient technical character, T1147/05 *RICOH/Environmental impact information*.[173]

We see, then, that business method patents generally receive short shrift in Europe. How does this compare with the position in the United States?

12.116   Compare and contrast the fate of Signature Financial Group Inc either side of the Atlantic when it tried to patent its data-processing system for managing financial services and portfolio returns across a variety of funds. In the EPO, the application was rejected by the Examining Division for lack of technical character. The importance of this example is the fact that it was essentially the same invention that lies at the heart of the dispute in *State Street Bank and Trust Co v Signature Financial Group*;[174] a decision that revolutionised business method patenting in the United States and set in motion a furore surrounding the practice worldwide.

12.117   In *State Street* the United States Court of Appeals for the Federal Circuit (CAFC) upheld the claims to this data-processing system and put an end to the speculation that a business method exception applies in the United States. Indeed, it is generally acknowledged that *State Street* in

---

[168] More recently, the Technical Board of Appeal applied *Hitachi* in T424/03 *Microsoft/Data Transfer* [2006] EPOR 40 and held that 'a computer system including a memory (clipboard) is a technical means and consequently the claimed method has technical character in accordance with established case law'.

[169] [2007] OJEPO 16.   [170] n 8 above, para 2.3.5.   [171] [2010] EPOR 3.   [172] [2010] EPOR 13.
[173] [2008] EPOR 34.   [174] 149 F 3d 1368 (Fed Cir 1998).

tandem with *AT&T Corp v Excel Communications Inc*,[175] went further in establishing the precedent that 'pure' business methods are patentable, that is, methods not dependent on software, although neither case involved such an example. While our remit does not extend to an analysis of US law where the statutory provisions and considerations are different, the disparity of approach towards the *State Street* invention—and in particular the need in Europe to establish technical character beyond the standard criteria—indicates that prospective patentees face more hurdles in this area in Europe compared to the experience across the Atlantic.

12.118   Some comments on *State Street* are, nonetheless, of assistance in our present discussion. US law requires a 'useful, concrete and tangible result' from an invention and the means to achieve this are irrelevant.[176] Although common law exclusions have grown up over the years, for example, in the realm of mathematical algorithms, formulae or calculations,[177] there are no statutory exclusions in US law,[178] and the common law measures have been interpreted in an increasingly narrower fashion.[179] Thus, while the *State Street* invention had been rejected by the lower court because it was an 'algorithm', the CAFC held that the system was a 'machine' in the proper sense of statutory subject matter, and that:

> 'every step-by-step process, be it electronic or chemical or mechanical, involves an algorithm in the broad sense of the term...[and] since §101 expressly includes processes as a category of invention which may be patentable...it follows that it is no ground for holding a claim is directed to non-statutory subject matter to say it includes or is directed to an algorithm. This is why the proscription against patenting has been limited to *mathematical* algorithms...'[180] [emphasis added].

12.119   The court went on to stress that the emphasis in patent examination should be on the essential characteristics of the subject matter, and most notably, whether it displays 'practical utility' in the sense of producing a 'useful, concrete and tangible result'. This renders an invention statutory subject matter, '...even if the useful result is expressed in numbers, such as price, profit, percentage, cost or loss.'[181] More recently, however, the approach of *State Street* has been directly challenged by an en banc decision of the CAFC *In re Bilski*.[182] It has been suggested that the 'useful, concrete and tangible result' test should be replaced by the 'transformation-machine test': that is, it must be shown that the invention transforms the nature of an article into a different state or thing, or that it is somehow connected to apparatus or a machine. In the instant case it was not possible to satisfy such a test and this led to the denial of patent protection. The application was for a method of hedging risk in the field of commodities trading and it was argued, and accepted, that this lacked patent-eligible subject matter. It was not suggested in *Bilski* that *State Street* should be overruled but rather that the approach was incorrect. The wider ramifications are eagerly awaited as the case has now been referred to the Supreme Court which heard oral argument in November 2009.

 Questions

[Reminder: *Pension Benefits Systems* and *State Street* were both denied protection in Europe yet were successful in the US.]

How approximate is the US need for 'practical utility' to the European requirement of 'technical contribution'? What impact does the continued existence of an express exclusion for methods of doing business have on European patent law and is it desirable that it should remain? What difference might a shift in approach mean for US patents?

---

[175] 172 F 3d 1352 (Fed Cir 1999).
[176] See USPTO Guidelines (2008), available at: http://www.uspto.gov/web/offices/pac/mpep/mpep.htm
[177] *Gottschalk v Benson* (1972) 409 US 63.   [178] 35 USC §101.   [179] See *In re Alappat* 33 F 3d 1526 (Fed Cir 1994).
[180] *State Street*, n 174 above, p 1375.   [181] ibid.   [182] 545 F 3d 943, 88 USPQ 2d 1385 (Fed Cir 2008)

UK–IPO Office guidelines

12.120 These rulings caused patent examiners in intellectual property offices around the world to sit up and take notice of the developments. Consider the current versions of the Guidelines that operate in the US, Europe, and Japan noting that each had to be amended in light of this case law. It is instructive to compare and contrast these provisions to gauge the different approaches.

The US Patent and Trademark Office

'Since a computer program is merely a set of instructions capable of being executed by a computer, the computer program itself is not a process and USPTO personnel should treat a claim for a computer program, without the computer-readable medium needed to realize the computer program's functionality, as non-statutory functional descriptive material. When a computer program is claimed in a process where the computer is executing the computer program's instructions, USPTO personnel should treat the claim as a process claim. When a computer program is recited in conjunction with a physical structure, such as a computer memory, USPTO personnel should treat the claim as a product claim.'[183]

12.121 Previous versions of the Guidelines instructed personnel to treat business method claims like any other process claims. In this latest version, this point is not even made. Quite simply then, US business method patents will be patentable so long as they meet the standard criteria for patentability. No distinction is drawn between computer-implemented methods and so-called 'pure' business methods.

Japanese Patent Office

'If a matter necessary to define an invention involves any means contrary to a law of nature, the claimed invention is not considered to be a statutory invention...If claimed inventions are any laws as such other than a law of nature (e.g. economic laws), arbitrary arrangements (e.g. a rule for playing a game as such), mathematical methods or mental activities, or utilize only these laws (e.g. methods for doing business as such), these inventions are not considered to be statutory because they do not utilize a law of nature...On the contrary, even if a part of matters defining an invention stated in a claim does not utilize a law of nature, when it is judged that the claimed invention as a whole utilizes a law of nature, the claimed invention is deemed as utilizing a law of nature...the characteristic of the technology is to be taken into account in judging whether a claimed invention as a whole utilizes a law of nature...For inventions relating to a method for doing business or playing a game, since there are cases in which the claimed invention a part of which utilizes an article, apparatus, device, system, etc., is judged as not utilizing a law of nature when considered as a whole, careful examination shall be required...There is possibility for an invention to be qualified as statutory where the invention is made not from a viewpoint of a method of doing business or playing a game but from a viewpoint of computer software-related inventions such as software used in doing business or in playing a game.'[184]

12.122 The outcome in Japan is that appropriately drafted technical claims that clearly define software-related means of carrying out business practices will be considered as patentable subject matter, but that pure business methods will not be so considered.

[183] USPTO Manual of Patent Examining Procedure, ß2106.01 Computer-Related non-statutory subject matter (2008), available at: http://www.uspto.gov/web/offices/pac/mpep/mpep_e8r6_2100.pdf

[184] JPO Examination Guidelines for Patent and Utility Model in Japan (2009), Part II: Requirements for Patentability, Chapter 1: Industrially Applicable Inventions, section 1.1. see: http://www.jpo.go.jp/tetuzuki_e/t_tokkyo_e/Guidelines/2_1.pdf

European Patent Office

'...if the claimed subject-matter specifies an apparatus or technical process for carrying out at least some part of the scheme, that scheme and the apparatus or process have to be examined as a whole. In particular, if the claim specifies computers, computer networks or other conventional programmable apparatus, or a program therefor, for carrying out at least some steps of a scheme, it is to be examined as a "computer-implemented invention".'[185]

12.123 The effect here then is to encourage business method-related claims to be drafted in line with software-related claims whereby they will be dealt with in the same fashion as is now represented post-the *IBM* decisions (see below). 'Pure' business methods, however, should be excluded to the extent that they are merely abstract and non-technical in nature.

12.124 The approach in the UK to computer-implemented inventions, including business methods, has been revised in light of the EPO approach and we will deal with it separately below.

Should business method patents be treated differently?

12.125 Business method patents have proved controversial for a number of reasons and below we recite some of the arguments that have been mounted against them.

From the UK–IPO:

(1) In what sense can a method of doing business be seen as an example of *industrial* property? That is, how can the protection of such a method achieve the original aims of the patent system which is to encourage *technological* innovation and development?

(2) What is a 'business method'? How can this be defined with sufficient precision to delimit clearly the scope of any patent monopoly? The problem is not just one of definition because indistinct and potentially broad claims necessarily impact on the scope of the monopoly granted. An ill-defined invention leads to an indeterminable monopoly calling its entire validity into question.

(3) A single business method could have applications across a very broad range of fields, thereby potentially leading to an excessively broad patent which might hinder rather than encourage innovation. Moreover, unlike other technical fields such as the biotechnology or pharmaceutical industries, the respective outlays in research and development costs are minimal for business methods and so the reward is disproportionate to the inventive effort. Yet the economic impact of such patents could be just as great or greater than other fields of technology.

(4) Many of the ways of doing business that form the subject of these patents have been around for a long time; a method of doing business does not become inventive simply because it is carried out on using computers or via the Internet.

(5) The prior art relating to business methods is difficult, if not impossible, to discern. This is partly because those employing effective methods kept them secret in the absence of other means of protection. It is also because of the infinite varieties of business methods that are being employed daily. If there is less evidence to reject applications this could result in an increase in patents leading to a plethora of potentially dubious monopolies. To complicate matters, patent examiners are not necessarily qualified in this field, and this too might lead to questionable and undeserving patents.

(6) To open up the categories of patentable subject matter will necessarily result in a restriction of material in the public domain.

(7) It can be very easy to infringe a business method patent leaving competitors uncertain about permissible acts and extremely vulnerable to infringement actions.

---

[185] European Patent Office Guidelines, Part C, Chapter IV, para 2.3.5: http://www.epo.org/patents/law/legal-texts/guidelines.html

rent EPO jurisprudence might be to prevent 'reverse engineering' of elements of programs and other activities considered legitimate within the industry and important to its development.

12.151   But this seemingly cautious approach was lambasted by the European Economic and Social Committee which called upon the Commission to rethink the proposal entirely anew.[244] The Committee dismissed as 'legal casuistry' the attempt to distinguish between protection of software itself and computer-implemented inventions and warned that the proposal would none the less 'open the way to the future patentability of the entire software field'. The Committee went on to challenge the economic case for patents in this field and to warn of the potentially adverse impact that patenting practice might have for our knowledge-based society, and in particular the internet and the free circulation of free/open source software. It called for a far more cautious approach still, based on more empirical evidence of the economic and employment consequences of various proposals, including leaving matters to the vagaries of the market.

12.152   This internal institutional wrangle over the proposal reflects broader, deeper, divides about the issue of software patenting. These are most evident in the European Parliament where the Directive was roundly defeated by an overwhelming majority of 648 to 14. Open Source and free software groups were particularly active in the lobbying process, arguing that the promised economic benefits were far from proven and that such a law would rather have a stifling and restricting effect on innovation and development. The triumph of these groups, and to an extent the triumph of the Parliament over the Commission, has led to broader questions being asked about the operation of the democratic process within the European Union. Who would have thought that intellectual property could be so political?

Further reading

Books

K Beresford, *Patenting Software Under the European Patent Convention* (2nd edn, 2010/11)

D Castle (ed), *The Role Of Intellectual Property Rights In Biotechnology Innovation* (2009)

A Plomer and P Torremans (eds), *Embryonic Stem Cell Patents: European Law and Ethics* (2009)

M Rimmer, *Intellectual Property and Biotechnology: Biological Inventions* (2008)

H Somsen (ed), *The Regulatory Challenge of Biotechnology* (2007)

GA Stobbs (ed), *Software Patents Worldwide* (2009)

G van Overwalle (ed), *Gene Patents and Public Health* (2007)

Reports

Department of Trade and Industry and the Intellectual Property Institute, *Patents for Genetic Sequences: the Competitiveness of Current UK Law and Practices* (2004)

European Group on Ethics, *Ethics of Synthetic Biology* (2009)

Nuffield Council on Bioethics, *Patenting DNA* (2002)

---

[244] Opinion of the Economic and Social Committee on the 'Proposal for a Directive of the European Parliament and of the Council on the patentability of computer-implemented inventions', OJ C61/154, 14 March 2003.

Articles

T Aplin, 'Patenting computer programs: a glimmer of convergence?' (2008) 30(9) EIPR 379

F Bor, 'Exemptions to Patent Infringement—Applied to Biotechnology Research Tools' [2006] EIPR 5

S Bostyn, 'How Biological is Essentially Biological? The Referrals to the Enlarged Board of Appeal G2/07 and G1/08' (2009) 31(11) EIPR 549

RS Crespi, 'The Human Embryo and Patent Law: A Major Challenge Ahead' [2006] EIPR 569

S Gaisser et al, 'The Phantom Menace of Gene Patents' (2009) 458(7237) Nature 407

CM Holman, 'Trends in Human Gene Patent Litigation' (2008) 322(5899) Science 198

A Huttermann and U Storz, 'A Comparison Between Biotech and Software Related Patents' (2009) 31(12) EIPR 589

G Laurie, 'Patenting Stem Cells of Human Origin' [2004] EIPR 59

K Liddell et al, 'Patents as incentives for translational and evaluative research: the case of genetic tests and their improved clinical performance' [2008]] 3 IPQ 286

K Moon, 'The Nature of Computer Programs: Tangible? Goods? Personal Property? Intellectual Property? (2008) 31(8) EIPR 396

A Odell-West, 'The Absence of Informed Consent to Commercial Exploitation for Inventions Developed from Human Biological Material: A Bar to Patentability?' [2009] 3 IPQ 273

M Rowlandson, 'WARF/Stem cells (G2/06): The ordre public and Morality Exception and its Impact on the Patentability of Human Embryonic Stem Cells' (2010) 32(2) EIPR 67

P Treichel, 'G2/06 and the Verdict of Immorality' (2009) 40(4) IIC 450

G van Overwalle, 'The Implementation of the Biotechnology Directive in Belgium and its After-Effects. The Introduction of a New Research Exemption and a Compulsory Licence for Public Health' (2006) IIC 889

Part V

Registered trade marks

Introduction

This Part of the book explains and discusses the law of registered trade marks within their international, European and domestic setting. Chapter 13 will explain the regulatory framework for the protection of trade marks, highlighting the international treaties and European Regulations and Directives which help shape trade mark law within the domestic arena. It will also discuss policy trends and the jurisprudence relevant to the function of a trade mark within the consumer society. Chapter 14 will consider the definition of a trade mark and deal with the rules pertaining to registration. Chapter 15 will examine the scope of trade mark protection, infringement and defences, bringing in current discussion on, inter alia, questions of use of a trade mark in the course of trade and comparative advertising. Chapter 16 will look at four contemporary issues in trade mark law: personality merchandising; domain names; the use of trade marks on the Internet; and geographical indications.

Sources of the law: key websites

- European Union Trade Mark Directives and Community Trade Mark Regulation for which, see the Commission's Internal Market Directorate General's website
  http://ec.europa.eu/internal_market/indprop/tm/index_en.htm

- Trade Marks Act 1994 as amended (the UK–IPO Office maintains a consolidated text), see
  http://www.ipo.gov.uk/tmact94.pdf

- Decisions of the Court of Justice of the European Union/ECJ (for which see the search form) at
  http://curia.europa.eu/jurisp/cgi-bin/form.pl?lang=en

- Office for the Harmonisation of the Internal Market (OHIM), for which see
  http://oami.europa.eu/

- Paris Convention for the Protection of Industrial Property, for which see the WIPO website
  http://www.wipo.int/treaties/en/ip/paris/trtdocs_wo020.html

- Madrid Agreement and Protocol, for which see the WIPO website http://www.wipo.int/madrid/en/legal_texts/
- The UK–IPO website has a useful section devoted to trade marks at http://www.ipo.gov.uk/tm.htm/

The function of a trade mark and the national, community and international regime

Introduction

Scope and overview of chapter

13.1   The purpose of this chapter is twofold. It is first to discuss policy tensions within trade mark law and to analyse the function of a trade mark as detailed in legislative enactments, case law and policy papers. Through this analysis it will be explained that the function of a trade mark is far from settled. As will be seen over the ensuing chapters, the lack of harmony in relation to the function has implications for the scope of protection conferred by the law. Key aspects of the trade mark system will be introduced and comment will be made on the interaction between registered trade marks and other intellectual property rights. The second purpose is to introduce the legal regime for the protection of trade marks from an international, community and national perspective. Through a series of agreements, treaties and legislation certain minimum standards for the protection of trade marks has been established as has a system by virtue of which traders can register and protect marks in many countries throughout the world.

13.2   **Learning objectives**

By the end of this chapter you should be able to describe and explain:

- the discussion surrounding the contemporary function of a trade mark;
- how registered trade marks fit in with other intellectual property rights;
- the major international, European and national instruments concerning trade marks;
- the routes a trader might choose to register a mark.

13.3   The rest of this chapter looks like this

- Trade marks: policy issues (13.4–13.8)
- Trade marks: function (13.9–13.20)
- Trade marks and other intellectual property rights (13.21–13.26)
- The regulatory framework (13.27–13.64)

Trade marks: policy issues

13.4   Trade marks are ubiquitous. In modern society the consumer is surrounded daily by images designed to distinguish the goods and services provided by one trader from those of another. The marks are designed to indicate the origin of the goods and services. But, as will be seen in the discussion below, it is argued that a mark plays other roles, including that of a quality indicator; a means of advertising goods and services; and a vehicle for investment. These functions are increasingly reflected in provisions in trade mark law enabling the registration of a broad variety of signs, and those which seek to protect the reputation of a mark against parasitic and damaging use of the same or a similar mark by third parties.

13.5   A key theme underpinning trade mark law concerns the extent of the monopoly conferred by a registered mark. As will been seen in the next two chapters, registration of a mark does not give the trader a monopoly in either the mark, or the underlying goods and services in connection with which the mark is registered, but only a monopoly over the use of the mark in conjunction with the goods and services for which it is registered. This leads to a constant tension between traders, as proprietors of trade marks, who would like to see the scope of that monopoly construed as broadly as possible so as to reserve to themselves as much exclusivity in the market as possible, and competitors wish to see the monopoly interpreted narrowly so as to enable them to encroach and 'free-ride' upon a successful registered trade mark. In determining where the boundaries lie, a number of interests require to be accommodated within the trade mark framework. Broadly they are of the trader, of competing traders, and of the consumer. A central question is as to how, and where, these respective interests should be taken into account and balanced. While the focus of the essential function of a trade mark remains on indicating the origin of goods and services and on consumer confusion, so the perception of the consumer is paramount. Registration and the scope of protection conferred by the mark are circumscribed by indications the consumer might find confusing, or which implicate the origin function of the mark. As the range of signs and symbols that can be registered expands, so concerns grow in some quarters as to the competitive disadvantage this may pose for other traders. The first comer may easily be able to establish a link between the more obvious mark in the mind of the consumer and the goods and services. This imposes a cost on the competing trader who will have to invest more in building a link between the less obvious mark and the consumer whilst trying to avoid allegations of consumer confusion. Once registered, and the broader functions of a mark are recognised, the interests of the consumer diminish. Consumer confusion is no longer relevant; the focus is instead on safeguarding the reputation of the mark against parasitic and detrimental uses by competing traders.

13.6   A related issue that permeates registered trade mark law is that of 'use'. A trade mark registration can be kept on the register indefinitely and so, unlike patents or copyright, a mark need not fall into the public domain after a specified time. In consequence a trade mark has to be used in order to maintain the registration. The obligation of use has been adopted in almost all juris-dictions.[1] Cornish has said that 'the conception of a trade mark registration as an entitlement dependent upon need—which has always underpinned the British approach to the subject, has become the major element in the EU system'.[2] As will be seen in the discussion in the fol-lowing chapters, there are many instances in which actual and genuine 'use' of a trade mark is essential. These include the need to put a registered mark to genuine use to retain it on the trade mark register, and whether a sign needs to be used 'as a trade mark' or 'in a trade mark sense' as opposed to descriptively before it will infringe the registered mark. These requirements seek to balance the interests of the trade mark proprietor and the competitor. Marks which are not put to genuine use will become free for competing traders as trade mark owners will not be able to stockpile marks putting competitors at a competitive disadvantage. The 'use' requirement for the purposes of infringement is vital in determining the scope of the rights granted to the trade mark holder. If any use of the same or similar mark by a competitor would infringe the registered mark whether or not that use is as a trade mark, so the rights of the owner are broader in scope than they would be if only use as a trade mark infringed.

13.7 Case law has at times sent inconsistent signals in recognising and balancing the interests. The current provisions on registered trade marks have spawned more case law at European level than any other area of intellectual property. This is not only because these central questions remain unsettled, but also because of the financial importance of trade marks to business. In 2008 Coca Cola was valued at $66,667 million, Intel at $31,261 million, and Disney at $29,251 million.[3] When such sums are at issue, trade mark owners and competitors are willing to litigate in seeking to ensure that they can obtain even the smallest competitive advantage over their rivals.

13.8 While the economic aspects of trade marks and the role that they play in the consumer society have always provided key justifications for their existence,[4] an increasingly rich discussion has developed from within related areas of the law supporting trade marks and seeking to limit their power. One of these is in relation to human rights. There is an academic literature reflect-ing upon the role of human rights as they impact upon all aspects of trade marks—including property rights and freedom of expression.[5] In *Anheuser-Busch v Portugal*[6] the European Court of Human Rights held that trade marks and applications are possessions for the purposes of Article 1, Protocol 1 ECHR. In the South African case of *Laugh It Off Promotions CC v South African Breweries International (Finance) BV*[7] freedom of expression and the censorship power

[1] See the comments by B Pretnar, 'Use and non-use in Trade Mark Law', in J Phillips and I Simon (eds) *Trade Marks Use* (2005) p 11.
[2] W Cornish & D Llewelyn, *Intellectual Property* (6th edn, 2007) p 728.
[3] See Business Week online at http://images.businessweek.com/ss/08/09/0918_best_brands/index.htm
[4] A rich literature examining the economic case for trade marks and trade mark law exists. See for example WM Landes, and RA Posner, *The Economic Structure of Intellectual Property Law* (2003); WM Landes and RA Posner, 'Trade Mark Law: An Economic Perspective' (1987) Journal of Law and Economics 268; NS Economides, 'The Economics of Trade Marks' (1988) 78 TMR 523; RW Holzhauer, 'Jenever and Jumping Wild Cats' (2002) in R Towse (ed) *III The Economics of Intellectual Property* p 418; IPL Png and D Reitman, 'Why are Some Products Branded and Others not?' (2002) in R Towse (ed) *III The Economics of Intellectual Property*, p 207; SL Carter, 'The Trouble with Trademark' (2002) in R Towse (ed) *III The Economics of Intellectual Property*, p 373.
[5] J Davis, 'European Trade Mark Law and the Enclosure of the Commons' (2002) 4 IPQ 342–67; LR Helfer, 'The New Innovation Frontier? Intellectual Property and the European Court of Human Rights' (2008) 49 Harvard International Law Journal 1; MA Naser Trademarks and Freedom of Expression 40 IIC 188 (2009)
[6] Application No 73049/01.KD Beiter, 'The Right to Property and the Protection of Interests in Intellectual Property—A Human Rights Perspective on the European Court of Human Rights' Decision in Anheuser-Busch v. Portugal' (2008) 39 IIC 714.
[7] [2005] FSR 30 Sup Ct (SA).

which could be wielded by the owner of a trade mark came into opposition.[8] Given the critical economic importance of trade marks in the consumer society it may be that there will be further developments in this area.

 Exercise

Find the trade mark cases in which human rights have featured. What is your assessment of the current state of the law in this area and how do you think it will develop?

Key points on policy issues

- A key theme underpinning trade mark law is as to the extent of the monopoly conferred by the mark
- The trade mark framework seeks to balance the interests of the trade mark proprietor, the competitor and the consumer

---

Trade marks: function

13.9   During the 19th century, when a consumer wanted to purchase particular goods, she had to rely heavily on the expertise of the shopkeeper for advice as to the origin of the goods and their quality.[9] It was not until 1875 that a register was first introduced in the UK partly in response to the growth in international trade where an increasing variety of goods were being traded under marks normally associated with British manufacturers, such as 'Sheffield' cutlery. Now, it is said that it is the association of a trade mark with goods and services (the origin) that sells products to the consumer, rather than the expertise of the shopkeeper.

13.10 The ability to register marks brought a number of benefits to traders. Not only could marks be registered, and thus protected, prior to being used, but in addition registration reduced the burden on the trader of the need to prove goodwill and distinctiveness necessary for an action in passing off.

 Question

What do you think is the function of a trade mark? Revisit your views once you have completed this Part.

13.11 In this symbiotic relationship between the supplier who owns the trade mark and the consumer, trade marks perform a vital function of indicating the *origin* of the goods and services

---

[8] ibid, para 15.93.
[9] A Vickery, *The Woman Who Shops 'Til She Drops: BBC Radio 4, Just Looking*, 3 September 2001 09:00–09:30.

being sold: in other words, the trade mark functions as a *badge of origin*. This function is at the heart of the existence of trade marks. It is noted in literature:

> 'The primary function of a trade mark, traditionally, has been to identify the commercial or trade origin of the goods (or services) to which it is applied'.[10]

In case law:

> '[T]he essential function of the mark, which is to give the consumer or final user a guarantee of the identity of the origin of the marked product by enabling him to distinguish, without any possible confusion, that product from others of a different provenance'.[11]

> 'Trade mark rights constitute an essential element in the system of undistorted competition which the Treaty is intended to establish and maintain. In such a system, undertakings must be able to attract and retain customers by the quality of their goods or services, which is made possible only by distinctive signs allowing them to be identified.[12]...In that context, the essential function of a trade mark is to guarantee the identity of origin of the marked goods or services to the consumer or end user by enabling him, without any possibility of confusion, to distinguish the goods or services from others which have another origin. For the trade mark to be able to fulfil its essential role in the system of undistorted competition which the Treaty seeks to establish and maintain, it must offer a guarantee that all the goods or services bearing it have been manufactured or supplied under the control of a single undertaking which is responsible for their quality'.[13]

And in formal documents:

> '[A trade mark] serves to distinguish trade marked products originating from a particular firm or group of firms from the products of other firms. From this basic function of the trade mark are derived all other functions which the trade mark fulfils in economic life'.[14]

Some examples of registered trade marks that fulfil this origin function include 'Tesco Value' owned by Tesco Stores Limited[15], and 'Rolls-Royce' owned by Rolls Royce plc.[16] Thus when a consumer sees one of the above registered marks used in conjunction with good or services, it gives an indication of the origin of those products.

13.12   However, that is not always the case. Consider the word mark 'Bambi' when it is used in conjunction with 'knitted articles of outer clothing for children', or the image shown in Figure 13.1.

Figure 13.1 Zoo

---

[10] S Ricketson, *The Law of Intellectual Property* (1984).   [11] *Centrafarm v American Home Products* [1979] FSR 189

[12] See, inter alia, Case C-10/89 *HAG GF* [1990] ECR I-3711, para 13, and Case C-517/99 *Merz & Krell* [2001] ECR I-6959, para 21.

[13] C-206/01 *Arsenal Football Club plc v Matthew Reed Case* [2003] ch 454, [2003] 3 All ER (EC) 1, [2003] 3 WLR 450, [2003] RPC 144, paras 47–48. Also Case 102/77 *Hoffman-La Roche* [1978] ECR 1139, para 7, and Case C-299/99 *Philips v Remington* [2002] ECR I-5475, para 30.

[14] Bulletin of the European Communities, Supplement 8/76 adopted by the Commission on 6th July 1976.

[15] UK Trade Mark No 2016874.   [16] UK Trade Mark No 291969.

This was used in connection with 'articles of outer-clothing for children'.[17] Perhaps only the most astute shopper would have known that the marks were also owned by Tesco Stores plc. However, what is important for those who buy children's clothes is to know the *quality* of the clothes they are purchasing. And this leads to the second important function of a trade mark, a sub-set of the origin function, and that is that a registered trade mark indicates to the consumer the *quality* of the particular goods or services sold in connection with a particular mark.

> '[T]he relevance of the trade mark's function as a guarantee of origin lies none the less in the fact that the trade mark conveys to the consumer certain perceptions as to the quality of the marked goods. The consumer is not interested in the commercial origin of goods out of idle curiosity; his interest is based on the assumption that goods of the same origin will be of the same quality. That is how trade mark protection achieves its fundamental justification of rewarding the manufacturer who consistently produces high-quality goods'.[18]

13.13   Returning to the first two examples of registered trade marks quoted above, not only do they give an indication of the origin of goods and services, but both 'Tesco Value' and 'Rolls-Royce' conjure up images of a certain differing quality in the mind of the consumer.

> 'Trade marks are able to achieve that effect because they act as a guarantee, to the consumer, that all goods bearing a particular mark have been produced by, or under the control of, the same manufacturer and are therefore likely to be of similar quality. The guarantee of quality offered by a trade mark is not of course absolute, for the manufacturer is at liberty to vary the quality; however, he does so at his own risk and he—not his competitors—will suffer the consequences if he allows the quality to decline. Thus, although trade marks do not provide any form of legal guarantee of quality the absence of which may have misled some to underestimate their significance they do in economic terms provide such a guarantee, which is acted upon daily by consumers'.[19]

This quality function has been emphasised by the House of Lords:

> 'The quality of goods on offer is at the heart of all trading activities. As long as trading has existed, buyers have sought information and assurance about the quality of the merchandise on display. The use of trade marks is an integral part of this activity'.[20]

13.14   A third function of a trade mark is that of *advertising* the goods or services sold by the trader in connection with the mark. Many traders invest not only time and effort, but also substantial sums in bringing a particular mark to the attention of the public. For many the hope will be that eventually such is the recognition of the mark on the consumer market it is then the mark that will sell the product.

> '[A trade mark is] a vehicle for communicating a message to the public, and itself represents financial value. This message is incorporated into the trade mark through use, especially for advertising purposes, which enables the trade mark to assume the message itself, whether informatively or symbolically. The message may refer to the product's qualities, or indeed to intangible values such as luxury, lifestyle, exclusivity, adventure, youth etc'.[21]

13.15   To this end, a trade mark can also be seen as an *investment*. Much time and money is spent on building consumer awareness of a particular mark, which can itself be sold, assigned, licensed and be the subject of a security

> 'The fact remains that a mark also acts as a means of conveying other messages concerning, inter alia, the qualities or particular characteristics of the goods or services which it covers or the images and

[17] UK Trade Mark No 1159971.   [18] Case C-10/89 *SA Cnl-Sucal NV v Hag GF AG* [1991] FSR 99 at 129/30.
[19] *Wagamama Ltd v City Centre Restaurants Plc* [1996] ETMR 23.
[20] *Scandecor Developments AB v Scandecor Marketing AB* [2001] UKHL 21; [2001] 2 CMLR 30; [2001] ETMR 74 Nichols LJ.
[21] *Souza Cruz SA v Hollywood SAS*, R283/1999–3 [2002] ETMR (64) 705, para 7.

feelings which it conveys, such as luxury, lifestyle, exclusivity, adventure, youth. To that effect the mark has an inherent economic value which is independent of and separate from that of the goods or services for which it is registered. The messages in question which are conveyed inter alia by a mark with a reputation or which are associated with it confer on that mark a significant value which deserves protection, particularly because, in most cases, the reputation of a mark is the result of considerable effort and investment on the part of its proprietor.'[22]

As with the quality function, these advertising and investment functions are considered by many as sub-sets of the basic function of indicating the origin of the goods and services:

'It is also argued that trade marks have other functions, which might be termed "communication", investment, or advertising functions. Those functions are said to arise from the fact that the investment in the promotion of a product is built around the mark. It is accordingly reasoned that those functions are values which deserve protection as such, even when there is no abuse arising from misrepresentations about either origin or quality. However, those functions seem to me to be merely derivatives of the origin function; there would be little purpose in advertising a mark if it were not for the function of that mark as an indicator of origin, distinguishing the trade mark owner's goods from those of his competitors'.[23]

13.16 These latter functions of a trade mark (advertisement, quality and investment) are sometimes referred to as the 'communicative functions' of a trade mark. They become particularly prominent when the scope of the protection conferred by the mark goes beyond the prevention of consumer confusion to protecting a mark with a reputation against the use of the same or similar mark in connection with the same or dissimilar goods and services. The effect on the consumer is no longer relevant. Rather the question becomes one of whether the use by the competitor of the sign dilutes the mark in the sense of taking unfair advantage of the reputation or being detrimental to the distinctive character or reputation of the earlier mark. The focus is on the value of the mark.[24]

Current trends

13.17 In recent years there has been something of a backlash in some sectors of society against the power that it is said trade marks can have over the daily life of a consumer. This campaign has been directed primarily against brands, rather than trade marks on their own. Although there seems to be some discussion and disagreement as to the definition, the terms 'brand' and 'branding' would appear to refer to the totality of the image that is portrayed in relation to or by a product in the marketplace, and the process of getting it there. A brand has been described thus:

'The intangible sum of a product's attributes: its name, packaging, and price, its history, its reputation, and the way it's advertised'.[25]

13.18 The process of branding can thus be applied to an entire corporate identity as well as to individual products and services.[26] And herein lies the nub of the controversy. In recent years com-

---

[22] *Mülhens GmbH & Co KG v OHIM* [2008] ETMR 69, para 36.

[23] Case C-337/95 *Parfums Christian Dior and Parfums Christina Dior BV v Evora BV* [1998] RPC 166.

[24] Case C-487/07 *L'Oréal v Bellure*. It seems that the communicative functions may extend to marks without a reputation at least in the case of comparative advertising. See para 15.128.

[25] Ogilvy at http://www.ogilvy.com/ See also *L'Oréal and others v Bellure and others* [2006] EWHC 2355 (Ch) in which a brand was described as 'a collection of intangible values as perceived by a consumer which are attributed to a name, symbol or design used to identify a product or group of products or services' (para 79).

[26] See eg http://www.interbrand.com

panies have attempted to build whole aspirations, images and lifestyles around a brand. Those that have achieved some success might include 'Bailey's Irish Cream', 'Pepsi Max', 'Levi' jeans and 'Absolut Vodka'. The message is that if you purchase this particular product, you too can have these experiences, this lifestyle and this success. The effect, so it is argued, is to offer a lifestyle that is dictated by the brand-owner, but which does not necessarily reflect 'real life'. The ultimate result is that it is the companies who own these brands who determine the way we live, the choices we make and the shape of the world in which we live.[27] This line of thinking underlies, at least in part, the activities of those involved in the anti-globalisation and anti-capitalist movement who disrupted attempts to hold meetings of G-8 leaders in, among other places, Prague, Seattle, Genoa and Gleneagles.

13.19   Suffice it to say that there is no single universally accepted function of a trade mark, although the weight of opinion tends, or at least has historically tended towards the origin function. However, the matter is by no means settled. As will be seen in the discussion in the ensuing chapters there is some confusion in the case law as to the function of a trade mark in particular with regards to registration and infringement. The matter is, however, of vital importance. It not only shapes what can be registered as a trade mark, but also helps to determine the scope of protection granted to the trade mark owner. It is an area of the law which is still taking shape and where the boundaries have, and will continue, to develop over time.

Exercise

Go into a supermarket and browse the goods on the shelves. Look at the trade marks on those products. What impressions do you get? Imagine then a supermarket full of products between which there is no differentiation. The shape of the goods and their packaging are alike. How do you make your choices?

Key points on functions of a trade mark

- A trade mark is said to have the following functions:
- A badge of origin
- An indication of quality
- A means of advertising
- An investment vehicle

The latter three are sometimes referred to as the 'communicative' functions

13.20   The following chapters will examine trade marks in detail. At this juncture it is useful to note the following points:

- Registered trade marks only have a function when they are actually used in the consumer society in conjunction with particular goods or services. They do not have a life of their

---

[27] A number of books have appeared recently which expound this theory. These include J Bove, F Dufour and A de Casparis, *The World is Not for Sale* (2001); N Klein, *No Logo: Taking Aim and the Brand Bullies* (2000).

own. This is reflected in the fact that a registered trade mark may be expunged in whole or in part[28] from the register if it has not been used for a period of five years.[29] However, a trade mark can be assigned separately from the goodwill of the business[30] to which it refers. It is also described as personal property (in Scotland, incorporeal property).[31]

- Marks have to be registered in a particular class of the trade mark register in connection with specified goods and services for which the mark is, or will be used. The trade mark register contains 45 classes altogether covering a diverse range of goods and services.[32] As examples, Class 1 encompasses inter alia chemicals used in industry, science and photography. Class 18 encompasses leather and imitations of leather, and goods made of these materials including umbrellas and parasols. Class 38 encompasses telecommunications.

- The classification[33] is based on the Nice International Arrangement on the International Classification of Goods and Services,[34] an international agreement administered by WIPO. The significance of having the register divided into these classes is that an applicant will need to apply for separate registration for the mark in each category of goods or services that are relevant to the use of the mark,[35] and a separate fee is payable for each.[36]

Weblink

You can find a copy of the Nice Classification at

http://www.wipo.int/classifications/nice/en/classifications.html

Question

What Nice classes cover the following goods/services: legal advice, spades, wine, tractors, paper?

---

[28] Section 46(1) (5) of the 1994 Act. Examples include *Premier Brands UK Limited v Typhoon Europe Ltd* [2000] FSR 767; *Minerva Trade Mark* [2000] FSR 734; *Mercury Communications Ltd v Mercury Interactive (UK) Ltd* [1995] FSR 850; *Decon Laboratories Ltd v Fred Baker Scientific Ltd* [2001] ETMR 46. See para 14.99ff.

[29] If a registered trade mark has not been put to genuine use in the UK within five years following the date of registration, or use of the trade mark has been suspended for a continuous period of five years, registration may be revoked. Section 46(1)(a), (b) and (c) of the 1994 Act. See para 14.99ff.

[30] TMA 1994, s 24(1).

[31] TMA 1994, s 22. The European Court of Human Rights has held that trade marks and applications are possessions for the purposes of Article 1, Protocol 1 ECHR: *Anheuser-Busch v Portugal* (Application No 73049/01). See para 13.8.

[32] The number of classes was increased from 42 to 45 on 1 January 2002: Trade Marks (Amendment) Rules 2001 (SI 2001/2832).

[33] TMA 1994, s 34.

[34] Full details of the classes can be found in the Trade Marks Rules 2000 as subsequently amended from time to time up to and including 2008. An unofficial consolidated version of the rules can be found on the UK–IPO website.

[35] TMA 1994, s 32 deals with applications for registration. Section 34 of the 1994 Act deals with the classification of goods and marks.

[36] It is also possible to apply for registration for a series of marks: s 41(1)(c) of the 1994 Act. A series of trade marks is defined as '…a number of trade marks which resemble each other as to their material particulars and differ only as to matters of a non-distinctive character not substantially affecting the identity of the trade mark': s 41(2) of the 1994 Act. See also Trade Marks (Fees) Rules 2008 (SI 2008/1958), r 28.

- A trader will gain protection for a trade mark in relation to the goods or services in which she deals, and for which the mark is registered. A similar mark registered in relation to a different class of goods by a different trader will not necessarily infringe the first if there is no *likelihood of confusion* between the two marks (see para 15.32 for a discussion on infringement). It follows that two or more traders can use identical marks in conjunction with similar or dissimilar goods and services, so long as the customer is not confused. For instance, the word 'Puffin' has been registered by United Biscuits (UK) Ltd, for use, among other things, in connection with coffee; tea; cocoa; sugar; rice and tapioca all in class 30, *and* by Kalon Limited (a company with no relationship with United Biscuits (UK) Ltd) in class 01 for adhesives, sealants, glue, bonding agents and fillers. If, however, a consumer is likely to be confused as to the origin or the goods or services sold under a mark, then either the application for registration will be turned down, or it will be opposed by the proprietor of the first registered mark, or, if a second person uses that mark as an unregistered sign, then the proprietor of the registered mark can challenge that use.

- Extended protection is granted to marks which have a reputation in the UK. Infringement may occur where the use of a similar sign by a competitor, without due cause, takes unfair advantage of, or is detrimental to the distinctive character or repute of the registered mark. This is so whether the sign is used in relation to the same or dissimilar goods or services. No consumer confusion is needed for infringement in these circumstances (for further discussion see para 15.68ff).

Trade marks and other intellectual property rights

13.21   Trade marks find their justification in the consumer society. As discussed above, the basic function of a trade mark is to denote the origin of particular goods or services and thus to reward the manufacturer who consistently produces goods of a particular quality using that mark. This stands in contrast with the justifications for the development of patents, copyright and designs, each of which seeks to encourage creativity and/or innovation and to reward the creator. This in turn stimulates further creation. If a trader manages to build up a good reputation in a mark, then a reward will also come in the form of economic return as the mark may ultimately sell the products. However, it will only do so because the mark is indicating to the consumer the origin (and quality) of those goods.

13.22   The nature of the monopoly granted by a registered trade mark also stands in contrast with the other intellectual property rights under discussion in this book. Patents give an absolute monopoly but for a limited period of time of 20 years.[37] Copyright gives a weaker monopoly, but for a longer period of up to 70 years after the death of the author.[38] Design right gives a monopoly of up to 25 years (registered designs).[39] Trade marks, by contrast can give a monopoly for an unlimited period of time. Registration of a trade mark in the UK lasts for 10 years from the date of registration.[40] Successive periods of registration thereafter for 10-year periods may

---

[37] For a discussion on patents see Chapter 11.
[38] For a discussion on copyright and duration of protection see Chapter 3.
[39] For a discussion on design right see Chapter 8.   [40] TMA 1994, s 42(1).

be applied for with the result that, if timeously renewed, registration may be perpetual.[41] Bass plc registered the red triangle shown below in Figure 13.2 on 1 January 1876.

Figure 13.2 Bass logo

It was the first mark to be registered in the UK trade mark register and is still a valid registered trade mark.

13.23   The Bass logo is registered in connection with pale ale (class 32). But the monopoly in that mark is limited in that registration does not prevent a competing trader from entering the market for beers. There are plenty of other examples of registered trade marks used in connection with beers. One example is Budweiser registered by Anheuser-Busch, Incorporated.[42] Neither does it prevent a competing trader from using a triangle in connection with other goods and services, such as that shown in Figure 13.3, which has been registered by The Society for Promoting Christian Knowledge for use in connection with inter alia computer programs in class 9, and printed matter in class 16.[43] Thus, a proprietor does not obtain a monopoly in the mark as such, nor in the goods and services to which it relates. The monopoly is limited to the use of the mark in connection with the same or similar goods and services for which it is registered.[44]

Figure 13.3 Triangle

TRIANGLE

---

[41] The date of registration for calculation of the period for renewal is the date of application for registration: TMA 1994, s 40(3).

[42] UK Trade Mark No 1125449. This is a rather unusual trade mark as the same word is registered by two different companies in respect of the same products—beer. This is because both companies have historically used the name, so neither has preference over the other. *Budweiser Trade Marks* [2000] RPC 906. The owners have engaged in extensive litigation as each tries to gain advantage over the other. See also UK Trade Mark No 1389680.

[43] UK Trade Mark No 2014176.

[44] This is subject to those circumstances in which the mark has a reputation. See para 15.65ff for discussion.

13.24   Finally, and in common with copyright, patents and designs, the rights conferred by a mark registered in the UK register are territorial.[45] This in turn contrasts with the EU-wide rights attached to a Community mark discussed in paras 13.34–13.40.

The overlap of trade marks with other intellectual property rights

13.25   Although registered trade marks occupy a particular place within the intellectual property family, as with the other rights, there is overlap between trade marks and the other areas. One such overlap is dealt with in the discussion of the Trade Marks Act 1994 (TMA 1994), section 3 in para 14.72ff. Thus, for example, it is not possible to register a trade mark where the shape is necessary to give a technical result. If registration of such shapes were permitted, then trade mark law might give an extensive monopoly in an area which is regarded as the province of the law of patents. As will be understood from the discussion on this section however, the parameters are yet to be fully settled.[46]

13.26   Equally, registered trade marks can be used in tandem with other rights to protect the same item. For example, the 'Work Mate' bench was protected by many patents when invented. Although patent protection has now expired, the words 'Work Mate' continue to be protected as a registered trade mark.[47] Thus, Black and Decker, the proprietors of the mark, are the only company able to market workbenches, vice benches, saw horses, and trestles, all made wholly or principally of wood, and tables, chairs and stools, in connection with the mark 'Work Mate'.

Discussion point   For answer guidance visit www.oxfordtextbooks.co.uk/orc/macqueen2e/

The area of registered trade marks has attracted more case law at European level than any other intellectual property right. Why do you think this is so? Note your views and return to them once you have finished this Part on registered trade marks to see if your reasoning has changed.

Key points on trade marks and other intellectual property rights

- Trade marks find their justification in the consumer society
- If renewed, a trade mark can last forever. This stands in contrast with other intellectual property rights which have limited duration

---

[45] TMA 1994, s 9(1), 107 and 108. In *Beautimatic International Ltd v Mitchell International Pharmaceuticals Ltd* [1999] ETMR 912, [2000] FSR 267, Beautimatic International owned the registered trade mark 'Lexus'. Mitchell marketed skin care products also under the name Lexus, but which were only available outside the UK. The 1994 Act, s 10(1) was therefore not infringed as use was not 'in the UK' as required by s 9(1).

[46] For a discussion on the interaction between registered trade marks and the law of passing off see *Inter Lotto (UK) Ltd v Camelot Group Plc* [2004] RPC 9, [2003] EWCA Civ 1132 (CA).   [47] UK Trade Mark No 938753.

The regulatory framework

13.27   The purpose of this part is to discuss the regulatory framework in depth to provide a foundation for discussion in the ensuing chapters on substantive trade mark law. In particular it is to enable the reader to appreciate how domestic law and procedure are shaped by both European Union and international requirements.

Institutions and measures for which they are responsible

National

UK Trade Marks Act 1994
implements Trade Mark Directive and obligations from international treaties (eg section 56 from the Paris Convention)

European

Community Trade Mark Regulation
Creation of supra national Community trade mark

Trade Marks Directive
Framework for protection of trade marks in member states

International

WTO
TRIPS
Substantive minimum standards
Makes reference to Paris
National treatment
Most favoured nation clause

WIPO
Paris Convention
Substantive minimum standards
National treatment
Madrid Agreement
Streamlined application process
NB central attack
Madrid Protocol
Streamlined application process
Conversion to national applications
Trade Mark Law Treaty
Procedural rules
Singapore Treaty
Procedural rules
Nice classification

The regulatory framework: domestic and European

UK trade marks

13.28   The current legislation in the UK governing registered trade marks is contained in the Trade Marks Act 1994 (TMA 1994). The TMA 1994 was introduced as a result of the EC Council Directive 89/104/EEC of 21 December 1988 to approximate the laws of the Member States relating to Trade Marks which was in turn codified as Directive 2008/95/EC of the European

Parliament and of the Council of 22 October 2008 to approximate the laws of the Member States relating to trade marks.[48] The 1994 Act repealed the earlier legislation relating to trade marks contained in the Trade Marks Act 1938[49] (the 1938 Act). The 1994 Act came into force on 31 October 1994,[50] and governs those trade marks registered in the UK Register with the UK Intellectual Property Office (IPO) in Newport, Gwent.

Weblink

The IPO has a website at http://www.ipo.gov.uk It has a section that is devoted entirely to trade marks, giving both general information on trade marks as well as access to a database containing details of registered marks, pending applications for registration, and information on applications which have been refused.

Exercise

To familiarise yourself with the site and in particular the trade mark database go to the IPO site and carry out a number of searches in the trade mark register. Can you find the Bass Logo mentioned above?

You will also notice that the trade mark section of the IPO website contains details of primary and secondary legislation affecting registered trade marks in the UK.

Question

What is the latest statutory instrument to have amended the Trade Marks Act 1994?

Place of application and procedure: UK

13.29   A UK trade mark has effect within the territory of the UK.[51] To apply for a UK registered trade mark, application is made to the office in Newport in Gwent (the application forms can be found on the IPO website). The application must include a request for registration, the name and address of the applicant, a statement of the goods or services in relation to which it is sought to register the mark, a representation of the trade mark[52] and the fee, which is currently £200 for one class of goods or services and £50 for every additional class. The applicant must also include a statement that the trade mark is being used or that the applicant has a bona fide intention to use it.[53] The date of filing is the date on which all the relevant information is given to the registrar.[54] The filing date is the one on which matters of priority under the Paris

---

[48] 89/104/EEC, OJ [1989] L40/1.

[49] As amended by, inter alia, the Trade Marks (Amendment) Act 1984, the Patents, Designs and Marks Act 1986, the Copyright, Designs and Patents Act 1988, and the Copyright, etc and Trade Marks (Offences and Enforcement) Act 2002.

[50] Trade Marks Act 1994 (Commencement) Order 1994 (SI 1994/2550) bringing the 1994 Act into force.

[51] TMA 1994, s 108: the Act extends to England and Wales, Scotland and Northern Ireland and to the Isle of Man.

[52] TMA 1994, s 32(2).   [53] ibid, s 32(3).   [54] ibid, s 33(1).

Convention may be settled[55] and those of seniority from prior use (for matters of priority and seniority see para 13.60 below).

13.30   When filed the examiners at the registry examine the application on absolute grounds[56] to see if it is registerable. Absolute in this context means that the examiners examine the mark to see whether it meets the criteria for registration set out in TMA 1994, section 3 including whether it meets the definition of a trade mark[57] whether it is devoid of distinctive character[58] or has become a word commonly used in the trade.[59] Previously marks were also examined on relative grounds, which meant that the examiners looked to other marks already on the register to see if the mark should be refused registration. For instance, if there was an earlier trade mark which was identical with[60] or similar to[61] the sign, the application for registration would be refused. This was changed in 2006 after a review by the IPO in which the office noted that the Office for the Harmonisation of the Internal Market (OHIM) (the office responsible for registering Community trade marks—see below at paras 13.37–13.40) only undertook examinations on absolute grounds for a Community trade mark (CTM). The procedure had resulted in an anomalous situation in that it was proving easier to register a mark as a CTM than it was as a UK mark via the IPO. Because OHIM only examined on absolute grounds, it was up to the trade mark owner with an earlier right to oppose an application for registration of a confusingly similar mark. The IPO concluded that the chance of a UK applicant obtaining a national registration had decreased because of the number of earlier CTMs and that a national applications were increasingly likely to fail due to the presence of earlier CTMs which had themselves not been examined on relative grounds. Hence the change to a formal examination on absolute grounds only. However, the examiners still monitor their records on relative grounds, and then inform both the applicant and the owner of the earlier right of potential conflicts. It now up to the owner of the conflicting right to oppose the application on relative grounds.[62] Once the application has been accepted it is published in the Trade Marks Journal.[63]

Weblink

You can access the Trade Marks Journal online at the IPO website at

http://www.ipo.gov.uk/tm/t-journal/t-tmj.htm

Thereafter there is a three-month period during which third parties can submit observations on the application or oppose the application. If the parties do not settle any disagreement on the application there may be a hearing and determination of registerability by the Registrar.

13.31   An appeal lies from a decision of the Registrar either to an 'appointed person' or to the court.[64] If an appeal is made to an appointed person, the appointed person may refer the matter to

---

[55] ibid, s 35.   [56] This has been the practice since October 2007. See PAN 1/08 for using the Internet for searches.
[57] TMA 1994, s 3(1)(a).   [58] ibid, s 3(1)(b).   [59] ibid, s 3(1)(d).   [60] ibid, s 5(1).
[61] ibid, s 5(2). Note that on application the grounds for a refusal under the Trade Mark Directive should not be ignored. See joined cases Case C-39/08 *Bild.T-Online.de AG & Co KG v President of the German Patent- und Markenamt* and Case C-43/08 *ZVS Zeitungsvertrieb Stuttgart GmbH v President of the German Patent- und Markenamt.*
[62] The legislative and administrative changes have been implemented as of 1 October 2007. See Practice Amendment Notice 8/07, available here: http://www.ipo.gov.uk/pro-types/pro-tm/t-law/t-pan/t-pan-807.htm
[63] TMA 1994, s 38.
[64] ibid, s 76(2). The 'appointed person' is appointed by the Lord Chancellor after consultation with the Lord Advocate.

the court if it appears that a matter of general legal importance is involved, or if the Registrar requests referral, or if such a request is made by any party to the proceedings.[65] If the appointed person hears the appeal, his decision is final.[66] If there is no effective opposition the trade mark will be registered[67] and the registration published in the Trade Marks Journal. The date of registration is the date of filing of the application[68] and is the date from which the rights of the owner are enforceable against third parties (although no enforcement action may be taken until such time as the trade mark is registered)[69] as well as the date from which the term of the trade mark is calculated.

13.32   The IPO website contains a 'Trade Marks Work Manual' giving full details of the application procedure and the forms necessary to make an application, oppose an application, appeal a decision and other formal and administrative steps in the registration procedure. The IPO regularly issues Practice Notices which give details of changes in procedures amending existing practices as case law develops.

13.33   The website also contains statistics on trade mark applications and registrations. In 2006 26,745 applications for registration were filed, compared with 28,083 in 2007. In 2006 18,492 applications were registered, compared with 21,350 in 2007 (for statistics on design registrations see Diagram 8.2).

Question

Can you find the most recent Practice Direction? What does it concern and what prompted its promulgation?

Community Trade Marks

13.34   Not only is it possible to obtain a trade mark covering the UK, but since 1994 it has been open to traders to register a Community trade mark (CTM), normally effective throughout the territory of member states of the EU. This was established in Council Regulation EC No 40/94 of 20 December 1993 (OJ [1994] L 11/1) on the Community trade mark establishing the Community Trade Mark Office situated in Alicante Spain. This came into force on 15 March 1994. The Regulation (CTMR) which governs the registration and enforcement of CTMs has been codified and can now be found as Council Regulation (EC) No 207/2009 of 26 February 2009 on the Community trade mark. The codification has entailed some changes in numbering of Articles. The codified numbering is referred to in the text and footnotes in this book but the numbering in case law is as in the original case.

Weblink

The database containing applications for and information on registered Community trade marks can be found at the Alicante website at http://oami.europa.eu/

---

[65] ibid, s 76(3).   [66] ibid, s 76(4).   [67] ibid, s 40.   [68] ibid, s 40(3).   [69] ibid, s 9(3).

Exercise

Familiarise yourself with the site by searching the database. Try searching for trade marks with the word 'Diana'. See what you come up with. Note that the site also contains much useful information concerning decisions made in relation to CTMs. Look under 'Legal Aspects' and you will see that you can access decisions of the Boards of Appeal, of the General Court (formerly the Court of First Instance) and of the Court of Justice of the European Union (formerly the European Court of Justice (ECJ)).

Question

You were given details of the first mark to be registered in the UK trade mark register in Figure 13.2 above. Find the first mark that was registered as a CTM.

The main features of the Community trade mark system

13.35   By contrast with a national trade mark, a CTM is effective throughout the member states of the EU. It was the first example of a supranational EU trade mark right. Whereas prior to the introduction of the CTM, a trader who wished to have a trade mark registration in each of the member states of the EU would have had to apply to each trade mark office in each state. Now, only one application needs to be made to the office in Alicante and the one mark is effective in all member states.

13.36   It has been stated in the previous paragraph that a CTM has effect throughout all the member states within the EU. However, there are circumstances in which that will not be the case, called by some the 'Emmental cheese' provisions because a hole may subsist in the unitary character of the CTM.[70] These 'holes' arise because Articles 110 and 111 CTMR preserve the right to invoke national or Union law to prevent the use of a later CTM in one or more member states. Annand and Norman give a number of examples of how these provisions may work in practice. Two of these are as follows:[71]

> 'A is the owner of a trade mark registered in France. A can oppose or apply to cancel a later conflicting CTM. Alternatively [and this is where the 'Emmental cheese' provisions arise] A can object to the use of the CTM in France by bringing an infringement action under French law before a French court'.

> 'B is the owner of an unregistered trade mark in the United Kingdom. B can oppose or apply to cancel a later conflicting CTM. Alternatively B can bring an action in passing-off before a United Kingdom court to prevent use in the United Kingdom.'

As can be seen from these examples, because the owner of the earlier right (that is, the one that subsists before the application for a CTM) chooses *not* to oppose the registration of the CTM, nor to apply for its cancellation, but instead to challenge the use of the CTM within the member state in question, the CTM is valid throughout the member states *except* in the one (or ones) where the earlier right subsists. Thus, the CTM is like a piece of cheese with a hole (or holes) in it.

---

[70]   RE Annand and HE Norman, *Blackstone's Guide to the Community Trade Mark* (1998) p 128.   [71]   ibid.

Place of application and procedure

13.37   The office in Alicante is called the Office for Harmonisation in the Internal Market (Trade Marks and Designs) or OHIM for short. This office is responsible for the registration procedures for the CTM. It maintains the public registers relating to the rights and rules on applications for declaration of invalidity of the rights after registration. The CTM process is available to nationals of the EU countries, countries that are parties to the Paris Convention and other countries granting reciprocal rights. A CTM applicant is not required to have a commercial establishment in the EU. Examiners in OHIM make decisions relating to conditions of filing of a CTM,[72] decisions on absolute grounds for refusal,[73] and refusal of a Community collective mark,[74] opposition decisions,[75] and decisions to revoke or declare invalid CTMs.[76] An appeal lies from any one of these decisions to the OHIM Boards of Appeal or in certain circumstances the Grand Board of Appeals.[77] Thereafter further appeal on specified grounds lies to the General Court.[78]

13.38   When an application has been examined, if accepted it is published in the Community Trade Marks Bulletin.[79] During a period of three months thereafter, third parties may make observations on, or oppose the application on relative grounds. If the application is rejected it may be converted to national applications retaining the OHIM filing date[80] (but not in those member states to which the ground of refusal relates). Where there is no opposition the mark will be registered[81] using the filing date as the effective date.

13.39   The matter of enforcement of a CTM is left to national law, subject to the applicable law being that of the CTMR.[82] Each member state has designated first and second instance national courts to deal with matters of litigation concerning the enforcement of the CTM. In the UK, the High Court is the court of first instance in England, Wales and Northern Ireland, and the Court of Session is the CTM court for Scotland.[83]

Weblink

The OHIM website contains a list of cases concerning the CTM which have been heard by national courts. The first, in a British court, was delivered in 1999. To mid-2009 over 400 cases had been disposed of in 12 different countries. For an archived list have a look at

http://oami.europa.eu/ows/rw/pages/CTM/caseLaw/judgementsCTMCourtsList.en.do

---

[72] Art 36 CTMR.

[73] Art 37 CTMR. Case T-317/05 *Kustom Musical Amplification, Inc v OHIM*. OHIM must inform an applicant at every stage of the process of the grounds which affect their rights and give an opportunity to present a case in reply. This obligation is not fulfilled by the mere provision of internet links to documentation without also supplying hard copies.

[74] Art 68 CTMR.   [75] Arts 41–43 CTMR.   [76] Arts 51–57 CTMR.

[77] Art 58 CTMR. See also Council Regulation (EC) No 422/2004 of 19 February 2004 amending Regulation (EC) No 40/94 on the Community Trade Mark; Commission Regulation (EC) No 2082/2004 of 6 December 2004 amending Regulation (EC) No 216/96 laying down the rules of procedure of the Boards of Appeal of the Office for Harmonisation in the Internal Market. On the boundaries of functions between Union and domestic level see the CFI in Case T-134/06 *Xentral LLC, v Office for Harmonisation in the Internal Market (Trade Marks and Designs) (OHIM)*, (CTMR Article 8(1)(b)) *Pagesjaune.com*.

[78] Art 65 CTMR.   [79] Art 39 CTMR.   [80] Art 112 CTMR.   [81] Art 45 CTMR.

[82] Arts 14 and 101 CTMR.

[83] CTM Regulations 2006 (SI 2006/1027). Jurisdiction of these courts: Art 96 CTMR. All infringement and threatened infringement actions relating to CTMs; actions for declarations of non-infringement; claims for damages brought under Art 9(3) CTMR; counterclaims for revocation or for a declaration of invalidity of a CTM. Any other dispute relating to a CTM is heard by a national court under the terms of Art 106 CTMR.

Question

What was the first case shown in the archive to have been heard in the English High Court? What was it about?

13.40 When an application is made for a CTM, a search is carried out by the Alicante office, as with the amended practice in the UK, on absolute grounds only. The application is forwarded to national registries (including that in the UK) for searches to be carried out in those databases. If any proprietor of an existing mark wishes to oppose the registration, then it is up to them to do this, although a copy of the application is sent to those parties who may be interested.[84]

Question

Why might a trader want to have a single registration effective throughout the community?

The advantages of the CTM over a portfolio of national marks

13.41 Procedural simplification:

- applying for a CTM greatly simplifies the procedure for trade mark owners. Only one application need be made in one language and one set of fees paid, resulting in a CTM, effective throughout the European Union.

- having a single CTM makes it much easier for trade mark owners to manage their portfolio of registered trade marks.

13.42 Single market benefits:

- Having trade marks registered in different member states by the same trader can cause problems for the internal market. Where a trade mark owner chooses different trade marks for different member states, it has the potential effect of partitioning the single market along territorial boundaries. A trade mark owner could maintain national registrations for the same mark in several member states with a view to keeping out parallel imports placed on the market by the trade mark owner or with his consent in another member state of the Union.

13.43 Over the years the problems have been dealt with in a number of ways, including the development by the Court of Justice of a distinction between the *existence* of a registered trade mark right and its *exercise*. One of the results has been that the rule has developed that once goods have been placed on the market in the EU by the trader or with consent of the trader, the rights arising from that mark may not be used to prohibit the further movement of those goods around the Union. Another mechanism, and one of the most potent ways of overcoming the potential for fragmentation of the single European market along national territories resulting from enforcement of national trade mark rights, was to create a single registered trade mark

---

[84] The OHIM guidelines are updated as new law and practices emerge.

effective throughout the Union: hence the CTM. For a discussion on the free movement of goods see Chapter 19.

Question

Why might a trader not want a CTM but prefer instead to maintain national registrations

13.44   The Community trade mark is becoming increasingly important, as more and more applications for registration are made. Over 43,000 applications were filed in 1996. While there were dips in 1997, 1998 and 2008, the numbers are increasing annually. There were over 87,000 applications in 2008.[85]

The regulatory framework: international

13.45   Both the World Intellectual Property Organisation (WIPO) and the World Trade Organisation (WTO) administer international treaties pertaining to trade marks.

WIPO: Paris Convention for the Protection of Industrial Property 1883 (Paris Convention)

13.46   The Paris Convention is one of the oldest international intellectual property treaties. It deals not only with registered trade marks, but also affects inter alia unregistered marks, patents and registered designs. It currently has 173 signatories.[86] The Convention is not directly effective in many countries: rather, those states which have signed the Treaty amend domestic laws to reflect the obligations imposed under the Treaty.[87] The basis of the Paris Convention is that of national treatment.[88] This means that contracting states are required to treat nationals (whether companies or individuals) of foreign contracting states as they would their own nationals. Thus, nationals of states who have signed the Convention must be able to register trade marks in the UK register and have the benefit of the law relating to those marks applied in the same way that it does to UK nationals.[89] Article 6 of the Convention provides that the conditions for filing and registration of a mark in a Convention country is to be determined according to domestic laws, but that any application in a Convention country may not be refused or registration annulled on the ground that filing, registration or renewal of the mark has not been effective in the country of origin.

13.47   The Paris Convention provides for a system of *priority*.[90] This means that those nationals who have registered their marks in their own contracting states have a period during which they may

---

[85] OHIM Annual report available at http://oami.europa.eu/ows/rw/pages/OHIM/OHIMPublications/annualReport. en.do See also the statistics for national registrations in para 13.33 and for registered designs in Diagram 8.3.

[86] As of November 2009.

[87] Case C-238/06 P *Develey Holding GmbH & Co Beteiligungs KG v Office for Harmonisation in the Internal Market (Trade Marks and Designs* [2008] ETMR 20. The provisions of the Paris Convention could not be relied on directly (para 40), 'while the direct effect of the Paris Convention could flow from the cross-reference made to it by Article 2(1) of the TRIPs Agreement, such a cross-reference cannot, in the absence of the direct applicability of the TRIPs Agreement, render the Paris Convention directly applicable' (para 43).

[88] Paris Convention, Art 2.

[89] National treatment extends also to companies and individuals who are not nationals of a contracting state, but who are domiciled or have a real and effective industrial and commercial establishment in the territory of one of the countries of the Union: Art 3.

[90] Paris Convention, Art 4.

file an application in other contracting states, and gain priority for that filing over and above other pending applications from unconnected third parties. This may be important for those entities who are attempting to protect trade marks in a number of different countries: it ensures that they may do so ahead of other pre-emptive applications. The Paris Convention *does not* provide for a central mechanism for filing trade marks. Nor does it give protection extending beyond the territory in which it is registered.

13.48   One important provision in the Paris Convention deals with unregistered marks[91] (rather than registered marks). This imposes an obligation on contracting states to protect well-known marks *even* where they have not been registered. The purpose is to protect those proprietors of well-known marks who have not commenced using their marks in a particular signatory state from activities of third parties who might attempt a pre-emptive registration. In determining whether a mark is a well-known mark within the meaning of the Paris Convention, 'the competent authority can take into account any circumstances from which it may be inferred that the mark is well known'.[92] The CFI considered some of the requirements in *El Corte Inglés v OHIM— Abril Sánchez and Ricote Saugar (BoomerangTV)*[93] and referred to Article 2 of the joint recommendation concerning the provisions on the protection of well-known trade marks, adopted by the Assembly of the Paris Union and the General Assembly of the World Intellectual Property Organisation (WIPO) at the 34th series of meetings of assemblies of the Member States of the WIPO (of 20 to 29 September 1999).

> 'In determining whether a mark is a well known mark within the meaning of the Paris Convention, the competent authority can take into account any circumstances from which it may be inferred that the mark is well known, including: the degree of knowledge or recognition of the mark in the relevant sector of the public; the duration, extent and geographical area of any use of the mark; the duration, extent and geographical area of any promotion of the mark, including advertising or publicity and the presentation, at fairs or exhibitions, of the goods and/or services to which the mark applies; the duration and geographical area of any registrations, and/or any applications for registration, of the mark, to the extent to which they reflect use or recognition of the mark; the record of successful enforcement of rights in the mark, in particular, the extent to which the mark has been recognised as well known by competent authorities; the value associated with the mark.'

In the instant case limited evidence of the use of a mark (a figurative mark including the word 'boomerang') in catalogues and a photograph of balloons was insufficient to prove that the marks were well known or even recognised in Ireland, Greece and/or the UK.

13.49   This section has been implemented in the UK in TMA 1994, section 56(2).[94] It was considered by Justice Arnold in the High Court in the following case.

■ *Hotel Cipriani SRL & Ors v Cipriani (Grosvenor Street) Ltd & Ors* [2008] EWHC 3032 (Ch)

In this case Justice Arnold drew heavily on his earlier decision in *Le Man Autoparts Ltd Trade Mark Application* (0/012/05) where he sat as Appointed Person and in which extensive reference was made to *General Motors*. Reference was also made to the 1999 Joint recommendation of

[91] Paris Convention, Art 6*bis*.
[92] *El Corte Inglés SA v Office for Harmonisation in the Internal Market (Trade Marks and Designs)* [2008] ETMR 71, para 80.
[93] Case T-420/03. The CFI was considering CTMR Article 8(1)(a) and (b) and Article 8(5) of Regulation No 40/94.
[94] This section provides protection for proprietors of well known trade marks which are already protected under the Paris Convention where it is proposed to use an identical or similar mark in relation to identical or similar goods where the use is likely to cause confusion.

WIPO. Applying these sources the judge came to the conclusion that the mark Cipriani was a well known trade mark for hotel and restaurant services among that sector of the public.

13.50   Section 56 provides protection to well-known unregistered marks even if there has been no trade in the UK.[95] Prior to the CFI's consideration of the meaning of well-known in *El Corte Inglés* (see para 13.48), the court in *Microsoft Corporation's Applications*[96] said that to show a mark was well-known 'there would need to be some independent evidence from the trade and, perhaps, more importantly the public as to the recognition accorded to the mark in this country'. *El Corte Inglés* suggests that the hurdle may be significantly higher.

13.51   The Paris Convention also requires Convention countries to prevent the use and registration of 'armorial bearings, flags and emblems' of the countries of the Convention,[97] to provide effective protection against unfair competition,[98] and to accept for registration any trade mark which has been duly registered in its country of origin.[99]

Exercise

Read the Paris Convention. Clarify in your own mind how the system of national treatment works.

WIPO: The Madrid Agreement and Protocol

13.52   The Madrid Agreement for the International Registration of Marks (1891) and the Madrid Protocol of 1989 are both administered by WIPO. In contrast with the Paris Convention, the Madrid Agreement and Protocol provide for a simplified mechanism for filing trade mark applications. However, and in common with the Paris Convention and by contrast with the CTM, no provision is made for a supranational right or a single application effective throughout a number of states.

- **Madrid Agreement:** The applicant must first file for or obtain a registration in the home state. Once this is done, an application may be made to WIPO for an international registration. It should however be noted that this is *not* an international trade mark. Rather the application is sent to those contracting states specified in the application to WIPO. Each state specified is then responsible for individual registrations as if it had been filed directly in that country. Importantly for traders, and in common with the Paris Convention, making the home application first gives a period of *priority* as regards the applications made in the other contracting states.

---

[95] TRIPS Agreement, Art 16(2) provides that in assessing whether a mark is well-known, account should be taken of the knowledge of the trade mark in the relevant sector of the public, including knowledge in the member country which had been obtained as a result of the promotion of the trade mark: TMA 1994, s 56.

[96] [1997–98] Information Technology Law Reports 361.

[97] Paris Convention, Art 6*ter*. This provision was recently considered in depth in Joined cases C-202/08 P and C-208/08 P *American Clothing Associates SA v OHIM* (2009), in which the Court confirmed that there is a broad protection for state emblems.

[98] Paris Convention, Art 10*bis*. It is debatable the extent to which the UK has fulfilled its obligations under this Article.

[99] Paris Convention, Art 6*quinquies*.

- **Madrid Protocol:** The UK is a party to the Madrid Protocol 1989 (but not the Madrid Agreement). Application for registration of a mark must be made in one of the countries which have signed up to the Madrid Protocol[100] and be based on a pre-existing application or registration filed in that office. The application for international registration under the Madrid Protocol must then be made through the national office, and not directly to WIPO.[101] Once the national office has satisfied itself that the application conforms with the existing application or registration it is forwarded to WIPO which will examine the application to confirm that it conforms to the requirements of the Protocol. When satisfied, the application is placed on the International Register of Trade Marks and details are passed to those countries named in the application. The application is then dealt with in each of the designated countries as if it had been made directly to that national office.[102] Any refusal of registration can only be based on grounds to be found in the Paris Convention.[103] If an application is made through this route and is successful, registration lasts for 10 years[104] and can be renewed for further periods of 10 years.[105] If a trader has registered a national trade mark, and later makes that mark the subject of an international registration under the Madrid Protocol, then the international registration replaces the national registration.[106]

- In 2004 the EC acceded to the Madrid Protocol. As a result, a CTM application or a registered CTM can be used as the basic mark for an international application and the EU can be designated in an international application via the Madrid Protocol.[107]

One of the problems with the Madrid Agreement, and why that Treaty attracted relatively few signatories, was because of the system known as *'central attack'*.[108] This means that if the home application for a trade mark is lost within five years from the date of international registration, perhaps through the national authority refusing the application, through a declaration of invalidity, or non-use for the requisite period, then all the other registrations are lost. This is not the case under the Madrid Protocol. In the event of the first registration being invalid, then the other registrations/applications may be turned into national or regional (ie CTM) applications,[109] which then stand independent of the original registration.

Exercise

Read both the Madrid Agreement and the Madrid Protocol.

Question

How many signatories are there to each? Can you find any examples of applications made under the Madrid Protocol in the UK or CTM register? How do you know which system the application has been made under?

---

[100] Madrid Protocol, Art 2(1).   [101] ibid, Art 2(2).   [102] ibid, Art 4.   [103] ibid, Art 5(1).
[104] ibid, Art 6(1).   [105] ibid, Art 7(1).   [106] ibid, Art 4*bis*.
[107] For an indication as to how the systems operate in practice see http://oami.europa.eu/en/mark/madrid/default.htm
[108] Madrid Agreement, Arts 6–7(1).   [109] Madrid Protocol, Art 9*quinquies*.

WIPO: The Trade Mark Law Treaty

13.53   The Trade Mark Law Treaty (TLT) was signed in Geneva on 28 October 1994. The scope of this Treaty is much more limited that the other treaties discussed above. The purpose of the TLT is to harmonise certain formalities in relation to the form and content of an application for registration and standardise the term of protection at 10-year renewable intervals. Article 1 of the TLT provides that its provisions apply to marks consisting of 'visible signs', and three-dimensional marks where contracting parties accept those for registration. The TLT does not apply to hologram marks, those 'not consisting of visible signs', for instance sound and olfactory marks, or collective, certification and guarantee marks. The TLT goes on to make provisions for the form and content of the application (Article 3), the filing date (Article 5), and other procedural formalities such as changing a name and address (Article 10) and correcting mistakes (Article 12).

The Treaty had 45 contracting states as of November 2009.

WIPO: Singapore Treaty on the Law of Trademarks

13.54   The purpose of the Singapore Treaty on the Law of Trademarks 2006 is to update the TLT. Not long after the adoption of the TLT it became apparent that it needed to be revised largely as a result of the 'dot.com' revolution, the introduction of e-mail and Internet based communications. For instance, the TLT contains provisions obliging states to accept communications in paper form. The Singapore Treaty also broadens the scope of the TLT which only covered visible marks. The Singapore Treaty encompasses any mark that a contracting party may offer. So, for example, if a contracting party, protects sound marks, the provisions of the Singapore Treaty apply, but if a contracting party does not allow for sound marks, that party has no obligation to provide for them.

13.55   The Singapore Treaty is separate from the TLT. The Treaties can be joined either together or individually. Article 27 of the Singapore Treaty governs the relationship between the two and provides that, between parties that are signatories to both treaties, the Singapore Treaty will govern. Unlike the TLT, the Singapore Treaty creates an 'Assembly of the Contracting Parties', which, among other powers, allows for modification of the treaty regulations and model forms used under the Treaty. The goal of this Assembly is to help keep the Singapore Treaty up-to-date.

13.56   This Treaty was finalised in March 2006. It came into force on March 2009, and as at November 2009, 56 members had signed this Treaty.

WIPO: Nice International Arrangement on the International Classification of Goods and Services

13.57   Note the comments on the Nice Agreement, a classification Treaty, in para 13.20 above.

WTO: Agreement on Trade-Related Aspects of Intellectual Property Rights including Trade in Counterfeited Goods (TRIPS)

13.58   The TRIPS Agreement resulted from the Uruguay round of the General Agreement on Tariffs and Trade (GATT) discussions held under the auspices of WTO. The Agreement, which is administered by the WTO, was passed in 1994. There are a number of points to note:[110]

- TRIPS does not provide either for its own mechanism for registration of marks, or for a mark to be registered in more than one territory (cf the CTM). TRIPS does provide for

---

[110] See also the discussion in Chapter 1.

certain minimum standards in relation to trade marks (and other intellectual property rights) which must be incorporated into national laws of contracting states. For instance, contracting states must apply the Paris Convention standards relating to trade marks;[111] TRIPS also adopts a broad definition of a sign which is capable of being registered as a trade mark; requires trade mark registration to extend to marks for services;[112] and defines the rights conferred by a registered mark.[113]

- As with other international conventions, the principle of national treatment is incorporated into the TRIPS Agreement.[114]

- Unlike other international conventions and Treaties, TRIPS includes a most favoured nation clause.[115] This broadly means that if any contracting state gives to any other contracting state preferential treatment, then that concession must also be given to all other contracting states.

- If a state fails to adhere to its obligations under any of the agreements administered by WIPO, then another state may bring a reference to the International Court of Justice. No such intellectual property reference has been made. By contrast, under TRIPS, failure by a state to adhere to its obligations may lead to GATT dispute settlement procedure and ultimately to sanctions withdrawing GATT privileges to that state. (For details of the enforcement procedure see paras 21.143–21.154.)

Exercise

Read the TRIPS Agreement and, in relation to trade marks, list five key points of similarity and/or difference between the provisions found in that agreement as compared with the CTMR and the UK TMA 1994.

The interaction between the systems concerning registration

13.59   As can be seen from the discussion above, there are a number of instruments that concern or affect the *registration* of trade marks. This has resulted in the construction of a complex framework where an application for registration of a mark in a particular trade mark register may be affected by a pending or registered mark in one of the other registers or by a claim to seniority arising from an earlier right. Full details on the registration processes and how to apply via the various routes are given in documentation available on each of the relevant websites. Each organisation maintains full and comprehensive practice manuals describing the procedures to be followed for registration. These are updated regularly to take account of the law as it develops through court decisions. It is however useful to be aware of the terminology that is used to manage the potentially competing claims of traders as these are often referred to in court cases.

Priority and seniority

13.60   *Priority* refers to the status a mark has on application for registration in relation to the registration systems and the Paris Convention.[116] Broadly, if a mark has already been registered

---

[111] TRIPS, Art 2(1).   [112] TRIPS, Art 15.   [113] TRIPS, Art 16(1).   [114] TRIPS, Art 2.   [115] TRIPS, Art 3.
[116] Paris Convention, Art 4.

or registration is applied for under one of the systems, then that mark will have priority over applications by other proprietors to register the same or similar marks in national registries or as a CTM for a period of six months from the date of the original filing of the application for registration.[117] *Seniority* by contrast allows a proprietor to claim the seniority of earlier national registrations in member states of the same mark when applying for a CTM.[118] The effect of a successful claim of seniority is that the trade mark proprietor can let the national registration lapse while at the same time have the same rights as if the national trade mark had continued to be registered.[119] The purpose is to permit trade mark owners to centralise ownership of trade marks in member states in a single mark (the CTM) without jeopardising rights accrued under individual trade marks.

13.61   These provisions have been incorporated into the TMA 1994 through the use of the terms 'earlier trade mark' and 'earlier right'.[120] An earlier trade mark[121] includes an existing registered trade mark (that is, one that is on the UK register whether by virtue of the 1938 or 1994 Act), an international trade mark (UK) (one for which registration is applied for under the Madrid Protocol), or a CTM. All of these earlier trade marks need a date of application for registration earlier than that for the mark under consideration, taking into account any priorities[122] or the seniority of a CTM.[123] A person who is entitled to prevent the use of a trade mark is referred to in the TMA 1994 as the proprietor of an earlier right in relation to the trade mark.[124]

Exercise

Read the Paris Convention, Article 4, CTMR, Articles 29–35 and Trade Marks Act 1994, section 6.

Opposition

13.62   The effect of these rules is that not only are there are a number of routes an applicant for a trade mark might choose in order to acquire registration, but also there are a series of grounds on which the registration of a mark in the UK register or CTM may be *opposed* by the proprietor of an earlier right. Opposition refers to the right of any person to oppose the registration of a

---

[117] ibid, Art 4C. TMA 1994, s 6(1)(c) provides for a trade mark which at the date of application for registration, in questions of the *priority* claimed in respect of the application, was entitled to protection under the Paris Convention as a well-known trade mark. TMA 1994, s 6(2) sets out the priority for applicants to be able to claim rights to an earlier trade mark. TMA 1994, s 35(1) provides that 'A person who has duly filed an application for protection of a trade mark in a [Paris] Convention country...has a right to priority for the purposes of registering the same trade mark under this Act for some or all of the same goods or services'.

[118] Art 34 CTMR. Section 6(1)(b) of the 1994 Act provides that a CTM is an *earlier mark* which has a valid claim to *seniority* due to an earlier registered trade mark or international trade mark (UK).

[119] The claim must be for the same sign, the same goods and services and the same proprietor as the CTM: CTMR, Art 34(1).

[120] See ss 5–8 of the TMA 1994. This means the date and not the time of filing if two applications are made on the same day, STAIGER Trade Mark [2004] RPC 33 2003 WL 23508814.

[121] See generally TMA 1994, s 6.   [122] ibid, s 6(1)(a).   [123] ibid, s 6(1)(b).   [124] ibid, s 5(4).

trade mark,[125] and generally occurs once the application has been accepted and published by the Registrar.[126]

13.63   Opposition grounds may include the existence of a UK, international (UK) or CTM registration; an earlier national, international or Community pending application; a Community trade mark with a later date of application but a valid claim of prior rights from a national or international registration (stemming from Article 34 of the CTMR); the existence of a well-known mark; an existing registered mark with a reputation;[127] the use of the mark which is likely to be prohibited by any rule of law, for example, passing off; the existence of an earlier copyright, design right or registered design right;[128] or there may be a Convention priority claim[129] deriving from the Paris Convention.

Exercise

Draw a diagram highlighting the various registration routes that can be taken by a trader who wishes to have a registered trade mark effective in the UK.

Conclusion

13.64   The international, European and domestic framework establishes a system in which the registration of trade marks can take place within an increasingly globalised trading structure and through which existing and pending rights of traders can be managed and balanced against the demands of competitors. The system is however complex and the choice of route to be taken to secure registration will depend on innumerable factors including the commercial aims of the trader, the costs of obtaining registration and the time taken for registration.

Key points on regulatory framework

- Domestic (UK) law is contained in the TMA 1994 and is shaped by European and international obligations
- The CTMR which establishes the CTM creates a supra-national trade mark right normally effective throughout the territories of the member states of the EU
- WIPO administers the Madrid Agreement and Protocol, which provide for a streamlined registration process for trade marks in different countries
- The Paris Convention (WIPO) and TRIPS (WTO) both contain substantive minimum obligations regarding trade marks
- The Trade Mark Law Treaty and the Singapore Treaty contain obligations relating to procedural matters for the registration of trade marks

---

[125]   ibid, s 38(2). Note the right of opposition to the registration of a CTM is limited to certain specified persons: CTMR, Art 41(1).

[126]   TMA 1994, s 38(1).   [127]   ibid, s 5(3).   [128]   ibid, s 5(4)(a) and (b).   [129]   ibid, s 35 and 60.

Further reading

Books

R Annand and H Norman, *Blackstone's Guide to the Trade Marks Act 1994*

R Annand and H Norman, *Blackstone's Guide to the Community Trade Mark 1998*

GB Dinwoodie and MD Janis (eds), *Trademark Law and Theory: A Handbook of Contemporary Research* (2008)

Kerly's Law of Trade Marks and Trade Names (14th edn, 2005)

C Morcom, A Roughton, and S Malynicz, *The Modern Law of Trade Marks* (3rd edn, 2008)

J Phillips, *Trade Mark Law: A Practical Anatomy* (2003)

N Pires de Carvalho, *The TRIPS Regime of Trademarks and Designs* (2006)

J Roberts, *International Trade Mark Classification: A Guide to the Nice Agreement* (3rd edn, 2007)

Articles

R Ashmead, 'International classification class headings: illustrative or exemplary? The scope of European Union registrations' (2007) 2(2) JIPLP 76–88

KD Beiter, 'The Right to Property and the Protection of Interests in Intellectual Property—A Human Rights Perspective on the European Court of Human Rights' Decision in Anheuser-Busch v. Portugal' (2008) 39 IIC 714

W Cornish, 'Intellectual Property: Omnipresent, Distracting, Irrelevant?' in *Clarendon Law Lectures* (2004), pp 73–110

J Davis, 'European Trade Mark Law and the Enclosure of the Commons' (2002) 4 IPQ 342–67

G Dinwoodie, 'Architecture of the International Intellectual Property System' (2002) 77 Chicago-Kent Law Review 993

G Dinwoodie, 'Trademarks and Territory: Detaching Trademark Law from the Nation-State' (2004) 41 Houston Law Review 885

A Folliard-Monguiral, and D Rogers, 'Significant 2007 case law on the Community trade mark from the ECJ and the CFI' (2008) 3(5) JIPLP 291

R Ghafele, 'Trade mark owners' perspectives on the Madrid System: practical experiences and theoretical underpinnings' (2007) 2(3) JIPLP 160–9.

LR Helfer, 'The New Innovation Frontier? Intellectual Property and the European Court of Human Rights' (2008) 49 Harvard International Law Journal 1

N Isaacs, 'Should the United Kingdom Adopt a European System for the registration of trade marks' [2006] EIPR 71–3

L Jaeschke, 'The quest for a superior registration system for registered trade marks in the UK and EU: an analysis of the current registration system in the UK, the CTM registration system and coming changes' [2008] EIPR 25

MA Leaffer, 'The New World of International Trademark Law' (1998) 2 Marq Intell Prop L Rev 1, 28

L Loughlan, 'Trade Marks: Arguments in a Continuing Contest' (2005) 3 IPQ 294–308

SM Maniatis and AK Sanders, 'A Consumer Trade Mark Protection Based on Origin and Quality' [1993] EIPR 406–15

FW Mostert, 'Is Goodwill Territorial or International? Protection of the Reputation of a Trade Mark Which has not been used in the Local Jurisdiction' [1989] 11(12) EIPR 440–48

FW Mostert, 'When is a Mark Well-Known?' (1997) 3 IPQ 377–83

MA Naser, 'Trademarks and Freedom of Expression' (2009) 40 IIC 188

H Rosler, 'The Rationale for European Trade Mark Protection' [2007] EIPR 100

F Schechter, 'The Rational Basis of Trade Mark Protection' (1927) 40 Harv LR 813

B Thompson and M Woodhouse, 'Use it or lose it!' [2006] 188 TW 22–3

J Weberndorfer, 'The Integration of the Office for Harmonization in the Internal Market into the Madrid System: A First Field Report' [2008] EIPR 216.

A Von Muhlendahl, 'Community Trade Mark Riddles: territoriality and unitary character' [2008] EIRP 6

Definition of a trade mark and registration

Introduction

Scope and overview of chapter

14.1 Since the Trade Marks Directive and the Community Trade Mark Regulation (CTMR) were enacted, the types of signs that can be registered as trade marks have expanded. Whereas traditionally registration was limited to words, pictures and similar signs, such is the breadth of the current legislation that all manner of two- and three-dimensional marks, sounds, gestures and other indicia now fall under the definition of a trade mark. Many questions have been raised before the Court of Justice of the European Union concerning the grounds on which registration or a trade mark should proceed or be refused by national trade mark registries and the Office for the Harmonisation of the Internal Market (OHIM). As the case law develops so it becomes possible to discern trends as to the perceived function of a trade mark; shifts in the balance among the varied interests represented within the registered trade mark framework; and fluctuations in the monopoly conferred by a mark. The purpose of this chapter is to examine the definition of a trade mark and to discuss the criteria for registration highlighting trends in the case law which shapes understanding as to the proper role of trade marks within the consumer society.

14.2 **Learning objectives**

By the end of this chapter you should be able to describe and explain:

- the definition of a trade mark and what may be registered;
- the conditions relating to graphic representation for the purposes of registration of a trade mark;
- the developing jurisprudence concerning the tests underlying the absolute grounds for refusing to register a trade mark;
- conditions under which a mark will become distinctive through use;
- details pertaining to the registration of collective and certification marks.

The rest of this chapter is broken into the following parts:

- The definition of a trade mark (14.6–14.24)
- Registration: absolute grounds for refusal (14.25–14.90)
- Collective and certification trade marks (14.91–14.93)
- Relative grounds for refusal of registration (14.94–14.97)
- Use requirements (14.98–14.110)

Preliminary matters[1]

14.3   As will be seen from a reading of the CTMR, the Trade Marks Directive and the TMA 1994, much of the wording dealing with the definition of a trade mark, registration and infringement is similar if not identical. As regards the interrelationship between the CTMR and the Directive this is because the definition and scope of what can be registered as a trade mark and the rights pertaining to a registered trade mark are intended to be the same, albeit that the geographical extent of the right differs. As was stated by the Advocate General in *SA Société LTJ Diffusion v SA Sadas*[2] concerning the parallel provisions of the Directive and the CTMR:

> '[I do not] agree that a directive and a regulation which use the same criteria and the same language in parallel contexts must be interpreted differently simply because they are different in nature. On the contrary, when the Community legislature takes care to express itself in that manner—as it clearly did in the field of trade marks—the presumption is very strong indeed that the two measures are intended to be interpreted in the same way. The fact that they will be applied in different legal and factual circumstances does not detract from that presumption,'[3] and in principle, therefore, I am of the view that the relevant parallel provisions of the Directive and the Regulation fall to be interpreted in the same way'.[4]

As between the Directive and the TMA 1994, this is because the purpose of the 1994 Act was, inter alia, to implement the Directive although it should be noted that the intention of the Directive is to approximate and not harmonise the laws of member states.[5] The Community trade mark regime is an autonomous system that applies independently of any national system. The legality of decisions of the Boards of Appeal must be evaluated solely on the basis of the CTMR, as it is interpreted by the Union Courts.[6] Similarly, the validity of a national trade mark cannot be called in question in proceedings for registration of a Community trade mark, only in cancellation proceedings brought in the member state concerned.[7] As the Court of Justice of the European Union (formerly the European Court of Justice (ECJ)) is the final arbiter in matters of interpretation relating both to the CTMR and to the Directive, reference will be made to, and judgments drawn from, cases concerning the CTMR, the Directive and TMA 1994 with particular reference to the jurisprudence of the Court of Justice. Also referred to will be judgments of the General Court (formerly the Court of First Instance) which hears appeals from the OHIM. In these circumstances the decision is highly persuasive, as is the judgment of the Court of Justice on further appeal.[8] National (UK) cases will also be incorporated into the discussion. Where a general reference is made to a court, then the new name (Court of Justice or General Court) will be used in the text. Where reference is made to a case or discussion of a case, the

---

[1] It was noted in paras 13.28 and 13.34 that both the Directive and the CTMR have been codified. The new provisions will be referred to in the text, but in case law the original provisions remain.

[2] Case C-291/00 [2003] ECR I-2799, [2003] ETMR 83, [2003] FSR 34.   [3] ibid, para 25.   [4] ibid, para 28.

[5] Recitals Trade Marks Directive.   [6] *L & D SA v OHIM* [2008] ETMR 62, para 58.

[7] Case T 134/06 *Xentral LLC, v OHIM*, para 36. Case T-328/05 *Apple Computer v OHIM—TKS-Teknosoft (QUARTZ)*.

[8] A Firth, G Lea, P Cornford, *Trade Marks: Law and Practice* (2nd edn, 2005), p 3.

name of the court at that time (European Court of Justice (ECJ) or Court of First Instance) will be used in the text.

14.4   In referring to sources of law in the text, in each heading reference will be made to the relevant section of the TMA 1994 as well as Articles of the Directive and of the CTMR where applicable. To avoid repetition, only the sections of the TMA 1994 will be referred to in the text (except where the case refers to the Directive or CTMR). The reader is strongly urged to read the relevant provision for each section including both the codified and uncodified versions of the Directive and CTMR as this will help considerably in understanding the discussion.

14.5   Where there are significant differences as between the application of the TMA 1994, the Directive and the CTMR, such as the geographical extent for fulfilling the requirement of distinctiveness through use, these will be specifically drawn to the attention of the reader.

The definition of a trade mark

 Exercise

Read TMA 1994, section 1; Directive, Article 2; and CTMR, Article 4.

'[A trade mark[9] is defined in section 1 of the TMA 1994 as:] any sign capable of being represented graphically which is capable of distinguishing goods or services of one undertaking from those of other undertakings. [The mark may] consist of words (including personal names), designs, letters, numerals or the shape of goods or their packaging'.[10]

14.6   There are thus three criteria the mark must meet:

- the mark must be a *sign*;

- the mark must be capable of being represented graphically;

- the mark must be capable of distinguishing goods or services of one undertaking from those of another.

Sign

14.7   The requirement that the mark should be a *sign* has not proved too problematic for the purposes of registration, and many different types of signs are now accepted for registration as trade marks.

- Simple word marks that have been registered include 'Rolls Royce' and 'Tesco'. Phrases which have been registered as trade marks include 'A Mars a day helps you work, rest and play'.[11] Many words are registered in combination with a device or a graphic such as that shown in Figure 14.1 below.[12]

---

[9] There is no distinction between a trade mark and a service mark under the TMA 1994.

[10] TMA 1994, s 1(1). Under the Regulation, the definition of a community mark is much the same: 'A Community trade mark may consist of any signs capable of being represented graphically, particularly words, including personal names, designs, letters, numerals, the shape of goods or of their packaging, provided that such signs are capable of distinguishing the goods or services of one undertaking from those of other undertakings' (CTMR, Art 4).

[11] UK Trade Mark No 1438989, class 30, proprietor: Mars UK Ltd.

[12] UK Trade Mark No 2101409, Classes 41 and 42, proprietor: The University Court of the University of Edinburgh.

Figure 14.1 Edinburgh Law School

EDINBURGH LAW SCHOOL

- Numbers have been registered, including the number '1010'.[13]
- Personal names (in signature form) have been registered including that of 'Marilyn Monroe'.[14]
- The shape of the packaging of goods has been registered:[15]

Figure 14.2 Coca-Cola bottle

as has the shape of goods such as the Mini shown in Figure 14.3 below.[16]

- Gestures: 'The Mark consists of a gesture made by a person which comprises tapping a pocket of an article of clothing worn below the waist of the person'.[17]
- Colours, such as that described in Figure 14.4.[18]
- Sounds have been registered: 'The mark consists of the sound of a dog barking'[19]; as have smells: 'The mark comprises the strong smell of bitter beer applied to flights for darts'.[20]

[13] UK Trade Mark No 2142860, classes 3.4.16.18 and 25, proprietor: Acheson and Acheson Limited.

[14] Trade Mark 1308828, the estate of Marilyn Monroe.

[15] UK Trade Mark No 2000546. The mark consists of a three-dimensional shape with the words 'Coca-Cola' appearing thereon, proprietor: The Coca-Cola Company. The Contour Bottle Design and Coca-Cola are registered trademarks of The Coca-Cola Company.

[16] UK Trade Mark No 2002390, Classes 6, 12, 16 and 28, proprietor: Bayerische Motoren Werke Aktiengesellschaft.

[17] UK Trade Mark No 2048673, classes 29, 30 and 31, proprietor: ASDA Stores Limited.

[18] UK Trade Mark No 2009633, class 3, proprietor: Chemisphere UK Ltd.

[19] UK Trade Mark No 2007456, class 2, proprietor: Imperial Chemical Industries plc.

[20] UK Trade Mark No 2000234, class 28—flights for darts, proprietor: Unicorn Products Limited.

Figure 14.3 BMW mini

Figure 14.4 Purple colour

PURPLE as a colour applied overall to and subsisting in the goods, the colour purple being definable within chromacity coordinate parameters, according to the CIELAB system, of L between o and 90, a between +5 and + 100, and b between –5 and –100.

> **? Question**
>
> How does the registered trade mark 'The mark comprises the strong smell of bitter beer applied to flights for darts' function as a trade mark?
>
> What other types of marks can you think of that might qualify as a trade mark under the definition given above?
>
> Consider the marks in the examples given above. Look at the representation of the mark in the trade mark database and note the date of registration. When you have finished reading this chapter consider whether all of these would now be registrable—or whether some may now be open to challenge.

14.8   While many signs have been accepted as meeting the need to be a mark, the judgment of the ECJ in *Dyson Ltd v Registrar of Trade Marks*[21] indicates that not every sign will pass this hurdle. In this case Dyson sought to register the shape of its vacuum cleaners in class 9 of the Nice Agreement for 'Apparatus for cleaning, polishing and shampooing floors and carpets; vacuum cleaners; carpet shampooers; floor polishers; parts and fittings for all the aforesaid goods.' A similar representation is shown in Figure 14.5.

This was accompanied by the text: 'The mark consists of a transparent bin or collection chamber forming part of the external surface of a vacuum cleaner as shown in the representation'. To

---

[21] Case C-321/03.

Figure 14.5 Dyson

see the second image, which was accompanied by the text 'The mark consists of a transparent bin or collection chamber forming part of the external surface of a vacuum cleaner as shown in the representation' have a look at the opinion of the Attorney General which is available on the Court of Justice of the European Union's website at http://curia.europa.eu/

The application was turned down by the Registry. On appeal to the High Court, that court referred a number of questions to the ECJ. Although the question referred to the Court was in relation to the conditions under which a sign can acquire a distinctive character within the meaning of Article 3(3) of the Directive where the trader had a de facto monopoly in the product bearing the sign prior to lodging an application for registration, the Court found it necessary to answer the prior question of whether the mark constituted a sign within the meaning of Article 2. The Court noted that it was common ground that the subject matter of the application was not a particular type of transparent collecting bin, but rather 'in a general and abstract manner, all the conceivable shapes of such a collecting bin.'[22] The sign was thus not specific. A consumer would not identify visually the subject matter of the application itself, but rather Dyson's graphic representations as contained in the application which in turn were merely examples of

---

[22] ibid, para 35.

the application.[23] The subject matter of the application was a mere property of the product and 'does not therefore constitute a "sign" within the meaning of Article 2 of the Directive'.[24]

14.9 Thus there are certain indicia that are unregistrable because they do not constitute a sign within the meaning of the legislation.[25]

 Question

Can you think of any other 'concepts' that might not meet the definition of a sign and would thus be unregistrable?

Graphic representation

14.10 There have been a number of cases over recent years elaborating on the requirement for graphic representation. In the early days of the 1994 Act there was some debate as to whether sounds and smells would be registrable.[26] In a series of cases the ECJ laid down a set of criteria which the more 'unusual' types of marks, including sounds, smells and colours must meet in order to satisfy the test of graphic representation.

Smells

14.11 The first case by the ECJ to consider an 'unusual' mark, *Sieckmann v Deutsches Patent- und Markenamt*[27] concerned a smell: a 'methyl cinnamate' scent, which the applicant had described as 'balsamically fruity with a slight hint of cinnamon' and given the formula as C6H5–CH = CHCOOCH3.

 Question

Do you know what 'balsamically fruity with a slight hint of cinnamon' smells like?

The question before the Court was whether Article 2 of the Directive included only signs which were capable of being represented visually, or whether it also encompassed signs that could be represented by some other means. If the latter, the question was whether the representation could include a description in words, by way of a chemical formula or a sample. The Court held that a trade mark could consist of a sign which itself may not be capable of being perceived visually (for example, a smell) provided that it could be represented graphically such as through the use of images, lines or characters. In particular the Court said the representation had to be:

- clear;
- precise;
- self contained;

---

[23] ibid, para 36.   [24] ibid, para 39.

[25] For further guidance on what constitutes a sign see Practice Amendment Notice (2007) 7/07.

[26] H Burton, 'The UK Trade Marks Act 1994: An Invitation to an Olfactory Occasion?' [1995] 8 EIPR 378.

[27] *Sieckmann v Deutsches Patent- und Markenamt* (C273/00) [2003] Ch 487, [2003] 3 WLR 424.

- easily accessible;
- intelligible;
- durable;
- objective.

These criteria have subsequently become known as the 'Sieckmann seven'. As regards the instant application it was not possible to register an odour by means of its chemical formula since such a formula was not representative of the odour but rather of the chemical substance itself. Neither would the requirement for graphic representation be satisfied by a written description or by the provision of an odour sample.

14.12 Quite how these criteria will be met in the future for smells remains to be seen. A quick search on the CTM database shows that as at July 2009, only one smell had been registered as a trade mark. This was 'The smell of fresh cut grass' in connection with tennis balls.[28] The application for this trade mark was filed in 1996 and was registered in 2000 (that is, before the judgment in *Sieckmann*). The other six marks shown in the database at the time of writing had all been refused registration.[29] This perhaps gives an indication that it is not going to be easy to register smells as trade marks due to the difficulties of meeting the criteria set out by the ECJ.

 Question

Do you think the mark: 'The mark comprises the strong smell of bitter beer applied to flights for darts' meets the *Sieckmann* seven criteria?

Colours

14.13 The next major case dealing with more unusual marks concerned an application to register a colour: *Libertel Groep BV v Benelux-Merkenbureau*.[30] Libertel applied to register the colour orange as a trade mark for telecommunications goods and services. The application contained an orange rectangle in the space for reproducing the trade mark, together with the word 'orange' in the space on the form for describing the trade mark. There was no reference to a colour code. When this was turned down by the office in the Netherlands, the Dutch court remitted the matter to the ECJ.

The Court held that a colour may, in respect of certain goods and services, have a distinctive character within the meaning of Article 3 of the Directive, provided that it can be represented graphically and repeated the Sieckmann seven criteria: it must be clear, precise, self-contained, equally accessible, intelligible, durable and objective. However this could not be satisfied by reproducing on paper the colour in question as it did not satisfy the requirement for durability that was one of the requirements for graphic representation. A sample with a description or which designated the colour using an internationally recognised identification code would however be sufficient to constitute a graphic representation.

---

[28] CTM No 000428870.
[29] Two went to appeal: El OLOR A LIMON in connection with footwear No 001254861; the smell of ripe strawberries in connection with inter alia bleaching preparations No 001122118. See also the discussion on passing off in para 17.23.
[30] Case C-104/01 [2004] Ch 83, [2004] 2 WLR 1081.

14.14   Further questions on the registerability of colours as trade marks were considered by the ECJ in *Heidelberger Bauchemie GmbH*.[31] These related to the registerability of two colours, blue and yellow, for a range of building products including glue, paint and cleaning, but where the inter-relationship between the two colours was left undefined. The Court said:

> 'The mere juxtaposition of two or more colours, without shape or contours, or a reference to two or more colours 'in every conceivable form', as is the case with the trade mark which is the subject of the main proceedings, does not exhibit the [necessary] qualities of precision and uniformity'.[32]

14.15   However, a colour combination without contours could constitute a trade mark where:

- it has been established that, in the context in which they are used, those colours or combinations of colours in fact represent a sign, and

- the application for registration includes a systematic arrangement associating the colours concerned in a predetermined and uniform way.

Thus colours may be sufficiently represented to constitute registered trade marks. Indeed there have now been a number of colours registered as CTMs. For example, a deep cranberry colour has been registered by Deutsche Telekom for inter alia merchandising and finance activities[33] (the pantone number is included with the application).

Sounds

14.16   The ECJ has also pronounced on the registerability of sounds as trade marks. In *Shield Mark BV v Joost Kist*,[34] Shield had registered a number of marks in the Benelux registry. These included:

- a musical stave depicting the first notes of Beethoven's *Für Elise*;

- the words 'the first nine notes of Für Elise';

- the sequence of notes 'E, D#, E, D#, E, B, D, C, A';

- the word 'Kukelekuuuuu' (the Dutch word for the English 'Cock-a-doodle-do');

- the words 'a cockcrow'.

The question arose as to whether these were valid trade marks given the requirements for graphic representation.

The Court basically reaffirmed its rulings in *Libertel* and *Sieckmann* repeating the Sieckmann seven and went on to say that those requirements were *not* met when the sound sign was represented by means of:

- a description such as the notes making up a musical work;

- an indication that it was the cry of animal;

- a simple onomatopoeia;

- a sequence of musical notes.

However, the requirements *were* satisfied where the sign was represented by a stave divided into measures and showing, in particular, a clef, musical notes and rests whose form indicated the relative values and, where necessary, accidentals.

---

[31] Case C-49/02 [2004] ETMR 99.   [32] ibid, para 34.   [33] CTM No 004636676.
[34] *Shield Mark BV v Kist (t/a Memex)* Case C- 283/01 [2004] Ch 97, [2004] 2 WLR 1117, [2004] All ER (EC) 277 RPC.

14.17   This ruling contemplates that musical notes can be registered as trade marks so long as correctly represented. One example is shown in Figure 14.6.

Figure 14.6 Musical notes

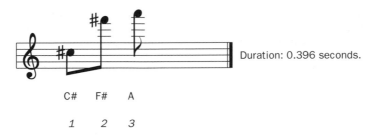

Duration: 0.396 seconds.

C#   F#   A

1   2   3

The description is: The sound of the trade mark consists of the tones above with a deviation as noted in the chart below where each tone is defined in Hz. – n°1: 1100Hz – tone C#;n°2: 1450Hz – tone F#;n°3: 1800Hz – tone A. seconds.[35]

14.18   More difficult will be the question of how other types of sounds, such as animal noises, might meet these criteria. 'Cock-a-doodle-doo' clearly will not do.

 Question

What representations in other languages are there for the crow of a cock? Try searching on Wikipedia and you might find some of the following: Arabic, KooKooKoo-koo; Chinese, goh-geh-goh-goh; Italian, chicchirichì; Korean, k'ok'iyo; Portuguese, Cócórócócó; Swahili, KokoRikoo koo; Swedish, kuckeliku; Gujarati, kuk-de-kuk. How might you go about satisfying the criteria for graphic representation if you wanted to register an animal noise as a trade mark?

Do you think that the mark 'The mark consists of the sound of a dog barking' (para 14.7) might be open to challenge?

Taste

14.19   An application to register a taste mark was made in *Eli Lilly & Co's Community Trade Mark Application*.[36] The application, for an artificial strawberry flavour for use in pharmaceutical products was refused by the OHIM second board of appeals partly on the grounds that it did not meet the criteria for graphic representation as laid out by the ECJ. It was also thought that consumers were likely to see the taste as a means to disguise the unpleasant flavour of medicine rather than as a trade mark—in other words there was doubt over whether it functioned as an indication of origin.[37] It is thus currently unclear as to whether tastes will be registrable as trade marks. It seems that it may be problematic to give sufficient information in an application to indicate precisely what is claimed within the parameters of the trade mark.[38]

[35] CTM No 002510345 by AB Electrolux in connection with lawn mowers and vacuum cleaners.
[36] *Eli Lilly and Company's Application* [2004] ETMR 4 OHIM (2nd Bd Appeal).   [37] ibid, para 15.
[38] At the time of writing it appeared that applications had been made but turned down for a number of 'position marks' where the positioning of certain features were key (Case T-152/07 *Lange Uhren v OHIM* (Figurative mark representing a watch) and R846/2008-4). No further information was available at the time of writing.

Exercise

Go to the OHIM site and find the CTM register. Have a search around some of the more unusual marks for which registration has been applied for. What is the most unusual you can find? Has the mark been registered? How do you know? If not, do you think the mark that you have found is likely to meet the criteria for graphic representation?

The purpose of the rules

14.20   In *Heidelberger Bauchemie Gmb*,[39] the ECJ stressed that the purpose of the requirement of graphic representation is to define the mark so that it is possible to determine the precise subject of the protection so that both the authorities and the general public know what is being claimed as a mark: the authorities so that they can carry out an examination of applications and maintain a 'precise' register of trade marks; and other traders so that they know what competitors' claim and their rights.[40]

Key points on graphic representation

- In order to be registrable a sign should be clear; precise; self contained; easily accessible; intelligible; durable; and objective
- This is so the subject of protection can be determined by both the authorities charged with maintaining a register, and competitors so they know what is being claimed

Service trade marks and retail trade

14.21   Service marks may be registered in connection with services. These are provided for in classes 35–45 of the Nice classification and include inter alia insurance and financial affairs;[41] education and the provision of training; sporting and cultural activities;[42] services for providing food and drink;[43] and medical and veterinary services.[44] Examples of service marks include 'Medacs. Giving you the option'[45] registered in classes 35 and 44 of the Nice Agreement, and the image of half a face along with the words 'Beautiful Smiles' in class 44.[46] (To see the image, go to the CTM register. The number is CTM E3275369.)

14.22   One question that has arisen is as to whether it would be possible to register a service mark for the ancillary services provided by retailers. Businesses will often provide a range of services to their customers in order to encourage the consumer to patronise their business. These may include not only the selection of the goods on offer but in addition those services that go towards consumer preferences in deciding where to shop including the provision of such services as car parking facilities and a crèche. Arguments against permitting such registrations included the view that services were only an adjunct of the retail trade, and not the main business of the retailer. An applicant for a service mark should be in the business of providing services. In addition there was the view that where the mark was to encompass the types of goods sold by the trader, these should be the subject of their own separate application. More recent thinking has suggested that

---

[39] Case C-49/02 [2004] ETMR 99.   [40] ibid, paras 28–30.   [41] Class 36.   [42] Class 41.   [43] Class 43.
[44] Class 44.   [45] UK Trade Mark No 2292972.   [46] CTM E3275369.

the economic trend towards a service society necessitates a reappraisal of retail trade as a service. The purchasing decisions made by the consumer are influenced not only by the availability and price of a product, but also by other aspects such as the variety and assortment of goods, their presentation, service levels, advertising, image and the location of the store. Services provided in connection with retail trade enable retailers to distinguish themselves from their competitors. As a result, such services ought to be eligible for protection by service marks.[47]

14.23　An application to register a service mark for retail activities was turned down under the 1938 Act by the Court of Appeal[48] on the grounds that they were not provided for money or money's worth: the costs were only indirectly passed on to the consumer. However the second Board of Appeal at the OHIM allowed the registration of a figurative mark in *Giacomelli Sport SpA*[49] for the 'bringing together for the benefit of others of a variety of goods...to enable consumers to view and buy the products' in class 35 for inter protective helmets and spectacles, all sporting articles, and the organisation of exhibitions in halls and showrooms for commercial or advertising purposes. The Board reasoned that the provision of a service was something over and above goods, and more in the form of labour expended to meet a particular need or want. As consumers prefer the services provided by some shops over others, so they met a certain need and were mutually beneficial to both the retailer and consumer.

14.24　This approach to permit the registration of retail service marks has been confirmed by the ECJ based on an appreciation that the provision of services by retail traders is a matter which influences consumer choice.

■ *Case C-418/02 **Praktiker Bau und Heimwerkermärkte AG v Deutsches Patent und Markenamt**[50]*

This case concerned a refusal by the German Patent and Trade Mark Office to register the word Praktiker for the service of 'retail trade in building, home improvement, gardening and other consumer goods for the do-it-yourself sector'. The office had refused the application considering that the concept of 'retail trade' claimed did not denote independent services having autonomous economic significance but related only to the distribution of goods as such. Trade mark protection could be achieved only by applying for registration of a trade mark in respect of the goods distributed in each case. On appeal the German court referred a number of questions to the ECJ, two of which were:

- Does retail trade in goods constitute a service within the meaning of Article 2 of the Directive?

- If the answer to this question is in the affirmative:

- To what extent must the content of such services provided by a retailer be specified in order to guarantee the certainty of the subject matter of trade mark protection that is required in order to:

  (a) fulfil the function of the trade mark, as defined in Article 2 of the Directive, namely, to distinguish the goods or services of one undertaking from those of other undertakings, and

  (b) define the scope of protection of such a trade mark in the event of a conflict?

---

[47] *Praktiker Bau- und Heimwerkermarkte AG v Deutsches Patent- und Markenamt* Case C-418/02 [2006] Ch 144, [2006] 2 WLR 195, [2005] ECR I-5873, [2005] ETMR 88.

[48] In *Re Dee Corporation's Application* [1990] RPC 159.　　[49] [2000] ETMR 277.

[50] *Praktiker Bau- und Heimwerkermarkte AG v Deutsches Patent- und Markenamt* Case C-418/02 [2006] Ch 144, [2006] 2 WLR 195, [2005] ECR I-5873, [2005] ETMR 88.

The Court saw no reason why retail services should be precluded from being covered by the concept of services under Article 2 of the Directive, pointing out that while the objective of retail trade is the sale of goods to consumers, part of that was the activity carried for the purpose of encouraging the conclusion of a transaction. This included selecting an assortment of goods offered for sale, and offering a variety of services.

On the question of what specification was necessary, the Court indicated that while it was not required to specify in detail the services for which registration was sought (it would be sufficient to use general wording such as 'bringing together of a variety of goods, enabling customers to conveniently view and purchase those goods')[51] it was necessary to specify the goods or types of goods to which those services relate.[52] The reason for this last requirement was that it would make it easier to apply the provisions in the Directive relating to conflicts with earlier trade marks and to determine the scope of the exclusive right conferred on the proprietor.[53] The High Court in England has suggested that where there was a registration application for a trade mark for a shopping centre, the word 'services' should be taken to mean those that are normally provided for remuneration, as described by the EC Treaty Art 50[54] (Art 57 TFEU) but it is not clear that the separate remuneration requirement could be justified in the light of the ECJ decision in *Praktiker Bau*.

Key point on retail services

- A service mark can be registered for retail services
- While it will not be necessary to specify in detail the services for which registration is sought, it will be necessary to specify the goods, or type of goods, to which the retail service relates

---

Registration: absolute grounds for refusal

14.25　The grounds on which application for registration of a trade mark can be refused are set out in TMA 1994, sections 3 and 5. Section 3 details the *absolute* grounds for refusal of registration, whereas section 5 looks to the *relative* grounds for refusal of registration. The term 'absolute' means that a mark is incapable of being registered as a trade mark because it does not meet the definition of a trade mark,[55] is devoid of distinctive character[56] is indicative of the characteristics of the goods or services[57] or has become a word commonly used in the trade.[58] In other words, the grounds for refusal look to the mark itself. By contrast, the term 'relative' means that account will be taken of other marks that are already registered to see whether the sign for which registration has been applied for can be accepted. The registrar can refuse registration on the grounds listed in section 5, if opposition on that ground is raised (successfully) by the proprietor of the earlier mark or sign.[59] Thus if there is an earlier trade mark which is identical

---

[51] ibid, para 49.　　[52] ibid, para 50.
[53] For difficulties that can arise in the intersection between the retail services and individual trade marks, see the CFI in Case T-116/06 *Oakley v OHMI*.
[54] *Land Securities plc v Registrar of Trade Marks* [2008] EWHC 1744 (Pat).　　[55] Trade Marks Act 1994, s 3(1)(a).
[56] ibid, s 3(1)(b).　　[57] ibid, s 3(1)(c).　　[58] ibid, s 3(1)(d).
[59] See Practice Amendment Notice 8/07, available here: http://www.ipo.gov.uk/pro-types/pro-tm/t-law/t-pan/t-pan-807.htm

with[60] or similar to[61] the sign, or if the registered mark has a reputation and the later registration would take unfair advantage of or be detrimental to the registered trade mark,[62] then the sign may not be registered.

Exercise

Read TMA 1994, sections 3, 5 and 10; Directive, Articles 3, 4 and 5; and CTMR, Articles 7, 8 and 9.

14.26   As will be seen from looking at TMA 1994, sections 5 and 10 (Directive, Articles 4 and 5; CTMR, Articles 8 and 9) almost mirror each other in the wording. This is because if a sign may not be registered as a trade mark under section 5, then the use of that sign (albeit unregistered) in the marketplace by another trader, will inevitably infringe the registered mark. Because the sections are the same, so the same considerations apply as to whether a mark may be registered under section 5, and whether the use of the sign will infringe under section 10. Therefore these two sections will be considered together in Chapter 15.

Non-distinctive, descriptive and customary marks

TMA 1994, sections 3(1)(b), (c), and (d); Directive, Article 3(1)(b)(c)(d); and CTMR, Article 7(1)(b)(c)(d))

14.27   Under these sections the following may not be registered as a trade mark:

- trade marks which are devoid of any distinctive character[63] (TMA 1994, section 3(1)(b)) (non-distinctive marks);

- trade marks which consist exclusively of signs or indications which may serve, in trade, to designate the kind, quality, quantity, intended purpose, value, geographical origin, or the time of production of the goods or of rendering of the service, or other characteristics of the goods or service[64] (TMA 1994, section 3(1)(c)) (descriptive marks);

- trade marks which consist exclusively of signs or indications which have become customary in the current language or in the bona fide and established practices of the trade[65] (TMA 1994, section 3(1)(d)) (customary marks).

Each of these sections yields to the proviso that, even though a mark may fail these tests, if it can be shown that the mark has acquired a distinctive character as a result of the *use* that has been made of it before the date of application, then the mark may be registrable.[66] So for example, if a mark is not inherently distinctive (distinctive by nature), if it is used, and it can

---

[60] ibid, s 10(1).   [61] ibid, s 10(2).   [62] ibid, s 10(3).

[63] ibid, s 3(1)(b). There are many examples under this subsection most of which do not proceed beyond the Trade Marks Registry. For instance *AD 2000 Trade Mark* [1997] RPC 168 (letters and numerals AD 2000); *Dualit Ltd's Trade Mark Application* [1999] RPC 890 (3d toaster); *Jane Austen Trade Mark* [2000] RPC 879 (name Jane Austen); *Ajlan Bin Abdullaziz Al-Ajlan & Bros Co's Trade Mark Application* [2000] ETMR 710 (the fact a mark is in common usage in Saudi Arabia does not make it devoid of distinctiveness in the UK); *Froot Loops Trade Mark* [1998] RPC 240 (Froot Loops for breakfast cereal); *Eurolamb Trade Mark* [1997] RPC 279. See also the comparison with passing off in para 17.23.

[64] TMA 1994, s 3(1)(c). *Siemens AG's Application* [1999] ETMR 146.   [65] TMA 1994, s 3(1)(d).

[66] When refusing registration of a mark under Article 3(1)(b) and (c) reasons must be given for each of the individual goods and services specified in the registration, see: *BVBA Management, Training en Consultancy v Benelux-Merkenbureau* [2007] ETMR 35, para 38.

be shown through that use to have become distinctive (distinctive by nurture), then it will be capable of registration (see para 14.62ff).

14.28   These subsections have spawned a good deal of case law, some conflicting. They are central to trade mark law in that, along with the provisions on graphic representation and relative grounds for refusal, application of these sections determines what can and what cannot be registered as a mark. The provisions have been described as essential to balancing the interests as between the would-be trade mark proprietor and the competing trader. The greater variety in the types of marks that can be registered, the fewer there are in the 'public domain' for competing traders to use. This is particularly so where the mark may be one that the competitor may wish, legitimately, to use in the course of her own trade, such as a descriptive term; where it is an indication of the characteristics of the goods and services on offer; or where the mark is one which is generally used to describe the characteristics of the goods.

'Distinguish' and 'distinctive'

14.29   It will be noted that TMA 1994, section 1 refers to the capacity of the mark to *distinguish* goods or services of one undertaking from those of another. By contrast section 3(1)(b) talks of trade marks which are devoid of any *distinctive character*. In the early case law there was some discussion as to whether these were separate tests; in other words, whether there was a category of marks which could not distinguish between goods and services, but at the same time might have a distinctive character and vice versa. This has been judicially considered by the ECJ in *Koninklijke Philips Electronics NV v Remington Consumer Products Ltd*[67] where one of the questions put before that court was whether there was 'a category of marks which is not excluded from registration by Art 3(1)(b), (c) and (d) and Art 3(3) of [the Directive] which is none the less excluded from registration by Art 3(1)(a) of the Directive as being incapable of distinguishing the goods of the proprietor from those [of] other undertakings?'

The Court held that was not so, saying:

> '...there is no class of marks having a distinctive character by their nature or by the use made of them which is not capable of distinguishing goods or services within the meaning of Art.2 of the Directive.'

14.30   So if a mark is distinctive by nature or by nurture, it must be capable of distinguishing goods and services. This has been applied by the Court of Appeal in *West (t/a Eastenders) v Fuller Smith & Turner*[68] which concerned the registration of the trade mark 'E.S.B' for bitter beers in class 32. Referring to the judgment of the ECJ in *Koninklijke*, the Court of Appeal said that the effect of the judgment was that 'the second half of the definition of "trade mark" in section 1(1) of the Act (corresponding to Article 2 of the Directive) must be viewed as imposing no distinctiveness requirement separate from that imposed by Articles 3(1)(b), (c) and (d) and 3(3). Thus, there is no requirement that the mark be both "capable of distinguishing" and "not devoid of any distinctive character".'[69]

The principles underlying the absolute grounds of refusal

14.31   There has been some discussion over recent years as to the principles underpinning the provisos in TMA 1994, section 3. One the one hand is the central provision of trade mark law that

---

[67] Case C-299/99 [2003] RPC 2.   [68] [2003] EWCA Civ 48 [2003] FSR 44.
[69] Arden LJ, para 62, see also paras 34–5.

a trade mark must be capable, for the consumer, of distinguishing goods and services of one trader from those of another. On the other hand is the need of competing traders to be able to use certain signs within the market place to compete fairly and to keep signs free from ownership to enable them to do so (the principle of availability). The debate has been as to what the underlying principles or tests are, which principle or test might be relevant to which section, and whether application of the underlying principles when applying one or other of the subsections should be independent or cumulative.

14.32   The paramount consideration when applying section 3(1)(b) is the need to ensure that a trade mark functions as an indication of origin—that a mark will be capable of distinguishing the goods and services of one trader from those of another. This criterion remains important for sections 3(1)(c) and (d) but both of those subsections encompass needs of competitors also—the need to keep certain marks available for competitors whether into the future (section 3(1)(c)) or at the point of application (section 3(1)(d)).[70] The different emphasis, or weight placed on the tests will have an impact on the range of marks which are registerable. Where the emphasis is on the consumer then it is likely that a broader spectrum of marks would be registrable than if the interests of competing traders was of greater weight. A consumer may perceive a mark as indicating origin even though it would be in the interests of competing traders to have that mark freely available for all to use. Where the tests are cumulative, then the range of marks registerable is likely to be narrowest.

14.33   When the focus is on the distinguishing function, the ECJ has made it clear that the range of goods and services for which application has been made must be considered as must, importantly, the perception of the consumer: '... distinctive character must be assessed, first, by reference to the products or services in respect of which registration has been applied for and, second, by reference to the perception of the relevant public, which consists of average consumers of the products or services in question, who are reasonably well informed and reasonably observant and circumspect'.[71]

14.34   By contrast, when the issue is more closely allied to the interests of competing traders, so their interests come to the fore. In an early case *Windsurfing Chiemsee*,[72] concerning the name Chiemsee (the name of a lake in Bavaria) the Court stressed the need to keep certain signs free for competitors:

> 'Article 3(1)(c) of the Directive pursues an aim which is in the public interest, namely that descriptive signs or indications relating to the categories of goods or services in respect of which registration is applied for may be freely used by all..., Article 3(1)(c) therefore prevents such signs and indications from being reserved to one undertaking alone because they have been registered as trade marks'.[73]

[70] Bently and Sherman refer to these as the distinguishing and protective functions (L Bently & B Sherman, *Intellectual Property Law* (3rd edn, 2009) p 822).

[71] See, inter alia, joined cases Case C-53/01 *Linde AG v Deutsches Patent- und Markenamt*; Case C-55/01 *Rado Uhren AG's Trade Mark Application*; Case C-54/01 *Winward Industrie Inc's Trade Mark Application* [2003] ECR I-3161, [2005] 2 CMLR 44, [2003] ETMR 78, [2003] RPC 45, para 41; Case C-363/99 *Koninklijke KPN Nederland NV v Benelux-Merkenbureau* [2005] 3 WLR 649, [2005] All ER (EC) 19, para 34; Joined Cases C-473/01 P and C-474/01 P *Procter & Gamble v OHIM* [2004] ECR I-5173 para 33; and Case C-25/05 P *Storck v OHIM* [2006] ECR I-5719, para 25.

[72] Joined cases Case C-108/97 and Case C-109/97 *Windsurfing Chiemsee Produktions- und Vertriebs GmbH v Boots- und Segelzubehor Walter Huber; Windsurfing Chiemsee Produktions und Vertriebs GmbH v Attenberger* (hereafter *Windsurfing Chiemsee*) [2000] Ch 523, [2000] 2 WLR 205, [1999] ECR I-2779, [1999] ETMR 585. See also Case C-53/01 *Linde AG, Winward Industries and Rado Watch Co Ltd* [2003] ECR I-3161, [2005] 2 CMLR 44, [2003] ETMR 78, [2003] RPC 45.

[73] ibid, para 25.

But the Court in the context of this case—geographical names—rejected the notion that there should be any differentiation as regards the perceived importance of keeping certain names free, thus rejecting the German doctrine of Freihaltungsbedürfnis.

14.35   In *Procter & Gamble Co v OHIM*[74] the ECJ reviewed a refusal to register the words 'Baby Dry' for nappies and caused some consternation when it said, in applying Article 7(1)(c) said that 'only signs that may serve in normal usage from a customer's point of view to designate…goods or services would be excluded from registration'.[75] This would have seemed to ignore the needs of competing traders to keep certain marks free focusing instead on the perception of the consumer.[76]

14.36   Despite spawning a vast academic literature, the case should be seen as an aberration as the approach has not been repeated. For instance, in the later case of *OHIM v Wrigley*[77] concerning an appeal from OHIMs refusal to register the word Doublemint for chewing gum on the basis that it was descriptive the ECJ did not mention *Baby Dry*. On whether a sign which could be used for descriptive purposes should be excluded from registration the Court said that was the case if 'at least one of its possible meanings designates a characteristic of the goods or services concerned' and that included whether the sign was capable of being used by other traders.

14.37   There has also been case law on whether the same test should apply to each of the subsections albeit separately considered. In a case concerning the registerability of the sign 'SAT.2' for services connected with satellite broadcasting[78] the ECJ said:

> '…it is important to observe that each of the grounds for refusal to register listed in Article 7(1) of the regulation is independent of the others and requires separate examination. Moreover, it is appropriate to interpret those grounds for refusal in the light of the general interest which underlies each of them. The general interest to be taken into consideration when examining each of those grounds for refusal may or even must reflect different considerations according to the ground for refusal in question'.[79]

The criterion relating to marks capable of being available for competitors was relevant in the context of CTMR, Article 7(1)(c) but not for Article 7(1)(b).[80]

14.38   This suggests that it is the distinguishing function that is paramount in relation to TMA 1994, section 3(1)(b), and the protective function that takes precedence in relation to TMA 1994, section 3(1)(c) and (d) and that each of the tests should be considered and applied separately. But other case law suggests that the application of the tests is much more nuanced and both tests may be reflected in consideration of each subsection albeit subject to different priority and weight in application. *Windsurfing Chiemsee* for example, considered above,[81] first considered the need to keep signs available for competing traders in the context of Article 7(1)(c) but then also considered the need to show that the mark does in fact do its job as a mark remains important, the question asked being whether there was an 'an association in the mind of the relevant class of persons between the geographic name and the category of goods in question'.[82] In other words, would the consumer see the mark as an indication of origin?

[74]   *Procter & Gamble Co v OHIM (Baby Dry)* Case C-383/99 [2001] ECR 1–6251, [2002] ETMR (3)(22).
[75]   ibid, para 39.   [76]   J Davis, 'European Trade Mark Law and the Enclosure of the Commons' [2002] IPQ 342.
[77]   *OHIM v Wrigley (Doublemint)* Case C-191/01 [2004] ETMR 88.
[78]   Case C-329/02 *SAT.1 Satellitenfernsehen GmbH v OHIM* [2005] 1 CMLR 57 [2005] ETMR 20 (hereafter *SAT.1*).
[79]   *SAT.1*, para 25. See Case C-456/01 P *Henkel KGaA v OHIM* [2004] ECR I-5089, [2005] ETMR 44, paras 45 and 46. Joined Cases C-456/01 P and C-457/01 P *Henkel v OHIM* [2004] ECR I-5089, para 45; Case C-64/02 P *OHIM v Erpo Möbelwerk* [2004] ECR I-10031, para 39; and Case C-173/04 P *Deutsche SiSi-Werke v OHIM* [2006] ECR I-551, para 59.
[80]   *SAT.1*, para 36. See also Case C-37/03 *BioID AG v OHIM* [2002] ECR II-5159, [2003] ETMR 60, paras 59–62.
[81]   *Windsurfing Chiemesee*.   [82]   *Windsurfing Chimesee*, para 37.

14.39 On the third issue, whether the subsections should be independent or interdependent, the ECJ has, as indicated above, stressed that each of the grounds for refusal to register listed in Article 7(1) is *independent* of the others and requires separate examination.[83] It has been argued that to read these subsections disjunctively may have superficial attraction in that it would appear to be logical in application. A first step would be to consider whether the sign is distinctive and functions as a badge of origin relying on the perception of the consumer. A second stage would then to be to consider whether the sign should be left free for use by other traders. However, the approach has been criticised.[84] A mark which may not describe the characteristics of goods and services and thus be acceptable under (c) may *not* indicate trade origin and thus fall under (b). But if a mark falls under (c) and describes the characteristics of the goods and services, it seems hard to imagine that it might be considered by the consumer to indicate trade origin. For these reasons it has been suggested that paragraphs (b), (c) and (d) should be considered as interdependent rather than independent and that the same tests of indicating origin and the need to leave marks free for other traders should be considered in relation to all three.[85]

Policy considerations

14.40 Much of this discussion which has arisen since the introduction of the Directive and the CTMR does so because of the wide variety of signs that may now be registered. There are only limited stocks of colours and shapes, around which much of this discussion has centred. In *Libertel*,[86] discussed above at para 14.13 the ECJ said of the application to register a colour:

> '[T]he fact that the number of colours actually available is limited means that a small number of trade mark registrations for certain services or goods could exhaust the entire range of colours available. Such a monopoly would be incompatible with a system of undistorted competition, in particular because it could have the effect of creating an unjustified competitive advantage for a single trader'.[87]

Given the breadth of the provisions on infringement (discussed in paras 15.21–15.103) if a trader was to secure a registration for a commonly used shape or colour, so other traders might have to rely on defences to infringement if a confusingly similar colour or shape were used in trade. Questions of monopolisation apart, the discussion also reflects the continuing uncertainty as to where the respective interests of the consumer, the trade mark owner and of competitors should be taken into account in the trade mark framework.

 Exercise

Read M Handler, 'The Distinctive Problem of European Trade Mark Law' (2005) 27(9) EIPR 306–12; Case C-329/02 P *SAT.1 Satellitenfernsehen GmbH v OHIM* [2005] 1 CMLR 57, [2005] ETMR 20; and Case C-109/97 *Windsurfing Chiemsee*.

What test(s) do you think should underpin the application of TMA 1994, sections 3(1)(b), (c) and (d) and why? In assessing whether certain marks should be left free for competing traders, are public interest considerations a part of this test, or a separate test?

---

[83] *Eurohypo AG v OHIM* [2008] ETMR 59, at para 60. In this case the court considered a mark composed of descriptive elements 'could meet the conditions for registration where the word has become a part of everyday language and has acquired a meaning of its own. But, while that criterion is relevant in the context of Article 7(1)(c) it cannot form a basis for the interpretation of Article 7(1)(b)', para 61.

[84] M Handler, 'The Distinctive Problem of European Trade Mark Law' [2005] EIPR 27(9), 306–12 at 309. See also CFI, Case T-230/05 *Golf USA, Inc v OHIM*, para 45.   [85] ibid. See Case T-230/05 *Golf USA Inc v OHIM*, para 45.

[86] Case C-104/01 *Libertel Groep BV v Benelux-Merkenbureau* [2003] ETMR 63.   [87] ibid, para 54.

> ## Key points on the test underlying the absolute grounds of refusal
>
> - Two policy considerations underpin the absolute grounds of refusal: that of ensuring that a mark can do its job of distinguishing goods and services of one trader from those of another; and the need to keep marks free for competing traders.
> - Jurisprudence from the Court of Justice in particular suggests that the subsections must be read independently and that the tests must be considered separately but both may apply to a single case.

Types of marks

14.41   Subject to the discussion above, some general comments can be made concerning the application of the absolute grounds for refusing to register a trade mark.

14.42   The reason for the exclusion of non-distinctive marks from registration under TMA 1994, section 3(1)(b) is because these marks are not seen as indications of origin.[88] In determining distinctiveness the overall impression given by the mark must be considered[89] first by reference to the goods and services and secondly the perception of the relevant consumers of the goods or services in question who are reasonably well informed and reasonably observant and circumspect.[90] In addition the criteria are the same for all categories of marks. Thus it is not permissible to have more stringent criteria in considering the distinctiveness of, for example, surnames (such as a search for the number of instances in which it appears in telephone books) than for any other category of mark.[91] However, and as will be seen in the discussion below, these rules have not been easy to apply at times particularly when considering three dimensional marks. It would appear that the perception of the ordinary consumer may differ when looking at these types of marks by comparison with words or figurative devices.

14.43   The reason for the exclusion of descriptive marks from registration is because these are the types of marks that another trader would normally wish to use in the course of trade. Thus under TMA 1994, section 3(1)(c) the trader needs to show that the sign is not, or may not be used by other traders as a description of the goods or services. Such use of a sign is likely to give an unfair competitive advantage to the trader who first registered the descriptive indication as a mark. The mark need not be in current use by other traders, but it will be unregistrable if it might be so used.[92] Further, a mark should be refused registration under this head even if there are more usual ways of designating the same characteristics in the trade.[93]

14.44   The reason for the exclusion of customary signs from registration under TMA 1994, section 3(1)(d) is that while such signs may have at one time been capable of distinguishing the goods and services of one trader from those of another, they have been used in such a way, either in the normal language, or in the trade, to mean those goods and services. They have thus become generic, can no longer perform a distinguishing function and are excluded from

---

[88] Joined Cases C-53/01, C-54/01, C-55/01 *Linde AG, Winward Industries, Rado Watch Co Ltd* [2003] RPC 45.
[89] See in relation to a word mark, Case C-104/00 *DKV v OHIM* [2002] ECR I-7561, para 24, and, in relation to a three-dimensional mark Joined Cases Cases C-468/01 to C-472/01 *Procter & Gamble v OHIM* [2004] ECR I-5141; Case C-136/02 *Mag Instrument Inc v OHIM* [2004] ECR I-9165, [2005] ETMR 46.
[90] Joined Cases C-456/01 and C-457/01 *Henkel v OHIM* [2004] ECR I-5089, para 35, and Case C-173/04 *Deutsche SiSi-Werke v OHIM* [2006] ECR I-551 (hereafter *SiSi-Werke*), para 25.
[91] Case C-404/02 *Nichols Plc v Registrar of Trade Marks* [2005] 1 WLR 1418, [2005] All ER (EC) 1.
[92] Case C-191/01 *Windsurfing Chiemsee* and *Wrigley v OHIM*, para 32.
[93] Case C-363/99 *Koninklijke KPN Nederland NV v Benelux-Merkenbureau* [2005] 3 WLR 649, [2005] All ER (EC) 19.

registration.[94] *In Merz & Krell GmbH*[95] it was stressed that it was immaterial whether the sign, the subject of the application, described the properties or characteristics of the goods or services. What was important was whether the mark had become customary in the language or in the trade to designate the goods or services in respect of which registration was sought.[96] While these types of marks will be unregistrable per se, care must also be taken that a mark once registered does not become generic lest it is revoked (see below para 14.107).

3d marks

14.45   Two points may be made in relation to three-dimensional marks. The first is that such marks tend to be considered as devoid of distinctiveness, and the second, related point is the importance of the perception of the average consumer.

Devoid of distinctiveness

14.46   While the ECJ emphasised, in joined cases *Henkel KGaA v OHIM*[97] that, in principle, 3d or shape marks are registrable[98] provided they are capable of being represented graphically, and of distinguishing the products or services of one undertaking from those of other undertakings,[99] a key question is as to how far the mark must be removed from the shape normally used in the trade. Often, and while registrable in principle, many three-dimensional shape signs prove to be unregistrable because, without having been used and the public having been educated that the mark is an indication of origin, they fall under the devoid of distinctiveness objection in TMA 1994, section 3(1)(b). In *Henkel*, the application was for the registration of the 3d shape of a tablet for washing machines in combination with an arrangement of colours. In these circumstances—where the shape for which registration is sought resembles the shape of the product in question—then it is likely to be considered devoid of distinctive character. 'Only a trade mark which departs significantly from the norm or customs of the sector and thereby fulfils its essential function of indicating origin, is not devoid of any distinctive character...' for the purposes of that provision.[100]

14.47   So there has to be some difference which departs significantly from the norm between the shape of the goods and the shape which is the subject of the application. Under this test, registration of the shape of a dishwasher tablet would not be permissible. However, that may not prevent the shape of a dishwasher tablet being registrable for completely different and unconnected goods and services. Nor indeed a shape which resembles but 'departs significantly' from the shape of a dishwasher tablet from being registrable for dishwasher tablets.

 Question

Why would a manufacturer of dishwasher tablets want to register the shape of a dishwasher tablets for marketing dishwasher tablets? What monopoly is the dishwasher tablet manufacturer hoping to obtain? Can you think of a shape which 'departs significantly' from the shape of a dishwasher tablet that a manufacturer of dishwasher tablets might want to register in connection with dishwasher tablets?

---

[94] Eg an image of a rose in connection with clothing by the Rugby Football Union: *RFU and Nike v Cotton Traders* [2002] ETMR (76) 861.

[95] Case C-517/99 [2001] ECR I-6959, [2002] ETMR (21) 231.   [96] ibid, para 41.

[97] Case C-456/01 *Henkel KGaA v OHIM* [2004] ECR I-5089, [2005] ETMR 44 (hereafter *Henkel*).

[98] ibid, para 31.   [99] ibid, para 30.   [100] ibid, para 39.

■ Case C-136/02 *Mag Instrument v OHIM* [2005] ETMR 46 ECJ (hereafter *Mag Instrument*)

This case concerned a refusal to register the shape of a torch as a trade mark. The Court emphasised that the overall impression of the mark must be considered and that the criteria for assessing distinctiveness of three-dimensional marks are no different from those applicable to other categories. However, the more closely the shape for which registration is sought resembles the shape of the product in question, the greater the likelihood of the shape being devoid of any distinctive character.[101] Only marks which depart 'significantly from the norm or customs of the sector and thereby fulfils its essential function of indicating origin, is not devoid of any distinctive character for the purposes of that provision'.[102]

14.48   A slightly different form of words was used in *August Storck KG v OHIM*[103] where the ECJ upheld the finding of the CFI that the application to register the shape of a sweet in class 30 for confectionary was unregistrable.

> 'The shape consists of a combination of presentational features which come naturally to mind and which are typical of the goods in question...the alleged differences are not readily perceptible, it follows that the shape in question cannot be sufficiently distinguished from other shapes commonly used for sweets and that it does not enable the relevant public to distinguish immediately and with certainty the appellant's sweets from those of another commercial origin'.[104]

14.49   So a second point here is that there must be differences between the way the mark would normally be used and the combination of elements which must be 'readily perceptible' from those used typically by other traders of the goods in question. This is to enable the consumer to distinguish immediately the mark from other goods in the marketplace. Many applications for 3d marks have been refused because of this difficulty of showing that such marks are distinctive. Where, however, there are other distinctive features included with the shape, this may be sufficient to confer distinctive capacity on the sign. In an unusual case, *Bang & Olufsen A/S v OHIM*, a picture of loud speakers was registerable as a CTM, because it departed significantly from the customs of the sector. The shape had a particular appearance which, having regard also to the aesthetic result of the whole, was such that it would retain the attention of the public concerned and enable it to distinguish the goods covered by the trade mark application from those of other commercial origins.[105] See Figure 14.7.

The average consumer

14.50   As was pointed out above (para 14.42), the ECJ has said that the criteria for distinctiveness is the same for all marks. However, and in relation to 3d marks the Court has stressed that as the average consumer is not in the habit of making assumptions about the origin of products on the basis of their shape or the shape of their packaging, in the absence of any graphic or word element it may prove difficult to establish distinctiveness.[106]

---

[101] *Mag Instrument*, para 31.
[102] ibid, para 31. Joined Cases T241/05, T262/05 to T264/05, T346/05, T347/05, T29/06 to T31/06 *The Procter & Gamble Company v OHIM* [2007] ECR II-01549, at para 44.
[103] Case C-25/05.   [104] ibid, para 29.
[105] *Bang & Olufsen A/S v OHIM* [2008] ETMR 46, at para 42.
[106] *Henkel*, para 38; *Mag Instrument*, para 30; and *SiSi-Werke*, para 28. *Develey Holding GmbH & Co Beteiligungs KG v OHIM* [2008] ETMR 20, at para 80.

Figure 14.7 Bang & Olufsen loud speaker

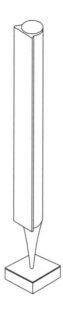

■ Case C-173/04 *Deutsche SiSi-Werke v OHIM*

In an appeal against a refusal to register 3d marks for packaging for drinks the ECJ considered that the CFI had not erred in law by holding, 'that the average consumer will see the form of drinks packaging as an indication of the product's commercial origin only if that form may be perceived immediately as such an indication'.[107] The packaging was unregistrable as a mark. (If you go to the CTM register and search by proprietor (Deutsche SiSi-Werke) you will see the applications that have been refused.)

Names

14.51   Personal names are regularly used by traders in the course of trade. For example, 'Cathy Philip' for a florist; 'Sutherland's' for a hairdresser; 'Emmanuel' for a clothes designer. There is however a problem in showing that a name, particularly in the absence of use, is distinctive and thus registrable. In *Nichols Plc v Registrar of Trade Marks*[108] concerning an appeal against a refusal to register the name Nichols for, inter alia, food and drink of the type normally sold through vending machines, the Court stressed that the distinctive character of a mark must be assessed in relation to the goods or services in respect of which registration is applied for and in relation to the perception of the relevant consumers,[109] and that no distinction is to be drawn between assessing distinctiveness of names and other categories of marks. Thus the practice of looking at telephone directories to determine how common a surname is, or of assessing how commonly surnames were used in the trade (a practice used by the UK Registry and Courts) could not be applied in assessing the distinctiveness of name marks. Neither could an application to register a name be refused because registration might give to the first comer a competitive advantage

---

[107] *SiSi-Werke*, para 30.   [108] Case C-404/02 [2005] 1 WLR 1418, [2005] All ER (EC) 1.
[109] Citing Case C-299/99 *Philips* [2002] ECR I-5475, paras 59 and 63, and *Henkel*, para 50.

since there is no provision to that effect in the Directive.[110] However, and as with 3d marks, the ECJ stressed that assessing distinctiveness for names might be more problematic than for other marks because the perception of the public differs as between categories of marks. For further discussion on the registration of names in the context of personality merchandising see paras 16.9–16.18.

Combinations of words

14.52   Much case law has revolved around the question as to whether and in what circumstances combinations of words can be registered where one or both words on their own might be taken to mean the kind, quality, quantity or intended purpose of the goods or services: in other words, a refusal would relate to TMA 1994, section 3(1)(c). In *Baby Dry*[111] discussed above (para 14.35), the ECJ said that the exclusion in (c) only related to marks serving in normal usage to describe the produce or its characteristics. How different a mark must be between the application and the use of the mark in the trade has been the subject of some debate. In *Baby Dry* the Court said that 'any perceptible difference between the combination of words submitted for registration and the terms used in common parlance of the relevant class of consumers to designate the goods or services or their essential characteristic is apt to confer distinctive character on the word combination enabling it to be registered as a trade mark'.[112] The Court said that the ground for refusal must be read in the light of the defences in Article 12 and of the definition of a trade mark. In other words, another trader wanting to use the words would need to look at the defences to an action of trade mark infringement if they used the mark, in trade, to describe their own goods or services.

14.53   There was some disquiet after this decision was handed down. Not only was it thought inappropriate that other traders would need to look to defences should they wish to use these marks descriptively, notably considering the disparity that often exists as between the resources of traders in the marketplace, but in addition it was considered that the Court had failed to appreciate the strength of the monopoly the first-comer would obtain over descriptive marks. Indeed it has been stressed that to prevent trade marks from being improperly registered, the grounds for refusal of registration should be applied independently of the defences that might be available to traders accused of infringement.[113]

14.54   However, and not long after this decision, the ECJ started to place parameters around what would be acceptable in relation to descriptive marks and what would not. In *Wrigley v OHIM*[114] discussed above at para 14.36 the ECJ said that a sign should be refused registration 'if at least one of its possible meanings designates a characteristic of the goods or services concerned.' This was so either at the time of application or could, at some later time be so used.[115]

---

[110]   Case C-404/02 *Nichols Plc v Registrar of Trade Marks* [2005] 1 WLR 1418, [2005] All ER (EC) 1, para 31.
[111]   Case C-383/99 *Procter & Gamble Co v OHIM* [2002] Ch 82, [2002] 2 WLR 485, [2002] All ER (EC) 29, [2001] ECR I-6251 (hereafter *Baby Dry*).
[112]   *Baby Dry*, para 40.
[113]   *Nichols Plc v Registrar of Trade Marks* Case C-404/02 [2005] 1 WLR 1418, [2005] All ER (EC) 1, paras 31–3.
[114]   Case C-191/01 [2004] 1 WLR 1728, [2004] All ER (EC) 1040, [2003] ECR I-12447, [2005] 3 CMLR 21, [2004] ETMR 9 (hereafter *Wrigley*).
[115]   *Wrigley*, para 32.

In attempting to draw a distinction between indications which designate a characteristic of the goods or services, and those which merely allude suggestively to those elements, AG Jacobs suggested three guidelines in *Wrigley v OHIM*:[116]

- The more factual and objective the relationship between the term and the product or one of its characteristics, the more likely it is that the term may be used as a designation in trade, so that registration will be precluded by Article 7(1)(c); conversely, the more imaginative and subjective the relationship the more acceptable the term will be for registration.

- The more ordinary, definite and down-to-earth a term is, the more readily a consumer will apprehend any designation of a characteristic and the more likely the term will be not to qualify for registration as a trade mark.

- Where the characteristic designated is essential or of particular importance to the product or choice of the consumer then the case for refusing registration is compelling; where the designation is of a characteristic that is purely incidental or arbitrary, the case is considerably weaker.[117]

In applying his criteria to the word Doublemint for chewing gum, the AG found that the word was 'a factual, objective reference to mint flavour in some way doubled'; that it was readily perceivable as such, and that such flavour is an important feature of the product: 'the term designates a characteristic of doubled mintiness'. The AG thus considered the mark to be unregistrable. While the ECJ did not make mention of the guidelines proposed by the AG, as indicated above that Court confirmed the AGs view that the mark was unregistrable.

14.55   Where a neologism is created, that may not necessarily be registrable if it does not differ from the sum of its parts.

■ Case C-265/00 *Campina Melkunie BV v Benelux-Merkenbureau* [2004] ECR I-1699; [2005] 2 CMLR 9

This case concerned an application to register the word Biomild for various foodstuffs, including milk products. The word 'Mild' means mild in the Netherlands where the applicant sought to market inter alia, a mild-flavoured yoghurt under the mark. In giving judgment the ECJ first reiterated the general rule that 'the mere combination of elements, each of which is descriptive of characteristics of the goods or services in respect of which registration is sought, itself remains descriptive of those characteristics within the meaning of Article 3(1)(c) of the Directive even if the combination creates a neologism'. However, if there was a perceptible difference between the neologism and the sum of its parts—enough to create an impression 'which is sufficiently far removed from that produced by the mere combination of meanings lent by the elements of which it is composed' then the mark may be registrable.[118] The criterion of 'sufficiently far removed' is not secondary to that of 'perceptible difference' but rather 'the existence of…a difference assumes that the combination resulting from the bringing together of the two word elements is sufficiently far removed from that produced by the simple juxtaposition of those elements'.[119] It would thus appear that, unlike the interpretation given to 'perceptible' in *Baby Dry*, the term 'perceptible' means 'appreciable' or 'definite'.

---

[116] Case C-191/01 [2003] ECR I-12447, [2003] ETMR 88.   [117] ibid, paras 63–4.
[118] Case C-265/00 *Campina Melkunie BV v Benelux-Merkenbureau* [2004] ECR I-1699, [2005] 2 CMLR 9, para 43.
[119] Case T-346/07 *Duro Sweden AB v OHIM*, para 43. See also Case C-80/09 *Volker Megel v OHIM*.

14.56   It is possible that a mark which is descriptive of some goods or services and thus unregistrable would be registrable in connection with other goods or services because for those it would be distinctive.[120] Thus it would not be possible to register 'giraffe' for toy giraffes, but 'Apple' for computers would be registrable.

14.57   The ECJ has also emphasised that in considering complex marks which may be made up of descriptive parts, it is essential to look at the mark as a whole and assess distinctiveness accordingly. Thus, in the appeal against the CFI's upholding of a refusal to register 'SAT.2' for satellite services on the grounds that each element was descriptive (para 14.37) the Court said:

> '...as regards a trade mark comprising words or a word and a digit, such as that which forms the subject-matter of the dispute, the distinctiveness of each of those terms or elements, taken separately, may be assessed, in part, but must, in any event, depend on an appraisal of the whole which they comprise. Indeed, the mere fact that each of those elements, considered separately, is devoid of distinctive character does not mean that their combination cannot present a distinctive character'.[121]

The Court had criticised the approach of the CFI which had been to look at each of the individual elements and when it had been determined neither were distinctive, the CFI considered the whole was not distinctive.[122] This was further considered in *OHIM v Celltech*, in which the Court confirmed that when a mark consists of a combination of elements, the mark can only be descriptive if the word combination itself is descriptive. It is not enough that each component is descriptive as where the combination creates an impression 'which is sufficiently far removed from that produced by the simple combination of those elements', such a combination may not be descriptive. It is therefore essential to look not only at the individual elements, but at the mark as a whole. The analysis of each of the elements of a mark is therefore not an essential step in this process, descriptiveness of the mark as a whole is what should be considered.[123]

Question

Given the above discussion, do you think the word 'BioID' would be registrable in classes 9, 38 and 42 of the Nice Agreement in connection with, inter alia, computer software including on the Internet and telecommunications? If so, why? If not, why not?[124]

---

[120] Case C-363/99 *Koninklijke KPN Nederland NV v Benelux-Merkenbureau* [2005] 3 WLR 649, [2005] All ER (EC) 19 EU.

[121] *SAT.1*, para 28. The Court also referred to *Campina Melkunie BV v Benelux-Merkenbureau* Case C-265/00 [2005] 2 CMLR 9, paras 40 and 41; and Case C-363/99 *Koninklijke Kpn Nederland NV v Benelux Merkenbureau* [2005] 3 WLR 649 paras 99 and 100. See also *OHIM v Celltech* [2007] ETMR 52, paras 76–80.

[122] The ECJ also said in this case that 'the frequent use of trade marks consisting of a word and a number in the telecommunications sector indicates that type of combination cannot be considered to be devoid, in principle, of distinctive character' (para 44). This has been criticised. See, eg, A Folliard-Monguiral and D Rogers, 'Significant Case Law from 2004 on the Community Trade Mark from the Court of First Instance, the European Court of Justice and OHIM' [2005] EIPR 133 at 135. Those authors point to subsequent case law of the ECJ in which that Court stresses the more closely the mark or the shape for which registration is sought resembles that most likely to be used in the trade, the greater the likelihood of the shape being devoid of distinctive character. And, 'Only a mark which departs significantly from the norm or customs of the sector and thereby fulfils its essential function of indicating origin, is not devoid of any distinctive character...' (Case C-468/01 *Procter & Gamble Co v OHIM* [2004] ECR I-5141, [2004] ETMR 88). The authors suggest that on this point, *SAT.1* should perhaps be seen as a 'one-off' case.

[123] *OHIM v Celltech* [2007] ETMR 52, paras 76–80. See also, inter alia, Case C-265/00 *Campina Melkunie* [2004] ECR I-1699; Case C-363/99 *Koninklijke KPN Nederland* [2004] ECR I-1619; Case C-329/02 P *SAT.1 v OHIM* [2004] ECR I-8317; C-37/03 P *BioID AG v OHIM* [2005] ECR I-7975. Case C-342/09 *Victor Guedes Industria e Comercia SA v OHIM*.

[124] Case T-91/01 *BioID AG v OHIM* [2002] ECR II-5159, [2003] ETM 60 to find the answer!

Geographical names

14.58   In *Windsurfing Chiemsee* (above, para 14.34) the ECJ made various comments in relation to the registerability of geographical indications as trade marks under Article 7(1)(c) of the CTMR. The purpose of the exclusion is that such signs should remain available not only because they may be an indication of the quality and other characteristics of the categories of goods, but in addition they may influence consumer taste because they give rise to a favourable response.[125] Registration will be refused where the name designates a specific geographical location which is already famous, or known and associated by consumers for the category of goods concerned, and where the geographical name is liable to be used by others as an indication of the geographical origin of the goods by others.[126] However, registration of a geographical name is not precluded where it is unknown to the relevant consumers as the designation of geographical origin or where, because of the place designated by the name, consumers are unlikely to believe that the category of goods concerned originates there or was conceived of there.[127] Descriptiveness of the geographical name is to be assessed by reference to the goods or services as well as by reference to the understanding which the relevant persons have of it.[128] In applying these rules the CFI found that the name 'Cloppenburg' (the name of a town in Lower Saxony in Germany) in connection with retail services falling within class 35 of the Nice Agreement to be registrable.[129]

Foreign word marks

14.59   An interesting issue arose in *Matratzen Concord AG v Hukla Germany SA*,[130] concerning the trade mark Matrazen, registered in Spain by Hukla Germany in class 20 of the Nice Agreement in respect of inter alia, furniture such as beds, sofa-beds, camp beds and cradles. Matratzen means mattress in German. Matratzen Concord AG, another German company, sought to have the registration revoked on the grounds that it was descriptive of the nature, quality, characteristics or geographic origin of the products or services that it purports to distinguish. The question referred to the ECJ was whether registration of a term borrowed from the language of another member state in which it is devoid of distinctive character or descriptive of the goods or services in respect of which registration is sought, must be refused in the member state of application. The ECJ said that this was not so and pointed out that because of linguistic, cultural, social and economic differences between the member states, a trade mark which is devoid of distinctive character or descriptive of the goods or services concerned in one member state may not be so in another member state.

> 'Consequently, Article 3(1)(b) and (c) of the Directive does not preclude the registration in a Member State, as a national trade mark, of a term borrowed from the language of another Member State in which it is devoid of distinctive character or descriptive of the goods or services in respect of which registration is sought'.[131]

The determining factor for registerability would be how the term would be understood by the relevant parties in the state where registration was sought. The relevant parties are the traders in, or average consumers of, the specified products.

---

[125] By analogy, *Windsurfing Chiemsee*, para 26 and *Peek & Cloppenburg KG, v OHIM* [2006] ETMR 33, para 33.
[126] By analogy, *Windsurfing Chiemsee*, paras 29 and 30.   [127] ibid, para 33.
[128] Case T-295/01 *Nordmilch v OHIM* (Oldenburger) [2003] ECR II-4365, paras 27–34). *Peek & Cloppenburg KG v OHIM* [2006] ETMR 33, para 37.
[129] *Peek & Cloppenburg KG v OHIM* [2006] ETMR 33.   [130] Case C-421/04 [2006] ETMR 48.   [131] ibid, para 26.

14.60   Although it is clear that foreign word marks, generic in their own country, can be registered as trade marks in another state, this proviso that the term must be distinctive among the relevant class of traders and consumers is perhaps likely to reduce the number of such applications destined to be successful. As goods move throughout the EU it may be likely that traders within the relevant trade are aware of the descriptions of goods in other countries, as may the well-travelled consumer.

Key points on the types of marks that can be registered

- Non-distinctive, descriptive and customary marks are all excluded from registration unless they have become distinctive through use

- The exclusions reflect the function of a trade mark as an indication of origin and provide a balance as between the interests of the would-be trade mark owner and competitors in the field

- The same factors are to be used in assessing the registerability of all types of marks

- For some marks (such as 3d marks) assessing distinctiveness may be more difficult given the perception of the public differs as between categories of marks

---

Quiz

14.61   As can be seen the jurisprudence in relation to those aspects of registerability discussed above has been developing rapidly in recent years. The above discussion has concentrated on the Court of Justice of the European Union cases. Beyond this there are a plethora of decisions and appeals from decisions made at national and European level as to the registerability or otherwise of signs as trade marks and which base themselves on the criteria laid down by the Court.

Weblinks

Cases determining the registerability of marks can be researched in a number of ways. Go to the Court of Justice website at http://www.curia.europa.eu and put intellectual property in the 'field'. This will bring up a number of hits where decisions relating to trade marks have been made at European level. Not all of these cases concern trade marks, and not all of those that do deal with registerability. But many do and this is a useful way to find them.

You can also look at the OHIM website at http://www.oami.europa.eu under case law of the Court of Justice of the European Union and of the General Court.

As was mentioned above the OHIM website contains a database showing all the marks which have been registered. In addition you will find on the site a database of marks which have been refused registration and the reasons for refusal (look under legal aspects on the site). If you are unsure of the contents of the particular classes of the Nice classification you can find a copy of the Treaty on the WIPO website at http://www.wipo.int/classifications/nice/en/classifications.html

Exercise

It is now your task to investigate the decisions and cases both at EU level (OHIM and General Court) and national level (Trade Marks Registry and courts) to ascertain how this jurisprudence of the Court of Justice is applied.

Do you think the following signs would be registrable? If so why? If not, why not? Note: there are plenty of clues in the footnotes as to the correct answers—test yourself before you look at these, and don't forget to supply reasons!

- Slogan mark

  'There is a difference':
  Nice classification 23.[132]

- Word mark

  'Everything is Possible'.
  Nice Classification 2, 9, 16, 35, 36, 37, 38 and 42.[133]

- Colour mark

  Where a representation of the colours and their juxtaposition is included in the application along with the description: Dark brown (Pantone 411 CVC); light brown (30% Pantone 411 CVC); dark green (Pantone 611); light green (40% Pantone 611 CVC); dark blue (Pantone 291 C); light blue (45% Pantone 291 CVC).
  Nice classification 18.[134]

- Word mark

  'DataCenterAlliance'
  Nice Classification 9, 11 and 40.[135]

- Sound mark (Figure 14.8 below)

  Nice classification 9, 38, 41, 42.[136]

Figure 14.8 Sound waves

- Olfactory mark

  The trade mark is a graphic representation of a particular fragrance. A lawn green note, citrus (bergamot, lemon), pink floral (orange blossom, hyacinth), musky in all shades of green and blue. Note: the graphic representation (a selection of colours) was included in the application.

[132] App No 002694123 (n). [133] App No 003514569 (n). [134] CTM 003678794 (y).
[135] App No 003892262 (n). [136] App No 000143891 (n).

> Nice classification 3, 5, 16, 18, 24.[137]
>
> • Word mark
>
> 'Drinkfresh'
> Nice classification 29 and 30.[138]

Distinctive through use

14.62   As was indicated above, TMA 1994, section 3(1) provides that each of these absolute grounds of refusal (except where a sign does not satisfy the requirement of TMA 1994, section 1) yields to the proviso that if a sign which is unregistrable becomes distinctive through use before the application is filed,[139] then it may be registered as a mark, Evidence of the mark becoming distinctive through use after the application is irrelevant as only the period before application is taken into account.[140] It should be noted that this is not an independent right to have a trade mark registered. Rather it is an exception to the grounds for refusal listed in section 3(1)(b)–(d). The scope is therefore to be interpreted in light of those grounds for refusal.[141]

14.63   Useful guidance on what evidence is required to show that a mark has become distinctive through use was given by the ECJ in joined cases *Windsurfing Chiemsee Produktions- und Vertriebs GmbH (WSC) v Boots- und Segelzubehör Walter Huber and Franz Attenberger.*[142] The court said that the following factors could be taken into account:

- the market share held by the mark;

- how intensive, geographically widespread and long-standing use of the mark has been;

- the amount invested by the undertaking in promoting the mark;

- the proportion of the relevant class of persons who, because of the mark, identify goods as originating from a particular undertaking;

- statements from chambers of commerce and industry or other trade and professional associations.[143]

The important factor is whether the 'relevant class of persons, or at least a significant proportion thereof, identify goods as originating from a particular undertaking because of the trade mark'.[144] The relevant class of persons can be made up of both professionals and the general public depending on the circumstance of the case.[145] In relation to geographical marks the ECJ has emphasised that such a mark can become distinctive through use where there has been 'long-standing and intensive use of the mark' and that the use of the mark 'is particularly well established'.[146]

---

[137] App No 000521914 (n).   [138] App No 003378692 (n).

[139] Case T-247/01 *eCopy Inc v OHIM* [2003] ETMR 99.

[140] *Imagination Technologies Ltd v OHIM* [2008] ETMR 10, para 77–79.

[141] *Bovemij Verzekeringen NV v Benelux-Merkenbureau* [2007] ETMR 29, para 21.

[142] Joined Cases C-108/97 and C-109/97.

[143] *Windsurfing Chiemsee*, para 51. See also Case C-299/99 *Koninklijke Philips Electronics NV v Remington Consumer Products Ltd* [2002] ECR I-5475, [2003] Ch 159 (hereafter *Philips*), para 60; Case C-353/03 *Société des Produits Nestlé SA v Mars UK Ltd* [2005] 3 CMLR 12, [2005] ETMR 96, [2006] FSR 2, para 31; Case C-25/05 *August Storck v OHIM*.

[144] *Windsurfing Chiemsee*, para 52.   [145] *AGC Flat Glass Europe SA formerly Glaverbel SA v OHIM* [2008] ETMR 37.

[146] ibid, para 50. See also the application in *Bovemij Verzekeringen NV v Benelux-Mekenbureau* (Benelux Trademarks Office) [2007] ETMR 29 for questions referred to the ECJ concerning geographic extent and language and para 14.65.

Geographical extent

14.64   A question arises as to the geographical extent of the territory in which a mark may become registrable through use. For a CTM it has been said that it is necessary to show that a mark has acquired distinctiveness in all of those countries of the Community (now Union) where it would be regarded as non-distinctive. Thus in *Ford Motor's Application*[147] the question arose over the registration of the word Options for insurance services. It was shown that the word had acquired distinctiveness in the UK but not in France. The CFI upheld the objection to registration on the grounds that a sign must possess distinctive character throughout the Community (now Union). The CFI pointed out that the CTMR (Article 1(2)) provides that the Community trade mark is to have 'a unitary character', which implies that '[i]t shall have equal effect throughout the Community'.[148] The conclusion was reinforced by CTMR Article 7(2) which provides that a trade mark is not to be registered 'notwithstanding that the grounds of non-registrability [laid down in Article 7(1)] obtain in only part of the Community'.[149] In *Glaverbel v OHIM*[150] concerning an application to register a piece of glass to which a design had been applied, the CFI said it was not enough that evidence was led in relation to 10 of the 15 member states. It had to be shown that the mark was considered distinctive through use in each territory. This is clearly a high (and expensive) hurdle for those seeking to prove distinctiveness through use for the purposes of registration of a CTM.

14.65   The geographical extent of acquired distinctiveness differs for a national trade mark and was considered in *Bovemij Verzekeringen NV v Benelux-Merkenbureau*.[151] The question was whether the sign 'Europolis' had acquired a distinctive character in the Benelux territory. The first two questions referred to the ECJ essentially asked which territory should be taken into account in order to assess whether a sign had acquired a distinctive character through use where a member state or group of member states (such as Benelux) have common legislation on trade marks. The Court stressed that registration of a trade mark could only be allowed if it was proven that the trade mark had acquired distinctive character through use throughout the territory of the member state or, in the case of Benelux, throughout the part of the territory of Benelux in which there exists a ground for refusal.[152] The third question the Court was asked was to what extent the linguistic areas in a member state should be taken into account in assessing the acquisition of a distinctive character through use where the trade mark consisted of one or more words in the official language of a member state or of Benelux. In the instant case the Dutch word 'polis' usually refers to an insurance contract and so the grounds for refusal existed only in that part of Benelux where Dutch is spoken. The Court ruled that it was necessary to take into account that part of Benelux where Dutch is spoken.[153]

14.66   Care must be taken in establishing that a mark which has become distinctive through use that it has not become customary. Thus in *Alcon Inc v OHIM*[154] the question concerned the mark 'BSS' which had been used but was found to have become customary for the target public concerned and hence the use made of the mark had not been able to confer distinctive character on it.[155] Relatedly, where a sign has been used for a particular purpose prior to it being used in a trade mark manner, that use may prevent the mark from being capable of signifying trade origin if

[147] Case T-91/99 [2000] 2 CMLR 276.   [148] ibid, para 23.   [149] ibid, para 25.   [150] [2008] ETMR 37.
[151] Case C-108/05.
[152] Case C-108/05, para 23. See also Case C-25/05 P *Storck v OHIM* [2006] ECR I-5719, para 83.
[153] ibid, para 26.   [154] Case C-192/03 P *Alcon Inc v OHIM* [2004] ECR I-8993, [2005] ETMR 69.
[155] ibid, para 31.

the first use still resonates in the mind of the relevant public as the sign would not be considered distinctive. So in *Score Draw Ltd v Alan Finch (CBD Trade Mark)*[156] the issue concerned a mark which had been used by the governing body for sport in Brazil, by the Brazilian football team until 1971, and had appeared on the shirts of historical football figures. In an appeal seeking to have the registration of the mark invalidated the court said what was important was to consider whether the prior use in connection with the football teams was so ingrained in the mind of the public that it was not possible for the badge to be distinctive of origin in relation to the person putting shirts on the market carrying the sign. In the instant case the prior use had indeed robbed the badge of its power to signify trade origin.[157]

Distinctiveness of part of a mark

14.67   It is possible for part of a mark to become distinctive through the use of the whole of the mark. In *OHIM v Erpo Möbelwerk*[158] the ECJ confirmed that slogans were registrable as trade marks (*Das prinzip der bequemlichkeit*). In *Société des produits Nestlé SA v Mars UK Ltd*[159] the question revolved around the slogan 'Have a break...Have a Kit Kat' and the name 'Kit Kat' which are both marks registered in the UK register in class 30 for chocolate, chocolate products, confectionery, candy and biscuits. When Nestle applied for registration of the words 'Have a Break' as a mark in respect of class 30 based on the acquisition of distinctive character through the use made of the whole of the mark, the Court said that the mark need not necessarily have been used independently;[160] 'of distinctive character' may be as a result both of the use as part of a registered trade mark (or of a component) and of the use of a separate mark in conjunction with a registered trade mark. In both cases it is sufficient that, in consequence of such use, the relevant class of persons actually perceive the product or service as originating from a given undertaking.[161]

> ### Key points on distinctiveness through use
>
> - A mark which is not inherently distinctive may become distinctive through use before the application is filed
> - This is an exception to the grounds for refusal listed in TMA 1994, section 3(1)(b) to (d) and not an independent right
> - For a CTM it is necessary to show that a mark has acquired distinctiveness throughout the Union and is considered to be so by a significant proportion of the relevant consumers
> - For a national mark it is necessary to show that it has become distinctive through use throughout the territory of the member state (or in the Benelux territory) in that part in which the objection subsists
> - Part of a mark may become distinctive through the use of the whole of a mark

---

[156] *Score Draw Ltd v Alan Finch (CBD Trade Mark)* [2007] EWHC 462 (Ch), [2007] FSR 20.
[157] See also the appeal before the ECJ concerning marks which include the words 'World Cup' (Cases T-444/08 to T-448/08 *FIFA v Ferrero*). Consider also the counteraction theory in the light of these cases discussed in para 15.47.
[158] Case C-64/02 [2004] ECR I-10031, [2005] ETMR 58. Case T-186/07 *Ashoka v OHIM (DREAM IT, DO IT!)*.
[159] Case C-353/03 *Société des Produits Nestlé SA v Mars UK Ltd* [2005] 3 CMLR 12, [2005] ETMR 96, [2006] FSR 2.
[160] ibid, para 27.   [161] ibid, para 30.

Exclusion from registration of certain shapes

TMA 1994, section 3(2); Directive, Article 3(1)(e); and CTMR, Article 7(1)(e)

14.68   Another important section dealing with absolute grounds for refusal is TMA 1994, section 3(2). This section provides that a sign will not be registered as a trade mark if it consists exclusively of:

- the shape which results from the nature of the goods themselves;
- the shape of the goods which is necessary to attain a technical result; or
- the shape which gives substantial value to the goods.

It should be noted that the ECJ has described these provisions as a 'preliminary obstacle' to registration saying: 'If any one of the criteria listed in Article 3(1)(e) is satisfied, a sign consisting exclusively of the shape of the product or of a graphic representation of that shape cannot be registered as a trade mark.'[162] In other words, if the sign falls under any one of these provisions, then it will not be registrable—and there is no need to go on to consider the other criteria as discussed above.

14.69   The prohibitions are included because to allow registration of the shapes under contemplation would mean that a monopoly would be created in the use of the shape as a trade mark *and* in the technical or functional characteristics of the goods themselves, a monopoly that would continue for as long as registration of the mark was renewed. To allow such registrations would 'form an obstacle preventing competitors from freely offering for sale products incorporating such technical solutions or functional characteristics in competition with the proprietor of the trade mark.'[163] As it would not be in the public interest to permit registration of such shapes it is not possible to overcome objections by showing that a shape falling under these provisions has become distinctive through use.[164]

Nature of the goods

14.70   Under TMA 1994, section 3(2)(a) (the shape which results from the nature of the goods themselves), it would not be possible to register the shape of a fork or a knife for cutlery as those shapes result from the nature of those implements. The first to register these shapes would have a monopoly not only over the shape as a mark, but over the shapes themselves. As was said in *Philips Electronics v Remington*.[165]

> 'No doubt an application to register a picture of a reel of cotton or a flag for coffee would succeed as they are not descriptive of the goods for which registration is sought; but that does not mean that a shape of an article is registrable in respect of the article shown in the application. To so hold would enable a few traders to obtain registrations of all the best designs of an article and thereby monopolise those designs. In my view a shape of an article cannot be registered in respect of the goods of that shape unless it contains some addition to the shape of the article which has trade mark significance. It is that addition which makes it capable of distinguishing the trade mark owner's goods from the same sort of goods sold by another trader'.

14.71   It would appear that the exclusion is relevant to generic shapes or basic shapes. As was also said in *Phillips Electronics v Remington*: 'Subsection 2(a) has to be construed in the context of

---

[162] *Philips*, para 76.   [163] *Philips*, para 78.
[164] *Lego Juris A/S v Mega Brands Inc* (Grand Board of Appeal) Case R 856/2004-G 10 July 2006. Upheld by the CFI: Case T-270/06 *Lego Juris A/S v OHIM*. Appealed to the ECJ: Case C-48/09.
[165] [1999] RPC 809 (CA) Aldous LJ p 818.

subsections (b) and (c). It is intended to exclude from registration basic shapes that should be available for use by the public at large. It is difficult to envisage such shapes, except those that are produced in nature such as bananas'. Thus, for example, the objection was not successful with regard to the shape of a three headed rotary electric shaver which was to be registered for inter alia electric shavers as electric shavers do not have to be of this shape.[166]

Functional features

14.72   Similar considerations underlie TMA 1994, section 3(2)(b), the operation of which is illustrated by the judgment of the ECJ in *Koninklijke Philips Electronics NV v Remington Consumer Products Ltd*.[167] Philips registered a trade mark consisting of a picture of a three-headed rotary electric shaver (the 208 mark). You can find an image of the trade mark if you look in the UK trade mark register available on the IPO website under TM (archived) No 1254208.

> ### Weblink
>
> The weblink to the mark is http://www.ipo.gov.uk/ tm/t-find/t-find-number?detailsrequested=c&trademark=1254208

Remington marketed three-headed rotary shavers. Philips accused Remington of infringing their registered trade mark. In turn Remington alleged that the Philips mark was invalid on a number of grounds including that it consisted exclusively of a shape which was necessary to obtain a technical result. At first instance the mark was held to be invalid and the court ordered the mark to be revoked. On appeal the Court of Appeal ordered a reference to be made to the ECJ on the grounds that the case raised difficult questions of construction of the Directive.[168] In addition, similar issues had arisen in a case pending before the Swedish Court of Appeal, in which the Swedish District Court had construed the Directive differently.

In giving judgment the ECJ made a number of important points.

- To allow registration of functional characteristics of a shape 'would limit the possibility of competitors supplying a product incorporating such a function or at least limit their freedom of choice in regard to the technical solution they wish to adopt in order to incorporate such a function in their product'.[169]

- The fact that some small element of the sign does not contribute to the technical performance but may serve, either alone or in combination, an aesthetic purpose, does not save a mark from the prohibition against registration under this measure.

- There is nothing in the provision that would allow registration of the shape of goods necessary to achieve a technical result even if other shapes could achieve the same technical result: 'where the essential functional characteristics of the shape of a product are attributable solely to the technical result, Article 3(1)(e), second indent, precludes registration of a sign consisting of that shape, even if that technical result can be achieved by other shapes'.[170]

---

[166] ibid Aldous LJ p 820.   [167] *Philips.*
[168] *Philips Electronics NV v Remington Consumer Products Limited* [1999] RPC 809 (CA).   [169] ibid, para 79.
[170] ibid, para 83.

14.73   This latter point was also emphasised in *Lego Juris A/S v Mega Brands Inc*[171] (subsequently upheld by the CFI in *Lego Juris A/S v OHIM*;[172] now appealed to the Court of Justice) in which the Grand Board of Appeal endorsed the finding of the Cancellation Division that if Article 7(1)(e)(ii) CTMR did not preclude monopolies on visual embodiments or designs of a technical solution, it would be possible to register not only the preferred embodiment of that solution (in this case of the Lego brick), but also every conceivable visual embodiment or design of that technical solution. 'This would necessarily result in a monopoly on a technical solution, so that Article 7(1)(e)(ii) CTMR would be circumvented'.[173]

14.74   While this seemed to provide a clear limitation on the registration of shape marks with technical features, the litigation concerning shavers has continued[174] in *Koninklijke Philips Electronics NV v Remington Consumer Products Ltd, Rayovac Europe Ltd*.[175] This case concerned a different mark—the 452 mark described as the overall shape of an inverted equilateral triangle, with three heads sitting within a raised faceplate of clover leaf design superimposed on a triangle. You can find an image of this trade mark if you look in the UK trade mark register available on the IPO website under TM No 1533452[176] as well as a series of device marks (see para 14.78).

14.75   When Philips brought infringement proceedings against Remington, Remington challenged the validity of the 452 mark on the ground that it consisted exclusively of features of the shape of the goods which were necessary to obtain a technical result under TMA 1994, section 3(2). In giving judgment the Court of Appeal made some comments on the interpretation of the section and in particular what is meant by essential feature and exclusively.

Essential feature

14.76   A central question was whether the addition of the clover leaf feature to the invalid 208 mark made the otherwise similar 452 mark a valid trade mark: was the clover leaf design an essential feature? The High Court had found that it was not, and the mark was invalid. The Court of Appeal agreed with this saying that the important factor was the impact of the mark on the eye of the average consumer who would not dissect and examine each feature. What is key is the feature which contributes most to the overall impression. Not every feature which contributes to the overall impression is an essential feature as not all features have the same visual impact. The question of essential feature is one of fact and degree. In the instant case the High Court had been entitled to find that the clover leaf did not have such eye impact as to make it an essential feature of the mark.

Exclusively

14.77   In order to decide whether the shape of the goods in question is exclusively necessary to obtain a technical result, the court must consider the mark as a whole as that is how the relevant section of the public would perceive it. In the instant case the trial judge, having decided that the clover leaf was not an essential feature of the mark, was entitled to conclude that the mark was in substance functional.[177] Although the point was not dealt with by the ECJ, AG Leger in

---

[171] Case R-856/2004-G [2007] ETMR 11.   [172] Cae T-270/06 [2009] ETMR 15.

[173] *Lego Juris A/S v Mega Brands Inc* (Grand Board of Appeal) Case R 856/2004-G 10 July 2006, para 58.

[174] Described by Mummery LJ in the Court of Appeal in *Koninklijke Philips Electronics NV v Remington Consumer Products Ltd, Rayovac Europe Ltd* [2006] ETMR 42, [2006] EWCA Civ 16 CA (Civ Div) as marathon litigation (para 1).

[175] [2006] ETMR 42, [2006] EWCA Civ 16 CA (Civ Div).

[176] Details can be found on the IPO website under TM No 1,533,452.

[177] *Koninklijke Philips Electronics NV v Remington Consumer Products Ltd, Rayovac Europe Ltd* [2006] ETMR 42, [2006] EWCA Civ 16 CA (Civ Div), para 62.

Dyson Ltd v Registrar of Trade Marks[178] (see above, para 14.8) took the view that the reasoning also applied to a functional feature which forms part of the appearance of a product. The functional feature in *Dyson* was the bagless vacuum cleaner. Granting a trade mark in respect of the application could extend to a multitude of shapes which that feature could take, with the result that competing undertakings could find themselves unable to determine precisely whether and how they may still use that feature.[179] In *Lego Juris v OHIM* the CFI considered that the word 'exclusively' should be read in the light of the expression 'essential characteristics which perform a technical function'.[180] In so doing, the 'addition of non-essential characteristics having no technical function does not prevent a shape from being caught by that absolute ground of refusal if all the essential characteristics of that shape perform such a function.'[181]

Device marks

14.78   In *Koninklijke Philips Electronics NV v Remington Consumer Products Ltd, Rayovac Europe Ltd*,[182] the court also had to consider the validity of further trade marks that the claimant had registered in class 8, each of which was a two-dimensional depiction of three circles arranged within an inverted equilateral triangle.[183] You can find an image of these trade marks if you look in the UK trade mark register available on the IPO website under TM No 1203652.

Registration had been declared invalid in the High Court on the basis that the signs were functional, but even if they were not, they were not distinctive. The Court of Appeal disagreed saying the marks which had eye appeal were of an abstract, non-technical and non-functional nature. None of them represented the shape of goods in the functional sense used in the legislation. They thus fell outwith the competition policy of the provisions and outside the scope of the functionality principle embodied in Article 3(1)(e) and section 3(2)(b) of the 1994 Act.[184] The Court of Appeal was careful to emphasise that no technical elements or details of the three-headed rotary electric shaver were depicted in the marks. Thus there was no question that the marks would give to Philips a monopoly over the technical features of three-headed razors.[185]

Substantial value

14.79   As regards the third ground, TMA 1994, section 3(2)(c), a shape which gives 'substantial' value to goods will not be registrable. It is suggested the type of shape which may fall under this proviso may be the cut of a diamond[186] or the shape of a crystal decanter, each of which will add substantial value to the goods. The Court of Appeal in *Philips Electronics NV v Remington Consumer Products Ltd (No 1)*[187] said that this section:

> '[W]as aimed at preventing a trader from monopolizing by way of a trade mark registration shapes which added a substantial value to the goods over other shapes, e.g. a lampshade, a telephone designed to appeal to the eye. Such designs should be protected as registered designs or the like protection, not by trade mark registration...There may be overlap between [TMA section 3(2)(c) and(b)] which excludes shapes necessary to obtain a technical result, but the purpose is different. The latter is intended to

---

[178] Case C-321/03.   [179] ibid, para 91.   [180] *Lego Juris v OHIM* [2009] ETMR 15, para 38   [181] ibid.
[182] [2006] ETMR 42, [2006] EWCA Civ 16 CA (Civ Div).
[183] TM Nos 1 080 316; 1 087 357, 1 124 415 and 1 203 652.
[184] *Koninklijke Philips Electronics NV v Remington Consumer Products Ltd, Rayovac Europe Ltd* [2006] ETMR 42, [2006] EWCA Civ 16 CA (Civ Div), para 94.
[185] ibid, para 95.   [186] J Phillips and A Firth, *Introduction to Intellectual Property Law* (4th edn, 2001), para 21.10.
[187] [1999] ETMR 816, [1999] RPC 809.

exclude functional shapes and the former aesthetic-type shapes. Thus the fact that the technical result of a shape is excellent and therefore the article can command a high price does not mean that it is excluded from registration by subsection (c)'.

14.80   In *Benetton Group SpA v G-Star International BV*[188] the ECJ emphasised that even where a mark has acquired distinctiveness through use, it may not be registered where the shape of the product adds substantial value to the goods.

 Question

Explain in your own words why you consider it important to define the boundaries of trade mark law by excluding certain signs from being registered as trade marks based on their functional features. What marks can you think of which, if registered, would preclude other traders from entering the market in a particular sector?

Key points on the exclusion from registration of certain shapes

- If the sign falls under any one of these provisions, then it will not be registrable
- It would not be in the interests of competitors to permit registration of these shapes as it would give to the registered holder an unfair competitive advantage

Public policy and morality

TMA 1994, section 3(3), Directive, Article 3(1) (f), (g); and CTMR, Article 7(1)(f), (g)

14.81   Public policy and morality and public deception also have a role to play in preventing signs that might prove problematic on these grounds from being registered as trade marks.

Under TMA 1994, section 3(3) a mark will not be registered if it is:

- contrary to public policy or to accepted principles of morality, or
- of such a nature as to deceive the public (for instance as to the nature, quality or geographical origin of the goods or service).

What is contrary to public policy[189] or accepted principles of morality may change over time. For instance, the word 'Hallelujah'[190] was refused registration for women's clothing under the 1938 Act on the grounds that is was offensive. Also considered offensive, in 1947, was the proposed use of 'Oomphies' for footwear.[191] Both would be likely to be immediately acceptable under the 1994 Act. Certain words do however still offend against morality. In 2001, an application to

---

[188] *Benetton Group SpA v G-Star International BV* [2008] ETMR 5.
[189] The expression 'public policy' referred to matters of the kind covered by the French legal term *'ordre public'*. *Philips Electronics NV v Remington Consumer Products Ltd* [1998] RPC 283.
[190] *Hallelujah Trade Mark* [1976] RPC 605.
[191] This was overturned on application to the court, and the name registered. *La Marquise's Footwear Application* (1947) 64 RPC 27. Apparently 'Oomphies' was derived from 'Oomph', denoting sex appeal, and had achieved significance, meaning those qualities in connection with a film actress with whom the word had originated.

register the words 'Tiny Penis' in connection with articles of clothing was turned down on the grounds that it offended against current principles of morality.[192]

14.82   In *Basic Trademark SA's Trade Mark Application*,[193] concerning an appeal against a refusal to register the word JESUS on the basis that to do so would be contrary to public policy, it was stressed that any objection on the grounds of public policy must relate to the intrinsic qualities of the mark and not to the personal qualities of the applicant for registration.[194] Further, mere offence to the public, such as that the public would consider the mark distasteful, is not enough: '. . . it is only in cases where it is plain that an accepted principle of morality is being offended against that registration should be denied'.[195] It is necessary to find the dividing line between distaste and outrage—where the latter is likely to undermine current religious, family or social values amongst an identifiable section of the public.[196] Words which contain profane language will not be registrable,[197] nor will signs that glorify terrorism.[198] The standard to be applied is that of the reasonable person with normal levels of sensitivity and tolerance.[199]

■ Case R 495/2005-G *Jebaraj Kenneth trading as Screw You*

The Grand Board of Appeal had the opportunity to consider what might be contrary to public policy or to accepted principles of morality in *Jebaraj Kenneth trading as Screw You* in which an application to register the words 'Screw you' as a CTM in classes 9, 10, 25, 28, 33 had been refused. The Grand Board started off by noting that for a CTM the grounds of non-registerability on the grounds of public policy and morality did not have to exist throughout the EU but that it was sufficient if they obtain in only part of the Community.[200] In the instant case objection was taken because of the way the term was likely to be perceived in the UK and Ireland. In balancing the rights of the trader to use words and signs as trade marks, and that of the public not to be offended, and looking to the standard of a reasonable person with normal levels of sensitivity and tolerance, the Board came to the view that 'Screw You' was registrable in respect of condoms, contraceptives, sex toys (vibrators, dolls), 'artificial breasts' and 'breast pumps' of a type normally sold exclusively in sex shops.

 Question

Do you think that the Appointed Person allowed registration of the word JESUS to proceed in Basic Trademark SA's Trade Mark Application, or do you think it was turned down?

 Exercise

Find out what marks have been refused registration as Community Marks on the grounds that to do so would be contrary to public policy or to accepted principles of morality. How are the different views of morality in Member States dealt with? How should they be dealt with?

---

[192] *Ghazilian's Trade Mark Application* [2002] ETMR 57   [193] [2005] RPC 25.
[194] [2005] RPC 25; see also Case T-140/02 *Sportwetten GmbH Gera v OHIM & Intertops Sportwetten GmbH* [2006] ETMR 15, para 14.83.
[195] *Ghazilian's Trade Mark Application* [2002] ETMR 57, at para 21.
[196] See also *CDW Graphic Design Ltd's Trade Mark Application* [2003] RPC 30 where the trade mark registry refused an application to register the domain name. http://www.standupifyouhatemanu.com/ as a trade mark on public policy grounds. It was enough to show that the normal and fair use of such a trade mark would be likely to lead to criminal or offensive behaviour.
[197] Case R 111/2002-4 DICK & FANNY.   [198] Case R 176/2004-2 BIN LADEN.   [199] ibid.
[200] CTMR, Art 7(2).

14.83 In *Sportwetten GmbH Gera v OHIM/Intertops Sportwetten GmbH*[201] a different question on public policy and morality arose concerning the validity of a CTM 'Intertops' registered for inter alia bookmaking and betting services of all kinds in class 42. The registration was challenged by Sportwetten on the basis that Intertops was not authorised to offer betting services in Germany and on that basis of non-authorisation the CTM was contrary to public policy and morality. No challenge was made alleging that either the sign or the services per se covered by the mark were contrary to public policy or accepted principles of morality. The CFI upheld the finding of the Board of Appeal in that such considerations were irrelevant when considering whether a CTM is contrary to public policy or accepted principles of morality within the meaning of Article 7(1)(f). The focus of enquiry must be on the sign in relation to the goods or services. It is also irrelevant to consider circumstances relating to the conduct of the applicant.[202]

Deceptive marks

14.84 A mark may be considered to be deceptive under TMA 1994, section 3(3)(b) if it suggests that the goods are made from specific materials if that is in fact not the case. An example would be the application to register the word 'Orlwoola'[203] for goods made from wool where the goods to be sold are not made solely from wool (the application was made under the 1938 Act).

14.85 In *Consorzio per la Tutela del Formaggio Gorgonzola v Käserei Champignon Hofmeister GmbH & Co KG and Eduard Bracharz GmbH*[204] the ECJ said that the prohibition presupposed the evidence of actual deceit or a sufficiently serious risk that the consumer will be deceived (that is, hypothetical deceit is not enough). This was re-emphasised in *Elizabeth Florence Emanuel v Continental Shelf 128 Ltd*[205] in which the Court in dealing with the name 'Elizabeth Emanuel' in connection with a dress design business said that even if a consumer was influenced into purchasing a garment because of the name and imagining that the individual was involved in the design, the 'characteristics and the qualities of that garment remain guaranteed by the undertaking which owns the trade mark'[206] and consequently the name was not of a nature to deceive the public as to the nature, quality or geographical origin of the product it designates. If there was an intention by the owner of the trade mark to make the consumer believe Ms Emanuel was the designer, that could be fraudulent behaviour and would be a matter for the national court but would not be deception for the purposes of Article 3.[207]

Question

Can you think of any sign which might be refused registration on the grounds that it might be deceptive?

Marks prohibited by law and protected emblems

TMA 1994, sections 3(4) and (5)

14.86 Further absolute grounds of refusal are to be found in TMA 1994, sections 3(4) and (5). These relate to non-registration of marks to the extent that its use would be prohibited in the UK or by

[201] Case T-140/02 [2006] ETMR 15.   [202] Case T-224/01 *Durferrit v OHIM—Kolene* [2003] ECR II-1589.
[203] (1909) 26 RPC 683 and 850.   [204] [1999] ETMR 454 ECJ.   [205] Case C-259/04   [206] ibid, para 48.
[207] Para 50. See also *Kraft Jacobs Suchard Limited's Application; Opposition by Nestlé UK Limited* [2001] ETMR 54 TMR.

a provision of Union law and to specially protected emblems. These would include, for example the Red Cross, the Union Jack and any sign that would lead to indicate a connection with the Royal Family. It will be recalled that the Paris Convention requires Convention countries to prohibit the registration of 'armorial bearings, flags and emblems' of the countries of the Union.[208]

Applications made in bad faith

TMA 1994, section 3(6); Directive, Article 3(2)(d); and CTMR, Article 52

14.87   An application to register a trade mark will be refused if or to the extent that it is made in bad faith. In *Gromax Plasticulture Ltd v Don & Low Nonwovens Ltd*[209] Lindsay J said this of bad faith:

> 'I shall not attempt to define bad faith in this context. Plainly it includes dishonesty and, as I would hold, includes also some dealings which fall short of the standards of acceptable commercial behaviour observed by reasonable and experienced men in the particular area being examined. Parliament has wisely not attempted to explain in detail what is or is not bad faith in this context: how far a dealing must so fall-short in order to amount to bad faith is a matter best left to be adjudged not by some paraphrase by the courts (which leads to the danger of the courts then construing not the Act but the paraphrase) but by reference to the words of the Act and upon a regard to all material surrounding circumstances'.[210]

14.88   Cases concerning bad faith applications have occurred where there has been an attempt to register a mark for which the applicant knows there is a competing claim,[211] where the applicant is an employee,[212] where there is an agreement to the contrary,[213] or where an application is made to register a trade mark based on an older trademark in which there is residual goodwill.[214]

14.89   *Harrison v Teton Valley*[215]concerned the name China White. The proprietors of a nightclub 'Chinawhite' had traded under the name for a number of years. As part of their business activity they discussed developing a cocktail with their bar manager—to be called China White. The bar manager informed Harrison of these developments who proceeded to apply for registration of the name. The Court of Appeal considered that the application had been made in bad faith. The test is a combined one of dishonesty[216] and acceptable commercial behaviour observed by reasonable and experienced persons in the commercial area under consideration:[217]

> 'dishonesty requires knowledge by the defendant that what he was doing would be regarded as dishonest by honest people, although he should not escape a finding of dishonesty because he sets his own standards of honesty and does not regard as dishonest what he knows would offend the normally accepted standards of honest conduct'.[218]

In *Harrison* the Court found that on the facts of the case—that the applicant knew of the night club, and that a drink, China White was sold at the club—the application was in bad faith. By contrast in *Hotel Cipriani SRL v Cipriani (Grosvenor Street) Limited*[219] Justice Arnold found that it was not bad faith on the part of one party who registered a mark when they knew that a third

---

[208] Paris Convention, Art 6*ter* (para 13.51). See also TMA 1994, ss 57 and 58.   [209] [1999] RPC 367, 379.
[210] Approved of by the Court of Appeal in *Harrison v Teton Valley Trading Co Ltd* [2004] EWCA Civ 1028, [2004] 1 WLR 2577, [2005] FSR 10 (hereafter *Harrison*).
[211] See, eg, *Harrison* (above).   [212] *Casson's Trade Mark* (1910) 27 RPC 65.
[213] *Mary Wilson Enterprises Inc's Trade Mark Application* [2003] EMLR 14.
[214] *Jules Rimet Cup Ltd v Football Association* [2007] EWHC 2376 (Ch).
[215] [2004] EWCA Civ 1028, [2004] 1 WLR 2577, [2005] FSR 10.   [216] *Twinsectra Ltd v Yardley* [2002] 2 AC 164.
[217] *Gromax Plasticulture Ltd v Don & Low Nonwovens Ltd* [1999] RPC 367. See also *Ajit Weekly Trade Mark* [2006] RPC 25.
[218] *Twinsectra Ltd v Yardley* [2002] UKHL 12, [2002] 2 AC 164, para 36.   [219] [2008] EWHC 3032 (Ch).

party used the same mark for similar goods and services elsewhere in the Community, a key difference being the applicant had used that mark for many years and it was one in which they had a reputation (Cipriani).

14.90   Just after this judgment was handed down the ECJ was asked to determine a similar case, this time concerning the registration as a CTM of a chocolate bunny and the challenge to the registration by other producers of chocolate bunnies in *Chocoladefabriken Lindt & Sprüngli AG v Franz Hauswirth GmbH.*[220]

In determining bad faith the Court said that the factors to be taken into account (which needed to be those relevant at the time of filing the application) were, in particular:

- the fact that the applicant knows or must know that a third party is using, in at least one member state, an identical or similar sign for an identical or similar product capable of being confused with the sign for which registration is sought;

- the applicant's intention to prevent that third party from continuing to use such a sign; and

- the degree of legal protection enjoyed by the third party's sign and by the sign for which registration is sought.[221]

Figure 14.9 Lindt bunny

[220] Case C-529/07 [2009] ECR I-04893.   [221] ibid

Figure 14.10 Franz Hauswirth bunny

 Question

Given the ruling of the ECJ, do you think that registration was, or should be, allowed to proceed?

> **Key points on the exclusion of registering a trade mark based on public policy and morality, deceptive marks and applications in bad faith**
>
> • Objections on the grounds of public policy must relate to the intrinsic qualities of the mark and not to the personal qualities of the applicant.
>
> • Mere offence to the public, such as that the public would consider the mark distasteful, is not enough.
>
> • The standard to be applied is that of the reasonable person with normal levels of sensitivity and tolerance for a mark to be considered deceptive there needs to be evidence of actual deceit or a sufficiently serious risk that the consumer will be deceived.
>
> • An application made in bad faith will be refused considering both dishonesty and acceptable commercial behaviour observed by reasonable and experienced persons in the commercial area under consideration.

Collective and certification trade marks

 Exercise

Read TMA 1994, sections 49, 50; Directive, Article 15; and CTMR, Article 66

14.91 The TMA 1994 provides for the registration of collective and certification marks. The Directive, Article 15 contains permissive provisions regarding these types of marks and under the CTMR it is possible to register a Community Collective Mark, but there is no such thing as a Community Certification Mark.

> '[A collective mark is defined in TMA section 49 as a] mark distinguishing the goods or services of members of the association which is the proprietor of the mark from those of other undertakings. [A certification mark is defined in TMA 1994, section 50 as] a mark indicating that the goods or services in connection with which it is used are certified by the proprietor of the mark in respect of origin, material, mode of manufacture of goods or performance of services, quality, accuracy or other characteristics'.[222]

It can be seen from the definition that collective and certification marks have different objectives. *Collective* marks are designed to indicate who can use the mark, for example members of a particular association. Quality standards are not necessarily a feature of a collective mark, but may be included by way of, for example, membership rules of the particular association. By comparison, a *certification* mark is designed to indicate that the quality of the goods or services meet with certain criteria, some examples of which are set out in the definition of a certification mark.

14.92 Because the function of collective and certification marks differ from ordinary trade marks, they have special rules that govern their use. In the case of a certification mark, the applicant

---

[222] The provisions of the 1994 Act apply to collective and certification marks, subject to Sch 1 and Sch 2 respectively.

must not itself carry on a business involving the supply of goods or services of the kind certified,[223] and in the case of both a collective and a certification mark, the applicant must file with the registrar regulations governing the use of the mark.[224] The regulations for collective marks must specify the persons authorised to use the mark, the conditions of membership of the association and the conditions of use of the mark including any sanctions against misuse.[225] The regulations governing the use of a certified mark require more information including who is authorised to use the mark; the characteristics to be certified by the mark; how the certifying body is to test the characteristics and supervise the use of the mark; the fees to be paid in connection with the operation of the mark and the procedures for resolving disputes.[226] As can be gathered from these rules, both collective and certification marks can be used by different entities: the purpose of a trader using one of these marks being either to signify membership of that group, or that certain standards are met by those who use the same mark in the marketplace.

14.93   Certification marks have been available in the United Kingdom for many years, well-known examples including the 'Woolmark' of the International Wool Secretariat.[227]

Figure 14.11 Woolmark certification mark

The 'Kite' mark of the British standards institute and the 'Stilton' mark.[228]

The mark shown in Figure 14.12 has been registered as a collective mark by the UK cartridge remanufacturers association.[229]

Figure 14.12 UK cartridge remanufacturers association collective mark

---

[223] TMA 1994, Sch 2, para 4.   [224] ibid, Sch 2, para 6(1) and Sch 1, para 5(1).   [225] ibid, Sch 1, para 5(2).
[226] ibid, Sch 2, para 6(2).   [227] UK Trade Mark No 2178977.   [228] *Stilton Trade Mark* [1967] RPC 173.
[229] UK Trade Mark No 2341823.

Question

Can you think of any certification and collective marks you have come across?

Key points on collective and certification marks

- Collective marks are designed to indicate who can use the mark, for example members of a particular association. Quality standards are not necessarily a feature of a collective mark, but may be included by way of, for example, membership rules of the particular association

- A certification mark is designed to indicate that the quality of the goods or services meet with certain criteria, examples of which are set out in the definition of a certification mark

Relative grounds for refusal of registration

 Exercise

Read TMA 1994, sections 5 and 10; Directive, Articles 4, 5; and CTMR, Articles 8, 9.

14.94   Section 5 of the 1994 Act concerns the *relative grounds* on which an application to register a trade mark might be refused if successful opposition is raised by the proprietor of an earlier mark or sign. These grounds thus look beyond the mark itself to other marks, and other goods and services to ensure that a registration does not conflict with pre-existing rights. As mentioned above, TMA 1994, section 5(1)–(3) virtually mirrors TMA 1994, section 10(1)–(3) which relates to infringement. For registration purposes a mark may not be registered if successful opposition is raised on the following grounds:

- it is identical to an earlier trade mark and the goods or services for which registration is sought are identical to the goods or services for which the earlier trade mark is protected;[230]

- it is identical with or similar to the earlier trade mark and the application is for registration in connection with identical or similar goods and services for which the earlier trade mark is protected, and there exists a likelihood of confusion on the part of the public which includes the likelihood of association with the earlier trade mark;[231]

- it is identical with or similar to an earlier trade mark and the earlier mark has a reputation and the use of the later mark without due cause would take unfair advantage of, or be detrimental to the distinctive character or the repute of the earlier mark.[232]

Logically, if a mark is registered, the later use of a sign in these circumstances will infringe the rights of the registered proprietor. To avoid repetition these relative grounds for refusal will be dealt with in the next chapter when examining infringement.

---

[230] TMA 1994, s 5(1).   [231] ibid, s 5(2).   [232] ibid, s 5(3).

14.95   The remaining parts of section 5 seek to ensure that a sign will not be registered as a trade mark looking to other factors, notably whether the registration would infringe the intellectual property rights belonging to others. For instance, if the use of the mark would amount to passing off,[233] or would infringe another's copyright or design right.[234] Thus, in a case decided under the equivalent provision in the 1938 Act, OSCAR Trade Mark,[235] the applicant sought to register the name 'Oscar' and a picture of the Oscar statuette. The application was rejected on the grounds that the applicant did not own the copyright in the statuette and registration as a trade mark would infringe the artistic copyright.

Earlier trade mark and earlier right

14.96   It will be noted that the legislation refers to 'earlier trade mark' and 'earlier right'. As was explained in para 13.61 an earlier trade mark[236] includes an existing registered trade mark (that is, one that is on the UK register whether by virtue of the 1938 or 1994 Act), an international trade mark (UK) (one for which registration is applied for under the Madrid Protocol) or a CTM. All of these earlier trade marks need a date of application for registration earlier than that for the mark under consideration, taking into account any priorities[237] or the seniority of a CTM.[238] A person who is entitled to prevent the use of a trade mark is referred to as the proprietor of an earlier right in relation to the trade mark.[239]

Consent of the earlier proprietor to registration

TMA 1994, section 5(5); Directive, Article 4(5)

14.97   All the provisions of section 5 of the 1994 Act are subject to the proviso in section 5(5) which states that where the proprietor of an earlier trade mark consents to the registration of the later mark, then registration may proceed.

Use requirements

14.98   Use provisions in the TMA 1994 arise in a number of circumstances. As has been discussed above, a trade mark which is not inherently distinctive can become distinctive through use, and thus registrable. In addition there are certain consequences if a registered trade mark is *not used* for a certain period of time, or if it is used in a particular manner[240] as well as questions relating to when a trade mark is *used for the purposes of infringement*. In this part the consequences of non-use will be discussed; matters relating to use for the purposes of infringement will be dealt with in the next chapter.

Exercise

Read TMA 1994, section 46; Directive, Article 10; and CTMR, Article 15.

---

[233] ibid, s 5(4)(a).   [234] ibid, s 5(4)(b).   [235] [1979] RPC 173.   [236] See generally TMA 1994, s 6.
[237] TMA 1994, s 6(1)(a).   [238] ibid, s 6(1)(b).   [239] ibid, s 5(4).   [240] ibid, s 46.

Non-use and revocation

14.99   The recitals of the Trade Marks Directive give an indication as to why a trade mark will be revoked if it is not used:

> 'Whereas in order to reduce the total number of trade marks registered and protected in the Community and, consequently, the number of conflicts which arise between them, it is essential to require that registered trade marks must actually be used or, if not used, be subject to revocation'

This objective reflects the basic principle that trade marks should be used, and if not used then a registration will be lost (see para 13.6).

Traders are thus precluded from stockpiling trade marks, keeping them from legitimate competitors. A concern also expressed in the recital is that the more registered trade marks on the register, the greater the potential for conflict with later applications for registration or for infringement to occur where confusingly similar signs are used by competing traders. The desire is thus to limit the potential for these conflicts.

> 'The purpose of revocation is to remove trade marks or parts of the specifications of trade marks where there has not been use. It is there to serve a purpose in trade; it is the Lipitor that stops the arteries of commerce being blocked with the cholesterol of unused trade marks'.[241]

14.100   An applicant for a UK trade mark requires to state that they have a bona fide intention to use the mark. If the applicant does not have this intention, then the mark may be revoked on the grounds of bad faith.[242] By contrast an applicant for a CTM does not have to state that they intend to use the mark.

14.101   A registered trade mark must be put to genuine use.[243] If a registered trade mark has not been put to genuine use within five years following the date of registration, or use of the trade mark has been suspended for a continuous period of five years, registration may be revoked.[244] Genuine use of a mark is to be judged against commercial criteria. Early UK cases suggested that even if there is no evidence of actual sales during the relevant five-year period, use can be shown where the mark had been employed in relation to goods offered for sale during that period,[245] and only limited use is necessary to maintain a mark on the register.[246] The ECJ has however indicated that token use will not be sufficient.[247] In *Ansul BV v Ajax Brandbeveiliging BV*[248] the court said that any use must be 'consistent with the essential function of a trade mark', in this case to guarantee origin'.[249] Such use must not be just internal use, but use of the mark, either by the proprietor or with consent, on the market or in relation to goods or services about to be marketed through such activities as advertising campaigns.[250] The use should be public and external.[251] Particular regard should be paid to whether the use is viewed as warranted in the economic sector concerned to maintain or create a share in the market for the goods or services. Regard must be had to the facts and circumstances relevant to establishing whether the commercial exploitation of

---

[241] Application for revocation *Nirvana Trade Mark*, O-030-06, para 75.   [242] TMA 1994, s 3(6).

[243] ibid, s 46(1)(a); Directive, Art 10; CTMR, Art 15.

[244] The period of non-use should be calculated from 'date of the completion of the registration procedure' within the meaning of Article 10(1) Directive and must be determined in each Member State in accordance with the procedural rules on registration in force in that State. See Case C-246/05 *Armin Häupl v Lidl Stiftung & Co KG* [2007] ECR I-04673.

[245] *Floris Trade Mark* [2001] RPC 19.

[246] *Zippo Trade Mark* [1999] RPC 173. But cf *Elle Trade Mark* [1997] FSR 529, [1997] ETMR 552.

[247] Genuine use does not include token use for the sole purpose of preserving the rights conferred by the registration: Case C-234/06 P *Il Ponte Finanziaria v OHIM* [2007] ECR I-7333, para 72; T-191/07 *Anheuser-Busch v OHIM* [2009] ECR II-00691, para 100.

[248] Case C-40/01 [2003] ECR I-2439, [2003] RPC 40 (hereafter *Ansul*).   [249] *Ansul*, para 36.

[250] ibid, para 37.   [251] Case T-174/01 *Goulbourn v OHIM—Redcats (Silk Cocoon)* [2003] ECR II-789, para 99.

the mark in the course of trade is real. It will not be enough to use a mark on free gifts as that does not create a commercial outlet for the goods[252] but it can be sufficient for a not-for-profit organisation to put a mark to genuine use through announcements of events, business advertising and so on.[253]

14.102   The Court of Appeal considered the genuine use requirement in a case concerning the registered mark 'Laboratoire de la Mer'[254] In this case the use comprised the sale of £800 worth of cosmetics containing seaweed to a firm in Banff, Scotland. There were five deliveries in 1997 where the items were packed in containers (bearing the mark) with recommended retail prices of between £5–£30. The goods were apparently to be sold by sub-agents but there was no evidence that any of the goods reached consumers. A reference was made to the ECJ asking inter alia for interpretation of the requirement of genuine use.[255] The Court noted that it had already answered the questions in *Ansul*.[256] The case was re-heard by the High Court and then appealed to the Court of Appeal.[257] That court considered that the owner of the mark in the UK wanted to create an outlet was sufficient to qualify as genuine use. The Court of Appeal came to the view that although internal use would not be relevant in assessing genuine use even if it was not token or sham, there was nothing in the ECJ judgment which indicated that the consumer or end user market was the only relevant market for determining whether use of a mark is genuine. In the instant case there were arm's length sales to a third party who imported the goods. The fact that the use was on the import market and was modest did not prevent that from being genuine use.

14.103   At the same time as *Laboratoire de la mer* had been progressing though the domestic courts, application was made for registration as a CTM the words 'La Mer'. Opposition was based on a likelihood of confusion with the earlier national word mark, 'Laboratoire de la mer'. The question also arose in this forum as to whether there had been genuine use of the national mark. The CFI stated that when examining whether there has been genuine use of an earlier trade mark, all relevant factors of the particular case must be considered. This assessment entails a degree of interdependence between the factors taken into account. The use of an earlier mark need not always be quantitatively significant in order to be deemed genuine and it is not possible to determine a priori and in the abstract what quantitative threshold should be chosen in order to determine whether use is genuine or not. Minimal use can be deemed genuine use, provided that this amount of use is warranted in the economic sector concerned to maintain or create a market share for the goods or services protected by the mark[258] so long as the use is 'outward facing' and grounded in the commercial sector.

14.104   Revocation will not occur on the grounds of non-use if there are 'proper reasons for non-use'.[259] This proviso has applied in circumstances where the registered proprietor had experienced protracted technical difficulties in setting up a satisfactory production method for a new product that has thus delayed the appearance of the product on the market for which

[252] Case C-495/07 *Silberquelle GmbH v Maselli-Strickmode GmbH* [2007] ECR I-00137.
[253] *Verein Radetzky-Orden v Bundesvereinigung Kameradschaft Feldmarschall Radetzky* [2009] ETMR 14, at 7.
[254] *Laboratoires Goëmar SA v La Mer Technology Inc* [2005] EWCA Civ 978; [2005] ETMR 114; [2006] FSR 5; 2005 WL 1801235 (CA (Civ Div)).
[255] Case C-259/02.   [256] Case C-40/01.
[257] [2005] EWCA Civ 978, [2005] ETMR 114, [2006] FSR 5, 2005 WL 1801235 (CA (Civ Div)).
[258] *La Mer Technology Inc v OHIM*, [2008] ETMR 9, at para 57–58.
[259] TMA 1994 s 46(1)(a) and (b). The onus is on the registered proprietor to prove that it has made genuine use of the trade mark in suit, or that there are proper reasons for non-use. TMA 1994, s 100 and application for revocation: *Nirvana Trade Mark* O-030-06.

the mark had been registered.[260] Generally however it would appear that lack of resources in setting up a business and using the trade mark would not amount to proper reasons for non-use as there are within the domain of the trade mark owner.[261] Other factors, outwith the trade mark proprietors control, may constitute proper reasons.[262] A question as to whether delayed implementation of the corporate strategy being pursued by the trade mark proprietor for reasons outside the control of the proprietor might constitute proper reasons was referred to the ECJ in *Armin Häupl v Lidl Stiftung & Co KG*[263] which also asked whether, in these circumstances, the trade mark proprietor is obliged to change his corporate strategy in order to be able to use the mark in good time. Here, the Court emphasised that in order to be taken into account any difficulties had to have a direct relationship with a trade mark making its use impossible or unreasonable. These difficulties had to be outwith the control of the proprietor of the mark. It was for the national court, when dealing with the facts of the case, to determine whether it would be unreasonable for the proprietor to change a business strategy in order to get around the difficulty.[264] It thus seems that the hurdle may be high to show non-use is reasonable.

Quality control and revocation

14.105   Revocation can also occur where the use of a mark is liable to mislead the public as to the nature, quality or geographical origin of the goods and services for which it is registered.[265]

14.106   It will be recalled from the discussion in para 14.84 a mark that is liable to mislead the public is precluded from registration. This section is the counterpart to the non-registerability of a mark in that if, once registered, a mark becomes likely to mislead the public then it can be revoked. The question of whether such circumstances might arise where a trade mark has been licensed to another but with no provisions for quality control over the goods or services produced under the mark in the licensing agreement was referred to the ECJ by the House of Lords in *Scandecor Developments AB v Scandecor Marketing AB*.[266] This is an interesting question which goes to the heart of the function accorded to a registered trade mark. One element of the function of a trade mark is that that of quality control (paras 13.9–13.16). If a trade mark is licensed with no possibility of such control by the trade mark owner, does the trade mark still fulfil its function? If not, must the mark then be revoked? Unfortunately the case settled before judgment was given by the ECJ and so this question remains unanswered to date.

 Exercise

If the case had proceeded, how do you think the Court should have decided it? If you are in favour of licensing with no quality controls, what then do you think is the function of a trade mark?

---

[260] *Magic Ball Trade Mark* [2000] ETMR 226, [2000] RPC 439. See also the discussion at para 14.109 in relation to revocation of a trade mark and whether it must be revoked in full or part.
[261] *Ecros SA v Banco Akros SpA* Decision No 3500/2002 (9 November 2002) Opposition Division.
[262] *Invermont Trade Mark* [1997] RPC 125.   [263] Case C-246/05.   [264] ibid, para 54.
[265] TMA 1994, s 46(1)(d).   [266] [2001] ETMR 74 HL.

Revocation and generic words

14.107   The proprietor of a registered trade mark should also take care that the use does not become generic. This is where the registered trade mark becomes the common name for the product or service for which it is registered. If a registered trade mark does become generic then it can be revoked.[267] Although the section refers to a mark being generic in the trade, the ECJ has said that the relevant classes of persons 'comprise principally consumers and end users. However, depending on the features of the product market concerned, the influence of intermediaries on decisions to purchase, and thus their perception of the trade mark, must also be taken into consideration'.[268] Examples of marks which have become generic in the UK include 'Thermos' for a vacuum flask and 'Escalator' for a moving staircase.[269]

14.108   The proprietor of a registered trade mark would thus be well advised to take certain self-help measures in order to ensure that his mark does not become generic. Such measure may include, for example, emphasising the mark in comparison with surrounding text; never using the mark as a noun or verb, only as a proper adjective, and using the ® symbol.[270] Proprietors of unregistered marks often add the initials TM to their marks. This may be an attempt to warn other traders that they are claiming common law rights in the sign. However, in terms of registered marks, and the TMA 1994, it has no legal significance.

 Question

Can you think of any other marks other that have become generic?

 Exercise

Find five examples of registered trade marks, identified by the ® symbol, and five examples of unregistered signs, identified by the TM symbol. Check the trade mark register to see if the marks showing the ® are on the register.

The extent of revocation

14.109   If a mark is to be revoked, then the question also arises as to the extent of that revocation. Must the mark be revoked altogether, or should the mark remain and only some of the goods or services in the specification be revoked? This was considered in *Premier Brands UK Limited v Typhoon Europe Ltd*[271] where Neuberger J said in applying this section:

> 'One simply looks at the list of items on the register whether or not the mark has been used in relation to or in connection with that item during the past five years. If the answer is in the affirmative then the mark can remain registered in respect of that item; if the answer is in the negative then, subject to any question of discretion the registration is revoked in respect of that item'.

---

[267] TMA 1994, s 46(1)(c).

[268] Case C-371/02 *Björnekulla Fruktindustrier AB v Procordia Food AB* [2004] ECR I-5791, [2005] 3 CMLR 16, [2004] ETMR 69, [2004] RPC 45, para 25.

[269] 'Spork' is a generic term in the catering trade: *D Green & Co (Stoke Newington) Ltd v Regalzone Ltd* [2001] EWCA Civ 639.

[270] TMA 1994, s 95(2) provides that it is an offence to represent that a mark is registered when it is not.

[271] [2000] FSR 767.

This test was considered too narrow in *Minerva Trade Mark*[272] where Jacob J was of the opinion that it did not deal adequately with huge classes of goods described by single phrases like 'computer software' or 'cleaning substances and preparations'. In these circumstances the mark could be partially revoked which itself is not limited to deletion of a single specified item, but could include a category of goods within a general description.[273]

14.110   The CFI considered this in *Mundipharma AG v OHIM*[274] in which it looked at the categories and extent of use for the purposes of revocation. It said:

> '. . . it is in practice impossible for the proprietor of a trade mark to prove that the mark has been used for all conceivable variations of the goods concerned by the registration. Consequently, the concept of 'part of the goods or services' cannot be taken to mean all the commercial variations of similar goods or services but merely goods or services which are sufficiently distinct to constitute coherent categories or sub-categories.'[275]

The desire is to be fair as between trade mark owner and competitor—to ensure that the proprietor is not stripped of protection with respect to all of the similar goods or services for which the trade mark has been used whilst ensuring space for the competitor in the market[276]

Key points on use requirements

- A registered trade mark must be put to genuine use: revocation may occur if it has not been put to genuine use within five years of registration

- Token use is not sufficient for genuine use

- Revocation will not occur if there are proper reasons for non-use

- Revocation can occur where the use of a mark is liable to mislead the public as to the nature, quality or geographical origin of the goods and services; if the use becomes misleading and if the mark becomes generic

---

Further reading

J Belson, 'Certification Marks, Guarantees and Trust' [2004] 24(7) EIPR 340–52

J Bergquist, and D Curley, 'Shape Trade Marks and Fast-moving Consumer Goods' [2008] EIPR 17

T Cohen Jehoram, and M Santman, 'Opel/Autec: does the ECJ realize what it has done?' (2008) 3(8) Journal of Intellectual Property Law and Practice 507

A Firth, 'Shapes as Trade Marks: Public Policy, Functional Considerations and Consumer Perception' [2001] 23(2) EIPR 86–99

---

[272] [2000] FSR 734.
[273] See also *Mercury Communications Ltd v Mercury Interactive (UK) Ltd* [1995] FSR 850; *Decon Laboratories Ltd v Fred Baker Scientific Ltd* [2001] ETMR 46; [2001] RPC 17; *Daimler Chrysler AG v Alavi (t/a Merc)* [2001] ETMR 98, [2001] RPC 42.
[274] Case T-256/04; Case T-483/04 *Armour Pharmaceutical Co v OHIM* [2006] ECR II-4109; Case T-126/03 *Reckitt Benckiser (Espana) SL v OHIM* [2005] ECR II-2861.
[275] Case T-256/04 *Mundipharma AG v OHIM* [2007] ECR II-00449 para 24.
[276] *Mundipharma*, ibid para 24.

A Folliard-Monguiral and D Rogers, 'Community trade mark case law round-up 2006' (2007) 2(4) JIPLP 215–33

A Folliard-Monguiral and D Rogers, 'Significant 2007 case law on the Community trade mark from the ECJ and the CFI' (2008) 3(5) JIPLP 291.

A Fox 'Does the Trade Mark Harmonisation Directive Recognise a Public Interest in Keeping non-distinctive Signs Free for Use?' [2000] 22(1) EIPR 1–6

C Gielen, 'adidas v Marca II: Undue Limitations of Trade Mark Owner's Rights by the European Court of Justice?' [2008] EIPR 254.

A Griffiths, 'Modernising Trade Mark Law and promoting Economic Efficiency: An Evaluation of the Baby Dry Judgement and its Aftermath' (2003) 1 IPQ 1–34

M Handler, 'The Distinctive Problem of a European Trade Mark' [2005] 27(9) EIPR 306–12

L Harrold, 'The genie in the bottle: brand 'free riding': what's permissible and what's not?' (2008) 3(8) Journal of Intellectual Property Law and Practice 511

G Humphreys, 'Deceit and immorality in trade mark matters: does it pay to be bad?' (2007) 2(2) JIPLP 89–96

A Kamperman Sanders, 'The return to Wagamama' [1996] EIPR 521

A Kamperman Sanders, 'The Wagamama Decision: Back to the Dark ages of Trade Mark Law' [1996] 1 EIPR 3

DT Keeling, 'About Kinetic Watches, Easy Banking and Nappies that keep A Baby Dry: A Review of Recent European Case Law on Absolute Grounds for Refusal to Register Trade Marks' (2003) 2 IPQ 131–62

P Prescott, 'Has Benelux Trade Mark Law been written into the Directive' [1997] EIPR 99

P Prescott, 'Think Before you Waga Finger: Comment' [1996] EIPR 317

P Reeskamp, 'Is Comparative Advertising a Trade Mark Issue?' [2008] EIPR 131.

C Schulze, 'Registering colour Trade Marks in the European Union' [2003] 25(2) EIPR 55–67

I Simon, 'Trade Marks in Trouble' [2005] 27(2) EIPR 71–5

C Thompson, B Ladas, 'How Green is my Trade Mark? Woolworths v BP' [2007] 29(1) EIPR 29–35

B Trimmer, 'An Increasingly Uneasy Relationship: The English Courts and the European Court of Justice in Trade Mark Disputes' [2008] EIPR 87.

P Yap, 'Honestly, neither Celine nor Gilette is defensible!' [2008] EIPR 286

Relative ground for refusing registration, infringement and defences

Introduction

Scope and overview of chapter

15.1   It is essential to understand the conditions under which a registered trade mark will be infringed by virtue of unauthorised use by a third party to appreciate the scope of the rights conferred by a trade mark. If a registered trade mark is infringed easily by competing traders, so the trade mark owner will have a broad monopoly in the market. On the other hand, if a competing trader can trade using a sign that is similar to that of the registered mark and in connection with similar goods as services so the monopoly conferred by the registered mark narrows—the greater the similarity the narrower the monopoly. As with other areas of trade mark law there is a constant tension between the desires of the trade mark owner, those of the competing trader and the interests of the consumer. One feature in this is the question as to whether a trade mark will be infringed only if it is used in the course of trade in a trade mark sense, or whether other unauthorised uses of a mark, such as descriptive uses, can be controlled by the trade mark owner. This is turn links to the discussion on defences to an action for trade mark infringement and the extent of permissible uses of a registered trade mark by a third party.

15.2   ### Learning objectives

By the end of this chapter you should be able to describe and explain:

- the current discussions on and relevance of the debate on the use of a trade mark during trade;
- the relative grounds for refusing to register a trade mark and those circumstances in which a trade mark will be infringed by unauthorised use by a third party;
- the scope of defences in relation to an action for trade mark infringement.

15.3   In this chapter, having examined the concept of use in the course of trade for the purposes of infringement, discussion will move to consider the relative grounds for refusal to register a trade mark and those circumstances in which a trade mark can be infringed and consider defences to an action of infringement. As was stated in the last chapter, those provisions on registration of a trade mark on relative grounds virtually mirror the provisions on infringement. The comments in relation to infringement are thus applicable to registration. The chapter will finish with an examination of the defences to an action for trade mark infringement including an analysis of comparative advertising.

So the rest of the chapter looks like this:

- Use of a trade mark for the purposes of infringement (15.4–15.20)
- Relative grounds for refusal of registration and infringement (15.21–15.103)
- Defences to an action of infringement (15.104–15.131)

Use of a trade mark for the purposes of infringement

 Exercise

Read TMA 1994, section 9; Directive, Article 5(3); and CTMR Article 9(2).

15.4   TMA 1994, section 9 provides that the proprietor of a registered trade mark has exclusive rights in the registered trade mark. Under the TMA 1994 these exclusive rights are infringed by the use of the trade mark in the UK without consent.[1] The acts of infringement are specified in TMA 1994, section 10. Infringement proceedings may be commenced on or after the date on which the mark is entered on the register.[2] This date appears on the front of the registration certificate.[3] As the rights conferred by the 1994 Act are territorial, the proprietor may only sue in respect of infringements occurring in the UK including the Isle of Man.[4] As was pointed out in para 13.34 the rights conferred by the CTM extend to all member states of the EU.

15.5   A non-exhaustive list of examples of when a sign which is identical to a registered trade mark is 'used' for the purposes of section 10 can be found in TMA 1994, section 10(4).

Under the 1994 Act, a sign is 'used' when a person:

- affixes it to goods or packaging;[5]
- offers to supply, stocks or markets goods or services under the sign;[6]

---

[1] TMA 1994, s 9(1).   [2] ibid, s 9(3)(a); CTMR, Art 9(3).

[3] Damages for infringement can be backdated and claimed from the date of the filing of the application for registration: TMA 1994, s 9(3).

[4] TMA 1994, ss 9(1), 107 and 108. An action for infringement may be brought by the proprietor of the trade mark: TMA 1994, s 14(1). An exclusive licensee may bring his own proceedings if permitted to do so by the licence: TMA 1994, s 14(1). Otherwise, a non-exclusive or sole licensee has the right to call upon the proprietor to take action, and may do so himself if the proprietor refuses or fails to do so within two months: TMA 1994, s 30(1)–(5).

[5] ibid, s 10(4)(a).   [6] ibid, s 10(4)(b).

- imports or exports goods under the sign;[7] or
- uses the sign on business paper or in advertising.[8]

15.6   TMA 1994, section 10(5) provides that a person who applies a registered trade mark to material which is intended to be used for labeling or packing goods, as a business paper, or for advertising goods, is to be treated as a party to any use of the material which infringes the registered trade mark. Thus, printers, advertisers and publishers can be treated as infringers, although there is a proviso in this section that a person who so applies the mark must have known, or had reason to believe that the application of the mark was not authorised by the licensee. In any unusual circumstances, printers, advertisers and publishers would be well advised to obtain authorisation for the particular application from the proprietor of the registered trade mark, or warranties and indemnities from the purchaser of the services that the activities of the publishers and printers will not infringe the rights attaching to the registered trade mark.

> **? Question**
>
> Can you think of any other circumstances in which the use of a sign might infringe a registered trade mark?

Use for the purposes of infringement: case law

15.7   Under the 1938 Act, a sign had to be used 'as a trade mark' also referred to as 'in a trade mark sense' before infringement occurred.[9] This meant that it actually had to be used as a trade mark, rather than for a descriptive purpose. Thus, for example, the travel writer who wrote an article about a fortnight's hillwalking in the Lake District and gave it the title 'Wet Wet Wet' would be using that mark in a non-trade mark sense because it was actually describing the walk.[10] Whether a trade mark has to be used 'in a trade mark sense' is important as the more uses that a trade mark owner can control, the greater the scope of the monopoly that is conferred on the holder, and the correspondingly greater cost imposed both on competitors and others who may wish to use or to allude to the mark otherwise than in trade. However, it was not clear from the 1994 Act that such use was actually necessary for infringement.[11] In *British Sugar v James Robertsons & Sons Ltd*[12] it was stated that use in a trade mark sense was not a necessary prerequisite to infringement. Subsequent case law from the British and European courts shows that the issue remains unsettled but is developing to tie the question of use to the function of a trade mark.

15.8   An early English case was:

■ *Trebor Bassett Ltd v Football Association Ltd* [1997] FSR 211

Trebor placed cards featuring photographs of England footballers in its packets of candy sticks. The England 'Three Lions' logo, in respect of which the football association owned

---

[7] ibid, s 10(4)(c).   [8] ibid, s 10(4)(d). See also Case C-62/08 *UDV North America Inc v Brandtraders NV.*
[9] *Bismag Ltd v Amblins (Chemists) Ltd* [1940] Ch 667.
[10] This example is taken from the case *Bravado Merchandising Services Ltd v Mainstream Publishing (Edinburgh) Ltd* [1996] FSR 205 OH.
[11] *Wagamama Ltd v City Centre Restaurants Plc* [1995] FSR 713 (Ch D).   [12] [1997] ETMR 118.

a registered trade mark, appeared on the England football shirts worn by the players in the photographs.[13]

The Football Association alleged that Trebor had infringed its trade mark by including these cards with the pictures in which the logo was apparent. The court gave this argument fairly short shrift saying that Trebor's act of publishing and marketing these cards in conjunction with the sweets did not in any sense amount to *using the logo* in respect of the cards on which the photographs appeared. 'Trebor Basset is not even arguably using the logo...in any real sense of the word "uses" and is certainly not, in my judgement, using it as a sign in respect of its cards'.[14]

Figure 15.1 Football Association three lions logo

15.9   This case must have given some comfort to those traders where they might include a registered trade mark belonging to another as an incidental part of their own marketing strategy. An example might be a supermarket advertising its own shops, pictures of which include the interior and thus goods with registered trade marks belonging to others.

15.10   However, as indicated, the ECJ has now had several opportunities to consider the issue. The question is not as simple as use as a trade mark or in a trade mark sense. Rather the question is as to whether the essential function of a mark is likely to be jeopardised through the unauthorised use of the mark by the third party.

■ *Arsenal Football Club Plc v Reed* [2001] 2 CMLR 23

The issue arose over the sale by Reed of souvenirs and memorabilia relating to the football club which incorporated registered trade marks 'Arsenal' and 'Gunners',[15] both marks registered by the club, and their logo, shown in Figure 15.2.

Arsenal football club argued that this use by Reed infringed their registered trade marks. The High Court, however, found that Reed's products did not state a trade origin. In other words,

---

[13] UK Trade Mark No 1104188, class 16, Proprietor: The Football Association Limited.

[14] *Trebor Bassett Ltd v Football Association Ltd* [1997] FSR 211 p 216. For an analysis of similar facts under the law of copyright see *The Football Association Premier League v Panini UK Ltd* [2003] EWCA Civ 995.

[15] UK Trade Mark No 1393206 classes 6 9 14 16 18 20 21 24 26 27 28, Proprietor: The Arsenal Football Club Public Limited Company.

Figure 15.2 Arsenal Football Club logo

Reed was not using the marks *'in a trade mark sense'* but merely in association with club souvenirs—as a badge of allegiance. However, it was felt that sufficient uncertainty surrounded the issued to ask the ECJ to adjudicate on the general question as to whether a registered mark would be infringed if it was being used in such a way that did not signify trade origin.[16] The Court[17] held that it was not a defence to an action for trade mark infringement to argue that a trade mark belonging to a third party was merely being used as a badge of allegiance or loyalty. That the trade mark was used in this manner did not mean that it did not affect the essential function of the mark—that of guaranteeing the identity of the origin of goods or services bearing that mark. The use of the Arsenal Marks in the instant case was 'such as to create the impression that there is a material link in the course of trade' between the goods and Arsenal: 'there is a clear possibility in the present case that some consumers, in particular if they come across the goods after they have been sold by Mr Reed and taken away from the stall where the notice appears, may interpret the sign as designating Arsenal FC as the undertaking of origin of the goods'.

15.11   Ultimately, when the judgment of the ECJ was applied to the case in the Court of Appeal,[18] that court interpreted the test laid down by the ECJ as being not about trade mark use, but whether the use of the sign was likely to affect or jeopardise the guarantee of origin. In the instant case the use of the Arsenal marks was such as to create an impression of a trade link between Arsenal and the goods: whether or not the signs were perceived as badges of affiliation was irrelevant to the function of the mark as a guarantee of origin.[19]

---

[16] The question was: '1. Where a trade mark is validly registered and (a) a third party uses in the course of trade a sign identical with that trade mark in relation to goods which are identical with those for whom the trade mark is registered; and (b) the third party has no defence to infringement by virtue of Article 6(1) of the Council Directive of December 21, 1988 to approximate the laws of the Member States relating to trade marks (89/104); does the third party have a defence to infringement on the ground that the use complained of does not indicate trade origin (i.e. a connection in the course of trade between the goods and the trade mark proprietor)? 2. If so, is the fact that the use in question would be perceived as a badge of support, loyalty or affiliation to the trade mark proprietor a sufficient connection?'

[17] Case C-206/01 *Arsenal Football Club v Matthew Reed* [2002] ECR I-10273.

[18] *Arsenal Football Club Plc v Reed* (No 2) [2003] EWCA Civ 696, [2003] 3 All ER 865, [2003] 2 CMLR 25, [2003] ETMR 73, [2003] RPC 39.

[19] But see the Scottish case *Dyer v Gallacher* [2006] GWD 7-136 where Gallacher was acquitted of criminally infringing the registered trade marks of Glasgow Rangers FC by selling hats and scarves bearing the word 'Rangers' or an 'RFC' monogram without any licence from the club to enable him to do so. See the discussion on passing off in para 17.35ff.

15.12   A somewhat different pronouncement on this question of use was made by the House of Lords in *R v Johnstone*[20] in which their Lordships came to the view that trade mark use was necessary for trade mark infringement and where the wider test of jeopardising the guarantee function was not considered. This case concerned bootleg CDs and the criminal provisions of the TMA 1994. The question was whether the fixation of the performers' names to the CDs amounted to trade mark infringement where those names were also registered trade marks. Having considered the ECJ judgement in the *Arsenal* case the House of Lords came to the conclusion that trade mark use in the sense of the use of a mark likely to be taken as an indication of trade origin was required. Whether the use was trade mark use or not would depend on 'how the use of the sign would be perceived by the average customer of the type of goods in question'. Non-trade mark use would not amount to infringement. The majority of the House *obiter* came to the view that the use in the instant case was not trade mark use.[21]

 Question

What difference does it make to the scope of the rights of the trade mark proprietor if a mark has to be used 'in a trade mark sense' before it will infringe the rights of the registered proprietor?

15.13   The matter returned to the ECJ in *Adam Opel AG v Autec AG*.[22] Opel had a registration of its trade mark not only for full scale motor vehicles, but also for toys. The manufacturer of toy cars, Autec, affixed Opel's registered trade marks to their own toy cars. The issue was thus the use of an identical mark by Autec in connection with identical goods for which Opel had a registration. A number of questions were referred to the Court which included the following:

- Does the use of a trade mark registered also for 'toys' constitute use as a trade mark for the purposes of Article 5(1)(a) of the Trade Mark Directive if the manufacturer of a toy model car copies a real car in a reduced scale, including the trade mark as applied to the real car, and markets it?

The Court reformulated the question as whether, 'when a trade mark is registered both for motor vehicles and for toys [as it was by Opel] the affixing by a third party, without authorisation from the trade mark proprietor, of a sign identical to that trade mark on scale models of that make of car, in order to reproduce it faithfully, and the marketing of those scale models constitutes, for the purposes of Article 5(1)(a) of the directive, a use which the trade mark proprietor is entitled to prevent'.[23] The Court reiterated its judgment in *Arsenal v Reed* stating that the exclusive right under Article 5(1) of the Directive 'was conferred in order to enable the trade mark proprietor to protect his specific interests as proprietor, that is, to ensure that the trade mark can fulfil its functions and that, therefore, the exercise of that right must be reserved to cases in which a third party's use of the sign affects or is liable to affect the functions of the

---

[20] [2003] UKHL 28, [2003] 1 WLR 1736, [2003] 3 All ER 884, [2003] 2 Cr App R 33, [2004] ETMR 2. Note *R v Boulter (Gary)* [2008] EWCA Crim 2375, [2009] ETMR 6 which involved counterfeit goods See para 21.122.
[21] See also *Regina v James Rupert Isaac* [2004] EWCA Crim 1082 CA (Crim Div) on difficulties that can arise in showing use of a cartoon as a trade mark in an action for revocation. Also *Animated Music Ltd's Trade Mark; Application for Revocation by Dash Music Co Ltd* [2004] ETMR 79 TMR.
[22] Case C-48/05.   [23] ibid, para 14.

trade mark, in particular its essential function of guaranteeing to consumers the origin of the goods'[24] so long as the use takes place in the course of trade[25] in the context of commercial activity with a view to economic advantage and not as a private matter.[26] The affixing of an identical sign to identical goods could thus not be prohibited unless it affects, or is liable to affect the function of the trade mark.[27] From this a key question is as to whether the function of a trade mark will be jeopardised—and that will be a matter for the national court to determine by reference to the average consumer of the type of products in question.[28]

15.14   Another question is as to which function of a mark needs to be jeopardised. In *Adam Opel* the question was over identical marks and identical goods and services. Here it has generally been thought that the function of the mark is to guarantee origin. An issue raised by the ECJ in *Adam Opel* (although not by the parties) was what the position would be had it been claimed that the use of the Opel trade mark by Autec diluted the extended functions of a mark. Here the Court said that the affixation of a well-known mark without authorisation would be a use the proprietor could prevent if, without due cause the use of that sign took unfair advantage of, or was detrimental to, the distinctive character or the repute of the trade mark as a trade mark registered for motor vehicles.[29] (For discussion on the extended functions of a mark see paras 13.12ff and 15.65ff).

15.15   The ECJ returned to this in *L'Oreal v Bellure*[30] where the issue was once again of identity of marks. In this case the Court spoke also of the functions of 'communication, investment or advertising'.[31] So it would seem that if these extended functions are implicated then there will be infringement. *L'Oreal* was in the context of comparative advertising (for a discussion see para 15.128). The extent to which these other functions might be relevant when considering use in cases concerning identical marks and goods beyond comparative advertising cases remains to be seen.

 Question

Where the question of the use of a trade mark jeopardising the function of a mark arises in relation to identity of goods and services and use, should the extended functions of a mark be a relevant consideration?[32] If yes, what does this mean for the trade mark owner and the competitor?

Use and company names

15.16   A different question has arisen concerning the adoption of a registered word mark by an unrelated third party without authorisation as a company or business name. Would such use of

---

[24] ibid, para 21.   [25] *Interflora v Marks and Spencer* [2009] EWHC 1095 (Ch)

[26] *Arsenal* fn 17, para 40. Case C-62/08 *UDV North America Inc v Brandtraders NV* para 44.   [27] ibid, para 22.

[28] For questions of use in the context of keyword advertising which were referred to the ECJ for preliminary rulings see Case C-278/08 *Die BergSpechte v Gunter Guni*; Case 236-08 *Google France v Louis Vuitton*; Case C-237/08 *Google v Viaticum*; Case C-238/08 *Google v CNRRH* and the discussion in para 16.67ff.

[29] Case C-48/05, para 37.   [30] Case C-487/07; [2007] EWCA Civ 936.   [31] Ibid, para 58

[32] For a case concerning the 'use' of a mark during the course of commercial negotiations see Case C-2/00 *Holterhoff v Freiesleben* [2002] All ER (EC) 665, [2002] ECR I-4187, [2002] ETMR 79, [2002] FSR 52.

the later sign would amount to use as a trade mark? In *Robelco v Robeco Groep*[33] the ECJ pointed out that the harmonisation brought about by Article 5(1)–(4) of the Directive does not affect national provisions relating to the protection of a sign against use other than for the purpose of distinguishing goods or services, where the use takes unfair advantage of, or is detrimental to the distinctive character or repute of the mark. Thus where a sign—such as a trade or company name—is used other than for distinguishing the goods or services (the origin function), it is necessary to look to the domestic law of the member states to determine the nature and extent of protection given to trade mark owners who claim to suffer damage as a result of such use.[34] This was also the conclusion of the ECJ in *Anheuser-Busch Inc v Budjeovický Budvar*[35] where the Court stressed that that the trade mark proprietor could oppose the later use of a company or business name so long as the later sign was used in the course of trade for goods. Where the mark was used otherwise than to distinguish the goods then relief would only be available where the use of the mark took advantage of, or was detrimental to, the distinctive character or repute of the mark, and where national law provided a remedy.

15.17   Although the Court appears to have been clear in saying that where the company or trade name which is identical or similar to the trade mark is used by the third party in the course of trade to distinguish the same or similar goods and services of that third party the use could be enjoined, a question on this point was again referred to the ECJ in *SARL Céline v SA Céline*[36] by the Cour d'Appel de Nancy France.

15.18   The Court re-iterated earlier case law and said that four factors had to be met:

- that use must be in the course of trade;
- it must be without the consent of the proprietor of the mark;
- it must be in relation to goods or services which are identical to those for which the mark is registered, and
- it must affect or be liable to affect the functions of the trade mark, in particular its essential function of guaranteeing to consumers the origin of the goods or services.

In the instant case the parties had agreed the names were identical. With respect to the third point above, the Court considered the concept 'in relation to' as important noting that within the meaning of Article 5(1) and (2) the phrase is used for the purpose of distinguishing the goods or services in question whereas Article 5(5) is directed at 'the use which is made of a sign for purposes other than distinguishing the goods or services…'.[37] In the instant case:

> 'the purpose of a company, trade or shop name is not, of itself, to distinguish goods or services…The purpose of a company name is to identify a company, whereas the purpose of a trade name or a shop name is to designate a business which is being carried on. accordingly, where the use of a company name, trade name or shop name is limited to identifying a company or designating a business which is being carried on, such use cannot be considered as being 'in relation to goods or services' within the meaning of Article 5(1) of the directive.'[38]

There would however be use in relation to goods within the meaning of Article 5(1) where a third party affixes the sign constituting his company name, trade name or shop name to the

---

[33] Case C-23/01 *Robelco v Robeco Groep NV* [2002] ECR I-10913.

[34] ibid, paras 30 and 34. Note the Tribunal set up at the IPO to deal with the registration of opportunistic company names which might include those where trade marks belong to third parties Companies Act 2006 s 69 and Company Names Adjudicator Rules 2008/1738. For details of decisions see http://www.ipo.gov.uk/cna.htm

[35] Case C-245/02.   [36] Case C-17/06.   [37] ibid, para 20.   [38] ibid, para 21.

goods which he markets[39] (see also para 15.108). Thus, use of a trade mark as a company name is not of itself infringing as it is not 'in relation to' goods and services. It is for the national court to decide in all of the circumstances whether the use should be enjoined.

15.19 In the context of comparative advertising, the Court of Appeal referred questions to the ECJ in *O2 Holdings Ltd, O2 (UK) Ltd v Hutchison 3g Ltd*[40] and *L'Oréal v Bellure*[41] asking whether the essential function of a trade mark in guaranteeing origin is jeopardised where, during the course of trade, a sign is used purely for the purpose of comparing the goods or services of the comparative advertiser with those of the trade mark owner. The judgments are discussed in paras 15.127ff.

Exercise

Critically consider the the decisions of the company names tribunal (on the IPO website) in the light of the judgment in *SARL Céline v SA Céline*.

15.20 As can be seen from the foregoing discussion the place of 'use' in relation to infringement within trade mark law continues to develop.[42] While the general direction of Court of Justice jurisprudence is to tie the question of use to the functions of a trade mark, it will take time to determine whether all functions are relevant in all cases of use and infringement, and more practically, for national courts to determine when the facts would support a finding that the functions had been jeopardised. The matter is important. The more functions that are recognised in an infringement action, and the easier it is to jeopardise a function, so the parameters of the monopoly expand. These issues are intimately linked with the balance within the registered trade mark framework as between the interests of the trader, of competitors and of the consumer.

Discussion point   For answer guidance visit www.oxfordtextbooks.co.uk/orc/macqueen2e/

What functions should be recognised when considering whether use by a third party is relevant to infringement? What are the parameters and what the implications and for whom?

Question

Does permission need to be obtained from the proprietor of the trade mark to use the images of registered trade marks in this book?

---

[39] ibid, para 22.   [40] Case C-533/06 [2006] EWCA Civ 1656.
[41] Case C-487/07 *L'Oréal v Bellure* [2007] EWCA Civ 968.
[42] For a detailed examination of use from a number of different perspectives see J Phillips and I Simon (eds), *Trade Mark Use* (2005).

> ## Key points on use
>
> - Court of Justice of the European Union jurisprudence is developing to tie the question of use for the question of trade mark infringement to the functions of a mark
> - The greater the scope for non-infringing uses by third parties the narrower the monopoly granted by the mark and vice versa

Relative grounds for refusal of registration and infringement

 Exercise

Read TMA 1994, sections 5 and 10; Directive, Articles 4 and 5; and CTMR, Articles 8 and 9.

15.21   The grounds on which an action for infringement of a registered trade mark may be taken under the 1994 Act are to be found mainly in section 10 (1)–(3). As discussed above, these provisions reflect section 5(1)–(3) of the 1994 Act which deal with the relative grounds for refusal of registration. In *LTJ Diffusion SA v Sadas Vertbaudet SA*[43] the ECJ said:

> 'the question submitted will be examined . . . solely in the light of Article 5(1)(a) of the Directive, but the interpretation adopted following that examination will also apply to Article 4(1)(a) of the Directive since that interpretation will be transposable, mutatis mutandis, to the latter provision'.[44]

In *10 Royal Berkshire Polo Club*[45] the appointed person noted:

> 'Objections under section 5(2) are conceptually indistinguishable from actions under section 10(2) of the Act (Article 5(1)(b) of the Directive). They serve to ensure that trade marks whose use could successfully be challenged before the courts are not registered'.[46]

These sections are therefore dealt with together in this part.[47]

Identity of goods and services and of marks

 Exercise

Read TMA 1994, sections 5(1) and 10(1); Directive, Articles 4(1)(a) and 5(1)(a); and CTMR, Article 8(1)(a) and 9(1)(a).

---

[43] Case C-291/00 [2003] ECR 1-2799.   [44] ibid, para 53.
[45] *10 Royal Berkshire Polo Club Trade Mark* [2001] RPC 32.   [46] ibid, para 17.
[47] Infringement proceedings for infringement of the exclusive rights of the proprietor of a registered trade mark can only be commenced once the trade mark appears on the Register: TMA 1994, s 9(3)(a). Damages, however, can be obtained from the date of the filing of the application for registration: TMA 1994, s 9(3). An infringement of the exclusive rights attaching to a registered trade mark is actionable by the proprietor: TMA 1994, s 14(1). The exclusive rights attaching to a registered trade mark can be infringed by non-graphic use, for example orally: TMA 1994, s 103(2).

> Section 5(1) of the 1994 Act provides that:
> • a trade mark shall not be registered if it is identical with an earlier trade mark and the goods or services for which the trade mark is applied for are identical with the goods or services for which the earlier trade mark is protected.
>
> Section 10(1) of the 1994 Act provides that:
> • a person infringes a registered trade mark if he uses in the course of trade a sign which is identical with the trade mark in relation to goods or services which are identical with those for which it is registered.

15.22   There are some important points arising from the wording:

• There is no need to show a likelihood of confusion amongst relevant consumers for registration to be refused, or for there to be infringement of the registered mark.

• Apart from those cases dealing with use (paras 15.13–15.19), comparative advertising (paras 15.127ff) and keyword advertising (paras 16.67ff) few cases have arisen under this section as it flies against the most fundamental tenets of trade mark law: that a trade mark is an indication of origin.[48] If two or more identical marks belonging to different proprietors are registered for identical goods or services (or if the specifications for which the goods and services are registered overlap),[49] then the consumer is bound to be confused as to the origin of those goods or services. Take the example of the Bass triangle given in para 13.22. That mark has been registered by Bass plc for beer. If another company making beer were able to register an *identical* trade mark for their beer, then how could the consumer identify the origin of the particular goods in the supermarket or pub? Thus registration would not be permitted, and looking to infringement one suspects (counterfeiting aside) that if an identical sign is used by a third party in relation to identical goods and services, a gentle warning by the trade mark owner would be sufficient to halt the unauthorised use.[50]

 Question

The section refers to identical marks, and identical goods and services. What therefore amounts to 'identical' in this sense?

Identity of marks

15.23   The question over what amounted to identity of marks arose in *Bravado Merchandising Services v Mainstream Publishing Ltd*.[51] Bravado Merchandising Services owned the registered trade mark 'Wet Wet Wet'. It was registered for inter alia printed matter, books and book covers. Mainstream Publishing produced a book about the pop group and included the name on the cover of the

---

[48] One case to consider s 10(1) was *Primark Stores Ltd v Lollypop Clothing Ltd* [2001] FSR 37 Ch D. Primark had the registered mark 'Primark' in respect of articles of clothing. Lollypop Clothing supplied a retailer with clothing apparently identical to that sold by Primark, and bearing the registered mark. S 10(1) of the 1994 Act was thus found to be infringed.
[49] *Galileo Brand Architecture Ltd Trade Mark Application* (No 2280603) [2005] RPC 22.
[50] But the owner needs to be careful about making threats. For details see para 21.77ff.   [51] [1996] FSR 205 OH.

the reputation of the earlier mark and regardless of the degree of identity or similarity of the goods or services concerned'.[104]

15.52   Thus if there is no similarity between marks then there can be no likelihood of confusion. However, and taking into account the Court's judgment in *Canon*, a *lesser* degree of similarity between the marks can be offset by a *greater* degree of similarity between the goods, and vice versa. There remains as question as to whether there is a threshold of similarity required in relation to goods, without which, however similar the marks, there could never be confusion. The CFI has suggested that this is indeed the case in *Commercy AG v OHIM*.[105]

Question

What do you think of the approach to link the question of similarity of goods and services with the distinctiveness of the mark? Do you think that there is a threshold of similarity required in relation to either marks or goods? Should there be?

15.53   One British case which considered similarity in respect of both marks and goods was *Pfizer Ltd v Eurofood Link (United Kingdom) Ltd*.[106] Pfizer was the owner of the UK trade mark 'Viagra' for a prescription-only pharmaceutical treatment for male impotence. Eurofood was seeking to launch Viagrene, a drink intended to be promoted as an aphrodisiac. Thus neither the marks 'Viagra' and 'Viagrene', nor the goods 'male impotence pills' and 'an aphrodisiac drink', were identical. When Pfizer sued for infringement under TMA 1994, section 10(2), the court found that a number of factors had to be taken into account. There had to be some similarity between the trade marks and goods, but there was no bar to a finding of infringement under TMA, section 10(2) merely because the goods were in some respects dissimilar.

> 'The correct comparison for the purposes of Section 10(2) is not merely a comparison of the use of the mark VIAGRA on a pharmaceutical product and VIAGRENE on a non-alcoholic beverage. It is between VIAGRA on a pharmaceutical product and VIAGRENE as proposed to be used on a beverage which was to be marketed as a drink capable of stimulating the libido of men and women by incorporating a natural herb which was thought to act directly upon the reproductive organs'.

15.54   On the facts the court found that there was a substantial similarity between the trade marks which were inherently likely to be confused if used in relation to similar goods. The goods themselves although superficially different, were similar in that they were both designed to appeal to men suffering from impotence. Pfizer's registered trade mark was thus infringed.

---

[104]   *Vedial*, para 55. See also *L'Oreal SA v Bellure NV* [2006] EWHC 2355, para 111.

[105]   Case T-316/07. See also Case C-398/07 *Waterford Wedgwood v Assembled Investment Ltd*. The Court of Appeal doubted there is a threshold of similarity required in relation to marks. *Esure v Direct Line Ltd* [2008] EWCA Civ 842.

[106]   [2000] ETMR 896, [2001] FSR 3.

Question

To what extent do you think you should abstract from the actual classification of the trade mark to determine whether the goods or services are similar?

Complementarity

15.55   One of the elements to be taken into account in assessing similarity of goods is whether they are complementary.[107] Some guidance on what amounts to complementary was given in *El Corte Inglés v OHIM - Bolaños Sabri*[108] concerning an application to register the word mark 'Piranha' in stylised form as a CTM which was opposed by the owner of the Spanish 'Piranha':

> '...goods are complementary if there is a close connection between them, in the sense that one is indispensable or important for the use of the other in such a way that customers may think that the responsibility for the production of those goods lies with the same undertaking...'.[109]

This narrow approach echoed the earlier case of *Mülhens GmbH & Co KG v OHIM*[110] concerning toiletries and where it was said that:

> 'this aesthetically complementary nature must involve a genuine aesthetic necessity, in that one product is indispensable or important for the use of the other and consumers consider it ordinary and natural to use these products together...'.[111]

Following this reasoning, wine glasses and wine were found not to be complementary.[112]

Likelihood of confusion

Consumer perception

15.56   To show there is a likelihood of confusion, there must be an association between the marks that causes the relevant consumers to believe wrongly that the goods or services come from the same or economically linked undertakings.[113] Thus there can be no objection to registration of a second trade mark under TMA 1994, section 5(2) or infringement under section 10(2) unless it can be shown that the public would believe goods and services come from the same producer or a linked undertaking, including licensed or joint venture arrangements,[114] or where there is a real risk that a significant number of people will believe that there is a connection between the marks.[115] Mere association, in the sense that the later mark brings the earlier mark to mind, is not sufficient (see below paras 15.59–15.64).[116] The principle of availability has no relevance in determining confusion.[117]

---

[107] *Canon*, para 35.   [108] Case T-443/05.   [109] ibid, para 48.   [110] Case T-150/04.   [111] Para 36.
[112] Case C-398/07 *Waterford Wedgwood v Assembled Investment Ltd.*   [113] *Canon*, para 29.
[114] *Canon*, para 29; *Raleigh International Trade Mark* [2001] RPC 11; *Lloyd*, para 17; Case T-104/01 *Oberhauser v OHIM-Petit Libero (Fifties)* [2002] ECR II-4359, para 25.
[115] *Betty's Kitchen Coronation Street Trade Mark* [2000] RPC 825; *Neil King's Trade Mark Application* [2000] ETMR 22.
[116] *Sabel*, para 26.
[117] Case C-102/07 *Adidas AG and Adidas Benelux BV v Marca Mode, C&A Nederland, H&M Hennes & Mauritz Netherlands BV and Vendex KBB Nederland BV.* For a discussion on the principle of availability on registration see para 14.31.

15.60   The argument that likelihood of association is a *separate* test has its origins in Benelux trade mark law and is exemplified by such cases as *Monopoly v Anti-Monopoly*.[127] In this case, registration was refused for the mark 'Anti-Monopoly', not because the consumer would be *confused* as to the origin of the goods, but because a link would be made in the minds of the public with the trade mark 'Monopoly' due to the similarities. In other words the consumer would *associate* the two marks.

15.61   This issue of likelihood of confusion and association has now been considered in a number of cases. In *Wagamama Limited v City Centre Restaurants plc and others*,[128] Wagamama owned the 'Wagamama' trade mark which was registered for restaurants. City Centre Restaurants decided to open a restaurant under the name Rajamama. Wagamama sued for infringement of the trade mark and passing off. The UK court held that there had been infringement and that a case of passing off had been made out. In the judgment much discussion revolved around the phrase 'likelihood of association'. The court found that the wording of the section clearly states that there must exist a likelihood of confusion in the minds of the public, and *included in*, but not separate to, that test was a likelihood of association. Nevertheless, the court concluded that there did exist confusion in the minds of the public as to the origin of the trade mark because it was shown that the public thought that the Rajamama restaurant might be connected with 'Wagamama'.

15.62   The matter was definitively settled by the ECJ in *Sabel BV v Puma AG*.[129] The issue concerned pictures of two 'bounding felines' (large cats). One of the marks included the word 'Sabel' in addition to the picture of the running cat. The question for the ECJ amounted to whether *mere association* between two marks, through the idea of a running cat, justified refusing protection of the later mark for products similar to those covered by the earlier mark. Puma had registered their mark for, inter alia, leather goods which was the same category applied for by Sabel. The Court held that the mere association alone *was not* enough to justify a finding of a likelihood of confusion. The Court also said that the more distinctive the earlier mark, the greater the likelihood of confusion. In the instant case, the earlier mark was not especially well known—the mere fact that the two marks were conceptually similar was not sufficient to give rise to a likelihood of confusion.[130]

15.63   This ruling was confirmed in *Marca Mode CV v Adidas AG*.[131] Adidas had a mark registered in the Benelux office consisting of three parallel stripes in connection with inter alia sports clothes and articles connected with sport. Marca Mode sold sports clothes in the Netherlands which bore two parallel stripes running longitudinally. When the question arose as to whether it was sufficient that consumers associated the mark, or whether there had also to be the likelihood of confusion the ECJ, referring to its judgment in *Sabel*, said that 'the concept of likelihood of association is not an alternative to that of likelihood of confusion, but serves to define its scope. The very terms of the provision exclude its application where there is no likelihood of confusion on the part of the public...'.[132] Further the Court said that 'the reputation of a mark does not give

[127]   *Edor Handelsonderneming BV v General Mills Fun Group*, Nederlands Jurisprudentie 1978, 83.

[128]   [1995] FSR 713.   [129]   Case C-251/95 [1998] 1 CMLR 445.

[130]   See also Case C-425/98 *Marca Mode CV Adidas AG and Adidas Benelux BV* [2000] All ER (EC) 694; *European Ltd v Economist Newspaper Ltd* [1998] FSR 283, [1998] EMLR 536, [1998] ETMR 307.

[131]   [2000] ETMR 723.

[132]   Case C-425/98 *Marca Mode CV Adidas AG and Adidas Benelux BV* [2000] ECR I-4861, [2000] All ER (EC) 694, para 34.

grounds for presuming a likelihood of confusion simply because of a likelihood of association in the strict sense'.[133]

15.64   Thus it is settled that the 'likelihood of association' test is a *subset* of the 'likelihood of confusion' test. It is therefore not sufficient for a consumer to associate two marks: confusion must also be present. The monopoly in the mark is thus kept in check to this extent.

Question

Do you think that the likelihood of association test should be a subset of the confusion test, or a separate test?

Key points on similarity and confusion

- In assessing similarity of marks account needs to be taken of the visual, phonetic or conceptual similarities including the distinctive or dominant component
- In assessing similarity of goods and services account must be taken of the nature of the goods and services, the end uses, the method of use and whether the use is in competition or complementary
- The more distinctive a mark, the broader the protection over progressively dissimilar goods and services
- To show confusion the consumer must wrongly believe that goods and services comes from the same or economically linked undertakings

Researching cases concerning registration and infringement on relative grounds:

Weblinks

As with the absolute grounds for refusal to register a mark, there is a plethora of cases from the national registry, OHIM registry, OHIM Board of Appeals and the General Court concerning in particular the relative grounds for refusing to register a mark and in addition infringement. To research these cases you can look at the databases available on the IPO website at http://www.ipo.gov.uk, at the OHIM website at http://www.oami.europa.eu, and at the Court of Justice website at http://www.curia.europa.eu.

---

[133] ibid, para 41.

Exercise

To understand the process that the examiners, registry and courts engage in when determining the similarities between goods and services, have a look at the reasoning of the CFI in Case T-115/02 *Avex Inc v OHIM*, para 26 and of the OHIM in the same case R 634/2002-1, para 32, and for marks have a look at the judgment of the CFI upholding the finding of the OHIM in Case T-355/02 *Mülhens v OHIM—Zirh International (ZIRH)* [2004] ECR II-791, paras 44–57.

Question

Do you think there are confusing similarities between the following marks? Explain your reasoning.

• EURODATA TV in, inter alia, class 35 for gathering and supply of commercial information, more especially opinion surveys and polls in the audiovisual realm, advising and assisting industrial or commercial undertakings; preparation and supply of trade statistics; marketing studies; market research and analysis'; and M + M EUROdATA in class 35 for market research, market analysis and trade research, services offering advice to businesses in the sphere of marketing and distribution'.[134]

Figure 15.6 HappyDog

• The mark shown above in Figure 15.6 and HAPPIDOG both for foodstuffs for dogs in Class 31.[135]

• PASH for clothing, also made of leather, belts for clothing, footwear, headgear in class 25 and BASS for footwear and clothing[136] in Class 25.

• BUD for clothing, footwear, headgear, sweatshirts, T-shirts, caps and socks, in Class 25 and BUDMEN for clothing, footwear, headgear in class 25.[137]

---

[134] Case T-317/01 *M+M Gesellschaft für Unternehmensberatung und Informationssysteme mbH/OHIM⊠Mediametrie SA* (R 698/2000-1).
[135] Case T-20/02 *Interquell GmbH/OHIM—Provimi Ltd & SCA Nutrition Ltd* (R 264/2000–2).
[136] Case T-292/01 *Phillips-Van Heusen Corp v OHIM* (Pash Textilvertrieb und Einzelhandel GmbH) (R 740/00–3).
[137] Case T-129/01 *Jose Alejandro SL/OHIM—Anheuser-Busch Inc* (R 230/2000-1).

Similar trade marks with a reputation

 Exercise

Read TMA 1994, sections 5(3) And 10(3); Directive, Article 4(4)(a) and 5(2); and CTMR Articles 8(5) and 9(1)(c).

15.65   Under section 5(3) of the 1994 Act when originally drafted a sign would not be registered if it was identical or similar to an earlier trade mark and was to be registered in respect of goods or services which are *not* similar to those for which the earlier trade mark was registered, if the earlier trade mark had a reputation in the UK, and the use of the later mark would take unfair advantage of, or be detrimental to the distinctive character or repute of, the earlier mark. The same provisions applied in relation to an infringement action under section 10(3) of the 1994 Act.

15.66   However, in 2003 in *Davidoff & Cie SA v Gofkid*,[138] the ECJ held that these provisions applied not only to those circumstances in which the goods were dissimilar, but also where the goods were similar or identical. In this case Davidoff who had a registration for a stylised mark, 'Davidoff', sought to have Gofkid's mark, 'Durfee', annulled. The referring court wanted to know whether Articles 4(4)(a) and 5(2) of the Directive were to be interpreted as entitling the member states to provide specific protection for registered trade marks with a reputation in cases where the later mark or sign, which is identical with or similar to the registered mark, is intended to be used or is used for goods or services *identical with or similar* to those covered by the registered mark. In other words, the relevant provisions of the Directive only referred to dissimilar goods and services. Were similar goods and services also covered?

15.67   The Court started off by noting that Article 5(2) of the Directive allows stronger protection to be given to marks with a reputation than that conferred under Article 5(1)[139] where the use of the sign without due cause takes unfair advantage of, or is detrimental to, the distinctive character or the repute of the mark. Where there was no likelihood of confusion, Article 5(1)(b) of the Directive could not be relied on by the proprietor of a mark with a reputation to protect himself against impairment of the distinctive character or repute of the mark.

> 'In those circumstances, . . . Articles 4(4)(a) and 5(2) of the Directive are to be interpreted as entitling the Member States to provide specific protection for registered trade marks with a reputation in cases where a later mark or sign, which is identical with or similar to the registered mark, is intended to be used or is used for goods or services identical with or similar to those covered by the registered mark'.[140]

15.68   As a result of this case the wording of the 1994 Act has been amended[141] and now reads as follows:

> A trade mark which:
>
> is identical with or similar to an earlier trade mark, shall not be registered if, or to the extent that, the earlier mark has a reputation in the United Kingdom (or, in the case of a Community trade mark, in the European Community) and the use of the later mark without due cause would take unfair advantage of, or be detrimental to, the distinctive character or the repute of the earlier trade mark.

---

[138] Case C-292/00 [2003] ECR I-389 (hereafter *Davidoff*).   [139] *Davidoff*, para 19.   [140] *Davidoff*, para 30.
[141] Trade Marks (Proof of Use, etc) Regulations 2004 (SI 2004/946).

Question

Can you explain why you think the Court ruled that similar goods and services should be covered under this section and that protection should not just extend to those circumstances in which they were dissimilar?

15.69   Section 10(3) of the 1994 Act has been amended similarly as has the relevant wording in the codified versions of the Directive and the CTMR

15.70   As explained above, under TMA 1994, sections 5(2) and 10(2) the relative grounds for refusing registration and infringement rest on the basis that there is a likelihood of consumer confusion. There is no requirement for consumer confusion in sections 5(3) and 10(3). It was the ECJs view in *Davidoff* that the protection accorded by this provision should be stronger than that afforded where consumer confusion was a prerequisite. The concern was that if sections 5(3) and 10(3) only covered dissimilar goods and services, then the protection would in essence be weaker. Any litigant who relied on the reputation of the mark under sections 5(3) and 10(3) would only be protected if the goods were *dissimilar.* If the goods were similar, then, even though the mark might have a reputation, protection would have to be sought under sections 5(2) and 10(2).

15.71   Whatever the merits or demerits of this argument, the effect was that the Court extended significantly the ambit of the measure. The judgment has been the subject of both support: J Cornwall,'The Davidoff v Gofkid Case' [2003] EIPR 537 and criticism: C Morcom, 'Extending Protection for Marks Having a Reputation' [2003] EIPR 279.

15.72   The Davidoff case has been affirmed by the ECJ in *Adidas-Salomon AG and Adidas Benelux BV v Fitnessworld.*[142]

 Exercise

Read the articles referred to above. What do you think of the judgment of the ECJ in the *Davidoff v Gofkid* case given the clear wording of the Directive which referred to dissimilar goods and services?

15.73   Returning to the provisions of the TMA 1994 it will be seen from the wording that the requirements of sections 5(3) and 10(3) are:

- the mark must have a reputation in the UK; and
- the use of the later mark without due cause would
- take unfair advantage of, or
- be detrimental to
- the distinctive character or the repute of the earlier trade mark.

---

[142] Case C-408/01 [2004] ETMR 10, ECJ.

Why are these sections included in the legislation?

Unfair advantage

15.74   Looking to the Directive, Recital 9, the purpose of these provisions is to provide *'extensive pro-*
tection to those trade marks which have a reputation'. By contrast with British law, other European
countries have a history of granting marks with a reputation greater protection than those
without. For instance in Germany, the Federal Supreme Court,[143] said that: 'The courts have
repeatedly held that it constitutes an act of unfair competition to associate the quality of one's
goods or services with that of prestigious competitive products for the purpose of exploiting
the good reputation of a competitor's goods or services in order to enhance one's promotional
efforts'. This is sometimes more generally called 'free-riding'. What the competitor is doing
here is attempting to 'take unfair advantage of' a mark with established substantial goodwill.
The advantage for the third party may be a substantial saving on investment in promotion and
publicity for its own mark, and it is unfair because it is done in a parasitic way.[144]

15.75   Referring to both the notion of 'advantage' and what might be unfair, the First Board of Appeal
of OHIM in *Mango Sport System Srl v Diknak*[145] said this:

> 'As to unfair advantage, which is in issue here since that was the condition for the rejection of the mark
> applied for, that is taken when another undertaking exploits the distinctive character or repute of the
> earlier mark to the benefit of its own marketing efforts. In that situation that undertaking effectively
> uses the renowned mark as a vehicle for generating consumer interest in its own products. The advan-
> tage for the third party arises in the substantial saving on investment in promotion and publicity for its
> own goods, since it is able to "free ride" on that already undertaken by the earlier reputed mark. It is
> unfair since the reward for the costs of promoting, maintaining and enhancing a particular trade mark
> should belong to the owner of the earlier trade mark in question'.[146]

15.76   In a similar vein in *L'Oreal v Bellure*[147] the ECJ summed up the notion of unfair advantage saying:

> 'As regards the concept of 'taking unfair advantage of the distinctive character or the repute of the trade
> mark', also referred to as 'parasitism' or 'free-riding', that concept relates not to the detriment caused
> to the mark but to the advantage taken by the third party as a result of the use of the identical or similar
> sign. It covers, in particular, cases where, by reason of a transfer of the image of the mark or of the
> characteristics which it projects to the goods identified by the identical or similar sign, there is clear
> exploitation on the coat-tails of the mark with a reputation.;[148]

Detriment

15.77   The issue of the use of a sign being *detrimental* to the distinctive character or reputation of a mark
has been referred to generally as 'dilution'. Dilution could be generally described as *the whittling*
away of the distinctive character of a trade mark and can be used to refer to both tarnishment and
blurring.[149] As with the notion of 'free-riding', and in contrast with British law, dilution has long

---

[143] *Dimple* [1985] GRUR 550.

[144] Case R 472/2001-1 *BIBA/BIBA* and Case R 552/2000-4 *Cosmopolitan cosmetics / Cosmopolitan.*

[145] Case R 308/2003-1 [2005] ETMR 5.

[146] ibid, para 19. See also Case R 1004/2000-1 *KinderCare*, para 26; *Société des Produits Nestlé SA v Mars Inc* [2005] ETMR 37 OHIM (2nd Bd App).

[147] Case C-487/07.   [148] Para 41.

[149] '[T]he essence [of dilution] is the blurring of distinctiveness of a mark such that it is no longer capable of arousing an immediate association with the goods or services for which it is registered and used'. Kerly's *Law of Trade Marks and Trade Names* (14th edn, 2005), para 9-118.

been a part of the law of other European countries. Its purpose was considered by the German Federal Supreme Court in *Quick*.[150]

> '[T]he owner of . . . a distinctive mark has a legitimate interest in continuing to maintain the position of exclusivity he acquired through large expenditures of time and money and that everything which could impair the originality and distinctive character of his distinctive mark, as well as the advertising effectiveness derived from its uniqueness, is to be avoided . . . Its basic purpose is not to prevent any form of confusion but to protect an acquired asset against impairment'.

Here the German court is referring to detriment to the distinctive character of the mark. The test looks to the impact that the use or proposed use of the second mark has on the existing mark with the reputation. Would that use be detrimental to the distinctive character or reputation of the first mark?

Detrimental to the reputation: tarnishment

15.78   The reputation of a mark can be *tarnished* where the use of the sign is detrimental to the reputation of the well known mark. An example might be by using a phonetically similar word for household cleaner as is registered for an expensive alcoholic beverage.[151]

15.79   As regards the detriment in *L'Oreal v Bellure*[152] the ECJ said that this is caused where a the sign is used by the third party in such a way that its power of attraction is reduced. This may be where the goods or services offered by the third party 'possess a characteristic or a quality which is liable to have a negative impact on the image of the mark'[153].

15.80   In an earlier case, the Third Board of Appeal of OHIM had used stronger language when it said that for detriment by tarnishing it would be necessary to show that a trade mark is 'sullied or debased by its association with something unseemly'[154] and the effect should be that the power of attraction of the trade mark is affected.[155] That might happen when 'the applied for trade mark, to which the mark with reputation may be associated, is used, on the one hand, in an unpleasant, obscene or degrading context or, on the other hand, in a context which is not inherently unpleasant but which proves to be incompatible with the trade mark's image'.[156]

15.81   In *Souza Cruz SA v Hollywood SAS OHIM*[157] the Second Board of Appeal said that this might happen in three ways. Where the mark is:

(1)   linked with goods of poor quality or which evoke undesirable or questionable mental associations which conflict with the associations or image generated by legitimate use of the trade mark by its proprietor;

(2)   linked with goods which are incompatible with the quality and prestige associated with the trade mark, even though it is not a matter of inappropriate use of the trade mark in itself;

(3)   amended or altered in a negative way.

---

[150]   [1959] GRUR 182.

[151]   *Claeryn/Klarein* (1976) 7 IIC 420, Nederlandse Jurisprudentie 1975, 472. Also in the UK, *Inlima SL's Application for a Three Dimensional Trade Mark* [2000] ETMR 325 aff'd [2000] RPC 661.

[152]   Case C-487/07.   [153]   para 40.   [154]   *Elleni Holding BV v Sigla SA* Case R 1127/2000-3 [2005] ETMR 7, para 43.

[155]   In *Adidas-Salomon AG v Fitnessworld Trading Ltd* [2004] Ch 120, ECJ, Jacobs A-G described it (para 38) as: 'the concept of detriment to the repute of a trade mark, often referred to as degradation or tarnishment of the mark, describes the situation where . . . the goods for which the infringing sign is used appeal to the public's senses in such a way that the trade mark's power of attraction is affected'. See also *Spa Monopole v OHIM* [2005] ETMR 109 (CFI).

[156]   *Souza Cruz SA v Hollywood SAS* OHIM Board of Appeal R 283/1999-3, para 85.   [157]   ibid.

The essence is that the mark with the reputation ceases to convey desirable messages to the public.

Detrimental to the distinctive character: blurring

15.82   Blurring has been described as 'the gradual whittling away or dispersion of the identity and hold upon the public mind of the mark or name by its use on non-competing goods'[158] such as the use of a prestige mark in association with T-shirts and window cleaning services. The CFI has said that there will be detriment to the distinctive character where the mark with a reputation is no longer capable of arousing immediate association with the goods for which it is registered and used.[159] The argument is thus that the original exclusive quality of the mark would be lost.[160] The concept has however been said to raise 'difficult conceptual issues'[161] and it has been suggested that where there is no tarnishment or confusion, then no real or verifiable damage would occur.[162] Bently and Sherman suggest that in order to show that the distinctive character of a mark will be blurred, it has to be shown that the earlier mark has a reputation for a limited category of goods. The result is that when the consumer thinks of the mark, they think of those goods. If a third party uses the same or similar mark for dissimilar goods or services so the 'singularity of that association' would be whittled away.[163]

15.83   Just one of these types of injury: taking unfair advantage, detrimental to the reputation and detrimental to the distinctive character is needed for an action,[164] and for Article 4(4)(a) of the Directive at least actual injury does not need to be shown: 'The proprietor of the earlier mark must, however, prove that there is a serious risk that such an injury will occur in the future'.[165]

The extended function

15.84   The inclusion of these provisions in domestic UK legislation marks a departure from the previous law. The provisions of the Directive are permissive: member states did not need to include them in their own laws but the UK chose to do so. As can be seen from the discussion above, the rationales justifying protection for marks with a reputation would seem to move away from the traditional origin function, to protecting the positive reputational 'aura' associated with the mark. As was emphasised by the Third Board of Appeal in *Elleni Holding BV,*[166] a trade mark is not only an indication of origin, but it can also serve as a communication tool. The message that the mark conveys could refer to the quality of the product 'or indeed to intangible values such as luxury, lifestyle, exclusivity, adventure, youth, etc'.[167] As these functions are recognised and protected within the scope of the mark, so the monopoly associated with the mark broadens.

---

[158] F Schechter, 'The Rational Basis of Trademark Protection' (1927) 40 HLR 813, 825. Case C-487/07 *L'Oréal v Bellure,* para 39. Case C-252/07 *Intel v CPM,* para 29.

[159] *Spa Monopole v OHIM* [2005] ETMR 109 (CFI).

[160] F Schechter, op cit; *Parfums Givenchy SA v Designer Alternative Ltd* [1994] RPC 243 where the court considered that damage could be caused by 'erosion of distinctiveness'.

[161] *DaimlerChrysler AG v Alavi* [2001] RPC 42, para 93.

[162] L Bently and B Sherman, *Intellectual Property Law* (3rd edn, 2009) p 886.

[163] ibid. Note that there is no head of damage that would constitute 'fettering' which is said to occur when the opportunities to further exploit the commercial value of an earlier mark are limited by the registration of a later mark: see UK Trade Marks Registry *Esure/Direct Line Insurance* 13 December 2006, para 148.

[164] Case C-252/07 *Intel v CPM,* para 28.   [165] Case C-252/07 *Intel v CPM,* para 38.

[166] Case R 1127/2000-3 *Elleni Holding BV v Sigla SA* [2005] ETMR 7.

[167] ibid, para 41. See also Case R 283/1999-3 *Hollywood/Hollywood,* paras 62–7. *Société des Produits Nestlé SA v Mars Inc* [2005] ETMR 37 OHIM (2nd Bd App).

No longer is it necessary that the consumer be confused: in other words, the mark is no longer limited to its traditional function as a badge of origin. Rather it is the investment in the mark in its ability to communicate a message that is protected. In considering the stakeholder interests that trade mark law accommodates, by protecting marks with a reputation the focus is on the mark and the interests of the trade mark owner. The issue then becomes one as to the scope of that protection, and where the interests of the competing trader and of the public are to be taken into account. Much will depend upon the interpretation of a 'mark with a reputation'; in deciding what amounts to unfair advantage or detriment; and when the use of the mark by a third party might be with 'due cause' thus removing use by a third party from the scope of infringement.

Case law

15.85   Because these concepts were only introduced into British registered trade mark law in the 1994 Act, the UK courts have struggled with the interpretation of the sections. In general, they have seemed ready to accept the notion of tarnishing but have had more difficulty with the other provisions. The task of the courts may now become easier given the opportunities the ECJ has had over recent years to hand down preliminary rulings on a number of matters in a diverse set of cases concerning inter alia sports gear, perfumes and computers. The British case law to date discussed below must be read in that light.

15.86   There are a number of steps to be followed when laying out a case:

- Does the proprietor's mark have a reputation?

- If so, is the defendant's sign sufficiently similar to it that the public are either deceived into the belief that the goods are associated with the proprietor so that the use of the sign takes unfair advantage of the mark, or alternatively cause detriment in their minds to either (a) the repute or (b) the distinctive character of the mark?

- Is the use complained of nonetheless with due cause?[168]

Mark with a reputation

15.87   The TMA 1994 states that the mark must have a *reputation in the UK*,[169] although the sections also provide for a CTM which has a reputation in the European Union. In *General Motors Corp v Yplon SA*[170] the ECJ, in considering the extent of the reputation needed for a trade mark under the Directive held that a mark had a 'reputation' if it was *known by a significant part of the public concerned by the product or services covered by that mark*.[171] Factors to be considered would include the market share held by the trade mark, the intensity, geographical extent and duration of its use, and the size of the investment made in promoting it. With regard to the extent of the territory in which a mark had a reputation, it need not have that reputation throughout the territory, but it is sufficient for it to be known by a significant part of the public concerned in a substantial part of that territory. In the instant case that test might consist of a part of one of the countries

---

[168] *Daimler Chrysler AG v Alavi (t/a Merc)* [2001] RPC 42, para 88.
[169] *Wannabee Trade Mark* 6 November, 2000 (Wannabee—insufficient reputation in the market to rely on s 5(3)).
[170] Case C-375/97 [1999] All ER (EC) 865, [1999] 3 CMLR 427.
[171] See also *Adidas-Salomon AG, Adidas Italy SpA v Gruppo Coin SpA, Oviesse* [2006] ETMR 39 Trib (Rome), para 15; Case T-8/03 *El Corte Inglés v OHIM—Pucci* [2004] ECR II-4297, para 67.

(Benelux) comprising that territory.[172] It is however not enough for a national mark if it is only known in a city and surrounding area; that is not a substantial part of the territory.[173] The question has yet to be resolved for a CTM. A related question has been referred to the Court of Justice in *PAGO v Tirolmilch*[174] asking if a CTM is protected in the whole Union as a trade mark with a reputation, if it has a reputation in only one member state. The issue is important since one of the tests of infringement is that unfair advantage is taken of the mark with a reputation. That would not be possible if a mark did not have a reputation.

Establishing a link

15.88   Unlike TMA 1994, sections 5(2) and 10(2), there is no requirement for confusion on the part of the public before registration is refused or infringement can occur.[175] A crucial point is that the relevant section of the public establishes a *link* between the sign and the mark although the public would not necessarily be confused.[176]

15.89   In *Electrocoin Automatics v Coinworld*[177] the High Court suggested that a relevant link should have an effect on economic behaviour in the marketplace.[178] In other words, it should transfer some benefit from the opponent to the applicant or the trade mark proprietor to the infringer.[179] However, where a mark was seen by the relevant public merely as an embellishment, that does not necessarily establish a link with the registered mark sufficient to satisfy the conditions in Article 5(2) of the Directive.[180] In *Adidas-Salomon AG & Adidas Benelux BV v Fitnessworld Trading Ltd*[181]when Adidas, the owner of the mark consisting of three vertical stripes running parallel down clothing complained of the use by Fitnessworld of a motif consisting of two parallel stripes on clothing it was for the national court to decide, as a finding of fact, whether the relevant public would view the sign purely as an embellishment or whether, notwithstanding the sign was viewed as an embellishment, the relevant link was also established.[182]

15.90   In the later case of *Intel*[183] the ECJ spent some time on the notion of a link. It said that the factors to be taken into account include:

- the degree of similarity between the conflicting marks. The more similar they are the more likely it is that the later mark will bring the earlier mark with a reputation to the

---

[172] The terms 'reputation', 'famous' and 'well-known' are all used in connection with trade marks, although there is little consensus on either what these terms mean, or when a mark will be considered to fall in to one or other category. Art 6*bis* of the Paris Convention gives protection to *well known* marks used in respect of identical or similar goods (not services). The TRIPS Agreement extended the provisions of Art 6*bis* to services (Art 16(2)). Further, Art 16(3) of TRIPS extended Art 6*bis* of the Paris Convention to goods or services which are not similar to those in respect of which a trademark is registered where the use would indicate a connection between the goods and services and the owner of the registered trade mark, and provided the interests of the owner of the registered trade mark are likely to be damaged by such use.

[173] Case C-328/06 *Nieto Nuno v Fraquet*.   [174] Case C-301/07.

[175] Some confusion arose in an early case to consider this subsection, *Baywatch Production Co Inc v Home Video Channel* [1997] FSR 22 where it was suggested that the likelihood of confusion was an essential element for infringement of this subsection. See also *BASF v EP* [1996] ETMR 51. However now, the ECJ in *General Motors v Yplon* Case C-375/97 [1999] 3 CMLR 427, the Trade Mark Registry in *Oasis Stores Ltd's Trade Mark Application* [1998] RPC 631, [1999] ETMR 531, the High Court in *Pfizer v Eurofood Link (UK)* [2000] ETMR 896, [2001] FSR 3, and the Court of Appeal in *BT v One in a Million* [1999] 4 All ER 476, [1999] RPC 1 have all indicated that confusion is not a necessary prerequisite.

[176] *Adidas-Salomon AG v Fitnessworld Trading Ltd* [2004] Ch 120, ECJ, para 31. The perception of the sign must call to mind the memory of the mark *O2 Holdings Limited, O2 (UK) Limited v Hutchison 3G Limited* [2006] EWHC 534 (Ch), para 136.

[177] [2005] ETMR 31, [2005] FSR 7, [2004] EWHC 1498.   [178] ibid, para 102.

[179] *Intel Corp Inc v Sihra* [2004] ETMR 44 [2003] EWHC 17 (Ch).   [180] ibid, para 41.

[181] Case C-408/01 [2004] Ch 120, [2004] 2 WLR 1095, [2004] ETMR 10.

[182] See also R 0506/2003-2 *Société des Produits Nestlé SA v Mars Inc* [2005] ETMR 37.

[183] Case C-252/07 *Intel Corporation Inc v CPM United Kingdom Ltd.* [2009] ETMR 13, [2009] RPC 15.

mind of the relevant public. But even if the marks are identical or very similar, that is not enough for a link.

- the nature of the goods or services for which the conflicting marks were registered, including the degree of closeness or dissimilarity between those goods or services, and the relevant section of the public must be taken into account when establishing a link. The marks may be registered for goods or services in respect of which the relevant publics do not overlap, in which case a link would not be established. Equally, if the goods or services are so dissimilar, the mark with a reputation may not be brought to mind.

- the strength of the earlier mark's reputation. If it is a very strong mark, the reputation may go well beyond the relevant public such that a link will be established;

- the degree of the earlier mark's distinctive character, whether inherent or acquired through use. The stronger a mark the more likely it is that the relevant public will call it to mind when confronted with a later identical or similar mark. If the mark is unique, the distinctive character will be strong.

- the existence of the likelihood of confusion on the part of the public. If confusion is established then a link is necessarily established although confusion is not required.[184]

Exercise

Read *Adidas-Salomon AG & Adidas Benelux BV v Fitnessworld Trading Ltd* in the light of what the Court has said about a link in *Intel*. Do you think there was sufficient to establish a link in *Adidas*? Or was the use of the sign pure embellishment?

Unfair advantage

15.91   The guidance from the ECJ will shape future national court decisions as they arise. It is however interesting to look at the British cases which have dealt with these points prior to the Court's ruling and the extent to which they anticipated the issues that arose. In *Oasis Stores Ltd's Trade Mark Application*[185] the Registrar was faced with an application to register 'Ever Ready' for condoms. This was opposed by Ever Ready plc who already had a registration for 'Eveready' in connection with inter alia batteries. Would the later registration take unfair advantage of the repute of the earlier trade mark? Here the Registrar said that 'simply being reminded of a similar trade mark with a reputation for dissimilar goods [does not] necessarily amount to taking unfair advantage of the repute of that mark'.[186]

15.92   The Registrar was clearly alive to the fact that if merely being *reminded* of an earlier mark with a reputation meant that a later mark could not be registered or the use of the same or a similar sign amounted to infringement, then the breadth of the monopoly enjoyed by the earlier mark would be very broad. Confusion may not be required but, as indicated in *Intel*, something else clearly is and that should be something that goes beyond being reminded of the earlier mark—in other words, the 'link'. In *L'Oreal v Bellure*[187] in the High Court it had been suggested there were three types of links, the third of which was 'where the public considers the sign to be similar to the mark and perception of the sign calls to mind the memory of the mark, although

---

[184] paras 42–58   [185] [1998] RPC 631.   [186] ibid, p 649.   [187] [2006] EWHC 2355 (Ch).

the two are not confused (likelihood of association in the strict sense)'—a matter also touched on by the ECJ in *Intel*.[188] So there is something of a struggle in the national courts to determine what this link actually is that does not require confusion, but which is not the same as the type of association in issue in *Sabel BV v Puma AG*[189] (para 15.62).

Question

Critically consider what you think is meant by 'likelihood of association in the strict sense' and how that differs from 'calling to mind the memory of the mark'.

15.93 Some suggestion of the Registry's view of what more was needed in the context of taking advantage of the repute of an existing mark is given in the case below.[190]

■ *Inlima SL's Application Opposition of Adidas AG*

The issue concerned the use of the three-stripe emblem owned by Adidas. Inlima applied to register a bottle in the shape of a boot that also had three stripes.

Figure 15.7 Inlima's boot shaped bottle with three stripes

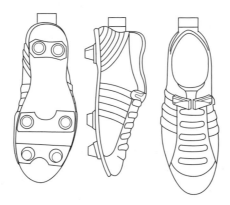

In rejecting the application, the Registry considered that the applicants get-up was designed to bring Adidas' mark to mind, and was thus 'precisely the sort of parasitic use that section 5(3) was intended to provide protection against'.[191] The Registry suggested that to establish benefit there must be some conceptual similarities between the reputation of the earlier mark and the goods in respect of which the sign was to be used. Here the connection between the stripes, isotonic drinks in the specification and sport was sufficient. As indicated above, the Court of Justice in *Intel* has now said that there is no need for the similarity—rather the test is nuanced as, for example, the reputation of a unique mark may cross many publics (para 15.90).

---

[188] Case C-252/07 *Intel v CPM*. [189] Case C-251/95 [1998] 1 CMLR 445. [190] [2000] ETMR 325.
[191] ibid, p 336.

15.94   Prior to the reference to the ECJ, the High Court in *Intel Corp Inc v CPM Technologies Ltd*[192] considered that in order to establish unfair advantage a link had to be made between the marks
which had economic consequences beneficial to the user of the later mark. In the event the
court found that link not to be established and so no declaration of invalidity made. Intel, as
indicated above, appealed to the Court of Appeal[193] which in turn referred questions to the
ECJ.[194] One of the questions put by the Court of Appeal was whether a link would be established
in the instant case. The ECJ declined to answer, repeating its mantra that it is for the national
court to decide on all of the facts of the case.

 Question

Looking at the facts in *Intel*, do you think a relevant link was established in this case? Or
was the High Court right in its assessment?

15.95   In *L'Oreal and others v Bellure and others*[195] which concerned packaging for perfumes, one of the
key questions was whether unfair advantage had been taken.

The High Court had found that certain of the packaging and bottles used for 'look- alike' perfumes infringed the registered marks as they took unfair advantage of the character or reputation of the registered marks. The court said that the extent of the similarity between certain
of the packaging was deliberate. 'It "winks at" the packaging of the premium brand'.[196] The
perfumes chosen as comparators were well promoted brands which were extensively advertised. The infringing perfumes benefited from the advertising and promotion of the expensive
perfumes. Thus 'the reward for the costs of promoting, maintaining and enhancing a particular
trade mark has been received by [the defendants]. That amounts to "free riding" and thus to
the taking of an unfair advantage'.[197] On appeal, the Court of Appeal[198] referred a number of
questions to the ECJ.[199] On the question of unfair advantage the Court of Appeal doubted the
test for unfair advantage laid down in *Mango Sport v Diknak*[200] (para 15.75) as that court had
focused on advantage and not what was unfair. So the Court of Appeal formulated a question
asking what amounted to unfair if advantage was taken. As indicated above, the ECJ stated that
unfair advantage refers to cases where there is exploitation on the coat-tails of the mark with a
reputation due to a 'transfer of the image of the mark or of the characteristics which it projects
to the goods identified by the identical or similar sign . . .'[201]. A global assessment needed to be
made of all of the facts, but in the instant case where a third party might benefit from the power
of attraction and prestige of a mark with a reputation without paying financial compensation
and using the marketing effort expended by the proprietor of the mark with a reputation, that
would amount to advantage unfairly taken of the distinctive character or repute of the mark. So
the focus of the unfairness is on the benefit to the free rider, rather than on the detriment to the
trade mark owner.

15.96   After *Intel* and *L'Oreal* were heard by the ECJ, the Court of Appeal had the opportunity to consider what might amount to unfair advantage in *Whirlpool Corporation v Kitchen Aid*.[202] Here

---

[192] [2006] EWHC 1878 (Ch). See also Case C-320/07 *Antartica Srl v OHIM* on the word 'Nasdaq'.
[193] [2007] EWCA Civ 431.   [194] Case C-252/07.   [195] [2006] EWHC 2355 (Ch).   [196] ibid, para 151.
[197] ibid, para 152.   [198] [2007] EWCA Civ 968.   [199] Case C-487/07.
[200] Case R 308/2003-1 [2005] ETMR 5.   [201] para 41.   [202] [2009] EWCA Civ 753.

Whirlpool argued that the shape of Kenwood's new mixer, Kkix, infringed its 3d CTM for the KitchenAid mixer. The question thus concerned similar publics and similar goods. The Court of Appeal in a lengthy judgment found that the CTM was a mark with a reputation but that no advantage had been taken of it by Kenwood, and even if advantage had been taken, it was not unfair. Unfortunately little further guidance was given on what might amount to *unfair* advantage suggesting that it may be challenging to plead a successful case on the grounds that unfair advantage has been taken of the distinctive character or repute of a mark.

Detrimental to the reputation: tarnishment

15.97   As indicated above, the ECJ in *L'Oreal v Bellure*[203] said that detriment through tarnishment or degradation is caused when the mark is used in such a way by the third party that the power of attraction of the mark may be reduced and this could arise, in particular where the goods or services offered by the third party have characteristics or qualities which are likely to have a negative impact on the image of the mark.[204]

15.98   The Registry and courts considered what amounts to tarnishment in a number of cases prior to the Court's judgment in *L'Oreal v Bellure*. In *Inlima SL's Application Opposition of Adidas AG*[205] (discussed, above para 15.93) although the Registry found a connection between the application and the mark with the reputation, the refusal to register concerned the extent to which detriment would be caused to the existing marks by use of the second. As the Registry pointed out: 'The applicants have alcohol included in their specification. Given the similarity of the applicants' mark to the goods of the opponents the use of the applicants mark on alcohol would, in my view, be detrimental to the opponents'.[206] A similar line was taken in *C A Sheimer (M) Sdn Bhd's Trade Mark Application*,[207] where the question was over the proposed registration of 'Visa' for condoms, opposed by Visa International. 'I think it is a fair inference from the evidence before me that so many people are so deeply imbued with Visa International's use of the word VISA as its trade mark that Sheimer's use of the word would to a significant extent trigger recollections of Visa International and its services'.[208] But something more was needed: 'Would it also exploit the distinctive character of the earlier trade mark positively (by taking unfair advantage of it) or negatively (by subjecting it to the effects of detrimental use)'?[209] In this case it was felt that the use by Scheimer of the word 'Visa' for condoms would damage the reputation of the earlier trade mark because it would 'burden Visa International's use of the mark with connotations of birth control and personal hygiene...Visa International should not have to carry the burden of advertising condoms and prophylactics at the same time as it promotes its own services'.[210] Registration was thus refused.[211] Similarly, Viagrene in relation to poor quality or ineffective goods (at least where male impotence was concerned) would tarnish Viagra;[212] and the use of 'Intel-Play' mark on inferior goods (toys) would 'almost certainly reduce the distinctive character of the Intel mark.[213]

---

[203] Case C-487/07   [204] Para 40   [205] [2000] ETMR 325.   [206] ibid, p 336.

[207] [2000] RPC 484, [2000] ETMR 1170.   [208] [2000] RPC 484, p 502.   [209] ibid, p 504/505.

[210] ibid, p 506.

[211] See *Mastercard International Inc v Hitachi Credit (UK) Plc* [2004] EWHC 1623, [2005] ETMR 10, [2005] RPC 21 where the question was whether the use of 'Credit Master' would be detrimental to the distinctive character or reputation of 'Mastercard'. The court found that there was insufficient similarity between the marks for the average consumer to make an association. Some proof of damage was required.

[212] *Pfizer Ltd and Pfizer Incorporated v Eurofood Link (United Kingdom) Ltd* [2000] ETMR 896, [2001] FSR 3, para 15.53.

[213] *Intel Corp Inc v Sihra* [2004] ETMR 44, [2003] EWHC 17 (Ch).

15.99   So, in the UK, while the use (or application for registration) of a sign which is the same or
similar to a mark with a reputation may be enjoined if it is used in connection with alcohol,
condoms or poor quality, ineffective or inferior goods, the use of a sign similar to a mark with
a reputation in connection with clothes aimed at mods, skinheads and casuals would seem not
to be sufficient to show detriment to the reputation of the mark.

■ *Daimler Chrysler AG v Alavi (t/a Merc) [2001] RPC 42*

Daimler brought an action under TMA 1994, section 10(3) against Alavi for the latters' use of
the word 'Merc' for a shop selling clothes and shoes. Alavi applied for the registration of the
mark in Figure 15.8 below.

Figure 15.8 Alavi's Merc mark

as a CTM. This was opposed by Daimler Chrysler arguing that the use of the word 'Merc' word
by Alavi for the shop damaged the reputation of Daimler's marks since Alavi's business was
targeted at *mods, skinheads and casuals*, none of which groups it wished to be associated with. In
other words, the claim was that the reputation of Daimler's marks would be damaged. The High
Court rejected the claim saying that:

> '[I]n order to succeed . . . it must be shown that there is established in the mind of the relevant public a
> connection between the mark with which they are familiar and the disparaging use. Thus, it is not suffi-
> cient to see the work MERC, note that this is the word which one uses to refer to Mercedes cars, see
> the disagreeable web site and register it as disagreeable, if nothing actually rubs off on the sign MERC
> itself or on MERCEDES, or on Daimler Chrysler. I was not satisfied that this was the case here, and so
> this allegation of infringement fails'.[214]

Detrimental to distinctive character: blurring

15.100   A number of cases have considered whether the use of (or application for) a sign might be detrimental to the distinctive character of the mark with a reputation. In other words, whether it
would lead to blurring. In one of the first hearings on this provision in the Registry, *AUDI-Med
Trade Mark*,[215] there was a clear concern to work out the parameters of the provision. 'Any use of
the same or similar mark for dissimilar goods or services is, to some extent, liable to dilute the
distinctiveness of the earlier mark. The provision is clearly not intended to have the sweeping
effect of preventing the registration of any mark which is the same as, or similar to a trade mark
with a reputation. It therefore appears to be a matter of degree'.[216] The Registry also indicated that

---

[214] [2001] RPC 42 at p 842.   [215] [1998] RPC 863, [1999] ETMR 1010.   [216] [1998] RPC 863, p 872.

it would be more difficult to show unfair advantage where the marks were descriptive ordinary words than if they were invented words. Other cases have perhaps been less clear in applying this provision. In *Premier Brands UK Ltd v Typhoon*[217] the attempted registration by Typhoon of the mark 'Typhoon' for kitchenware, was opposed by Premier Brands, who had the registration of 'TY.PHOO' for tea.[218] The court opined that: 'The use of the sign in such circumstances will lead to blurring, as it will reduce the uniqueness of the TY.PHOO mark as a brand name in the kitchen'.[219] This was however subject to the proviso that the association had to be such as to be 'detrimental as to the character or repute of the mark'. In this case, the existence of the association in the minds of a limited proportion of members of the public would not result in a 'lessening of the capacity of [the TY.PHOO] mark to identify and distinguish goods'[220], nor would it impinge upon 'the position of exclusivity [Premier] acquired through large expenditure of time and money', nor could it 'impair the originality and distinctive character of [the TY.PHOO] mark'.[221]

15.101   In *Julius Sämann Ltd, Julius Sämann Ltd, H Young (Operations) Limited v Tetrosyl Limited*[222] the High Court found a case to be made out. The question was whether the production by Tetrosyl of an air freshener in the shape of a fir tree diluted the earlier tree shaped marks for inter alia air fresheners belonging to Julius Samann Ltd. The court found that the tree marks had a substantial reputation in the UK and that there was 'a real probability that members of the public seeing the Christmas Tree product will think that it is another product in the Magic Tree range or a Christmas version of the Tree products'. On the evidence the average consumer would make a link between the sign and the Tree marks 'and that this will inevitably damage the distinctiveness of the Tree marks. Their capacity to denote the products of the claimants exclusively will be diminished'.[223]

As the sign used by Tetrosyl was both similar to Samann's mark and used in connection with similar goods for which it was registered it might be questionable whether the use by Tetrosyl of the tree mark would result in the registered mark owned by Samann being no longer capable of arousing immediate association with the goods for which it was registered and used.

Discussion point   For answer guidance visit www.oxfordtextbooks.co.uk/orc/macqueen2e/

Read *Julius Sämann Ltd, Julius Sämann Ltd, H Young (Operations) Limited v Tetrosyl Limited* [2006] EWHC 529 (Ch) Ch D. Do you think that the use of the sign by Tetrosyl was:

- taking advantage
- detrimental to the distinctive character
- detrimental to the reputation

of the earlier mark owned by Samann? Justify your response.

If you want to see the registered tree mark you can find it on the trade mark database at the IPO. You could compare the case with the findings of the CFI in Case T-168/04 *L & D, SA, v OHIM/ Julius Sämann Ltd*, in which L&D had applied to register the same mark as a CTM. This was opposed by Julius Samann on the basis of its earlier marks. There the CFI found that the marks and goods (apart from Class 35 services) were similar, and that there was a likelihood of confusion. This was upheld by the ECJ.[224]

---

[217] [2000] ETMR 1071, [2000] FSR 767.   [218] In class 30.   [219] [2000] FSR 767, p 793.   [220] ibid, p 787.
[221] ibid, p 801.   [222] [2006] EWHC 529 (Ch).   [223] ibid, para 84.   [224] Case C-488/06P.

15.102   So as can be seen, there has been some difficulty evidenced in the registry and courts as to what is required by this provision. This may well be as a result of the conceptual confusion underlying the provision as discussed in para 15.82. As the ECJ has now had the opportunity to consider what might amount to detriment to the distinctive character in the *Intel* case discussed above the guidance given might alleviate some of the difficulties. The relevant questions on this part referred to the Court asked whether it only applied to a unique mark; whether a first use of a mark by a third party would be sufficient; and whether the economic behaviour of the consumer had to alter to satisfy the test. The Court responded saying that a mark does not necessarily need to be unique to establish the link but the stronger the reputation of the first mark the easier it may be to show that link; that first use of a later mark might sometimes be sufficient; and that evidence is needed of a 'change in the economic behaviour of the average consumer of the goods or services for which the earlier mark was registered consequent on the use of the later mark, or a serious likelihood that such a change will occur in the future'[225] although not relevant is whether the proprietor of the later mark gets commercial benefit from the distinctive character of the earlier mark.[226] It is for the national court to make a global assessment based on all of the factors. So in terms of future cases based on this head of dilution, the Court has given valuable guidance although there will continue to be difficulties for national courts and applicants. It will not, for instance, be easy to show that the economic behaviour of the consumer has changed due to the later use of the mark by the third party.

Question

Explain when you think it could successfully be shown that an application or use of a sign could be detrimental to the distinctive character of the earlier mark with a reputation.

Discussion point   For answer guidance visit www.oxfordtextbooks.co.uk/orc/macqueen2e/

Do you see any bright line distinctions between the likelihood of association test which, for TMA 1994, sections 5(2) and 10(2) is only a subset of the likelihood of confusion test, and what is meant by 'taking advantage' of in relation to TMA 1994, sections 5(3) and 10(3)?

Without due cause

15.103   It will be noted from the legislation that the use of the sign and the taking of unfair advantage of, or being detrimental to the earlier mark must be without *due cause*. In *Premier Brands v Typhoon*[227] the court emphasised that regard should be had to the purpose of the provision which is to protect the value and goodwill of well-known trade marks from being unfairly taken advantage of or unfairly harmed. The burden of proof is on the defendant to show that the use complained of is 'with due cause' and that the taking of unfair advantage or causing of detriment are not 'without due cause'. In *Julius Sämann Ltd, Julius Sämann Ltd, H Young (Operations) Limited v Tetrosyl Limited*[228] the court thought that 'All of these matters point to a relatively stringent test'.[229] Beyond these comments there is little guidance as to what may amount to 'due

---

[225] Intel para 77   [226] Intel para 78   [227] [2000] FSR 767.   [228] [2006] EWHC 529 (Ch) Ch D.
[229] ibid, para 84.

cause' and hence when the use of a well known mark which otherwise takes unfair advantage of, or causes detriment to the earlier mark might be excused.

 Question

Can you think of any circumstances where the use of a later mark might be with due cause and when the taking of unfair advantage or causing of detriment would not be without due cause?

 Exercise

For a case heard by the Supreme Court of Appeal in South Africa on matters of dilution see *Laugh It Off Promotions CC v South African Breweries International (Finance) BV*[230] in which a parody by Laugh It Off Promotions on a T-shirt of Carling Black Label's trade mark was considered. In giving judgment the court weighed the right to freedom of speech (the parody of the trade mark) against the intellectual property rights in the mark and considered that placing the onus on the trade mark holder to adduce evidence to prove the likelihood of substantial economic harm as a result of this parody was an appropriate balance of these rights. The court found that harm to the mark had not been proven. Read and summarise the case which you will find at http//:www.saflii.org/za/cases/ZASCA/2004/76.pdf (you will find images of the T shirt and of the beer label in the text). Give your opinion of the balance the court found between freedom of expression and trade mark rights.

Key points on similar trade marks with a reputation

- These provisions protect the extended functions of a mark
- No consumer confusion is required
- The public must establish a link between the mark with the reputation and the application or allegedly infringing sign (which must affect economic behaviour)
- The use of the later mark must be without due cause

Defences to an action of infringement

 Exercise

Read Trade Marks Act 1994, section 11; Directive, Article 6; and CTMR, Article 12.

---

[230] [2005] FSR 30 Sup Ct (SA).

Question

When do you think a registered trade mark should be able to be lawfully used by an unconnected third party? Revisit your views once you have read this section.

15.104   Defences to an action for infringement of a trade mark are vital to balance the interests of the trade mark owner and the honest competitor. In the *Baby Dry* case[231] (discussed in paras 14.35 and 14.52) it will be recalled that the ECJ appeared to endorse the registration of marks that appeared to some to be no more than descriptive. In so doing the Court linked registration to the defences for an action of infringement. What the court appeared to suggest was that although marks were not to be registered if they consisted exclusively the characteristics of the goods or service, in the next paragraph the court pointed out that the rights conferred by the trade mark would not permit the proprietor to prohibit a third party from using those same indications in the course of trade by reference to the defences in the Directive.[232] It appeared to commentators that, by linking the two, the Court was permitting the registration of a broader category of marks but indicating that a defence would be available for legitimate third party use. This however did not take account of the respective strengths of parties within the marketplace. A small trader might have had great difficulty in resisting calls by Proctor and Gamble to cease using the words '*Baby Dry*' in literature describing the properties of nappies. Since then it appears that the tendency to link the two (registration and infringement) is less common. As was said in *AD2000*,[233] to protect the legitimate interests of honest traders, the first line of protection is to refuse registration of signs which are excluded under TMA 1994, section 3.[234] When a mark has been registered, the honest trader may then point to the defences to excuse certain legitimate uses.

The statutory provisions

15.105   TMA 1994, section 11 contains provisions dealing with circumstances in which the use of a registered trade mark will not infringe the rights of the registered proprietor. The most important are in section 11(2) which contains three circumstances in which a registered trade mark will not be infringed. These are:

- the use by a person of his own name or address;
- the use of indications concerning the kind, quality, quantity, intended purpose, value, geographical origin, the time of production of goods or of rendering of services, or other characteristics of goods or services; or
- the use of the trade mark where it is necessary to indicate the intended purpose of a product or service (in particular, as accessories or spare parts).

Honest practices

15.106   Use for section 11 must be 'in accordance with honest practices in industrial or commercial matters'.[235] The ECJ has said that honest practice constitutes a duty to act fairly in relation to the

---

[231] Case C-383/99 *Procter & Gamble Co v OHIM (Baby Dry)* [2001] ECR 1-6251, [2002] ETMR (3)(22).
[232] ibid, paras 35 and 36.   [233] [1997] RPC 168.   [234] See also *Nichols Plc's Trade Mark Application* [2003] RPC 16.
[235] Trade Marks Act 1994, s 11(2).

legitimate interests of the trade mark owner.[236] In assessing whether this condition is satisfied account must firstly be taken of the extent to which the use of the third party's trade name is understood by the relevant public as indicating a link between the third party's goods and the trade-mark proprietor or a person authorised to use the trade mark; and secondly of the extent to which the third party ought to have been aware of that.

15.107   In *The Gillette Company v LA-Laboratories Ltd Oy*[237] the ECJ had the opportunity to consider what would meet the test of honest practices. Gillette had registered in Finland the trade marks 'Gillette' and 'Sensor' for, inter alia, razors and had marketed razors under this sign comprised of a handle and replaceable blades. LA-Laboratories also sold razors in Finland comprised of a handle and replaceable blades, but under the mark 'Parason Flexor'. This packaging bore a sticker stating: 'All Parason Flexor and Gillette Sensor handles are compatible with this blade'. Gillette objected to this affixing of its trade mark to the packaging. The ECJ confirmed that honest practices constitute a duty to act fairly in relation to the legitimate interests of the trade mark owner. As such, the use of a trade mark would not be in accordance with this test where:

- it is done in such a manner that it may give the impression that there is a commercial connection between the reseller and the trade mark proprietor;[238]
- where the use would affect the value of the trade mark by taking unfair advantage of its distinctive character or repute;[239]
- if the use discredits or denigrates that mark;[240]
- the third party presents its product as an imitation or replica of the product bearing the trade mark of which it is not the owner.[241]

The own name defence

15.108   With regard to TMA 1994 section 11(2)(a) (the 'own name defence'), it will be a matter for consideration in each case as to whether the use by a person of his own name in connection with particular goods or services is in accordance with honest practices. One may question the motives of a software programmer called James Microsoft who wanted to start producing his own software and sell it under the name 'Microsoft'.[242]

15.109   In the Court of Appeal the registration by Mr Adlem of his own name for, inter alia, funeral services was considered in *IN Newman Limited v Richard T Adlem*.[243] In the years prior to the registration Mr Adlem had carried on business as a funeral director, trading under his own name, but had sold that business along with the goodwill. Once the restrictive covenant expired he recommenced the business and registered his name Richard T Adlem. The owners of the original business objected to this registration. Mr Adlem claimed, inter alia, the own name defence.

---

[236] Case C-100/02 *Gerolsteiner Brunnen GmbH & Co v Putsch GmbH* [2004] RPC 39; Case C-17/06 *SARL Céline v SA Céline*; *Bravado Merchandising Services Ltd v Mainstream Publishing (Edinburgh) Ltd* [1996] FSR 205 in which the use of the words 'Wet Wet Wet' as the title of a book was registered but third party use was in accordance with honest practices in industrial and commercial matters.
[237] Case C-228/03 [2005] All ER (EC) 940, [2005] 2 CMLR 62, [2005] ECR I-2337 (hereafter *Gillette*).
[238] *Gillette*, para 42.   [239] ibid, para 43.   [240] ibid, para 44.   [241] ibid, para 45.
[242] In Case C-404/02 *Nichols Plc v Registrar of Trade Marks* [2005] 1 WLR 1418 the ECJ made it clear that the fact that the effects of registration of a trade mark are limited by the own name defence has no impact the assessment of the existence or otherwise of the distinctive character of a name as a mark.
[243] *IN Newmans Limited v Richard T Adlem* [2005] EWCA Civ 741.

The Court of Appeal found that the sale of the business included the goodwill and it was not open to Mr Adlem, even after the expiry of the restrictive covenant, to start a fresh business under exactly the same name. Accordingly the trade mark registration was invalid, Mr Adlem being unable to rely on the own name defence.[244]

15.110   The own name defence applies both to individual names and to company and trade names.[245] While in principle a third party can use a trade name which is identical or similar to a trade name, the use will be subject to the condition of honest practice. As such account should be first of the extent to which the use of the third party's trade name is understood by the relevant public as indicating a link between the third party's goods and the trade mark proprietor, and secondly of the extent to which the third party ought to have been aware of that. Another factor to be taken into account when making the assessment is whether the trade mark concerned enjoys a certain reputation in the Member State in which it is registered and its protection is sought, from which the third party might profit in selling his goods.[246] The Court of Appeal ruled in *Asprey & Garrard Ltd v WRA (Guns) Ltd (t/a William R Asprey Esquire)*,[247] that the use by William Asprey of his own name to carry out a trade the same as Asprey & Garrard did not have to be tackled because it was not William Asprey who was trading, but rather the limited company, WRA (Guns) Ltd. The court added the proviso: 'however honest his subjective intentions may be, any use of his own name which amounts to passing off cannot be in accordance with honest practice in industrial or commercial matters'. In *Hotel Cipriani v Cipriani (Grovesnor Street) Limited*[248] the question was in whether the use of the name 'Cipriani' by Cipriani (Grovesnor Street) could be excused under the own name defence. The High Court considered it was bound by Asprey & Garrard in that the own name defence would not apply as Cipriani was not its own name.[249]

For further discussion on the use of trade names see para 15.16.

The use of indications concerning, inter alia, the characteristics of products

15.111   Section 11(2)(b) of the 1994 Act is designed to allow traders to use registered trade marks where they might wish to describe some of the characteristics of their own products or services. As indicated above, these provisions mirror the grounds for refusing registration under section 3 of the 1994 Act. An indication of the quality, etc, of goods may not be registered as a trade mark. If it is, then a third party using the mark in the course of trade in connection with its own goods or services will have a defence. For example, the maker of chairs might want to describe the fabric in which they were covered, and to do so may use a registered trade mark belonging to the maker of the fabric. As with the first subsection however, the use must be in accordance with honest practices.

---

[244] It is unlikely that a formal change of name (whether personal or company) to take advantage of the own name defence will be look on favourably by the courts: *International Business Machines Corp, IBM United Kingdom Ltd v Web-Sphere Ltd, Richard de Serville, David Markson* [2004] ETMR 94, [2004] EWHC 529 (Ch).

[245] See the opinion of AG Sharpston in Case C-17/06 *SARL Céline v SA Céline* discussed above at para 15.17.

[246] ibid, para 82.   [247] [2002] FSR 31, [2001] EWCA Civ 1499 (CA).

[248] [2008] EWHC 3032. See also para 14.89 and note the judgment of the CA and ECJ.   [249] Para 137.

15.112   The ECJ has indicated that the use of a geographical indication may be in accordance with honest practices even where it is registered as a word mark and even if there exists a likelihood of aural confusion between the mark and the indication of geographical origin.

■ Case C-100/02 *Gerolsteiner Brunnen GmbH & Co v Putsch GmbH* [2004] RPC 39 ECJ

This case concerned bottles of mineral water marketed in Germany under the registered trade mark 'Gerri', and bottles of Irish mineral water also marketed in Germany under the mark 'Kerry Spring' (Kerry Spring seemingly being an indication of geographical origin). The owner of the 'Gerri' mark brought trade mark infringement proceedings against the owner of the 'Kerry Spring' mark. The ECJ held that the relevant test is whether or not the use of the geographical indication is used in accordance with honest practices in industrial or commercial matters. 'The mere fact that there was a likelihood of aural confusion between a word mark registered in one Member State and a geographical indication from another Member State was insufficient to conclude that the use of the geographical indication was not in accordance with honest practices'.

15.113   This finding seemed at least in part as a result of the recognition that in a Community of then 15 states (now enlarged) there was a real possibility of phonetic similarity between a trade mark registered in one state and a geographical indication from another. Thus the use of a geographical name as a sign can fall within this defence.

15.114   In *Adam Opel AG v Autec AG*[250] (discussed above, para 15.13) questions were also referred to the ECJ concerning defences. In particular the Court was asked:

- Whether the affixation and use of a trade mark in the circumstances described is an indication of the kind or quality of the model car within the meaning of Article 6(1)(a) of the Trade Mark Directive?

- If yes: what are the decisive criteria to be applied in assessing whether the trade mark corresponds to honest practices in industrial or commercial matters?

- What is the effect of the toy manufacturer applying his own recognisable trade mark to the packaging?

The Court, having pointed out that the relevant provision was actually Article 6(1)(b) of the Directive, said that while it was intended to prevent the owner of a trade mark prohibiting competitors from using one or more descriptive terms forming part of the registered mark to indicate certain characteristics of their products, it was not limited to such a situation.[251] However, in the instant case, the affixation of a sign identical to a trade mark registered in respect of models of that make of vehicle in order to reproduce the vehicles was not an indication of the characteristics of the scale models but rather part of the faithful reproduction of the vehicle. In view of the answer given to this question, and the question on use, the Court found it unnecessary to reply to the other points.

15.115   Although the ECJ has suggested that the parameters of the defence in Article 6(1)(b) might be broader than suggested by the wording, the defence will not be applicable where an identical

---

[250] Case C-48/05.   [251] ibid, para 42.

sign is used in a reproduction of an original albeit designed for a different market where the origin function is compromised.

? Question

Given the ECJ's judgment in *Adam Opel AG v Autec AG* both in relation to the question of 'use' of the trade mark, and the defences, how do you think the national court should have decided the case? If the use jeopardises the essential function of the mark, and the toy manufacturer has no defence to the infringement, what does that say about the monopoly conferred by the trade mark and the function performed by the trade mark? (You might like to have a look at the opinion of the AG to see what was said there.) You will remember that in *AD2000* the court said that the first line of protection for the legitimate interests of honest traders is to refuse registration of signs which are excluded under TMA 1994, section 3. By analogy, at what point could, or should, the legitimate interests of the honest trader be protected in this scenario?

The use of the trade mark where it is necessary to indicate the intended purpose of a product or service (in particular, as accessories or spare parts)

15.116   Section 11(2)(c) of the 1994 Act is particularly important for those who manufacture spare parts for goods, for example consumer goods, agricultural machinery and cars. This section provides that the use of a registered trade mark will not infringe that mark where it is necessary to indicate the intended purpose of a product or service (in particular, as accessories or spare parts). It may be that a computer programmer selling computer software wants to advertise by stating 'compatible with Microsoft 95 software'. So long as the use is necessary and in accordance with honest practices such use of the registered trade mark should be permitted.

15.117   In *The Gillette Company v LA-Laboratories Ltd Oy*[252] (above, para 15.107) the ECJ had the opportunity to consider what was meant by 'necessary' to indicate the intended purpose of a product'.[253] A use would be necessary where the trade mark was used 'to indicate the intended purpose of a product marketed by that third party where such use in practice constitutes the only means of providing the public with comprehensible and complete information on that intended purpose in order to preserve the undistorted system of competition in the market for that product'.

15.118   The Court has stressed that a trade mark can be used by a third party when advertising goods for sale. However, in relation to luxury marks the Court said in *Parfums Christian Dior SA v Evora BV*,[254] that the reseller could not act to the detriment of the trade mark owner. A balance has to be struck between the interests of resellers on the one hand, and of the trade mark proprietors on the other who will always have a desire to preserve the prestige of the trade mark.

15.119   In assessing whether the defence is available, the whole circumstances of the case should be considered. If the use of the mark suggests that there is a connection between the third party and the trade mark owner, then the use is likely to be enjoined.

---

[252] [2005] 2 CMLR 62, [2005] ECR I-2337.   [253] *Gillette*, para 39.   [254] Case C-337/95 [1998] RPC 166.

■ *Aktiebolaget Volvo v Heritage (Leicester) Ltd* [2000] FSR 253

Heritage had been an approved Volvo dealer, but that approval had been withdrawn. Heritage became a member of the Association of Independent Volvo Specialists, a group consisting of other motor dealers in the same situation. Heritage replaced a Volvo sign outside its premises with a new sign that read 'Independent Volvo Specialist', the word 'Volvo' being written in larger script than the other two. In addition, Heritage sent letters to customers that failed to indicate the true status of the relationship with Volvo. When challenged, Heritage argued that the use of the word 'Volvo' was necessary to describe the type of service being offered. The High Court found that while the use of the word Volvo was necessary to describe the service, such use had to be in accordance with honest commercial practices in which the *whole* circumstances of the use must be considered. Both the letters and the sign could be seen as deliberate attempts to cause confusion in the minds of its customers by indicating that a trading relationship still existed. The use was therefore *not* an honest use in the context of the motor trade.

15.120   Similarly in *Bayerische Motorenwerke AG v Deenik*,[255] the ECJ stressed that if the use of the mark makes customers believe that there is a commercial connection between that other party and the trade mark owner when in fact this does not exist, then such use would *not* be in accordance with honest commercial practices.

 Question

Give three examples from your observations of the use by third parties of registered trade marks that you consider would not be deemed to be in accordance with honest commercial practices and three examples where you think it would be deemed to be in accordance with this test.

To what extent do you think that resellers and other parties should be able to use registered marks belonging to others in their businesses? Do you think that the parameters that are being hammered out represent a fair compromise between the interests of the trader and of the third party?

Key points on defences to an action of infringement

- Each of the defences (own name, use of indications concerning quality, etc, use of a mark to indicate the intended purpose) is subject to the proviso that it must be in accordance with honest practices in industrial or commercial matters

- A trader may not indicate a false commercial connection with the proprietor, take unfair advantage of the mark nor denigrate the mark.

Comparative advertising

15.121   Comparative advertising is the use of another's trade mark in advertising which compares the relative advantages and disadvantages of the products with that of the rival. In the words of

[255] Case C-63/97 [1999] All ER (EC) 235, [1999] 1 CMLR 1099.

the ECJ in *Pippig Augenoptik v Hartlauer*[256] 'All comparative advertising is designed to highlight the advantages of the goods or services offered by the advertiser in comparison with those of a competitor. In order to achieve that, the message must necessarily underline the differences between the goods or services compared by describing their main characteristics. The comparison made by the advertiser will necessarily flow from such a description'.

15.122   The practice of comparative advertising has been the subject of much debate. Those who are in favour of it argue that comparative advertising is the only reasonable way in which consumers can make informed judgements about the products and services that they wish to purchase. If, in one advertisement, the relative merits and demerits of two competing products are described, the consumer has more of an opportunity to choose the best or most appropriate for themselves. Those who are against comparative advertising argue that those who engage in the practice do so for one of two reasons: either to trade off the positive reputation that is associated with the 'superior' product (for example by comparing a Skoda with a Mercedes) or to denigrate the competing product. Despite the hesitations, comparative advertising is now permitted, and the policy of the courts seems to be in favour of the practice. The boundaries of the law, however, are constantly being tested by traders.

15.123   There are two main sources for the rules on comparative advertising. One is the TMA 1994 and the other is the EC Directive on Comparative Advertising.

Trade Marks Act 1994

15.124   Under the TMA 1994, section 10(6) a trader is given a defence for the use of a trade mark in a comparative advertising campaign. In order to take advantage of the defence the comparative advertiser must show that the trade mark is used for the purpose of identifying the goods or services of the proprietor or licensee; that the use is in accordance with honest practices in industrial or commercial matters; and that the use does not, without due cause, take unfair advantage of, and is not detrimental to, the distinctive character or repute of the trade mark.[257]

EC Directive on Misleading and Comparative Advertising

15.125   In 1997, EC Directive 97/55/EEC on Misleading and Comparative Advertising (amending an earlier Directive[258]) required member states to permit comparative advertising under the conditions in Article 3a. The provisions concerning misleading and comparative advertising were codified in Directive 2006/114/EC which came into force in December 2007.[259] The conditions for comparative advertising are set out in Article 4:

- it is not misleading within the meaning of Articles 2(b), 3 and 8(1) of this Directive or Articles 6 and 7 of Directive 2005/29/EC of the European Parliament and of the Council of 11 May 2005 concerning unfair business-to-consumer commercial practices in the internal market ('Unfair Commercial Practices Directive');
- it compares goods or services meeting the same needs or intended for the same purpose;

---

[256] Case C-44/01 [2004] All ER (EC) 1156, [2004] 1 CMLR 39, [2003] ECR I-3095, para 36. See the discussion on passing off in para 17.49.

[257] TMA 1994, s 10(6).   [258] Directive 84/450/EEC.

[259] The Directive includes provisions from the Unfair Commercial Practices Directive 2005/29/EC. Case C-44/01 *Pippig Augenoptik v Hartlauer* [2004] All ER (EC) 1156, [2004] 1 CMLR 39, [2003] ECR I-3095.

- it objectively compares one or more material, relevant, verifiable and representative features of those goods and services, which may include price;

- it does not discredit or denigrate the trade marks, trade names, other distinguishing marks, goods, services, activities or circumstances of a competitor;

- for products with designation of origin, it relates in each case to products with the same designation;

- it does not take unfair advantage of the reputation of a trade mark, trade name or other distinguishing marks of a competitor or of the designation of origin of competing products;[260]

- it does not present goods or services as imitations or replicas of goods or services bearing a protected trade mark or trade name;

- it does not create confusion among traders, between the advertiser and a competitor or between the advertiser's trade marks, trade names, other distinguishing marks, goods or services and those of a competitor.

- Comparative advertising is defined as 'any advertising which explicitly or by implication identifies a competitor or goods or services offered by a competitor.'

15.126   The ECJ has said that the test, as regards the comparative nature of advertising, is that it identi-fies, explicitly or by implication, a competitor or goods or services offered by a competitor. It is sufficient that a representation be made in any form which refers, even by implication, to a competitor or to the goods or services on offer.[261]

Weblink

You can find a copy of the codifying Directive 2006/114/EC at http://www.eur-lex. europa.eu/LexUriServ/site/en/oj/2006/l_376/l_37620061227en00210027.pdf

The relationship between the Trade Marks Act and Comparative Advertising Directive

15.127   In *O2 Holdings Ltd, O2 (UK) Ltd v Hutchison 3G Ltd*[262] (see also the discussion in para 15.19) the question arose as to whether, to be non-infringing under the TMA 1994, a comparative advertisement must also comply with the Comparative Advertising Directive. The High Court came to the conclusion that the Directive harmonised those circumstances in which compara-tive advertising is permitted, 'whether comparative advertising is lawful is to be determined 'solely' in accordance with the Directive.' On the relationship between the TMA 1994, section 10(6) and the Directive the court concluded that the 1994 Act: 'must be interpreted as permit-ting comparative advertising, so long as it is conducted in accordance with honest practices, as those practices have been defined for the purposes of the Comparative Advertising Directive.

---

[260] In Case C-59/05 *Siemens AG v VIPA Gesellschaft für Visualisierung und Prozeßautomatisierung GmbH*, the ECJ found, in the circumstances of the case, that the use by a competing supplier of a manufacturer's distinguishing mark known in specialist circles does not take unfair advantage of the reputation of the distinguishing mark.

[261] Case C-112/99 *Toshiba Europe v Katun Germany* [2001] ECR I-7945, para 29–31. See also the opinion of the AG in Case C-381/05 *De Landtsheer Emmanuel SA v Comité Interprofessionnel du Vin de Champagne*, para 28.

[262] *O2 Holdings Ltd, O2 (UK) Ltd v Hutchison 3G Ltd* [2006] ETMR 55, [2006] EWHC 534 Ch D.

Accordingly, in my judgment the defence under [TMA 1994] s.10(6), in the case of comparative advertising, is the same defence as the defence under the Comparative Advertising Directive itself'.[263]

When in the Court of Appeal, that court considered the defences in Article 6(1)(b) of the Directive rather than section 10(6) of the TMA 1994. While it was considered that the former dovetailed with the provisions in the Comparative Advertising Directive in that any comparison would be an indication concerning the kind, quality, quantity, etc of the goods or service, and that any advertisement that was not compliant with Article 3a of the Comparative Advertising Directive would not be in accordance with honest practices, section 10(6) was called 'a pointless provision' which 'should be repealed as an unnecessary distraction in an already complicated branch of the law'.[264]

Questions from the *O2* case were referred to the ECJ.[265] In dealing with the Directive and the Comparative Advertising Directive the Court said that in order to reconcile the protection of registered marks and the use of comparative advertising, Article 5(1) and (2) of Directive 89/104 and Article 3a(1) of Directive 84/450 mean that the proprietor of a registered mark may not prevent use by a third party of an identical or similar sign in a comparative advertisement which satisfied the conditions of Article 3a(1). However where those conditions required under Article 5(1)(b) of Directive 89/104 preventing the use of the same or similar sign are met a comparative advertisement using the sign cannot meet the condition in Article 3a(1)(d). In other words, if there is a likelihood of confusion, the conditions permitting comparative advertising will not be met.

Comparative advertising and the function of a mark

15.128 This jurisprudence on the interrelationship between the Comparative Advertising Directive and the Directive deals also with the function of the mark and whether that is jeopardised. So in in *L'Oreal v Bellure*[266] the same question arose but this time in relation to identical marks rather than similar marks as in O2. The ECJ noted the interrelationship between the Trade Marks Directive and Comparative Advertising Directive laid out above. It went on to state that the exclusive right under Article 5(1)(a) was conferred to ensure that the trade mark can fulfill its functions.

> 'These functions include not only the essential function of the trade mark, which is to guarantee to consumers the origin of the goods or services, but also its other functions, in particular that of guaranteeing the quality of the goods or services in question and those of communication, investment or advertising'.[267]

So it would seem that the extended functions of a mark are relevant to determine infringement where marks and goods/services are identical—at least in comparative advertising cases. It remains to be seen whether these extended functions would also be relevant where marks/goods are similar rather than identical. In the instant case it was for the referring court to decide whether the comparative advertising in question was such as to affect one of the extended functions.

[263] ibid, para 170.   [264] *O2 Holdings Ltd, O2 (UK) Ltd v Hutchison 3G Ltd* [2006] EWCA Civ 1656, para 58.
[265] Case C-533/06 *O2 Holdings Limited v Hutchison 3G UK Limited* [2008] 3 CMLR 14, [2008] ETMR 55, [2008] RPC 33.
[266] Case C-487/07   [267] Para 58.

Exercise

Read the *O2* cases. What do you think of the view the various courts have come to on the interrelationship between the practice of comparative advertising, the Comparative Advertising Directive, the Trade Mark Directive and TMA 1994, section 10(6)?

15.129   Once again there had been cases which arose in front of the British courts before the *O2* and *L'Oreal* cases in which they showed themselves willing to accept the practice of comparative advertising albeit within certain parameters.

■ *Barclays Bank plc v RBS Advanta* [1996] RPC 307

RBS Advanta advertised a new credit card and in the advertisement made adverse comparisons with Barclaycard and in so doing used the registered trade mark. The court refused to grant an injunction considering that the primary objective of section 10(6) of the 1994 Act was to allow comparative advertising so long as the use of the competitor's mark would be considered honest by a reasonable audience. Honesty was to be tested against what was reasonably to be expected of advertisements for that kind of goods or services by the relevant public.

■ *Vodafone Group plc and Vodafone Ltd v Orange Personal Communications* [1997] FSR 34

Orange launched an advertising campaign which proclaimed that Orange users saved £20 per month in comparison to Vodafones's equivalent tariffs. The court found that the advertisement was neither malicious nor false. It was shown that the calculation of the figures used was fair and the advertisement was not misleading. Accordingly the claim for trade mark infringement failed.

15.130   It can be seen how important this question of fairness is in connection with comparative advertising. One case that might be considered to be on the margins is *British Airways Plc v Ryanair Ltd*.[268] An advertisement by Ryanair headed 'Expensive BA – DS' and 'Expensive BA' was found to constitute honest comparative advertising. In considering the actual wording of the slogan itself, the court found that this amounted to no more than vulgar abuse.

15.131   There are those traders who overstep the boundaries, and the courts have shown themselves willing to step in to moderate the practice particularly where false representations may be made in the comparison.

■ *Emaco Ltd v Dyson Appliances Ltd* [1999] ETMR 903

Both parties alleged trade mark infringement in relation to a flyer and graph in which vacuum cleaners manufactured by the other party were described unfavourably. The court found that although neither the graph nor the flyer had been published maliciously, they both contained a number of false representations and were thoroughly misleading. On an objective test this was 'otherwise than in accordance with honest practices in industrial or commercial matters'.[269]

---

[268] [2001] ETMR 24, [2001] FSR 32.
[269] See also *Cable & Wireless Plc v British Telecommunications Plc* [1998] FSR 383. On price comparisons see Case C-356/04 *Lidl Belgium GmbH & Co KG v Etablissementen Franz Colruyt NV.*

> ### Key points on comparative advertising
>
> - Provisions on comparative advertising are to be found in the 1994 Act and in the Comparative Advertising Directive although the continuing relevance of TMA 1994, section 10(6) remains open to question
> - Courts seem generally in favour of comparative advertising where it is considered honest by a reasonable audience
> - The extended functions of a mark may be a relevant factor to consider whether there is infringement in comparative advertising cases where identical marks are used in connection with identical goods and services

Further reading

Books

J Phillips (ed) *Trade Marks at the Limit* (2006)

Articles

JN Adams, 'Court Endorses Rent Seeking: Arsenal Football Club v Reed (Adidas-Salomon AG v Fitness Trading Ltd En Passant' (2004) 1 IPQ 114–20

G Anagnostaras, 'The application of the harmonised standards on comparative advertising: some recent developments' (2007) 32(2) EL Rev 246–59

Z Ballantyne, 'Legal Loophole: UK companies may not be able to rely on their well-known marks under the Paris Convention' [2002] 24(8) 415–17

M Boote, 'What's in a Name?' [2006] 28(6) EIPR 349–52

A Breitschaft, 'Intel, Adidas & Co—is the jurisprudence of the European Court of Justice on dilution law in compliance with the underlying rationales and fit for the future?' [2009] EIPR 497 I

A Carboni, 'Two Stripes and You're Out! Added Protection for Trade marks with a reputation' [2004] 26(5) EIPR 229–33

N Dawson, 'Famous and Well-Known Trade Marks usurping a Corner of the Giant's Robe' [1998] 4 IPQ 350–82

A Folliard-Monguiral, 'Coexistence in Community trade mark disputes: conditions and implications' (2006) 1(11) JIPLP 703–13

A Folliard-Monguiral and D Rogers, 'Community trade mark case law round-up 2006' (2007) 2(4) JIPLP 215–33

A Folliard-Monguiral and D Rogers, 'Significant 2007 case law on the Community trade mark from the ECJ and the CFI' (2008) 3(5) JIPLP 291

A Griffiths, 'The trade mark monopoly: an analysis of the core zone of absolute protection under Art.5(1)(a)' (2007) 3 IPQ 312–49

S Harper and D Curley, 'Bubble Confusion—the O2 Decision' [2006] 28(9) EIPR 499–504

H Norman, 'Time to Blow the Whistle on Trade Mark Use' (2004) 1 IPQ 1–34

FW Mostert, 'When is a Mark Well-Known?' (1997) 3 IPQ 377–83

OHIM Boards of Appeal, Case Law overview of cases decided during 2007, available at http://
oami.europa.eu/en/office/aspects/pdf/BoAcaseLaw2007_en.pdf

M Rimmer, 'The Black Label: Trade Mark Dilution, Culture Jamming and the No Logo
Movement', (2008) 5:1 SCRIPTed 70 @: http://www.law.ed.ac.uk/ahrc/script-ed/vol5-1/
rimmer.asp

C Rutz, 'After Arsenal and Electrocoin: can the opinions on trade mark use be reconciled?'
(2005) 36(6) IIC 682–705

N Shemtov, 'Trade mark use in Europe: revisiting Arsenal in the light of Opel and Picasso'
(2007) 2(8) JIPLP 557

I Simon, 'Embellishment: Trade Mark use Triumph or Decorative Disaster' [2006] 28(6) EIPR
321–8

I Simon, 'Nominative use and honest practices in industrial and commercial matters—a very
European history' (2007) 2 IPQ 117–47

I Simon, 'Trade Marks in Trouble' [2005] 27(2) EIPR 71–5

WH Tatham, 'WIPO Resolution on Well Known Marks: A Small Step or a Giant Leap' [2000]
2 IPQ 127–37

B Thompson and M Woodhouse, 'Use it or lose it!' [2006] 188 TW 22–3.

P Yap, 'Making sense of trade mark use' (2007) 29(10) EIPR 420–7

Contemporary issues in trade mark law

Introduction

Scope and overview of chapter

16.1 This chapter will give an overview of four topical areas. The first is trade marks and personality merchandising; the second is trade marks and domain names; the third is the use of trade marks in connection with Internet related activities including in websites, in metatags, and for the purposes of keyword advertising; and the fourth is in the related area of geographical indications. The purpose is to highlight the contemporary tensions and trends in these areas.

Trade marks and personality merchandising

Introduction

16.2 Personality merchandising has been described as 'the use of the true identity of an individual . . . in the marketing or advertising of goods or services'[1] It is one aspect of a broader phenomenon of character merchandising that looks not only to merchandising 'real' characters (personality merchandising), but also to fictional characters such as cartoon characters, or to fictional characters played by real personalities, such as Superman or Harry Potter.[2]

The focus in this part will be on personality merchandising as it is the area that has proved problematic and in which developments might be expected in the near future both within trade mark law and other areas (for example, breach of confidence for which see Chapter 18).

---

[1] JN Adams, *Character Merchandising* (2nd edn, 1996) p xiv.

[2] HE Ruijsenaars, 'The WIPO Report on Character Merchandising' (1994) Vol 25 IIC 532. The International Association for the Protection of Industrial Property (AIPPI) has called character merchandising 'the use, among other things, of names or images of characters, real or fictional persons, events, groups, entities of the most varied kinds, literary and artistic works, their titles and other distinctive elements, in order to enhance the promotion or sale of products and services. This comprises four aspects; character merchandising, personality merchandising, event merchandising and brand merchandising': HE Ruijsenaars, 'Legal Aspects of Merchandising: The AIPPI Resolution' [1996] 6 EIPR 330. Adams defines character merchandising to mean 'the use in the marketing or advertising of goods or services of a fictional personality or situation'. 'Personality merchandising involves the use of the true identity of an individual . . . in the marketing or advertising of goods or services . . . [and] between these two types lies a rather unclear area where fictional characters played by real actors are used': JN Adams, *Character Merchandising* (2nd edn, 1996) p xiv.

The rest of this part contains the following sections

- Personality merchandising (16.4–16.8)
- Personality: signature and name (16.9–16.18)
- Personality: image (16.19–16.22)

16.3

Learning objectives

By the end of this part of the chapter you should be able to describe and explain:

- the circumstances under which the name, signature and image of a celebrity may be registered as a trade mark;
- the scope of protection for famous names;
- developments in assignation of a trade mark consisting of the name of a celebrity.

Personality merchandising

16.4   The practice whereby celebrities use their name and image to endorse and associate themselves with products and services is increasingly common. Elvis Presley, Marilyn Monroe, Posh and Becks, the late Diana, Princess of Wales and Ali G are, or were, all examples of celebrity characters who others imitate, or whose likeness and/or name could be used in connection with the sale of goods and services. In other words, the personality is merchandised. But a problem might arise. For instance, a fan of David Beckham might take a photograph as he was walking down the street, and apply that picture to the front of a T-shirt to be sold in market stalls. If a photograph of David Beckham had been registered as a trade mark in connection with articles of clothing, that might prevent any picture of him being applied to a T-shirt by another: one picture of David Beckham is likely to be similar to another. Equally, if the name of Marilyn Monroe had been registered in connection with T-shirts, that might prevent any other trader from using the name on a T-shirt which also had a picture of the late star.

Question

Read this last example again. What defence from registered trade mark law might the T-shirt vendor have in the given circumstances? You could have a look at para 15.104ff.

Exercise

Choose the name of a well-known celebrity. Search both the UK register and the CTM register to see if you can find any registered trade marks consisting of or including that name.

The policy issues

16.5   A key question underlying the protection of personality, and which to an extent explains the UK courts' reluctance to embrace a fully fledged personality right, lies in the justifications, or absence of justifications, for such protection. It is accepted that personality merchandising is a common feature of daily commercial life, and much money is made by individuals and organisations through these activities, but it does not thereby follow that the individual should be given an enforceable right in personality. It cannot, for example, be argued that a property right is necessary to encourage creativity because an ability to exploit personality tends to be a by-product of another facet of the personality—such as being a film star or famous athlete. Granting a personality right would add nothing more to the innovation/incentive/reward cycle. It also begs the question as to who precisely has created the 'celebrity'. Is it the individual or the inevitable media attention that attaches itself to certain 'personalities'?[3] Suffice to say that protection of personality in the UK is piecemeal. Trade mark law, passing off (para 17.30), copyright and the law of confidence (paras 18.25, 18.72) all have some role to play in this area. The focus in this part is on trade marks, and discusses the extent to which elements of a personality, in particular a name/signature and an image, can be protected by this area of the law.

The protection of elements of personality

16.6   To date there has been very little case law on attempts to protect facets of real personalities using registered trade mark law although the incidents are growing. Where a picture of a celebrity has been used by a third party, arguments by the celebrity to try and enjoin this use have been made under the law of passing-off, but with little success. A key issue is whether the use of the indicia of celebrity indicates the origin of the goods and services sold under the name or image.

■ *Lyngstad v Anabas Products* [1977] FSR 62

The pop group ABBA sued Lyngstrad for selling T-shirts and other goods which bore a picture of the group. The court refused to grant relief, stating that it was unlikely that anyone would imagine that the consent of the group would have been given to the activity. The defendants were doing no more than catering for a popular demand among teenagers for effigies of their idols.

16.7   In response, some have argued that pictures and other memorabilia depicting celebrities should incorporate the word 'unofficial' when produced without the consent of the individual or group concerned. Others have argued that memorabilia produced with consent should have the words 'official' added.

[3] There is an extensive literature focussing on the protection of personality. For examples see H Beverly-Smith, *The Commercial Appropriation of Personality* (2002); H Beverley-Smith, A Ohly, A Lucas-Schloetter, *Privacy, Property and Personality: Civil Law Perspectives on Commercial Appropriation* (2005); H Carty, 'Passing off and the Concept of Goodwill' (1995) JBL 139–154; G Phillipson, 'Transforming breach of confidence? Towards a common law of privacy under the Human Rights Act' (2003) 66 MLR 726; D Howarth, 'Privacy, Confidentiality and the Cult of Celebrity' [2002] CLJ 264; H Carty, 'Advertising, Publicity Rights and English Law' [2004] IPQ 209; T Frazer, 'Appropriation of Personality—a New Tort?' (1993) 99 LQR 281; P Jaffey, 'Merchandising and the Law of Trade Marks' [1998] IPQ 240; A Story, 'Owning Diana: From People's Princess to Private Property' [1998] 5 Web JCLI http://webjcli.ncl.ac.uk/1998/issue5/story5.html; G Scanlan, 'Personality, Endorsement and Everything' [2003] EIPR 563; G Davies, 'The Cult of Celebrity and Trade Mark: The Next Installment' (2004) 1(2) SCRIPT-ed; N R Whitty, R Zimmermann (eds) *Rights of Personality in Scots Law: A Comparative Perspective* (Dundee University Press, 2009).

■ *Halliwell v Panini* Unreported, 9 July 1997 (Ch D)

This case concerned an application for an injunction to prevent an unauthorised trader selling 'Spice Girls' sticker collections. The court rejected arguments that the *absence* of the word 'unofficial' was sufficient to influence the public's perception of the origin of the goods:

> 'I shall only say that I am far from satisfied that the absence of any disavowal of authorisations by the plaintiffs can reasonably lead members of the public to the defendants' product on the basis or in the belief that it was authorised by the plaintiffs. It is to be noted that in a number of their products the plaintiffs state their own products to be official, indicating by that as it seems to me, that that is not something which is necessarily implicit'.

16.8 The legal landscape in relation to passing off has altered since the case of *Irvine v Talksport*[4] where a case of passing off through false endorsement was made out. This arose as a result of the manipulation of a photograph of Eddie Irvine by Talksport to make it appear as if Irvine endorsed Talksport's 'Talk Radio.' For a full discussion of this case see para 17.34.

Personality: signature and name

16.9 Signatures of celebrities, both alive and dead have been registered as trade marks in the UK. Thus, the example is given in para 14.7 of Marilyn Monroe's signature, registered in class 3 in connection with cosmetics; soaps; shampoos and foamable preparations for the bath.[5] The signature of James Dean has also been registered in a number of classes, including class 3[6] in connection with cosmetics and toiletries.

 Question

When you see the signature of Marilyn Monroe or James Dean, what do you think of?

16.10 So a signature might be distinctive for the purposes of trade mark law[7] because of the script used and thus registerable. However the registration of celebrity names as such has proved more problematic and has been called into question since the appeal in *Elvis Presley Enterprises Inc v Sid Shaw Elvisly Yours*.[8] In this case the Court of Appeal upheld the decision to overturn registrations of a variety of styles of the name 'Elvis Presley'. The court decided that a celebrity name was not registrable as a trade mark as it was not *distinctive*. The court appeared aware of the broad monopoly power that could be conferred on traders if celebrity names could be registered as trade marks. In the words of Simon Brown LJ:

> '...there should be no a priori assumption that only a celebrity or his successors may ever market (or licence the marketing of) his own character. Monopolies should not be so readily created'.

---

[4] [2002] FSR 60.   [5] UK Trade Mark No 1308828, the estate of Marilyn Monroe.
[6] UK Trade Mark No 1289838, the James Dean Foundation, USA.
[7] In *Elvis Presley Enterprises Inc v Sid Shaw Elvisly Yours* [1999] RPC 567 the Court of Appeal found that Elvis Presley's signature to be distinctive but was not registered because opposition based on a confusing similarity to an earlier mark used by a third party merchandiser succeeded.
[8] *Elvis Presley Enterprises Inc v Sid Shaw Elvisly Yours* [1999] RPC 567. See also *Corsair Toiletries's Appn* [1999] ETMR 1038 (Jane Austen for toiletries refused because it lacked distinctiveness).

It had been argued by Counsel for the appellants (Elvis Presley Enterprises Inc) that the general public would assume that the use of the signature of a celebrity in connection with goods and services meant that there would be a connection between the celebrity and the goods and services, and that the only reason that another trader would want to use an image or signature of the celebrity would be to take advantage of the commercial value in the name.

As was pointed out, again by Simon Brown LJ, if this was accepted:

> 'it would apply virtually irrespective of the products being exploited...irrespective of when registration were applied for...irrespective of whether it was sought by the personality himself or his legal successors...and irrespective of what if any trading in the relevant products has previously been effected either by whoever seeks registration or by competing traders'.

16.11   The *Elvis Presley* case dealt with the law as it stood under the 1938 Act. Would the same result be achieved had the 1994 Act been in operation? Some writers argue not. Nonetheless it has been followed in the decision by the trade mark registry to turn down the application to register the name Diana, Princess of Wales as a trade mark.[9] In refusing the application, the registry emphasised that a name unique to a particular person did not of itself have distinctive character as a trade mark. The essential function of a trade mark was to guarantee that the items bearing it had originated under the control of a single undertaking responsible for their quality. Unless, therefore, such control could be shown, the use of a famous name to endorse a product was not a trade mark use. It would thus seem that the better known the personality, the less likely it is that a name will be registered as a trade mark because the name is not considered distinctive in the trade mark sense.

16.12   Even where a name is made up, and thus may be thought distinctive for the purposes of registration, it will not be registerable for certain goods and services where it is to be used descriptively.

■ *Linkin Park LLC's Application* [2005] ETMR 17

The applicant sought to register the words 'Linkin Park' as a trade mark for inter alia printed matter, posters and poster books in class 16. An objection was raised on the grounds that the words Linkin Park were devoid of distinctiveness under the Trade Marks Act 1994, section 3(1)(b). Although the name was made up by the group, by the time application was made for registration it had acquired a well established meaning. As the name was capable of being used descriptively, it would be impossible for other traders to sell posters of the group without using the mark. 'The name Linkin Park appearing on posters, etc. is the subject matter of the goods which itself is an essential characteristic of such goods'.

It is interesting however to note that the name Linkin Park has been registered as a CTM for, inter alia, posters.[10]

16.13   Where the goods are seen as 'mere image carriers', then the name will be unregisterable.

■ *In the matter of Application No 2323092B to register a trade mark in Class 16 by Sir Alexander Chapman Ferguson Trade Mark Decision o/26605*

The application by Alex Ferguson, the manager of Manchester United football team, to register his name in, inter alia, class 16 (printed matter; posters; photographs; transfers; stickers;

[9] *Diana, Princess of Wales Trade Mark* [2001] ETMR 25. See also C Waelde, 'Commercialising the Personality of the late Diana, Princess of Wales Censorship by the Back Door?' in N Dawson, A Firth (eds), *Perspectives on Intellectual Property: Trade Marks Retrospective* Vol 7 (2000).
[10] CTM App No 002517720.

decalcomanias; stickers relating to football) was turned down. The Registry pointed out that registration of a famous name could take place where the consumer would believe that the goods bearing the name are under the control of one undertaking. However, the use of a name or image of a famous person on posters, photos, stickers and figurines would merely be seen as descriptive of the subject matter of those goods. These items are merely 'image carriers'[11] and as such cannot be registered.

The refusal to register the name was upheld on appeal to the Lord Chancellor's Appointed Person, where reference was made to the Trade Marks Registry Works Manual and to *Linkin Park*: 'The more famous the personage(s) or event(s), the more likely it is that there will be a market for such goods and the less likely it is that the name will be regarded as acceptable for registration in relation to goods of that kind on the basis of the approach currently applied by the Registry in the United Kingdom'.[12]

Exercise

Have a look at the Trade Marks Registry Works Manual, Chapter 3. What does it say about the registration of: famous names, badges of allegiance, names of deceased individuals or defunct groups, pictures of famous persons?

Weblink

Don't forget that you can find the Trade Marks Registry Works Manual on the IPO website at

http://www.ipo.gov.uk

16.14 The names of living and dead well-known personalities which have become distinctive can and indeed have been registered as trade marks: Gucci, Dior, Versace and Naomi Campbell[13] are all examples.

Exercise

Note the story in *The Guardian*, 14 October 2006 in which it was reported that the former Beatle, Paul McCartney applied to register the name 'McCartney' for a wide range of products including vegetarian foods and meat products. Apparently the application in respect of the meat products was defensive to give McCartney protection against the name being used in connection with products of which he does not approve. Was the application successful? Might a registration be subject to challenge at a later date? If so, on what grounds?

[11] Para 19.   [12] Para 4.   [13] International Madrid (UK) Case M706887.

> ### Key points on signature and name of celebrities
>
> * The signature of a celebrity may be considered as sufficiently distinctive for registration as a trade mark
> * Where the name of a celebrity is seen as purely descriptive of the subject matter of goods it will be unregisterable as a trade mark

Scope of protection for famous names

16.15   Where registration has taken place case law suggests that the names of celebrities and other well- known people will have a more limited scope of protection than other trade marks (see also para 15.44).

■ **Case C-361/04** *Ruiz-Picasso v OHIM* (hereinafter *Picasso*)

An application was made by DaimlerChrysler to register 'Picaro' for vehicles.[14] This was objected to by the estate of Picasso, owners of the Picasso CTM registered for vehicles shown below in Figure 16.1.

Figure 16.1 Picasso mark

The Picasso estate argued that although there were conceptual differences between the two signs, these should not be found to be increased by virtue of the fact that the meaning of one (Picasso) was so clear and specific such that the general public would immediately recognise the mark. Further, any analysis of confusion between the marks should take place within the context of the goods for which registration is applied for and for which registration has been obtained. Any other meaning of the mark—including the name of Picasso as a famous artist—should not be relevant. The ECJ rejected the appeal and agreed with the CFI. Where the meaning of at least one of the two signs at issue is clear and specific so that it can be grasped immediately by the relevant public, the conceptual differences observed between those signs may counteract any visual and phonetic similarities between them.[15] When confronted with the word sign 'Picasso', the relevant

---

[14] CTM App No 000927764.   [15] *Picasso*, para 20.

public inevitably sees in it a reference to the painter and that, 'given the painter's renown with that public, that particularly rich conceptual reference is such as greatly to reduce the resonance with which, in this case, the sign is endowed as a mark, among others, of motor vehicles'.[16]

16.16   Thus it would appear that when the names of well-known people have been registered as trade marks, the better known the name the narrower the scope of protection will be granted as against similar marks, and the lower the distinguishing capacity of the mark in relation to the goods for which it is registered.[17]

 Question

To what extent do you think the well-known status of a name will be able to displace any likelihood of confusion between the name and the use of the name as a mark?

Key point on well-known names

- The better known a name, the more likely it is that any confusion due to visual, aural or conceptual similarities as between similar names may be displaced

Assignation of trade marks consisting of the names of well-known individuals

16.17   Questions have been raised before the ECJ concerning the assignation of trade marks which consist of the names of well-known individuals. In particular as to whether where such an assignation occurs, but the individual does not remain involved with the business, whether consumer deception would result. *Elizabeth Emanuel v Continental Shelf*[18] concerned the assignation, by Elizabeth Emanuel, of the trade mark bearing her name along with a crest made up of two 'E's back to back. After ownership of the trade mark had changed hands several times, Ms Emanuel opposed a proposed amendment to the registered trade mark and applied for revocation of the existing mark on the grounds that to let the mark stay on the register would be to deceive the public within the meaning of Article 3(1)(g) of the Directive. It was argued that a significant proportion of the relevant public would believe that use of the trade mark indicated that the individual remained involved with the design or creation of the goods in relation to which the marks was used, and so using the name mark in a business in which the individual was not concerned would be deceptive. The Court did not accept this argument. The Court ruled that a trade mark which corresponds to the name of the designer and first manufacturer of the goods is not, for that reason, liable to revocation on the ground that that mark would mislead the public. This was particularly so where the goodwill associated with that mark has been assigned together with the business making the goods to which the mark relates.

16.18   Thus a trade mark consisting of a well-known name can be assigned even if the individual does not thereafter remain associated with the business. Although this might seem an odd result if

[16] *Picasso*, para 27.   [17] See also Case C-16/06 P *Les Editions Albert Rene Sarl v OHIM* [2009] ETMR 21.
[18] Case C-259/04 [2006] ECR I-3089; [2006] ETMR 56.

the view is taken that a consumer might be confused that the named individual designer had not actually had a hand in designing the goods, it undoubtedly reflects what happens in commercial life. To what extent, for example, does Naomi Campbell have a hand in developing perfumes sold under her name? As the Attorney General had argued: 'a user is aware of the possibility of divergences between personal names used as trade marks and the participation of those persons in the production of the goods or the provision of the services which they cover. All consumers know that a fashion designer is entitled to transfer his or her business at any time'.[19]

Question

Why is it that some names can be registered as trade marks? What comes first? The use of the name of the personality in association with the products followed by the personality becoming well-known? Or the personality becoming well-known followed by the use of the name in association with certain products?

Key point on assignation of trade marks which consist the names of well known individuals

- An assignation of a trade mark consisting of the name of a well-known celebrity is not liable to be revoked purely on the grounds that the celebrity no longer remains involved with the business carried on under the mark

Personality: image

16.19   The second facet of a well-known personality that a merchandiser (whether the celebrity him-self[20] or a third party) might want to protect is the celebrity image. Early cases suggested that reg-istration would be permissible on the grounds that an image is distinctive. As was said in 1897:

'it is difficult to suppose anything could be more distinctive than the portraiture of the man who was professing to be the manufacturer of that particular article'.[21]

Thus, pictures of celebrities have been registered as trade marks, such as that of Eric Cantona[22] and Damon Hill.[23] To see the picture of Eric Cantona look at the UK trade mark register under Trade Mark No 2120277 and for Damon Hill the number is 2036489.

16.20   However, the IPO refused to register images of the late Diana Princess of Wales as trade marks.[24] Applications were made to register 52 different images for a wide variety of goods and services.

---

[19] Case C–259/04 *Elizabeth Florence Emanuel v Continental Shelf*, AG Opinion para 63.
[20] Of course a celebrity may want to protect his image for reasons of privacy also (see Chapter 18).
[21] *Rowland v Mitchell* (1897) 14 RPC 37.
[22] UK Trade Mark No 2120277, classes 16 and 25, proprietor: Eric Cantona c/o Manchester United plc.
[23] UK Trade Mark No 2036489, classes 06, 09, 16, 25, 28, proprietor: Damon Hill Grand Prix Limited.
[24] http://news.bbc.co.uk/1/hi/uk/272380.stm The application was to register 52 images of Diana and was turned down by the Patent Office in February 1999. The reasons for declining the application have not been made public (except for journalistic reporting). It is understood that had the Fund decided to appeal the decision, then the reason for the initial refusal would have been publicly available.

Unfortunately the reasoning behind the refusal has not been made public, so one can only speculate as to what they might have been. In trade mark terms, the registry may have decided that the images were not distinctive. Diana was, after all, one of the most photographed people in the world for a number of years. Another ground for refusal might have been that there was no trade connection between the images and the goods and services they were to be registered in connection with: the intention might merely have been to indicate sponsorship, such as the use of her name on tubs of margarine, rather than trade origin. Equally, there may have been a lack of any form of quality control over those products and services: an argument similar to that used to turn down the application to register her name as a trade mark.

Question

Why do you think that the application to register the image of the late Diana Princess of Wales as a trade mark was turned down by the Trade Mark Registry?

Exercise

Have a look at the Trade Marks Registry Works Manual, Chapter 3. What does it say about the registration of pictures of famous persons?

The implications for personality merchandising

16.21   It thus appears that neither the name (as opposed to the signature) nor the image of a well-known celebrity will be accepted in the UK for registration as a trade mark for certain goods unless the mark has acquired distinctiveness through use. For some goods the signs will be unregisterable. For those names and images that are already registered it may be that in any dispute with a third party the scope of protection will be narrow or the registration vulnerable to being declared invalid as being merely descriptive of the goods for which it is registered.

16.22   Under the current state of the law it will not be possible for a well-known personality comprehensively to protect her personality under trade mark law for the purposes of merchandising.

Exercise

Should a personality be able to protect elements of her personality as a registered trade mark? What justifications would you give? If it were possible, what effect might this have on the availability of consumer goods in the marketplace?

Weblinks

The protection of personality in general differs markedly as between jurisdictions. For a comparative project examining elements of personality protection carried out by the

SCRIPT: the AHRC Research Centre for Studies in Intellectual Property and Technology Law comprising responses to personality case studies from a number of different jurisdictions and a wiki containing a variety of information on the protection of personality see http://www.law.ed.ac.uk/ahrc/files/92_pppcasestudiesfinaljan07.pdf and http://www.personalityrightsdatabase.com

> ## Key points on celebrity image
>
> - The name and image of a celebrity can be registered as trade marks in certain cicumstances
> - For some goods the signs will be unregisterable as they will not be considered as indicating origin
> - It is not possible comprehensively to protect personality under registered trade mark law

Trade marks and domain names

Introduction

16.23   The purpose of this part of the chapter is to discuss the interaction between trade marks and domain names. While trade marks have been around for a long time, domain names have attracted public attention only since the rise in popularity of the Internet. The legal interface between trade marks and domain names has been the subject of much analysis. When the potential for conflict between the two first arose, there was the potential for a wave of cross border litigation as trade mark owners and domain name holders battled for the control of domain names. In the event, an alternative dispute resolution mechanism was established which, in terms of dealing with a large number of domain name disputes and keeping these disputes out of the courts, has been a great success. Some cases are still litigated in UK courts, primarily by reference to the law of passing off and trade marks. The area remains one of intense practical importance given the numbers of disputes that are still heard via the dispute resolution mechanism coupled with the anticipated significant increase in the numbers of domain names available for registration. At international policy level, its importance is illustrated by the fact that WIPO placed the topic of domain names on its General Assembly meeting agenda for October 2009.

16.24   Having explained the basis for the disputes between trade marks and domain names and considered how the law of trade marks has been applied by domestic courts to these disputes, the alternative dispute mechanism developed to cope with disagreements over domain names and trade marks will be described.

The rest of this part contains the following sections:

- What is a domain name? (16.26–16.27)
- The registration of a domain name as a trade mark (16.28–16.29)

- Conflicts over domain names and trade marks (16.30–16.32)
- Resolution of disputes (16.33–16.48)

16.25

> ## Learning objectives
>
> By the end of this chapter you should be able to describe and explain:
>
> - the constituent parts of a domain name;
> - how conflicts arise between trade marks and domain names;
> - the application of trade mark law to domain name disputes in the British courts;
> - the operation of the Uniform Dispute Resolution Policy to domain name disputes.

What is a domain name?

16.26   A domain name is part of the address of the location of a site on the Internet. For instance harrods. com is the domain name of the London department store, Harrods. The portion of the address taken by 'harrods' is sometimes the part that equates to the registered (or unregistered) trade mark of the person seeking to use the domain name: for instance, 'virgin' or 'caesers-palace'. The next part is the top level domain (TLD)—.com, .net and .org are all generic Top Level Domains (gTLDs). Until 2000 these were the main generic gTLDs. Over the ensuing years new gTLDs were approved by the Internet body Internet Corporation for Assigned Names and Numbers (ICANN), for example, .aero, .biz, .cat, .com, .coop, .info, .jobs, .mobi, .museum, .name, .net, .org, .pro, and .travel. Agreement has been reached on the introduction of new gTLDs, including Internationalised Domain Names (IDNs) (those which use local language characters or equivalents). It is as yet unknown how many may emerge from this process – with some estimates suggesting there could be many thousand new gTLDs and IDNs created over the coming years. There are also Country Code Top Level Domains (ccTLDs) which include .uk, .de and .fr and more recently a .eu domain.[25] Different rules apply to registration of a domain name in the gTLDs[26] and the ccTLDs.[27]

16.27   The .com, .net and.org gTLDs are 'open' in the sense that any business or individual can make an application to register a domain name using those gTLDs. The policy is broadly to register on a first come first served basis. It is however different for some of the newer or sponsored gTLDs, each of which has a number of rules attached to registration. For instance the .biz gTLD must be used primarily for bona fide business or commercial purposes and not exclusively for personal use; while the .name gTLD is intended to be for individual use. Most registries operate dispute resolution policies in the event of a conflict between the holder of a trade mark, and the holder of a domain name. Those who register in the gTLDs all operate the same dispute resolution policy[28] which is known as the ICANN Uniform Domain Name Dispute Resolution Policy (UDRP)[29] and has been in operation since late 1999. Nominet, the register for the .uk ccTLD,

---

[25] For information see http://www.eurid.eu/en/. The reservation of the domain name 'galileo.eu' by the Commission was challenged by Galileo Lebensmittel GmbH but the application was declared inadmissible by the ECJ on the grounds that the applicant was not directly and individually concerned Case C-483/07P *Galileo Lebensmittel GmbH & Co KG v Commission of the European Communities*.

[26] For Nominet's rules see http://www.nominet.org.uk/ref/terms.html

[27] For links to the eligibility criteria in each of the gTLDs see http://www.icann.org/udrp/

[28] http://www.icann.org   [29] For the policy see http://www.icann.org/udrp/

has had a dispute resolution procedure in place since December 2001, the terms of which were updated in July 2009.[30]

Weblinks

You will find much information about ICANN at http://www.icann.org

Each domain name is maintained by a registry (for instance .name is managed by www.nic.name, .uk is managed by Nominet www.nominet.org.uk). Applications for registration of a domain name are made by competing registrars. To become a registrar for the gTLDs, accreditation is required from ICANN. There are also resellers of domain names (go to Google and type in 'domain name reseller' for examples) who may also offer hosting facilities to clients. You can check to see if a domain name is registered in a number of the cc or gTLDs by going to http://www.whois.org.net

---

 ### Exercise

Try seeing if SCRIPT is available as a domain name in any of the gTLDs.

The registration of a domain name as a trade mark

16.28   The question of whether an Internet address which includes 'www' (as opposed to a domain name) can be registered as a CTM has been considered by OHIM. In *Nationsbanc Montgomery Securities LLC's Application*[31] the application by Nationsbanc to register http://www.primebroker.com in connection with goods and services in class 9 (computer hardware and software) and class 42 (online services) was refused on the grounds that it was devoid of distinctive character. The appeal was dismissed. It was found that the trade mark as a whole represented an e-mail address. The element 'www' represented the 'world wide web' and '.com' a top level domain name. The whole sign was likely to be seen by the relevant public as an electronic mail address for a broker engaged in the services set out in the application and not in any way distinctive.

16.29   Despite this ruling, domain names have been registered as CTMs, albeit with added material rendering the domain name distinctive, such as http://www.bigsave.com shown below in Figure 16.2.[32]

Figure 16.2 www.bigsave.com

---

[30] Substantive changes included clarification of the wording to make it clear that rights can exist in descriptive terms that have acquired a secondary meaning; confirmation that some activities are not in an of themselves abusive registration; the introduction of a likelihood of confusion factor and made clear that threatened use of a domain name may be evidence of an abusive registration.

[31] [2000] ETMR 245.   [32] CTM No 1632140. Proprietor Bigsave.com Ltd.

The UK–IPO issued a Practice Amendment Notice[33] (a statement of the practice that will be followed at the IPO) in which they said that subject to the usual criteria of the 1994 Act, the Office will permit domain names to be registered as trade marks. The TLD part of the domain name (.com or .uk) is, however, considered to be totally non-distinctive. Therefore consideration is given as to whether the remainder of the mark is descriptive or non-distinctive. If that is the case, then registration may be refused under section 3(1)(b) of the 1994 Act.

As a result of this policy, a number of domain names have been registered as illustrated in Figure 16.3. For instance:

Figure 16.3 www.bags123.com

with the text www.bags123.com[34]

> **Key point on registering a domain name as a trade mark**
>
> • A domain name can be registered as a trade mark although the gTLD or ccTLD will be considered non-distinctive

Conflicts over domain names and trade marks

16.30   Disputes over ownership of domain names have arisen for a number of reasons. A domain name has been considered as akin to a trade mark (whether registered or unregistered). Therefore those who own the mark for the non-Internet business will wish to use the same name on the Internet: it is seen as a valuable addition to the branding of goods and services, or of the business as a whole. However, as discussed above, trade mark law is territorial whereas the Internet is global. Therefore different businesses trading under the same mark in various parts of the world may have what they consider to be the same legitimate claim to a particular domain name. As no two domain names can be identical, only one business can have a particular name. 'prince.com' is a good example in that it was the subject of a dispute between Prince plc in the UK and Prince Sports Inc in the US. Prince plc registered the domain name first and was challenged by

---

[33] PAN 1/08. See BL O/008/07 Application by FSTC Ltd Foundation for Science Technology and Civilisation, for the mark MuslimHeritage.com, and the decision of the Second Board of Appeal Case R 338/2006-2, DNI Holdings Ltd for the mark Sportsbetting.com

[34] In class 35. Interestingly, the specification is 'The bringing together, for the benefit of others, of a variety of goods, enabling customers to conveniently view and purchase those goods from an Internet website specialising in the marketing of luggage, fashion handbags, and leather goods'. UK TM No 2268716, proprietor: Boros Leathergoods Ltd.

Prince Sports Inc.[35] The name remained with Prince plc. This type of dispute might be viewed as 'domain name envy'.

16.31   Disputes have also arisen where Internet users, with a degree of entrepreneurial spirit, have registered domain names which are the same as or very similar to the trading name or registered trade mark of a company that is well-known or famous, or which has a reputation. Generally the intent has been to do one of two things. One option might be to offer it to the owner of the registered trade mark or trading company in return for some payment. Alternatively, if it is a name that is similar to a well-known name, such as porschegirls.com, the intention might be to use the domain name in an effort, not necessarily to confuse, but to draw people to the site. In other words, to draw on the magnetism that attaches to the mark. The name that has been given to this type of activity is 'domain name hijacking' or more commonly *'cyber-squatting'*. Parallels can be seen with the notion of dilution discussed above.

16.32   And finally, there are the disputes where the owners of trade marks who have aggressively pursued policies to prevent other Internet participants from using any rendition of a name that includes or alludes to their registered trade mark, in some cases quite unjustifiably. This is sometimes termed *reverse domain name hijacking*.

Question 1

There is a Mrs McDonald who lives in the Highlands of Scotland and operates a small bed and breakfast. McDonald is also the name of an electrical distributor in Florida, of a garden centre in France and of a multi-national corporation which sells, among other things, beefburgers. Who should own the domain name mcdonald.com?

Question 2

What are the most common types of disputes that arise as between domain names and trade marks?

Resolution of disputes

16.33   There have been remarkably few domain name disputes that have been referred to the UK courts for resolution. This may be for a number of reasons:

- First, many domain names disputes which arise concerning the gTLDs are referred to the ICANN Uniform Dispute Resolution Policy (UDRP) (discussed below). For disputes concerning the ccTLDs, many registrars operate dispute resolution policies of their own (eg Nominet in the UK). Some ccTLD registrars have adopted the UDRP on a voluntary basis.

- Second, one of the earliest cases, *BT v One in a Million*[36] made clear the disapproval of the court of the practice of *cyber-squatting*. This may have resulted in similar cases being settled out of court.

---

[35] *Prince plc v Prince Sports Group Inc* [1998] FSR 21.   [36] [1999] 4 All ER 476, [1999] RPC 1.

- Finally, it is very expensive to take a case to court. Either of the parties to a potential dispute may not have the means to fund expensive litigation. By comparison, using the ICANN UDRP or one of the cc dispute resolution procedures is relatively cheap.[37]

Resolution of disputes in British courts

Trade Marks Act 1994, section 10(1)

16.34   Of those disputes that have been heard in the UK courts, section 10(1) of the 1994 Act was considered in *Avnet Inc v Isoact Limited (Avnet)*[38] (see also the discussion of this case in para 15.29). Avnet Inc, a US company ran a business selling goods by catalogue and in so doing carried advertisements for different manufacturers.[39] It registered the trade mark 'Avnet' in the UK in class 35 for advertising and promotional services. Isoact Limited, by contrast was an Internet Service Provider with a particular interest in aviation. It used the words Aviation Network and Avnet in connection with its interests. Isoact Limited registered the domain name 'avnet.co.uk' and allowed customers to display their own advertisements on their site.

Avnet argued that Isoact infringed its registered trade mark by using the word 'avnet' in its domain name. Section 10(1) TMA 1994 was relied upon as the ground of infringement. So Avnet Inc argued that the sign used by Isoact was *identical* to its registered mark and used in connection with *identical* goods and services. Jacob J disagreed with Avnet. Judgment was given purely by looking to the terms of what was covered by the registration of the mark 'Avnet'. Jacob J decided that in substance Isoact were not providing advertising and promotional services within class 35 of the Trade Mark Register, but rather provided the services of an Internet Service Provider. These activities would (if registered) probably fall within class 42. In other words, the services provided were different. Therefore there was no infringement under section 10(1) and Isoact had a right to keep and use the domain name.

16.35   For anyone who alleges infringement of their trade mark through the use by another of a domain name, and relying on section 10(1) of the 1994 Act, the specification of the goods and services in connection with which the mark is registered is going to have to be identical with that used in connection with the domain name. If this is not the case, there will be no infringement under section 10(1).

 Question

Would the mark have to be absolutely identical with the domain name for section 10(1) of the TMA 1994 to be relevant, or might slight variations in the mark and the name be permitted? See para 15.23ff for a discussion on what is meant by the identity of marks.

---

[37] Where they do reach court now it is generally part of a wider dispute; eg *Evans and Evans v Focal Point Fires* [2009] EWCH 2784 (Ch).

[38] [1998] FSR 16.

[39] Jacob J doubted that this activity actually fell within class 35 of the Trade Mark Register and thought the activity was more akin to retail sales, but did not decide the point.

Trade Marks Act 1994, section 10(2)

16.36   Section 10(2) of the TMA 1994 was considered in *Phones4U Ltd v Phone4u.co.uk Ltd*[40] albeit, for the reasons explained below, it was found that there was no infringement of this section. Phones4U Ltd had been in business for a number of years. Mr Heykali, who had no connection with Phones4U Ltd, registered the domain name phone4u.co.uk. Phones4U Ltd alleged passing off and trade mark infringement. The High Court had found that passing off had not been established—a finding which was overturned in the Court of Appeal. Infringement of the registered trade mark was also considered. Phones4u Ltd had registered its trade mark in 1999[41] in the form of a logo. It included the statement that 'the mark is limited to the colours red, white and blue'. The key question was the effect of this limitation.

Section 13 of the 1994 Act describes the limitation of a mark as follows:

> '(1) An applicant for registration of a trade mark, or the proprietor of a registered trade mark, may—
> (a) disclaim any right to the exclusive use of any specified element of the trade mark, or
> (b) agree that the rights conferred by the registration shall be subject to a specified territorial or other limitation; and where the registration of a trade mark is subject to a disclaimer or limitation, the rights conferred by section 9 (rights conferred by registered trade mark) are restricted accordingly
> (2) Provision shall be made by rules as to the publication and entry in the register of a disclaimer or limitation.'

The reason for including the limitation was that when the application was made for registration, the Registry had taken the view that the sign was not distinctive in black and white. The addition of the limitation made the non-distinctive sign distinctive for the purposes of registration. The Court of Appeal found that section 13 meant that the rights in the logo mark were limited to the colours red, white and blue.[42] As a result, there was no infringement of section 10(2) of the TMA 1994 by the registration of the domain name Phone4u.co.uk. Had the limitation not been included, then the registered mark would have been infringed. The Court of Appeal noted that where a mark had been registered through the inclusion of a limitation to make that mark distinctive, but later and through use the mark gained a broader distinctive appeal (distinctive through use), then the mark with wider rights could be registered.[43]

16.37   This holding clearly places quite a significant restriction on marks subject to a limitation where it is alleged, as in this case, that the registration and use of a similar domain name infringes the registered mark under section 10(2) of the TMA 1994. Although the courts seem willing to find passing off to be proved in these type of domain name cases (as was the position in the instant case), trade mark owners may want the comfort of being able to rely on the law of registered trade marks. As a result, where marks have been registered with a limitation, owners would do well to consider whether the mark has sufficient acquired distinctiveness to make a further application for registration of the mark without the limitation.

---

[40] [2006] EWCA Civ 244; [2007] RPC 5;. See the discussion on passing off and domain names at para 17.63.

[41] No 2185824 as of the date 8 January 1999.

[42] See also the discussion on limitations and disclaimers in the High Court in *L'Oréal SA & Ors v Bellure NV & Ors* [2006] EWHC 2355 (Ch) paras 84–90. *Nestlé SA's Trade Mark Application* [2005] RPC 5, [2004] EWCA Civ 1008. *Imagination Technologies Ltd v OHIM* [2008] ETMR 10, in which the CFI stated that where a mark contains an element that is not distinctive and its inclusion might give rise to doubts about the scope of protection, the OHIM may request as a condition of registration that the applicant disclaims rights to the element (para 63).

[43] Para 57.

16.38 Section 10(2) of the TMA 1994 was also considered in *Ellerman Investments Limited v Elizabeth C-Vanci*[44] where, in an application for summary judgment the court found that domain names including ritzypoker.co.uk, ritzypoker.net, ritzpoker.org, ritzpoker.info, and ritzpoker.biz to be confusingly similar to the claimant's registered trade mark 'Ritz' registered as a UK and CTM for inter alia gaming services.

Trade Marks Act 1994, section 10(3)

16.39 Section 10(3) of TMA 1994 has been considered in a number of cases including *BT v One in a Million*,[45] and *Global Projects Management Ltd v Citigroup Inc and others*.[46]

16.40 In *One in a Million*[47] a number of domain names including marksandspencer.com, bt.org, britishtelecommunication.net were registered by, among others, One in a Million. These they, inter alia, offered for sale to the claimants. The case was decided primarily by looking to the law of passing off, and by some extension of existing principles the court determined that by registering the domain names the defendants had created *instruments of fraud*.[48] Thus the domain names had to be handed back to the trade mark and brand owners. The judgment has been criticised.[49] It is said that the bounds of the tort of passing off were extended—by implication possibly too far; and that it is not at all clear that even if a case of passing off is made out, that would necessarily provide the remedy required.

In dealing with Trade Marks Act 1994, section 10(3), the court was relatively brief as to its application of the law to the facts. In the High Court it had been said that on the detriment requirement under section 10(3): 'It seems to me to be equally clear that the defendant's use of it is detrimental to the trade mark, if only by damaging the plaintiff's exclusivity'. This was confirmed in the Court of Appeal where it was said 'The domain names were registered to take advantage of the distinctive character and reputation of the marks. That is unfair and detrimental'. There was thus infringement under this section.

16.41 Although the case did not do much to aid understanding of the law of trade marks in relation to these types of disputes, consideration was given to the ruling in the case below.

■ *Global Projects Management v Citigroup* [2005] EWHC 2663 (Ch)

In this case the High Court was faced with a scenario where an individual registered citigroup.co.uk after an announcement had been made concerning the merger of two financial companies to form Citigroup Inc. The court referred extensively to *BT v One in a Million*, but went further in that it found against Global Projects Management even though no attempt had been made to sell the domain name to Citigroup or anyone else, nor was there any evidence of a track record of cyber-squatting (as there had been in *BT v One in a Million*). The court said that the mere registration and maintenance in force of a domain name which led people to believe that the holder of the domain name was linked with a person was enough to make the domain name

---

[44] [2006] EWHC 1442 (Ch).   [45] [1999] 4 All ER 476, [1999] RPC 1.
[46] [2006] FSR 39, [2005] EWHC 2663 (Ch).   [47] [1999] 4 All ER 476, [1999] RPC 1.
[48] See also *Radio Taxicab (London) Ltd v Owner Drivers Radio Taxis Services* [2004] RPC 19 Ch D 12 October 2001, Chancery Division TLC 1024/00; *Phones 4U Ltd v Phone4U.co.uk Internet Ltd* [2005] EWHC 334 (Ch); *Easyjet Airline Co Ltd v Dainty (t/a EasyRealestate)* [2002] FSR 6 Ch D.
[49] See, for example, C Thorne and S Bennett, "Domain Names—Internet Warehousing: Has protection of well-known names on the Internet Gone too Far?" [1998] EIPR 468.

a potential 'instrument of fraud' and amounted to passing off.[50] As with *BT v One in a Million* the court did not consider infringement of section 10(3) in detail merely saying that: 'It is admitted that Citicorp is the holder of registered trade marks of which one is the name and mark "Citigroup", and that GPM, by virtue of obtaining and maintaining in force the citigroup.co.uk domain name, has used or may use a sign which is similar to the registered mark, and which is used in relation to services that are not similar to those for which the trademark is registered. Thus far, paras (b) and (c) of s.10(3) are satisfied'.[51] The court noted that interesting arguments had been raised to suggest that not all of the rest of the conditions in section 10(3) were satisfied, but that the arguments were contrary to the holding in *One in a Million*. It therefore found that Citigroup were entitled to summary judgment on this claim.

16.42   The courts have made clear their dislike of these practices but have not really elaborated on how section 10(3) of the 1994 Act is relevant to the facts. How, for instance, could the section be relevant when the trade mark was not actually *used* (for example, offered for sale), but merely registered? To what extent does mere registration of the domain name *free-ride* upon or *dilute* an existing mark with a reputation?

16.43   What is interesting is reliance on the creation of an *instrument of fraud* as a basis of liability rather than registered trade mark law. Clearly registered trade mark law can only be relevant where there is a registered trade mark in existence. Nevertheless, in both *One in a Million* and *Global Projects Management*, the courts found much safer ground in the related area of passing off. This does have the merit that there is less need to stretch the boundaries of trade mark law in directions to which it may be little suited. That is not, however, to say that trade mark law is not used in negotiations between parties arguing for transfer or retention of a domain name.[52]

Key points on resolution of disputes in British courts

- Trade Marks Act 1994, section 10(1), (2) and (3) have all been used by the courts as a basis for settling domain name disputes
- The proper boundaries for finding of infringement of the TMA 1994, section 10(3) in domain name disputes are at present unclear.

 Discussion point   For answer guidance visit www.oxfordtextbooks.co.uk/orc/macqueen2e/

How do you think traditional trade mark law should apply to domain name disputes, if indeed it should?

Resolution of disputes under the ICANN UDRP

16.44   A reason why not many disputes may have been heard in the courts is because numerous cases are referred for resolution to the ICANN UDRP (or to one of the cc dispute resolution registrars).

---

[50] *Global Projects Management Ltd v Citigroup Inc* [2006] FSR 39, [2005] EWHC 2663 (Ch) Ch D para 40.
[51] ibid, para 58.
[52] For a case basing itself on free speech arguments see *Patel v Allos Therapeutics Inc.* 2008 WL 2442985 (Ch).

As mentioned above, the ICANN UDRP applies to domain names registered in the gTLDs.[53] The rules governing dispute resolution were drawn up as a result of a document initially prepared by WIPO following a series of meetings with interested parties around the globe and then amended by ICANN.

The important part of the dispute policy is to be found in Article 4 (where 'you' have registered the domain name that is contested by the Complainant).

4 a. Applicable Disputes. You are required to submit to a mandatory administrative proceeding in the event that a third party (a 'complainant') asserts to the applicable Provider, in compliance with the Rules of Procedure, that

(i) your domain name is identical or confusingly similar to a trademark or service mark in which the complainant has rights; and

(ii) you have no rights or legitimate interests in respect of the domain name; and

(iii) your domain name has been registered and is being used in bad faith.

In the administrative proceeding, the complainant must prove that each of these three elements are present.

b. Evidence of Registration and Use in Bad Faith. For the purposes of Paragraph 4(a)(iii), the following circumstances, in particular but without limitation, if found by the Panel to be present, shall be evidence of the registration and use of a domain name in bad faith:

(i) circumstances indicating that you have registered or you have acquired the domain name primarily for the purpose of selling, renting, or otherwise transferring the domain name registration to the complainant who is the owner of the trademark or service mark or to a competitor of that complainant, for valuable consideration in excess of your documented out-of-pocket costs directly related to the domain name; or

(ii) you have registered the domain name in order to prevent the owner of the trademark or service mark from reflecting the mark in a corresponding domain name, provided that you have engaged in a pattern of such conduct; or

(iii) you have registered the domain name primarily for the purpose of disrupting the business of a competitor; or

(iv) by using the domain name, you have intentionally attempted to attract, for commercial gain, Internet users to your web site or other on-line location, by creating a likelihood of confusion with the complainant's mark as to the source, sponsorship, affiliation, or endorsement of your web site or location or of a product or service on your web site or location.[54]

16.45   Each of the competing registrars authorised to register domain names in the gTLD's[55] must sign up to this dispute resolution process.[56] Those who register domain names then agree to be bound when registering a domain name. At the time of writing four providers are accredited as recognised to hear disputes arising under this dispute resolution process:[57] WIPO, the National Arbitration Forum (NAF), the Asian Domain Name Dispute Resolution Centre (ADNDRC) and

---

[53] Individual countries may however elect to use one of the arbitration providers under the ICANN UDRP and to apply the terms of the UDRP to registrations in their ccTLDs. For example, Trinidad and Tobago .tt and Ecuador .ec (http://www.wipo.int/amc/en/domains/cctld/index.html).

[54] http://www.icann.org/udrp/udrp-policy-24oct99.htm

[55] For details see http://www.icann.org/registrars/accredited-list.html

[56] A full list of these registries can be found at http://www.icann.org   [57] http://www.icann.org

the Czech Arbitration Court.[58] In December 2001 eResolution withdrew from providing services under the UDRP followed by CPR (the International Institute for Conflict Prevention and Resolution) in January 2007.

 Question

Why did eRes withdraw from providing arbitration services under the ICANN UDRP?
- Have a look at:
- M Geist, 'Fair.com?: An Examination of the Allegations of Systemic Unfairness in the ICANN UDRP', http://aix1.uottawa.ca/~geist/geistudrp.pdf and 'Fundamentally Fair. com? An Update on Bias Allegations an the ICANN UDRP', http://aix1.uottawa. ca/~geist/fairupdate.pdf
- M Mueller, 'Rough Justice: An Analysis of ICANN's Uniform Dispute Resolution Policy', http://www.acm.org/usacm/IG/roughjustice.pdf
- MS Donahey, 'The UDRP: Fundamentally Fair, But Far From Perfect Electronic Commerce & Law Reports' (2001) 6(34) Electronic Commerce & Law Reports (August 29), available from http://www.scottdonahey.com/Publications/UDRP_far_from_perfect.pdf
- See also A Kur, 'A Study on the UDRP' at http://www.zar.uni-karlsruhe.de/admin/get_data.php?resID=95

16.46   While statistics giving details of the absolute numbers of proceedings are difficult to come by, to June 2007 there were, since inception, 18,754 proceedings many of which concerned multiple domain names. WIPO holds statistics on the cases heard through their system which show increases year on year in the number of domain names in dispute with 4685 in 2008 involving an average of 2.2 domain names per case. These names included generic names such as Allocation, concierge and cello, place names such as Barcelona and Heathrow, personal names such as BillyConnolly, Madonna, and Juliaroberts, business names such as BankofNewZealand and Easyjet, and additions such as Directlinesucks, Easymaterial and Nokiagirls.

Weblink

WIPOs Arbitration and Mediation Centre have developed a most useful search tool for domain name disputes available at http://www.wipo.int/amc/en/domains/search/legalindex.jsp

In addition WIPO has compiled an overview of WIPO Panel Views on selected UDRP questions available at http://www.wipo.int/amc/en/domains/search/overview/

---

[58] The ADR.eu Centre is attached to the Czech Arbitration Court. For a hearing concerning the .eu domain see *Game Group Plc v First Internet Technology Ltd Case* 04014 ADR [2007] ETMR 78.

16.47   Looking to the cases, a number of broad factors can be suggested which tend to militate against the respondent, and if found, could mean that the domain name is transferred to the complainant—although it should be noted that there are inconsistencies in approach. Important factors (UDRP, Article 4) include whether the respondent has offered the domain name for sale: this is likely to be frowned upon, particularly if the sum is large.[59] Registering more than one domain name can be seen as an indication of the intention to profit from that name.[60] Failure to develop a website using the name can also cost the respondent the name, being seen as an indication of bad faith.[61]

16.48   While it is not the intention to discuss the cases in detail, it should be noted that the process represents an interesting exercise in Internet self-regulation—a solution to a global problem that was escalating, and which appeared to have no reasonable resolution on a national basis. Taking the disputes away from individual territories and trade mark laws has meant that a body of decisions has been developed specific to these disputes, however difficult it may be to draw consistent lessons. As noted, disputes may still be referred to national courts, and indeed a number are so referred resulting in a body of decisions which are interesting for their insights into the interaction between the UDRP process and the approach of national courts. One suspects that there would be more were the costs not prohibitive.

 Exercise

Investigate at least 10 different decisions made by the arbitrators in the domain name disputes in each of the following categories. Choose the cases from at least three different dispute resolution providers.

Categories:

- Generic names (eg Allocation, concierge, cello)
- Place names (eg Barcelona)
- Personal names (eg BillyConnolly, Madonna)
- Business names (eg BankofNewZealand, Easyjet)
- Additions (eg Directlinesucks, Easymaterial, Nokiagirls)
- Do you consider that there is consistent application of the rules in the UDRP?

Key points on resolution of disputes under the ICANN UDRP

- The number of disputes over domain names referred to the ICANN UDRP suggests that the system has been successful in minimising the volume of disputes referred to national courts.

- The dispute resolution process is intended to be limited to bad faith abusive domain name registrations

---

[59] billyconnolly.com; chickhere.com; hotmetal.com; topdog.com; herstyle.com; bridgetjones.com.
[60] nicholekidman.com (2) danmarino.com (50) clickhere.net (250) jimihendrix (2000).
[61] zero.com, timekeeper.com.

- The continuing importance of domain names and the issues that arise under the dispute settlement processes can be seen when considering the prominence WIPO gave to this subject in its General Assembly in Geneva in September to October 2009 where it devoted some time to considering the current state of play[62] which preceded a conference held by WIPO, '10 Years UDRP—What's next?'. The contributions to the conference suggest that participants considered the system is working but there are several areas which could be much improved including such matters as reverse domain name hijacking; matters of identity of participants; and the ever vexed question of what will happen when new gTLDs are introduced.[63]

The use of trade marks on the Internet

Introduction

16.49   The use of registered trade marks on the Internet raises many different questions over the interaction of such use with registered trade mark law. One issue concerns the co-existence of marks when the same or similar mark registered for the same or similar goods is used by traders based in different countries, but where that trade mark becomes accessible in other countries by virtue of being used on web pages. Other difficulties have arisen where trade marks are used by an unauthorised third party in metatags or in banner advertisements. More recent challenges have concerned the use of trade marks in keyword advertising campaigns. This part will discuss some of the cases that have arisen in the British courts dealing with co-existence of trade marks on the Internet; discuss the response of the courts to the use of trade marks as meta tags and in banner advertisements; and briefly introduce the keyword advertising disputes.

This part contains the following sections

- Territorial scope of protection: accessibility and disclaimers (16.51–16.62)
- Banners and metatags (16.63–16.66)
- Keyword advertising (16.67–16.73)

16.50
Learning objectives

By the end of this chapter you should be able to describe and explain:

- why and in what circumstances conflicts can arise over the use of trade marks on the Internet;
- the response of the British courts to co-existence of marks on the Internet and the suggestions made by WIPO to enable co-existence of marks on the Internet;
- how the courts have applied trade mark law to meta tags, banner advertisement and to keyword advertising.

---

[62] WIPO paper WO/GA/38/12

[63] For full details of the conference and copies of the presentations see http://www.wipo.int/amc/en/events/workshops/2009/10yrs-udrp/program/index.html

Territorial scope of protection: accessibility and disclaimers

16.51 The scope of protection available under a trade mark is, as with any other intellectual property rights, limited to the geographical territory where protection has been obtained. The main consequence of this principle of territoriality is that a domestic court would only be able to find an infringement in case of a domestic right being infringed. In other words, infringing acts may occur on the Internet, yet in order to be actionable, have to manifest itself as a right that subsists within the territory in respect of which action is taken. It follows from that there should be no automatic case of *infringement* if an identical or similar mark is used on the Internet as such. However, where different owners own identical or similar marks in different countries, and those marks are accessible in the territory where the 'competing' mark is registered, then infringement could occur. For example, if the owner of mark 'X' in country A advertises on the Internet, and mark 'X' is owned by a different person in country B for the same goods, then conflicts are likely to arise, especially if courts view mere *accessibility* of a trade mark on the Internet as infringing use.

16.52 According to EU jurisprudence, where there are the same or similar marks owned by different persons, there is no right of importation of goods bearing the mark from member state A to member state B.[64] As was pointed out by the ECJ in *IHT International Heiztechnik v Ideal Standard*:

> 'There is no unlawful restriction on trade between member states within the meaning of Arts. 30 and 36 where a subsidiary operating in Member State A of a manufacturer established in Member State B is to be enjoined from using as a trade mark the name "Ideal Standard" because of the risk of confusion with a device having the same origin, even if the manufacturer is lawfully using that mark in his country of origin under a trade mark protected there, he acquired that trade mark by assignment and the trade mark originally belonged to a company affiliated to the undertaking which, in Member State A, opposes the importation of goods bearing the trade mark "Ideal Standard" '.[65]

16.53 How then can valid and competing claims between unrelated traders be reconciled when those traders wish to use their registered marks on websites?

Two avenues have been suggested:

- the first deals with accessibility or use of a trade mark on the Internet, and whether mere accessibility would amount to infringement;
- the second is whether there might be room to argue for the use of disclaimers in the event that claims appear irreconcilable.

Accessibility and use of a trade mark on the Internet: British case law

16.54 In relation to the first avenue it has been suggested that the mere use of a trade mark on a website should not be sufficient to qualify as 'use' under domestic trade mark law, and thus the trade mark in the country of importation (or accessibility) would not be infringed. The relevant

---

[64] Neither is there a right to import goods from outwith the territory of the EU and re-sell over the Internet even where the trade mark may not be seen until after the sale (1) *Kabushiki Kaisha Sony Computer Entertainment (Also T/A Sony Computer Entertainment Inc*; (2) *Sony Computer Entertainment Europe Ltd (collectively 'Sony') v Nuplayer Ltd* [2006] FSR 9, [2005] EWHC 1522.

[65] Case C-9/93 *IHT International Heiztechnik v Ideal Standard* [1994] 3 CMLR 857, [1994] ECR I-2789, [1995] FSR 59.

country? Under present trade mark law, the trade marks are identical, and therefore there would be infringement where one was soliciting business in the territory of the other. To solve this conundrum it may be appropriate to introduce the use of disclaimers. If 'Ritz' Barcelona' and 'Ritz' Paris made it clear that they were not associated with each other through the use of a disclaimer then there would be no infringement.

16.60 It is acknowledged that such a rule would be inconsistent with established trade mark principles in many jurisdictions.[74] There may also be questions as to the extent to which the use of such disclaimers might be considered anti-competitive and/or disguised restrictions on trade. Nonetheless, if trade marks are to co-exist on the Internet, and trade is to be facilitated rather than hampered, then the avenues above might help to alleviate the difficulties faced by traders.

Key points on territorial scope of protection: accessibility and disclaimers

- The accessibility of trade marks on websites require legitimate interests of owners to be balanced
- The accessibility of a trade mark on a website may not necessarily amount to use in another territory
- Suggestions have been made that disclaimers might be utilised to resolve conflicts

---

International strategies

16.61 In 1988 WIPO published a study concerning the use of trade marks on the Internet. This study was wide ranging in its terms, and covered not only registered trade marks, but also unregistered rights. The report summarised a number of possible principles for discussion, notably concerning use of trade marks on the Internet.[75]

16.62 On the question of *use* WIPO suggested:

'There seems to be a general understanding that the mere appearance of a sign or a mark on the Internet is not sufficient to establish a connection between that sign or mark and a given territory. Many comments suggest that a relationship between a sign used on the Internet and a given territory is only established through commercial use of that sign in respect of that territory or, as it was expressed in one comment, whether the sign used on the Internet has 'commercial effect' in a territory'.

The report went on to outline a number of factors which could contribute to a finding of use. These included servicing of customers in the particular territory or country; entering into other commercially motivated relationships with persons in the particular territory or country; and actual visits to the website for which or on which the sign is used from persons in the particular territory or country.[76]

---

[74] Note the general discussion on 'use of a trade mark' in Chapter 15.
[75] WIPO Standing Committee on the Law of Trade Marks Industrial Designs and Geographical Indications Study concerning the use of trade marks on the Internet Second Session. SCT/2/9 Available on the WIPO website.
[76] ibid, Summary, p 14.

Question

What rules do you think should govern the co-existence of legitimate trade marks on the Internet?

Banners and metatags

16.63 In the case of *Reed Executive Plc v Reed Business Information Ltd*[77] the Court of Appeal made some observations on the interaction between trade mark infringement, banners and metatags. Reed Executive (RE) had registered the word 'Reed' for employment agency services in Class 35. They also operated a website at reed.co.uk. An unconnected business, Reed Business Information (RBI), ran a recruitment website called totaljobs.com.

RBI used the word Reed as follows:

- on their website they used the words 'Reed Business Information' with their logo and the statement 'Contact Reed Business Information if you would like to advertise your company's job vacancies';

- as metatags leading to the totaljobs.com site;

- in banner advertising on search engine home pages linking to the totaljobs.com site.

RE sued for trade mark infringement and passing off, arguing that RBI's activities amounted to a use of a sign identical or similar to their mark which was likely to lead to public confusion.

The Banner argument

16.64 At first instance the court had found that when the banner was triggered by the word 'Reed' REs trade mark was infringed. The Court of Appeal disagreed saying that the banner itself referred only to totaljobs, there being no visible appearance of the word Reed. The appearance of the banner when a search for Reed or Reed jobs was undertaken could not amount to infringement of the registered trade mark as there was no consumer confusion.

> 'The idea that a search under the name Reed would make anyone think there was a trade connection between a totaljobs banner making no reference to the word "Reed" and Reed Employment is fanciful. No likelihood of confusion was established'.[78]

The court also raised the question (but did not answer it) as to whether the use of the word Reed by the search engine at the instance of RBI would amount to use 'in the course of trade' a matter which would have been considered had the basis for trade mark infringement been on identity of marks rather than similarity. The court simply noted that: 'It may be that an invisible use of this sort is not use at all for the purposes of this trade mark legislation—the computers who "read" sets of letters merely "look for" patterns of 0s and 1s—there is no meaning being conveyed to anyone—no "sign" '.[79]

---

[77] [2004] ETMR 56.   [78] ibid, para 140.   [79] ibid, para 143.

The Metatag argument

16.65   Metatags which are used by search engines to index Internet content may never be visible to the eye. RBI had used the words 'Reed Business Information' in their metatags and RE alleged that this amounted to trade mark infringement in that there would be consumer confusion. The Court of Appeal disagreed indicating that even if the use of a mark as a metatag amounted to trade mark use, there was no consumer confusion: causing a site to appear in a search result does not suggest any connection with anyone else.

16.66   As on the matter of banner use, interesting questions were raised but not answered by the court:

- Does metatag use count as use of a trade mark?

- If it does, is there infringement if the marks and goods or services are identical?

- If metatag use does amount to infringement, do any of the defences such as the own name defence apply?

- On matters of use, and given the Court of Justices's developing jurisprudence in this area, the question arising now would be likely to be framed to ask whether the use implicated one of the functions of a mark (paras 15.4ff).

 Question

How would you answer these points? Give reasons for your views.

Why do you think that there have been few reported cases in the UK dealing with trade marks and their use in the internet context?

Key points on banners and metatags

- Questions concerning 'use' of a trade mark seem central to matters of infringement concerning banners and metatags.

Keyword advertising[80]

16.67   In *Reed Executive Plc v Reed Business Information Ltd*[81] Jacob LJ noted, obiter that use as a keyword is invisible use having no meaning denoting origin or source—suggesting there was no trade mark infringement. These arguments have now come to the fore in a series of cases in the UK and throughout Europe challenging the practice. On the one hand is the desire of the trade mark owner to keep control of all uses of their trade mark in relation to internet usage. On the other is the business model on which search engines and other intermediaries depend—that

---

[80] Note that this section draws from the book chapter *'Search Engines, Keyword Advertising and Trade Marks: Fair Innovation or Free Riding?'*, T Bednarz and C Waelde, in 'Law and the Internet', L Edwards and C Waelde (eds) (3rd edn, 2009).
[81] ibid, n 76.

of the income generated through keyword advertising. As an example, in 2008, 97 per cent of Google's revenue came from advertising (21.1 billion USD): 66 per cent of this from Google's own websites (keyword advertising activities); 31 per cent from network sites; and 3 per cent from other licensing and revenue.[82]

The mechanics of keyword advertising

16.68   Every time a search engine is used to find something on the Internet, it not only returns results pertinent to the search terms entered by the user, but it also displays small advertisements, also called sponsored links, most commonly above or beside the actual search results. The display of these advertisements is by no means random. Rather, each advertisement is associated with certain keywords and is triggered every time the search term(s) match one of the keywords. It is the advertisers who specify the keywords. The advertiser can also indicate where those advertisements should be placed on the search page, whether at the top or along the right hand side. Revenue comes from the advertisers who pay to the search engine a specified amount each time an internet user clicks on a sponsored advertisement (click through). The ranking of the advertisements on the page depends on a combination of factors. For Google it includes other advertisers' bids; the quality score of advertisements in any particular search calculated by the click through rate; the relevance of the advertisers' text and keywords; and account history. The minimum bid for a keyword takes into account the quality of the landing page (where the user gets to when she clicks on the advertisement) including the relevancy and originality of the content.[83]

16.69   Key to the legal disputes is that search engines permit advertisers to 'buy' keywords that are the same as or similar to trade marks registered by third parties. So when a user searches for 'coca cola', advertisements for 'Pepsi cola' might appear if Pepsi cola has bid on the 'coca cola' trade mark. This, it is argued by the trade mark owners, causes consumer confusion, dilution of the trade mark, unfair competition (passing off) and leads to misleading advertising. Search engines on the other hand argue that their business model does not make use of the trade mark, and even if it did, it does not lead to consumer confusion or to the dilution of well-known trade marks. Further, if there is a problem for trade mark law it is the advertisers who are responsible as it is they who choose the keyword, not the search engine.

16.70   There have been two cases to date in the UK looking at these arguments. The first, *Wilson v Yahoo!*,[84] concerned the CTM 'Mr Spicy' which Mr Wilson had registered in classes 29, 30 and 42 of the CTM register. Mr Wilson brought an action against Yahoo! arguing that when 'Mr Spicy' was typed into Yahoo!'s search bar the first return to come up was for Sainsbury's and 'Delicious meal ideas for all occasions www.sainsbury's.co.uk, food news, inspiration and recipes from Sainsbury's on-line', and second for Pricegrabber where the entry began with the word 'spicy' followed by 'www.pricegrabber.co.uk, compare prices on a variety of products at Pricegrabber'. (as at 14 December 2006). The High Court was asked about, and dealt with, the question of use as a trade mark. According to the court

> [t]he trade mark in this case is not used by anyone other than the browser [Internet user] who enters the phrase 'Mr. Spicy' as a search query in the defendants' search engine. In particular, the trade mark is

---

[82] Unaudited accounts available at http://investor.google.com/releases/2008Q4_google_earnings.html

[83] See the instructions at http://www.google.co.uk/intl/en/ads/. See also the description by J Grimmelmann, 'Rescuecom Oral Argument Report' (laboratorium.net, 4 April 2008) http://laboratorium.net/archive/2008/04/04/rescuecom_oral_argument_report

[84] *Wilson v Yahoo! UK Ltd* [2008] EWHC 361 (Ch), [2008] ETMR 33.

not used by [Yahoo!]. The response of the defendants to the use of the trade mark by the browser is not use of the trade mark by the defendants. That is enough to decide the case in the defendants' favour.[85]

The High Court went on to apply the ECJ's ruling in *Arsenal* saying:

[i]n my judgment, this case, very comfortably and clearly, comes within paragraph 54 of the decision in that case; that is, Mr. Wilson is not able to prohibit the use of the words 'Mr. Spicy' even when they are being applied to goods identical to those for which the mark is registered if that use cannot affect his own interest as proprietor of the mark having regard to its functions. That is satisfied here.[86]

Thus there was no infringement. It is notable in the instant case that the advertisers had only paid for 'spicy' as a descriptive term.[87] Yahoo!'s service, however, functioned so as to display the advertisement every time an internet user searched for the term 'spicy' or any other phrase containing it. This is why Morgan J came to the conclusion that only the Internet user searching for 'Mr. Spicy' used this term and therefore Mr Wilson's trade mark, but not the advertiser or the search engine provider. *Wilson v Yahoo!* is therefore not typical case of keyword advertising and it cannot be assumed that UK courts would thereby reject the notion of use as a trade mark if the search engine had sold a distinctive third party trade mark as a keyword. In the second, *Interflora v Marks and Spencer*,[88] the trade mark owner, Interflora, sued the advertiser, Marks and Spencer. Interflora not only claimed that Marks and Spencer had infringed its trade mark, but in addition that Google had committed acts for which Marks and Spencer were jointly liable.[89] The court noted that the implications of keyword advertising were currently subject of very different treatment in member states of the EU and summarised the existing six national references to the ECJ for a preliminary ruling. Ultimately, the court held that there was a 'real possibility that the rulings by the [Court] on the existing references will not clearly resolve all the issues of law which arise in the present case' and without giving any view of what the possible answer to any of the questions might be, ordered a reference to be made—making this the seventh reference to the ECJ on this topic.

16.71   To November 2009, the Court of Justice had received seven requests for a preliminary ruling on matters relating to keyword advertising. From France these are *Google v Viaticum*, *Google v CNRRH*, and *Google v. Louis Vuitton Malletier*[90] each involving the search engine, Google (rather than individual advertisers); from Austria, *BergSpechte v trekking.at*, a case in which the trade mark owner sued an advertiser who offered competing services;[91] the *Hoge Raad der Nederlanden* referred questions in *Portakabin v Primakabin*, a dispute between a trade mark owner and an advertiser;[92] the German *Bundesgerichtshof* in the *bananabay* case, a conflict between trade mark owner and advertiser;[93] and finally, as mentioned above, *Interflora Inc v Marks and Spencer plc*.[94]

16.72   On trade marks matters most ask whether the use of a third party trade mark by the search engine is an infringing use for the purposes of TMD Art 5(1)(a) and (b) and CTMR Art 9(1)(a) and (b). In addition questions include whether the trade mark owner's exclusive right is infringed

---

[85] ibid, para 64.   [86] ibid, para 65.   [87] ibid, paras 31 and 68.   [88] [2009] EWHC 1095 (Ch).

[89] *Wilson v Yahoo! UK Ltd* [2008] EWHC 361 (Ch), [2008] ETMR 33.was not mentioned.

[90] Cass comm., 20 mai 2008, *Sté Google France c/ Sté Viaticum et Sté Luteciel*; Cass Comm, 20 mai 2008, *Sté Google c/ Sté CNRRH et autres*; Cass comm., 20 mai 2008, *Sté Google France et Sté Google Inc. c/ Sté Louis Vuitton Malletier*. These cases were joined for hearing in the Court of Justice.

[91] OGH (20.05.2008 – 17 Ob 3/08b); the decision can be found at http://www.ris.bka.gv.at/Jus/.

[92] Hoge Raad der Nederlanden (12.12.2008 – C 07/056 HR); available at http://zoeken.rechtspraak.nl/.

[93] BGH *bananabay* (22.01.2009 – I ZR 125/07); available at http://www.bundesgerichtshof.de/index.

[94] Case C-323/09.

'regardless of whether the accessed advertisement appears in the list of hits or in a separate advertising block and whether it is marked as a "sponsored link" ';[95] where an identical sign is used for similar goods and services or a sign similar to the trade mark is used for identical or similar goods and services (ie those envisaged in TMD Art 5(1)(b)) 'is the fact that the advertisement is marked as a 'sponsored link' and/or appears not in the list of hits but in a separate advertising block sufficient to exclude any likelihood of confusion?'[96] whether it made a difference in this regard if the advertiser offered similar or identical goods or services (a) in the advertisement itself and (b) on the site to which Internet users are directed when clicking on the sponsored link.

16.73 The fact of the lawsuits has been argued by some to threaten the viability of the search engine as a business model: if a search engine cannot raise revenue via keyword advertising, the search engine will cease to exist. It seems that might be an overly simplistic approach to the complexities involved in keyword advertising, and the very different and multi-varied questions that can and do arise with regard to the place of and potential liability in relation to unauthorised use of trade marks in relation to that activity. At the time of writing the Attorney General had handled down this opinion. Broadly he has advised that the selection by an advertiser of a keyword does not constitute an infringement of a trade mark and that a trade mark proprietor may not prevent a search engine from making available keywords that constitute registered trade marks whether the mark has a reputation or not. The judgment of the full court is expected in early 2010.

Discussion point For answer guidance visit www.oxfordtextbooks.co.uk/orc/macqueen2e/

Read the questions referred to the Court of Justice of the European Union in the seven cases highlighted above and the opinions of the Attorney General. How do you think the Court will respond?

Geographical indications

Introduction

16.74 Geographical indications (GIs) are a form of intellectual property[97] rooted in agricultural policy and designed to highlight a link between the natural geographical advantages or the reputation associated with a place and the foodstuffs produced in that place. There are treaties at international level dealing with geographical indications although the most developed regime is at EU level. This was enhanced as part of the reform of the common agricultural policy designed to mark a move from mass produced to quality food products. A series of bilateral treaties has extended the protection as between various countries.

16.75 On the one hand a GI serves to give the consumer information as to the quality of the produce marketed under the GI. But critics see a danger in that if protection is overbroad and tied to reputation, innovation may be hampered. The GI may become a means to shield against

---

[95] Case C-278/08 *Die BergSpechte Outdoor Reisen und Alpinschule Edi Koblmüller GmbH v Günter Guni and trekking.at Reisen GmbH*, reference for a preliminary ruling [2008] OJ C223/30.
[96] ibid.   [97] *Consorzio del Prosciutto di Parma v Asda Stores Ltd* [2002] FSR 3, para 6.

competition from new entrants to the market[98] rather than a genuine means for indicating the quality and provenance of a product.

Scope of this part

16.76   In this part, having considered some of the terminology used when referring to GIs, the scheme of protection at international level will be briefly described followed by an examination of the EU Regulation on the protection of geographical indications and designations of origin for agricultural products and foodstuffs. In its original form this Regulation came into force in 1993.[99]

16.77

> ### Learning objectives
>
> By the end of this chapter you should be able to describe and explain:
>
> - the terminology and definitions used in connection with GIs;
> - the framework of international and regional protection;
> - the EU regime from the protection of geographical indications and designations of origin.

The rest of this part looks like this:

- Terminology (16.78–16.79)
- International protection (16.80–16.84)
- The EU regime (16.85–16.112)

Terminology

16.78   A number of different expressions are used to define GIs, each of which has different characteristics. The common factor is that all are designed to give protection to indications which have some link with a location. While there is no definition of a GI in the Paris Convention for the Protection of Industrial Property (the Paris Convention), that instrument refers to indications of the source of the goods, and to locality, region and country.[100] Similarly the Madrid Agreement for the Repression of False or Misleading Indications of Source on Goods 1891 (the Madrid Agreement) refers to indications of the country or place of origin.[101] Extrapolating from these provisions it has been said that 'an indication of source can be defined as an indication

---

[98] T Josling, 'The War on Terroir: Geographical indications as a Transatlantic Trade Conflict' (2006) 57 Journal of Agricultural Economics 537.

[99] Originally Regulation No 2081/92 of 14 July 1992 as amended several times and most recently replaced by Council Regulation (EC) No 510/2006 of 20 March 2006 on the protection of geographical indications and designations of origin for agricultural products and foodstuffs. This followed a WTO Panel decision on the compatibility of Regulation 2081/92 with the national treatment clause in TRIPS.

[100] Paris Convention, Arts 10(1) and (2).   [101] Madrid Agreement, Art 1.

referring to a country, or to a place in that country, as being the country or place of origin of a product'.[102]

16.79   For the purposes of the TRIPS Agreement, GIs are defined as 'indications which identify a good as originating in the territory of a Member, or a region or locality in that territory, where a given quality, reputation or other characteristic of the good is essentially attributable to its geographical origin'.[103] The Lisbon Agreement for the protection of appellations of origin and their international registration (the Lisbon Agreement) talks of appellations of origin. These are 'the geographical name of a country, region, or locality, which serves to designate a product originating therein, the quality and characteristics of which are due exclusively or essentially to the geographical environment, including natural and human factors'. Regulation 510/2006 refers to designations of origin as being the name of a region, place or country used to describe an agricultural product or foodstuff originating in that place and which exhibits characteristics due to the environment, and to geographical indications as the name of a region where there is a particular quality attributable to the origin and the production, processing or preparation taking place in that area.

> **Key point on terminology**
>
> • The extent of protection for a GI will depend on the scope of protection under each of these instruments and is linked to the definition to be found in the instrument

International protection

16.80   There is patchwork protection for GIs at international level. The Paris Convention and the Madrid Agreement both provide for the seizure of goods on importation where there is a false indication as to the source of the goods, irrespective of the intent of the user.

Weblinks

The Madrid Agreement is administered by WIPO and can be found at
http://www.wipo.int/treaties/en/ip/madrid/

The Paris Convention also administered by WIPO can be found at
http://www.wipo.int/treaties/en/ip/paris/

16.81   The Lisbon Agreement, by contrast, established a registration system for appellations of origin. Where an appellation of origin is protected in a signatory state to the Treaty, this can be

[102] WIPO Standing Committee On The Law Of Trademarks, Industrial Designs And Geographical Indications Sixth Session Geneva, 12–16 March, 2001, *Geographical Indications: Historical Background, Nature Of Rights, Existing Systems For Protection And Obtaining Effective Protection In Other Countries* available at http://www.wipo.int/edocs/mdocs/sct/en/sct_6/sct_6_3.pdf
[103] TRIPS Agreement, Art 22(1).

used to apply for international registration via WIPO.[104] This means that the Lisbon system of registration is only applicable to appellations of origin where they are already protected on the national level in the country of origin. Application must be made by an administrative body on behalf of the group entitled to use the appellation. When an application for registration is made, other member states who are a party to the agreement have 12 months to indicate whether they are able to protect the appellation in their home country. If no objection is lodged, the appellation must be protected for as long as it is protected in the country of origin. Once registered, the Lisbon Agreement requires an appellation to be protected against misleading use even if a consumer may not be confused or deceived by such use. The agreement also requires member states to protect against imitation of the appellation of origin even where the origin of the product is indicated or where it is accompanied by terms such as 'kind', 'type', 'make' or 'imitation'. Examples of appellations of origin registered under the Lisbon Agreement include 'Bordeaux' for wine, 'Noix de Grenoble' for nuts, 'Tequila' for spirit drinks, and 'Jaffa' for oranges.

Weblinks

You will find the Lisbon Agreement at
http://www.wipo.int/lisbon/en/legal_texts/lisbon_agreement.htm#P22_1099

You can also search the Lisbon Register on the WIPO website
http://www.wipo.int/ipdl/en/search/lisbon/search-struct.jsp

16.82   The TRIPS Agreement contains measures relating to geographical indications which apply to all products (not just agricultural products and foodstuffs). The Agreement requires member states to prevent the use of any means that indicates or suggests that a good originates in a geographic area other than the true place of origin such that it misleads the public as to the geographical origin.[105] It also requires member states to protect against a use that constitutes an act of unfair competition within the meaning of Article 10*bis* of the Paris Convention.[106] For wines and spirits, and as with the Lisbon Agreement, member states must also protect against the use of a GI where products do not originate in that location even where the true origin of the goods is indicated (that is, they are literally true) although they falsely represent to the public that the goods on which they are used come from a different territory,[107] or where the GI is used in translation or accompanied by expression such as 'kind', 'type', 'style', 'imitation' or the like.[108]

16.83   As can be seen, these instruments exhibit differences in approach to the protection of GIs. From the prohibition of the use of false and deceptive indications of source (Paris Convention and Madrid Agreement) to a more general prohibition of the use of GI which constitutes an act of unfair competition within the meaning of Article 10*bis* of the Paris Convention (TRIPS Agreement). The discussion below will examine the EU approach.

16.84   There are also a number of bilateral agreements in the field of GIs most notably dealing with wines. For example bilateral agreements between the EU and other countries include the

---

[104] WIPO held a conference in 2009 on the subject of GIs and during which there was detailed examination of the Lisbon Agreement. See WIPO Symposium Bulgaria June 2009 Perspectives for Geographical Indications WIPO/GEO/SOF/09/1.
[105] TRIPS Agreement, Art 22(2)(a).   [106] ibid, Art 22(2)(b).   [107] ibid, Art 22(4).   [108] ibid, Art 23(1).

Australia EU Agreement (Concerning the Conclusion of an Agreement between the European Community and Australia on Trade in Wine);[109] and an Agreement between the European Community and the United States of America on Trade in Wine.[110] Such agreements may provide for a prohibition on the use of a GI not having that origin, or provide for changes to the local laws to protect GIs within the territory.[111]

Key points on international regime

- Patchwork protection exists for GIs at international level
- The instruments take varying approaches to definitions of protected subject matter and scope of protection

---

The EU regime

16.85 The EU operates four systems for the protection of geographical indications: for wines;[112] spirit drinks;[113] agricultural products and foodstuffs (which will be examined below);[114] and for agricultural products and foodstuffs for Traditional Specialties Guaranteed (TSGs).[115] National laws of Member States apply to all non-agricultural geographical indications. In its *Communication on agricultural product quality policy* adopted on 28 May 2009, the Commission announced its intention to bring together the different systems into a single register.

Weblink

Regulation 510/2006 can be found at

http://eur-lex.europa.eu/LexUriServ/site/en/oj/2006/l_093/l_09320060331en00120025.pdf

---

16.86 Regulation 510/2006 protects designations of origin and geographical indications of foodstuffs and agricultural products as stipulated in the Annex:

- foodstuffs:
  - beers
  - beverages made from plant extracts

---

[109] 94/184/EC [1994] OJ L86/1.   [110] [2006] OJ L87/2.

[111] For an ECJ case on the compatibility of a bilateral agreement between two individual countries with Regulation 2081/92 see Case C-216/01 *Budejovicky Budvar Narodni Podnik v Rudolf Ammersin GmbH* [2005] 1 CMLR 56, [2003] ECR I-13617, [2004] ETMR 21

[112] Regulation (EC) No 479/2008 on the common organisation of the market in wine.

[113] Regulation (EC) No 110/2008 on the definition, description, presentation, labelling and protection of geographical indications of spirit drinks.

[114] Regulation (EC) No 510/2006 on the protection of geographical indications and designations of origin for agricultural products and foodstuffs.

[115] Regulation 509/2006.

  – bread, pastry, cakes, confectionery and other baker's wares
  – natural gums and resins
  – mustard paste
  – pasta
- agricultural products:
  – hay
  – essential oils
  – cork
  – cochineal (raw product of animal origin)
  – flowers and ornamental plants
  – wool
  – wicker
  – scutched flax

The Regulation does not apply to wine-sector products (except wine vinegars) or to spirits.[116]

Protected designations of origin and protected geographical indications

16.87   Regulation 510/2006 provides for the protection of Designations of Origin (DO) and Geographical Indications (GI). Once these are registered they are called Protected Designations of Origin (PDO) and Protected Geographical Indications (PGI) respectively.

A designation of origin is defined in Article 2:

> '(a) the name of a region, a specific place or, in exceptional cases, a country, used to describe an agricultural product or a foodstuff:
>
>   – originating in that region, specific place or country,
>   – the quality or characteristics of which are essentially or exclusively due to a particular geographical environment with its inherent natural and human factors, and
>   – the production, processing and preparation of which take place in the defined geographical area;'

A geographical indication is also defined in Article 2 as:

> '(b) the name of a region, a specific place or, in exceptional cases, a country, used to describe an agricultural product or a foodstuff:
>
>   – originating in that region, specific place or country, and
>   – which possesses a specific quality, reputation or other characteristics attributable to that geographical origin, and
>   – the production and/or processing and/or preparation of which take place in the defined geographical area.'

The purpose of giving protection to PDOs and PGIs is said to be twofold. It is intended both to protect producers of the products from unfair competition and to protect consumers from being misled by the application to products of false or misleading descriptions.[117]

---

[116] Regulation 510/2006, Art 1.   [117] *Consorzio del Prosciutto di Parma v Asda Stores Ltd* [2002] FSR 3, para 58.

Question

What similarities and distinctions can you see as between the definitions of a PDO and a PGI?

16.88   As can be seen there are both similarities and distinctions between the definitions.

- PDO: The characteristics must be essentially or exclusively due to the geographical environment.

- PGI: The quality, reputation or other characteristics must be attributable to the geographical origin—that is, a reputation based link.

- PDO: The production, processing and preparation must take place in the defined geographical area.

- PGI: The production or processing or preparation must take place in the defined geographic area.

In *Consorzio del Prosciutto di Parma v Asda Stores Ltd*[118] it was said that 'A PDO is similar to a PGI except that the causal link between the place of origin and the quality of the product may be a matter of reputation rather than verifiable fact'.

Traditional geographical or non-geographical names

16.89   Article 2(3) of Regulation 510/2006 also protects certain traditional geographical or non-geographical names which designate an agricultural product or a foodstuff and which originates is a region or a specific place, and fulfils the conditions in the definition of a designation of origin.

16.90   Protection of a non-geographic name was considered in *Germany v Commission of the European Communities*[119] where the question was over the protection of the word 'feta'. The ECJ accepted that the word feta was derived from the Italian word 'fetta', meaning 'slice', which had entered the Greek language in the 17th century and that 'feta' is not the name of a region, place or country. However where the produce came from a 'geographical environment with specific natural and human factors and which is capable of giving an agricultural product or foodstuff its specific characteristics' and where homogenous natural factors distinguished it from the areas adjoining it, that would be sufficient to fall under the criterion in Article 2(3).[120]

Key point on non-geographical names

- A non-geographic name can be protected as a PDO if it originates in a geographical environment which gives it specific characteristics

---

[118] *Consorzio del Prosciutto di Parma v Asda Stores Ltd* [2002] FSR 3, para 8. See also Case C-343/07 *Bavaria NV, Bavaria Italia Srl v Bayerischer Brauerbund eV*, for mention of the link between 'on the one hand, the geographical origin of the product and, on the other hand, a specific quality of that product, its reputation or another characteristic of the product, attributable to that origin ...', para 107.

[119] Case C-465/02 *Germany v Commission of the European Communities* [2005] ECR I-9115, [2006] ETMR 16.

[120] ibid, para 50.

Generic names

16.91   Regulation 510/2006 prohibits the registration of generic names. A name that has become generic means:

> 'the name of an agricultural product or a foodstuff which, although it relates to the place or the region where this product or foodstuff was originally produced or marketed, has become the common name of an agricultural product or a foodstuff in the Community.'[121]

The Regulation sets out a series of non-exhaustive factors to be taken into account in determining whether a name has become generic. These include factors concerning the existing situation in the member states and in areas of consumption; and the relevant national or Union laws.

16.92   The generic character of a name was considered by the ECJ in *Germany v Commission of the European Communities*[122] where the Court noted that the fact that a product has been lawfully marketed under a name in some member states may constitute a factor which must be taken into account in the assessment of whether that name has become generic.[123] Other factors to be considered were listed by the Court when considering the PDO Parmigiano Reggiano and the user of the name Parmesan. These included the places of production of the product both inside and outside the member state where the name was registered; the consumption of the product and how it is perceived by consumers both in and beyond the member state; and any national legislation relating to the product[124] In *Bavaria NV, Bavaria Italia Srl v Bayerischer Brauerbund eV*,[125] the Court said that 'as regards a PGI, a name becomes generic only if the direct link between, on the one hand, the geographical origin of the product and, on the other hand, a specific quality of that product, its reputation or another characteristic of the product, attributable to that origin, has disappeared, and that the name does no more than describe a style or type of product'.[126]

16.93   Regulation 510/2006 provides that a protected name may not become generic.[127]

Plant varieties, animal breeds, homonymous names

16.94   Regulation 510/2006 provides that a name may not be registered as a DO or a GI where it conflicts with the name of a plant variety or an animal breed and as a result is likely to mislead the consumer as to the true origin of the product.[128] As regards homonymous names (words having the same name or designation) the Regulation provides that a name which is wholly or partially homonymous with that of a name already registered can be registered after having due regard to local and traditional usage and the actual risk of confusion. Where a consumer will be misled into believing that products come from another territory then the name may not be registered even if the name is accurate as far as the actual territory of origin is concerned. In addition there must be sufficient distinction between the homonym and the name already on the register having regard to the need to treat producers equitably and not mislead consumers.[129]

---

[121] Regulation 510/2006, Art 3(1).   [122] Case C-465/02 [2005] ECR I-9115; [2006] ETMR 16.
[123] ibid, para 79.   [124] Case C-132/05 *Commission of the European Communities v Germany*.
[125] Case C-343/07 para 107.
[126] ibid para 107. See also Case C-446/07 *Alberto Severi v Regione Emilia Romagna*.
[127] Art 13(2).   [128] Art 3(2).   [129] Art 3(3)(a) and (b).

The specifications

16.95 Article 4 of the Regulation 510/2006 contains the specifications with which a PDO or PGI must comply. These specifications set out the information used to determine whether a name should be registered; once registered it sets out the standard with which users must comply if they wish to use the PDO or PGI; it also determines the scope of protection accorded by the PDO or PGI.[130]

The list of what must be contained in the specifications, which is not exhaustive, includes the following:

(1) the name of the agricultural product or foodstuff comprising the designation of origin or the geographical indication;
(2) a description of the agricultural product or foodstuff, including the raw materials, if appropriate, and principal physical, chemical, microbiological or organoleptic characteristics of the product or the foodstuff;
(3) the definition of the geographical area;
(4) evidence that the agricultural product or the foodstuff originates in the defined geographical area;
(5) a description of the method of obtaining the agricultural product or foodstuff and, if appropriate, the authentic and unvarying local methods as well as information concerning packaging, if the applicant group within the meaning of Article 5(1) so determines and gives reasons why the packaging must take place in the defined geographical area to safeguard quality or ensure the origin or ensure control;
(6) details bearing out the following:
  (i) the link between the quality or characteristics of the agricultural product or foodstuff and the geographical environment or, as the case may be,
  (ii) the link between a specific quality, the reputation or other characteristic of the agricultural product or foodstuff and the geographical origin
(7) the name and address of the authorities or bodies verifying compliance with the provisions of the specification and their specific tasks;
(8) any specific labelling rule for the agricultural product or foodstuff in question.

The specification has been described as a 'discursive document.'[131] Not everything that is contained in the specification is protected. Only those matters that impact upon the quality of the product[132] are relevant to the scope of protection.

Key points on specifications

The specifications are central to the protection of GIs.

- They set out the information used to determine whether a name should be registered
- Once registered the specifications set out the standard with which users must comply if they wish to use the PDO or PGI
- The specifications determine the scope of protection accorded by the PDO or PGI.

---

[130] L Bently and B Sherman, *Intellectual Property Law* (3rd edn, 2009) p 985.
[131] *Consorzio del Prosciutto di Parma v Asda Stores Ltd* [2002] FSR 3, para 29.
[132] L Bently and B Sherman, *Intellectual Property Law* (3rd edn, 2009) p 994.

16.96   One of the key questions that arise is as to the definition of the geographical area (Article 4(2)(c)) in particular where it is the reputation of the product that is to be protected (PGI) rather than a product tied to the particular characteristics of the local environment (PDO). This question arose in the *Melton Mowbray pork pie* case in which a number of questions were referred to the ECJ relating to the geographical scope.[133]

When Melton Mowbray pork pie was registered as a PGI, Northern Foods objected as it was a producer of the pies but was based outwith the geographical area in the specifications. It argued that there had never been a consistent recipe for pork pies; that the pork pies had, since at least the mid-1800s, been made outside the area detailed in the specifications; and, in any event, Melton Mowbray was considered as a generic name for a quality pork pie. When the objections were turned down, Northern Foods sought judicial review. The High Court[134] found that Melton Mowbray pork pie satisfied the definition of a PGI on account of it being a convenient short hand term for a geographical area shown through historical analysis to be the place most likely to have been where the pies were produced in the 1900s. The High Court found that the defined geographical area for the purposes of Articles 2(2)(b) and 4(2) of the Regulation may be different from a named specific place or region where the foodstuff originated. Permission to appeal was granted as was a stay of the proceedings for a referral to the ECJ.

The following questions were referred to the Court:

'Where the specification in an application for a protected geographical indication (PGI) in respect of 'Melton Mowbray Pork Pies' made pursuant to Council Regulation 2081/92/EEC on the protection of geographical indications and designations of origin for agricultural products and foodstuffs ('the Regulation') defines the relevant geographical area pursuant to Article 4(2)(c) of the Regulation as 'the town of Melton Mowbray and its surrounding region bounded as follows:'

– to the North by the A52 from the M1 and the A1 and including the city of Nottingham;
– to the East by the A1 from the A52 to the A45 and including the towns of Grantham and Stamford;
– to the West by the M1 from the A52 and the A45; and
– to the South by the A45 from the M1 and the A1 and including the town of Northampton

1. are the requirements of Article 2(2)(b) of the Regulation capable of being satisfied insofar as the proposed PGI would apply to products produced and/or processed and/or prepared in places other than that whose name appears in the PGI;
2. if so, what criteria must be applied in delimiting the defined geographical area referred to in Articles 2(2)(b) and 4(2)(c) of the Regulation?'[135]

Where protection is based on specific geographical characteristics, such as the type of soil or the quality of water, geographical origin may be demarcated by those particular qualities. However, and where protection is based on reputation 'constructed around cultural, historical or socio-economic moorings rather than scientifically verifiable natural features',[136] the danger is that the monopoly conferred by the PGI has arbitrary boundaries. The justifications for the monopoly (consumer information and quality associated with provenance) become hard to sustain and a GI may be seen as no more than a commercially and politically expedient monopoly.

---

[133] *R (On the application of Northern Foods Plc) v Department for Environment, Food and Rural Affairs and the MMPPA Minute of Order* (14 March, 2006).
[134] *R (On the application of Northern Foods Plc) v Department for Environment, Food and Rural Affairs* [2005] EWHC 2971.
[135] Case C-169/06.
[136] Dev S Gangjee, 'Melton Mowbray and the GI Pie in the Sky: exploring the cartographies of protection' [2006] 3 IPQ 291–309, 300.

Unfortunately the reference was withdrawn.[137] On the EU granting PGI status for Melton Mowbray pork pies, Northern Foods had been given a period of five years to transfer production thus prompting Northern Foods to drop its action and withdraw the reference. PGI protection for Melton Mowbray has now been granted.[138]

Exercise

Read Dev S Gangjee, 'Melton Mowbray and the GI Pie in the Sky: exploring the cartographies of protection' (2006) 3 IPQ 291–309, and the questions that were referred to the Court of Justice. If the application had proceeded, how do you think the Court should have answered these questions? From your analysis, what do you consider to be the justifications for protection of a GI under the European regime? What should the justifications for protection be?

Preparation of foodstuffs

16.97   Of historic interest is the question that arose in relation to the way in which the foodstuff is prepared and whether the preparation, such as the grating of cheese or the slicing of ham, could be limited to the region. These issues came before the Court of Justice in *Consorzio del Prosciutto di Parma, Salumificio S. Rita SpA v Asda Stores Ltd*,[139] concerning the slicing of Parma ham, and in *Ravil SARL v Bellon import SARL, Biraghi SpA*[140] concerning the grating of Grana Padano cheese.

16.98   In *Consorzio*, Asda sold Parma ham bought from Hygrade who in turn sourced the ham boned but not sliced from an Italian producer, a member of the Consorzio. Hygrade sliced and packed the ham. The packaging bore the words 'ASDA A taste of Italy PARMA HAM Genuine Italian Parma Ham'. Consorzio argued that the slicing and packaging was contrary to the rules and the specifications applicable to Parma ham. The following question was referred to the ECJ:

> '...does Council Regulation (EEC) No 2081/92 read with Commission Regulation (EC) No 1107/96 and the specification for the PDO 'Prosciutto di Parma' create a valid Community right, directly enforceable in the court of a Member State, to restrain the retail sale as 'Parma ham' of sliced and packaged ham derived from hams duly exported from Parma in compliance with the conditions of the PDO but which have not been thereafter sliced, packaged and labelled in accordance with the specification'?

The Court started off by pointing out that by requiring the slicing and packaging to be carried out in the region of production, the intention is to allow the persons entitled to use the PDO to keep under their control one of the ways in which the product appears on the market. In particular it aimed at safeguarding the quality and authenticity of the product, and consequently

---

[137] Transitional relief granted to Northern Foods in Melton Mowbray Pork Pie battle, 3 November 2006, see http://www.northern-foods.co.uk/media/press-releases/2006/62/transitional-relief-granted-to-northern-foods-in-melton-mowbray-pork-pie-battle.htm
[138] Commission Regulation (EC) No 566/2009 of 29 June 2009 entering a name in the register of protected designations of origin and protected geographical indications (Melton Mowbray Pork Pie (PGI)).
[139] Case C-108/01 *Consorzio del Prosciutto di Parma, Salumificio S Rita SpA v Asda Stores Ltd*, [2003] 2 CMLR 21, [2003] ECR I-5121, [2004] ETMR 23.
[140] Case C-469/00 *Ravil SARL v Bellon import SARL, Biraghi SpA* [2003] ECR I-5053, [2004] ETMR 22.

the reputation of the PDO.[141] Where it has been sliced and packaged outside the region, so there was a greater risk to the quality and authenticity of the product than there would be had this been done within the region.[142] Therefore the Regulation (No 2081/92) did not preclude the use of a PDO from being subject to the condition that operations such as the slicing and packaging of the product take place in the region of production, where the condition enters the specification.[143]

16.99   The Regulation was subsequently amended[144] to include Article 4(2)(e):

> '(e) a description of the method of obtaining the agricultural product or foodstuff and, if appropriate, the authentic and unvarying local methods as well as information concerning packaging, if the applicant group within the meaning of Article 5(1) so determines and gives reasons why the packaging must take place in the defined geographical area to safeguard quality or ensure the origin or ensure control.'

As can be seen above in para 16.95 this is also included in Regulation 510/2006.

 Question

If adequate notice is given to economic operators, do you think that the specifications could extend to the slicing of ham in restaurants and delicatessens? Have a look at *Consorzio Del Prosciutto di Parma v Asda Stores Ltd* [2002] FSR 3, Lord Scott of Foscote at p 62.

Procedure for registration

16.100   Articles 5 to 7 of Regulation 510/2006 detail the procedure for registration. The application may be made by a group of producers and/or processors or, subject to certain conditions, a natural or legal person. The application must include the specification and addressed to the member state in which the geographical area concerned is located. When the member state is satisfied that the requirements have been fulfilled, the application is forwarded to the Commission. Within six months the Commission will check whether the application includes all the particulars required. If the Commission concludes that the name qualifies for protection, a notice will be published in the Official Journal. Member states have six months to lodge objections. If none are forthcoming the name is entered on the Register of protected designations of origin and protected geographical indications and published in the Official Journal.

Weblink

To consult the Register of PDOs and PDIs (and traditional speciality guaranteed) see

http://ec.europa.eu/agriculture/quality/database/index_en.htm

---

[141] Case C-108/01 *Consorzio del Prosciutto di Parma, Salumificio S Rita SpA v Asda Stores Ltd*, [2003] 2 CMLR 21, [2003] ECR I-5121, [2004] ETMR 23, para 65.

[142] ibid, para 76.

[143] ibid, para 50. In the event Consorzio could not stop Asda using the name for Parma Ham sliced outside the region because the PDO had been registered under the fast track procedure in Regulation 2081/92 which only required the publication of limited information about the conditions pertaining to the PDO. As the information in relation to slicing and packaging had not been published, 'this could not be relied on as against economic operators, as it was not brought to their attention by adequate publicity in Community legislation'. Para 99.

[144] Added by Art 1(2), Regulation 692/2003 (8 April 2003) OJ L 99/1.

16.101   Any operator marketing agricultural product or foodstuffs conforming to the corresponding specification[145] may use the registered name and the logo associated with the PDO[146] or PGI illustrated below in Figures 16.4 and 16.5.

Figure 16.4 Protected designation of origin logo

Figure 16.5 Protected geographical indication logo

Scope of protection

16.102   Article 13 details the scope of protection of a PDO or PGI as follows:

'1. Registered names shall be protected against:

(a) any direct or indirect commercial use of a registered name in respect of products not covered by the registration in so far as those products are comparable to the products registered under that name or in so far as using the name exploits the reputation of the protected name;

(b) any misuse, imitation or evocation, even if the true origin of the product is indicated or if the protected name is translated or accompanied by an expression such as 'style', 'type','method', 'as produced in', 'imitation' or similar;

(c) any other false or misleading indication as to the provenance, origin, nature or essential qualities of the product, on the inner or outer packaging, advertising material or documents relating to the

---

[145] Regulation 510/2006, Art 8(1).
[146] New logo as from 1 May 2009 (subject to transnational provisions until 1 May 2010). Commission Regulation (EC) 628/2008.

product concerned, and the packing of the product in a container liable to convey a false impression as to its origin;

(d) any other practice liable to mislead the consumer as to the true origin of the product.'

16.103   As can be seen, the scope of protection is broad. A registered name is protected against both direct and indirect commercial use where the products are comparable to the products registered under the name. In assessing the scope, much will depend on the interpretation of a 'comparable product'. The more dissimilar the product, the greater the scope of protection conferred by the registration. In addition a registered name is to be protected where the use would exploit the reputation of the protected name. Here the scope of protection will depend on what amounts to exploiting the reputation—matters that resonate with the issues that arise in the protection of well-known marks with a reputation and the use of a sign where that takes advantage of the reputation (see the discussion in para 15.74). Protection against misuse, imitation or invocation even if the true origin of the product is stated would cover uses such as 'Beacon Fell traditional Lancashire cheese made in Somerset', or 'tastes like white Stilton Cheese', or perhaps 'raised using the same methods as Scotch beef '.

16.104   In relation to what constitutes evocation, the ECJ said that this 'covers a situation where the term used to designate a product incorporates part of a protected designation, so that when the consumer is confronted with the name of the product, the image triggered in his mind is that of the product whose designation is protected'.[147] Further, for evocation there is no need to show a likelihood of confusion as between the products. In addition, evocation may take place even where no Union protection extends to the parts of that designation which are echoed in the term or terms at issue.[148] The case in hand concerned the name Cambozola used for 'soft blue cheese' and whether it infringed the PDO 'Gorgonzola'. The Court concluded that:

'Since the product at issue is a soft blue cheese which is not dissimilar in appearance to Gorgonzola, it would seem reasonable to conclude that a protected name is indeed evoked where the term used to designate that product ends in the same two syllables and contains the same number of syllables, with the result that the phonetic and visual similarity between the two terms is obvious.'[149]

Key points on scope of protection

- Protection extends to both direct and indirect commercial use where the products are comparable to the products registered under the name
- Evocation occurs where the consumer, when faced with a product, thinks of the product whose designation is protected

---

Cancellation

16.105   Under Article 12 of Regulation 510/2006 where the Commission takes the view that compliance with the conditions of the specification for an agricultural product or foodstuff covered

---

[147] Case C-87/97 *Consorzio per la Tutela del Formaggio Gorgonzola v Käserei Champignon Hofmeister GmbH & Co KG, Eduard Bracharz GmbH* [1999] 1 CMLR 1203, ECJ, para 25. See also Case C-132/05 *Commission v Germany*, para 44.
[148] ibid, para 26.   [149] ibid, para 27.

by a protected name is no longer ensured, it can initiate a cancellation procedure published in the Official Journal. Detailed rules are laid out in the Regulation as to the procedure to be followed. Any natural or legal person having a legitimate interest may also request cancellation of the registration, giving reasons for the request.

16.106   A request for cancellation of a PGI, 'Newcastle Brown Ale', was made by Scottish and Newcastle plc.[150] The reasons for the cancellation request were twofold. The first was that production at the site in Newcastle-upon-Tyne named in the PGI specification was no longer commercially viable. The second was that the PGI, which was requested by a single producer, was granted on condition that the producer may not prevent others within the area from producing the products in accordance with the specification. The specification however included ingredients (the strain of yeast, the blend of water and salt) which were secret to Scottish and Newcastle plc. No other producer was thus entitled to use the name without the consent of Scottish and Newcastle, who made it clear that they would not make public details of the ingredients, nor given consent to any other producer to use them.[151]

Exercise

Given the requirements of the specifications discussed above, why do you think Newcastle Brown Ale was accorded PGI status without disclosing the raw materials that determined the nature of the beer?

Conflicts between PDOs, PGIs and trade marks

16.107   Regulation 510/2006 provides for the possible (and inevitable) conflicts that could arise as between PDOs, PGIs and registered trade marks. Article 3(4) of the Regulation states that a DO or GI is not to be registered if there exists a trade mark, and in light of the reputation, renown and length of time for which the trade mark has been used, registration of the DO or GI is likely to mislead consumers as to the identity of the product.

16.108   Article 14(1) of the Regulation deals with competition between applications for registration and stipulates that a trade mark application which, if registered and used within the same class of product would infringe the PDO or PDI, will not be registered where the application for registration is submitted after the date of submission of the application of the registration of the PDO or PGI.

16.109   Article 14(2) provides that where a PDO or PGI is registered and there exists a trade mark which has been applied for, registered, or established by use before the date of protection of the PDO or PGI, or 1 January 1996, then the trade mark may continue to be used notwithstanding the registration of the PDO or PGI.[152]

---

[150] Official Journal 18.11.2006, C 280/13.
[151] The cancellation came into effect in August 2007. Commission Regulation 952/2007.
[152] For a discussion on PDOs, PDIs and trade marks under Regulation No 2081/92 see Case C-343/07 *Bavaria NV v Bayerischer Brauerbund eV*.

Regulation 2081/92 and TRIPS

16.110   In 1999 the US (joined by Australia) contended that Regulation 2081/92, as amended was not in conformity with the EC's obligations under the TRIPs Agreement. Specifically the allegation was that the Regulation did not provide national treatment with respect to GIs and did not provide sufficient protection to pre-existing trademarks that are similar or identical to a GI. The WTO Panel[153]agreed with the US and Australia on the matter of national treatment for the following reasons:

- registration of a GI from a country outside the European Union was contingent upon the Government of that country adopting a system of GI protection equivalent to the EC's system and offering reciprocal protection to EC GIs; and

- the Regulation's procedures required applications and objections from other WTO Members to be examined and transmitted by the governments of those Members, and require those governments to operate systems of product inspection like EC member States. Therefore, foreign nationals do not have guaranteed access to the EC's system for their GIs, unlike EC nationals.

The Panel did however find that a system of GI protection that requires product inspection is not inconsistent with WTO obligations; and that although the Regulation permits the registration of GIs where they conflict with a prior trade mark, the Regulation, qualifies as a 'limited exception' to trade mark rights.

16.111   As a result the EC implemented Regulation 510/2006. However this would not have appeared to have satisfied the concerns of either Australia or the United States. Specifically the anxiety would appear to relate to the interaction between trade marks and GIs. Regulation 2081/92 provided for the continued use of trade marks that acquire rights before the submission to the EC of a registration application for a conflicting GI.[154] In Regulation 510/2006 the wording has been changed from 'or the date of submission to the Commission of the application for registration of the designation of origin or geographical indication,' to 'or before 1 January 1996'. The argument is that this leaves any additional trade marks acquiring rights after 1 January, 1996, potentially vulnerable. The matter appears to be still under discussion between the respective authorities.

Development and reform of the system

16.112   Geographical indications remain on the policy agenda at international (WTO and WIPO), regional (EU) and national levels. Arguments continue between proponents and opponents as to the benefits or otherwise of geographical indications, a divide which tends, geographically to be East/West rather than the more usual North/South. The arguments, legal, economic, social, and political echo those which reverberate around the broader IP framework.

Further reading

Books

Personality

John Adams, Julian Hickey and Guy Tritton, *Merchandising Intellectual Property*, (3rd edn, 2007)

H Beverley-Smith, *The Commercial Appropriation of Personality* (2002)

H Beverley-Smith, A Ohly, A Lucas-Schloetter, *Privacy, Property and Personality: Civil Law Perspectives on Commercial Appropriation* (2005)

Articles

Personality

K Assaf Zakharov, *'The scope of protection of trade mark image—including comments on a recent decision of the Israeli Supreme Court'* (2005) IIC 36(7), 787–808

I Blackshaw, 'Protecting the images of sporting celebrities' (2004) 36 Euro Law 12–13

S Boyd, 'Does English law recognise the concept of an image or personality right?' (2002) 13(1) Ent LR 1–7

A Jooss, 'Life after death? Post mortem protection of name, image and likeness under German law with specific reference to "Marlene Dietrich" ' (2001) 12(5) Ent LR 141–4

J Klink, '50 years of publicity rights in the United States and the never ending hassle with intellectual property and personality rights in Europe' (2003) 4 IPQ 363–387

S Lane, 'The Problems of Personality Merchandising in English Law—The King, the Princess and the Penguins', in Year Book of Media and Entertainment Law 1998 28, 30.

P Masiyakurima, 'The trouble with moral rights' (2005) 68(3) MLR 411–34

J Mitchiner, 'Intellectual Property in Image—A Mere Inconvenience' (2003) 2 IPQ 168–203

R Moscona, 'What really matters: the Designer's name or the name on the label?' [2007] EIPR 152

A Taubman, 'Is there a right of collective personality?' (2006) 28(9) EIPR 485–92

A Wood, 'Sewing up "Personality" Brands: The Implications of Case C-259/04 Elizabeth Emanuel v Continental Shelf 128 Ltd' [2006] 17(8) Ent LR 232–3

Domain names

M Boote, 'What's in a Name?' [2006] 28(6) EIPR 349–52

S Chapman, J Holmen, 'New gTLDs—protection or threat for IP owners?' (2006) 28(6) EIPR 315–20

W Chik, 'Lord of your domain, but master of none: the need to harmonize and recalibrate the domain name regime of ownership and control' (2008) 16(1) IJL & IT 8–72

HA Deveci, 'Domain names: has trade mark law strayed from its path?' (2003) 11(3) IJL & IT 203–25

F Gurry, 'Internet domain name disputes' (2006) 17(2) EBL Rev 413–16

G Jacobs, 'Internet specific collisions of trade marks in the domain name system—an economic analysis based on US law' (2006) 37(2) IIC 156–79

C McLeod, 'WIPO: Trade and Service Marks—Rights in Domain Name' [2006] 17(6) Ent LR N56–57

SM Maniatis, 'Trade Mark Law and Domain Names: Back to Basics' [2002] 24(8) EIPR 397–408

T Varas, 'Sealing the cracks: a proposal to update the anti-cybersquatting regime to combat advertising-based cybersquatting' (2008) 3(4) JIPLP 246

C Wilson 'Internationalised domain names: problems and opportunities' (2004) 10(7) CTLR 174–81

Trade mark use on the Internet

D Bainbridge, 'Infringement of trademarks on web pages' (2003) 19(2) CLSR 124–30

D Bainbridge, 'Trademark infringement, the Internet and jurisdiction' (2003) 1 JILT http://www2.warwick.ac.uk/fac/soc/law/elj/jilt/2003_1/bainbridge/

L Curtis, 'Shades—of greytrademark law and the world wide web' (2004) 6(5) ECL & P 5–7

R Garnett, 'Cross-border internet trade mark litigation: towards a model of co-existence and parallel use' (2006) 28(4) EIPR 213–19

A Kur, 'Use of trade marks on the internet—the WIPO recommendations' (2002) 33(1) IIC 41–7

Geographical indications

D Ampollini, 'Cheese for Thought for the European Court of First Instance' (2008) 3(1) JIPLP 16

M Blakeney, 'Geographical indications and trade' (2000) 6(2) Int TLR 48–55

R Chesmond, 'Protection or Privatisation of Culture? The Cultural Dimension of the International Intellectual Property Debate on Geographical Indications of Origin' [2007] EIPR 379

GE Evans, M Blakeney, 'The protection of geographical indications after Doha: Quo Vadis?' (2006) 9(3) JIEL 575–614

D Gangjee, 'Melton Mowbray and the GI pie in the sky: exploring cartographies of protection' (2006) 3 IPQ 291–309

D Gangjee, 'Say Cheese! A Sharper Image of Generic Use Through the Lens of Feta', [2007] EIPR 172

M Handler, 'The WTO geographical indications dispute' (2006) 69(1) MLR 70–80

C Heath, 'Parmiggiano Reggiano by Another Name—on the ECJ's Parmesan Decision' (2008) 39 IIC 951

B O'Connor, 'The legal protection of geographical indications' (2004) 1 IPQ 35–57

B O'Connor, 'The EC Need not be Isolated on GIs', Opinion: [2007] EIPR 303.

D Rangnekar, 'Geographical Indications A Review of Proposals at the TRIPS Council: Extending Article 23 to Products other than Wines and Spirits' UNCTAD-ICTSD 'Project on Intellectual Property Rights and Sustainable Development'

J Reed, 'Feta: a cheese or a fudge? Federal Republic of Germany v Commission' (2006) 28(10) EIPR 535–8

N Resinek, 'Geographical Indications and Trade Marks: Coexistence or 'First in Time, First in Right' principle?' [2007] EIPR 447

AF Ribeiro de Almeida, 'The TRIPS Agreement, the bilateral agreements concerning geographical indications and the philosophy of the *WTO*' (2005) 27(4) EIPR 150–3

M Ricolfi, 'Is the European IGs Policy in Need of Rethinking?' (2009) 40 IIC 123

S Stern, 'Are GIs IP?' (2007) 29(2) EIPR 39–42

W Van Caenegem, 'Registered GIs: intellectual property, agricultural policy and international Trade' (2004) 26(4) EIPR 170–81

Part VI

Common law protection of intellectual property

Introduction

The various forms of intellectual property discussed in the previous chapters have all had their roots in statute. This Part of the book turns to consider the protection afforded to certain forms of intellectual property at common law: that is, the law developed in the decisions of the English and Scottish courts over the centuries with the assistance of jurists analysing those judgments in textbooks and treatises. There are two main forms of common law protection: *passing off*, which can be most readily equated with registered trade marks, and *breach of confidence*, which has close links to both copyright and patents. But it is important to emphasise that despite these relationships with statutory intellectual property, the common law protections each have their own independent character and scope. A further point is that English and Scots law in the two fields, while very similar, are not necessarily identical and may still develop in slightly different ways.

The chapter on *passing off* explores the three elements which have classically been taken to amount to the legal wrong (tort or delict) in question—goodwill, misrepresentation and damage—as well as the defences which may be available to the person defending an action based upon such a claim. The chapter then moves to consider two contemporary issues that have arisen in the modern law of passing off: its use against 'cyber-squatting', and the possibility of the action developing into one against a much more general wrong of unfair competition, such as is found in some other EU member states.

The chapter on *breach of confidence* examines the history and basic principles of the law of confidence in the two main jurisdictions in the UK, with reference to personal information, national security and employment and post-employment scenarios, and a balance between the public interests in preserving confidence and in disclosure. The chapter then considers the impact of the Human Rights Act 1998, and Articles 8 and 10 European Convention on Human Rights, first in moving towards protection of privacy, secondly in respect of other types of information and the public interest. Finally, the chapter considers the relationship between confidential information and IP.

Because common law rights arise without registration, and are based upon court decisions, it is necessary to refer to the court websites for freely accessible source material on the Internet. These are most conveniently gathered together on the British and Irish Legal Information website:

http://www.bailii.org/

Also important in respect of breach of confidence are decisions of the European Court of Human Rights, for which see the court website

http://www.echr.coe.int/ECHR/EN/Header/Case-Law/HUDOC/HUDOC+database/

Reference will also be made to the following legislation and instruments:

- Human Rights Act 1998
  http://www.opsi.gov.uk/acts/acts1998/19980042.htm

- Data Protection Act 1998
  http://www.opsi.gov.uk/acts/acts1998/19980029.htm

- The European Convention on Human Rights 1950
  http://www.hri.org/docs/ECHR50.html

- TRIPS
  http://www.wto.org/english/tratop_e/trips_e/t_agm0_e.htm

Passing off

Introduction

Scope and overview of chapter

17.1   This chapter considers the action of passing off, the means by which one trader may prevent another from misleading customers by representing (or 'passing off') goods or services as emanating from the former party. Although conceptually this part of the law is closely linked to the statutory trade mark law, and it will offer protection to unregistered trade marks which are nonetheless badges of identity in the market place, in some ways passing off goes further than trade mark law, and extends to other acts of unfair competition.

17.2

> ### Learning objectives
>
> By the end of this chapter you should be able to:
>
> - define and explain the scope of the action of passing off;
> - define and explain each of the principal elements of passing off, namely, goodwill, misrepresentation, and damage;
> - differentiate passing off from other, closely related aspects of intellectual property protection, such as registered trade marks;
> - understand and explain the modern extensions of the scope of passing off known as 'extended passing off';
> - understand and explain the use of passing off to control 'cyber-squatting';
> - discuss the relationship between passing off and concepts of unfair competition.

17.3   After an introductory discussion, the chapter analyses the leading judicial definitions of passing off, from which emerge the key elements of goodwill, misrepresentation and damage. These elements are then taken in turn for more detailed discussion. The chapter concludes with discussion of key issues regarding the future of passing off, in particular its use to attack the practice of 'cyber-squatting' and its possible development as a law against unfair competition. So the chapter looks like this:

- Overview of passing off (17.4–17.9)
- Definitions (17.10–17.13)
- Goodwill (17.14–17.34)
- Misrepresentation (17.35–17.56)
- Damage (17.57–17.61)
- Defences (17.62)
- Cyber-squatting and passing off (17.63–17.68)
- Unfair competition and passing off (17.69–17.72)

Overview of passing off

17.4   The action of 'passing off' is well established in the various jurisdictions of the UK, having first developed in English common law and then been received in the early 19th century in the Scottish courts.[1] Today there is little if any difference in the two laws on the subject. The usual question in passing off actions is whether in marketing goods or services one party has employed an identifying device or badge associated in the market with another party or parties. In its most typical form the action concerns the use of words or names as trade marks.

> 'The remedy which the law gives to a person who has used a particular name in trade is that he is entitled to prevent others from using the same name in such a way as is likely to mislead the public into thinking that the business or the goods so described is or are the business or goods of the claimant.'[2]

However, as long ago as 1842 Lord Langdale MR suggested that the action was of broader scope than merely the misleading use of names:

> 'A man is not to sell his own goods under the pretence that they are the goods of another man; he cannot be permitted to practise such a deception, nor to use the means which contribute to that end. He cannot therefore be allowed to use names, marks, letters or other indicia, by which he may induce purchasers to believe, that the goods he is selling are the manufacture of another person.'[3]

In modern times, and especially in England, the action has been applied to stop a variety of forms of passing off, using not only names, but also a wide variety of other ways in which traders enable customers to identify their products and distinguish them from those of competitors. One way of thinking about passing off is as a form of protection for unregistered trade marks;[4] but the scope of protection offered by the common law extends beyond trade marks as such.

---

[1] See on English law C Wadlow, *The Law of Passing Off: Unfair Competition by Misrepresentation* (3rd edn, 2004); H Carty, *An Analysis of the Economic Torts* (2001), Ch 8; M Spence, 'Passing off and the misappropriation of valuable intangibles' (1996) 112 LQR 472. On the development of English law see H Carty, 'The development of passing off in the twentieth century', and C Morcom, 'Leading cases in passing off', both in N Dawson and A Firth (eds), *Trade Marks Retrospective* (2000). For Scots law see EM Clive, 'The action of passing off: its scope and basis' 1963 JR 117.

[2] *Kinnell v Ballantyne* 1910 SC 246 at 251 per Lord President Dunedin.

[3] *Perry v Truefitt* (1842) 6 Beav 66 at 73 (49 ER 749 at 752). Note that although Lord Langdale refers only to selling goods, it is clear that passing off also applies to the supply of services. There seems no reason why it should not also apply to the supply of incorporeals and of land and buildings.

[4] Trade Marks Act 1994, s 2(2): 'No proceedings lie to prevent or recover damages for the infringement of an unregistered trade mark as such; but nothing in this Act affects the law relating to passing off.'

Basis of action: misrepresentation and goodwill

17.5   At one time Scots and English lawyers flirted with the idea that the right to prevent passing off arose because the claimant or petitioner had by exclusive appropriation acquired a right of property in his marketing device. This theory became discredited because it was unacceptable to suppose that there could be rights of property in names or words, or that use alone could create such property rights. In England, the action came to be seen as based rather on two elements:

- the existence of trading *goodwill* or reputation, the desire of customers to buy from one trader rather than another, which was conceived of as a right of property of the first trader, especially as it had market value in the buying and selling of the business itself;
- the invasion of that right of property by means of a *misrepresentation*.

Marketing devices are an important element in goodwill because their use enables customers to identify the products of particular traders and to distinguish them from those of competitors. The association between device and trader means that use of the device by another may mislead the customer who believes he is obtaining the goods and services of one trader while in fact receiving those of another. The typical injury for which the action of passing off provides a remedy is therefore loss of custom to a competitor, while the wrong which leads to the injury is the false statement by the competitor. In Scotland, 'the action for passing off is based on the general right which everyone possesses not to have published about him or his goods, statements which are both untrue and prejudicial to his pecuniary interests.'[5]

 Question

What are the key concepts in passing off?

17.6   As a result of its being rooted in the protection of goodwill, passing off is no longer confined to the case of one trader representing his goods as those of another. Wherever there is a misrepresentation damaging goodwill—for example, creating injurious associations in the public mind—there may be a claim for passing off. This is not to say that passing off has become a general law of unfair competition such as is found in various European jurisdictions. Like other items of property, the value of goodwill may fluctuate or even be destroyed as a result of the operations of the market, without giving its owner any legal remedies; the element of misrepresentation is the key which unlocks the door.

Key points on general development of passing off

- Passing off starts with the idea that one person may not represent his goods or services as those of another and so gain business which should have gone to that other
- In modern law, passing off is seen as protecting trading goodwill against misrepresentations in general, and this has been a basis for extending the scope of the action considerably
- A question therefore arises about the extent to which passing off is becoming a law against unfair competition generally, similar to actions of this kind found in other European countries

---

[5] Clive, 1963 JR 117, 134.

Lord Fraser said (at pp 755–6):

'It is essential for the plaintiff in a passing off action to show at least the following facts:

(1) That his business consists of, or includes, selling in England a class of goods to which the particular trade name applies;

(2) That the class of goods is clearly defined, and that in the minds of the public, or a section of the public, in England, the trade name distinguishes that class from other similar goods;

(3) That because of the reputation of the goods, there is goodwill attached to the name;

(4) That he, the plaintiff, as a member of the class of those who sell the goods, is the owner of goodwill in England which is of substantial value;

(5) That he has suffered, or is really likely to suffer, substantial damage to his property in the goodwill by reason of the defendant's selling goods which are falsely described by the trade name to which the goodwill is attached.'

17.12   These two statements are not easily reconciled in all respects. Lord Fraser appears to confine passing off to the misuse of trade names in relation to goods, while Lord Diplock speaks simply of misrepresentations in the course of trade, without limiting the ways in which such misrepresentations may be made. It has long been clear, however, that services may be passed off as well as goods and that the form which the misrepresentation may take includes statements other than trade names. Lord Fraser's stress on activity and goodwill in England is also important but it is not thought that by this he meant to indicate that the law would be different in Scotland. In general it appears best to treat his remarks as directed entirely at the very special kind of case which he was then deciding, namely, one involving misuse of a trade name in which many traders, some from outside the UK, shared goodwill, and not as intended to restrict the scope of the action in other cases, or in Scotland. Lord Diplock's definition, on the other hand, comprehends not only such trade name cases but also all the other situations in which passing off has been held to have taken place.

 Exercise

What are the differences between (i) Lord Oliver's definition of passing off and (ii) those of Lords Diplock and Fraser; or between the definitions of Lords Diplock and Fraser? Does it matter, and if so why? What do the definitions have in common? Consider this exercise now, and again when you have completed your study of this chapter.

Business context

17.13   The three definitions by Lords Oliver, Diplock and Fraser have in common that passing off must take place in a business context. Although 'business context' has been widely interpreted in the courts to include, for example, charities,[10] in some cases an action has failed because the context has not been one of commercial activity. In *Kean v McGivan*[11] an action on behalf of a political party regarding the use of the initials 'SDP' failed because the plaintiff was not carrying on a business. Similarly it may not be possible to prevent another person using the name of one's house.[12] Trade associations such as the Scotch Whisky Association can only sue in respect

---

[10] See eg *British Diabetic Association v Diabetic Society Ltd* [1995] 4 All ER 812.
[11] [1982] FSR 119.   [12] *Day v Brownrigg* (1878) 10 Ch D 294.

of their own trading activities as distinct from those of their members, although the members may sue together as individual organisations.[13]

 Discussion point   For answer guidance visit www.oxfordtextbooks.co.uk/orc/macqueen2e/

Can you conceive of circumstances in which use of the name of another person's house might be passing off? Is a political party any less in business than a charity? What about a school? Or a university?

> **Key points about the definition of passing off**
>
> - There are three major elements to be established in a passing off action:
>   (1) goodwill
>   (2) misrepresentation
>   (3) damage
> - This must all occur in a business context

Goodwill

Definition of goodwill[14]

17.14   It is essential that the party claiming passing off should enjoy goodwill before any action can succeed.

> Goodwill is 'the attractive force which brings in custom', or, 'whatever adds value to a business by reason of situation, name and reputation' (*IRC v Muller & Co's Margarine Ltd* [1901] AC 217 per Lord Macnaghten at 223 and per Lord Lindley at 235).

These definitions focus attention first on the existence of *customers* as the starting point for understanding the concept, and explain goodwill as that composite of *elements which lead to customers choosing to give their business to a particular trader, or to acquire that trader's product*. Reputation as such is not enough; customers must be attracted to the business. For there to be protectable goodwill in a device, it must be established that in the relevant market there is an association between it and a particular trader or class of traders. This association requires to be established by evidence. The trader's actual identity need not be known to the public, so long as the device is known to distinguish his product or services in the market.[15] The test for the

---

[13] See *Consorzio Prosciutto di Parma v Marks & Spencer* [1991] RPC 351; *Chocosuisse Union des Fabricants Suisses de Chocolat v Cadbury* [1999] RPC 826. It is assumed that similar rules would apply in Scotland.

[14] See further H Carty, 'Passing off and the concept of goodwill' [1995] JBL 139.

[15] *Birmingham Vinegar Brewery Co v Powell* [1897] AC 710; *Hoffmann La Roche v DDSA* [1969] FSR 410.

existence of goodwill is less demanding than that of distinctiveness in relation to registered trade marks.[16]

 Question

How may goodwill be defined?

17.15   In general the public's *association* of device with trader should *arise from use* of the device. The period of use need not have been long—three weeks was sufficient to justify the granting of an interlocutory injunction in one English case,[17] a few hours in an Australian one.[18] Publicity prior to the launch of a business may in exceptional circumstances create sufficient goodwill to permit the raising of an action of passing off.[19] Goodwill may survive the cessation of use if there is an intention appropriately manifested to return to business,[20] but if the goodwill is disposed of when the business is abandoned, then there can be no claim of subsequent passing off.[21] The purchaser of goodwill is entitled to protect it by actions of passing off, even against the former owner.[22] Goodwill may be lost over time where there is a cessation or significant reduction in activity and reputation.[23]

◼ *Knight v Beyond Properties Pty Ltd* [2007] FSR 34 (Ch)

'Mythbusters' was the title of a series of primary school-age children's books published in the first half of the 1990s. From late 2003 'Mythbusters' was used by others as the title for a 'dads and lads' TV series. The author of the book series sued the TV producers for passing off. The claim was dismissed. Although the title 'Mythbusters' was capable of generating exclusive goodwill, and the claimant had established a reputation in the UK sufficient to attract passing off protection between 1993 and 1996, it thereafter diminished so that it was no longer significant by 2003.

◼ *Wise Property Care Ltd v White Thomson Preservation Ltd* [2008] CSIH 44

In 1976 W and T set up a company called WTP Ltd, carrying out business in property preservation services. In 1983 W and T went their separate ways, trading respectively as WTP (Northern) Ltd (WTPNL) and WTP (Southern) Ltd in different regions of Scotland. W was joined in WTPNL by his three sons, E, G1 and G2. In 2002 the sons left and set up a new company called White Preservation Ltd (WPL); E left this in 2004. In 2005 W retired and WTPNL was dissolved. In 2006 G1 and G2 sold the business and assets of WPL to Wise Property Care Ltd; Wise successfully ran the business until late 2007 as 'White Preservation, a division of Wise Property Care Ltd'. WPL's name was first changed to 'Gragav Ltd', then the company was dissolved. Wise separately set up a company called WPL but it never traded. In 2007 E set up a new company called

---

[16] *Phones 4U Ltd v Phone4U.co.uk Internet Ltd* [2007] RPC 5. For the registered trade mark test of distinctiveness, see above, para 14.27ff.

[17] *Stannard v Reay* [1967] RPC 589.

[18] *Fletcher Challenge v Fletcher Challenge Pty* [1982] FSR 1.

[19] *BBC v Talbot* [1981] FSR 228; *My Kinda Bones v Dr Peppers Stove Co* [1984] FSR 289.

[20] *Norman Kark Publications Ltd v Odhams Press Ltd* [1962] 1 WLR 380; *Ad-Lib Club Ltd v Granville* [1972] RPC 673.

[21] *Star Industrial v Yap Kwee Kor* [1976] FSR 256 (PC).

[22] *Melrose Drover Ltd v Heddle* (1902) 4F 1120; see also *Cowan v Millar* (1895) 22R 833.

[23] *Alexander Fergusson & Co Ltd v Matthews McClay & Manson Ltd* 1989 SLT 795.

WTP Ltd, adopting the business get-up of his father's former company and undertaking to honour its guarantees. The court accepted that in effect E was reviving a dormant business. Wise sued E's company for passing off. Interim interdict was granted on the balance of convenience. Wise had built up goodwill in the 'White Preservation' name; the companies were trading in the same business and region; consumers were confused, although local property professionals such as solicitors were not; and WTP Ltd was effectively a newcomer or interloper, the interests of which should be given less weight than those of the established business. Note that although the defender was a 'newcomer' it was in fact the only one of the two companies involved which had within its operation a member of the W family which had given its name to the business acquired by the pursuers.[24]

Goodwill and reputation: the problem of foreign goodwill

17.16 There are two problems:

(1) the goodwill which a trader here may enjoy abroad, and

(2) that which a foreigner may have in this country.

It is clear with regard to (1) that a home trader may protect foreign goodwill by means of the action of passing off.[25] So far as concerns (2), the foreigner claiming to protect goodwill here, however, a complex series of English cases before the Trade Marks Act 1994 established that where there was *reputation but no trading activity in England* no action lay.[26] The usual situation was that of a well-known foreign trader whose distinctive indicia had been adopted by another party in England. The foreign plaintiff's passing off action would succeed only if he could show business activity generating goodwill in England; merely being known there will not suffice. Business activity did not necessarily mean having a place of business in England, but might arise through export or other activities, or through the fact that English customers went to the claimant in the latter's country.[27]

■ *Hotel Cipriani SRL v Cipriani (Grosvenor Street) Ltd* [2009] RPC 9; [2010] EWCA Civ 110

The Community trade mark 'Cipriani' was used for hotels in Venice, Lisbon and Madeira by HC, members of the Orient Express Hotels Group. CGSL used the name on a sign for their restaurant in London. It was held that the claimant had to own goodwill in the UK, rather than a mere reputation in the UK. In demonstrating this, it was immaterial whether or not HC had a branch in the UK or traded through intermediaries (provided the importers or distributors did not own the goodwill). In the case of a claimant providing services abroad, as here, it was sufficient to establish UK goodwill that the services were booked by customers in the UK. In principle ownership of concurrent goodwill could in appropriate circumstances constitute a defence to a passing off claim. However, the defence failed on the facts here. As to the existence of a misrepresentation, it was held that the use of the names Cipriani and Cipriani London

---

[24] For comment on this case see CW Ng, 'A common law of passing-off? English and Scottish perspectives' (2009) 13 Edin LR 134.

[25] See further below, para 17.46.

[26] *Anheuser-Busch Inc v Budejovicky Budvar* [1984] FSR 413; note Lord Fraser's speech in *Advocaat*, with its reference to trade in England.

[27] See also *Peter Waterman v CBS* [1993] EMLR 27 and *Jian Tools v Roderick Manhattan Group Ltd* [1995] FSR 924.

was likely to mislead a substantial number of members of the public into believing that the restaurant was in some way connected with HC. In demonstrating this, no evidence of actual confusion was required, though its presence would be influential. The judgment was upheld on appeal.

17.17   It is submitted that with the development, not only of European and international markets in many fields of business in general, but also of cross-border e-commerce by way of the Internet, it would be unfortunate if the law did not recognise that goodwill may cross national frontiers, and fail in consequence to grant appropriate protection.[28] That danger may have been avoided, however, by the enactment in section 56 of the Trade Mark Act 1994 of the 'well-known mark' protection under the Paris Convention; under this, mere reputation is enough for the foreign trader to be able to protect its badge of identity in this country.[29]

> ## Question
>
> What is the significance of 'well-known mark protection for the modern development of passing off?

England and Scotland

17.18   Since England and Scotland are independent legal systems, each is a foreign country in the other's legal system, and the problem of foreign goodwill thus takes on a particular character in this context. In *Flaxcell v Freedman*[30] a London trader using the name 'Dirty Dick's' was held entitled to interdict a Glasgow trader from trading as 'Dicky Dirts', but there was mail order business in Scotland for the London company. In *Pegasus Security Ltd v Gilbert*[31] an English company commencing business in Scotland obtained interim interdict against an existing Scottish business which had been using a similar name. In both cases it was established that the English trader had goodwill in Scotland despite not having an actual place of business there.

Regional goodwill

17.19   Just as goodwill may cross national boundaries, so it may not extend over the whole country but instead be confined to a particular locality. It is not clear whether protection in such cases is also confined to the locality in question, so that another trader may set up in another area using the same badges of identity as the first. In the leading English decision, the plaintiffs' operations were local in character but they were nonetheless granted an injunction covering the whole country.[32] There are other cases, however, where only restricted injunctions were obtained.[33] There seems to be no Scottish discussion in point, but the grant of a limited interdict in an appropriate case would seem consistent with the general principles of passing off.

---

[28] See further F Mostert, 'Is goodwill territorial or international?' [1989] EIPR 440; D Rose, 'Season of goodwill: passing off and overseas traders' [1995] EIPR 356. Note the recognition of international goodwill in the Australian case of *ConAgra v McCain Foods (Australia)* (1992) 23 IPR 193 (Fed Ct Aus).

[29] Note however *Microsoft Corporation's Applications* [1997–8] Information Technology Law Reports 361, in which 'Windows' was held not to be a well-known mark, at least in May 1991.

[30] 1981 SLT (Notes) 131.   [31] 1989 GWD 26–1186.

[32] *Chelsea Man Menswear Ltd v Chelsea Girl Ltd* [1987] RPC 189.   [33] *Brestian v Try* [1958] RPC 161 (CA).

The question of what constitutes an appropriate case is difficult, however. A business which can only offer services at a fixed location, such as a hotel, club or restaurant, can nonetheless develop widespread goodwill as the result of passing custom, although its existence may be difficult to prove or disprove.

> ## Key points on goodwill
>
> - Goodwill is about bringing in customers, and in the law of passing off is to be distinguished from mere reputation
> - Goodwill is increasingly recognised as an international phenomenon, so that foreign traders may be able to raise actions of passing off in England & Wales or Scotland. The 'well-known mark' provision of the Paris Convention, enacted in this country by the Trade Marks Act 1994, section 56, has been important in this development
> - Traders in this country may also be able to raise actions in this country in respect of passing off abroad: see further below, para 17.46
> - Goodwill may also be regional or local in character

Product goodwill: 'extended passing off'

17.20   The classical definitions of goodwill as the attractive force which brings in custom do not refer directly to what has been termed *'product goodwill'*, that is, *the reputation which a product has, as distinct from its manufacturer or seller.* Passing off nevertheless now protects goodwill of this kind, by finding that certain named products—typically, but not exclusively, alcoholic drinks—are associated with particular characteristics in the marketplace and form a reason why they are bought. This goodwill will be damaged if products without these characteristics can be marketed under the name of the genuine article.[34] But the goodwill in such cases, unlike that protected by classical passing off, is not limited to one trader; instead it is shared by all who produce goods having the characteristics in question, and all have the right to claim passing off protection. Because the protection reaches further in this way, this is often known as *'extended passing off'*. It is to this form of passing off that the definitions of Lords Diplock and Fraser in the *Advocaat* case, quoted above at para 17.11, are now typically applied.

> **Question**
>
> How does our previous definition of goodwill (above, para 17.14) now need to be revised?

Examples of product goodwill recognised by the courts in extended passing off actions include the following.

(1) Champagne

'The region in which the Champagne vineyards are found is about 100 miles east of Paris around Rheims and Epernay, where there is a chalky, flinty soil and the climate is subject to extreme

---

[34] See further S Naresh, 'Passing off, goodwill and false advertising: new wine in old bottles' (1986) 45 CLJ 97.

variations of heat and cold. It appears that these factors give to the wine its particular qualities.... [S]ince 1927 the Champagne Viticole district has been strictly limited by [French] law, and
only certain vineyards are allowed in France to use the name 'champagne'.... The wine is naturally
sparkling wine made from grapes produced in the Champagne district by a process of double
fermentation which requires a considerable amount of care.... [I]n the UK... champagne is a wine
specially associated with occasions of celebration so that (in addition to sales to persons who
regularly buy wine), it is purchased on such occasions from time to time by many persons who are
not in the habit of buying wine for consumption and are not educated in the nature or qualities of
different kinds of wine.'

(*Bollinger v Costa Brava Wine Co Ltd* [1961] 1 WLR 277, per Danckwerts J, at pp 281–2)

(2) Scotch whisky

' "Scotch whisky" as a description has obtained a particular standing.... It may only be applied to a
spirit distilled in Scotland from a mash of cereal grain saccharified by the diastase of malt. To such a
spirit many individual brand names are applied but, irrespective of that, all producers satisfying the
conditions applicable are entitled to describe their product as 'Scotch whisky' and to take action to
protect the advantages conferred by such a right from improper use of that trade description.'

(*John Walker & Sons v Douglas McGibbon* 1972 SLT 128 per Lord Avonside at p 128)

(3) Harris Tweed

'Harris Tweed means a Tweed made from pure virgin wool produced in Scotland, spun, dyed and
finished in the Outer Hebrides and handwoven by the Islanders at their own homes in the Islands of
Lewis, Harris, Uist, Barra, and their several purtenances and all known as the Outer Hebrides.'

(Harris Tweed Association 1934 definition of Harris Tweed, approved in *Argyllshire Weavers Ltd v A
Macaulay Tweeds Ltd* 1965 SLT 21 per Lord Hunter at p 33)

(4) Sherry

'Since 1935 the use of the words "Jerez" or "Xeres" or "sherry" in connection with wine has been
regulated by Spanish law. To be entitled to be so described the wine has to have been made of
grapes of certain kinds grown in certain areas and has to have been matured and blended in
"bodegas" situated in certain places. There is a board of control whose duty it is to secure that
nobody offers wine for sale under those names without complying with the regulations.... [T]he
word "sherry" standing alone still ordinarily means, in the context of buying and selling, a wine from
the Jerez district of Spain and not a type of wine or alcoholic liquid which may be produced anywhere
or in any way.'

(*Vine Products Ltd v Mackenzie & Co Ltd* [1969] RPC 1 per Cross J at pp 16, 25.)

(5) Advocaat

'The composition of Dutch advocaat (and therefore, in effect, of all the advocaat sold in England)
is regulated by Dutch law and consists of hens' eggs, sugar flavouring and spirit. The spirit used is
called in Dutch "brandewijn". Brandewijn is ethyl alcohol derived from grain or molasses. It is not the
same as brandy which, at least in modern English usage, means a spirit derived from grapes.'

(*Erven Warnink BV v J Townend & Sons (Hull) Ltd* [1979] AC 731, per Lord Fraser at p 749)

(6) Swiss chocolate

'The term "Swiss chocolate" is the designation which has been used, save for very minor exceptions, only on chocolate made in Switzerland in accordance with Swiss food regulations. Subject
to the restrictions imposed by these regulations, those chocolates have been made to very different recipes. They taste different from each other and are no doubt of different qualities inter se.
Notwithstanding these differences, together they have acquired a reputation for quality.'

(*Chocosuisse Union des Fabricants Suisses de Chocolat v Cadbury Ltd* [1998] RPC 117, per Laddie J,
at p 135; aff'd [1999] RPC 826)

In the *Chocosuisse* case, Laddie J pointed out that the protection of product goodwill was not available only to 'superior' products.[35] What mattered was the public's *perception* of a distinctive quality about the product, and this was regardless of whether there was any difference in quality and ingredients between goods sold under the name and competing goods. The point arose because Swiss chocolate was not necessarily unique in its recipes or taste, and there might be chocolates made elsewhere which were indistinguishable on a blind tasting.

Discussion point   For answer guidance visit www.oxfordtextbooks.co.uk/orc/macqueen2e/

Can you think of any other products on the market in which the goodwill attaches to the product, whoever and no matter how many, manufacture it? From a commercial point of view, what features might the products mentioned be thought to have in common, and how important are they for the protection given?

Exercise

Consider the Parma Ham case (*Consorzio del Prosciutto di Parma v Marks and Spencer plc* [1991] RPC 351), in which a claim of passing off was rejected, and discuss whether in the light of the ECJ decision, C-108/01 *Consorzio del Prosciutto di Parma v Asda Stores Ltd* [2003] ECR I-5121, Parma ham should now be held to enjoy product goodwill for the purposes of protection by actions of passing off in the UK. And what about Feta cheese? (see C-465/02 *Germany v Commission of the European Communities* [2006] ETMR 16 ECJ).

Key points on product goodwill

- Some products may enjoy goodwill in their own right, as possessing certain characteristics no matter which trader produces and sells them

- Examples include champagne, Scotch whisky, sherry and Swiss chocolate

- Such goodwill in a product's descriptive name can be protected by actions of passing off, even although it does not belong to any one trader and is instead shared by many

Other types of shared goodwill: (a) groups of companies

17.21   Issues about the possibility of shared goodwill may arise in contexts other than those of product goodwill. In *Habib Bank Ltd v Habib Bank AG Zurich*,[36] it was held that the English subsidiary of a multi-national group of companies had the exclusive rights in England to the goodwill in the group's 'Habib' name, so that when it became independent it was able to sue its former holding company for passing off when the latter used the 'Habib' name in England. Similarly in *Scandecor Development v Scandecor Marketing*,[37] the UK subsidiary of an international business originating from Sweden was held to own exclusive goodwill in England in the name 'Scandecor', so that it was able to resist successfully an attempt to stop it doing so by the company which had taken

---

[35] [1998] RPC 117 at 128–9.   [36] [1981] 1 WLR 1265 (CA).   [37] [1999] FSR 27.

over the holding company in Sweden. But in *Revlon Inc v Cripps & Lee*,[38] the English subsidiary of a multi-national group (Revlon) was unable to prevent the defendant's importation of products manufactured by the US parent company in the group and marked with the Revlon name. It was held that the public, being unaware of the Revlon group's internal structure, did not distinguish amongst the various companies, and that the sale of the imported products was not passing off by the defendants. It is not clear, however, whether this means that the goodwill in the group name is shared amongst the members of the group and, if so, what the nature of each company's property right is. The changing approach to foreign goodwill described above may also have implications in this context, especially given that there is no need for public awareness of the precise identity of the person using the badge of identity in issue.

 Question

How may a group of companies share goodwill?

Other types of shared goodwill: (b) franchises

17.22   Franchising operations, under which a franchisor licenses other traders (franchisees) to make use of particular formats under which to do business—for example, in restaurants and dry-cleaning—present similar problems. Clearly the initial goodwill is that of the franchisor, but a successful franchisee (which will be a legally independent undertaking) may be able to generate further goodwill at his particular outlet. Does that goodwill belong to the franchisor, the franchisee, or to both of them, and can it be protected by an action for passing off? The problem is even more acute where the franchisor has no goodwill in England or Scotland when he first licenses his franchisees there. Clearly the activity of the franchisees is what generates the protectable goodwill in this country. It is suggested nonetheless that in general the franchisor is the owner of the goodwill. The public is usually unaware of the legal arrangements lying behind a franchise outlet, and the goodwill will tend to be attributed to the group as a whole, where the franchisor is in control. The principle that there may be goodwill even when the public does not know the actual identity of its owner is also helpful to the franchisor's claim. Finally, such case law as there is on conflicts between franchisor and franchisee has held for the former's right to sue the latter for passing off when the licensee attempts to break away and trade independently under the same indicia.[39] Again, a particular problem is where a foreign franchisor seeks to grant franchises within a particular jurisdiction, but finds that the name or other indicia which constitute the franchise have already been appropriated by someone in that market. A number of cases where the franchisor's action has failed illustrate the point that goodwill, not just mere reputation, is required to found an action of passing off.[40]

 Question

How do franchisor and franchisee share goodwill?

---

[38] [1980] FSR 85 (CA).

[39] *J H Coles Pty Ltd v Need* [1934] AC 82; *British Legion v British Legion Club (Street) Ltd* (1931) 48 RPC 555.

[40] *Athletes Foot Marketing Associates Inc v Cobra Sports Ltd* [1980] RPC 343; *Wienerwald Holding AG v Kwan Wong Tan and Fong* [1979] FSR 381 (Hong Kong). For a Scottish example of a foreign franchisor encountering difficulty of this kind, see *Salon Services (Hairdressing Supplies) Ltd v Direct Salon Services Ltd* 1988 SLT 417.

> **Key points on shared goodwill**
>
> - In certain circumstances the action of passing off can be used to protect goodwill which is shared by a number of different persons (eg groups of companies and the group name)
> - This aspect of the law is often linked to problems of foreign goodwill and reputation in this country

Focusing the goodwill: protectable devices

17.23   Traders turn customer satisfaction with their goods and services into repeat business—and so goodwill—by enabling the customer to recognise the product again, and to distinguish it from competing products by the use of some device in association with the product. The range of devices which the law has been prepared to recognise as constituting badges of identity in the marketplace now stretches very widely, and carries passing off well beyond the scope of traditional trade mark law.[41] In this section of the chapter, we will consider the range of devices which the law has recognised as badges of identity for the purposes of passing off actions, and some of the rules which limit the scope of the protection offered. In particular, we will consider:

- words (including personal, geographical and business names, titles, and invented words),
- get-up (the packaging or dress in which goods are presented to the public),
- use of personalities and characters, and
- advertising techniques and themes.

Protectable devices: words

17.24   The cases show a series of distinctions which the courts have evolved to enable them to test whether a word may be protected by passing off action. The central issue is the trader's freedom to use the language, in particular to provide the customer with a description of the goods or services being offered. No-one should be able to claim an exclusive right to use words in use in ordinary English language, unless there is very good reason (that is, deception or confusion of customers) to allow them to do so.[42] The courts have thus come up with some distinctions to help determine when there is such an exclusive right.

'Invented' or 'fancy' words
Invented or fancy words are much easier to protect by means of the action of passing off because it is more likely that such words will be distinctive of the party making the claim—are contrasted with *words already established in the English language.*

---

[41] In *L'Oreal SA v Bellure NV* [2006] EWHC 2355 (Ch), para 164, however, Lewison J states that the smell of a perfume does not form of its goodwill protectable by the action of passing off. Contrast registered trade marks: above, para 14.11.

[42] See eg *Reddaway v Banham* [1896] AC 199; and in Scotland *Cellular Clothing Co v Maxton & Murray* (1899) 1 F (HL) 29; *Bile Bean Manufacturing Co v Davidson* (1906) 8F 1181; *Kinnell v Ballantine* 1910 SC 246; *Salon Services (Hairdressing Supplies) Ltd v Direct Salon Services Ltd* 1988 SLT 417.

Examples of invented words:

(1) Kodak

(2) FiloFax

(3) Linoleum

(4) Sellotape

(5) Nike

(6) Adidas

(7) Mondeo

Descriptive or self-laudatory words with secondary meaning through use

This covers *merely descriptive or self-laudatory words*, giving rise to no rights of exclusive use, and those which, *although descriptive, have acquired a secondary meaning through use*, whereby they serve to distinguish the goods or services of a particular trader in the market and whose use by others may as a result constitute passing off.

Examples of descriptive words acquiring secondary meanings:

(1) Camel hair (for belts) in *Reddaway v Banham* [1896] AC 199

(2) Special Brew (for beer) in *Carlsberg v Tennant Caledonian Breweries Ltd* [1972] RPC 847

(3) Oven chips (to be oven-cooked rather than fried) in *McCain International v County Fair Foods* [1981] RPC 69

(4) Mothercare (shop and clothing for expectant mothers and young children) in *Mothercare v Penguin Books* [1988] RPC 113

Example of descriptive words without secondary meaning:

(1) Office Cleaning Services as the name of a company providing office cleaning services (*Office Cleaning Services Ltd v Westminster Window and General Cleaning Cleaners Ltd* (1946) 63 RPC 39)

Where words are merely laudatory, however, it may be extremely difficult to show that any secondary meaning has arisen.

Personal and geographical names

In general, no one can claim an exclusive right in personal and geographical names, but again a particular name (including a surname, nickname, or an assumed name) or a geographical location or descriptor may, like ordinarily descriptive words, acquire a *secondary meaning through use* in a particular trading context. The name adopted does not have to be the name of a person concerned with the business in order to gain protection, and its scope may extend to the names of fictional characters, although the scope of this protection is unclear.

Examples of personal and geographical names acquiring secondary meaning:

(1) Scotch in the context of whisky (note also its use in the context of adhesive tape, however)

(2) Johnny Walker in *John Walker & Sons Ltd v Henry Ost & Co Ltd* [1970] RPC 489

(3) John Haig in *John Haig & Co Ltd v John D D Haig Ltd* 1957 SLT (Notes) 36

(4) Grant in *William Grant & Sons Ltd v Glen Catrine Bonded Warehouse Ltd* 2001 SC 901 (whisky, vodka, gin)

(5) any number of distillery locations, all in the context of whisky (see eg *Highland Distilleries Co plc v Speymalt Whisky Distributors Ltd* 1985 SC 1 (Bunnahabhain, Islay); *William Grant & Sons Ltd v William Cadenhead Ltd* 1985 SC 121 (Glenfiddich))

(6) Thistle (surname of sole trader trading as Thistle Communications—*Thistle v Thistle Telecom Ltd* 2000 SLT 262)

(7) Swiss in the context of chocolate in *Chocosuisse Union des Fabricants Suisses de Chocolat v Cadbury Ltd* [1998] RPC 117

(8) the name of an author or artist or performer in their respective fields in eg *Carrick Jewellery Ltd v Ortak* 1989 GWD 35–1624 (Charles Rennie Mackintosh); *Clark v Associated Newspapers* [1998] RPC 261 (Alan Clark).

Titles

Titles, whether of books, TV and radio programmes, newspapers, magazines, or websites, may again often consist of words and names in use in ordinary language all the time. But if it can be shown that distinctiveness has been acquired in the marketplace, then exclusive rights may be asserted by way of passing off

Examples of protected titles:

(1) *The Times* newspaper in *Walter v Ashton* [1902] 2 Ch 282 (the newspaper could stop sales of *Times* bicycles)

(2) *East Enders* TV programme (*BBC v Celebrity Centre* (1988) 15 IPR 333—an injunction granted to stop book entitled *A to Z of East Enders*)

Contrast:

(1) *County Sound plc v Ocean Sound plc* [1991] FSR 367 ('Gold AM' not distinctive for a radio station playing 'golden oldies')

(2) *GTG Sports Publications Ltd v Fitness Shop (Publications) Ltd* 1983 SC 115 (magazines on Scottish rugby: the title 'Scottish Rugby' held not distinctive, being merely descriptive of the magazine contents, and so 'Rugby Scotland' could not be stopped)

Note also cases about English newspapers adopting the titles of Scottish ones. In the two leading cases the English courts refused to grant injunctions to the Scottish plaintiffs on the grounds of lack of confusion between the newspapers concerned (*George Outram v London Evening Newspapers* (1911) 28 RPC 308—Evening Times in Glasgow and London; *D & C Thompson v Kent Messenger* [1975] RPC 191—Sunday Post in Scotland and south-east England).

Business names

Business names may often consist of personal names, descriptive words, or invented words, or some combination of these; again, if distinctiveness in the marketplace is achieved, then the name may be protected by way of passing off. The cases illustrate this with regard to clubs, hotels, restaurants, professional associations, and musical bands, as well as those of partnerships and companies.

Examples of distinctive business names:

(1) Annabel's in *Annabels v Shock* [1972] RPC 838 (club)

(2) Maxim's in *Maxims Ltd v Dye* [1977] FSR 364 (restaurant)

(3) Dr Crock and his Crackpots in *Hines v Winnick* [1947] Ch 708 (musical band)

(4) The Drifters in *Treadwell's Drifters Inc v RCL Ltd* 1996 SLT 1048 (musical group)

(5) Radio Rentals in *Radio Rentals Ltd v Rentals Ltd* (1934) 51 RPC 407

But it may be very difficult to show distinctiveness in certain words in certain contexts: for example, *International* in the case of hotels (*Park Court Hotel Ltd v Trans-World Hotels Ltd* [1970] FSR 89), or *Drive Yourself* in the case of car hire (*Drive Yourself Hire Co (London) Ltd v Parish (trading as 'Self Drive Cars')* [1957] RPC 307), or *Salon Service* for hairdressing supplies (*Salon Services (Hairdressing Supplies) Ltd v Direct Salon Services Ltd* 1988 SLT 414).

Abbreviations and combinations of letters and numbers

If ordinary words might be thought normally open for use by all, this is even more so for the individual letters which go to make them up; and also numerals. But in a world where acronyms and short, eye-catching abbreviations or combinations of letters and numbers are ever more important badges of identity, passing off can be used to protect such identifiers if they have become distinctive.

Examples of distinctive abbreviations, initials and numerals:

(1) CA in *Society of Accountants in Edinburgh v Corporation of Accountants* (1893) 20R 750

(2) CB in *Bayer v Baird* (1898) 25R 1142

(3) BMA in *British Medical Association v Marsh* (1931) 48 RPC 565

(4) 1001 in *PC Products v Dalton* [1957] RPC 199(5) 4711 in *Reuter v Muhlens* (1953) 70 RPC 235

But not:

(1) FCUK in *French Connection v Sutton* [2000] ETMR 341

17.25   What appears to be most important overall, therefore, is the creation or acquisition of distinctiveness in the marketplace in a word or combination of words (or letters and numerals). But the distinctiveness thus created or acquired can also be lost.[43] So a trader who invents a word for a product will have to be vigilant to prevent its use by other traders for similar products, since if this is not stopped the word will cease to be distinctive of the original product and become a *generic* term for all products of that particular kind. A well-known example is the word *Linoleum* for a certain type of floor-covering, originally manufactured under a patent and using the name Linoleum by the patent holder alone. But once the patent had expired, other manufacturers moved into the market, also using the name Linoleum. The former patent holder's attempt to stop this was unsuccessful, on the grounds that the word had become a generic term for floor-covering of this type, and had ceased to be distinctive of the original manufacturer.[44]

 Question

Explain how an initially distinctive product name may become 'generic'. How can passing off actions help to prevent this?

---

[43] *Burberry v Cording* (1909) 26 RPC 693.   [44] *Linoleum Manufacturing Co v Nairn* (1878) 7 Ch D 834.

17.26 On the other hand, in many extended passing off cases, initially descriptive words came also to indicate goods of a particular quality or set of characteristics, so that many traders making goods of that quality or with those characteristics may use the name without its necessarily losing its secondary and distinctive meaning.[45]

> **Key points about descriptive words and secondary meanings**
>
> - The use of ordinary words in the English language as part of a business identity can become associated with a particular trader in the marketplace, so that exclusive use can be claimed by way of the action for passing off. The words are then said to have acquired a 'secondary meaning'
>
> - Just as words can acquire a secondary meaning, so they can lose it if the trader fails to defend its exclusivity in the marketplace
>
> - Even invented words can become generic, that is, descriptive of all goods or services of a particular kind, if their exclusivity is not defended quickly enough

 Discussion point   For answer guidance visit www.oxfordtextbooks.co.uk/orc/macqueen2e/

Why do extended passing off cases (the ones about product goodwill—above, para 17.20) allow for the protection of a generic name for a product? What is the difference from cases where words are held to be merely descriptive or to lack a secondary meaning associating it with a particular trader?

Protectable devices: get-up

17.27 Get-up is *'the dress in which the goods are offered to the public'.*[46] If distinctive of the goods, a feature by which customers distinguish the product from those of competitors, it may be protected by an action of passing off. Get up will usually be the packaging of the goods, either in whole or in part. Some examples are as follows.

(1) The *whole packaging* such as:

- the Coca Cola or the Haig 'Dimple' bottles in *Coca Cola v Barr* [1961] RPC 387; *John Haig & Co v Forth Blending Co* 1954 SC 35

- containers for fruit in *Plix Products v Winstone* [1986] FSR 608

- the lemon-shaped container of lemon juice in *Reckitt & Colman Products v Borden Inc* [1990] 1 All ER 873.

(2) Some feature of the packaging:

- colouring in *Hoffmann La Roche v DDSA* [1969] FSR 410 (black and green colours of Librium capsules)

- stylised typeface of writing appearing on the goods in *Carrick Jewellery Ltd v Ortak* 1989 GWD 35–1624

---

[45] *Erven Warnink v Townend* [1979] AC 731.
[46] *John Haig & Co v Forth Blending Co* 1954 SC 35 per Lord Hill Watson at p 38.

However, the *shape of the product itself* generally *cannot* be a badge of identity and goodwill, although some part thereof may be. An example of a product shape denied protection was Cadbury's chocolate flake in *Cadbury Ltd v Ulmer GmbH* [1988] FSR 385. Contrast that case with the following.

■ *Edge v Nicchols* [1911] AC 693

The product was a device for parcelling up blue or other colour in a porous calico bag with a wooden handle attached to it so that the colour could be dissolved in water without staining the hands of the operator. The handle was a distinctive feature but the bag bore no name. It was held that the producer of this bag could prevent a competitor from marketing their blue colour in a bag with an identical handle, and that the placing of the competitor's name on their bags was not enough to avoid passing off.

 Exercise

Consider the distinction between 'get-up' and the shape of the product in the light of the cases where a container gives shape to an otherwise formless product, as in the drinks and lemon juice decisions. See the comments of Lord Oliver in *Reckitt & Colman Products v Borden Inc* [1990] RPC 341 at 410; [1990] 1 WLR 491 at 503; [1990] 1 All ER 873 at 884.

Key points about get-up

- Passing off will protect distinctive packaging, or distinctive aspects of the packaging, of goods
- But the shape of the *product itself* cannot generally be a basis for a claim, although some distinctive part of the product may be

17.28 Features of the way in which goods or services are offered to the public, other than packaging or shape, could be protected by the action of passing off: for example, the ambience or decor of a restaurant,[47] or the nature of 'back up' services offered by authorised dealers in the goods of particular manufacturers,[48] or the conduct of business over the Internet in a particular format and style.[49] Distinctions similar to those found in the cases about words may apply in assessing distinctiveness, in particular that a prima facie descriptive get-up—such as a lemon-shaped container for lemon juice—may acquire a secondary meaning and become distinctive of a particular trader through unchallenged use.[50] The smell of a fine fragrance has been held not to form part of its goodwill protectable by passing off. In the Court of Appeal Jacob LJ said that a fragrance might be a source of goodwill, 'but that does not mean that anyone who seeks to emulate the fragrance is guilty of any wrong.'[51]

---

[47] See *My Kinda Town v Soll* [1983] RPC 407.   [48] *Sony v Saray* [1983] FSR 302.
[49] *easyJet v Dainty* [2002] FSR 111.   [50] *Reckitt & Colman Products v Borden Inc* [1990].
[51] *L'Oreal SA v Bellure NV* [2007] RPC 14 (Lewison J); [2008] RPC 9 (CA), para 127.

■ *easyJet v Dainty* [2002] FSR 6

In this case, the judge (at p 114) described the way in which easyJet and the other 'easy-' businesses carried in their image:

'the following distinctive combination of features. First of all, the name "easy" together with another word which alludes to the service in question being offered, so as to form one new word, such as the word "easyJet" in the case of the airline, or "easyRentacar" in the case of the third claimant. Secondly, the word 'easy' in this formulation is in lower case in the case of every one of the uses of the combination. Thirdly, in every combination the first letter of the second word is displayed as a capital letter so that easyJet has a capital J, easyEverything a capital E and easyRentacar a capital R. Fourthly, in every case the get-up is against a bright orange background with plain white lettering except on occasions where the colouring is reversed so that the background is white and the lettering is in the same distinctive orange colour, as has usually been associated with the product in question....[O]ne of the distinctive features is that business is either with, to do with, or conducted over the Internet so that the evidence suggests something of the order of 75, sometimes 81% of bookings on an individual day might be done and conducted over the Internet, although it is possible for business to be conducted by telephone and I daresay by other means as well. But it is a highly Internet organised business and this is a matter which also needs to be taken into account'.

Key point on business image

- Passing off can protect the equivalent of 'get-up' for services, the image of a business.

Advertising themes and techniques

17.29   In *Cadbury Schweppes Pty Ltd v Pub Squash Co Pty Ltd*[52] Cadbury marketed their non-alcoholic soft drink 'Solo' in Australia with a theme of rugged masculine endeavour, showing dynamic young men quenching the thirst arising from their activities by drinking 'Solo'. Pub Squash began to market their rival soft drink product with a similar campaign. Cadbury's claim that this was passing off was rejected by the Privy Council because the original advertising campaign had not achieved exclusive goodwill for them. But Lord Scarman stated one effect of the *Advocaat* case as follows:[53]

'[T]he tort is no longer anchored, as in its early nineteenth century formulation, to the name or trade mark of a product or business. It is wide enough to encompass other descriptive material, such as slogans or visual images, which radio, television or newspaper advertising campaigns can lead the market to associate with a plaintiff's product, provided always that such descriptive material has become part of the goodwill of the product. And the test is whether the product has derived from the advertising a distinctive character which the market recognises.'

Key point on advertising themes

- The *Pub Squash* case recognises the possibility of an advertising theme or slogan being part of the image of a business protectable by way of passing off

---

[52] [1981] 1 WLR 193 (PC).   [53] ibid, at 200.

Personalities and characters

17.30   A long-established marketing technique is the use in association with goods or services of the names and characters of well-known personalities. Such personalities may be real—for example a well-known sportsman such as the footballer David Beckham, or a popular singer such as Elvis Presley—or entirely fictitious—for example, cartoon or puppet characters in a television series such as *The Simpsons* or *Teletubbies*. It is frequently the case that the popularity of a particular personality or character is exploited by putting on the market a variety of products bearing the name or image of the person or character, or reproducing the image in either two- or three-dimensional form. This form of marketing is known as *spin off* or *character merchandising* when applied to fictional characters, *personality merchandising* when the character is a real person. The boundary may become blurred when, for example, the personality of an actor well-known in a particular role is exploited in this sort of way. A good example was the way in which the actor Telly Savalas developed the personality of his character, Kojak the New York detective, in his own right; other instances may be found with actors involved in long-running TV series such as 'soap operas'.

> **Question**
>
> What is the difference between character and personality merchandising?

17.31   There have been a number of cases in which courts in Britain and elsewhere in the Common Law world have recognised that a character or personality associated with goods may become a device distinguishing those goods in the market.

■ *Mirage Studios v Counter-Feat Clothing Co Ltd* [1991] FSR 145

This was the Teenage Mutant Ninja Turtles case in England. The defendants applied the images of the Turtles, cartoon characters, humanoid creatures with some of the features of turtles (notably half-shells), to their clothing products without having a licence to do so from the creators of the characters. Browne-Wilkinson V-C held that this was passing off. A substantial section of the public knew that the reproduction of well-known characters on goods was generally licensed by the originators of the characters; that the public would therefore assume that the goods so marketed had the approval of the originators for quality, and that the images used came from the originators rather than being copies; and that the public would therefore be misled by such unlicensed reproductions, even although the plaintiffs did not themselves market or manufacture goods in this way in the UK.

■ *Shaw Bros v Golden Harvest* [1972] RPC 559

In this Hong Kong case it was held that an author may claim goodwill in a fictional character and that a film producer who has a licence to use the story creating the character can also build up a goodwill in it which may be protected by a passing off action.

Note also the 'Crocodile Dundee' cases in Australia, which illustrate how the image of an actor and his character may coalesce:

■ *Hogan v Koala Dundee (1988) 12 IPR 508; Hogan v Pacific Dunlop (1989) 12 IPR 225*

Hogan played the character, Crocodile Dundee in a series of films which he also wrote. These cases involved the defendants' sale of goods making use of the Crocodile Dundee name and image, and the Australian courts held that there was passing off.

17.32   However, *Mirage Studios* apart, the English courts have been reluctant to recognise that the use of characters or personalities can be stopped by their originator, especially if he himself has not yet commenced trading operations using them. The argument is that goodwill, as distinct from reputation, is necessary before there can be a claim of passing off. Examples of unsuccessful claims include the following:

- Uncle Mac, children's radio character in *McCulloch v May* (1948) 65 RPC 58
- Sherlock Holmes in *Conan Doyle v London Mystery Magazine Ltd* (1949) 66 RPC 312
- Wombles of Wimbledon in *Wombles v Womble Skip* [1977] RPC 99
- ABBA pop group in *Lyngstad v Anabas* [1977] FSR 62
- Teletubbies in *BBC Worldwide v Pally Screen Printing* [1998] FSR 665

Even where the character or personality is already being used under licence to market goods, English judges have argued that the use of the image is *not* seen by the public as a representation of a connection with, or authorisation by, the originator of the character in question, or by the personality. If there is a false claim of authorisation—for example, a claim that the merchandise is 'official'—then, but only then, may there be a misrepresentation.[54]

17.33   Much may depend on the facts of the individual case, in particular the extent to which the character or personality is already in merchandising use, and on the availability of other remedies through, for example, copyright, trade marks, and perhaps defamation; but in policy terms it can be said that the approach so far of the English courts in the law of passing off fails to recognise the extent to which 'character' and 'personality' merchandising has become an established form of trading supported by complex licensing arrangements, all of which will be baseless unless the law is prepared to recognise the goodwill which does attach to characters even before they have been employed in a merchandising context.[55]

Exercise

How far should the law follow commercial practice in its development?

Key point on character and personality merchandising

- Although passing off is now recognised as reaching the unauthorised use of fictional characters and real persons in the marketing of products, the English courts have

---

[54] *Elvis Presley Trade Marks* [1997] RPC 543 at 558, per Laddie J. This would also cover the Scottish case of *Wilkie v McCulloch* (1823) 2 S 413. See also *Arsenal FC plc v Reed* [2001] RPC 922 (Laddie J), where the defendant who made clear that his goods were *not* official Arsenal merchandise was not guilty of passing off.

[55] See further H Carty, 'Character merchandising and the limits of passing off' (1993) 13 Legal Studies 289.

been reluctant to allow the action unless the claimant is actually trading using the character/personality in question, or where there is a false claim by the defendants that their use is authorised or 'official'

 Exercise

Consider the case of *Taverner Rutledge v Trexapalm* [1977] RPC 275. Is it anomalous that in this case the UK licensees of the originators of 'Kojak' lollipops found themselves unsuccessfully defending a passing off action brought by an unlicensed trader who had reached the English market first with his own 'Kojakpops'? 'Kojak', a character in an American TV detective series who liked lollipops and whose catchphrase was 'Who loves ya, baby?', was played by Telly Savalas.

17.34   Character and personality merchandising should be distinguished from *endorsement*. As Laddie J explained in *Irvine v Talksport Ltd*:[56]

> 'When someone endorses a product or service he tells the relevant public that he approves of the product or service or is happy to be associated with it. In effect he adds his name as an encouragement to members of the relevant public to buy or use the service or product. Merchandising is rather different. It involves exploiting images, themes or articles which have become famous. . . . It is not a necessary feature of merchandising that members of the public will think the products are in any sense endorsed [by the personalities or characters concerned].'

False endorsements by real persons tended to be dealt with in the English courts, if at all, by means other than passing off, for example, defamation.[57] The view seemed to be that, even if there was appropriation of goodwill by the false endorsement, the business being made by the defendant from its activities was not custom that would otherwise have gone to the person represented as making the endorsement.[58] The law did not recognise any character or personality right. By contrast, in the early Scottish decision of *Wilkie v McCulloch*,[59] a firm was stopped from representing that its ploughs were made under the inspection and authority of an individual who had developed a new kind of plough. In more recent times, the Australian courts also took a rather different approach:

■ *Henderson v Radio Corporation Pty Ltd* [1969] RPC 218 (High Court of New South Wales)

The unauthorised appearance of a photograph of two well-known professional ballroom dancers on the sleeve of a dance music record was held to constitute passing off as a misrepresentation of the dancers' endorsement of the record.[60]

---

[56] [2002] 2 All ER 414; [2002] FSR 60 [para 9].
[57] *Tolley v Fry* [1931] AC 333 (champion amateur golfer portrayed with Fry's chocolate bar in advertisement for that product; defamation in implication that he had been paid for an endorsement of the product).
[58] *McCulloch v May* (1948) 65 RPC 58; *Elvis Presley Trade Marks* [1999] RPC 567 at 597 per Simon Brown LJ.
[59] (1823) 2S 413.
[60] See also *Campomar Sociedad Limitada v Nike International Ltd* (2000) 46 IPR 481 (High Court of Australia).

The law in England appears to have changed, however, as a result of the judgment of Laddie J in *Irvine v Talksport Ltd*, which was approved by the Court of Appeal on appeal.[61]

■ *Irvine v Talksport Ltd* [2002] 2 All ER 414 (Laddie J); [2003] EWCA Civ 423

Eddie Irvine, the leading Formula 1 racing driver, was shown in a promotional brochure for Talksport Radio wearing his Ferrari racing gear and apparently listening intently to a radio marked with the Talksport insignia. This was however the result of manipulation of a photograph (lawfully acquired for reproduction by Talksport) which actually showed Irvine using a mobile telephone. It was held that this was passing off. Laddie J said (at para 39):

'[I]t is common for famous people to exploit their names and images by way of endorsement. They do it not only in their own field of expertise but, depending on the extent of their fame or notoriety, wider afield also. It is common knowledge that for many sportsmen, for example, income received from endorsing a variety of products and services represent a very substantial part of their total income. The reason large sums are paid for endorsement is because, no matter how irrational it may seem to a lawyer, those in business have reason to believe that the lustre of a famous personality, if attached to their goods and services, will enhance the attractiveness of those goods or services to their target market. In this respect, the endorsee is taking the benefit of the attractive force which is the reputation or goodwill of the famous person.'

Laddie J justified his approach by reference to the realities of modern commerce, but he also indicated that he might have been willing to proceed by way of an argument under Article 8 of the European Convention on Human Rights, which requires respect for privacy and family life.

Key point on endorsement

- *Irvine* is authority that false endorsement is passing off because endorsement is established as a lucrative way in which personalities may exploit their fame.

Question

What is the difference between endorsement, on the one hand, and personality merchandising on the other?

Discussion point   For answer guidance visit www.oxfordtextbooks.co.uk/orc/macqueen2e/

Do you agree that the endorsement of a well-known personality can be a source of goodwill? Does Article 8 of the European Convention on Human Rights (privacy) require the protection of such goodwill? Whose goodwill—the trader whose products are endorsed or the personality doing the endorsing? Is it false endorsement and passing off for a political party to create a compilation CD of songs without the approval of the artists featured in the material (who also disagree strongly with the political party's aims and beliefs)? See http://www.timesonline.co.uk/tol/comment/letters/article6374280.ece See also http://the1709blog.blogspot.com/2009/06/it-is-golfers-and-racing-drivers-who.html

---

[61] See further M Learmouth, 'Eddie, are you OK? Product endorsement and passing off' [2002] IPQ 306.

Misrepresentation

17.35   Passing off provides a remedy for *misrepresentation* appropriating or otherwise diminishing the goodwill of another trader. A misrepresentation is a false statement of fact. In passing off, the false representation is that the goods or services in which the defendant trades are those of the claimant, or in some way have a business connection with the claimant, or have the particular qualities of the claimant's goods or services. It is comparatively easy to determine that this is what the defendant has done when he uses exactly the same device as the claimant in connection with an identical or similar product,[62] but even there it must be clear that the claimant's goodwill will be damaged.

■ *Mothercare UK Ltd v Penguin Books Ltd* [1988] RPC 113 (CA)

The claimant, a well-known retailer of goods for mothers, babies and small children, failed to establish that the use of the phrase 'Mother Care' in the title of a controversial book would lead the public to take the book as a publication of the retailer.

Even when the defendant has *copied* the claimant's badge of identity, passing off will not provide a remedy unless the latter's goodwill has been damaged.[63]

 Question

What is the typical misrepresentation in a passing off case?

17.36   Generally, however, the representation is of a more subtle kind than exact reproduction of a badge of identity, with either the nature of the defendant's statement, or the nature of the goods or services provided by him, or the way in which the defendant conducts himself in relation to the goods and services, or some combination of these things, being different in some way from that of the claimant. The key factor is *the way in which the market reacts to the defendant's activities*. It must be shown that there has been, or that there is likely to be, *confusion about the existence of a trading link between the defendant's product and the claimant* as a result of what the defendant has done. In approaching this question it is important to remember that the confused public need not be aware of the claimant's actual identity (see above, para 17.14).

■ *United Biscuits (UK) Ltd v Asda Stores Ltd* [1997] RPC 513

Asda began to market 'Puffin' biscuits to compete with UB's 'Penguin' biscuits. Asda were careful to design their packaging to avoid deception of customers, but at the same time sought to match, or challenge, or parody, the 'Penguin' style, using the image of the relevant bird and the name in black lettering alongside on the packaging, as well as similar colours and wrapping materials. See the report at p 516 for colour images of the competing wrappers. It was held that

---

[62]   See eg *Kinnell v Ballantine* 1910 SC 246 ('Horseshoe' for boilers); *Carlsberg v Tennant Caledonian Breweries Ltd* [1972] RPC 847 ('Special Brew' for lager); *Thistle v Thistle Telecom Ltd* 2000 SLT 262 ('Thistle' in relation to telecoms hardware and services).

[63]   See eg *County Sound plc v Ocean Sound plc* [1991] FSR 367; *Arsenal FC plc v Reed* [2001] RPC 922.

there was passing off, in that customers might be led by the similarities of get-up to suppose that the two biscuits came from the same manufacturing source.

17.37 The courts have adopted an increasingly broad approach to what kinds of misrepresentation constitute passing off. The definitions of passing off in the *Advocaat* case (see above, para 17.11) do not confine relevant misrepresentation to statements about the trading source of the goods or services, but extend to statements, express or implied, about distinctive characteristics of the goods or services themselves.

■ *Lang Brothers v Goldwell* 1980 SC 237

This case held that it was misrepresentation to attach indicia of Scottishness (appearance on the bottle label of the name 'Wee McGlen', a tartan background, and a thistle device, and the deployment in newspaper advertisements of a caricature of a be-tartaned Scotsman) to a whisky-based product not wholly produced in Scotland.

■ *Associated Newspapers plc v Insert Media Ltd* [1991] FSR 380

A business which inserted advertising material between the pages of national newspapers without the authority of the newspaper publishers was held to misrepresent that such authority had been obtained.

■ *British Sky Broadcasting Group plc v Sky Home Services Ltd* [2007] FSR 14 (Briggs J)

The claimant BSB provided extended warranty services under the name 'Sky Repair Protection Plan' in respect of satellite broadcast reception equipment on which its Sky satellite broadcasts were viewed. The defendant SHS also marketed and supplied extended warranty contracts using corporate names including the word 'Sky' or confusingly similar words. Held that there was passing off by way of implied misrepresentations, including failure of the SHS sales force to correct the misapprehensions held by customers as to their links with BSB. BSB had held a de facto monopoly in their services, and in entering such a market SHS had a duty to take care that their marketing methods did not convey the implicit message of a connection with the existing monopolist.

17.38 It is no longer the law that the misrepresentation should have been fraudulent. In England, once passing off was explained as a protection of property in goodwill, the importance of fraud waned as an element in the action, although it is still occasionally mentioned. Fraud was never important in Scotland. Intention to deceive may make proof of confusion and damage to goodwill easier, but intention not to deceive, as in the *Puffin/Penguin* case (above, para 17.36), will not prevent a successful action of passing off action if nevertheless customers are confused. Again, the claimant will have a remedy if the defendant's statement falsely suggests a trading connection between them, even if in other respects the defendant's statement is a true description of his goods or services. In this aspect, the problem most commonly arises over the use of descriptive words or geographical and personal names, where the issue is whether the words used are merely descriptive, available to all whose goods or services meet the description, or have that name, or whether they have become distinctive of the claimant's goods and services in the marketplace. With regard to the use of one's own name in relation to one's business, it is no longer (if it ever was) the law that there is a right to use one's own name which can be used to fend off a claim of passing off: 'a man is entitled to carry on his business in his own name so long as he does not do anything more than that to cause confusion with the business of another, and so long as he does it honestly.'[64]

◼ *Reddaway v Banham* [1896] AC 199

The defendant sold belting made of the yarn of camel's hair under the name 'Camel Hair Belting'. The plaintiff had already established a reputation in the market using that name and was held entitled to an injunction against the defendant.

◼ *Dunlop Pneumatic Tyre Co v Dunlop Motor Co* 1907 SC (HL) 15

The Court of Session and the House of Lords agreed that car dealers were entitled to use their surnames as a business name, even though it was already the company name of the tyre manufacturer claimants.

◼ *Parker-Knoll Ltd v Knoll International Ltd* [1962] RPC 265 (HL)

Parker-Knoll, manufacturers of furniture, became so named after the English company Parker & Sons purchased a springing system for chairs invented by Wilhelm Knoll. Wilhelm's nephew, Hans Knoll, developed Knoll International as an international furniture business from the USA, and sought to enter the UK market. It was held that Knoll International could not enter the UK furniture market using the word 'Knoll', even although it was the personal name of their founder. A name may be used as a mark under which a person's good are sold so that the name comes to mean goods sold by that person and not those of anyone else, even when that other has the same name.

◼ *Watts v O'Briens* 1987 SLT 101

A married woman may not be able to use her maiden name in business if that name already has goodwill pertaining to another (here, a firm of solicitors).

◼ *BIBA Group v Biba Boutique* [1980] RPC 143

An individual may not be free to use her nickname if that name is already associated in the public mind with an existing trader.

◼ *John Haig & Co Ltd v John D D Haig Ltd* 1957 SLT (Notes) 36

A man may be unable to give his name to his company if that name is already associated in the public mind with an existing trader in a relevant market. Here the new trader manufactured whisky liqueur chocolates, which was too close to the existing trader's whisky business.

◼ *Office Cleaning Services Ltd v Westminster Window & General Cleaners Ltd* (1946) 63 RPC 39 (HL)

The plaintiffs, who traded as 'Office Cleaning Services', were held unable to prevent the defendants carrying on business as 'Office Cleaning Association'. The term 'office cleaning' described

---

[64] *Joseph Rodgers & Sons Ltd v W N Rodgers & Co* (1924) 41 RPC 277 per Romer J; approved in *Parker-Knoll Ltd v Knoll International Ltd* [1962] RPC 265 (HL), and quoted in *Reed Executive plc v Reed Business Information Ltd* [2004] RPC 40 (CA), at para 109, per Jacob LJ.

the nature of the activity carried on and only a small differentiation between the two names was therefore required to avoid passing off.

But minor differentiation between descriptive words may not be enough where there is evidence of confusion:

■ *Chill Foods (Scotland) Ltd v Cool Foods Ltd* 1977 SLT 38

It was held that on this basis (see further para 17.39 below) that Chill Foods, traders in frozen foodstuffs, were entitled to prevent the use of the name Cool Foods by competitors.

 Question

To what extent may a trader use his own name in business?

Is fraud or intent to deceive a necessary element of the misrepresentation required for passing off?

Key points on misrepresentation

- The misrepresentation is a statement that the goods or services in which the defendant trades are those of, or have a business connection with, the claimant, or have the particular qualities of the claimant's goods or services
- The misrepresentation must have damaged the claimant's goodwill by causing confusion in the marketplace for the goods or services
- The misrepresentation need not have been fraudulent
- Traders are not entitled to use their personal names as those of their businesses if that would cause confusion with another's business

Confusion

17.39   Confusion of the public as to the source of the goods or services, or as to their qualities in appropriate cases, is at the heart of passing off. It is not necessary that the whole of the public is confused, while it is not fatal to a claim that many members—even the majority[65]—of the public are not confused by the defendant's conduct. What matters is that there is, or there is likely to be, confusion amongst significant numbers of the public in the market where the parties operate.[66]

■ *Clark v Associated Newspapers* [1998] 1 All ER 959

The London *Evening Standard* carried a weekly parody of the famous diaries of Alan Clark, a well-known Conservative MP. The articles were entitled 'Alan Clark's Secret Political Diaries'.

---

[65] See eg *Chocosuisse Union des Fabricants Suisses de Chocolat v Cadbury* [1998] RPC 117; [1999] RPC 826.
[66] For an argument about the point of time at which confusion must take place in order to be legally actionable, see P O'Byrne and B Allgrove, 'Post-sale confusion' [2007] 2 JIPLP 315.

Each article had a photograph of Clark and a byline indicating that it was in fact written by a journalist imagining how Clark would be recording events. It was held that this was passing off even though many readers would not be misled; but as an evening paper read by commuters on their homeward journeys, a substantial number would be confused, and that was enough. See also para 3.47 on moral right aspects of this case.

■ *Topps Company Inc v Tom Hannah Agencies Ltd* 1999 GWD 40–1957

This was a case about children's confectionery. Lord Nimmo Smith said: 'I have to consider what impression might be made on a child who goes into a typical corner shop clutching a 50p coin and gazes up at the whole range of confectionery on display, all competing by various forms of get-up and other attraction for the child's attention and purchasing power.'

■ *Irvine v Talksport Ltd* [2002] 2 All ER 414 (Laddie J); [2003] EWCA Civ 423

For the facts, see above, para 17.34. The brochure containing the manipulated image of Eddie Irvine listening avidly to Talksport Radio was a trade rather than a public promotion. It was held that a not insignificant number of recipients of the brochure would have concluded that Irvine was endorsing the radio station, making it a more attractive medium in which to place advertisements, given the public following enjoyed by the racing driver.

It is permissible to lead evidence that members of the public have been confused. So, for example, in *Great North of Scotland Railway Co v Mann*,[67] which concerned the names of hotels, there was evidence that customers seeking one hotel had been taken to the other. In *Chill Foods (Scotland) Ltd v Cool Foods Ltd*,[68] a letter from a supplier was used as evidence that there was confusion between the parties as a result of their similar trading names. In *Phones 4U Ltd v Phone4U.co.uk Internet Ltd*,[69] emails from customers to the defendant's website showed that these people thought they were communicating with the claimant's business, even after visiting the website.

■ *Flaxcell v Freedman* 1981 SLT (Notes) 131

This case concerned the names 'Dirty Dicks' and 'Dicky Dirts'. The petitioners, who sold jeans from a shop in London under the name 'Dirty Dicks', referred to their own practice of listing their business under both names in the telephone directory as evidence of the precautions necessary against confusion. The defenders, who were employed by Lee Jeans, had formed a workers' cooperative to occupy their factory in protest against its closure by Lee Jeans, and there was also evidence that the petitioners had been congratulated on their support of this action.

■ *D Jacobson & Sons Ltd v Globe GB Ltd and another* [2008] EWHC 88 (Ch)

G marketed footwear by the name of 'Globe Finale', 'Globe Wedge' and 'Globe Motto'. DJ, who owned the IP rights in Gola footwear, alleged, *inter alia*, that G was passing off the Gola footwear brand. The Globe shoes featured a stripe design on the sides similar to that featured on the Gola footwear. Held that there was passing off. Copious evidence in the form of, *inter alia*, consumer surveys, advertisements and the product's long history was relied upon to reach the conclusion that DJ's shoes enjoyed significant goodwill and a strong reputation. The side design

---

[67] (1892) 19R 1035.   [68] 1977 SLT 38.   [69] [2007] RPC 5 (CA).

on G's shoes was held to misrepresent to the public that they were DJ's shoes. While there was no evidence of actual loss or damage resulting from confusion generated by the Globe footwear, the confusion that resulted between the two brands put DJ's goodwill at risk as it could not control G's use of the designs.

17.40   Where it is averred that the passing off consists of supplying one type of goods when another type has been asked for, the evidence gleaned from placing 'trap orders' may also be accepted by the courts. A systematic survey of the public may be used as evidence of the confusion caused by the defendant's activities,[70] but will often be subject to methodological challenge, since it is usually produced at the behest of one or other or the contending parties. Expert evidence may also be led to help the court understand such matters as the nature of the marketplace and the attention which the typical customer gives to aspects of the appearance of a product in that marketplace.[71] In *Arsenal FC plc v Reed*,[72] which concerned the sale of unlicensed merchandise bearing Arsenal insignia outside the club's ground, Laddie J suggested that the club could have set up a mock stall with the type of products sold only by the defendant and then interviewed customers to find out their motives and beliefs when purchasing Arsenal memorabilia. But the decision on whether or not there is confusion is for the judge ultimately. In the *Arsenal* case, Laddie J was unwilling to infer confusion in the absence of evidence that it existed, because the defendant had been trading in the way complained of for 30 years, quite openly and extensively.[73]

 Question

What level of public confusion must be shown for misrepresentation and a claim of passing off to be made out?

17.41   In many cases, the claimant will be seeking to prevent the defendant's activities, not on the basis that the public is already confused, but rather because of concern that the public is *likely* to be confused if the defendant's activities are allowed to continue unchecked. In testing the likelihood of confusion, two points must be borne in mind. One is the conditions in the market where the parties operate. 'Thirsty folk want beer, not explanations.'[74] Accordingly the differences between the devices of claimant and defendant, or any disclaimers which may be attached to the defendant's product, should only be given the degree of attention which the typical customer would use.

[70] See eg *Coca Cola v Struthers* 1968 SLT 353; *Chocosuisse Union des Fabricants Suisses de Chocolat v Cadbury Ltd* [1999] RPC 826.
[71] See eg *Reckitt & Colman Properties Ltd v Borden Inc* [1990] 1 WLR 491; *Chocosuisse Union des Fabricants Suisses de Chocolat v Cadbury Ltd* [1999] RPC 826.
[72] [2001] RPC 922.
[73] Arsenal did not appeal against Laddie J's judgment on passing off. The case proceeded to other courts on issues about registered trade marks infringement: see further [2003] RPC 9 (ECJ); [2002] EWHC 2695 (Ch, Laddie J); [2003] RPC 39 (CA); and para 15.10ff. But note the *obiter* comment of Aldous LJ in the Court of Appeal that he was unconvinced by Laddie J's rejection of the passing off claim ([2003] RPC 39, para 70). In *L'Oreal SA v Bellure NV* [2007] RPC 14 Lewison J held that English law still requires misrepresentation and deception, and did not follow Aldous LJ in the *Arsenal* case. This view was upheld in the Court of Appeal ([2008] RPC 9).
[74] *Montgomery v Thompson* [1891] AC 217 per Lord Macnaghten at p 225.

■ *Haig & Co v Forth Blending Co* 1954 SC 35

This case concerned the use of 'dimple'-shaped bottles for whisky. The defender's labelling was different from the pursuer's and the bottles were closed with corks rather than patent stoppers. There was little likelihood of confusion while the bottles remained unopened. But the whisky was sold in pubs, with the bottles open and a pourer attached to the top. With evidence that even barmen might confuse the rival products in the atmosphere of a pub, it was held that the defender's bottle was likely to cause confusion sufficient to amount to passing off.

■ *Reckitt & Coleman Products v Borden Inc* [1990] RPC 341; [1990] 1 WLR 491; [1990] 1 All ER 873

This case concerned the lemon-shaped containers of lemon juice sold typically in supermarkets. The shape, size and colour of the containers were the same, but the neck-labels on the two products were different, and the word 'Jif' was embossed on the side of the plaintiffs' container. For colour photos of the competing 'lemons' see [1990] RPC at p 343. There was evidence that members of the public picking up the defendants' lemon juice from open shelves in supermarkets would think that they were getting Jif lemon juice. The trial judge, Walton J, had said: 'One is typically dealing with a shopper in a supermarket, in something of a hurry, accustomed to selecting between various brands when there is such a choice, but increasingly having to choose in relation to a wide range of items between the supermarket's 'own brand' and one other brand, and no more' ([1987] FSR 505 at p 512). Lord Oliver said: 'The crucial point of reference for the shopper requiring Jif juice is the natural lemon-shape and size which had for many years, with only immaterial exceptions, been utilised solely by the respondents in the context of this particular trade' ([1990] 1 WLR at p 503).

■ Joined Cases T-114/07 and 115/07 *Last Minute Network v OHIM—Last Minute Tour*

Article 18(4) of the Community Trade Mark Regulation[75] provides that the owner of a non-registered national trade mark may obtain the removal of a more recent Community trade mark where national law provides a right to prohibit the use of such a mark. The law of passing off was used in this way. OHIM had rejected a trade mark application in 2000 for 'lastminute.com'. Three years later, however, a trade mark was granted to another company for Last Minute Tour. The claimants sought a declaration before OHIM that the 'Last Minute Tour' trade mark was invalid. OHIM rejected this, on the basis that the relevant public, which it deemed to be the average consumer in the UK, would think that the 'Last Minute Tour' mark referred to a company offering last minute holidays, without considering that the offers originate from the proprietor of Lastminute.com. OHIM opined that the company lastminute.com had its reputation in 'lastminute.com' rather than the more generic phrase 'last minute' and that the '.com' element was distinctive and would concentrate the public's mind. However, the Court of First Instance, relying on *Reckitt & Coleman Products v Borden Inc* (above), stated that OHIM had misinterpreted national law by applying the wrong concept of the relevant public. Instead, the CFI ruled, OHIM should have applied the test with the relevant public being the claimant's customers, as the owner of the non-registered national mark. Furthermore, the CFI held that the law of passing off in the UK meant that a mark may acquire an independent reputation following from the way it is used, even where the mark is descriptive or lacking a distinctive

---

[75] Council Regulation (EC) No 40/94 of 20 December 1993 on the Community trade mark

character. Therefore, the CFI reasoned, OHIM had to consider the possibility that the words 'last minute' had an independent reputation solely due to their generic nature. The CFI concluded that OHIM's comparison of the marks was too formal. The application for cancellation of the Last Minute Tour registered trade mark was remitted back to OHIM for reconsideration. It should be noted, therefore, that confusion under trade mark law and misrepresentation under passing off do not necessarily lead to the same result.

17.42 The second point is, however, the consideration that if the defendant's activities would confuse or deceive only 'a moron in a hurry',[76] or 'a very small, unobservant section of society',[77] then there is no passing off. The court must adopt the stance of the reasonable person in all the circumstances (personified in one Scottish case as 'the average citizen of Kilmarnock'[78]) and consider the likelihood of his being confused. But it is important also to remember the diversity of customers in the marketplace, and that reasonableness is not some absolute objective standard in this context.

■ *Knight v Beyond Properties Pty Ltd* [2007] FSR 34 (Ch)

The 'Mythbusters' case (for the facts see above para 17.15). Had there still been goodwill in the children's book series, there would none the less probably not be confusion about the source of the very different 'dads and lads' TV series of the same name.

■ *William Grant & Sons Ltd v William Cadenhead Ltd* 1985 SC 121

This was a decision about passing off malt whisky. Interim interdict was refused on the ground, inter alios, that the 'cognoscenti' of malts would not be deceived by the defender's conduct.

But this test is inappropriate, since the market for malt whisky is not confined to the 'cognoscenti'. See further:

■ *Taittinger SA v Allbev Ltd* [1993] FSR 641

This was a decision about passing off a carbonated, non-alcoholic soft drink as champagne by naming it 'Elderflower Champagne', selling it in outlets which also sold champagne, in bottles of the same shape, size and colour as champagne, with labels and wired corks like those used for champagne. 'Elderflower Champagne' sold for £2.45 per bottle, while champagne was normally three or four times that amount at the time. It was held that there was passing off. The average person would not be deceived. 'But there is another section of the public. There is the simple unworldly man who has in mind a family celebration and knows that champagne is drunk for celebrations. He may know nothing of elderflower champagne as an old cottage drink. Seeing 'Elderflower' on a label with below the word 'Champagne' he may well suppose that he is seeing champagne. Since the simple man I have in mind will know little of champagne prices, he is likely to suppose that he has found champagne at a price of £2.45. I do not mean that I now refer to any majority part of the public or even to any very substantial section of the public, but to my mind there must be many members of the public who would suppose that the defendants' 'Elderflower' is champagne.' (per Sir Mervyn Davies, at p 654). In the Court of Appeal, Peter Gibson LJ quoted this passage and added (at p 667): 'It seems to me at least as

---

[76] *Morning Star Co-operative Society v Express Newspapers* [1979] FSR 113 per Foster J at 117.
[77] *Newsweek Inc v BBC* [1979] RPC 441 per Lord Denning MR, at p 447.
[78] *Dunlop Pneumatic Tyre Co v Dunlop Motor Co* 1907 SC (HL) 15 per Lord James of Hereford at 17.

likely that a not insignificant number of members of the public would think it had some association with champagne, if it was not actually champagne...It is right not to base any test on
whether a moron in a hurry would be confused, but it is proper to take into account the ignorant
and unwary.'

See further on this case para 17.55, below. See also:

■ *Chocosuisse Union des Fabricants Suisses de Chocolat v Cadbury Ltd* [1998]
RPC 117

This was a passing off action by manufacturers of Swiss chocolate against the UK company
Cadbury, which was marketing a new chocolate product called 'Swiss Chalet'. The report has
five pages of slightly fuzzy black and white photos of the chocolate wrappers at issue in this
case. It was held that there was sufficient confusion for passing off. 'I think it is clear that for
many people, including some of those for whom the words Swiss chocolate mean a product of
quality from Switzerland, the prominent use of the famous Cadbury name and get up will be
enough to prevent them thinking that Swiss Chalet is a Swiss chocolate. Furthermore there are
very many for whom the origin or connections of Swiss Chalet will be irrelevant....Many people, and particularly those who are more observant, would not be confused. For them the words
'Swiss Chalet' will signify nothing but a pretty sounding name for a bar of chocolate...However,
I have come to the conclusion that there are some who will be struck by the largest and most
prominent word on the defendant's packaging, namely 'Swiss', and think it is a reference to
an attribute of the product itself. I think it is likely that some will think that it is an indication
that the product is Swiss chocolate...It is likely that the number who think that will be smaller
than the number for whom there will be no confusion but, in my view, it is still likely to be a
substantial number.' (per Laddie J, at p 143).

In the Court of Appeal, Chadwick LJ said that the above conclusion of Laddie J on the evidence
before him 'cannot be regarded as perverse' ([1999] RPC at p 838).

Key points on confusion

- The confusion required must involve significant numbers of the public in the market
  where the parties operate

- Confusion may be shown by a variety of forms of evidence (eg surveys, trap orders)

- Likelihood of confusion is also a basis for preventive action

- The court must take account of conditions in the world where the goods or services are
  bought and sold—pubs, supermarkets, etc

- The approach should not be from the perspective of either the sophisticated or the
  stupid person; but the ignorant and unwary can be taken into account

---

'Common field of activity'

17.43   It has sometimes been said that there can be no relevant confusion between the parties unless
both are trading in a 'common field of activity'. The phrase was first used by Wynn Parry J in

McCulloch v May,[79] to define what he thought was an essential element for a successful passing off action. He went on to hold that, because there was no common field of activity between the radio broadcaster plaintiff (known as Uncle Mac) and the cereal manufacturer defendant, it was not passing off for the latter to use the name of the former's radio character (Uncle Mac) in connection with his product Puffed Wheat. The concept has been applied in a number of subsequent English cases, notably those relating to character and personality merchandising.[80] But it has also been criticised.[81] Probably it is best explained in the words of Oliver J in *Lyngstad v Anabas*: 'not a term of art…a convenient shorthand term for indicating…the need for a real possibility of confusion'.[82] This seems to be the present approach of the English courts, and although passing off actions may fail on the factual basis that there has been no confusion between two different types of business, it is clear that a common field of activity between the parties is not an essential element in law.[83] It is not referred to as such in the classic definitions of passing off (see above, paras 17.10–17.17), and indeed appears to have been rejected by Lord Diplock in *Advocaat*.[84]

17.44   The cases which recognise the variety of types of damage which can be done to goodwill apart from deprivation of customers—for instance, association with activities tending to lower a trader's reputation—provide good examples of situations where there has been no common field of activity.[85]

■ *Lego System A/S v Lego M Lemelstrich Ltd* [1983] FSR 155

A passing off action was successfully brought by a toy manufacturer against the manufacturer of irrigation equipment, concerning the use of the name LEGO. Falconer J held that the LEGO name was so well-known that even on irrigation equipment it was bound to be associated with the plaintiffs, whose goodwill might be damaged in respect of any move that they might make into the defendants' line of business. A distinction was drawn between the use of household names and other less well-known names and it was said that with regard to the former the absence of a common field of activity would probably be irrelevant.

17.45   The Scottish courts have not evolved any 'common field of activity' test. There have been cases where the fact that the parties were engaging in different types of business has led the court to hold no passing off.[86] But this has clearly been on the basis that no confusion had been shown, rather than on the assumption that there was a substantive rule precluding the possibility of passing off.

---

[79] [1947] 2 All ER 845.

[80] See *Wombles Ltd v Wombles Skips* [1975] FSR 488.

[81] See J Phillips and A Coleman, 'Passing off and the common field of activity' (1985) 101 LQR 242.

[82] [1977] FSR 62 at 67.

[83] See *Stringfellow v McCain Foods* [1984] FSR 413; *Miss World v James Street* [1981] FSR 309; *Mirage Studios v Counter-Feat Clothing* [1991] FSR 145.

[84] [1979] AC at 741–2.

[85] See *Dr Barnardo's Homes v Barnardo Amalgamated Industries* (1949) 66 RPC 103; *Annabels v Schock* [1972] RPC 838.

[86] *Dunlop Pneumatic Tyre Co v Dunlop Motor Co* 1907 SC (HL) 15 (tyre manufacturer and motor dealer); *Scottish Union & National Insurance* 1909 SC 318 (marine insurance and fire and life insurance); *Scottish Milk Marketing Board v Drybroughs* 1985 SLT 253 (milk products and beer); *Pebble Beach Co v Lombard Brands Ltd* 2002 SLT 1312 (golf course and whisky marketing).

> ## Key point on 'common field of activity'
>
> • It is not necessary that the parties to a passing off action be in the same field of business

Deception in foreign markets

17.46 It is possible to sue any party in this country (whether England or Scotland) who is involved as an exporter of the means of practising the deception in the foreign country, such as raw materials, distinctive shapes of bottles and labels. This follows from *Johnston & Co v Orr-Ewing & Co*,[87] in which the House of Lords held that an exporting business might restrain another from passing off its goods as the plaintiff's in a foreign market. The wrong lay, not in the actual misrepresentation in the foreign market, but in export of the goods from England, enabling the misrepresentation and deception in the foreign market. This has since been applied in several Scottish and English cases concerning the use of the trade name 'Scotch Whisky' in overseas markets, in which it was held that producers of Scotch whisky were entitled to prevent the export of whisky to be used abroad in the production and sale of blended drinks under the name 'Scotch Whisky'.[88] The *former* possibility of suing in the courts of this country in respect of activities in a foreign country (as distinct from exporting from Britain) constituting passing off, provided that the defendant was subject to a jurisdiction in the UK and that what was done was also a wrong under the law of the other country concerned,[89] was abolished by Part III of the Private International Law (Miscellaneous Provisions) Act 1995.[90] The general rule in such cases now is that, while an action may be raised in this country if there is jurisdiction over the defendant, the applicable law will be that of the country in which the activity took place.[91] The rule may be displaced if there are factors linking the case to another country (for example, England or Scotland) which make it *substantially* more appropriate for the law of that country to be the applicable law. The factors that may be taken into account include, in particular, factors relating to the parties, to any of the events which constitute the wrong in question, or to any of the circumstances or consequences of those events.[92]

> ## Key point on deception in foreign markets
>
> • It is sometimes possible to sue in England or Scotland in relation to passing off occurring overseas

---

[87] (1882) 7 App Cas 219.

[88] *John Walker v Ost* [1970] RPC 489; *John Walker v Douglas McGibbon* 1972 SLT 128; *John Walker & Sons Ltd v Douglas Laing & Co Ltd* 1993 SLT 156 (decided 19 Oct 1976); *White Horse Distillers Ltd v Gregson Associates Ltd* [1984] RPC 61; *William Grant & Sons Ltd v Glen Catrine Bonded Warehouse Ltd* 1995 SLT 936, aff'd 2001 SC 901, 2001 SLT 1419.

[89] *James Burroughs (Distillers) plc v Speymalt Whisky Distributors Ltd* 1989 SLT 561.

[90] c. 42, s 10.   [91] ibid, s 11.   [92] ibid, s 12.

Can A supply goods which enable B to pass other goods off as C's?

17.47   Despite the case law above on deception on foreign markets, it seems in general not to be passing off for a trader to supply another trader with the means enabling the latter to pass off other goods as those of a third trader. Examples of the situation might include the supply of labels, containers or raw materials which the second trader requires to pass off his goods. Such supply may be a civil wrong in extreme circumstances, such as where the supplier knew of his customer's intentions or has actively participated in the customer's deceptive marketing; but there is no obligation to ensure that supplies are not used deceptively.[93]

Substitution selling as passing off

17.48   The simple case of passing off involves the defendant passing off his own goods and services as those of the claimant. This includes responding to a customer's order for particular goods of another trader by sending one's own, unless the customer is aware of what is done.[94] However the law also provides a remedy where an intermediary between manufacturer or producer and the ultimate consumer, such as a retailer or publican, is responsible for presenting the goods or services as those of the claimant. It is passing off, for example, to sell beer as Bass when it is not.[95] The problem which a claimant may have to overcome here is the passage of his product name into the language as a generic term for that particular type of goods.[96]

> ### Key point on substitution selling
>
> * Supplying your own goods in response to an order of another's may be passing off

Inverse passing off: A passes off B's goods as his own

17.49   English law has had some difficulty with the situation where the defendant, instead of representing his goods or services to be those of another, claims that goods and services in fact produced by another come from him.

■ *Lucasfilm Ltd v Ainsworth* [2009] FSR 2

For the facts of this case (the 'Star Wars' case), see also paras 2.77, 2.86, 9.90 and 9.94. It illustrates well the distinction between classic and inverse passing off. L relied on the goodwill and reputation generated by the film, asserting that this extended to the business of licensing toys, models and other goods reproducing facets of the film, including the fictional characters in

---

[93]   *Paterson Zochonis Ltd v Merfarken Packaging Ltd* [1983] FSR 273.

[94]   *Purefoy Engineering Co Ltd v Sykes Boxall & Co Ltd* (1955) 72 RPC 89. Sending a catalogue or statement about the substitution with the goods comes too late; the customer should be told in advance.

[95]   *Bass v Laidlaw* (1886) 13R 898; *Thomson v Robertson* (1888) 15R 880; *Thomson v Dailly* (1897) 24R 1173; *Bayer v Baird* (1898) 25R 1142; (1898) 6 SLT 98; *Bass v Laidlaw* (1908) 16 SLT 660.

[96]   See eg *Havana Cigar & Tobacco Factories Ltd v Oddenino* [1924] 1 Ch 179 ('Corona' describes shape and size of cigars generally).

the film and their costumes. L's claim in passing off stemmed primarily from publicity on A's website which stressed the authenticity of his products (see para 172):

'Andrew Ainsworth and Shepperton Design Studios created the original helmets and armour for the greatest sci-fi fantasy film of all time. Now, almost 30 years on and for the FIRST time ever, YOU can own an exclusive 1:1 collectible replica of the original movie helmets. **Made by the original prop-maker from the original moulds** (*emboldening in original*). Produced and endorsed by Andrew Ainsworth at Shepperton Design Studios, these unique props offer collectors a rare opportunity of owning some of the most iconic designs of modern cinema. These unique collectibles are the ONLY helmets ever produced from the original moulds used to create the screen-used helmets...' (para 172).

L argued that this would mislead members of the public into thinking that it had licensed or somehow approved the manufacture and sale of the helmets and armour. Furthermore, it was claimed that members of the public would be misled into thinking that A was the creator or designer of the helmets and body armour. Finally, L alleged that A's claims amounted to inverse passing off because he was passing off L's work as his own. It was held that A's website did not either expressly or impliedly suggest that A had the consent of L. References to authenticity were to the products' fidelity to the original designs. Despite A claiming incorrectly that he had been the original creator of the designs, this did not amount to misrepresentation about licensing. As there was no relevant misrepresentation, the claim in passing off failed. The inverse passing off claim also failed. A had not pretended that L's goods actually belonged to him, or that the goods he was selling were L's. His statement as to the origin of the goods was true. Though it was false to state that the creation of the original design was A's, this did not amount to a misappropriation of L's goodwill sufficient to satisfy the requirements of a claim of passing off as any misstatement made related only to A himself and not the goods he was selling.

◼ *Bristol Conservatories v Conservatories Custom Built* [1989] RPC 455

The parties each supplied conservatories. CCB's salesmen showed photographs of BC's conservatories to potential customers, inducing them to think that they were CCB products. It was held at first instance that representing another's goods as your own was not passing off; but the decision was reversed in the Court of Appeal: there was passing off, but because CCB were representing that their own products were of the same quality as BC's (see para 17.50 below), rather than because the photographs showed CCB products.

There is Scottish authority, however, that this kind of inverse passing off is actionable as such.[97]

◼ *Henderson & Co v Munro & Co* (1905) 7 F 636

M had once been managing director of H &Co, artesian well engineers and mineral boring prospectors, and commenced a similar business, M & Co, on his own account. He issued an advertising circular referring to his experience with H & Co, giving lists of clients for whom wells had been put down, and contracts and work completed under his supervision. The circular did not state that the work had been done by H & Co when M was a managing director thereof. It was held that the circular was likely to mislead an ordinary reader into thinking that the work had been done by M & Co and not by H & Co, and that H & Co was entitled to an interdict against M & Co.

---

[97] *Henderson v Munro* (1905) 7F 636.

This appears to be in line with the definition of passing off in the *Advocaat* case: there is a misrepresentation, calculated to injure the goodwill of another trader in the sense that it is appropriated by the misrepresenting trader for his own purposes.[98]

Question

What is the difference between substitution selling (para 17.48) and 'inverse passing off'?

Is representing another's goods or services as yours passing off? See further on this H Carty, 'Inverse passing off: a suitable addition to passing off?' [1993] EIPR 370.

Passing off one quality of goods or services for another

17.50   The discussion thus far has been concerned with misrepresentations as to the trading source of goods or services. But it has been clear law since *Spalding v Gamage*[99] that misrepresentations as to the quality of goods or services may also constitute passing off, even when the trading source is accurately represented. If the source's goodwill would be damaged by its association with goods or services not of the quality with which it is identified in the market, then action may be taken.

■ *Spalding v Gamage* (1915) 32 RPC 273 (HL)

The plaintiffs manufactured and sold the 'Improved Sewn Orb' football. The defendants obtained a supply of the plaintiffs' rejected moulded balls, and sold them as 'Improved Sewn Orbs'. The House of Lords held that this was passing off.

■ *Lang Brothers v Goldwell* 1980 SC 237

It was held that misleading indicia of a Scottish origin—the appearance on the bottle label of the name 'Wee McGlen', a tartan background, and a thistle device, and the deployment in newspaper advertisements of a caricature of a be-tartaned Scotsman—used in the marketing of a whisky-based drink in fact manufactured in England, was passing off. This case goes further than many, however, as it is not clear that the quality in question was necessarily an exclusive part of the petitioners' goodwill. (cf *Wee McGlen Trade Mark* [1980] RPC 115.)

Selling secondhand goods as new is passing off, as is the sale of altered, repaired, modified or deteriorated goods.[100]

Discussion point   For answer guidance visit www.oxfordtextbooks.co.uk/orc/macqueen2e/

How may this form of passing off be linked to the 'extended' form of the action (above, para 17.20; see also below, para 17.55)?

---

[98] See further J Griffiths, 'Misattribution and misrepresentation: the claim for reverse passing off as 'paternity' right' [2006] IPQ 34.

[99] (1915) 32 RPC 273 (HL).   [100] *Gillette v Franks* (1924) 41 RPC 499.

17.51   A recurrent problem in this area of passing off concerns *parallel importing*, where goods are sold
by the manufacturer under the same trade mark in several countries around the world, and then
some sold in one country are imported to another for re-sale there, usually at a price lower than
that at which they are sold ordinarily in the importing country. Where there is a difference in
quality between the imported and the 'home' goods, the English courts have held that putting
the imports on the market may be passing off.[101] But where the goods are of the same quality,
then it is irrelevant that the imported goods were made by another company in the same group
as the company raising the action in this country; no deception as to source or quality can be
said to have occurred.[102]

17.52   It is also possible to pass off services as having qualities which they do not possess. Thus it is
passing off for a retailer to state that he is an authorised dealer in a particular product when he
is not and is unable to offer the services which such a dealer should do.[103] Unauthorised 'insert
advertising' in newspapers is passing off as an implied representation that it has been vetted by
the newspaper publishers in accordance with its usual procedures for the acceptance of advertisements.[104] The quality in question might be that of being connected to or under the control of the claimant, where that party enjoys a good reputation of some kind. Thus the British
Legion, a charitable organisation for the benefit of First World War veterans, could prevent a
local social club calling itself 'British Legion Club (Street)' when it had no connection with the
Legion.[105] But the representation must be such as to suggest a connection in which the claimant has responsibility for or control over the quality of what the defendant offers. This can also
apply to goods, as the following, more recent cases show.

■ *Harrods v Harrodian School* [1996] RPC 697

Harrods, the well-known London department store, sued a school which was operating from
a site known as 'The Harrodian Club' (because the store had once run a social club there for
its employees under that name). The aim of the action was to stop the school calling itself 'The
Harrodian School'. It was held that there was no passing off. Millett LJ said (at p 713): 'It is not
in my opinion sufficient to demonstrate that there must be a connection between the defendant and the plaintiff, if it is not a connection which would lead the public to suppose that the
plaintiff has made himself responsible for the quality of the defendant's goods or services.
A belief that the plaintiff has sponsored or given financial support to the defendant will not
ordinarily give the public that impression.'

■ *Arsenal FC plc v Reed* [2001] RPC 922

R had sold merchandise outside the Arsenal football club ground for about 30 years. The merchandise bore insignia associating it with the club, such as its name, nickname ('the Gunners'),
its crest and a logo of a cannon. From about 1987 the club began to license traders (but not R)
to use these insignia on merchandise, which was then marketed as 'official' club merchandise.
The club sued R in passing off to prevent his continued unlicensed operations. It was held that
there was no passing off. Use of the Arsenal insignia did not carry any message of trade origin.
Some fans wanted to purchase only 'official' merchandise, but it did not follow that all Arsenal
memorabilia would be taken by fans to have come from or be licensed by the club. There would

---

[101] *Wilkinson Sword v Cripps & Lee* [1982] FSR 16; *Colgate-Palmolive v Markwell Finance* [1989] RPC 497.
[102] *Revlon Inc v Cripps & Lee* [1980] FSR 85.   [103] *Sony v Saray* [1983] FSR 302.
[104] *Associated Newspapers plc v Insert Media Ltd* [1991] FSR 380.
[105] *British Legion v British Legion Club (Street)* (1931) 63 RPC 555.

have to be something more than the mere use of the insignia to make that statement, and here R actually made clear that his activities were unofficial.[106]

 Discussion point   For answer guidance visit www.oxfordtextbooks.co.uk/orc/macqueen2e/

Consider the above cases in the light of *Irvine v Talksport* [2002] 2 All ER 414 (above, para 17.34). Are they mutually consistent?

Key points on misrepresentations about the quality of one's goods or services

- Falsely representing one's goods or services as possessed of qualities associated in the market with another trader may amount to passing off
- This can include cases where the representation (express or implied) is that the claimant exercises some form of quality control over the defendant's goods or services

Comparative advertising

17.53   It is generally legitimate for a manufacturer or retailer marketing goods or services to make comparisons of his product with others, or to draw attention to the compatibility of his product with that of another trader, for example as a replacement or an additional part. In no sense is the advertiser stating that his goods come from another trading source. Indeed, the whole purpose of comparative advertising in particular is to differentiate competing products in the public mind. In the *Advocaat* case Lord Diplock remarked that:

> 'advertisements are not on affidavit; exaggerated claims by a trader about the quality of his wares, assertions that they are better than those of his rivals, even though he knows this to be untrue, have been permitted by the common law as venial 'puffing' which gives no cause of action to a competitor even though he can show that he has suffered actual damage in his business as a result'. (*Erven Warnink v Townend* [1979] AC 731 at p 742.)

But if the comparison involves making specific and false claims of equivalent or greater quality for the advertised product, or false denigration of the quality of its rival, then the damage to the competitor's goodwill arising from the misrepresentation may be remedied through passing off. The situation seems to fall within the scope of the general tests stated in the *Advocaat* case (above, para 17.11), in that they are misrepresentations calculated to damage the goodwill of another trader. Lord Diplock's further remarks in the case, quoted above, are immediately followed by a passage in which he discusses how the common law may develop following the general policy line of Parliament to protect consumers by imposing higher standards on traders. Most of the cases on this matter to date have concerned infringement of registered trade marks,[107] but there are some examples in passing off:

---

[106]   Note however the *obiter* comment of Aldous LJ in the Court of Appeal that he was unconvinced by Laddie J's rejection of the passing off claim ([2003] RPC 39, para 70), commented upon by S Middlemiss and S Warner, 'Is there still a hole in this bucket? Confusion and misrepresentation in passing off' (2006) 1 JIPLP 131, and C Wadlow, 'One more outing for *Arsenal*: a case of dilution or one for restitution?' (2006) 1 JIPLP 143. See further n 73 above.

[107]   See above, para 15.130ff.

■ *McDonalds Hamburgers Ltd v Burger King UK Ltd* [1986] FSR 45 (aff'd on other points [1987] FSR 112)

McDonalds sold hamburgers called 'Big Macs'. Burger King advertised their competing product (the 'Whopper'), using the slogan 'It's Not Just Big Mac'. Evidence showed that the public thought this meant that Big Macs were available at Burger King and that they could go to Burger King stores for them. It was held that, as the defendant's advertisement referring to the plaintiff's hamburgers had failed adequately to distinguish the two products from each other, there was passing off. The decision is not so much about false comparisons, however, as about the borderline between comparing products and representing that they come from the same trade source.

■ *Kimberly Clark v Fort Sterling* [1997] FSR 877

FS promoted their 'Nouvelle' toilet roll with the phrase, 'Softness guaranteed (or we'll exchange it for Andrex)'. It was held that this was passing off; there was a misrepresentation in that the statement would induce customers to think, wrongly, that Nouvelle was an Andrex brand.

Professional associations

17.54   Somewhat akin to the cases on misleading representations as to quality of goods and services are the decisions holding that misleading use of initials and letters which indicate membership of professional associations is passing off, for example, BMA for the British Medical Association.[108] Thus in Scotland members of the Corporation of Accountants Ltd and the Corporation itself were held not entitled to use the letters 'CA' and 'MCA' as an abbreviation of the qualification to be obtained from the Corporation, since the public associated them with the qualification of the members of the Society of Accountants in Edinburgh.[109]

Exercise

Consider whether pre-sale misrepresentations can be remedied in passing off. See B Allgrove and P O'Byrne, 'Pre-sale misrepresentations in passing off: an idea whose time has come or unfair competition by the back door?' (2006) 1 JIPLP 413.

Key points on misrepresentations as to quality

- While comparative advertising is generally legitimate, specific and false claims of equivalent or greater quality for one's own goods or services, or false denigration of a competitor's, can be passing off
- False use in business of initials and letters indicating a status or membership of a professional association is passing off

---

[108] *British Medical Association v Marsh* (1931) 48 RPC 565.
[109] *Society of Accountants in Edinburgh v Corporation of Accountants* (1893) 20R 750; *Corporation of Accountants v Society of Accountants in Edinburgh* (1903) 11 SLT 424.

Improper use of descriptive class designation: extended passing off

17.55 A very particular type of misrepresentation is found in the 'product goodwill' or 'extended passing off' cases, where what is protected is the goodwill attached to products of a particular kind rather than to a specific trader (see above, para 17.20). In such cases the representation is that the product in question belongs to a particular class of goods, and arises through the use of a name for that class which is recognised by the public as identifying goods of that class and no others. The development of the law began in *Bollinger v Costa Brava Wine Co*.[110]

■ *Bollinger v Costa Brava Wine Co* [1961] 1 Ch 262

The producers of champagne sought and obtained an injunction to prevent the defendants from marketing a sparkling wine as 'Spanish Champagne'. The judge held that the word 'Champagne' could be used accurately only of sparkling wines produced in the Champagne district of France and that this was how it had come to be understood in the market. The name was thus a source of goodwill to those who produced such a drink. The inaccurate application of the name to a drink which lacked the necessary characteristics was therefore a misrepresentation which injured the goodwill of the genuine trader, and so constituted passing off.

Bollinger was approved and applied in a number of subsequent cases: for example, regarding the use of 'Sherry',[111] and 'Scotch whisky',[112] as well as further cases on 'Champagne'.[113] In *Argyllshire Weavers v Macaulay Tweeds*,[114] it was held that mill-spun tweed could not be marketed as Harris tweed. Full confirmation of *Bollinger's* place in the law was finally given by the House of Lords in *Erven Warnink v Townend* (the *Advocaat* case):[115]

■ *Erven Warnink v Townend* [1979] AC 731

This case concerned the use of 'Advocaat' as a name for an alcoholic drink. An English firm was enjoined from marketing its product as 'Keeling's Old English Advocaat', since the drink was made up, not of brandewijn, egg yolks and sugar, but rather of dried egg powder mixed with Cyprus sherry. It was also ruled that a name's lack of geographical connotations was immaterial to this form of misrepresentation; the action lay because the defendant's product was not made up of the correct ingredients, not because the correct ingredients came from a particular locality.

Since the Advocaat case, the most important decisions are *Taittinger SA v Allbev Ltd*[116] (the *Elderflower Champagne* case) and *Chocosuiise Union des Fabricants Suisses de Chocolat v Cadbury*,[117] on Swiss chocolate. In the *Elderflower Champagne* case, where the eponymous product was sold at a very low price but in a get-up akin to that of real champagne, it was held that the misrepresentation was either that the drink was champagne or that it was in some way associated with the French champagne houses. In *Chocosuisse* it was held that 'Swiss chocolate' was a designation of a particular class of chocolate which could only be used by manufacturers of chocolate

[110] [1961] 1 Ch 262.   [111] *Vine Products v Mackenzie* [1969] RPC 1.
[112] *John Walker & Sons v Henry Ost* [1970] 1 WLR 917; *John Walker v Douglas McGibbon* 1972 SLT 128; *Lang Brothers v Goldwell* 1980 SC 237.
[113] *Bulmer (H P) Ltd v Bollinger (J) SA* [1978] RPC 79; *Taittinger SA v Allbev Ltd* [1993] FSR 641.
[114] 1965 SLT 21.   [115] [1979] AC 731.
[116] [1993] FSR 641.   [117] [1998] RPC 117, aff'd [1999] RPC 826.

made in Switzerland in accordance with certain standards laid down by regulation in that country, meaning that its use on a non-conforming product was a misrepresentation. The case is also important for its discussion of the nature of the confusion which must be caused by the misrepresentation to make it actionable (see above, para 17.42).

> ## Key point on misrepresentation in extended passing off cases
>
> * In such cases the representation is that the product in question belongs to a particular class of goods, and arises through the use of a name for that class which is recognised by the public as identifying goods of that class and no others

Authorship and personality

17.56   It is passing off for the author of any creative work to attach to it the name of another author, perhaps especially if that name is a nom de plume.[118] It may also be noted that the actors' trade union Equity insists that none of its members may use the name of another professionally, so possibly it is passing off for an actor to use the professional name of another. There may be passing off if the fanciful name of a musical band is used by another band.[119] The unauthorised association with goods or services of the real name of a living person (false endorsement) may constitute such an appropriation of the goodwill attached to the name as to be passing off.

■ *Wilkie v McCulloch* (1823) 2 S 413

A early Scottish case where a firm was interdicted from representing that ploughs were made under the inspection and authority of an individual who had developed a new kind of plough.

■ *Samuelson v Producers Distributing Co* [1932] 1 Ch 201

A more recent English case where the author of a highly successful dramatic sketch was able to prevent a film being publicised as a version of his sketch.

■ *Clark v Associated Newspapers Ltd* [1998] 1 All ER 959

A weekly feature in the London *Evening Standard* was entitled 'Alan Clark's Secret Political Diary' and bore a photograph of Alan Clark, the well-known MP and author of notorious published diaries. But the feature was actually a work of imagination by a *Standard* journalist. It was held that there was passing off by the linking of the work with Clark, with not enough being done by the newspaper to remove the possibility of confusion in the mind of the typical reader. See also para 3.47 on moral right aspects of this case.

---

[118] *Marengo v Daily Sketch* (1948) 65 RPC 242 (HL). Note also the right to prevent false attribution in CDPA 1988, s 85 (see above para 3.47).
[119] *Hines v Winnick* [1947] 1 Ch 708 (Doctor Crock and his Crackpots); *Treadwell's Drifters Inc v RCL Ltd* 1996 SLT 1048 (The Drifters).

■ *Irvine v Talksport Ltd* [2002] 2 All ER 414 (Laddie J); [2003] EWCA Civ 423

A promotional brochure for Talksport contained a manipulated image of the racing driver Eddie Irvine apparently listening to the radio station. It was held that this was a representation of an endorsement of the radio station by Irvine, and constituted passing off.

The authority of some other decisions in this area may now be doubtful:

■ *Serville v Constance* [1954] 1 All ER 662

The welterweight boxing champion of Trinidad sought to enjoin the defendant from passing himself off as holder of that title. His action failed on the basis of lack of reputation and lack of confusion in the UK; however, the case seems to leave open the possibility that, if these elements had been present, the defendant would have been held to have been passing himself off as the plaintiff.

■ *Sim v H J Heinz & Co* [1959] 1 WLR 313

The defendant used an unauthorised imitation of the voice of a well-known actor (Alastair Sim) to advertise its goods, but the court refused an interlocutory injunction. Possibly with the wider view now current of what constitutes a misrepresentation and notwithstanding the character merchandising cases (above, para 17.30–17.33), this case might be decided differently today.

In the USA, the singer and comedian Bette Midler was held able to prevent unauthorised imitation and use of her voice in television commercials.[120]

 Discussion point   For answer guidance visit www.oxfordtextbooks.co.uk/orc/macqueen2e/

How far does and should the law of passing off go in offering protection to aspects of individual personality against use by others constituting misrepresentation? What aspects of personality in addition to name, designation and voice used in one's trade or profession might be covered?

Damage

Damage to goodwill

17.57 The courts have recognised a variety of ways in which the goodwill of a trader may be damaged by the representations of another trader in connection with his goods and services. The most obvious form of damage is loss of custom, actual or potential, arising from confusion. Closely related to this is the attraction of custom by the defendant using the goodwill associated with the claimant. It may not be possible to show that the customer bought goods from the defendant which he would otherwise have bought from the claimant—for example, because the parties do not trade in the same field—but nonetheless an action of passing off will lie if

---

[120] *Midler v Ford Motor Co Inc* 849 F 2d 460 (1988).

the customer will associate the goods with the claimant to his potential detriment.[121] In *Knight v Beyond Properties Pty Ltd*,[122] the 'Mythbusters' case (for the facts see above para 17.15), it was recognised that the claimant might have been able to claim for loss of opportunity to convert his books into a TV series had the evidence supported that as a real possibility (which it did not).

■ *Annabel's (Berkeley Square) Ltd v Shock* [1972] RPC 838

Annabel's was a well-known nightclub. S started an unconnected escort agency under the same name. It was held that there was passing off. Escort agencies did not have a good public image and, while S's agency was above reproach, it was inevitable that the two businesses would be associated in the public mind and that the nightclub's good reputation would be damaged, attracting to it the wrong kind of goodwill.

17.58   Damage to trading relationships with business customers, suppliers, distributors and retailers, which have been recognised as part of goodwill, can also result from passing off activities, and so be a basis for action.[123]

> ### Key points on main forms of damage relevant to passing off
>
> - The main traditional forms of damage relevant to passing off are:
> - Loss of custom, actual and potential
> - Attraction of custom by defendant using claimant's goodwill
> - Damage to claimant's reputation, and thence goodwill, through false associations
> - Damage to claimant's trading relations

Dilution of a name

17.59   The defendant's activities may have the effect of diminishing goodwill by lessening the distinctive associations and reputation of the claimant's device ('dilution').[124] This has been especially important in the product goodwill cases (above, paras 17.20, 17.55), where the action of passing off has been used to ensure that a name retains a particular meaning in the market and cannot be attached to any other product.[125] Here again it may well not be possible to show that the claimant has been deprived of custom, but the reputation of his product is endangered by the defendant's activities and so there can be a remedy. This kind of damage is often referred to as 'dilution'. The scope of dilution as a kind of damage has been the subject of controversy in the courts.[126]

[121] See eg *Eastman Photographic Materials Ltd v Griffiths Cycle Corp* (1898) 15 RPC 105; *Walter v Ashton* [1902] 2 Ch 282; *Harrods Ltd v R Harrod Ltd* (1924) 41 RPC 74; *Dr Barnardos Homes v Barnardo Amalgamated Industries* (1949) 66 RPC 103; *Annabels (Berkeley Square) Ltd v Schock* [1972] RPC 838; *Dash Ltd v Philip King Tailoring Ltd* 1988 GWD 7-304 (rev'd on other points 1989 SLT 39); *Phones4u Ltd v Phone4u.co.uk Internet Ltd* [2007] RPC 5.
[122] [2007] FSR 34 (Ch).
[123] See eg *Chelsea Man Menswear Ltd v Chelsea Girl Ltd* [1987] RPC 189; *Highland Distilleries Co plc v Speymalt Whisky Distributors Ltd* 1985 SC 1; *Associated Newspapers plc v Insert Media Ltd* [1991] FSR 380.
[124] See eg *Rolls Royce v Dodd* [1981] FSR 517.
[125] See above all *Erven Warnink v Townend* [1979] AC 731; also *Macallan-Glenlivet plc v Speymalt Whisky Distributors Ltd* 1983 SLT 348; and *Highland Distilleries Co plc v Speymalt Whisky Distributors* Ltd 1985 SC 1.
[126] See further H Carty, 'Heads of damage in passing off' [1996] EIPR 487; A Murray, 'A distinct lack of goodwill' [1997] EIPR 345.

■ *Taittinger SA v Allbev Ltd* [1993] FSR 641

This was the so-called *Elderflower Champagne* case (see above, paras 17.42, 17.55). In this case, only some of the public would be deceived by the defendant's use of the name 'Elderflower Champagne' that his product was champagne. But the judges of the Court of Appeal all thought that the damage extended beyond loss of custom to the blurring or erosion of the uniqueness attendant upon the word 'champagne'; to a gradual debasement or dilution not demonstrable in figures of lost sales, but diminishing the goodwill. The clearest statement was by Sir Thomas Bingham MR (at p 678): 'Any product which is not Champagne but is allowed to describe itself as such must inevitably, in my view, erode the singularity and exclusiveness of the description Champagne and so cause the first plaintiffs damage of an insidious but serious kind.... [A] reference to champagne imports nuances of quality and celebration, a sense of something privileged and special. But this is the reputation which the Champagne houses have built up over the years, and in which they have a property right. It is not in my view unfair to deny the defendants the opportunity to exploit, share or (in the vernacular) cash in on that reputation, which they have done nothing to establish. It would be very unfair to allow them to do so if the consequence was, as I am satisfied it would be, to debase and cheapen that very reputation.'

But contrast Millett LJ in:

■ *Harrods Ltd v Harrodian School Ltd* [1996] RPC 697

An action by the well-known London department store, Harrods, to prevent a school from trading as the 'Harrodian School' was unsuccessful (see above, para 17.52). On damage and the possibility of dilution of the Harrods name, Millett LJ said (at p 716): 'To date the law has not sought to protect the value of the brand name as such, but the value of the goodwill which it generates; and it insists on proof of confusion to justify its intervention. But the erosion of the distinctiveness of a brand name which occurs by reason of its degeneration into common use as a generic term is not necessarily dependent on confusion at all.... I have an intellectual difficulty in accepting the concept that the law insists upon the presence of both confusion and damage and yet recognises as sufficient a head of damage which does not depend upon confusion. Counsel for the plaintiffs relied strongly on the possibility of damage of this nature, but it is in my opinion not necessary to consider it further in the present case. There is no danger of "Harrods" becoming a generic term for a retail emporium in the luxury class, and if such a danger existed the use of a different name in connection with an institution of a different kind would not advance the process.' Note however Sir Michael Kerr, dissenting, at p 726: 'The use of the adjectival form of their own name will become lost to the plaintiffs; but the false impression of a connection between the plaintiffs and unconnected businesses using the name 'Harrodian' will proliferate. The plaintiffs' reputation will become involved with their fortunes or misfortunes, and become a hostage to them.'

 Question

How far, if at all, does 'dilution' differ from the more traditional forms of damage recognised in passing off actions?

Does the concept of dilution blur the distinction between 'goodwill' and 'reputation' (above, para 17.14)?

Dilution of a personal reputation

17.60   In a judgment later approved by the Court of Appeal, Laddie J in *Irvine v Talksport Ltd* extended the notion of dilution to the personal reputation of a well-known public figure whose image had been included without authorisation in a trade promotion (for the facts see above para 17.34). He said:

> 'If someone acquires a valuable reputation or goodwill, the law of passing off will protect it from unlicensed use by other parties. Such use will frequently be damaging in the direct sense that it will involve selling inferior goods or services under the guise that they are from the claimant. But the action is not restricted to protecting against that sort of damage. The law will vindicate the claimant's exclusive right to the reputation or goodwill. It will not allow others to so use goodwill as to reduce, blur or diminish its exclusivity. It follows that it is not necessary to show that the claimant and the defendant share a common field of activity or that sales of products or services will be diminished either substantially or directly, at least in the short term. Of course there is still a need to demonstrate a misrepresentation because it is that misrepresentation which enables the defendant to make use or take advantage of the claimant's reputation.'[127]

In cases of this kind there is again no loss of custom to the party raising the action, merely an insidious diminution of the person's reputation and its exclusivity as a trading commodity.

Key points on dilution as a form of damage

- Dilution is a form of damage in which the defendant's activities in some way weaken or diminish the distinctive associations and reputation of the claimant's marketing device (typically a name), without necessarily depriving the claimant of customers

- Dilution appears to be important in 'product goodwill' or 'extended passing off' cases, but has also been deployed in the false endorsement case to protect the personal reputation of a public figure

- Dilution is a controversial form of damage, since it seems to weaken the requirement of goodwill and lead passing off into the protection of reputation

---

Damage need only be prospective

17.61   It is clear law that in general damage (of whatever kind) need not have been actually suffered before the action is brought. An injunction or an interdict can certainly be obtained because damage is reasonably to be anticipated. It has been said that there is a presumption of damage in cases where the defendant has sold goods as those of the claimant.[128] In cases of fraud, the burden of proving damage will be light.[129]

Defences

17.62   All the requirements of passing off as discussed so far in this chapter may be present, yet the party sued may have a defence. Some defences are of course implicit in the requirements of

---

[127] [2002] 2 All ER 414, para 38.   [128] See *Draper v Trist* (1939) 56 RPC 429.
[129] *Bulmer v Bollinger* [1978] RPC 79.

passing off, for example, lack of goodwill, absence of confusion, that one is making honest use of one's own name. But there are some defences in passing off which arise even if all the other requirements of the claim are met. The scope of some of these is rather uncertain: for example, parody, as when it was held that there was no passing off by title in a film called 'Alternative Miss World' satirising the well-known beauty competition.[130] But a defence of parody was of no avail in *Clark v Associated Newspapers Ltd*,[131] where the parodist had not done enough to prevent confusion as to the authorship of the work amongst readers; while in *Irvine v Talksport Ltd*[132] the suggestion that the manipulated picture of Irvine listening intently to a radio marked with Talksport insignia would be seen as a joke by its intended audience was rejected by the court. One of the most important defences in practice is *delay*—technically known as acquiescence, or taciturnity and mora—on the part of the person raising the action of passing off: that is to say, despite knowing of the other party's activities, taking no steps to prevent them for a significant period of time. Thus, for example, in the extended passing off case about sherry, the plaintiffs were unable to prevent the continued use of the phrase 'British sherry', which had been in use for many years,[133] while in *Bulmer v Bollinger*[134]champagne houses were unable, after 18 years of use, to prevent cider being marketed as 'champagne perry'. In *Arsenal FC plc v Reed*,[135] the defendant traded openly outside the Arsenal ground for 30 years, and in such circumstances, especially when there was no evidence of actual confusion in the marketplace for the goods in question, the failure of the club's passing off action was unsurprising.[136] An important recent discussion of the defence is in a Scottish case where it was rejected.

■ *William Grant & Sons Ltd v Glen Catrine Bonded Warehouse Ltd* 2001 SC 901

WG sought to prevent GC from using the name 'Grant's' in connection with the sale of gin, vodka and other alcoholic drinks. WG had been selling whisky products under the name 'Grant's' since the 1920s, and gin and vodka since 1963. GC began using the name on gin in 1972 and on vodka in 1974. From 1986 GC's sales began to increase dramatically. GC believed they could use the name 'Grant's' as it had been the name of a company they acquired in 1972. GC defended WG's claim of passing off on the basis of acquiescence. The action was raised in 1992, although there had been communication between the parties since WG became aware of GC's activities in 1986. It was held that WG were not barred by acquiescence from a remedy for passing off. GC had exploited the name 'Grant's', not because they believed WG had consented, but because they believed they had a historical right to use the name. Further, acquiescence was being invoked to bar action in respect of future wrongs (that is, continued passing off), but the evidence did not justify an inference that WG had consented irrevocably to GC passing their products off as WG's in the future. Knowledge was not the same as acquiescence. The court, although relying principally on Scottish authorities on personal bar (anglicé estoppel),[137] found support for its approach in the English case of *Farmers Build Ltd v Carier Bulk Materials Handling Ltd* [1999] RPC 461 (see para 9.35).

---

[130] *Miss World v James Street* [1981] FSR 309.   [131] [1998] RPC 261.

[132] [2003] EWCA Civ 423.   [133] *Vine Products Ltd v Mackenzie* [1969] RPC 1.

[134] [1971] FSR 405.   [135] [2001] RPC 922.

[136] It is therefore difficult to see why Aldous LJ in the Court of Appeal was unconvinced (*obiter*) by Laddie J's rejection of the passing off claim ([2003] RPC 39, para 70). In *L'Oreal SA v Bellure NV* [2007] RPC 14 Lewison J holds that English law still requires misrepresentation and deception and does not follow Aldous LJ in the *Arsenal* case. This view was upheld in the Court of Appeal ([2008] RPC 9).

[137] On this aspect of the case see E Reid, 'Acquiescence in the air' 2002 JR 191.

Question

What constitutes acquiescence or delay sufficient to prevent a party succeeding in a passing off action?

Key point on defences

- A defendant who can show that his activity went on for many years unchecked before the raising of the action has a good defence against an action of passing off
- The technical names for this defence are *acquiescence, taciturnity, mora* and *delay*
- It follows that claimants should take prompt action when they learn of possible passing off

Cyber-squatters and passing off

17.63   An important development is the use of passing off to control the phenomenon known as 'cyber-squatting'. This is an example of a commercial practice made possible by the Internet, and is also revealing about the sluggish response of major British companies to the trading potential of the Internet. Domain names identifying and locating organisations on the Internet are a crucial part of what is needed to do business there. There is a non-official, self-regulatory system for allocating domain names, which operates on a first-come, first-served basis (see above, para 16.23ff). In the 1990s businesses were established which registered domain names comprising well-known trade marks and corporate and other names without the consent of the person owning the trade mark or goodwill in the name in question. These businesses then offered the domain names to the owners of the trade marks or goodwill, usually for very substantial sums, but typically did not themselves make much, if any, commercial use of the domain name on the Internet. It was far from clear that this activity constituted infringement of any trade mark rights there might be in the name, although the phrase 'cyber-squatting' conveyed a sense that the businesses concerned had occupied the name without permission, and only because the real owners had left this particular part of their property vacant. So the owners turned to the law of passing off as a way of evicting the squatters. They gained their way in *British Telecommunications plc v One in a Million Ltd*.[138]

■ *British Telecommunications plc v One in a Million Ltd* [1999] 1 WLR 903 (CA)

One in a Million were dealers in domain names who had registered the following names; *ladbrokes.com; sainsbury.com; sainsburys.com; j-sainsbury.com; marksandspencer.com; cellnet.net; bt.org; virgin.org*. Other dealers who were co-defendants in the case had registered *marksandspencer.co.uk; britishtelecom.co.uk; britishtelecom.net*, and *britishtelecom.com*. They were sued for passing off by Marks and Spencer plc, J Sainsbury plc, Virgin Enterprises Ltd, British Telecommunications plc, Telecom Cellular Radio Ltd and Ladbrokes plc. The Court of Appeal held that there was passing off and that the plaintiffs were entitled to *quia timet* injunctions. Analysis of previous case law

[138]   [1999] 1 WLR 903 (CA).

showed that an injunction could be granted against a defendant equipped with or intending to equip another with an instrument of fraud. A name which would, by reason of its similarity to the name of another, inherently lead to passing off, is such an instrument. The court could infer an intention to appropriate goodwill or enable others to do so, even if there was a possibility that such appropriation would not take place (the importance of this point being that there was little evidence that the 'cyber-squatters' intended actually to trade under the domain names or to sell the names to anyone other than the plaintiffs, although there were threats, express or implied, to do so contained in the communications between them and the owners).

17.64 The decision builds on earlier cases, mostly concerned with exporting material which would be used in the destination country to pass off goods as coming from a particular source in this country (above, para 17.46). In general, supply of the means by which another trader might pass off goods or services—for example, providing materials for bottling or labelling—is not passing off unless there is fraud or at any rate intention and knowledge on the part of the supplier (see para 17.47). The difficulty in the *One in a Million* case is that the domain names held by the cybersquatters were of very little value in the hands of anyone other than the cyber-squatters and the companies whose names had been used. Had the cyber-squatters attempted themselves to trade under the domain names, or sold them to third parties so to trade, then there would have been passing off in the ordinary sense. So it is difficult to see how the cyber-squat is really analogous to the earlier 'instruments of fraud' cases. The decision is also difficult to reconcile with the classic definitions of passing off by Lords Diplock, Fraser and Oliver quoted at the outset of this chapter (see paras 17.10, 17.11). The court clearly did not like the behaviour of the cyber-squatters, in particular the threatening way in which they advanced their offers to sell the domain names to the well-known companies; but in order to remedy that wrong, the law of passing off was probably extended further than ever before.

 Question

What is cyber-squatting? Does this activity constitute passing off as usually understood?

17.65 The courts of both England and Scotland have however followed the *One in a Million* decision without much quibble.[139] Scottish cases, all unreported, have dealt with cyber-squatting in relation to the domain names for Scottish Widows, the leading insurance company, and Haggis Backpackers, an Edinburgh touring hostel. In *easyJet v Dainty*,[140] the defendant registered the domain name *easyRealestate.co.uk* and set up a website offering estate agency services; but he did no significant business through the site. He attempted to interest easyJet in his proposition, made use of 'easy-' style livery on the website, and ultimately attempted to sell his domain name to easyJet while threatening to sell to third parties. He was held liable for passing off, which was constituted in both its traditional form and in its 'instruments of deception' form. The judge ordered that the defendant's domain name be transferred to easyJet. In *Phones 4U Ltd v Phone4U. co.uk Internet Ltd*,[141] the defendant commenced Internet trading under the domain name as well

---

[139] For critical commentary see C Thorne and S Bennett, 'Domain names—Internet warehousing: has protection of well known names on the Internet gone too far?' [1998] EIPR 468; C Colston, 'Passing off: the right solution to domain names?' [2000] LMCLQ 523; H Carty, 'Passing off and instruments of deception: the need for clarity' [2003] EIPR 188.

[140] [2002] FSR 6. See also *Easygroup IP Licensing Ltd v Sermbezis* [2003] All ER (D) 25 (car rental websites).

[141] [2007] RPC 5 (CA). See also *Tesco Stores Ltd v Elogicom Ltd* [2007] FSR 4 (Ch).

as offering it for sale after learning of the claimant's existence and use of the trade name; the Court of Appeal thought this not materially different from the *One in a Million* case.

17.66   *One in a Million* was distinguished, however, in *French Connection v Sutton*.[142] French Connection, a chain of fashion stores, began in 1997 to use the word FCUK in a widespread advertising campaign as well as registering it as a trade mark. Sutton, an Internet consultant, registered *FCUK.com* as a domain name, and set up a website at which he would advertise his consultancy. This was challenged by French Connection on the basis of the *One in a Million* case, and the evidence showed that Sutton had subsequently tried to sell his domain name to the company. However Rattee J refused summary judgment, on the basis that FCUK was not a household name—or indeed the name of anything—in any way like the names involved in the *One in a Million* case; Sutton's website had offered services quite different from those of French Connection; and the registration of FCUK as a domain name had not been merely for the purpose of extracting money from French Connection but had rather been to draw the attention of Internet users to Sutton's site:

> 'According to the defendant's evidence, the letters FCUK together in that order was a well-known alternative used by people on the Internet as a means of circumventing various filters which were imposed by certain Internet Service Providers to prevent the use of the expletive FUCK in the material placed on the Internet. It is also the defendant's evidence that at the time he registered his domain name and, I think, still, FCUK is also known to a certain class of Internet users as indicating pornographic subject matter...[H]e thought that it might improve the level of custom for [his] business if he attracted to it unsuspecting persons interested in accessing a pornographic site.'[143]

17.67   In *L'Oreal SA v Bellure NV*,[144] the claimants complained of the defendants' importation, distribution and sale of what were alleged to be copies—'smell-alikes'—of the former's perfumes, and argued that the defendants' products were instruments of fraud and deception, making their activities passing off. The argument was supported by the way in which the products were advertised on the Internet, albeit by third parties as well as by their names and packaging. The claim was rejected by Lewison J: to be an instrument of deception the product had to be so inherently defective that its mere existence made it passing off waiting to happen. The names and packaging of the defendants' products did not fall into that category, while third party advertising could not be laid at the defendants' door.

17.68   A further issue about passing off on the Internet was raised in *Reed Executive plc v Reed Business Information Ltd*.[145] RE, an employment agency which had been in business using the name REED since 1960, operated a website, *reed.co.uk*. RBI were publishers who had used the REED name since 1983 and who in 1999 began to run a recruitment website called *totaljobs.com*. There was visible use of the word REED on the site, and also invisible use, as the word REED had been used as a metatag in the creation of the site. Metatags are elements of the HTML language used to provide structured metadata about a webpage, that is, data about the material contained in the webpage. Metatags permit discovery of the website by search engines such as Google and Yahoo, and also the generation of various forms of web advertising.[146] There was some evidence of confusion between the two websites in the *Reed* case, and RBI had made efforts by the date of trial to remove both visible and invisible uses of the word REED. Pumfrey J held that, while the

---

[142] [2000] ETMR 341.   [143] [2000] ETMR at p 345.
[144] [2007] RPC 14; affd on instruments of deception and the activities of third parties [2008] RPC 9 (CA).
[145] [2003] RPC 12 (Pumfrey J), aff'd [2004] RPC 40 (CA).
[146] See further A Murray, 'The use of trade marks as meta tags: defining the boundaries' (2000) 8 International Jnl of Law and Information Technology 263.

visible uses of REED could constitute passing off, this was not so for the invisible metatags. The Court of Appeal held that there was no passing off at all, pointing to evidence that had been led about the results of searches under the phrase 'Reed jobs'. Jacob LJ said of this evidence:

'In all cases where totaljobs was listed, it came below the Reed employment site in the search results (which, as is usual, included many other results, irrelevant to both sides). Obviously anyone looking for Reed Employment would find them rather than totaljobs. I am unable to see how there could be passing off. No one is likely to be misled—there is no misrepresentation. This is equally so whether the search engine itself rendered visible the metatag or not.'[147]

 Question

What are metatags? Why do they create problems relevant to the law of passing off? What is the law on these problems as a result of the cases discussed above?

Unfair competition and passing off

17.69   As pointed out at the beginning of this chapter (para 17.7), passing off is as near as the laws of England and Scotland come to having a law of unfair competition such as is commonly found in the laws of other member states of the EU, and it is usually taken to satisfy the requirements of the Paris Convention in this regard. It has sometimes been suggested that the expansion of passing off from the simple case of representing one's goods as those of another and thereby damaging that other's goodwill, means that it would be better to speak now of unfair competition rather than passing off. A particularly strong instance of this development has been the growth of protection of product goodwill, with its ability to prevent dilution of a valuable reputation in trade. But other developments, such as the broadening concept of misrepresentation, the decreasing emphasis on confusion and the recognition of 'dilution', are taking the law increasingly towards a basis in *misappropriation* of another's *reputation* (as distinct from goodwill), to enable one to reap profit and enrichment where another has sown the seed.[148] Laddie J has gone so far as to say that the 'underlying principle' of passing off is 'the maintenance of what is currently regarded as fair trading',[149] while Aldous LJ, unconvinced by Laddie J's rejection of the claim of passing off in the *Arsenal* case, suggested at the same time that the modern extensions of passing meant that it was 'perhaps best referred to as unfair competition'.[150] If we consider the prohibitions listed in Article 10*bis*(3) of the Paris Convention article:

'1.   all acts of such nature as to create confusion by any means whatever with the establishment, the goods, or the industrial or commercial activities, of a competitor;

---

[147] [2004] RPC 40 (CA), para 147. For further comment see R Sumroy and C Badger, 'Infringing 'use in the course of trade': trade mark use and the essential function of a trade mark', and S Maniatis, 'Trade mark use on the Internet', both in J Phillips and I Simon (eds), *Trade Mark Use* (2005), paras 10.29–30, 15.18–21.

[148] A Kamperman Sanders, *Unjust Enrichment: the New Paradigm for Unfair Competition Law?* (1996).

[149] *Irvine v Talksport Ltd* [2002] 2 All ER 414, para 17.

[150] *Arsenal FC plc v Matthew Reed* [2003] RPC 39, para 70; commented upon by S Middlemiss and S Warner, 'Is there still a hole in this bucket? Confusion and misrepresentation in passing off' (2006) 1 JIPLP 131, and C Wadlow, 'One more outing for *Arsenal*: a case of dilution or one for restitution?' (2006) 1 JIPLP 143. The dictum is also discussed by Lewison J in *L'Oreal SA v Bellure SA* [2006] EWHC 2355 (Ch), paras 165–167 (the perfume 'smell-alike' case), holding that misrepresentation is still required in the modern law whether or not it has moved in the direction of unfair competition. This view was upheld in the Court of Appeal ([2000] RPC 9).

2. false allegations in the course of trade of such a nature as to discredit the establishment, the goods, or the industrial or commercial activities, of a competitor;

3. indications or allegations the use of which in the course of trade is liable to mislead the public as to the nature, the manufacturing process, the characteristics, the suitability for their purpose, or the quantity, of the goods'

—then we can see that passing off is capable of dealing with all three. Indeed, passing off goes further in several respects. It would not be straightforward to say, for example, that the use of passing off to prevent false endorsement or cyber-squatting comes squarely within these prohibitions. In *L'Oreal SA v Bellure NV*[151] the Court of Appeal was invited to develop a tort of unfair competition, either because the present law was in derogation from the Paris Convention or as an evolution of the common law. The Court held (correctly, it is submitted) that there was no derogation from the Convention and vigorously rejected the argument that it could develop passing off to become a tort of unfair competition. Given that competition was not only lawful but also the mainspring of the economy, it was for Parliament rather than the judges to legislate for restraints upon competition. Jacob LJ was highly critical of the concept of misappropriation as the means of further developing the law; he thought it 'very unhelpful . . . at best muddling and at worst tendentious.'[152]

 Exercise

Consider how each of the three prohibitions in the Paris Convention article on unfair competition is dealt with by the law of passing off.

17.70   There are those, however, who argue that passing off still does not go far enough to deal with all forms of unfair competition in the market place. In the mid-1990s the issue was focused by the debate about supermarkets' 'own brand' products and the competition which they offered to branded products in their fields. The supermarket brand generally bore some similarity of name and get-up to a well-known branded product, but sold at a significantly lower price. The owners of the brands argued that this was unfair, derivative, trading, which made use of their goodwill but which would be difficult to prevent as passing off because the supermarket customers were not confused by the practice.[153] While this argument was to some extent confounded by the outcome of the *Penguin/Puffin* case (see above, para 17.36), the brand owners lobby has sought legislative intervention to remove the requirement of confusion and so create a much wider law of unfair competition. During the Parliamentary passage of what is now the Trade Marks Act 1994, the following additional section was proposed, although ultimately the amendment was withdrawn:

'After Clause 56, insert the following clause:

Unfair Competition

(1) Where any goods of the proprietor of a trade mark bearing the trade mark are associated in the course of trade with any label, packaging or container having an overall appearance of a distinctive

---

[151] [2008] RPC 9 (CA).

[152] Ibid, para 160. See further L Harrold, 'The genie in the bottle: brand "free riding": what's permissible and what's not?' (2008) 3 JIPLP 511, and T Alkin, 'Should there be a tort of "unfair competition" in English law?' (2008) 3 JIPLP 48.

[153] See further B Mills, 'Own label products and the "lookalike" phenomenon: a lack of trade dress and unfair competition protection?' [1995] EIPR 116.

character, it shall be an act of unfair competition, actionable as such, for any person in the course of trade to supply or offer to supply any such goods with or in any label, packaging or container which is similar in overall appearance, whether by reason of name, shape, colour, design or any combination thereof or otherwise, to the overall appearance of that of the proprietor's goods if the use of the label, packaging or container either—

(a) is likely to cause confusion, which includes a likelihood of association with the proprietor or the proprietor's goods; or

(b) without due cause takes unfair advantage of, or is detrimental to, the distinctive character or repute of the appearance of the proprietor's goods or trade mark.'

17.71   In March 2000 Lord McNally laid a Copyright and Trade Marks Bill before the House of Lords, which was again withdrawn, but which contained a clause described as follows by the noble Lord:[154]

'Clause 3 seeks to tighten up the currently weak laws on competitive imitation. It is intended to prevent business from dressing up products so as to resemble competing goods, thereby taking unfair advantage of the original's reputation for quality and safety and investment in innovation and marketing. Such legislation is necessary because the imitation is designed deliberately to mislead consumers by stealing the identity and reputation of the rival product. When I was at the Retail Consortium I noted that it was not only the back-street trader who indulged in such copycat retailing. I believe that to steal a brand image is unfair to the initiator who over decades may have made an investment to win customer confidence in a particular product. At the moment, imitation is governed by passing-off law that dates from the 18th and 19th centuries. It is very vague and has proved ineffective in providing protection to rights owners. The required standard of proof under passing-off law is extreme and gives copycats immense freedom to copy designs in a way that misleads consumers. It is unrealistic to ask industry to fight legal actions and to lose just to prove a point. The lack of legal cases demonstrates the difficulty in bringing actions. I am proposing that courts are in the best position to decide what constitutes imitation. The Bill also gives the wronged party a chance to seek damages in cases where imitation is proven. The present laws, like so many others in this area, present a barrier to innovation by industry and consumers continue to be deceived.'

Exercise

What difference, if any, would the amendment to the Trade Marks Bill have made to the law of passing off? Comment on Lord McNally's criticism of the law of passing off. Should there be a law of unfair competition to prevent imitative trading even if customers are not confused between the competing products?

17.72   While the idea of replacing passing off with a more general law against unfair competition is attractive in some ways—in bringing the law in the UK into line with that of our fellow member states of the EU, in stopping the need to strain the basic concepts of passing off to meet new forms of unfair trading, and in enabling those who invest time, creativity and labour in generating products and services attracting good will to gain appropriate rewards without quite so much risk of free-riding by less innovative or would-be competitors—there are countervailing arguments.[155] Perhaps the most potent is that, while a law of unfair competition would be justified ultimately as a protection of consumers, it would be administered through

---

[154] *Parliamentary Debates*, House of Lords, vol 610, 17 March 2000, cols 1888–9. The whole debate on the Bill can be found at cols 1885–1906.

[155] See especially H Carty, *An Analysis of the Economic Torts* (2001), Ch 8.

the courts and by way of litigation involving, not the consumer directly, but rather the suppliers competing for the consumer's custom. It is not immediately clear that this would be the most efficient or effective way of protecting the consumer from unfair trading practices. The instruments of market regulation would be dependent on the competitive interests of the market players. Again, a law of unfair competition might be overly inhibiting upon the free play of market forces and competition generally, and the most effective form of consumer protection is arguably a competitive market place. If we take the own brand example, for instance, the consumer who had benefited from the lower prices of the supermarkets' products would not be pleased if told that this facility, being unfair competition, was no longer available.

Further reading

Books

General

L Bently and B Sherman, *Intellectual Property Law* (3rd edn, 2009) Chs 31–34

H Carty, *An Analysis of the Economic Torts* (2001), Ch 8

WR Cornish and D Llewelyn, *Intellectual Property* (6th edn, 2007), Ch 17.1

C Wadlow, *The Law of Passing Off: Unfair Competition by Misrepresentation* (3rd edn, 2004)

Unfair competition

A Kamperman Sanders, *Unjust Enrichment: the New Paradigm for Unfair Competition Law?* (1996)

Articles and chapters

General

H Carty, 'The common law and the quest for the IP effect' [2007] IPQ 237

M Spence, 'Passing off and the misappropriation of valuable intangibles' (1996) 112 LQR 472

Development of the law

H Carty, 'The development of passing off in the twentieth century', and C Morcom, 'Leading cases in passing off', both in N Dawson and A Firth (eds), *Trade Marks Retrospective* (2000)

EM Clive, 'The action of passing off: its scope and basis', 1963 Juridical Review 117 (Scots law)

Goodwill

M Learmouth, 'Eddie, are you OK? Product endorsement and passing off' [2002] IPQ 306

F Mostert, 'Is goodwill territorial or international?' [1989] EIPR 440

S Naresh, 'Passing off, goodwill and false advertising: new wine in old bottles' (1986) 45 CLJ 97

D Rose, 'Season of goodwill: passing off and overseas traders' [1995] EIPR 356

Misrepresentation

J Griffiths, 'Misattribution and misrepresentation: the claim for reverse passing off as "paternity" right' [2006] IPQ 34

J Phillips and A Coleman, 'Passing off and the common field of activity' (1985) 101 LQR 242

Cyber-squatting

C Colston, 'Passing off: the right solution to domain names?' [2000] LMCLQ 523

R Sumroy and C Badger, 'Infringing "use in the course of trade": trade mark use and the essential function of a trade mark', and S Maniatis 'Trade mark use on the Internet', both in J Phillips and I Simon (eds), *Trade Mark Use* (2005)

Breach of confidence

Introduction

Scope and overview of chapter

18.1   This chapter considers contemporary law and policy relating to the protection of confidential information. The chapter begins with an overview of confidential information, including its legal basis and international relevance. The chapter summarises some key cases to give examples of the issues which arise, and the approaches which are adopted by the court. The chapter then reviews the action for breach of confidence. This has a long history, which is traced through scenarios involving personal secrets, national security, employment, post-employment and regulation. The controversial impact of the action on the public domain and free expression, and the public interest defence, are also considered.

18.2   From this starting point, the chapter considers the significant impact the Human Rights Act 1998 (HRA 1998) had on this established action, in respect of what can loosely be termed 'privacy'. The HRA 1998 required courts to consider the right to respect for private life found in Article 8 European Convention on Human Rights (ECHR). As a result, courts developed the breach of confidence action to protect information in respect of which there was a reasonable expectation of privacy. However, the HRA 1998 also required regard to be had to the rights in Article 10 ECHR—freedom of expression. A new balancing act was therefore developed by the courts when considering these two rights, and in carrying this out the courts are making increasing reference to decisions of the European Court of Human Rights (ECtHR).

18.3   The chapter next evaluates the present and potential impact of the HRA 1998, ECHR and ECtHR on other aspects of breach of confidence—notably commercial and regulatory information—and also on the public interest defence. Finally, after reviewing more practical questions relating to enforcement, the chapter considers the interaction between breach of confidence and enforcement of IP rights; the extent to which reliance on confidentiality can be used as an alternative and complement to IP protection and exploitation; and the implications of this for the public domain and other human rights. Note that this chapter will not consider questions of remedy save in respect of Springboard orders, nor will it discuss the grant of injunctions in the light of HRA 1998, section 12. These are considered in Chapter 21.[1]

18.4   **Learning objectives**

By the end of this chapter you should be able to describe and explain:

- when information can be confidential and/or private, such as to be the subject of the action;
- when the courts will find that there is an obligation not to disclose information, or other basis for information not to be disclosed;
- who can complain about use of confidential or private information, and against whom;
- industries and situations where breach of confidence questions arise frequently;
- the impact of the HRA 1998 on privacy, freedom of expression and the public interest;
- the relationship between breach of confidence and IP in the commercial and adversarial contexts; and
- the policy implications of breach of confidence as an alternative to and adjunct of IP in respect of innovation and creativity.

18.5   Control and use of information lies at the heart of breach of confidence. However, these questions are also addressed, from a different perspective, in the Data Protection Act 1998, the Regulation of Investigatory Powers Act 1998, the Freedom of Information Act 2000[2] and legislation and developments relating to e-commerce and new technologies. These matters are not considered here, although details of further reading are included at the end of this chapter.

18.6   So the rest of the chapter looks like this:

- Overview (18.7–18.17)
- Breach of confidence (18.18–18.66)
- Private information (18.67–18.84)
- Convergence? (18.85–18.91)
- Parties to action (18.92–18.95)
- Confidence and IP (18.96–18.102)
- Conclusions and the future (18.103)

---

[1] See in particular paras 21.87, 21.88, 21.101ff, 21.105.

[2] For examples of direct interfaces with breach of confidence see eg *Campbell v Mirror Group Newspapers Ltd* [2004] UKHL 22, [2004] 2 AC 457, [2004] 2 WLR 1232, [2004] 2 All ER 995, [2004] EMLR 15 (House of Lords) ('*Campbell*'), *Re C's Application for Judicial Review* [2009] UKHL 15, [2009] 1 AC 908, [2009] 2 WLR 782, [2009] 4 All ER 335, [2009] 2 CrAppR 1, [2009] EMLR 19, [2009] HRLR 20, [2009] UKHRR 853, [2009] CrimLR 525, and *Bluck v Information Commissioner* EA/2006/0090 (2007) 98 BMLR 1, [2008] WTLR 1.

Overview

Basics

18.7   Breach of confidence prevents use and disclosure of confidential information, if there is an obligation of confidence. The obligation might arise under a contract, say of employment, or may be implied. The obligation could be implied from the circumstances of receipt of information (for example, through eavesdropping, or finding documents marked 'confidential' in a dustbin), or from the relationship between the parties involved in disclosure of information (solicitor/client or wife/husband). However, not all confidential information will be protected in all circumstances; and not all information which people might wish to keep secret (say, a celebrity bad hair day captured in the street and then posted on a social networking site) will be considered to be confidential.

18.8   The HRA 1998 created a new role for breach of confidence, with courts moulding a cause of action which the House of Lords in 2004 termed 'misuse of private information.' This provided new protection in the privacy field, although the House of Lords stressed that there was still no over-arching action for breach of privacy.[3] The foundation of this action lay in the fact that the information was private—as opposed to confidential. 'Private information' was information in respect of which there was a reasonable expectation of privacy; and courts have made it clear that even public figures are entitled to such an expectation of privacy in some situations.

When will a claim succeed?

18.9   It is not always enough for a person complaining to establish these initial requirements. Other factors often need to be taken into account. For example, in employment cases there is a careful balance between protecting trade secrets of the employer (for example, proposals for developing new products, marketing plans, customer lists and source codes) after the employee has left, and the ability of the employee to move on and utilise their acquired skill and knowledge. Freedom of expression is also relevant. Before the HRA 1998, there was a public interest defence based on freedom of expression, which was considered particularly in national security cases. This defence required a balancing of the countervailing public interests in first, the continuing confidentiality of material, and second, the disclosure proposed.

18.10   The HRA 1998 provided a different basis for freedom of expression to be considered and by relying on Article 10 ECHR, courts have developed a more methodical approach. The question is: would the restriction on freedom of expression involved, by preventing publication of the information, be proportionate? This test is now used in respect of all aspects of breach of confidence (including misuse of private information). It will be interesting to observe how this use of human rights together with breach of confidence develops. Could human rights (for example, to life and expression under the ECHR) be relied upon by a company wishing access to details of a new secret (and unpatented) cancer drug or climate change technology?

18.11   Note that when evaluating an action, misuse of private information should not be seen as distinct from a claim for breach of confidence. The Court of Appeal stressed this in 2006, when it

---

[3] *Campbell*, paras 11, 14.

considered the publication of diaries of the Prince of Wales which commented on the handover of Hong Kong.[4] The Court of Appeal summarised the framework of the action as follows:

> '(a) there must be (i) confidential information and a relationship of confidence, (ii) private information in respect of which there was reasonable expectation of privacy in the light of article 8 or (iii) both; and
>
> (b) each of these must then be balanced against article 10.'[5]

Confidence and IP

18.12 Protection of information by breach of confidence differs importantly from protection conferred by IP rights. IP protects the expression of an idea, an invention as claimed, or a design. In contrast, breach of confidence protects the basic underlying information. Thus, use of information in creating a valuable new product might be in breach of confidence, even if there is no IP infringement because of differences between 'old' and 'new' products. Likewise, removing customer lists and business plans (rather than copying them) might avoid copyright infringement—but their use in a new venture could be in breach of confidence.

18.13 Further, by relying on trade secrets, rather than seeking patent protection, it would be possible for an inventor to have permanent control[6] over the use of the technology. This would not prevent third party reverse engineering attempts[7] nor independent development. However, the almost mythical status according to the Coca-cola formula suggests that it is not always possible to discover that which others wish to keep secret.

What is breach of confidence (legally)?

18.14 The legal nature of breach of confidence in the UK jurisdictions is unclear.[8] Some argue that as information can be property (or intellectual property),[9] the action is one of property. Others argue the action to be based on contract, the English concept of equity[10] (which does not exist in Scotland), or something else again.[11] This debate is likely to continue.

---

[4] *HRH Prince of Wales v Associated Newspapers Ltd* [2006] EWCA Civ 1776, [2008] Ch 57, [2007] 3 WLR 222, [2007] 2 All ER 139, [2008] EMLR 4 ('HRH CA') paras 64–5. Note consideration of this case in respect of copyright at paras 4.43, 5.32 and 5.35 above. See also *HRH Prince of Wales v Associated Newspapers Ltd* [2007] EWHC 1685 (Ch) which brought the matter finally to an end.

[5] *HRH CA*, para 65.   [6] See para 18.34.

[7] See para 4.22 above regarding reverse engineering and copyright.

[8] See general consideration of the Scots position in *Laws of Scotland: Stair Memorial Encyclopaedia*, Vol 18, Part II, paras 1451 *et seq* ('Stair'); see also F Gurry, (1984) *Breach of Confidence* ('Gurry'), 46–56; and WR Cornish and D Llewellyn, *Intellectual Property: Patents, Copyright, Trade Marks and Allied Rights* (6th edn, 2007) ('Cornish/Llewellyn'), paras 8.06 *et seq*.

[9] See Senior Courts Act 1981, s 72 and Law Reform (Miscellaneous Provisions) (Scotland) Act 1985, s 15 and consideration in the Report of the UK Commission on Intellectual Property Rights 'Integrating Intellectual Property Rights and Development Policy' (http://www.iprcommission.org/), *R v Licensing Authority ex parte Smith Kline & French Laboratories Ltd* (No. 1) [1990] 1 AC 64, 79–80, 88 ('SKF'). For an analysis of property in respect of virtual worlds, which have information and intellectual property as their base, see FG Lastowka and D Hunter, 'The Laws of the Virtual Worlds' (2004) 92 Calif L Rev, 1, January.

[10] See recent consideration by the Court of Appeal in *Napier v Pressdram Ltd* [2009] EWCA Civ 443, [2009] EMLR 21 ('Napier'), paras 16–19.

[11] See consideration in N Witzleb, 'Justifying gain-based remedies for invasions of privacy' (2009) OJLS 325–63. A different Scots' cause of action, the *actio in iniuriam* has also been considered in respect of non information privacy. See HL MacQueen, 'Searching for Privacy in a Mixed Jurisdiction' (2006) 21 Tulane European & Civil Law Forum 73.

18.15   Notwithstanding this uncertainty, and its reflection in court decisions,[12] the set of principles considered in this chapter has emerged. Most of these come from decisions of the English courts. However, there is also strong authority for the existence of a general obligation of confidence in Scots law, which is at least similar to that in England.[13] Further, the UK wide impact of the HRA 1998 suggests that, at least at the outset of an action, the same principles should be considered in each jurisdiction. It also suggests that there may be some convergence between decisions.

The international angle

18.16   Confidential information is covered by two international agreements:

- TRIPS, Article 39(1) and (2)—which provide that undisclosed information shall be protected in particular situations (similar to those explored here); and Article 39(3)—which provides that undisclosed data submitted for regulatory clearance shall be protected against unfair commercial use.

- Paris Convention, Article 10*bis*—which provides that there shall be protection from unfair competition, including by acts contrary to honest practices in industrial and commercial matters.[14]

- Courts in the UK have not considered TRIPS and the Paris Convention in any depth.[15] These provisions have received some scholarly attention in relation to regulatory data.[16]

How does it work in practice?—some important examples

■ *Coco v AN Clark Engineers Ltd* [1968] FSR 415 [1969] RPC 41
(High Court of Justice—Ch D) ('Coco v Clark')

Coco designed a moped engine and then negotiated with Clark about its manufacture. These discussions broke down and Clark designed an engine very similar to Coco's. In proceedings for breach of confidence (copyright was not alleged), it was held that for an action in breach of confidence to succeed, there must be (i) a contract imposing an obligation of confidence or information received in circumstances where the reasonable person would think they were under an obligation of confidence, and (ii) use of the information. The court was willing to find an obligation of confidence, but was not satisfied that there was use of confidential information. Undertakings regarding future use were provided.

---

[12] See Gurry, 46–56. Although there are frequent references in cases to protection of property in information, this seems almost a form of shorthand, eg *Roger Bullivant Ltd v Ellis* [1987] FSR 172 ('*Bullivant*'), headnote para 2, *SBJ Stephenson v Mandy* [2000] FSR 286 ('*Stephenson*') headnote 2, 298, referring to *Printers & Finishers Ltd v Holloway* [1965] 1 WLR 1 ('*Printers & Finishers*') at 5.

[13] *Lord Advocate v Scotsman Publications Ltd* 1989 SLT 705 ('*Scotsman*'), 708 and 1988 SLT 490 ('*Scotsman Second Division*') at 503. See also Stair. Scottish courts have been reluctant, however to accept that the position would necessarily always be so, given the evolving nature of the field *Quilty v Windsor* 1999 SLT 346, 347, 355. See also para 19.53, n 91 regarding the independent approach of the Scottish courts.

[14] Notes to TRIPS in respect of Art 39(2) consider this Article of the Paris Convention to cover breach of confidence.

[15] For some detailed analysis, see NP de Carvalho, *The TRIPS Regime of Antitrust and Undisclosed Information* (2008), Section 7 and J De Werra, 'What legal framework for promoting the cross-border flow of intellectual assets (trade secrets and music)? A view from Europe towards Asia (China and Japan)' (2009) 1 IPQ 27–76.

[16] C Wadlow, 'Regulatory data protection under TRIPs Article 39(3) and Article 10bis of the Paris Convention: is there a doctor in the house?' (2008) 4 IPQ 355–415. See also n 108 below.

■ *Roger Bullivant Ltd v Ellis* [1987] FSR 172 (Court of Appeal) (*'Bullivant'*)

An employee moved to a rival and took with him a copy set of index cards with customer details from his former employer. Some of the information in the cards was publicly available, and the employee would have remembered some of it anyway. However, as the cards had been taken, an injunction was granted preventing use of the information for a reasonable period.

■ *London Regional Transport v Mayor of London* [2001] EWCA Civ 1491, 2001 WL 825728, [2003] EMLR 4 (Court of Appeal) (*'LRT'*)

This concerned proposed disclosure of a report critical of Private Public Partnerships in respect of the London Underground. The Court of Appeal balanced the interests of non disclosure of confidential and commercially sensitive information, and the interests of the public in being informed as to serious problems with this method of funding. It carried out a careful balance, considering the pressing and recognised social need for restriction of any right; whether the proposed restriction was greater than necessary; and whether there were logical reasons for it. Ultimately a proposed compromise with some information blanked out was found to be acceptable.

■ *Campbell v MGN Ltd* [2004] 2 AC 457[17] (House of Lords) (*'Campbell'*)

This involved the newspaper publication of a photograph of supermodel Naomi Campbell in a public place, leaving a confidential Narcotics Anonymous meeting. The House of Lords considered breach of confidence was better named 'misuse of private information.' It held that the photographs were private information. The right for this to be respected was then balanced against rights to freedom of expression, considering the nature of expression involved and of the information, and the extent to which Campbell was a public figure. The House of Lords split 3:2[18] in favour of Campbell. Significant weight was attached to her seeking medical treatment, and it was considered that restriction on freedom of expression in such circumstances was necessary and proportionate.

 Exercise

> Devise a scenario which you think might involve breach of confidence in the context of an innovation business. You might get some ideas from other exercises in this chapter.

18.17 The next section reviews in more detail the traditional action for breach of confidence. The section which follows that reviews misuse of private information and the impact of the HRA 1998.

Breach of confidence

18.18 The starting point is the three-step test set out in *Coco v Clark* considered above:[19]

- information to be of a confidential nature;

---

[17] For other references of case reports see para 18.5, n 2.

[18] The House of Lords claimed to be united, however, on the questions of principle they considered. See *Campbell*, para 36, per Lord Hoffmann.

[19] The decision, treated as a landmark, built on existing authorities, particularly *Saltman Engineering Co Ltd v Campbell Engineering Co Ltd* (1948) 65 RPC 203 (*'Saltman'*)—see *Coco v Clark*, 415, 419.

- information to be communicated in circumstances of confidence such that the reasonable man in the position of the recipient would realise that the information was given to him in confidence;

- unauthorised use of the information—(possibly) to the detriment of the confider.

What type of information is protected?

18.19   Over the years, cases have dealt with all manner of information: from the highly personal about individuals, through sports, trade, business and technical information, ideas for television shows, and political and historical information about government. The essential question is whether the information is confidential. Whether this is so is, perhaps surprisingly, not always clear.

Discussion point   For answer guidance visit www.oxfordtextbooks.co.uk/orc/macqueen2e/

Write down three types of information you think of as confidential. Review your answer after reading the next sections.

When is information confidential?

General points

18.20   Not all information can be confidential. From decided cases, it can be discerned that to qualify, information need not be complex[20] nor of commercial value,[21] although some form of creativity[22] would likely be required. Courts have been reluctant to protect mere 'tittle tattle';[23] but some personal information, such as private diaries and details of sexual activities, has been found confidential.[24] Although as noted claims are frequent in the employment context, not all details of workplace activities will be confidential.[25]

Already in the public domain?

18.21   The content of information (isolated or in combination)[26] or its value[27] likely must not be public knowledge. Yet, unlike with patents, absolute novelty is not required—the key is the level of accessibility of the information. Accordingly, a claim in confidence has in the past survived

---

[20] *Cranleigh Precision Engineering Ltd v Bryant* [1965] 1 WLR 1293 ('*Cranleigh*'), 1310; *Coco v Clark*, 420.

[21] *Nichrotherm Electrical Co Ltd v Percy* [1956] RPC 272; aff'd [1957] RPC 207.

[22] *Coco v Clark*, at 419–20

[23] *Coco v Clark*, 421. It has been argued however that this point was made to avoid awarding relief, rather than to avoid confidential status—*Stephens v Avery* [1988] 2 WLR 1280, [1988] 2 All ER 477, [1988] FSR 510, [1988] Ch 449 ('*Stephens*'), 454 finding wholesale revelation of sexual activity not to be tittle tattle.

[24] *Argyll v Argyll* [1967] Ch 302 ('*Argyll*'); *Stephens; X (HA) v Y* [1988] 2 All ER 648, [1988] RPC 379 ('*X v Y*'), *Barrymore v News Group Newspapers Ltd* [1997] FSR 600. See also *Mosley v News Group Newspapers Limited* [2008] EWHC 1777 (QB), [2008] EMLR 20 ('*Mosley*') paras 5,6,105–8. See further consideration below at para 18.83.

[25] *Tillery Valley Foods v Channel Four Television Corporation* 2004 WL 1074218 ('*Tillery*') (films of frozen meals for hospitals made by someone working undercover as employee), para 11.

[26] *Coco v Clark*, 420. *Saltman*, 215.   [27] Gurry, 78–81.

publication of the information overseas.[28] However, this approach would likely not be taken now, given increased global communication technologies.

18.22   Information might still be confidential even if it is published to a finite group, say passengers on an aeroplane, or a small number of readers.[29] When more than one person is involved in the subject matter of information (say a sexual relationship) and only one wants to disclose it, the other might still claim the information to be confidential. Both attitudes will be relevant to the court.[30] Information shared with a friend in confidence will be confidential to that friend.[31]

18.23   If information has been disclosed for limited, specified purposes, it will remain confidential in respect of other purposes. The Prince of Wales providing confidential access to his diaries to his authorised biographer did not mean that they were no longer confidential.[32] If information is disclosed as part of a project, then when the project is completed the information must be treated as confidential.[33]

18.24   A photograph may be confidential even if it has been published, has the same subject as a photograph proposed to be published, or was taken in public. The fact that one can take a photograph in public does not mean one can publish it, if the subject matter is clearly controlled. For example photographs of the set for the album cover of the band Oasis were confidential, as there was a clear indication that photography was not permitted.[34]

18.25   In *Douglas v Hello!*[35] regarding photographs of the wedding of Michael Douglas and Catherine Zeta-Jones, a freelance photographer managed to attend the wedding and take photographs to sell to Hello! magazine. The wedding party permitted no unofficial photography, and had an exclusive deal with OK! magazine. There, special treatment was considered appropriate for photographs (as opposed to other information potentially in the public domain) because of the invasive nature of photographs, and impact of their republication.[36] The photographs were found to disclose private information, and the fact that there was a contract for publication of other photographs of the wedding did not change this.[37] Further, the publisher who had entered into a contract to publish the photographs was considered by the House of Lords to have the right to

---

[28]   *Franchi v Franchi* [1967] RPC 149 regarding publication in foreign patent.

[29]   Gurry, 75–6. See also *Woodward v Hutchins* [1977] 1 WLR 760, [1977] 2 AllER 751, 764 (disgraceful conduct of pop-stars on aeroplane might have been confidential, if there had been slightly different facts), *HRH CA*, paras 41–2 (practice of limited sharing of information long established without previous breach). Compare *Scotsman* which left open whether small number of copies distributed privately meant the work was not confidential. On this issue see *McKennitt v Ash* [2006] EWCA Civ 1714, 2006 WL 3609995, [2008] QB 73, [2007] 3 WLR 194, [2007] EMLR 4 ('*Ash CA*') regarding memoirs of a friend of a Canadian folk singer; singer had herself previously published some of the information privately, paras 79–80.

[30]   *A v B plc* [2002] EWCA 337, 2003 QB 195, [2002] 3 WLR 542, [2002] 2 All ER 545, [2002] EMLR 21, 2002 WL 237087(CA) ('*A v B plc*'), para 43(iii), 79–80.

[31]   *Ash CA*, para 29–32.   [32]   *HRH CA*, paras 21, 43.

[33]   See *Torrington Manufacturing Co. v Smith & Sons (England) Ltd* [1966] RPC 285, *Regina Glass Fibre Ltd v Werner Schuller* [1972] FSR 141[1972] RPC 229 and Gurry, 134–5.

[34]   In *Creation Records Ltd v News Group Newspapers Ltd* [1997] EMLR 444 ('*Creation*'), paras 461–4 and *Shelley Films Ltd v Rex Features Ltd* [1994] EMLR 134, ('*Shelley*') 148–9 it is unclear whether the basis for order preventing further publication was confidentiality or to prevent a springboard benefit—see paras 18.65ff.

[35]   *Douglas and others v Hello! Ltd No 3* [2005] EWCA Civ 595, [2005] 3 WLR 881, [2005] 4 All ER 128 [2005] EMLR 28, [2006] QB 125 ('*Douglas v Hello!*').

[36]   *Campbell*, paras 31, 73–75, *Douglas v Hello!* headnote 1, and paras 85–88, 105–8 (referring paras 40–1, 77–80 to *Theakston v MGN Ltd* [2002] EWHC 137, [2002] EMLR 22, 2002 WL 45379 ('*Theakston*') when injunction had been granted regarding photos but not words, and also referring to *Von Hannover v Germany* (59320100) [2004] EMLR 21, (2005) 40 EHRR 1 ('*Hannover*') para 59). See further *Mosley*, paras 16–23. Note also special rules in respect of photographs regarding moral rights, see para 3.48.

[37]   *Douglas v Hello!*, para 95. See paras 16.19ff regarding circumstances in which image can be protected.

control the information in the photographs.[38] Regarding photographs of more public conduct, in *Campbell* the photographs of the supermodel were found to be worthy of protection,[39] and the Court of Appeal in *Murray v Express Newspapers Plc ('Murray')*[40] found this was also so regarding photographs taken in the street of the infant son of a well known author.

18.26   Further, information which is disclosed in breach of confidence may not in fact enter the public domain. *Speed Seal Products v Paddington ('Speed Seal')*[41] suggested that confidentiality was lost only if information was published with the consent of the person to whom an obligation of confidence was owed. This case drew heavily, however, from a decision which although it involved published information, was more likely based on breach of fiduciary duty.[42] The House of Lords considered the issue in *Attorney General v Guardian Newspapers Ltd (No 2), ('Spycatcher')*.[43] The case concerned the diaries of former member of the security services Peter Wright, which had already been published abroad. The House of Lords indicated that they might have been prepared to grant an injunction against Wright (who was not a party). However, some Law Lords suggested that this would not have been based on breach of a continuing obligation of confidence.[44]

18.27   More recently, in the aftermath of the financial difficulties of Northern Rock in 2007, a court granted a short injunction ordering that information which had been published on the website of the Financial Times be removed from that site. It considered that there should be a qualitative, not quantitative, assessment of information which had already been disclosed and its future impact.[45] In 2009, however, Arnold J considered that there was no general principle that injunctions could be granted in relation to breach of confidence once information was in the public domain.[46]

18.28   Information disclosed in open court or read by the judge is not confidential.[47] However, confidentiality is not lost if hearings do not take place in open court, or are behind a locked door, with restricted access to information, and excerpted judgments.[48]

[38] And as such, to treat them as any other trade secret. The decision of the House of Lords is reported at *OBG Ltd v Allan* [2007] UKHL 21 [2002] 1 AC 1, [2007] 2 WLR 920, [2007] Bus LR 1600, [2007] 4 All ER 545 ('Hello! HL'). See paras 117–122, 278, 307, 310, 325–9 cf 255–9, 298–300. For detailed consideration of different approaches taken by the House of Lords, see G Black, 'Douglas v Hello!—An OK! Result' (2007) 4(2) SCRIPT-ed page 161 @ http://www.law.ed.ac.uk/ahrc/scripted/vol4-2/editorial.asp

[39] See further discussion at paras 18.74–18.75.

[40] *Murray v Express Newspapers Plc* [2008] EWCA Civ 446, [2008] 3 WLR 1360, [2008] ECDR 12, [2008] ECDR 12, [2008] EMLR 12.

[41] *Speed Seal Products Ltd v Paddington* [1986] 1 All ER 91, [1985], 1 WLR 1327, 1332–3.

[42] *Cranleigh*, 93. *Speed Seal* was agreed with by *Scotsman Second Division* at 491–4.

[43] [1988] 3 WLR 776 at 785–6, 789, 791, 795–6, 809, 817.

[44] Other possibilities considered were Crown copyright, profiting from own wrong and Springboard. See *Spycatcher* 786, 796, compare 791, 809–812, 818. Injunction was granted only against Peter Wright and connected parties. Regarding Crown copyright, see also para 3.29. In *EPI Environmental Technologies Inc v Symphony Plastic Technologies* plc [2006] EWCA Civ 3, 2006 WL 421838, [2006] 1 WLR 495 (Note) ('EPI') paras 46–50, 73, the Court of Appeal declined to consider ongoing questions of confidentiality, seeing this as an academic question, partially because of its complexity.

[45] *Northern Rock PLC v The Financial Times Limited* [2007] EWHC 2677 (QB) 2007 WL 3389581 ('Northern Rock'), in particular paras 15, 19–20, 25. Compare *Attorney-General v Blake* [2001] 1 AC 268 (HL), [2000] 3 WLR 625; [2000] 4 All ER 385, for an extreme case of remedies awarded for publication when information is no longer confidential and *Schering Chemicals Ltd v Falkman Ltd* [1982] QB 1 including an overview of earlier cases, see pp 36, 37, 39, 40 and per Lord Denning pp 15–17, 21–2.

[46] *Vestergaard Frandsen A/S v BestNet Europe Ltd* [2009] EWHC 1456 (Ch), [2010] FSR 2 (*Vestergaard*), notably paras 22, 68–76. Compare para 18.65.

[47] Including where only read by the judge in advance, and not referred to in court; *Smithkline Beecham Biologicals SA v Connaught Laboratories Inc (Disclosure of Documents)* [2000] FSR 1. See also *Crossley v Newsquest (Midlands South) Ltd* [2008] EWHC 3054 (QB).

[48] See *EPI* for example of a redacted judgment.

Government information

18.29 For government information to be confidential, the government must satisfy the court that the public interest in confidentiality exceeds the public interest in the information being available.[49] This is a special hurdle, given the importance of government information being available.

Key points on when information is confidential

- Not all information can be confidential
- It is possible for information to be confidential if there has been limited sharing or some disclosure
- There is a special public interest test in respect of government information

---

What *is* the information?

18.30 An important legal and practical question is whether, and how well, the information can be identified.[50] If it cannot be clearly identified and distinguished from other information, the court will be unable to determine if it is in fact confidential; also, any court order could not be set out with sufficient clarity.[51] This raises two different problems for the party complaining: the necessary detail might not be available (eg if information was communicated orally or developed in someone's head); and overspecification might reveal more than had previously been known by the other side.

Key point

- It is important to specify information, to enable liability to be determined and remedy to be properly framed

---

 Exercise

The box below contains a list of scenarios. Split them into three groups: is this information confidential: YES, NO, MAYBE? Is further information required?

- 'Just what you did last summer'—even if you have already put it on a social networking site which does/does not have some form of 'privacy protection'.
- The formula for a new product which had been kept locked in a safe.

---

[49] *Spycatcher*, 783, 785, 796, 807 and in *Australia Cth v Jonathan Fairfax & Sons Ltd* (180) 147 CLR 39 and *Smith Kline & French Laboratories (Australia) v Secretary to the Department of Community Services and Health* [1990] FSR 617 ('*SKF Australia*') paras 21–2, 29.

[50] *Inline Logistics v UCI Logistics* [2002] RPC 32 ('*Inline Logistics*') For an example of a case where information was not identified with the necessary precision, see *FSS Travel & Leisure Systems v Johnson* [1999] FSR 505 (CA) ('*FSS Travel*'), 513.

[51] Compare, however, broad approach to framing of order preventing future disclosure in *Levin v Farmers Supply Association of Scotland* 1973 SLT (Notes) 43, 44. Detail considered important, however, in *Ocular Sciences Ltd v Aspect Vision Care (No 2)* [1997] RPC 289 ('*OSI*'), 359. This case is considered in respect of unregistered design rights at paras 9.45 and 9.47.

- The formula for an industry staple product, which was launched years ago, is easy to reverse engineer—but is locked in a safe.
- Next year's exam papers.
- Details of the proposed use of illegal immigrants as guinea pigs for unlicensed drug tests.

 Discussion point   For answer guidance visit www.oxfordtextbooks.co.uk/orc/macqueen2e/

Is posting on an Internet chat site the equivalent of speaking to a friend on the phone? Should postings be treated as confidential? How appropriate are established principles given new technology?

An obligation: circumstances of confidence

When will the obligation exist?

18.31   An obligation of confidence is required for breach of confidence. The obligation can be based on contract, but it need not be. *Coco v Clark* set out an objective test to be applied when there is no contract; would the reasonable man realise that the information was given in confidence: how would the circumstances of receipt of information impact upon the conscience of the reasonable person?[52] There have been cases questioning whether a subjective test might also be appropriate given the reference to 'conscience'. However, so far this has not proved significant in identifying obligations.[53]

18.32   Accordingly, there might be an obligation when a confidentiality agreement is signed as part of a research and development project; or in less formal situations, such as information obtained after hacking into a password protected website,[54] during a heartfelt confession from a friend,[55] or by using illegal means to listen to phone calls.[56]

Scope

18.33   Even if there is an obligation, its scope must be established in each case. For example, it might be acceptable to use, but not disclose, information.[57] In 2001 in relation to disclosure of

---

[52] *Coco v Clark*, 419–425, see also *Spycatcher*, 805, *Kavanagh Balloons Pty Ld v Cameron Balloons Ltd* [2004] RPC 5 ('*Kavanagh*') para 46 and *Napier*, para 42.

[53] This was considered in *Carflow Products (UK) Ltd v Linwood Securities (Birmingham) Ltd* [1996] FSR 424 ('*Carflow*'), 424, 429 and *Vestergaard*, para 24. See also para 18.49.

[54] Although merely encrypting information, without more, has been held not to create an obligation of confidence: *Mars UK Ltd v Teknowledge Ltd (No 1)* The Times, 23 June 1999 (Ch D). See J Watts, 'Copyright: reverse engineering and encryption' (1999) 21(9) EIPR N158.

[55] Eg *Stephens*, 451, 453, 456.

[56] In *Francome v Mirror Group* [1984] 2 All ER 408, [1984] 1 WLR 892, ('*Francome*'). Compare *Malone v Commissioner of Police of the Metropolis (No 2)* [1979] 2 All ER 620, [1979] 2 WLR 700 ('*Malone*') (information obtained from official wire tap was not a breach of confidence). See also para 18.56–18.57. Compare the finding that the making of a complaint to the Law Society, and its investigation, did not give rise to an obligation of confidence: *Napier*, paras 48–9, 52–7.

[57] *Coco v Clark*, 419, 421.

anonymised medical data by pharmacists to marketing companies, the Court of Appeal said the key question as to scope was the conscience of the reasonable pharmacist.[58]

 Discussion point   For answer guidance visit www.oxfordtextbooks.co.uk/orc/macqueen2e/

Plans for the University of Edingow to take over the University of Glasburgh (which are being met with riots in the streets) are posted on a blog clearly described as 'Private to Members of the University of Edingow', but which required no password. Ross, a student at Sydbourne, finds the information and sends it to Hamish at a newspaper. Was Ross under an obligation of confidence? If so, how wide was this obligation?

Key points on bases of obligation of confidence

- Obligation can arise under contract
- Obligation can arise from circumstances of receipt, assessed (likely) using an objective test
- Scope of an obligation is to be assessed in each case, using an objective test

Duration

18.34   Provided the information in question remains confidential, the obligation is infinite. Contractually imposed obligations (if they are not otherwise objectionable) can continue after the contract term[59]—provided the information remains confidential. This is one appeal for business of relying on confidential information, rather than, say, patents[60] in respect of vaccines or copyright[61] in respect of customer lists.

18.35   With Government information, the obligation depends upon the public interest balance, and so the obligation may cease if this balance changes.[62] Different balances have been reached in respect of members of the security services[63] and government ministers.[64]

 Question

Would you prefer patents or confidential information for your business?

Key point on duration

- There is no time limit, provided the information remains confidential

---

[58] *R v Department of Health ex parte Source Infomatics (No 1)*, [2001] QB 424, [2000] 2 WLR 940, [2001] 1 All ER 786 (CA) ('*Source*') para 31.

[59] *Lady Archer v Williams* [2003] EWHC 1670, [2003] EMLR 38, para 47. Regarding the likely limited impact of a breach of the contract, see *Rock Refrigeration Ltd v Jones* [1997] 1 All ER 1, [1998] ICR 938 (CA) and *Campbell v Frisbee* [2002] EWHC 328 (Ch), EWCA (Civ) 1375, [2002] EMLR 31.

[60] See para 11.137ff.   [61] See paras 3.49ff.   [62] See para 18.29, *Douglas v Hello!*, para 104.

[63] *Spycatcher*, 782, 790–1, 794, 808; *Scotsman*, 709 (lifelong obligation of confidence).

[64] *Attorney General v Jonathan Cape Ltd* [1976] QB 752, [1975] 3 WLR 606 (diaries of Cabinet discussions can be published after a decent interval).

18.36   Two categories merit further consideration: particular types of obligation (including, importantly, employment) and indirect recipients of information.

Special relationships

Employment

18.37   There is an obligation of confidence during a period of employment. If the contract is silent the court will imply an obligation, on the basis of good faith and fidelity. The nature of the obligation will vary,[65] however courts have implied terms preventing injury to employer's interests.[66] Courts have found that this would cover disclosure of secret information to the competitors[67] or to a trade union.[68]

18.38   Regarding preparations for the period after employment, courts have implied terms preventing making or memorising lists of customers[69] (although there are difficulties of proof if the information was publicly available)[70] or soliciting customers to join a new venture.[71] Not all preliminary activity will necessarily be prohibited: it is a question of fact and degree.[72]

18.39   After the employment term has ended, courts will imply a further, more limited, obligation. According to the leading case *Faccenda Chicken Ltd v Fowler* ('*Faccenda*'),[73] former employers must not use or disclose information which is a trade secret or which in all the circumstances is so confidential that it requires the same level of protection.

18.40   *Faccenda* suggests that a trade secret must not be the skill, know how and general knowledge of the employee.[74] Decided cases suggest that it will also depend upon:

- the nature of the employment (if an employee frequently works with confidential information, for example, in a locked lab);[75]

- the nature of the information (possibilities include secret processes or designs,[76] and customer lists);[77]

- whether the employer impressed the confidentiality of the information on the employee (eg locked doors, training sessions, or is information openly available and discussed);[78]

---

[65]   *Faccenda Chicken Ltd v Fowler* [1987] Ch 117, [1986] 3 WLR 288 1986 FSR 291 ('*Faccenda*'), 302.
[66]   Including work done outside office hours—see Gurry, 188ff and *Hivac Ltd v Royal Park Scientific Instruments Ltd* [1946] 1 Ch 169. Note also the Public Interest Disclosure Act 1989.
[67]   *Printers & Finishers* and *Bullivant*.   [68]   *Bents Brewery v Hogan* [1945] 2 A11 ER 570.
[69]   *Robb v Green* [1895] 2 QB 315; *Faccenda*, 302; *Bullivant* 175–181, *JN Dairies Ltd v Johal Dairies Ltd* [2009] EWHC 1331 (Ch).
[70]   See also *Bullivant*, 183. Followed in *Bradford & Bingley Plc v Holden* [2002] EWHC 2445, [2002] WL 31962007 ('*Holden*') but compare *Universal Thermosensors v Hibben* [1992] 1 WLR 840 ('*Hibben*') and *Stephenson*, 298. See also *Sectrack NV v Satamatics* [2007] EWHC 3003 (Comm).
[71]   *Faccenda*, 302, *Bullivant*.   [72]   *ABK v Foxwell* [2002] EWHC 9, 2002 WL 499040.
[73]   Followed in Scotland in *Harben Pumps (Scotland) Ltd v Lafferty* 1989 SLT 752.
[74]   *Faccenda*, 303, *FSS Travel*, 516 and see *Lansing Linde v Kerr*, [1991] 1 All ER 418, [1991] 1 WLR 251 (CA) ('*Lansing*'). *Faccenda*, 306 left open the question of whether it would be breach of confidence if the employee simply passed on or sold information, rather than used it themselves. See also *Crowson Fabrics Ltd v Rider* [2007] EWHC 2942 (Ch), [2008] FSR 17.
[75]   *Faccenda*, 304.
[76]   *Faccenda*, 303–4, *Littlewoods Organisation Ltd v Harris* [1978] 1 All ER 1026, [1977] 1 WLR 1472.
[77]   See also *AT Poeton (Gloucester Plating) Ltd v Horton* [2001] FSR 14.
[78]   *Faccenda*, 305.

- whether the information could be readily isolated from other information;[79]
- whether there would be real or significant harm if the information were disclosed.[80]

18.41 Given some uncertainties in applying these principles in practice, an employer could choose to be proactive and clarify information status in the contract; it might also include a clause preventing the employee working in the same field, possibly in the same geographic area, for a period. These clauses, known as restrictive covenants, will not be implied into contracts. They are also scrutinised carefully by courts.[81]

18.42 *Faccenda* provides that a restrictive covenant will not be enforced unless the protection sought was reasonable and necessary to protect trade secrets or prevent abuse of personal influence over customers.[82] It is a difficult balance. Is an employer protecting legitimate business information which cannot be erased from memory, and might require a special protection for a time? Or is the employer placing an unreasonable restriction on the employee's ability to work elsewhere, exploiting their skill and know how?[83]

18.43 Laddie J was more succinct in *Polymasc Pharmaceuticals v Charles*:[84] is the clause 'too greedy'?

Key points on employment relationship and beyond

- There is obligation of confidence in the course of employment
- After employment, there is an obligation not to disclose trade secrets or equivalent
- Restrictive covenants are only enforced to the extent reasonable and necessary, balancing the interests of employer and employee
- Problem areas are new product ideas, business plans, know how sets and customer lists

---

Exercise

Katie is headhunted to join Eversogood Ltd. Katie has been in charge of developing a new chocolate bar for FunFunFun Ltd. FunFunFun gave her no support, she worked on her own, and wrote nothing down. On joining Eversogood, Liz, her line manager, offered a team of researchers to develop a new chocolate bar. Being conscientious, Katie shared some ideas with her new team. They developed a much improved third generation product. Discuss.

---

[79] *Faccenda*, 305. See also *FSS Travel*, 516.   [80] *Lansing*, 270.

[81] This was stressed by the Court of Appeal in *Faccenda*, 304–5. Regarding garden leave as well as or instead of a restrictive covenant, see *GFI Group Inc v Eaglestone* [1994] FSR 535 (but compare *Provident Finance Group v Hayward* [1989] 3 All ER 298). In relation to England and Wales, section 4 Fraud Act 2006 may also have some impact: see consideration in B Allgrove and S Sellers, 'The Fraud Act 2006: is breach of confidence now a crime?' (2009) 4(4) JIPLP 278–282.

[82] *Faccenda*, 303–4.

[83] *Lock International plc v Beswick* [1989] 1 WLR 1268 [1989] 3 All ER 373; *Balston v Headline Filters Ltd (No 2)* [1990] FSR 385 (CA). See also *Hinton & Higgs (UK) Ltd v Murphy* 1989 SLT 450, *Bullivant, Basic Solutions Ltd v Sands* [2008] EWHC 1388 (QB), *Wrn Ltd v Ayris* [2008] EWHC 1080 (QB), [2008] IRLR 889, *Mantis Surgical Ltd v Tregenza* 2007 EWHC 1545 (QB) and *Thomas v Farr plc and Hanover Park Commercial Limited* [2007] EWCA Civ 118, [2007] ICR 932, [2007] IRLR 419.

[84] [1999] FSR 711, 719.

Other special situations

18.44   Obligations of confidence exist where there is a particular relationship, as, for example, between professional adviser and client or doctor and patient.[85] Difficulties can arise when professionals move or firms merge—although the obligations do continue.[86]

18.45   There are often specific restrictions on when information obtained on a particular statutory or regulatory basis, can be used or passed to others. This could involve information obtained pursuant to, for example, Police and Criminal Evidence Act 1984 or Banking Act 1987, or for regulatory product clearance.[87] The outcome in each case will depend on the proposed conduct, the wording of the legislation and the function of the regulator.

18.46   There is an obligation of confidence in marriage and in stable relationships. The scope and indeed existence of this declines with the level of involvement.[88]

> ### Key points on special situations
>
> * Obligation within marriage or equivalent
> * Obligation between professional adviser and client

>   ### Question
>
> Does your best friend owe you an obligation of confidence? Consider in the light of *McKennitt v Ash* 2006 WL 3609995, [2008] QB 73, [2007] 3 WLR 194, [2007] EMLR 4.

Indirect recipient

18.47   An employee might take information with them to a new employer, but may be unable to use the information without the colleagues and resources available with that new employer. Or a memory stick left in a laptop found on a bus might mean nothing to the 'finder', who then passes it to a friend in the IT industry. What is the position of these new recipients? This distinction can be important in practice—as the real concern of the original holder of the information might be what another business might do with it.

18.48   The principles in *Coco v Clark* apply here: would a reasonable person believe that the information was received subject to an obligation.[89] Third parties were considered in *Spycatcher*,[90] suggesting an obligation of confidence not only in:

> 'those cases where a third party receives information from a person who is under a duty of confidence in respect of it, knowing that it has been disclosed by that person to him in breach of his duty of confidence, but also to include certain situations, beloved of law teachers—where an obviously confidential

---

[85] See Gurry, 143–162 for further details regarding positions of Bankers, Dentists, Counsel and Fiduciaries.
[86] See *Surface Technology v Young* [2002] FSR 25 ('*Surface Technology*').
[87] Compare *SKF*, 70–8, 81–2, 84–5, 86–7, 89–90 and on the same facts *SKF Australia*.
[88] *Argyll v Argyll* [1967] Ch 302 ('*Argyll*'), 322, 329–330. Post-HRA 1998 authorities are also relevant here: *A v B plc* paras 11(xi), 29, 43, 47, *Ash CA*, paras 29–30, *Theakston*, paras 57–61, 74, 76 and *Mosley*, paras 105–109. See also para 18.80.
[89] In *Shelley*, the photographic agency was found to have knowledge of restrictions so was under an obligation not to publish, 149–151.
[90] *Spycatcher*, 806.

document is wafted by an electric fan out of a window into a crowded street, or where an obviously confidential document, such as a private diary, is dropped in a public place, and is then picked up by a passer-by.'

18.49   The more intervening recipients there have been in respect of the information, the less likely it is that there will be an obligation:[91] say, a former employee tells a new colleague who later takes information to a third employer, or the finder on the bus passes it to a colleague with a plausible explanation. The key test for such recipients has been held to be dishonest conduct. Carelessness, stupidity or naivety (such as believing the explanation without question) would not suffice.[92]

18.50   If there is no obligation, there can be no liability. However, if someone is subsequently told that information is confidential, there will be an obligation from that time.[93]

> ### Key point on indirect recipients of confidential information
>
> * Indirect recipients may be subject to obligations of confidence

Exercise

Go back to Hamish, Ross and Edingow (after para 18.33). Is Hamish under an obligation of confidence? What about Hamish's editor? Draw a diagram setting out when there will be obligations of confidence, noting relevant factors.

Relevant conduct

What is required?

18.51   There must be some conduct for there to be a breach of confidence. However, the nature of the breach is closely tied to the scope of the obligation; not all activities in relation to relevant information will constitute a breach.

18.52   Thus it can be breach of confidence to use or disclose information, including doing more with information than that to which the subject consented.[94] The disclosure of anonymised medical information by pharmacists to marketing companies was not a breach of their obligation of confidence. The interest of the subject was held to be in not being identified, rather in the confidentiality of the underlying information.[95]

---

[91] See Gurry, 270ff.

[92] *Thomas v Pearce* [2000] FSR 718 (CA), 719, 721 which includes careful analysis of objective and subjective tests. See also *Carflow*.

[93] See Gurry, 275ff and see *Surface Technology*. It is likely, given the equitable nature of the obligation, that even if someone pays for information, there will still be an obligation if there is the necessary knowledge: *Stephenson Jordan & Harrison Ltd v Macdonald & Evans* (1952) 69 RPC 10 ('*Stephenson Jordan*'), 16.

[94] *Cornelius v De Taranto* (2001) 68 BMLR 62 involved overly wide disclosure of medical information in the circumstances.

[95] *Source*, paras 34–5.

however, starting with *Fraser v Evans*,[111] this concept developed into broader defence of 'just cause for breaking confidence.' The House of Lords in *Spycatcher*[112] said

> 'although the basis of the law's protection of confidence is that there is a public interest that confidences should be preserved and protected by the law, nevertheless that public interest may be outweighed by some countervailing public interest which favours disclosure.... It is this limiting principle which may require a court to carry out a balancing operation, weighing against the public interest in maintaining the confidence against a countervailing public interest favouring disclosure.'

18.60   The application of the public interest defence and balancing act has been criticised as open to 'idiosyncracy'.[113] The public interest defence was an important weapon for the free press, but its application was invariably controversial.[114] Further, disclosure in the public interest did not necessarily mean disclosure to the press. The police or a regulator would likely be deemed more appropriate by courts,[115] however this would depend on the nature of the information and those involved.[116]

18.61   There are interesting examples of how this balance was carried out in the medical field. In 1988 identification of doctors being treated for AIDS was found not to be in the public interest, given the countervailing interest in encouraging seeking of treatment and in the confidentiality of medical records.[117] However in 1989, the doctor–patient relationship was overridden by the public interest in public safety. A report on mental health regarding a person suffering from schizophrenia was sent ultimately to the Home Secretary and this was held not to be breach of confidence.[118]

18.62   Finally, the public interest defence might be available if public bodies are discharging their public function—for example, phone tapping by the police.[119]

> ### Key points on public interest defence
>
> - This has developed from 'no confidence in iniquity' to a careful balance of important public interests in both confidence and disclosure
> - The identity and function of both parties may be important

Unclean hands

18.63   If breach of confidence is based in equity, the complainant must, in accordance with standard principles, come with 'clean hands', having behaved properly themselves in respect of the relevant information. If not, the court may in its discretion refuse relief—even if the public interest did not favour disclosure.[120]

---

[111] [1968] 3 WLR 1172 [1969] 1 QB 349 at 362 (this case is considered in respect of copyright at para 5.32). Followed in *Hubbard v Vosper* [1972] 2 WLR 389, [1972] 2 QB 84 (CA) (regarding publication of the confidential works of the Church of Scientology).
[112] *Spycatcher* 807. See also 785, 794–5, 798, 800–1, 812. See also *Scotsman* at 709, 710 and 712–3.
[113] *SKF, Australia*, 663.   [114] See Gurry, 325ff.
[115] *Initial Services Ltd v Putterill* [1967] 3 WLR 1032, [1968] 1 QB 396, 405; *Malone*, 376–8; *Francome*, 898. See also *Butler v Board of Trade* [1970] 3 WLR 822, [1971] Ch 680, 690 regarding the public interest in availability of information to authorities for use in criminal proceedings.
[116] *Lion Laboratories v Evans* 1985] QB 526, [1984] 3 WLR 539.
[117] *X v Y*, 395–6. See also the decision of the ECtHR in *I v Finland* (2009) 48 EHRR 31.
[118] *W v Egdell* [1989] 2 WLR 689, [1989] 1 All ER 1089.   [119] *Malone*, 362, 367.
[120] See *Stephenson Jordan*, 196 and *Church of Scientology v Kaufman* [1973] RPC 627, [1972] FSR 591. Note that there is no doctrine of equity in Scotland, see para 18.14.

Prior knowledge

18.64   A more apparently mundane defence is that the information received in confidence was already known.[121] It is difficult to distinguish between two sets of information and similar problems to those considered above in the employment context might arise here.[122]

Springboard

18.65   If someone subject to an obligation discloses or uses information in breach of this, and the information is then in the public domain[123]—are they free to use it? Special rules can apply, although they have not gone unchallenged.[124] This is called the springboard doctrine: preventing (at least for a short period) persons who have breached confidence from getting a head start on others, and by avoiding doing preparatory work. This doctrine could apply to new theories and product designs, and also to lists of customer details. An early and still helpful summary of the doctrine is:[125]

> 'a person who has obtained information in confidence is not allowed to use it as a springboard for activities detrimental to the person who made the confidential communication, and springboard it remains even when all the features have been published or can be ascertained by actual inspection by any member of the public." *Terrapin Ltd v Builders Supply Co (Hayes) Ltd* [1960] RPC 128 at 130.

18.66   The controversial question is how long one must be subject to restraint when others can use the information freely. The aim is not to punish but to protect and to prevent unfair advantage;[126] and situations will vary, with courts reluctant to impose permanent restrictions.[127] A key question is how easily the information could have been obtained?[128] Much will depend, however, on the view of the court: sinister behaviour is never viewed kindly:[129] 'having made deliberate and unlawful use of the plaintiff's property, he cannot complain if he finds that the eye of the law is unable to distinguish between those he could, if he chose, have contacted lawfully and those he could not.'

Exercise

Back at Eversogood they are doing well in the market, building on Katie's good relationships with the supermarkets' area sales managers. They all went to university together and keep in touch through industry training courses. Just yesterday, however, Katie realised that she had left her FunFunFun contacts book in the bottom of her handbag. Eversogood's in-house legal counsel Graeme is concerned. Discuss.

---

[121] See for example *Johnson v Heat and Air Systems Ltd* (1941) 58 RPC 229.
[122] See also Stair, para 1486.
[123] Note debate considered in para 18.26 as to whether the information does enter the public domain.
[124] See *OSI*, 401 and *Vestergaard*, notably paras 67–93.
[125] See also Scottish case, *Levin v Farmers Supply Association of Scotland* 1973 SLT (Notes) 43.
[126] *Bullivant*, headnote para 3, 183ff; *Sun Valley Foods Ltd v Vincent* [2000] FSR 825 and *UBS Wealth Management (UK) Ltd v Vestra Wealth LLP* [2008] EWHC 1974 (QB), [2008] IRLR 965.
[127] *Bullivant*, 183–4, 186–7.
[128] See eg *Hibben* which concerned a small market, and information could have been obtained from trade journals.
[129] Eg *Bullivant*, 181, *Holden*.

Private information

18.67   This section will trace the use of breach of confidence to protect some aspects of personal privacy, and note the significant impact of the HRA 1998.

The pre-HRA 1998 position

18.68   On several occasions, courts had found details of extramarital affairs, private artwork or sexual activities to be confidential, and for there to be obligations of confidence on the basis set out above.[130] There is a continuum, however, between private diaries kept under lock and key, details of sexually transmitted disease, an illegitimate child of a campaigner for family values, a trip to the shop in old clothes by a minor celebrity, or a visit to the park of a stereotypical family of four. Are all these really confidential? Yet publication of details of each, and photographs, might all cause distress.

18.69   In 1988 in *Spycatcher* the House of Lords stated 'the right to personal privacy is clearly one which the law should in this field seek to protect'.[131] This did not mean, however, that it did—or does—so protect. A 1990 report[132] recommended against the introduction of a statutory tort of infringement of privacy. But when a photographer gained unauthorised access to a hospital in the early 1990s and photographed a celebrity patient,[133] the law was found to have no means of response.[134]

> ### Key points on pre-HRA 1998 position
>
> - Some private information was considered confidential for the purposes of breach of confidence
> - Obligations of confidence have been identified when there is no pre-existing relationship
> - But there was still a gap and no legislation was proposed

The HRA 1998 and actions between persons

18.70   Article 8 ECHR provides the right to respect for private life, subject to exceptions. This would seem to cover situations such as publication of photographs of private events. Although the UK was a signatory to the ECHR, however, the ECHR was not part of the laws of the UK. What was the impact of the HRA 1998 in respect of Article 8?

18.71   The HRA 1998 did not in fact incorporate the ECHR into the laws of the UK. However, it created possibilities for use of human rights in combination with existing causes of action. Section 6

---

[130] *Prince Albert v Strange* (1849) 1 H & T 1(*'Albert'*); *Argyll*; *Stephens*; *X v Y*. See also paras 18.20 and 18.32.
[131] *Spycatcher*, 782.
[132] Calcutt Report on Privacy and Related Matters June 1990: Cmnd 1102.
[133] *Kaye v Robertson* [1991] FSR 62.
[134] There was voluntary regulation of print media by the Press Complaints Commission which continues (http://www.pcc.org.uk/). Courts are unwilling to intervene in its operation and to grant judicial review: see *R (on application of Ford) v Press Complaints Commission* [2001] EWHC Admin 683, 2002 EMLR 5.

of the Act prohibits a public authority (stated to include a court) from acting in a manner incompatible with Convention rights when, essentially, an alternative approach is available.[135] Convention rights are defined to include Article 8 ECHR. However, another Convention right is Article 10 ECHR. This protects freedom of expression, albeit with exceptions—which include breach of confidence.[136] The relationship between these two ECHR rights is a constant theme in the ongoing development of breach of confidence and privacy.

18.72 Early concerns that the ECHR could be of limited impact in actions between individuals, as it is addressed to states,[137] were not realised. Articles 8 and 10 had a central role in decisions of the Court of Appeal in *A v B plc* in 2002 (regarding publication of the extramarital activities of a footballer), the House of Lords in *Campbell* in 2004,[138] and the Court of Appeal in *Douglas v Hello!* in 2005.[139] Indeed in 2004 the ECtHR in *Hannover* (regarding photographs taken of Princess Caroline of Monaco, mainly in public places) found that states might have positive obligations to introduce measures for exploration by individuals amongst themselves.[140]

Weblinks

Here is the link to the text of the ECHR in its entirety

http://conventions.coe.int/Treaty/en/Treaties/Html/005.htm

and to the HRA 1998

http://www.opsi.gov.uk/acts/acts1998/19980042.htm

Article 8 ECHR

(1) Everyone has the right to respect for his private and family life, his home and his correspondence.

(2) There shall be no interference by a public authority with the exercise of this right except such as is in accordance with the law and is necessary in a democratic society in the interests of national security, public safety or the economic well-being of the country, for the prevention of disorder or crime, for the protection of health or morals, or for the protection of the rights and freedoms of others

Article 10 ECHR

(1) Everyone has the right to freedom of expression. This right shall include freedom . . . to receive and impart information and ideas without interference by public authority and regardless of frontiers . . .

(2) The exercise of these freedoms, since it carries with it duties and responsibilities, may be subject to such formalities, conditions, restrictions or penalties as are prescribed by law and are necessary in a democratic society . . . for the protection of the reputation or rights of others, for preventing the disclosure of information received in confidence . . .

---

[135] See also para 5.49, with reference to HRA 1998, s 3 and interpretation of legislation.

[136] In *Douglas v Hello!* the Court of Appeal confirmed that the action for breach of confidence, although still evolving with the human rights perspective, was also sufficiently precise to come within the prescribed by law restriction on free expression in Art 10: see paras 141–51.

[137] See for example G Phillipson, 'Transforming Breach of Confidence? Towards a Common Law Right of Privacy Under the Human Rights Act' (2003) 66 MLR 726.

[138] *Campbell*, paras 17–8, 49, 50.   [139] *Douglas v Hello!* paras 47–9.

[140] *Hannover*, paras 57 and 72. Considered also in 2006 in *Ash CA*, paras 9–11 and *Reklos v Greece* [2009] EMLR 16 ('*Reklos*'), para 35.

> **Key point on HRA and individual actions**
>
> • National courts can use Articles 8 and 10 ECHR when considering actions for breach of confidence

The HRA 1998, courts and privacy

18.73   In *A v B plc* in 2002 the Court of Appeal set out guidelines for breach of confidence in the light of the HRA 1998. These required assessment of Articles 8 and 10 ECHR in each case and called for only limited reference to be made to pre-HRA cases.[141]

18.74   The key development then came in 2004 when the House of Lords considered the question in *Campbell*, which has been summarised above. Although different approaches are adopted by Law Lords, key principles can be extracted for present purposes. It was held that there was still no overarching claim for invasion of privacy;[142] that breach of confidence could and did deal with personal information;[143] and that pursuant to existing case law, the necessary relationship of confidence might be identified in personal information cases. However, it was felt to be still 'awkward' to have to distinguish information from relationship.[144]

18.75   In the light of this, the House of Lords considered that breach of confidence in this field would be better referred to as misuse of private information.[145] The correct question was whether the information was private, such that Article 8 was engaged. Information would be private if there was a reasonable expectation of privacy.[146]

 Discussion point   For answer guidance visit www.oxfordtextbooks.co.uk/orc/macqueen2e/

Lord Hoffmann in *Campbell* considered there to have been a 'shift in the centre of gravity' of breach of confidence regarding personal information, based not on extended duties of confidence and good faith but on autonomy and dignity.[147] Do you agree? Review your answer after you have considered subsequent cases, which are discussed below.

---

[141] *A v B plc* paras 4, 6, 9, 11 (vi), (xi), (xii) and (xiii). The Court of Appeal did not, however, address ECHR authorities. The Court of Appeal in 2006 held *A v B plc* not to be binding on it in respect of how to conduct the balance in a case on similar facts: *Ash CA*, paras 60–3.

[142] Unlike the position in the US: see *Campbell*, para 11. The limits of the action in respect of non information matters are evident in the House of Lords decision, *Wainwright v Home Office* [2003] UKHL 53, [2004] 2 AC 406, [2003] 3 WLR 1137 regarding strip searching of prison visitors. The UK was subsequently found to have been in breach of its ECHR obligation by the ECtHR, *Wainwright v United Kingdom* (12350/04) 2006 WL 2794071, (2007) 44 EHRR 40. See also *Peck v United Kingdom* (44647/98) [2003] EMLR 15, (2003) 36 EHRR 41 and consideration in M Bhogal, 'United Kingdom Privacy Update 2003' (2004) 1(1) *SCRIPTed* 205, < http://www.law.ed.ac.uk/ahrc/script-ed/docs/privacy_comment.asp and E Reid, 'Wainwright v United Kingdom: Bringing Human Rights Home' (2007) 11(1) EdinLR 83–88. The UK was again found to have failed to comply with its obligations under Article 8 ECHR in *Copland v United Kingdom* (62617/00) (2007) 45 EHRR 37, regarding the monitoring by a public body of an employee's phone calls and Internet usage.

[143] *Campbell*, paras 43–5, 47, 51, referring to *Albert* and *Spycatcher*.

[144] ibid, para. 14, 49.   [145] ibid, para. 14.

[146] ibid, paras 20–21.   [147] ibid, para 51.

A reasonable expectation of privacy

18.76   The House of Lords in *Campbell* considered that it would usually be obvious when there was a reasonable expectation of privacy. More involved tests, such as whether disclosure would be 'grossly offensive', were rejected.[148] It was also stressed that questions of proportionality are not relevant at this stage.[149] But case law suggests that the 'reasonable expectation of privacy' will frequently give rise to uncertainty. For example, blogging has been found to be a public activity, and that the identity of bloggers was not information in respect of which there is a reasonable expectation of privacy.[150] More generally, the Court of Appeal in *Douglas v Hello!* in 2005 considered that the test must cover information personal to the person possessing it, which they do not intend to be shared with the general public; and that this might be clear from the nature or form of the information.[151] The ECtHR in *Hannover* in 2004 considered that private life within Article 8 covered physical and psychological integrity; and that even in public, public figures might engage in private acts in respect of particular zones of life.[152]

18.77   In 2008 in the Court of Appeal considered the issue in *Murray*.[153] The case involved the publication of a photograph of the son of JK Rowling, the author of the Harry Potter books. The photograph was taken, without consent, with a long range lens when the child was being pushed along an Edinburgh street in his buggy. The court at first instance[154] considered this to be an attempt by JK Rowling to exercise her own rights, and held that she could not have rights in respect of walking down the street. The Court of Appeal considered, however, that her son David had his own rights and reasonable expectation of privacy[155] and that these may, in some circumstances, be greater than those of his well known mother.

18.78   Of wider interest is the statement by the Court of Appeal in *Murray* that the reasonable expectation of privacy must always be assessed on the basis of the facts of each case and there could be no guarantees of privacy,[156] but that the following questions could be taken into account:

> 'the attributes of the claimant, the nature of the activity in which the claimant was engaged, the place at which it was happening, the nature and purpose of the intrusion, the absence of consent and whether it was known or could be inferred, the effect on the claimant and the circumstances in which and the purposes for which the information came into the hands of the publisher.'[157]

18.79   The focus on the rights of the child was also seen in the decision of the ECtHR in 2009 in *Reklos v Greece*[158] regarding photographs of a newborn baby taken in a supposedly secure unit.[159] The child was in a place where, unlike the facts in *Murray*, there should have been no prospect of a photograph being taken. The Article 8 right to private life was again considered not to be

---

[148] ibid paras 22, 92–4, 135 (and referring to *Australian Broadcasting Corporation v Lenah* (2001) 208 CLR 199, para 42, which has been considered at first instance, see paras 22, 93, 135, 166).

[149] ibid, para 21.

[150] *The Author of a Blog v Times Newspapers Ltd* [2009] EWHC 1358 (QB), [2009] EMLR 22, paras 2–11, 33

[151] *Douglas v Hello!*, para 83. The Court of Appeal had reviewed authorities which had developed the concept of protection of some information on the basis on its nature (see paras 63–9, referring to *Spycatcher* and *Venables v News Group Newspapers Ltd* [2001] Fam 430). The Court of Appeal went on to apply this approach in *Ash CA*, paras 12–14. Compare Lord Hoffmann in *Hello! HL*, para 118, who focussed more on the question of control, see also n 38 above.

[152] *Hannover*, para 50. In England, see also *X v Persons Unknown* [2006] EWHC 2783 (QB), [2007] EMLR 10, [2007] HRLR 4.

[153] See para 18.25.

[154] *Murray v Express Newspapers Plc* [2007] EWHC 1908 (Ch), [2007] ECDR 20, [2007] EMLR 22 reviewed in paras 13 and 44 of *Murray*.

[155] *Murray*, para 12.   [156] *Murray*, paras 14–20, 27 37, 45 55–8.

[157] *Murray*, para 36.   [158] See n 140 above.   [159] *Reklos*, para 37.

848

Commercial secrets

T Aplin, 'A right of privacy for corporations?', Chapter 19 in P Torremans *Intellectual Property and Human Rights. An Enhanced Edition of Copyright and Human Rights* (2008)

T Aplin, 'Commercial confidences after the Human Rights Act' (2007) 29(10) EIPR 411–19

H Carty, 'An analysis of the modern action for breach of commercial confidence: when is protection merited?' (2008) 4 IPQ 416–455

J Lang, 'The protection of commercial trade secrets' (2003) 25(10) EIPR 462–71

Regulatory data and article 39 TRIPS

P Ganguli, 'Complying with article 39 of TRIPS…a myth or evolving reality?' (2003) 25(4) World Patent Information 329–33

A.Taubman, 'Unfair competition and the financing of public-knowledge goods: the problem of test data protection' (2008) 3(9) JIPLP 591–606

Scotland

Laws of Scotland: Stair Memorial Encyclopaedia (1993), Vol 18, Part II, paras 1451 *et seq.*

R Goldberg, 'Breach of Confidence' in *Delict*, (Scottish Universities Law Institute, 2008)

Other information regimes

P Carey, *Data Protection. A Practical Guide to UK and EU Law* (3rd edn, 2009)

H Fenwick, *Civil Liberties and Human Rights* (4th edn, 2007), Chs 4, 5, 6, 7, 8, 9, 10

R Jay and A Hamilton, *Data Protection Law and Practice* (3rd edn, 2007)

I Lloyd, *Information Technology Law* (5th edn 2008), Part I and Ch 13

J Macdonald QC, R Crail, C Jones, *The Law of Freedom of Information* (2nd edn, 2009)

C Reed and J Angel (eds), *Computer Law. The Law and Regulation of Information Technology* (6th edn, 2007), Chs 10, 11, 12

J Wadham, J Griffiths and K Harris, *Blackstone's Guide to the Freedom of Information Act* (3rd edn, 2007)

VO Benjamin, 'Interception of internet communications and the right to privacy: an evaluation of some provisions of the Regulation of Investigatory Powers Act against the jurisprudence of the European Court of Human Rights' (2007) 6 EHRLR 637–648

C Prins, 'When personal data, behavior and virtual identities become a commodity: Would a property rights approach matter?', (2006) 3(4) SCRIPTed 270 http://www.law.ed.ac.uk/ahrc/script-ed/vol3-4/prins.asp

J Rauhofer, 'Privacy is dead—get over it' (2008) 17(3) ICLT 185–197

Useful websites

Pangloss blog http://blogscript.blogspot.com/

Light Blue Touchpaper blog http://www.lightbluetouchpaper.org/

UK Information Commissioner's Office http://www.ico.gov.uk/

Part VII

Intellectual property, free movement of goods and competition law in Europe

Introduction

This Part of the book has two chapters. The first chapter explains and discusses the interaction between free movement of goods and intellectual property rights and the second the interaction between intellectual property rights and EU competition law.

There are four fundamental freedoms prescribed in the Treaty of Rome: freedom of movement of goods, persons, services and capital. The goal is to establish the common market of the Union: there should not be any trade barriers or obstacles as between the member states. However, in the domain of IP, the exercise of the rights can, and do, pose problems for the free movement of goods and thus the creation of the common market. A key theme in Chapter 19 is as to how the tensions between the exercise of intellectual property by right holders and the achievement of a common market have been reconciled. Intellectual property rights also confer a monopoly on the holder, albeit a carefully crafted monopoly designed to provide a balance between innovation and other public interest goals. But sometimes the exercise of IP rights can produce unexpected outcomes, conferring on the holder an over-strong monopoly through which the right holder may occupy a position of strength which may in turn hamper competition in the marketplace; or owners of IPRs may enter into agreements which may not, ultimately, be to the benefit of consumers. Chapter 20 contains a discussion on when EU competition law may be used to curb the anti-competitive effects of the exercise of IPRs within the marketplace.

Sources of the law: key websites

- Consolidated versions of the founding treaties of the European Union
  http://eur-lex.europa.eu/en/treaties/index.htm
- For the case law of the Court of Justice of the European Union/ECJ and General Court/CFI see
  http://www.curia.europa.eu/

- For decisions of the courts in the various jurisdictions of the UK see BAILII
  http://www.bailii.org/
- For a full list of the various notices issued by the Commission relating to competition rules see
  http://ec.europa.eu/competition/antitrust/legislation/entente3_en.html
- For details of the notices and communications issued by the Commission in relation to the
  modernisation of EU competition rules and procedures (the 'Modernisation Package') see
  http://ec.europa.eu/competition/antitrust/legislation/legislation.html
- The Technology Transfer Block Exemption Regulation ((EC) No 772/2004 of 27 April 2004)
  http://eur-lex.europa.eu/LexUriServ/LexUriServ.do?uri=OJ:L:2004:123:0011:0017:EN:PDF

Free movement of goods and intellectual property rights

Introduction

19.1 The purpose of this chapter is to discuss the European rules on the free movement of goods as they impact on intellectual property rights.

There are four fundamental freedoms in European Union trade law: the freedom of movement of goods, persons, services and capital. The achievement of these freedoms is prescribed in the Treaty of Rome as a means to establish the common market of the Community (and now the Union): there should not be any trade barriers or obstacles as between the member states.

However, in the domain of intellectual property, the existence and exercise of the rights can, and do, pose problems for the free movement of goods and thus the creation of the common market. How then should the aim of establishing and maintaining a common market be reconciled with the existence and exercise of intellectual property rights?

19.2 **Learning objectives**

By the end of this chapter you should be able to describe and explain:

- the competing interests and pressures that underlie this area of the law;
- what is meant by 'consent' as it relates to free movement of goods and how it operates in particular cases;
- when a trade mark proprietor might have a legitimate interest to oppose the free circulation of goods;
- the rules on international exhaustion;
- the differences between free movement of goods and services.

Scope and overview of chapter

19.3   The first part of this chapter explains the tensions that arise between the aims of creating a common market and intellectual property with particular reference to the Treaty provisions relevant to this area, and then moves to examine the competing interests that underlie this area. The next part will focus on case law development, and in particular how the ECJ has sought to reconcile the tensions between the owner of the IPR and the parallel importer. A particularly important facet in this is the notion of consent by the intellectual property owner to the placing of the protected goods on the market. While the IP owner will often not be able to oppose the movement of protected goods once they have been placed on the market, there are circumstances in which the IP owner will have legitimate reasons to prevent further dealings. These will be examined in the next part of the chapter. Discussion will then move to the concept of international exhaustion and examine whether exhaustion applies only within the EU, or whether it extends beyond the borders of the territory. Finally the chapter will consider the free movement of services with a particular focus on how those rules differ from the free movement of goods. As will be seen, the majority of the cases have arisen in relation to registered trade marks.

So the rest of the chapter looks like this:

- Tensions between the aims of the common market and those of intellectual property (19.4–19.10)
- Free movement of goods: case law development (19.11–19.33)
- Legitimate reasons for using a trade mark to prevent further dealing (19.34–19.48)
- International exhaustion (19.49–19.66)
- Free movement of services (19.67–19.72)

Tensions between the aims of the common market and those of intellectual property

19.4   The purpose of Article 34 TFEU (ex Art 28 EC) is to ensure that restrictions to be found within member states that would inhibit the free movement of goods throughout the Community, and thus the creation of a common market, are prohibited.

> 'Quantitative restrictions on imports and all measures having equivalent effect shall be prohibited between Member States.'

This is subject to certain provisos to be found in Article 36 TFEU (ex Art 30 EC). These include measures that would restrict the free movement of goods justified on the grounds of the protection of industrial and commercial property.

> 'The provisions of Articles 34 and 35 shall not preclude prohibitions or restrictions on imports, exports or goods in transit justified on grounds of public morality, public policy or public security; the protection of health and life of humans, animals or plants; the protection of national treasures possessing artistic, historic or archaeological value; or the protection of industrial and commercial property. Such prohibitions or restrictions shall not, however, constitute a means of arbitrary discrimination or a disguised restriction on trade between Member States.'

Early case law concerning Article 28 of the EC Treaty (post Lisbon Article 34 TFEU) showed a determination by the ECJ to prioritise the goal of the creation of a single market. In 1979 in *Cassis de Dijon*[1] the ECJ laid down the general rule:

> 'In the absence of common rules, obstacles to movement within the Community resulting from dispari-ties between the national laws relating to the marketing of a product must be accepted in so far as those provisions may be recognized as being necessary in order to satisfy mandatory requirements relating in particular to the effectiveness of fiscal supervision, the protection of public health, the fairness of commercial transactions and the defence of the consumer.'[2]

One of the difficulties the Court has faced in application of Article 28 (post Lisbon Article 34 TFEU) to the intellectual property sphere is Article 345 TFEU (ex Art 295 EC).

> 'This Treaty shall in no way prejudice the rules in Member States governing the system of property ownership...'

The rules granting IPRs to those entitled is a system of property ownership. The task for the Court was thus to reconcile these tensions.

Overview of the competing interests

19.5   The essence of an IPR is that it gives to the owner a monopoly in the subject matter of the right for a defined period of time. In addition, and as has been explained in preceding chapters, the rights are mostly limited to a single territory. Thus the owner of a particular IPR in one territory (for example, a trade mark, patent or copyright) could use that right to prevent goods bearing the same or a similar mark, an invention which would infringe the patent, or a work protected by copyright, from entering another territory in which the right subsists. That is so even if the IPR is owned by the same person in the two different territories.

For example, if Company X has a registered trade mark in country A, and the same registered trade mark for the same goods in country B, the nature of the right conferred by the trade mark could enable Company X to prevent goods sold in country B from being imported into country A and sold there. Thus the owner of the IPR could partition the market by virtue of the owner-ship of the right in the various different territories.

This partitioning of the market could lead to price differentials as between the territories. In country A, company X could sell the product for £10, but in country B for £5. An entrepreneur (parallel importer) might look at these price differentials and decide that if the goods were bought in country B, imported into country A, the goods could be sold below the price nor-mally charged in country A whilst still giving the parallel importer a profit. If Company X, as the right holder, were able to prevent the importation of the goods into country A, so the com-mon market would be partitioned. This could lead to consumers paying different prices for the same goods depending on where they were purchased.[3]

19.6   The rules on free movement of goods, as they have been developed at European level, are designed to avoid this outcome whilst taking into account Article 345 TFEU (ex Art 295 EC). This has been achieved primarily by the ECJ (now Court of Justice) looking behind the

---

[1] Case 120/78 *Rewe-Zentral AG v Bundesmonopolverwaltung fur Branntwein* [1979] ECR 649.

[2] ibid, para 8.

[3] There are of course many reasons, from the perspective of the IP owner, why the goods may be put onto the territories at different prices. Each national market has its own characteristics: the tax system; regulatory requirements (in par-ticular in the pharmaceutical industry); costs of manufacture; exchange rate fluctuations, etc. W Cornish & D Llewelyn, *Intellectual Property: Patents, Copyright, Trade Marks and Allied Rights* (6th edn, 2007), paras 1–48, 19–02.

monopolistic nature of IPRs to the reason for their existence and the specific subject matter. It was argued that reason for the existence of IPRs is to obtain an economic return. Therefore right holders are given the exclusive right to place the goods which are the subject of the IPR on the market within the Community for the first time. Thereafter the right holder is unable to prevent further circulation of those goods throughout the Community. The right holder is said to have *exhausted* the rights associated with the IPR. However it is important to note that the rights are only exhausted in relation to further movement of those goods throughout the market, and not in respect of other rights associated with the IP.

Policy arguments

19.7   Application of the rules on free movement of goods and their interface with intellectual property takes place against a background containing diverse views—political, social and economic—as well as differing national regulatory regimes designed to achieve domestic goals but which can conflict with European strategies. At its most basic the exhaustion rule states that where goods which are the subject of the IPR are put on the market within the EEA by the right holder or with his consent, then the right holder may not object to movement of the physical object around the territory of the EEA. Right holders can however stop the import of goods into the EEA where those goods have been placed on the market outwith the Community.

The market

19.8   An IP owner will often argue that maintaining price differences as between territories is an essential part of any business strategy. In some circumstances, there may be no choice, for instance in the case of pharmaceuticals the price may be set by the national regulatory authority. In other cases, consumers in one jurisdiction may be more willing to pay more for goods than in others: some freedom for the IP owner to cross subsidise costs as between jurisdictions may be seen as fundamental to economic survival. Other factors, such as labour and material costs also have a bearing on the eventual price to be charged to the consumer. In addition, IP owners (in particular trade mark proprietors) like to control the way in which their goods are presented and sold to the consumer. If this control is absent, so the brand image may be undermined as where luxury items are sold in what are perceived to be shoddy surroundings. If that happens, then the IP owner may be discouraged from developing new products. This in turn will reduce consumer choice.

Parallel traders on the other hand team up with the consumer to argue that the exhaustion rule actually benefits consumers. In a market with no barriers, prices will fall and so consumers pay less for the goods.

As between the IP owner and the parallel trader, the conflicts arise because of the profits that can be made from moving goods from one market (the cheaper market) to another (the more expensive market). Who should profit from the differentials in prices? Should the IP owner be able to maintain the price differences? Or should the parallel trader be able to take advantage of them to their financial benefit?

The governments

19.9   But just as there are disagreements between those who operate within the markets, so there are disagreements at political level. One conflict looks to the domestic interests of the member states. To what extent should governments be able to rely on national interests in any one sector (such as health care) to undermine the fundamental goal of the creation of a single market? Another discussion looks to the Community as a whole. Should the exhaustion rule only apply within the Community, or should a broad, international rule of exhaustion be favoured? If consumer interests are at the forefront of thinking, then that might (but not necessarily) call for a rule of international exhaustion if the effect would be a reduction in prices. If on the other hand it is the interests of economic entities within the Community together with promoting investment within its boundaries that is of prime concern, then is it not preferable to maintain barriers at the boundaries of the territory?

The theorists

19.10   And then there are the theoretical and philosophical underpinnings of the various IPRs. The exhaustion rule applies to all IPRs, although, and as will be discussed below, it is in the realm of patents, and in particular trade marks, that most problems arise. The application of an exhaustion rule to the exercise of IPRs raises the question as to how the existence of the right is justified, and whether a tension arises as between the justification of the right and the rules on free movement of goods. For those IPRs which rest on the incentive/innovation/reward theories, should the owner not be the one to have control over movement of protected goods so that the reward can be gained in the manner in which the IP owner anticipated? But what of those IPRs, notably trade marks, where the existence of the right is as a guarantee of origin to the consumer? What justification could there be for the right holder to control movement of goods to which the mark has been affixed once they have been placed on the market anywhere in the world with the consent of the rightholder? And why should the exhaustion rule operate in the context of tangible articles embodying the intellectual property, but not in relation to transient rights such as the performance right in copyright?

 Question

As will be noted in the discussion below, many of the cases which have shaped this area of the law have concerned trade marks, with patents coming in second place. Fewer cases have been brought in the domain of copyright. Why might this be the case? Revisit your answer when you have finished this chapter.

Key points on the goals of free movement of goods

- The rules on free movement of goods seek to reconcile the tensions between Articles 34 TFEU (ex Art 28 EC), 36 TFEU (ex Art 30 EC) and 345 TFEU (ex Art 295 EC)

Free movement of goods: case law development

19.11   Through a series of cases starting in 1971, the ECJ and national courts sought to develop rules which balance the interests of the IP holder with those of the parallel trader and the creation of a common market.

Some of the terms that are used in case law in this area include:

- Existence
- Exercise
- Specific subject matter
- Exhaustion
- Free movement of goods

 Exercise

Explain what you think might be meant by these terms. Revisit your definitions when you have completed this chapter.

Note that the numbering of the relevant articles has changed twice: Article 34 TFEU (ex Art 28, ex Art 30); Article 36 TFEU (ex Art 30, ex Art 36); Article 345 TFEU (ex Art 295, ex Art 222). The article numbering which applies following the changes made by the Treaty of Lisbon will be used in this chapter except where the discussion relates to historical events and/or where quotations from cases are used in the text.

19.12 The first case to consider the interaction between IPRs and the free movement of goods was *Deutsche Grammophon GmbH v Metro SB Grossmarkte GmbH & Co.*[4] Deutsche Grammophon (DG) produced records. In Germany it supplied them under the 'Polydor' mark to retailers. In the agreement with the retailers DG not only controlled retail prices, but also required an undertaking from the retailers that they would only import goods from elsewhere with the agreement of DG which would only be given if the retailers agreed to sell the goods at the maintained price. DG exported records to a subsidiary in Paris. These goods were re-exported and imported into Germany where Metro, not part of DG and not part of the distribution chain, sold them below the price fixed in Germany.

Diagram 19.1 *Deutsche Grammophon GmbH v Metro SB Grossmarkte GmbH & Co*

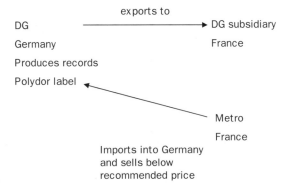

---

[4] [1971] CMLR 631.

The effect of this was to undermine the system that DG had put into place to maintain retail prices in Germany. The case was ultimately referred to the ECJ. In passing judgment the Court said:

> '...the Treaty does not affect the existence of the industrial property rights conferred by the national legislation of a member-State, the exercise of these rights may come within the prohibitions of the Treaty. Although Article 36 permits prohibitions or restrictions on the free movement of goods that are justified for the protection of industrial and commercial property, it only allows such restrictions on the freedom of trade to the extent that they are justified for the protection of the rights that form the specific object of this property'.[5]

Existence, exercise and specific subject matter

19.13   So here we see the ECJ making a distinction between the existence of an IPR, the exercise of that right, and the specific object or subject matter of the right. These have been further developed in subsequent case law.

19.14   In *Centrafarm v Sterling & Winthrop*[6] the ECJ was faced with questions concerning the movement of patented drugs between Holland and the UK. Sterling held parallel patents for a drug in Holland and the UK and had placed drugs protected by the patent on both markets. Centrafarm, without the permission of Sterling, purchased the patented drugs in the UK and imported them into Holland where prices were higher. This was challenged by Sterling.

Diagram 19.2 *Centrafarm v Sterling & Winthrop*

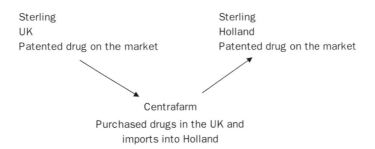

The ECJ said that the use of an exclusive right granted by a patent to prevent imports was an exercise of rights which was incompatible with the provisions of the Treaty on free movement of goods.

The specific subject matter of industrial property is to reward the creative effort of the inventor. The inventor thus has the exclusive right to use an invention with a view to manufacturing industrial products and to put them into circulation for the fist time either directly or by way of a grant of a licence to a third party. In addition the inventor has the right to oppose infringements.[7] Any derogation from the principle of free movement of goods is not justified where the product, protected by the right, has been put onto the market by the patentee himself or with his consent.[8]

⁵ ibid, para 11.   ⁶ [1974] ECR 1147, [1974] 2 CMLR 480.
⁷ ibid, para 9.   ⁸ ibid, para 11.

So in this case the ECJ alluded to the specific subject matter of industrial property as being the economic reward that can be obtained from exploitation. However, once that has been obtained—through putting the goods on the market for the first time—the right to prevent further circulation is exhausted. In addition the ECJ mentioned consent. This is central to the concept of free movement of goods: the goods must have been placed on the market by the right holder or with his consent. Subsequent case law has helped to refine what is meant by consent.

19.15   It should be noted that the existence/exercise dichotomy has been criticised by commentators who have pointed out that it is not the exercise of rights that inhibits the free movement of goods, but measures to be found in national legislations. Further, the existence of an IPR could be considered worthless unless the owner is able to exercise it. It is a concept that has been less mentioned in the more recent case law, where focus is on the specific object or the specific subject matter of the right.[9]

Consent

19.16   A central feature in this area relates to the notion of consent. The ECJ has repeatedly said that where protected goods have been placed on the market by the rightholder or with the consent of the right holder, then no objection may be made to further movement of the goods throughout the territory of the common market.

For example and in relation to patents:

'Articles 30 and 36 of the EEC Treaty prevent national legislation from applying to give a patentee the right to prohibit the import and marketing of a product which was legally placed on the market of another member-State by the proprietor of the patent himself or with his consent or by a person connected to him by a relationship of legal or economic dependence'.[10]

The justification lies in the need to prevent the artificial partitioning of the market:

'In fact, if the patentee were able to prohibit the import of products covered by the patent which had been marketed in another member-State by him or with his consent he would be enabled to partition the national markets and thus to put into effect a restriction on trade between member-States without such restriction being necessary to ensure that he obtains the substance of the exclusive rights arising under parallel patents'.[11]

19.17   Consent by the proprietor of a trade mark to marketing goods in the EEA by a third party who has no economic link may be implied where it can be inferred from facts and circumstances prior to, simultaneous with, or subsequent to the marketing where it can be unequivocally demonstrated that the proprietor has renounced his exclusive rights.[12]

Common origin and consent

19.18   An early case where a trade mark, originally held by one proprietor but later by different proprietors for different territories, concerned coffee and the Hag trade mark: *Van Zuylen Freres v Hag*

[9] W Cornish & D Llewelyn, *Intellectual Property: Patents, Copyright, Trade Marks and Allied Rights* (6th edn, 2007) para 19-05.
[10] Case C-19/84 *Pharmon v Hoescht BV* [1985] 3 CMLR 775 ECJ, para 22.
[11] ibid, para 23.
[12] Case C-324/08 *Makro Zelfbedieningsgroothandel e.a. v Diesel S.p.a.* See also para 19.57.

AC.[13] The Hag mark was owned both in Germany and in Belgium by the same company. During the war, the Belgian mark was sequestrated and ownership passed to a third party. The owner of the Hag mark in Germany wanted to import coffee bearing the mark into Belgium.

Diagram 19.3 *Van zuylen Freres v Hag Ac*

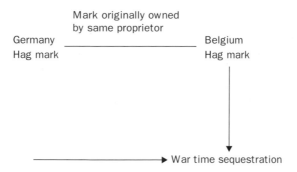

Van Zuylen was held entitled to import goods into Benelux countries as the mark had a common origin.

The ECJ found that by virtue of the fact that the mark was originally held by the one proprietor (a common origin), this entitled the German owner to market the goods in the Benelux countries.

There was much disquiet amongst commentators as a result of this case.[14] If the facts—where the trade mark had been passed to a third party and there remained no control with the original owner—entitled the owner to market goods bearing the mark in the country, why not then permit any unconnected third party to market goods in a country where the same (or similar) IPR might belong to a totally independent unconnected third party?

19.19   The ECJ had a chance to revisit its judgment in 1990 in *SA CNL-Sucal NV v Hag GV*.[15] By this time CNL owned the Hag mark for its business in Belgium. CNL sought to import its products bearing the Hag mark into Germany. The ECJ, reversing its earlier judgment, said that CNL had no right to go into the German market. No consent had been given by the German proprietor of the trade mark.

19.20   This, more sophisticated appreciation of the function of a trade mark, was further refined in *IHT Internationale Heiztechnik GmbH v Ideal Standard GmbH*[16] (Ideal Standard) where a question arose over the import of bathroom accessories from France into Germany. The Ideal Standard trade mark was owned by an American firm. This firm had subsidiaries in both Germany and France which held the trade marks for those territories. The Ideal Standard trade mark in France was assigned to a third party which had no legal or economic ties with either the American firm or with the German subsidiary of the American firm. IHT then sought to import goods

---

[13] [1974] ECR 731, [1974] 2 CMLR 127.

[14] W Cornish & D Llewelyn, *Intellectual Property: Patents, Copyright, Trade Marks and Allied Rights* (6th edn, 2007) para 19–06.

[15] [1990] ECR I-3711, [1990] 3 CMLR 571.

[16] [1994] ECR I-2789, [1994] 3 CMLR 857, [1995] FSR 59.

bearing the mark from France into Germany. The German subsidiary objected and brought proceedings for infringement.

Diagram 19.4 *IHT Internationale Heiztechnik GmbH v Ideal Standard GmbH*

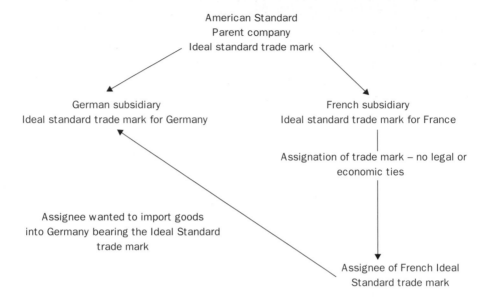

The ECJ said that the German subsidiary could indeed keep the goods bearing the trade mark from being imported into Germany. A trade mark is a guarantee of quality. There was no control by the German subsidiary or the American parent company over the goods manufactured by the French assignee under the Ideal Standard trade mark. The division of the mark through the assignation had the effect of depriving the original proprietor (the American firm) of any form of quality control over the goods manufactured under the mark.

> 'This principle known as exhaustion of rights applies where the owner of the trade mark in the import-ing State and the owner of the trade mark in the exporting State are the same or where even if they are separate persons they are economically linked. A number of situations are covered: products put into circulation by the same undertaking, but a licensee, a parent company, a subsidiary of the same group or by an exclusive distributor'.[17]

Specifically relating to trade marks, the ECJ said in *Ideal Standard* that the decisive factor is whether the trade mark owner has the possibility of control over goods to which the mark is affixed to the country of exportation and the quality of goods that were placed on the market. If it did have such control, then it would be seen as having consented to the marketing.

 Exercise

What would have been the position if the agreement between the French subsidiary and the French assignee was not at arms length thus enabling both the German subsidiary and the French assignee to keep goods belonging to the other out of their respective territories?

[17] ibid, para 34.

Might competition law be relevant to challenge such an agreement? Consider *Consten and Grundig v Commission* (1966) ECR 299 where Grundig, a manufacturer of electrical goods, appointed Consten as its exclusive distributor in France. The distributor was permitted to register the trade mark 'Gint' under which goods were distributed. The intention was to ensure that the distributors could prevent parallel traders from importing goods from other member states thus reserving exclusive territories to the distributor. When challenged under Article 81 the ECJ found that the Gint trade mark could not be enforced to prevent parallel imports as that would amount to an arbitrary distortion of trade within the EU.[18] See also the discussion of *Doncaster Pharmaceuticals Group Ltd v The Bolton Pharmaceutical Company Ltd* [2006] EWCA Civ 661 in para 20.63.

19.21   Consent thus refers to the consent by the rightholder to the placing of the protected goods onto the common market for the first time. However, and as can be seen from *Ideal Standard*, consent is not limited to the right holder as such, but extends also to circumstances where a right holder and the person placing the goods on the market, are economically linked.

Differing levels of protection in member states and no consent

19.22   Circumstances arise in which there may be differing levels of protection for IPRs in member states, or protection may exist in one country but not in another. If the owner of the IPR has not consented to the marketing, then he may invoke his right to prevent importation into the country where the right exists.

19.23   In *EMI Electrola GmbH v Patricia Im- und Export*[19] the sound recording right in Cliff Richard's songs was extant under German law but had expired in Denmark. Patricia attempted to import the sound recordings from Denmark into Germany.

Diagram 19.5 *EMI Electrola GmbH v Patricia Im- und Export*

Cliff Richard songs

Germany   Denmark
Sound recording right extant   ◄————   Sound recordings right expired
Owned by EMI   Patricia sought to import into
                                                    Germany

The Court held that as the copyright owner, the manufacturer and importer were unconnected parties, no consent had been given to the marketing of the recordings in Germany. EMI could invoke its copyright in the sound recording in Germany to prevent the importation as its rights had not been exhausted.

---

[18] Note the emergence of the existence/exercise dichotomy later directly applied to free movement of goods cases in *Deutsche Grammophon GmbH v Metro SB Grossmarkte GmbH & Co* [1971] 1 CMLR 631.
[19] [1989] ECR 79.

Question

This case led to the enactment of an EU Directive. Which one?[20]

19.24   A not dissimilar set of circumstances arose in *Sony Music Entertainment (Germany) GmbH v Falcon Neue Medien Vertrieb GmbH*[21] but with the twist that copyright was argued to subsist with respect to US recordings made before 1 January 1966 by Bob Dylan. Sony sought to enjoin Falcon from copying and distributing two Bob Dylan songs in Germany. Falcon argued that those songs were never subject to copyright protection in Germany. The ECJ ruled that 'the term of protection laid down in Directive 2006/116 [the Directive on the term of protection of copyright and related rights] is also applicable…where the subject matter at issue has at no time been protected in the Member State in which the protection is sought'. This is so because the Bob Dylan recordings were subject to copyright protection in the UK, which affords protection to American recordings made before 1 January 1966. According to the court, since the American recordings of Bob Dylan's songs were protected in at least one Member State (the UK), Sony, as the current rights holder, could sue for copyright infringement in any Member State (such as Germany) even though the recordings were never protected under the national copyright laws of Germany.

Different levels of protection in member states and consent

19.25   The ECJ has also considered circumstances in which no protection exists in one country but the owner has consented to the marketing of products protected by IP.

19.26   In *Merck & Co Inc v Stephar BV*,[22] Merck put drugs on the market in Italy, a country in which no patent protection for the drugs could be obtained at the relevant time. Merck did have a patent for the drugs in the Netherlands. Stephar purchased the drugs in the Italy and sought to import them into the Netherlands. Merck invoked its patent rights in the Netherlands to prevent the importation. Merck acknowledged that it had consented to the marketing of the drugs in Italy, but argued that since no patent protection could be obtained there, it should not be seen as having exhausted its rights.

Stephar purchased in Italy and sought to import into Netherlands. The ECJ said that since consent had been given to the marketing of the drugs in Italy, Merck could not invoke its patent to prevent their importation into the Netherlands.

Diagram 19.6 *Merck & Co Inc v Stephar BV*

Merck   Merck
Italy – no protection possible   Netherlands – patent protection
Drugs on the market with consent

———————————————————————▶

---

[20] See also *Warner Bros v Christiansen* [1988] ECR 2605 dealing with the rental of videos in Denmark which had been manufactured in the UK where no rental right subsisted.

[21] Case C-240/07 [2009] ECDR 12.

[22] [1981] ECR 2063.

19.27   This view was subsequently reaffirmed in *Merck & Co v Primecrown Ltd.*[23] Merck held patents in the UK for drugs which they also marketed in Spain and Portugal where protection was not obtainable. The price of the drugs was fixed by the respective governments. Merck argued that they had ethical obligations to place the drugs on the market in these countries to meet the requirements of the population. However, the ECJ did not find this argument sufficient to change the rule in *Merck v Stephar*. The Court pointed out that any anomalies that existed as between member states arising from differences in protection in the territories were disappearing with the harmonisation programme. The Court did however note that if legal compulsion exists which requires marketing in a particular country, then the patent owner would not be deemed to have consented to the marketing.[24] However, ethical considerations did not provide sufficient certainty to determine when an IP owner is deprived of the power to determine how to market a product.

 Question

What do you think of the argument deployed by Merck that it had ethical obligations to place the drugs on the territories in which no protection existed? Could ethical obligations ever give sufficient basis to enable an IP owner to argue successfully that there was no consent in relation to the marketing of a product?

Consent and the pharmaceutical industry

19.28   Both of the *Merck* cases involved the pharmaceutical industry. Health care is a domain in which much governmental regulation exists in member states in relation to prices, packaging and availability of drugs and many other aspects of the industry. The ECJ has long held that price differences as between member states resulting from governmental measures makes no difference to the rules on exhaustion and the goal of attaining a common market.[25] But questions continue to be raised and referred to the ECJ in this area. One concerning the interaction between competition law and free movement of goods first arose in *Syfait v GSK*[26] (see also para 20.56). The Greek Government requires that medicines sold in Greece are so sold at the lowest price prevailing on the European market. GSK supplied wholesalers with drugs but found that many batches were being onward sold by parallel traders in other territories where the price was higher. GSK decided to limit the supply of these products to the Greek wholesalers to the quantities needed to fulfil local need. The question arose as to whether it was an abuse of a dominant position (Article 82 EC ([ex 86] post Lisbon, Article 102 TFEU) for GSK to refuse to fill the wholesalers' orders where the intention was to limit parallel trade?[27]

---

²³ [1996] ECR I-6285.
²⁴ See also Case C-19/84 *Pharmon BV v Hoechst AG* [1985] ECR 2281 where drugs produced under a compulsory licence were not subject to exhaustion; also Case C-24/67 *Parke Davis & Co v Probel & Centrafarm* [1968] ECR 55 where goods were placed on a market without the consent of the trade mark owner where no protection existed.
²⁵ Case C-15/74 *Centrafarm v Sterling* (1974) ECR 1147.
²⁶ *Synetairismos Farmakopoion Aitolias & Akarnanias (Syfait) and Others v GlaxoSmithKline plc* [2005] 5 CMLR 1.
²⁷ For discussion on EU competition law under Art 101 TFEU (ex Art 81 EC) see Chapter 20.

In the event, the ECJ declined jurisdiction, as the questions had not been referred by a competent tribunal within the meaning of Article 234 of the EC Treaty (post Lisbon, Article 267 TFEU). But that was not before the Advocate General Francis Jacob (AG) issued his opinion.

The AG noted that an intention to restrain parallel trade would probably be a reason to condemn a refusal to supply, but that in certain circumstances it might be permitted. There were instances where parallel trade might result in inadequate supplies being available. Because parallel importers sourced products from the cheapest country, pharmaceutical companies might delay or stop the supply of drugs in countries where the price was lowest. The benefits of parallel trade would go to the wholesalers in the countries were prices were limited at the lowest level and not to the patients nor to those paying for their treatment. It was thus the effect of the national law in fixing the price that would be paid for the drugs that segregated the market and not, in the instant case, the behaviour of GSK.

19.29   While the ECJ declined jurisdiction in *Syfait*, the same questions were referred to the court by the Efetio Athinon in joined cases *Sot. Lelos Kai Sia EE and Others v Glaxosmith-Kline Aeve Farmadeftikon Proionton (formerly Glaxowellcome Aeve).*[28] (see also para 20.56) The ECJ ruled that a dominant undertaking that refuses to meet ordinary orders from wholesalers in order to put a stop to parallel exports carried out by those wholesalers from one member state to another abuses its dominant position, it being for the national court to decide whether the orders are ordinary. A company could however counter, in a reasonable and proportionate manner, orders where the supplies were destined for the parallel market. So it is clear from this ruling that a company may act to limit orders where parallel markets are being supplied, the key difficulty being to determine what might be ordinary, and in the event it is thought that an order does not fall within this category, the need to respond in a reasonable and proportionate manner. As with repackaging cases, there is much grey area between what is permissible from the perspective of the company and what it not. It is likely that there will be further case law to clarify the boundaries.[29]

 Question

Read the opinion of the AG in *Syfait v GSK* [2005] 5 CMLR 1 and of the ECJ in the *Sot. Lelos Kai* case. Read also Chapter 20 on competition law. Do you think it should be permissible for an entity in a dominant position to limit supply in order to prevent parallel trade? What weight should be placed on the right of a company to take reasonable and proportional steps to protect its own commercial interests? Who benefits from this, and who might be prejudiced? Should the rule be limited to the pharmaceutical industry or be more widely applicable?

Licence terms and consent

19.30   A question arises as to the interaction between licence terms and consent. Specifically whether exhaustion applies where a licensee of a trade mark places goods on the market in contravention of the licence terms.

---

[28] Joined Cases C-468/06 to C-478/06 [2008] 5 CMLR 20.
[29] For a case concerning competition, copyright and conditional access services see para 19.69.

■ *Case C-59/08 Copad SA v Christian Dior Couture SA [2009] ETMR 40*

Christian Dior (Dior) entered into a trade mark licence agreement with Societe industrielle lingerie (SIL) to manufacture and distribute luxury corsetry goods bearing the Christian Dior trade mark. In contravention of an express provision in the licence agreement, SIL sold goods bearing the Christina Dior trade mark to Copad, which operated discount stores and was outside Dior's selective distribution network. Dior sued SIL and Copad for trade mark infringement. The ECJ ruled that a 'licensee who puts goods bearing a trade mark on the market in disregard of a provision in a licence agreement does so without the consent of the proprietor of the trade mark where it is established that the provision in question is included in those listed in art.8(2) of... [the Trade Marks] Directive'.[30]

The list in Article 8(2), which the Court said was exhaustive, provides:

> 'The proprietor of a trade mark may invoke the rights conferred by that trade mark against a licensee who contravenes any provision in his licensing contract with regard to its duration, the form covered by the registration in which the trade mark may be used, the scope of the goods or services for which the licence is granted, the territory in which the trade mark may be affixed, or the quality of the goods manufactured or of the services provided by the licensee.'

Thus if a breach of contract falls within Article 8(2), consent will be considered to have been withdrawn and the licensee will infringe the trade mark.

Absence of consent

19.31   There have been examples of cases where no consent by or on behalf of the IP owner has been given and hence the IP owner can prohibit the movement of the goods. One example is given above (para 19.23) in *EMI Electrola v Patricia*.[31] Another example was in *Terrapin (Overseas) Ltd v Terranova Industrie C A Kapferer & Co*.[32] The question there was whether the German firm, Terranova Industrie, could prevent the importation into Germany from Britain of prefabricated houses bearing the mark 'Terrapin'. The German firm had registration of the mark 'Terranova' in Germany for construction materials. Thus both the marks and the goods were similar. As there had never been a connection between the firms, the ECJ ruled that the German firm could indeed keep the products bearing the Terrapin mark out of Germany.

The ECJ pointed out that 'If in such a case the principle of the free movement of goods were to prevail over the protection given by the respective national laws, the specific objective of industrial and commercial property rights would be undermined'. Protection thus had to be ensured for the 'legitimate use' of the rights conferred by national laws.[33] However such protection would be denied where improper exercise would be of such a nature as to maintain or effect artificial partitions within the common market.

19.32   Where the right owner has been required to place goods on the market as under a compulsory licence, the goods will not be seen as having been placed on the market by or with the consent of the IP owner who will be able to prevent further movement of the goods.

---

[30] Case C-59/08 *Copad SA v Christian Dior Couture SA* [2009] ETMR 40, para 51.

[31] [1989] ECR 79.

[32] Case C-119/75 [1976] 2 CMLR 482 ECJ. See also Case T-168/01 *GlaxoSmithKline Services Unlimited v Commission of the European Communities* [2006] 5 CMLR 29 for a differential pricing system for drugs in Spain and questions of competition law.

[33] ibid, para 7.

■ *Case C-19/84 Pharmon v Hoescht* [1985] 3 CMLR 775, ECJ

Hoescht held a drug patent in the UK and the Netherlands. A compulsory licence was obtained
in the UK by DDSA Pharmaceuticals Ltd to manufacture the drug in the UK, but subject to
a prohibition on export. DDSA ignored the prohibition and sold the drug to Pharmon who
intended to market it in the Netherlands. Hoescht challenged this on the basis of its patent in
the Netherlands. As Hoescht had not consented to the manufacture and marketing in the UK,
there was no consent, and thus the sale of the drugs in the Netherlands could be prevented.

> 'It should be emphasised in this respect that when the competent authorities in a member-State, . . . grant
> a compulsory licence to a third party which allows him to carry out manufacturing and marketing opera-
> tions which the patentee would normally have the power to prohibit, the patentee cannot be regarded
> as having consented to the actions of the third party. In fact, the holder of the patent is deprived by
> such an official act of his right to decide freely on the conditions under which he will place his product
> on the market'.[34]

Consent and transfer of ownership

19.33   The issue of transfer of ownership arose in the copyright case, *Peek & Cloppenburg KG v Cassina
SpA*,[35] in which the ECJ was asked to rule on whether the display and use of items in a shop
infringed an IP owner's distribution right. Chairs had been manufactured in Italy and imported
into Germany without the consent of the copyright owner, Cassina, at a time when copyright
protection did not subsist for chairs in Italy. Cassina alleged infringement of the distribution
right. The ECJ held that the concept of distribution to the public, otherwise than through sale,
of the original of a work or of a copy, for the purpose of Article 4(1) of the Infosoc Directive
2001/29, covers acts which entail, and only acts which entail, a transfer of the ownership of that
object.[36] The display of the chairs and their use by the public in the shops was not a transfer of
ownership and thus not an infringement.

Key points on consent

- Consent by the rightholder is fundamental to free movement of goods
- Consent means consent to placing goods on the common market for the first time,
  thereafter the right holder may not object to further distribution of those goods

---

Legitimate reasons for using a trade mark to prevent further dealing

19.34   A key question is as to when a trade mark proprietor may legitimately oppose the further dealing with goods placed on the market with their consent.

The wording of Article 7.2 of Directive 2008/95/CE to approximate the laws of the member
states relating to trade marks[37] is:

---

[34] Para 26.   [35] Case C-456/06.   [36] ibid, para 36.
[37] Version 2008/95/CE consolidated version previously First Council Directive 89/104/EEC of 21 December 1988 to
approximate the laws of the member states relating to trade marks (Trade Marks Directive).

'Paragraph 1 shall not apply where there exist legitimate reasons for the proprietor to oppose further commercialisation of the goods, especially where the condition of the goods is changed or impaired after they have been put on the market.'

The issue of legitimate reasons has arisen in two broad areas. The first concerns repackaging, most notably in the pharmaceutical industry, and the second concerns advertising where the IP is used by a third party in a promotional campaign.

The pharmaceutical industry, trade marks and repackaging by parallel importers

19.35   The pharmaceutical industry is one of the main industries at the centre of cases on repackaging and parallel imports. When drugs are imported from one member state into another, the parallel importers often repackage, re-box or over-sticker the drug containers. The majority of the cases below deal with the pharmaceutical industry—although it should be noted that the rulings are not limited to that industry but would appear to apply whenever the facts are relevant within other industry sectors.[38]

Some terminology:

- *Repackaging:* a parallel importer acquires a product placed on the market, replaces the container in which the products were sold, and reaffixes the trade mark before marketing.

- *Re-labelling:* a parallel importer replaces the outer packaging and reaffixes another trade mark, under which the very product is sold in the member state where it is going to be marketed.

- *Re-boxing:* a parallel importer retains the original internal packaging but adds a new exterior carton printed in the language of the member state of importation.

- *Over-stickering:* a parallel importer retains the original internal and external packaging but adds an additional external label printed in the language of the member state of importation.

- *De-branding:* a parallel importer sells the goods after their original trade marks have been removed and not replaced.

 Exercise

Have a look at the article by N Gross and L Harrold, 'Fighting for Pharmaceutical Profits: the Decision of the ECJ in *Boehringer Ingelheim v Swingward*' [2002] EIPR 497 to get an idea of what the packages look like once some of these activities have occurred.

19.36   Parallel importers argue that such actions are necessary for the drugs to be accepted in the member state of importation. National rules and consumer expectation may require drugs to be purchased and presented in a particular way and in specified quantities. However repackaging and re-labelling invariably involve the affixing of the drug companies trade mark back onto the re-packaged product or the removal altogether of that trade mark. In addition, the trade mark of the parallel importer may be affixed to the packaging.

[38] *F Loendersloot Internationale Expeditie v George Ballantine & Son Ltd* [1998] 1 CMLR 1015.

19.37   It will be recalled that the Trade Mark Directive provides that a trade mark owner can prevent a third party from using, in the course of trade, a sign which is identical or similar to the registered mark.[39] Use includes fixing the sign to the goods or other packaging, importing the goods and offering the goods for sale or putting them on the market.[40] Thus, the drug companies argue that the activities of the parallel importers constitute an infringement of their trade marks and that they may legitimately oppose such activities. As regards re-boxing and over-stickering, the trade mark proprietors argue that the parallel importers are not only free riding on the goodwill they have built up, but in addition, and when the parallel importers use their own generic name for a drug on the packaging, this gives them an advantage when the patent expires in that the generic name can easily be substituted as the name of the drug.

19.38   There have been many cases brought before the ECJ dealing with repackaging.[41] Four of the key ones are *Hoffmann-La Roche v Centrafarm*;[42] *Bristol-Myers Squibb v Paranova*;[43] *Loendersloot v Ballantine*,[44] and *Upjohn v Paranova*.[45]

From these cases it is apparent that a trade mark owner may legitimately oppose the further marketing of a pharmaceutical product where the importer has repackaged the product and reaffixed the trade mark unless:

- the reliance by the trade mark owner on the IPR to oppose the marketing of the repackaged goods contributes to the artificial partitioning of the markets between member states (that is, the repackaging must be necessary for market access). This may be the case where the trade mark owner places identical drugs on the market in different member states but in different packaging;

- it is shown that the repackaging has not affected the original condition of the goods. Such might be the case where new instructions in the language of importation are added to the goods;

- the new packaging includes information on who repackaged the product and the name of the manufacturer in legible print;

- the presentation of the repackaged product is not such as to be liable to damage the reputation of the trade mark and of its owner;

- the parallel importer gives notice to the trade mark owner before the repackaged product is put on sale and, on demand, supplies him with a specimen of the repackaged product.

Thus the parallel importer who repackages the goods and re-applies the mark will need to satisfy these conditions if there is to be no infringement.

Artificial partitioning of the market

19.39   One of the key questions concerns when the reliance on the IPR by the owner might contribute to the artificial partitioning of the market between member states. There have been a number of cases elaborating on those circumstances where the result may be such artificial partitioning and in particular where repackaging might be necessary for market access.

---

[39] Trade Mark Directive, Art 5.   [40] ibid, Art 5(3).
[41] See Jacob LJ in *Boehringer Ingelheim v Swingward Ltd* [2004] ETMR 65, [2004] EWCA Civ 129 (CA).
[42] Case C-102/77 [1978] ECR 1139.
[43] Joined Cases C-427/93, C-429/93 and C-436/93, [1996] ECR I-3457.
[44] Case C-349/95 [1997] ECR I-6227, [1998] 1 CMLR 1015, [1998] ETMR 10.
[45] Case C-379/97 [2000] Ch 571, [2000] 3 WLR 303, [1999] All ER (EC) 880.

Test of necessity

19.40   In *Bristol-Myers Squibb v Paranova*[46] the ECJ stressed that the power of the trade mark owner to oppose the marketing of repacked products should be limited only in so far as the repackaging is necessary to market the product in the member state of importation.[47] The justification is the risk inherent in the change that is brought about by the repackaging during which there could be interference with the original product. Thus the repackaging must be necessary to enable the marketing of the product, but is limited to what is necessary in order to ensure that the legitimate interests of the right owner are safeguarded.

19.41   The meaning was explored in *Upjohn v Paranova*.[48] Paranova marketed an antibiotic under the name Dalacin C in all member states except Denmark, Germany and Spain. In these countries it used the name Dalacin, and in France it used Dalacine. Paranova justified the differences by reference to the rules pertaining to registration of trade marks in the various countries. Upjohn bought goods in both Greece and France, repackaged them under the name Dalacin and marketed them in Denmark. A reference was made to the ECJ asking when it was necessary to repackage the drugs.

The ECJ said that the test of necessity would be satisfied where:

> 'the rules or practices in the importing Member States prevent the product in question from being marketed in that State under its trade mark in the exporting Member State. This is so where a rule for the protection of consumers prohibits the use, in the importing Member State, of that trade mark used in the exporting Member State on the ground that it is liable to mislead consumers. In contrast, the condition of necessity will not be satisfied if replacement of the trade mark is explicable solely by the parallel importer's attempt to secure a commercial advantage'.[49]

19.42   Thus where products purchased by the parallel importer cannot be placed on the market in the member state of importation in their original packaging by reason of national rules or practices relating to packaging, or where sickness insurance rules make reimbursement of medical expenses depend on a certain packaging or where well-established medical prescription practices are based, inter alia, on standard sizes recommended by professional groups and sickness insurance institutions repackaging would be necessary.[50] It would not however be necessary where the parallel importer can reuse the original packaging for the purpose of marketing in the member state of importation by affixing labels to that packaging.[51]

Necessity, consumer preferences, poor quality packaging and minimum intervention

19.43   Consumer preference on a particular market might result in repackaging being necessary. *Boehringer Ingelheim v Swingward Ltd*[52] concerned a variety of different methods of repackaging: the inclusion of English language information sheets; replacing of the trade mark onto the boxes and leaflets; the inclusion, with the trade mark, of packaging which was distinctive of the parallel importer; the use of the generic name of the drug but not the trade mark. The ECJ held that replacement packaging of drugs is objectively necessary if, without such repackaging, effective access to the market or to a substantial part of the market would be hindered

---

[46] Joined Cases C-427/93, C-429/93 and C-436/93, [1996] ECR I-3457.   [47] ibid, para 56.
[48] Case C-379/97 [1999] ECR I-6927, [2000] Ch 571, [2000] 3 WLR 303.   [49] ibid, para 43.
[50] Joined Cases C-427/93, C-429/93 and C-436/93 *Bristol-Myers Squibb and Others* [1996] ECR I-3457, paras 53 and 54.
[51] ibid, para 55.   [52] Case C-143/00 [2002] All ER (EC) 581, [2003] Ch 27, [2002] 3 WLR 1697.

as the result of strong resistance from a significant proportion of consumers to relabelled drugs.[53]

When this ruling was applied by the High Court it was found that the respective trade marks had been infringed.[54] This resulted in a further appeal and cross appeal being taken to the Court of Appeal.[55] That court found that the High Court had been wrong to suggest that the ECJ had created an irrebuttable presumption that repackaging was prejudicial to the specific subject matter of the trade mark right. The Court of Appeal found that there was a strong resistance to the purchase of over-stickered drugs as it had a less neat and professional look than repackaging. Re-boxing was therefore necessary.

19.44   On the extent of repackaging and whether the necessity test applies only to the act of repackaging or whether it also extends to the presentation of the repackaged product in particular where the reputation of the mark might be damaged, some conflicting views arise. In *Bristol-Myers Squibb v Paranova*[56] the ECJ recognised that where repackaging was poor and untidy, the reputation of the mark might suffer. Poor presentation could thus be a legitimate reason to oppose the further circulation of goods. In *Glaxo Group v Dowelhurst*[57] Laddie J suggested that repackaging was only to be tolerated to the extent that it could be shown to inflict the minimum possible damage on the mark. By contrast, in *Paranova AS v Merck*[58] the EFTA court said that once it was shown that repackaging was necessary the importer has the right to repackage. Thereafter the focus should be on whether the mark's ability to guarantee origin or its reputation was compromised.

19.45   As a result a second reference was made to the ECJ in *Boehringer Ingelheim KG v Swingward Ltd*.[59] The ECJ's judgment appeared to make parallel importing more onerous for parallel importers than had been thought might be the case in the aftermath of the AG's opinion in this case.[60] While the ruling has clarified some matters, for instance that the conditions in *Bristol Myers Squibb* apply to re-labelling, re-boxing and over-stickering—other elements of the judgment will no doubt provoke further debate—for instance as to what is meant by an 'inappropriately repackaged product' which could damage the reputation of a trade mark.

   • The Court started by noting that the specific subject matter of a mark is to guarantee the origin of the product bearing the mark and that repackaging by a third party without authorisation is likely to create real risks for that guarantee of origin.[61] Case law has indicated that it is the repackaging which is in itself prejudicial to the specific subject-matter of the mark and it is not necessary in that context to assess the actual effects of the repackaging by the parallel importer.[62] However, opposition to repackaging contributes to artificial partitioning of the market where it is necessary to enable the product to be marketed in the importing state.[63] A change brought about by repackaging may be prohibited unless it is necessary to enable

---

[53] ibid, para 54.   [54] [2003] EWHC 2109 (Ch) Ch D.
[55] [2004] ETMR 65, [2004] EWCA Civ 129 CA.
[56] Joined Cases C-427/93, C-429/93 and C-436/93, [1996] ECR I-3457.
[57] *Glaxo Group Ltd v Dowelhurst Ltd (No 2)* [2000] IP&T 502.   [58] Case E-3/02.
[59] Case C-348/04. Reference for a preliminary ruling by the Court of Appeal (England & Wales) (Civil Division), 17 June 2004, in the case of *Boehringer Ingelheim KG v Swingward Ltd.*
[60] Opinion of AG Sharpston Case C-348/04, 6 April 2006.   [61] Case 348/04, para 14.
[62] ibid, para 15.   [63] ibid, para 18.

the marketing of the products and the legitimate interests of the proprietor are safeguarded.[64] Notice must be given that a re-packaged product is being put on sale.[65]

- The ECJ noted that in the instant case the packaging of the pharmaceutical products and instruction leaflets had been altered for importation into the UK. In some cases labels identifying the parallel importer had been added but the trade mark and languages other than English were visible. Other products had been re-boxed and the trade mark reproduced and in yet others which were re-boxed, the trade mark was not visible but the generic name was and in others the trade mark inside the box was over-stickered with information on the parallel importer and the generic name. The information leaflet, written in English, contained the trade mark.

- *The concept of repackaging.* The court considered that both re-labelling and re-boxing are prejudicial to the specific subject matter of the mark and create a risk to the guarantee of origin.[66] A change may thus be prohibited unless it is necessary for marketing and the legitimate interests of the trade mark owner are safeguarded.[67] Thus if the requirements set out in *Bristol Myers Squibb* are met, the proprietor may not oppose further commercialisation whether through repackaging or over-stickering.

- *The manner and style of repackaging.* The key question was whether the requirement that re-packaging was necessary was directed at the fact of repackaging rather than the manner and style of that re-packaging. Here the ECJ considered that the necessity test is directed only at the fact of re-packaging and the choice of style of re-packaging and not to the manner or style in which it is re-packaged.[68]

- *The presentation of the re-packaged product and the reputation of the mark.* Here the ECJ noted that the five conditions to be fulfilled include the condition that the presentation of the repackaged product must not be such as to be liable to damage the reputation of the trade mark and of the proprietor: it must not be defective, of poor quality or untidy.[69] In addition, an inappropriately repackaged product could damage the reputation of the mark where it detracted from the image of reliability and quality attaching to the product and the confidence it could inspire in the public.[70]

- *The circumstances in which the reputation of the trade mark may be damaged.* De-branding, co-branding, over-stickering such as to obscure the trade mark, a failure to state that the trade mark belongs to the proprietor or where the name of the parallel importer is printed in capital letters are in principle liable to damage the reputation of the trade mark. These are questions of fact for the national court.[71]

- *Burden of proof.* It is for the parallel importer to prove the existence of the conditions under which parallel importation is permitted and which, if fulfilled, would prevent the proprietor from opposing further commercialisation of the products. Where it must be shown that the re-packaging does not affect the original condition of the product in the packaging,

---

[64] ibid, para 19.   [65] ibid, para 20.

[66] ibid, para 29.   [67] ibid, para 30.

[68] See also Case C-276/05 *Wellcome Foundation v Paranova* [2009] ETMR 20 in which the ECJ ruled that 'the condition of necessity is directed only at the fact of re-packaging the product inter alia by re-boxing it, and not the presentation of that new packaging'.

[69] Case 348/04 para 40.   [70] ibid, para 44.

[71] In Case C-276/05 *Wellcome Foundation v Paranova* [2009] ETMR 20, the ECJ held that in cases where the 'repackaging of the pharmaceutical product is necessary for its further marketing in a Member State of importation, the presentation of the packaging should be assessed only against the condition that it should not be as to be liable to damage the reputation of the trade mark or that of its proprietor', para 30.

the parallel importer must furnish evidence which leads to a reasonable presumption that is the case. That applies also to the presentation of the repackaged product such that it must not be such as to damage the reputation of the trade mark. The parallel importer must furnish initial evidence. It is then for the trade mark owner to prove that the reputation of the owner and that of the trade mark have been damaged.

• In applying the judgment of the ECJ, Jacob LJ found that 'the defendants have complied with BMS condition 4 and in particular that their activities by way of re-boxing and re-labelling have not caused and will not cause damage to the reputation of the claimants' trade marks.'[72]

Discussion point   For answer guidance visit www.oxfordtextbooks.co.uk/orc/macqueen2e/

In *Boehringer Ingelheim* Jacob LJ gave his view of the current state of trade mark law: 'Notwithstanding the two references to the ECJ and its answers, each "side" (there are several claimant drug companies as claimants and two parallel importers as defendants) claims to have won. That is a sorry state of affairs. European trade mark law seems to have arrived at such a state of uncertainty that no one really knows what the rules are, outside the obviously core case of straightforward infringement (the use of a mark as a trade mark for the defendant's goods which is the same as or confusingly similar to a plaintiff's registered mark registered for the same or similar goods). Big brand owners want bigger rights; smaller players, no change or less. The compromises which have emerged have very fuzzy lines. So it is that in this case, notwithstanding two references (and a host of cases about relabelling parallel imports going back at least 30 years, see *Hoffmann-La Roche v Centrafarm*, Case 102/77 [1978] ECR 1139), there is still room for argument'.[73]
Do you agree with Jacob LJ? How would you suggest the law be clarified in this area?

Notice

19.46   As can be seen above (para 19.38), to comply with the conditions the parallel importer must give notice to the trade mark owner and supply samples of the packaging. The ECJ has said that it is for the parallel importer to give notice.[74] In *Boehringer v Swingward*[75] the ECJ said that on the evidence before it a period of 15 days would seem reasonable where the parallel importer chose to give notice by supplying a sample of the repackaged product. The court did however say that the period was purely indicative and it was open to the parallel importer to allow a shorter time, and to the proprietor to ask for a longer time to react than that proffered by the parallel importer.[76] Where a parallel importer has not given prior notice, every importation of the product is in infringement until notice is given. The sanction should be proportionate and effective and may be treated in the same manner for those circumstances in which the goods were spurious.[77] It is for the national court to assess in the light of the circumstances whether the proprietor has had a reasonable time to react to the intended packaging.

---

[72] [2008] EWCA Civ 83, para 67. For further questions that have been referred to the Court of Justice on repackaging, see Case C-400/09 *Orifarm and others v Merck & Co Inc*.

[73] ibid, para 2.

[74] Case C-102/77 *Hoffmann-La Roche*, para 12 and *Boehringer Ingelheim v Swingward Ltd* [2003] Ch 27, [2002] 3 WLR 1697.

[75] Case C-143/00 [2002] All ER (EC) 581, [2003] Ch 27, [2002] 3 WLR 1697.

[76] ibid, para 57.   [77] Case 348/04, para 64.

Comment on repackaging cases

19.47   The number of cases to come before the courts dealing with trade mark infringement, parallel imports and repackaging appears to have prompted a growing sense of frustration amongst the judiciary. In the Court of Appeal in *Boehringer Ingelheim v Swingward Ltd*[78] Jacob LJ highlighted the assumption made in the cases that the reaffixing of the trade mark to the goods, unless permitted by free circulation rules, infringes the registered trade mark. He pointed out that most people would not assume that a mark would be infringed simply by reaffixing the original trade mark to the goods or using a mark when marketing the goods. Such practices are a daily occurrence in commerce where shop keepers use signs to advertise goods which bear the trade mark of another and second hand goods are sold by reference to the trade mark.

> 'Sometimes I think the law may be losing a sense of reality in this area—we are, after all, only considering the use of the owner's trade mark for his goods in perfect condition. The pickle the law has got into would, I think, astonish the average consumer'.[79]

Jacob LJ suggested that the law of registered trade marks was being stretched to deal with conduct that would more happily sit under general unfair competition rules: 'There is more than one way to skin a cat'.[80] In her opinion, AG Sharpston has indicated that after 30 years of case law on repackaging of pharmaceutical products, 'it should be possible to distil sufficient principles to enable national courts to apply the law to the constantly replayed litigation between manufacturers and parallel importers'.[81] Whether these comments will have any impact on the number of cases brought before the courts remains to be seen. That there are so many cases to come before the courts is perhaps an indication of the commercial importance of these fine distinctions that are being litigated between the parties.

 Question

What do you think of the suggestion by Jacob LJ that trade mark law might not be relevant to the activities of parallel importers? Revisit the functions of a trade mark. Are the arguments of the trade mark proprietors justified by reference to these functions?

Use of marks in advertising

19.48   As can be seen from the discussion above, a concern of trade mark proprietors as goods are repackaged is as to safeguarding the reputation of their marks. This also arises in the context of advertising. If a parallel importer wishes to re-sell the goods, then they would want to use the mark in advertising them. Where the re-seller makes those goods available to a different market, for instance where luxury goods are re-sold in supermarkets, then the trade mark owner may wish to control the way in which they are advertised over concern for the reputation of the mark. The question then arises as to whether the trade mark owner has a legitimate reason to do so: is safeguarding the reputation of the mark a legitimate reason for opposing certain styles of advertising? Such an issue arose in *Parfums Christian Dior SA v Evora BV*.[82] Dior owned trade marks for, inter alia, perfumes sold to the luxury market. Evora owned a chain of chemist shops

---

[78] [2004] ETMR 65, [2004] EWCA Civ 129 (CA).   [79] ibid, para 79.
[80] ibid, para 20.   [81] Opinion of AG Sharpston Case C-348/04, para 3.
[82] Case C-337/95 *Parfums Christian Dior SA v Evora BV* [1997] ECR I-6013.

in which it sold Dior products which were parallel imports. Evora carried out a promotion and in the literature it showed pictures of the packaging and of the bottles. Dior argued that such literature did not present the goods in the way that they wished: it did not conform to the prestige image Dior was keen to promote so brought an action for trade mark infringement.

The ECJ considered that the damage done to the reputation of a mark might be a legitimate reason to enable the proprietor to oppose further commercialisation.[83]

However a balance had to be struck between the legitimate interests of the trade mark owner from a re-seller using the mark in such a manner that might damage the mark, and the re-seller's legitimate interest in being able to re-sell the goods in question by using advertising methods which are customary in his sector of trade.[84] Where luxury goods were resold, the re-seller should try to prevent the advertising from affecting the value of the mark by detracting from the aura of luxury.[85]

The ECJ did go on to note that where the re-seller used advertising methods common in the trade, even if those were not the methods the trade mark owner would have used, that was not a legitimate reason for the trade mark owner to oppose the use of the mark by the re-seller unless it could be established that the use would seriously damage the reputation of the mark. As an example, such damage could occur where the re-seller put the mark on an advertising leaflet in a context which would detract from the aura of luxury.[86]

Key points on legitimate reasons

- A trade mark owner may legitimately oppose further marketing of a pharmaceutical product where the importer has repackaged the product and reaffixed the trade mark unless the points in para 19.38 arise

- A court will look to see if the repackaging by the parallel importer is necessary

- A trade mark owner may oppose the use of a mark by an advertiser if the reputation of the mark is likely to be damaged

---

International exhaustion

19.49   It will be recalled that Article 7(1) of the Trade Mark Directive provides that a 'trade mark shall not entitle the proprietor to prohibit its use in relation to goods which have been put on the market in the Community under the trade mark by the proprietor or with his consent'.

This would appear to limit the operation of the exhaustion doctrine to the Community (now Union). Is this then a minimum standard, or are member states free to apply a doctrine of international exhaustion?

TRIPS, Article 6 leaves this open to signatory states:

'. . . nothing in this Agreement shall be used to address the issue of the exhaustion of intellectual property rights'.

---

[83] ibid, para 43.   [84] ibid, para 44.
[85] See also Case C-59/08 *Copad SA v Christian Dior Couture SA* [2009] ETMR 40, para 37.
[86] ibid, para 46.

? Question

If one member state applied the doctrine of international exhaustion, what impact would this have on the movement of goods throughout the Union where goods are imported from outwith the EEA and placed on the market in that member state?

19.50   The ECJ had a chance to rule on the question of international exhaustion in 1988.

■ *Case C-355/96 Silhouette International Schmied GmbH & Co KG v Hartlauer Handelsgesellschaft GmbH [1998] All ER (EC) 769*

Silhouette (S) manufactured designer spectacles under its trade mark, 'Silhouette'. It sold a number of outdated designs to a Bulgarian company on the condition that they would only be sold in Bulgaria and the former Soviet Union states. Hartlauer, an Austrian retailer, obtained some of these frames and sold them in their shops. S claimed that their trade mark had been infringed.

Diagram 19.7 *Silhouette International Schmied GmbH & Co KG v Hartlauer Handelsgesellschaft*

The Court, proceeding on the basis that no consent had been given to the sunglasses to be sold in Austria, held that national rules which provided for exhaustion of rights in respect of goods which were put onto the market outwith the EC by the proprietor or with his consent were contrary to Article 7(1). A member state had no discretion in this. The Court took the view that the Directive provided for full harmonisation of those rules which affect the functioning of the internal market.[87] Member states are thus not free to apply a regime of international exhaustion.[88]

19.51   Parallel importers have sought to argue around the rule on international exhaustion by arguing that the mark owner had consented to the importation of goods into the Union.

---

[87] ibid, para 23.

[88] In an Advisory Opinion in Case E-9/07 *L'Oréal Norge AS v Per Aarskog AS and Others*, and reversing its earlier Advisory Opinion in Case E-2/97 *Mag Instrument Inc v California Trading Company Norway* [1997] EFTA Ct Rep 129, the EFTA court said that '...Article 7(1) of the Trade Mark Directive is to be interpreted to the effect that it precludes the unilateral introduction or maintenance of international exhaustion of rights conferred by a trade mark regardless of the origin of the goods in question.'

Consent and batches of goods

19.52   In *Sebago Inc and Ancienne Maison Dubois v GB Unic SA*,[89] GB Unic imported shoes from El Salvador into Belgium bearing the 'Sebago' trade mark and sold them in retail outlets. GB Unic argued that whenever a trade mark owner consented to the placing of goods onto the market bearing a trade mark, then that consent extended to all goods of that type. In giving judgment the ECJ said that consent in the sense of Article 7(1) of the Trade Marks Directive must relate to each individual item in respect of which exhaustion is pleaded. A trade mark owner does not place a whole stock of goods on the market through the act of selling one batch.

Implied consent

19.53   In a number of joined cases[90] concerning, inter alia, perfume and jeans, an argument arose over implied consent.

■ *Case C-414/99 Zino Davidoff v A&G Imports* [2002] All ER (EC)

Zino Davidoff (ZD) wanted to prevent the import into England of goods bearing the marks 'Cool Water' and 'Davidoff Cool Water' which had been marketed with consent in Singapore. A&G argued that by marketing the goods in Singapore, ZD had given implied consent to their free circulation. The chain of distribution included a standard agreement in terms of which distributors undertook not to sell any products outside their assigned territories. However, no such term was imposed on distributors further down the chain. In the High Court Laddie J had held that the rule of community exhaustion did not prevent trade mark owners from consenting to importation. Interpretation of the contract under the applicable law (in this case English law) meant that consent could be implied. There was a rebuttable presumption that, in the absence of full and explicit restrictions being imposed on purchaser at the time of purchase, the proprietor is treated as consenting to the goods being imported into and sold in the EEA.[91] When the case reached the ECJ, the Court ruled that consent could be implied:

- only where the facts and circumstances were such that the proprietor could be considered to have unequivocally demonstrated to have renounced his right to oppose the subsequent importation of those goods into the EEA.

Consent could not be implied from:

- the failure of the proprietor to communicate to subsequent purchasers of the goods that he did not consent to their subsequent importation into the EEA;
- the fact the fact that there was nothing on the goods to suggest that they were not be imported into the EEA;
- the fact that the proprietor had transferred ownership without imposing any restrictions.

---

[89] Case C-173/98 [1999] 2 CMLR 1317, [1999] ETMR 681.

[90] Joined cases C-414/99, C-415/99 and C-416/99 *Zino Davidoff SA v A&G Imports Ltd; Levi Strauss & Co Levi Strauss (UK) Ltd v Tesco Stores Ltd, Tesco plc; Levi Strauss & Co, Levi Strauss (UK) Ltd v Costco Wholesale UK Ltd* [2002] Ch 109, [2002] 2 WLR 321, [2002] All ER (EC) 55. See also *Honda Motor Co Ltd v Neesam* [2008] EWHC 338 (Ch).

[91] [1999] RPC 631 Ch D, [1999] ETMR 700 Ch D, para 38.8. At the same time *JOOP! GmbH and Zino Davidoff SA v M&S Toiletries Ltd* [1999] 2 CMLR 1056 was heard in the Scottish Court of Session—an almost identical case. Lord Kingarth noted that not only would the approach taken in the High Court mean that unless the trade mark owner blocked every avenue, he could be held as having consenting to importation (an almost impossible task) but in addition, making the issue of consent dependent on the law of contract would offend against the purpose of harmonisation in the Directive and lead to uncertainly in application. It was unclear that the reference to presumed consent would be applied in the same way in Scotland as in England.

In addition the Court said that it was irrelevant that the importer was unaware the proprietor objected to their importation, or that authorised retailers had not imposed on their purchasers any contractual restrictions even if those retailers were aware of the proprietor's objection.

19.54   The Court of Appeal had the opportunity to consider when implied consent might be relevant in *Mastercigars Direct Ltd v Hunters & Frankau Ltd*.[92] This appeal concerned the importation into the UK of cigars from Cuba by Mastercigars. The Cuban company, Corporacion Habanos, had an exclusive UK distributor Hunters & Frankau. It was claimed that a consignment of cigars were counterfeit and infringed the trade mark in that no consent had been given to the placing of the goods on the market in the EEA. As no express consent had been given to the importation of the cigars, the key question was as to whether consent could be implied. In order to show implied consent the factors had to 'demonstrate unequivocally' that the trade mark proprietor had renounced any intention to enforce his rights. Unequivocal is not about the standard of proof; a proved act which is consistent with consent and consistent with its absence is not enough to draw the conclusion that goods had been marketed with the consent of the trade mark owner.[93]

The facts of the case—and in particular that when cigars were sold in Cuba they were sold by encouraging sales of up to $25000, a level far too high for individual use, and that the purchaser was given appropriate customs documentation—showed that the sellers must have known that they would be used for onwards resale in the end market. This was sufficient on the facts to demonstrate implied consent.

On who should give consent, the Court of Appeal said that it is insufficient for consent to be given by a licensee or connected company. What matters is the 'point of control' shown through actual knowledge and the actual practical control or right to exercise that control by the trade mark owner.[94] In this case Corporacion Habanos exercised that control through the sale of cigars in retail outlets in Cuba.

19.55   From *Zino Davidoff* it appeared the level for showing consent to importation into the EEA by the proprietor was high requiring a positive renunciation of the right to oppose importation, rather than a negative inference to be gleaned from the facts of the relationship between the various parties.[95] However the Court of Appeal's ruling in Mastercigars Direct suggests the standard is by no means insurmountable on the evidence.

 Question

Mastercigars gives an example of certain facts that will be taken to 'unequivocally demonstrate' that a trade mark proprietor had consented to importation of goods into the EEA. Can you think of other examples?

---

[92] *Corporacion Habanos SA v Mastercigars Direct Ltd* [2007] EWCA Civ 176, [2007] ETMR 44
[93] ibid, para 19.   [94] Op cit para 30.
[95] For other UK cases see *Kabushiki Kaisha Sony Computer Entertainment Europe Ltd v Nuplayer Ltd* [2005] EWHC 1522 (ChD); *Sony Computer Entertainment Ltd v Electricbirdland Ltd* [2005] EWHC 2296 (Ch D); *Hewlett-Packard Development Co LP v Expansys UK Ltd* [2005] EWHC 1495 (Ch D); *KK Sony Computer Entertainment & Anor v Pacific Game Technology (Holding) Ltd* [2006] EWHC 2509. Note that the ECJ dealt with implied consent to marketing within the EEA in Case C-324/08 *Makro Zelfbedieningsgroothandel e.a. v Diesel S.p.a.* For further discussion see para 19.17.

When are goods placed on the market?

19.56   For a trade mark owner's rights to be exhausted goods must be put on the market within the EEA by or with the consent of the trade mark owner. What is meant by being 'put on the market' was considered by the ECJ in *Peak Holding AB v Axolin-Elinor AB*.[96] Peak Holding granted the right to use the trade mark, 'Peak Performance', to Peak Performance Production AB (PPP) in Sweden. Certain goods were offered for sale in PPP's shops within the EU but were not sold. PPP sold these to a French company. The agreement contained a clause prohibiting the French company from selling more than 5 per cent of the goods in France. Of the remainder, the only European countries that could be supplied were Russia and Slovenia. None of the goods actually left the EEA. A large number of items were subsequently offered for sale in Sweden through Factory Outlet (FO). When sued for trade mark infringement, FO argued that PPP's rights had been exhausted by the sale to the French company and that the clause which prohibited resale in the EEA was of no effect.

The ECJ was asked:

- Had PPP had put the goods on the market by importing them into the EU and offering them for sale in their shops?

If the answer was in the negative:

- Had the goods had been put on the market and the rights exhausted when they were sold to the French company? If this was the case, what was the impact of the restriction on re-sale in Europe?

The ECJ confirmed that an actual sale of goods to a third party within the EEA resulted in putting the goods on the market in the EEA. However, where the goods are imported, or offered for sale in the proprietor's shops or in those of an associated company but without actually selling any of the goods, the rights in respect of those goods are not exhausted.[97] This is because at this stage the economic value of the mark in respect of the goods has not been realised. The ECJ went on to say that any transaction which transfers the right to dispose of the goods amounts to putting the goods on the market in the EEA regardless of any agreement prohibiting re-sale within the EEA. This is because the sale itself is enough to realise the economic value of the mark. Any third party acquiring the goods could not be sued for infringement of the trade mark.[98]

It will be for the national court to apply the ruling of the ECJ to the facts of the case. However, it would appear that the offer for sale of the goods by PPP did not exhaust the trade mark rights as the goods remained unsold, but sale of the goods to the French company did and thus the goods could thereafter move freely around the EEA. The contract limiting resale within France to 5 per cent of the assignment was of no effect and FO could not be sued for trade mark infringement for reselling the goods in Sweden.[99]

---

[96]   Case C-16/03 [2005] Ch 261 ECJ, [2005] ETMR 28 ECJ.
[97]   ibid, paras 40–4.   [98]   ibid, paras 54–6.
[99]   See also Case C-405/03*Class International BV v Colgate-Palmolive Co and others* ECJ, discussed below, on importation and goods in transit.

Question 1

Consider the facts of the above case. If you were a trade mark owner, had unsold goods and did not want them to be marketed within the Union, what would you do?

Question 2

Consider perfume testers which are made available without transfer of ownership to contractually bound intermediaries. Do you think these have been 'put on to the market' within the meaning of Article 13(1) of Regulation 207/2009 and Article 7(1) of Directive 2008/95/EC where there was a prohibition on sale and the tester displayed a notice to that effect and the goods may be recalled by the manufacturer/trade mark owner at any time?[100]

19.57   There are circumstances in which public opinion might support attempts by a trade mark owner to prevent the circulation of goods within the EEA. In *Glaxo Group Limited v Dowelhurst Ltd*[101] Glaxo had sold pharmaceuticals within the EEA at cheap rates based on the understanding that they would only be used for humanitarian purposes in Africa. The drugs were sold to a Swiss company who sold them on to a parallel importer. The drugs then found their way onto the UK market where the importer was sued for trade mark infringement. Much of the discussion in the court revolved around the question of as to when goods were put onto the market in the EEA (some clarity in relation to this question now exists given the ruling of the ECJ in *Peak Holding v Axolin-Elinor* (para 19.56)). Given the facts of the *Glaxo* case, it seems possible that the consignment of drugs was sold within the EEA and thus subject to the rules on exhaustion—which was the view taken by the Court of Appeal. However, it is unlikely that the arguments will be further aired in court as it is understood that the case between the parties has settled.[102] That does not detract from the fact that at times it may be just to enable right holders to control the movement of their products without fear of falling on the wrong side of complex and often unsettled rules in relation to free movement and exhaustion within the EU.[103]

Consent and goods in transit

19.58   A question as to whether a trade mark proprietor had to consent to goods being brought into the EC for transit or customs storage arose in *Class International BV v Colgate-Palmolive Co and others*.[104] The Beecham group owns the 'Aquafresh' CTM for, inter alia, toothpastes. Class International, a parallel importer, brought into Rotterdam a container load of toothpaste products bearing the Aquafresh trade mark, purchased from Kapex International, a South African undertaking. The Beecham group believed them to be counterfeit but a subsequent examination showed they were genuine goods. The ECJ said that the trade mark owner could not stop (that is, consent was not needed) the goods being brought into the EC for the

---

[100] For the ECJ view in due course see Case C-127/09 *Coty Prestige Lancaster Group GmbH v Simex Trading* AG. For contractual restrictions see also Case C-59/08 *Copad SA v Christian Dior Couture SA*, para 19.30.

[101] *Glaxo Group Limited v Dowelhurst Limited* [2004] EWCA Civ 290 CA; [2005] ETMR 104.

[102] http://news.bbc.co.uk/1/hi/uk/4476329.stm

[103] For other initiatives impacting on this area see C Davies, 'Glaxo v Dowelhurst—A New Twist in the Tale!' [2005] EIPR 127.

[104] Case C-405/03 [2006] Ch 154, [2006] 2 WLR 507.

purposes of transit or customs storage. 'Importing'...requires introduction of those goods into the Community for the purposes of putting them on the market therein.'[105] Neither could the proprietor stop the goods from being offered for sale in a third county unless it was clear that they would subsequently be put on the market in the Community.[106]

19.59   A related question arose in *Montex Holdings Ltd v Diesel SpA*.[107] Here, Diesel objected to the transit through Germany of goods destined for Ireland bearing the Diesel mark. The goods had been assembled in Poland; there was no trade mark protection for the Diesel trade marks in Ireland. Referring to *Class International*, the ECJ held that a trade mark owner could only prohibit transit of goods through a member state in which the mark was protected and placed under the external transit procedure if the goods were subject to the act of a third party whilst in this procedure which would necessarily entail their being put on the market in the member state of transit.[108] A theoretical risk that the goods could fail to reach their destination and that they would be marketed fraudulently in the state where trade mark protection existed was insufficient to reach the conclusion that the transit infringed the rights of the trade mark proprietor.[109]

19.60   A further twist arose in *Nokia Corporation v Her Majesty's Commissioners of Revenue & Customs*.[110] In this case Her Majesty's Commissioners of Revenue & Customs (HMRC) refused to continue to detain a consignment of allegedly counterfeit mobile phones and accessories bearing the Nokia trade mark that HMRC had seized at Heathrow Airport and were in transit from Hong Kong to Columbia. The High Court reiterated the principle that 'infringement of a registered trade mark requires goods to be placed on the market and that goods in transit and subject to suspensive customs procedures do not, without more, satisfy this requirement'.[111] In order for there to be infringement of allegedly counterfeit goods under the Counterfeit Goods Regulation, the goods must in fact infringe someone's trade mark in the territory in question. The court also said that the mere risk that the goods may be diverted into the internal market is not enough to constitute infringement. In coming to this conclusion the court exposed a gap in the law which would prevent these allegedly counterfeit goods from being seized. The ruling has produced much anxious blogging. Questions have now been referred to the Court of Justice.[112]

Parallel importing and the burden of proof

19.61   The ECJ has said that the burden of proof lies on the person alleging consent to prove it, and not for the trade mark owner to prove its absence. This left parallel importers in something of a quandary. If a parallel importer had to prove consent to marketing within the EEA, then that may involve giving information on the distribution system through which the goods had been sourced. Once the trade mark owner had details of that source, then they could act to close it—thus leaving the parallel importer without supplies. The question over who should

[105]   ibid, para 34.
[106]   See also *Eli Lilly and Co and another v 8PM Chemist Ltd* [2008] EWCA Civ 24. In Case C-115/02 *Administration des Douanes, Droits Indirects v Rioglass SA* [2006] 1 CMLR 12, the ECJ held that where goods, lawfully manufactured in one member state are in transit in the Community with the destination being a non-member country, that does not involve any marketing of the goods in question.
[107]   Case C-281/05 [2007] ETMR 13. Cf the Dutch case *Sisvel v Sosecal* (July 18, 2008).
[108]   Para 23.   [109]   Para 24.
[110]   [2009] EWHC 1903 (Ch), 2009 WL 2207339.   [111]   ibid, para 49.
[112]   Case C-495/09 *Nokia Corporation v Her Majesty's Commissioners of Revenue and Customs*. See also *Eli Lilly and Co and another v 8PM Chemist Ltd* [2008] EWCA Civ 24. The use of a mark in the course of trade requires the goods being in the Community for the purposes of putting them on the market. Mere physical introduction under a customs approved procedure was not importing and was not using the mark in the course of trade.

bear the burden of proof and at what stage in the proceedings has been the subject of further consideration.

■ *Case C-244/00 Van Doren + Q GmbH v Lifestyle + Sportswear Handelsgesellschaft GmbH* [2004] All ER (EC) 912[113]

Van Doren (VD) was the exclusive German distributor of goods bearing the 'Stussy' trade mark, owned by a Californian company. VD sued Lifestyle for selling goods bearing the trade mark in Germany. VD alleged that those goods were first put on the market in the USA. No consent had been given to their distribution in Germany. Lifestyle argued that the trade mark rights had been exhausted because the goods were sourced in the EEA where they had been put on the market by the trade mark owner or with his consent. As German law provides that exhaustion operates as a defence to trade mark infringement, it was for the parallel importer to prove where the goods were sourced.

The ECJ held that a rule of evidence that required a defendant relying on a plea of exhaustion to prove the conditions existed for the defence to be successful was consistent with Community law.[114] However, that rule might have to be qualified.

- It was for the parallel importer to show that there would be a real risk of partitioning the markets if the burden of proof lay on him. This would be particularly so where the trade mark owner operated an exclusive distribution system.

If he was successful then:

- it was for the trade mark owner to establish that the products were placed on the market outside the EEA by him or with his consent.

If such evidence was forthcoming:

- the burden shifted back to the parallel importer to prove the trade mark owner's consent to subsequent marketing of the products in the EEA.[115]

19.62 Although this ruling provides some guidance, questions remain. For instance: what evidence would be required to show there is a real risk of market partitioning? Would it be enough to show that the trade mark owner operates an exclusive distribution system? Might price differences as between member states be sufficient? Suffice it to say there will no doubt be more references to the ECJ before clarity is achieved.

19.63 A question over what a trader might have to do to show that reasonable steps had been taken to ascertain that goods had been placed on the market in the EU arose in the English High Court in *Sun Microsystems Inc v Amtec Computer Corporation Ltd.*[116] Amtec was sued by Sun for trade mark infringement in relation to servers that Amtec had purchased from a Danish intermediary. It transpired that the servers had not been put onto the market in the EEA by Sun or with Sun's consent. In seeking to discharge their burden of proof, Amtec argued that the Danish intermediary was known as a reputable European source of Sun products and that a term in the contract as between Amtec and the Danish intermediary had stipulated that the goods should be of EU origin (which they were). Amtec also believed that the goods had originally been supplied by a distributor known to be an authorised seller of Sun products—thus adding

[113] [2003] ECR I-3051, [2003] 2 CMLR 6.   [114] ibid, para 36.
[115] ibid, paras 41 and 42.   [116] [2006] EWHC 62 (Ch).

to the belief that they had originally been put on the market with the authorisation of Sun. When the servers arrived they were in boxes marked with the words 'Origin: United Kingdom' and the servers themselves had UK serial numbers. On investigation of the facts it transpired that the servers had not actually been put on the market in the EU by Sun or with their consent (they were destined for Israel) and Amtec accepted that they had infringed Sun's trade marks but said that it had occurred innocently.

The court found that this was no defence to trade mark infringement saying:

- 'There is no requirement of knowledge on the part of an infringing trader that he is infringing. To put that proposition another way, lack of knowledge is not a defence to infringement proceedings;

- It is not a defence for the trader to show that he took all reasonable steps open to him to establish that goods were put on the market by, or with the consent, of the trade mark proprietor'.[117]

The court did however limit the scope of the injunction recognising that, without Sun's assistance, Amtec could do nothing to ensure that the goods it acquired had been placed on the market in the EEA with the consent of Sun.[118]

 Question

What do you think you would have to do to be absolutely sure that the goods in question had been placed on the market in the EEA by or with the consent of the owner of the trade mark?

Should there be a system of international exhaustion?

19.64   An issue that has troubled policy makers within the EU for many years is whether a system for international exhaustion should be introduced. The debate has focussed on trade marks and was galvanised after the judgment of the ECJ in *Silhouette* in 1998 (para 19.50). In order to obtain a clearer picture of the economic aspects of a possible change to the exhaustion regime, the Commission commissioned a study in 1999 from the NERA Institute in London. The conclusions of that study are as follows.

- The short term effects on consumer pricing of a change of exhaustion regime would vary from small (less than 2 per cent price reduction) for certain products to 'negligible' (0 per cent price reduction) for other products.

- The long term effects of a change of exhaustion are more difficult to predict. It is however likely that the marginal, positive effect on consumer pricing in the long run will disappear.

- A change in the exhaustion regime may have an impact not only on pricing, but for example, also on product quality, product availability, after-sales services and employment in Europe.

---

[117] ibid, para 21.   [118] For discussion on the scope of the injunction see para 21.105.

- Trade mark policy has only a marginal effect on parallel trade: other elements like distribution arrangements, transport costs, health and safety legislation and technical standards and labelling differences may have a greater, and more direct impact.

19.65   In June 2000 a communiqué was issued by the Commission indicating that, taking into account the findings in the report, there was to be no change to the rule of Community exhaustion.

Weblink

You will find the Communiqué from Commissioner Bolkestein on the issue of exhaustion of trade mark rights, 7 June 2000

http://ec.europa.eu/internal_market/indprop/docs/tm/comexhaust_en.pdf

19.66   In May 2003 the issue was revisited resulting in a Commission working paper 'Possible abuses of trade mark rights within the EU in the context of Community exhaustion'.[119]

Weblink

You will find this document on the Commission's Industrial Property section of the Europa website at

http://ec.europa.eu/internal_market/indprop/tm/index_en.htm

Set against the question as to whether the Community should move to a system of international exhaustion, the paper sought to identify whether there were any abuses of trade mark rights, to explain how they might have been addressed, and to identify deficiencies that may exist in the current legal provision.

Having examined selective distribution systems, abuse of a dominant position involving trade marks and trade mark infringements, the conclusion of the report was that there was no evidence of deficiencies in current legal provision relating to possible abuses of trade marks within the EU. Thus it is unlikely that there will be any changes to the rules on Community wide exhaustion in the near term.

Key points on international exhaustion

- The exhaustion doctrine is limited to the Community
- Consent relates to batches of goods put onto the market and not to goods of a particular type
- The level for showing consent appears high and suggests a positive renunciation of the right to oppose importation
- Importing requires introduction of goods into the Community for the purposes of putting them on the market.
- The burden of proving consent may shift between the parallel importer and trade mark owner

---

[119] SEC (2003) 575.

Free movement of services

19.67   The doctrine of exhaustion, as discussed above, applies to the right to control distribution. Within copyright it does not however apply to the right to rent, to perform or to show a copy of a work in public. Here the specific subject matter of the right is to obtain a return from the exercise of the right which includes performance of a work. Thus the owner may control these uses. In *Coditel v Cine Vog (No 1)*[120] the owner of the copyright in a film, Le Boucher, granted cinema and television rights in Belgium to Cine Vog for a period of seven years. During this period a German version of the film was transmitted by cable into Belgium by Coditel. Cine Vog sued Coditel for an infringement of their exclusive rights. The ECJ held that 'the right of a copyright owner and his assigns to require fees for any showing of a film is part of the essential function of copyright in this type of literary and artistic work'[121] and accepted that the copyright owner could place geographic restrictions on the exploitation of performing rights.

19.68   Similar questions were raised in respect of the rental right[122] and the sound recording right[123] which received comparable rulings from the ECJ.

 Question

Explain in your own words why there is a distinction between the movement of goods around the Community and the movement of services. What policy goals underlie this distinction?

19.69   As always, the law continues to evolve—most notably when challenged by new technologies. The law is now coming under pressure with questions going to the heart of the interactions between copyright, free movement of goods and competition law.[124] In *Murphy v Media Protection Services*[125] and *FA Premier League v QC Leisure & Ors*[126] the new technology in question was decoders. The issue was the receipt of broadcasts of football matches via a decoder supplied by a supplier furth of the UK where the broadcaster had the IP right to broadcast within a defined territory which did not include the UK. The recipient (Murphy) purchased the decoder and used it to show the matches within licensed premises in the UK. The sale of the decoder in the third country was subject to the restriction that it could only be sold to a person who had an address in that country and was subject to an export ban as between the manufacturer and broadcaster. Looking to the current state of the law, copyright would support the argument that the right was territorially defined, and receipt of the signal in an unlicensed territory an infringement. The rules underpinning free movement of goods should uphold the right of the individual to purchase the decoder for use within the territory of the common market. Competition law may find that agreements between the manufacturer and broadcaster to place an export ban on the decoders to be in contravention of the competition rules on market sharing in Article 101 TFEU (ex Art 81 EC).

120   Case C-62/79 [1980] ECR 881.   121   ibid, para 14.
122   Case C-158/86 *Warner Bros v Christiansen* [1988] ECR 2605, [1990] 3 CMLR 684.
123   Case C-402/85 *Basset v Sacem* [1987] ECR 1747, [1987] 3 CMLR 173.
124   Media law is also relevant to the cases in that they involve the broadcasting of live football matches.
125   Case C-429/08 [2008] EWHC 1666.
126   Case C-403/08. Joined with Case 429/08 in order of the President of the Court 3 December 2008.

The High Court in *Murphy* found the key question to concern Directive 98/84/EC, the Conditional Access Directive and the definition of 'illicit device'.[127] Is an illicit device one which has been manufactured unlawfully and has not been put on to the market by or with the consent of the manufacturer? Or is it one that has been manufactured and placed on to the market with consent but which is being used in a manner contrary to the wishes of the broadcaster?[128]

On the one hand it was argued that Article 81 EC Treaty was irrelevant, pointing to *Coditel (No 2) Coditel SA v Ciné-Vog Films SA*[129] in which the ECJ held:

> ...the mere fact that the owner of the copyright in a film has granted to a sole licensee the exclusive right to exhibit that film in the territory of a Member State and, consequently, to prohibit during a specified period, its showing by others, is not sufficient to justify the finding that such a contract must be regarded as the purpose, the means or the result of an agreement, decision or concerted practice prohibited by the Treaty.'[130]

On the other hand it was argued that the instant case is distinct from the facts in *Coditel (No 2)*. Far from being governed by copyright law, the case is governed by competition law. Of relevance is *Nungesser v Commission*[131] where the Court distinguished between open and closed exclusive licences and said:

> The court has consistently held...that absolute territorial protection granted to a licensee in order to enable parallel imports to be controlled and prevented results in the artificial maintenance of separate national markets, contrary to the Treaty.[132]

The ECJ has difficult issues to resolve. It is perhaps difficult to conceive that a decision would be made that would in any way distort the established position that copyright is a territorial right. It may be that, pointing to such cases as *Consten & Grundig v Commission*[133] and *Sot. Lelos Kai Sia EE v Glaxosmith-Kline Aeve Farmadeftikon Proionton*[134] that there are limited derogations from the rules on free movement of goods and competition law and this is one of them. The more difficult question over the longer term then becomes as to whether increasing numbers of exceptions from the norm require the underlying premises to be re-thought.

 Exercise

How do you think the Court of Justice will decide the questions in *Murphy* and *Premier League*? How should they be decided? Is a re-think required of the underlying premises on which the laws are based?

Exhaustion and the Infosoc Directive

19.70 The Directive on the harmonisation of certain aspects of copyright and related rights in the information society[135] (Infosoc Directive) makes it clear that community exhaustion applies with respect to the movement of tangible copies of works incorporating copyright material.

---

[127] 'Illicit device' is defined in Article 2(e): 'illicit device shall mean any equipment or software designed or adapted to give access to a protected service in an intelligible form without the authorisation of the service provider.'
[128] *Murphy*, para 26.   [129] Case 262/81 [1982] ECR 3381.
[130] Para 57.   [131] Case 258/78 *Nungesser v Commission* [1982] ECR 2015.   [132] Para 58.
[133] Joined Cases 56 and 58/64 *Consten & Grundig v Commission* [1966] ECR 299, [1966] CMLR 418.
[134] Joined Cases C-468/06 to C-478/06 [2008] 5 CMLR 20. See para 19.29.
[135] Directive 2001/29/EC of the European Parliament and of the Council of 22 May 2001 on the harmonisation of certain aspects of copyright and related rights in the information society.

Recital 28 of the Directive states:

> 'Copyright protection under this Directive includes the exclusive right to control distribution of the work incorporated in a tangible article. The first sale in the Community of the original of a work or copies thereof by the rightholder or with his consent exhausts the right to control resale of that object in the Community. This right should not be exhausted in respect of the original or of copies thereof sold by the rightholder or with his consent outside the Community'.

Article 4(2) provides:

> 'The distribution right shall not be exhausted within the Community in respect of the original or copies of the work, except where the first sale or other transfer of ownership in the Community of that object is made by the right holder or with his consent'.

However, where a work protected by copyright is delivered online, then the rights are not exhausted as expressed in recital 29:

> 'The question of exhaustion does not arise in the case of services and on-line services in particular. This also applies with regard to a material copy of a work or other subject-matter made by a user of such a service with the consent of the rightholder . . . Unlike CD-ROM or CD-I, where the intellectual property is incorporated in a material medium, namely an item of goods, every on-line service is in fact an act which should be subject to authorisation where the copyright or related right so provides'.

19.71   Thus the act of uploading a work on to the Internet does not exhaust the right, nor does the act of downloading. Permission is thus needed to download (a reproduction), print (a reproduction) or further distribute any copies of a work obtained from the Internet. Even where a copy of a work has been printed down, exhaustion will not occur in relation to the printed copy; thus the copy could not, for example, be lent for commercial gain or resold to a third party. The matter becomes one of the terms of the contract as between the copyright owner and the downloader (For a discussion on the interaction between copyright and contract see Chapter 5.)

19.72   A case concerning the validity of Article 4(2) and whether it precludes member states from retaining international exhaustion in domestic legislation was referred to the ECJ by a Danish court, *Laserdisken ApS v Kulturministeriet*.[136] On the second point the ECJ held that, in conformity with recital 28, and Article 4(2) of the Directive, it is not open to member states to provide for a rule of exhaustion other than the Community wide exhaustion rule.[137] On the first question, on the validity of the measure, the ECJ found that it was consistent with obligations to be found in the EC Treaty, and other international obligations (including the WIPO Copyright Treaty and the WIPO Performances and Phonograms Treaty both of 1996).

Laserdisken had also argued that the maintenance of a Community wide principle of exhaustion was anti-competitive, contrary to the principle of proportionality and breached the right to freedom of expression. None of these arguments were accepted by the ECJ.

 Question

Do you think that arguments concerning cultural diversity and freedom of expression should hold sway over a rule that precludes international exhaustion?

---

[136] Case C-479/04 [2006] ECR I-8089.   [137] ibid, para 24.

> ## Key point on free movement of services
>
> - Copyright gives to the owner the right to control distribution of a work incorporated in a tangible article. First sale in the Community exhausts that right within the Community. There is no exhaustion in respect of the rights to rent, show or perform a work in public, nor by on-line distribution.

Further reading

Books

T Hays, *Parallel importation in European Union Law* (2004)

DT Keeling, *Intellectual Property Rights in EU Law* (2003)

Articles

AEL Brown, 'Post-harmonised Europe: United, Divided or Unimportant' [2001] 3 IPQ 275–86

T Cottier The Exhaustion of Intellectual Property Rights—A Fresh Look (2008) 39 IIC 755

P Dyrberg, 'For EEA Exhaustion to apply, who has to prove the marketing of the trade marked goods in the EEA—the Trade Mark Owner or the Defendant' [2004] 26(2) EIPR 81–4

D Edward, 'Trade Marks, Descriptions of Origin and the Internal Market: the Stephen Stewart Memorial Lecture 2000' [2001] 2 IPQ 135–45

S Enchelmaier, 'The inexhaustible question—free movement of goods and intellectual property in the European Court of Justice's case law, 2002–2006' (2007) 38(4) IIC 453–470.

N Gross and L Harrold, 'Fighting for Pharmaceutical Profits: The Decision of the ECJ in Boehringer Ingelheim v Swingward' [2002] EIPR 497 and see also [2003] EIPR 582

I Karet and I Britton, 'Parallel Imports Continue. The Patent Exhaustion Principle Upheld' (1997) 19(4) EIPR 207–9

V Korah, 'The exhaustion of patents by sale in a member state where monopoly profit could not be earned' (1997) 18(4) ECLR 265–73

Y Marinova 'The European Court of Justice on external parallel trade: interpreting the law or constructing an implied trade mark infringement' (2009) 2 IPQ 254–280

H MacQueen, 'International Exhaustion of Trade Mark Rights: A Scottish Contribution to the Debate' [2000] 4 IPQ 357–66

A van der Merwe, 'The exhaustion of rights in patent law with specific emphasis on the issue of parallel importation' (2000) 3 IPQ 286–94

G Petursson and P Dyrberg, 'What is Consent? A Note on Davidoff and Levi Strauss' (2002) 27(4) EL Rev 464–71

J Slaven, 'Sony keeps a tight grip on its hand-held Playstation Console' (2005) 16(8) Ent LR 233–4

IA Stamatoudi, 'From drugs to spirits and from boxes to publicity (decided and undecided cases in relation to trade marks and copyright exhaustion)' [1999] 1 IPQ 95–113

Intellectual property and EU competition law

Introduction

20.1 It will have been apparent from reading previous chapters that there is an unending tension between those who would argue for expansion of intellectual property rights (IPRs) on the ground that such are needed to encourage creators, and those who seek to limit, and even to roll back the parameters of the rights on the ground that over-strong rights can harm innovation. Wherever these boundaries lie, those parts within them give to the right holder exclusive rights to deal with the subject matter in the market.

20.2 It will be recalled that one of the underlying justifications for the grant of IPRs is that innovation will be encouraged. The monopoly granted by the IPRs has been carefully crafted to ensure that, despite the extent of the right, competition will thrive in the marketplace ultimately for the benefit of consumers and users. But sometimes the exercise of IPRs can produce unexpected outcomes: perhaps an over-strong monopoly is acquired due to the popularity of a particular product protected by IPRs, the rightholder may then occupy a position of strength which may hamper competition in the marketplace; or owners of IPRs may enter into agreements which may not, ultimately, be to the benefit of consumers. Competition law, operated at national (UK) and European level, may then be used to regulate the behaviour of these entities in the marketplace.

Scope and overview of chapter

20.3 The purpose of this chapter, concentrating on European competition law, is to provide an overview of some of the more common circumstances in which the Commission and the Court of Justice may intervene to regulate the exercise of IPRs by undertakings within the Common Market. The focus is on European competition law as there is no international regime of competition rules. TRIPS authorises members to provide for national competition rules within certain limits,[1] but does not oblige them to do so. Competition law (called anti-trust in the US)

---

[1] TRIPS Agreement, Arts 8(2), 31 and 40.

emanates from regional (EU) and national rules which, in the UK, are now modelled on the European standards.

20.4

Learning objectives

By the end of this chapter you should be able to describe and explain:

- the tension between the application of competition law and the exercise of IPRs and how that relates to the underlying justifications for the grant of IPRs;
- those circumstances in which competition law may be applied to moderate the exercise of IPRs in the relevant market;
- clauses in IP licensing agreements between undertakings that might be permissible in terms of EU competition law and those which are not;
- the conditions under which a refusal to supply products protected by an IPR might constitute an abuse of a dominant position by the right holder;
- the ongoing debate concerning the relevance of competition law to the exercise of IPRs.

The rest of the chapter looks like this:

- Theory of competition (20.5–20.10)
- Competition law and IP (20.11–20.20)
- Intellectual property and agreements between undertakings: Article 101 TFEU (20.21–20.43)
- Intellectual property and abuse of a dominant position: Article 102 TFEU (20.44–20.58)
- EU competition law in the British courts: Eurodefences (20.59–20.64)
- *Commission v Microsoft* (20.65–20.74)

Theory of competition

20.5   Competition law seeks to regulate the behaviour of firms in the marketplace. In capitalist economies there is a belief that where there is competition between firms, this will ultimately be of benefit to consumers. This is because firms will:

- be unable to charge artificially high prices;
- continuously innovate to create new goods;
- make available those products necessary to meet consumer demand.

20.6   There is a theory that consumer welfare is maximised when there is *perfect competition*. In this model, available resources are *allocated efficiently*. This means that the consumer can buy the goods that they wish to buy, for the price they are prepared to pay, with this price not being above the marginal cost of production of the goods. Firms also work to *productive efficiency*. This means that the manufacturer makes goods for as low a cost as possible, while still making a profit. Such market conditions foster innovation or *dynamic efficiency* in which the firm is constantly striving to create new, and better, products to meet consumer demand.

20.7   At the heart of this economic analysis of competition lies the concept of *market power*. If any one firm (or number of firms acting in concert) has the ability to reduce output and raise prices without concern that competitors might enter the market and fill consumer demand at lower prices, then the firm is said to be able to exercise market power. A single firm which can act substantially independently of its competitors and without regard to consumers is said to be able to exercise monopoly power and to be a *monopolist*. Two or more firms which, consciously or subconsciously, act in furtherance of a common goal in pursuit of which they deviate from competitive behaviour are termed *oligopolists*. Firms which collude to alter the competitive structure of a market to their own advantage, by, for example, fixing prices or limiting production, are said to form a *cartel*.

 ### Question

Can you think of any flaws that might exist in this theory of perfect competition?

Can you think of any firm which you think is a monopolist through ownership and/or exercise of IPRs? Analyse your response. Why have you thought of the particular firm? What factors have you considered important in your decision? Revisit this question once you have finished this chapter and see if your analysis changes.

Workable competition

20.8   There are many flaws in the theory of perfect competition. Not only does it presuppose that decisions are made rationally by those decision-makers responsible for directing corporate strategy and behaviour in the marketplace, but it also assumes that consumers have perfect knowledge of market conditions and will also make rational decisions when it comes to purchases.

20.9   The deficiencies have led to the development of a theory of 'workable' or 'effective competition':[2]

> '[e]ffective competition does connote the idea...that firms should be subject to a reasonable degree of competitive constraint, from actual and potential competitors and from customers, and that the role of a competition authority is to be that such constraints are present on the market'.[3]

The goal of EU and UK competition policy would appear to be predicated on this notion of effective competition[4] and is to maintain competition within the internal market.

Cartels and monopolies

20.10   In order to maintain a state of effective or workable competition, competition law is directed towards dealing with abuses that can occur to upset that state. These are:

- preventing agreements between firms that have the effect of restricting competition between them;

---

[2] R Whish, *Competition Law* (6th edn, 2008) p 14–16.   [3] R Whish (6th edn, 2008) p 16.
[4] W Cornish & D Llewelyn, *Intellectual Property: Patents, Copyright, Trade Marks and Allied Rights* (6th edn, 2007) paras 1-39–1-47;

- checking behaviour by monopolists who might abuse their dominant position and prevent new competition emerging;
- ensuring workable competition is maintained between oligopolists;
- monitoring mergers between independent firms the effect of which may be to concentrate the market and diminish competitive pressures.[5]

This chapter will consider the first two of those as they relate to the exercise of IPRs and as regulated by Articles 101 (ex Art 81 EC) and 102 (ex Art 82 EC) TFEU. Note that the article numbering which applies following the changes made by the Treaty of Lisbon will be used in this chapter except where the discussion relates to historical events and/or where quotations from cases are used in the text.

Competition law and IP

20.11   As IP laws confer on the owner exclusive rights, so the owner can prevent competition in relation to the subject matter of the right. However, there is a constant tension between the grant of those exclusive rights and the application of competition law. The aim is to find the balance between IPRs and competitive markets. On the interaction between IP and competition law, the Commission has stated:

> 'The fact that intellectual property laws grant exclusive rights of exploitation does not imply that intellectual property rights are immune from competition law intervention. Articles 81 and 82 are in particular applicable to agreements whereby the holder licenses another undertaking to exploit his intellectual property rights. Nor does it imply that there is an inherent conflict between intellectual property rights and the Community competition rules. Indeed, both bodies of law share the same basic objective of promoting consumer welfare and an efficient allocation of resources. Innovation constitutes an essential and dynamic component of an open and competitive market economy. Intellectual property rights promote dynamic competition by encouraging undertakings to invest in developing new or improved products and processes. So does competition by putting pressure on undertakings to innovate. Therefore, both intellectual property rights and competition are necessary to promote innovation and ensure a competitive exploitation thereof'.[6]

 Exercise

Familiarise yourself with the terms of both Articles 101 and 102 TFEU. Consider the mischief they are aimed at and see if you can think of any examples where they might apply to the exercise of IPRs.

20.12   Some concepts are common in any discussion of competition law. The purpose of this next section is to introduce some of these to assist the reader in understanding this chapter.

---

[5] R Whish (6th edn, 2008) p 17.

[6] Commission Notice, Guidelines on the application of Article 81 of the EC Treaty to technology transfer agreements, OJ 2004/C 101/02. The Commission issued a Report on Competition Policy 2008 COM(2009) 374. For a report on Regulation 1/2003 and enforcement see COM(2009) 206.

The relevant market

20.13   The term *market* is usually understood as the place where business is done between companies. As was discussed above, in a state of workable competition, firms will compete against each other in this market to the ultimate benefit of consumers. If a number of firms enter into an agreement which upsets competitive market conditions, or a monopolist is able to, and does, act independently of either competitors or consumers, then the market is said to be distorted.

20.14   But it is only behaviour on the *relevant market* that is taken into account when looking to the behaviour of these entities. This immediately leads to questions as to how the relevant market should be defined. The starting point is generally to look at those products which are in competition. But within these confines if a market is defined too widely, then it is unlikely that anti-competitive conduct will have an adverse effect. For example, if there is an agreement between manufacturers to increase the retail price of wine, this would be unlikely to affect competition in the manufacture, distribution and sale of all drinks, both alcoholic and non-alcoholic. A narrowing of this definition might look to alcoholic drinks. Narrowing it still further might concentrate on wines; or wines from a particular region. But taking a definition that is overly narrow can be equally problematic. For instance raising the price of one brand of children's clothing might be considered an abuse of a dominant position if the market is defined as that particular brand.

■ Case C-22/78 *Hugin v Commission* [1979] ECR 1869, [1979] 3 CMLR 345[7]

In this case the relevant market was defined very narrowly. Hugin made cash register machines in London and had a 13 per cent share of the cash register market; Lipton, a small firm in South East England serviced the registers. Hugin wanted to get into the servicing market and as part of that strategy it refused to supply spare parts to Liptons. In looking to the relevant market both the Commission and the ECJ found that it was in spare parts for the machines (although ultimately the court found that there was no effect on inter state trade). Had the market been defined as that of the product (the cash register) *and* the spare parts, then Hugin would not have been dominant.

20.15   The EC Commission has published a Notice on Market Definition.[8] This sets out the factors that are taken into account in defining the relevant market. The Commission focuses on demand and supply product substitutability and potential competition. To determine the relevant market it is necessary to investigate both the relevant product market and the relevant geographical market. The relevant product market includes those products which are regarded as interchangeable or substitutable by the consumer. This may be because of the characteristics of the products, the price and intended use. The relevant geographical market refers to the area in which the businesses are involved in the supply and demand of products or services.

Weblink

Read the Commission's Notice on Market Definition, which can be found at

http://europa.eu/legislation_summaries/competition/firms/l26073_en.htm

---

[7] Case C-22/78 *Hugin Kassaregister AB and Hugin Cash Registers Limited v Commission of the European Communities* [1979] ECR 1869, [1979] 3 CMLR 345.

[8] Commission Notice on the definition of the relevant market for the purposes of Community competition law, OJ 1997/C 372.

Intra brand competition

20.16   Competition exists at different levels between businesses in the marketplace. A manufacturer may produce a particular product, for example, soap powder. Wholesalers who purchase the soap powder from the manufacturer, and retailers who sell the soap powder to the consumer may then compete with each other in the downstream market. This is called *intra brand* competition—competition between distributors of the same brand. Here the goods are the same and therefore quality is an irrelevant factor. The price at which the product is sold, availability on the market and the conditions under which it is sold may however be important. For example, the soap powder may be sold at a lower price in a discount store as compared with a more upmarket supermarket, but often without the amenities and services that the latter provides.

Inter brand competition

20.17   *Inter brand* competition is where competition exists between suppliers of competing products, for example two differently branded soap powders. Such competition is normally between different firms that have developed brands or labels for their products in order to distinguish them from other brands sold in the same market segment, although sometimes the same manufacturer may develop a number of differently branded products of the same kind. Ariel versus Persil is an example of inter brand competition. Consumers are interested in the quality and the price of the goods as well as, for many products, after sales service.

Horizontal agreements

Weblink

For the Commission Guidelines on the applicability of Article 81 EC (post Lisbon Article 101 TFEU) to horizontal cooperation agreements see

http://europa.eu/legislation_summaries/competition/firms/l26062_en.htm

20.18   A horizontal agreement is one between actual or potential competitors, operating at the same level of the production or distribution chain. Such an agreement may cover, for example, research and development, production or purchasing. Horizontal agreements may restrict competition where they involve price fixing or market sharing, or where the market power resulting from the horizontal co-operation causes negative market effects with respect to prices, output, innovation or the variety and quality of products. On the other hand, horizontal cooperation can be a means to share risk, save costs, pool know how and launch innovation faster. In particular for small and medium-sized enterprises cooperation can be important means to adapt to the changing market place.[9]

---

[9] For discussion of IP and competition issues relating to the development of technology standards see M Lemley, 'Intellectual Property Rights and Standard-Setting Organizations' (2002) 90 California Law Review 1889. See also White Paper 'Modernising ICT Standardisation in the EU: the Way Forward' COM(2009) 324 final.

Vertical agreements

20.19   A vertical agreement is one entered into between two or more undertakings each of which operates at a different level of the production or distribution chain. Vertical agreements tend to be less able to affect other parties and thus foreclose competition on the relevant market. However, where either party has a large market share in the relevant market, vertical agreements can affect third parties who supply the same or substitutable goods. An example would be an agreement between a distributor and manufacturer which prevented other manufacturers from competing to sell goods to that distributor. The effect may be to foreclose competition in the downstream market.

20.20   The Commission has issued a number of notices on vertical and horizontal agreements the purpose of which is to set out the principles that will be used in assessing the impact of these agreements on the relevant market. These include guidelines on vertical restraints[10] and on horizontal cooperation agreements.[11]

> ### Weblink
>
> For a full list of the various notices issued by the Commission relating to competition rules see
> http://ec.europa.eu/competition/antitrust/legislation/entente3_en.html

Intellectual property and agreements between undertakings: Article 101 TFEU

20.21   Article 101 TFEU concerns agreements between undertaking which have the object or effect of preventing, restricting or distorting competition within the common market, and which may affect trade between member states. The interpretation and application of this Article is central in determining the acceptable boundaries of agreements and the clauses they contain entered into between parties which relate to the exploitation of IP.

> **Article 101 TFEU (ex Art 81 EC)**
>
> 'The following shall be prohibited as incompatible with the common market: all agreements between undertakings, decisions by associations of undertakings and concerted practices which may affect trade between Member States and which have as their object or effect the prevention, restriction or distortion of competition within the common market, and in particular those which:
> (a) directly or indirectly fix purchase or selling prices or any other trading conditions;
> (b) limit or control production, markets, technical development, or investment;
> (c) share markets or sources of supply;

[10] Commission Notice, Guidelines on Vertical Restraints, OJ 2000/C 291/01.

[11] Guidelines on the applicability of Article 81 to horizontal co-operation agreements, OJ 2001/C 3/02. See *Re CISAC Agreement Case* COMP/C2/38.698 [2009] 4 CMLR 12 which has been appealed to the CFI, Case T-442/08 *CISAC v Commission*. For an in-depth discussion on the problems caused by segmentation of the internal market see the European Commission's Online Commerce Roundtable Report on Opportunities and barriers to online retailing at http://ec.europa.eu/competition/consultations/2009_online_commerce/roundtable_report_en.pdf

(d) apply dissimilar conditions to equivalent transactions with other trading parties, thereby placing them at a competitive disadvantage;

(e) make the conclusion of contracts subject to acceptance by the other parties of supplementary obligations which, by their nature or according to commercial usage, have no connection with the subject of such contracts. Any agreements or decisions prohibited pursuant to this Article shall be automatically void.

2. The provisions of paragraph 1 may, however, be declared inapplicable in the case of:
  – any agreement or category of agreements between undertakings;
  – any decision or category of decisions by associations of undertakings; – any concerted practice or category of concerted practices,

which contributes to improving the production or distribution of goods or to promoting technical or economic progress, while allowing consumers a fair share of the resulting benefit, and which does not:

(a) impose on the undertakings concerned restrictions which are not indispensable to the attainment of these objectives;

(b) afford such undertakings the possibility of eliminating competition in respect of a substantial part of the products in question.'

20.22   The Commission has said that, in the context of the single market programme, the objective of Article 101 TFEU (at that time Art 81 EC) is to protect competition on the market as a means of enhancing consumer welfare and of ensuring an efficient allocation of resources.[12] It will be noted from the text of the Article that agreements which are prohibited by Article 101 TFEU are void Article 101(2) TFEU. However, Article 101(3) TFEU provides that the provisions of Article 101(1) TFEU may be declared inapplicable in specified circumstances—in other words an agreement would not be in breach of Article 101(1) TFEU. This Article will be discussed below.

Article 101 TFEU and licensing agreements

20.23   A common way of exploiting intellectual property is through a licensing agreement (paras 21.7–21.57). The holder of a patent might not have the financial resources to develop and exploit the patent, and so may enter into an agreement with a third party. A singer may need the help of a record company to record, market and distribute recordings of performances, or of a collecting society to ingather sums due for the performance of that song in public. Such an agreement with one entity may well foreclose the IP owner from dealing with other parties, at least within the scope of the first arrangement, and thus be restrictive of competition as regards third parties. Equally, a licensing agreement may be pro-competitive. A licensee is permitted to do something that would otherwise be an infringement of another's rights. The owner will get a financial return while others can improve efficiency in terms of both manufacture and distribution of the products. The question then is as to when and where might the prohibitions on anti-competitive conduct found in Article 101(1) TFEU apply to licensing agreements concerning IP to render an agreement void and unenforceable?

As will be seen from the text of Article 101 TFEU, an agreement is not within its scope unless:

• it has the object or effect of preventing, distorting or restricting competition. Where an agreement has the object of preventing competition, for example through absolute territorial exclusivity, then there will be no need to examine the economic effect of the agreement in the market. Where it is not intended to foreclose competition, then the effect of the agreement in the market will have to be analysed;

[12] Guidelines on the application of Article 81(3) of the Treaty (2004/C 101/08).

> - it may affect trade between member states. Trade must be affected to an appreciable extent. To help businesses assess whether Article 101 TFEU (ex Art 81 EC) may be applicable the Commission has published a Notice on Agreements of Minor Importance which sets out the market share thresholds below which an agreement will be regarded as de minimis.[13] These are set at 10 per cent market share for agreements between competitors and to 15 per cent for agreements between non-competitors.

It should also be noted that any type of agreement between two or more entities might fall under Article 101 TFEU. An agreement does not have to be in writing and can extend to 'informal' understandings (concerted practices) between undertakings in the market, for instance an understanding not to enter the territory of another competitor.

Weblink

For a series of model licensing agreements see:

http://www.innovation.gov.uk/lambertagreements/index.asp?lvl1=2&lvl2=0&lvl3=0&lvl4=0

These agreements have been drafted by the Lambert committee which was charged with developing model agreements for use where one of the parties to the agreement is an educational institution. Read through some of the agreements to familiarise yourself with the type of provisions to be found in these documents. In what ways do you think Article 101(1) TFEU might need to be considered? Revisit your answer when you have finished this section.

ECJ case law, Article 101 TFEU and IP agreements

20.24   In the early development of case law on the application of Article 81(1) EC to IP licences, the ECJ followed a fairly restrictive approach to what it considered may fall foul of the Treaty. This was a consequence of the pursuit of the goal of bringing about a free market between member states. This approach tended to be followed irrespective of broader economic benefits that may have been brought about through an agreement. In so doing, the ECJ developed a distinction between the *existence* and *exercise* of an IPR which in turn led to a consideration of the *specific subject matter*. The existence/exercise dichotomy can be seen in *Consten & Grundig v EEC Commission*.

■ Case C-56/64 *Consten & Grundig v EEC Commission* [1966] ECR 299, [1966] CMLR 418

A German manufacturer, Grundig, made electrical goods in Germany. Grundig entered into an agreement with Consten, a French distributor, whereby Consten would distribute Grundig's products in France under both *Grundig* and *Gint* trade marks. The intention was to grant Consten absolute territorial protection for the distribution of Grundig's products in France. Grundig sought to achieve this by:

---

[13] Commission Notice on agreements of minor importance which do not appreciably restrict competition under Article 81(1) of the Treaty establishing the European Community (de minimis), OJ 2001/ C 368/13.

- imposing certain terms on other wholesalers and distributors including re-export bans and express terms prohibiting distribution of Grundig products in France; and

- entering into a licence agreement which authorised the exclusive use by Consten of Grundig's trade mark, *Gint*, in France which would be assigned to Consten once the agreement came to an end.

The Commission condemned these agreements as a breach of Article 81(1). Both parties sought annulment of the Commission decision.

The ECJ said:

- Article 81 applies to both horizontal and vertical agreements.

- An agreement between a manufacturer and distributor who are not in competition might have an adverse effect on competition between one of them and a third party. It is thus distortive of competition to make an agreement designed to insulate national markets.

The Court went on to say that the injunction contained in the contested decision to refrain from using rights in national trade mark law in order to set an obstacle in the way of parallel imports *does not affect the grant* of those rights, but only *limits their exercise* to the extent necessary to give effect to the prohibition under Article 81.

Points to note:

- The Court considered the licensing of the trade mark a material factor in the attempt to ensure for Consten absolute territorial exclusivity. This caused the agreement to fall foul of Article 81. (Note however that the approach to territorial exclusivity has changed over time—see for example the *Maize Seeds* case discussed below.)

- The purpose of registration of the trade mark in France was to increase the protection against parallel imports into France of Grundig products. In other words, it was to give Consten its own means of repelling the parallel imports of genuine Grundig products from other member states.

The specific subject matter

20.25   In *Windsurfing International v Commission*,[14] the Commission and the ECJ used the concept of *specific subject matter* to determine the compatibility of Article 81 EC with a patent licensing agreement.

■ **Case C-193/83 *Windsurfing International v Commission* [1986] ECR 611, [1986] 3 CMLR 489**

Windsurfing invented a rig for a sailboard. Patents were applied for in several countries including Germany. Windsurfing entered into a number of agreements with licensees in Germany. The provisions in the licence included:

- Clauses tying patented goods to unpatented goods. The patent itself only covered the rig. The licence tied exploitation of the rig to exploitation of the sail board. In other words, if a licensee wanted a licence to manufacturer and sell the patented rig mechanism, they also had to manufacture and sell the sail board.

[14] Case C-193/83 [1986] ECR 611, [1986] 3 CMLR 489.

- Royalties were to be calculated on the basis of sales of final assembled goods. This included both patented and unpatented products.

- A requirement to fix patent attribution and the logo to both patented and unpatented goods.

- A 'no-challenge' clause.

The Commission and then the ECJ found that a number of these clauses went beyond the *specific subject matter* of the patent. In other words there was an attempt by the patentee to extend the patent monopoly.

The ECJ said:

> 'the clauses contained in the licensing agreements, in so far as they relate to parts of the sailboard not covered by the German patent or include the complete sailboard within their terms of reference, can therefore find no justification on grounds of the protection of an industrial property right'.[15]

20.26   Little use has been made of the existence/exercise and specific subject matter doctrine by either the Commission or ECJ during the 1990s. However, one of the leading writers in this area, Tritton, has said that: 'It is probable it will be relied on in the future in Article 81 to the extent that [clauses in licences] which are related to the specific subject matter of an IPR will be permissible without further analysis'.[16] Such clauses may include an obligation to pay royalties and relate to quality control.

Question

What is a 'no-challenge' clause?

Exercise 1

Compare the emergence of the existence/exercise/specific subject matter doctrines used in the application of Article 101 TFEU to IP agreements with those developed in relation to the free movement of goods (see Chapter 19).

Exercise 2

Consider ways in which you think agreements between undertakings dealing with IP might fall under the prohibitions in Article 101 TFEU.

20.27   The ECJ has also used an economic or *'rule of reason'* approach in its application of Article 81 EC to IP agreements. Broadly this consists of an economic analysis of an agreement on the relevant market. If the agreement has pro-competitive effects which outweigh the anti-competitive effects, then it should not be prohibited by competition laws.[17] This approach can be seen in

---

[15] ibid, at point 36.   [16] G Tritton, *Intellectual Property in Europe* (2nd edn, 2002) para 8–062.
[17] G Tritton, (2nd edn, 2002) paras 8–010 and 8–071.

Nungesser v Commission[18] otherwise known as the *Maize Seed* case in which the central question was whether an exclusive licence of plant breeders rights infringed Article 81(1).

■ Case C-258/78 *Nungesser v Commission* [1981] ECR 45, [1982] ECR 2015

A French Institute developed varieties of maize seeds for which it held plant breeders rights in French and German law. By a series of agreements the German rights were partly licensed and partly assigned to a German undertaking. The French Institute agreed to ensure absolute territorial exclusivity for the production and sale of the seeds in Germany. It did so by pursuing the following strategy:

The French Institute agreed:

- not to license another undertaking in Germany to produce or sell the seeds;
- not itself to produce the seeds in Germany; and
- not itself to export seeds to Germany, and to obtain agreement from other licensees in other territories that they would not export seeds to Germany.

The Commission took a rigid view of Article 81(1) and held that the grant of exclusive rights contravened its provisions. When the case was heard by the ECJ, the court took a different approach. The ECJ sought to reconcile the objectives of free competition between member states and the wider competitive benefits of exclusive licences of IP rights. It did so by drawing a distinction between:

- *'open exclusive licences'* where exclusive rights are granted for one territory; and
- *'closed licences'* in terms of which steps are taken to ensure there is no competition from entities in other territories.

The ECJ said that open licences were acceptable. Some exclusivity may be essential to encourage a potential licensee to invest in a new product. Therefore the agreement not to license another German undertaking, and not to produce the seeds in Germany itself were acceptable. However, that part of the agreement by virtue of which the French Institute was to seek agreement from other licensees not to import into Germany was void as it affected the position of third parties such as parallel importers.

20.28   After some hesitation this economic balancing approach seems now also to be pursued by the Commission:

'The aim of the Community competition rules is to protect competition on the market as a means of enhancing consumer welfare and of ensuring an efficient allocation of resources. Agreements that restrict competition may at the same time have pro-competitive effects by way of efficiency gains. Efficiencies may create additional value by lowering the cost of producing an output, improving the quality of the product or creating a new product. When the pro-competitive effects of an agreement outweigh its anti-competitive effects the agreement is on balance pro-competitive and compatible with the objectives of the Community competition rules. The net effect of such agreements is to promote the very essence of the competitive process, namely to win customers by offering better products or better prices than those offered by rivals'.[19]

---

[18] Case C-258/78 [1981] ECR 45, [1982] ECR 2015.
[19] Commission Notice, Guidelines on the application of Article 81 of the EC Treaty to technology transfer agreements, OJ 2004/C 101/02, para 33. See also the discussion in Chapter 21 on collective licensing and Article 101. *Re CISAC Agreement Case* COMP/C2/38.698 [2009] 4 CMLR 12, which has been appealed to the General Court, Case T-442/08 *CISAC v Commission*.

Exercise

Can you see any drawbacks in the adoption of an economic rule of reason approach? How easy or difficult do you think it is for companies operating in the marketplace to carry out a detailed economic analysis of the effect of an agreement in the relevant market?

20.29   This line of reasoning may be further explored in joined cases *Murphy v Media Protection Services*[20] and *FA Premier League v QC Leisure & Ors*[21] concerning the supply of decoders and receipt of broadcasts of football matches (see also para 19.69). The case looks to the interfaces between Article 81, IP and free movement of goods. The competition law point focuses on the agreements between the manufacturer and broadcaster to place an export ban on the decoders to be in contravention of the competition rules on market sharing in Article 81. It has been argued that the *Nungesser v Commission*[22] is the relevant line of law to be followed with its distinction between open and closed exclusive licences and those circumstances under which a certain degree of exclusivity may be needed to encourage and nurture competition.

Article 101(2) TFEU

20.30   If an agreement falls within Article 101(1) TFEU then it is void. A national court may determine if a particular clause is severable and those parts of the agreement not caught may continue.

Article 101(3) TFEU

20.31   Even if an agreement does fall under Article 101(1) TFEU, it may be exempted under Article 101(3) TFEU. This Article exempts agreements which improve production or distribution of products, or which contribute to technical or economic progress. This is subject to the proviso that consumers must gain a share of the benefit. However, any restrictions should only be such as are indispensable and not eliminate competition in respect of a substantial part of the products in question.

20.32   A new procedural regime came into force on 1 May 2004 for the application of Article 81(3) EC (now Article 101(3) TFEU). Under the old regime[23] application could be made to the Commission for exemption under this Article unless the agreement fell within one of the block exemption regulations (discussed below). In 2004 a new Regulation came into force under which Article 81(3) became directly applicable.[24] It is now for businesses to self-assess as to whether an agreement falls under Article 101(1) TFEU. A ruling on the legality of an agreement will only be required if a dispute or complaint arises. At that point national competition authorities and national courts will have concurrent jurisdiction with the Commission including the right to rule on the legality of an agreement under Article 101(3) TFEU.

[20] Case C-429/08 [2008] EWHC 1666.
[21] Case C-403/08. Joined with Case 429/08 in order of the President of the Court, 3 December 2008.
[22] Case 258/78 *Nungesser v Commission* [1982] ECR 2015, para 20.27.
[23] Council Regulation No 17/62 of 6 February 1962.
[24] Council Regulation (EC) No 1/2003 of 16 December 2002 on the implementation of the rules on competition laid down in Arts 81 and 82 of the Treaty.

Question

What does direct applicability mean?

20.33 Alongside this new procedure the Commission issued a set of guidelines which set out the Commission's interpretation of the conditions for application of the exception contained in Article 101(3) TFEU, and to provide guidance on how the Commission will apply Article 101 TFEU in individual cases. In so doing the Commission has indicated that it will weigh the pro- and anti-competitive effects of agreements between undertakings.

> 'The assessment under Article 81 . . . consists of two parts. The first step is to assess whether an agreement between undertakings, which is capable of affecting trade between Member States, has an anti-competitive object or actual or potential anti competitive effects. The second step, which only becomes relevant when an agreement is found to be restrictive of competition, is to determine the pro-competitive benefits produced by that agreement and to assess whether these pro-competitive effects outweigh the anti-competitive effects'.[25]

Weblink

The Commission has issued a raft of notices and communications resulting from their programme designed to update and modernise EU competition (anti-trust) rules and procedures. These documents are collectively termed the 'Modernisation Package' and can be found at

http://ec.europa.eu/competition/antitrust/legislation/legislation.html

Note in particular the Guidelines on the application of Article 81(3) of the Treaty (2004/ C 101/08).

Block exemption regulations

20.34 The Commission (acting on delegated authority from the EU Council of Ministers) may, pursuant to Article 101(3) TFEU issue block exemptions relating to the licensing and sharing of IP. A block exemption specifies those conditions under which certain types of agreements are exempted from the prohibition laid down in Article 101(1) TFEU. When an agreement fulfils the conditions set out in a block exemption regulation, the agreement is automatically valid and enforceable. Block exemption regulations exist in a number of sectors including for vertical agreements,[26] research and development (R&D) agreements,[27] technology transfer agreements[28] and car distribution agreements[29] and have become a valuable tool for businesses.

---

[25] Commission Notice, Guidelines on the application of Article 81(3) of the Treaty, OJ 2004/C 101/08, para 11.

[26] Commission Regulation (EC) No 2790/1999 of 22 December 1999 on the application of Art 81(3) of the Treaty to categories of vertical agreements and concerted practices. Note that this Regulation expires in May 2010. A consultation on the functioning of this Regulation closed in September 2009. A draft Regulation has been issued which may be amended in the light of comments received during the consultation.

[27] Commission Regulation (EC) No 2659/2000 of 29 November 2000 on the application of Art 81(3) of the Treaty to categories of research and development agreements.

[28] See now, Commission Regulation (EC) No 772/2004 of 27 April 2004 on the application of Art 81(3) of the Treaty to categories of technology transfer agreements.

[29] Commission Regulation (EC) No 1400/2002 of 31 July 2002 on the application of Art 81(3) of the Treaty to categories of vertical agreements and concerted practices in the motor vehicle sector.

The most important for current purposes is the Technology Transfer Block Exemption Regulation.

Technology Transfer Block Exemption Regulation

20.35   The initial IP block exemptions promulgated by the Commission dealt separately with the licensing of patents[30] and know how.[31] These block exemptions were replaced in 1996 by one instrument, the Technology Transfer Block Exemption (TTBE),[32] covering technology transfer agreements generally. Following extensive consultation the TTBE has now been replaced by a revised Technology Transfer Block Exemption Regulation, the TTBER, which came into force on 1 May 2004[33] and which is accompanied by a set of guidelines[34] on the application of Article 101 TFEU to technology transfer agreements.

20.36   The TTBER is relevant to undertakings which enter into technology transfer (licensing) agreements where those agreements deal with patents, know how, software copyright or a mixture of these IPRs. The TTBER also covers those agreements which include other IPRs, so long as those are not the primary object of the agreement.[35]

20.37   The TTBER distinguishes between licensing arrangements between competitors and non-competitors: the question is whether the agreement restricts actual or potential competition that would have existed without the agreement.[36] Competing undertakings (horizontal agreements) may benefit from the exemptions only where the combined market share[37] of the parties does not exceed 20 per cent of either a relevant technology market or a relevant product market;[38] non-competing undertakings (vertical agreements) may benefit from the exemptions only where the market share of each party does not exceed 30 per cent on the relevant technology and product markets.[39] If parties have a market share in excess of that specified, then any contractual restrictions will be subject to analysis.

The Regulation works on the premise that any clauses which are not forbidden are exempt. Two classes of restrictions are set out and detail those clauses that would, or might (unless severable), cause the agreement to be non-exempt.

Hardcore restrictions[40]

20.38   Hardcore restrictions will, if included, mean that the agreement falls outwith the TTBER.[41] These are based on the nature of the restriction and have, through experience been found to be anticompetitive.[42] They vary depending on whether the agreement is one between competitors or non-competitors.

---

[30] Regulation 2349/84, OJ 1984 L219, amended by Regulation 151/93, OJ 1993 L21/8 and Regulation 2131/95, OJ 1995 L214/6.
[31] Regulation 556/89, OJ 1989 L61, amended by Regulation 151/93, OJ 1993 L21/8.
[32] Regulation 240/96, OJ 1996 L31/2.
[33] Commission Regulation (EC) No 772/2004 of 27 April 2004 on the application of Art 81(3) of the Treaty to categories of technology transfer agreements (TTBER).
[34] Guidelines on the application of Art 81 of the EC Treaty to technology transfer agreements (2004/C 101/02) (TTBER Guidelines).
[35] TTBER, Art 1(b).   [36] TTBER Guidelines, para 12.
[37] Market share is defined in terms of presence of the licensed technology on the relevant technology market and includes the licensor's and all its current licensees share of the market. TTBER, Art 1(j).
[38] TTBER, Art 3(1).   [39] ibid, Art 3(2).   [40] ibid, Art 4.   [41] ibid, Art 4(1) and (2).
[42] TTBER Guidelines, para 74.

- Where the parties are competitors, then prohibited clauses include:
(a) the restriction of a party's ability to determine its prices when selling products to third parties—for instance by setting the exact price at which the products can be sold, or the range of prices with maximum rebates;
(b) the limitation of output, except limitations on the output of contract products imposed on the licensee in a non-reciprocal agreement or imposed on only one of the licensees in a reciprocal agreement;
(c) the allocation of markets or customers except:
    (i)   the obligation on the licensee(s) to produce with the licensed technology only within one or more technical fields of use or one or more product markets,
    (ii) the obligation on the licensor and/or the licensee, in a non-reciprocal agreement, not to produce with the licensed technology within one or more technical fields of use or one or more product markets or one or more exclusive territories reserved for the other party,
    (iii) the obligation on the licensor not to license the technology to another licensee in a particular territory,
    (iv) the restriction, in a non-reciprocal agreement, of active and/or passive sales by the licensee and/or the licensor into the exclusive territory or to the exclusive customer group reserved for the other party,
    (v)   the restriction, in a non-reciprocal agreement, of active sales by the licensee into the exclusive territory or to the exclusive customer group allocated by the licensor to another licensee provided the latter was not a competing undertaking of the licensor at the time of the conclusion of its own licence,
    (vi) the obligation on the licensee to produce the contract products only for its own use provided that the licensee is not restricted in selling the contract products actively and passively as spare parts for its own products,
    (vii) the obligation on the licensee, in a non-reciprocal agreement, to produce the contract products only for a particular customer, where the licence was granted in order to create an alternative source of supply for that customer.
(d) the restriction of the licensee's ability to exploit its own technology or the restriction of the ability of any of the parties to the agreement to carry out research and development, unless such latter restriction is indispensable to prevent the disclosure of the licensed know how to third parties.
- Where the parties are not in competition then prohibited clauses include:
(a) the restriction of a party's ability to determine its prices when selling products to third parties, without prejudice to the possibility of imposing a maximum sale price or recommending a sale price, provided that it does not amount to a fixed or minimum sale price as a result of pressure from, or incentives offered by, any of the parties;
(b) the restriction of the territory into which, or of the customers to whom, the licensee may passively sell the contract products, except:
    (i)   the restriction of passive sales into an exclusive territory or to an exclusive customer group reserved for the licensor,
    (ii) the restriction of passive sales into an exclusive territory or to an exclusive customer group allocated by the licensor to another licensee during the first two years that this other licensee is selling the contract products in that territory or to that customer group,
    (iii) the obligation to produce the contract products only for its own use provided that the licensee is not restricted in selling the contract products actively and passively as spare parts for its own products,
    (iv) the obligation to produce the contract products only for a particular customer, where the licence was granted in order to create an alternative source of supply for that customer,
    (v)   the restriction of sales to end-users by a licensee operating at the wholesale level of trade,
    (vi) the restriction of sales to unauthorised distributors by the members of a selective distribution system.
(c) the restriction of active or passive sales to end-users by a licensee which is a member of a selective distribution system and which operates at the retail level, without prejudice to the possibility of prohibiting a member of the system from operating out of an unauthorised place of establishment.

Exercise

Read the TTBER and the Guidelines. Explain why these particular clauses are considered to be restrictive of competition and thus prohibited in IP agreements.

Excluded restrictions

20.39   The TTBER also contains excluded restrictions.[43] These are clauses that do not fall under the TTBER and thus require individual assessment as to their pro- or anti-competitive effect. Their inclusion in an agreement does not prevent the TTBER applying to the rest of the agreement. Excluded restrictions include:

- obligations on the licensee to grant exclusive licences-back (or assignments back) of severable improvements or new applications to the licensor or a third party. A severable improvement is one which can be exploited without infringing the licensed technology. The underlying concern is that such grant-backs will reduce the licencee's incentive to innovate as severable improvements cannot be exploited;[44]

- no-challenge clauses—although the licensor can include a provision for termination of the licence in the event a challenge to the validity of the intellectual property right is made;

- obligations limiting the ability of the licensee to exploit its own technology;

- restrictions on either party's R&D activities.

Question

What do you understand to be the differences between hardcore and excluded restrictions, and why does the treatment of the latter differ to the former?

20.40   The Guidelines state that analysis of the potential anti-competitive effect of an agreement should focus on the actual or potential competition that would have existed without the agreement. An example is given relating to inter-technology competition is where two undertakings established in different member states cross licence competing technologies and undertake not to sell products in each other's home markets. Potential competition existing prior to the agreement is thus restricted. Equally where a licensor places obligations on his licensees not to use competing technologies, the technology belonging to third parties would not be used. The result is that actual or potential competition that would have existed in the absence of the agreement is restricted.

20.41   On intra technology competition a licensor might restrict its licensees from competing with each other. Any potential competition that could have existed between the licensees is restricted. Examples of restrictions would include vertical price fixing and territorial or customer sales restrictions between licensees.[45]

---

[43] TTBER, Art 5.   [44] TTBER Guidelines, para 109.   [45] TTBER Guidelines, Part 2.

Consequences of an agreement being in breach of Article 101(1) TFEU

20.42   If an agreement is in breach of Article 101(1) TFEU and does not benefit from the block exemption then:

- the agreement is automatically void and unenforceable;
- the Commission can impose a fine on the parties;[46]
- in the UK, directors of companies risk being disqualified under the Enterprise Act 2002, s 204.

Exercise

Construct a decision tree showing the steps that need to be taken to ascertain whether clauses in an IP licensing agreement would fall within the parameters of the TTBER and explain the questions that would need to be asked at each step.

20.43   A number of concerns have been expressed over the application of the TTBER. These include the following.

- The need for parties (and their advisors) to assess their relevant market share to see if they can benefit from the block exemption.
- Agreements which are initially exempt can cease to be so if the market shares of the parties increases. This might occur if cutting edge technology is involved.
- The new regime will be implemented by national courts and competition authorities. This may lead to inconsistencies in approach.
- The Commission can withdraw the benefit of the block exemption if it considers that it offends Article 101(1) TFEU. This could lead to uncertainty for the parties.

Question

Can you think of any other difficulties that may be experienced with the application of the TTBER? What advantages do you think it has?

---

[46] See Guidelines on the method of setting fines imposed pursuant to Art 23(2)(a) of Regulation No 1/2003 (2006/ C 210/02).

> ### Key points on intellectual property and agreements between undertakings: Article 101 TFEU
>
> - Article 101 TFEU concerns agreements between undertakings which have the object or effect of preventing, restricting or distorting competition within the common market, and which may affect trade between member states
> - The TTBER is relevant to undertakings which enter into technology transfer (licensing) agreements where those agreements deal with patents, know how, software copyright or a mixture of these IPRs
> - Where an agreement contains hardcore restrictions, it will fall outwith the TTBER
> - The pro- and anti-competitive effect of excluded restrictions need to be assessed on a case-by-case basis

Intellectual property and abuse of a dominant position: Article 102 TFEU

20.44   Article 102 TFEU concerns the prevention of abuse of market power by undertakings which occupy a dominant position within the common market.

> Article 102 TFEU (ex Art 82 EC)
>
> 'Any abuse by one or more undertakings of a dominant position within the common market or in a sub-stantial part of it shall be prohibited as incompatible with the common market insofar as it may affect trade between Member States.
>
> Such abuse may, in particular, consist in:
> (a) directly or indirectly imposing unfair purchase or selling prices or other unfair trading conditions;
> (b) limiting production, markets or technical development to the prejudice of consumers;
> (c) applying dissimilar conditions to equivalent transactions with other trading parties, thereby plac-ing them at a competitive disadvantage;
> (d) making the conclusion of contracts subject to acceptance by the other parties of supplementary obligations which, by their nature or according to commercial usage, have no connection with the subject of such contracts.'

20.45   All IPRs give some form of exclusive right to the owner. But it does not follow that the IP owner occupies a dominant position and is able to exert market power. Market power implies that a consumer will have no choice but to deal with the dominant entity—the monopolist: in other words, that there will be no substitutes for the product or services on offer by the monopolist. That is often not the case for the subject matter of IP. If the price of a painting by a favoured art-ist exceeds what most can afford, then another less well-known but more affordable artist may find favour; if the price of a patented remedy for a headache increases, then alternative therapies may have to be found; if the price of a well-advertised branded product exceeds reasonable expectations, then the consumer may look for other varieties. The extent to which alternatives cannot be found or will not find favour with a consumer may depend on, for example, technical advances or fashion.[47]

---

[47] W Cornish & D Llewelyn, *Intellectual Property: Patents, Copyright, Trade Marks and Allied rights* (6th edn, 2007) para 1-45.

20.46   However, it is with the expansion of both the scope and subject matter of IPRs to cover, for example, new technological advances used by consumers in daily life; medicines essential to human health; and to compilations of information that cannot be obtained elsewhere that increasing attention is now being focused on the extent to which Article 82 may, in particular, be used to require the owner of an IPR to license its IP to a third party.

Dominant position

20.47   Article 102 TFEU refers to undertakings which occupy a dominant position. A dominant position relates to a position of economic strength enjoyed by an undertaking on the relevant market. A dominant position in and of itself does not cause an entity to fall under the prohibition in Article 102 TFEU.[48] However, when that dominant position is *abused*, perhaps by foreclosing effective competition on the relevant market brought about by the firm having the power to behave to an appreciable extent independently of its competitors, customers, and ultimately of its consumers, then Article 102 TFEU may be brought into play.

20.48   Generally, abuse has been described as conduct by a dominant firm which seriously and unjustifiably distorts competition or causes it further to weaken.[49] This is an objective test, and may impose burdens on dominant undertakings not faced by others.

ECJ case law

20.49   In the early cases, the ECJ made it clear that mere ownership of an IPR, and exercising it, for example to gain higher prices, would not necessarily involve a breach of Article 82 EC (now Article 102 TFEU).[50]

■ Case C-24/67 *Parke Davis v Probel* [1968] ECR 55; [1968] CMLR 47

The ECJ considered whether the exercise of patent rights could be an abuse of a dominant position. Parke Davis, a US company, held a patent in the Netherlands for a certain chemical process. Probel delivered chloramphenicol to the Netherlands which had been sold freely in Italy. Parke Davis used its patent to complain.

The ECJ held:

- the existence of IPRs are not affected by Article 82;
- the exercise of rights cannot fall under Article 82 in the absence of abuse of a dominant position;
- a higher sale price does not necessarily constitute abuse.

The Court went on to say:

'For this prohibition to apply it is thus necessary that three elements shall be present together: the existence of a dominant position, the abuse of this position and the possibility that trade between

---

[48] *Deutsche Grammophon v Metro* Case C-78/70 [1971] ECR 487. In *Kanal 5 Ltd v Föreningen Svenska Tonsättares Internationella Musikbyrå (STIM) UPA* Case C-52/07 [2009] 5 CMLR 18 the ECJ held that, while a copyright management organisation has a de facto monopoly in Sweden for licensing music for broadcast television, it does not mean that its mere use of a remuneration model amounts to an abuse of a dominant position under Art 82 EC. See also para 21.25ff.

[49] C Bellamy & G Child, (5th edn, 2001) p 717.

[50] Case C-24/67 *Parke, Davis v Probel* [1968] ECR 55, [1968] CMLR 47. See also Case C-78/70 *Deutsche Grammophon v Metro* [1971] ECR 487, [1971] CMLR 631.

Member States may be affected thereby. Although a patent confers on its holder a special protection at national level, it does not follow that the exercise of the rights thus conferred implies the presence together of all three elements in question. It could only do so if the use of the patent were to degenerate into an abuse of the abovementioned protection.'[51]

Thus, the mere exercise of IPRs does not constitute an abuse. However, the exercise of IPRs when used as an instrument of abuse, and where trade between member states may be affected, may be enjoined under this Article.

Article 102 TFEU and the refusal to supply

20.50   One of the most interesting areas in which the interaction between Article 102 TFEU and the exercise of IPRs has occurred in relation to the refusal to supply. When, if at all, can the owner of an IPR be required to supply a third party on the basis that a refusal to supply would amount to the abuse of a dominant position? IPRs after all, by their nature give to the owner exclusive rights. Could, or should the application of competition law be used to limit the exercise of the right? Or should the IP owner have the absolute right, within the parameters of the monopoly, to decide not to licence that right to a third party?

■ Case C-238/87 *Volvo v Veng* [1988] ECR 6211, [1989] 4 CMLR 122

A refusal to licence was considered in *Volvo v Veng*. Volvo held the design right in the UK over front wings for cars. Veng imported panels into the UK from Italy and Denmark where they had been manufactured without Volvo's consent. Volvo alleged infringement of its UK registered designs. Veng's defence was that Volvo's refusal to grant a licence was an abuse of a dominant position when Veng was willing to pay a reasonable royalty for a licence.
The question for this discussion that was put before the ECJ related to Volvo's refusal to grant a licence to others. Was this an abuse of a dominant position?

The ECJ said:

'It must also be emphasised that the right of the proprietor of a protected design to prevent third parties from manufacturing and selling or importing, without its consent, products incorporating the design constitutes the very subject-matter of his exclusive right. It follows that an obligation imposed upon the proprietor of a protected design to grant to third parties, even in return for a reasonable royalty, a licence for the supply of products incorporating the design would lead to the proprietor thereof being deprived of the substance of his exclusive right, and that a refusal to grant such a licence cannot in itself constitute an abuse of a dominant position'.[52]

So a refusal in and of itself would not be an abuse of a dominant position as a refusal to license others is part of the *'very subject-matter'* of an IPR. There has to be something more. The question is what more is needed? The ECJ went on to indicate those circumstances in which the exercise of an IPR may go beyond the subject matter of an IPR, and thus constitute an abuse of a dominant position:

'...the exercise by the proprietor of an exclusive right in a registered design in respect of car body panels my be prohibited by Article 82 if it involves, on the part of an undertaking holding a dominant position, certain abusive conduct such as the arbitrary refusal to supply spare parts to independent repairers, the fixing of prices for spare parts at an unfair level, or a decision no longer to produce spare

---

[51] ibid, para 4.   [52] ibid, para 8.

parts for a particular model even though many cars of that model are still in circulation, provided that such conduct is liable to affect trade between Member States'.[53]

20.51   The examples given by the Court are interesting, and can be seen as related to the prohibitions laid down in Article 102 TFEU. So, for example, a decision no longer to produce spare parts for a particular model even though cars of that model were still in circulation would certainly prejudice consumers and thus fall under Article 102(b) TFEU. Nevertheless, the mere refusal to license a third party (as opposed to an arbitrary refusal to supply spare parts to independent repairers) did not, at this stage, amount to an abuse of a dominant position.

 Question

> Why might a refusal to license be a contentious issue both for the IP owner and for the third party seeking the licence? In what circumstances (if any) could you imagine a refusal to license constituting an abuse of a dominant position?

20.52   Despite the position taken by the ECJ in *Volvo v Veng*, the question as to when and if a refusal to license a third party might amount to an abuse of a dominant position has come up in subsequent case law. In 1995, for the first time, the ECJ held that in *exceptional circumstances* a refusal to license might constitute an abuse of a dominant position. The case in which this arose was *RTE and ITP v Commission* (*Magill*).

■ **Joined Cases C-241/91 P and C-242/91 P** *RTE and ITP v Commission (Magill)* **[1995] ECR I-743**

Television programmes were (and are) broadcast by different companies in the UK and Ireland, and only they held the details of the programmes to be broadcast each week. They disseminated weekly listings of their own output. Given the low level of originality in each jurisdiction the listings were protected by copyright. Magill, a Dublin company, put out a publication listing channels received in most Irish households. Almost immediately it was enjoined for copyright infringement. Magill complained to the Commission which found the conduct of the Irish broadcasters to be an abuse of a dominant position. The Commission ordered them to supply all third parties with weekly listings in advance.

The ECJ upheld the decision of the Commission saying:

- mere ownership of an IPR cannot confer a dominant position;
- in the absence of harmonisation the conditions for granting protection of IPRs is a matter for national rules;
- the exclusive right of reproduction is part of the author's right so that a refusal to grant a licence, even if it is the act of an undertaking holding a dominant position, cannot in itself constitute abuse of a dominant position;
- however, the exercise of an exclusive right by the proprietor may in *exceptional circumstances* involve abusive conduct.

The ECJ emphasised that the television companies were the only sources of the basic information on programme scheduling which is the indispensable raw material for compiling a weekly

---

[53] ibid, para 10. See also *CICRA v Renault* [1990] 4 CMLR 265.

The tying (bundling) of Windows Media Player and Windows client PC operating system

20.74   The CFI upheld the part of the Commission decision relating to the bundling of windows media player. The CFI agreed that Microsoft had a dominant position on the client PC operating systems market; that there was separate consumer demand for media players; that different companies were present in the market supplying the products; and that consumers continue to acquire competing media players separately. However, a consumer could not acquire the Windows operating system without simultaneously acquiring Windows Media Player. Through this there was a significant risk that competition would be weakened in such a way that an effective competitive structure could not be ensured in the near future. Microsoft had demonstrated no objective justification for this bundling. Consequently the remedy imposed by the Commission was proportionate. Microsoft retained the right to continue to offer the version of Windows bundled with Windows Media Player and was required only to make it possible for consumers to obtain the operating system without that media player, a measure which does not mean any change in Microsoft's current technical practice other than the development of that version of Windows.

 Exercise

Read in full the judgment of the ECJ in *IMS* and the decision of the CFI in the *Microsoft* case. What factors strike you in the discussions concerning secondary markets?

Do you think it correct that Microsoft be compelled to grant what is in effect a compulsory licence of its IP and to what extent do you think this would be consistent with the compulsory licensing provisions in the Berne Convention and in TRIPS?

Read Microsoft's arguments concerning Article 6 of the Software Directive (Directive 91/250) that were made before the Commission and the CFI. You will recall that Article is designed to require owners of programs to disclose interfaces where competitors wish to develop a competing but interoperable program. What was Microsoft's interpretation of those provisions in this case? What is your view?

Further reading

Books

S Anderman, *EC Competition Law and Intellectual Property Rights* (2000)

C Bellamy and G Child, *European Community Law of Competition* (6th edn, 2007)

S Bishop and M Walker, *The Economics of EC Competition Law: Concepts, Applications and Measurement* (2nd edn, 2002)

V Korah, *Intellectual Property Rights and the EC Competition Rules* (2006)

G Tritton, *Intellectual Property in Europe* (3rd edn, 2008)

R Whish, *Competition Law* (6th edn, 2008)

Articles

B Batchelor, 'Application of the technology transfer block exemption to software licensing agreements' [2004] 10(7) CTLR 166–73

B Bird and A Toutoungi, 'The New EC Technology Transfer Regulation: One Year On [2006]' 28(5) EIPR 292–6

D Curley, 'Value judgments' (2009) 31(10) EIPR 491–496

J Drexl, 'IMS Health and Trinko—Antitrust Placebo for Consumers Instead of Sound Economics in Refusal-to-Deal Cases' (2004) 35(7) IIC 788

I Eagles and L Longdin, 'Microsoft's refusal to disclose software interoperability information and the Court of First Instance' (2008) 30(5) EIPR 205–8

T Eilmansberger, 'How to Distinguish Good from Bad Competition Under Article 82 EC: In Search of Clearer and More Coherent Standards for Anti-competitive Abuses' (2005) CLMR 129

H First, 'Microsoft's tenth anniversary' (2008) 39(4) IIC 381–3

G Ghidini, 'Intellectual Property and Competition Law—The Innovation Nexus (Conde Gallego)' (2008) 39 IIC 879

T Heide, 'Trade marks and competition law after Davidoff' (2003) 25(4) EIPR 163–168

F Houwen and R Neville, 'Risky business: current challenges in the relationship between competition law and copyright' (2009) 8(1) Comp LJ 18–36.

D Howarth and K McMahon, ' "Windows has performed an illegal operation": the Court of First Instance's judgment in the Microsoft v Commission' (2008) 29(2) ECLR 117–134

D Kallay, 'Levi Strauss v Tesco: at a difficult juncture of competition, IP and free trade policies' (2002) 23(4) ECLR 193–9

B Ong, 'Anti-Competitive Refusals to Grant Copyright Licences: Reflections on the IMS Saga' (2004) 26(11) EIPR 505–24

D Ridyard, 'Compulsory Access under EC Competition Law—a new doctrine of convenient facilities and the case for price regulation' (2004) 25(11) ECLR 669–73

C Stothers, 'The End of Exclusivity? Abuse of Intellectual Property Rights in the EU' (2002) 24(2) EIPR 86–93

C Stothers, 'Who needs intellectual property? Competition law and restrictions on parallel trade within the European Economic Area' (2005) 27(12) EIPR 458–66

J Temple Lang, 'Defining Legitimate Competition: Companies' Duties to Supply Competitors and Access to Essential Facilites' (1994) 18 Fordham Int Law Journal 439

P Treacy, 'Intellectual property transactions and block exemptions—the future?' (2005) 11(6) CTLR 191–3

P Treacy and T Heide, 'The New EC Technology Transfer Block Exemption' (2004) 25(9) EIPR 414–20

Part VIII

Exploitation, enforcement, remedies and cross border litigation

Introduction

This Part of the book explains and discusses exploitation, enforcement, remedies and cross border litigation of intellectual property rights. It has two chapters. The first, Chapter 21, considers exploitation of intellectual property rights (IPRs), enforcement and remedies. In looking to this area the purpose is in particular to highlight contemporary exploitation strategies, enforcement and remedies with a particular emphasis on copyright, patents and trade marks. As will be seen from the discussion, new modes of exploitation are challenging the traditional ways in which IPRs were exploited and enforced. For instance, both digitisation and globalisation have respectively resulted in innovative exploitation strategies, and increasing prevalence of counterfeited and pirated works moving across borders. Much activity has taken place within Europe to streamline exploitation strategies and enforcement procedures which, in turn, impact upon domestic law. In addition, the chapter will briefly consider enforcement via the TRIPS Agreement where there are increasing numbers of cases concerning IPRs brought before the Dispute Settlement Body. The second, Chapter 22, considers intellectual property and international private law with a particular focus on infringement actions. As digital works and works protected by IPRs increasingly move across borders, so litigants are faced with problems in selecting the appropriate jurisdiction, determining the law to be applied, and enforcing judgments. The chapter discusses contemporary thinking on cross border infringement.

Sources of the law: key websites

- For judgments of the Court of Justice of the European Union/ECJ see
  http://curia.europa.eu/
- Decisions of the courts in the various jurisdictions of the UK see BAILII
  http://www.bailii.org/

- The UK–IPO website has a section devoted to enforcement

  http://www.ipo.gov.uk/types/copy/c-manage/c-useenforce/c-enforce.htm
- The EC website has a section dealing with counterfeiting and piracy

  http://ec.europa.eu/taxation_customs/customs/customs_controls/counterfeit_piracy/index_en.htm
- and one devoted to enforcement

  http://ec.europa.eu/internal_market/iprenforcement/index_en.htm
- For the Gowers Review Report see

  http://www.hm-treasury.gov.uk/media/583/91/pbr06_gowers_report_755.pdf
- The text of the Brussels Regulation can be found at

  http://europa.eu./legislation_summaries/justice_freedom_security/judicial_cooperative_in_civil_matters/133054_en.htm

  Details about the Hague Conference on Private International Law and the text of the Convention can be found at

  http://www.hcch.net/index_en.php

Exploitation of intellectual property rights, enforcement and remedies

Introduction

Scope and overview of chapter

21.1 Exploitation of IPRs takes place within the context of a general framework of legislative and regulatory initiatives reflecting the policies of any particular country (such as employment and health and safety laws). Beyond that a number of specific rules arise in the sphere of IPRs. These include rules on assignments; general contract rules determining fairness as between parties to a bargain; controls on licensing within specific pieces of IP legislation; measures on compulsory licensing and controls on collective licensing. As well as being aware of the rules within which exploitation takes place, a right holder will want a means of enforcing the right and a remedy should the right be infringed by a third party. The intellectual property system provides for a web of civil, criminal and administrative rules and procedures which can be used in the event of an infringement.

21.2 The first half of this chapter will discuss specific examples of exploitation practices and controls on those practices primarily within the domains of copyright, patents and trade marks, and highlight a number of topical exploitation strategies focusing on the policy and regulatory issues that arise. The second half will discuss enforcement procedures and remedies available to an intellectual property right holder in the event of an infringement of a right highlighting the tensions that arise in crafting remedies appropriate to a transgression.

For an explanation of the application of the rules on free movement of goods and of EU competition law on exploitation practices, see Chapters 19 and 20.

21.3

Learning objectives

By the end of this chapter you should be able to describe and explain:

- the rules on assignment for registered intellectual property rights;
- common exploitation strategies used for copyright, patents and trade marks;
- the regulatory controls on exploitation and their purpose;
- circumstances in which compulsory licences might be granted for the exploitation of intellectual property rights;
- emergent exploitation strategies in the light of expansion of the scope and subject matter of IPRs;
- the matrix of civil and criminal enforcement procedures and remedies available for infringement of IPRs;
- recent developments and proposals on enforcement and remedies emanating from the EU and how these fit into, and may complement, the current framework;
- the measures to be found in TRIPS and their contribution to global intellectual property enforcement.

The rest of the chapter looks like this:

- Assignment (21.4–21.6)
- Licensing (21.7–21.57)
- Contemporary exploitation strategies (21.58–21.74)
- Enforcement and remedies (21.75–21.155)

Assignment

21.4   The owner of an IPR may choose to assign that right to a third party. An assignment (known as assignation in Scotland) is the transfer of ownership of an intellectual property right from one party to another.[1] When an IPR is assigned, the assignee stands in the shoes of the assignor and can deal with the right as they wish.[2]

21.5   Different rules apply for assignment of intellectual property right, requiring care to ensure that an assignation is valid. An assignment of a patent and a CTM must be in writing and signed by or on behalf of all of the parties to the transaction.[3] Where a patent or application for a patent is owned by more than one party all the co-owners must consent to the assignment.[4] Only

---

[1] In *Siemens Schweiz AG v Thorn Security Ltd* [2008] EWCA Civ 1161, [2009] Bus LR D67 the Court of Appeal, in relation to the Patents Act 1977 s 33(3) said 'The term "assignment" is inherently capable of more than one meaning. It may refer to the passing of ownership or, where parties may only transfer property by executing a particular form it can mean that instrument as executed in relation to particular property...there is no reason why the word "assignment" should not receive a wide meaning in section 33(3)' (para 88).

[2] For matters of contract interpretation see *JHP Ltd v BBC Worldwide Ltd & Anor* [2008] EWHC 757 (Ch)

[3] Patents Act 1977, s 30(6) (England), s 31 (Scotland). CTMR, Art 17(3).   [4] ibid, s 36(3).

the assignor need sign an assignment of copyright and a UK trade mark,[5] and a prospective copyright owner can assign future copyright.[6] A trade mark can be assigned without a corresponding assignment of goodwill or business,[7] but the owner of an unregistered mark can only assign that mark along with the goodwill of the business. Where there are co-owners of a CTM, the assignment must be signed by all parties to the transaction.[8] For UK trade marks owned by more than one party, each co-owner can only assign their share, and then only if the others consent to the assignment.[9] Assignment of a trade mark can be partial, that is in respect of some of the goods covered by the trade mark registration, limited geographically, or limited in manner of use,[10] whereas a CTM must be dealt with 'in its entirety and for the whole area of the Community'.[11]

Question

What is the policy that underlies the rule that a CTM be dealt with 'in its entirety and for the whole area of the Community' while dealing with a national UK trade mark may be in respect of some but not all of the right? (See para 13.35.)

Registration

21.6   An assignment of an unregistered right, such as copyright and unregistered design right, does not require to be registered to be effective. Indeed there is no register on which assignment could be placed. By contrast, assignments of registered rights, such as patents and trade marks can, but need not be registered. However, it would appear that it is policy to encourage registration. This is apparent from the rules that lay down the consequences of non-registration.

- *Registered designs:* If no entry has been made on the design register, then any document recording an assignation may not be admitted as evidence of title unless the court otherwise directs.[12] An assignation of a registered community design must be entered in the register to permit the successor in title to invoke the rights arising from the registration of the community design.[13] As with CTMs, community designs are unitary and so can only be assigned for the whole Community.

- *Trade marks:* If a transaction concerning a UK trade mark is not registered, it will be ineffective as against a person acquiring a conflicting interest in or under the mark who does not know of the transaction.[14] An assignee who does not register within six months of the transaction in respect of acts of infringement that occur prior to registration cannot recover costs in the event that the mark is infringed.[15] As regards a CTM, as long as the transfer has not been entered on the CTM register the assignee may not invoke the rights arising from registration of the CTM.[16]

---

[5] CDPA 1988, s 90(3), TMA 1994, s 24(3). See also Registered Designs Act 1949, s 15B.   [6] CDPA 1988, s 91(1).
[7] TMA 1994, s 24(1); CTMR, Art 17.   [8] CTMR, Art 17(3).   [9] TMA 1994, s 23(4).
[10] TMA 1994, s 24(2).   [11] CTMR, Art 16(1).   [12] Registered Designs Act 1949, s 19(5).
[13] Community Design Regulations, Art 28(b).   [14] TMA 1994, s 25(3).   [15] ibid, s 25(4).
[16] Art 17(6).

- *Patents:* Registration gives the registrant priority against anyone who has an earlier unregistered right so long as the registrant had no notice of the earlier right;[17] (as with trade marks) cost or expenses are withheld from assignees who do not register within six months of the transaction in respect of acts of infringement that occur prior to registration.[18]

Question

Why do you think there are different rules on execution of assignations and consequences of non-registration for the various registered IPRs? Do you think this area of the law should be rationalised?

Key point on assignment

- Different rules exist for the assignation of the various IPRs rights and registration (where applicable) of those assignations. Care must be taken to ensure the correct rules are followed

Licensing

General

21.7   Licensing is a central feature of the exploitation of intellectual property. An IP owner may not have the resources or the expertise to exploit a work protected by intellectual property. For instance, the inventor of a new type of ceramic kettle may need to enter into a licensing agreement with a manufacturer to develop the product and bring it to the market. A music band may need the help of a record label to produce and market a song. Literary authors may need the assistance of a collecting society to enable them to monitor use of a work and to receive a return from exploitation. If the owner of the intellectual property right does not assign the work, then he will need to enter into a licence to permit such exploitation and management of the right.

Licences can be exclusive, non-exclusive or sole. An exclusive licence means that the owner licences a third party to carry out some or all of the restricted acts to the exclusion of all others including the owner. A non-exclusive licence permits the owner to licence as many other people as he wishes to carry out the same act. A sole licence permits the owner of the IPR to exploit the right as well as the person to whom he has licensed the work.[19]

---

[17] Patents Act 1977, s 33.   [18] ibid, s 68.

[19] For a complex case on the construction of a trade mark licence see *Leofelis SA and Leeside srl v Lonsdale Sports Ltd, Trade Mark Licensing Co Ltd and Sports World International Ltd* [2008] EWCA Civ 640.

Exercise

Imagine scenarios where these different types of licence might be used and consider why it might be appropriate to use one type of licence rather than another in any given set of circumstances. Consider the interests that require to be met when making a choice.

21.8 Licences for some intellectual property rights, notably copyright, tend to cover some, but not all of the rights pertaining to a particular work. For example, the author of a book might licence the right to one publisher to publish the book in hardback, but another publisher may be granted the serial rights. One director might be given permission to turn a work into a play, another to turn the work into a film.[20] Patents tend to be exploited in a more unitary fashion, the right to exploit the bundle of rights protected by a patent being given to one or more parties.[21] Under the Trade Marks Act 1994, a trade mark licence may be limited to one or more class of goods or services and limited in respect of territory. However there is an important caveat in that if a trade mark becomes liable to deceive through such licensing practices, so it may be revoked.[22]

Assignment or licence?

21.9 Sometimes a question can arise as to whether a document is an assignment or a licence. In a case involving rights to the song 'A Whiter Shade of Pale', the House of Lords stated that in order for there to be an implied assignment: '(a) it would have been obvious to the [assignor] (as well as [the record company]) that his interests in the musical copyright was being, or had to be, assigned to [the record company], or, which may amount to the same thing, (b) the commercial relationship between the parties could not sensibly have functioned without such an agreement'.[23] The House of Lords ruled that there was no implied assignment and that the recording contract merely granted the record company the right to exploit the original recording.[24]

21.10 If a reverter clause is present in an agreement, a question may arise as to whether the agreement is a licence or an assignation. In *JHP Ltd v BBC Worldwide Ltd*[25] the court reviewed the authorities. In *Chaplin v Frewin*[26] an agreement in a publishers' contract whereby the publishers should, during the legal term of the copyright, have the exclusive right of producing, publishing and selling a work in volume form in any language throughout the world was held to be an assignment of copyright. In *Messager v BBC*[27] the grant by composers and authors of an opera to the proprietor of the theatre for the sole and exclusive right of representing a play, in which it was provided that the copyright in the music of the play should remain the property of the composer and in certain events the right of representation should 'revert to and become again the absolute property of [the composer and the authors]'. The court in that case said that there had been use of 'inept language in which to describe the mere cessation of a licence and...much more apt to describe the reversion to the licensors of rights which had been assigned'. The court in *JHP* came to the conclusion that 'the concept of reverter (rather than of termination or cessation) is strongly suggestive of the assignment or a transfer of a property right that does not depend for its existence on the very agreement which contains the reverter provision itself. But...there is no general principle that a reverter clause automatically indicates an assignment.'

---

[20] Note that both the rules on free movement of goods and competition law will prevent the licensing of rights that have the effect of partitioning the market. For more information see Chapters 19 and 20.
[21] See below in the discussion on Genetic Inventions, Intellectual Property Rights and Licensing Practices: OECD, para 21.40.   [22] Discussed in para 14.105.
[23] *Fisher v Brooker and another* [2009] UKHL 41, [2009] 1 WLR 1764, para 50.   [24] ibid, para 78 and 79.
[25] [2008] EWHC 757 (Ch).   [26] [1966] Ch 71.   [27] [1929] AC 151.

Copyright

Copyright contract practices UK: the music company and the musician

21.11   Perhaps the most well-known examples of controls on copyright licences as between the author and exploiter arise in the entertainment field, most particularly in the music sector. Recording companies have long argued that their business model is predicated on the success of a minority of musicians. The financial return that the companies receive from this minority enables them in turn to engage other musicians. To ensure that the record company can profit from the future success of the few, it is in the interests of the record company to enter into a relationship with a musician for as long as possible. Equally, the record company will not want to be bound to the unsuccessful musician, and in particular it does not want to be under any obligation to publish and distribute music that may not have found favour in the market. This has caused some problems where record companies have signed musicians in the early stages of their career, and where the musicians have not had the benefit of independent advice in relation to the contract into which they entered. General principles of contract law have, in some circumstances, been called upon to give relief to the musician.

Restraint of trade

21.12   In *Schroeder Music Publishing v Macaulay*,[28] Macaulay entered into a standard form agreement with Schroeder Music Publishing in which he agreed to assign the copyright in his works to the publisher for five years and, if the royalties exceeded £5,000, for a further five-year period. However, Schroeder was not required to exploit the works. The House of Lords held this agreement was invalid as it was in restraint of trade. Lord Reid was particularly concerned as to the one-sided nature of the contract which assigned the copyright in the work to the publisher, but which did not require the publisher to exploit that work:

> '...it appears to me to be an unreasonable restraint to tie the composer for this period of years so that his work will be sterilised and he can earn nothing from his abilities as a composer if the publisher chooses not to publish. If there had been...any provision entitling the composer to terminate the agreement in such an event the case might have had a very different appearance. But as the agreement stands not only is the composer tied but he cannot recover the copyright of work which the publisher refuses to publish'.[29]

21.13   The doctrine is however not without its limits. Georgios Panayiotou (aka George Michael) challenged his contract with Sony Music Entertainment[30] from which he wanted to resile on the grounds that it was in restraint of trade. The history between the parties was complex, and a number of changes to their contractual relationship had occurred during the 1980s, the last of which was in 1988. The High Court refused to set aside the agreement largely because it was considered that to do so would be contrary to public policy.

 Question

If you were the publishing company, how might you draft a clause that would meet the concerns of Lord Reid?

---

28   [1974] 1 WLR 1308, [1974] 3 All ER 616. See also *Elton John v James* (1983) [1991] FSR 397.
29   [1974] 1 WLR 1308 at 1315.   30   *Panayiotou and Others v Sony Music Entertainment* [1994] EMLR 229.

Undue influence

21.14 In *O'Sullivan and Another v Management Agency*[31] Gilbert O'Sullivan had entered into various contracts with a management agency and publishing company without receiving any independent advice. The Court of Appeal held that the onus was on those asserting that the agreements were valid to show that they had been entered into with full information as to the nature of the transaction—which was not so in this case.[32]

 Question

Despite these examples, there have been few other cases in which the contractual arrangement between a musician and a record company has been challenged in court. Why do you think this is the case? When considering this question you might like to browse the Musicians' Union website at http://www.musiciansunion.org.uk/ What activities does the Musicians' Union undertake on behalf of its members?

21.15 It is not only in the music industry that difficulties may be encountered due to the inequality of bargaining power as between the author and the exploiter. To assist a number of different societies representing the interests of the author have developed style agreements that an author can use in negotiations. For instance the Writers' Guild has negotiated a raft of agreements applicable as between their members and organisations such as the BBC, ITV and the Producers Alliance for Cinema and Television (PACT); Equity does the same for performers with respect to the exploitation of performances in, for example, cinema and on television.

Weblinks

A number of the Writers' Guild agreements can be found at
http://www.writersguild.org.uk/public/index.html
and the Equity agreements at
http://www.equity.org.uk/

Copyright, performers and equitable remuneration

21.16 In some jurisdictions measures can be found within copyright and related rights legislation which are protective of the author. For example, in Germany the Copyright Act provides that an author is entitled to reasonable remuneration for the exploitation of a work, to be judged by the standard of the prevailing levels in the industry.[33] In UK law by contrast there are few statutory controls on contracts negotiated between individual authors and exploiters in the field of copyright and related rights. An exception is in relation to the rental right in a film or sound recording belonging to the author or performer. When the right is voluntarily or is presumed to be transferred to a producer,[34] the author or performer has a right to equitable remuneration.[35]

---

[31] [1985] QB 428.
[32] The doctrines of restraint of trade and undue influence may be subject to acquiescence: *Zang Tumb Tuum Records Ltd v Johnson* [1993] EMLR 61.   [33] German Copyright Act, Arts 32 and 36.
[34] CDPA 1988, s 93A; CDPA 1988, s 191(G)(1).
[35] A performer also has a right to equitable remuneration where a commercially published sound recording is played in public or otherwise communicated to the public (CDPA 1988, s 182D).

This right cannot be transferred or waived although it can be assigned to a collecting society or may transfer by testamentary disposition or operation of law. The level of remuneration is to be determined by agreement or, failing agreement, by the copyright tribunal. Thus the author or performer has an unwaivable right to benefit from successful exploitation of the work, albeit in these relatively narrow areas. (See also para 6.39.)

 Exercise

Do you think that a right to equitable remuneration should be extended in the area of copyright? For instance, if a literary work becomes a best seller, should the author, who might have assigned or licensed exclusive rights to the publisher, be entitled to benefit from the financial success of the work? Would a system such as that to be found in Germany where the copyright law provides that an author may benefit from financial success of a work be appropriate for the UK? (for information see WR Cornish, 'The Author as Risk-Sharer' (2003) 26(1) Columbia Journal of Law and the Arts 1). Note also the European Directive on the resale right for the benefit of the author of an original work of art.[36]

Copyright and compulsory licences

21.17   International obligations under the Berne and Rome Conventions mean that compulsory licences will be granted in respect of the exploitation of copyright in only limited circumstances under UK law. The Berne Convention allows for the grant of compulsory licences for jukeboxes, and mechanical licences for musical works, both subject to conditions. However, the UK does not take advantage of either of these relaxations.[37] Under the Rome Convention compulsory licences may only be granted as regards broadcasting or communication to the public of phonograms.[38]

21.18   A topical challenge to the narrow scope of compulsory licences in copyright law is currently being considered in the context of 'orphan works'. If an author wishes to use a substantial part of an existing protected work in a new work, then permission must be obtained from the owner of the copyright. However tracing copyright owners can be a complex, costly and time consuming activity particularly where a work may be out of print, the copyright may have devolved amongst countless heirs or the work may simply have been forgotten about. Where an owner cannot be located after reasonable enquiry, some term the work an 'orphan work'. Orphan works have been the subject of an enquiry by the US Copyright Office. During the course of the investigation much evidence was submitted on behalf of copyright owners arguing that the introduction of a scheme which would permit the use of protected works without permission even where the author could not reasonably be traced would amount to the imposition of a compulsory licence and thus contrary to international obligations. The Copyright Office sought to avoid this outcome by suggesting a limitation on remedies: where a work is used after a reasonable enquiry during which the owner could not be traced damages for commercial

---

[36] Directive 2001/84/EC of the European Parliament and of the Council of 27 September 2001 on the resale right for the benefit of the author of an original work of art.
[37] The jukebox licence: Berne Convention, Art 11*bis* (2), and the mechanical licence: Berne Convention, Art 13.
[38] Rome Convention, Art 12.

use would be limited to reasonable compensation for the use. It is perhaps open to argument whether such a scheme does, in essence, amount to a compulsory licence.[39]

Weblinks

Have a look at the US website discussing this issue at
http://www.copyright.gov/orphan/
Look in particular at the comments submitted by Paul Goldstein and Jane Ginsburg at
http://www.copyright.gov/orphan/comments/OW0519-Goldstein-Ginsburg.pdf

What do they say about orphan works and compulsory licences?

In the EU, the i2010 EU High Level Expert Group (Copyright Subgroup) in their 'Final Report on Digital Preservation, Orphan Works and Out-of-Print Work'[40] recommended that a key aspect to deal with across member states would be mutual understanding of levels of due diligence required when searching for rightholders. Thereafter there are suggestions for collating information and linking databases across member states. In the UK, in the Digital Britain Report,[41] the UK Government states that it intends to put into place mechanisms necessary for the use of orphan works for those who follow a process including obtaining permission from the Government, making reasonable searches and provision for reimbursement for owners who may subsequently come forwards and claim payment. A further consultation paper is currently open through which the parameters of the orphan works provisions will be shaped.[42]

Collective licensing

21.19   Exploiting works protected by copyright can cause practical problems for both the copyright owner and the prospective licensee. A copyright owner can find it difficult to keep track of third parties who wish to exploit those works in one form or another. Similarly, a licensee may wish to incorporate a large number of works protected by copyright into their repertoire, but have difficulty in tracing the copyright owners to obtain permission. For example, educational establishments and businesses often make copies of published literary works which do not fall under the fair dealing provisions in the copyright legislation;[43] broadcasters frequently use musical works which are protected by copyright. In order to facilitate the management of these rights, collecting societies were introduced.[44] Authors of works protected by copyright are able to assign or licence their rights to the collecting societies (or the collecting society will act as agent on their behalf) who then manage the rights on behalf of their members. Thus, the

---

[39] The progress of this initiative has, at the time of writing, stalled as the attention of the legislators has focussed on managing the economic crisis.   [40] 3 June 2008.

[41] Digital Britain Final Report June 2009. ISBN: 9780101765022. This followed on from the recommendation in the Gowers Review of Intellectual Property that a proposal should be put to the European Commission to introduce a provision on orphan works in the form of a Directive.   [42] paras 39–47.

[43] See Chapter 5.

[44] Note the reference made to the Court of Justice in Case C-393/09 *Bezpecnostni Softwarova Asociace v Svaz Softwarove Ochrany* asking whether an application for authorisation for the collective administration of copyright in computer programs can include rights to use computer programs as works by means of cable transmission and by television broadcasts.

authors are saved from having to spend a lot of time on administration, and those who wish to exploit the works have one place from which they can seek permission to use them.

21.20   Examples of collecting societies currently operating in the UK include the Copyright Licensing Agency (CLA), the PRS for Music (formerly the Performing Right Society (PRS) and the Mechanical Copyright Protection Society (MCPS)). Different societies operate in different ways. PRS for Music, which represents composers, authors and publishers of music, has copyright assigned to it and administers licences and enforces copyright as the owner of the copyright. Royalties are distributed to the members in proportion to the use made of a particular work. In contrast, the MCPS is authorised by the composer, author or publisher of a work to licence the recording of the work on his behalf—there is no assignment of the copyright.

21.21   In 2008 a consultation was carried out on proposed changes to exemptions from public performance rights in sound recordings and performers' rights managed by the PPL (originally called Phonographic Performance Limited).[45] The consultation considered two exemptions in the CDPA 1988 which apply to rights managed by the PPL:

- where charitable bodies play CDs or other recorded music if certain conditions are met; and

- where not-for-profit bodies play radios or TVs if the broadcasts include recorded music and the audience has not been charged entry.

After consultation, the Government has stated that it intends to introduce measures to repeal the exemptions, giving right holders exclusive rights over the public playing of sound recordings in all the circumstances which are currently exempt and said that the Secretary of State should no longer be able to refer PPL licences or licensing schemes to the Copyright Tribunal (CDPA 1988, section 128A). Given the more organisations will now require to obtain a licence, PPL has said that it will not charge for certain uses of music including domestic/family occasions such as weddings, music as part of divine worship and music played in residential homes and hospices.

Weblinks

Have a look at the websites of the CLA http://www.cla.co.uk/ PRS and MCPS http://www.prsformusic.com Can you envisage any regulatory problems that might arise in their management and administration? Can you find any similar organisations in other jurisdictions?

Oversight of activities of collecting societies: the UK

21.22   Because collecting societies occupy a powerful role, both in relation to the authors of the works, and in relation to users, some oversight of their activities has been found to be essential. If a collecting society manages a number of copyright works on behalf of their copyright owners, the collecting society may refuse to license the work to a particular individual or group, or it might seek to extract unreasonable royalties. These dangers were recognised after the first collecting society, the Performing Right Society which came into being in 1914, had been in operation for

---

[45] See http://www.ppluk.com

a number of years. As a result, a regulatory framework for the oversight of collecting societies has been developed.

21.23 The Competition Commission has oversight of the activities of a society in relation to matters that might operate against the public interest.[46] If the Commission finds that there are certain matters which operate against the public interest, including, for example, conditions in licences which restrict the use of a work by the licensee,[47] or a refusal of the copyright owner to grant licences on reasonable terms,[48] there are powers to cancel or modify the conditions and to provide licences in respect of the copyright to be made available as of right.[49] One example of a reference to the Monopolies and Mergers Commission (MMC) (the predecessor of the Competition Commission) concerned the PRS (discussed above).[50] The MMC found that a number of the rules which the Society had in place operated against the interests of its members. The PRS was required to alter its rules in accordance with the recommendations in the report.

21.24 The Copyright Tribunal exists to monitor the activities of collecting societies.[51] Thus, for instance, those parties who wish to take a licence from the collecting society but who feel that the terms are unfair, or where the society might have refused to grant them a licence, may take a complaint and have it heard by the Tribunal.[52]

■ *CT 71/00, CT 72/00, CT 73/00, CT 74/00 and CT 75/01 Universities UK (formerly the Committee of Vice Chancellors and Principals) v The Copyright Licensing Agency (Intervenors: Design and Artists Copyright Society) [2002] RPC 36*

In this case, universities within the UK asked the Copyright Tribunal to rule on the terms of the Higher Education Copying Accord promulgated by the CLA and which allows, inter alia, students within higher education institutions to make copies up to a certain amount of published works during the currency of their educational courses. Negotiations had broken down on matters concerning both the scope of and the fee for the licence. The Copyright Tribunal made an order referring to both of these matters: the course pack provision (which had required separate negotiation each time a 'course pack' was provided to a class of students) so disliked in education was to be abolished, artistic works were to be included in the licence, and the fee was to be set at £4.00 per full time enrolled student.

Exercise

Have a look at the final decision of the Copyright Tribunal. What do you think of the outcome of the hearing? What price do you think should be paid to authors and publishers for photocopying materials for educational purposes? What difference (if any) do you think digitisation might make to the debate?

---

[46] CDPA 1988, s 144. [47] ibid, s 144(1)(a). [48] ibid, s 144(1)(b).

[49] ibid, s 144 specifies what powers are available under Part I of Schedule 8 to the Fair Trading Act 1973 in the event of an adverse finding by the Competition Commission.

[50] A report on the supply in the UK of the services of administering performing rights and film synchronisation rights. Cmnd 3147 (1995).

[51] See CDPA 1988, ss 118–122. See also the discussion in para 7.17. *In Respect of the Appeal of Phonographic Performance Limited v The Appeal of The British Hospitality Association and Other Interested Parties* [2008] EWHC 2715 (Ch), 2008 WL 4975450.

[52] eg Copyright Tribunal Interim Decision CT84-90/05 confirming that songwriters, composers and publishers should receive 8 per cent of gross revenues from online music service providers for on-demand services including downloads and subscription streaming services, 6.5 per cent of revenues for interactive webcasting services and 5.75 per cent for non-interactive webcasting.

Oversight of collecting societies' activities: the EU

21.25   Collecting societies are to be found in most jurisdictions and whereas, to date, they have tended to be largely concerned with activities within a particular territory,[53] they have operated between territories by means of reciprocal agreements. EU competition law has been applied to collecting societies by both the ECJ and by the Commission. Three broad issues have been addressed: the relationship between collecting societies and users;[54] the relationship between collecting societies and their members (right holders);[55] and the reciprocal relationship between different collecting societies.[56]

21.26   On the relationship between collecting societies and users the ECJ has ruled that as a dominant undertaking, a collecting society cannot refuse—under Article 82 EC (now Art 102 TFEU) Treaty—to license a user in its own territory without a legitimate reason (for a discussion on Article 102 TFEU and a refusal to supply see para 20.50ff). Neither may collecting societies engage in collective action, the effect of which is to refuse to license the use of their repertoires to users in other territories arguing that it would be impractical to set up a monitoring system in another territory.[57] The ECJ has also been vexed as to the differences in administrative costs of running a society and the level of royalties remitted to right holders as between societies located in different member states. It has been suggested that it may be the lack of competition in the market that leads to this result.[58]

21.27   On the relationship between collecting societies and right holders, both the Commission and the ECJ have had the opportunity to consider different aspects of the relationship. The Commission has said that a collecting society in a dominant position is not permitted to exclude members from other member states;[59] and that a requirement that an author assign all rights to a society, including online exploitation rights, amounts to an abuse of a dominant position in that it is the imposition of an unfair trading condition.[60] The ECJ has held[61] that mere application of a remuneration model on commercial broadcasters that is tied to the revenues of those television stations is not an abuse of a dominant position provided that the royalties are 'proportionate overall to the quality of musical works protected by copyright actually broadcast or likely to be broadcast . . .'.[62] On the claim that it was an abuse of position to apply a different royalty calculation for commercial television stations and the public service broadcaster, STV, the ECJ ruled that the imposition of different manner of computing the royalties could possibly be an abuse of a dominant position 'if it applies with respect to those companies dissimilar conditions to equivalent services and if it places them as a result at a competitive disadvantage, unless such a practice may be objectively justified'.[63]

---

[53] In Case C-425/07P *AEPI Elliniki Etaireia pros Prostasian tis Pneumatikis Idioktisias AE v Commission of the European Communities* [2009] 5 CMLR 2 the ECJ upheld a Commission Decision rejecting the complaint made by AEPI that Greece and the three main Greek collective management bodies (Erato, Apollon and Grammo) were in breach of Articles 81 and 82 EC. In refusing the complaint, the Commission stated that 'the alleged infringement is unlikely to seriously impede the proper functioning of the common market, given that all the parties involved are established in Greece and pursue their activities in that country alone. It is not foreseeable that that situation will change, that is to say, that the three . . . bodies will start to pursue their activities in other countries in the near future . . . The case does not, therefore, present the level of Community interest necessary for the Commission to open an investigation' (para 11).

[54] Case 395/87 *Ministere Public v Tournier* [1989] ECR 2521.

[55] *Re GEMA No 1* [1971] CMLR D35; Case C-127/73 *BRT v SABAM* [1974] ECR 313.

[56] Case C-395/87 *Ministère Public v Tournier* [1989] ECR 2521; Cases C-110/88 *Lucazeau v SACEM*, 241/88 and 242/88, 13 July 1989, [1989] ECR 2811   [57] Op cit, n 40.

[58] ibid.   [59] *GEMA I*, Decision of 20.06.1971, OJ L134/15; *GVL*, Decision of 29.10.1981, OJ L370/49.

[60] *Banghalter et Homem Christo v Sacem* Case COMP/C2/37.219, Decision of 06.08.2002.

[61] Case C-52/07 *Kanal 5 Ltd v Föreningen Svenska Tonsättares Internationella Musikbyrå (STIM) UPA* [2009] 5 CMLR 18.

[62] Para 41.   [63] Para 48.

21.28   On reciprocal agreements between collecting societies, in 1989 the ECJ concluded that reciprocal representation agreements as such do not fall under Article 81 (now Art 102 TFEU) provided they were not accompanied by concerted action or exclusivity.[64] One area in which reciprocal agreements have been discussed at length is the music industry as attempts are made to streamline the licensing processes which enable cross border exploitation of music over many varied platforms. This is discussed below, para 21.34ff.

21.29   The Commission has been actively considering the wider framework for the collective management of copyright and related rights. In 2004[65] it was suggested that the regulation of collecting societies under general competition rules should be complemented by a legislative framework and that the following areas should be the target of regulation.

The establishment and status of collecting societies

Collecting societies are formed using a number of different business models including both for and not for profit and using both corporate and charitable vehicles. Given that these societies have responsibilities with regard to the economic, cultural and social functions they fulfil the Commission has suggested there should be common rules as regards their establishment and status including in relation to the persons who may establish a society; the status of the society; the economic viability of a society and the representation of right holders within the society.

The relation of collecting societies to users

The Commission would like to see societies under an obligation to publish their tariffs and to grant licences on reasonable terms with redress for the user for instance through the courts or a specially constituted tribunal being available in the event of a dispute.

The relation of collecting societies to right holders

On the relationship between collecting societies and right holders, the Commission would like to see principles of good governance, non-discrimination, transparency and accountability being imposed which would apply to the acquisition of rights, the conditions of membership and to representation within the society.

External control of collecting societies

Finally, and on the external control of collecting societies, practice diverges as among member states. The Commission would like to see harmonisation of the public control of collecting societies.

21.30   While initiatives concerning the regulation of collective licensing in general have been under consideration, the specific challenges posed by the regulation of collective licensing in the music industry have been of particular moment. Over recent years the Commission has investigated and made a number of decisions on music licensing. In 2001 the Commission investigated an agreement concerning simulcasting proposed by the International Federation of the Phonographic Industry (IFPI).[66] The IFPI brokered an agreement between a number of collecting societies from within Europe and beyond, each of which concerned the administration of the neighbouring rights of their record producer members for the purposes of broadcasting and public performance. This included the licensing of rights in sound recording of their members

---

[64] Case C-395/87 *Ministère public v Tournier* [1989] ECR 2521; Cases C-110/88, 241/88 and 242/88 *Lucazeau v SACEM*, 13 July 1989 [1989] ECR 2811.

[65] Communication from the Commission to the Council, the European Parliament and the European Economic and Social Committee, *The Management of Copyright and Related Rights in the Internal Market* COM/2004/0261 final.

[66] Commission Decision of 8 October 2002 relating to a proceeding under Art 81 of the EC Treaty and Art 53 of the EEA Agreement, Case No COMP/C2/38.014 (IFPI simulcasting). OJ C 231/18 – C 231/21 (17 August 2001).

to users, determining tariffs, collecting and distributing royalties and monitoring use.[67] As simulcasting involves the simultaneous transmission by radio and TV stations via the Internet of sound recordings[68] and this crosses boundaries, the scope and the extent of the licences had to be re-thought most notably to provide for the fact that the signals would be transmitted into several territories at the same time. A new multi-repertoire and multi-territorial licence was proposed. IFPI, on behalf of the collecting societies sought an individual exemption under Article 81(3) of the Treaty. After some hesitation and the imposition of requirements that would ensure that competition between the collecting societies would extend to pricing[69] and that there would be sufficient transparency in the relationship between the societies and their users by splitting the copyright and administrative fees,[70] the Commission granted an exemption under Article 81(3) until 31 December 2004. This has now expired.

> ### Weblink
>
> The text of the Commission decision can be found at
> http://ec.europa.eu/comm/competition/antitrust/cases/decisions/38014/en.pdf

21.31   This was followed in 2005 by consideration by the Commission of the terms of 'the Santiago Agreement' also concerning collective exploitation of music. In terms of the agreement each society could grant non-exclusive licences for the communication right from the repertoires of other societies. The society responsible for granting the licence would be the one in the country in which the content provider had its economic seat or which corresponded to the URL of the country of the website where the content provider is incorporated. The Commission believed that this arrangement would lead to an 'effective lock up of national territories'. Although just the one collecting society could grant rights for several different states (that is, a one stop shop for the user) the content provider would have no choice as to which collecting society to use: thus there would be no competition as between the collecting societies. After extensive consultations the Commission issued a notice[71] indicating that as the parties had agreed to undertake, amongst other things and for a period of three years, 'not to be party to any agreement on licensing of public performance rights for online use with other copyright management societies containing an economic residency clause',[72] a condition designed to meet the competition concerns.

> ### Exercise
>
> Do you think the concerns of the Commission in relation to the Santiago Agreement are valid? What sort of conditions might you want to see in an agreement between collecting societies to encourage competition?

---

[67] ibid, para 2.   [68] ibid, para 2.   [69] ibid, para 120.   [70] ibid, para 121.
[71] Notice published pursuant to Art 27(4) of Council Regulation (EC) No 1/2003 in Cases COMP/C2/39152—*BUMA* and COMP/C2/39151—*SABAM* (Santiago Agreement COMP/C2/38126) (2005/C 200/05).   [72] ibid, para 9.

21.32   The most recent decision by the Commission concerning anticompetitive practices of music collecting societies is *Re CISAC Agreement*.[73] Broadly the decision stipulates that the collecting societies may no longer apply a membership clause whereby authors are prevented from choosing
or moving to another collecting society. Neither may the territorial restriction which prevents
a collecting society from offering licences to commercial users outside their domestic territory
be applied. These territorial restrictions tend to include an exclusivity clause which contains
authorisation by one collecting society in favour of another to administer its repertoire on a
given territory on an exclusive basis and thus result in segmentation of the market on a national
basis. As such a commercial user wishing to offer a pan-European media service could not obtain
a licence which covers several member states, but has had, up to now, to negotiate with each individual national collecting society. At the time of writing the decision is under appeal.

21.33   In tandem with these decisions, the Commission made a recommendation in 2005 seeking
to facilitate cross border music licensing.[74] As a result major music publishers withdrew the
mechanical online rights for their Anglo-American repertoire from the traditional system of
collective management and offered them individually on a pan-European, basis thus fundamentally changing the shape of on-line music licensing.[75] This was followed by Commission
Communication of 3 January 2008 on Creative Content Online in the Single Market[76] in which
it was sought to identify and address the most pressing challenges related to the distribution of
on-line creative content. Given the value of the creative industries in general to the European
economies it is likely that the debate over how best to manage cross border licensing within a
competitive environment will continue apace over the coming years.[77]

Weblink

You will find an overview of the developments in on-line music licensing 'Collecting societies
and cultural diversity in the music sector', (study for the European Parliament, DG Internal
Policies, Policy Department B, Brussels June 2009)[78] at
http://www.eliamep.gr/en/wp-content/uploads/2009/12/Collecting_Societies_EN.pdf
You will see that one of the conclusions is that there is no there is no 'truly multi-territorial and
multi-repertoire system in place. Repertoire fragmentation is one of the principal results of EU
action in the field of music rights management.'[79]

---

[73] Case COMP/C2/38.698 [2009] 4 CMLR 12. See also Case T-411/08 *R Artisjus v Commission of the European Communities*
[2009] 4 CMLR 8 where interim measures were sought from the CFI by Artisjus, a Hungarian collective management
association, to suspend the operation of the Commission's Decision on the CISAC Agreement Case on the ground that
'the system of reciprocal representation agreements…might be destroyed completely and the present network of those
agreements disappear if the model envisaged by the Commission were applied' (para 38). The application was dismissed
due to lack of urgency.
[74] Commission Recommendation of 18 October 2005 on collective cross-border management of copyright and related
rights for legitimate online music services (2005/737/EC).
[75] For details see 'Creative Content in a European Digital Single Market: Challenges for the Future', Response from the
Intellectual Property Foresight Forum to the Reflection Document of DG INGSO and DG MARKT of 22 October 2009.
[76] (COM(2007)0836).
[77] For a judgment of the ECJ concerning the enforcement of music copyright on the Internet and the disclosure of personal information about the infringers see Case C-275/06 *Productores de Música de España v Telefónica de España SAU*.
[78] IP/B/CULT/IC/2008_136
[79] Page 10. Note also the earlier comment, 'Music copyright: Study on a community initiative on the cross- border collective management of copyright' at http://ec.europa.eu/internal_market/copyright/management/management_en.
htm. For a discussion on, inter alia, the difficulties encountered in cross border exploitation of music because of the territorial nature of the rights see 'The Recasting of Copyright & Related Rights for the Knowledge Economy' IViR (the

Exercise

Can you devise a system which would result in a multi-territorial and multi-repertoire system of licensing while respecting traditional forms of copyright ownership and exploitation and encouraging competition?

Collective licensing and digitisation

21.34   Beyond the music sector is interesting to speculate as to how the market for collective licensing might develop. One of the advantages of digital rights management is that it facilitates one to one licensing. Hence it makes it easier for the right holder to reach out directly to the user, and to enforce rights (and payments) against the user without necessarily needing to employ the assistance of an intermediary. The dissemination of literary works over the Internet where they are used in educational establishments is a case in point. In traditional hardcopy form a licence has been needed from the CLA to make copies for educational use—and indeed it still is. However, it would now appear that more and more publishers are making their works directly available to the user subject to payment and various terms and conditions. Along the way, those successful digital publishers (such as Sweet & Maxwell (Westlaw) and Butterworths (Lexis) in the legal domain) have acquired the rights to make available portfolios of works from other publishers. In some ways these publishers now become their own collecting societies, except that they are not subject to the controls of the Copyright Tribunal. That is not, however, to say that competition law may not be applied to their activities. On this last point, the Secretary of State for Trade and Industry referred to the Competition Commission for investigation and report under the merger provisions of the Fair Trading Act 1973 the proposed acquisition of Harcourt General, Inc by Reed Elsevier plc.[80] Three aspects of the merger were considered as they may have caused some public interest concerns:

- arrangements for providing customers with access to electronic versions of STM journals;
- arrangements under which other access mechanisms would be able to establish links with RE's and Harcourt's electronic platforms; and
- the pricing of annual subscriptions to STM journals.[81]

While two of the reporting group did find these aspects to be of some worry, they did not consider that they would operate against the public interest. By contrast the third member of the group did consider the merger would operate against the public interest. Although the merger did proceed, interesting observations were made in the report with regard to competition in this market and which may have implications for future dealings in this area.

Exercise

What do you think is the future of collective licensing as regards the dissemination of creative works over the Internet? How do you see this segment of the market developing?

Institute for Information Law at the University of Amsterdam), November 2006 available at http://ec.europa.eu/internal_market/copyright/docs/studies/etd2005imd195recast_report_2006.pdf

[80] Reed Elsevier plc and Harcourt General, Inc. A report on the proposed merger presented to Parliament by the Secretary of State for Trade and Industry July 2001.   [81] ibid, para 1.7.

Individual online licensing schemes

21.35 The opportunities for making creative works available over the Internet, coupled with the uncertain nature of the fair dealing provisions in copyright law have led to a proliferation of licensing schemes applicable for the dissemination and re-use of creative works. These initiatives are interesting in that they operate within the existing copyright framework but are designed to meet the challenges imposed by what many perceive to be the opaque boundaries of the law on re-use of works protected by copyright.

Creative Commons

21.36 Perhaps the best known of these is Creative Commons (CC). The aim of this licensing scheme is to offer a limited range of licenses containing restrictions and permissions that can be used by authors and artists. Started in the US it has now become international with licences offered in over 21 jurisdictions (including nine EU countries) with more in preparation, and several others in prospect. In the UK, licences are available for England and Wales[82] and for Scotland.[83]

Creative Commons offers several licences enabling authors (or other rights holders) to select which rights they wish to reserve and which they wish to offer. All Creative Commons (CC) licences have a baseline set of features which are:

- Licensees are granted the right to copy, distribute, display, digitally perform and make verbatim copies of the work into another format.

- Licensees may incorporate the work into collective works (that is when the work, in its entirety in unmodified form, along with a number of other separate and independent works, is assembled into a collective whole).

- The licences have worldwide application that lasts for the entire duration of copyright and are irrevocable.

- Licensees cannot use technological protection measures to restrict access to the work.

- Copyright notices should not be removed from copies of the work.

- Every copy of the work should maintain a link to the licence.

- The right holder must be attributed.

- The work must not be subjected to any derogatory treatment as defined in the Copyright, Designs and Patents Act 1988 (England and Wales jurisdiction, and planned in Scottish version).

Beyond these baseline features it is possible to choose between several options:

- *Non-commercial:* The work can be copied displayed and distributed by the public but only if these actions are for non-commercial purposes.

- *No derivative works:* The licence grants baseline rights, but it does not allow derivative works to be created from the original.

- *Share-alike:* Derivative works can be created and distributed based on the original, but only if they are published under the same licence.

For a critique of Creative Commons see N Elkin-Koren, 'What Contracts Cannot Do: The Limits of Private Ordering in Facilitating a Creative Commons' (2006) 74 Fordham L Rev 375.

---

[82] http://creativecommons.org/international/uk/   [83] http://creativecommons.org/international/scotland

Other schemes

21.37 Other licensing schemes, some of which have been trialed and some of which have been estab-lished to meet similar ends include AE ShareNet[84] run by a nonprofit company in Australia to streamline the licensing of intellectual property within the education sector; the Creative Archive[85] licence which was used by the BBC to make available programmes from its archive (the pilot ended in 2006); and BC Commons[86] (offered by the BC (British Columbia) Campus organisation in Canada) for post secondary institutions developing online content.

Each of these was conceived of and developed in response to the complexities which arise when licensing digital content on-line. Each aims to make the process of licensing works simple and efficient and, importantly, to set out clearly the parameters on re-use. The number of licences granted in particular under the CC licence scheme is large (a statistics generator on the CC web-site gives some indication of the numbers of works licensed under CC licences) and seems set to grow over the coming years.

Copyright in the Knowledge Economy

21.38 In 2008 the European Commission released a Green Paper on Copyright in the Knowledge Economy which focused on how 'knowledge for research, science and education can best be dis-seminated in the online environment'.[87] After consultation the final report was released in October 2009[88] in which it was stated that copyright policy must be geared towards meeting the needs of the Internet-based knowledge economy whilst at the same time respecting intellectual property rights. Four specific areas were highlighted as in need of further action. First, on libraries and archives, it was acknowledged that there was pressing need to streamline permissions processes; second, on orphan rights the need to establish agreed standards of due diligence was reiterated; third, on teaching and learning the desire to move towards open access for the results of publicly funded research was restated as was the need to streamline licensing process and facilitate a space for distance learning; and finally the needs of disabled people were highlighted alongside the rec-ognition that their special needs should be more fully met within the copyright framework. The Commission will be working to take these areas forwards over the coming years.

 Exercise

Read the Report from the Commission on Copyright in the Knowledge Economy. How does what is proposed fit with other initiatives at European and domestic levels? Do you consider these as being the most pressing areas for copyright policy reform in the areas of research, science and education?

Key points on copyright licensing

- The doctrines of restraint of trade and undue influence can sometimes control copyright licensing practices

---

[84] http://www.aesharenet.com.au/   [85] http://creativearchive.bbc.co.uk/
[86] http://solr.bccampus.ca/cms2/   [87] COM (2008) 466 final, 16 July 2008.
[88] COM (2009) 532 final. Communication from the Commission 'Copyright in the Knowledge Economy'.

- Equitable remuneration is available for authors or performers who transfer the rental right in a sound recording or film
- Compulsory licenses may be granted in respect of copyright in only very limited circumstances laid down in the Berne and Rome Conventions
- Collective licensing is a notable feature in copyright exploitation
- Collecting societies are subject to regulatory oversight by the competition commission, the copyright tribunal and competition law
- The EU is currently considering the regulation of collecting societies
- Several licensing schemes have emerged in recent years to facilitate the licensing of digital works protected by copyright, the most well-known of which is Creative Commons

Patents

Exploitation

21.39   In contrast with works protected by copyright, patents tend to be exploited in a unitary fashion where the licensee is given the right to exploit the bundle of rights that make up the patent. As this mode of exploitation makes the relationship between the patent owner and the licensee easier to manage, collecting societies do not exist in this area. Rather the terms of the bargain will be the subject of negotiation between the parties. However it has long been realised that the terms of a licence may have anti-competitive impacts, and so competition law regulates certain clauses that may be found in exploitation agreements. Chapter 20 contains a discussion of the application of the Technology Transfer Block Exemption Regulation to, inter alia, patent agreements.

Compulsory licences

21.40   In contrast with copyright, patent law does contain provisions for compulsory licences. They are included because it is considered to be in the public interest for an invention protected by a patent to be worked. A patent could be misused if it was not worked or licensed, in particular where there was a demand that was not being met. UK law was amended in 1999 to take account of the measures to be found in TRIPS[89] which contains obligations concerning compulsory licences. The UK Patents Act 1977[90] now contains two different procedures for the grant of compulsory licences. One of these is for WTO proprietors, and the other for non-WTO proprietors. A WTO proprietor is a person who is a national of, or domiciled in a country which is a member of the WTO, or who has a real and effective industrial or commercial establishment in a WTO country.[91] There are fewer occasions on which a compulsory licence will be granted in respect of a WTO proprietor as compared with a non-WTO proprietor.

21.41   For example, those grounds on which a compulsory licence will be granted in respect of a WTO proprietor include circumstances where:

- the demand for a patented product in the UK is not being met on reasonable terms;[92]

[89]   Patents and Trade Marks (WTO) Regulations 1999 (SI 1999/1899).
[90]   Patents Act 1977, s 48.   [91]   ibid, s 48(5)(a) and (b).   [92]   ibid, s 48A(1)(a).

- the owner's failure to license a patent on reasonable terms has a blocking effect on future improvements;[93]

- the failure to license a patent on reasonable terms unfairly prejudices the establishment or development of commercial or industrial activities in the UK;[94]

- as a consequence of terms in the licence the manufacture, use or disposal of materials in the UK not protected by the patent or the development of industrial activities in the UK is unfairly prejudiced.[95]

21.42   A compulsory licence will be granted in respect of a non-WTO proprietor include circumstances where:[96]

- the patented invention is capable of being commercially worked in the UK is not being so worked, or not worked to its fullest extent as is reasonably practicable;[97]

- the patented invention is a product and the demand in the UK is not being met on reasonable terms, or is being met by way of importation from a country that is not a member state of the WTO.[98]

21.43   Few applications are made for compulsory licenses. Most commentators do not see this as indicating that the provisions are not working. Rather the fact that the measures are present in the law may serve as a necessary backdrop against which patent owners licence third parties in circumstances where they might otherwise be tempted to refuse.[99]

 Question

Do you think that this last proposition is correct? Justify your response.

Access to medicines: compulsory licences

21.44   For a discussion on access to medicines and compulsory licences see para 10.48ff.

Genetic inventions, patents and licensing practices

21.45   Remaining with public health, but moving away from compulsory licences, interesting issues have been raised over the ways in which patented genetic inventions are licensed. Concern has been expressed, in both the public and private sectors, as to the impact of granting patents over DNA sequences, and the consequent effect that might have for researchers, firms and clinical users on legal access to genetic inventions. To explore these issues the OECD Working Party on Biotechnology held an expert group meeting 'Genetic Inventions, IPR, and Licensing Practices'[100] in early 2002. The aim of the group was to:

- assess the impact of patents on genetic inventions and on access to the information and technologies covered by DNA patents;

---

[93] ibid, s 48A(1)(b)(i).   [94] ibid, s 48A(1)(b)(ii).   [95] ibid, s 48A(1)(c).   [96] ibid, s 48B.
[97] ibid, s 48B(a).   [98] ibid, s 48B(b).
[99] Note also the Patents and Plant Variety Rights (Compulsory Licensing) Regulations 2002 (SI 2002/247).
[100] OECD, Genetic Inventions, Intellectual Property Rights and Licensing Practices: Evidence and Policies, 2002 available at: http://www.oecd.org/dataoecd/42/21/2491084.pdf

- discuss the challenges patents on genetic inventions pose for scientists, industrialists and medical practitioners.[101]

21.46   The workshop came to a number of interesting conclusions. Not only was it found, perhaps contrary to popular perception, that the patentability of genetic inventions is not fundamentally in question among the users of the system whether from the public or private sectors or from the medical establishment, but also that the evidence available to the group did not suggest a systematic breakdown in the licensing of genetic inventions. Whereas fears were expressed as to the potential for licensing practices to over-fragment patent rights, block exploitation and result in monopoly positions being abused, these appeared not to be borne out in practice.

Some perceived problems did however seem to have substance in practice. This was particularly so where the numbers and breadth of gene patents being issued was considered alongside the rise of patents with reach through claims. Other areas included problems arising over access to diagnostic genetic tests, although the cause of the problems appears not to have been fully explained.

 Question

What is a reach through claim?

21.47   The Report concluded that continued monitoring of patenting and licensing of genetic inventions is necessary, as is the collection and analysis of economic data. The purpose of such research would be to ensure that access does not become a problem in the future. However, as regards the present, it was suggested that more rigorous and data-intensive studies of licensing practices should be carried out prior to embarking on any significant reform of the present system.[102]

21.48   As a follow-up, the OECD drafted a series of 'Principles for the licensing of healthcare genetics'.[103] Noting that research thrives on collaboration and that getting the most out of the genetics revolution will rely increasingly on efficient and effective exchange between those researching and developing new innovations, the guidelines are drafted so as to try and facilitate licensing grounded in economic principles, to eliminate excessive transactions costs, and on a basis which ultimately will serve the interests of society, shareholders and other stakeholders.[104]

No information is available as yet to indicate whether the Principles have been adopted by those involved in licensing healthcare genetics.

Weblink

Look at the OECD Report which can be found at
http://www.oecd.org/dataoecd/42/21/2491084.pdf
Do you agree with the conclusions? What measures do you think might be necessary at international, EU or domestic level to ensure that all interests are taken into account?

---

[101] ibid, p 77.   [102] ibid.
[103] The Principles, 'Licensing genetic information' can be found at http://www.oecd.org/document/26/0,2340,en_264
9_34537_34317658_1_1_1_1,00.html   [104] ibid, para 8.

> ### Key points on patent licensing
>
> • Compulsory licensing provisions exist for patents the extent of which depends on whether the proprietor is a member of the WTO
>
> • Concerns over exploitation of patents in the health care domain have resulted in the promulgation of a series of Principles designed to facilitate licensing

Trade marks

Exploitation

21.49   Trade mark licensing has been said to underpin 'a multi-billion dollar activity that pervades the ways in which goods and services are distributed, marketed and sold, both domestically and internationally'.[105] The proprietor of a trade mark may itself sell goods or services under the mark. Equally it may devise any number of different trading mechanisms that would permit subsidiaries, related companies and third parties to manufacture, distribute and sell goods bearing that mark. A well-known exploitation strategy is by way of franchising where an independent business is permitted to use the trade mark under strict conditions often extending to the 'look and feel' of the business: McDonalds, Dyno-Rod and Kall Kwik are all examples of this model.[106] Another is merchandising, where third parties are licensed to make goods and services available bearing (usually) a well-known mark, such as Coca Cola or Disney. In each of these examples a trade mark licensing agreement would need to be negotiated to permit the lawful use of the mark.

21.50   The Trade Marks Act 1994 does not contain express provisions concerning licensing of a trade mark by the right holder to a third party. In other words, the trade mark owner is, subject to competition law, free to licence the mark in any way she likes. However it is possible under the Trade Mark Act 1994 to revoke a trade mark if its use becomes generic or deceptive.[107] The power of revocation was discussed in para 14.99ff. To avoid such an outcome, the trade mark owner may want to exert control over the use of the trade mark by a licensee. For instance, quality control mechanisms might be included in a licence agreement detailing how the mark is to appear on packaging and providing for the quality of the goods to be sold in association with the mark. If a trade mark owner chooses not to include any provisions regarding the quality of the goods sold under a licence and so has no control over the licensee in this respect (known as a bare[108] licence) the question has arisen as to whether this would be objectionable in that it may deceive potential customers. (For further discussion see para 14.105, *Scandecor Developments AB v Scandecor Marketing AB and Others*.[109])

Compulsory licences

21.51   There are no compulsory licensing provisions in trade mark law.[110]

---

[105] N Wilkof, *Trade Mark Licensing* (1995), 1.

[106] For termination of a franchise and a non-compete clause see *ChipsAway International Ltd v Errol Kerr* [2008] EWHC 1887 (Ch).   [107] TMA 1994, s 46.

[108] A bare licence is one under which the owner of the trade mark has no power to control the quality of the good sold.

[109] [2001] UKHL 21.

[110] For completeness sake it should be noted that compulsory licences are available for both registered designs; Registered Designs Act 1949, s 10; and for plant breeders' rights: CVPR, Art 29.

Trade mark licensing and EU competition law

21.52 The Technology Transfer Block Exemption Regulation (TTBER),[111] discussed in Chapter 20 on competition law may be relevant to licence agreements which include elements dealing with licensing of trade marks, but only where the trade mark licence is not the primary object of the agreement. Also of relevance may be the Vertical Agreements Block Exemption.

The Vertical Agreements Block Exemption[112]

21.53 As with the TTBER the Vertical Agreements Block Exemption (VABE) exempts agreements falling within its terms from the application of Article 101(1) TFEU (ex Art 81(1) EC).

Article 1 provides:

'Pursuant to Article 81(3) of the Treaty and subject to the provisions of this Regulation, it is hereby declared that Article 81(1) shall not apply to agreements or concerted practices entered into between two or more undertakings each of which operates, for the purposes of the agreement, at a different level of the production or distribution chain, and relating to the conditions under which the parties may purchase, sell or resell certain goods or services ("vertical agreements").'

Thus the relationship between the parties must be at different levels of the production or distribution chain (such as manufacturing and retailing).

21.54 Any provisions which relate to the licensing of IPRs (including trade marks) must comply with the following conditions. They must:

- relate to use by the buyer of intellectual property rights;
- not constitute the primary object of the agreement;
- be directly related to the use, sale or resale of the goods or services by the buyer or its customers; and
- in relation to the contract goods or services, not contain restrictions that have the same object or effect as vertical restraints which are not exempted under the block exemption.

21.55 The exemption provided for in Article 2 of the VABE will not apply where the market share of the licensor exceeds 30 per cent of the relevant market (or in the case of the licensee where it is an exclusive supply agreement) nor where the agreement contains one or more of the 'hardcore restrictions' found in Article 4. These include restrictions on:

- the ability of the licensee to determine its sale price;
- the territory into which the licensee can sell or customers to whom the licensee can sell;
- active or passive sales by members of a selective distribution system operating at the retail level;
- cross supplies between distributors operating at the same level of trade;
- the resale of components to retailers outwith the distribution chain.

21.56 A number of these are subject to provisos. So, for example, on the matter of determination of sale price, the licensor can impose a maximum sale price or recommend a sale price; and on the matter of restricting active sales, these can be limited where a second licensee has been granted exclusive territory for the same products.

---

[111] Commission Regulation (EC) No 772/2004 of 27 April 2004 on the application of Art 81(3) of the Treaty to categories of technology transfer agreements (TTBER).

[112] Commission Regulation (EC) No 2790/1999 of 22 December 1999 on the application of Art 81(3) of the Treaty to categories of vertical agreements and concerted practices.

21.57   The VABE also contains a number of excluded obligations in Article 5 which will not benefit from the exemption in the VABE if contained in a licensing agreement. That would not however prevent the VABE applying to the remainder of the agreement. These excluded restrictions include any direct or indirect non-compete obligation during the currency of the agreement, the duration of which is indefinite or exceeds five years; any non-compete obligation after the expiry of the agreement; and obligations not to sell competing brands in a selective distribution system.

Because the existing Block Exemption Regulations on vertical restraints ends in May 2010, the European Commission in July 2009 launched a consultation for a review of the competition rules applicable to vertical agreements.[113] This closed in late 2009 and the Commission expects to issue a draft regulation for comment prior to the expiry of the current measure.

> ### Key points on trade mark licensing
>
> - There are no compulsory licensing provisions in trade mark law
> - Both the TTBER and the VABE may apply to licensing practices in the trade mark arena

Contemporary exploitation strategies

21.58   As will have been seen from the discussion above, policy and regulatory responses to exploitation strategies have been developing over the years. Much of the regulatory oversight has been in response to the potential and actual anti-competitive impacts of exploitation in the market place and in response to the real (or perceived) ways in which exploitation could operate against the public interest. Self-regulatory initiatives are also apparent, particularly in relation to exploitation of copyright.

Over recent years there have been other notable developments in the IP sector. This section will examine the debate in relation to access to data, the database right and competition law; and the exploitation of public sector information.[114]

Access to data, the database right and competition law

21.59   The application of competition law to the exercise of the *sui generis* database right is an area in which a number of issues are raised. The database right has been discussed in Chapter 6. Neither the Database Directive nor UK law contain any compulsory licensing provisions as regards the database right. Compulsory licensing provisions were contained in an early draft,[115] but did not enter the final text.

---

[113]   See at http://ec.europa.eu/competition/consultations/2009_vertical_agreements/index.html

[114]   Another interesting area concerns patent pools and trolls. See S Subramanian, 'Patent trolls in thickets: who is fishing under the bridge?' (2008) 30(5) EIPR 182–188.

[115]   Proposal for a Council Directive on the Legal Protection of Databases, COM (92)24 final, Brussels, 13 May 1992, OJ 1992 C156/4, Art 8(1) and (2). The draft text read: '(1) Notwithstanding the right provided for in Article 2(5) to prevent the unauthorized extraction and re-utilization of the contents of a database, if the works or materials contained in a database which is made publicly available cannot be independently created, collected or obtained from any other source, the right to extract and re-utilize, in whole or substantial part, works or materials from that database for commercial purposes, shall be licensed on fair and non-discriminatory terms. (2) The right to extract and re-utilize the contents of a database shall also be licensed on fair and non-discriminatory terms if the database is made publicly available by a pub-

21.60   While the recent case law from the ECJ has suggested that the database right is not as strong as was anticipated by many commentators and does not go so far as to protect information per se, nonetheless the owner of the database right is placed in a strong position vis-à-vis third parties particularly so where the owner is the sole source of the information within the database or where, economically, it may not be viable for the third party to collate that information independently.[116] Merely because the contents of the database do not attract the database right it does not thereby follow that access can be gained to the contents. Tariffs, technological protection measures, and contract may all be common features surrounding access to databases.

Tariffs

21.61   That charges may be made for access to data contained within a database whether or not the database right subsists was acknowledged by the ECJ in *British Horseracing Board v William Hill*.[117]

> 'The fact that a database can be consulted by third parties through someone who has authorisation for re-utilisation from the maker of the database does not … prevent the maker from recovering the costs of his investment. It is legitimate for the maker to charge a fee for the re-utilisation of the whole or a part of his database which reflects, inter alia, the prospect of subsequent consultation and thus guarantees him a sufficient return on his investment'.[118]

Access may come at a high price, particularly for first comers, to reflect the lack of control thereafter. The purpose of the database right is to reward investment, so charging for access to information that has been collated and made available in a useful form would seem a sensible reward. However, it would seem that only the market will determine the price of access, which may mean that for many access may be unaffordable.

Technological protection measures

21.62   As with creative works, technological protection measures are likely to be used to guard access to the content of a database, allowing access only to those who have fulfilled relevant criteria laid down by the maker and use for only those purposes specified by the maker. See para 5.50ff.

Contract

21.63   Contract terms could be imposed on the 'first-taker' of data from a database to prevent the data being passed on to third parties. The maker may also try to impost contractual conditions concerning use and ongoing control of the data whether by that third party or by another with whom the third party might contract: in other words, the maker may use contract to exert control over downstream innovations.

21.64   The inclusion of compulsory licensing provisions within the Database Directive and thus into the laws of member states may have alleviated a number of these concerns—although the debate over control of the re-use of data by contract would no doubt continue. The failure to include the provision now means that it will be left to competition law to regulate the behaviour of makers.

---

lic body which is either established to assemble or disclose information pursuant to legislation, or is under a general duty to do so'.

[116] On the scope of 'extraction' see Case C-304/07 *Directmedia Publishing GmbH v Albert-Ludwigs-Universitat Freiburg* and Case C-545/07 *Apis-Hristovich EOOD v Lakorda AD*.   [117] [2005] EWCA Civ 863 (hereafter *BHB*).

[118] *BHB*, para 57.

Question

Do you think that the absence of compulsory licensing provisions covering the *sui generis* database right will cause problems? If so, what measures would you introduce to deal with them?

21.65   There have been interesting developments in the horse racing field in the aftermath of the decision by the ECJ in the database cases.. The Court of Appeal gave its judgment in *British Horseracing Board v William Hill*[119] in light of the decision by the ECJ. The Court unanimously agreed that the *sui generis* database right did not subsist in the database compiled by the British Horseracing Board (BHB): the information contained in the database was created by BHB and did not exist as independent materials. This ruling, in conjunction with the uncertainty caused by the references to the ECJ, caused several of the organisations to whom BHB supplied data to challenge the terms of their licence agreements with the result that BHB threatened to cease supplying these third parties with data. The major concern appeared to be the price charged by BHB for the use of the data. The basis of the challenges, bolstered by the absence of any form of intellectual property right in the data, was under competition law, both UK and EU.

Victor Chandler (International) Ltd ('VCI') (a bookmaker) took the view that their agreement with BHB for the supply of racing data was unenforceable given the ruling by the ECJ.[120] VCI stopped paying for data as was required under its agreement with BHB claiming the prices charged were excessive and the agreement void. BHB sought damages from VCI for breach of contract making it clear that unless the data was paid for, the agreement to supply the data (via the intermediary company, PA Ltd) would be terminated.

VCI sought an order preventing the cessation of supply of the data, claiming that BHB was abusing its dominant position under Competition Act 1998[121] and Article 82 EC Treaty (now Art 102 TFEU). The application was dismissed by the High Court. Laddie J held that, irrespective of the decision by the ECJ, BHB was entitled to continue to charge for the service for compiling the pre-race data and making it available to VCI. In addition, for an abuse of a dominant position to subsist, it was unfair prices, and not high prices, that constituted the relevant criterion. The instant case showed no basis on which it could be claimed that the prices charged by BHB were unfair.

21.66   A similar challenge, also using competition law, was made in a second case, *Attheraces Ltd v The British Horseracing Board Ltd*.[122] Attheraces challenged the basis on which BHB charged for data; BHB in turn threatened to cease supplying Attheraces. On the contravention of competition law, Atteraces alleged that BHB's threat to cease supply was an abuse of dominance contrary to the UK Competition Act 1998, section 18 and Article 82 EC Treaty (now Art 102 TFEU) and that the fees for the licence were excessive, unfair, unreasonable and discriminatory and in themselves abuses of BHB's dominance. The High Court[123] found the BHB did indeed occupy a dominant position in the market for the market for the supply of UK pre-race data to those in the horse racing industry outside of the UK and Ireland, and that BHB had abused that position by charging excessive and unfair prices which bore no relation to the cost to BHB of its database plus a reasonable return. However the Court of Appeal, while agreeing with the assessment

[119] [2005] EWCA Civ 863.   [120] *BHB Enterprises plc v Victor Chandler (International) Ltd* [2005] EWHC 1074 (Ch).
[121] Competition Act 1998, s 18.   [122] [2007] EWCA Civ 38   [123] [2005] EWHC 3015 (Ch).

of dominance, disagreed that BHB abused its position. On the issue of excessive pricing the Court of Appeal found that the method of ascertaining the economic value of the data—its competitive price based on cost plus—was too narrow in that it did not take sufficient account of the value of the pre-race data to Attheraces and that it tied the costs allowable in cost plus too closely to the costs of producing the pre-race data.

21.67   As *Attheraces v BHB* did not concern excessive pricing of a work or product protected by an intellectual property right (the *sui generis* database right did not exist in the part of the BHB database under discussion), it is a matter for speculation whether the same conclusion would have been reached had the database right subsisted. It is possible that competition law will be used with increasing frequency to challenge price and other licensing terms for the supply of data most particularly where the holder of the data is in the public sector.[124]

 Exercise

Have a look at the database licences available at http://www.opendatacommons.org/ What do these licences seek to do, and do you think they meet their goals?

Exploitation of public sector information

21.68   In June 2002, the Commission presented a proposal for a Directive on the re-use and commercial exploitation of public sector documents (subsequently changed to public sector information).[125] The purpose of this proposal was to form the basis on which information created by the public sector could be used by third parties, the intention being that such re-use of information will contribute to the eEurope Action Plan in particular in the areas of eGovernment and digital content.[126] The Directive was adopted on 17 November 2003[127] and the UK implementing Regulations entered into force on 1 July 2005.

The purpose of the measure is set out in recital 8. It is to provide:

‘A general framework for the conditions governing reuse of public sector documents . . . in order to ensure fair, proportionate and non-discriminatory conditions for the re-use of such information’.

21.69   The Directive does not affect the existence of intellectual property rights in public sector information, nor the way in which public sector bodies can themselves exercise their intellectual property rights. It does however set boundaries on the exercise of those rights vis-à-vis third parties. Further, the Directive does not require public sector bodies to permit the re-use of information, but where such a body does so, it will be subject to the obligations to be found in the Directive.[128]

---

[124]   See, eg, OFT Report: The commercial use of public information (CUPI) December 2006 OFT861; OPSI report on its investigation of a complaint (SO 42/8/4): Intelligent Addressing and Ordnance Survey.

[125]   Proposal for a Directive of the European Parliament and of the Council on the re-use and commercial exploitation of public sector documents COM (2002) 207 final Brussels, 5.6.2002. 2002/0123 (COD). Subsequently changed to ‘public sector information’ COM (2003) 119 final. 2002/0123 (COD).

[126]   eEurope 2002 Action Plan *‘An Information Society for All’* (COM(2000) 330 final).

[127]   Directive 2003/98/EC of the European Parliament and of the Council of 17 November 2003 on the re-use of public sector information (Re-use Directive).   [128]   Re-use Directive, Art 3.

21.70   At first glance the measure seems to be wide in scope. 'Document' is defined in the Directive to mean 'any content whatever its medium (written on paper or stored in electronic form or as a sound, visual or audiovisual recording) and any part of such content.[129] However, the coverage is narrowed both by reference to the type of documents to which the Directive applies, and to the body to whom it applies. Thus, it does not apply to the supply of documents generated by an activity falling outside the scope of the public task of the public sector body, to documents in which third parties hold intellectual property rights, or to documents containing personal data unless the re-use of such data is permitted under Union or national law. Neither does it apply to documents which can be dealt with by public sector broadcasters and their subsidiaries, to those held by educational and research establishments such as universities, research facilities, archives and libraries, nor to those held by cultural establishments such as museums, libraries, archives, orchestras, operas, ballets and theatres.[130]

21.71   Where a public sector body does allow the re-use of documents and a request is made for re-use then it should be supplied through electronic means where possible and appropriate,[131] within 20 days where possible[132], on non-discriminatory conditions,[133] and on a non-exclusive basis.[134] The information can be charged for, but the total income should not exceed the cost of producing, reproducing and disseminating the information, together with a reasonable return on investment.[135]

21.72   It is clear from the wording of the Directive that it does not impose compulsory licensing measures in relation to public sector information. There is no compulsion for public sector bodies to grant licences to third parties, and member states are merely 'invited to stimulate public sector bodies to make the information available for re-use'.[136] A review of the Directive was published in 2009[137] in which the Commission surveyed progress in member states with regard to the implementation of the Directive and attainment of the Directive's objectives. Noting that a number of members states had been tardy in implementing the Directive and it was thus too early to suggest amendments to its terms, improvements could none the less be made in ensuring that exclusive agreements for re-use were terminated; developing licensing and charging models that facilitate the availability and re-use of public sector information, and ensuring equality of use as between the originating organisation and third parties. Each of these is designed to encourage competition.

21.73   In the UK, a body—the Office of Public Sector Information (OPSI)—was established (which replaced Her Majesty's Stationery Office (HMSO)) to manage the re-use of public sector information processes. OPSI, the regulator of public sector information holders for their information trading activities provides a Click-Use system through which licences can be obtained for the re-use of Crown copyright and public sector material[138] and has been developing an information asset register to record details of unpublished documents emanating from Government departments falling under the auspices of the Directive.

---

[129] ibid, Art 2(3).   [130] See generally ibid, Art 1(2).   [131] ibid, Art 4.   [132] ibid, Art 4(2).   [133] ibid, Art 10.
[134] ibid, Art 11.   [135] ibid, Art 6.
[136] Proposal for a Directive of the European Parliament and of the Council on the re-use and commercial exploitation of public sector documents COM(2002) 207 final Brussels, 5.6.2002. 2002/0123 (COD) p 10 referring to the general principle in Art 3.
[137] See Communication from the Commission to the European Parliament, the Council, the European Economic and Social Committee and the Committee of the Regions—Re-use of Public Sector Information: review of Directive 2003/98/EC— [SEC(2009) 597] COM(2009) 212, 7 May 2009.
[138] OPSI is in the course of changing its licensing model to one more closely based on Creative Commons.

21.74   In recent years there have been some significant changes in the way the UK Government holds and manages public sector information. In 2009 a report was produced on public sector information in the UK.[139] Driven by the belief that significant economic gains are to be had through the liberalisation of the public sector information, the thrust of the report is towards increasing commercial use of information by third parties underpinned by transparent, easily understood and non-discriminatory licensing terms.

> ### Weblink
>
> For information on OPSI and the current initiatives taking place see
> http://www.opsi.gov.uk/about/index.htm

 Exercise

Could intellectual property rights be exercised by public sector bodies in a manner inconsistent with the aims of the Directive? If so how, and to what extent?

Enforcement and remedies

21.75   Of importance to a right holder is a means of enforcing a right and a remedy if the right is infringed—each of which should be appropriate to a particular transgression. For instance, an owner of copyright, faced with an enterprise churning out pirated copies of a music CD is most likely to want the production of the unlawful CDs halted, the copies destroyed and the transgressor subject to criminal penalties. The right holder might like to bring a civil action for damages or account of profits, but whether such an enterprise would be in a position to pay might be a moot point. By contrast, the owner of a patent, where the subject of the patent has been unlawfully worked by another, is likely to want to receive damages for the wrong, as well as an order prohibiting such conduct in the future. On the other side of the coin, it is equally as important that the enforcement procedure and remedy should be proportionate to the infringement. If the user of a protected work or invention unintentionally infringes the right, it would seem disproportionate if criminal sanctions were imposed where an order prohibiting the continued infringement and discretionary damages would suffice.[140]

21.76   To deal with the variety of intellectual property infringements that can occur, a raft of enforcement procedures and remedies have been developed and which can be deployed to assist the right holder in appropriate circumstances. These can be found in obligations in international agreements (TRIPS, Part III), at European level (for instance in the measures for combating counterfeiting and piracy as well as the EU Enforcement Directive) and at national level in the

---

[139] For recent developments on the re-use of public information in the UK see The United Kingdom Report on the Re-use of Public Sector Information 2009 at http://www.official-documents.gov.uk/document/cm76/7672/7672.pdf See also R Pollock, D Newbery and L Bently *Models of Public Sector Information Provision via Trading Funds* (2008). Published by BERR (commissioned by HM Treasury and BERR) and the OFT report on the Commercial Use of Public Sector Information available at http://www.oft.gov.uk/shared_oft/reports/consumer_protection/oft861.pdf

[140] Although note that damages are not available for innocent infringement of a number of IPRs. See para 21.108.

measures both within the respective intellectual property statutes, in general rules and procedures pertaining to court actions, and at common law.

21.77   The majority of enforcement procedures are civil. Intellectual property rights are private rights; hence it is for the owner to take action where infringement occurs. Civil cases generally need no knowledge on behalf of the infringer and require that a case be proved on the balance of probabilities. By contrast, criminal cases require knowledge on behalf of the infringer, proof beyond reasonable doubt and may not carry the same remedies as those available in civil disputes. As civil litigation over intellectual property disputes becomes ever more complex, lengthy and expensive, so the use of alternative dispute resolution systems is increasing in importance. Perhaps the best known is that for domain name disputes (see paras 16.23ff). Beyond that there exist a number of specialised intellectual property mediation and arbitration services which may be used in this field.

21.78   In response to the increased incidence of counterfeiting and piracy a raft of criminal procedures have been introduced and developed over the past years. In the areas of copyright, performers' rights and trade marks, civil actions are boosted by criminal sanctions for those cases in which infringement is carried out on a commercial scale, such as the use of trade marks on counterfeit goods, or the production of pirated copies of CDs and DVDs. Recognising that counterfeiting and piracy extend well beyond individual jurisdictions and to combat what some perceive to be organised crime, a number of measures updated over recent years now exist at European level to deal with infringers and infringing goods. These are enforced and supplemented by way of a network of administrative procedures in terms of which enforcement agencies (such as trading standards departments and customs and excise officers) are charged with apprehending intellectual property infringers.

21.79   At international level, and as between states, TRIPS contains enforcement procedures expedited by way of its Dispute Resolution System. This allows one state to take action against another if the TRIPS obligations have either not been implemented, or have been incorrectly implemented into domestic law of contracting states.

Suspected infringements: unjustified threats

21.80   If an IP owner suspects that there has been an infringement of an IPR it can be easy to issue threats alleging infringement. This can be particularly damaging to a small or developing business that may not have the resources to respond or to take advice as to whether there has been an infringement. To give some protection each industrial property right (patents,[141] trade marks,[142] registered designs[143] and unregistered design right[144]) provides a remedy for those who receive groundless threats of infringement proceedings.

Unjustified threats and trade marks

21.81   An example from the domain of registered trade marks illustrates both the procedure and some of the pitfalls that can trap the unwary. If a claimant wants to bring an action for unjustified threats, it must be shown that an actionable threat has been made, that the claimant is

---

[141]   Patents Act 1977, s 70 as amended by Patents Act 2004, s 12.   [142]   TMA 1994, s 21.
[143]   Registered Designs Act 1949, s 26. See also para 21.78 for Community registered and unregistered design right.
[144]   CDPA 1988, s 253.

aggrieved and that the threat was groundless. The relief to which a claimant is entitled (in the absence of a successful action for infringement) includes a declaration that the threats are unjustifiable,[145] an injunction against the continuation of the threats,[146] and damages in respect of any loss sustained by the threats.[147]

21.82　Unjustified threats can be made in a number of ways. Often it is by way of letter and some thought should be given to the contents.

■ *L'Oréal (UK) Limited and Golden Limited v Johnson & Johnson* [2000] ETMR 691, [2000] FSR 686[148]

This case illustrates the type of content to which courts will take exception. L'Oréal launched a range of shampoos for children called 'L'Oréal Kids'. They used the words 'No Tears' on the packaging. Johnson's owned registered trade marks for 'No More Tears' for baby shampoos. Solicitors for L'Oréal wrote to Johnson and Johnson seeking confirmation that no proceedings would be raised in the UK. Johnson replied that while they had not received instructions to commence infringement proceedings, they could offer no comfort as to future litigation. The letter included the following text:

> 'No decision has yet been made on whether to make a claim of trade mark infringement. You should, however, be aware that, at the same time as L'Oreal is commencing use of the mark, others in the UK market who had been using the mark...have now agreed to respect Johnson & Johnson's position and are stopping their use...Our clients do, after all, have six years in which they could commence proceedings...Bearing this in mind, we cannot give L'Oreal comfort at this stage and accordingly we must reserve all of Johnson & Johnson's rights'.

Calling the letter a 'work of a master of Delphic utterances' the court found it to constitute a threat of legal proceedings on the basis that it would be understood as such by the ordinary recipient. According to the judge, the author of the letter was one who 'uses all his skill to say everything and nothing and to convey an enigmatic message which has the same effect on the recipient as a threat...'

 Question

As an advisor to Johnson & Johnson how would you have drafted the letter to L'Oréal in order to avoid liability?

Unjustified threats and patents

21.83　The unjustified threats provisions in patent law were amended in 2004 to deal with some of the perceived shortcomings of the existing legislation. The Patents Act 2004 amended the Patents Act 1977 in a number of ways including those measures dealing with threats of infringement proceedings.[149]

---

[145] TMA 1994, s 21(2)(a).　　[146] ibid, s 21(2)(b).　　[147] ibid, s 21(2)(c).

[148] Design right: *Frayling v Premier Upholstery Ltd and others* (6 November 1998, unreported). Trade Marks: *Prince Plc v Prince Sports Group Ltd* [1998] FSR 21.

[149] Patents Act 2004, s 12 amending Patents Act 1977 s 70(2) brought into force by the Patents Act 2004 (Commencement No 2 and Consequential, etc and Transitional Provisions) Order 2004 (SI 2004/3205).

Old law: A patent owner who thought he had a valid patent and on that basis approached an alleged infringer would be liable for making unjustified threats if the patent on which he relied turned out to be invalid.

New law: Even if the patent turns out to be invalid, the patent owner will not be liable so long as he had no reason to suspect that the patent was invalid when the approach to the alleged infringer was made.

Old law: The patent owner could only discuss primary infringements with the alleged infringer. If secondary infringements were discussed, such as stocking and selling the products, this could lead to a claim for unjustified threats.

New law: The patent holder can discuss both primary and secondary infringing acts.

Old law: The patent owner could only approach the alleged primary infringer (such as the manufacturer) to discuss alleged primary infringements. An approach to an alleged secondary infringer (such as a retailer) could lead to a claim for unjustified threats.

New law: If the patent owner, despite using best endeavours cannot locate the primary infringer, he may approach the alleged secondary infringer without being found liable for making unjustified threats to the retailer.

As can be seen there are subtle shifts in these provisions in favour of the right holder, most notably that the patent owner may now approach the alleged secondary infringer without being liable for making unjustified threats.[150] It remains to be seen whether this will cause problems for retailers. Much may turn on the interpretation of the phrase 'best endeavours'.

Groundless threats and design rights

21.84   Section 253 of the Copyright, Designs and Patents Act 1988 contains measures dealing with groundless threats for unregistered design right, and section 26 of the Registered Designs Act 1949 for registered design right. These have been extended to Community registered and unregistered design rights in the Community Design Regulations 2005[151] (the Regulations). Regulation 2 of the Regulations allows anyone aggrieved by a threat of proceedings for an infringement of a Community design may bring an action for (a) a declaration the threats are unjustifiable; (b) an injunction against the continuance of the threats; and (c) damages. There is an exception for threats relating to primary infringing (making or importing).[152]

21.85   A case on the groundless threats provisions arose in *Quads 4 Kids v Campbell*[153] illustrating the many ways in which unjustified threats may be made. eBay operates a policy whereby IP owners may notify eBay of alleged infringements of intellectual property rights by way of filling in an online form. On receipt of a notice eBay will remove the allegedly infringing items, and then inform the seller. Campbell notified eBay in this way of the sale of quad bikes by Quads 4 Kids which Campbell alleged infringed his community design right. An interim injunction was sought to stop Campbell interfering with Quad 4 Kids business of selling quad bikes on eBay. Campbell took no further proceedings with regard to infringement action against Quad 4 Kids once the goods had been removed from eBay. The court had to decide whether the submission of the online form could be regarded as a threat to bring infringement proceedings.

---

[150] *Zeno Corporation (incorporated under the laws of the state of Texas, USA, & formerly known as Tyrell Inc), Adept Scientific Plc v BSM-Bionic Solutions Management GmbH, Riemser Arzneimittel AG* [2009] EWHC 1829 (Pat), Patents Act 1977, s 50(5)(b): a finding of unjustified threats was upheld. *LB Europe Ltd (t/a DuPont Liquid Packaging Systems) v Smurfit Bag In A Box SA* [2008] EWHC 1231: the appropriate level of damages if a patentee made groundless threats of patent infringement to a competitor's customer.   [151] SI 2005/2339.

[152] Community Design Regulations 2005 (SI 2005/2339), reg 2.5.   [153] [2006] EWHC 2482 (Ch).

The court said that the test to apply was whether a reasonable person, in the position of the person allegedly threatened, would have understood that he might have been subject to infringement proceedings at some point in the future. Filling in of eBay's form did not necessarily mean that infringement proceedings were a possibility. However, the effect in this case was to enable Campbell to stop Quads 4 Kids from selling bikes by completing the form. The proper test was thus whether eBay would have understood that it could be subject to future infringement proceedings if it had not adopted the policy of removing any allegedly infringing items. As the answer to that was affirmative the balance of convenience meant the injunction should be granted.

Other intellectual property rights

21.86   There are no unjustified threats provisions for other intellectual property rights such as copyright, passing off, database right and breach of confidence. It is however possible to apply for a declaration that a threat of legal action of any kind is unjustified.

■ *Point Solutions Ltd v Focus Business Solutions Ltd* [2006] FSR 31

This case concerned an application by Point for a declaration that its computer software did not infringe the copyright in the source code produced by Focus. Focus had not commenced a claim for copyright infringement, but Point alleged that Focus had alleged, both expressly and by implication that Point's software infringed Focus's copyright through correspondence between the parties, and by statements to clients of Point. The court found that while Point had established that Focus had made the assertions, there was insufficient evidence to establish that Point had developed the software independently, no evidence that there was any impact on Point's business and a concern that a grant of declaratory relief would foreclose a future claim for Focus. The declaration was thus refused. The judgment was affirmed on appeal.[154]

 Exercise

Do you think there should be unjustified threats provisions in copyright law? If so, why? If not, why not?

Key points on unjustified threats

- Unjustified threats actions are available for trade marks, patents and registered and unregistered design right
- The test is whether a reasonable person, in the position of the person allegedly threatened, would think that he might be subject to infringement proceedings at some point in the future

---

[154] *Point Solutions Ltd v Focus Business Solutions Ltd* [2007] EWCA Civ 14.

Preparing a case: obtaining evidence: Freezing (Mareva) and Search (Anton Piller) Orders

21.87   If an infringement of an IPR is suspected, then it will be imperative for the owner to gather evidence of that infringement. In common with other areas, in intellectual property cases it would be easy for a defendant to destroy much needed evidence, particularly if in digital form, or to move assets abroad should it be feared that action is pending. To counter this problem the courts in England and Wales have developed two types of orders: a search order, authorising a search of the defendant's premises and to photograph, seize or copy allegedly infringing material; and a freezing order, freezing the assets of the defendant. In Scotland similar procedures exist under the Administration of Justice (Scotland) Act 1972, section 1 (search order) and an arrestment to found jurisdiction under the Civil Jurisdiction and Judgments Act 1982, Schedule 8.

Although these types of orders can be of vital importance to a claimant to allow him to gain the evidence needed to prove a case, or to ensure that the illicit proceeds made from pirated copies of works are not lost prior to trial, they are potent orders, and so checks and balances exist to ensure they are granted only when appropriate and that their terms are not exceeded.

21.88   There are three essential pre-requisites for the grant of a search order:

- There must be a strong prima facie case.

- The damage, potential or actual must be serious for the applicant.

- There must be clear evidence that the defendants have incriminating documents or things in their possession and a real possibility must exist that they may destroy the evidence.[155]

Given that a search order is most often granted in secret and without the defendant appearing or being represented it was apparent that procedural safeguards were needed. Updated in 1994,[156] these safeguards include: the need for the claimant to give a cross undertaking in damages; time for the defendant to consider the order and seek independent legal advice; time for the defendant to seek a discharge of the order; the claimant's solicitor and an independent solicitor to accompany the search team; records to be kept of all material removed from the premises; a date on which to report back to the court to facilitate claims for compensation to be made by the defendant.

21.89   A freezing order may also be granted without the defendant being heard. If granted, the court orders that the assets of the defendant remain within the jurisdiction and that they may not be disposed of. As with a search order, there are safeguards to ensure that the procedure is fair to the defendant.[157] Thus the claimant must show a good arguable case; reason to believe that the assets may be removed; give a cross undertaking in damages; serve notice of the order on the defendant and any third party who may be affected by the order; and undertake to indemnify third parties against costs, expenses and fees incurred in complying with the order.

---

[155] *Anton Piller KG v Manufacturing Process Ltd* [1976] Ch 55 (CA), Omrod LJ.
[156] Practice Direction (Mareva Injunctions and Anton Piller Orders) (1994).
[157] *Z v A* [1982] 1 All ER 556; *CBS v Lambert* [1983] FSR 127.

Exercise

Give examples of those types of infringements of intellectual property you think would justify the grant of a freezing and/or search order.

Self help

21.90 An interesting measure, found in copyright legislation permits copyright owners to seize infringing copies of protected works from market stalls and car boot sales (a similar measure exists in relation to illicit recordings).[158] A copyright owner is not, however, allowed to seize infringing goods from premises where the infringer has a permanent place of business. If an infringing copy of a work is found for sale or hire and it is one that would entitle the copyright owner to apply for an order for delivery up, then he may detain the copies, or authorise others to do so on his behalf. Certain conditions are attached to the procedure.[159] These are that:

- a notice of the time and place of the proposed seizure must be given to a local police station,[160]

- nothing may be seized that is in the possession, custody or control of a person operating from a permanent or regular place of business;

- no force may be used;[161]

- at the time when anything is seized a notice must be left in the prescribed term at the place where the infringing copy is seized.[162]

21.91 In practical terms a copyright owner may not have the courage to seize infringing copies of works from the stalls of market traders. In those circumstances he may feel it necessary to authorise another to do so on his behalf such as trading standards officers or FACT, the Federation Against Copyright Theft.

An activity report[163] prepared by FACT gives an insight into the numbers of infringing copies of works in circulation. It also serves to demonstrate how useful the seizure procedures can be. Thus in 2006, 1546895 seizures of infringing articles (VHS, DVD DVD-R, VCD) were made, which increased to 2823449 seizures in 2007. These numbers may be just the tip of the iceberg but as such do serve to indicate something of the scale of the problem faced by copyright owners concerning pirated goods, and the numbers of these infringing goods that must be in circulation across the country.

Weblinks

Have a look at the FACT website http://www.fact-uk.org.uk Why was this organisation set up and who does it represent? Note also FAST (the Federation against Software Theft) at http://www.fastiis.org/ and the Alliance Against IP Theft http://www.allianceagainstiptheft. co.uk/ Can you find any other similar organisations?

---

[158] CDPA, s 196.   [159] ibid, s 100.   [160] ibid, s 100(2).   [161] ibid, s 100(3).
[162] ibid, s 100(4). Copyright and Rights in Performances (Notice of Seizure) Order 1989 (SI 1989/1006).
[163] http://www.fact-uk.org.uk It seems that FACT have now stopped making their activity reports publicly available.

Survey evidence

21.92 In preparing a case concerning passing off or registered trade marks, survey evidence may be used to show that the public has been deceived by the misrepresentation, that the trade mark has become distinctive through use for registration purposes, or that the public is likely to be confused by the use of a sign that is similar to an already registered mark. Dealing with the question of distinctiveness for trade marks the ECJ in *Windsurfing Chiemsee*[164] said that 'Community law does not prevent the competent authority, where it has particular difficulty in that connection, from having recourse, under the conditions laid down by its own national law, to an opinion poll as guidance for its judgement'.[165]

21.93 However care needs to be taken over preparation of survey evidence. A number of guidelines were laid down in *Imperial Group v Philip Morris*,[166] a case in which passing off was alleged:

- The selection of interviewees must include a relevant cross-section of the public.

- The survey must be of a size to produce a statistically relevant result.

- Full details must be disclosed of the number of surveys carried out, how they were conducted and the number of persons involved.

- The totality of all answers given to all surveys must be disclosed along with the exact answers given to the questions, the instructions given to the interviewers as to how to carry out the survey and any computer coding instructions where the answers are coded for computer input.

- The questions themselves must not be leading nor should they lead the person answering into a field of speculation he would never have embarked upon had the question not been put.

21.94 There have been a number of cases in which survey evidence has failed to establish what it set out to do. For instance in *GMG Radio Holdings v Tokyo Project Limited*[167] the survey evidence did establish that interviewees recognised similarities between the claimant's get up and that of the defendant's products, but not that it was the right kind of association to establish passing off.[168] In *esure Insurance Ltd v Direct Line Insurance plc*[169] the Court of Appeal said that there was much to be said for the practice initiated by the late Pumfrey J[170] where the parties sought the direction of the court as to the scope or methodology of any proposed consumer survey.[171]

[164] Case C-108/97 *Windsurfing Chiemsee Produktions- und Vertriebs GmbH v Boots- und Segelzubehor Walter Huber* [2000] Ch 523 [2000] 2 WLR 205.   [165] ibid, para 53.

[166] [1984] RPC 293.   [167] [2006] FSR 15.

[168] Eg also *Mothercare (UK) Ltd v Penguin Books* [1988] RPC 113 where the evidence did not establish that the term was being used 'in a trade mark sense'; *Quorn Hunt's Application v Opposition of Marlow Foods Ltd* [2005] ETMR 11 TMR where the attempt to use survey evidence to show that the reputation of the registered mark, 'Quorn', would be damaged by the registration of 'Quorn Hunt' might have shown that interviewees made an association between the marks but could not have achieved the desired result—to show that the registered mark would be tarnished.

[169] [2008] EWCA Civ 842.

[170] *O2 Ltd v Hutchison 3G Ltd* [2005] ETMR 61, and subsequently followed by Rimer J in *UK Channel Management Ltd v E! Entertainment Television Inc* [2008] FSR 5.   [171] Para 63.

Exercise

How might you frame a question to be used in a survey which would elicit responses designed to show that the reputation of a mark would be damaged if a second were to be registered?

21.95   The introduction of expert evidence has also caused some difficulties in IP cases. In an application by esure for leave to appeal against a decision of the High Court, Arden LJ commented on the use of experts to determine consumer confusion.

> '...given that the critical issue of confusion of any kind is to be assessed from the viewpoint of the average consumer, it is difficult to see what is gained from the evidence of an expert as to his own opinion where the tribunal is in a position to form its own view...I note that in *The European Ltd v. The Economist Newspaper Ltd* [1998] FSR 283 at 290–291...considered that the evidence of trade witnesses who gave their opinion of the likelihood of confusion was "almost entirely inadmissible...."'[172]

Remedies

Interim injunctions (England and Wales) and interdicts (Scotland)

21.96   In intellectual property disputes it is often of vital importance to the aggrieved party to have a case heard as quickly as possible with the aim to have the allegedly infringing act halted before full trial. Thus, many civil intellectual property actions are applications for interim relief.[173] However, care needs to be taken prior to granting interim orders such as an interim injunction or interim interdict, as, if granted, it can determine the outcome of the case if it does not proceed to full trial. A defendant, prohibited from carrying out a particular act, may choose an alternative business strategy rather than wait for a number of years for a full hearing of the case. For instance if a dispute is over whether a substantial part of a work has been reproduced (copyright) or a sign is confusingly similar to a registered mark, then the defendant may decide to cease dealing in the goods that allegedly infringe the existing rights. Further, the grant of such an order may be enough to close down a business if it there are insufficient resources to defend the action. For these reasons the courts have developed guidelines to be applied in cases where interim relief is sought.[174]

21.97   The leading case on interim injunctions in England and Wales is *American Cyanamid Co v Ethicon Ltd*.[175] The House of Lords enunciated a number of factors to be taken into account when deciding whether an interim injunction should be granted the steps of which are represented in Diagram 21.1.

21.98   In *Series 5 Software v Ltd v Clarke*[176] Laddie J reformulated the principles stressing the importance of assessing the relative strengths of each of the parties' cases. That however did not require

---

[172] Para 62.

[173] On guidelines as to cross undertakings and compensation of loss, *Lilly Icos LLC and Another, Pfizer Enterprises SARL and Others, Merck & Co Inc and Others, AstraZeneca AB and Others v 8PM Chemists Limited, Vinesh Aggarwal, RDA Kollektif Sirketi* [2009] EWHC 1905 (Ch) 2009 WL 2392200; for a discussion on fairness and the grant of interim relief see *Riemann and Co v Linco Care Ltd.* [2007] EWHC 3466 (Ch); for circumstances in which an injunction will not be granted *Landor & Hawa International Ltd v Azure Designs Ltd* [2007] FSR 9.

[174] For a case in which an injunction was conditioned on a cross undertaking see *Wake Forest University Health Sciences v Smith & Newphew Plc* [2009] EWHC 45 (Pat), [2009] FSR 11.   [175] [1975] AC 396.

[176] *Series 5 Software Ltd v Clarke* [1996] 1 All ER 853, [1996], FSR 273.

Diagram 21.1 *American Cyanamid Co v Ethicon Ltd*

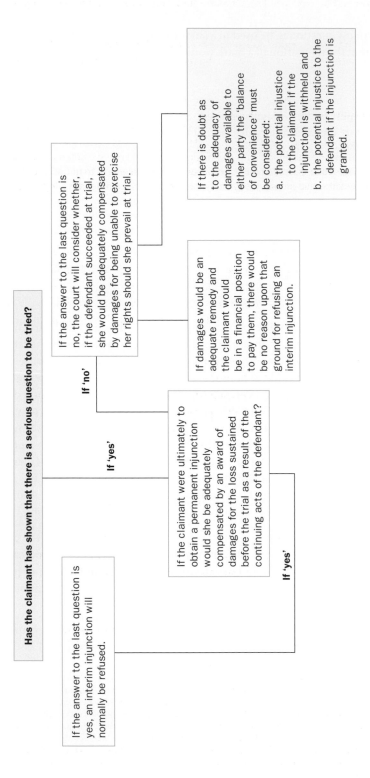

General Comment:

The course to be taken is that which would involve the least risk of ultimate injustice, having regard to the actual and potential rights and liabilities of the parties on both sides.

a mini trial on the facts. The case has been much cited, but is yet to be affirmed by a higher court.[177]

21.99 In Scotland the courts have had regard to the relative strength of the cases put forward by the parties at interlocutory stage as one of the factors that go to make up the balance of convenience for many years.

> 'Whether the likelihood of success should be regarded as one of the elements of the balance of convenience or as a separate matter seems to me an academic question of no real importance, but my inclination is in favour of the former alternative. It seems to make good sense: if the pursuer or petitioner appears very likely to succeed at the end of the day, it will tend to be convenient to grant interim interdict and thus prevent the defender or respondent from infringing his rights, but if the defender or respondent appears very likely to succeed at the end of the day it will tend to be convenient to refuse interim interdict because an interim interdict would probably only delay the exercise of the defender's legal activities'.[178]

Freedom of expression, privacy and interim relief

21.100 Of particular note in applications for interim relief are developments on the interaction between freedom of expression and privacy. Section 12(3) of the Human Rights Act 1998 provides that no relief should be granted that restrains publication prior to trial where such relief might affect the exercise of the right to freedom of expression as enshrined in the European Convention on Human Rights unless the applicant is *likely* to establish that publication should not be allowed.

21.101 There has been much discussion as to the correct interpretation of the word 'likely' in this context. It was suggested in *Imutran Ltd v Uncaged Campaigns Ltd*[179] that it implies a higher test than enunciated in *American Cyanamid*; that there should be a real prospect of success rather than success on a balance of probabilities. Subsequently in *Cream Holdings Ltd v Banerjee*[180] the House of Lords confirmed that approach but left leeway for a court to do away with that higher standard where the circumstances make it necessary. The court emphasised that the Human Rights Act 1998, section 12(3) made the 'likelihood of success' at trial an essential element in considering whether to make an interim order.[181]

21.102 The interaction between section 12(3) of the HRA 1998 and an application to have an interim injunction lifted has been considered by the Court of Appeal in *Douglas v Hello!*[182] For full details of this case see Chapter 18. The High Court initially granted an order restraining the publication by *Hello!* of a number of photographs taken at the wedding of Catherine Zeta Jones and Michael Douglas allegedly in breach of obligations of confidentiality and a 'right of privacy'.

---

[177] Eg *Guardian Media Group Plc v Associated Newspapers Ltd* 2000 WL 331035, para 18; *Gadget Shop Limited v Bug Com Limited* [2001] CP Rep 13 Ch D; *Berry Birch & Noble Financial Planning Limited v Berwick & Others* 2005 WL 1991635.

[178] *NWL Ltd v Woods* [1979] 3 All ER 614, p 628. See also *Boehringer Ingelheim Pharma GmbH & Co KG v Munro Wholesale Medical Supplies Ltd* 2004 SC 468, [2004] ETMR 66.   [179] [2002] FSR 2.

[180] [2004] UKHL 44, [2004] 3 WLR 918, para 20.

[181] *Miss World Limited v Channel 4 Television Corporation* [2007] EWHC 982 (Pat). It was 'likely' for the purposes of HRA 1998, s 12(3) that the claimant would succeed in showing that the proposed broadcast of a programme called 'Mr Miss World' would infringe the registered trade mark 'Miss World' in terms of TMA 1994, ss 10(1) and 10(2). *Response Handling v BBC* [2007] CSOH 102 information on bank account details had been obtained in breach of confidence by an employee of the BBC, the court was not satisfied that the pursuers were more likely than not to succeed at proof to restrain publication of the resultant television programme. See also *Red Dot Technologies Ltd v Apollo Fire Detectors Ltd* [2007] EWHC 1166 (Ch). *Boehringer Ingelheim Limited v VetPlus Limited* [2007] EWCA Civ 583: the general threshold under HRA 1998, s 12(3) that a claimant will probably succeed at trial applies also to trade mark infringement in comparative advertising cases.

[182] [2001] 2 All ER 289, [2001] QB 967.

The order was subsequently lifted by the Court of Appeal who considered that preventing Hello! magazine from publishing the pictures before a full trial could, potentially, lead to incalculable damages, whereas the damage that *OK!* magazine might suffer was capable of calculation.[183]

However, this result was subsequently criticised in the next round of the case when the appeal was heard in the Court of Appeal. Here the court thought there was no public interest (as opposed to public curiosity) grounds that justified lifting the interlocutory injunction.[184] Insufficient consideration had been given by the lower court to the likely level of damages which the Douglases would recover if an interlocutory injunction was refused and publication of the unauthorised photographs infringed their rights.[185]

On the question as to whether the Douglases would be *likely* to succeed at trial, the Court of Appeal took particular note of the reasoning in *Campbell v MGN*[186] in the House of Lords, and *von Hannover v Germany*[187] in the European Court of Human Rights, both of which were handed down after the interlocutory injunction in *Douglas v Hello!* had been lifted. The appeal court considered that the 'likelihood of success' threshold had been satisfied by the Douglases who appeared to have 'a virtually unanswerable case for contending that publication of the unauthorised photographs would infringe their privacy'.[188] Only by granting an interlocutory injunction could the Douglases rights have been protected. By contrast the financial interests of *Hello!* could have been satisfied by an undertaking by the Douglases to pay damages should they not be successful at trial.[189]

21.103   The courts are clearly alive to the tensions that arise at the stage of requesting interim relief in cases concerning both freedom of expression and privacy. After the comments on the harm done to the Douglases in allowing publication in *Hello!* courts may be more willing to grant interim relief where it is clear that there would be no satisfactory remedy should publication go ahead.[190]

Exercise

The case of *Douglas v Hello!* was a particularly challenging one for the courts to deal with. The substantive law on breach of confidence has been developing apace in recent years, making it difficult to decide when it might be appropriate to grant an interim order. Do you think that the Court of Appeal was correct in its assessment of where the balance between freedom of expression and confidentiality lay when considering the grant of an interim injunction? Would the same arguments apply in copyright infringement cases? Consider *Ashdown v Telegraph Group Ltd* [2001] 2 All ER 370 (see para 5.47).

---

[183] For the High Court decision on the merits see [2003] EWHC 786 and for the appeal (No 3) [2005] EWCA Civ 595.

[184] (No 3) [2005] EWCA Civ 595 para 254.   [185] ibid, para 255.

[186] [2004] UKHL 22, [2004] 2 AC 457, [2004] 2 WLR 1232, [2004] 2 All ER 995.

[187] *Von Hannover v Germany* (59320/00) [2004] EMLR 21, (2005) 40 EHRR 16.

[188] (No 3) [2005] EWCA Civ 595, para 253.   [189] ibid, para 259.

[190] Eg *Ms Elizabeth Jagger v John Darling & Others* [2005] EWHC 683 (Ch) Ch D. Note also HRA 1998, s 12(4)(b) which provides: 'The court must have particular regard to the importance of the Convention right to freedom of expression and, where the proceedings relate to material which the respondent claims, or which appears to the court, to be journalistic, literary or artistic material (or to conduct connected with such material), to (a) the extent to which (i) the material has, or is about to, become available to the public; or (ii) it is, or would be, in the public interest for the material to be published; (b) any relevant privacy code.' Guidance was given in interpreting this subsection by Woolf CJ in *A v B Plc* [2002] EWCA Civ 337, para 11. In *Browne v Associated Newspapers Ltd* [2007] EWHC 202 (QB) various categories of information reviewed in coming to the decision that, considering the factors under HRA 1998, s 12(3) an injunction prohibiting the publication of information in the press would remain in force but to a limited degree.

There are however times when the information may be so widely available that court would feel the grant of an interim order to be inappropriate. In *Max Mosley v News Group Newspapers Limited*[191] the High Court had to decide whether to grant an interim injunction prohibiting further publication of videos of Mosley engaged in sexual activity with prostitutes. While the court had little difficulty in deciding Mosley would prevail at trial, preventing further publication at the interim stage was judged to be unlikely to make any practical difference because it was so widely available it was, in essence, 'in the public domain'.[192] Allied to that was the argument that the view that it would be inappropriate to restrain one organisation from publishing material when it was open to other media outlets including competitors to publish the same information.[193] As a result, '…the granting of an order against this Respondent at the present juncture would merely be a futile gesture'.[194]

Injunctions and interdicts

21.104   A final injunction or interdict may be granted to a claimant who proves his case at trial unless the claimant does not come with clean hands, the right is nearing its end or repetition is unlikely. The scope of an injunction in intellectual property cases has been the subject of some debate. (For a discussion on the territorial scope of an injunction (cross border injunctions) see para 22.60ff). An injunction is normally worded so as to prevent repetition of the infringement in issue. However there are times when an injunction might prevent activities which do not relate to the infringement in question, and which may prevent other lawful activities. In *Coflexip v Stolt Comex Seaway*[195] concerning infringement of a patent, Laddie J suggested that the objective of an injunction should be to:

- protect the claimant from a continuation of the infringement of its rights by the threatened activities of the defendant; and
- be fair to the defendant.

The reason given in *Coflexip* for the grant of an injunction narrow in scope was because the grant of a broad injunction might result in restraining a defendant from doing things he had not threatened to do, may never have thought of doing, or may be incapable of doing. This was, however, overturned by Aldous J in the Court of Appeal who agreed that, while an injunction should set out with clarity what may not be done, such a test would be met by issuing the standard form of injunction. However, prior to the appeal being heard, the narrower formulation was followed in other cases, including one concerning copyright and computer software[196] and another concerning patents.[197] As both of these were heard prior to the appeal in *Coflexip*, the precise scope of an injunction to be granted in intellectual property cases, and to which intellectual property rights, is at present unclear.[198]

21.105   The matter has been considered again in the case below.

■ *Sun Microsystems Inc v Amtec Computer Corporation Ltd* [2006] EWHC 62

This concerned the sale of Sun computers in the EEA by Amtec—computers which had not been put on the market in the EEA with the consent of Sun. Sun thus took action against Amtec

[191] *Max Mosley v News Group Newspapers Limited* [2008] EWHC 687 (QB), 2008 WL 925042.   [192] ibid, para 33.
[193] Op cit, para 35. Citing *Attorney-General v Times Newspapers Ltd* [2001] 1 WLR 885 , 895–6,   [194] Op cit, para 36.
[195] [1999] FSR 473.   [196] *Microsoft Corporation v Plato Technology Limited* [1999] FSR 834.
[197] *Nutrinova Nutrition Specialties & Food Ingredients GmbH v Scanchem UK Limited (No 2)* [2001] FSR 43.
[198] H Hurdle, 'What should be the Scope of a Permanent Injunction in UK Patent Infringement Actions? An Update' (2000) (November) Patent World 1.

alleging trade mark infringement.[199] Before selling computers in the EEA Amtec had been to some lengths to ensure the goods they resold had been lawfully placed on the market. They used only a reputable supplier and included a term in their contract with that supplier stipulating that supplies should be of EU origin. The court accepted that a broad injunction, prohibiting Amtec dealing in Sun products, would have the practical effect of closing their legitimate business, a solution which would not be proportionate to protect Sun's business. Further, it was impossible for Amtec to know that the Sun products that it dealt with had been put on the market with consent unless Sun provided information on the products. Thus a qualified injunction would be granted which would allow Amtec to deal in Sun products if:

- Amtec informed Sun by writing or by email of the serial numbers of products they were going to sell together with a description of the product indicating whether it was new or secondhand;

- Sun had not responded within a defined period (between 7 to 14 days) indicating that its records showed to its satisfaction that the product had not been put on the market in the EEA by it or with its consent; provided that

- Amtec did not know or believe that the product had not been put on the market in the EEA by, or with the consent of, Sun.[200]

It is interesting to note that this type of limited injunction requires Sun and Amtec to work together to identify potentially infringing goods. Whether more limited injunctions of this type are granted will depend on the facts of individual cases.

 Exercise

Can you think of cases other than those dealing with parallel imports in which the scope of an injunction should be narrow? Do you think such limited injunctions are fair to both claimant and defendant?

Delivery up

21.106   A court may order delivery up or destruction of infringing articles.[201] The purpose of such an order is to ensure that the infringing goods do not enter circulation. Where a person has committed a secondary infringement of copyright, trade mark, performers' rights and unregistered design right, in other words the infringement has been committed in the course of a business, then the court may order delivery up to the right owner pending a further order for destruction or forfeiture.[202]

Damages

21.107   The most common form of remedy available in intellectual property cases is that of damages. The purpose of an award of damages is (in common with other actions in tort and delict) to put the claimant back in the position he would have been had the infringement not occurred.

---

[199] See also para 19.63.   [200] Op cit, n 158, para 46.
[201] Patents Act 1977, s 61(1)(b); TMA 1994, s 16; Registered Designs Act 1949, s 24C.
[202] TMA 1994, s 16, CDPA 1988, ss 99, 108, 195, 199, 204, 230, 231.

21.108   It may not be possible to obtain an award of damages against an 'innocent infringer'. In cases of copyright, UK unregistered design right and rights in performances, damages will not be awarded in an infringement action where, at the time of the infringement, the defendant did not know, and had no reason to believe, that a right subsisted in the work to which the action relates.[203] In the case of patents and UK registered designs, damages will not be awarded where the defendant proves that at the date of infringement they were not aware and had no reasonable grounds for supposing that the patent existed or the design was registered.[204] No innocent infringement defence exists to an infringement of registered or unregistered community design right.[205] The fact that an article is accompanied by the words 'registered' or 'patented' does not thereby mean that the defendant has knowledge. However, that does not apply if the number of the registration is included. Therefore, the owner of a patent or registered design would be well advised to include the words 'registered' or 'patented' and the relevant number. For trade marks and passing off it would appear that damages can be awarded against an innocent infringer.[206]

21.109   The method of calculation of an award of damages for economic loss in an intellectual property infringement claim was considered in *Ultraframe (UK) Limited v Eurocell Building Plastics Limited, Eurocell Profiles Limited*[207] (note that this case was decided before the regulations implementing the Enforcement Directive were in force—see para 21.130). The guidelines put forwards by the High Court included the following:

'The claimant can recover loss which was (i) foreseeable, (ii) caused by the wrong, and (iii) not excluded from recovery by public or social policy. It is not enough that the loss would not have occurred but for the tort. The tort must be, as a matter of common sense, a cause of the loss.

The burden of proof rests on the claimant. Damages are to be assessed liberally. But the object is to compensate the claimant and not to punish the defendant.

Where a claimant has exploited his patent by manufacture and sale he can claim (a) lost profit on sales by the defendant that he would have made otherwise; (b) lost profit on his own sales to the extent that he was forced by the infringement to reduce his own price; and (c) a reasonable royalty on sales by the defendant which he would not have made.

The assessment of damages for lost profits should take into account the fact that the lost sales are of "extra production" and that only certain specific extra costs (marginal costs) have been incurred in making the additional sales. Nevertheless, in practice costs go up and so it may be appropriate to temper the approach somewhat in making the assessment.

The reasonable royalty is to be assessed as the royalty that a willing licensor and a willing licensee would have agreed. Where there are truly comparable licences in the relevant field these are the most useful guidance for the court as to the reasonable royalty. Another approach is the profits available approach. This involves an assessment of the profits that would be available to the licensee, absent a licence, and apportioning them between the licensor and the licensee.

---

[203] CDPA 1988, ss 97(1), 191J, 233(1). Under the 2004 Directive on the Enforcement of Intellectual property rights (EC Directive 2004/48) damages are mandatorily to be recoverable where there is knowing infringement.

[204] Patents Act 1977, s 62(1); Registered Designs Act 1949, s 24B.

[205] Council Regulation 6/2002 on registered and unregistered Community designs. EC Directive of 2004 on the Enforcement of Intellectual Property Rights, Art 13. Community Design Regulations 2005 as amended by the Intellectual Property Enforcement Regulations 2006. *J Choo (Jersey) Limited v Towerstone Limited & Others* [2008] EWHC 346 (Ch).

[206] L Bently and B Sherman, *Intellectual Property Law* (2nd edn, 2004) p 1024.

[207] [2006] EWHC 1344. For the general principles for patents see *Gerber Garment Technology v Lectra Systems* [1997] RPC 443.

Where damages are difficult to assess with precision, the court should make the best estimate it can, having regard to all the circumstances of the case and dealing with the matter broadly, with common sense and fairness.'[208]

21.110   The Department for Constitutional Affairs (DCA) launched a consultation on 'The law on damages' dealing inter alia with Recommendation 38 from the Gowers Review of Intellectual Property which states that the DCA should review the issues raised in its forthcoming consultation paper on damages and seek further evidence to ensure that an effective and dissuasive system of damages exists for civil IP cases and that it is operating effectively.[209] Views were submitted by a range of stakeholders. The Government has indicated that it does not consider the introduction of exemplary or pre-established damages is appropriate; that measures to facilitate publicity measures have been put into place; and that the provisions as they stand do meet the requirements of TRIPs. On measure of damages the Government has said that it will clarify that additional damages are included within aggravated and restitutionary damages and that that these, along with account of profit are intended to be within Article 13.1 of the Enforcement Directive.[210]

 Question

In what circumstances do you think that a person who infringes a right could successfully claim to be an 'innocent infringer'?
What, if any, liability would an individual face if the word 'registered' or 'patented' was used in connection with articles that were not registered or patented? (See also para 14.107.)

Additional damages

21.111   Additional damages may be awarded by a court in an action for infringement of copyright,[211] rights in performances[212] and unregistered design right.[213] The Court is required to have regard to all the circumstances, and in and particular to the flagrancy of the infringement[214] and any benefit which may accrue to the defendant by reason of the infringement.[215] Additional damages are in addition to an award of 'normal' damages[216] and so a claimant can only elect for additional damages if normal damages are claimed.[217] This means that it is not possible to claim additional damages with an account of profits (for which see below), where the claimant has to elect either an account of profits or damages. Neither are additional damages available where ordinary damages are not granted, for instance in cases of innocent infringement.

21.112   The nature of the award of additional damages was considered at some length by Pumfrey J in the following case.

---

[208]   [2006] EWHC 1344, para 47.

[209]   The consultation can be found at http://www.dca.gov.uk/consult/damages/cp0907.pdf

[210]   Ministry of Justice, The Law on Damages, Response to consultation CP(R) 9/07. 1 July 2009.

[211]   CDPA 1988, s 97(2). An infringement of copyright commited in breach of an injunction restraining such infringement could found an award of additional damages. *Kabushi Kaisha Sony Computer Ent. Inc. v Owen* [2002] EWHC 45. Also *PPL v Reader* [2005] EWHC 416 (Ch).   [212]   ibid, s 191J.

[213]   ibid, s 229(3).

[214]   Flagrancy can include sales in breach of a court order: *Sony Computer Entertainment v Owen* [2002] EWHC 45.

[215]   CDPA 1988, s 97(2).   [216]   *Ravenscroft v Herbert* [1980] RPC 193.

[217]   *Redrow Homes Ltd v Bett Brothers Plc* [1999] 1 AC 197, [1998] 1 All ER 385, [1998] FSR 345.

■ *Nottinghamshire Healthcare NHS Trust v News Group Newspapers Ltd* [2002] EWHC 409

The case concerned the infringement of copyright in a photograph of a patient at Rampton Hospital published by the Sun newspaper. Copyright in the photograph belonged to the NHS Trust. While the measure of damages was to be calculated on the basis of infringement of copyright, the fact that the photograph was confidential, being part of a patient's medical records, does appear to have had a bearing on the decision. It was clear that the court wished to award additional damages taking into account the 'flagrancy of the infringement.'[218] But what did this phrase mean and what should the award of additional damages reflect? Should damages be exemplary in that an award would be intended both to compensate the claimant for the loss, and to teach the defendant that infringement does not pay? Or should they rather be aggravated, which would compensate the claimant for the loss, but would also take into account the injury to the claimant's feelings of pride and dignity, humiliation, distress, insult, or pain?[219] After much deliberation the court decided that an award of additional damages should not be punitive or exemplary in nature, pointing to the difficulties that would occur if this was not the case particularly where an infringer was sued by successive claimants each seeking punishment for their respective interests. The example was given of a counterfeiter who had produced numerous compact discs.[220] Pumphrey J did however consider that the section permitted an aggravation of an award of damages 'on a basis far wider than the factors admitted as aggravation at common law'.[221] In particular, it permitted an element of restitution. In the event £450 was awarded as the fee that would have been negotiated between a willing copyright owner and the newspaper and, having regard to the flagrancy and the need to do justice in the case, the total damages were set at £10,000.[222]

In the words of the judge: 'If this [sum of £10,000] exceeds the sum appropriate under section 97(2) having regard to the benefit to the Defendant, then no further infringements of this kind will take place. If further infringements consisting of the publishing of stolen photographs from medical records do take place, it will show the advantage to the newspaper still exceeds the award of damages'.[223]

 Discussion point   For answer guidance visit www.oxfordtextbooks.co.uk/orc/macqueen2e/

Do you think that this finding will deter newspapers in the future from publishing information without consent that is confidential and protected by copyright?

Account of profits

21.113   An account of profits is available for infringement of most intellectual property rights.[224] The remedy is based on the principle that the infringer has carried out the infringing act on behalf of the right owner. The owner is therefore entitled to the profits made from the infringement. Once liability is established, the owner can opt for either damages or an account of profits but

---

[218] CDPA 1988, s 97(2)(a).
[219] *Nottinghamshire Healthcare NHS Trust v News Group Newspapers Ltd* [2002] EWHC 409, para 33.
[220] ibid, para 51.   [221] ibid.   [222] ibid, para 60.   [223] ibid. See also *PPL v Reader* [2005] EWHC 416 (Ch).
[224] CDPA 1988, s 96; Patents Act 1977, s 61; TMA1994, s 14.

not both. The net profits, after deducting the profit attributable to the infringers efforts, is the measure of damages that is awarded.[225]

> ## Key points on remedies
>
> - Both interim and final injunctions (interdicts) are available in IP infringement actions
> - The scope of a final injunction is currently a matter of debate
> - Delivery up and damages are both available as remedies
> - Damages are not available against innocent infringers (except possibly for trade marks, passing off, registered and unregistered community design right)
> - Additional damages are available for copyright, rights in performances and unregistered design right

(For discussion on implementation of the Enforcement Directive and the impact on calculation of damages, see para 21.133.)

Alternative dispute resolution

21.114 Taking intellectual property disputes to court can be time consuming and expensive, factors that may have contributed towards the increasing interest shown in recent years in alternative forms of dispute resolution. The most notable amongst these is the procedure that has been put into place for domain name disputes. Further information on this can be found in Chapter 16.

21.115 But it is not only domain name disputes that are referred to alternative dispute resolution. The number of organisations offering mediation and arbitration services in the sphere of intellectual property disputes have been increasing over the past years. WIPO has an arbitration and mediation service which was established in 1994. Apparently it took several years after establishment for disputes to be referred to the Centre, but it would appear that it is now increasing in popularity. As of 2009, 80 mediation and 110 arbitration disputes had been referred to the Centre's service.

21.116 The IPO launched an intellectual property mediation service in early 2006 partly in response to the Woolf Report, 'Access to Justice' which identified the need for mechanisms to promote the speedy and cheap resolution of disputes.

Weblinks

Details of the WIPO Arbitration and Mediation Center can be found at http://www.wipo.int/ amc/en/index.html Details of the IPO mediation service can be found at http://www.ipo.gov. uk/types/patent/p-dispute/p-mediation.htm

---

[225] *Delfe v Delamotte* (1857) 3 K & J 581.

Criminal enforcement

21.117 In the UK a number of criminal sanctions exist in the fields of copyright, performers' rights and trade mark infringement. The offences relate to those circumstances where the infringer makes for sale, hire, or otherwise deals in the course of a business with infringing materials in the following circumstances, each of which is predicated on knowledge or reason to believe by the infringer (in contrast to civil actions where liability is strict).

Copyright

21.118 Making for sale, hire or otherwise dealing with in the course of a business:

- copies of works that have been made without the authorisation of the copyright owner;[226]
- articles that are specifically designed or adapted for making infringing copies of copyright material;[227]
- communications of a work to the public;[228]
- performances of a work in public;[229]
- unauthorised decoders;[230]
- devices, products or components which are primarily designed, produced or adapted for the purpose of enabling or facilitation the circumvention of effective technological measures.[231]

In addition, criminal sanctions are also placed on those who distribute infringing articles otherwise than in the course of a business to such an extent as to *affect prejudicially* the owner of the copyright in the following circumstances:

- distribution of an article which is, and which the infringer knows or has reason to believe, infringes copyright in a work;
- communication of the work to the public;[232]
- distribution of any device product or component designed produced or adapted for the purpose of enabling or facilitating the circumvention of effective technological measures;[233]
- promotion or advertisement of a service the purpose of which is to enable or facilitate the circumvention of effective technological measures.[234]

Exercise

What do you think of the inclusion of criminal sanctions being used against those who do not infringe in the course of a business, but do infringe to the extent that the interests of the owner are prejudicially affected? What do you think the test 'affect prejudicially' means? What do you think of the inclusion of criminal sanctions against those who distribute devices which could circumvent technological protection measures? Does it make any difference that copyright need not be infringed for the sanction to attach?

---

[226] CDPA 1988, s 107(1).   [227] ibid, s 107(2).   [228] ibid, s 107(2A).   [229] ibid, s 107(4).
[230] Defined as 'Devices or other apparatus, including software, that allow people to access encrypted transmissions without paying the normal fee for their reception': ibid, s 297A. Case C-429/08 *Murphy v Media Protection Services* [2008] EWHC 1666; see para 19.69 for a discussion on the free movement elements of the case.   [231] ibid, s 296ZB(1)(d).
[232] ibid, s 107(2A).   [233] ibid, s 296ZB(1)(d).   [234] ibid, s 296ZB(2).

21.119 Offences can be committed not just by individuals but also by corporate entities. In *Thames Hudson Ltd v Design and Artists Copyright Society Ltd*[235] a criminal action[236] was brought against the directors of Thames Hudson Ltd by the Design and Artists Copyright Society (DACS). The matter concerned the publication and distribution of a book which contained an infringing copy of a painting. The case was allowed to proceed at the same time as civil action was being taken. The criminal court suggested that that the magistrate might, if the civil proceedings were found to be carried out with due diligence, use discretion to adjourn the final disposal of the criminal aspects of the case pending the decision in the Chancery Division.

Performers' rights

21.120 In relation to infringement of performers' rights, the following criminal sanctions exist:

- where copies of recordings of performances have been made without the authorisation of the performer(s) or a person having recording rights in the performance, that is, illicit or bootleg recordings;[237]

- where a performer's making available right is infringed.[238]

Trade marks

21.121 Under the Trade Marks Act 1994 criminal sanctions are available where:

- a trade mark has been applied without the consent of the owner to goods, on packaging or on labels (that is, counterfeit goods);

- articles are specifically designed or adapted for making unauthorised copies of a trade mark for use on such goods and other material.[239]

21.122 An interesting question concerning criminal liability fell to be decided by the House of Lords in *R v Johnstone*.[240] (See also para 15.12.) Johnstone had been making and disseminating CDs containing copies of bootleg recordings containing the name of the performer which had been registered as a trade mark. Johnstone was charged under section 92(1) of the Trade Marks Act 1994 for falsely applying and using a trade mark. It was argued that, to be liable, civil infringement had first to be established which was not so in the instant case as the performers' names had not been used as indications of origin[241] but merely to identify the artists. The House of Lords found this argument to be correct: as a matter of principle if a name of an artist was used exclusively as an indication of the name of the performer in connection with the performance this was merely descriptive and not an indication of the trade origin. Johnstone was therefore not guilty of this offence.

A different defence was raised in *R v Boulter (Gary)*.[242] The applicant was charged with selling counterfeit and pirated music CDs bearing the logos of EMI and other recording companies. He raised the defence that the CDs that bore the trade marks were of such poor quality that no one would think that its trade origin was that of the trade mark owners. In other words, there would be no confusion. The Court of Appeal ruled that no confusion was needed to be guilty of the offence in section 92 because the issue was identity, and not similarity, of the marks. Regardless of how badly the marks were copied they were identical to those registered to the recording

---

[235] [1995] FSR 153.   [236] Pursuant to CDPA 1988, ss 107 and 110.   [237] ibid, s 198(1).
[238] ibid, s 198(1A).   [239] TMA 1994, s 92.
[240] [2003] UKHL 28, [2003] 3 All ER 884, [2003] 2 Cr App Rep 493, [2004] Crim LR 244.
[241] TMA 1994, s 11(2)(b).   [242] [2008] EWCA Crim 2375, [2009] ETMR 6.

companies, and used on identical goods. A counterfeiter could not avoid criminal liability by claiming that the goods are 'genuine fakes'.[243]

Copyright, etc and Trade Marks (Offences and Enforcement) Act 2002

21.123   In 2002, the Copyright, Etc And Trade Marks (Offences and Enforcement) Act 2002[244] amended the criminal provisions relating to copyright, rights in performances, fraudulent reception of conditional access transmissions by use of unauthorised decoders and trade marks. The purpose of this act was to rationalise the criminal procedures in these areas. It did so by:

- providing for maximum penalties for certain offences: the new maximum penalty for offences for conviction on indictment for copyright cases is an unlimited fine and/or up to 10 years in prison, and on summary conviction a fine (up to the statutory maximum) and/or up to 6 months in prison (previously only a fine could be imposed);[245]

- rationalising police search and seizure powers relating to copyright and trade mark offences;[246]

- making provision for court orders on forfeiture of illegal material that may have been seized during investigation of copyright and trade mark offences.[247]

The 2002 Act made no changes to the scope of criminal offences.

In a document narrating the details of the consultation on penalties for copyright infringement that took place as a result of Recommendation 36 of the Gowers review, the majority view was that exceptional statutory maxima of £50,000 for all IP offences should be introduced albeit some concern was expressed that the options offered did not meet the Gowers recommendation.[248]

Counterfeiting and piracy

21.124   Counterfeiting and piracy have been the subject of a number of European initiatives to harmonise the rules as within member states of the EU. In particular procedures relating to border control of the movement of goods infringing intellectual property rights have been strengthened and sanctions available within member states bolstered.[249]

21.125   The movement of goods infringing intellectual property rights across borders has long troubled right holders. In recent years there appears to have been a significant increase in this activity, certainly into Europe. The Commission published statistics on counterfeiting and piracy in 2007. The report shows that seizures were up 17 per cent on 2006; a decrease in the overall

---

[243] ibid, para 9. For a discussion on whether a person charged with trade mark infringement believed on objectively reasonable grounds that the goods he was selling were genuine see *Essex Trading Standards v Wallati Singh* [2009] EWHC 520 (Admin), 2009 WL 392234. In this case the High Court ruled that the respondent was not able to discharge the burden under TMA 1994, s 92(5).

[244] Copyright, etc and Trade Marks (Offences and Enforcement) Act 2002 (Commencement) Order 2002 (SI 2002/2749).   [245] CDPA 1988, ss 107(4), 198(5), 297A(2), 297A(2).

[246] ibid, ss 109, 200, 297B, 297A; TMA 1994, s 92A.

[247] TMA 1994, ss 97 and 98 allowing forfeiture of infringing goods, are inserted into the CDPA 1988 in respect of the offences in ss 107(1) and (2), 198(1) and 297A and offences under the Trade Descriptions Act 1968 and those involving dishonesty or deception. Section 97 of the TMA 1994 relates to forfeiture in England, Wales and Northern Ireland and s 98 is a modified version relating to forfeiture in Scotland.   [248] http://www.ipo.gov.uk/response-gowers36.pdf

[249] *Beecham Group plc, SmithKline Beecham plc, Glaxo Group Ltd, Stafford-Miller Ltd, GlaxoSmithKline Consumer Healthcare NV and GlaxoSmithKline Consumer Healthcare BV v Andacon NV Case* C-132/07 for questions concerning powers of customs officers under Regulation (EC) No 1891/04 and Regulation (EC) No 1383/03.

number of counterfeit and pirated goods seized by customs (79 million compared to 128 million in 2006) due to fewer cigarettes and CD/DVDs in particular being seized; increases in certain sectors including 264 per cent in cosmetics and personal care, 98 per cent in toys and 51 per cent in medicines.[250]

 Exercise

It can sometimes be very difficult to distinguish between a genuine article and a fake. Go to eBay and type in Mulberry handbag (or the name of any other designer goods you would like). Which are the genuine articles?

21.126   In July 2004 a new European Regulation was brought into force concerning action to be taken by customs officials with respect to goods suspected of infringing certain intellectual property rights and measures to be taken against goods found to infringe such rights.[251] It replaced a Regulation promulgated in 1994 which in turn replaced a Regulation of 1986[252] dealing with the same subject matter. In the 2004 Regulation counterfeit goods are defined as:

'goods or trade mark symbols or packaging presented separately, bearing without authorisation a trademark identical to another trademark validly registered, or which cannot be distinguished in its essential aspects and which thereby infringes the trademark-holder's rights.'

And pirated goods as:

'goods that are or contain copies made without the consent of the holder of a copyright or related right or design right.'

21.127   The new Regulation is broad in scope and covers:

- patents
- supplementary protection certificates
- designs and models
- copyright and related rights
- trade marks[253]
- designations of origin
- new plant varieties

---

[250] For details see http://ec.europa.eu/taxation_customs/customs/customs_controls/counterfeit_piracy/statistics/index_en.htm

[251] Council Regulation (EC) No 1383/2003 of 22 July 2003 concerning customs action against goods suspected of infringing certain intellectual property rights and measures to be taken against goods found to have infringed such rights came into force. Referred to by CDPA 1988, s 111(3B); TMA 1994, s 89(3). See also Commission Regulation 1891/2004 of 21.10.2004 laying down provisions for the implementation of this Council Regulation. For a number of questions that have arisen concerning Article 11 Regulation No 1383/20031 see Case C-93/08 *SIA Schenker v Valsts ienēmumu dienests.*

[252] Council Regulation (EEC) No 3842/86 of 1 December 1986 laying down measures to prohibit the release for free circulation of counterfeit goods.

[253] Case C-302/08 *Zino Davidoff SA v Bundesfinanzdirektion Südos* the ECJ ruled that the Regulation also covers international trade marks. The ECJ explained that, following the assimilation of internationally registered trade marks into Community trade marks pursuant to Article 146 of Council Regulation (EC) No 40/94 as amended by Council Regulation (EC) No 1992/2003, Article 5(4) of the Regulation allows 'the holder of an international registered trade mark to secure action by the customs authorities of one or more other Member State, besides that of the Member State in which it is lodged, just like the proprietor of a Community trade mark'.

- geographical indications
- any mould or matrix designed or adapted for the manufacture of goods infringing an intellectual property right

The purpose of the Regulation is to facilitate the seizure and destruction of infringing goods (according to the law of the member state in which the goods are found) with the intention of preventing them from entering circulation in the EU. The Regulation sets out the procedure by which notice should be given to the relevant customs authorities and the action to be taken thereafter; although for difficulties that arose in the UK where Commissioners of Revenue & Customs (HMRC) refused to continue to detain a consignment of allegedly counterfeit mobile phones and accessories bearing the Nokia trade mark because they had not been placed on the market (see para 19.60 and *Nokia Corporation v Her Majesty's Commissioners of Revenue & Customs*.[254]) Under the Regulation measures may also be taken to deprive the persons concerned of the economic benefits of the transaction.[255]

21.128 National governments have also been busy in developing responses to the increased incidence of counterfeiting and piracy. Not only do trading standards officers have some responsibility for the enforcement of legislation in this area, but in addition, the UK Government has established an IP Crime Group which has produced and IP Crime Strategy designed to coordinate the efforts of public bodies in this area.[256] IPO publishes as annual Intellectual Property Crime Report. The 2008–2009 report shows that during the period under review 106182 DVD/software units were confiscated, 45,000 perfumes and 5,359 CDs.

Weblink

If you look at the IPO website at http://www.ipo.gov.uk/crime.htm you will find documents relating to the IP Crime Strategy, the 2008 Report along with a number of documents concerning the activities of the Office and other organisations involved in measures aimed at tackling piracy and counterfeiting.

21.129 A network of organisations, such as FAST, the British Software Alliance and FACT, monitor markets and alert the relevant regulatory authorities to incidents of counterfeiting and piracy. Counterfeiting and piracy were subjects also discussed at the G8 meeting held at Gleneagles in Scotland in 2005. The Ministers issued a document pledging to work together to draw up a plan to reduce the incidence of these activities over the coming years.[257] In 2006 the EU and the US agreed to work together to develop approaches to defeat the rising tide of counterfeit and pirated goods coming from China and Russia, to be followed by Latin America and the Middle

---

[254] [2009] EWHC 1903 (Ch), 2009 WL 2207339 and the reference to the Court of Justice in Case C-495/09. See also the reference in Case C-446/09 *Koninklijke Philips Electronics NV v Lucheng Meijing Industrial Company Ltd*.

[255] Art 17(1)(b) Council Regulation (EC) No. 1383/2003. Domestic procedures relating to copyright and trade marks are also available but are narrower than those to be found under the Regulation. CDPA 1988, ss 111, 112; TMA 1994, s 89. In September 2008 the European Council adopted a Resolution on a comprehensive European anti-counterfeiting and anti-piracy plan: OJ C253, 04/10/2008 p 1. In March 2009 the Council adopted a Resolution on the EU Customs Action Plan to combat IPR infringements for the years 2009 to 2012: OJ C 71, 25/03/2009 p. 1

[256] For information see http://www.ipo.gov.uk/enforcereport2005.pdf

[257] At Gleneagles in July 2005 the G8 statement 'Reducing IPR Piracy and Counterfeiting through more effective enforcement' was issued.

East.[258] This may have heralded the start of the negotiations for a proposed new international treaty designed to combat counterfeiting although about which there are, at the time for writing, few hard facts. In 2007 the European Commission stated that it intended to seek a mandate from member states to negotiate a new Anti Counterfeiting Trade Agreement (ACTA) with major trading partners, including the US, Japan, Korea, Mexico and New Zealand.[259] Three particular avenues would be pursued:

- building international cooperation leading to harmonised standards and better communication between authorities;

- establishing common enforcement practices to promote strong intellectual property protection in coordination with right holders and trading partners; and

- creating a strong modern legal framework which reflects the changing nature of intellectual property theft in the global economy, including the rise of easy-to-copy digital storage mediums and the increasing danger of health threats from counterfeit food and pharmaceutical drugs.

There has been little further information forthcoming from the negotiating bodies. At the time of writing many stories have been circulating as to some of the powers that may be sought to combat counterfeiting, but very little authoritative information as to the proposed scope of the Treaty.[260]

 Exercise

The definitions of counterfeiting and piracy have changed and would appear to have expanded in scope over the years. See how many different definitions you can find used in both European and UK instruments. What do you think of the use of the term 'piracy' in connection with individuals who download music files from the Internet?

EU Enforcement Directive

21.130   Also in response to the rising levels of counterfeiting and piracy a European Directive on the Enforcement of Intellectual Property Rights was agreed in 2004.[261] The purpose of the Directive, which contains measures and procedures concerning civil sanctions and remedies, is to create a level playing field for right holders while acting as a deterrent to those engaged in counterfeiting and piracy. The focus of the measure is on infringements carried out for commercial purposes or those which cause significant harm to the right holder. The Directive which required implementation into member states legislation by the end of April 2006 covers the following IP areas:

- copyright

- rights related to copyright

---

[258] 'US and EU Pledge to take action over fake Goods', *Financial Times*, 18 June 2006. See SABIP Report (Number EC001) 'IP Enforcement in the UK and Beyond: A Literature Review' 18 May 2009.   [259] See IP/07/1573.

[260] See the Electronic Frontier Foundation's opinion on ACTA at http://www.eff.org/issues/acta. See also 'Fact Sheet: Anti-Counterfeiting Trade Agreement' at http://ec.europa.eu/trade/issues/sectoral/intell_property/fs231007_en.htm But see M Blakeney, 'Trade mark survey: ACTA gives hope to trade mark owners' (2009) IPQ 2009, 1–6.

[261] Directive 2004/48/EC of the European Parliament and of the Council of 29 April 2004 on the enforcement of intellectual property rights (Enforcement Directive).

- *sui generis* right of a database maker
- rights of the creator of the topographies of a semiconductor product
- trade mark rights
- design rights
- patent rights, including rights derived from supplementary protection certificates
- geographical indications
- utility model rights
- plant variety rights
- trade names, in so far as these are protected as exclusive property rights in the national law concerned.[262]

21.131 The substantive provisions of the Directive are drawn from a variety of national legislations of member states of the EU. For example, Article 5 provides that in addition to individual right holders, representatives of right holders such as trade association and rights management bodies should be entitled to sue for infringement of a right. This is said to be based on Article 98 of the Belgian Consumer Protection Law 1991, and Article IL-331-1(2) of the French Intellectual Property Code. On this point it should be noted that in England,[263] the High Court has concluded that various claimants were allowed to bring a claim on behalf of other members of the music industry as well as themselves; in other words, in a representative capacity.

21.132 Turning back to the Directive, the provisions on seizure[264] and evidence[265] take inspiration from the search (Anton Pillar) order in the UK and the saisie-contrefaçon system in France and Belgium. These procedures require that evidence found in the control of the opposing party be produced, and provide for the seizure of banking, financial and commercial documents subject to guarantees being lodged should the action be unfounded at the end of the day.

21.133 Other Articles in the Directive require that judicial authorities be given the power to order information to be disclosed as to the origin of the infringing goods and services and distribution mechanisms, personal details of producers, distributors, suppliers, wholesalers and retailers.[266] Interlocutory injunctions should be available,[267] as well as orders requiring the recall and destruction of infringing goods. In addition, the Directive sets out a formula for calculating damages to be awarded to injured parties. This can either be a fixed payment equal to double the amount of royalties or fees which would have been due if the infringer had requested authorisation, or damages which correspond to the losses suffered by the right holder, including loss of earnings. In this the Directive suggests that factors such as 'moral prejudice' caused to the right holder could be taken into account.[268]

21.134 During gestation the Directive was the subject of much criticism—both from those who said that its provisions did not go far enough, and from those who argued that it went too far. At one time the draft was significantly broader than the text as finally agreed, and seemingly went beyond infringements of IPRs carried out on a commercial scale to be relevant to individual

---

[262] Statement by the Commission concerning Art 2 of Directive 2004/48/EC of the European Parliament and of the Council on the enforcement of intellectual property rights (2005/295/EC) (13 April 2005). Both Sweden and Germany were found to have failed to transpose Directive 2004/48/EC on the Enforcement of intellectual property rights into domestic law within the prescribed period (Cases C-395/07 and C-341/07).

[263] *Independiente Ltd and Others v Music Trading On-Line (HK) Ltd* [2003] EWHC 470 (Ch).

[264] Enforcement Directive, Art 9.   [265] ibid, Art 7.   [266] ibid, Art 8.   [267] ibid, Art 9.

[268] ibid, Art 13. For the UK Government's view that it has largely implemented these obligations, see para 21.118.

acts of infringement, such as downloading music files from the Internet. After criticism the Directive was amended to its current form.

21.135   Following both formal and informal consultations (most notable were concerns that there should be a balance between the legitimate interests of right holders and the public interest) the Directive has now been implemented in the UK in regulations that came into force on 6 April 2006.[269] Of particular note is regulation 3 which sets out the grounds on which damages should be assessed and includes an obligation to take into account the knowledge (actual or reasonable grounds for) of the defendant, and that the damages should be appropriate to the actual prejudice suffered taking into account the negative economic consequences the claimant has suffered. This may include unfair profits made by the defendant and the moral prejudice caused to the claimant. Alternatively damages may be awarded on the basis of what the claimant would have got as a fee or licence (note the discussion in para 21.130).

21.136   Regulation 4 introduces a new type of court order into Scotland enabling a pursuer (claimant) to ask the court to require the defendant to disclose information about distribution networks of goods or services which infringe intellectual property rights. As always this is subject to a number of checks and balances in particular that a court may only grant such an order where it is considered just and proportionate. If granted the order can be the subject of such conditions as the court deems fit.[270] This type of order is already available in the English courts.[271]

21.137   Beyond that the Regulations make a number of amendments to other primary and subordinate measures including the Patents Act 1977, the Copyright, Designs and Patents Act 1988, the Registered Designs Act 1949 and the Community Designs Regulations 2005, relating to such matters as orders for the disposal of infringing articles and orders for delivery up.[272]

 Discussion point   For answer guidance visit www.oxfordtextbooks.co.uk/orc/macqueen2e/

The Directive and implementing regulations refer to taking into account the 'moral prejudice' caused to the claimant when assessing damages. What moral prejudice do you think might be relevant under this heading and for whom might it be applicable?

EU proposals on enforcement

21.138   In June 2005 the Commission promulgated a proposal for a further Directive, this time aimed at criminal sanctions and remedies along with a proposal for a council framework decision to strengthen the criminal law framework to combat intellectual property offences.[273] This proposal, couched in language referring to obligations under TRIPS and Article 17(2) of the

---

[269] Intellectual Property (Enforcement, etc) Regulations 2006 (SI 2006/1028) (Enforcement Regulations) and the related Community Trade Mark Regulations 2006 (SI 2006/1027).   [270] Enforcement Regulations, reg 4(3).
[271] *Norwich Pharmacal v Customs and Excise Commissioners* [1974] AC 133.
[272] For a discussion on the laws of England and Wales and the Directive see K Huniar, 'The Enforcement Directive: Its Effects on UK Law' [2006] EIPR 92. The second sentence of Article 11 of the Directive was considered in *L'Oréal SA v eBay International* [2009] EWHC 1094 (Ch); [2009] ETMR 53; [2009] RPC 21. This requires the possibility of the grant of an injunction against an intermediary whose services are used by third parties to infringe IP rights. The court considered that it was not clear as to the extent of the obligation and reference should be made to the ECJ.
[273] 2005/0127(COD), 2005/0128(CNS).

Charter of Fundamental Rights (which states that 'Intellectual property shall be protected') would extend criminal sanctions to all intentional infringements of an intellectual property right carried out on a commercial scale, as well as for attempting, aiding or abetting and inciting such offences. The proposal for a framework decision set a threshold for criminal penalties of at least four years' imprisonment if the offence involved a criminal organisation or if it jeopardised public health and safety. The fine had to be at least 100,000 euros to 300,000 euros for cases involving criminal organisations or posing a risk to public health and safety, although member states could apply tougher penalties.

21.139   The proposal was withdrawn after uncertainty as to the competence of the EC to legislate in the arena of criminal sanctions. That they did was (arguably) affirmed by the ECJ in *Commission v Council*[274] where it was held that provisions of criminal law required for the effective implementation of Community law (in the instant case, criminal sanctions for environmental issues) fell under the EC Treaty.[275] The draft Directive was re-issued in amended form and adopted in April 2007 by the European Parliament. Concerns remain as to the scope of the measure and of the competence of the Commission to harmonise criminal sanctions.[276] The proposal apparently remains under discussion.

21.140   While there may be sympathy for the fight against organised crime and its relationship to counterfeiting and piracy, a general anxiety is that, as it stands, the draft Directive could reach far beyond this domain most notably by reference to the rather vague standards of 'attempting, aiding, abetting and inciting' infringements. What is notable are the grounds on which the proposal is justified. As with the original proposal, TRIPS is referred to. However, that Agreement only requires criminal sanctions to be applied in the area of wilful trademark counterfeiting or copyright piracy on a commercial scale.[277] This measure, by contrast, would apply across the IP domains. Reference to the Charter of Fundamental Rights remains, cited as evidencing the obligation to protect intellectual property and thus justify the proposal: human rights standards have most often in the past been used as arguments for limiting the exercise of IPRs rather than providing a justification for tougher enforcement measures.

21.141   Given the concerns over increasing levels of counterfeiting and piracy, it seems likely that moves will continue aimed at introducing criminal sanctions. However it may be that should ACTA materialise, then the need for the Directive passes. Whatever the legal basis, the anxiety must be as to whether the result will represent a balance as between the legitimate concerns of right holders and those who fear for public health and the economy, whilst providing safeguards for non-commercial infringers and the general public interest.

Weblink

The amended draft Directive COM(2006) 168 final can be found at http://eur-lex.europa.eu/ LexUriServ/site/en/com/2006/com2006_0168en01.pdf **Read the draft. What do you think of the proposals and the basis on which they have been justified?**

---

[274] *Commission v Council* Case C 176/03.
[275] For comment see P Treacy and A Wray, 'IP Crimes: The Prospect for EU-Wide Criminal Sanctions—A Long Road Ahead?' [2006] EIPR 1.
[276] See House of Lords European Union Committee 11th Report of Session 2006–07: The Criminal Law Competence of the EC, follow-up Report, 13 March 2007.   [277] TRIPS, Art 61.

21.142   Although civil, criminal and border procedures and remedies are independent they are designed to work together in an integrated system. From border measures through to the receipt of an award of damages or a criminal prosecution, a right owner should be able to call upon appropriate procedures to vindicate a claim and receive a remedy for an infringement of a right.

 Exercise

You are the owner of the copyright in a film. You have heard that DVDs featuring the film and copied without your consent or authorisation have been made in an Eastern European country, not part of the EU. Some of these DVDs have been found in a market stall in Glasgow, others in retail shops in the Borders. You have heard that a further consignment is due to arrive at Rosyth within the next two weeks. What do you do?

TRIPS

21.143   On enforcement matters, TRIPS is important for two reasons.

- TRIPS calls for effective enforcement measures to be available at the domestic level to allow action to be taken by intellectual property owners where rights are infringed. This includes the availability of certain remedies which should be considered a deterrent to further infringement.

- TRIPS provides a mechanism (through the WTO) whereby disputes between member states may be settled. This is particularly so where one country alleges that another is not adhering to its obligations to incorporate the minimum standards of intellectual property protection and enforcement mechanisms into domestic law as laid down in the Agreement.

Effective enforcement measures

21.144   TRIPS is the first international treaty in the IP sector to place obligations on member states relating to the enforcement of intellectual property rights. Three areas of enforcement activity are laid down in the Agreement: civil and administrative procedures including remedies,[278] border measures[279] and criminal procedures.[280]

21.145   Member states are to make available to right holders civil judicial procedures concerning the enforcement of any intellectual property right including rules relating to representation,[281] evidence,[282] and the availability of injunctions and damages.[283] Border measures must be available to enable a right holder to prevent the importation of counterfeit trade mark and pirated copyright goods.[284] Criminal procedures and penalties must be applied in cases of wilful trademark counterfeiting or copyright piracy on a commercial scale.[285]

---

[278] ibid, Part III, s 2.   [279] ibid, Part III, s 4.   [280] ibid, Part III, s 5.   [281] ibid, Art 42.   [282] ibid, Art 43.
[283] ibid, Arts 44 and 45.   [284] ibid, Art 51.   [285] ibid, Art 61.

21.146   Four principles underlie each type of enforcement measure. These are that the action should be effective,[286] procedures should be fair and equitable,[287] decisions should be reasoned[288] and there should be the opportunity to seek judicial review.[289] In addition, the measures should be applied in a manner that avoids creating barriers to legitimate trade and which provides safeguards against their abuse.[290]

21.147   The UK meets all the requirements imposed by TRIPS, and indeed some aspects of domestic enforcement procedures and remedies go beyond those to be found in that Agreement.

 Exercise

Look at TRIPS and compare the procedures laid down in that Agreement with the provisions in the EU Enforcement Directive. Which, if any, of those measures in the Directive go beyond what is required by TRIPS?

21.148   However, not all states who are members of TRIPS have been, or are in compliance with the obligations to be found in that Agreement, including those on enforcement and remedies. This highlights the second, and important, aspect of TRIPS. If a member does not comply with its obligations, then a complaint may be taken to the Dispute Settlement Body (DSB) established by the WTO Agreement. Representatives of every WTO member sit on the DSB which was created to deal with disputes arising under the WTO Agreements. This it does in accordance with the provisions of the Dispute Settlement Understanding (DSU). Member states or trading groups recognised by the WTO may bring an action before a WTO Dispute Settlement Panel if they believe that another country or trading group has failed to meet its obligations under TRIPS. If a country or group is found not to have complied with TRIPS, trade sanctions can be imposed.[291] This mechanism has been used in a number of intellectual property cases both where member states have not incorporated minimum standards on enforcement and remedies into their domestic law, as well as in cases concerning alleged failures to implement the correct substantive level of intellectual property protection.

21.149   On enforcement and remedies the US has brought complaints against, inter alia, Denmark[292] and Sweden[293] arguing that their domestic laws did not provide for provisional measures in civil proceedings as required by TRIPS. Both the actions settled when a mutually agreed solution was found.

21.150   Other complaints concerning the failure of member states' domestic substantive law to reflect obligations imposed by the Agreement have been heard by the full WTO Panel. The first in the copyright field was based on a complaint against the US brought by the EC concerning section 110(5)(B) of the US Copyright Act.[294] This section exempts eating, drinking and retail establishments of a certain size from liability for the public performance of music played from radio and television. It was alleged that this section was incompatible with obligations under both the

---

[286] ibid, Art 41.   [287] ibid, Art 41.2.   [288] ibid, Art 41.3.   [289] ibid, Art 41.4.
[290] See generally ibid, Arts 41, 42, 43, 48.
[291] The WTO Agreement provides that 'Each Member shall ensure the conformity of its laws, regulations and administrative procedures with its obligations as provided in the annexed Agreements'. Art XVI:4.   [292] US DS83.
[293] US DS86.   [294] As amended by the US Fairness in Music Licensing Act 1988.

Berne Convention and TRIPS.[295] In a lengthy decision the Panel analysed the compatibility of section 110(5)(B) with the three-step test to be found in both of those Treaties.[296] On the first step of the test, the Panel found that section 110(5)(B) was not limited to certain special cases: it had been estimated that 70 per cent of eating establishments, 73 per cent of drinking establishments and 45 per cent of retail establishments fell under the exemption. On the second part of the test the Panel found that section 110(5)(B) conflicted with a normal exploitation of a work. This was based on the principle that exempted uses may not compete with actual or potential means of economic exploitation: there would be a conflict between an exemption and normal exploitation if the exemption interfered with the ways in which a right holder would 'normally extract economic value' from a particular use of a work. On the third part of the test, the Panel found that the legitimate interests of the right holder were prejudiced saying that prejudice becomes unreasonable when an exception causes, or has the potential to cause, an unreasonable loss of income to the authors; that actual and potential prejudice to the right holder should be taken into account; and that in analysing unreasonable prejudice the legitimate interests of copyright holders at large should be taken into account and not only the interests of right holders of the WTO member that initiated the complaint. In conclusion the Panel Report found that section 110(5)(B) was indeed incompatible with obligations to be found in TRIPS and recommended that the DSB request the US to amend its legislation.[297]

21.151   Patent disputes have also been heard by the Panel. The EU challenged various aspects of Canadian patent law including the provision that would have meant that it was not an infringement of a patent to make a patented product during the life of the patent for the purpose of stockpiling it for sale after the patent expired. The Panel found this to be a violation of Canada's obligations under TRIPS saying that the manufacture for commercial sale is a commercial activity and that the character of that activity is not altered by mere delay of the commercial reward. Thus, and in practical terms, the enforcement of the right to exclude others from 'making' and 'using' a patented product during the patent term will necessarily give all patent owners a short period of extended exclusivity after the patent expires. Therefore the stockpiling provision in the Canadian patent law was in breach of TRIPS and the Panel concluded that Canada should be required to amend its law to remove this provision.[298]

21.152   Many of the complaints settle prior to being heard by the Panel. For instance a complaint was made by the US against Ireland alleging that Irish legislation did not conform with inter alia obligations concerning rental rights for producers of phonograms.[299] The request for the establishment of the panel was withdrawn after agreement was reached that Ireland would amend its copyright laws.

21.153   To 2009, 27 complaints had been brought before the DSB concerning TRIPS. It is difficult to know at this stage whether this number is likely to increase as states recognise the power of making a complaint in obtaining compliance with obligations under the WTO, or whether the fact that the procedure is available—and indeed will be used—will encourage members voluntarily to ensure that their domestic legislation is in line with obligations in TRIPS.

---

[295] Arts 11*bis*(1)(iii) and 11(1)(ii) of the Berne Convention concerning rights of public performance and communication to the public incorporated into TRIPS by virtue of Art 9(1) and with the three-step test in Art 13 of TRIPS.

[296] For a discussion of the three-step test see Chapter 5.

[297] For the subsequent action see R Owens, 'TRIPS and the Fairness in Music Arbitration: The Repercussions' [2003] EIPR 49. In an action against China DS362 the Panel found that China needed to amend certain of its laws relating to copyright and customs measures so as to conform with obligations under TRIPs.   [298] WT/DS1114/13.

[299] WT DS82/3, WT/DS115/3, IP/D/8/Add.1, IP/D/12/Add.1.

21.154 A different strategy concerning IP rights is being used by some States. Where a State had been found to be in violation of its obligations under TRIPs the Arbitrator may impose sanctions in an unrelated field. So when the US was found in violation of its WTO obligations in respect of gambling and betting services, the Arbitrator found that Antigua may request authorisation from the DSB, to suspend the obligations under the TRIPS Agreement in the areas of copyright and related rights; trade marks; industrial designs; patents and undisclosed information at a level not exceeding US$21 million annually.[300]

Weblink

The WTO web pages can be difficult to navigate until you find your way around. Go to the home page and see if you can find information about disputes that have arisen concerning TRIPS. If in difficulty look at

http://www.wto.org/english/tratop_e/dispu_e/dispu_agreements_index_e.htm?id=A26#selected_agreement

In the list of headings you will find Intellectual Property (TRIPs). Go to these pages and browse though the documents. Re-visit the pages at regular intervals to keep abreast of developments.

 ### Exercise

Would you recommend establishing a procedure akin to that available for disputes arising under TRIPS to hear complaints made under other international treaties such as the Berne Convention? If so, why? If not, why not?

Key points on TRIPS and enforcement

- TRIPS places obligations on member states to implement into their national laws certain minimum standards concerning remedies and sanctions for infringement of intellectual property rights (as well as substantive provisions)

- TRIPS provides a mechanism (through the WTO) whereby disputes between member states as to their adherence or otherwise to obligations laid down in TRIPS may be raised and settled. TRIPS is the only international treaty to contain such an enforcement mechanism

---

[300] See WT/DS285/ARB. United States—Measures Affecting The Cross-Border Supply Of Gambling And Betting Services. Recourse to Arbitration by the United States under Article 22.6 of the DSU. Decision by the Arbitrator. The holding has prompted a great deal of discussion. See eg I Wohl, 'The United States–Antigua Online Gambling Dispute', Journal of International Commerce and Economics, Web Version July 2009 available at http://www.usitc.gov/publications/332/journals/online_gambling_dispute.pdf. See also DS267 United States—Subsidies on Upland Cotton in which Brazil may 'suspend' certain US IP rights.

Future developments

21.155   As will have been seen from this chapter, in common with all areas of IP, policy tensions are evident in this domain. New modes of exploitation are challenging the existing framework both in terms exploitation and enforcement. In civil matters the key concern is to ensure that the interests of the IP owner are sufficiently but not over protected at the expense of innovation. In criminal matters the articulated strategy is to combat counterfeiting and piracy not only because of its links with organised crime, but also because of the anxiety over consumer welfare. This has resulted in the enactment of a number of recent measures in the field of enforcement as discussed in the text, as well as further proposals to strengthen the regime. Although many initiatives emanate from Europe, the Gowers Review of Intellectual Property also made several recommendations in the field of enforcement including: the introduction of matching penalties for online and physical copyright infringement; reviewing the award of damages to ensure that an effective and dissuasive system exists for civil IP cases; the introduction of measures to tighten regulation of occasional sales and markets; and giving Trading Standards the power to enforce copyright infringement.[301] Developments are thus likely over the coming years.

Further reading

Books and papers

S Anderman et al (eds), *The Interface between Intellectual Property Rights and Competition Policy Cambridge University Press* (2007)

C Correa, *Intellectual Property and Competition Law: Exploration of Some Issues of Relevance to Developing Countries, ICTSD IPRs and Sustainable Development Programme* (2007) Issue Paper No 21, International Centre for Trade and Sustainable Development, Geneva, Switzerland.

O Vrins and M Scheider (eds), *Enforcement of Intellectual Property Rights through Border Measures— Law and Practice in the EU* (2006)

Articles

'Statement of the Max Planck Institute for Intellectual Property, Competition and Tax Law on the Proposal for a Directive of the European Parliament and of the Council on criminal measures aimed at ensuring the enforcement of intellectual property rights' (2006) 37(8) IIC 970–7

A Andreangeli 'Interoperability as an "essential facility" in the Microsoft case—encouraging competition or stifling innovation?' (2009) EL Rev 584

L Blakeney, and M Blakeney, 'Counterfeiting and Piracy—Removing the Incentives through Confiscation' [2008] EIPR 348.

M Blakeney, 'International proposals for the criminal enforcement of intellectual property rights: international concern with counterfeiting and piracy' (2009) IPQ 1

V Bomhard, H O'Neill and A Paz, 'Licences in OHIM practice' (2007) 2(11) JIPLP 756

---

301   Gowers Review of Intellectual Property, December 2006.

E Bonadio, 'Remedies and sanctions for the infringement of intellectual property rights under EC law' (2008) 30(8) EIPR 320–7.

O Brand, 'The dawn of compulsory patent licensing' (2007) 2 IPQ 216–35

P Chaudhry, 'Managing intellectual property rights: Government tactics to curtail counterfeit trade' (2006) 17(4) EBL Rev 939–58

WJ Davey, 'The WTO Dispute Settlement System: The first ten years' (2005) 8 J Int'l Econ L 17A

I Davies and T Scourfield, 'Threats: is the current regime still justified?' E.I.P.R. 2007, 29(7), 259–265

GB Dinwoodie, 'International Intellectual Property Litigation:. A Vehicle for Resurgent Comparativist Thought?' (2001) 49 Am J Comp L 429

S Dusollier, 'Technology as an imperative for regulating copyright: from the public exploitation to the private use of the work' (2005) 27(6) EIPR 201–04

D Ehrlich, 'Trade mark warranties in M & A transactions' (2008) 3(8) JIPLP 501

M Elsmore, 'Trade Mark Coexistence Agreements: What is all the (lack of) fuss about?', (2008) 5:1 SCRIPTed 7 @: http://www.law.ed.ac.uk/ahrc/script-ed/vol5-1/elsmore.asp

A Endeshaw, 'Free trade agreements as surrogates for TRIPs-Plus' (2006) 28(7) EIPR 374–80

G Evans, 'University patent licensing for the research and development of pharmaceuticals in developing countries' (2009) 3 IPQ 311–44

J Farchy, 'Are free licences suitable for cultural works?' (2009) EIPR 255

A Gagliardi, 'Trade Mark Assignments Under EC Law' (1998) EIPR 371

G Grassie, 'The Scottish Courts—the tartan alternative for resolving IP disputes?' (2004) 33(7) CIPAJ 406–08

K Huniar, 'The Enforcement Directive—Its Effects on UK Law' (2006) 28(2) EIPR 92–9

M T Landova, 'Public policy exception to recognition and enforcement of judgments in cases of copyright infringement' (2009) IIC 642

S Lane, 'Goodwill Hunting: Assignments and Licenses in Gross after Scandecor' (1999) 2 IPQ 264–79

S Lawrance, 'Attheraces v British Horseracing Board: What price abuse of dominance?' (2007) 2(9) JIPLP 605

V Lowe, 'The law of unintended consequences—a perspective on the draft Directive on criminal measures to enforce intellectual property rights' (2006) Crim Law 163, 3–5

D Matthews, 'The Lisbon Treaty, trade agreements and the enforcement of intellectual property rights' (2010) EIPR 104

G Mengistie, 'Intellectual property as a tool for development: the Ethiopian Fine Coffee designations and trade marking and licensing experience' (2010) Int TLR 1

M Mercedes, 'Frabboni Old monopolies versus new technologies—the CISAC decision in context' (2009) Ent LR 77

TT Nguyen, Competition Rules in the TRIPS Agreement—The CFI's Ruling in Microsoft v. Commission and Implications for Developing Countries' (2008) 39 IIC 558

A Niedermann, 'Surveys as evidence in proceedings before OHIM' (2006) 37(3) IIC 260–76

R Owens, 'TRIPs and the Fairness in Music Arbitration: The repercussions' (2003) 25(2) EIPR 49–54

E Reid, 'No sex please, we're European: Mosley v News Group Newspapers Ltd' (2009) Edin LR 116

E Smith, 'The bowl with the bitter taste' (2007) 2(8) JIPLP 510

C Stothers, 'Copyright and the EC Treaty: music, films and football' (2009) 31(5) EIPR 272–82

P Sugden, 'How long is a piece of string? The meaning of "commercial scale" in copyright piracy' (2009) 31(4) EIPR 202–12

P Treacy and A Wray, 'IP crimes: the prospect for EU-wide criminal sanctions—a long road ahead?' (2006) 28(1) EIPR 1–4

Yu-Lin Tsai, 'Compulsory licenses for access to medicines, expropriation and investor-state arbitration under bilateral investment agreements—are there issues beyond the TRIPS Agreement?' (2009) 40(2) IIC 152–73

B Ubertazzi, 'Licence agreements relating to IP rights and the EC Regulation on Jurisdiction' (2009) 40(8) IIC 912–939

G Urbanchuk, and J Tumbridge, 'Patent damages: the European landscape' (2008) 3(9) JIPLP 576

J van Hezewijk, 'Montex and Rolex—Irreconcilable Differences? A Call for a Better Definition of Counterfeit Goods' (2008) 39 IIC 775

NJ Wilkoff, 'A Wake Up Call for UK Law on Trade Mark Licensing' [1998] 20(10) EIPR 386–90

Intellectual property and international private law

Introduction

22.1 As has been suggested throughout this work, although intellectual property law is territorial, the expansion of commerce means that various goods and services (the whole or some element of which may be protected by IP) can be traded in numerous different countries throughout the world. With this increase in international exchange where there are many opportunities for infringement it becomes increasingly difficult to apply the principle of territoriality which forms the basis of intellectual property law. If a music file protected by copyright, and owned by a recording company in the US is 'shared' by users in many different countries using P2P software, who can be sued and where can they be sued? What law would apply to determine the matter? Would a judgment given in one country be recognised in another? When a trade mark is used in a website, that is the same as or similar to a trade mark registered by a separate entity in another country, would the second trade mark be infringed by its mere accessibility in a website? Can one country issue an order that would affect a registered right, such as a patent, in another (a cross border injunction)?

22.2 Of these issues, those concerning copyright and trade marks have become particularly pressing due to the expansion of the Internet. For copyright the dissemination of perfect copies of creative works across the net, out of the control of the right holders, has stretched the capabilities of the territorially based law. Similarly, the conflicting rights that may arise when trade mark owners of identical or similar registered marks in different territories use their respective marks within websites have given rise to some difficulties which are likely to increase with the further expansion of e-commerce. Patents too have had their share of transnational problems; although to date this has not been as a result of Internet use. Rather the cases have concerned cross border injunctions; where one court issues an injunction that can affect a patent in another.

Scope and overview of chapter

22.3 The purpose of this chapter is to discuss the application of the rules of international private law as they affect cross border infringements of intellectual property rights in Europe. The prime focus will be on copyright and trade marks, but reference will also be made to cross border patent litigation. It is not the intention to discuss the rules in depth, but to explain those which are applicable to infringement and to highlight a number of (mainly) UK cases that have applied the rules in intellectual property cases.

22.4

Learning objectives

By the end of this chapter you should be able to describe and explain:

- why UK courts have been unwilling to hear a dispute concerning an infringement of intellectual property rights that occurred abroad, and what legislative changes have occurred to alter that approach;
- how the rules on international private law apply to cross border intellectual property infringements within Europe and the attendant difficulties in applying those rules in an era of globalisation and digital dissemination;
- contemporary developments.

The rest of the chapter looks like this:

- International private law (22.5–22.39)
- Copyright (22.40–22.43)
- Trade marks: registered and unregistered (22.44–22.52)
- Patents (22.53–22.64)
- Contemporary developments (22.65–22.76)

International private law

22.5   The object of international private law (IPL) is to ensure, so far as possible, that disputes involving a foreign element are adjudicated by the court best placed to do justice to both parties, and that the appropriate law is applied to the dispute.

The rules of IPL thus determine:

- which court should hear a dispute (jurisdiction);
- which law governs the dispute (choice of law);
- what should be done to recognise and enforce a judgment.

It is important to note that although one court may have jurisdiction to hear a dispute, this does not mean that the law of that forum must necessarily be applied to the matter in hand.

  Question

Do any of the cases considered in other chapters of this book concern cross border infringement of intellectual property rights? If so, which ones?

Historical development of the rules

22.6 Unlike some other areas of the law (such as family law or succession), there has been a reluctance by courts in one jurisdiction to hear a case concerning an infringement of intellectual property which took place in another jurisdiction.

Why have courts been reluctant to hear cross border disputes?

22.7 The reluctance to hear cross border disputes stems in part from the development of the international treaties on intellectual property law, in particular the Paris[1] and Berne Conventions.[2] It will be recalled that there are two main principles underlying these conventions. The first is of national treatment where, as a general rule, a signatory state is obliged to offer protection to nationals of other signatory states in accordance to the protection afforded to its own nationals.[3] The second requirement is for signatory states to provide, in domestic law, certain substantive minimum levels of intellectual property protection. For example, signatories to the Berne Convention are required to afford owners of copyright a minimum term of protection of 50 years pma[4]—although many offer considerably more.[5] The international conventions do not, however, directly address or affect the question of IPL.

This has meant that, for example, when a copyright infringement dispute arose in one State party to the Berne Convention (State X) that concerned an author who hailed from another signatory state (State Y), on hearing the case the court in State X would apply and interpret national law. Intellectual property rights thus remained territorial. Where a case did arise before a court which concerned a foreign intellectual property right, the courts were reluctant to intervene.

22.8 In the UK, these concerns were reflected in rules which made it particularly difficult for an English or Scottish court to hear a case concerning an infringement of a foreign intellectual property right. The first was the public policy rule concerning jurisdiction. It was enunciated in *British South Africa Co v Companhia de Moçambique*[6] (the Moçambique rule). This rule classified torts (delicts) occurring in foreign lands as local in the sense that they had a particular connection with the territory on which they occurred. This in turn meant that it was appropriate for any action in relation to this tort to be heard in the local forum, that is, the place where the wrong occurred. So where an infringement of a patent, occurred in one of the states in Australia, that was the appropriate forum in which the dispute should be heard.[7] The second rule concerned a choice of law rule, the 'double actionability rule'.[8] This stipulated that the tort which occurred abroad should be classified as a tort in both the country where it occurred *and* in England or Scotland under English or Scots law. In effect, this meant that the laws of two different territories had to be applied to determine whether the infringement in question was unlawful. Both of these rules meant that the English and Scottish courts refused to entertain actions concerning foreign intellectual property rights.

22.9 Two useful, often cited examples from the UK can be given.

---

[1] Paris Convention for the Protection of Industrial Property 1883.
[2] Berne Convention for the Protection of Literary and Artistic Works 1886.
[3] Paris Convention, Art 2; Berne Convention, Art 5. [4] Berne Convention, Art 7.
[5] See Chapter 3 (copyright term). [6] [1893] AC 602.
[7] ibid. Note also *Satyam Computer Services Ltd v Upaid Systems Ltd* [2008] EWHC 31, para 95 where the court, in discussing the Moçambique rule, did not think that it supported a wider proposition than the English courts should not make inquiry into the validity of a foreign patent or similar foreign intellectual property rights.
[8] *Phillips v Eyre* (1870) LR 6 QB 1; *Boys v Chaplin* [1971] AC 356.

■ *Def Lepp Music v Stuart-Brown* [1986] RPC 273

In this case, the claimants, Deff Lepp, brought an action against a number of defendants for what they argued was an infringement of their copyright in the form of a tape recording that had been pirated, copied, and thereafter sold on under the control of entities located in Luxembourg and Holland. Leave to serve the defendants outside the jurisdiction had been obtained. The defendants then applied to have the order set aside arguing that acts carried out by them outside the UK could not constitute infringements of UK copyright in the tape recording. Browne Wilkinson VC agreed saying: 'It is therefore clear that copyright under the English Act is strictly defined in terms of territory. The intangible right which is copyright is merely a right to do certain acts exclusively in the United Kingdom: only acts done in the United Kingdom constitute infringement, either direct or indirect of such right'.[9] Further, 'In my judgment, therefore, a successful action cannot be brought in England for alleged infringement of United Kingdom copyright by acts done outside the United Kingdom'.[10]

■ *Tyburn Productions Ltd v Conan Doyle* [1991] Ch 75, [1990] 1 All ER 909, [1990] 3 WLR 167, [1990] RPC 185

In the second and later case, the claimant was an English company who wished to distribute a television film featuring 'Sherlock Holmes' in the US. Tyburn Productions were concerned that the defendant, who was the only surviving relative of Conan Doyle, author of the Sherlock Holmes books, would repeat previous assertions that she had the copyright in these characters. Tyburn thus applied to the English court for a declaration that the defendant had no rights under copyright, unfair competition or trade marks of the US to entitle her to prevent the distribution. Tyburn also sought an injunction preventing her from so doing. Having reviewed a number of previous authorities including *British South Africa Co v Cia de Moçambique*,[11] *Boys v Chaplin*,[12] and *Def Lepp Music v Stuart-Brown*[13] Vinelott J concluded:

> 'In my judgment therefore the question whether Lady Bromet is entitled to copyright under the law of the United States of America or of any of the states of the United States of America is not justiciable in the English courts'.[14]

Points to note:

- Had an injunction been granted it would have had cross-border effect. In other words it would, (if recognised), have taken effect in another territory. In *Tyburn*, there was no evidence that if the validity of the rights claimed were justiciable in the English courts, the decision of the English courts would be treated as binding on any of the states of the US.

- The recognition by the English court that had it accepted jurisdiction, it would not be domestic law which applied to the question under consideration: 'which raises complex issues which may require a survey by the English courts with the assistance of experts of the laws of each of the states of the United States of America'.[15]

22.10   In 2009 this approach was upheld by the Court of Appeal in *Lucasfilm Limited v Andrew Ainsworth*.[16] In this case, the High Court had suggested that there were circumstances in which the English courts may be willing to adjudicate on foreign copyright infringement claims emanating from jurisdictions beyond those which are a party to the Brussels Regulation. This was overturned by the Court of Appeal.

---

[9] ibid at 275.   [10] ibid at 277.   [11] [1893] AC 602.
[12] [1969] 2 All ER 1085, [1971] AC 356, [1969] 3 WLR 322, HL.   [13] [1986] RPC 273.   [14] ibid.   [15] ibid.
[16] [2009] EWCA Civ 1328.

■ *Lucasfilm Limited v Andrew Ainsworth* [2009] EWCA Civ 1328

The case concerned alleged infringement of copyright in the designs of costumes for Star Wars characters. Mr Justice Mann in the High Court was required inter alia to decide on whether an English court could hear an action to enforce a foreign copyright in respect of infringements that took place abroad. As the Brussels Regulation did not apply in this case, the court had to consider whether the IPL rules would allow a claim for infringement of copyright in the US to be litigated in England. Mann J reviewed the authorities including those cited above and came to the conclusion that:

'(i) The discussion reveals a tendency to move away from a strict and absolute application of the Moçambique rule to all intellectual property cases, and in particular copyright cases.
(ii) The statutory modification of the Mocambique rule itself, and the principles of the Brussels and Lugano conventions that between them draw a distinction between title (for land) and validity and regis-tration aspects (for registrable intellectual property rights) on the one hand and trespass/infringement on the other, justify the conclusion that at least infringement of foreign copyright should be justiciable here, whether or not subsistence is also justiciable.
(iii) There is nothing in the cases which binds me to a contrary conclusion.
(iv) The rule (if any) which underpins the extent to which an English court should not embark on a consid-eration of aspects of intellectual property rights is a public policy rule, not an actionability rule—see Coin Controls.'[17]

As a result English courts could, and should in appropriate circumstances determine questions of infringement of foreign copyright claims.[18]

As said, this was overturned by the Court of Appeal. That court comprehensively reviewed the decision of Mann J concerning the justiciability of the foreign copyright claim and the authori-ties on which it rested and ruled that: there was no authority that would require the court to determine such questions, and on grounds of judicial comity it should not; that the matter was non-justiciable on the grounds, inter alia of the Mocambique rule; concerning the potential clash between domestic IP policies, there is no distinction between subsistence and registration of a right for the purposes of infringement.[19]

'We accordingly conclude that for sound policy reasons the supposed international jurisdiction over copyright infringement claims does not exist. If it is ever to be created it should be by Treaty with all the necessary rules about mutual recognition, lis pendens and so on. It is not for judges to arrogate to themselves such a jurisdiction'.[20]

Neither was the US judgement enforceable in the English courts:

'On the contrary, it might be said that the sheer omnipresence of the internet would suggest that it does not easily create, outside the jurisdiction or jurisdictions in which its website owners are on established principle already to be found, that presence, partaking in some sense of allegiance, which has been recognised by our jurisprudence and rules of private international law as a necessary ingredient in the enforceability of foreign judgments.'[21]

The Court of Appeal judgement therefore affirms the position that that foreign intellectual property claims are not justiciable in the English courts in the absence of any specific legislative provision to the contrary.[22]

---

[17] *Lucasfilm Limited v Andrew Ainsworth* [2008] EWHC 1878 (Ch), para 265.
[18] G Austin, 'The concept of "justiciability" in foreign copyright infringement cases' (2009) 40(4) IIC 393–412.
[19] op cit, n 17 above, paras 174–182.   [20] ibid, para 183.   [21] ibid, para 194.
[22] The principles in the draft convention on jurisdiction and choice of law as endorsed by the American Law Institute (see n 113 below) was discussed in Lucasfilm where court said: 'Mr Bloch also prayed in aid the recent American Law Institute "Principles Governing Jurisdiction, Choice of Law, and Judgments in Transnational Disputes" (2008) which suggests that a national court should have subject-matter jurisdiction over IP disputes in other countries. We acknowledge

Exercise

List five points you consider were instrumental in the decisions by the courts to refuse jurisdiction in *Def Lepp Music*, *Tyburn Productions Ltd*, and *Lucasfilm*.

As will be seen below, the rules have changed in a number of jurisdictions where the litigants are party to the Brussels Regulation and where the courts will adjudicate on foreign intellectual property claims.

Key points on historical development of the rules

- English and Scottish courts are reluctant to hear disputes concerning infringement of an IP right in a foreign country in the absence of a specific direction to do so

- Torts (delicts) are classified as local

- The tort has to be classified as such both in the place where it occurred and in England or Scotland

Legislative developments

22.11   As indicated above, time has not stood still. Two legislative developments have required UK courts to re-think their attitude on the hearing of infringements of IPRs which occur in certain jurisdictions abroad; the first concerning jurisdiction, and the second concerning the applicable law. These, combined with the increasing number of infringements (both potentially and actually possible in the intellectual property sphere as a result of the rise of Internet usage) have resulted in courts taking some interesting and creative approaches in particular in relation to matters of jurisdiction.

The following section will consider the provisions of the Brussels Regulation concerning jurisdiction and enforcement of judgments and the Private International Law (Miscellaneous Provisions) Act 1995 as these relate to copyright, trade mark, patent and common law infringement actions. Thereafter some specific examples will be given.

Jurisdiction

The Brussels Regulation

22.12   Matters governing jurisdiction and recognition of judgments in the EU fall under the Brussels Regulation which came into force on 1 March 2002.[23] This Regulation replaced the Brussels

that is what it says, and it may, from an academic point of view, seem a good idea. For the reasons we give below we do not think it is a good idea in practice given the current, essentially national, nature of IP rights and their enforcement. As the court in Voda said, this is not a matter for the unilateral decision of the judges of a particular State.' (para 173).

[23]   The Brussels Regulation on jurisdiction and the recognition and enforcement of judgments in civil and commercial matters Council Regulation (EC) No 44/2001 of 22 December 2000.

Convention.[24] However, as the majority of the cases that have been decided to date were concerned with facts that occurred and the law that was in force prior to the Brussels Regulation, the judgments generally refer to the older measure, as well as to the Lugano Convention which is a parallel Convention to the Brussels Convention but extending to EFTA states.[25] The wording of the Brussels Regulation is almost identical to that of the Brussels and Lugano Conventions, save only a few minor variations. In the following discussion, the wording of the Regulation will be referred to. Where there are important differences in the wording these will be highlighted.[26]

22.13   The original reason for harmonisation in this area was to ensure that judgments would be recognised and enforced throughout the EU. In order to facilitate this goal, the rules on jurisdiction were also synchronised.

Weblink

The text of the Brussels Regulation can be found at http://europa.eu/legislation_summaries/justice_freedom_security/judicial_cooperation_in_civil_matters/l33054_en.htm Read in particular Articles 2, 5, 6 and 22.

Scope of the Regulation

22.14   If the defendant is domiciled in the EU, and the dispute concerns a civil or commercial matter, then the Brussels Regulation will apply to determine jurisdiction. The Regulation does not apply to defendants domiciled outwith the EU, where the domestic rules of the forum continue to apply.[27] The location of the claimant is irrelevant. Therefore the Brussels Regulation will apply if the claimant is outside the EU but the defendant within. No national rules providing for additional bases of jurisdiction can be applied against the defendant.

Article 2

22.15   The basic rule in the Regulation is that the defendant should be sued in the state in which he is domiciled.

'Subject to this Regulation, persons domiciled in a Member State shall, whatever their nationality, be sued in the courts of that Member State'.[28]

---

[24] The Brussels Convention on Jurisdiction and the Enforcement of Judgements in Civil and Commercial Matters 72/454, 1972 OJ (L299) 32.

[25] The Lugano Convention on Jurisdiction and Enforcement of Judgements in Civil and Commercial Matters Convention 88/592, 1988 OJ (L319) 9.

[26] The rules have been enacted in the UK in the Civil Jurisdiction and Judgments Act 1982 as amended to reflect the Brussels Regulation. The Civil Jurisdiction and Judgments Act 1982, Sch 1 contains rules for the United Kingdom; Sch 4 which only applies when Sch 1 rules do not; and Scottish rules on jurisdiction, Sch 8, which only applies when neither Sch 1 nor Sch 4 applies.

[27] Brussels Regulation, Art 4. For a case examining whether jurisdiction could be claimed in the English courts in relation to a matter concerning ownership of copyright in Australia see *R Griggs Group Ltd and Others v Evans and Others* [2005] Ch 153 [2004], EWHC 1088 (Ch), [2005] 2 WLR 513 Ch D.

[28] Case C-281/02 *Owusu* established that where Article 2 confers personal jurisdiction in a court of a member state by reason of the defendant's domicile in that State, the court cannot refuse to hear the case because there is a more appropriate forum abroad.

Article 5(1)

22.16   Article 5(1)(a) of the Regulation provides that in matters relating to contracts, a person domiciled in a Member States may be sued 'in the courts of the place of performance of the obligation in question'.

There has been some case law on the meaning of the place of the performance of the obligation in relation to intellectual property. *Falco v Weller-Lindhorst* concerned the issue of 'whether a contract under which the owner of an intellectual property right grants its contractual partner the right to use that right in return for remuneration is a contract for the provision of services'.[29] The ECJ ruled that this type of contract is not a contract for services under the Regulation, and that reference must be made to the ECJ case law relating to Article 5(1) of the Brussels Convention in order to determine which court has jurisdiction. The court explained that the concept of service implies the carrying out of a particular activity in return for remuneration. However, in the case of a licence to exploit intellectual property rights in particular Member States, 'the owner of an intellectual property right does not perform any service in granting a right to use that property and undertakes merely to permit the licensee to exploit that right freely'.[30] In *JS Swan v Kall Kwik*,[31] a company based in Scotland sued an English franchising company for breach of a franchise agreement before a court in Scotland. Citing the principles laid down by the ECJ in relation to the Brussels Regulation, the Scottish court ruled that it had no jurisdiction to hear the case because the franchise agreement did not explicitly state that the obligations should be performed exclusively in Scotland, and certain obligations that could be performed in Scotland were merely implied in their agreement. The court also said that following the ECJ's interpretations of the Regulation, Article 5 grounds for jurisdiction should be interpreted restrictively so as not to derogate the general rule that the defender must be sued in its domicile.

Article 5(3)

22.17   Under the title 'Special Jurisdiction', Article 5(3) of the Regulation provides that a defendant domiciled in a contracting state may be sued in another contracting state:

> 'in matters relating to tort, delict or quasi-delict, in the courts for the place where the harmful event occurred or may occur'.

22.18   A number of issues have arisen in relation to this Article. In *Kalfelis v Schröder*[32] the ECJ said that the expression 'matters relating to tort, delict or quasi-delict' has an autonomous meaning; covering all actions which seek to hold a defendant liable and which are not related to a 'contract' within the meaning of Article 5(1) of the Regulation. As the measure is an exception to the general rule in Article 2 of the Regulation a court only has jurisdiction over an action *insofar as* it is based on tort.[33]

22.19   As can be seen from the wording, Article 5(3) directs the claimant to the courts, or the place where the harmful event occurred or may occur. Under this rule, if the defendant is sued in the place which gives rise to the harmful event, he can be sued in those courts for the harm in its entirety. If, however, the claimant chooses to sue the defendant in the courts where the harm

---

[29]   Case C-533/07 [2009] ECDR 14.
[30]   ibid, para 31. B Ubertazzi, 'Licence agreements relating to IP rights and the EC Regulation on Jurisdiction' (2009) 40(8) IIC 912–939.
[31]   [2009] CSOH 99, 2009 WL 1949468.   [32]   [1988] ECR 5565.
[33]   Referred to by the court in *Mackie T/A 197 Aerial Photography v Askew 2009* SLT (Sh Ct) 146, para 31.

is felt, he can sue only for the damage that is felt in that place. This rule was articulated in a case concerning defamation, *Shevill and Others v Presse Alliance*.[34] The ECJ held that the courts of each contracting state where a defamatory publication was received, and where the claimant was injured, were limited to only awarding damages for injury sustained within their own borders.[35] If however the defendant was sued in the place of the event giving rise to the damage, that forum is competent to award damages for the full harm.

22.20   The wording of the equivalent provision in the Brussels Convention (and the wording in the Lugano Convention) referred to the place where the harmful event *occurred*. That raised the question under those Conventions as to whether the basis of jurisdiction in Article 5(3) only applied to a claim based on an existing tort, rather than one to restrain the threatened commission of a tort in the future. This has been resolved by the ECJ in *Verein Fur Konsumenteninformation v Henkel*[36] where the Court said:

> 'The courts for the place where the harmful event occurred are usually the most appropriate for deciding the case, in particular on the grounds of proximity and ease of taking evidence. These considerations are equally relevant whether the dispute concerns compensation for damage which has already occurred or relates to an action seeking to prevent the occurrence of damage'.[37]

22.21   The Brussels Regulation Article 5(3) refers to 'the place where the harmful event occurred or may occur'. Thus the question should not arise under the Regulation.

22.22   What is meant by the 'harmful event' in the phrase 'the place where the harmful event occurred'? If construed broadly, this could result in jurisdiction being claimed in many different fora. This is particularly so as torts with economic consequences can affect a claimant where she is domiciled and has property, goodwill and a reputation. However, the ECJ has been keen to place limits on the applicability of Article 5(3) notably where a claimant would be enabled to sue in a home forum for consequential damage.

22.23   Some guidance on what might amount to consequential damage was given in *Marinari v Lloyds Bank plc*[38] where an Italian domiciled claimant was arrested and had promissory notes sequestrated at the instance of the Manchester Branch of Lloyds Bank. The claimant sued in Italy for the exchange value of the notes and the damage to his reputation which he alleged he had suffered in Italy. The question for the ECJ was: 'In applying the jurisdiction rule laid down in Article 5(3) of the Brussels Convention . . . is the expression "place where the harmful event occurred" to be taken to mean only the place in which physical harm was caused to persons or things, or also the place in which the damage to the plaintiff's assets occurred?' The ECJ held that the Article should not be construed so extensively so 'as to encompass any place where the adverse consequences of an event that has already caused actual damage elsewhere can be felt'. Further it could not be construed 'as including the place where, as in the present case, the victim claims to have suffered financial damage consequential on initial damage arising and suffered by him in another contracting state'. Thus the actual answer to the question was that Article 5(3) should be interpreted 'as *not* referring to the place where the victim claims to have suffered financial loss consequential on initial damage arising and suffered by him in another contracting state'

---

[34] [1995] 2 WLR 499.
[35] The courts have allowed a plaintiff to sue for injury to feelings within a jurisdiction in a case of aggravated damages where the aggravating conduct occurred outside of the jurisdiction: *Clarke v Bain* [2008] EWHC 2636 (QB), 2008 WL 4963094.
[36] [2003] ILPr 1 ECJ (6th Chamber).   [37] ibid, para 46.   [38] [1996] QB 217.

(emphasis added).[39] Thus, a claimant is limited in the number of jurisdictions in which she can seek to bring an action based on the occurrence of the harmful event. For intellectual property cases this may mean that a claimant could not claim jurisdiction on the grounds of, say, loss of profits flowing from an infringement of copyright in a different territory.[40]

22.24   For any case in which claims for infringement of copyright in other jurisdictions are included, the claims 'would have to be pleaded out territory by territory by setting out the law relied on, and, if necessary, the facts and due damages'.[41]

Article 6(1)

22.25   In Article 6(1), also under the title 'Special Jurisdiction', the Regulation provides that:

> 'A person domiciled in a Contracting State may also be sued:(1) where he is one of a number of defendants, in the courts for the place where any one of them is domiciled, provided that the claims are so closely connected that it is expedient to hear and determine them together to avoid the risk of irreconcilable judgments resulting from separate proceedings'.

22.26   This Article thus permits joint defendants to be sued in one go at the place where one of them is domiciled. However, for this Article to be relevant, there has to be a sufficient connection between the defendants that to do otherwise might mean that irreconcilable judgments were handed down. As emphasised by the ECJ in *Kalfelis v Schröder*,[42] there must 'exist between the various actions brought by the same plaintiff against different defendants a connection of such a kind that it is expedient to determine the actions together in order to avoid the risk of irreconcilable judgments resulting from separate proceedings'[43] (see further para 22.53).

22.27   The Article also brings further complexity into questions of jurisdiction in particular in that it gives scope for forum shopping in intellectual property cases. This was recognised in *Research in Motion UK Ltd v Visto Corporation*:[44]

> 'Intellectual property also adds three further complications. Firstly there is a range of potential defendants extending from the source of the allegedly infringing goods (manufacturer or importer) right down to the ultimate users. Each will generally infringe and the right holder can elect whom to sue. One crude way to achieve forum selection is to sue a consumer or dealer domiciled in the country of the IP holder's choice (jurisdiction conferred by Art. 2.1) and then to join in his supplier—the ultimate EU manufacturer or importer into the EU if the product comes from outside. Jurisdiction for this is conferred by Art. 6.

---

[39] In an action arising furth of the countries party to the Brussels Regulation the High Court has ruled that it was wrong to strike out libel actions filed by a resident of England against publishers based in the United States as an abuse of process on the ground that the extent of publication within England was very small (ie, the online publication only had less than a dozen hits and merely 177 hard copies of the publication were made available in England). According to the High Court in *Mardas v New York Times* [2008] EWHC 3135 (QB), [2009] EMLR 8 'What matters is whether there has been a real and substantial tort within the jurisdiction...This cannot depend upon a numbers game, with the court fixing an arbitrary minimum according to the facts of the case' (para 15). The High Court, however, noted that the claimant could only claim for damages sustained in England and not in the United States where the publications had a larger circulation.

[40] See also Case C-220/88 *Dumez France v Hessische Landesbank* [1990] ECR I-49. *Mazur Media Limited and Another v Mazur Media GmbH* [2004] EWHC 1566 (Ch), [2005] 1 Lloyd's Rep 41, [2005] 1 BCLC 305, [2004] BPIR 1253. A claimant could not rely on Art 5(3) where the alleged loss flowed from an assignation of copyright but not the title to master recordings which could have been exploited in England among other countries. The damage in England was found to be indirect: 'I consider that for the purposes of Art 5(3) damage flowing from inability to exploit the copyright as a result of not having physical possession of the masters would be, for the purposes of Art 5(3), the kind of financial loss which the decision in *Marinari v Lloyds Bank plc (Zubadi Trading Co intervening)* [1995] ECR I-2719 rules out' (para 52).

[41] *Madonna Ciccone v Associated Newspapers* [2009] EWHC 1107 (Ch), 2009 WL 1949637.   [42] [1988] ECR 5565.

[43] ibid, at 5584.   [44] *Research in Motion UK Ltd v Visto Corporation* [2008] EWCA Civ 153.

Thus there is considerable scope for forum shopping—the very thing the scheme of the Regulation is basically intended to avoid'.[45]

 Exercise

'Formally the appeal [in Research in Motion] is now only about costs, but it involves much more than that. The case is yet another illustrating the unsatisfactory state of the current arrangements for deciding European wide patent disputes. Too often one finds parties litigating as much about where and when disputes should be heard and decided as about the real underlying dispute'.[46] Critically comment on this statement.

Article 22(4) (Article 16(4) of the Brussels Convention)

22.28   In Article 22(4) under the heading 'Exclusive jurisdiction' the Regulation provides:

'The following courts shall have exclusive jurisdiction regardless of domicile:

. . . 4. in proceedings concerned with the registration or validity of patents, trade marks, designs, or other similar rights required to be deposited or registered, the courts of the Member State in which the deposit or registration has been applied for, has taken place or is under the terms of a Community instrument or an international convention deemed to have taken place.'

22.29   Article 22(4) reflects the understanding that the *validity* of registered intellectual property rights can only be challenged in the state for which the right is registered. It is generally accepted that a state has autonomy over the grant of a property right, and only the state in which the property right exists should have the competence to adjudicate on its validity. Although this Article is of relevance to the validity of registered intellectual property rights, and whereas this chapter is primarily concerned with infringement, matters relevant to the interpretation and extent of this provision have arisen in connection with infringement actions as discussed below in para 22.54ff.

Review of Brussels Regulation

22.30   There have been moves to review the Brussels Regulation. The European Commission has released a Green Paper on the Review of Council Regulation (EC) No 44/2001.[47] This was supplemented by the Commission's Report on the application of Council Regulation (EC) No 44/2001 on jurisdiction and the recognition and enforcement of judgments in civil and commercial matters.[48] Generally the reports find that the working of the Regulation is highly satisfactory and has facilitated cross border litigation. Some suggestions are made for reform including: the operation of the Regulation in a broader international context and its operation in connection with intellectual property cases in particular.

---

[45] ibid, para 6.   [46] [2008] EWCA Civ 153, para 3.
[47] Commission (EC), 'Green Paper on the Review of the Council Regulation (EC) No 44 on jurisdiction and the recognition and enforcement of judgments in civil and commercial matters' COM(2009) 175 final, 21 April 2009.
[48] COM(2009) 174, 21 April 2009.

> ## Key points on the Brussels Regulation
>
> - The Regulation applies where the dispute concerns a civil or commercial matter
> - Jurisdiction is in the state:
>   - where the defendant is domiciled
>   - where the harmful event occurred
>   - where the defendant is one of a number of defendants
> - Where the question concerns the registration or validity of the right then those courts have exclusive jurisdiction

Choice of law

22.31   The main choice of law approach in intellectual property *infringement* actions is determined by the territorial nature of intellectual property rights.

22.32   Neither the Paris Convention nor TRIPS provides any detailed guidance in matters of trade mark or patent law. As noted these Conventions are premised on principles of national treatment and territoriality of laws. This notion of territoriality has been seen as the basis for the application of the law of the place where protection is claimed.[49] This has caused few problems for registered rights. Whether an infringement has occurred will be judged in accordance with the law of the place where the right is registered. That law will also govern the extent of the infringement. More discussion has arisen with copyright and other unregistered rights such as passing off.

22.33   In relation to copyright, the Berne Convention contains a measure that some commentators have argued is a choice of law provision. Article 5(2) provides that:

> '...the extent of protection, as well as the means of redress afforded to the author to protect his rights, shall be governed exclusively by the laws of the country where protection is claimed'.

22.34   What is meant by the phrase *'the country where protection is claimed'*? Some have argued that it should be interpreted as the law of the forum, as that is where the claimant seeks protection. Others argue it is rather to be interpreted as the country 'for which' protection is claimed against infringing acts occurring there. Most commentators now agree that the second interpretation is the one to be preferred,[50] and indeed, it is the interpretation that is consistent with the accepted notion that there is no such thing as international copyright law, but rather a collection of local laws.[51] For infringement cases, therefore, the law to be applied is the law of the place of the infringement.

---

[49]   J Facwett and P Torremans, *Intellectual Property and Private International Law* (1998), pp 477–8.

[50]   J Ginsburg, 'Private International Law Aspects of the Protection of Works and Objects of Related Rights Transmitted Through Digital Networks', available on the WIPO website as Paper GCPIC/2 (30 November 1998) p 35 (hereafter Ginsburg 1988).

[51]   Case C-28/04 *Tod's SpA and Tod's France SARL v Heyraud SA*. A question arose over shoes protected in Italy as designs. Could protection under the law of copyright be claimed in France? The ECJ said that: 'Article 12 EC, which lays down the general principle of non-discrimination on grounds of nationality, must be interpreted as meaning that the right of an author to claim in a Member State the copyright protection afforded by the law of that State may not be subject to a distinguishing criterion based on the country of origin of the work'. Thus the rights enforceable by claimants in one country cannot be withheld from claimants from another.

22.35   For unregistered rights, as will be discussed below,[52] there has been a tendency to apply domestic UK law to two situations:

- where a wrong which takes effect or is likely to take effect abroad is threatened or committed in the UK;
- where a wrong is threatened or committed abroad and the effect of the wrong or threatened wrong is felt in the UK.

22.36   As indicated above,[53] pursuing a tort or delict in the English or Scottish courts where that tort occurred in a territory abroad has been an almost impossible task thanks to the double actionability rule.[54] An exception to this rule was introduced in 1995 in *Red Sea Insurance v Bouygues*[55] which provided that where an issue between the parties had its most significant relationship with an occurrence in another country, then the law of that country should be applied to it. UK law has since changed, however. The Private International Law (Miscellaneous Provisions) Act 1995 governs questions of choice of law in tort and delict. The Act abolishes the double actionability rule[56] (except for defamation cases)[57] and now provides that the applicable law is the law of the country in which the events constituting the tort or delict in question occur.[58] Where elements of those events occur in different countries, the applicable law under the general rule is to be the law of the country in which the most significant element or elements of those events occurred.[59] For infringement actions the focus will now be on deciding which events constitute the tort, and applying the law of that country in the proceedings.[60]

22.37   Regulation (EC) No 864/2007 of the European Parliament and of the Council of 11 July 2007 on the law applicable to non-contractual obligations came into effect from 11 January 2009. This Regulation, also known as Rome II, deals, as the title suggests, with non-contractual obligations and has specific provisions concerning intellectual property.

22.38   Article 6 deals with unfair competition and Article 8 with intellectual property rights. Article 8 provides:

'Infringement of intellectual property rights

1. The law applicable to a non-contractual obligation arising from an infringement of an intellectual property right shall be the law of the country for which protection is claimed.

2. In the case of a non-contractual obligation arising from an infringement of a unitary Community intellectual property right, the law applicable shall, for any question that is not governed by the relevant Community instrument, be the law of the country in which the act of infringement was committed.

3. The law applicable under this Article may not be derogated from by an agreement pursuant to Article 14'.

While it seems that this measure may codify the current law, questions no doubt will arise over such matters as the country 'for which protection is claimed', as they have under the Berne Convention, and 'the country in which the infringement is committed', among others.

---

[52] See below para 22.44ff.   [53] See para 22.8.
[54] *Phillips v Eyre* (1870) LR 6 QB 1; *Boys v Chaplin* [1971] AC 356.   [55] [1995] AC 190.
[56] Private International Law (Miscellaneous Provisions) Act 1995, s 10.   [57] ibid, s 13.   [58] ibid, s 11(1).
[59] ibid.
[60] It is possible to displace the general rule under the Private International Law (Miscellaneous Provisions) Act 1995, s 12. It has however been argued that this section should not apply to infringements of intellectual property. If it did it 'would mean that there would be two IP rights competing in one country which appears contrary to the principle of national treatment upon which the IP Conventions and legislation are based...' (W Cornish in AV Dicey and JHC Morris, *Private International Law*, 4th Supplement (2004) p 231; Supplementary Memorandum in HL Paper 36 (1995) p 62 Annex by W Cornish, p 64).

> **Key points on choice of law**
>
> • The double actionability rule has been abolished
> • The applicable law is that of the place where the events constituting the tort or delict occur

Recognition and enforcement of judgments

22.39 As indicated above, one of the main reasons for the introduction of the Brussels Convention and now the Brussels Regulation was to streamline the procedure for the recognition and enforcement of a judgment granted by one member state, but which would take effect in another. It was, in other words, to encourage the free flow of judgments. Recognition of a judgment of a court in another member state requires no special formality. Under the Regulation, the first stage of the enforcement procedure in the State in which enforcement is sought is virtually automatic. Under Article 33 of the Regulation, '[a] judgment given in a Member State shall be recognised in the other Member States without any special procedure being required'. A member state can however refuse to recognise a judgment given by another member state (Article 34) if 'such recognition is manifestly contrary to public policy in the Member State in which recognition is sought'.[61] However, a foreign judgment may not, under any circumstances, be reviewed as to its substance.[62]

Copyright

22.40 The first UK case in the copyright field to arise after the introduction of the Brussels Regulation and enactment of the Private International Law (Miscellaneous Provisions) Act 1995 was *Pearce v Ove Arup*.

■ *Pearce v Ove Arup* [2000] Ch 403, [2000] 3 WLR 332, [1999] 1 All ER 769, [1999] FSR 525

The claimant (Pearce) was an architectural student in London in 1986. He worked on a project to produce drawings and plans for a town hall in Docklands. He brought an action against a firm of civil engineers based in the UK who had been commissioned to construct a building in Rotterdam, two further defendants who had designed the building and the City of Rotterdam as owners of the building. Pearce claimed infringement of his UK and Dutch copyright in the drawings. He alleged that the second and third defendants had taken copies of his drawings in 1986 and made graphic copies of elements of his plans in designing the building in Rotterdam.

One of the main questions was as to whether jurisdiction could be claimed in the UK. The court found that this was satisfied under the Brussels Convention Article 2 (the domicile of the defendant rule) and Article 6(1), on the basis of multiple defendants.

The court considered that the Convention overrode the Moçambique rule and thus there was no longer a bar on an English court hearing a claim in respect of an infringement of a foreign

---

[61] Brussels Regulation, Art 34(1).   [62] ibid, Art 36.

copyright. In addition the Private International Law (Miscellaneous Provisions) Act 1995, section 11 swept away the double actionability rule. The alleged infringement of copyright in the plans would be decided in accordance with Dutch copyright law, as that was where the alleged infringement took place—the construction of the building to the plans.

22.41 Thus it would appear that there are now no barriers to a court in England or Scotland (assuming that Scottish courts follow the *Pearce* rule), hearing an action against a foreign defendant in relation to an infringement of copyright that has occurred in a foreign territory.[63]

22.42 A second case to come before the English courts this time concerned Article 5(3) of the Lugano Convention.

■ *IBS Technologies (PVT) Ltd v APM Technologies SA and another* [2003] All ER (D) 105

The claimant was an Indian corporation and owner (by virtue of a number of assignments) of the copyright in a piece of software known as TopAir. This was used to support planning and control procedures for small and medium airlines operating on a charter basis. The first defendant was a Swiss corporation and the second defendant its chairman who was also domiciled in Switzerland. The original creator of the software was the Swiss chairman, the copyright was subsequently assigned to IBS Technologies. The main question of relevance to this discussion was whether IBS could sue the Swiss defendants in the English courts. The English court came to the conclusion that this was possible based on Article 5(3) of the Lugano Convention, but that the court would be limited to deciding on the damage which had occurred or which was threatened in the UK:

> 'In my judgement Article 5(3) of the Lugano convention does enable the claimant to sue the defendants in this Court, but only in relation to damage which can properly be said to have been caused, or to be threatened, against the claimant in the United Kingdom. This limitation applies both to the claim for damages for past infringement and to the claim for an injunction to restrain threatened infringement'.[64]

The actual damage in this case was the testing of the software in Manchester. The threatened damage was the potential future marketing by the defendants of the software system in the UK.

The court referred to the *Marinari* case[65] but said that it did not apply to the current action. In *Marinari* the only damage suffered in Italy was pure economic loss *consequential upon* the suffering of actual damage and economic loss in England. By contrast, in the instant case the actual and threatened damage was original damage: 'flowing directly from acts of infringement rather than loss consequential upon the claimant having suffered or having threatened against it, damage elsewhere'.[66]

22.43 The first of these two cases indicates a change in the attitude of the English courts in their willingness to accept jurisdiction for a copyright infringement that has been committed abroad, and in their readiness to apply a foreign law. The second case is more in keeping with the view that jurisdiction will be accepted where an infringement is committed within the territory.[67]

---

[63] See generally W Cornish and D Llewellyn, *Intellectual Property* (6th edn, 2007) para 2–72.   [64] ibid, para 55.
[65] Case C-364/93 *Marinari v Lloyds Bank plc* [1996] QB 217, [1996] All ER (EC) 84.
[66] [2003] All ER (D) 105, para 59.
[67] For questions concerning the justiciability of foreign copyright in a country not a party to the Brussels Regulation see paras 22.6–22.10.

> **Key points in relation to copyright**
>
> • English courts have accepted jurisdiction where an infringement occurred abroad: the law to be applied is that of the place of infringement
>
> • Jurisdiction has also been accepted on the basis of damage done or threatened in the UK limited to the damage caused or threatened in the UK

Trade marks: registered and unregistered

22.44   Some of the problems that have arisen with the registration and use of domain names have been considered in Chapter 16. The purpose of this part is to consider the use of registered and unregistered trade marks within websites.

22.45   It is perfectly possible and indeed likely that different traders in different jurisdictions own the same mark for the same goods and services. For instance, the mark 'ABC' might be owned by A in country Z, registered for X goods. That same mark might be owned by B in country Y, also registered for X goods. Given that trade mark law is territorial that is perfectly acceptable. What then happens when those marks are used on the Internet? The main question has revolved around whether the mere *accessibility* of a web page containing a mark in any country of the world also means that the mark is *used* in that country in a manner sufficient to ground jurisdiction or to amount to infringement? (See also the discussion in para 16.52ff.) On matters of jurisdiction the rules in the Brussels Convention will determine whether a court will hear a case. As regards the law to be applied, for cases concerning infringement of registered marks, it has generally been accepted that the place of the infringement determines the law to be applied. For passing off actions the Private International Law (Miscellaneous Provisions) Act 1995 mandates that the governing law is the lex loci (unless displaced by a more appropriate 'proper law of the tort').[68]

A wrong committed in the UK which has, or is likely to take effect abroad

22.46   It has long been recognised that an English Court has jurisdiction over acts done in the UK comprising supply of instruments of fraud which facilitate passing off abroad.

■ *John Walker & Sons Ltd v Ost* [1970] 2 All ER 106

The claimants who were blenders and exporters in Scotland and England of 'Scotch whisky' raised an action for passing off against the defendants who had shipped quantities of single malt whisky along with bottles labels and cartons for White Abbey and Scottish Archer whisky to a firm in Ecuador. The defendants knew that the whisky would be sold in Ecuador under these labels after having been mixed with local cane spirit. The court found that the tort of passing off had been committed in England because the defendant not only knew that local cane spirit was to be added to the whisky and sold as 'Scotch Whisky' but also that the labels would

---

[68] Private International Law (Miscellaneous Provisions) Act 1995, s 12.

be put on the bottles describing it as such. Thus the acts in the UK were sufficient to found jurisdiction even although the tort had effect in Ecuador.

22.47   English law may also be applied to decide whether conduct constitutes a tort which gives rise to a claim in damages. This approach can be seen in *Modus Vivendi (Ronson) v Keen*[69] which concerned allegations of passing off arising from the manufacture of goods in England for supply in China. Lightman J stated:

> '...since the "instruments of deception"...were put into circulation in this jurisdiction, under English law the tort of passing-off has been committed in England, though the damage, in respect of which compensation is sought in this action, has been suffered outside the jurisdiction, i.e. in China. Accordingly, not only is United Kingdom the proper forum for the trial, but English law is the proper law to apply in deciding whether [the defendant's] conduct constitutes a tort giving rise to a claim in damages'.

A wrong committed abroad which has, or is likely to take effect in the UK

22.48   English courts will also seize jurisdiction under Article 5(3) of the Brussels Regulation where a wrong is threatened or is committed abroad that has or is likely to have effect in the UK.

■ *Mecklermedia Corp v DC Congress GmbH* [1998] Ch 40, [1997] FSR 627

This case concerned use of the Internet. The claimants argued they had goodwill in the name 'Internet World' in the UK. They also used the domain names internetworld.com and iworld.com. The defendant had a German registered trade mark for 'Internet World' and domain name internetworld.de. The defendants has also organised two trade shows (in Germany and Austria) under the Internet World banner. Evidence showed the defendant had targeted promotional activities for its shows in the UK. The claimants argued that this amounted to passing off in the UK. The defendant disputed this saying that since all its activities took place in Germany and Austria, it was inappropriate for action to be taken in the UK. The judge did not accept this and concluded:

> '...when an enterprise [the defendant] wants to use a mark or word throughout the world (and that may include an internet address or domain name) it must take into account that in some places, if not others, there may be confusion. Here it is clear DC knew that Mecklermedia used the name "Internet World" and I do not think it is surprising that it is met with actions in places where confusion is considered likely'.[70]

The use of a mark within a website

22.49   This idea of the availability or use of a mark within a territory where it is placed within a website has been echoed in subsequent cases also discussed in para 16.55. Both of these revolved around the question as to whether a mark in a website had been used in the UK. In the first of these, *1–800 Flowers Inc v Phonenames Ltd*[71] the issue was whether the defendant had *used* or had the *intention to use* the trade mark 800 FLOWERS in the UK for the purposes of registration. The applicant had argued that the trade mark had been used in the UK by its use on a website. The court considered that merely because an Internet website could be accessed from anywhere in

[69] Unreported, Ch D 5 July 1995.

[70] The defendants also argued that the UK action should be stayed on the basis that the case was already being heard in Germany. The Chancery Division found that it was appropriate for the passing off claim to be pursued in the UK and dismissed the application.

[71] [2000] ETMR 369, [2000] FSR 697.

the world, that of itself did not mean that it should be regarded as having been *used* everywhere in the world. *Use*, for trade mark purposes, depended on all the circumstances of a particular case, particularly the intention of the owner of the website and the understanding that a person using the Internet would gain from reading the website. On the facts of this case, there was insufficient intention shown of use the mark in the UK.

22.50   *Euromarket Designs Inc v Peters*,[72] concerned alleged acts of infringement of a registered trade mark in the UK by the use of a sign by Peters on a website emanating from Ireland. Euromarket had a UK and CTM for 'Crate & Barrel' in class 21.[73] Peters ran a store in Dublin called 'Crate & Barrel'. Peters advertised their shop in Dublin on a website. It was alleged that two kinds of goods sold in the Irish store, a hurricane lamp and a beaded coaster, fell within the specification of Euromarket's trade mark. On the question of use, the court considered that an apt analogy was that of peering down a telescope towards Dublin, and being invited to visit the shop in Dublin. This would not amount to *use* in the UK. This was different to other Internet selling activities, such as those carried out by Amazon.com, who had gone out actively seeking worldwide custom. In those circumstances, a sign would be 'used' on a website.[74]

22.51   In some circumstances when a mark owned and used on a website by one entity that will infringe competing rights belonging to another but in a different territory. This is illustrated by the following case.

▣ *Bonnier Media Limited v Greg Lloyd Smith and Kestrel Trading Corporation* 2002 SCLR 977 OH Court of Session[75]

Bonnier Media were the owners, printers and publishers of a newspaper known as 'business a.m.'. They had a registered mark that included the name 'business a.m.'. They also ran a website using the domain name www.businessam.co.uk. Lloyd was resident and domiciled in Greece and the managing director of Kestrel, a company incorporated in Mauritius. The defenders registered a number of domain names including businessam.uk.com and businessam.info. The claimants feared that the defenders would set up and run a website passing themselves off as the claimants, as well as infringing their registered trade mark. In accepting jurisdiction based on Article 5(3) of the Brussels Convention the court said that: 'the person who sets up the website can be regarded as potentially committing a delict in any country where the website can be seen, in other words in any country in the world'.[76] Thus the marks could be considered as potentially being used in any country in the world. However, the court went on to narrow this by saying that a website should not be regarded as having delictual (tortious) consequences where it is unlikely to be of significant interest to consumers. In this case, there had been a history of some animosity between the parties. Bonnier had run a series of stories about the defender as a result of which libel proceedings were under way in the England. As a consequence it was considered likely that the domain name and website would be used to confuse customers of Bonnier, resulting in both trade mark infringement and passing off.

---

[72] [2001] FSR 20 Ch D.   [73] Trade Mark No 1331917.

[74] The case was also litigated in the US where a federal court asserted personal jurisdiction over the Irish based website because the site sold products priced in US dollars and requested that shipping and billing information included state and zip code fields: *Euromarket Designs Inc v Crate & Barrel Ltd* 96F Supp 824 (ND I11 2000). See also *KK Sony Computer Entertainment & Anor v Pacific Game Technology (Holding) Ltd* [2006] EWHC 2509.

[75] See also *L'Oréal SA v eBay International AG* [2009] EWHC 1094 (Ch), [2009] ETMR 53, (2009) IPD 32050, (2009) 106(23) LSG 18.

[76] *Bonnier Media*, para 19.

22.52   The implications of this case—that a trade mark is used in any country where the website is accessible—is thus narrowed by the need to show that there is likely to be a threatened wrong in the country where jurisdiction is claimed. Nonetheless, the case does illustrate what might happen if there are competing claims in different countries. It should however be stressed that the external factors in this case (the animosity between the parties, the litigation in England) appeared to have a powerful influence on the decision.

Key points on trade marks: registered and unregistered

- Courts will accept jurisdiction where a wrong in committed in the UK has or is likely to take effect abroad and where a wrong committed abroad has or is likely to take effect in the UK

- In Internet-related matters a court may ask whether the mark has been used in the UK to determine whether jurisdiction should be seized

---

Patents

22.53   In the patents arena two problems have been encountered. The first is the operation of Article 22(4) of the Brussels Regulation (previously Article 16(4) of the Brussels Convention), and the second is the effect of issuing a cross border injunction on the autonomy of the state in which it is to have effect.

Brussels Regulation, Article 22(4)

22.54   It will be recalled that for questions concerning validity and registration Article 22(4) provides for exclusive jurisdiction for the court in the state in which the right is registered. This is because an action concerning the validity of a registered right concerns the competence of the national authority to grant such a right. Any judgment rendered by a court outwith that territory therefore will have both private law implications in that it will affect the individual litigants and the property of one of those litigants, and public interest ramifications which have, in a patent action, been described thus:

> 'Although patent actions appear on their face to be disputes between two parties, in reality they also concern the public. A finding of infringement is a finding that a monopoly granted by the state is to be enforced. The result is invariably that the public have to pay higher prices than if the monopoly did not exist. If that be the proper result, then that result should, I believe, come about from a decision of a court situated in the state where the public have to pay the higher prices'.[77]

22.55   However, that exclusive jurisdiction is granted to national courts in cases concerning the registration and validity of a registered right has prompted some litigants to engage in forum shopping exercises. If a defendant is faced with infringement proceedings one tactic may be to call into question the validity of the right. Thus jurisdictional competence is shifted to the state where the right has been registered.

---

[77]   *Plastus Kreativ AB v Minnesota Mining and Manufacturing Co* [1995] RPC 438 at 447.

22.56 This is illustrated by the case of *Coin Controls v Suzo International*[78] where the English Patent Court was requested to enforce British, German and Spanish patents that had all originated from the same European Patent, against defendants domiciled in England, Germany and Spain. Jurisdiction had been based on Article 6(1) of the Brussels Convention. The court struck out the pleadings insofar as they applied to the foreign patents. In so doing the court said that if the conditions of Article 6(1) applied, the court had jurisdiction to deal with infringement of the German and Spanish patents. However, once the validity of the patents had been challenged, the provisions of Article 16(4) of the Brussels Convention (now Article 22(4) of the Brussels Regulation) came into play.

> 'The court cannot decline jurisdiction on the basis of mere suspicions as to what defence may be run. But once the defendant raises validity the court must hand the proceedings over to the courts having exclusive jurisdiction over that issue...infringement and validity of an intellectual property right...are so closely interrelated that they should be treated for jurisdictional purposes as one and the same issue'.[79]

22.57 The problem with this rule is that a defendant can easily block any infringement action based on foreign patent by raising a defence of invalidity. The ECJ was asked to rule on the interpretation of Article 16(4) (now Article 22(4)) by the Court of Appeal in *Fort Dodge v Akzo*.[80] The defendant challenged a UK patent before an English court claiming that this court had exclusive jurisdiction for the action based on the UK patent. The effect would have been to bar a Dutch court from issuing a cross-border injunction based on the same English patent (for cross border injunctions see below para 22.60ff). Unfortunately the *Fort Dodge* case settled prior to being heard by the ECJ.

22.58 The matter has now been considered by the ECJ in the following case.

▪ Case C-4/03 *Gat, Gesellschaft Für Antriebstechnik MBH & Co KG v Luk Lamellen Und Kupplungsbau Beteiligungs KG (Gat v Luk)*

The case concerned patents in a number of countries including France for parts of motor vehicles. The case was brought by the applicant before a German court in Dusseldorf seeking a declaration that the defendant did not have any claims arising from the French patents. It was claimed that the French patents were invalid due to a prior sale of the allegedly infringing parts. On appeal the question was raised as to whether the German courts had jurisdiction on the basis of Article 16(4) (now Article 22(4) of the Regulation). Proceedings were stayed to refer a question to the ECJ as to whether Article 16(4) was to be interpreted as meaning that the exclusive jurisdiction conferred by that provision only applies if proceedings are brought to declare a patent invalid, or whether the Article was also relevant where a plea is made that a patent is invalid but in the course of infringement proceedings.[81]

The ECJ, in a relatively short judgment has said the Article must be construed in accordance with the objective it pursues: that is that the rules seek to ensure that jurisdiction rests with courts closely linked to the proceedings in fact and law.[82] Article 16(4) means that the exclusive jurisdiction rule it lays down concerns all proceedings 'whatever the form of proceedings in which the issue of a patent's validity is raised, be it by way of an action or a plea in objection, at the time the case is brought or at a later stage in the proceedings'.[83]

---

[78] [1997] 3 All ER 45.   [79] ibid, p 60–1.   [80] [1998] FSR 222.
[81] OJ C 55, 08.03.2003, p 14. GAT Judgments Convention/Enforcement of judgments.   [82] Case C-4/03, para 21.
[83] ibid, para 25. See also *Research in Motion UK Ltd v Visto Corporation* [2008] EWCA Civ 153.

22.59   The English courts have considered a variety of factors where the possibility of irreconcilable judgments has been raised. In *Kitfix Swallow Group Ltd v Great Gizmos Ltd*,[84] a trade mark case, the High Court refused to stay proceedings. In favour of a stay were the higher costs in the English courts; the remote possibility of only a partial finding; and the possibility of irreconcilable judgments. Against a stay were arguments that a decision from the English courts was likely to be rendered months sooner; the prospect of appeals delaying proceedings in OHIM were much greater than before the English courts and the prospect of ultimate finality taking into account appeals is greater in England than before the OHIM. The interests of justice required that the claimant be permitted to continue proceedings before the High Court.[85]

Cross border injunctions[86]

22.60   As with copyright[87] and trade mark cases, it is open to claimants in patent infringement cases to base jurisdiction on Article 5(3) of the Regulation. This is because damage will occur wherever an infringing product reaches the market. For example, an infringement action can be based on a sale to a buyer located in a particular territory. In line with the *Shevill* ruling, a court in that jurisdiction can then hear the action for that particular damage. The difficulty however with filing a series of infringement actions under Article 5(3) is not only that it will be expensive, but an unfavourable ruling by one court in one location in relation to what might be essentially the same facts that arise in another location (for example, where patents have been obtained under the procedure in the European Patent Convention (EPC), and goods protected by a patent have been manufactured in the same place) might influence a decision made by the court in the second location. To try and solve these problems some claimants have attempted to combine defendants under Article 6(1) of the Brussels Regulation. It will be recalled that this Article provides for jurisdiction of a court in one state over a defendant in another state 'where he is one of a number of defendants in the courts for the place where any of them is domiciled'. The problem with this is that, if the claimant is successful, it will result in the court granting a cross border injunction. In other words an injunction issued by a court in one territory that has effect in another as regards the patent infringement.

22.61   The English courts have had some difficulty with the practice of granting of cross-border injunctions. In the High Court Aldous J said that 'it would not be right for this Court to grant an injunction which had effect outside the United Kingdom'.[88] Other national courts within Europe have been less circumspect. Dutch courts in particular have been quite active in this area. Dutch courts applied Article 6(1) to join not only a Dutch company, but also the foreign parent company and affiliated companies in the same proceedings for infringement of the Dutch patent and patents granted in other territories, each of which had been granted under the same EPC application.[89]

22.62   However there are potential injustices arising from this practice. If defendants are joined under Article 6(1) in cases where they merely infringe the same European patent by selling the same product, not only does the claimant have opportunities for forum shopping leaving

---

[84]   [2007] EWHC 2668 (Ch),

[85]   Speed of judgment was a factor in *Glaxo Group Ltd v Genentech Inc and Biogen Idec Inc* [2008] EWCA Civ 23.

[86]   See in general the discussion by F Blumer, *Patent Law and International Private Law on Both Sides of the Atlantic*, available on the WIPO website, Paper WIPO/PIL/01/3.

[87]   For a case concerning the geographic extent of an injunction claim based on copyright law see *Re Bill the Dog*, Federal Supreme Court (Germany) 8 July 2004, Doc No 1 ZR 25/02 commented on at [2005] EIPR N-102.

[88]   [1995] FSR 325, 338.   [89]   Op cit, n 70, p 16.

the defendant uncertain as to which court they may be required to appear before, but also the potential defendants may not know of each other's activities, and thus their risk of being joined under Article 6(1).

22.63   Perhaps aware of these concerns the Dutch courts took a step back from what may have seemed to some as expansive jurisdiction under this Article. The Dutch Court of Appeal ruled in 1998 that Article 6(1) does not permit a Dutch infringer (for infringement of the Dutch patent) and a foreign infringer (for the infringement of the foreign patents belonging to the European bundle) to be sued as joint defendants. One exception, however, was accepted. Foreign defendants could be joined with Dutch defendants under Article 6(1) if the foreign defendants belong to the same group of companies and the European headquarters of that group of companies is located on the territory of the court.[90] This approach has been named the *'spider in the web'* theory; the defendants can be sued as joint defendants if they form a web among themselves. The action has to be brought before a court located in the centre of the web.[91]

22.64   The ECJ has now ruled on this question in the following case.

■ Case C-539/03 *Roche Nederland BV v Frederick Primus, Milton Goldenberg*

Primus brought an action in the Netherlands against Roche Nederland BV and eight other companies in the Roche group established in other countries. Primus claimed that the companies had infringed their European patent by placing on the market goods in the countries where they were established. The Roche group companies which were not established in the Netherlands contested the jurisdiction of the Netherlands court arguing that there was no infringement of the patent in question and that it was invalid. The following questions were referred to the ECJ:

'(1) Is there a connection, as required for the application of Article 6(1) of the Brussels Convention, between a patent infringement action brought by a holder of a European patent against a defendant having its registered office in the State of the court in which the proceedings are brought, on the one hand, and against various defendants having their registered offices in Contracting States other than that of the State of the court in which the proceedings are brought, on the other hand, who, according to the patent holder, are infringing that patent in one or more other Contracting States?

(2) If the answer to Question 1 is not or not unreservedly in the affirmative, in what circumstances is such a connection deemed to exist, and is it relevant in this context whether, for example,

– the defendants form part of one and the same group of companies?
– the defendants are acting together on the basis of a common policy, and if so is the place from which that policy originates relevant?
– the alleged infringing acts of the various defendants are the same or virtually the same?'

The ECJ said that the national court was asking whether Article 6(1) of the Brussels Convention must be interpreted as meaning that it is to apply to European patent infringement proceedings involving a number of companies established in various contracting states in respect of acts committed in one or more of those states and, in particular, where those companies, which

[90] *Expandable Grafts Partnership v Boston Scientific et al* Court of Appeal The Hague, 23 April 1998, [1998] EIPR N-132.
[91] *Boston Scientific BV and Others v Cordis Corporation* [2000] ENPR 87 Hof (Den Haag): 'In the view of the Court…only the court of the domicile of the key defendant has jurisdiction…[it] thus avoids the result that several fora have jurisdiction and this reduces the possibilities of forum shopping', p 95. For an article discussing the spider in the web theory and related cases see P De Jong, 'The Belgian Torpedo: From Self Propelled Armament to Jaded Sandwich' [2005] EIPR 27(2), 75–81. Note also that the English High Court has issued a Community-wide injunction in respect of Community trade marks. See *Kabushiki Kaisha Sony Computer Entertainment & Anr v Electricbirdland Ltd* 2005 WL 1942171, [2005] EWHC 2296 (Ch) Ch D.

belong to the same group, have acted in an identical or similar manner in accordance with a common policy elaborated by one of them.[92]

The ECJ pointed to the decision *Kalfelis*[93] (para 22.18) where it had been held that for Article 6(1) of the Brussels Convention to apply there must exist, between the various actions brought by the same plaintiff against different defendants, 'a connection of such a kind that it is expedient to determine the actions together in order to avoid the risk of irreconcilable judgments resulting from separate proceedings'.

The ECJ pointed to the EPC which lays down common rules on the grant of European patents which are adjudicated according to national laws.[94] From this the court concluded that any diverging decisions could not, therefore, be treated as contradictory.[95]

> 'In those circumstances, even if the broadest interpretation of "irreconcilable" judgments, in the sense of contradictory, were accepted as the criterion for the existence of the connection required for the application of Article 6(1) of the Brussels Convention, it is clear that such a connection could not be established between actions for infringement of the same European patent where each action was brought against a company established in a different Contracting State in respect of acts which it had committed in that State'.[96]

Even where the defendant companies had acted in an identical or similar manner in accordance with a common policy thus the factual situation may be the same, the legal situation would not and therefore there would be no risk of contradictory decisions.[97]

See the related discussion in paras 10.29ff on development of a unitary patent right and Community Patent Court.

Question

Are there any intellectual property rights for which it might be appropriate to issue a cross border injunction? See for example *Kabushiki Kaisha Sony Computer Entertainment & Anr v Electricbirdland Ltd* 2005 WL 1942171, [2005] EWHC 2296 (Ch) Ch D. Note also that the question as to whether a CTM court can issue an EU wide injunction is currently before the ECJ in Case C-235/09 *DHL Express France v Chronopost SA*.[98]

Key points on patents

- National courts have exclusive jurisdiction where the validity of a registered right is in issue whether the action concerns invalidity or whether it is raised as a defence to infringement
- Article 16(4) (now 22(4)) does not apply to multiple infringements of a patent granted under the EPC

---

[92] ibid, para 18.   [93] Case 189/87 *Kalfelis* [1988] ECR 5565.   [94] Case C-539/03, paras 29 and 30.
[95] ibid, para 32.   [96] ibid, para 33.   [97] ibid, para 35.
[98] Note also the questions referred to the Court of Justice in Case C-496/09 *Realchemie Nederland BV v Bayer Cropscience AG*.

Contemporary developments

22.65   There has been increasing discussion in recent years as to the problems posed by the ubiquitous nature of the Internet, the territorial nature of intellectual property rights and the rules of international private law. The rules on jurisdiction, choice of law and recognition and enforcement of judgments have been discussed above. That discussion focused on the European approach with particular reference to the case law that has arisen in the UK and from the ECJ. Other jurisdictions operate their own rules concerning international private law matters. In addition, if a defendant is not domiciled within the EU, then national laws of member states will apply to trans-national disputes. The result, on an international scale, is a complex maze of rules, the operation of which can result in conflicting solutions to international private law questions concerning infringement of intellectual property rights. In an attempt to deal with these conflicts, proposals have been made to try and rationalise international private law rules particularly in relation to copyright and trade mark infringement cases.

The Hague Conference on Private International Law and the Convention on Choice of Court Agreements

22.66   For a number of years the Hague Conference on Private International Law has been working on the text of a Convention that would harmonise jurisdiction and enforcement of judgments for commercial matters. However the proposals have proved controversial, not least in the area of intellectual property. From ambitious beginnings in 1996: '. . . to include in the Agenda of the Nineteenth Session the question of jurisdiction, and recognition and enforcement of foreign judgments in civil and commercial matters'[99] the Convention, as finally agreed on 30 June 2005 concerns only agreed exclusive choice of court clauses[100] in civil or commercial matters and the enforcement of judgments.[101] The measures on intellectual property proved to be consistently difficult to negotiate. Questions arose as to whether intellectual property should be included at all, and if so, whether questions as to the validity of registered rights should be excluded.

22.67   On intellectual property matters the Convention does not apply to:

- the validity of intellectual property rights other than copyright and related rights;[102]

- infringement of intellectual property rights other than copyright and related rights, except where infringement proceedings are brought for breach of a contract between the parties relating to such rights, or could have been brought for breach of that contract;[103]

- the validity of entries in public registers.[104]

But Article 2.3 goes on to state that notwithstanding what is said in Article 2 if an excluded matter arises 'merely as a preliminary question and not as an object of the proceedings' in particular if it arises by way of defence, then proceedings are not excluded from the Convention 'if that matter is not an object of the proceedings'.

The European Council issued a Council Decision 2009/397/EC signing, on behalf of the European Community, the Convention. The Convention is not yet in force (November 2009).

---

[99] Eighteenth Session of the Hague Conference on Private International Law Part B No 1.
[100] Hague Convention, Art 3.   [101] ibid, Art 1.   [102] ibid, Art 2 n.   [103] ibid, Art 2 o.   [104] ibid, Art 2 p.

Exercise

What sort of issues might arise in connection with the 'validity of copyright and related
rights'? What sort of preliminary questions in relation to patents and trade marks might
arise that could be covered under the Convention? What sort of argument in relation to
patents or trade marks might be raised by way of defence that could be covered under the
Convention?

Rome I

22.68   Work has been on-going over the years to update the rules on the law applicable to contractual
obligations. The 1980 Rome Convention on the law applicable to contractual obligations was
implemented into UK law by the Contracts (Applicable Law) Act 1990. This was updated and
replaced by Regulation (EC) No 593/2008 of the European Parliament and of the Council of
on the law applicable to contractual obligations, also called Rome I. This was published in the
Official Journal of the EU in July 2008 and came into force in December 2009. It applies to relations between parties to contracts which involve intellectual property. The main thrust is that
of freedom of choice: parties are free to choose the law governing their contract[105] subject to a
number of provisos including overriding mandatory provisions.[106] Of greater importance for
intellectual property is Rome II, discussed above at para 22.37.

Copyright reform proposals

22.69   Specific proposals that are directed towards the international arena have been made in relation to copyright. The purpose behind many of the suggestions is to streamline choices in
relation to forum and of the law to be applied where many infringements occur as a result of
the dissemination of a protected work over the Internet. In other words the aim of the rules is
to designate one applicable forum that would be competent to hear an action for infringement
for all the subsequent loss, and one law that would be applicable to an infringement action.
It is accepted that many different reproductions and therefore infringements occur of a work
protected by copyright if it is digitised, uploaded on to a server and further made available over
the Internet. Under current rules, it may not be possible to consolidate claims for infringement
in one place. The location and identity of the defendant may be unknown. The harm resulting
from an initial act of digitisation and uploading an infringing work on to a server (which may
itself be located in a copyright haven) is likely to be felt in many different fora. Which court, out

---

[105] Article 2.   [106] Article 9.

of many possible options, should have jurisdiction to hear the case, and for what harm? Where, for the applicable law, is the place of the infringement? Is it where the initial infringing copy was made? Where it was uploaded on to a server? Downloaded onto a users computer? Further communicated between individual surfers? Under present laws, and reflecting the territorial nature of copyright not only may many different courts have jurisdiction to hear a case on the harm arising from the one initial act of infringement, but in addition many different laws may apply to the various infringements that occur.

22.70   Proposals to designate one single forum competent to hear an action for all the harm that arises range from choosing the courts located at the domicile of the defendant, to the courts in the place of the uplink (the server), to 'a court other than that of the place of emission which would be recognised to be competent to make good the full prejudice suffered at world wide level.' Such a tribunal would be the one 'having the closest link with the prejudice, with a presumption in favour of the court where the victim has his place of residence or principal establishment'.[107]

22.71   In the quest to apply a single law to all the infringements occurring over the Internet as a result of the unauthorised communication of a work, suggestions range from applying the law of the place where the author is domiciled;[108] the law of the country that affords the greatest protection among all countries having access to the network disseminating the infringing materials; to the law of the place where the server is situated[109] subject to the application of a number of sub-rules intended to ensure that the minimum standards mandated by Berne (and TRIPS) and the WIPO Copyright Treaty are part of the law applied to the problem.[110]

22.72   Suffice it to say that no changes have, as yet, been made to the rules. Proposals that have been made in this area by two US academics, Professors Dreyfuss[111] and Ginsburg[112] did seem to be gaining some ground. Their work focuses on jurisdiction and enforcement of judgments in intellectual property disputes. They have suggested that these areas should be the subject of a discrete convention (with the possible exception of patents). The authors prepared a draft treaty that would be open to signature only by countries that have joined the WTO and who are obliged to fully implement the TRIPS Agreement. The thrust of the proposal, first presented at a WIPO meeting in 2001[113] is to enable a single forum to hear a case for harm that arises in a number of different jurisdictions as a result of multiple infringements. The Dreyfuss and Ginsburg proposals on jurisdiction, choice of law, and the enforcement of judgments abroad in international IP were presented to and approved by the American Law Institute in May 2007.[114]

---

[107] Internet el les reseaux numeriques, Rapport du Conseil d'Etat prec Note 50, p 151, 1988 quoted in A Lucas, 'Aspects de Droit International Privé de la Protection d'Oeuvres et d'Objets de Droits Connexes Transmis par Réseaux Numériques Mondiaux', WIPO paper, November 1998. Available as GCPIC/1 paper on the WIPO website.

[108] F Dessemontet, 'Internet, la propriete intellectuelle et le droit international prive' in F Boele-Woelki et C Kessedjan (eds), *Which Court Decides? Which Law Applies?* (1998) '…finally infringement of intellectual property rights—of the author or his successors in title, for example—happens in a specific place: that of the economic harm', p 47.

[109] Other commentators argue for a solution which finds its origins in the Satellite Directive: Ginsburg 1998, p 42.

[110] Ginsburg 1998, p 42; P Torremans, 'Private International Law Aspects of Internet—IP disputes', in L Edwards and C Waelde (eds), *Law and the Internet: A Framework for Electronic Commerce* (2000).

[111] New York University.   [112] Columbia University.

[113] R Dreyfuss and J Ginsburg, 'Draft Convention on Jurisdiction and Recognition of Judgments', available as paper WIPO/PIL/01/7 on the WIPO website.

[114] http://www.ali.org/doc/2007_intellectualproperty.pdf. See the comments by the Court of Appeal in *Lucasfilm Limited v Andrew Ainsworth* [2009] EWCA Civ 1328, para 22.10 above.

The Treaty remains in draft form; whether it gains sufficient support in the intellectual property community to develop yet further remains to be seen.[115]

 Discussion point   For answer guidance visit www.oxfordtextbooks.co.uk/orc/macqueen2e/

Do you think that a single law should be applied in multi-territorial copyright infringement disputes? If yes, which law should apply?

Trade mark reform proposals

22.73   As indicated above, discussions for reform of the rules of international private law in the copyright realm have largely focused on proposals where the difficulties associated with infringements on an international scale can be streamlined by designating one forum competent to hear all the harm, and one law to be applied to the infringements.

22.74   Reform proposals in the trade mark arena have a different focus. Instead of seeking consolidation, there is greater concern to find ways in which competing rights can co-exist when used in connection with the Internet. This difference in approach stems from the different nature of the rights. Copyright is an unregistered right. Because many states are bound together by virtue of the obligations undertaken in the Berne Convention and TRIPS, a copyright owner in one country will equally be the owner of copyright in the same work in another country so long as that country is also a signatory to the Berne Convention and/or TRIPS. By contrast, registered trade mark and unregistered rights are limited to the territory in which they are registered or used (subject to a mark being famous or well-known). Therefore the concern has been to allow competing and equally legitimate rights co-exist on the Internet.

22.75   Some flavour of the discussion on jurisdiction is apparent from the cases discussed in paras 16.63ff, notably in relation to the question of use for infringement purposes. When a mark is used on the Internet, does the fact that it is accessible almost anywhere in the world mean that it is used everywhere in the world for the purposes of infringement?

WIPO proposals for use

22.76   Over the past few years the WIPO Standing Committee on the law of Trademarks, Industrial Designs and Geographical Indications has been working on proposals to harmonise national approaches to questions of 'use' of marks on the Internet.[116] The purpose is first to reduce the number of likely conflicts through restricting what may qualify as 'use' of a mark on the internet and second to provide a mechanism for mediating conflicts that do occur. These proposals have been discussed in paras 16.64–16.66.

---

[115] M Landova, 'Public policy exception to recognition and enforcement of judgments in cases of copyright infringement' (2009) 40(6) IIC 642–65.

[116] World Intellectual Property Organisation Standing Committee on the Law of Trademarks Industrial Designs and Geographical Indications, Second Session, Second Part Geneva 7–12 June 1999, Study Concerning the use of Trade Marks on the Internet SCT/2/9 Prov.

Further reading

Books

For general information about International Private Law see:

P North and J Fawcett, *Cheshire and North's Private International Law* (13th edn, 1999)

For information about International Private Law and Intellectual Property see:

J Fawcett and P Torremans, *Intellectual Property and Private International Law* (1998)

C Wadlow, *Enforcement of Intellectual Property in European and International Law* (1998)

Articles

For a series of online articles see:

Generally *Wipo Forum on Private International Law and Intellectual Property* Geneva, 30 and 31 January 2001

GW Austin, *Private International Law and Intellectual Property Rights—A Common Law Overview.* Paper WIPO/PIL/01/5

F Blumer, *Patent Law and International Private Law on Both Sides of the Atlantic.* Paper WIPO/PIL/01/3

GB Dinwoodie, *Private International Aspects of the Protection of Trademarks.* Paper WIPO/PIL/01/4

RC Dreyfuss and JC Ginsburg, *Draft Convention on Jurisdiction and Recognition of Judgments in Intellectual Property Matters.* Paper WIPO/PIL/01/7

JC Ginsburg, *Private International Law Aspects of the Protection of Works and Objects of Related Rights Transmitted Through Digital Networks (2000 Update).* Paper WIPO/PIL/01/2

A Lucas, *Private International Law Aspects of the Protection of Works and of the Subject Matter of Related Rights Transmitted Over Digital Networks.* Paper WIPO/PIL/01/1

Others

G Austin, 'The concept of "justiciability" in foreign copyright infringement cases' (2009) 40(4) IIC 393–412

A Dickinson, 'The Rome II Regulation: The Law Applicable to Non-Contractual Obligations' (2009) IJL & IT

MAC Dizon, 'The symbiotic relationship between global contracts and the international IP regime' (2009) 4(8) JIPLP 559–65

P Johnson, 'Court of Justice plucks the spider from the web' (2006) 1(11) JIPLP 689–90

P Joseph, 'The rise and fall of cross-border jurisdiction and remedies in IP disputes' (2006) 1(13) JIPLP 850–7

A Kur, 'A farewell to cross-border injunctions? The ECJ decisions GAT v LuK and Roche Nederland v Primus and Goldenberg' (2006) 37(7) IIC 844–55

M Landova, 'Public policy exception to recognition and enforcement of judgments in cases of copyright infringement' (2009) 40(6) IIC 642–665

P Morris, 'Pirates of the internet, at intellectual property's end with torrents and challenges for choice of law' (2009) 17(3) IJL & IT 282–303

P Torremans, 'Exclusive jurisdiction and cross-border IP (patent) infringement: suggestions for amendment of the Brussels I Regulation' (2007) EIPR 195

B Ubertazzi, 'Licence agreements relating to IP rights and the EC Regulation on Jurisdiction' (2009) 40(8) IIC 912–939

C Wadlow, 'Bugs, spies and paparazzi: jurisdiction over actions for breach of confidence in private international law' (2008) EIPR 269

C Wadlow, 'Trade secrets and the Rome II Regulation on the law applicable to non-contractual obligations' (2008) EIPR 309

Index